Foreword

Our yearbook *Europe in figures* provides you with a selection of the most important and interesting statistics on Europe. Drawing from the huge amount of data available at Eurostat, we aim to give an insight into the European economy, society and environment — for example, how the population of the European Union is changing, how the economy is performing in comparison with the USA or Japan, or how living conditions vary between Member States. I hope that you will find information of interest both for your work and for your daily life.

You can find the content of this book updated online in *Statistics Explained* as the continuously updated virtual publication *Europe in figures — Eurostat yearbook*. As usual, the latest and most complete versions of all the data can be downloaded from the Eurostat website.

Eurostat is the statistical office of the European Union. Working together with national statistical authorities in the European Statistical System, we produce official statistics which meet the highest possible standards of quality.

I wish you an enjoyable reading experience!

Walter Radermacher

Director-General, Eurostat
Chief Statistician of the European Union

Abstract

Europe in figures — Eurostat yearbook 2012 presents a comprehensive selection of statistical data on Europe. The yearbook may be viewed as an introduction to European statistics and provides guidance to the vast range of data freely available from the Eurostat website at: http://ec.europa.eu/eurostat.

Most data cover the period 2000-2010 for the European Union and some indicators are provided for other countries, such as members of EFTA, acceding and candidate countries to the European Union, Japan or the United States (subject to availability). With more than 470 statistical tables, figures and maps, the yearbook treats the following areas: economy and finance; population; health; education and training; labour market; living conditions and social protection; industry, trade and services; agriculture, forestry and fisheries; international trade; transport; environment; energy; and science and technology.

The continuously updated virtual yearbook is available at http://bit.ly/Eurostat_yearbook

Editor-in-chief

Ulrich Wieland
Eurostat, Unit B6 – Dissemination

Principal editor

Jukka Piirto
Eurostat, Unit B6 – Dissemination

Editors

Annika Johansson and Veronika Lang
Eurostat, Unit B6 – Dissemination

Contact details

Eurostat
Bâtiment Joseph Bech
5, rue Alphonse Weicker
2721 Luxembourg
LUXEMBOURG
E-mail: estat-user-support@ec.europa.eu

Production

This publication was produced by Giovanni Albertone, Simon Allen, Andrew Redpath (Informa sàrl)

For more information please consult

Internet: http://ec.europa.eu/eurostat

Data extracted

July to September 2011 (unless otherwise noted)

Virtual yearbook
English edition

Contents

Acknowledgements

The editor-in-chief and the editors of the Eurostat yearbook would like to thank all those who were involved in its preparation. The yearbook could only be published thanks to the support of the following colleagues:

Eurostat, the statistical office of the European Union

Eurostat had a reorganisation on 1 January 2012. The contributors are given according to the new structure.

Deputy Director-General

Marie Bohatá

Laboratory for developments in cross-cutting statistical domains

Helene Strandell

Directorate A: Cooperation in the European Statistical System; international cooperation; resources

A1 European Statistical System governance and external relations: Heli Lehtimäki, Astrid Meesters, Cristina Pereira de Sá

A2 Human resources management: Maria Isabel Lazaro, Matthias Lipps

Directorate B: Corporate statistical and IT services

B5 Management of statistical data and metadata: Håkan Lindén, Michael Mietzner, Barbara Rychel

B6 Dissemination: John Allen, Henric Anselm, Marc Debusschere, Isabelle Fiasse, Matthias Fritz

Directorate C: National accounts, prices and key indicators

C1 National accounts methodology. Sector accounts. Financial indicators: Ismael Ahamdanech Zarco, Boryana Milusheva, Peter Parlasca, Gilles Thouvenin

C2 National and regional accounts production. Balance of payments: Jeanne De Cannière, Christine Gerstberger, Andreas Krüger, Olaf Nowak, Isabelle Remond-Tiedrez

C3 Statistics for administrative purposes: Ian Dennis

C4 Key indicators for European policies: Viktoria Bolla, Graham Lock, Gian Luigi Mazzi, Rosa Ruggeri Cannata, Iliyana Savova, Vincent Tronet

C5 Price statistics. Purchasing power parities. Housing statistics: Paul Konijn, Jarko Pasanen

Directorate D: Government finance statistics (GFS)

D1: GFS methodology, data collection and dissemination: Isabel Gancedo Vallina, Irena Tvarijonavičiūtė, Laura Wahrig

D2: Excessive deficit procedure (EDP) 1: Rasa Jurkonienė

D3: Excessive deficit procedure (EDP) 2: John Verrinder

Directorate E: Sectoral and regional statistics

E1 Agriculture and fisheries: Marco Artico, Ludivine Baudouin, Steffie Bos, Fausto Cardoso, Catherine Coyette, Giovanni Dore, Matthew Elliott, Henri-François Fank, Annabelle Jansen, Jean-Claude Jeanty, Werner Kerschenbauer, Garry Mahon, Pol Marquer, Carla Martins, Arcangelo Milella, Gaetana Montana, Iulia Pop, Henri Risch, Herta Schenk, Darko Vrančić, Franco Zampogna

E2 Environmental accounts and climate change: Stephan Moll, Velina Pendolovska, Cristina Popescu, Stela Stamatova, Annamaria Szirony

E3 Environment and forestry: Karin Blumenthal, Lene Bochaton, Manon Elsen, Evangelia Ford-Alexandraki, Jürgen Förster, Christian Freudenberger, Christian Heidorn, Jean Klein, Rajmund Laczkó, Csaba Mózes, Hartmut Schrör, Marilise Wolf-Crowther

E4 Regional statistics and geographical information: César de Diego Díez, Paolo Dominici, Marjo Kasanko, Alessandra Palmieri, Daniela Sciranková

E5 Energy: Daniel Ganea, Antigone Gikas, John Görten

E6 Transport: Hubertus Cloodt, Luciano De Angelis, Franz Justen, Vidar Lund, Hans Strelow

Directorate F: Social statistics

F1 Social statistics – modernisation and coordination: Fernando Reis

F2 Population: Piotr Juchno, Monica Marcu, Fabio Sartori, Katya Vasileva

F3 Labour market: Eusebio Bezzina, Simone Casali, Beate Czech, Arturo de la Fuente Nuño, Didier Dupré, Sabine Gagel, Hannah Kiiver, Hubertus Vreeswijk

F4 Quality of life: Paulina Hojny, Anna Rybkowska, Cynthia Tavares, Geoffrey Thomas

F5 Education, health and social protection: Lucian Agafiței, Gemma Asero, Marta Beck-Domżalska, Sadiq Kwesi Boateng, Hartmut Buchow, Elodie Cayotte, Bart De Norre, Sorin-Florin Gheorghiu, Dominique Groenez, Sylvain Jouhette, Dorota Kawiorska, Ana María Martínez Palou, Lene Mejer, Luiza Cristina Munteanu, Jean-Marc Pascal Schaefer, Paolo Turchetti

Directorate G: Global business statistics

G2 Competitiveness of European businesses: Thierry Courtel, Stefaan Eeckels, Tatiana Mrlianová, Christine Nicasi, Aleksandra Stawińska

G3 Short-term statistics; tourism: Christophe Demunter, Thomas Jaegers

G4 Global transactions: Luis Antonio de la Fuente, Franca Faes-Cannito

G5 International trade in goods: Gilberto Gambini

G6 Innovation and information society: Ilcho Bechev, Silvia Crintea Rotaru, Bernard Félix, Konstantinos Giannakouris, Anna Lööf, Peter Pospíšil, Petronela Reinecke, Heidi Seybert, Maria Smihily, Albrecht Wirthmann

European Free Trade Association (EFTA)

Directorate-General for Translation of the European Commission

Publications Office of the European Union

01/06

UNIVERSITY OF
WOLVERHAMPTON
ENTERPRISE LTD.

ONE WEEK LOAN

Telephone Renewals: 01902 321333 or 0845 408 1631
Please RETURN this item on or before the last date shown above.
Fines will be charged if items are returned late.
See tariff of fines displayed at the Counter.   (L2)

Europe in figures

Eurostat yearbook 2012

2012 edition

eurostat
EUROPEAN COMMISSION

*Europe Direct is a service to help you find answers
to your questions about the European Union.*

Freephone number (*):

00 800 6 7 8 9 10 11

(*) Certain mobile telephone operators do not allow access to
     00 800 numbers or these calls may be billed.

More information on the European Union is available on the Internet (http://europa.eu).

Cataloguing data can be found at the end of this publication.

Luxembourg: Publications Office of the European Union, 2012

ISBN 978-92-79-22085-2
doi:10.2785/20539
Cat. KS-CD-12-001-EN-C

Theme: General and regional statistics
Collection: Statistical books

Printed in Belgium

PRINTED ON ELEMENTAL CHLORINE-FREE BLEACHED PAPER (ECF)

Introduction

The Eurostat yearbook

Europe in figures — Eurostat yearbook 2012 provides users of official statistics with an overview of the wealth of information that is available on Eurostat's website and within its online databases. It belongs to a set of general compendium publications and, of these, it provides the most extensive set of analyses and detailed data. *Europe in figures* has been conceived as a publication that provides a balanced set of indicators, with a broad cross-section of information, covering all of the main areas in which official European statistics are available.

Different formats, their language versions and MS Excel files of the Eurostat yearbook

PDF file and printed book

The *Eurostat yearbook* is released as a PDF file and on paper in English.

The virtual Eurostat yearbook

The most up-to-date version in English is available on *Statistics Explained* (part of Eurostat's website) as an online publication, the *virtual Eurostat yearbook*. It is translated once a year into German and French. During the course of a year, the virtual English yearbook is gradually updated and therefore the virtual German and French yearbooks are sometimes not as up-to-date as the English one. The translations of the 2012 edition are foreseen to become gradually available on *Statistics Explained* by the end of September 2012. The three language versions of the *virtual Eurostat yearbook* are accessible through the short URLs:

http://bit.ly/Eurostat_yearbook;

http://bit.ly/Eurostat-Jahrbuch, and;

http://bit.ly/Annuaire_Eurostat.

MS Excel files of the yearbook

The MS Excel files of the tables, figures and maps are available on the Eurostat website within each *Statistics Explained* article.

Related Eurostat publications

Pocketbook Key figures on Europe

The pocketbook *Key figures on Europe* (2012 edition foreseen to be published in June 2012) is derived from the *Eurostat yearbook* and presents the core content of the *Eurostat yearbook*. It is available in English, German and French both as a PDF file and on paper.

Eurostat regional yearbook

The *Eurostat yearbook*'s sister publication, the *Eurostat regional yearbook* (2011 edition published in December 2011) supplements the information provided for the EU-27 and the Member States in the *Eurostat yearbook* by providing data at a sub-national level to give an overview of key statistics that are available for the regions of Europe. The *Eurostat regional yearbook* is published in the same formats and language versions as the *Eurostat yearbook* (see above). The three language versions of the *virtual Eurostat regional yearbook* are accessible through the short URLs:

http://bit.ly/Eurostat_regional_yearbook;

http://bit.ly/Eurostat_Jahrbuch_der_Regionen, and;

http://bit.ly/Annuaire_regional_Eurostat.

Multilingual articles in *Statistics Explained*

A selection of *Eurostat yearbook* and *Eurostat regional yearbook* statistical articles will gradually become available by the end of June 2012 in *Statistics Explained* in 18 additional languages: Bulgarian, Spanish, Czech, Danish, Estonian, Greek, Italian, Latvian, Lithuanian, Hungarian, Dutch, Polish, Portuguese, Romanian, Slovak, Slovenian, Finnish and Swedish.

Structure of the publication

Europe in figures is divided into an introduction, 13 main chapters and a set of annexes. The main chapters contain data and/or background information relating to a very wide range of Eurostat data. After a brief introduction, each subchapter starts with a commentary on the main findings, continues with some details regarding data sources and data collection methods, and finishes with a section that details the context of the information presented. The core of each subchapter is a set of tables and figures that have been selected to illustrate the wide variety of data available for that particular topic; often these include information on how important benchmark indicators have developed during recent years within the European Union (EU), the euro area (EA) and the

Member States. Users will find a great deal more information when consulting Eurostat's website, which contains subject-specific publications and online databases. The publication closes with a set of annexes that contain details of classifications, a list of statistical symbols, abbreviations and acronyms, and a subject index.

Data extraction, updates and coverage

Data extraction

The statistical data presented in the yearbook were mainly extracted during September 2011 although some were extracted a few months later; for example, most of the data relating to government finances were extracted in April 2012. The accompanying text was drafted between September and November 2011 (and in April 2012 for government finances).

The collection, processing and subsequent release of data to the public (either online as a PDF or database files, or on paper) is a complex process that results in a certain amount of time elapsing; this can vary from a few weeks in the case of short-term monthly indicators to several years for complex, ad-hoc surveys. There is a release calendar, which provides details of the schedule for releasing euro-indicators (a collection of important monthly and quarterly indicators), available at: http://epp.eurostat.ec.europa.eu/portal/page/portal/release_calendars/news_releases. For other data sets, the metadata provided on the Eurostat website gives information relating to the frequency of surveys and the time that may elapse before data is published/released.

Data updates

The Eurostat website is continuously being updated and so it is likely that fresher data will have become available since the data was extracted for this publication. It is possible to access the latest version of each data set through data codes that are provided as part of the source under each table, figure and map. A description on the use of the data codes is given somewhat later in 'A practical guide to accessing European statistics'/'Access to data'/'Eurostat online data code(s) – easy access to the freshest data'. The yearbook's MS Excel files contain bookmarks to the specific, tailor-made extractions that were used to create each table, figure or map.

Spatial data coverage

The yearbook usually presents information for the EU-27 (the 27 Member States of the EU), the euro area (based on 17 members), as well as the individual Member States. The order of the Member States used in the yearbook generally follows their order of protocol; in other words, the alphabetical order of the countries' names in their respective original languages; in some of the tables or figures the data are ranked according to the values of a particular indicator.

The EU-27 and euro area (EA-17) aggregates are normally only provided when information for all of the countries is available, or if an estimate has been made for missing information. Any incomplete totals that are created are systematically footnoted. Time-series for these geographical aggregates are based on a consistent set of countries for the whole of the time period (unless otherwise indicated). In other words, although the EU only had 25 Member States since early 2004 and has only had 27 Member States since the start of 2007, the time-series for EU-27 refer to a sum or an average for all 27 countries for the whole of the period presented, as if all 27 Member States had been part of the EU in earlier periods. In a similar vein, the data for the euro area are consistently presented for the 17 members (as of January 2011), despite the later accessions of Greece, Slovenia, Cyprus and Malta, Slovakia and most recently, Estonia, to the euro area. Unless

otherwise stated, the data for the euro area covers the 17 Member States that shared the euro as a common currency as of January 2011 (Belgium, Germany, Estonia, Greece, Spain, France, Ireland, Italy, Cyprus, Luxembourg, Malta, the Netherlands, Austria, Portugal, Slovenia, Slovakia and Finland).

When available, information is also presented for EFTA countries (including Iceland that is also a candidate country) and the candidate countries ([1]) of Montenegro, Croatia ([2]), the former Yugoslav Republic of Macedonia ([3]) and Turkey, as well as for Japan and the United States. In the event that data for any of these non-member countries does not exist, then these have been excluded from tables and figures; however, the full set of 27 Member States is maintained in tables, with footnotes being added in figures for those Member States for which information is missing.

Temporal data coverage

In addition to presenting the data for the latest year (or reference period) available, the yearbook often presents earlier year(s) too in its tables and figures; this may be either one additional year, a couple of years or a full time-series covering a ten-year period. The interval between the years presented in tables and figures is often restricted to five or ten year comparisons in order to highlight slower, structural changes.

If data for a reference period are not available for a particular country, then efforts have been made to fill tables and figures with data for previous reference years (these exceptions are footnoted); generally, an effort has been made to go back at least two reference periods.

([1]) As Serbia was granted candidate country status on 2 March 2012, it was not possible to include it in this edition.

([2]) The EU and Croatian leaders signed Croatia's EU Accession Treaty on 9 December 2011. Croatia is called thereafter an 'acceding country' (instead of a 'candidate country'). Subject to ratification of the Treaty by all the Member States and Croatia, Croatia will become the EU's 28th Member State on 1 July 2013.

([3]) The name of the former Yugoslav Republic of Macedonia is shown in tables and figures in this publication as FYR of Macedonia – this does not prejudge in any way the definitive nomenclature for this country, which is to be agreed following the conclusion of negotiations currently taking place on this subject at the United Nations.

Eurostat – the statistical office of the European Union

Eurostat is the statistical office of the European Union, situated in Luxembourg. Its task is to provide the EU with statistics at a European level that enable comparisons between countries and regions.

Eurostat's mission, structure, staff and budget

Eurostat's mission is '*to be the leading provider of high quality statistics on Europe*'.

As one of the Directorate-Generals of the European Commission, Eurostat is headed by a Director-General. Under him are seven Directors responsible for different areas of activity (Directorates as of January 2012):

- Cooperation in the European Statistical System; international cooperation; resources;
- Corporate statistical and IT services;
- National accounts, prices and key indicators;
- Government finance statistics (GFS);
- Sectoral and regional statistics;
- Social statistics;
- Global business statistics.

In 2011, Eurostat had around 880 persons working for it; of these some 74 % were civil servants or temporary agents, while contract agents and seconded national experts represented 19 % of the staff, leaving 7 % with other types of contract. Eurostat's executed budget amounted to EUR 85 million in 2011 (excluding costs of statutory staff and administrative expenses) of which around EUR 55 million was used for the implementation of the Community statistical programme 2008-2012, almost EUR 9 million was used for the implementation of the modernisation of European enterprise and trade statistics (MEETS), while EUR 21 million was sub-delegated to Eurostat by other Directorates-General.

European Statistical System (ESS)

Since the creation of a European statistical office in 1952, there has always been a realisation that the planning and implementation of European policies must be based on reliable and comparable statistics. As a result, the European Statistical System (ESS) was built-up gradually to provide comparable statistics at EU-level.

The ESS is the partnership between the Union statistical authority, which is the European Commission (Eurostat), and the national statistical institutes (NSIs) and other national authorities responsible in each Member State for the development, production and dissemination of European statistics. This partnership also includes the EEA and EFTA countries. Member States collect data and compile statistics for national and EU purposes. The ESS functions as a network in which Eurostat's role is to lead the way in the harmonisation of statistics in close cooperation with the national statistical authorities. ESS work concentrates mainly on EU policy areas – but, with the extension of EU policies, harmonisation has been extended to nearly all statistical fields.

The ESS also coordinates its work with candidate countries and at European level with other European Commission services, agencies and the ECB and international organisations such as OECD, the UN, the International Monetary Fund and the World Bank.

Legal framework and ESSC

Regulation (EC) No 223/2009 of the European Parliament and of the Council of 11 March 2009 on European statistics established a new legal framework for the development, production and dissemination of European statistics. The Regulation states that European statistics shall be developed in conformity with the statistical principles set out in Article 338 of the Treaty on the functioning of the European Union and further elaborated in the European Statistics Code of Practice, namely, that: '*the production of Union statistics shall conform to impartiality, reliability, objectivity, scientific independence, cost-effectiveness and statistical confidentiality; it shall not entail excessive burdens on economic operators*'.

Article 7 of Regulation (EC) No 223/2009 establishes the European Statistical System Committee (ESSC), which is at the heart of the ESS, stating the Committee *'shall provide professional guidance to the ESS for developing, producing and disseminating European statistics'*. The ESSC is chaired by the European Commission (Eurostat) and composed of representatives from the national statistical institutes of the Member States. The national statistical institutes of EEA and EFTA countries participate as observers, as may representatives of other European / international bodies, for example, the ECB, the OECD or UNECE.

Objectives and means

To meet the challenges associated with the adoption of the Regulation, Eurostat aims:

- to provide other European institutions and the governments of the Member States with the information needed to design, implement, monitor and evaluate Community policies;
- to disseminate statistics to the European public and enterprises and to all economic and social agents involved in decision-making;
- to implement a set of standards, methods and organisational structures which allow comparable, reliable and relevant statistics to be produced throughout the Union, in line with the principles of the European statistics Code of Practice;
- to improve the functioning of the ESS, to support the Member States, and to assist in the development of statistical systems on international level.

Eurostat and its partners in the ESS aim to provide relevant, impartial, reliable and comparable statistical data. Indeed, access to high-quality statistics and Eurostat's obligation for trustworthiness is enshrined in law. European statistics should be provided to all types of users on the basis of equal opportunities, such that public administrations, researchers, trade unions, students, businesses and non-governmental organisations (NGOs), among others, can access data freely and easily. Access to the most recent statistics, as well as an expanding archive of information, is guaranteed through free access to Eurostat databases on its website.

The data collected and reported to Eurostat have been agreed through a well-defined political process at the European level in which the Member States are deeply involved. Most data collections and statistics are based on European regulations that are legally binding. In order to be able to produce comparable statistics between countries concepts and definitions, as well as technical standards and infrastructures are needed. Indeed, this is one of Eurostat's key roles – leading and facilitating these harmonisation and standardisation processes.

ESGAB and ESAC

In order to enhance accountability of the ESS, the European Statistical Governance Advisory Board (ESGAB, set up in 2008) prepares an annual report for the European Parliament and the Council on the implementation of the Code of Practice by Eurostat and by the ESS as a whole. It is composed of seven independent members. ESGAB's annual reports are available at: http://ec.europa.eu/esgab.

The European Statistical Advisory Committee (ESAC) is composed of 24 members representing users, respondents and other stakeholders of European statistics (including the scientific community, social partners and civil society), as well as institutional users (for example the European Council and the European Parliament). This committee is entrusted with ensuring that user requirements as well as the response burden on information providers and producers are taken into account when developing statistical programmes. For further information, please see: http://epp.eurostat.ec.europa.eu/portal/page/portal/esac/introduction.

A practical guide to accessing European statistics

The simplest way to access Eurostat's broad range of statistical information is through the Eurostat website (http://ec.europa.eu). Eurostat provides users with free access to its databases and all of its publications in PDF format via the Internet. The website is updated daily and gives access to the latest and most comprehensive statistical information available on the EU, its Member States, EFTA countries, and candidate countries.

For full access to all of the services available through Eurostat's website, it is recommended that users should take a few minutes to register from the homepage. Registration is free of charge and allows access to:

- tailor-made e-mail alerts providing information on new publications or statistics as soon as they are online;
- enhanced functionalities of the databases (for example, user are able to save data queries and make bulk downloads).

The information on Eurostat's website under the 'Statistics' tab that is always present near the top of each webpage provides links to:

- EU policy indicators (see the end of this introduction for more details);
- Statistics by theme, broken down into:
  - general and regional statistics;
  - economy and finance;
  - population and social conditions;
  - industry, trade and services;
  - agriculture and fisheries;
  - external trade;
  - transport;
  - environment and energy;
  - science and technology.

For each of these themes, the user is presented with a range of different sub-topics – for example, within the population and social conditions theme there are sub-topics for: population; health; education and training; labour market; income, social inclusion and living conditions; social protection; household budget surveys; crime and criminal justice; and culture. These sub-topics are presented as hyperlinks that take the user to a dedicated section on the subject, with information generally presented for data (main tables and databases), legislation, methodology, publications and other background information.

Access to data

Data navigation tree

The majority of Eurostat's statistics may be accessed from the data navigation tree, at: http://epp.eurostat.ec.europa.eu/portal/page/portal/statistics/search_database; alternatively, there is an icon at the right-hand end of the top menu bar ⬇ on most webpages that can be used to switch to the data navigation tree.

The data navigation tree is based on the statistical themes presented above and is collapsible and expandable. It has three main branches:

- Database by themes which contains the full range of public data available on the Eurostat website. These data are presented in multi-dimensional tables with selection features that allow tailor-made presentations and extractions. The interface for databases is called the Data Explorer (icon 🖉) and this provides an intuitive way to select and organise information. Data can be downloaded (icon 🖫) from the Data Explorer in various formats (XLS, CSV, HTML, PC AXIS, SPSS, TSV and PDF).
- Tables by themes which offers a selection of the most important Eurostat data in a user-friendly way. All data are presented in simple two- or three-dimensional tables, generally with European aggregates and data for the Member States on the y-axis and time on the x-axis. Tables can be viewed using an interface called TGM – tables, graphs and maps (icon 📊) – where data can be visualised as graphs or maps in addition to a standard, tabular presentation. Data can be downloaded (icon 🖫) from TGM in various formats (XLS, HTML, XML and TSV).

- Tables on EU policy which also provide access to pre-defined tables; these have particular relevance for tracking the progress being made in relation to some of the important policy areas. This section of the website covers indicators in relation to Euro-indicators / Principal European Economic Indicators (PEEIs), Europe 2020 indicators, sustainable development indicators, globalisation indicators, structural (Lisbon) indicators, and employment and social policy indicators. The tools for viewing and extracting data are the same as those described above for tables by themes.

The data navigation tree also has two special branches, where new items or recently updated items (from all databases and tables) can be displayed according to a set of user preferences (criteria set by the user).

Eurostat online data code(s) – easy access to the freshest data

Eurostat online data codes, such as tps00001 and nama_gdp_c (⁴), allow the reader to easily access the most recent data on Eurostat's website. In this yearbook these online data codes are given as part of the source below each table and figure.

In the PDF version of this publication, the reader is led directly to the freshest data when clicking on the hyper-links that form part of each online data code. Readers of the paper version can access the freshest data by typing a standardised hyper-link into a web browser – http://ec.europa.eu/eurostat/product?code=<data_code>&mode=view – where <data_code> is to be replaced by the online data code printed under the table or figure in question. The data is presented either in the TGM or the Data Explorer interface.

Online data codes can also be fed into the 'Search' function on Eurostat's website, which is found in the upper-right corner of the Eurostat homepage, at http://ec.europa.eu/eurostat.

The results from such a search present related dataset(s) and possibly publication(s) and metadata. By clicking on these hyper-links users are taken to product page(s) (⁵), which provide some background information about each dataset / publication or set of metadata. For example, it is possible to move directly to the data from the data product page by clicking the TGM or Data Explorer icons presented under the 'View table' sub-heading.

Note that the data on Eurostat's website is frequently updated.

Note also that the description above presents the situation as of the end of November 2011.

Statistics Explained

Statistics Explained is part of Eurostat's website – it provides easy access to Eurostat's statistical information. It can be accessed via a link on the right-hand side of Eurostat's homepage, or directly at http://epp.eurostat.ec.europa.eu/statistics_explained.

Statistics Explained is a wiki-based system that presents statistical topics. Together, the articles make up an encyclopaedia of European statistics, which is completed by a statistical glossary that clarifies the terms used. In addition, numerous links are provided to the latest data and metadata and to further information, making *Statistics Explained* a portal for regular and occasional users alike.

At present *Statistics Explained* contains well over 500 statistical and background articles and some 1 200 glossary pages in English; their number is continuously growing. About 100 of these articles, the content of the *Eurostat yearbook* (by the end of September 2012) and *Eurostat regional yearbook* are available in French and German, and

---

(⁴) There are two types of online data codes:
Tables (accessed using the TGM interface) have 8-character codes, which consist of 3 or 5 letters – the first of which is 't' – followed by 5 or 3 digits, e.g. tps00001 and tsdph220.
Databases (accessed using the Data Explorer interface) have codes that use an underscore '_' within the syntax of the code, e.g. nama_gdp_c and proj_08c2150p.

(⁵) The product page can also be accessed by using a hyper-link, for example, http://ec.europa.eu/eurostat/product?code=<data_code>, where <data_code> is to be replaced by the online data code in question.

20 representative ones have been translated into 18 other EU languages. As a result, 570 articles in 20 languages besides English can be consulted.

Users can search for articles using navigational features in the left-hand menu. The top-right menu bar of *Statistics Explained* offers tools, among others, to print, forward, cite, blog or share content easily.

Country profiles interface

The *country profiles interface* offers the possibility to visualise key statistical indicators, of different countries and / or EU aggregates, in a user-friendly map-based presentation. The interface can be accessed via the following link: http://epp.eurostat. ec.europa.eu/guip/introAction.do.

In 2011, Eurostat developed its first mobile device version of the Country profiles interface. The app runs on iPhone/iPad and Android mobile devices. It can be downloaded from the Apple App Store (see http://itunes.apple.com/en/app/country-profile/ id490077702?mt=8) and from Google Play store (previous Android market; see https://play.google. com/store/apps/details?id=eurostat.ec.europa. eu.country.profils&feature=search_result#?t=-W251bGwsMSwxLDEsImV1cm9zdGF0LmVjLm V1cm9wYS5ldS5jb3VudHJ5LnByb2ZpbHMiXQ).

The application gives mobile access to key statistical data for the EU and its Member States, the euro area, EFTA countries, in many cases EU candidate countries and a few other countries in the world. The latest data available from Eurostat can be viewed in table, graph and map format. An update function allows downloading of data twice a day. The user interface is available in English, French and German.

Publications

Eurostat produces a variety of publications, which all are available on the Eurostat website in PDF format (except some compact guides), free of charge. As with the 'Statistics' tab for accessing data, there is a 'Publications' tab that is accessible from the top menu bar.

There are a variety of different types of publication, ranging from pocketbooks and news releases to more in-depth analyses in the form of statistical books and statistics in focus.

Eurostat's publications programme consists of the following collections:

News releases provide the most recent information, designed to be of interest for journalists and for a broad audience;

Statistical books are larger publications with statistical analysis and data;

Pocketbooks are free-of-charge publications aiming to give users a set of basic figures on a specific topic;

Statistics in focus are short publications providing the most recent statistical data and complementary statistical analysis;

Methodologies and working papers are technical publications for statistical experts working in a particular field;

Compact guides are leaflets offering basic figures and guidance on how to obtain more information from the Eurostat website.

Large amounts of Eurostat's information are also available in *Statistics Explained*, a user-friendly online publishing system using a wiki-like format (http://epp.eurostat.ec.europa.eu/ statistics_explained).

Some Eurostat publications, including this publication, are also printed; these can be ordered from the website of the EU bookshop (http://bookshop. europa.eu).

Reference metadata

The ESMS (Euro SDMX Metadata Structure) is a format based on the Statistical Data and Metadata eXchange (SDMX) Content Oriented Guidelines, which were adopted in January 2009 by seven international organisations at a worldwide level. The ESMS uses a subset of 21 cross domain concepts (plus sub-concepts) and is the new standard for reference metadata in the ESS. It puts emphasis on quality-related information (containing concepts such as accuracy, comparability, coherence and timeliness).

Reference metadata may be accessed from the heading 'Metadata' which appears in the left-hand menu after selecting the 'Statistics' tab, or directly from the data navigation tree, where the following icon ▥ is used to signify its availability, or through the interfaces for viewing databases and tables.

In addition, since 2011 there has been national reference metadata in ESMS format available within the data navigation tree for the harmonised indices of consumer prices (prc_hicp_esms). From the first quarter of 2012 more national ESMS files from other statistical domains will be made available.

Quality profiles

Quality profiles are user-oriented summaries of the main quality features of indicators. These have been introduced for some sets of indicators linking statistics to European policies (see later), for example for the Europe 2020 indicators and the sustainable development indicators (SDI).

Through these profiles Eurostat provides guidance for the use and analysis of the indicators as well as input to the selection processes of structural indicators. In line with the Eurostat quality concept, quality is defined along several dimensions. The quality profile aims at a quick overview on how far an indicator is deemed 'fit for use' with regard to its key objectives.

The Eurostat quality profile for Europe 2020 indicators covers the following quality dimensions: feasibility by looking at timeliness and coverage; technical soundness, comprising overall accuracy, comparability (over time and across countries). For each of these components a brief overall assessment (high/restricted) is provided, substantiated by further qualitative information, if considered useful.

For SDIs the quality profile includes information on timeliness, accuracy, comparability and relevance, as well as information on how the indicator could be improved.

User support

Eurostat and the other members of the ESS have set up a system of user support centres – European Statistical Data Support (ESDS). These exist for nearly all of the EU's official languages and for a range of languages spoken in the EFTA, candidate and western Balkan countries.

In order to offer the best possible and personalised support, requests should, whenever possible, be addressed to the relevant language support centre. The mission of each centre is to provide free of charge additional help and guidance to users who are having difficulty in finding the statistical data they require. The contact information for the support centres is on the 'User support' tab on Eurostat's website (http://epp.eurostat.ec.europa.eu/portal/page/portal/help/user_support).

Eurostat's service for journalists

Statistics make news and they are essential to many reports, features and in-depth analyses. Printed media, as well as radio and television, use Eurostat data intensively. Eurostat's press office puts out user-friendly news releases on a key selection of data covering the EU, the euro area, the Member States and their partners. All Eurostat news releases are available free of charge on the Eurostat website at 11 a.m. (C.E.T.) on the day they are released. Around 200 news releases were published in 2011, of which approximately three quarters were based on monthly or quarterly euro-indicators; other releases covered major international events and important Eurostat publications.

Eurostat's press centre helps professional journalists find data on all kinds of topics. Journalists can contact media support for further information on news releases and other data (tel. (352) 4301-33408; e-mail: eurostat-mediasupport@ec.europa.eu).

Linking statistics to European policies

Effective economic and political decision-making depends on the regular supply of reliable information. Statistics are one of the principal sources of such information, providing quantitative support to the development and implementation of policies. Statistics are also a powerful tool for communicating with the general public.

Information needs for policy purposes require constant interaction between policymakers and statisticians: the former formulate their needs for data, and the latter attempt to adapt the statistical production system so as to fulfil those needs. In this way, policies can lead to improvements in statistical production, both in terms of enhancing the quality of existing indicators and of creating new ones.

Policymakers often require highly aggregated indicators which provide a synthetic and clear picture of the different phenomena in which they are interested. Statisticians therefore have to filter and aggregate basic, detailed data in order to increase data readability and extract information (or indicators).

Over recent years, a number of policies have substantially influenced Eurostat's priorities and activities:

- economic and monetary union (EMU) and the creation of the euro area (1999);
- the Lisbon strategy (2000, revised in 2005), including for example the open method of coordination on social inclusion and social protection;
- the EU's sustainable development strategy, EU SDS (2001, renewed in 2006);
- the Europe 2020 strategy (2010), the successor to the Lisbon strategy.

Economic and monetary union and the setting-up of the European Central Bank (ECB) required a broad range of infra-annual short-term statistics to measure economic and monetary developments within the euro area and to assist in the implementation of a common monetary policy. Effective monetary policy depends on timely, reliable and comprehensive economic statistics giving an overview of the economic situation. These infra-annual short-term statistics are also needed for the assessment of the business cycle.

Europeans place a high value on their quality of life, including aspects such as a clean environment, social protection, prosperity and equity. In recent years the European Council has focused on a number of key areas intended to shape the future social, economic and environmental development of the EU. While Europe 2020 is the EU's strategy for smart, sustainable and inclusive growth for the next decade, the sustainable development strategy is concerned with improving the quality of life and well-being, both for current and future generations, through seeking a balance between economic development, social cohesion and protection of the environment.

Eurostat has responded to politicians needs in these areas by developing four sets of 'EU policy indicators' that may be accessed through dedicated sections on the Eurostat website either directly from the homepage or from the 'Statistics' tab that appears near the top of every webpage:

- Europe 2020 indicators;
- Euro-indicators and Principal European Economic Indicators (PEEIs);
- Sustainable development indicators;
- Employment and social policy and equality indicators.

Europe 2020 indicators

The Europe 2020 strategy designed as the successor to the Lisbon strategy was adopted by the European Council on 17 June 2010. It is the EU's common agenda for the next decade – it puts an emphasis on the need for a new growth path that can lead to a smart, sustainable and inclusive economy, a path that can overcome the structural weaknesses in Europe's economy, improve its competitiveness and productivity and underpin a sustainable social market economy.

The key areas of the strategy where action is needed are limited to five headline targets on the EU level, which are being translated into national targets for each EU country, reflecting the specific situation of its economy. The European Commission adopted seven flagship initiatives in addition to the headline targets, in order to drive progress towards the Europe 2020 goals.

Eurostat provides the statistical support for measuring the progress towards the strategy objectives.

Employment:

- 75 % of the population aged 20-64 should be employed.

R&D / innovation:

- 3 % of the EU's GDP (public and private combined) should be invested in R & D.

Climate change / energy:

- greenhouse gas emissions should be reduced by at least 20 % compared with 1990;
- the share of renewable energy sources in final energy consumption should increase to 20 %;
- there should be a 20 % increase in energy efficiency.

Education:

- the share of early school leavers from education and training should be under 10 %;
- at least 40 % of 30-34 year olds should have completed a tertiary (or equivalent) education.

Poverty and social exclusion:

- at least 20 million people should be lifted out of the risk of poverty or social exclusion.

Europe 2020 strategy

The Europe 2020 strategy is part of the European semester (see MEMO/11/14 at http://europa.eu/rapid/pressReleasesAction.do?reference=MEMO/11/14). This process of enhanced economic coordination was launched in the beginning of 2011. Under the new governance architecture the European Commission assesses each year the main economic challenges for the EU and identifies priority actions to address them. The Member States and the European Commission have first collective discussions at an EU level (on economic and budgetary policies) and then the national decisions follow.

The European Commission's assessment is presented in the Annual Growth Survey (AGS) (see: http://ec.europa.eu/europe2020/tools/monitoring/annual_growth_survey_2011/index_en.htm). The first AGS was published in January 2011.

To ensure each EU country implements the Europe 2020 strategy in a way that fits its particular situation, the five EU-level targets are being translated into national targets. Countries set their final national targets in National Reform Programmes (NRP) and their macro-economic policies to ensure balanced budgets and financial stability in Stability or Convergence Programmes (SCP) (see http://ec.europa.eu/economy_finance/sgp/convergence/programmes/2011_en.htm and http://ec.europa.eu/europe2020/reaching-the-goals/monitoring-progress/recommendations-2011/index_en.htm).

Based on the National Reform and Stability and Convergence Programmes, the Council concluded the first semester in July 2011 by agreeing on a set of country-specific recommendations, highlighting areas where Member States needed to take further action (see: COM(2011) 400 of 7.6.2011).

In March 2011, Eurostat organised an international conference on 'statistics for policymakers: Europe 2020'. The aim of the conference was to bring together policymakers and statisticians in a dialogue on how to shape statistics that underpin policymaking. The conference underlined the importance of good interaction and understanding between policy makers and statisticians in order to be able to correctly measure the political targets set.

More information

More information regarding the Europe 2020 indicators may be found on the Eurostat website: http://epp.eurostat.ec.europa.eu/portal/page/portal/europe_2020_indicators/headline_indicators.

For more information on this strategy, please refer to European Commission's website, at: http://ec.europa.eu/europe2020/index_en.htm.

Euro-indicators / PEEIs

Since October 2001 the euro-indicators / PEEIs web pages have been a reference point for all users of official statistics dealing with short-term data.

Euro-indicators / PEEIs aim to supply business-cycle analysts, policymakers, media, researchers, students, and other interested users with a comprehensive, well structured and high quality set of information which is useful for their daily activities. The core of Euro-indicators / PEEIs comprises a set of statistical indicators giving an accurate and as timely as possible overview of the economic evolution of the euro area, the EU, and the individual Member States. The Euro-indicators / PEEIs dedicated section contains the following additional products and services intended to assist in the understanding and analysis of data:

- selected Principal European Economic Indicators (PEEIs);
- background;
- Economic and Financial Committee Status Reports;
- news releases;
- data;
- publications;
- information relating to seminars / conferences.

Data

The data presented in Euro-indicators / PEEIs are built around a set of the most relevant statistics, called Principal European Economic Indicators (PEEIs), a list of which can be found in the European Commission's Communication (2002) 661 ([6]). They are presented in three main parts:

- a selected Principal European Economic Indicators webpage (containing an overview on a set of 22 most relevant and timely short-term economic indicators for the euro area and the EU) directly accessible on the Euro-indicators / PEEIs homepage;
- Euro-indicators tables (included as the first branch of the 'Tables on EU policy' section of the data navigation tree as short-term indicators);
- European and national short-term statistics database (included as the first branch of the 'Database by themes' section of the data navigation tree – under the heading of 'General and regional statistics' – as European and national short term indicators – Euroind).

([6]) For more information: http://eur-lex.europa.eu/LexUriServ/LexUriServ.do?uri=CELEX:52002DC0661:EN:NOT.

◎ **European Union** *
◉ **Euro Area** **

	Release date latest	next	Unit	Reference period					
				2010q4	2011q1	2011q2	2011q3	2011q4	2012q1
GDP in volume	06/06/2012	04/07/2012	% (Q/Q-1)	0.3	0.7	0.1	0.1	-0.3	0.0
			% (Q/Q-4)	2.0	2.6	1.8	1.3	0.3	0.3
Private final consumption in volume	06/06/2012	04/07/2012	% (Q/Q-1)	0.4	-0.1	-0.4	0.3	-0.5	0.0
			% (Q/Q-4)	1.1	0.7	0.6	0.2	-0.7	-0.1
Investments in volume	06/06/2012	04/07/2012	% (Q/Q-1)	-0.6	1.8	-0.1	-0.3	-0.4	-1.4
			% (Q/Q-4)	1.7	3.8	1.1	0.6	0.4	-1.7
				2011m12	2012m1	2012m2	2012m3	2012m4	2012m5
External trade balance	15/06/2012	16/07/2012	mio euro	6855.6	5217.1	3857.3	3742.7	6205.9	(:)
Current account - Total	23/05/2012	21/06/2012	mio euro	21640	-10111	-5632	7543	(:)	(:)
				2011m12	2012m1	2012m2	2012m3	2012m4	2012m5
Inflation (HICP all items)	14/06/2012	29/06/2012	% (M/M-1)	0.3	-0.8	0.5	1.3	0.5	-0.1
			% (M/M-12)	2.7	2.7	2.7	2.7	2.6	2.4
				2011m12	2012m1	2012m2	2012m3	2012m4	2012m5
Unemployment rate - Total	01/06/2012	02/07/2012	%	10.7	10.8	10.9	11.0	11.0	(:)
Unemployment rate - 15-24 years	01/06/2012	02/07/2012	%	21.6	21.8	21.9	22.2	22.2	(:)
Unemployment rate - above 24 years	01/06/2012	02/07/2012	%	9.5	9.6	9.7	9.8	9.8	(:)
				2010q4	2011q1	2011q2	2011q3	2011q4	2012q1
Labour Cost Index	14/06/2012	13/09/2012	% (Q/Q-1)	0.5	1.1	1.0	0.0	0.7	0.3
			% (Q/Q-4)	1.6	2.5	3.3	2.5	2.8	2.0
Employment	15/06/2012	14/09/2012	% (Q/Q-1)	0.1	0.0	0.2	-0.2	-0.3	-0.2
			% (Q/Q-4)	0.0	0.2	0.4	0.2	-0.2	-0.5
				2011m12	2012m1	2012m2	2012m3	2012m4	2012m5
Industrial producer prices	04/06/2012	03/07/2012	% (M/M-1)	-0.2	0.9	0.6	0.5	0.0	(:)
			% (M/M-12)	4.3	3.9	3.7	3.5	2.6	(:)

Both the main tables for Euro-indicators and the Euroind database are divided into the following eight domains:

- balance of payments;
- business and consumer surveys;
- consumer prices;
- external trade;
- industry, commerce and services;
- labour market;
- monetary and financial indicators;
- national accounts.

Publications and working papers

The main publication in this domain is called 'Eurostatistics'. It is a monthly release that presents a synthetic picture of the macro-economic situation together with detailed statistical analysis of the latest economic events for the euro area, the EU, and the Member States. It is based on PEEIs, which are complemented by some business cycle indicators. The latest issue of 'Eurostatistics' is accessible from the homepage of the Euro-indicators / PEEIs dedicated section. Previous issues are also accessible – by selecting the 'publications' entry in the left-hand menu of the euro-indicators / PEEIs dedicated section and then clicking on the link to 'Official publications'. Under the same heading of 'publications', users may, for example, access a collection of 'selected readings' and 'working papers', containing both methodological and empirical studies on statistical activities and analyses of European data.

Quality reports

Since 2001, the Euroind database has been subject to monthly quality monitoring. The results of this assessment are presented in a detailed online publication called 'State of affairs', also accessible from the 'publications' link in the left-hand menu of the Euro-indicators / PEEIs dedicated section. A synthesis of the assessment is presented in another publication, entitled the 'Monitoring report', accessible from the same location.

Economic and Financial Committee Status Reports

PEEIs were designed together with timeliness targets. Since 2002, the progress achieved and the remaining challenges have been constantly monitored. Each year Eurostat, in cooperation with the European Central Bank, drafts a Status Report on Information Requirements in the European monetary union (EMU) which is first submitted to the Economic and Financial Committee (EFC) and then to the Economic and Financial Affairs Council (ECOFIN). The EFC Status Reports from 2005 onwards can be found in the Euro-indicators / PEEIs dedicated section by selecting the 'PEEIs' entry in the left-hand menu and then clicking on the link 'EFC Status Report'.

More information

It is possible to access Euro-indicators / PEEIs data directly via the Euro-indicators / PEEIs dedicated section at: http://ec.europa.eu/eurostat/euroindicators. It is also possible to contact the Euro-indicators team by e-mail at: ESTAT-EUROINDICATORS@ec.europa.eu.

Sustainable development indicators

The EU sustainable development strategy (EU SDS), adopted by the European Council in Gothenburg in June 2001, and renewed in June 2006, aims to continuously improve the quality of life, for both current and future generations, through reconciling economic development, social cohesion and protection of the environment. A set of sustainable development indicators (SDIs) has been developed to monitor progress in the implementation of the strategy. The indicators are organised within ten themes (and sub-themes) that reflect different political priorities (see first column of Table 2). The set of indicators has been built as a four-level pyramid.

Table 1: Framework for sustainable development indicators

Indicator level	Hierarchical framework	Indicator types
Level 1	Lead objectives	11 headline indicators are at the top of the pyramid. They are intended to monitor the 'overall objectives' of the strategy. They are well-known indicators with a high communication value. They are robust and available for most EU Member States for a period of at least five years.
Level 2	SDS priority objectives	The second level of the pyramid consists of ca. 30 indicators related to the operational objectives of the strategy. They are the lead indicators in their respective subthemes. They are robust and available for most EU Member States for a period of at least three years.
Level 3	Actions/explanatory variables	The third level consists of ca. 80 indicators related to actions outlined in the strategy or to other issues which are useful to analyse progress towards the SDS objectives. Breakdowns of level-1 or -2 indicators are usually also found at level 3.
Contextual indicators	Background	Contextual indicators are part of the SDI set, but they either do not monitor directly any of the strategy's objectives or they are not policy responsive. Generally they are difficult to interpret in a normative way. However, they provide valuable background information on issues having direct relevance for sustainable development policies and are useful for the analysis.

The distinction between the top three levels of indicators reflects the structure of the renewed strategy (overall lead objectives, operational priority objectives, and actions / explanatory variables) and also responds to different kinds of user needs. These three levels of the pyramid are complemented with contextual indicators, which do not monitor directly the strategy's objectives, but provide valuable background information for analysis. The SDI data set also describes indicators which are not yet fully developed but which will, in the future, be necessary to get a more complete picture of progress, differentiating between indicators that are expected to become available within some years, with sufficient quality ('indicators under development'), and those to be developed in the longer term ('indicators to be developed').

The table below presents the situation as regards the progress made with respect to the headline indicators, as presented in the 2011 edition of the Eurostat monitoring report of the EU sustainable development strategy (the weather symbols reflect in most cases the progress towards the EU objectives or targets between 2000 and 2009-2010).

Table 2: Headline sustainable development indicators and progress being made within the EU

SDI theme	Headline indicator	EU-27 evaluation of change (since 2000)
Socioeconomic development	Real GDP per capita	
Climate change and energy	Greenhouse gas emissions	
	Consumption of renewables (¹)	
Sustainable transport	Energy consumption of transport relative to GDP	
Sustainable consumption and production	Resource productivity	
Natural resources	Abundance of common birds (²)	
	Conservation of fish stocks	
Public health	Life expectancy and healthy life years (³)	
Social inclusion	Risk of poverty or social exclusion (⁴)	
Demographic changes	Employment rate of older workers	
Global partnership	Official development assistance	
Good governance	[No headline indicator]	:

 Clearly favourable change / on target path   Moderately unfavourable change / far from target path

 No or moderately favourable change / close to target path   Clearly unfavourable change / moving away from target path

(¹) From 2005.
(²) Based on 19 Member States.
(³) From 2002.
(⁴) From 2006.

Source: Eurostat

More information

More information on the set of sustainable development indicators may be found on the Eurostat website: http://ec.europa.eu/eurostat/sustainabledevelopment, or by contacting: estat-sdi@ec.europa.eu. There is also a comprehensive publication on the subject, 'Sustainable development in the European Union: 2011 monitoring report of the EU sustainable development strategy', available at: http://ec.europa.eu/product?code=KS-31-11-224&mode=view.

Employment and social policy and equality indicators

This collection of indicators covers various aspects of employment and social policy and equality issues. The indicators are used to monitor and report upon progress being made as regards EU policies relating to:

- employment;
- social inclusion and social protection;
- education and training;
- information society;
- youth policy;
- equality issues.

European Employment Strategy

Since the launch of the European Employment Strategy (EES) in 1997 indicators have been used for the assessment of Member States' progress on implementing the employment guidelines that have been developed under the EES, and that are proposed by the European Commission and approved by the European Council. The guidelines were most recently revised in 2010 as part of the Europe 2020 strategy (⁷). The EES seeks to create more and better jobs throughout the EU and encourages measures that are designed to meet three headline target objectives, namely, that:

- 75 % of the population aged 20-64 should be employed;
- the share of early school leavers from education and training should be under 10 %; at least 40 %

of 30-34 year olds should have completed a tertiary (or equivalent) education;
- at least 20 million people should be lifted out of the risk of poverty or social exclusion.

Most of the indicators for monitoring and analysis of the employment guidelines are provided by Eurostat. For more information on the list of indicators as well as the EES, please refer to the Directorate-General for Employment, Social Affairs and Inclusion website, at: http://ec.europa.eu/social/main.jsp?catId=101&langId=en.

Joint assessment framework

A joint assessment framework (JAF) for the employment guidelines within the context of the Europe 2020 strategy has been developed. Among other points this includes a quantitative monitoring of progress towards the relevant EU headline target and related national targets (see Europe 2020 indicators above). This aims to provide a quantitative tracking of progress with respect to these targets, as well as for the labour market participation and social inclusion of specific groups. The results should contribute to an 'employment performance monitor', an easy to communicate summary that can be used to identify at a glance the main challenges.

Open method of coordination on social inclusion and social protection

The Lisbon strategy gave rise to the open method of coordination (OMC) that provides a framework for political coordination (without legal constraints) in relation to social inclusion and social protection issues; this framework continues under the Europe 2020 strategy. The OMC is a flexible and decentralised method, which involves:

- agreeing on common objectives which set out high-level, shared goals to underpin the entire process;
- agreeing to a set of common indicators which show how progress towards these goals can be measured;

(⁷) For more information see part II of: http://ec.europa.eu/eu2020/pdf/Brochure%20Integrated%20Guidelines.pdf.

- preparing national strategic reports, in which Member States set out how they will plan policies over an agreed period to meet the common objectives;
- evaluating these strategies jointly through the European Commission and the Member States.

Indicators that form part of the open method of coordination on social inclusion and social protection (OMC) can be accessed directly from the Eurostat website, through the left-hand menu of the dedicated section covering employment and social policy and equality indicators, that may be found by clicking on the 'Statistics' tab near the top of the screen on each webpage. The indicators are currently divided into four strands, covering:

- overarching indicators;
- indicators of the social inclusion strand;
- indicators of the pension strand;
- indicators of the health and long term care strand.

Common indicators allow a comparison of best practices to be made and also measure progress being made towards common objectives. For more information about the open method of coordination on social inclusion and social protection, please refer to the Directorate-General for Employment, Social Affairs and Inclusion website, at: http://ec.europa.eu/social/main.jsp?catId=753&langId=en.

Education and training

To ensure their contribution to the Lisbon strategy, the ministers of education from the Member States adopted in 2001 a report on the future objectives of education and training systems agreeing for the first time on shared objectives to be achieved by 2010; a year later in 2002, a ten-year work programme was endorsed.

On 25 May 2007 the Council adopted conclusions on a coherent framework of 16 core indicators for monitoring progress towards the Lisbon objectives in education and training. Indicators and methodology are available on the Eurostat website as part of the dedicated section covering employment and social policy and equality.

The programme was subsequently extended to cover the period through to 2020. The long-term

strategic objectives of EU education and training policies are:

- making lifelong learning and mobility a reality;
- improving the quality and efficiency of education and training;
- promoting equity, social cohesion and active citizenship;
- enhancing creativity and innovation, including entrepreneurship, at all levels of education and training.

Five new goals have already been defined for 2020, through a strategic framework for European cooperation in education and training (ET 2020), by when:

- an average of at least 15 % of adults (aged 25-64) should participate in lifelong learning;
- the share of low-achieving 15-years olds in reading, mathematics and science should be less than 15 %;
- the share of 30-34 year olds with tertiary educational attainment should be at least 40 %;
- the share of early leavers from education and training should be less than 10 %;
- at least 95 % of children between four years of age and the age for starting compulsory primary education should participate in early childhood education.

For more information on these programmes, please refer to Directorate-General for Education and Culture website, at: http://ec.europa.eu/education/lifelong-learning-policy/doc28_en.htm.

European Information Society for growth and employment

Within the context of the renewed Lisbon agenda, a strategic framework for a European information society for growth and employment (i2010) was launched. This was succeeded, in 2010, by the Digital Agenda for Europe, one of the seven flagship initiatives within the Europe 2020 strategy.

The benchmarking framework for measuring progress in relation to the i2010 strategy was set up and approved in April 2006; it contained a set of core indicators and provided for flexible modules on specific issues to be defined each year. On

9 November 2009 a new benchmarking initiative was endorsed, providing the conceptual framework for the collection of statistics and the development of a list of core indicators to cover the period through to 2015. For more information, please refer to: http://ec.europa.eu/information_society/eeurope/i2010/docs/benchmarking/benchmarking_digital_europe_2011-2015.pdf.

Annual Community surveys on ICT usage in households and by individuals are a major source of information for the Digital Agenda scoreboard. The data presented on Eurostat's website as part of the dedicated section covering employment and social policy indicators is divided into four main themes:

* developments of broadband;
* advanced services;
* inclusion;
* public services.

For more information on the Digital Agenda and its scoreboard, please refer to the Directorate-General for Information Society website, at: http://ec.europa.eu/information_society/digital-agenda/index_en.htm.

Youth policy

The EU's youth strategy (2010-2018) seeks to promote better educational and job opportunities for young people, as well as active citizenship, social inclusion and solidarity. A list of EU Youth Indicators has been developed by an expert group. This contains a set of contextual indicators as well as more specific indicators.

Indicators have already been agreed in certain policy fields:

* education and training;
* employment and entrepreneurship;
* social inclusion;
* health and well-being.

New indicators have been proposed in fields where they do not currently exist or where no youth perspective is apparent:

* culture and creativity;
* youth participation;

* volunteering;
* youth and the world.

The indicators presented in the dedicated section on Youth on Eurostat's website are those based on data from Eurostat. Other indicators (for example from Eurobarometer surveys) are accessible from the youth domain of the website of the Directorate-General Education and Culture, as is more information on the EU's youth policy: http://ec.europa.eu/youth/youth-policies/overview_en.htm.

Equality

This final heading covers equality issues: although EU law prohibits discrimination in a number of areas, statistics show that various types of inequalities still exist. The Lisbon Treaty proposed taking action to combat discrimination based on gender, race or ethnic origin, religion or belief, disability, age and sexual orientation. In some of these areas, it is difficult to gauge from statistics how far equality has been achieved, but for others information is being developed. Eurostat therefore intends to expand its collection of data in order to cover the different forms of equality as and when suitable indicators become available. At the time of writing, there are two main strands of equality indicators – those relating to gender issues and those relating to age issues. For the former, the information is split into the following headings:

* education;
* labour market;
* earnings and social inclusion;
* childcare;
* health.

A similar list is used to categorise the information that has been collected for age equality measures, although this does not include childcare, but is extended to cover the population and the use of information technology.

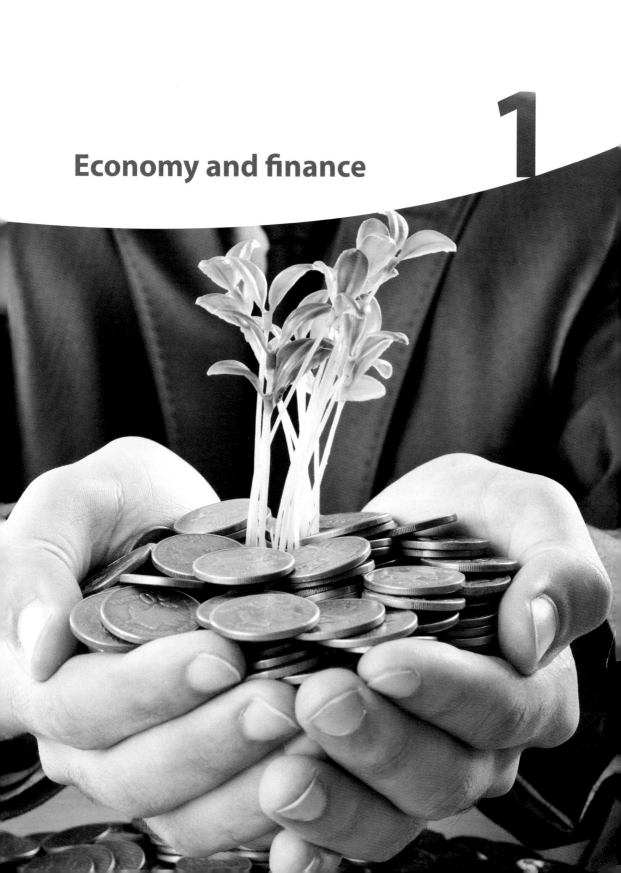

Economy and finance

1

Introduction

Indicators from various areas, such as national accounts, government finance, exchange rates and interest rates, consumer prices, and the balance of payments support analysis of the economic situation. These indicators are also used in the design, implementation and monitoring of the European Union's (EU's) policies.

The EU is active in a wide range of policy areas, but economic policies have traditionally played a dominant role. Starting from a rather narrow focus on introducing common policies for coal and steel, atomic energy and agriculture as well as the creation of a customs union over 50 years ago, European economic policies progressively extended their scope to a multitude of domains.

Since 1993, the European single market has enhanced the possibilities for people, goods, services and money to move around the EU as freely as within a single country. The start of economic and monetary union (EMU) in 1999 gave economic and market integration further stimulus. The euro has become a symbol for Europe, and the number of countries that have adopted the single currency increased from an original 11 to 17 countries by 2011.

Fostering economic and social progress has been a key objective of European policies. In March 2010, the European Commission launched the Europe

2020 strategy for smart, sustainable and inclusive growth to follow up the 2000 Lisbon strategy. Its declared objective is to overcome the effects of the 2008 financial and economic crisis and prepare the EU's economy for the next decade; integrated economic and employment guidelines have been revised within the context of this new strategy.

Following actions to stabilise the financial system and the economy, the recent crisis also prompted a reinforced economic agenda with closer EU surveillance, as well as agreement over a range of policy priorities and a set of targets as part of the Europe 2020 strategy. Tighter EU surveillance of economic and fiscal policies has been introduced as part of the stability and growth pact, while new tools to tackle macro-economic imbalances and a new working method – the European semester – have also been introduced in order to promote discussions concerning economic and budgetary priorities at the same time every year.

In October 2011, the Council adopted an EU economic governance package of six new legislative acts that comes into force by the end of 2011. This puts much more emphasis on debt reduction, sets minimum requirements for national budgetary frameworks and installs a new procedure to prevent and correct macro-economic imbalances including a scoreboard of economic and financial indicators that the European Commission will monitor.

1.1 National accounts – GDP

National accounts are the source for a multitude of well-known economic indicators which are presented in this subchapter. Gross domestic product (GDP) is the most frequently used measure for the overall size of an economy, while derived indicators such as GDP per capita – for example, in euro or adjusted for differences in price levels – are widely used for a comparison of living standards, or to monitor the process of convergence across the European Union (EU).

Moreover, the development of specific GDP components and related indicators, such as those for

economic output, imports and exports, domestic (private and public) consumption or investments, as well as data on the distribution of income and savings, can give valuable insights into the driving forces in an economy and thus be the basis for the design, monitoring and evaluation of specific EU policies. Economic developments in production, income generation and (re)distribution, consumption and investment may be better understood when analysed by institutional sector. In particular, sector accounts provide several key indicators for

households and non-financial corporations, like the household saving rate and business profit share.

Main statistical findings

Developments in GDP

In 2010, the EU-27's GDP recovered partly from the effects of the 2008 global financial and economic crisis. It increased to EUR 12 268 000 million in 2010 from EUR 11 770 000 million in 2009 (see Figure 1.1.1 and Table 1.1.1). This was however still below the pre-crisis level of EUR 12 479 000 million in 2008 and even below the level of 12 390 000 million reached in 2007. The euro area accounted for 74.9 % of this total in 2010, while the sum of the five largest EU economies (Germany, France, the United Kingdom, Italy and Spain) was 71.2 %. However, cross-country comparisons should be made with caution as notably exchange rate fluctuations may significantly influence the development of nominal GDP figures for Member States which have not adopted the euro.

To evaluate standards of living, it is more appropriate to use GDP per capita in purchasing power standards (PPS), in other words adjusted for the size of an economy in terms of population and also for differences in price levels across countries. The average GDP per capita within the EU-27 in 2010 was PPS 24 500, which was higher than in 2009 (PPS 23 500) but lower than in 2008 and 2007 (both PPS 25 000). The relative position of individual countries can be expressed through a comparison with this average, with the EU-27 value set to equal 100. The highest relative value among EU Member States was recorded for Luxembourg, where GDP per capita in PPS was more than 2.8 times the EU-27 average in 2010 (which is partly explained by the importance of cross-border workers from Belgium, France and Germany). On the other hand, GDP per capita was less than half the EU-27 average in Romania and Bulgaria.

Although PPS figures should, in principle, be used for cross-country comparisons in a single year rather than over time, the development of these figures over the past decade suggests that some convergence in living standards took place as Member States that joined the EU in 2004 or 2007 moved closer to the EU average despite some setback in relation to the 2008 financial and economic crisis. Whereas Luxembourg moved further ahead of the EU-27 average, Spain and Ireland moved back towards the EU-27 average after 2007; comparing the situation in 2010 with that in 2000 several other EU-15 Member States, notably Italy, Belgium, Denmark and France, as well as Austria, the United Kingdom, Sweden and Ireland, moved closer to the EU-27 average (see Figure 1.1.2). From a position below the EU-27 average in 2000, Slovakia, Estonia, Lithuania and Romania made the greatest moves towards the EU-27 average by 2010.

Economic growth within the EU suffered from the 2008 global financial and economic crisis. A severe recession in most countries in 2009 was followed by a partial recovery in 2010. Real GDP increased by 1.8 % in the EU-27 and in the euro area in 2010 after a contraction of 4.3 % and 4.2 % respectively in 2009. In Japan and the United States, the respective figures were growth of 4.0 % and 3.0 % in 2010 following –contractions of 6.3 % and 3.5 % in 2009 (see Figure 1.1.3 and Table 1.1.2).

Among EU Member States, real GDP growth varied significantly. Nevertheless, after a contraction in all EU Member Stares except Poland in 2009, economic growth resumed in 22 of the EU Member States in 2010. The highest growth rates in 2010 were recorded in Sweden (5.7 %), Slovakia (4.0 %) and Poland (3.8 %). The economies of Spain (– 0.1 %), Latvia (– 0.3 %), Ireland (– 0.4 %) and Romania (– 1.3 %) continued to contract – but Greece was the only Member State where the recession deepened as Greek GDP contracted by 2.0 % in 2009 and 4.5 % in 2010.

The global recession has also significantly lowered Member State's growth performance over the past decade. The average annual growth rates of the EU-27 and the euro area between 2001 and 2010 were 1.3 % and 1.1 % respectively. The highest growth by this measure was recorded for Slovakia (4.9 %), followed by Lithuania (4.6 %) and Romania (4.2 %). The other Baltic Member States as well as Bulgaria and Poland also had average growth rates close to 4 %. In contrast, average growth was lowest

for Italy (0.3 %), Portugal and Denmark (both 0.7 %), Germany (0.9 %) and France (1.1 %).

Main GDP aggregates

Looking at GDP from the output side, the analysis reveals some shifts in the economic structure of the EU-27 economy over the last ten years (see Table 1.1.3). The comparison of 2000 and 2010 figures shows that the proportion of gross value added accounted for by agriculture (hunting, forestry and fishing) and industry fell, as did the proportion from trade, transport and communication services. In contrast, the proportion of GDP from construction, business activities and financial services, as well as other services rose. This structural change is, at least in part, a result of phenomena such as technological change, developments in relative prices, outsourcing, and globalisation, often resulting in manufacturing activities being moved to lower labour-cost regions, both within and outside the EU. However, the impact of the financial and economic crisis on industry, construction, and trade, transport and communication services was clearly reflected in the sharp decline in of their gross value added in 2009 (see Figure 1.1.4); in fact, gross value added for construction fell in 2008, 2009 and 2010, while for industry it fell in 2008 and 2009.

Among the six activities presented in Table 1.1.3, by 2010 the three largest were all service activities and together contributed close to three quarters (73.6 %) of the EU-27's total gross value added in 2010. Business activities and financial services accounted for 29.0 % of the EU-27's gross value added, followed by other services (largely made-up of public administrations, education and health services, as well as other community, social and personal service activities (23.8 %) and trade, transport and communication services (20.8 %). The smallest contributions came from agriculture, hunting, forestry and fishing (1.7 %) and construction (6.0 %). The relative importance of services was particularly high in Luxembourg, Cyprus, France (2009 data), Greece, Malta, the United Kingdom, Belgium and Denmark, as services accounted for more than three quarters of total value added in each of these Member States.

An analysis of labour productivity per person employed over the same ten-year period (2000 to 2010) shows increases for all activities, ranging from about 20% in trade, transport and communication services as well as business activities and financial services, to 33 % in construction (see Figure 1.1.5). To eliminate the effects of inflation, labour productivity per person can also be calculated using constant price output figures. More detailed data on the development of productivity measured either per person employed or per hour worked show that labour productivity in those Member States that joined the EU in 2004 or 2007 converged towards the EU-27 average during the last decade (see Table 1.1.4). Notably, labour productivity per person employed in Romania increased from 24 % to 48 % of the EU-27 average between 2000 and 2010; Estonia, Lithuania, Slovakia, Latvia and Bulgaria also recorded substantial movements towards the EU-27 average. On the other hand, Italy, recorded a substantial decline in its labour productivity per person in relation to the EU-27 average, as did Belgium and Austria to a lesser extent.

Turning to an analysis of the development of GDP components from the expenditure side it can be noted that final consumption expenditure across the EU-27 rose by 16 % in volume (constant price) terms between 2000 and 2010 (see Figure 1.1.6) while final consumption expenditure of general government rose by 21%. The growth in GDP during the same period was lower (14 %) as overall growth in gross capital formation was just 2.0 % due in large part to a sharp fall in 2009.

In current prices, consumption expenditure by households and non-profit institutions serving households recovered from its fall in 2009 and contributed 58.5 % of the EU-27's GDP in 2010. General government expenditure in the EU-27 continued to expand and accounted for a 22.2 % share of total GDP in 2010. By 2010 gross fixed capital formation, had not recovered from its sharp fall in 2009 and remained only slightly above its 2005 level: it accounted for an 18.5 % share of GDP in 2010. The external balance of goods and services represented 0.8 % of the EU-27's GDP in 2010 (see Figures 1.1.7 and 1.1.8).

Among Member States there was a wide variation in the overall investment intensity (public and private combined) and this may, in part, reflect the different stages of economic development as well as growth dynamics over recent years (see Table 1.1.5 and Figure 1.1.9). In 2010 gross fixed capital formation (total investment) as a share of GDP was 18.5 % in the EU-27 and 19.1 % in the euro area. It was highest in Bulgaria (23.5 %), Romania (22.7 %) and Spain (22.5 %) and lowest in Ireland (11.5 %), the United Kingdom and Greece (both 14.7 %). The vast majority of investment was made by the private sector: in 2010 private investment accounted for 15.9 % of the EU-27's GDP, whereas the equivalent figure for public sector investment was 2.7 %, so that total investment reached 18.5 % of the EU-27's GDP. With 5.6 %and 5.5 %, public investment was highest in Poland and Romania, while private investment was highest in Austria (19.6 %).

An analysis of GDP within the EU-27 from the income side shows that the distribution between the production factors of income resulting from the production process was dominated by the compensation of employees, which was 49.4 % of GDP in 2010. The share of gross operating surplus and mixed income was 38.8 % of GDP while the share of taxes on production and imports less subsidies was 11.8 % (see Figure 1.1.10). The development of the respective aggregates over the past years shows a partial recovery in 2010 from the effects of the global financial and economic crisis (see Figure 1.1.11).

Household consumption

The consumption expenditure of households accounted for at least half of GDP in the majority of Member States in 2010. This share was highest in Greece (75.4 %), Cyprus (74.6 %) (both 2009 data), and Malta (69.5 %). In contrast, it was lowest in Luxembourg (37.2 %, 2009 data) which had, nevertheless, by far the highest average household consumption expenditure per capita (PPS 23 800, 2009 data) (see Table 1.1.6).

More detailed data on the structure of total household consumption expenditure in the EU-27 in 2009 show that nearly a quarter (22.9 %) was devoted to housing, water, electricity, gas and other fuels (see Figure 1.1.12). Transport expenditure (13.2 %) and expenditure on food and non-alcoholic beverages (13.1 %) were the next important expenditure categories. All other consumption expenditure together accounted for about half of the total.

National savings

Gross national saving as a proportion of national disposable income averaged 19.6 % in the euro area (of 13 countries) in 2010 and among the EU Member States reached its highest in Austria (25.0 %) and Romania (24.9 %) and lowest in Greece (4.0 %). Compared with 2000, there was a relative decline in gross national savings for the euro area and most of its members, the exceptions being Germany, Estonia and Austria where savings increased. The most substantial decreases (in percentage point terms) were in Ireland, Portugal, Finland and Greece where savings as a proportion of disposable income fell by 7 percentage points or more, while the largest increases were recorded in Bulgaria and Romania where the proportion increased by 11 points and 9 points respectively.

Sector accounts

Table 1.1.7 shows that the household saving rate in 2010 was 1.4 percentage points higher in the euro area (13.7 %) than in the EU-27 (12.3 %). This gap is mainly explained by the relatively low saving rate of the United Kingdom (6.0 %, 2009 data) and the high rates in Spain (18.1 %, 2009 data) and Germany (17.1 %). Among the Member States within the euro area, eight (including two with data from 2009) had household saving rates above the EU-27 average and seven below, with two (Greece and Malta) not available (see Figure 1.1.14). The highest household savings rate among the EU Member States not in the euro area was recorded in Sweden (13.4 %).

The EU-27 household saving rate decreased in 2010 by 1.4 percentage points, which was fractionally less than the decrease recorded within the euro area (– 1.5 points). The largest increase in savings between 2009 and 2010 was observed in Slovakia (3.5 points), while the largest decrease was in Latvia

(– 6.1 points); changes in the other Member States ranged from a decrease of 2.3 points to an increase of 0.8 points.

In 2010, the household investment rate was 8.1 % in the EU-27. This rate ranged from 5.0 % in the United Kingdom to 10 % or more in Belgium, the Czech Republic, the Netherlands and Finland, with Latvia (3.8 %) and Lithuania (3.2 %) below this range (see Figure 1.1.15). The household investment rate was relatively unchanged in the EU-27 and the euro area in 2010, when compared with the year before: it fell by 1 percentage point or more in six Member States (for which data are available), most notably in Ireland where the reduction was 2.9 percentage points. The household investment rate increased by 1 percentage point or more in Finland and the Czech Republic between 2009 and 2010.

In 2010, the household debt-to-income ratio varied considerably between Member States. While it was close to or below 50 % in Lithuania, Slovenia, Poland and the Czech Republic (2008 data), it exceeded 200 % in Ireland, the Netherlands and Denmark (2009 data): a rate of 200 % indicates that it would take two years of disposable income for households to repay their debt. A comparatively high debt-to-income ratio was recorded in several north western European Member States. In contrast, in central and eastern Europe, the debt-to-income ratio was comparatively low with household debt never greater than annual disposable income. It should be borne in mind that high household debt may to some extent mirror high levels of financial assets, as shown in the analysis of the household net financial wealth-to-income ratio. It may also mirror the ownership of non-financial assets such as dwellings or be impacted by national provisions that foster borrowing (for example, the deduction of interest from taxes).

In 2010, the household debt-to-income ratio increased (compared with 2009) most notably in the Netherlands (7.3 points), Sweden (6.7 points) and Hungary (5.4 points), while it fell most in Ireland (– 3.8 points).

Like the debt-to-income ratio, the household net financial wealth-to-income ratio differed considerably between Member States. The Netherlands and

Belgium recorded ratios around 325 %, the highest among the EU Member States in 2010, and high values were also observed in the United Kingdom (2009 data) and Italy, as well as in Switzerland. Latvia and Slovakia (2008 data) had remarkably low net financial assets-to-income ratios, as did Norway (see Figure 1.1.16).

Figure 1.1.17 shows that in 2010, the business investment rate was 20.0 % in the EU-27. The highest rates among the Member States were recorded in Slovakia, Austria, Spain (2009 data) and Slovenia, all above 25 %; the lowest rate, by far, was recorded in Ireland (8.6 %). The business investment rates of the five largest EU-27 economies diverged quite significantly: in Spain and Italy the rates were clearly above the EU-27 average, while in France, Germany and the United Kingdom they were clearly below the average. The business investment rate fell in nearly all EU Member States (with 2009 and 2010 data available); however, it increased by 3.1 percentage points in Slovakia, by 1.5 points in Italy and by smaller amounts in France and Germany. Overall, the rate fell by 0.3 percentage points in the EU-27 between 2009 and 2010, with particularly large reductions in Ireland and Hungary (4 points or more) – see Table 1.1.8.

The profit share of non-financial corporations was 37.4 % in the EU-27 in 2010. The lowest shares were recorded in France and Slovenia, around 30 %, while profit shares above 50 % were posted in Malta, Ireland, Slovakia, Latvia and Lithuania, as well as in Norway. Profit shares rose in the EU-27 by 1.2 percentage points between 2009 and 2010. Estonia recorded the highest percentage point increase between 2009 and 2010, up by 7.0 points, while Lithuania, Hungary and Sweden all recorded increases of more than 4 points. Slovenia and the Czech Republic were the only Member States (with 2009 and 2010 data available) to experience reductions in their profit shares.

Data sources and availability

The European system of national and regional accounts (ESA) provides the methodology for national accounts in the EU. The current version, ESA95, was fully consistent with worldwide

guidelines for national accounts, the 1993 SNA. Following international agreement on an updated version of the SNA in 2008, a respective update of the ESA is, at the time of writing, close to finalisation.

GDP and main components

The main aggregates of national accounts are compiled from institutional units, namely non-financial or financial corporations, general government, households, and non-profit institutions serving households (NPISH).

Data within the national accounts domain encompasses information on GDP components, employment, final consumption aggregates and savings. Many of these variables are calculated on an annual and on a quarterly basis.

GDP is the central measure of national accounts, which summarises the economic position of a country (or region). It can be calculated using different approaches: the output approach; the expenditure approach; and the income approach.

An analysis of GDP per capita removes the influence of the absolute size of the population, making comparisons between different countries easier. GDP per capita is a broad economic indicator of living standards. GDP data in national currencies can be converted into purchasing power standards (PPS) using purchasing power parities (PPPs) that reflect the purchasing power of each currency, rather than using market exchange rates; in this way differences in price levels between countries are eliminated. The volume index of GDP per capita in PPS is expressed in relation to the EU-27 average (set to equal 100). If the index of a country is higher/lower than 100, this country's level of GDP per head is above/below the EU-27 average; this index is intended for cross-country comparisons rather than temporal comparisons.

The calculation of the annual growth rate of GDP at constant prices, in other words the change of GDP in volume terms, is intended to allow comparisons of the dynamics of economic development both over time and between economies of different sizes, irrespective of price levels.

Complementary data

Economic output can also be analysed by activity: at the most aggregated level of analysis six NACE Rev. 1.1 headings are identified: agriculture, hunting and fishing; industry; construction; trade, transport and communication services; business activities and financial services; and other services. An analysis of output over time can be facilitated by using a volume measure of output – in other words, by deflating the value of output to remove the impact of price changes; each activity is deflated individually to reflect the changes in the prices of its associated products.

A further set of national accounts data is used within the context of competitiveness analyses, namely indicators relating to the productivity of the workforce, such as labour productivity measures. Productivity measures expressed in PPS are particularly useful for cross-country comparisons. GDP in PPS per person employed is intended to give an overall impression of the productivity of national economies. It should be kept in mind, though, that this measure depends on the structure of total employment and may, for instance, be lowered by a shift from full-time to part-time work. GDP in PPS per hour worked gives a clearer picture of productivity as the incidence of part-time employment varies greatly between countries and activities. The data are presented in the form of an index in relation to the EU average: if the index rises above 100, then labour productivity is above the EU average.

Data on consumption expenditure may be broken down according to the classification of individual consumption according to purpose (COICOP), which identifies 12 different headings at its most aggregated level. Annual information on household expenditure is available from national accounts compiled through a macro-economic approach. An alternative source for analysing household expenditure is the Household budget survey (HBS): this information is obtained by asking households to keep a diary of their purchases and is much more detailed in its coverage of goods and services as well as the types of socio-economic breakdown that are made available. HBS is only carried out and

published every five years – the latest reference year currently available is 2005.

Household saving is the main domestic source of funds to finance capital investment. The system of accounts provides for both disposable income and saving to be shown on a gross basis, in other words, with both aggregates including the consumption of fixed capital.

Sector accounts

Sector accounts group together economic subjects with similar behaviour into institutional sectors, such as: households, non-financial corporations, financial corporations and government. Grouping economic subjects in this way greatly helps to understand the functioning of the economy. The behaviour of households and non-financial corporations is particularly relevant in this respect.

The households sector covers individuals or groups of individuals acting as consumers and entrepreneurs provided, in the latter case, that their activities as market producers are not carried out by separate entities. For the purpose of the analysis within this subchapter, this sector has been merged with the relatively small sector of non-profit institutions serving households (for example, associations and charities).

Non-financial corporations cover enterprises whose principal activity is the production of goods and non-financial services to be sold on the market. It includes incorporated enterprises, but also unincorporated enterprises as long as they keep a complete set of accounts and have an economic and financial behaviour which is similar to that of corporations. Small businesses (such as sole traders and entrepreneurs operating on their own) are recorded under the households sector.

Sector accounts record, in principle, every transaction between economic subjects during a certain period and can also be used to show the opening and closing stocks of financial assets and liabilities in financial balance sheets. These transactions are grouped into various categories that have a distinct economic meaning, such as the compensation of employees (comprising wages and salaries, before taxes and social contributions are deducted, and social contributions paid by employers).

In turn, these categories of transactions are shown in a sequence of accounts, each of which covers a specific economic process. This ranges from production, income generation and income (re)distribution, through the use of income, for consumption and saving, and investment, as shown in the capital account, to financial transactions such as borrowing and lending. Each non-financial transaction is recorded as an increase in the resources of a certain sector and an increase in the uses of another sector. For instance, the resources side of the interest transaction category records the amounts of interest receivable by different sectors of the economy, whereas the uses side shows interest payable. For each type of transaction, total resources of all sectors and the rest of the world equal total uses. Each account leads to a meaningful balancing item, the value of which equals total resources minus total uses. Typically, such balancing items, such as GDP or net saving, are important economic indicators; they are carried over to the next account.

The analysis in this subchapter focuses on a selection of indicators from the wealth of sector accounts data. Households' behaviour is described through indicators covering saving and investment rate, as well as debt-to-income and net financial wealth-to-income ratios. The analysis of non-financial corporations is based on the business investment rate and business profit share.

Context

European institutions, governments, central banks as well as other economic and social bodies in the public and private sectors need a set of comparable and reliable statistics on which to base their decisions. National accounts can be used for various types of analysis and evaluation. The use of internationally accepted concepts and definitions permits an analysis of different economies, such as the interdependencies between the economies of the EU Member States, or a comparison between the EU and non-member countries.

Business cycle and macro-economic policy analysis

One of the main uses of national accounts data relates to the need to support European economic policy decisions and the achievement of economic and monetary union (EMU) objectives with high-quality short-term statistics that allow the monitoring of macro-economic developments and the derivation of macro-economic policy advice. For instance, one of the most basic and long-standing uses of national accounts is to quantify the rate of growth of an economy, in simple terms the growth of GDP. Core national accounts figures are notably used to develop and monitor macro-economic policies, while detailed national accounts data can also be used to develop sectoral or industrial policies, particularly through an analysis of input-output tables.

Since the beginning of the EMU in 1999, the European Central Bank (ECB) has been one of the main users of national accounts. The ECB's strategy for assessing the risks to price stability is based on two analytical perspectives, referred to as the 'two pillars': economic analysis and monetary analysis. A large number of monetary and financial indicators are thus evaluated in relation to other relevant data that allow the combination of monetary, financial and economic analysis, for example, key national accounts aggregates and sector accounts. In this way monetary and financial indicators can be analysed within the context of the rest of the economy.

The Directorate-General for Economic and Financial Affairs produces the European Commission's macro-economic forecasts twice a year, in the spring and autumn. These forecasts cover all EU Member States in order to derive forecasts for the euro area and the EU-27, but they also include outlooks for candidate countries, as well as some non-member countries.

The analysis of public finances through national accounts is another well established use of these statistics. Within the EU a specific application was developed in relation to the convergence criteria for EMU, two of which refer directly to public finances. These criteria have been defined in terms of national accounts figures, namely, government deficit and government debt relative to GDP. See the subchapter on government finance statistics for more information.

Regional, structural and sectoral policies

As well as business cycle and macro-economic policy analysis, there are other policy-related uses of European national and regional accounts data, notably concerning regional, structural and sectoral issues.

The allocation of expenditure for the structural funds is partly based on regional accounts. Furthermore, regional statistics are used for ex-post assessment of the results of regional and cohesion policy.

Encouraging more growth and more jobs is a strategic priority for both the EU and the Member States, and is part of the Europe 2020 strategy. In support of these strategic priorities, common policies are implemented across all sectors of the EU economy while the Member States implement their own national structural reforms. To ensure that this is as beneficial as possible, and to prepare for the challenges that lie ahead, the European Commission analyses these policies.

The European Commission conducts economic analysis contributing to the development of the common agricultural policy (CAP) by analysing the efficiency of its various support mechanisms and developing a long-term perspective. This includes research, analysis and impact assessments on topics related to agriculture and the rural economy in the EU and non-member countries, in part using the economic accounts for agriculture.

Target setting, benchmarking and contributions

Policies within the EU are increasingly setting medium or long-term targets, whether binding or not. For some of these, the level of GDP is used as a benchmark denominator, for example, setting a target for expenditure on research and development at a level of 3 % of GDP.

National accounts are also used to determine EU resources, with the basic rules laid down in a Council Decision. The overall amount of own resources

needed to finance the EU budget is determined by total expenditure less other revenue, and the maximum size of the own resources are linked to the gross national income of the EU.

As well as being used to determine budgetary contributions within the EU, national accounts data are also used to determine contributions to other international organisations, such as the United Nations (UN). Contributions to the UN budget are based on gross national income along with a variety of adjustments and limits.

Analysts and forecasters

National accounts are also widely used by analysts and researchers to examine the economic situation and developments. Financial institutions' interest in national accounts may range from a broad analysis of the economy to specific information concerning savings, investment or debt among households, non-financial corporations or other institutional sectors. Social partners, such as representatives of businesses (for example, trade associations) or representatives of workers (for example, trade unions), also have an interest in national accounts for the purpose of analysing developments that affect industrial relations. Among other uses, researchers and analysts use national accounts for business cycle analysis and analysing long-term economic cycles and relating these to economic, political or technological developments.

Figure 1.1.1: GDP at current market prices, 2000-2010
(EUR 1 000 million)

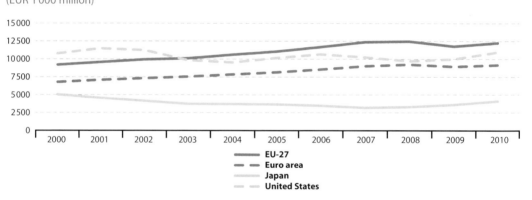

Source: Eurostat (online data codes: nama_gdp_c or tec00001)

Table 1.1.1: GDP at current market prices, 2000, 2009 and 2010

	GDP						GDP per capita			
	(EUR 1 000 million)			(PPS 1 000 million)			(PPS, EU-27 = 100)			(PPS)
	2000	2009	2010	2000	2009	2010	2000	2009	2010	2010
EU-27	9 208	11 770	12 268	9 208	11 770	12 268	100	100	100	24 500
Euro area	6 789	8 953	9 191	6 715	8 435	8 760	112	109	108	26 400
Belgium	252	339	353	246	295	314	126	116	118	28 900
Bulgaria	14	35	36	44	79	80	28	44	43	10 600
Czech Republic	61	137	145	134	202	205	68	82	80	19 500
Denmark	174	222	234	134	157	169	132	121	124	30 400
Germany	2 063	2 397	2 499	1 855	2 241	2 369	118	116	118	29 000
Estonia	6	14	15	12	20	21	45	64	65	15 900
Ireland	106	161	156	96	134	139	132	127	127	31 100
Greece	*138*	*235*	*230*	*175*	*249*	*246*	*84*	*94*	*89*	*21 700*
Spain	630	1 054	1 063	747	1 116	1 140	97	103	101	24 700
France	1 440	1 889	1 933	1 333	1 622	1 692	115	107	107	26 100
Italy	1 191	1 520	1 549	1 268	1 470	1 472	117	104	100	24 300
Cyprus	10	17	17	12	19	19	89	98	98	24 000
Latvia	8	19	18	17	27	28	37	52	52	12 600
Lithuania	12	27	27	26	43	47	39	55	58	14 200
Luxembourg	22	38	42	20	32	35	245	272	283	69 100
Hungary	51	93	98	108	153	157	55	65	64	15 700
Malta	4	6	6	6	8	8	84	81	83	20 400
Netherlands	418	572	591	407	508	544	134	131	134	32 800
Austria	208	274	284	200	245	257	131	124	125	30 700
Poland	186	310	354	352	544	583	48	61	62	15 300
Portugal	127	169	173	158	201	210	81	80	81	19 800
Romania	41	117	122	111	233	236	26	46	45	11 000
Slovenia	22	35	36	30	42	44	80	88	87	21 200
Slovakia	22	63	66	52	93	98	50	73	74	18 100
Finland	132	173	180	116	143	152	117	114	116	28 300
Sweden	268	291	347	216	260	282	128	119	123	30 100
United Kingdom	1 602	1 566	1 697	1 335	1 636	1 723	119	113	114	27 800
Iceland	9	9	10	7	9	9	132	117	110	*26 800*
Liechtenstein	3	3	:	:	:	:	:	:	:	:
Norway	183	267	312	141	198	214	165	175	179	43 700
Switzerland	271	355	396	198	264	279	144	144	147	35 800
Croatia	23	*46*	*46*	42	*67*	*67*	50	*64*	*61*	*15 000*
FYR of Macedonia	4	7	*7*	10	17	*18*	27	36	35	*8 600*
Turkey	290	440	554	512	770	861	42	45	48	11 800
Japan	5 057	3 613	4 122	2 827	3 094	*3 318*	117	103	107	*26 000*
United States	10 775	9 994	10 958	8 655	10 502	*11 204*	161	145	149	*36 500*

Source: Eurostat (online data codes: nama_gdp_c and tec00001)

Figure 1.1.2: GDP per capita at current market prices, 2000 and 2010
(EU-27 = 100; based on PPS per inhabitant)

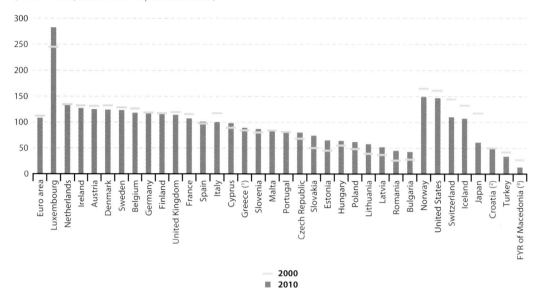

_2000_
_2010_

(¹) Provisional.
(²) 2010, provisional.
(³) Forecast.

Source: Eurostat (online data codes: nama_gdp_c and tec00001)

Figure 1.1.3: Real GDP growth, 2000-2010
(% change compared with the previous year)

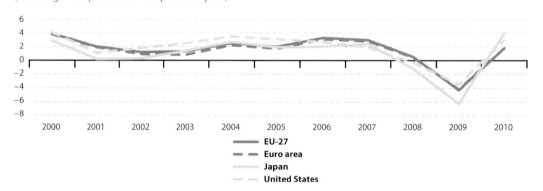

_____ EU-27
_ _ _ Euro area
_____ Japan
_ _ _ United States

Source: Eurostat (online data codes: nama_gdp_c or tsieb020)

Table 1.1.2: Real GDP growth, 2001-2010
(% change compared with the previous year; average 2001-2010)

	2001	2002	2003	2004	2005	2006	2007	2008	2009	2010	Average 2001-10
EU-27	2.0	1.2	1.3	2.5	2.0	3.3	3.0	0.5	−4.3	1.8	1.3
Euro area	1.9	0.9	0.8	2.2	1.7	3.1	2.8	0.4	−4.2	1.8	1.1
Belgium	0.8	1.4	0.8	3.2	1.7	2.7	2.9	1.0	−2.8	2.2	1.4
Bulgaria	4.2	4.7	5.5	6.7	6.4	6.5	6.4	6.2	−5.5	0.2	4.1
Czech Republic	2.5	1.9	3.6	4.5	6.3	6.8	6.1	2.5	−4.1	2.3	3.2
Denmark	0.7	0.5	0.4	2.3	2.4	3.4	1.6	−1.1	−5.2	1.7	0.7
Germany	1.2	0.0	−0.2	1.2	0.8	3.4	2.7	1.0	−4.7	3.6	0.9
Estonia	7.5	7.9	7.6	7.2	9.4	10.6	6.9	−5.1	−13.9	3.1	4.1
Ireland	4.8	5.9	4.2	4.5	5.3	5.3	5.2	−3.0	−7.0	−0.4	2.5
Greece	4.2	3.4	5.9	4.4	2.3	5.2	4.3	1.0	−2.0	−4.5	2.4
Spain	3.6	2.7	3.1	3.3	3.6	4.0	3.6	0.9	−3.7	−0.1	2.1
France	1.8	0.9	0.9	2.5	1.8	2.5	2.3	−0.1	−2.7	1.5	1.1
Italy	1.8	0.5	0.0	1.5	0.7	2.0	1.5	−1.3	−5.2	1.3	0.3
Cyprus	4.0	2.1	1.9	4.2	3.9	4.1	5.1	3.6	−1.7	1.0	2.8
Latvia	8.0	6.5	7.2	8.7	10.6	12.2	10.0	−4.2	−18.0	−0.3	4.1
Lithuania	6.7	6.9	10.2	7.4	7.8	7.8	9.8	2.9	−14.7	1.3	4.6
Luxembourg	2.5	4.1	1.5	4.4	5.4	5.0	6.6	1.4	−3.6	3.5	3.1
Hungary	3.8	4.1	4.0	4.5	3.2	3.6	0.8	0.8	−6.7	1.2	1.9
Malta	−1.6	2.6	−0.3	1.8	4.2	1.9	4.6	5.4	−3.3	3.2	1.9
Netherlands	1.9	0.1	0.3	2.2	2.0	3.4	3.9	1.9	−3.9	1.8	1.4
Austria	0.5	1.6	0.8	2.5	2.5	3.6	3.7	2.2	−3.9	2.1	1.6
Poland	1.2	1.4	3.9	5.3	3.6	6.2	6.8	5.1	1.6	3.8	3.9
Portugal	2.0	0.7	−0.9	1.6	0.8	1.4	2.4	0.0	−2.5	1.3	0.7
Romania	5.7	5.1	5.2	8.5	4.2	7.9	6.3	7.3	−7.1	−1.3	4.2
Slovenia	2.9	3.8	2.9	4.4	4.0	5.8	6.8	3.7	−8.1	1.2	2.7
Slovakia	3.5	4.6	4.8	5.1	6.7	8.5	10.5	5.8	−4.8	4.0	4.9
Finland	2.3	1.8	2.0	4.1	2.9	4.4	5.3	1.0	−8.2	3.6	1.9
Sweden	1.3	2.5	2.3	4.2	3.2	4.3	3.3	−0.6	−5.3	5.7	2.1
United Kingdom	2.5	2.1	2.8	3.0	2.2	2.8	2.7	−0.1	−4.9	1.4	1.5
Iceland	3.9	0.1	2.4	7.7	7.5	4.6	6.0	1.4	−6.9	−3.5	2.3
Norway	2.0	1.5	1.0	3.9	2.7	2.3	2.7	0.7	−1.7	0.3	1.5
Switzerland	1.2	0.4	−0.2	2.5	2.6	3.6	3.6	2.1	−1.9	2.6	1.7
Montenegro	1.1	1.9	2.4	4.4	14.7	8.6	10.6	6.9	−5.7	2.5	4.7
Croatia	3.7	4.9	5.4	4.1	4.3	4.9	5.1	2.2	−6.0	−1.2	2.7
FYR of Macedonia	−4.5	0.9	2.8	4.6	4.4	5.0	6.1	5.0	−0.9	0.7	2.4
Turkey	−5.7	6.6	4.9	9.4	8.4	6.9	4.7	0.4	−4.5	8.9	4.0
Japan	0.2	0.3	1.4	2.7	1.9	2.0	2.4	−1.2	−6.3	4.0	0.7
United States	1.1	1.8	2.5	3.5	3.1	2.7	1.9	−0.3	−3.5	3.0	1.6

Source: Eurostat (online data codes: nama_gdp_k or tsieb020)

Figure 1.1.4: Gross value added, EU-27, 2000-2010
(2000 = 100)

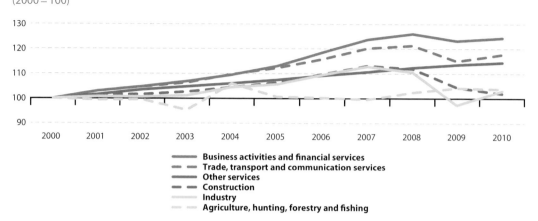

Legend:
- Business activities and financial services
- Trade, transport and communication services
- Other services
- Construction
- Industry
- Agriculture, hunting, forestry and fishing

Source: Eurostat (online data code: nama_nace06_k)

Table 1.1.3: Gross value added at basic prices, 2000 and 2010
(% share of total gross value added)

	Agriculture, hunting, forestry & fishing		Industry		Construction		Trade, transport & communication services		Business activities & financial services		Other services	
	2000	2010	2000	2010	2000	2010	2000	2010	2000	2010	2000	2010
EU-27	2.3	1.7	22.4	18.8	5.6	6.0	21.5	20.8	26.2	29.0	22.0	23.8
Euro area	2.4	1.7	22.2	18.6	5.6	5.9	21.0	20.5	26.6	29.3	22.1	24.0
Belgium	1.4	0.7	22.1	16.6	5.0	5.3	21.2	21.8	27.8	30.3	22.5	25.3
Bulgaria	13.6	5.3	21.3	23.2	4.6	8.1	23.5	23.6	19.3	23.6	17.7	16.3
Czech Republic	3.9	2.4	31.6	30.5	6.5	7.2	25.8	24.0	16.2	18.4	16.0	17.5
Denmark	2.6	1.2	21.3	17.8	5.5	4.3	21.8	20.7	22.3	26.8	26.4	29.3
Germany	1.3	0.9	25.1	23.7	5.2	4.1	18.2	17.2	27.5	30.5	22.8	23.6
Estonia	4.8	3.5	22.0	22.7	5.6	5.7	28.3	25.2	22.4	23.8	17.0	19.1
Ireland	3.2	1.0	34.3	26.3	7.5	5.6	17.9	17.2	21.3	27.2	15.8	22.8
Greece	6.6	3.3	13.9	13.8	7.0	4.1	30.1	33.3	20.6	20.5	21.7	25.1
Spain	4.4	2.7	20.9	15.6	8.3	10.1	26.1	25.3	19.5	22.8	20.8	23.5
France (¹)	2.8	1.8	17.8	12.5	5.2	6.5	18.9	19.2	30.7	34.1	24.8	27.0
Italy	2.8	1.9	23.4	19.4	5.0	6.0	23.9	22.2	24.7	28.4	20.1	22.2
Cyprus	3.6	2.3	12.2	9.2	6.8	7.2	31.2	25.5	23.8	29.9	22.3	25.9
Latvia	4.6	4.1	17.4	16.8	6.2	5.0	32.0	30.2	18.9	23.6	20.9	20.2
Lithuania	6.3	3.4	23.8	22.3	6.0	5.7	30.2	33.5	12.5	16.1	21.2	19.1
Luxembourg	0.7	0.3	12.6	8.1	5.7	4.9	21.8	22.1	43.8	48.4	15.4	16.2
Hungary	5.4	3.5	26.6	26.8	5.0	4.0	20.1	20.4	20.9	23.3	22.0	22.1
Malta	2.3	1.9	24.4	15.8	4.1	3.5	30.2	23.6	18.5	24.9	20.4	30.3
Netherlands	2.6	1.9	19.3	18.4	5.6	5.3	23.1	20.5	27.3	27.7	22.1	26.1
Austria	2.0	1.5	23.3	22.3	7.5	6.9	24.6	23.3	21.5	24.1	21.1	21.9
Poland	5.0	3.5	24.0	24.6	7.7	7.1	27.3	27.5	18.1	18.2	18.0	19.2
Portugal	3.7	2.4	20.4	17.0	7.6	6.0	25.3	25.5	20.3	23.1	22.7	26.0
Romania	12.1	6.7	29.0	29.7	5.4	10.0	23.8	23.8	16.4	15.7	13.4	14.1
Slovenia	3.3	2.4	29.0	24.3	6.7	6.7	20.4	22.2	20.2	23.4	20.0	21.3
Slovakia	4.5	3.8	29.1	25.8	7.0	9.0	25.2	24.2	17.1	19.1	17.0	18.0
Finland	3.5	2.9	28.4	22.3	6.2	6.6	20.2	19.8	20.9	24.1	20.7	24.2
Sweden	2.1	1.9	24.5	21.1	4.3	5.5	18.9	19.6	24.9	24.6	25.3	27.4
United Kingdom	1.0	0.7	22.0	15.7	5.3	6.1	22.9	20.6	27.0	33.7	21.8	23.2
Iceland (¹)	9.0	7.1	17.3	20.3	8.6	5.0	21.8	18.4	19.7	25.7	23.6	23.7
Norway	2.1	1.6	37.8	35.7	4.1	4.9	18.8	15.3	16.9	19.7	20.3	22.8
Switzerland	1.6	1.1	21.8	21.0	5.5	5.7	21.4	22.0	24.0	23.6	25.7	26.5
Croatia	6.5	5.5	23.4	19.0	5.1	6.7	23.7	22.8	19.4	27.3	21.9	18.7
FYR of Macedonia (¹)	12.0	11.2	26.9	21.5	6.8	5.9	25.4	25.3	10.2	15.7	18.6	20.4
Turkey	10.8	9.4	24.6	21.5	5.4	4.6	29.1	30.1	19.5	22.2	10.6	12.3

(¹) 2009 instead of 2010.

Source: Eurostat (online data codes: nama_nace06_c or tec00003, tec00004, tec00005, tec00006, tec00007 and tec00008)

Figure 1.1.5: Labour productivity, EU-27, 2000 and 2010
(EUR 1 000 per person employed)

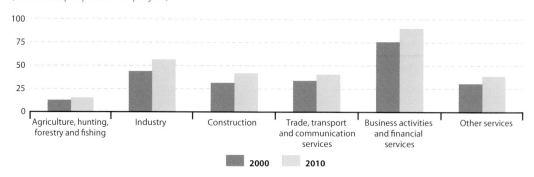

Source: Eurostat (online data codes: nama_nace06_c and nama_nace06_e)

Table 1.1.4: Labour productivity (based on PPS), 2000-2010 (^{1})

	Per person employed (EU-27 = 100)						Per hour worked (EU-27 = 100)					
	2000	2002	2004	2006	2008	2010	2000	2002	2004	2006	2008	2010
EU-27	100	100	100	100	100	100	100	100	100	100	100	100
Euro area	112	111	109	109	109	109	117	115	113	114	114	114
Belgium	138	137	133	129	126	128	152	146	144	138	134	:
Bulgaria	31	34	35	37	40	42	33	35	35	37	40	42
Czech Republic	62	63	68	70	73	72	52	55	59	59	62	62
Denmark	111	109	109	107	104	109	122	118	118	115	113	118
Germany	107	106	108	109	107	105	124	124	126	128	126	124
Estonia	47	51	58	63	65	70	41	44	49	52	55	62
Ireland	130	135	137	137	129	137	113	119	122	121	117	125
Greece	94	100	101	99	100	96	76	80	82	77	79	75
Spain	104	105	103	103	105	110	103	103	102	104	106	:
France	126	126	121	121	120	120	135	138	130	132	128	:
Italy	127	118	113	111	112	108	116	109	104	102	104	101
Cyprus	86	85	83	84	89	89	76	74	74	76	80	81
Latvia	40	43	46	49	52	55	31	34	37	39	43	47
Lithuania	43	48	54	57	62	63	40	45	50	51	54	55
Luxembourg	177	164	171	180	179	178	:	172	181	193	191	:
Hungary	58	65	68	68	72	71	49	55	57	57	60	60
Malta	97	93	91	90	91	93	85	82	80	81	81	:
Netherlands	115	114	113	115	115	115	137	136	135	137	139	138
Austria	121	118	118	117	115	113	120	115	116	115	115	115
Poland	56	59	62	61	62	67	46	48	50	49	50	54
Portugal	72	71	70	73	73	77	62	61	60	63	64	65
Romania	24	30	35	40	49	48	22	27	32	36	44	42
Slovenia	76	78	82	84	84	81	76	76	79	84	84	80
Slovakia	58	63	66	72	80	83	55	61	64	69	75	78
Finland	116	112	114	111	113	114	113	109	111	108	111	111
Sweden	115	109	116	113	114	113	120	115	121	118	117	116
United Kingdom	111	113	114	113	109	108	111	112	115	113	110	:
Iceland	104	105	108	99	100	93	:	:	:	:	:	:
Norway	140	132	143	158	157	149	164	157	170	186	184	175
Switzerland	111	107	105	105	110	111	113	111	106	107	113	:
Croatia	62	67	71	74	79	79	:	:	:	:	:	:
FYR of Macedonia	49	47	53	57	59	58	:	:	:	:	:	:
Turkey	54	49	54	62	65	62	:	:	:	:	:	:
Japan	99	99	100	98	96	96	:	:	:	:	:	:
United States	143	141	144	141	138	144	132	131	135	133	131	:

(^{1}) 2005, break in series.

Source: Eurostat (online data codes: tsieb030 and tsieb040), OECD

Figure 1.1.6: Consumption expenditure and gross capital formation at constant prices, EU-27, 2000-2010
(2000 = 100)

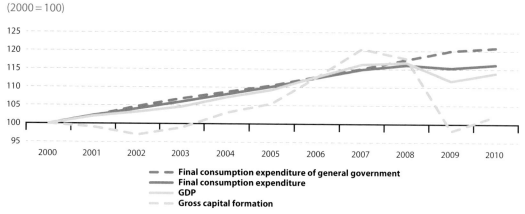

Source: Eurostat (online data code: nama_gdp_k)

Figure 1.1.7: Expenditure components of GDP, EU-27, 2000-2010
(EUR 1 000 million)

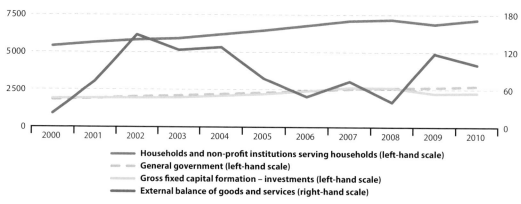

Source: Eurostat (online data codes: nama_gdp_c or tec00009, tec00010, tec00011 and tec00110)

Figure 1.1.8: Expenditure components of GDP, EU-27, 2010
(% share of GDP)

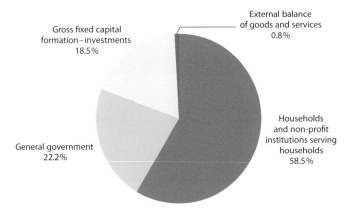

External balance
of goods and services
0.8%

Gross fixed capital
formation – investments
18.5%

Households
and non-profit
institutions serving
households
58.5%

General government
22.2%

Source: Eurostat (online data codes: nama_gdp_c or tec00009, tec00010, tec00011 and tec00110)

Table 1.1.5: Investment, 2000, 2005 and 2010
(% share of GDP)

	Total investment			Public investment			Business investment		
	2000	2005	2010	2000	2005	2010	2000	2005	2010
EU-27	20.6	19.9	18.5	2.3	2.2	2.7	18.4	17.8	15.9
Euro area	21.4	20.6	19.1	2.5	2.5	2.5	19.0	18.3	16.7
Belgium	21.1	20.6	20.3	2.0	1.7	1.7	19.1	19.0	18.6
Bulgaria	15.8	25.7	23.5	3.6	3.4	4.6	12.2	22.3	18.9
Czech Republic	28.0	24.9	21.3	3.6	4.9	4.6	24.4	20.0	16.4
Denmark	20.2	19.5	16.6	1.7	1.8	2.2	18.5	17.7	14.1
Germany	21.5	17.3	17.5	1.8	1.3	1.6	19.8	16.2	16.5
Estonia	25.7	32.1	18.6	3.7	4.0	3.6	22.0	28.1	15.0
Ireland	23.1	26.6	11.5	3.4	3.5	3.9	19.6	23.0	7.4
Greece	21.6	20.0	14.7	3.6	2.8	2.8	17.9	17.1	11.9
Spain	25.8	29.4	22.5	3.2	3.6	3.7	22.7	25.8	18.8
France	18.9	19.3	19.3	3.1	3.3	3.0	16.4	16.8	17.2
Italy	20.3	20.7	19.5	2.3	2.4	2.1	18.0	18.4	17.4
Cyprus	17.0	19.3	18.4	2.9	3.1	3.6	14.0	16.1	14.8
Latvia	24.2	30.6	18.0	1.3	3.1	3.6	22.9	27.5	14.4
Lithuania	18.8	22.8	16.1	2.4	3.4	4.6	16.4	19.3	11.5
Luxembourg	20.8	20.5	16.4	3.8	4.5	4.1	17.0	16.0	12.4
Hungary	23.4	23.1	19.3	3.2	4.0	3.2	20.2	19.1	16.1
Malta	22.9	21.7	16.7	3.9	4.7	2.1	18.8	17.0	14.2
Netherlands	21.9	18.9	17.7	3.1	3.3	3.7	18.8	15.6	14.0
Austria	24.0	21.7	20.8	1.6	1.2	1.2	22.4	20.5	19.6
Poland	23.7	18.2	19.7	2.4	3.4	5.6	21.4	14.8	13.9
Portugal	27.7	23.0	19.0	3.7	3.0	3.3	24.1	20.0	15.7
Romania	18.8	23.7	22.7	3.4	3.9	5.5	15.4	19.9	17.2
Slovenia	26.2	25.4	21.6	3.2	3.2	4.3	22.3	22.3	18.3
Slovakia	25.8	26.5	20.3	2.8	2.1	2.6	23.8	24.9	17.7
Finland	20.0	20.1	18.8	2.4	2.5	2.7	17.6	17.5	15.8
Sweden	18.0	17.9	17.9	2.8	3.0	3.5	15.2	14.9	14.3
United Kingdom	17.1	16.7	14.7	1.2	0.7	2.5	15.9	16.0	12.1
Iceland	22.9	28.4	12.9	4.1	3.1	2.6	18.8	25.3	10.3
Norway	18.4	18.8	20.3	2.6	2.7	3.2	15.8	16.1	16.6
Switzerland (¹)	22.7	21.2	20.9	2.7	2.2	2.0	19.9	19.0	18.2
Croatia	19.0	24.7	21.6	:	:	:	:	:	:
FYR of Macedonia	16.2	16.6	18.8	:	:	:	:	:	:
Turkey	20.4	21.0	18.7	:	:	:	:	:	:
Japan	25.2	23.3	20.5	:	:	:	:	:	:
United States	20.3	19.9	15.4	:	:	:	:	:	:

(¹) 2009 instead of 2010.

Source: Eurostat (online data codes: nama_gdp_c, tsdec210, tec00022 and tsier140)

Figure 1.1.9: Gross fixed capital formation, 2010
(% share of GDP)

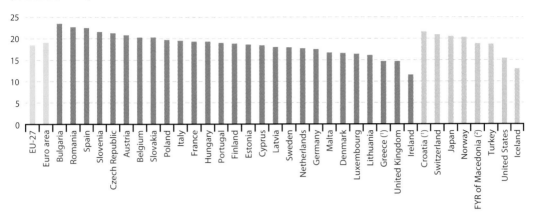

(¹) Provisional.
(²) Forecast.

Source: Eurostat (online data code: nama_gdp_c)

Figure 1.1.10: Distribution of income, 2010
(% share of GDP)

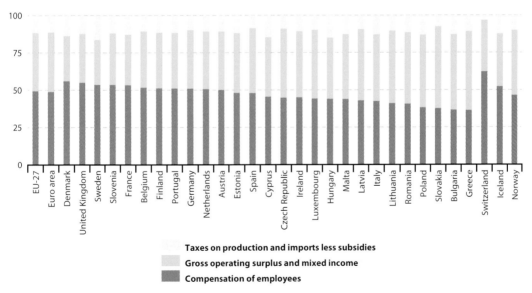

Taxes on production and imports less subsidies

Gross operating surplus and mixed income

Compensation of employees

Source: Eurostat (online data codes: nama_gdp_c or tec00016, tec00015 and tec00013)

Figure 1.1.11: Distribution of income, EU-27, 2000-2010
(2000 = 100)

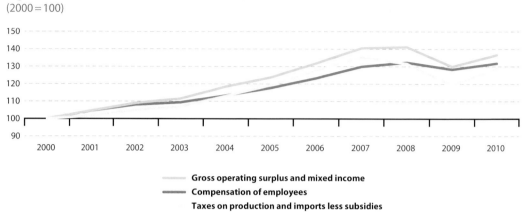

Gross operating surplus and mixed income
Compensation of employees
Taxes on production and imports less subsidies

Source: Eurostat (online data codes: nama_gdp_c or tec00016, tec00015 and tec00013)

Table 1.1.6: Consumption expenditure of households (domestic concept), 2000, 2005 and 2010

	As a proportion of GDP (%)			Per capita (PPS)		
	2000	2005	2010	2000	2005 (¹)	2010 (²)
Belgium (³)	51.8	49.7	50.7	12400	13400	13900
Bulgaria	71.3	69.5	:	3900	5700	:
Czech Republic (³)	54.5	50.8	51.9	7100	8700	10000
Denmark	47.0	47.6	48.1	11800	13200	13700
Germany (³)	56.2	56.5	56.4	12600	14700	15300
Estonia (³)	60.0	58.4	52.9	5100	8100	7900
Ireland	47.1	43.7	46.5	11900	14200	13900
Greece (³)	*75.7*	*75.5*	*75.4*	*12100*	*15500*	*16600*
Spain (³)	63.1	60.1	58.3	11700	13800	14200
France	55.1	55.6	56.4	12100	13800	14200
Italy (³)	61.1	59.7	60.4	13600	14100	14800
Cyprus (³)	83.4	75.8	74.6	14100	15500	17300
Latvia (³)	60.7	60.3	60.3	4200	6600	7300
Lithuania (³)	65.6	65.3	67.9	4900	7800	8700
Luxembourg (³)	46.6	41.6	37.2	21700	23800	23800
Hungary (³)	56.4	55.3	53.4	5900	7800	8200
Malta	76.5	75.1	69.5	12200	13300	13200
Netherlands	49.2	47.7	44.8	12600	14000	13800
Austria (³)	55.8	56.0	55.4	14000	15600	16200
Poland (³)	63.8	62.7	60.6	5900	7200	8600
Portugal	64.6	65.5	:	10000	11700	:
Romania (³)	67.5	68.5	61.1	3300	5400	6600
Slovenia	59.2	57.1	58.5	9000	11200	12100
Slovakia (³)	56.1	56.4	59.6	5400	7600	10300
Finland	47.7	49.4	51.6	10600	12700	13900
Sweden	47.0	46.5	48.3	11400	12700	13500
United Kingdom	62.4	61.6	62.0	14200	16900	16400
Iceland	55.6	53.9	48.8	13900	15800	13500
Norway	40.9	39.5	40.3	12800	15600	16600
Switzerland (³)	58.8	58.3	56.8	16200	17300	19200
FYR of Macedonia (³)	76.9	78.7	78.5	3900	5200	6600
Turkey	74.9	75.6	75.0	6000	7200	8000

(¹) 2005, break in series.
(²) Slovenia, break in series.
(³) 2009 instead of 2010 data.

Source: Eurostat (online data code: nama_fcs_c)

Figure 1.1.12: Consumption expenditure of households, EU-27, 2009
(% of total household consumption expenditure)

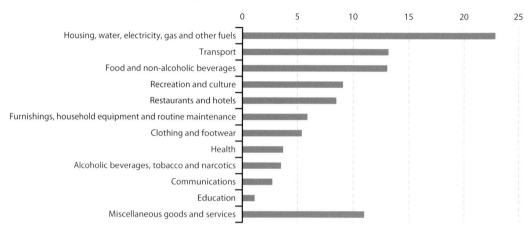

Source: Eurostat (online data code: nama_co3_c)

Figure 1.1.13: Gross national savings, 2000 and 2010 (¹)
(% of gross national disposable income)

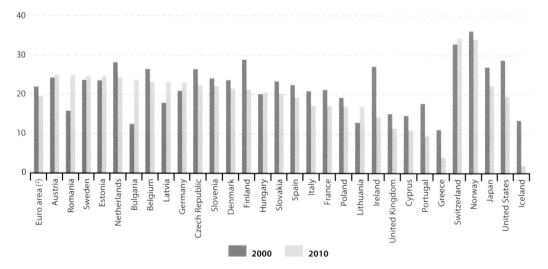

(¹) EU-27, Luxembourg and Malta, not available.
(²) EA-13 instead of EA-17.

Source: Eurostat (online data code: nama_inc_c)

Table 1.1.7: Key ratios of sector accounts, households, 2010 (¹)

	Saving rate (²)	Investment rate (²)	Debt-to-income ratio (³)	Net financial wealth-to-income ratio (⁴)	Saving rate	Investment rate	Debt-to-income ratio	Net financial wealth-to-income ratio
	(%)				Change from 2009 (percentage points)			
EU-27	12.3	8.1	:	:	−1.4	−0.1	:	:
Euro area	13.7	8.8	99.3	197.5	−1.5	0.0	1.8	5.2
Belgium	16.2	10.0	84.2	324.4	−2.3	0.0	4.0	14.9
Bulgaria	:	:	:	:	:	:	:	:
Czech Republic	10.3	10.2	49.1	86.3	−0.4	1.4	:	:
Denmark	7.7	9.7	275.1	151.7	:	:	:	:
Germany	17.1	8.5	88.9	180.7	0.0	0.2	−2.0	7.8
Estonia	9.6	7.6	:	:	−2.0	0.2	:	:
Ireland	13.4	5.7	202.6	128.0	−1.4	−2.9	−3.8	25.6
Greece	:	:	:	:	:	:	:	:
Spain	18.1	9.2	124.6	113.1	:	:	:	:
France	15.6	9.0	78.3	191.8	−0.5	−0.1	:	:
Italy	12.1	8.9	65.9	256.1	−1.4	0.3	2.5	−8.6
Cyprus	11.6	9.6	:	176.6	0.2	−1.9	:	−14.8
Latvia	4.2	3.8	74.3	16.7	−6.1	−1.4	−0.8	2.0
Lithuania	7.9	3.2	43.6	56.9	0.8	−1.7	−1.2	4.0
Luxembourg	13.6	9.8	131.0	202.3	:	:	:	:
Hungary	8.2	6.9	68.4	115.4	−1.8	−1.6	5.4	5.8
Malta	:	:	:	:	:	:	:	:
Netherlands	10.9	10.8	249.5	325.4	−2.0	−0.7	7.3	32.9
Austria	13.5	7.4	90.1	190.9	−2.2	−0.2	2.6	3.9
Poland	9.9	7.5	47.6	63.3	:	:	:	:
Portugal	9.8	6.5	128.6	165.9	−1.0	−0.2	−1.2	−2.3
Romania	:	:	:	:	:	:	:	:
Slovenia	15.7	6.6	46.7	124.3	0.7	−1.3	2.3	3.4
Slovakia	11.3	7.3	51.2	18.9	3.5	−0.8	:	:
Finland	11.3	11.4	102.1	106.0	−0.6	1.1	2.3	6.5
Sweden	13.4	5.1	146.5	203.5	−2.2	0.4	6.7	18.7
United Kingdom	6.0	5.0	149.0	265.7	:	:	:	:
Norway	12.4	8.2	178.1	26.3	0.0	−0.3	1.1	1.4
Switzerland	17.1	6.7	168.5	293.0	:	:	:	:

(¹) Including non-profit institutions serving households.
(²) Denmark, Spain, Luxembourg, Poland, the United Kingdom and Switzerland, 2009.
(³) Denmark, Spain, France, Luxembourg, Poland, Slovakia and the United Kingdom, 2009; Czech Republic and Switzerland, 2008.
(⁴) Denmark, Spain, France, Luxembourg, Poland and the United Kingdom, 2009; Czech Republic, Slovakia and Switzerland, 2008.

Source: Eurostat (online data code: nasa_ki)

Figure 1.1.14: Household saving rate (gross), 2010 (¹)
(%)

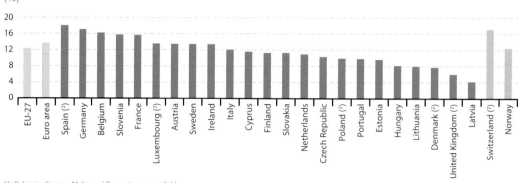

(¹) Bulgaria, Greece, Malta and Romania, not available.
(²) 2009.

Source: Eurostat (online data code: nasa_ki)

Figure 1.1.15: Household investment rate (gross), 2010 (¹)
(%)

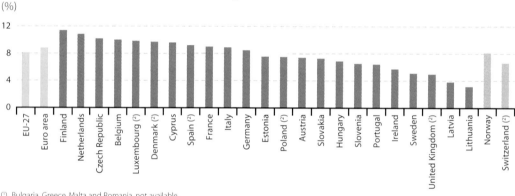

(¹) Bulgaria, Greece, Malta and Romania, not available.
(²) 2009.

Source: Eurostat (online data code: nasa_ki)

Figure 1.1.16: Household net financial wealth-to-income ratio, 2010 (¹)
(%)

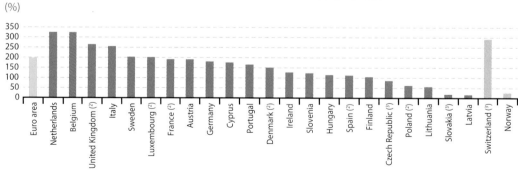

(¹) EU-27, Bulgaria, Estonia, Greece, Malta and Romania, not available.
(²) 2009.
(³) 2008.

Source: Eurostat (online data code: nasa_ki)

Table 1.1.8: Key ratios of sector accounts, non-financial corporations, 2010

	Investment rate	Profit share	Investment rate	Profit share
	(%)		Change from 2009 (percentage points)	
EU-27	20.0	37.4	−0.3	1.2
Euro area	20.6	38.6	0.1	1.3
Belgium	21.4	37.7	−0.7	1.5
Bulgaria	:	:	:	:
Czech Republic	24.6	47.1	−0.8	−0.6
Denmark (¹)	22.2	31.2	:	:
Germany	17.8	41.3	0.4	1.6
Estonia	17.8	45.2	−1.7	7.0
Ireland	8.6	51.2	−4.7	3.3
Greece	:	:	:	:
Spain (¹)	26.0	36.6	:	:
France	18.7	30.2	0.2	0.9
Italy	23.8	41.5	1.5	0.5
Cyprus	17.3	43.8	−0.6	0.8
Latvia	21.3	52.3	−1.3	3.6
Lithuania	14.9	56.1	−0.8	4.7
Luxembourg (¹)	19.7	42.5	:	:
Hungary	20.0	45.1	−4.0	4.7
Malta	:	51.1	:	1.4
Netherlands	15.7	38.6	−0.1	0.9
Austria	27.3	41.0	−0.1	1.5
Poland (¹)	23.8	49.5	:	:
Portugal	20.9	34.2	−3.3	0.7
Romania	:	:	:	:
Slovenia	25.1	30.4	−1.1	−1.1
Slovakia	31.1	51.6	3.1	2.1
Finland	17.1	39.7	−2.3	1.8
Sweden	19.2	33.1	−0.8	4.5
United Kingdom (¹)	14.9	32.4	:	:
Norway	22.5	52.6	−1.9	2.2
Switzerland (¹)	21.0	33.6	:	:

(¹) 2009.

Source: Eurostat (online data code: nasa_ki)

Figure 1.1.17: Investment rate (gross) of non-financial corporations, 2010 (¹)
(%)

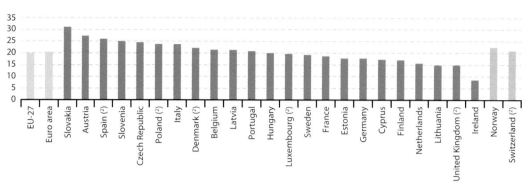

(¹) Bulgaria, Greece, Malta and Romania, not available.
(²) 2009.

Source: Eurostat (online data code: nasa_ki)

1.2 Government finances

This subchapter examines how key government finance indicators have evolved in the European Union (EU) and the euro area (EA-17). Specifically, it considers public (general government) deficits, general government gross debt, revenue and expenditure of general government, as well as taxes and social contributions, which are the main sources of government revenue.

These statistics are crucial indicators for determining the health of a Member State's economy and under the terms of the EU's stability and growth pact (SGP), Member States pledged to keep their deficits and debt below certain limits: a Member State's government deficit may not exceed – 3 % of its gross domestic product (GDP), while its debt may not exceed 60 % of GDP. If a Member State does not respect these limits, the so-called excessive deficit procedure is triggered. This entails several steps – including the possibility of sanctions – to encourage the Member State concerned to take appropriate measures to rectify the situation. The same deficit and debt limits are also criteria for economic and monetary union (EMU) and hence for joining the euro. Furthermore, the latest revision of the integrated economic and employment guidelines (revised as part of the Europe 2020 strategy for

smart, sustainable and inclusive growth) includes a guideline to ensure the quality and the sustainability of public finances. The financial and economic crisis has resulted in serious challenges being posed to many European governments. The main concerns are linked to the ability of national administrations to be able to service their debt repayments, take the necessary action to ensure that their public spending is brought under control, while at the same time trying to promote economic growth.

Main statistical findings

In 2011, the government deficit (net borrowing or lending of the consolidated general government sector, as a share of GDP) of both the EU-27 and the euro area (EA-17) decreased compared with 2010, while general government debt increased.

Government deficit

In the EU-27 the government deficit-to-GDP ratio decreased from – 6.5 % in 2010 to – 4.5 % in 2011, and in the euro area it decreased from – 6.2 % to – 4.1 %. Deficit ratios were greater than the reference threshold of – 3 % of GDP in 17 of the Member States in 2011. Ten Member States had a

government deficit exceeding the – 3 % threshold for the whole of the reporting period 2008 to 2011. The largest government deficits (as a percentage of GDP) in 2011 were recorded by Ireland (– 13.1 %), Greece (– 9.1 %), Spain (– 8.5 %) and the United Kingdom (– 8.3 %). Twenty-five Member States saw their government deficit (in relation to GDP) reduced, or saw their government surplus expand in 2011 compared to 2010. Hungary, Estonia and Sweden registered a government surplus in 2011. There were seven Member States, namely Bulgaria, Denmark, Germany, Luxembourg, Malta, Austria and Finland which recorded deficits in 2011 that were lower than the – 3 % threshold (see Figure 1.2.1). Two Member States – Cyprus and Slovenia – recorded larger deficits in 2011 than in 2010.

Government debt

In the EU-27 the government debt-to-GDP ratio increased from 80.0 % at the end of 2010 to 82.5 % at the end of 2011, and in the euro area from 85.3 % to 87.2 %. A total of 14 Member States reported a debt ratio above 60 % of GDP in 2011. At the end of 2011, the lowest ratios of government debt-to-GDP were recorded in Estonia (6.0 %), Bulgaria (16.3 %) and Luxembourg (18.2 %) – see Figure 1.2.2. In 2011, government debt-to-GDP ratios increased for 21 EU Member States when compared with 2010, while government debt ratios decreased for six Member States: Germany, Estonia, Latvia, Luxembourg, Hungary and Sweden. The highest increases of debt ratios from 2010 to 2011 were observed in Greece (20.4 percentage points), Ireland (15.7 points), Portugal (14.4 points) and Cyprus (10.2 points).

Government revenue and expenditure

The importance of the general government sector in the economy may be measured in terms of total general government revenue and expenditure as a percentage of GDP. In the EU-27, total government revenue in 2011 amounted to 44.6 % of GDP (up from 44.1 % of GDP in 2010), and expenditure to 49.1 % of GDP (down from 50.6 % in 2010). In the euro area total general government expenditure amounted to 49.4 % of GDP in 2011 and total revenue to 45.3 % of GDP – see Figure 1.2.3.

In absolute terms, total general government expenditure grew steadily over the period from 2001 to 2010 – both in the EU-27 and in the euro area (see Figure 1.2.4). From 2010 to 2011 total general government expenditure decreased slightly in absolute terms both in the EU-27 and in the euro area. Revenues also grew steadily through to 2007 in the EU-27 and the euro area, remained relatively unchanged in 2008, decreased in 2009 and then increased again in 2010 and 2011.

The level of general government expenditure and revenue varies considerably between the EU Member States (see Figure 1.2.5). In 2011, the countries with the highest levels of combined government expenditure and revenue as a proportion of GDP (in excess of 100 %), were Denmark, Finland, France, Belgium, Sweden and Hungary, as well as Norway among the EFTA countries. Seven Member States reported relatively low combined ratios (less than 80 % of GDP); they were Bulgaria, Lithuania, Slovakia, Romania, Latvia, Estonia and Spain, while Switzerland reported the lowest ratio (68.9 % in 2010, latest year available) among the EFTA members.

Across the EU-27, the main components of total general government revenue are taxes and social contributions (see Figure 1.2.6). In 2011, taxes made up 58.2 % of total revenue in the EU-27 (55.1 % in the euro area), while social contributions amounted to 31.2 % of total revenue (34.6 % in the euro area). Looking at each Member State, the relative importance of the different revenue categories varies widely. For example, taxes made up less than 50 % of government revenue in Hungary, the Czech Republic and Slovakia in 2011, but almost 85 % of government revenue in Denmark (see Figure 1.2.7).

The largest proportion of EU-27 government expenditure in 2011 concerned the redistribution of income in the form of social transfers in cash or in kind (see Figures 1.2.8 and 1.2.9). Social transfers made up 43.4 % of total expenditure in the EU-27 (46.8 % in the euro area). Compensation of employees accounted for 22.0 % of government expenditure (21.5 % in the euro area). Property income paid – of which by far the largest part is made up of interest payments – accounted for 6.0 % of government

expenditure in the EU-27 (6.2 % in the euro area), a share which rose to 13.9 % of total expenditure in Greece and 10.1 % in Iceland.

General government expenditure can be analysed in more detail using the classification of the functions of government (COFOG). In 2010 social protection measures accounted for the highest proportion of government expenditure in all EU Member States, with an EU-27 average of 19.9 % of GDP. This pattern held across all Member States except Ireland, where capital transfers to sustain the Irish banking sector influenced the high share of the 'economic affairs' function. The share of the 'social protection' function ranged from 25.4 % of GDP in Denmark, 24.2 % in France and 23.9 % in Finland to 11.7 % in Cyprus and 11.2 % in Iceland. The next COFOG functions, in order of their relative importance within the EU-27, were health (7.5 % of GDP), general public services (6.5 %) and education (5.5 %). Spending on economic affairs in the EU-27 stood at 4.7 % of GDP in 2010, while less than 2 % of GDP was devoted to defence, public order and safety, environmental protection, housing and community affairs, recreation, or religion and culture (all of these functions are grouped together under the heading of 'others' in Figure 1.2.10).

The main types of government revenue are current taxes on income and wealth, etc., taxes on production and imports, and social contributions, with capital taxes making up just 0.6 % of total revenue in the EU-27 in 2011. There was an increase in the relative importance of receipts from social contributions in the EU-27 during the period from 2007 to 2009, however, this pattern was reversed in 2010, with social contributions then remaining almost stable from 2010 to 2011 (at 13.9 % of GDP in 2010 and 2011). The relative importance of current taxes on income and wealth, etc. decreased from 2007 to 2009, then remained stable from 2009 to 2010, before increasing to 12.6 % of GDP in 2011. Taxes on production and imports increased by 0.4 percentage points of GDP from a low point in 2009 to stand at 13.1 % of GDP in 2011 (see Figure 1.2.11).

There was considerable variation in the structure of tax revenues across the EU Member States in 2011 (see Figure 1.2.12). As may be expected, those countries that reported relatively high levels

of expenditure tended to be those that also raised more taxes (as a proportion of GDP). For example, in 2011 the highest return from the main categories of taxes and social contributions was 48.8 % of GDP recorded in Denmark, with France and Belgium recording the next highest shares (45.3 % and 45.2 % respectively), while the proportion of GDP accounted for by such revenue was below 30 % in six of the Member States: Ireland, Slovakia, Latvia, Romania, Bulgaria and Lithuania (where the lowest share was recorded at 26.2 % of GDP). Switzerland also recorded a share below 30 %.

In 2009 the value of public procurement which is openly advertised reached 12.2 % of GDP in Bulgaria, more than three times as high as the 3.6 % average for the EU-27 (see Figure 1.2.13). None of the Member States that joined the EU in 2004 or 2007 recorded ratios below the EU-27 average in 2009. Among the EU-15 Member States, the United Kingdom (6.2 %) and Finland (4.9 %) recorded the highest ratios of openly advertised public procurement to GDP, while Germany (1.4 %) and Luxembourg (1.5 %) reported the lowest.

Total state aid in the EU-27 stood at 3.5 % in 2009; a relatively high level reflecting responses to the financial and economic crisis – by means of comparison the same ratio had remained relatively stable during the run-up to the crisis, at around 0.4 to 0.5 % of GDP. The EU-27 average masks significant disparities among Member States (see Figure 1.2.14).

Data sources and availability

Under the terms of the excessive deficit procedure, EU Member States are required to provide the European Commission with their government deficit and debt statistics before 1 April and 1 October of each year. In addition, Eurostat collects more detailed data on government finances within the framework of the ESA transmission programme which results in the submission of national accounts data. The main aggregates collected for general government are provided to Eurostat twice a year, whereas statistics on the functions of government (COFOG) and detailed tax and social contribution receipts should be transmitted within one year after the end of the

reference period and within nine months after the end of the reference period, respectively.

The data presented in this subchapter correspond to the main revenue and expenditure items of the general government sector, which are compiled on a national accounts (ESA 95) basis. The difference between total revenue and total expenditure – including capital expenditure (in particular, gross fixed capital formation) – equals net lending/net borrowing of general government, which is also the balancing item of the government non-financial accounts.

Delineation of general government

The general government sector includes all institutional units whose output is intended for individual and collective consumption and mainly financed by compulsory payments made by units belonging to other sectors, and/or all institutional units principally engaged in the redistribution of national income and wealth. The general government sector is subdivided into four subsectors: central government, state government – where applicable, local government, and social security funds – where applicable.

Definition of main indicators

The public balance is defined as general government net borrowing/net lending reported for the excessive deficit procedure and is expressed in relation to GDP. According to the protocol on the excessive deficit procedure, government debt is the gross debt outstanding at the end of the year of the general government sector measured at nominal (face) value and consolidated.

The main revenue of general government consists of taxes, social contributions, sales and property income. It is defined in ESA95 by reference to a list of categories: market output, output for own final use, payments for the other non-market output, taxes on production and imports, other subsidies on production, receivable property income, current taxes on income, wealth, etc., social contributions, other current transfers and capital transfers.

The main expenditure items consist of the compensation of civil servants, social benefits, interest on the public debt, subsidies, and gross fixed capital formation. Total general government expenditure

is defined in ESA95 by reference to a list of categories: intermediate consumption, gross capital formation, compensation of employees, other taxes on production, subsidies, payable property income, current taxes on income, wealth, social benefits, some social transfers, other current transfers, some adjustments, capital transfers, and transactions on non-produced assets.

General government data reported for main aggregates of general government and for expenditure of general government by function in the ESA95 framework must be consolidated, meaning that specific transactions between institutional units within the general government sector – 'property income', 'other current transfers' and 'capital transfers' – are eliminated or cancelled out. Sub-sector data should be consolidated within each sub-sector but not between sub-sectors. Thus data at sector level should equal the sum of sub-sector data, except for items 'property income', 'other current transfers' and 'capital transfers', which are consolidated. For these latter items and consequently total revenue and total expenditure, the sum of the sub-sectors should exceed the value of the sector.

Taxes and social contributions correspond to revenues which are levied (in cash or in kind) by central, state and local governments, and social security funds. These levies (generally referred to as taxes) are organised into three main areas, covered by the following headings:

- taxes on income and wealth, etc. including all compulsory payments levied periodically by general government on the income and wealth of enterprises and households;
- taxes on production and imports, including all compulsory payments levied by general government with respect to the production and importation of goods and services, the employment of labour, the ownership or use of land, buildings or other assets used in production;
- social contributions, including all employers' and employees' social contributions, as well as imputed social contributions that represent the counterpart to social benefits paid directly by employers.

Data on public procurement are based on information contained in the calls for competition and contract award notices submitted for publication

in the Official Journal of the European Communities (the S series). The numerator is the value of public procurement, which is openly advertised. For each of the sectors – works, supplies and services – the number of calls for competition published is multiplied by an average based, in general, on all the prices provided in the contract award notices published in the Official Journal during the relevant year. The value of public procurement is then expressed relative to GDP.

State aid is made up of sectoral state aid (given to specific activities, such as agriculture, fisheries, manufacturing, mining, services), ad-hoc state aid (given to individual enterprises, for example, for rescue or restructuring), and state aid for cross-cutting (horizontal) objectives, such as research and development, safeguarding the environment, support to small and medium-sized enterprises, employment creation or training, including aid for regional development. The first two of these (sectoral and ad-hoc state aid) are considered potentially more distortive to competition.

Context

The disciplines of the stability and growth pact (SGP) are intended to keep economic developments in

the EU, and the euro area countries in particular, broadly synchronised. Furthermore, the SGP is intended to prevent Member States from taking policy measures which would unduly benefit their own economies at the expense of others. There are two key principles to the SGP: namely, that the deficit (planned or actual) must not exceed – 3 % of GDP and that the debt-to-GDP ratio should not be more than (or should be falling towards) 60 %. The SGP was substantially reinforced in 2011, as was EU economic governance in general.

Each year, Member States provide the European Commission with detailed information on their economic policies and the state of their public finances. Euro area countries provide this information in the context of the stability programmes, while other Member States do so in the form of convergence programmes. The European Commission assesses whether the policies are in line with agreed economic, social and environmental objectives and may choose to issue a warning if it believes a deficit is becoming abnormally high. This action can lead to the Council finding the existence of an excessive deficit, which requires a deadline to be set for its correction.

Figure 1.2.1: Public balance, 2010 and 2011 (¹)
(net borrowing or lending of consolidated general government sector, % of GDP)

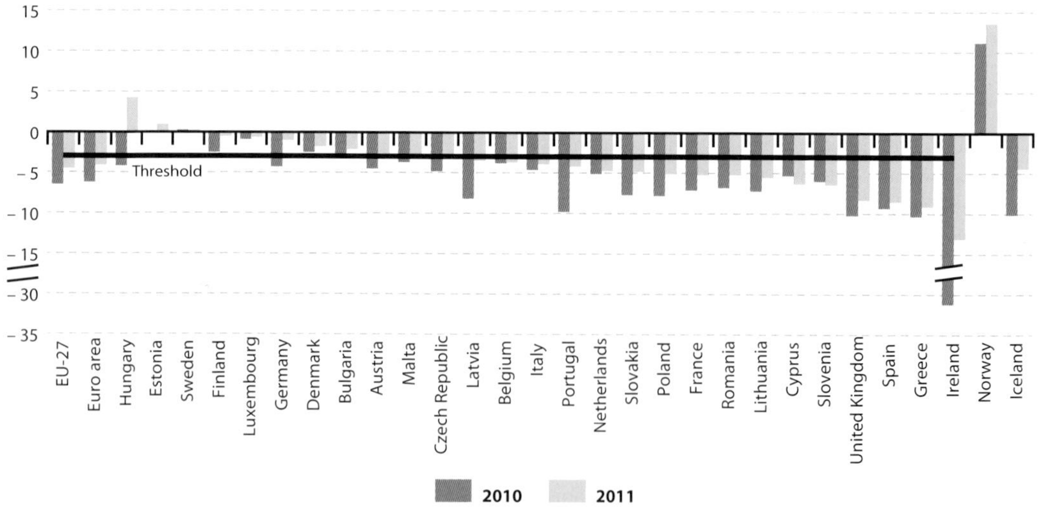

(¹) Data extracted on 23.04.2012.
Source: Eurostat (online data code: tsieb080)

Table 1.2.1: Public balance and general government debt, 2008-2011 (¹)
(% of GDP)

	Public balance (net borrowing/lending of consolidated general government sector)				General government debt (general government consolidated gross debt)			
	2008	2009	2010	2011	2008	2009	2010	2011
EU-27	−2.4	−6.9	−6.5	−4.5	62.5	74.8	80.0	82.5
Euro area	−2.1	−6.4	−6.2	−4.1	70.1	79.9	85.3	87.2
Belgium	−1.0	−5.6	−3.8	−3.7	89.3	95.8	96.0	98.0
Bulgaria	1.7	−4.3	−3.1	−2.1	13.7	14.6	16.3	16.3
Czech Republic	−2.2	−5.8	−4.8	−3.1	28.7	34.4	38.1	41.2
Denmark	3.2	−2.7	−2.5	−1.8	33.4	40.6	42.9	46.5
Germany	−0.1	−3.2	−4.3	−1.0	66.7	74.4	83.0	81.2
Estonia	−2.9	−2.0	0.2	1.0	4.5	7.2	6.7	6.0
Ireland	−7.3	−14.0	−31.2	−13.1	44.2	65.1	92.5	108.2
Greece	−9.8	−15.6	−10.3	−9.1	113.0	129.4	145.0	165.3
Spain	−4.5	−11.2	−9.3	−8.5	40.2	53.9	61.2	68.5
France	−3.3	−7.5	−7.1	−5.2	68.2	79.2	82.3	85.8
Italy	−2.7	−5.4	−4.6	−3.9	105.7	116.0	118.6	120.1
Cyprus	0.9	−6.1	−5.3	−6.3	48.9	58.5	61.5	71.6
Latvia	−4.2	−9.8	−8.2	−3.5	19.8	36.7	44.7	42.6
Lithuania	−3.3	−9.4	−7.2	−5.5	15.5	29.4	38.0	38.5
Luxembourg	3.0	−0.8	−0.9	−0.6	13.7	14.8	19.1	18.2
Hungary	−3.7	−4.6	−4.2	4.3	73.0	79.8	81.4	80.6
Malta	−4.6	−3.8	−3.7	−2.7	62.3	68.1	69.4	72.0
Netherlands	0.5	−5.6	−5.1	−4.7	58.5	60.8	62.9	65.2
Austria	−0.9	−4.1	−4.5	−2.6	63.8	69.5	71.9	72.2
Poland	−3.7	−7.4	−7.8	−5.1	47.1	50.9	54.8	56.3
Portugal	−3.6	−10.2	−9.8	−4.2	71.6	83.1	93.3	107.8
Romania	−5.7	−9.0	−6.8	−5.2	13.4	23.6	30.5	33.3
Slovenia	−1.9	−6.1	−6.0	−6.4	21.9	35.3	38.8	47.6
Slovakia	−2.1	−8.0	−7.7	−4.8	27.9	35.6	41.1	43.3
Finland	4.3	−2.5	−2.5	−0.5	33.9	43.5	48.4	48.6
Sweden	2.2	−0.7	0.3	0.3	38.8	42.6	39.4	38.4
United Kingdom	−5.0	−11.5	−10.2	−8.3	54.8	69.6	79.6	85.7
Iceland	−13.5	−10.0	−10.1	−4.4	70.3	87.9	93.1	98.8
Norway	18.8	10.6	11.2	13.6	48.2	43.5	43.7	29.0
Croatia	−1.4	−4.1	:	:	28.9	35.3	:	:
Turkey	−2.2	−6.7	:	:	39.5	45.4	:	:

(¹) Data extracted on 23.04.2012.

Source: Eurostat (online data codes: tsieb080 and tsieb090)

Figure 1.2.2: General government debt, 2010 and 2011 (^{1})
(general government consolidated gross debt, % of GDP)

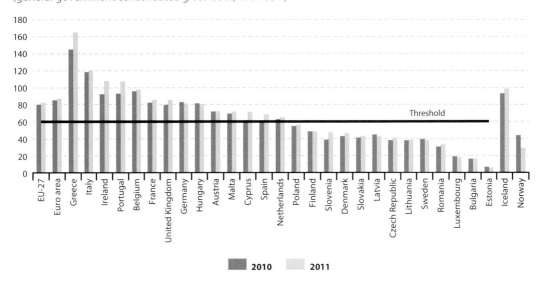

(^{1}) Data extracted on 23.04.2012.

Source: Eurostat (online data code: tsieb090)

Figure 1.2.3: Development of total expenditure and total revenue, 2001-2011 (^{1})
(% of GDP)

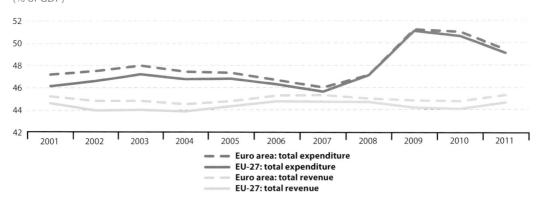

(^{1}) Data extracted on 23.04.2012; note that the y-axis is cut.

Source: Eurostat (online data code: gov_a_main)

Figure 1.2.4: Development of total expenditure and total revenue, 2001-2011 (¹)
(EUR 1 000 million)

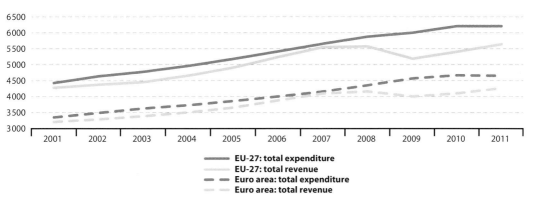

- EU-27: total expenditure
- EU-27: total revenue
- Euro area: total expenditure
- Euro area: total revenue

(¹) Data extracted on 23.04.2012; note that the y-axis is cut.

Source: Eurostat (online data code: gov_a_main)

Figure 1.2.5: Government revenue and expenditure, 2011 (¹)
(% of GDP)

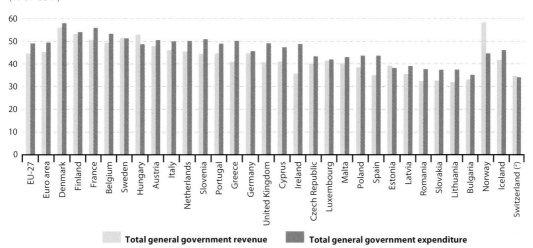

Total general government revenue   Total general government expenditure

(¹) Data ranked in descending order according to the average of total revenue and expenditure; data extracted on 23.04.2012.
(²) 2010.

Source: Eurostat (online data code: gov_a_main)

Figure 1.2.6: Composition of total revenue, 2011
(% of total revenue) (¹)

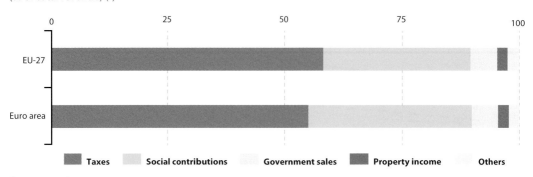

(¹) Data extracted on 23.04.2012.
Source: Eurostat (gov_a_main)

Figure 1.2.7: Main components of government revenue, 2011 (¹)
(% of total revenue)

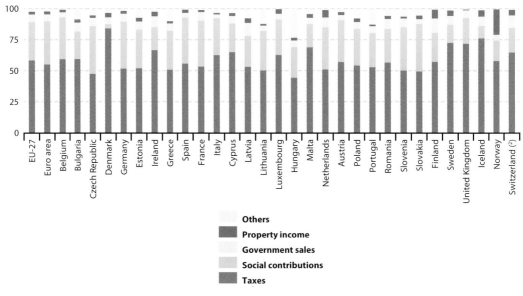

(¹) Data extracted on 23.04.2012.
(²) 2010.
Source: Eurostat (online data code: gov_a_main)

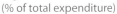

Figure 1.2.8: Composition of total expenditure, 2011 (¹)
(% of total expenditure)

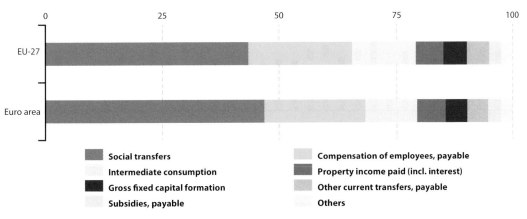

Legend:
- Social transfers
- Intermediate consumption
- Gross fixed capital formation
- Subsidies, payable
- Compensation of employees, payable
- Property income paid (incl. interest)
- Other current transfers, payable
- Others

(¹) Data extracted on 23.04.2012.

Source: Eurostat (gov_a_main)

Figure 1.2.9: Main components of government expenditure, 2011 (¹)
(% of total expenditure)

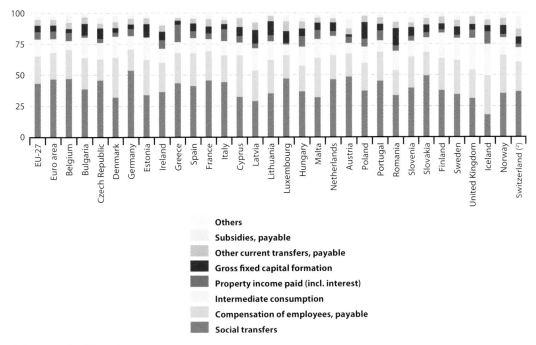

Legend:
- Others
- Subsidies, payable
- Other current transfers, payable
- Gross fixed capital formation
- Property income paid (incl. interest)
- Intermediate consumption
- Compensation of employees, payable
- Social transfers

(¹) Data extracted on 23.04.2012.
(²) 2010.

Source: Eurostat (online data code: gov_a_main)

Figure 1.2.10: General government expenditure by COFOG function, 2010 ([1])
(% of GDP)

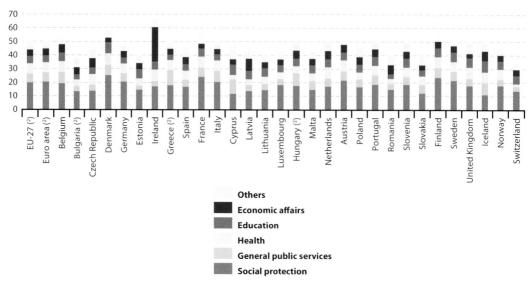

Others

Economic affairs

Education

Health

General public services

Social protection

([1]) COFOG: classification of the functions of government; data extracted on 23.04.2012.
([2]) Provisional.

Source: Eurostat (online data code: gov_a_exp)

Figure 1.2.11: Main categories of taxes and social contributions, EU-27, 2001-2011 ([1])
(% of GDP)

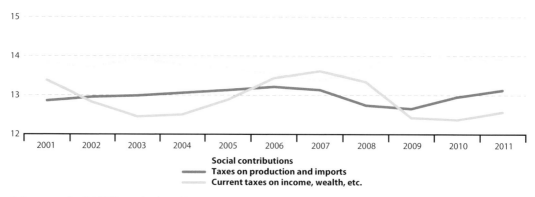

Social contributions
Taxes on production and imports
Current taxes on income, wealth, etc.

([1]) Data extracted on 23.04.2012; note that the y-axis is cut.

Source: Eurostat (online data code: gov_a_main)

Figure 1.2.12: Main categories of taxes and social contributions, 2011 (¹)
(% of GDP)

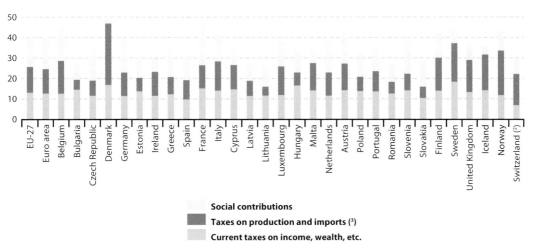

    Social contributions
    Taxes on production and imports (³)
    Current taxes on income, wealth, etc.

(¹) Data extracted on 23.04.2012.
(²) 2010.
(³) Denmark, includes taxes on production and imports paid to the institutions of the European Union.

Source: Eurostat (online data code: gov_a_main)

Figure 1.2.13: Public procurement, 2004 and 2009 (¹)
(value of public procurement which is openly advertised, as % of GDP)

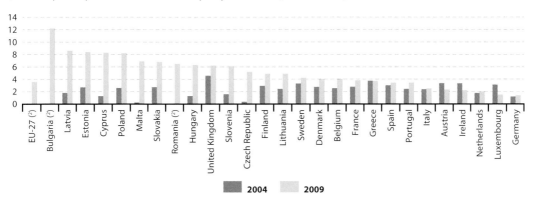

    2004   **2009**

(¹) Data extracted on 12.08.2011.
(²) 2004, not available.

Source: Eurostat (online data codes: gov_oth_procur), European Commission services

Figure 1.2.14: State aid, 2009 (¹)
(% of GDP)

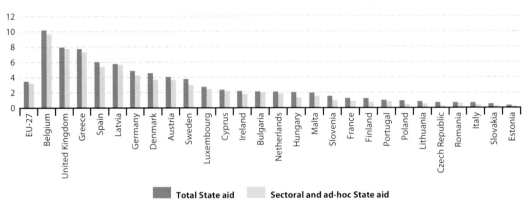

Total State aid   **Sectoral and ad-hoc State aid**

(¹) Data ranked in descending order according to the sum of total State aid and sectoral and ad-hoc State aid; data extracted on 12.08.2011.
Source: Eurostat (online data code: gov_oth_staid), European Commission services

1.3 Exchange rates and interest rates

This subchapter presents an analysis of exchange rates and interest rates; these indicators change quite frequently and the latest data can be consulted through Eurostat's website. The analysis starts by considering the development of exchange rates across the European Union (EU), as well as exchange rate fluctuations between the euro, the Japanese yen, the Swiss franc and the United States dollar (all of which are important reserve currencies).

The second half of the subchapter examines interest rates – in other words, the cost of borrowing and/or lending money. At the macro-economic level, key interest rates are generally set by central banks, as a primary tool for monetary policy with the goal of maintaining price stability and controlling inflation.

Main statistical findings

It is important to note that practically all of Eurostat's data presented in monetary terms (including statistics for those Member States that are not part of the euro area and data for non-member countries) have been converted from national currencies to euro (EUR – see currency codes). When making

comparisons across different countries for indicators denominated in euro terms, it is necessary to bear in mind the possible effect of currency fluctuations, in particular when analysing time series.

The index of annual average exchange rates presented in Figure 1.3.1 starts in 2001, as the euro was starting to appreciate from historically low levels against many currencies. There was a marked appreciation in the value of the euro compared with the Japanese yen during the period from 2000 to 2007, while a similar pattern was observed against the United States dollar from 2001 to 2008. In contrast, there was considerably less variation in exchange rates between the euro and the Swiss franc; no more than +/– 4 % overall between 2000 and 2006 after which the euro appreciated more strongly in 2007 (4.4 %), before depreciating at an accelerating pace in 2008 (– 3.4 %), 2009 (– 4.9 %) and 2010 (– 8.6 %).

A more detailed analysis – using average daily exchange rates – shows that the euro reached a relative high against the Swiss franc on 12 October 2007 (EUR 1 = CHF 1.6803). In the summer of 2008 the euro rose to its most recent relative highs against the currencies of the United States and

Japan, peaking against the dollar on 15 July 2008 (EUR 1 = USD 1.599) and against the yen only eight days later (EUR 1 = JPY 169.75).

Since these relative peaks, the value of the euro has generally depreciated against both the Swiss franc and the Japanese yen. On 4 October 2011 (as this subchapter was in the process of being drafted), the latest exchange rates available showed that one euro was worth CHF 1.2169, or JPY 101.08. A comparison between the relative highs of 2007/2008 and the latest euro exchange rates shows that the value of the euro depreciated against the yen by almost two fifths (40.5 %), while the value of the euro fell against the Swiss franc by 27.6 %. In relation to the United States dollar the developments were more complex: from the aforementioned peak of USD 1.599 in July 2008 the value of one euro fell to a low of USD 1.1942 on 8 June 2010; it subsequently rose to USD 1.4882 on 4 May 2011 and stabilised in a range from USD 1.40 to USD 1.46 until the end of August 2011; since 29 August 2011 the euro has generally depreciated against the dollar and its latest rate (at the time of drafting) was USD 1.381, which was 11.4 % below its May 2011 peak.

Table 1.3.1 shows the development of exchange rates between the euro and a broader range of currencies. Between 2001 and 2010, the euro appreciated strongly against the Turkish lira, and also against the Icelandic króna (particularly between 2007 and 2009). The euro also appreciated against the currencies of Latvia, Hungary, Poland, Romania, Sweden and the United Kingdom. In contrast, the national currencies of the Czech Republic and to a lesser extent Lithuania appreciated against the euro during the period 2001 to 2010, as did those of Switzerland and Norway (among non-member countries). Note that some non-euro area members have fixed their exchange rates against the euro, as part of the exchange rate mechanism (ERM II) in preparation for joining the euro area.

The overall pattern in bond yields (see Table 1.3.2) for the EU-27 (weighted) average was that yields were highest at the beginning of the decade (2000), lowest in the middle of the decade (2005), increased in 2006 and 2007 before declining through to the end of the decade (2010) without quite returning to their lowest levels recorded in 2005; this pattern of high yields at the beginning of the decade, low yields in the middle of the decade (2005 or 2006) and yields at the end of the decade somewhat above the mid-decade lows was broadly repeated in ten of the Member States. The largest group of exceptions, containing several of the larger Member States, saw yields at the end of the decade fall below their mid-decade lows. This group included a mixture of euro area and non-euro area members, namely: Denmark, Germany, France, Malta, the Netherlands, Austria, Finland, Sweden and the United Kingdom. Another group saw their yields climb towards the end of the decade and reach their highest levels for the decade in either 2009 or 2010 – this group was composed of Bulgaria, Ireland, Greece, Latvia, Lithuania, Hungary and Romania.

Money market rates, also known as inter-bank rates, are interest rates used by banks for operations among themselves. In the money market, banks are able to trade their surpluses and deficits. Table 1.3.3 shows three-month interbank rates for the euro area and for EU Member States that are not in the euro area, as well as for some non-member countries. As was the case for yields, money market rates tended to fall during the first half of the decade and then rose through to 2008 or 2009 before falling again, with rates in the United Kingdom and the United States peaking one year earlier in 2007.

Tables 1.3.5 and 1.3.6 provide information on interest rates for housing loans for households and overdrafts for non-financial corporations (businesses). In broad terms these followed a similar progression to that observed for bond yields and money market rates, falling in the first half of the decade and then rising for a couple of years before falling again. Among the Member States for which data are available, interest rates on new loans for housing ranged in 2010 from less than 3 % in Austria and Spain to nearly 10 % in Romania and Hungary. For new bank overdrafts rates ranged from less than 3 % in Finland, the Czech Republic and France to 10.5 % in Romania.

Data sources and availability

Exchange rates

Eurostat publishes a number of different data sets concerning exchange rates. Three main data sets can be distinguished, with statistics on:

- bilateral exchange rates between currencies, including some special conversion factors for countries that have adopted the euro;
- fluctuations in the exchange rate mechanism (ERM and ERM II) of the EU;
- effective exchange rate indices.

Bilateral exchange rates are available with reference to the euro, although before 1999 they were given in relation to the European currency unit (ECU). The ECU ceased to exist on 1 January 1999 when it was replaced by the euro at an exchange rate of 1:1. From that date, the currencies of the euro area became subdivisions of the euro at irrevocably fixed rates of conversion.

Daily exchange rates are available from 1974 onwards against a large number of currencies. These daily values are used to construct monthly and annual averages, which are based on business day rates; alternatively, month-end and year-end rates are also published.

Interest rates

Interest rates provide information on the cost or price of borrowing, or the gain from lending. Traditionally, interest rates are expressed in annual percentage terms, although the period for lending/borrowing can be anything from overnight to a period of many years. Different types of interest rates are distinguished either by the period of lending/borrowing involved, or by the parties involved in the transaction (business, consumers, governments or interbank operations).

Long-term interest rates are one of the convergence criteria for European economic and monetary union (EMU). In order to comply, Member States need to demonstrate an average nominal long-term interest rate that does not exceed by more than 2 percentage points that of, at most, the three best-performing Member States. Long-term interest rates are based upon central government bond yields (or comparable securities), taking into account differences in national definitions, on the secondary market, gross of tax, with a residual maturity of around ten years.

Eurostat also publishes a number of short-term interest rates, with different maturities (overnight, 1 to 12 months). Other interest rates that are published include retail bank interest rates which are lending and deposit rates (non-harmonised and historical series), and harmonised monetary financial institutions (MFI) interest rates, such as loans to households or non-financial corporations.

A yield curve, also known as term structure of interest rates, represents the relationship between market remuneration (interest) rates and the remaining time to maturity of government bonds.

Context

Interest rates, inflation rates and exchange rates are highly linked: the interaction between these economic phenomena is often complicated by a range of additional factors such as levels of government debt, the sentiment of financial markets, terms of trade, political stability, and overall economic performance.

Central banks seek to exert influence over both inflation and exchange rates, through controlling monetary policy – their main tool for this purpose is the setting of key interest rates.

An exchange rate is the price or value of one currency in relation to another. Those countries with relatively stable and low inflation rates tend to display an appreciation in their currencies, as their purchasing power increases relative to other currencies, whereas higher inflation typically leads to a depreciation of the local currency. When the value of one currency appreciates against another, then that country's exports become more expensive and its imports become cheaper.

The exchange rate mechanism (ERM II) was set up on 1 January 1999, with the goal of ensuring that exchange rate fluctuations between the euro and other EU currencies did not disrupt economic stability within the single market, and to help non-euro area countries prepare themselves for participation in the euro area. The convergence criteria (Maastricht criteria) on exchange rate stability requires participation in ERM II, with exchange rates of non-euro area Member

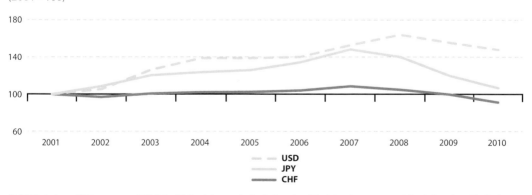

States fixed against the euro such that these may only fluctuate by 15 % above or below an agreed central rate. If necessary, the currencies are supported by intervention (buying or selling) to keep the exchange rate against the euro within the agreed fluctuation band; such intervention is coordinated by the European Central Bank (ECB) and the central bank of the non-euro area Member State. The general council of the ECB monitors the operation of ERM II and ensures coordination of monetary and exchange rate policies, as well as administering the intervention mechanisms with the central banks of the Member States.

All economic and monetary union participants are eligible to adopt the euro. Aside from demonstrating two years of exchange rate stability (via membership of ERM II), those Member States wishing to join the euro area also need to adhere to a number of additional criteria relating to interest rates, budget deficits, inflation rates, and debt-to-GDP ratios.

Through using a common currency, the countries of the euro area have removed exchange rates and, therefore, hope to benefit from the elimination of currency exchange costs, lower transaction costs and the promotion of trade and investment resulting from the scale of the euro area market. Furthermore, the use of a single currency increases price transparency for consumers across the euro area.

From 1 January 2002, notes and coins entered circulation across the euro area, as 12 Member States – Belgium, Germany, Ireland, Greece, Spain, France, Italy, Luxembourg, the Netherlands, Austria, Portugal and Finland – adopted the euro as their common currency. Slovenia subsequently joined the euro area at the start of 2007, and was followed by Cyprus and Malta on 1 January 2008, Slovakia on 1 January 2009 and Estonia on 1 January 2011, bringing the total number of countries using the euro as their common currency to 17.

In joining the euro each Member States has agreed to allow the ECB to act as an independent authority responsible for maintaining price stability through the implementation of monetary policy. As of 1999, the ECB started to set benchmark interest rates and manage the euro area's foreign exchange reserves. The ECB has defined price stability as a year-on-year increase in the harmonised index of consumer prices (HICP) for the euro area below, but close to, 2 % over the medium term (see the subchapter on consumer prices – inflation and comparative price levels). Monetary policy decisions are taken by the ECB's governing council which meets every month to analyse and assess economic and monetary developments and the risks to price stability and thereafter to decide upon the appropriate level of key interest rates.

Figure 1.3.1: Exchange rates against the euro, 2001-2010 (¹)
(2001 = 100)

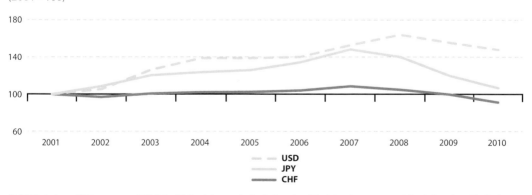

(¹) CHF, Swiss franc; JPY, Japanese yen; USD, United States dollar; a reduction in the value of the index shows an appreciation in the value of the foreign currency and a depreciation in the value of the euro.

Source: Eurostat (online data code: tec00033), ECB

Table 1.3.1: Exchange rates against the euro, 2001-2010 (^{1})
(1 EUR = ... national currency)

	2001	2002	2003	2004	2005	2006	2007	2008	2009	2010
Bulgaria	1.9482	1.9492	1.9490	1.9533	1.9558	1.9558	1.9558	1.9558	1.9558	1.9558
Czech Republic	34.068	30.804	31.846	31.891	29.782	28.342	27.766	24.946	26.435	25.284
Denmark	7.4521	7.4305	7.4307	7.4399	7.4518	7.4591	7.4506	7.4560	7.4462	7.4473
Latvia	0.5601	0.5810	0.6407	0.6652	0.6962	0.6962	0.7001	0.7027	0.7057	0.7087
Lithuania	3.5823	3.4594	3.4527	3.4529	3.4528	3.4528	3.4528	3.4528	3.4528	3.4528
Hungary	256.59	242.96	253.62	251.66	248.05	264.26	251.35	251.51	280.33	275.48
Poland	3.6721	3.8574	4.3996	4.5268	4.0230	3.8959	3.7837	3.5121	4.3276	3.9947
Romania	2.6004	3.1270	3.7551	4.0510	3.6209	3.5258	3.3353	3.6826	4.2399	4.2122
Sweden	9.2551	9.1611	9.1242	9.1243	9.2822	9.2544	9.2501	9.6152	10.6191	9.5373
United Kingdom	0.62187	0.62883	0.69199	0.67866	0.68380	0.68173	0.68434	0.79628	0.89094	0.85784
Iceland	87.42	86.18	86.65	87.14	78.23	87.76	87.63	143.83	172.67	161.89
Norway	8.0484	7.5086	8.0033	8.3697	8.0092	8.0472	8.0165	8.2237	8.7278	8.0043
Switzerland	1.5105	1.4670	1.5212	1.5438	1.5483	1.5729	1.6427	1.5874	1.5100	1.3803
Croatia	7.4820	7.4130	7.5688	7.4967	7.4008	7.3247	7.3376	7.2239	7.3400	7.2891
FYR of Macedonia	60.9131	60.9786	61.2631	61.3372	61.2970	61.1896	61.1730	61.5201	61.2815	61.4800
Turkey	1.1024	1.4397	1.6949	1.7771	1.6771	1.8090	1.7865	1.9064	2.1631	1.9965
Japan	108.68	118.06	130.97	134.44	136.85	146.02	161.25	152.45	130.34	116.24
United States	0.8956	0.9456	1.1312	1.2439	1.2441	1.2556	1.3705	1.4708	1.3948	1.3257

(^{1}) The euro replaced the ecu on 1 January 1999; on 1 January 2002, it also replaced the notes and coins of 12 Community currencies with the introduction of the euro to the euro area (EA-12) members; on 1 January 2007, the euro came into circulation in Slovenia; on 1 January 2008, the euro came into circulation in Cyprus and Malta; on 1 January 2009, the euro came into circulation in Slovakia; on 1 January 2011, the euro came into circulation in Estonia; as of 1 January 2009 the official rate for the Icelandic króna is shown for indicative purposes.

Source: Eurostat (online data codes: tec00033 and ert_bil_eur_a), ECB

Table 1.3.2: EMU convergence criterion bond yields (Maastricht criterion), 2000-2010 ([1])
(%)

	2000	2001	2002	2003	2004	2005	2006	2007	2008	2009	2010
EU-27	:	5.00	4.92	4.23	4.38	3.70	4.03	4.56	4.54	4.13	3.82
Euro area ([2])	5.44	5.00	4.91	4.14	4.12	3.42	3.84	4.32	4.31	3.82	3.62
Belgium	5.59	5.13	4.99	4.18	4.15	3.43	3.81	4.33	4.42	3.90	3.46
Bulgaria	:	:	:	6.45	5.36	3.87	4.18	4.54	5.38	7.22	6.01
Czech Republic	:	6.31	4.88	4.12	4.82	3.54	3.80	4.30	4.63	4.84	3.88
Denmark	5.64	5.08	5.06	4.31	4.30	3.40	3.81	4.29	4.28	3.59	2.93
Germany	5.26	4.80	4.78	4.07	4.04	3.35	3.76	4.22	3.98	3.22	2.74
Estonia	:	:	:	:	:	:	:	:	:	:	:
Ireland	5.51	5.01	5.01	4.13	4.08	3.33	3.76	4.31	4.53	5.23	5.74
Greece	6.10	5.30	5.12	4.27	4.26	3.59	4.07	4.50	4.80	5.17	9.09
Spain	5.53	5.12	4.96	4.12	4.10	3.39	3.78	4.31	4.37	3.98	4.25
France	5.39	4.94	4.86	4.13	4.10	3.41	3.80	4.30	4.23	3.65	3.12
Italy	5.58	5.19	5.03	4.25	4.26	3.56	4.05	4.49	4.68	4.31	4.04
Cyprus	:	7.62	5.70	4.74	5.80	5.16	4.13	4.48	4.60	4.60	4.60
Latvia	:	7.57	5.41	4.90	4.86	3.88	4.13	5.28	6.43	12.36	10.34
Lithuania	:	8.15	6.06	5.32	4.50	3.70	4.08	4.55	5.61	14.00	5.57
Luxembourg	5.52	4.86	4.70	3.32	2.84	2.41	3.30	4.46	4.61	4.23	3.17
Hungary	:	7.95	7.09	6.82	8.19	6.60	7.12	6.74	8.24	9.12	7.28
Malta	:	6.19	5.82	5.04	4.69	4.56	4.32	4.72	4.81	4.54	4.19
Netherlands	5.40	4.96	4.89	4.12	4.10	3.37	3.78	4.29	4.23	3.69	2.99
Austria	5.56	5.08	4.96	4.14	4.13	3.39	3.80	4.30	4.36	3.94	3.23
Poland	:	10.68	7.36	5.78	6.90	5.22	5.23	5.48	6.07	6.12	5.78
Portugal	5.59	5.16	5.01	4.18	4.14	3.44	3.91	4.42	4.52	4.21	5.40
Romania	:	:	:	:	:	:	7.23	7.13	7.70	9.69	7.34
Slovenia	:	:	8.72	6.40	4.68	3.81	3.85	4.53	4.61	4.38	3.83
Slovakia	:	8.04	6.94	4.99	5.03	3.52	4.41	4.49	4.72	4.71	3.87
Finland	5.48	5.04	4.98	4.13	4.11	3.35	3.78	4.29	4.29	3.74	3.01
Sweden	5.37	5.11	5.30	4.64	4.42	3.38	3.70	4.17	3.89	3.25	2.89
United Kingdom	5.33	5.01	4.91	4.58	4.93	4.46	4.37	5.06	4.50	3.36	3.36

([1]) The indicator for Luxembourg is based on a basket of long-term bonds, which have an average residual maturity close to ten years; the bonds are issued by a private credit institution.
([2]) EA-11, 2000; EA-12, 2001-2006; EA-13, 2007; EA-15, 2008; EA-16, 2009-2010.

Source: Eurostat (online data code: tec00097), ECB

Table 1.3.3: Short-term interest rates – three-month interbank rates (annual average), 2000-2010 (%)

	2000	2001	2002	2003	2004	2005	2006	2007	2008	2009	2010
Euro area (¹)	4.4	4.3	3.3	2.3	2.1	2.2	3.1	4.3	4.6	1.2	0.8
Bulgaria	4.6	5.1	4.9	3.7	3.7	3.6	3.7	4.9	7.1	5.7	4.1
Czech Republic	5.4	5.2	3.5	2.3	2.4	2.0	2.3	3.1	4.0	2.2	1.3
Denmark	5.0	4.7	3.5	2.4	2.2	2.2	3.2	4.4	5.3	2.5	1.3
Latvia	5.4	6.9	4.4	3.8	4.2	3.1	4.4	8.7	8.0	13.1	2.0
Lithuania	8.6	5.9	3.7	2.8	2.7	2.4	3.1	5.1	6.0	7.1	1.8
Hungary	11.4	10.9	9.2	8.5	11.4	7.2	7.0	7.9	8.7	9.3	6.2
Poland	18.8	16.1	9.0	5.7	6.2	5.3	4.2	4.7	6.4	4.4	3.9
Romania	50.7	41.3	27.3	17.7	19.1	8.4	8.1	7.2	12.3	11.3	6.5
Sweden	4.1	4.1	4.3	3.2	2.3	1.9	2.6	3.9	4.7	0.9	0.9
United Kingdom	6.2	5.0	4.1	3.7	4.6	4.8	4.9	6.0	5.5	1.2	0.7
Japan	0.3	0.2	0.1	0.1	0.1	0.1	0.3	0.8	0.9	0.5	0.2
United States	6.5	3.8	1.8	1.2	1.6	3.6	5.2	5.3	2.9	0.7	0.3

(¹) EA-11, 2000; EA-12, 2001-2006; EA-13, 2007; EA-15, 2008; EA-16, 2009-2010; Euribor.

Source: Eurostat (online data code: tec00035), ECB

Table 1.3.4: Euro yield curve, 2006-2010 ([1])
(%)

	2006	2007	2008	2009	2010
1 year until maturity	3.22	3.99	3.61	0.91	0.59
2 years until maturity	3.37	4.04	3.59	1.51	0.94
3 years until maturity	3.43	4.05	3.65	2.00	1.31
4 years until maturity	3.48	4.06	3.74	2.41	1.68
5 years until maturity	3.53	4.08	3.83	2.75	2.01
6 years until maturity	3.58	4.11	3.93	3.03	2.31
7 years until maturity	3.63	4.14	4.02	3.28	2.58
8 years until maturity	3.68	4.17	4.10	3.49	2.80
9 years until maturity	3.72	4.20	4.18	3.67	2.99
10 years until maturity	3.76	4.23	4.25	3.82	3.15
11 years until maturity	3.79	4.26	4.31	3.95	3.28
12 years until maturity	3.82	4.28	4.36	4.06	3.39
13 years until maturity	3.85	4.30	4.41	4.15	3.47
14 years until maturity	3.88	4.32	4.45	4.22	3.54
15 years until maturity	3.90	4.34	4.48	4.28	3.60
16 years until maturity	3.92	4.36	4.52	4.33	3.64
17 years until maturity	3.93	4.37	4.54	4.37	3.67
18 years until maturity	3.95	4.39	4.57	4.40	3.69
19 years until maturity	3.96	4.40	4.59	4.42	3.70
20 years until maturity	3.98	4.41	4.61	4.43	3.71
21 years until maturity	3.99	4.42	4.63	4.43	3.72
22 years until maturity	4.00	4.43	4.64	4.43	3.72
23 years until maturity	4.01	4.44	4.66	4.43	3.71
24 years until maturity	4.02	4.45	4.67	4.42	3.71
25 years until maturity	4.03	4.46	4.68	4.40	3.70
26 years until maturity	4.03	4.46	4.69	4.39	3.69
27 years until maturity	4.04	4.47	4.70	4.37	3.68
28 years until maturity	4.05	4.47	4.70	4.35	3.66
29 years until maturity	4.05	4.48	4.71	4.32	3.65
30 years until maturity	4.06	4.49	4.72	4.30	3.64

([1]) Zero-coupon yield curve spot rate for AAA rated euro area central government bonds; EA-12, 2006; EA-13, 2007; EA-15, 2008; EA-16, 2009-2010.

Source: Eurostat (online data code: irt_euryld_a), ECB

Table 1.3.5: MFI interest rates on new loans to households for housing, maturity of 1 to 5 years, 2003-2010
(%, annualised agreed percentage rate)

	2003	2004	2005	2006	2007	2008	2009	2010
Euro area (¹)	4.18	3.95	3.85	4.56	5.03	5.06	3.96	3.52
Belgium	4.37	4.12	3.80	4.44	5.18	4.99	3.98	3.55
Bulgaria	:	:	:	:	6.12	9.84	8.30	5.53
Czech Republic	:	5.13	4.34	4.66	5.34	5.67	5.68	4.51
Denmark	:	:	:	:	:	:	:	:
Germany	4.75	4.29	4.25	4.86	5.33	4.84	3.76	3.31
Estonia	:	:	5.72	6.70	12.08	17.01	16.00	7.00
Ireland	:	:	:	:	:	:	:	:
Greece	5.83	5.19	4.92	4.37	4.21	5.53	4.60	3.95
Spain	3.27	3.47	3.59	4.78	5.65	5.71	3.06	2.94
France	4.01	3.85	3.46	4.04	4.77	5.21	3.80	3.15
Italy	3.73	3.80	3.28	4.09	4.99	4.98	3.35	3.48
Cyprus	:	:	:	:	:	:	:	4.08
Latvia	:	7.70	7.16	7.59	12.63	7.01	7.18	6.39
Lithuania	:	:	:	:	:	:	:	:
Luxembourg	.	.	:	:	:	:	:	:
Hungary	12.81	11.40	8.93	10.14	9.69	11.11	10.99	9.86
Malta	:	:	:	:	:	:	:	:
Netherlands	4.38	3.87	3.85	4.65	5.18	5.32	4.87	4.19
Austria	4.05	3.15	2.98	3.47	4.26	4.82	2.94	2.38
Poland	:	:	9.21	6.95	8.04	8.68	7.43	7.76
Portugal	:	:	:	:	:	:	:	:
Romania	:	:	:	:	9.25	8.99	11.60	9.99
Slovenia	5.10	:	:	5.13	6.30	7.30	5.17	5.46
Slovakia	:	:	:	:	:	6.36	5.57	4.68
Finland	4.18	3.66	3.76	4.53	5.03	3.96	3.47	3.27
Sweden	:	:	:	:	:	:	:	:
United Kingdom	:	:	:	:	:	:	:	:

(¹) EA-12, 2003-2006; EA-13, 2007; EA-15, 2008-2009; EA-16, 2010.

Source: Eurostat (online data code: irt_rtl_lhh), ECB

Table 1.3.6: MFI interest rates to non-financial corporations for (new) bank overdrafts, 2003-2010
(%, annualised agreed percentage rate)

	2003	2004	2005	2006	2007	2008	2009	2010
Euro area (¹)	5.49	5.23	5.12	5.80	6.61	6.24	4.06	3.86
Belgium	8.09	8.17	6.46	7.34	7.31	8.20	6.95	6.69
Bulgaria	:	:	:	:	9.24	10.36	9.31	8.79
Czech Republic	:	4.15	5.34	4.82	5.31	5.37	2.52	2.39
Denmark	:	:	:	:	:	:	:	:
Germany	6.44	6.01	5.79	6.54	7.15	6.35	4.84	4.86
Estonia	:	:	4.93	5.26	6.44	8.03	6.17	9.55
Ireland	6.58	5.69	6.37	7.78	8.81	7.66	5.75	5.33
Greece	6.78	6.97	7.00	7.35	7.56	7.13	5.81	6.78
Spain	13.63	19.51	16.29	12.69	18.26	20.66	19.99	3.41
France	4.21	3.81	3.97	4.74	5.74	5.15	2.57	2.49
Italy	5.62	5.49	5.35	5.95	6.83	6.64	4.28	4.08
Cyprus	:	:	:	:	:	7.19	6.69	6.68
Latvia	:	6.90	5.57	6.02	9.97	11.39	12.53	4.13
Lithuania	:	4.20	4.11	5.29	7.22	6.87	5.73	4.28
Luxembourg	:	:	:	:	:	:	:	:
Hungary	13.78	11.93	8.06	10.01	9.86	12.85	10.02	8.88
Malta	:	:	:	:	5.27	5.14	5.08	5.04
Netherlands	4.98	4.63	4.68	5.17	5.93	5.08	3.31	3.15
Austria	4.85	4.30	4.17	5.09	5.97	6.00	3.07	3.13
Poland	:	:	6.11	5.62	6.36	7.53	5.94	5.92
Portugal	4.29	4.26	4.28	5.55	6.57	6.33	4.06	4.70
Romania	:	:	:	:	11.97	18.33	15.18	10.50
Slovenia	:	:	3.31	4.78	6.29	6.88	5.96	5.54
Slovakia	:	:	:	:	:	4.36	3.31	3.56
Finland	4.34	4.21	4.33	5.40	5.71	4.37	2.55	2.37
Sweden	:	:	:	:	:	:	:	:
United Kingdom	:	:	:	:	:	:	:	:

(¹) EA-12, 2003-2006; EA-13, 2007; EA-15, 2008-2009; EA-16, 2010.

Source: Eurostat (online data code: irt_rtl_lnfc), ECB

1.4 Consumer prices – inflation and comparative price levels

An increase in the general level of prices of goods and services in an economy is called inflation that is usually measured by consumer price indices or retail price indices. Within the European Union (EU) a specific consumer price index for the purpose of tracing price developments has been developed — it is called the harmonised index of consumer prices (HICP).

If there is inflation within an economy, then the purchasing power of money falls as consumers are no longer able to purchase the same amount of goods and services (for the same amount of money). In contrast, if prices fall, then consumers should be able to purchase more goods and services; this is often referred to as deflation. When there is no change in prices (or relatively low rates of inflation) this is often referred to as a period of price stability.

A comparison of prices between countries depends not only on movements in price levels, but also on changes in exchange rates – together, these two forces impact on the price and cost competitiveness of individual Member States.

Purchasing power parities estimate price level differences between countries and these can be used to calculate price level indices. Price level indices may also be used as a starting point for analysing price convergence.

Main statistical findings

Compared with historical trends, consumer price indices rose only at a moderate pace during the last two decades. The EU's (evolving aggregate based upon EU membership) inflation rate decreased during the 1990s, reaching 1.2 % by 1999, after which the pace of price increases settled at around 2 % per annum during the period 2000 to 2007.

In 2008, an annual average inflation rate of 3.7 % was recorded for the EU. This sharp rise in price inflation can be largely attributed to rapid increases in energy and food prices between the autumn of 2007 and the autumn of 2008. Indeed, consumer prices for food recorded historically high inflation rates in 2008 with prices rising on average by 6.7 % in the EU; the increase was particularly associated with steep price rises for dairy products, oils and fats.

In 2009, annual inflation for the EU was 1.0 % – on the back of decreasing food prices between the summers of 2008 and 2009. Energy prices fell from December 2008 until November 2009, with their biggest reduction in July 2009 (– 10.4 %, on the basis of a comparison with July 2008).

In 2010 there was some evidence of a modest expansion in the pace at which prices were rising in the EU as annual inflation was 2.1 %, in other words around the same level experienced in the years leading up to the financial and economic crisis. In April 2011 the inflation rate (compared to 12 months earlier) reached 3.3 % and the latest information available at the time of writing shows a rate of 2.9 % in August 2011. In 2010 annual inflation for two main headings was over 5 %, namely transport, and alcohol and tobacco – see Figure 1.4.2 – while almost no change was recorded for communications (– 0.1 %).

Ireland (– 1.6 %) and Latvia (– 1.2 %) recorded a fall in prices in 2010, while the fastest price increase among the Member States was recorded in Romania (6.1 %); higher price rises were recorded in Turkey and Iceland – see Table 1.4.1.

Comparative price levels of private household consumption vary considerably across the EU Member States. In 2010, they ranged from 51 in Bulgaria to 143 in Denmark (EU-27 = 100). Over the ten years from 2000 to 2010, several of the Member States that joined the EU in 2004 or 2007 recorded substantial increases in their comparative price levels, notably Slovakia, the Czech Republic, Estonia, Hungary and Romania, as did Luxembourg. In contrast, only a few Member States recorded a fall in their comparative price levels, notably the United Kingdom which moved from 20 % above the EU-27 average in 2000 to parity in 2010. There was a convergence of price levels within the EU-27 as a whole during these

years; the coefficient of variation of comparative price levels declined from 33.3 % in 2000 to 23.9 % by 2008, before rising in 2009 to 25.7 % and then declining again slightly in 2010 to 25.1 %. Price levels were more homogeneous across the euro area than the EU-27 throughout the period from 2000 to 2010.

Data sources and availability

Inflation

The harmonised index of consumer prices (HICP) is constructed to measure, over time, the change in prices of consumer goods and services that are acquired by households. These indices cover practically every good and service that may be purchased by households in monetary transactions; owner-occupied housing is, however, not yet included. Goods and services are classified according to the international classification of individual consumption by purpose, adapted to the compilation of the harmonised indices of consumer prices (COICOP/HICP). At its most disaggregated level, Eurostat publishes around 100 sub-indices for consumer prices, which can be aggregated to broad categories of goods and services. The inflation rate is one such example – it is calculated as the rate of change of the all-items harmonised index of consumer prices.

The indices are calculated according to a common approach with a single set of definitions, providing comparable measures of consumer price inflation across countries, as well as for different country groupings such as the EU, the euro area, or the European Economic Area (EEA). There are three key HICP aggregates: the Monetary Union Index of Consumer Prices (MUICP) covering the euro area countries, the European Index of Consumer Prices (EICP) covering all EU Member States, and the European Economic Area Index of Consumer Prices (EEAICP), which includes the EU Member States as well as Iceland and Norway. Note that these aggregates reflect changes over time in their country composition through the use of a chain index formula – for example, the MUICP includes Slovenia only from 2007 onwards, Cyprus and Malta only from 2008 onwards, Slovakia only

from 2009 onwards and Estonia only from 2011 onwards.

Harmonised indices of consumer prices are presented with a common reference year (currently 2005 = 100). Normally the indices are used to calculate percentage changes that show price increases/decreases. Although the rates of change shown in the tables and figures for this subchapter are annual averages, the basic indices are compiled on a monthly basis and are published at this frequency by Eurostat. Harmonised indices of consumer prices are published some 14 to 16 days after the end of the reporting month. The majority of the data is available with series starting in the mid-1990s.

Comparative price levels

Within the framework of the Eurostat-OECD purchasing power parities (PPP) programme, surveys on prices of household goods and services are carried out cyclically in the EU Member States, EFTA countries, candidate countries (Montenegro, Croatia, the former Yugoslav Republic of Macedonia and Turkey) and three western Balkan countries (Albania, Bosnia and Herzegovina, and Serbia). Each survey cycle comprises six surveys that are related to a particular group of household consumption products; with two surveys per year the whole cycle takes three years to conclude. The latest surveys were carried out in 2008, 2009 and 2010, and the prices collected in 2008 and 2009 were updated to 2010 using detailed consumer price indices.

PPPs estimate price level differences across countries; they are aggregated price ratios calculated from price comparisons of a large number of goods and services. They may be used to calculate price level indices, the latter are calculated as the ratio of purchasing power parities to exchange rates. Price level indices may be constructed for a number of expenditure aggregates based on the expenditure classification of national accounts. The differences in price levels of consumer goods and services should be analysed on the basis of household final consumption expenditure (HFCE); Eurostat publishes detailed information on price level

indices for more than 30 different groups of goods and services. Comparative price level indices for the EU Member States are expressed relative to the average price level for the EU-27. If the price level index of a given Member State is above 100, then prices in that Member State are, on average, higher than in the EU as a whole. On the other hand, a price level index below 100 shows that prices are, on average, lower than the EU-27 as a whole.

Context

Harmonised indices of consumer prices are, among other things, used for the purposes of monetary policy and assessing inflation convergence as required in the Treaty on the functioning of the European Union. In particular, they are used for measuring inflation in the euro area; the primary objective of the European Central Bank's (ECB) monetary policy is to maintain price stability. The ECB has defined price stability as a year-on-year increase in the harmonised index of consumer prices for the euro area of below, but close to 2 % over the medium-term.

Purchasing power parities (PPPs) are indicators of price level differences across countries. They indicate how many currency units a particular quantity of goods and services costs in different countries. PPPs can be used as currency conversion rates to convert expenditures expressed in national currencies into an artificial common

currency (the purchasing power standard or PPS), thus eliminating the effect of price level differences across countries. In this way PPPs can be used to convert national accounts aggregates into comparable volume aggregates – for example, to compare the gross domestic product (GDP) of different countries without the figures being distorted by differing price levels in those countries. One particularly important use of PPPs is for the European Commission to establish both the list of regions that could benefit from EU structural funds, as well as the amount of funds to be allocated to each region. One criterion for allocating these funds is based on GDP converted by PPPs and then expressed in PPS per capita.

PPPs can also be used to analyse relative price levels across countries. For this purpose, PPPs are divided by the current nominal exchange rate to obtain a price level index (PLI) which expresses the price level of a given country relative to others: comparative price levels across EU Member States are shown as price level indices expressed relative to the average price level of the EU-27. Price level indices may also be used as a starting point for analysing price convergence. For this purpose, the coefficient of variation of price level indices across any number of countries (for example, the EU Member States) is calculated. A decreasing coefficient over time indicates that price levels are converging. Eurostat publishes an annual estimate of price convergence based on the temporal development of the coefficient of variation.

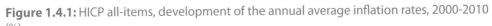

Figure 1.4.1: HICP all-items, development of the annual average inflation rates, 2000-2010
(%)

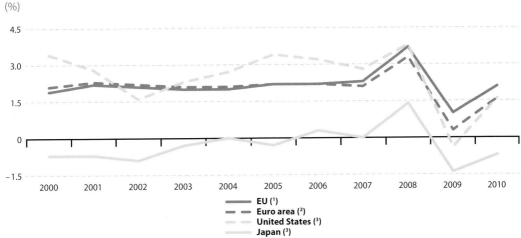

(¹) The data refer to the official EU aggregate, its country coverage changes in line with the addition of new EU Member States and integrates them using a chain-linked index formula.
(²) The data refer to the official euro area aggregate, its country coverage changes in line with the addition of new EA Member States and integrates them using a chain-linked index formula.
(³) National CPI: not strictly comparable with the HICP.

Source: Eurostat (online data codes: prc_hicp_aind and prc_ipc_a)

Table 1.4.1: HICP all-items, annual average inflation rates, 2000-2010
(%)

	2000	2001	2002	2003	2004	2005	2006	2007	2008	2009	2010
EU (¹)	1.9	2.2	2.1	2.0	2.0	2.2	2.2	2.3	3.7	1.0	2.1
Euro area (²)	2.1	2.3	2.2	2.1	2.1	2.2	2.2	2.1	3.3	0.3	1.6
Belgium	2.7	2.4	1.6	1.5	1.9	2.5	2.3	1.8	4.5	0.0	2.3
Bulgaria	10.3	7.4	5.8	2.3	6.1	6.0	7.4	7.6	12.0	2.5	3.0
Czech Republic	3.9	4.5	1.4	−0.1	2.6	1.6	2.1	3.0	6.3	0.6	1.2
Denmark	2.7	2.3	2.4	2.0	0.9	1.7	1.9	1.7	3.6	1.1	2.2
Germany	1.4	1.9	1.4	1.0	1.8	1.9	1.8	2.3	2.8	0.2	1.2
Estonia	3.9	5.6	3.6	1.4	3.0	4.1	4.4	6.7	10.6	0.2	2.7
Ireland	5.3	4.0	4.7	4.0	2.3	2.2	2.7	2.9	3.1	−1.7	−1.6
Greece	2.9	3.7	3.9	3.4	3.0	3.5	3.3	3.0	4.2	1.3	4.7
Spain	3.5	2.8	3.6	3.1	3.1	3.4	3.6	2.8	4.1	−0.2	2.0
France	1.8	1.8	1.9	2.2	2.3	1.9	1.9	1.6	3.2	0.1	1.7
Italy	2.6	2.3	2.6	2.8	2.3	2.2	2.2	2.0	3.5	0.8	1.6
Cyprus	4.9	2.0	2.8	4.0	1.9	2.0	2.2	2.2	4.4	0.2	2.6
Latvia	2.6	2.5	2.0	2.9	6.2	6.9	6.6	10.1	15.3	3.3	−1.2
Lithuania	1.1	1.6	0.3	−1.1	1.2	2.7	3.8	5.8	11.1	4.2	1.2
Luxembourg	3.8	2.4	2.1	2.5	3.2	3.8	3.0	2.7	4.1	0.0	2.8
Hungary	10.0	9.1	5.2	4.7	6.8	3.5	4.0	7.9	6.0	4.0	4.7
Malta	3.0	2.5	2.6	1.9	2.7	2.5	2.6	0.7	4.7	1.8	2.0
Netherlands	2.3	5.1	3.9	2.2	1.4	1.5	1.7	1.6	2.2	1.0	0.9
Austria	2.0	2.3	1.7	1.3	2.0	2.1	1.7	2.2	3.2	0.4	1.7
Poland	10.1	5.3	1.9	0.7	3.6	2.2	1.3	2.6	4.2	4.0	2.7
Portugal	2.8	4.4	3.7	3.3	2.5	2.1	3.0	2.4	2.7	−0.9	1.4
Romania	45.7	34.5	22.5	15.3	11.9	9.1	6.6	4.9	7.9	5.6	6.1
Slovenia	8.9	8.6	7.5	5.7	3.7	2.5	2.5	3.8	5.5	0.9	2.1
Slovakia	12.2	7.2	3.5	8.4	7.5	2.8	4.3	1.9	3.9	0.9	0.7
Finland	2.9	2.7	2.0	1.3	0.1	0.8	1.3	1.6	3.9	1.6	1.7
Sweden	1.3	2.7	1.9	2.3	1.0	0.8	1.5	1.7	3.3	1.9	1.9
United Kingdom	0.8	1.2	1.3	1.4	1.3	2.1	2.3	2.3	3.6	2.2	3.3
Iceland	4.4	6.6	5.3	1.4	2.3	1.4	4.6	3.6	12.8	16.3	7.5
Norway	3.0	2.7	0.8	2.0	0.6	1.5	2.5	0.7	3.4	2.3	2.3
Switzerland	:	:	:	:	:	:	1.0	0.8	2.3	−0.7	0.6
Croatia	4.5	4.3	2.5	2.4	2.1	3.0	3.3	2.7	5.8	2.2	1.1
Turkey	53.2	56.8	47.0	25.3	10.1	8.1	9.3	8.8	10.4	6.3	8.6
Japan (³)	−0.7	−0.7	−0.9	−0.3	0.0	−0.3	0.3	0.0	1.4	−1.4	−0.7
United States (³)	3.4	2.8	1.6	2.3	2.7	3.4	3.2	2.8	3.8	−0.4	1.6

(¹) The data refer to the official EU aggregate, its country coverage changes in line with the addition of new EU Member States and integrates them using a chain-linked index formula.
(²) The data refer to the official euro area aggregate, its country coverage changes in line with the addition of new EA Member States and integrates them using a chain-linked index formula.
(³) National CPI: not strictly comparable with the HICP.

Source: Eurostat (online data codes: prc_hicp_aind and prc_ipc_a)

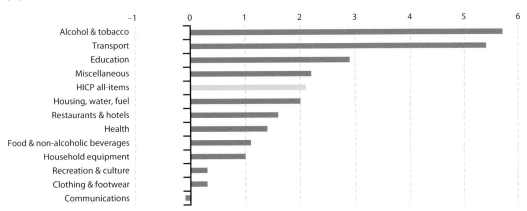

Figure 1.4.2: HICP main headings, annual average inflation rates, EU-27, 2010
(%)

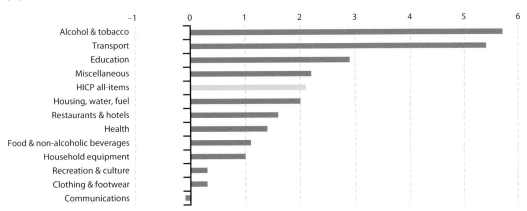

Source: Eurostat (online data code: prc_hicp_aind)

Table 1.4.2: Comparative price levels, 2000-2010 (^{1})
(final consumption by private households including indirect taxes, EU-27 = 100)

	2000	2001	2002	2003	2004	2005	2006	2007	2008	2009	2010
EU-27	100	100	100	100	100	100	100	100	100	100	100
Euro area	100	100	100	103	103	102	102	101	104	106	104
Belgium	102	103	102	107	107	106	108	107	110	113	112
Bulgaria	39	41	41	41	42	43	45	46	49	50	51
Czech Republic	48	50	57	55	55	58	61	62	72	70	72
Denmark	130	135	134	141	140	140	138	137	140	145	143
Germany	107	107	107	106	105	103	103	102	104	106	104
Estonia	57	61	61	62	63	65	69	73	78	77	75
Ireland	115	119	125	126	126	124	125	124	129	126	118
Greece	85	82	80	86	88	88	89	90	91	97	96
Spain	85	85	85	88	91	91	92	93	95	98	97
France	106	104	104	110	110	108	109	108	112	114	112
Italy	98	100	103	104	105	105	104	103	103	106	104
Cyprus	88	89	89	91	91	90	90	88	89	90	89
Latvia	59	59	57	54	56	57	61	67	75	74	69
Lithuania	53	54	54	52	54	55	57	60	66	66	64
Luxembourg	102	104	102	103	103	112	111	115	118	121	120
Hungary	49	53	57	58	62	63	61	67	69	64	66
Malta	73	75	75	72	73	73	75	76	77	80	79
Netherlands	100	103	103	108	106	105	104	102	105	109	106
Austria	102	105	103	103	103	103	102	103	105	108	107
Poland	58	65	61	54	53	61	63	62	69	58	63
Portugal	83	84	86	86	87	85	85	86	88	89	88
Romania	43	42	43	43	43	55	58	64	63	58	59
Slovenia	73	74	74	76	76	76	77	79	82	84	84
Slovakia	44	43	45	51	55	55	58	63	70	72	71
Finland	121	125	124	127	124	124	123	120	121	125	123
Sweden	128	120	122	124	121	119	119	116	113	108	120
United Kingdom	120	117	117	108	109	110	111	114	102	95	100
Iceland	144	128	135	139	138	153	145	149	117	99	111
Norway	138	142	151	142	135	141	140	138	140	136	147
Switzerland	143	146	147	144	141	138	135	125	129	139	148
Montenegro	:	:	:	:	:	56	56	56	60	60	59
Croatia	:	:	:	65	67	69	73	72	75	74	74
FYR of Macedonia	:	:	:	44	44	43	45	45	46	45	44
Turkey	63	48	52	57	59	67	67	70	69	64	73
Japan	198	178	156	137	130	120	110	96	102	120	129
United States	121	126	120	101	93	93	93	85	82	89	92

(^{1}) Break in series in 2005 for all countries except for Japan and the United States.

Source: Eurostat (online data code: tsier010)

Figure 1.4.3: Price convergence between Member States, 2000-2010
(%, coefficient of variation of comparative price levels of final consumption by private households including indirect taxes)

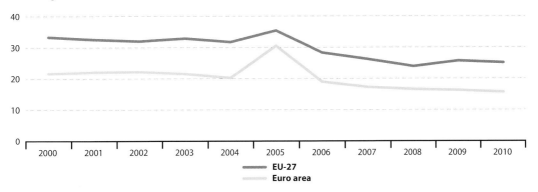

Source: Eurostat (online data code: tsier020)

1.5 Balance of payments

The balance of payments records all economic transactions between resident and non-resident entities during a given period. This subchapter presents data on the current and financial accounts of the balance of payments for the European Union (EU) and its Member States.

The current account balance determines the exposure of an economy to the rest of the world, whereas the capital and financial account explains how it is financed. A subchapter on foreign direct investment provides more information on one component of the financial account and another on international trade in services focuses on one component of the current account.

Main statistical findings

The current account deficit of the EU-27 was EUR 95 700 million in 2010 (see Figure 1.5.1), corresponding to 0.8 % of gross domestic product (GDP); the current account deficit in 2009 (EUR 99 500 million) was at a similar level to that recorded in 2010, while both of these deficits were about 60 % lower than in 2008, when the deficit corresponded to about 2.0 % of GDP. The current account deficit for 2010 comprised deficits in the

current account for goods (– 1.0 % of GDP) and current transfers (– 0.5 %), alongside a positive balance for services (0.6 %) and for the income account (0.2 %) (see Table 1.5.2).

There were a total of 14 Member States that reported current account deficits in 2010 (see Table 1.5.1): the largest of these (relative to GDP) were in Greece and Portugal (both – 10.0 %); Luxembourg (7.4 %), Sweden (6.6 %) and the Netherlands (6.5 %) reported the largest current account surpluses. Ireland, Slovakia, Germany, Italy and Romania were the only EU Member States to report a current account deficit for services in 2010, while Luxembourg (54.5 % of GDP), Cyprus 20.5 %) and Malta (19.2 %) reported relatively large surpluses. A total of 18 Member States reported a deficit for goods – most notably Cyprus (– 26.7 % of GDP), while Ireland reported the largest surplus relative to GDP (23.4 %).

Among those countries shown in Figure 1.5.2, the EU-27's current account deficit with China was EUR 144 550 million in 2010, more than three times as large as the deficit with Russia and five and half times the deficit with Japan (these two countries accounted for the second and third largest EU-27 current account deficits). The highest current

account surplus was recorded with the United States (EUR 51 850 million), followed by Switzerland; with surpluses also registered with Brazil, Hong Kong, Canada and India.

Three types of investment (foreign direct investment (FDI), portfolio and other) make-up the financial account, along with financial derivatives and official reserve assets. A positive value for the financial account indicates that inward investment flows (inward FDI, portfolio and other investment liabilities) exceed outward investment flows (outward FDI, portfolio and other investment assets). This was the case for the euro area in 2010, where the financial account was equivalent to 0.5 % of GDP, mainly due to high value of portfolio investment liabilities.

As can be seen in Table 1.5.3, the EU-27 continued to be a net direct investor vis-à-vis the rest of the world in 2010. Inward flows of FDI represented 0.8 % of GDP, while outward flows of FDI represented 1.4 % of GDP, making FDI the main form of outward investment from the EU-27 in 2010. Luxembourg recorded by far the highest levels of both inward and outward FDI (in relation to GDP) with the rest of the world, followed by Belgium and Ireland. Luxembourg also recorded the highest level of FDI transactions in absolute terms, followed by Germany and France in relation to outward flows of FDI, and Belgium and United Kingdom in relation to inward flows of FDI.

While the value of FDI flows continued to fall for the third consecutive year in 2010 having peaked in 2007, flows in portfolio and other investment exceeded amounts of FDI transactions. The EU-27 recorded investment in portfolio investment assets (outward investment) equivalent to 2.5 % of GDP in 2010. EU-27 portfolio investment liabilities (inward investment) were valued at 4.7 % of GDP, almost six times as high as the level of inward FDI. Seven of the Member States recorded disinvestment for portfolio assets, with Ireland recording relatively large flows (12.0 % of GDP). The largest investments in portfolio assets (in relative terms) were recorded in Luxembourg (home to a large fund management activity), Malta and Cyprus. Disinvestment in portfolio liabilities was also relatively common, with Greece, Portugal, Spain and Belgium reporting

negative flows in excess of 2 % of GDP. Luxembourg again reported the largest positive flows (relative to GDP), followed by Ireland and Finland.

For other assets and liabilities (such as currency and deposits, loans and trade credit) the EU-27 recorded in 2010 net capital outflows equivalent to 0.9 % of GDP. Investment in other assets was equal to 3.0 % of the EU-27's GDP in 2010, with the largest investments (in relative terms) recorded in Luxembourg and the United Kingdom. Inward investment in other liabilities was equivalent to 2.1 % of GDP in the EU-27. Again the largest investments in relative terms were recorded in Luxembourg, followed at some distance by Malta, Greece, the United Kingdom, Portugal and Finland, with substantial disinvestment recorded in Cyprus and Ireland. In contrast to the overall EU-27 situation of net outflows of other investments, a small number of Member States recorded net investment inflows for other investment assets and liabilities, most notably Greece and Portugal.

Data sources and availability

The main methodological references used for the production of balance of payment statistics is the fifth balance of payments manual (BPM5) of the International Monetary Fund (IMF). The sixth edition of this manual (BPM6) was finalised in December 2008 with implementation planned in 2014. This new set of international standards has been developed, partly in response to important economic developments, including an increased role for globalisation, rising innovation and complexity in financial markets, and an greater emphasis on using the balance sheet as a tool for understanding economic activity.

The transmission of balance of payments data to Eurostat is covered by Regulation 184/2005 on Community statistics concerning balance of payments, international trade in services and foreign direct investment (of which there is a consolidated version, dating from 9 May 2006).

Current account

The current account of the balance of payments provides information not only on international trade in goods (generally the largest category), but also on international transactions in services, income and current transfers. For all these transactions, the balance of payments registers the value of credits (exports) and debits (imports). A negative balance – a current account deficit – shows that a country is spending abroad more than it is earning from transactions with other economies, and is therefore a net debtor towards the rest of the world.

The current account gauges a country's economic position in the world, covering all transactions that occur between resident and non-resident entities. More specifically, the four main components of the current account are defined as follows:

- Trade in goods covers general merchandise, goods for processing, repairs on goods, goods procured in ports by carriers, and non-monetary gold. Exports and imports of goods are recorded on a so-called fob/fob basis – in other words, at market value at the customs frontiers of exporting economies, including charges for insurance and transport services up to the frontier of the exporting country.
- Trade in services consists of the following items: transport services performed by EU residents for non-EU residents, or vice versa, involving the carriage of passengers, the movement of goods, rentals of carriers with crew and related supporting and auxiliary services; travel, which includes primarily the goods and services EU travellers acquire from non-EU residents, or vice versa; and other services, which include communication services, construction services, insurance services, financial services, computer and information services, royalties and licence fees, other business services (which comprise merchanting and other trade-related services, operational leasing services and miscellaneous business, professional and technical services), personal, cultural and recreational services, and government services not included elsewhere.
- Income covers two types of transactions: compensation of employees paid to non-resident workers or received from non-resident employers, and investment income accrued on external financial assets and liabilities.

- Current transfers include general government current transfers, for example transfers related to international cooperation between governments, payments of current taxes on income and wealth, and other current transfers, such as workers' remittances, insurance premiums (less service charges), and claims on non-life insurance companies.

Under the balance of payment conventions, transactions which represent an inflow of real resources, an increase in assets, or a decrease in liabilities (such as exports of goods) are recorded as credits, and transactions representing an outflow of real resources, a decrease in assets or an increase in liabilities (such as imports of goods) are recorded as debits. Net is the balance (credits minus debits) of all transactions with each partner.

Financial account

The financial account of the balance of payments covers all transactions associated with changes of ownership in the foreign financial assets and liabilities of an economy. The financial account is broken down into five basic components: direct investment, portfolio investment, financial derivatives, other investment, and official reserve assets. Direct investment implies that a resident investor in one economy has a lasting interest in, and a degree of influence over the management of, a business enterprise resident in another economy. Direct investment is classified primarily on a directional basis: resident direct investment abroad and non-resident direct investment in the reporting economy. Within this classification three main components are distinguished: equity capital, reinvested earnings, and other capital; these are discussed in more detail in a subchapter on foreign direct investment.

Portfolio investment records the transactions in negotiable securities with the exception of the transactions which fall within the definition of direct investment or reserve assets. Several components are identified: equity securities, bonds and notes, money market instruments. Financial derivatives are financial instruments that are linked to, and whose value is contingent to, a specific financial instrument, indicator or commodity, and

through which specific financial risks can be traded in financial markets in their own right. Transactions in financial derivatives are treated as separate transactions, rather than integral parts of the value of underlying transactions to which they may be linked.

Reserve assets are foreign financial assets available to, and controlled by, monetary authorities; they are used for financing and regulating payments imbalances or for other purposes.

Other investment is a residual category, which is not recorded under the other headings of the financial account (direct investment, portfolio investment, financial derivatives or reserve assets). It also encompasses the offsetting entries for accrued income on instruments classified under other investment. Four types of instruments are identified: currency and deposits (in general, the most significant item), trade credits, loans, other assets and liabilities.

Context

The EU is a major player in the global economy for international trade in goods and services, as well as foreign investment. Balance of payments statistics give a complete picture of all external transactions for the EU and its individual Member States.

These statistics may be used as a tool to study the international exposure of different parts of the EU's economy, indicating its comparative advantages and disadvantages with the rest of the world. The financial and economic crisis underlined the importance of such economic statistics insofar as improvements in the availability of data on the real and financial economies of the world may have helped as the crisis unfolded, if internationally comparable information about financial asset and liability flows and their impact on production, employment, and income had been available.

Figure 1.5.1: Current account transactions, EU-27, 2001-2010 (¹)
(EUR 1 000 million)

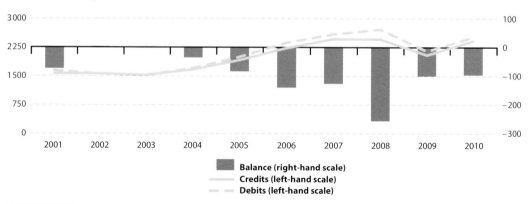

(¹) EU-25, 2001-2003.

Source: Eurostat (online data code: bop_q_eu)

Table 1.5.1: Current account balance with the rest of the world, 2004-2010 (¹)
(EUR 1 000 million)

	2004	2005	2006	2007	2008	2009	2010
EU-27	− 35.7	− 83.5	− 139.6	− 125.9	− 255.4	− 99.5	− 95.7
Euro area	60.8	10.8	− 12.6	7.4	− 143.5	− 25.9	− 42.2
Belgium	9.3	6.0	5.9	5.4	− 5.7	− 5.7	5.2
Bulgaria	− 1.3	− 2.7	− 4.6	− 7.8	− 8.2	− 3.1	− 0.5
Czech Republic	− 4.7	− 1.0	− 2.4	− 5.7	− 3.3	− 3.4	− 4.7
Denmark	5.9	9.0	6.5	3.1	6.8	7.3	13.0
Germany	102.8	112.9	145.0	181.2	154.8	133.7	141.5
Estonia	− 1.1	− 1.1	− 2.1	− 2.6	− 1.6	0.5	0.5
Ireland	− 0.9	− 5.7	− 6.3	− 10.1	− 10.2	− 4.7	0.8
Greece	− 10.7	− 14.7	− 23.8	− 32.6	− 34.8	− 25.8	− 23.0
Spain	− 44.2	− 66.9	− 88.3	− 105.3	− 104.7	− 54.5	− 48.4
France	9.0	− 8.3	− 10.3	− 18.9	− 33.7	− 28.4	− 33.7
Italy	− 4.6	− 12.6	− 22.3	− 19.9	− 45.2	− 30.1	− 54.1
Cyprus	− 0.6	− 0.8	− 1.0	− 1.9	− 2.7	− 1.8	− 1.7
Latvia	− 1.4	− 1.6	− 3.6	− 4.7	− 3.0	1.6	0.5
Lithuania	− 1.4	− 1.5	− 2.6	− 4.1	− 4.2	1.2	0.4
Luxembourg	3.3	3.5	3.5	3.8	2.0	2.4	3.1
Hungary	− 6.8	− 6.4	− 6.6	− 7.2	− 7.7	− 0.2	1.1
Malta	− 0.3	− 0.4	− 0.5	− 0.3	− 0.3	− 0.4	− 0.2
Netherlands	37.5	38.0	50.4	38.4	25.5	24.3	38.6
Austria	5.2	5.3	7.3	9.6	13.8	7.5	8.5
Poland	− 10.8	− 5.9	− 10.4	− 19.3	− 23.8	− 12.1	− 16.5
Portugal	− 12.4	− 15.9	− 17.2	− 17.1	− 21.7	− 18.4	− 17.2
Romania	− 5.1	− 6.9	− 10.2	− 16.8	− 16.2	− 4.9	− 4.9
Slovenia	− 0.7	− 0.5	− 0.8	− 1.6	− 2.6	− 0.5	− 0.3
Slovakia	− 2.7	− 3.3	− 3.5	− 2.9	− 4.0	− 1.6	− 2.3
Finland	9.4	5.3	7.0	7.7	4.7	3.4	3.3
Sweden	19.1	20.2	26.6	31.2	29.4	20.5	23.0
United Kingdom	− 36.9	− 47.8	− 63.3	− 51.3	− 24.6	− 23.0	− 42.9
Iceland	− 1.1	− 2.2	− 3.2	− 2.3	− 2.8	− 1.1	− 1.1
Norway	26.5	39.7	46.2	40.1	54.5	35.8	38.7
Croatia	− 1.5	− 2.0	− 2.7	− 3.2	− 4.4	− 2.4	− 0.6
Turkey	− 11.5	− 17.8	− 25.6	− 27.9	− 28.1	− 10.0	− 35.9
Japan	138.5	133.3	136.0	154.0	105.1	101.6	147.6
United States	− 505.4	− 602.2	− 637.1	− 519.7	− 460.5	− 269.2	− 357.0

(¹) EU-27, extra EU-27 flows; euro area, extra EA-17 flows; Member States and other countries, flows with the rest of the world.

Source: Eurostat (online data codes: bop_q_eu, bop_q_euro and bop_q_c), ECB

Table 1.5.2: Main components of the current account balance, 2010 (¹)
(% of GDP)

	Current account	Goods	Services	Income	Current transfers
EU-27	−0.8	−1.0	0.6	0.2	−0.5
Euro area	−0.5	0.1	0.5	0.0	−1.1
Belgium	1.5	−1.0	1.8	2.4	−1.8
Bulgaria	−1.3	−7.7	5.6	−3.5	4.3
Czech Republic	−3.2	1.4	2.0	−7.0	0.2
Denmark	5.6	2.8	2.8	1.9	−1.9
Germany	5.7	6.4	−0.9*	1.8	−1.5
Estonia	3.5	−1.7	9.1	−5.6	1.8
Ireland	0.5	23.4	−4.5	−17.6	−0.8
Greece	−10.0	−12.3	5.8	−3.5	0.1
Spain	−4.6	−4.4	2.6	−2.1	−0.7
France	−1.7	−2.8	0.5	1.9	−1.4
Italy	−3.5	−1.3	−0.6	−0.6	−1.0
Cyprus	−9.8	−26.7	20.5	−2.2	−0.7
Latvia	3.0	−7.1	6.1	0.3	3.6
Lithuania	1.5	−4.6	3.6	−2.3	4.9
Luxembourg	7.4	−9.9	54.5	−35.6	−1.6
Hungary	1.1	3.3	3.0	−5.6	0.4
Malta	−3.9	−15.4	19.2	−8.1	0.5
Netherlands	6.5	6.6	1.3	0.4	−1.8
Austria	3.0	−1.1	4.6	0.2	−0.7
Poland	−4.7	−2.5	0.7	−3.6	0.8
Portugal	−10.0	−10.5	3.9	−4.6	1.3
Romania	−4.0	−4.8	−0.5	−1.6	2.8
Slovenia	−0.8	−3.4	3.7	−1.4	0.3
Slovakia	−3.5	0.2	−1.1	−1.9	−0.6
Finland	1.8	1.7	0.1	1.0	−0.9
Sweden	6.6	2.4	3.9	1.7	−1.4
United Kingdom	−2.5	−6.7	4.0	1.6	−1.4
Iceland	−11.3	7.8	2.3	−20.8	−0.5
Norway	12.4	14.1	−0.8	0.3	−1.1
Croatia	−1.2	−13.0	12.8	−3.3	2.2
Turkey	−6.5	−7.7	2.0	−1.0	0.2
Japan	3.6	1.7	−0.3	2.4	−0.2
United States	−3.3	−4.4	1.0	1.1	−0.9

(¹) EU-27, extra EU-27 flows; euro area, extra EA-17 flows; Member States and other countries, flows with the rest of the world.

Source: Eurostat (online data codes: bop_q_eu, bop_q_euro, bop_q_c and nama_gdp_c), ECB

Figure 1.5.2: Current account balance with selected partners, EU-27, 2010
(EUR 1 000 million)

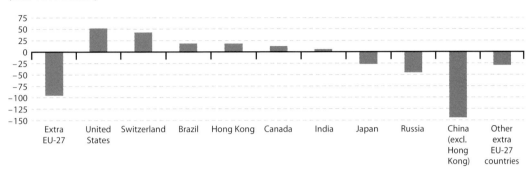

Source: Eurostat (online data code: bop_q_eu)

Table 1.5.3: Main components of the financial account balance, 2010 (¹)
(% of GDP)

	Financial account	Outward foreign direct investment	Inward foreign direct investment	Portfolio investment, assets	Portfolio investment, liabilities	Other investment, assets	Other investment, liabilities
EU-27	:	−1.4	0.8	−2.5	4.7	−3.0	2.1
Euro area	0.5	−1.9	1.4	−1.6	3.2	−1.9	1.3
Belgium	−1.5	−10.4	15.4	1.9	−2.0	1.8	−8.3
Bulgaria	0.6	−0.5	4.9	−1.6	−0.2	−0.1	−2.9
Czech Republic	3.9	−0.9	3.5	0.4	3.9	−2.4	0.6
Denmark	−1.1	−1.1	−2.4	−4.9	3.4	−2.6	6.7
Germany	−5.7	−3.3	1.4	−6.9	1.9	−5.2	7.2
Estonia	−5.6	−0.7	8.0	−2.0	−1.0	−8.9	−6.9
Ireland	7.9	−8.6	12.7	12.0	48.3	−10.2	−38.7
Greece	9.3	−0.3	0.1	5.6	−14.8	3.3	15.2
Spain	4.2	−1.5	1.7	6.6	−3.2	−1.5	1.4
France	0.9	−3.3	1.3	1.2	5.0	−6.1	1.4
Italy	5.6	−1.6	0.4	−2.0	4.5	3.2	1.4
Cyprus	9.4	−2.9	3.3	−14.7	3.6	77.3	−58.0
Latvia	−5.5	−0.1	1.6	−0.8	−0.1	−3.6	2.5
Lithuania	−4.2	−0.2	2.1	−1.5	6.6	−1.1	−7.9
Luxembourg	−6.4	−334.5	373.6	−238.2	353.1	−305.0	101.8
Hungary	−1.7	−1.0	1.4	−0.4	0.2	−0.1	0.5
Malta	−2.2	−1.1	12.7	−51.8	0.0	8.4	29.6
Netherlands	−3.1	−6.4	−1.7	1.6	6.1	−5.4	4.8
Austria	−0.9	−2.2	1.0	−2.3	−0.2	5.2	−2.0
Poland	4.8	−1.2	1.9	−0.2	5.7	−0.8	2.8
Portugal	9.1	3.7	0.6	−1.4	−4.2	−3.9	14.7
Romania	4.7	0.0	1.8	−0.3	1.0	0.1	4.8
Slovenia	0.9	0.2	0.8	−1.1	6.6	1.9	−7.2
Slovakia	−0.8	−0.4	0.5	−3.9	2.1	−0.6	1.6
Finland	−0.8	−4.4	2.9	−12.1	8.6	−10.8	14.2
Sweden	−9.2	−7.0	1.3	−4.0	8.3	−6.5	−2.3
United Kingdom	2.9	−0.5	2.0	−5.8	6.5	−16.0	15.0
Iceland	26.2	20.8	3.8	−0.4	−83.5	18.5	82.6
Norway	−11.3	−3.0	2.9	−12.7	7.9	−6.8	1.4
Croatia	2.6	0.2	0.5	−0.8	1.7	1.4	0.3
Turkey	5.9	−0.2	1.3	−0.5	2.7	1.0	3.4
Japan	−3.2	−1.0	0.0	−4.9	2.1	−2.5	3.7
United States	1.8	−2.4	1.6	−1.1	4.9	−3.4	2.1

(¹) EU-27, extra EU-27 flows; euro area, extra EA-17 flows; Member States and other countries, flows with the rest of the world; note that according to the balance of payments sign convention, increases in assets and decreases in liabilities are shown with a negative sign, whereas decreases in assets and increases in liabilities are shown as positive.

Source: Eurostat (online data codes: bop_q_eu, bop_q_euro, bop_q_c and nama_gdp_c), ECB

1.6 Foreign direct investment

This subchapter examines the developments of foreign direct investment (FDI) in the European Union (EU), through an analysis of inward and outward flows, information on the origin and destination of these flows, important investment activities, as well as stocks of FDI at the end of the year.

FDI is the category of international investment made by an entity resident in one economy (the direct investor) to acquire a lasting interest in an enterprise operating in another economy (the direct investment enterprise). The lasting interest is deemed to exist if the direct investor acquires at least 10 % of the voting power of the direct investment enterprise. FDI is a component of the balance of payments, showing all financial transactions between one country or areas – such as the EU-27 – and all other countries.

Main statistical findings

Effects of the financial and economic crisis

Flows of FDI (new investments made during the reference period) fluctuate considerably from one year to the next, partly as a function of economic fortunes. FDI flows generally increase during times of rapid economic growth, while disinvestment is more likely during periods of recession as businesses are more likely to focus on core activities in their domestic market.

In 2008, total EU-27 FDI outflows dropped by 30 %, mainly due to a sharp decline in equity capital and reinvested earnings. A similar trend was observed in 2009, as all types of FDI flows contributed to a negative development, with outflows falling by a further 28 %.

Following a sharp decrease of 60 % in 2008, EU-27 FDI inflows recovered in 2009 (up 26 %) largely as a result of growth in equity capital and reinvested earnings.

Provisional figures for 2010 show a sharp drop in EU-27 FDI, for both outward and inward flows of investment, thereby confirming the continued impact of the global financial and economic crisis.

EU-27 outward flows of FDI decreased for the third consecutive year, falling by 62 % in 2010 when compared with the year before. At the same time, EU-27 inward flows of FDI decreased by 75 %. FDI flows channelled through special-purpose entities (SPEs) played a significant role in the results for 2010.

EU-27 FDI flows by partner country

EU-27 FDI flows with a range of economic partners have been considerably affected by the global financial and economic crisis. The decline in EU-27 outflows in 2009 could be largely attributed to a fall in investment to the United States — from EUR 148 200 million in 2008 to EUR 79 200 million in 2009. During the same period, investment from the United States in the EU-27 recovered, rising to EUR 97 300 million, which was more than twice the figure recorded in 2008 (EUR 44 400 million). Provisional figures for 2010 show a considerable decrease in both flows with respect to the United States.

EU-27 outward FDI to Canada fell to such a degree that there was disinvestment in both 2009 and 2010. Incoming FDI from Canada, after decreasing by 14 % in 2009, seems to have recovered in 2010, rising to EUR 27 700 million.

EU-27 investment flows to emerging economies, such as China, were generally less affected than flows to other economic partners. Having fallen to EUR 5 200 million in 2008, EU-27 outward FDI flows to China rose by 11 % in 2009. Preliminary results for 2010 suggest that FDI flows from the EU-27 to China fell by 16 %. Outward flows of FDI from the EU-27 to Brazil decreased for three successive years after peaking in 2007; however, the pace of decline was less marked than the average reduction in outflows for all EU-27 partners.

There was some evidence of an increase in inward investment into the EU-27 from Asia in 2010, as inward FDI flows from China (EUR 900 million) and Hong Kong (EUR 11 300 million) rose in relation to 2009. In a similar manner, there was a

considerable increase in the level of inward flows from Brazil in 2010.

EU-27 outward investment in Russia dropped considerably in 2009 and then fell again in 2010, such that there was slight disinvestment in 2010. There was a similar pattern as regards Russian investment in the EU-27: having peaked in 2007 (EUR 10 500 million) much lower levels were recorded during the period 2008 to 2010, with a modest degree of disinvestment in 2010 (EUR 400 million).

EU-27 FDI outflows to Africa remained relatively unchanged during the period from 2007 to 2009, averaging EUR 20 707 million; this pattern was in stark contrast to that recorded for the other continents, where EU-27 outflows of FDI were considerably reduced.

There was a wide variation from one year to the next as regards the development of FDI for offshore financial centres. These played a considerable role in FDI flows in 2007 both with respect to outward and inward flows – accounting for around one quarter of the total flows to and from extra-EU partners. The financial and economic crisis saw the role played by offshore financial centres being reduced considerably, such that in 2008 they accounted for around one tenth of EU-27 inward and outward FDI flows. Although there was an increase in FDI flows to offshore financial centres in 2009, this was immediately reversed in 2010.

Principal EU Member States for outward flows of FDI

FDI flows can oscillate considerably from one year to the next, influenced mainly by large mergers and acquisitions. Luxembourg's share (24 %) of EU-27 outward flows of FDI during the period 2007 to 2009 may be explained by the activities of special-purpose entities (SPEs) that represented about 85 % of total direct investments. SPEs also played an important role in a number of other EU Member States; this was especially the case in the Netherlands and Hungary. There was a 42 % increase in outward flows of FDI from Luxembourg between 2008 and 2009. As a result, Luxembourg became the principal EU-27 investor in non-member countries. The four main partner destinations of FDI

from Luxembourg included Switzerland, the United States, Bermuda and the Bahamas, thereby revealing the importance of the financial sector.

Although the United Kingdom accounted for the second highest share of outward FDI among the EU Member States between 2007 and 2009, outward investment to non-member countries from the United Kingdom was almost cut in half in 2009. The reduction in investment flows was particularly marked for traditional partners such as the United States, Canada or Australia, while higher levels of investment were destined for the United Arab Emirates, New Zealand, Japan and India.

Changes in FDI positions (stocks)

EU-27 outward and inward stocks (or positions) grew in 2009: outward stocks rose by 10 % and inward stocks by 7 %. In 2008, both inward and outward stocks had increased at a slower pace, rising by 3 % (see Table 1.6.4).

At the end of 2009, the biggest share (30.9 %) of EU-27 outward stocks of FDI was recorded for the United States, valued at some EUR 1 134 000 million. The services sector represented 70 % of EU-27 stocks held in the United States, and most of these were from financial intermediation (39 %), real estate and other business activities or manufacturing (both 22 %); for the latter, the main area of investment activity was the manufacturing of chemicals and chemical products. At the end of 2009, the main holder of EU-27 FDI stocks in the United States continued to be the United Kingdom, accounting around one quarter of the total. Switzerland was the second most important outward partner as regards EU-27 FDI positions in 2009, accounting for 14 % of total stocks; financial intermediation was the main activity for EU-27 investment in Switzerland. EU-27 stocks of FDI in Russia grew by 24 % between 2007 and 2009. Financial intermediation and manufacturing were the main areas of EU-27 investment in Russia, and FDI stocks in these two sectors were maintained during the period under consideration.

In Asia, the main positions for EU-27 stocks of FDI were found in Singapore, Hong Kong and Japan, while EU-27 stocks of FDI in China continued

to grow in 2009 (up 11 % on the 2008 figure); the fastest expansions in EU-27 outward stocks of FDI across Asia were recorded in Malaysia, India and Indonesia (up by 82 %, 56 % and 22 % respectively between the end of 2008 and the end of 2009).

In Africa, the main positions for EU-27 stocks of FDI were found in South Africa (EUR 77 000 million), Nigeria (EUR 30 300 million) and Egypt (EUR 26 400 million). EU-27 outward positions in South Africa grew by 40 % between the end of 2008 and the end of 2009, such that South Africa became one of the EU-27's top ten FDI partners.

In 2009, the United States held 39 % of inward stocks of FDI in the EU-27; this share was valued at EUR 1 044 100 million at the end of 2009. The United States therefore consolidated its position as the main investor in the EU-27, with the main area of investment being the services sector, which accounted for 79 % of investment positions held by the United States in the EU-27 at the end of 2008. Switzerland was the second biggest holder of EU-27 FDI stocks, with EUR 347 900 million at the end of 2009, which was 10 % higher than a year before. Other countries with significant shares of EU-27 inward stocks included Japan, Canada, Brazil and Singapore. The relative importance of EU-27 FDI inward stocks was 10 % higher for Japan and 11 % higher for Canada at the end of 2009 (compared with a year before). The position of Brazilian investment in the EU-27 also rose, climbing 7 % between the end of 2008 and the end of 2009 – although this was a relatively modest increase when compared with far higher growth rates recorded during the period from the end of 2006 to the end of 2008.

Analysis of FDI by economic activity

The structure of the EU-27's FDI stocks according to economic activity is shown in Table 1.6.5. Services provided by far the largest contribution both to outward (72 %) and to inward (83 %) stocks of FDI at the end of 2008; almost two thirds of the stock of EU-27 FDI in services was held in the financial intermediation sector (for both inward and outward FDI).

Income and rates of return

The financial and economic crisis had a persistent impact on the EU-27's income from FDI, with the income from inward and outward FDI stocks falling in 2008 and 2009. The EU-27's investment income from stocks of FDI in non-member countries fell by 13 % between the end of 2008 and the end of 2009 to stand at EUR 169 000 million, while the income paid to non-member countries remained relatively unchanged, falling just 2 %, to EUR 104 000 million. The resulting net income from the rest of the world amounted to EUR 65 300 million, which was 27 % lower than at the end of 2008. As such, the EU-27's net income from FDI was valued at 0.55 % of GDP in 2009, compared with 0.72 % in 2008.

The rate of return from stocks of EU-27 outward investment declined for the third consecutive year to the end of 2009, reaching 5.1 %; the return from inward investments remained relatively stable at 4.1 %. As a result, the latest rates of return on outward and inward FDI stocks fell to their lowest level in recent years (see Figure 1.6.3).

Data sources and methodology

FDI statistics in the EU are collected according to Regulation 0184/2005 on Community statistics concerning balance of payments, international trade in services and foreign direct investment.

The methodological framework used is that of the OECD's benchmark definition of foreign direct investment (third edition), which provides a detailed operational definition that is fully consistent with the IMF's balance of payments manual (fifth edition).

Annual EU FDI statistics give a detailed presentation of FDI flows and stocks, showing which Member States invest in which partner countries and in which economic sectors. Eurostat collects FDI statistics for quarterly and annual flows, as well as for positions/stocks at the end of the year. FDI stocks (assets and liabilities) are part of the international investment position of an economy.

Through outward FDI flows, an investor country builds up FDI assets abroad (outward FDI stocks). Correspondingly, inward FDI flows cumulate into liabilities towards foreign investors (inward FDI stocks). However, changes in FDI stocks differ from FDI flows because of the impact of revaluation (changes in prices and, for outward stocks, exchange rates) and other adjustments such as catastrophic losses, cancellation of loans, reclassification of existing assets or liabilities.

FDI flows are components of the financial account of the balance of payments, while FDI assets and liabilities are components of the international investment position. FDI income consists of the income accruing to the direct investor from its affiliates abroad. Income earned from outward FDI is recorded among credits in the current account of the balance of payments, while income paid to foreign owners of inward FDI stocks is recorded among debits.

FDI flows and positions are recorded according to the immediate host/investing country criterion. The economic activity for both flows abroad and flows in the reporting economy are classified according to the economic activity of the resident enterprise; the same applies to FDI positions.

FDI flows are new investments made during the reference period, whereas FDI stocks provide information on the position, in terms of value, of all previous investments at the end of the reference period. The intensity of FDI can be measured by averaging the value of inward and outward flows during a particular reference period and expressing this in relation to GDP. The sign convention adopted for the data shown in this subchapter, for both flows and stocks, is that investment is always recorded with a positive sign, and a disinvestment with a negative sign.

European aggregates (such as the EU-27) include special-purpose entities (SPEs), which are a particular class of enterprises (often empty shells or holding companies) not included in all countries' national statistics. Therefore, European aggregates (for the EU or euro area) are not simply equal to the sum of the requisite national figures.

Context

In a world of increasing globalisation, where political, economic and technological barriers are rapidly disappearing, the ability of a country to participate in global activity is an important indicator of its performance and competitiveness. In order to remain competitive, modern-day business relationships extend well beyond the traditional foreign exchange of goods and services, as witnessed by the increasing reliance of enterprises on mergers, partnerships, joint ventures, licensing agreements, and other forms of business co-operation.

FDI may be seen as an alternative economic strategy, adopted by those enterprises that invest to establish a new plant/office, or alternatively, purchase existing assets of a foreign enterprise. These enterprises seek to complement or substitute external trade, by producing (and often selling) goods and services in countries other than where the enterprise was first established.

There are two kinds of FDI: namely, the creation of productive assets by foreigners or the purchase of existing assets by foreigners (acquisitions, mergers, takeovers, etc.). FDI differs from portfolio investments because it is made with the purpose of having control or an effective voice in management and a lasting interest in the enterprise. Direct investment not only includes the initial acquisition of equity capital, but also subsequent capital transactions between the foreign investor and domestic and affiliated enterprises.

Conventional trade is less important for services than for goods. While trade in services has been growing, the share of services in total intra-EU trade has changed little during the last decade. However, FDI is expanding more rapidly for services than for goods, increasing at a more rapid pace than conventional trade in services. As a result, the share of services in total FDI flows and positions has increased substantially, as the service sector within the EU-27 has become increasingly international.

Table 1.6.1: FDI outward flows by main partner, 2010 (¹)
(EUR 1 000 million)

	Extra EU-27	of which:									
		United States	Canada	Switz-erland	Russia	Japan	China	Hong Kong	India	Brazil	Offshore financial centres
EU-27 (²)	106.7	11.9	−4.1	−7.4	−0.4	−4.1	4.9	3.0	3.0	6.2	21.1
Belgium	35.9	24.0	0.6	–	1.3	−0.1	–	0.5	–	1.0	1.5
Bulgaria	0.1	–	–	–	–	–	–	–	–	–	0.1
Czech Republic	0.1	–	–	–	0.1	–	–	–	0.1	–	–
Denmark	−0.3	0.9	–	−4.3	0.1	0.1	0.4	0.5	0.2	0.3	1.2
Germany	28.7	10.7	0.4	2.6	0.3	1.8	1.6	0.9	0.7	0.9	2.2
Estonia	–	–	:	:	–	:	:	:	:	:	–
Ireland	7.4	1.6	:	−0.7	:	:	–	0.1	−0.1	–	10.2
Greece	0.3	–	–	–	–	–	–	0.1	–	–	0.1
Spain	7.9	2.4	0.7	0.4	0.1	:	1.4	0.4	0.1	−0.8	0.5
France	22.7	1.2	−1.6	7.8	1.7	−0.4	1.3	0.9	0.2	2.1	3.0
Italy	6.0	0.8	0.1	−3.0	0.8	−0.2	0.5	0.1	0.4	−0.2	0.1
Cyprus	2.3	–	–	0.1	1.1	–	–	–	–	–	0.5
Latvia	–	–	–	–	–	–	–	–	–	–	–
Lithuania	–	–	–	–	–	–	–	–	–	–	–
Luxembourg	38.3	5.7	3.9	0.4	0.7	0.2	−3.2	0.4	–	6.6	24.3
Hungary (³)	0.5	0.2	−0.1	0.3	–	–	–	–	–	–	1.0
Malta	–	–	:	:	:	–	:	–	:	–	–
Netherlands (³)	13.5	−9.5	0.5	6.7	−0.5	0.8	–	−0.1	0.1	0.6	11.0
Austria (³)	5.3	0.2	–	:	0.7	–	−0.2	–	0.1	0.1	0.5
Poland	0.6	0.2	–	0.9	−0.2	–	–	−0.2	–	−0.1	−0.5
Portugal	−0.7	0.2	–	–	–	–	–	:	–	−0.6	0.2
Romania	–	–	–	–	–	–	–	–	–	–	–
Slovenia	0.2	–	–	–	0.1	–	–	–	–	–	–
Slovakia	0.1	–	–	–	–	–	–	–	–	–	–
Finland	1.2	−0.8	–	−1.2	0.4	–	1.4	–	0.3	–	0.6
Sweden	16.2	7.4	–	0.5	1.8	−0.2	0.4	−0.2	0.1	0.2	0.1
United Kingdom	12.5	−20.9	−9.2	9.4	:	0.4	:	−0.4	0.2	:	17.6

(¹) Minus sign stands for disinvestment; "–" indicates less than EUR 50 million.
(²) Takes into account confidential data, estimates for Member States missing data and data for special purpose entities (SPEs) that in some cases are additionally collected by Eurostat and the ECB from Member States not including SPEs foreign direct investment in national data (see footnote 3).
(³) Excluding SPEs.

Source: Eurostat (online data code: bop_fdi_main)

Table 1.6.2: FDI inward flows by main partner, 2010 ([1])
(EUR 1 000 million)

	Extra EU-27	of which:									
		United States	Canada	Switz-erland	Russia	Japan	China	Hong Kong	India	Brazil	Offshore financial centres
EU-27 ([2])	54.2	28.5	27.7	6.2	−0.4	1.5	0.9	11.3	0.6	3.8	−3.9
Belgium	−2.4	−1.6	–	2.4	–	−0.2	–	0.9	–	–	−0.1
Bulgaria	0.2	0.1	–	–	0.1	–	–	–	–	–	−0.1
Czech Republic	0.2	–	–	0.3	0.1	–	–	–	–	–	–
Denmark	1.9	0.9	–	0.3	–	–	–	0.2	–	−0.1	0.4
Germany	14.5	5.3	−0.7	1.4	0.3	0.2	0.3	0.3	0.1	0.1	6.0
Estonia	–	–	:	:	–	:	:	:	:	:	–
Ireland	21.5	8.3	:	−0.3	0.1	:	:	0.5	−0.1	0.1	13.5
Greece	0.1	–	–	–	–	–	–	–	–	–	–
Spain	5.6	1.4	−0.2	1.7	0.5	:	:	:	:	0.7	−0.1
France	8.0	0.2	1.0	1.2	0.3	−0.3	0.1	0.3	–	–	2.9
Italy	2.5	0.5	–	0.8	0.1	0.2	0.1	–	–	0.1	–
Cyprus	2.4	0.1	–	–	0.6	–	–	–	–	–	1.6
Latvia	0.1	–	–	0.1	–	–	–	–	–	–	–
Lithuania	0.1	−0.1	–	–	0.2	–	–	–	–	–	–
Luxembourg	47.6	23.2	21.8	3.8	−1.7	−0.2	–	5.7	–	1.3	−3.8
Hungary ([3])	0.4	0.2	0.1	0.3	0.2	–	0.1	−0.1	–	–	0.1
Malta	0.5	–	–	:	:	–	–	–	–	:	–
Netherlands ([3])	−5.3	−3.0	0.4	−1.5	–	0.1	0.2	−0.5	0.1	–	−2.1
Austria ([3])	−0.7	−0.6	–	−0.1	–	–	–	–	–	0.1	−1.1
Poland	1.3	–	–	0.5	–	−0.2	–	–	–	−0.1	0.3
Portugal	1.1	−0.2	0.2	–	–	–	–	–	:	0.8	0.1
Romania	−0.3	–	–	−0.3	0.1	–	–	–	–	–	–
Slovenia	0.2	–	–	−0.1	–	–	–	–	–	–	–
Slovakia	−0.2	−0.1	–	–	−0.1	0.1	–	–	–	−0.2	–
Finland	−0.1	−0.1	–	–	–	0.1	–	–	–	–	−0.2
Sweden	−5.5	−3.3	−0.5	0.3	−0.3	−0.2	0.8	–	–	–	−2.6
United Kingdom	28.5	20.6	14.2	2.4	:	3.2	:	3.8	0.2	:	13.5

([1]) Minus sign stands for disinvestment; "–" indicates less than EUR 50 million.
([2]) Takes into account confidential data, estimates for Member States missing data and data for special purpose entities (SPEs) that in some cases
    are additionally collected by Eurostat and the ECB from Member States not including SPEs foreign direct investment in national data (see footnote 3).
([3]) Excluding SPEs.

Source: Eurostat (online data code: bop_fdi_main)

Figure 1.6.1: FDI flows and stocks, EU-27, 2004-2010
(EUR 1 000 million)

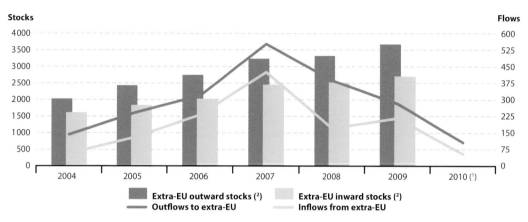

Stocks

Flows

	Extra-EU outward stocks (²)	Extra-EU inward stocks (²)
	Outflows to extra-EU	Inflows from extra-EU

(¹) Provisional.
(²) 2010, not available.

Source: Eurostat (online data code: bop_fdi_main)

Table 1.6.3: Foreign direct investment, EU-27, 2007-2010 ([1])
(EUR 1 000 million)

	Outward FDI flows					Inward FDI flows				
	2007	2008	2009	2010	Share in 2009 (%)	2007	2008	2009	2010	Share in 2009 (%)
Extra EU-27	550.7	387.3	280.6	*106.7*	100.0	423.8	170.7	215.7	*54.2*	100.0
Europe (non-EU), *of which*	85.2	65.3	38.8	:	13.8	20.7	29.0	16.8	:	7.8
Switzerland	39.6	25.2	43.9	− 7.4	15.6	29.6	8.4	24.7	*6.2*	11.5
Russia	18.2	27.3	0.7	− 0.4	0.2	10.5	0.5	2.7	− 0.4	1.3
Croatia	2.5	2.2	2.5	:	0.9	0.0	− 0.1	− 0.1	:	0.0
Turkey	15.7	6.5	4.2	:	1.5	0.6	− 0.3	1.2	:	0.5
Ukraine	5.3	7.3	3.0	:	1.1	0.4	0.5	0.0	:	0.0
Africa, *of which*	17.0	24.1	21.0	:	7.5	3.9	7.2	0.9	:	0.4
Egypt	1.5	10.6	2.1	:	0.8	− 0.5	0.8	0.1	:	0.1
South Africa	5.1	3.0	5.9	:	2.1	1.9	2.5	1.0	:	0.5
North America, *of which*	204.4	154.9	78.3	:	27.9	201.3	57.7	108.8	:	50.4
Canada	30.6	6.7	− 0.9	− 4.1	− 0.3	6.3	13.3	11.5	*27.7*	5.3
United States	173.8	148.2	79.2	*11.9*	28.2	195.0	44.4	97.3	*28.5*	45.1
Central America, *of which*	108.5	0.0	61.0	:	21.7	78.2	− 15.3	30.7	:	14.2
Mexico	5.8	5.6	4.0	:	1.4	0.4	0.7	2.7	:	1.2
South America, *of which*	19.2	19.1	9.4	:	3.3	27.9	12.0	0.8	:	0.3
Argentina	2.4	4.1	0.8	:	0.3	− 0.2	− 0.3	0.4	:	0.2
Brazil	14.9	9.1	8.8	*6.2*	3.1	24.7	10.0	0.4	*3.8*	0.2
Asia, *of which*	55.0	72.9	28.1	:	10.0	39.9	72.5	18.2	:	8.4
Arabian Gulf countries	4.7	19.5	3.9	:	1.4	2.7	51.2	10.6	:	4.9
China (excl. Hong Kong)	7.2	5.2	5.8	*4.9*	2.1	0.8	− 0.2	0.3	*0.9*	0.1
Hong Kong	7.2	5.6	2.0	*3.0*	0.7	5.9	2.7	1.3	*11.3*	0.6
Japan	10.2	2.5	− 0.2	− 4.1	− 0.1	18.6	2.8	− 0.8	*1.5*	− 0.4
India	4.6	3.7	3.4	*3.0*	1.2	1.2	3.6	0.9	*0.6*	0.4
Singapore	8.7	21.7	1.7	:	0.6	10.6	2.2	2.8	:	1.3
Oceania, *of which*	10.2	18.5	− 1.6	:	− 0.6	7.1	− 0.4	5.8	:	2.7
Australia	9.6	17.3	− 2.7	:	− 1.0	7.1	− 0.3	5.8	:	2.7
Offshore financial centres	158.4	39.4	89.5	*21.1*	31.9	105.8	16.8	46.1	− 3.9	21.4

([1]) 2007-2009 annual FDI data; preliminary figures for 2010 are based on annualised quarterly data; the sum of continents does not always equal the extra-EU total because of non-allocated flows.

Source: Eurostat (online data code: bop_fdi_main)

Figure 1.6.2: FDI outward flows, 2007 to 2009 average
(% of total EU-27 outward flows)

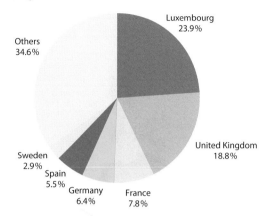

Luxembourg
23.9%

Others
34.6%

United Kingdom
18.8%

Sweden
2.9%

Spain
5.5%

Germany
6.4%

France
7.8%

Source: Eurostat (online data code: bop_fdi_main)

Table 1.6.4: Top 10 countries as extra EU-27 partners for FDI positions, EU-27, 2007-2009
(EUR 1 000 million)

	Outward				Inward			
	2007	2008	2009	Growth rate 2007-2009 (%)	2007	2008	2009	Growth rate 2007-2009 (%)
Extra EU-27	*3 231.6*	*3 319.8*	*3 665.6*	*13.4*	*2 447.9*	*2 522.3*	*2 707.2*	*10.6*
United States	1 027.1	1 089.5	1 134.0	10.4	1 027.2	1 014.6	1 044.1	1.6
Switzerland	458.0	462.9	503.3	9.9	323.6	315.7	347.9	7.5
Canada	142.6	142.7	157.5	10.4	103.0	108.1	119.5	16.1
Brazil	107.7	108.5	132.2	22.7	41.2	52.5	56.3	36.7
Singapore	66.7	89.2	95.8	43.7	45.0	39.3	50.2	11.4
Hong Kong	89.3	89.3	92.9	4.0	17.2	25.5	26.8	55.9
Russia	71.5	83.2	88.8	24.2	24.7	26.4	27.5	11.4
Japan	74.8	78.4	84.0	12.3	122.3	122.6	135.3	10.6
Australia	69.9	70.3	82.8	18.5	25.7	21.2	30.2	17.3
South Africa	55.1	55.1	77.0	39.7	6.0	6.8	6.2	4.1

Source: Eurostat (online data code: bop_fdi_pos)

Map 1.6.1: Outward stocks of FDI, EU-27, end 2009
(EUR 1 000 million (share in extra-EU-27))

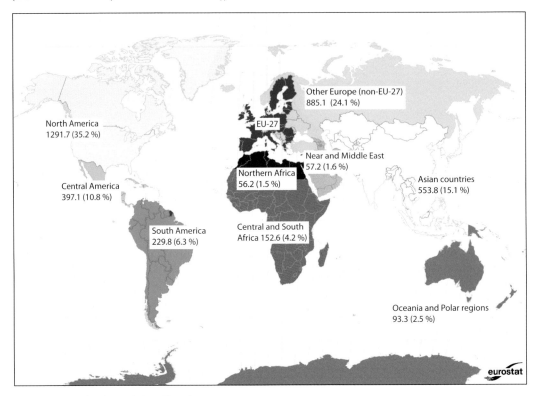

Other Europe (non-EU-27)
885.1 (24.1 %)

North America
1291.7 (35.2 %)

EU-27

Near and Middle East
57.2 (1.6 %)

Northern Africa
56.2 (1.5 %)

Asian countries
553.8 (15.1 %)

Central America
397.1 (10.8 %)

South America
229.8 (6.3 %)

Central and South
Africa 152.6 (4.2 %)

Oceania and Polar regions
93.3 (2.5 %)

Source: Eurostat (online data code: bop_fdi_pos)

Table 1.6.5: Extra EU-27 FDI stocks by economic activity, EU-27, end 2008
(EUR 1 000 million)

	Outward	Inward
Total	3 319.8	2 522.3
Agriculture, hunting and fishing	1.0	1.4
Mining and quarrying	187.1	40.0
Manufacturing	645.0	330.3
Food products	70.6	53.3
Textiles and wood activities	29.3	33.2
Petroleum, chemical, rubber, plastic products	262.9	124.5
Metal and mechanical products	125.7	46.1
Machinery, computers, RTV, communication	20.4	14.1
Vehicles and other transport equipment	60.4	22.9
Electricity, gas and water	57.2	18.2
Construction	16.0	13.4
Services	2 374.7	2 088.4
Trade and repairs	126.9	139.0
Hotels and restaurants	11.6	13.4
Transport and communications	122.0	41.8
Financial Intermediation	1 550.9	1 356.9
Real estate and business services	535.9	514.3
Other services	27.4	23.0
Other sectors	38.6	30.7

Source: Eurostat (online data code: bop_fdi_pos)

Figure 1.6.3: FDI income and rates of return, EU-27, 2004-2009 (¹)

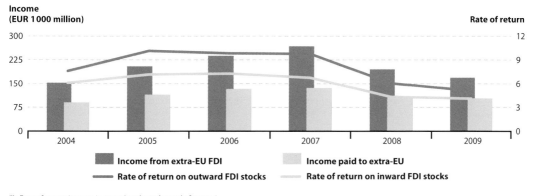

(¹) Rate of return: income in year t/stocks at the end of year t-1.

Source: Eurostat (online data code: bop_fdi_inc)

Population

Introduction

As the population of the European Union (EU) grew beyond 500 million inhabitants in 2010, its structure continued to change. Recent demographic developments show that the EU's population is increasing, while its age structure is becoming older as post-war baby-boom generations reach retirement age. Furthermore, people are living longer, as life expectancy continues to increase. On the other hand, while fertility is increasing slowly, it remains well below a level that would keep the size of the population constant in the absence of inward or outward migration. As a result, the EU will, in the coming decades, face a number of challenges associated with an ageing society which will impact on a range of areas, including labour markets, pensions and provisions for healthcare, housing and social services.

Population change and the structure of the population are gaining importance in the political, economic, social and cultural context of demographic behaviour. Demographic trends in population growth, fertility, mortality and migration are closely followed by policymakers. EU policies, notably in social and economic

fields, use demographic data for planning and for programme monitoring and evaluation.

Eurostat provides a wide range of demographic data, including statistics on populations at national and regional level, as well as for various demographic factors (births, deaths, marriages and divorces, immigration and emigration) influencing the size, the structure and the specific characteristics of these populations. Eurostat also collects detailed information on different areas related to migration and asylum: foreign resident populations, annual flows of immigrants and emigrants, persons acquiring citizenship, monthly and quarterly information on asylum applicants and on asylum decisions, residence permits issued to non-EU nationals and information on persons found illegally present in EU Member States. These statistics concerning migration and asylum provide the basis for the development and monitoring of EU policy initiatives in several areas, including: the impact of migration on labour markets, the promotion of migrant integration, the development of a common asylum system, the prevention of unauthorised migration, and trafficking in human beings.

2.1 European population compared with world population

This subchapter gives an overview of the European Union's (EU's) population in relation to the rest of the world by looking at several key demographic indicators; it includes information on population levels, population density, fertility, life expectancy and old-age dependency ratios. The figures presented portray a diverse range of developments: with slow or even diminishing population numbers in some developed economies in contrast to rapid population increases in certain developing countries.

Main statistical findings

The world's population reached 7 000 million inhabitants towards the end of 2011 and continues

to grow. Asia accounted for the majority of the world's population (just over 60 % in 2010) with 4 164 million inhabitants, while Africa was the next most populous continent with 1 022 million inhabitants, or 14.8 % of the world total.

The world's population more than doubled between 1960 and 2010. The increase in global population between 1960 and 2010 can be largely attributed to growth in Asia, Africa and Latin America.

The most populous countries in the world in 2010 were China (19.5 % of world's population) and India (17.8 %), followed at some distance by the United States (4.5 %), Indonesia (3.5 %) and Brazil (2.8 %). The share of the EU-27 in the world's population was 7.3 %.

Population density within the EU-27 was 116.7 persons per km² in 2010, more than 3.5 times as high as in the United States, but below the values recorded for Indonesia, China, Japan, India and South Korea.

The latest United Nations (UN) population projections (World Population Prospects, the 2010 Revision) suggest that the pace at which the world's population is expanding will slow somewhat in the coming decades; however, the total number of inhabitants is nevertheless projected to reach more than 9 600 million by 2060. According to these projections (the medium variant), the world's population will also be relatively older (in other words, with a higher median age) in 2060 than it is now.

Ageing societies

Ageing society represents a major demographic challenge and is linked to several issues, including, persistently low fertility rates and significant increases in life expectancy during recent decades (see Table 2.1.3). Improvements in the quality and availability of healthcare are likely, at least in part, to explain the latter, alongside other factors such as increased awareness of health issues, higher standards of living, or changes in workplace occupations from predominantly manual labour to tertiary activities. The average life expectancy of a new-born baby in the world was estimated at 67.9 years (for the period 2005 to 2010): the value of this indicator increased by 3.5 years compared with the period 1990 to 1995. In the EU-27, life expectancy at birth is generally higher than in most other regions of the world.

The old-age dependency ratio is used as indicator of the level of support of the old population (aged 65 years and over) by the working age population (those aged between 15 to 64 years). Both the UN's and Eurostat's population projections suggest that the population of older persons in the EU-27 will increase to such an extent that there will be fewer than two persons of working age for each person aged 65 or more by the year 2050.

Data sources and availability

The data in this subchapter is based on information from two sources: Eurostat and the United Nations Population Division (World Population Prospects, the 2010 Revision).

The UN is involved in several multi-national survey programmes whose results provide key information about fertility, mortality, maternal and child health. UN population data is often based on registers or estimates of mid-year population; this may be contrasted with Eurostat's data that generally reflect the situation as of 1 January in each reference year.

UN population projections are used in this subchapter to provide comparisons between EU and non-EU countries; within this subchapter use was made of the medium variant projections. Eurostat regularly produces population projections at a national level for the EU Member States. The latest Eurostat Population Projections were made in 2010 (EUROPOP2010).

Context

Europe's ageing society and its relatively static number of inhabitants may be contrasted against a rapid expansion in the world's population, driven largely by population growth in developing countries. However, the demographic challenge that the EU-27 is confronted with is by no means unique. Most developed, and also some emerging economies, will undergo changes in their demographic composition in the next five decades. Shrinking working age populations, a higher proportion of elderly persons, and increasing old-age dependency rates suggest that there will be a considerable burden to provide social expenditure related to population ageing (pensions, healthcare, institutional care). The challenges associated with an ageing society are likely to be even more acute in countries such as Japan and South Korea where this dependency ratio will rise rapidly and to a very high level, while the share of older persons in the total population is also expected to increase at a rapid pace in China.

Figure 2.1.1: World population, 2010
(% of total)

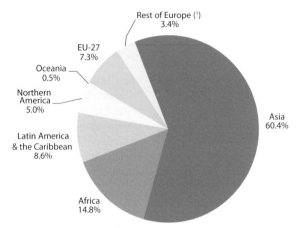

(¹) Albania, Andorra, Belarus, Bosnia and Herzegovina, Croatia, Faeroe Islands, Iceland, Liechtenstein, the former Yugoslav Republic of Macedonia, Moldova, Montenegro, Norway, Russia, Serbia, Switzerland and Ukraine.

Source: United Nations, Department of Economic and Social Affairs, Population: World Population Prospects, 2010 revision

Table 2.1.1: World population, 1960-2010

	1960	1965	1970	1975	1980	1985	1990	1995	2000	2005	2010
						(million)					
World	3 038	3 333	3 696	4 076	4 453	4 863	5 306	5 726	6 123	6 507	6 896
Europe (¹)	604	634	656	676	693	707	720	727	727	731	738
Africa	287	324	368	420	483	555	635	721	811	911	1 022
Asia	1 708	1 886	2 135	2 393	2 638	2 907	3 199	3 470	3 719	3 945	4 164
Latin America and the Caribbean	220	253	286	323	362	402	443	483	521	557	590
Northern America	204	219	231	242	254	267	281	296	313	329	345
Oceania	16	17	20	21	23	25	27	29	31	34	37
					(% of the world population)						
Europe (¹)	19.9	19.0	17.7	16.6	15.6	14.5	13.6	12.7	11.9	11.2	10.7
Africa	9.4	9.7	10.0	10.3	10.8	11.4	12.0	12.6	13.2	14.0	14.8
Asia	56.2	56.6	57.8	58.7	59.2	59.8	60.3	60.6	60.7	60.6	60.4
Latin America and the Caribbean	7.2	7.6	7.7	7.9	8.1	8.3	8.3	8.4	8.5	8.6	8.6
Northern America	6.7	6.6	6.3	5.9	5.7	5.5	5.3	5.2	5.1	5.1	5.0
Oceania	0.5	0.5	0.5	0.5	0.5	0.5	0.5	0.5	0.5	0.5	0.5

(¹) EU-27, Albania, Andorra, Belarus, Bosnia and Herzegovina, Croatia, Faeroe Islands, Iceland, Liechtenstein, the former Yugoslav Republic of Macedonia, Moldova, Montenegro, Norway, Russia, Serbia, Switzerland and Ukraine.

Source: United Nations, Department of Economic and Social Affairs, Population: World Population Prospects, 2010 revision

Table 2.1.2: Population and population density, 1960 and 2010

	Population (million)		Population density (persons per km²)	
	1960	**2010**	**1960**	**2010**
EU-27 (¹)	402.6	501.1	94.0	116.7
Argentina	20.6	40.4	7.4	14.5
Australia	10.3	22.3	1.3	2.9
Brazil	72.8	194.9	8.5	22.9
Canada	17.9	34.0	1.8	3.4
China	658.3	1 341.3	68.6	139.8
India	447.8	1 224.6	136.2	372.5
Indonesia	91.9	239.9	48.3	125.9
Japan	92.5	126.5	244.8	334.9
South Korea	25.1	48.2	251.9	484.1
Mexico	38.4	113.4	19.6	57.9
Russia	119.9	143.0	7.0	8.4
Saudi Arabia	4.0	27.4	1.9	12.8
South Africa	17.4	50.1	14.2	41.1
Turkey	28.2	72.8	35.9	92.8
United States	186.3	310.4	19.4	32.2
World	3 038.4	6 895.9	22.3	50.6

(¹) Excluding French overseas departments for 1960; population density is calculated as the ratio between (annual average) population and the surface (land) area; whenever land area was not available, the total surface area was used instead.

Source: Eurostat (online data codes: demo_pjan and demo_r_d3area); United Nations, Department of Economic and Social Affairs, Population: World Population Prospects, 2010 revision

Figure 2.1.2: Population, 1960-2060 (¹)
(1960 = 100)

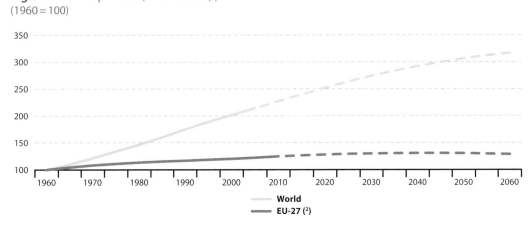

(¹) Population projections are shown as a dotted line.
(²) Excluding French overseas departments up to and including 1997.

Source: Eurostat (online data codes: demo_pjan and proj_10c2150p); United Nations, Department of Economic and Social Affairs, Population: World Population Prospects, 2010 revision

Table 2.1.3: Fertility and mortality, 1990 and 2008 (¹)

	Total fertility rate (live births per woman)		Life expectancy at birth (years)	
	1990	**2008**	**1990**	**2008**
EU-27	:	1.60	:	79.4
Argentina	2.90	2.25	72.1	75.3
Australia	1.86	1.93	77.5	81.4
Brazil	2.60	1.90	67.3	72.2
Canada	1.69	1.65	77.8	80.5
China	2.01	1.64	69.9	72.7
India	3.72	2.73	59.0	64.2
Indonesia	2.90	2.19	63.1	67.9
Japan	1.48	1.32	79.5	82.7
South Korea	1.70	1.29	72.9	80.0
Mexico	3.19	2.41	71.8	76.2
Russia	1.55	1.44	66.6	67.7
Saudi Arabia	5.45	3.03	69.6	73.1
South Africa	3.34	2.55	61.2	51.2
Turkey	2.90	2.15	64.4	73.0
United States	1.99	2.07	75.6	78.0
World	3.04	2.52	64.4	67.9

(¹) World and non-member countries, averages for 1990-95 and 2005-2010.

Source: Eurostat (online data codes: demo_frate and demo_mlexpec); United Nations, Department of Economic and Social Affairs, Population: World Population Prospects, 2010 revision

Table 2.1.4: Old-age dependency ratio, 1960-2060 (¹)
(population aged 65 years and over as % of population aged 15-64)

	1960	**1970**	**1980**	**1990**	**2000**	**2010**	**2020**	**2030**	**2040**	**2050**	**2060**
EU-27 (²)	:	:	:	20.6	23.2	25.9	31.4	38.3	45.5	50.2	52.6
Argentina	8.7	10.8	13.1	14.8	15.8	16.4	18.5	20.8	24.1	30.3	35.9
Australia	14.0	13.3	14.8	16.8	18.6	19.9	25.5	31.5	35.9	39.0	42.8
Brazil	5.9	6.5	6.9	7.4	8.5	10.4	13.8	20.0	26.6	35.8	43.6
Canada	12.7	12.7	13.9	16.6	18.4	20.3	27.7	37.8	41.0	42.3	44.9
China	7.1	7.1	8.7	9.0	10.4	11.3	16.8	23.9	36.9	41.9	51.8
India	5.4	5.8	6.3	6.5	6.9	7.6	9.5	12.2	15.4	19.9	25.4
Indonesia	6.3	6.2	6.4	6.3	7.1	8.2	10.0	15.1	22.2	30.0	36.1
Japan	8.9	10.2	13.4	17.1	25.2	35.5	48.2	52.9	63.3	69.6	68.6
South Korea	6.8	6.1	6.2	7.2	10.2	15.4	22.4	37.3	52.0	60.7	64.3
Mexico	6.4	7.5	7.4	7.6	8.6	9.8	12.5	17.4	24.8	31.3	38.6
Russia	9.9	11.7	15.0	15.3	17.9	17.7	22.5	29.4	31.2	38.5	42.4
Saudi Arabia	7.0	6.7	5.6	4.8	5.8	4.4	6.6	9.0	13.0	22.2	32.1
South Africa	7.0	6.3	5.6	5.5	5.9	7.1	9.4	11.7	12.5	14.6	18.7
Turkey	5.5	6.8	7.3	6.3	8.0	8.8	11.7	16.5	22.5	30.5	36.9
United States	15.3	15.9	17.1	19.0	18.7	19.5	25.3	32.7	34.7	35.4	36.8
World	8.8	9.3	10.1	10.2	10.9	11.6	14.3	18.0	22.2	25.7	29.6

(¹) From 2020 onwards: Eurostat's population projections Europop2010 for EU-27 and UN's medium variant for the world total and non-member countries.
(²) Excluding French overseas departments in 1990.

Source: Eurostat (online data codes: demo_pjanind and proj_10c2150p); United Nations, Department of Economic and Social Affairs, Population: World Population Prospects, 2010 revision

2.2 Population structure and ageing

The impact of demographic ageing within the European Union (EU) is likely to be of major significance in the coming decades. Consistently low birth rates and higher life expectancy will transform the shape of the EU-27's age pyramid; probably the most important change will be the marked transition towards a much older population structure and this development is already becoming apparent in several Member States. As a result, the proportion of people of working age in the EU-27 is shrinking while the relative number of those retired is expanding. The share of older persons in the total population will increase significantly in the coming decades, as a greater proportion of the post-war baby-boom generation reaches retirement. This will, in turn, lead to an increased burden on those of working age to provide for the social expenditure required by the ageing population for a range of related services.

Main statistical findings

Population structure in 2010

Young people (0 to 14 years old) made up 15.6 % of the EU-27's population in 2010, while persons considered to be of working age (15 to 64 years old) accounted for 67.0 % of the population, and older persons (65 or more years old) had a 17.4 % share (see Table 2.2.1). Across the EU Member States, the highest share of young people in the total population was observed in Ireland (21.3 %), while the lowest share was recorded in Germany (13.5 %). The reverse situation was observed for the proportion of older persons in the total population, where Germany recorded the highest proportion (20.7 %) and Ireland had the lowest share (11.3 %).

The median age of the EU-27's population was 40.9 years in 2010: this means that half of the EU-27's population was older than 40.9 years, while half was younger (see Table 2.2.2). The median age of populations across the EU Member States ranged between 34.3 years in Ireland and 44.2 years in Germany, confirming the relatively young and relatively old population structures recorded in each of these two countries.

Age dependency ratios may be used to study the level of support given to young and/or older persons by the working age population; these ratios are expressed in terms of the relative size of young and/or older populations relative to the working age population. The old-age dependency ratio for the EU-27 was 25.9 % in 2010; as such, there were around four persons of working age for every person aged 65 or over. The old-age dependency ratio ranged across the EU Member States from 16.8 % in Ireland to 31.4 % in Germany.

The combination of young and old age dependency ratios provides the total age dependency ratio, which in 2010 was 49.3 % in the EU-27, indicating that there were about two working age persons for every dependent person. The lowest total age dependency ratio was observed in Slovakia (38.1 %) and the highest in France (54.2 %).

Population pyramids (see Figures 2.2.1 and 2.2.2) show the distribution of population by sex and by five-year age groups. Each bar corresponds to the share of the given sex and age group in the total (men and women combined) population. The population pyramid for the EU-27 in 2010 is narrow at the bottom and is shaped more as a rhomboid due to the baby-boom cohorts of the 1960s. The baby-boom was a phenomenon characterised by high fertility rates in several European countries in the middle of the 1960s. Baby boomers currently represent an important part of the working age population and the first of these large cohorts, born over a period of 20-30 years, are now getting close to retirement (this may be observed by comparing the 2010 population pyramid with a previous year – in Figure 2.2.1 a comparison is made with 1990).

Past and current trends of population ageing in the EU

Population ageing is a long-term trend which began several decades ago in the EU. This ageing is visible in the development of the age structure of the population and is reflected in an increasing share of older persons and a declining share of working age persons in the total population.

In the past two decades, the share of the working age population in the EU-27 increased by 0.3 percentage points, while the share of the older population increased by 3.7 percentage points; as a result, the top of the EU-27 age pyramid for 2010 became larger as compared with 1990 (see Figure 2.2.1). The growth in the relative share of older people may be explained by increased longevity – a pattern that has been evident for several decades as life expectancy has risen (see mortality and life expectancy statistics) – this development is often referred to as 'ageing at the top' of the population pyramid.

On the other hand, low levels of fertility have been maintained across most of the EU (see fertility statistics); this has resulted in a decreasing share of young people in the total population. This process, known as 'ageing at the bottom', is visible in the population pyramids through a reduction at the base of the age pyramids, as seen between 1990 and 2010.

The development of the median age of the EU-27 population also provides an illustration of population ageing. The median age increased from 35.2 years in 1990 to 40.9 years by 2010 (see Figure 2.2.4). Over the period from 1990 to 2010, the median age increased in all of the EU Member States, rising by at least six years in Slovenia, Portugal, Lithuania, Germany, Spain, Malta, Italy, the Netherlands and Austria (see Figure 2.2.5).

Future trends in population ageing

Eurostat's latest set of population projections (EUROPOP2010) were made covering the period from 2011 to 2060 – and show that population ageing is likely to affect all EU Member States over this period. The convergence scenario is one of several possible population change scenarios that aim to provide information about the likely future size and structure of the population. According to this scenario, the EU's population will be slightly higher in 2060, while the age structure of the population will be much older than it is now.

According to the convergence scenario of EUROPOP2010, the EU-27's population is projected to increase to 525 million by 2035, peaking at 526 million around 2040, and thereafter gradually declining to 517 million by 2060. During the same period, the median age of the EU-27's population is projected to rise to 47.6 years. The population of working age is expected to decline steadily, while older persons will likely account for an increasing share of the total population – those aged 65 years or over will account for 29.5 % of the EU-27's population by 2060 (17.4 % in 2010).

Another aspect of population ageing is the progressive ageing of the older population itself, as the relative importance of the oldest people is growing at a faster pace than any other age segment of the EU's population. The share of those aged 80 years or above in the EU-27's population is projected to almost triple between 2010 and 2060 (see Figure 2.2.6).

As a result of the population movement between age groups, the EU-27's old age dependency ratio is projected to more than double from 25.9 % in 2010 to 52.6 % by 2060. The total age dependency ratio (calculated as the ratio of dependent people, young and old, compared with the population aged 15 to 64 years old) is projected to rise from 49.3 % in 2010 to 77.9 % by 2060.

Age pyramids for 2010 and 2060 (see Figure 2.2.2) show that the EU-27's population is projected to continue to age. In the coming decades, the high number of baby boomers will swell the number of elderly people. The population pyramid shows how the baby boomer bulge is moving up while the middle and the base of the pyramid (those of working age and children) are projected to narrow considerably by 2060.

Data sources and availability

Eurostat provides information for a wide range of demographic data. Data on population includes breakdowns by several characteristics, such as age and sex. Eurostat produces population projections at a national level every three years. These projections are what-if scenarios that aim to provide information about the likely future size and age structure of the population based on assumptions of future trends in fertility, life expectancy and migration; the latest projection exercise was EUROPOP2010.

Context

Eurostat's population projections are used by the European Commission to analyse the likely impact of ageing populations on public spending. Increased social expenditure related to population ageing, in the form of pensions, healthcare and institutional or private (health)care, is likely to result in a higher burden for working age populations.

A number of important policies, notably in social and economic fields, use demographic data for planning actions, monitoring and evaluating programmes – for example, population ageing and its likely effects on the sustainability of public finance and welfare provisions, or the economic and social impact of demographic change.

Table 2.2.1: Population age structure by major age groups, 1990 and 2010
(% of the total population)

	0-14 years old		15-64 years old		65 years old or over	
	1990	2010	1990	2010	1990	2010
EU-27	19.5	15.6	66.7	67.0	13.7	17.4
Belgium	18.1	16.9	67.1	65.9	14.8	17.2
Bulgaria	20.5	13.6	66.5	68.9	13.0	17.5
Czech Republic	21.7	14.2	65.8	70.6	12.5	15.2
Denmark	17.1	18.1	67.3	65.6	15.6	16.3
Germany	16.0	13.5	69.2	65.9	14.9	20.7
Estonia (¹)	22.3	15.1	66.1	67.8	11.6	17.1
Ireland	27.4	21.3	61.3	67.3	11.4	11.3
Greece	19.5	14.4	66.8	66.7	13.7	18.9
Spain	20.2	14.9	66.3	68.2	13.4	16.8
France (²)	20.1	18.5	65.9	64.8	13.9	16.6
Italy	16.8	14.1	68.5	65.7	14.7	20.2
Cyprus	26.0	16.9	63.1	70.1	10.8	13.1
Latvia	21.4	13.8	66.7	68.9	11.8	17.4
Lithuania	22.6	15.0	66.6	68.9	10.8	16.1
Luxembourg	17.2	17.7	69.4	68.3	13.4	14.0
Hungary	20.5	14.7	66.2	68.6	13.2	16.6
Malta	23.6	15.6	66.0	69.6	10.4	14.8
Netherlands	18.2	17.6	69.0	67.1	12.8	15.3
Austria	17.5	14.9	67.6	67.5	14.9	17.6
Poland	25.3	15.2	64.8	71.3	10.0	13.5
Portugal	20.8	15.2	66.0	66.9	13.2	17.9
Romania	23.7	15.2	66.0	69.9	10.3	14.9
Slovenia	20.9	14.0	68.5	69.4	10.6	16.5
Slovakia	25.5	15.3	64.3	72.4	10.3	12.3
Finland	19.3	16.6	67.4	66.4	13.3	17.0
Sweden	17.8	16.6	64.4	65.3	17.8	18.1
United Kingdom	19.0	17.5	65.3	66.1	15.7	16.5
Iceland	25.0	20.9	64.4	67.1	10.6	12.0
Liechtenstein	19.4	16.4	70.6	70.1	10.0	13.5
Norway	18.9	18.9	64.8	66.2	16.3	14.9
Switzerland	17.0	15.2	68.4	68.0	14.6	16.8
Montenegro (¹)	:	19.6	:	67.7	:	12.7
Croatia (¹)	:	15.3	:	67.5	:	17.3
FYR of Macedonia (¹)	:	17.7	:	70.7	:	11.6
Turkey	35.0	26.0	60.7	67.0	4.3	7.0

(¹) The population of unknown age is redistributed for calculating the age structure.
(²) Excluding French overseas departments in 1990.

Source: Eurostat (online data code: demo_pjanind)

Table 2.2.2: Population age structure indicators, 2010

	Median age	Young age dependency ratio	Old age dependency ratio	Total age dependency ratio	Share of population aged 80 or over
	(years)	(%)			
EU-27	*40.9*	*23.3*	*25.9*	*49.3*	*4.7*
Belgium	40.9	25.6	26.0	51.7	4.9
Bulgaria	41.4	19.7	25.4	45.1	3.8
Czech Republic	39.4	20.2	21.6	41.7	3.6
Denmark	40.5	27.6	24.9	52.4	4.1
Germany	44.2	20.5	31.4	51.8	5.1
Estonia	39.5	22.3	25.2	47.5	4.1
Ireland	34.3	31.7	16.8	48.5	2.8
Greece	41.7	21.5	28.4	49.9	4.6
Spain	39.9	21.9	24.7	46.6	4.9
France	*39.8*	*28.6*	*25.6*	*54.2*	*5.2*
Italy	43.1	21.4	30.8	52.2	5.8
Cyprus	36.2	24.1	18.6	42.7	2.9
Latvia	40.0	20.0	25.2	45.1	3.9
Lithuania	39.2	21.8	23.3	45.0	3.6
Luxembourg	38.9	26.0	20.4	46.4	3.6
Hungary	39.8	21.5	24.2	45.7	3.9
Malta	39.2	22.4	21.2	43.6	3.3
Netherlands	40.6	26.2	22.8	49.0	3.9
Austria	41.7	22.0	26.1	48.1	4.8
Poland	37.7	21.2	19.0	40.2	3.3
Portugal	40.7	22.7	26.7	49.4	4.5
Romania	38.3	21.7	21.4	43.0	3.1
Slovenia	41.4	20.2	23.8	44.0	3.9
Slovakia	36.9	21.2	16.9	38.1	2.7
Finland	42.0	25.0	25.6	50.6	4.6
Sweden	40.7	25.4	27.7	53.1	5.3
United Kingdom	*39.6*	*26.4*	*24.9*	*51.3*	*4.6*
Iceland	34.8	31.2	17.9	49.1	3.3
Liechtenstein	40.8	23.4	19.3	42.7	3.2
Norway	38.6	28.5	22.5	51.0	4.5
Switzerland	41.5	22.3	24.7	47.0	4.8
Montenegro	36.2	29.0	18.8	47.8	2.1
Croatia	41.3	22.7	25.6	48.3	3.5
FYR of Macedonia	35.8	25.1	16.4	41.5	1.8
Turkey	28.8	38.8	10.5	49.2	1.2

Source: Eurostat (online data code: demo_pjanind)

Figure 2.2.1: Population pyramids, EU-27, 1990 and 2010 (¹)
(% of the total population)

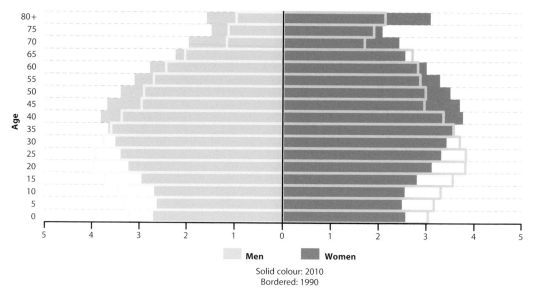

Men   Women

Solid colour: 2010
Bordered: 1990

(¹) Excluding French overseas departments in 1990; 2010, provisional.

Source: Eurostat (online data code: demo_pjangroup)

Figure 2.2.2: Population pyramids, EU-27, 2010 and 2060 (¹)
(% of the total population)

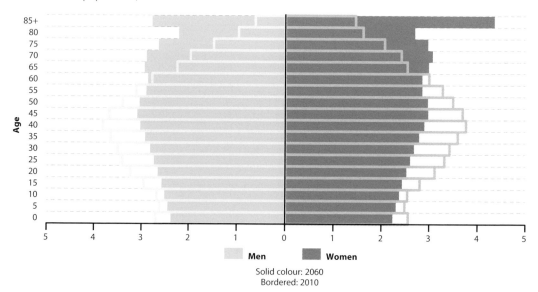

Men   Women

Solid colour: 2060
Bordered: 2010

(¹) 2010, provisional; 2060 data are projections (EUROPOP2010 convergence scenario).

Source: Eurostat (online data codes: demo_pjangroup and proj_10c2150p)

Figure 2.2.3: Change in the share of the population aged 65 years or over between 1990 and 2010 (percentage points)

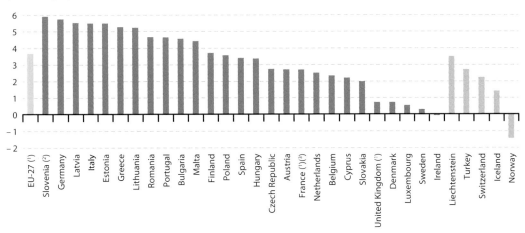

(¹) Provisional.
(²) Data may be affected by the change of population definition in 2008.
(³) Excluding French overseas departments in 1990.

Source: Eurostat (online data code: demo_pjanind)

Figure 2.2.4: Median age of population, EU-27, 1990-2010 (¹)
(years)

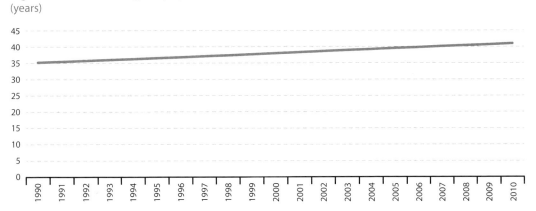

(¹) Excluding French overseas departments before 1998; 2008-2010, provisional.

Source: Eurostat (online data code: demo_pjanind)

Figure 2.2.5: Median age of population, 1990 and 2010
(years)

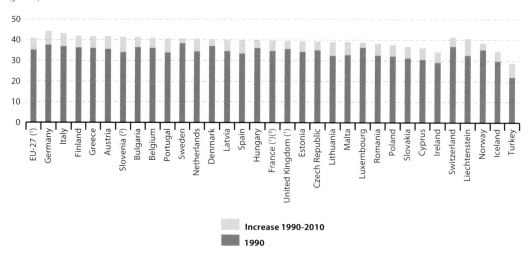

(¹) Increase 1990-2010, provisional.
(²) Data may be affected by the change of population definition in 2008.
(³) Excluding French overseas departments in 1990.

Source: Eurostat (online data code: demo_pjanind)

Figure 2.2.6: Population structure by major age groups, EU-27, 1990-2060 (¹)
(% of total population)

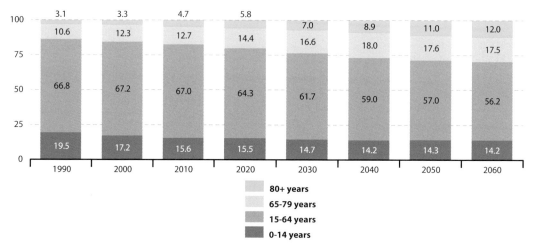

(¹) Excluding French overseas departments in 1990; 2010, provisional; 2020-2060 data are projections (EUROPOP2010 convergence scenario).

Source: Eurostat (online data codes: demo_pjanind and proj_10c2150p)

2.3 Population and population change

This subchapter gives an overview of the development of European Union (EU) population statistics, detailing the two components of population change: natural population change and net migration plus statistical adjustment. More information on net migration is provided within a subchapter on migration and migrant population statistics.

Main statistical findings

EU-27 population continues to grow

On 1 January 2011 the population of the EU-27 was estimated at 502.5 million; this was 1.4 million people more than the year before and therefore continued a pattern of uninterrupted EU-27 population growth that has been apparent since 1960. The number of inhabitants in the EU-27 grew from 402.6 million in 1960, rising by almost 100 million persons through to 2011 (see Figure 2.3.1).

Natural population growth in the EU-27 is slowly increasing in importance

Just over one third (36.8 %) of the population increase in the EU-27 during 2010 resulted from natural growth (the positive difference between live births and deaths). Net migration plus statistical adjustment continued to be the main determinant of population growth in the EU-27, accounting for 63.2 % of the population increase during 2010.

The contribution of net migration plus statistical adjustment to the total population change in the EU-27 has been greater than that of natural change since 1992 (see Figure 2.3.2). The share of net migration plus statistical adjustment in total population growth peaked, in relative terms, in 2003 (95.1 % of total change). Since this date, the contribution of net migration plus statistical adjustment decreased somewhat. Thus, the share of natural change in total population growth followed an upward development over the most recent period (from 2004 onwards).

The relatively low contribution of natural change to total population growth is the result of two

factors: net migration in the EU-27 increased considerably from the mid-1980s onwards; secondly, the number of live births fell, while the number of deaths increased.

The gap between live births and deaths in the EU-27 narrowed considerably from 1960 onwards (see Figure 2.3.3), almost reaching parity in 2003 before diverging again somewhat. Since the number of deaths is expected to increase as the baby-boom generation moves into retirement, and, assuming that the fertility rate continues to remain at a relatively low level, negative natural change (more deaths than births) cannot be excluded in the future. In this event, the extent of population decline or population growth is likely to depend on the contribution made by migration.

Population change at a national level

The number of inhabitants in EU Member States on 1 January 2011 ranged from 81.8 million in Germany to 0.4 million in Malta. Germany together with France, the United Kingdom and Italy comprised more than half (53.7 %) of the total EU-27 population in 2011 (see Table 2.3.1).

Although the population of the EU-27 increased during 2010, population growth was unevenly distributed across the Member States. A total of 20 Member States observed an increase in their respective populations, while the number of inhabitants fell in Lithuania, Latvia, Bulgaria, Hungary, Romania, Germany and Portugal.

Analysing the two components of population change at a national level, eight types of population change can be distinguished, separating growth from decline, and the relative weights of natural change and net migration – see Table 2.3.3 for the full typology. Luxembourg, Belgium, Sweden, Malta and the United Kingdom recorded the highest population growth rates in 2010 (more than 6 persons per 1 000 inhabitants), which was more than twice the EU-27 average of 2.8 persons per 1 000 inhabitants (see Table 2.3.2). The highest rates of natural change were registered in Ireland (10.4 persons per 1 000 inhabitants) and Cyprus (5.7 per 1000 inhabitants), while the highest net migration plus statistical adjustment was recorded in Luxembourg, followed by Belgium, Malta, Sweden, and Italy (all above 5 persons per 1000 inhabitants).

Data sources and availability

The demographic balance provides an overview of annual demographic developments in the EU Member States; statistics on population change are available in absolute figures and as crude rates.

Population change – or population growth – in a given year is the difference between the population size on 1 January of the given year and the corresponding level from 1 January of the previous year. It consists of two components: natural change and net migration plus statistical adjustment. Natural population change is the difference between the number of live births and the number of deaths. If natural change is positive then it is often referred to as a natural increase. Net migration is the difference between the number of immigrants and the number of emigrants. In the context of the annual demographic balance, Eurostat produces net migration figures by taking the difference between total

population change and natural change; this concept is referred to as net migration plus statistical adjustment.

Context

Statistics on population change and the structure of population are increasingly used to support policymaking and to provide the opportunity to monitor demographic behaviour within political, economic, social and cultural contexts. In particular, this concerns demographic developments that focus on a likely reduction in the relative importance of the working age population and a corresponding increase in the number of older persons. These statistics may be used to support a range of different analyses, including studies relating to population ageing and its effects on the sustainability of public finance and welfare, the evaluation of fertility as a background for family policies, or the economic and social impact of demographic change. The European Commission assessed many of these issues in a Communication titled, 'The demographic future of Europe – from challenge to opportunity' (COM(2006) 571 final).

Figure 2.3.1: Population, EU-27, 1960-2011 (¹)
(at 1 January, million persons)

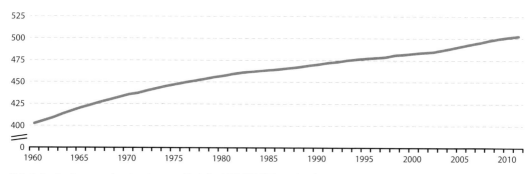

(¹) Excluding French overseas departments up to and including 1997; 2009-2011, provisional.

Source: Eurostat (online data code: demo_gind)

Figure 2.3.2: Population change by component (annual crude rates), EU-27, 1960-2010 (¹)
(per 1 000 inhabitants)

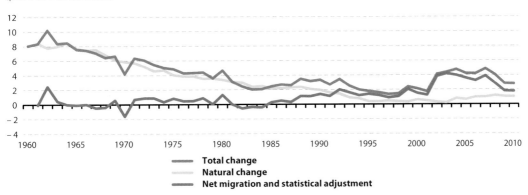

(¹) Excluding French overseas departments up to and including 1997; net migration and natural change, not available for 1960.

Source: Eurostat (online data code: demo_gind)

Figure 2.3.3: Births and deaths, EU-27, 1961-2010 (¹)
(million persons)

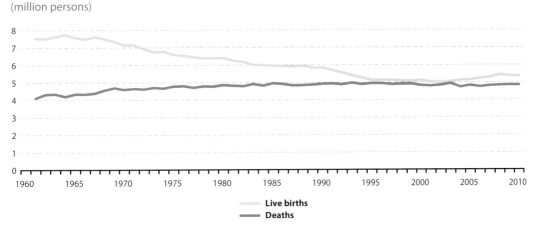

(¹) Excluding French overseas departments up to and including 1997; 2009-2010, provisional.

Source: Eurostat (online data code: demo_gind)

Table 2.3.1: Demographic balance, 2010
(1 000 persons)

	Population, 1 January 2010	Live births	Deaths	Natural change (¹)	Net migration and statistical adjustment (²)	Total change between 1 January 2010 and 2011	Population, 1 January 2011
EU-27	*501 125.9*	*5 358.7*	*4 845.4*	*513.3*	*880.8*	*1 394.1*	*502 520.0*
Belgium	10 839.9	127.0	104.5	22.5	89.3	*111.8*	*10 951.7*
Bulgaria	7 563.7	75.5	110.2	− 34.7	− 24.2	*− 58.8*	*7 504.9*
Czech Republic	10 506.8	117.2	106.8	10.3	15.6	*26.0*	*10 532.8*
Denmark	5 534.7	63.4	54.4	9.0	16.8	*25.9*	*5 560.6*
Germany	81 802.3	677.9	858.8	− 180.8	130.2	*− 50.7*	*81 751.6*
Estonia	1 340.1	15.8	15.8	0.0	0.0	*0.1*	*1 340.2*
Ireland	4 467.9	73.7	27.1	46.6	− 33.6	*13.0*	*4 480.9*
Greece	11 305.1	110.0	106.7	3.3	17.5	*20.8*	*11 325.9*
Spain	45 989.0	485.6	381.4	104.2	59.8	*163.9*	*46 152.9*
France	*64 716.2*	829.0	545.0	284.0	75.2	*359.2*	*65 075.4*
Italy	60 340.3	561.9	587.5	− 25.5	311.7	*286.1*	*60 626.4*
Cyprus	803.1	10.0	5.4	4.6	− 3.3	*1.3*	*804.4*
Latvia	2 248.4	19.2	30.0	− 10.8	− 7.9	*− 18.7*	*2 229.6*
Lithuania	3 329.0	35.6	42.1	− 6.5	− 77.9	*− 84.4*	*3 244.6*
Luxembourg	502.1	5.9	3.8	2.1	7.7	*9.8*	*511.8*
Hungary	10 014.3	90.3	130.5	− 40.1	11.5	*− 28.6*	*9 985.7*
Malta	414.4	4.0	3.0	1.0	2.2	*3.2*	*417.6*
Netherlands	16 575.0	184.4	136.1	48.3	32.5	*80.8*	*16 655.8*
Austria	8 375.3	78.7	77.2	1.5	27.4	*29.0*	*8 404.3*
Poland	38 167.3	413.3	378.5	34.8	− 2.1	*32.7*	*38 200.0*
Portugal	10 637.7	101.3	105.9	− 4.5	3.8	*− 0.7*	*10 637.0*
Romania	*21 462.2*	212.2	259.7	− 47.5	− 0.8	*− 48.4*	*21 413.8*
Slovenia	2 047.0	22.3	18.6	3.7	− 0.5	*3.2*	*2 050.2*
Slovakia	5 424.9	60.4	53.4	7.0	3.4	*10.3*	*5 435.3*
Finland	5 351.4	61.0	50.9	10.1	13.8	*23.8*	*5 375.3*
Sweden	9 340.7	115.6	90.5	25.2	49.7	*74.9*	*9 415.6*
United Kingdom	*62 027.0*	807.3	561.7	245.6	163.1	*408.7*	*62 435.7*
Iceland	317.6	4.9	2.0	2.9	− 2.1	*0.8*	*318.5*
Liechtenstein	35.9	0.3	0.2	0.1	0.2	*0.3*	*36.1*
Norway	4 858.2	61.4	41.5	19.9	42.2	*62.1*	*4 920.3*
Switzerland	*7 785.8*	80.3	62.6	17.6	63.1	*80.7*	*7 866.5*
Montenegro	616.4	7.4	5.6	1.8	0.0	*1.8*	*618.2*
Croatia	4 425.7	43.4	52.1	− 8.7	− 4.9	*− 13.6*	*4 412.1*
FYR of Macedonia	2 052.7	24.3	19.1	5.2	− 0.6	*4.6*	*2 057.3*
Turkey	72 561.3	1 279.0	459.0	820.0	341.7	*1 161.7*	*73 723.0*

(¹) Live births minus deaths.
(²) Total change minus natural change.

Source: Eurostat (online data code: demo_gind)

Table 2.3.2: Crude rates of population change, 2008-2010
(per 1 000 inhabitants)

	Total change			Natural change			Net migration and statistical adjustment		
	2008	**2009**	**2010**	**2008**	**2009**	**2010**	**2008**	**2009**	**2010**
EU-27	4.0	2.8	2.8	1.2	1.0	1.0	2.9	1.8	1.8
Belgium	8.0	8.0	10.3	2.2	2.1	2.1	5.9	5.9	8.2
Bulgaria	−4.4	−5.6	−7.8	−4.3	−3.6	−4.6	−0.1	−2.1	−3.2
Czech Republic	8.3	3.7	2.5	1.4	1.0	1.0	6.9	2.7	1.5
Denmark	6.5	4.2	4.7	1.9	1.4	1.6	4.6	2.8	3.0
Germany	−2.6	−2.4	−0.6	−2.0	−2.3	−2.2	−0.7	−0.1	1.6
Estonia	−0.4	−0.2	0.0	−0.5	−0.2	0.0	0.1	0.0	0.0
Ireland	11.0	4.0	2.9	10.3	10.2	10.4	0.7	−6.2	−7.5
Greece	4.1	4.0	1.8	0.9	0.9	0.3	3.2	3.1	1.5
Spain	12.0	3.5	3.6	2.9	2.4	2.3	9.0	1.1	1.3
France	5.6	5.4	5.5	4.5	4.3	4.4	1.2	1.1	1.2
Italy	7.1	4.9	4.7	0.0	−0.4	−0.4	7.1	5.3	5.2
Cyprus	9.6	7.8	1.6	5.1	5.5	5.7	4.5	2.3	−4.1
Latvia	−4.2	−5.7	−8.4	−3.1	−3.6	−4.8	−1.1	−2.1	−3.5
Lithuania (¹)	−4.9	−6.2	−25.7	−2.6	−1.6	−2.0	−2.3	−4.6	−23.7
Luxembourg	19.9	17.2	19.3	4.1	4.0	4.2	15.8	13.2	15.1
Hungary	−1.4	−1.7	−2.9	−3.1	−3.4	−4.0	1.6	1.7	1.2
Malta	8.1	1.8	7.8	2.1	2.2	2.4	5.9	−0.4	5.4
Netherlands	4.9	5.4	4.9	3.0	3.1	2.9	1.9	2.3	2.0
Austria	4.4	2.4	3.5	0.3	−0.1	0.2	4.1	2.5	3.3
Poland	0.5	0.8	0.9	0.9	0.9	0.9	−0.4	0.0	−0.1
Portugal	0.9	1.0	−0.1	0.0	−0.5	−0.4	0.9	1.4	0.4
Romania	−1.4	−1.7	−2.3	−1.5	−1.6	−2.2	0.1	−0.1	0.0
Slovenia	10.9	7.2	1.6	1.7	1.5	1.8	9.2	5.6	−0.3
Slovakia	2.1	2.3	1.9	0.8	1.5	1.3	1.3	0.8	0.6
Finland	4.9	4.7	4.4	2.0	2.0	1.9	2.9	2.7	2.6
Sweden	8.0	9.1	8.0	1.9	2.3	2.7	6.0	6.7	5.3
United Kingdom	6.6	7.0	6.6	3.5	3.7	3.9	3.1	3.3	2.6
Iceland	12.3	−5.5	2.6	9.0	9.5	9.1	3.3	−15.0	−6.5
Liechtenstein	6.6	8.5	7.1	4.1	5.0	2.5	2.5	3.6	4.6
Norway	13.0	12.2	12.7	3.9	4.2	4.1	9.1	8.0	8.6
Switzerland	14.2	10.8	10.3	2.0	2.0	2.3	12.1	8.8	8.1
Montenegro (²)	4.2	4.4	2.9	4.1	4.4	2.9	0.1	0.0	0.0
Croatia	−0.3	−2.1	−3.1	−1.9	−1.8	−2.0	1.6	−0.3	−1.1
FYR of Macedonia	1.7	2.0	2.2	1.9	2.3	2.5	−0.3	−0.3	−0.3
Turkey	13.1	14.5	15.9	11.4	10.8	11.2	1.7	3.7	4.7

(¹) Due to administrative reasons emigration recorded in Lithuania in 2010 may include emigration that took place over previous years.
(²) Break in series in 2010.

Source: Eurostat (online data code: demo_gind)

Table 2.3.3: Contribution of natural change and net migration (and statistical adjustment) to population change, 2010

Demographic drivers	Member States
Growth due to:	
Only natural change	Ireland, Cyprus, Poland, Slovenia
Mostly natural change	Estonia, Spain, France, Netherlands, Slovakia, United Kingdom
Mostly net migration (and adjustment)	Belgium, Czech Republic, Denmark, Greece, Luxembourg, Malta, Austria, Finland, Sweden
Only net migration (and adjustment)	Italy
Decline due to:	
Only natural change	Hungary, Portugal
Mostly natural change	Bulgaria, Germany, Latvia, Romania
Mostly net migration (and adjustment)	Lithuania
Only net migration (and adjustment)	–

Source: Eurostat (online data code: demo_gind)

2.4 Marriage and divorce

This subchapter presents developments that have taken place in relation to family formation and dissolution through an analysis of marriage and divorce indicators. Marriage, as recognised by the law of each country, has long been considered to mark the formation of a family unit. Recent demographic data show that the number of marriages per 1 000 inhabitants has decreased within the EU-27 in recent years, while the number of divorces has increased – this has generally led to an increase in the number of children who are born to unmarried women.

Main statistical findings

Fewer marriages, more divorces

The number of marriages that took place in the EU-27 in 2009 was 2.3 million, while around 1.0 million divorces were recorded in 2008. The crude marriage rate, in other words the number of marriages per 1 000 inhabitants, was 4.5, and the crude divorce rate was 2.0.

The crude marriage rate in the EU-27 declined from 7.9 marriages per 1 000 inhabitants in 1970 to 4.5 marriages in 2009, an overall reduction of 34 % in the number of marriages. Over the same period, marriages

became less stable, as reflected by the increase in the crude divorce rate, which doubled from 1.0 divorce per 1 000 inhabitants in 1970 to 2.0 divorces by 2008. When considering the increase in the divorce rate it should be noted that national laws did not allow divorce in several countries until recently; thus, the increased number of divorces in the EU-27 may, at least in part, reflect the addition of divorces in those Member States where divorce was not previously possible (for example, Italy, Spain, Ireland or Malta).

Table 2.4.1 shows that in 2010 the crude marriage rate was highest in Cyprus (7.9 marriages per 1 000 inhabitants in 2009) and Poland (6.0); the lowest crude marriage rates were reported by Slovenia and Bulgaria (both with 3.2 marriages per 1 000 inhabitants).

The lowest crude divorce rates were recorded in Ireland (0.7 divorces per 1 000 inhabitants in 2010) and Italy (0.9 in 2009). A number of other southern Member States also recorded relatively low crude divorce rates, including Slovenia and Greece (in 2008). The highest crude divorce rates were recorded in Lithuania and Belgium (3.0 divorces per 1 000 inhabitants in 2010), ahead of the Czech Republic (2.9) – see Table 2.4.2.

A rise in births outside marriage

The proportion of live births outside marriage increased across the EU-27 over the last two decades, reflecting a change in the pattern of traditional family formation, away from the model of parenthood following marriage; children born outside of marriage may be born to a couple in a non-marital relationship (for example, cohabiting couples) or to a single mother.

In the EU-27 some 37.4 % of children were born outside marriage in 2010, while the corresponding figure for 1990 was 17.4 % (see Table 2.4.3). The share of extra-marital births has been on the rise in recent years in almost every Member State. Indeed, extra-marital births accounted for the majority of live births in Estonia, Slovenia, Bulgaria, Sweden and France. The number of births outside of marriage was lowest in Greece (6.9 % in 2010) and Cyprus (11.7 % in 2009), while more than one in every five births was outside of marriage in Poland (the EU Member State with the third lowest proportion of births outside of marriage).

Data sources and availability

Eurostat compiles information on a wide range of demographic data, including data on the number of marriages by sex and previous marital status and statistics relating to the number of divorces. Data on the number of live births according to the mother's marital status may be used to derive the share of births outside marriage.

Context

The family unit is a changing concept: what it means to be a member of a family and the expectations people have of family relationships vary with time and space, making it difficult to find a universally agreed and applied definition. Legal alternatives to marriage, like registered partnership, have become more widespread and national legislation has evolved to confer more rights to unmarried couples. Alongside these new legal forms, other forms of non-marital relationships have appeared, making it more difficult for statisticians to collect data within this domain that can be compared across countries.

Due to differences in the timing and formal recognition of changing patterns of family formation and dissolution, these concepts have become more difficult to measure in practice. Analysts of demographic statistics therefore have access to relatively few complete and reliable datasets with which to make comparisons over time and between or within countries.

Figure 2.4.1: Crude marriage and divorce rates, EU-27, 1970-2009
(per 1 000 inhabitants)

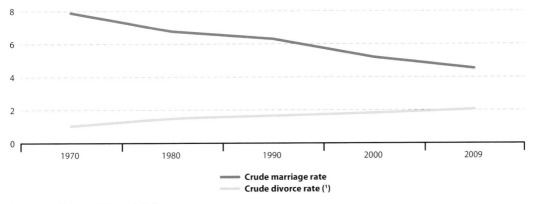

Crude marriage rate
Crude divorce rate (¹)

(¹) 1971 instead of 1970; 2008 instead of 2009.
Source: Eurostat (online data codes: demo_nind and demo_ndivind)

Table 2.4.1: Crude marriage rate, 1960-2010
(per 1 000 inhabitants)

	1960	1970	1980	1990	2000	2010
EU-27 (¹)	:	7.9	6.8	6.3	5.2	4.5
Belgium	7.1	7.6	6.7	6.5	4.4	4.2
Bulgaria	8.8	8.6	7.9	6.9	4.3	3.2
Czech Republic	7.7	9.2	7.6	8.8	5.4	4.4
Denmark	7.8	7.4	5.2	6.1	7.2	5.6
Germany	9.5	7.4	6.3	6.5	5.1	4.7
Estonia	10.0	9.1	8.8	7.5	4.0	3.8
Ireland	5.5	7.0	6.4	5.1	5.0	4.6
Greece	7.0	7.7	6.5	5.8	4.5	5.1
Spain	7.8	7.3	5.9	5.7	5.4	3.6
France (²)	7.0	7.8	6.2	5.1	5.0	3.8
Italy	7.7	7.4	5.7	5.6	5.0	3.6
Cyprus (¹)(³)	:	8.6	7.7	9.7	13.4	7.9
Latvia	11.0	10.2	9.8	8.9	3.9	4.2
Lithuania	10.1	9.5	9.2	9.8	4.8	5.7
Luxembourg	7.1	6.4	5.9	6.1	4.9	3.5
Hungary	8.9	9.4	7.5	6.4	4.7	3.6
Malta	6.0	7.9	8.8	7.1	6.7	6.2
Netherlands (¹)	7.7	9.5	6.4	6.5	5.5	4.4
Austria	8.3	7.1	6.2	5.9	4.9	4.5
Poland	8.2	8.6	8.6	6.7	5.5	6.0
Portugal	7.8	9.4	7.4	7.2	6.2	3.7
Romania	10.7	7.2	8.2	8.3	6.1	5.4
Slovenia	8.8	8.3	6.5	4.3	3.6	3.2
Slovakia	7.9	7.9	8.0	7.6	4.8	4.7
Finland	7.4	8.8	6.2	5.0	5.1	5.6
Sweden	6.7	5.4	4.5	4.7	4.5	5.3
United Kingdom (¹)	7.5	8.5	7.4	6.6	5.2	4.3
Iceland	7.5	7.8	5.7	4.5	6.3	4.9
Liechtenstein	5.7	5.9	7.1	5.6	7.2	5.0
Norway	6.6	7.6	5.4	5.2	5.0	4.8
Switzerland	7.8	7.6	5.7	6.9	5.5	5.5
Montenegro	:	:	:	:	:	6.0
Croatia	8.9	8.5	7.2	5.9	4.9	4.8
FYR of Macedonia	8.6	9.0	8.5	8.3	7.0	6.9
Turkey	:	:	8.2	:	:	8.0

(¹) 2009 instead of 2010.
(²) Excluding French overseas departments for 1960 to 1990.
(³) Up to and including 2002, data refer to total marriages contracted in the country, including marriages between non-residents; from 2003 onwards, data refer to marriages in which at least one spouse was resident in the country.

Source: Eurostat (online data code: demo_nind)

Table 2.4.2: Crude divorce rate, 1960-2010 (¹)
(per 1 000 inhabitants)

	1960	1970	1980	1990	2000	2010
EU-27 (²)(³)	:	1.0	1.5	1.6	1.8	2.0
Belgium	0.5	0.7	1.5	2.0	2.6	3.0
Bulgaria	:	1.2	1.5	1.3	1.3	1.5
Czech Republic	1.4	2.2	2.6	3.1	2.9	2.9
Denmark	1.5	1.9	2.7	2.7	2.7	2.6
Germany	1.0	1.3	1.8	1.9	2.4	2.3
Estonia	2.1	3.2	4.1	3.7	3.1	2.2
Ireland	–	–	–	–	0.7	0.7
Greece (³)	0.3	0.4	0.7	0.6	1.0	1.2
Spain	–	–	–	0.6	0.9	2.2
France (³)(⁴)	0.7	0.8	1.5	1.9	1.9	2.1
Italy (²)(⁵)	–	0.3	0.2	0.5	0.7	0.9
Cyprus (⁵)	:	0.2	0.3	0.6	1.7	2.2
Latvia	2.4	4.6	5.0	4.0	2.6	2.2
Lithuania	0.9	2.2	3.2	3.4	3.1	3.0
Luxembourg	0.5	0.6	1.6	2.0	2.4	2.1
Hungary	1.7	2.2	2.6	2.4	2.3	2.4
Malta	–	–	–	–	–	–
Netherlands (⁵)	0.5	0.8	1.8	1.9	2.2	1.9
Austria	1.1	1.4	1.8	2.1	2.4	2.1
Poland	0.5	1.1	1.1	1.1	1.1	1.6
Portugal (⁵)	0.1	0.1	0.6	0.9	1.9	2.5
Romania	2.0	0.4	1.5	1.4	1.4	1.5
Slovenia	1.0	1.1	1.2	0.9	1.1	1.2
Slovakia	0.6	0.8	1.3	1.7	1.7	2.2
Finland	0.8	1.3	2.0	2.6	2.7	2.5
Sweden	1.2	1.6	2.4	2.3	2.4	2.5
United Kingdom (⁵)	:	1.0	2.6	2.7	2.6	2.0
Iceland	0.7	1.2	1.9	1.9	1.9	1.8
Liechtenstein	–	–	:	:	3.9	2.4
Norway	0.7	0.9	1.6	2.4	2.2	2.1
Switzerland	0.9	1.0	1.7	2.0	1.5	2.8
Montenegro	:	:	:	:	:	0.8
Croatia	1.2	1.2	1.2	1.1	1.0	1.1
FYR of Macedonia	0.7	0.3	0.5	0.4	0.7	0.8
Turkey	:	:	:	:	:	1.6

(¹) Divorce was not possible by law in Italy until 1970, in Spain until 1981, in Ireland until 1995 and in Malta until 2011.
(²) 1971 instead of 1970.
(³) 2008 instead of 2010.
(⁴) Excluding French overseas departments for 1970 to 1990.
(⁵) 2009 instead of 2010.

Source: Eurostat (online data code: demo_ndivind)

Table 2.4.3: Live births outside marriage, 1960-2010
(% share of total live births)

	1960	1970	1980	1990	2000	2010
EU-27 (¹)	:	:	:	17.4	27.4	37.4
Belgium	2.1	2.8	4.1	11.6	28.0	47.0
Bulgaria	8.0	8.5	10.9	12.4	38.4	54.1
Czech Republic	4.9	5.4	5.6	8.6	21.8	40.3
Denmark	7.8	11.0	33.2	46.4	44.6	47.0
Germany	7.6	7.2	11.9	15.3	23.4	33.3
Estonia	:	:	:	27.2	54.5	59.1
Ireland	1.6	2.7	5.9	14.6	31.5	33.6
Greece	1.2	1.1	1.5	2.2	4.0	6.9
Spain	2.3	1.4	3.9	9.6	17.7	33.1
France (²)(³)	6.1	6.8	11.4	30.1	43.6	53.7
Italy	2.4	2.2	4.3	6.5	9.7	25.4
Cyprus (³)	:	0.2	0.6	0.7	2.3	11.7
Latvia	11.9	11.4	12.5	16.9	40.3	44.1
Lithuania	:	3.7	6.3	7.0	22.6	28.7
Luxembourg	3.2	4.0	6.0	12.8	21.9	34.0
Hungary	5.5	5.4	7.1	13.1	29.0	40.8
Malta	0.7	1.5	1.1	1.8	10.6	25.2
Netherlands (³)	1.4	2.1	4.1	11.4	24.9	43.3
Austria	13.0	12.8	17.8	23.6	31.3	40.1
Poland	:	5.0	4.8	6.2	12.1	20.6
Portugal (³)	9.5	7.3	9.2	14.7	22.2	38.1
Romania	:	:	:	:	25.5	27.7
Slovenia	9.1	8.5	13.1	24.5	37.1	55.0
Slovakia	4.7	6.2	5.7	7.6	18.3	33.0
Finland	4.0	5.8	13.1	25.2	39.2	41.1
Sweden	11.3	18.6	39.7	47.0	55.3	54.1
United Kingdom	5.2	8.0	11.5	27.9	39.5	46.9
Iceland	25.3	29.9	39.7	55.2	65.2	64.3
Liechtenstein	3.7	4.5	5.3	6.9	15.7	21.3
Norway	3.7	6.9	14.5	38.6	49.6	54.8
Switzerland	3.8	3.8	4.7	6.1	10.7	18.5
Montenegro (³)	:	:	:	:	:	15.7
Croatia	7.4	5.4	5.1	7.0	9.0	13.3
FYR of Macedonia	5.1	6.2	6.1	7.1	9.8	12.2

(¹) Excluding French overseas departments and Romania for 1990; 2009 instead of 2010.
(²) Excluding French overseas departments for 1960 to 1990.
(³) 2009 instead of 2010.

Source: Eurostat (online data code: demo_find)

2.5 Fertility

This subchapter looks at the development of a range of indicators concerning the number of births and fertility across European Union (EU). Fertility steadily declined from the mid-1960s through to the turn of the century in those countries which form the EU. However, in recent years the total fertility rate in the EU-27 showed some signs of rising slightly.

Main statistical findings

From the 1960s up to the beginning of the 21st century, the number of live births in the EU-27 declined sharply from 7.5 million to a low of 5.0 million in 2002 (see Figure 2.5.1). Since then there has been a modest rebound in the number of live births, with 5.4 million children born in the EU-27 in each of the last three years for which data are available (2008-2010).

In recent decades Europeans have generally been having fewer children, and this can partly explain the slowdown in the EU-27's population growth (see population and population change statistics). A total fertility rate of around 2.1 live births per woman is considered to be the replacement level: in other words, the average number of live births per woman required to keep the population size constant if there were no inward or outward migration is 2.1.

The total fertility rate in the EU-27 declined to a level well below this replacement level in recent decades. The lowest total fertility rate of 1.45 live births per woman was registered in the EU-27 in 2002, according to the available aggregated information. A slight recovery in the fertility rate was subsequently observed in most of the Member States, such that the EU-27 average had increased to 1.59 live births per woman by 2009.

The slight increase in the total fertility rate observed in recent years may, in part, be attributed to a catching-up process following a general pattern of postponing the decision to have children. When women give birth later in life, the total fertility rate tends to decrease at first, before a subsequent recovery.

Total fertility rates across EU Member States tended to converge during the last few decades. In 1980, the gap between the highest rate (3.2 live births per woman in Ireland) and the lowest rate (1.5 live births per woman in Luxembourg) was 1.7 live births per woman (see Table 2.5.1). By 1990 the difference had decreased to 1.1 live births per woman, and by 2009 it had narrowed still further to 0.8. Ireland continued to report the highest fertility rate in 2009, with an average of 2.1 live births per woman, just ahead of France (which was the only other EU Member State to report a fertility rate in excess of 2.0 children per woman). In contrast, the lowest fertility rates were recorded in Latvia, Portugal and Hungary (all 1.3 live births per woman).

As noted above, another reason that partly explains the downward development of fertility rates within the EU Member States is the decision of many parents to delay starting a family. While only a relatively short time series is available for the EU-27 aggregate, Table 2.5.2 shows that the mean age of women at childbirth continued to rise between 2003 and 2009, when it stood at 29.8 years.

Data sources and availability

Eurostat compiles information for a large range of demographic data, including statistics on the number of live births by sex, by the mother's age, education and marital status. Fertility statistics are also collected in relation to the number of births by the rank of the child (first, second, third child and so on). A series of fertility indicators are produced from the information collected, including the total fertility rate and fertility rates according to the mother's age, the mean age of women at childbirth, the crude birth rate or the relative proportion of births outside of marriage.

Context

The EU's social policy does not include a specific strand for family issues. Policymaking in this area remains the exclusive responsibility of Member States, reflecting different family structures, historical developments, social attitudes and traditions from one Member State to another. Nevertheless, policymakers may well evaluate fertility statistics as a background for family policymaking. Furthermore, a number of common demographic themes are apparent across the whole of the EU, such as a reduction in the average number of children being born per woman and an increasing mean age of mothers at childbirth.

Figure 2.5.1: Number of live births, EU-27, 1961-2010 ([1])
(million)

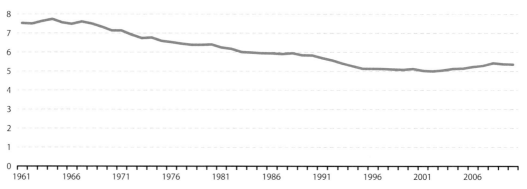

([1]) Excluding French overseas departments before 1998; provisional values for 2009 and 2010.
Source: Eurostat (online data code: demo_gind)

Table 2.5.1: Total fertility rate, 1960-2009
(live births per woman)

	1960	1970	1980	1990	2000	2003	2009
EU-27	:	:	:	:	:	1.47	1.59
Belgium	2.54	2.25	1.68	1.62	1.67	1.66	1.84
Bulgaria	2.31	2.17	2.05	1.82	1.26	1.23	1.57
Czech Republic	2.09	1.92	2.08	1.90	1.14	1.18	1.49
Denmark	2.57	1.95	1.55	1.67	1.77	1.76	1.84
Germany	:	:	:	:	1.38	1.34	1.36
Estonia	:	:	:	2.05	1.38	1.37	1.62
Ireland	3.78	3.85	3.21	2.11	1.89	1.96	2.07
Greece	2.23	2.40	2.23	1.40	1.26	1.28	1.52
Spain	:	:	2.20	1.36	1.23	1.31	1.40
France ([1])	2.73	2.47	1.95	1.78	1.89	1.89	2.00
Italy	2.37	2.38	1.64	1.33	1.26	1.29	1.41
Cyprus	:	:	:	2.41	1.64	1.50	1.51
Latvia	:	:	:	:	:	1.29	1.31
Lithuania	:	2.40	1.99	2.03	1.39	1.26	1.55
Luxembourg	2.29	1.97	1.50	1.60	1.76	1.62	1.59
Hungary	2.02	1.98	1.91	1.87	1.32	1.27	1.32
Malta	:	:	1.99	2.04	1.70	1.48	1.43
Netherlands	3.12	2.57	1.60	1.62	1.72	1.75	1.79
Austria	2.69	2.29	1.65	1.46	1.36	1.38	1.39
Poland	:	:	:	2.06	1.35	1.22	1.40
Portugal	3.16	3.01	2.25	1.56	1.55	1.44	1.32
Romania	:	:	2.43	1.83	1.31	1.27	1.38
Slovenia	:	:	:	1.46	1.26	1.20	1.53
Slovakia	3.04	2.41	2.32	2.09	1.30	1.20	1.41
Finland	2.72	1.83	1.63	1.78	1.73	1.76	1.86
Sweden	:	1.92	1.68	2.13	1.54	1.71	1.94
United Kingdom	:	:	1.90	1.83	1.64	1.71	1.94
Iceland	:	2.81	2.48	2.30	2.08	1.99	2.23
Liechtenstein	:	:	:	:	1.57	1.36	1.71
Norway	:	2.50	1.72	1.93	1.85	1.80	1.98
Switzerland	2.44	2.10	1.55	1.58	1.50	1.39	1.50
Montenegro ([2])	:	:	:	:	:	:	1.77
Croatia	:	:	:	:	:	1.32	1.49
FYR of Macedonia	:	:	:	:	1.88	1.77	1.52
Turkey ([2])	:	:	:	:	:	:	2.10

([1]) Excluding French overseas departments, up to and including 1990.
([2]) 2008 instead of 2009.
Source: Eurostat (online data code: demo_frate)

Table 2.5.2: Fertility indicators, EU-27, 2002-2009

	2002	2003	2004	2005	2006	2007	2008	2009
Total fertility rate (live births per woman)	1.45	1.47	1.50	1.51	1.54	1.56	1.60	1.59
Mean age of women at childbirth (years)	:	29.3	29.4	29.5	29.6	29.7	29.7	29.8

Source: Eurostat (online data code: demo_find)

2.6 Mortality and life expectancy

This subchapter provides information relating to mortality in the European Union (EU). Life expectancy at birth rose rapidly during the last century due to a number of factors, including reductions in infant mortality, rising living standards, improved lifestyles and better education, as well as advances in healthcare and medicine.

Main statistical findings

Some 4.85 million persons died in the EU-27 in 2010 – this was broadly in line with the number of deaths recorded over the previous 40 years.

Life expectancy is increasing

The most commonly used indicator for analysing mortality is that of life expectancy at birth. Improvements in living standards and the establishment and improvement in health systems across Europe have led to a continuous increase in life expectancy at birth. Indeed, life expectancy at birth in the EU-27 increased over the last 50 years by about ten years. Even in the last six years for which data at an aggregated EU-27 level are available (2002 to 2008) there was an increase in life expectancy of 1.5 years for women and 1.9 years for men (see Figure 2.6.2).

Life expectancy in the EU-27 is generally higher than in most other regions of the world. Based on EU-27 observations for 2008, a new born male is expected to live, on average, to 76.4 years old, while a new born female is expected to live to 82.4 years old (see Table 2.6.1).

Significant differences in life expectancy at birth are nevertheless observed between the EU Member States. Looking at the extremes of the ranges (2009 data for the majority of countries), a woman born in 2009 is expected to live between 77.4 years

(Bulgaria) and 85.0 years (France), a range of 7.6 years. A man born in 2009 can be expected to live between 67.5 years (Lithuania) and 79.4 years (Sweden), a range of 11.9 years.

The gender gap is shrinking

With a gender gap of six years of life in 2008, women generally outlive men in the EU-27. However, the gap between male and female life expectancies at birth varied substantially between Member States. In 2009, the largest difference between the sexes was found in Lithuania (11.2 years) and the smallest in Sweden (4.1 years) – see Figure 2.6.3.

Infant mortality

Improvements in life expectancy at birth are achieved through reductions in the probability of dying. One of the most significant changes in recent decades has been a reduction in infant mortality rates. During the 15 years from 1994 to 2009 the infant mortality rate in the EU-27 was almost halved. The biggest reductions in infant mortality were generally recorded within those Member States which tended to record higher than average levels of infant mortality in 1994. The lowest infant mortality rate within the EU-27 in 2009 occurred in Slovenia (2.4 deaths per 1 000 live births), Luxembourg, Sweden (both 2.5 ‰) and Finland (2.6 ‰). In contrast, infant mortality rates were approximately four times higher in Romania (10.1 ‰) and Bulgaria (9.0 ‰).

Data sources and availability

Eurostat provides information on a wide range of demographic data, including statistics on the number of deaths by age, deaths by year of birth, deaths according to sex, and deaths according to educational attainment, while statistics are also collected for infant mortality and late foetal deaths. A series of mortality indicators are produced, which may be used to derive a range of information on subjects such as crude death rates or life expectancy measures by age, sex or educational attainment.

Context

The gradual increase in life expectancy is one of the contributing factors to the ageing of the EU-27's population – alongside relatively low levels of fertility that have persisted for decades (see the subchapters on population structure and ageing and fertility statistics).

Figure 2.6.1: Number of deaths, EU-27, 1961-2010 (¹)
(million)

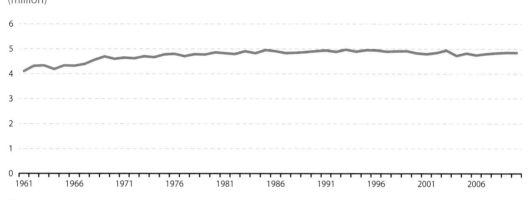

(¹) Excluding French overseas departments up to 1997; provisional, 2009 and 2010.

Source: Eurostat (online data code: demo_gind)

Figure 2.6.2: Life expectancy at birth, EU-27, 2002-2008
(years)

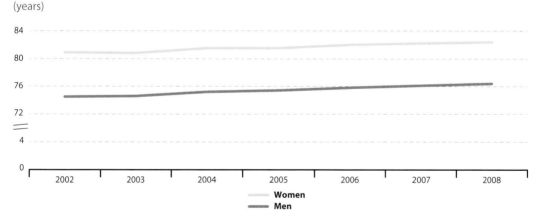

Source: Eurostat (online data code: demo_mlexpec)

Table 2.6.1: Life expectancy at birth, 1994 and 2009
(years)

	Total		Men		Women	
	1994	**2009**	**1994**	**2009**	**1994**	**2009**
EU-27 (¹)	:	79.4	:	76.4	:	82.4
Belgium	76.8	80.1	73.4	77.3	80.2	82.8
Bulgaria	70.9	73.7	67.3	70.1	74.8	77.4
Czech Republic	73.2	77.4	69.6	74.2	76.8	80.5
Denmark	75.5	79.0	72.8	76.9	78.2	81.1
Germany	76.6	80.3	73.1	77.8	79.7	82.8
Estonia	66.6	75.2	60.6	69.8	72.9	80.2
Ireland	75.8	79.9	73.1	77.4	78.6	82.5
Greece	77.5	80.2	75.1	77.8	80.0	82.7
Spain	78.1	81.8	74.4	78.6	81.8	84.9
France (²)	78.0	81.6	73.8	78.0	82.2	85.0
Italy (¹)	78.1	81.9	74.8	79.1	81.2	84.5
Cyprus	77.2	81.1	75.0	78.6	79.3	83.6
Latvia	:	73.3	:	68.1	:	78.0
Lithuania	68.6	73.2	62.6	67.5	74.9	78.7
Luxembourg	76.7	80.8	73.2	78.1	79.9	83.3
Hungary	69.6	74.4	65.0	70.3	74.5	78.4
Malta (³)	77.2	80.3	74.8	77.9	79.6	82.7
Netherlands	77.6	80.9	74.6	78.7	80.4	82.9
Austria	76.7	80.5	73.2	77.6	79.8	83.2
Poland	71.8	75.9	67.5	71.5	76.1	80.1
Portugal	75.5	79.6	72.0	76.5	79.0	82.6
Romania	69.4	73.5	65.7	69.8	73.3	77.4
Slovenia	74.0	79.4	70.1	75.9	77.8	82.7
Slovakia	72.5	75.3	68.4	71.4	76.7	79.1
Finland	76.7	80.1	72.9	76.6	80.3	83.5
Sweden	78.9	81.5	76.2	79.4	81.6	83.5
United Kingdom	76.8	80.5	74.1	78.3	79.5	82.5
Iceland	79.3	81.8	77.1	79.8	81.5	83.8
Liechtenstein	78.7	81.7	75.3	79.5	81.8	83.6
Norway	77.9	81.0	74.9	78.7	80.8	83.2
Switzerland	78.7	82.3	75.2	79.9	82.0	84.6
Montenegro (¹)	:	75.3	:	74.4	:	76.6
Croatia	:	76.4	:	73.0	:	79.7
FYR of Macedonia	71.7	74.4	69.4	72.3	74.1	76.7

(¹) 2008 instead of 2009.
(²) Excluding French overseas departments in 1994.
(³) 1995 instead of 1994.

Source: Eurostat (online data code: demo_mlexpec)

Figure 2.6.3: Life expectancy at birth, gender gap, 2009
(years, female life expectancy – male life expectancy)

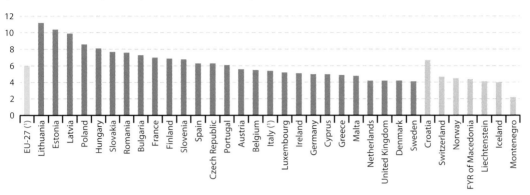

(¹) 2008 instead of 2009.

Source: Eurostat (online data code: demo_mlexpec)

Table 2.6.2: Life expectancy at age 65, 1994 and 2009
(years)

	Total		Men		Women	
	1994	2009	1994	2009	1994	2009
EU-27 (¹)	:	19.1	:	17.2	:	20.7
Belgium	17.3	19.5	14.8	17.5	19.3	21.1
Bulgaria	14.2	15.5	12.9	13.8	15.5	17.0
Czech Republic	14.7	17.2	12.7	15.2	16.1	18.8
Denmark	16.2	18.2	14.3	16.8	17.9	19.5
Germany	17.0	19.3	14.7	17.6	18.6	20.8
Estonia	14.1	17.1	11.6	14.0	15.7	19.2
Ireland	15.7	19.0	13.8	17.2	17.4	20.6
Greece	17.2	19.2	16.0	18.1	18.2	20.2
Spain	18.3	20.5	16.2	18.3	20.1	22.4
France (²)	18.9	21.2	16.3	18.7	21.0	23.2
Italy (¹)	17.8	20.2	15.7	18.2	19.6	22.0
Cyprus	17.1	19.5	16.1	18.1	18.0	20.9
Latvia	:	16.3	:	13.4	:	18.2
Lithuania	15.1	16.4	12.7	13.4	16.8	18.4
Luxembourg	17.1	19.7	14.7	17.6	19.0	21.4
Hungary	14.2	16.4	12.1	14.0	15.9	18.2
Malta (³)	16.6	18.8	15.5	16.8	17.6	20.6
Netherlands	17.2	19.4	14.8	17.6	19.2	21.0
Austria	17.2	19.6	15.0	17.7	18.7	21.2
Poland	14.9	17.3	12.8	14.8	16.4	19.2
Portugal	16.6	18.9	14.8	17.1	18.2	20.5
Romania	14.2	15.8	12.8	14.0	15.3	17.2
Slovenia	15.8	18.8	13.6	16.4	17.3	20.5
Slovakia	14.8	16.3	12.8	14.1	16.4	18.0
Finland	17.1	19.6	14.7	17.3	18.7	21.5
Sweden	18.2	19.8	16.1	18.2	20.0	21.2
United Kingdom	16.7	19.6	14.7	18.1	18.4	20.8
Iceland	18.5	19.8	16.8	18.6	20.0	21.0
Liechtenstein	18.0	20.4	16.4	18.4	19.2	22.0
Norway	17.4	19.6	15.3	18.0	19.4	21.1
Switzerland	18.6	20.8	16.2	19.0	20.6	22.2
Montenegro	:	15.9	:	16.5	:	15.7
Croatia	:	16.4	:	14.5	:	17.9
FYR of Macedonia	14.1	14.9	13.2	13.9	15.0	15.8

(¹) 2008 instead of 2009.
(²) Excluding French overseas departments in 1994.
(³) 1995 instead of 1994.

Source: Eurostat (online data code: demo_mlexpec)

Figure 2.6.4: Life expectancy at age 65, 2009
(years)

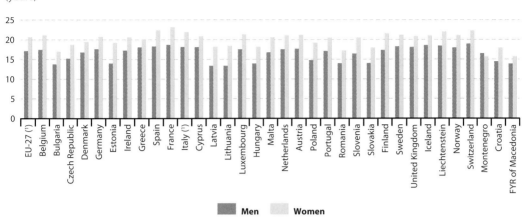

Men **Women**

(¹) 2008 instead of 2009.

Source: Eurostat (online data code: demo_mlexpec)

Figure 2.6.5: Infant mortality, 1994 and 2009
(deaths per 1 000 live births)

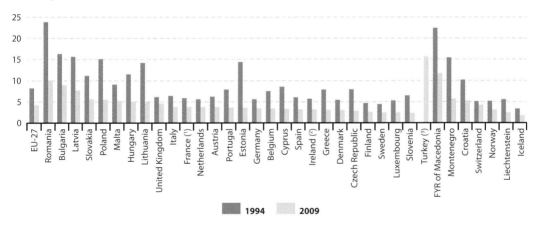

1994 **2009**

(¹) Excluding French overseas departments in 1994.
(²) 2009, provisional.
(³) 1994, not available.

Source: Eurostat (online data code: demo_minfind)

2.7 Migration and migrant population

This subchapter presents European Union (EU) statistics on international migration, population stocks of national and foreign (non-national) citizens, and the acquisition of citizenship. Migration is influenced by a combination of economic, political and social factors, either in a migrant's country of origin (push factors) or in the country of destination (pull factors); historically, the relative economic prosperity and political stability of the EU are thought to have exerted a considerable pull effect on immigrants.

In destination countries, international migration may be used as a tool to solve specific labour market shortages. However, international migration alone will almost certainly not reverse the ongoing trend of population ageing experienced in many parts of the EU.

Main statistical findings

Migration flows

During 2009, about 3.0 million people immigrated into one of the EU Member States (see Table 2.7.1), while at least 1.9 million emigrants were reported to have left an EU Member State. The latest figures available reveal a substantial decline in immigration in 2009 as compared with 2008. However, it is difficult to quantify exactly the magnitude of this decline as some countries (including Germany, Austria and the Netherlands) have modified the underlying definitions of migration (for example, immigration into Germany in 2009 was 347 000, but the level would have been more than double under the earlier definition).

It should be noted that these figures do not represent the migration flows to/from the EU as a whole, since they also include flows between different EU Member States. However, more than half of the immigrants into the EU Member States, an estimated 1.6 million people in 2009, were previously residing outside the EU.

The United Kingdom reported the largest number of immigrants (566 500) in 2009, followed by Spain (499 000) and Italy (442 900); just over half (50.3 %) of all immigrants into EU Member States were recorded in these three countries.

The United Kingdom also reported the highest number of emigrants in 2009 (368 000), followed by Spain with 324 000 and Germany with 287 000. Most EU Member States reported more immigration than emigration in 2009, but in Ireland, Malta and the three Baltic Member States emigrants outnumbered immigrants.

Relative to the size of the resident population (see Figure 2.7.1), Luxembourg recorded the highest number of immigrants in 2009 (31 immigrants per 1 000 inhabitants), followed by Malta (17), Slovenia and Cyprus (both 15); immigration was also high in the EFTA countries, greatly exceeding the EU average of 6.1 immigrants per 1 000 inhabitants.

Among EU Member States, Luxembourg (20 emigrants per 1 000 inhabitants) and Malta (16) reported the highest rate of emigration in 2009; these levels were surpassed in Iceland, where almost 29 residents per 1 000 inhabitants left the country.

Immigrants include both nationals (former emigrants returning 'home' and citizens born abroad who are immigrating for the first time) and non-nationals (people who are not citizens of the destination country). Among all immigrants into EU Member States in 2009, 18 % were nationals (see Figure 2.7.2), 31 % were citizens of other EU Member States, and 51 % were third-country nationals, that is citizens of non-member countries. These third-country nationals can be differentiated according to the level of development of their country of citizenship, based on the human development index (HDI) calculated by the United Nations (UN) under the UN Development Programme. According to this analysis, the largest share (28 %) of immigrants into the EU came from medium HDI countries, while relatively low shares came from low HDI countries (5 %), candidate countries (2 %) or EFTA countries (1 %).

The relative importance of nationals within the total number of immigrants was highest in Lithuania

(74 %) and Portugal (56 %) in 2009. In contrast, Spain, Luxembourg, Slovakia, Italy, Hungary and Slovenia reported relatively low shares, with nationals accounting for less than 10 % of all immigrants.

Regarding the gender distribution of immigrants in 2009, there was a slight prevalence for more men than women to immigrate into the EU as a whole (52 % compared with 48 %). The country reporting the highest share of male immigrants was Slovenia (76 %); in contrast, the highest share of female immigrants was reported by Cyprus (58 %).

Immigrants into EU Member States in 2009 were, on average, much younger than the population already resident in their country of destination. On 1 January 2010, the median age of the EU-27 population was 40.9 years. The median age of immigrants in 2009 ranged from 24.9 years (in Portugal) to 33.7 years (in Latvia).

Non-national population

The total number of non-nationals (people who are not citizens of their country of residence) living on the territory of an EU Member State on 1 January 2010 was 32.5 million persons, representing 6.5 % of the EU-27 population (see Table 2.7.2). More than one third (a total of 12.3 million persons) of all non-nationals living in the EU-27 on 1 January 2010 were citizens of another EU Member State.

In absolute terms, the largest numbers of non-nationals living in the EU were found in Germany (7.1 million persons on 1 January 2010), Spain (5.7 million), the United Kingdom (4.4 million), Italy (4.2 million) and France (3.8 million). Non-nationals in these five Member States collectively represented 77.4 % of the total number of non-nationals living in the EU-27, while the same five Member States had a 62.8 % share of the whole of the EU-27 population. In relative terms, the EU Member State with the highest share of non-nationals was Luxembourg, as they accounted for 43.0 % of the total population at the beginning of 2010. The vast majority (86.3 %) of non-nationals living in Luxembourg were citizens of other EU Member States. As of 1 January 2010, a high proportion of non-nationals (10 % or more of the resident

population) was also observed in Latvia, Cyprus, Estonia, Spain and Austria.

In most Member States the majority of non-nationals are citizens of non-member countries (third-country nationals). At the beginning of 2010 citizens of other EU Member States represented the majority of non-nationals living in Luxembourg, Ireland, Belgium, Slovakia, Cyprus and Hungary. In the case of Latvia and Estonia, the proportion of citizens from non-member countries is particularly large due to the high number of recognised non-citizens; these are mainly former Soviet Union citizens, who are permanently resident in these countries but have not acquired Latvian/Estonian citizenship or any other citizenship.

Looking at the distribution by continent of origin of third-country nationals living in the EU, the largest proportion (36.5 %) were citizens of a European country outside the EU-27 (see Figure 2.7.5), a total of 7.2 million people; among these more than half were citizens of Turkey, Albania or Ukraine. The second biggest group was from Africa (25.2 %), followed by Asia (20.9 %), the Americas (16.4 %) and Oceania (0.9 %). More than half of the citizens of African countries that were living in the EU were from North Africa, often from Morocco or Algeria. Many Asian non-nationals living in the EU came from southern or eastern Asia, in particular from India or China. Citizens of Ecuador, Brazil and Colombia made up the largest share of non-nationals from the Americas living in the EU.

Among the nationals from non-member countries living in the EU-27 in 2010, some 45.8 % possessed the citizenship of a high HDI country (with Turkey, Albania and Russia accounting for almost half of these), while a slightly higher share (46.6 %) came from medium HDI countries (one fifth of whom were citizens of Morocco, with nationals of China and Ukraine the next largest groups), the remaining 7.6 % of nationals of non-member countries living in the EU were from low HDI countries (30 % of whom had Nigerian or Iraqi citizenship). In order to give some perspective, a breakdown of the world's population (outside of the EU) shows that the medium HDI group accounted for by far the largest share (68.4 %) of global inhabitants, followed

by those living in the high HDI group (21.3 %) and the low HDI group (10.4 %).

The citizenship structure of the population of non-nationals living in the EU varies greatly between Member States; it is influenced by factors such as labour migration, historical links between origin and destination countries, and established networks in destination countries. Turkish citizens made up the biggest group of non-nationals (see Figure 2.7.7) living in the EU in 2010, comprising 2.4 million people, or 7.2 % of all non-nationals. The second largest group was Romanians living in another EU Member State (6.6 % of the non-national population), followed by Moroccans (5.7 %). The group of non-nationals living in the EU with the most significant increase over the period from 2001 to 2010 was Romanians, their numbers increasing seven-fold from 0.3 million in 2001 to 2.1 million by 2010. The number of Polish and Chinese citizens also increased significantly during this period, and citizens from both of these countries figured among the ten largest non-national groups in 2010.

An analysis of the age structure of the resident population shows that, for the EU-27 as a whole, the non-national population was younger than the national population. The distribution by age of non-nationals shows, with respect to nationals, a greater representation of adults aged between 20 and 47; this feature is evident when looking at the corresponding population pyramids (see Figure 2.7.8). In 2010, the median age of the EU-27 total population was 40.9 years, while the median age of non-nationals living in the EU was 34.4 years.

Acquisition of citizenship

The number of people acquiring the citizenship of an EU Member State was 776 000 in 2009, corresponding to an 11.1 % increase with respect to 2008 (see Figure 2.7.9). The main contribution to this increase came from the United Kingdom, where acquisitions rose from 129 000 in 2008 to 204 000 in 2009 (see Table 2.7.3); this was largely due to a relatively low number of acquisitions in the United Kingdom in 2008, which was a consequence of changes in staff allocation within the responsible national authority.

Several other EU Member States recorded an increase in the number of acquisitions of citizenship between 2008 and 2009. In absolute terms, the highest increases, after the United Kingdom, were observed in Italy (5 700 more), Romania (3 800), Portugal (3 200) and Luxembourg (2 800). In some cases (such as Luxembourg, Portugal and Romania) these increases are due to recent reforms of the respective nationality laws, which had the effect of boosting the number of applications.

Relative to the size of the resident population, Luxembourg granted the highest number of citizenships: 8.1 per 1 000 inhabitants, followed by Cyprus (5.1), the United Kingdom (3.3) and Sweden (3.2).

One indicator which is commonly used to measure the effect of national policies concerning citizenship is the 'naturalisation rate', in other words, the ratio between the total number of citizenships granted and the stock of foreign residents in each country at the beginning of the year (see Figure 2.7.10). The country with the highest naturalisation rate in the EU-27 in 2009 was Portugal (5.8 acquisitions per 100 foreign residents), followed by Sweden (5.3) and the United Kingdom (4.8). On the other hand, Luxembourg, due to its large share of foreign residents (43.0 % on 1 January 2010) had a naturalisation rate below the EU-27 average, despite being the EU Member State with the highest number of citizenship acquisitions per inhabitant.

More than 90 % of those who acquired the citizenship of an EU Member State in 2009 were previously citizens of a non-member country; this was the case in nearly all of the Member States. However, in Luxembourg and Hungary the majority of new citizenships granted were to citizens of another EU Member State. In the case of Luxembourg, the largest share (almost half of those from EU Member States that were granted citizenship) was that of Portuguese citizens, while in the case of Hungary almost exclusively that of Romanian citizens.

As in previous years, the highest number of new citizens in the EU Member States in 2009 was composed of citizens of Morocco (59 700, corresponding to 8 % of all citizenships granted) and Turkey (51 800, or 7 %). Compared with 2008, the number of citizens from Morocco acquiring citizenship of

an EU Member State fell by 6 %, while the number of Turkish citizens rose by 5 %. The largest share of Moroccans acquired their new citizenship in France (43 %), Italy (15 %) or Spain (11 %), while the largest shares of Turkish people acquired their new citizenship in Germany (48 %) or France (18 %).

Data sources and availability

Eurostat produces statistics on a range of issues related to international migration flows, non-national population stocks and acquisition of citizenship. Data are collected on an annual basis and are supplied to Eurostat by the national statistical authorities of the Member States.

Since 2008 the collection of data has been based on Regulation 862/2007. This defines a core set of statistics on international migration flows, non-national population stocks, acquisition of citizenship, residence permits, asylum and measures against illegal entry and stay. Although Member States are able to continue to use any appropriate data according to national availability and practice, the statistics collected under the Regulation must be based on common definitions and concepts. Most Member States base their statistics on administrative data sources such as population registers, registers of non-nationals, registers of residence or work permits. Some countries use sample surveys or estimation methods to produce migration statistics. The data on the acquisition of citizenship are normally produced from administrative systems. The implementation of the Regulation is expected to result in increased availability and comparability of migration and citizenship statistics.

Previously statistics on migration flows, non-national population stocks and the acquisition of citizenship were sent to Eurostat on a voluntary basis, as part of a joint migration data collection organised by Eurostat in cooperation with a series of international organisations, for example the United Nations Statistical Division (UNSD), the United Nations Economic Commission for Europe (UNECE) and the International Labour Organisation (ILO). The recent changes in methodology, definitions and data sources used to produce migration and citizenship statistics may result, for some

Member States, in a lack of comparability over time for their respective series.

Emigration is particularly difficult to measure; it is harder to count people leaving a country than those arriving. An analysis comparing 2008 immigration and emigration data from the EU Member States (mirror statistics) confirmed that this was true in many countries. As a result, this subchapter focuses mainly on immigration data.

Context

Migration policies within the EU are increasingly concerned with attracting a particular migrant profile, often in an attempt to alleviate specific skills shortages. Selection can be carried out on the basis of language proficiency, work experience, education and age. Alternatively, employers can make the selection so that migrants already have a job upon their arrival.

Besides policies to encourage labour recruitment, immigration policy is often focused on two areas: preventing unauthorised migration and the illegal employment of migrants who are not permitted to work, and promoting the integration of immigrants into society. In the EU, significant resources have been mobilised to fight people smuggling and trafficking networks.

Some of the most important legal texts adopted in the area of immigration include:

* Directive 2003/86/EC on the right to family reunification;
* Directive 2003/109/EC on a long-term resident status for non-member nationals;
* Directive 2004/114/EC on the admission of students;
* Directive 2005/71/EC for the facilitation of the admission of researchers into the EU;
* Directive 2008/115/EC for returning illegally staying third-country nationals;
* Directive 2009/50/EC concerning the admission of highly skilled migrants.

Within the European Commission, the Directorate-General for Home Affairs is responsible for immigration policy. In 2005, the European Commission relaunched the debate on the need for a common set of rules for the admission of economic migrants with a Green paper on an EU approach to managing economic migration (COM(2004) 811 final) which led to the adoption of a policy plan on legal migration (COM(2005) 669 final) at the end of 2005. In July 2006, the European Commission adopted a Communication on policy priorities in the fight against illegal immigration of third-country nationals (COM(2006) 402 final), which aims to strike a balance between security and an individuals' basic rights during all stages of the illegal immigration process. In September 2007, the European Commission presented its third annual report on migration and integration (COM(2007) 512 final). A European Commission Communication adopted in October 2008 emphasised the importance of strengthening the global approach to migration: increasing coordination, coherence and synergies (COM(2008) 611 final) as an aspect of external and development policy. The Stockholm programme, adopted by EU heads of state and government in December 2009,

sets a framework and series of principles for the ongoing development of European policies on justice and home affairs for the period 2010 to 2014; migration-related issues are a central part of this programme. In order to bring about the changes agreed upon, the European Commission enacted an action plan implementing the Stockholm programme – delivering an area of freedom, security and justice for Europe's citizens in 2010 (COM(2010) 171 final). The action plan foresees a number of priority areas, providing measures for:

- evaluating justice, freedom and security policies and mechanisms;
- training legal and security professionals as well as judicial and law enforcement authorities;
- public awareness-raising activities;
- dialogue with civil society;
- new financial programmes.

Table 2.7.1: Immigration by main citizenship group, 2009 (¹)

	Total immigrants (1 000)	Nationals		Non-nationals					
				Total		Citizens of other EU Member States		Citizens of non-member countries	
		(1 000)	(%)	(1 000)	(%)	(1 000)	(%)	(1 000)	(%)
EU-27	*3 000.0*	*600.0*	*18.0*	*2 500.0*	*81.0*	*1 000.0*	*31.0*	*1 500.0*	*50.0*
Belgium	:	:	:	:	:	:	:	:	:
Bulgaria	:	:	:	:	:	:	:	:	:
Czech Republic	75.6	21.7	28.8	53.9	71.2	15.5	20.5	38.4	50.7
Denmark	51.8	19.3	37.2	32.5	62.8	16.2	31.3	16.3	31.4
Germany	347.3	79.2	22.8	267.2	76.9	126.8	36.5	140.4	40.4
Estonia	3.9	1.7	42.6	2.2	57.4	1.0	26.8	1.2	30.5
Ireland	37.4	14.7	39.4	22.5	60.1	16.0	42.7	6.5	17.4
Greece	:	:	:	84.2	:	29.5	:	54.6	:
Spain	499.0	29.6	5.9	469.3	94.1	144.9	29.0	324.5	65.0
France	:	:	:	:	:	:	:	:	:
Italy	442.9	36.2	8.2	406.7	91.8	136.1	30.7	270.6	61.1
Cyprus	11.7	:	:	:	:	:	:	:	:
Latvia	2.7	0.5	19.4	2.2	80.6	1.1	40.2	1.1	40.4
Lithuania	6.5	4.8	74.3	1.7	25.7	0.3	4.0	1.4	21.7
Luxembourg	15.8	1.1	7.1	14.6	92.7	11.9	75.7	2.7	16.9
Hungary	27.9	2.3	8.3	25.6	91.7	14.2	51.1	11.3	40.6
Malta	7.2	1.2	17.0	6.0	83.0	4.0	54.7	2.0	28.3
Netherlands	128.8	36.9	28.7	81.9	63.6	47.3	36.7	34.6	26.8
Austria	73.3	9.5	13.0	63.6	86.9	39.1	53.3	24.6	33.5
Poland	:	:	:	:	:	:	:	:	:
Portugal	32.3	18.0	55.9	14.3	44.1	4.0	12.4	10.3	31.8
Romania	:	:	:	:	:	:	:	:	:
Slovenia	30.3	2.9	9.6	27.4	90.3	1.9	6.2	25.5	84.1
Slovakia	15.6	1.2	7.7	14.4	92.3	6.9	43.9	7.6	48.4
Finland	26.7	8.6	32.3	17.8	66.7	6.5	24.2	11.3	42.4
Sweden	102.3	18.5	18.1	83.5	81.6	26.9	26.3	56.6	55.4
United Kingdom	566.5	96.0	16.9	470.5	83.1	167.4	29.6	303.1	53.5
Iceland	3.9	1.4	36.0	2.5	64.0	2.0	51.3	0.5	12.6
Liechtenstein	:	:	:	:	:	:	:	:	:
Norway	56.0	7.3	13.1	48.6	86.9	26.9	48.0	21.8	38.9
Switzerland	160.6	22.4	13.9	138.3	86.1	91.1	56.7	47.1	29.3

(¹) EU-27 rounded totals are based on estimates; the individual values do not add up to the total due to rounding and the exclusion of the 'unknown' citizenship group from the table.

Source: Eurostat (online data code: migr_imm1ctz)

Figure 2.7.1: Immigrants, 2009 (¹)
(per 1 000 inhabitants)

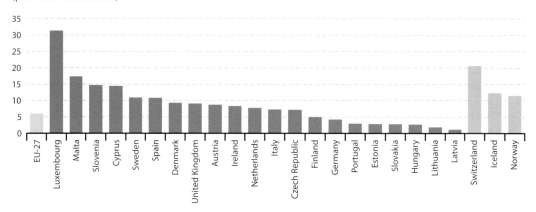

(¹) Data on the number of inhabitants refer to 1 January 2010; Belgium, Bulgaria, Greece, France, Poland and Romania, not available.
Source: Eurostat (online data codes: migr_imm1ctz and migr_pop1ctz)

Figure 2.7.2: Share of immigrants by citizenship group, EU-27, 2009
(%)

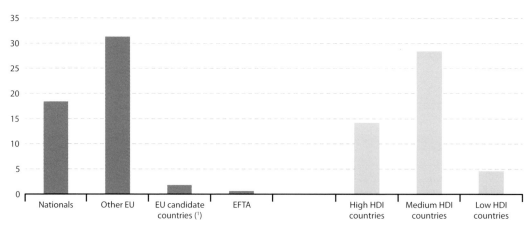

(¹) Candidate countries as of 1 January 2009: Croatia, former Yugoslav Republic of Macedonia and Turkey.
Source: Eurostat (online data code: migr_imm1ctz)

Figure 2.7.3: Share of nationals and non-nationals among immigrants, 2009 (¹)
(%)

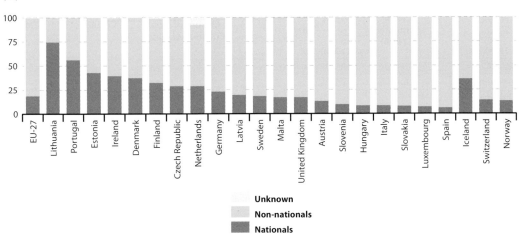

	Unknown
	Non-nationals
	Nationals

(¹) Data for Belgium, Bulgaria, Greece, Cyprus, France, Poland and Romania, not available.

Source: Eurostat (online data code: migr_imm1ctz)

Table 2.7.2: Total population and resident non-national population by group of citizenship, 2010 (¹)

	Total population (1 000)	Non-nationals					
		Total		Citizens of other EU Member States		Citizens of non-member countries	
		(1 000)	(%)	(1 000)	(%)	(1 000)	(%)
EU-27	*501 100.0*	*32 500.0*	*6.5*	*12 300.0*	*2.5*	*20 200.0*	*4.0*
Belgium	*10 839.9*	*1 052.8*	*9.7*	*715.1*	*6.6*	*337.7*	*3.1*
Bulgaria	:	:	:	:	:	:	:
Czech Republic	10 506.8	424.4	4.0	137.0	1.3	287.4	2.7
Denmark	5 534.7	329.8	6.0	115.5	2.1	214.3	3.9
Germany	81 802.3	7 130.9	8.7	2 546.3	3.1	4 584.7	5.6
Estonia	1 340.1	212.7	15.9	11.0	0.8	201.7	15.1
Ireland	4 467.9	384.4	8.6	309.4	6.9	75.0	1.7
Greece	11 305.1	954.8	8.4	163.1	1.4	791.7	7.0
Spain	45 989.0	5 663.5	12.3	2 327.8	5.1	3 335.7	7.3
France	64 716.3	3 769.0	5.8	1 317.6	2.0	2 451.4	3.8
Italy	60 340.3	4 235.1	7.0	1 241.3	2.1	2 993.7	5.0
Cyprus	803.1	127.3	15.9	83.5	10.4	43.8	5.5
Latvia	2 248.4	392.2	17.4	9.7	0.4	382.4	17.0
Lithuania	3 329.0	37.0	1.1	2.4	0.1	34.6	1.0
Luxembourg	502.1	215.7	43.0	186.2	37.1	29.5	5.9
Hungary	10 014.3	200.0	2.0	118.9	1.2	81.1	0.8
Malta	414.4	18.1	4.4	7.3	1.8	10.8	2.6
Netherlands	16 575.0	652.2	3.9	310.9	1.9	341.3	2.1
Austria	8 367.7	876.4	10.5	328.3	3.9	548.0	6.5
Poland	38 167.3	45.5	0.1	14.8	0.0	30.7	0.1
Portugal	10 637.7	457.3	4.3	94.2	0.9	363.1	3.4
Romania	:	:	:	:	:	:	:
Slovenia	2 047.0	82.2	4.0	4.6	0.2	77.6	3.8
Slovakia	5 424.9	62.9	1.2	38.7	0.7	24.2	0.4
Finland	5 351.4	154.6	2.9	56.1	1.0	98.5	1.8
Sweden	9 340.7	590.5	6.3	265.8	2.8	324.7	3.5
United Kingdom	62 027.0	4 362.0	7.0	1 919.9	3.1	2 442.1	3.9
Iceland	317.6	21.7	6.8	17.2	5.4	4.5	1.4
Liechtenstein	35.9	:	:	:	:	:	:
Norway	4 854.5	331.6	6.8	185.6	3.8	146.0	3.0
Switzerland	7 785.8	1 714.0	22.0	1 073.7	13.8	640.3	8.2

(¹) EU-27 rounded totals are based on estimates; the individual values do not add up to the total due to rounding.

Source: Eurostat (online data code: migr_pop1ctz)

Figure 2.7.4: Share of non-nationals in the resident population, 2010 (¹)
(%)

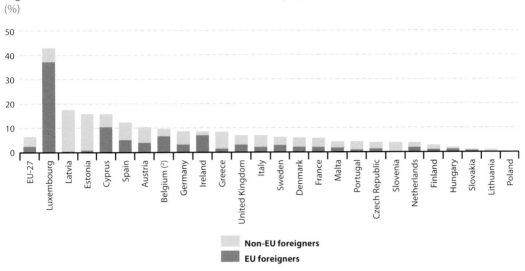

■ **Non-EU foreigners**
■ **EU foreigners**

(¹) Excluding Bulgaria and Romania.
(²) Provisional.

Source: Eurostat (online data code: migr_pop1ctz)

Figure 2.7.5: Citizens of non-member countries resident in the EU-27 by continent of origin, 2010
(%)

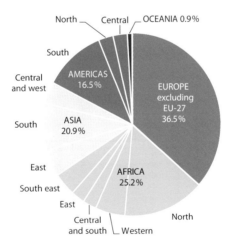

Source: Eurostat (online data code: migr_pop1ctz)

Figure 2.7.6: Non-EU citizens analysed by level of human development index (HDI), 2010
(%)

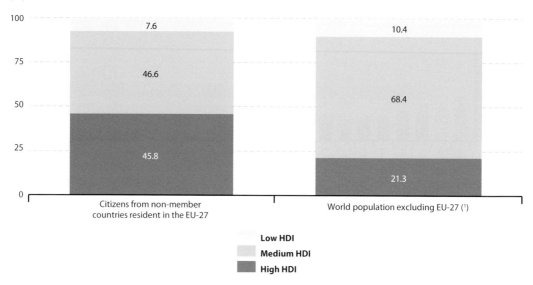

(¹) UN 2009 mid-year population estimates.

Source: Eurostat (online data code: migr_pop1ctz)

Figure 2.7.7: Main countries of origin of non-nationals, EU-27, 2010
(million)

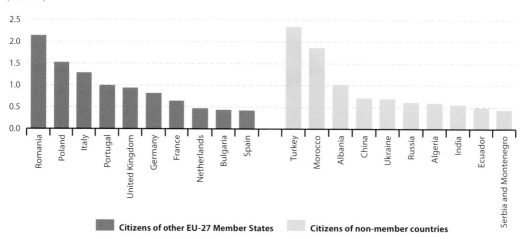

Source: Eurostat (online data code: migr_pop1ctz)

Figure 2.7.8: Age structure of the national and non-national populations, EU, 2010 (¹)
(%)

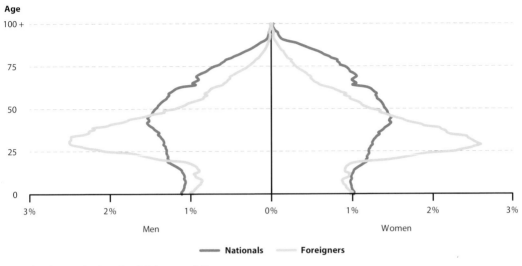

(¹) Based on those Member States for which data are available.

Source: Eurostat (online data code: migr_pop2ctz)

Figure 2.7.9: Number of persons having acquired the citizenship of an EU Member State, 1999-2009
(1 000)

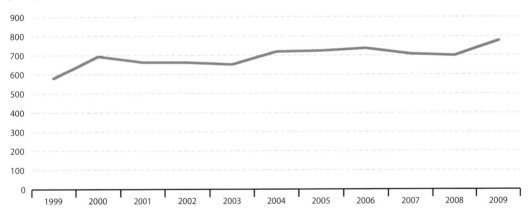

Source: Eurostat (online data code: migr_acq)

Table 2.7.3: Number of persons having acquired the citizenship of the reporting country, 2001-2009 (1 000)

	1999	2000	2001	2002	2003	2004	2005	2006	2007	2008	2009
EU-27	*579.7*	*693.9*	*663.3*	*662.5*	*651.9*	*719.1*	*723.6*	*735.9*	*707.1*	*698.7*	*776.1*
Belgium	24.2	62.0	62.2	46.4	33.7	34.8	31.5	31.9	36.1	37.7	32.8
Bulgaria	:	:	4.4	3.5	4.4	5.8	5.9	6.7	6.0	7.1	9.2
Czech Republic	7.3	6.4	6.3	3.3	2.2	5.0	2.6	2.3	2.4	1.2	1.1
Denmark	12.4	18.8	11.9	17.3	6.6	15.0	10.2	8.0	3.6	6.0	6.9
Germany	143.1	186.7	180.3	154.5	140.7	127.2	117.2	124.6	113.0	94.5	96.1
Estonia	4.5	3.4	3.1	4.1	3.7	6.5	7.1	4.8	4.2	2.1	1.7
Ireland	1.4	1.1	2.8	3.4	4.0	3.8	4.1	5.8	4.6	3.2	4.5
Greece	:	:	1.5	1.7	1.9	1.4	1.7	2.0	3.9	16.9	17.0
Spain	16.4	16.7	16.7	21.8	26.5	38.2	42.9	62.4	71.9	84.2	79.6
France	147.5	150.0	127.5	128.1	144.6	168.8	154.8	147.9	132.0	137.5	135.8
Italy	11.3	9.6	10.4	10.7	13.4	19.1	28.7	35.3	45.5	53.7	59.4
Cyprus	0.1	0.3	0.2	0.1	0.2	4.5	4.0	2.9	2.8	3.2	4.1
Latvia	12.9	13.5	9.9	9.4	10.0	17.2	20.1	19.0	8.3	4.2	3.2
Lithuania	0.6	0.5	0.5	0.5	0.5	0.6	0.4	0.5	0.4	0.3	0.2
Luxembourg	0.5	0.7	0.5	0.8	0.8	0.8	1.0	1.1	1.2	1.2	4.0
Hungary	6.1	5.4	8.6	3.4	5.3	5.4	9.9	6.1	8.4	8.1	5.8
Malta	0.1	0.6	1.2	0.8	0.6	0.6	0.6	0.5	0.6	0.6	0.8
Netherlands	62.1	50.0	46.7	45.3	28.8	26.2	28.5	29.1	30.7	28.2	29.8
Austria	:	24.3	31.7	36.0	44.7	41.6	34.9	25.7	14.0	10.3	8.0
Poland	:	1.4	1.1	1.2	1.7	1.9	2.9	1.1	1.5	1.8	2.5
Portugal	1.2	1.6	2.2	2.7	2.4	2.9	3.0	4.4	9.8	22.4	25.6
Romania	0.2	:	0.4	0.2	0.1	0.3	0.8	0.0	0.0	5.6	9.4
Slovenia	2.3	2.1	1.3	2.8	3.3	3.3	2.7	3.2	1.6	1.7	1.8
Slovakia	1.3	4.5	2.9	3.5	3.5	4.0	1.4	1.1	1.5	0.5	0.3
Finland	4.7	3.0	2.7	3.0	4.5	6.9	5.7	4.4	4.8	6.7	3.4
Sweden	37.8	43.5	36.4	37.8	33.2	28.9	39.6	51.2	33.6	30.5	29.5
United Kingdom	54.9	82.2	89.8	120.1	130.5	148.3	161.8	154.0	164.5	129.3	203.6
Iceland	0.3	0.3	0.4	0.4	:	:	:	:	0.6	0.9	0.7
Liechtenstein	0.6	:	:	0.2	0.2	0.2	0.2	0.2	0.2	0.3	0.1
Norway	8.0	9.5	10.8	9.0	7.9	8.2	12.7	12.0	14.9	10.3	11.4
Switzerland	20.4	28.7	27.6	36.5	35.4	35.7	38.4	46.7	43.9	44.4	43.4
Croatia	:	:	:	:	12.7	8.9	:	12.3	13.2	7.6	5.3
FYR of Macedonia	:	2.0	1.7	1.9	:	2.6	2.7	2.1	1.7	1.1	0.8
Turkey	:	:	:	:	24.8	8.2	6.9	5.1	4.4	6.0	8.1

Source: Eurostat (online data code: migr_acq)

Figure 2.7.10: Naturalisation rate – number of persons having acquired the citizenship of an EU Member State, 2009 (¹)
(per 100 non-nationals)

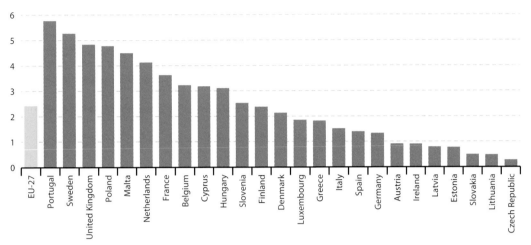

(¹) Number of inhabitants refers to 1 January 2010; Bulgaria and Romania, not available, as foreign population stocks are not fully comparable.

Source: Eurostat (online data codes: migr_acq and migr_pop1ctz)

2.8 Asylum

This subchapter describes recent developments in international protection, presenting information on the numbers of asylum applicants and decisions on asylum applications in the European Union (EU).

The analysis focuses on characteristics of asylum applicants (country of origin, age and sex) as well as decisions on asylum applications. Most of the statistics displayed in this subchapter were collected under the regulatory framework of Regulation (EC) 862/2007 on migration and international protection statistics.

Main statistical findings

Asylum applications

In recent years, there has been a sharp decrease in the number of asylum applicants in the EU. Having peaked in 1992 (670 000 applications in the EU-15) and again in 2001 (424 200 applications in the EU-27), there were an estimated 258 950 asylum

applications received in the EU-27 in 2010 (see Figure 2.8.1).

This figure constituted a slight decrease of 5 050 applicants when compared with the year before, in part due to a lower number of applications from Zimbabwe, Somalia, Georgia, Nigeria and Iraq (see Table 2.8.1). In contrast, there was a sizeable increase of more than 12 000 Serbian applicants between 2009 and 2010 and of more than 6 000 applicants from the former Yugoslav Republic of Macedonia; as a result, both of these countries moved into the top ten countries of origin of asylum seekers in the EU-27. Nevertheless, Afghanistan and Russia remained the two most common countries of origin for asylum seekers in the EU.

The number of asylum applications and their relative importance (for example, as a percentage of the total population) vary considerably between Member States. The highest number of applications for asylum in 2010 was lodged in France, while

Germany, Sweden, Belgium and the United Kingdom, were the other main recipients of applications (see Table 2.8.2). The number of asylum claims lodged in these five Member States accounted for more than two thirds (70.6 %) of the total number of applications lodged in the EU-27.

Out of each 20 asylum applicants in the EU-27 in 2010, on average close to 6 were minors, of which 1 was unaccompanied, 10 were young adults aged between 18 and 34 years and the remaining 4 persons were aged 35 and older (see Table 2.8.2). An unaccompanied minor is a person below the age of 18 who arrives on the territory of a Member State unaccompanied by an adult responsible for them or a minor who is left unaccompanied after having entered the territory of a Member State. Out of the 71 350 asylum applicants in the EU-27 who were minors in 2010, some 10 700 (excluding the Czech Republic) were unaccompanied.

Across the EU-27 as a whole, the gender distribution tends to be more balanced for asylum applicants aged less than 14 than for asylum applicants aged 14-17 or 18-34 for which around 14 out of 20 applicants were men. Male applicants were even more represented when considering the group of unaccompanied minors (see Figure 2.8.2) as approximately four in every five unaccompanied minors were male. Women outnumbered men only in the group of asylum seekers aged 65 and over though this group is relatively small and accounted for around 1 930 individuals in 2010.

The historical ties between countries of origin and destination, former colonies for instance, which often implies a certain knowledge of the language used in the host country, the presence of established ethnic communities, and the economic situation of countries may also be taken into consideration by asylum seekers. These pull factors largely overlap with the drivers of other non-asylum migration flows. However, other factors such as the perceived likelihood that the destination country will grant a protection status or the benefits connected to a protection status in the country of destination are specific to asylum seekers. Table 2.8.3 provides an overview of the five main citizenships of asylum applicants in each Member State.

Decisions on asylum applications

In 2010, a quarter (25.0 %) of EU-27 first instance asylum decisions resulted in positive outcomes with the grants of a refugee, subsidiary protection status or authorisation to stay for humanitarian reasons, while the share was slightly lower (21.5 %) for final decisions (based on appeal or review). For first instance decisions, close to half (48.7 %) of all positive decisions granted in the EU-27 in 2010 consisted of refugee status, while for final decisions the share was notably higher, over two thirds (70.7 %). In absolute numbers, some 41 180 persons were granted refugee status, 24 695 subsidiary protection and 9 674 authorisation to stay for humanitarian reasons. A wide diversity in the handling of asylum applications between Member States may be observed which is partly due to the differing citizenships of applicants in each Member State but may also reflect the current asylum and migration policies applied in each country.

In absolute terms, the highest number of positive asylum decisions in 2010 was recorded in the United Kingdom (14 070), followed by Germany (12 910), France (10 375), Sweden (9 760) and the Netherlands (8 680). Altogether, these five Member States represented close to three quarter (73.9 %) of the total number of positive decisions issued in EU Member States. Though refugee and subsidiary protection status are defined by EU law, humanitarian reasons are specific to the national legislation and relate to authorisation to stay for humanitarian reasons under national law concerning international protection, which explains why this latter protection status is not applicable in certain Member States.

Data sources and availability

Eurostat produces statistics on a range of issues relating to international migration. Between 1986 and 2007, data on asylum was collected on the basis

of a gentlemen's agreement. Since 2008 data have been provided to Eurostat under the provisions of Article 4 of Regulation (EC) 862/2007. Data are provided to Eurostat with a monthly frequency (for asylum application statistics), quarterly frequency (for first instance decisions) or annual frequency (for final decisions based on appeal or review, resettlement and unaccompanied minors). The statistics are based on administrative sources and are supplied to Eurostat by statistical authorities, home office ministries/ministries of the interior, or related immigration agencies in the Member States.

Two different categories of persons should be taken into account when analysing asylum statistics. The first includes asylum-seekers who have lodged a claim (asylum applications) and whose claim is under consideration by a relevant authority. The second is composed of persons who have been recognised, after consideration, as refugees or have been granted another kind of international protection (subsidiary protection) or were granted protection on the basis of the national law related to international protection (authorisations to stay for humanitarian reasons) or were rejected from having any form of protection. Since the entry into force of Regulation (EC) 862/2007, asylum decisions statistics have been made available at difference stages of the asylum procedure. First instance decisions are decisions granted by the respective authority acting as a first instance of the administrative/judicial asylum procedure in the receiving country. In contrast, final decisions in appeal or review relate to decision granted at the final instance of administrative/judicial asylum procedure and which result from an appeal lodged by an asylum seeker rejected in the preceding stage. Since asylum procedures and the number/levels of decision making bodies differ among the Member States, the true final instance may be, according to the national legislation and administrative procedures, a decision of the highest national court. However, the applied methodology defines that final decisions should refer to what is effectively a final decision in the vast majority of cases: in other words, that all normal routes of appeal have been exhausted.

Context

The 1951 Geneva Convention relating to the status of refugees (as amended by the 1967 New York Protocol) has for almost 60 years defined who is a refugee, and laid down a common approach towards refugees that has been one of the cornerstones for the development of a common asylum system within the EU. Asylum is a form of protection given by a state on its territory. It is granted to a person who is unable to seek protection in his/her country of citizenship and/or residence, in particular for fear of being persecuted for reasons of race, religion, nationality, membership of a particular social group, or political opinion. Since 1999, the EU has worked towards creating a common European asylum regime in accordance with the Geneva Convention and other applicable international instruments. A number of directives in this area have been developed, the four main legal instruments on asylum including:

- the Reception Conditions Directive 2003/9/EC laying down minimum standards for the reception of asylum seekers;
- the Asylum Procedures Directive 2005/85/EC on minimum standards on procedures in Member States for granting and withdrawing refugee status;
- the Qualification Directive 2004/83/EC on minimum standards for the qualification and status of third-country nationals or stateless persons as refugees or as persons who otherwise need international protection and the content of the protection granted;
- the Dublin Regulation (EC) 343/2003 establishing the criteria and mechanisms for determining the Member State responsible for examining an asylum application lodged in one of the Member States by a third-country national.

The Hague programme was adopted by heads of state and government on 5 November 2004. It puts forward the idea of a common European asylum system (CEAS), in particular, it raises the challenge to establish common procedures and uniform status for those granted asylum or subsidiary protection. The European Commission) adopted on 17 February 2006 a Communication on 'strengthened practical cooperation' (COM(2006) 67 final), presenting a vision of how Member States could further cooperate on asylum.

The European Commission's policy plan on asylum (COM(2008) 360) was presented in June 2008 which included three pillars to underpin the development of the CEAS:

- bringing more harmonisation to standards of protection by further aligning the Member States' asylum legislation;
- effective and well-supported practical cooperation;

- increased solidarity and sense of responsibility among EU Member States, and between the EU and non-member countries.

In May 2010, the European Commission presented an action plan for unaccompanied minors (COM(2010) 213), who are the most exposed and vulnerable victims of migration. This plan aims to set-up a coordinated approach and commits all Member States to grant high standards of reception, protection and integration for unaccompanied minors. As a complement to this action plan, the European migration network has produced a comprehensive EU study on reception policies, as well as return and integration arrangements for unaccompanied minors.

Figure 2.8.1: Asylum applications (non-EU-27) in the EU-27 Member States, 2000-2010 (¹) (1 000)

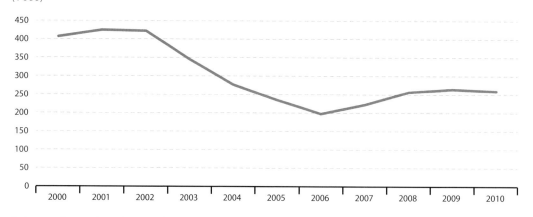

(¹) Cyprus, applications relate to the main applicant only; United Kingdom, 2008 data refers to new asylum applicants.
Source: Eurostat (online data codes: migr_asyctz and migr_asyappctza)

Table 2.8.1: Countries of origin of (non-EU-27) asylum seekers in the EU-27 Member States, 2009 and 2010 (^{1})
(number)

| | 2010 | 2009 | Change 2009 to 2010 | | Ranking | | |
			Absolute (number)	Relative (%)	2010	2009	Change
Non-EU-27 total	258 945	263 990	− 5 045	− 1.9	–	–	–
Afghanistan	20 590	20 455	135	0.7	1	1	0
Russia	18 590	20 110	− 1 520	− 7.6	2	2	0
Serbia	17 745	5 460	12 285	225.0	3	16	+ 13
Iraq	15 800	18 845	− 3 045	− 16.2	4	4	0
Somalia	14 355	19 000	− 4 645	− 24.4	5	3	− 2
Kosovo (UNSCR 1244/99)	14 310	14 275	35	0.2	6	5	− 1
Iran	10 315	8 565	1 750	20.4	7	9	+ 2
Pakistan	9 180	9 925	− 745	− 7.5	8	8	0
FYR of Macedonia	7 550	930	6 620	711.8	9	47	+ 38
Georgia	6 860	10 500	− 3 640	− 34.7	10	6	− 4
Nigeria	6 750	10 270	− 3 520	− 34.3	11	7	− 4
Sri Lanka	6 470	7 380	− 910	− 12.3	12	11	− 1
Turkey	6 350	7 030	− 680	− 9.7	13	12	− 1
Bangladesh	6 190	5 970	220	3.7	14	14	0
China	5 655	5 800	− 145	− 2.5	15	15	0
Armenia	5 525	6 855	− 1 330	− 19.4	16	13	− 3
Dem. Rep. of Congo	5 515	4 950	565	11.4	17	18	+ 1
Syria	5 010	4 750	260	5.5	18	19	+ 1
Guinea	4 895	4 485	410	9.1	19	20	+ 1
Eritrea	4 525	5 230	− 705	− 13.5	20	17	− 3
Algeria	3 575	3 405	170	5.0	21	21	0
India	3 175	3 030	145	4.8	22	22	0
Zimbabwe	2 615	8 050	− 5 435	− 67.5	23	10	− 13
Haiti	2 345	1 840	505	27.4	24	30	+ 6
Vietnam	2 320	2 460	− 140	− 5.7	25	24	− 1
Sudan	2 295	1 955	340	17.4	26	27	+ 1
Bosnia and Herzegovina	2 105	1 330	775	58.3	27	34	+ 7
Azerbaijan	2 060	2 585	− 525	− 20.3	28	23	− 5
Albania	1 905	2 065	− 160	− 7.7	29	25	− 4
Mongolia	1 680	2 030	− 350	− 17.2	30	26	− 4
Other non-EU-27	42 690	44 455	–	–	–	–	–

(^{1}) Cyprus, data relates to applications instead of applicants.

Source: Eurostat (online data code: migr_asyappctza)

Table 2.8.2: Number of (non-EU-27) asylum applicants in the EU and EFTA Member States and their age distribution, 2010

	Total (number)	Minors (%)					Aged 18 and over (%)			Age un-known (%)
		All minors	Accom-panied	Unaccom-panied	0-13	14-17	18-34	35-64	65 and over	
EU-27 (¹)	258 945	27.6	23.4	4.1	20.4	7.2	51.5	19.9	0.7	0.3
Belgium	26 130	31.1	27.0	4.1	23.7	7.4	48.5	19.8	0.6	0.0
Bulgaria	1 025	11.2	9.3	2.0	6.8	4.4	60.5	26.3	2.0	0.0
Czech Republic	780	20.5	:	:	18.6	1.9	44.2	34.6	0.6	0.0
Denmark	5 070	29.5	21.4	8.1	14.6	14.9	53.1	16.6	0.9	0.0
Germany	48 490	34.4	30.4	4.0	25.3	9.1	46.9	17.8	0.9	0.0
Estonia	35	14.3	14.3	0.0	14.3	0.0	57.1	14.3	0.0	0.0
Ireland	1 940	29.6	27.8	1.8	25.5	4.1	53.1	17.0	0.0	0.0
Greece	10 275	4.5	3.1	1.4	1.7	2.8	77.4	17.8	0.0	0.2
Spain	2 740	13.9	13.3	0.5	11.5	2.4	60.8	23.9	1.3	0.0
France	52 725	21.9	20.7	1.2	18.4	3.5	54.0	23.3	0.7	0.0
Italy	10 050	20.9	17.9	3.0	15.9	5.0	64.3	14.5	0.2	0.0
Cyprus (²)	2 875	9.0	7.8	1.2	6.3	2.8	66.3	24.0	0.3	0.3
Latvia	65	23.1	15.4	7.7	7.7	15.4	53.8	23.1	0.0	0.0
Lithuania	495	18.2	16.2	2.0	13.1	5.1	54.5	27.3	1.0	0.0
Luxembourg	780	26.3	23.7	2.6	19.9	6.4	51.9	21.2	0.0	0.0
Hungary	2 095	22.2	15.0	7.2	13.4	8.8	64.0	13.6	0.0	0.0
Malta	175	17.1	14.3	2.9	11.4	5.7	62.9	14.3	0.0	2.9
Netherlands	15 100	35.9	31.3	4.6	26.1	9.8	44.5	18.6	1.0	0.1
Austria	11 050	37.2	31.8	5.4	27.1	10.1	46.3	16.2	0.4	0.0
Poland	6 540	40.2	36.7	3.5	35.8	4.4	37.5	21.6	0.8	0.0
Portugal	160	15.6	12.5	3.1	9.4	6.3	59.4	25.0	0.0	0.0
Romania	885	11.9	7.9	4.0	6.8	5.1	68.4	19.2	0.6	0.0
Slovenia	245	26.5	16.3	10.2	10.2	16.3	51.0	22.4	0.0	0.0
Slovakia	540	10.2	9.3	0.9	6.5	3.7	68.5	20.4	0.9	0.0
Finland	3 090	24.3	14.1	10.2	14.6	9.7	57.3	17.5	0.3	0.8
Sweden	31 875	33.3	25.8	7.5	23.3	10.0	46.3	19.3	1.1	0.0
United Kingdom	23 715	20.4	13.6	6.7	13.2	7.2	53.2	22.7	0.8	2.9
Iceland (³)	35	0.0	0.0	0.0	0.0	0.0	57.1	28.6	0.0	0.0
Liechtenstein	105	28.6	28.6	0.0	23.8	4.8	47.6	23.8	0.0	0.0
Norway	10 025	28.8	19.9	8.9	19.6	9.2	53.7	17.0	0.5	0.0
Switzerland	15 435	26.8	25.4	1.4	22.3	4.5	58.5	14.2	0.3	0.1

(¹) The analysis of accompanied and unaccompanied minors excludes the Czech Republic.
(²) Applications instead of applicants.
(³) 2009.

Source: Eurostat (online data codes: migr_asyappctza and migr_asyunaa)

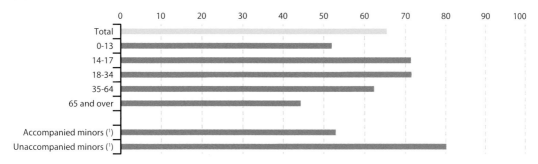

Figure 2.8.2: Share of male (non-EU-27) asylum applicants in the EU-27, by age group and status of minors, 2010
(%)

(¹) Excluding the Czech Republic.

Source: Eurostat (online data codes: migr_asyappctza and migr_asyunaa)

Table 2.8.3: Five main citizenships of (non-EU-27) asylum applicants, 2010 (¹)
(number, rounded figures)

EU-27	
Afghanistan	20 590
Russia	18 590
Serbia	17 745
Iraq	15 800
Somalia	14 355
Other	171 865

Belgium	
Kosovo (UNSCR 1244/99)	3 230
Russia	2 725
Serbia	2 220
Iraq	1 990
Afghanistan	1 830
Other	14 135

Bulgaria	
Iraq	450
Stateless	100
Iran	60
Afghanistan	60
Armenia	60
Other	295

Czech Republic	
Ukraine	115
Mongolia	95
Belarus	55
Turkey	50
Stateless	50
Other	415

Denmark	
Afghanistan	1 465
Syria	815
Iran	655
Russia	400
Serbia	265
Other	1 470

Germany	
Serbia	6 795
Afghanistan	6 065
Iraq	5 945
FYR of Macedonia	3 545
Iran	2 970
Other	23 170

Estonia	
Afghanistan	10
Sri Lanka	5
Russia	5
Nigeria	5
Zimbabwe	*
Other	10

Ireland	
Nigeria	385
China (incl. Hong Kong)	230
Pakistan	200
Afghanistan	70
Dem. Rep. of Congo	70
Other	985

Greece	
Pakistan	2 750
Georgia	1 160
Bangladesh	985
Albania	695
China (incl. Hong Kong)	545
Other	4 140

Spain	
Cuba	405
Nigeria	240
Algeria	175
Guinea	165
Cameroon	155
Other	1 600

France	
Kosovo (UNSCR 1244/99)	5 285
Russia	4 695
Dem. Rep. of Congo	3 715
Bangladesh	3 695
Sri Lanka	3 410
Other	31 925

Italy	
Nigeria	1 385
Pakistan	930
Afghanistan	875
Turkey	855
Bosnia and Herzegovina	815
Other	5 190

Cyprus (²)	
Iraq	340
India	320
Vietnam	225
Egypt	210
Sri Lanka	185
Other	1 595

Latvia	
Afghanistan	25
Russia	5
Kyrgyzstan	5
Ghana	5
Dem. Rep. of Congo	5
Other	20

Lithuania	
Georgia	250
Russia	110
Afghanistan	40
Armenia	20
Belarus	15
Other	60

Luxembourg	
Kosovo (UNSCR 1244/99)	160
Serbia	150
Iraq	95
Algeria	45
Somalia	30
Other	300

Hungary	
Afghanistan	700
Kosovo (UNSCR 1244/99)	380
Palestinian territory	225
Georgia	70
Serbia	65
Other	655

Malta	
Somalia	35
Pakistan	15
India	15
Eritrea	15
Syria	10
Other	85

Netherlands	
Somalia	3 670
Iraq	1 905
Afghanistan	1 585
Iran	865
Unknown	660
Other	6 415

Austria	
Russia	2 330
Afghanistan	1 590
Kosovo (UNSCR 1244/99)	610
Nigeria	555
India	435
Other	5 530

(¹) A * indicates 2 or fewer applicants.
(²) Applications instead of applicants.

Source: Eurostat (online data code: migr_asyappctza)

Table 2.8.3 (continued): Five main citizenships of (non-EU-27) asylum applicants, 2010 (¹)
(number, rounded figures)

Poland		Portugal		Romania		Slovenia	
Russia	4 795	Guinea	45	Afghanistan	115	Turkey	30
Georgia	1 085	Colombia	15	Moldova	110	Afghanistan	30
Armenia	105	Guinea-Bissau	10	Turkey	70	Bosnia and Herzegovina	30
Vietnam	45	Dem. Rep. of Congo	10	Iraq	65	Kosovo (UNSCR 1244/99)	20
Ukraine	45	Angola	10	China (incl. Hong Kong)	65	Serbia	15
Other	465	Other	70	Other	460	Other	120

Slovakia		Finland		Sweden		United Kingdom	
Afghanistan	75	Somalia	520	Serbia	6 255	Zimbabwe	2 435
Russia	65	Iraq	515	Somalia	5 630	Iran	2 350
Georgia	65	Russia	395	Afghanistan	2 400	Pakistan	2 185
India	45	Afghanistan	240	Iraq	1 995	Afghanistan	1 975
Moldova	40	Serbia	155	Kosovo (UNSCR 1244/99)	1 715	Sri Lanka	1 660
Other	250	Other	1 265	Other	13 880	Other	13 110

Iceland (²)		Liechtenstein		Norway		Switzerland	
Syria	5	FYR of Macedonia	40	Eritrea	1 710	Nigeria	1 970
Albania	5	Russia	30	Somalia	1 395	Eritrea	1 800
Iraq	5	Nigeria	10	Afghanistan	980	Sri Lanka	940
Iran	5	Somalia	5	Russia	630	Serbia	910
Zimbabwe	*	Serbia	5	Ethiopia	505	Afghanistan	670
Other	15	Other	15	Other	4 805	Other	9 145

(¹) A * indicates 2 or fewer applicants.
(²) 2009.

Source: Eurostat (online data code: migr_asyappctza)

Table 2.8.4: First instance decisions on (non-EU-27) asylum applications, 2010
(number)

	Total number of decisions	Positive decisions				Rejected
		Total	Refugee status	Subsidiary protection	Humani-tarian reasons	
EU-27 (¹)	222070	55460	27035	20410	8090	167025
Belgium	16245	3510	2700	805	–	12740
Bulgaria	515	140	20	120	–	375
Czech Republic	500	175	75	75	20	330
Denmark	3280	1345	660	520	170	1935
Germany	45310	10445	7755	545	2145	34865
Estonia	40	15	10	5	–	25
Ireland	1600	25	25	5	–	1575
Greece	3455	105	60	20	30	3350
Spain	2785	610	245	350	15	2175
France	37610	5095	4080	1015	–	32515
Italy	11325	4305	1615	1465	1225	7015
Cyprus	2440	425	30	370	25	2015
Latvia	50	25	5	20	–	25
Lithuania	190	15	0	15	–	175
Luxembourg	:	:	55	15	–	405
Hungary	1040	260	75	115	70	785
Malta	350	220	45	165	15	125
Netherlands	17580	8005	810	4010	3180	9575
Austria	13770	3445	2055	1390	–	10325
Poland	4420	510	80	195	230	3910
Portugal	130	55	5	50	–	75
Romania	425	70	40	30	0	355
Slovenia	115	25	20	0	–	95
Slovakia	295	90	5	55	30	205
Finland	4260	1595	165	1240	190	2665
Sweden	27650	8510	1935	5970	605	19140
United Kingdom	26690	6440	4445	1850	140	20250
Iceland (²)	25	5	0	0	5	25
Liechtenstein	85	0	0	:	0	85
Norway	15180	5300	2975	1565	760	9955
Switzerland	18475	7815	3380	1155	3280	10660

(¹) Total number of decisions and total number of positive decisions, excluding Luxembourg.
(²) 2009.

Source: Eurostat (online data code: migr_asydcfsta)

Table 2.8.5: Final decisions on (non-EU-27) asylum applications, 2010
(number)

	Total number of decisions	Positive decisions				Rejected
		Total	Refugee status	Subsidiary protection	Humani-tarian reasons	
EU-27 (¹)	93 280	20 015	14 145	4 285	1 585	73 265
Belgium	7 985	280	195	85	–	7 705
Bulgaria	35	20	0	20	–	15
Czech Republic (¹)	415	25	0	0	25	390
Denmark (¹)	440	130	65	70	0	310
Germany	7 775	2 465	1 220	235	1 005	5 315
Estonia	5	0	0	0	–	5
Ireland	2 785	130	130	–	–	2 655
Greece (¹)	2 105	40	30	15	0	2 065
Spain	1 545	15	15	5	–	1 530
France	23 080	5 280	4 245	1 035	–	17 800
Italy	1 530	275	70	0	200	1 260
Cyprus	2 975	110	25	5	80	2 870
Latvia	15	0	0	0	–	15
Lithuania	65	0	0	0	–	65
Luxembourg	190	35	30	5	–	160
Hungary	190	25	10	15	0	165
Malta	325	0	0	0	0	325
Netherlands	1 350	675	90	390	195	675
Austria	10 540	1 435	1 060	375	–	9 105
Poland	110	50	0	35	15	60
Portugal	20	0	0	0	–	20
Romania	530	110	85	30	0	420
Slovenia	15	0	0	0	0	15
Slovakia	40	5	0	5	0	35
Finland	115	70	5	35	30	45
Sweden	12 830	1 250	285	710	255	11 580
United Kingdom	21 975	7 630	6 010	1 405	210	14 345
Iceland (¹)	30	5	0	0	5	30
Liechtenstein	60	0	0	:	0	60
Norway	10 100	410	165	70	170	9 690
Switzerland	5 575	435	70	40	325	5 140

(¹) 2009.

Source: Eurostat (online data code: migr_asydcfina)

EUROPE IN FIGURES — Eurostat yearbook 2012

List of abbreviations and acronyms

Statistical symbols

Italic	data value is forecasted, provisional or estimated and is likely to change
:	not available, confidential or unreliable value
–	not applicable

Breaks in series are indicated in the footnotes provided under each table and figure

Geographical aggregates and names

EU	European Union
EU-27	European Union of 27 Member States including Belgium, Bulgaria, the Czech Republic, Denmark, Germany, Estonia, Ireland, Greece, Spain, France, Italy, Cyprus, Latvia, Lithuania, Luxembourg, Hungary, Malta, the Netherlands, Austria, Poland, Portugal, Romania, Slovenia, Slovakia, Finland, Sweden and the United Kingdom. Note that unless otherwise stated, the EU aggregate in this publication refers to 27 countries, as if all 27 of these had been part of the EU in periods prior to 1 January 2007
EU-25	EU-27 without Bulgaria and Romania (from 1 May 2004 to 31 December 2006)
EU-15	Belgium, Denmark, Germany, Ireland, Greece, Spain, France, Italy, Luxembourg, the Netherlands, Austria, Portugal, Finland, Sweden and the United Kingdom (from 1 January 1995 to 30 April 2004)
Euro area	Note that unless otherwise stated, the euro area (EA) aggregate in this publication refers to 17 countries, as if all 17 of these had been part of the euro area in periods prior to 1 January 2011
EA-17	Belgium, Germany, Estonia, Ireland, Greece, Spain, France, Italy, Cyprus, Luxembourg, Malta, the Netherlands, Austria, Portugal, Slovenia, Slovakia and Finland; EA-16 plus Estonia (since 1 January 2011)
EA-16	EA-15 plus Slovakia (from 1 January 2009 to 31 December 2010)
EA-15	EA-13 plus Cyprus and Malta (from 1 January 2008 to 31 December 2008)
EA-13	EA-12 plus Slovenia (from 1 January 2007 to 31 December 2007)
EA-12	EA-11 plus Greece (from 1 January 2001 to 31 December 2006)
EA-11	Belgium, Germany, Ireland, Spain, France, Italy, Luxembourg, the Netherlands, Austria, Portugal and Finland (from 1 January 1999 to 31 December 2000)
FYR of Macedonia (¹)	the former Yugoslav Republic of Macedonia

Units of measurement

%	per cent
AWU	annual work unit
CHF	Swiss franc
cm³	cubic centimetre
CO_2 equivalent	carbon dioxide equivalent
ECU	European currency unit
ESU	economic size unit
EUR	euro
FTE	full-time equivalent
GJ	gigajoule
GRT	gross registered tonnage
GT	gross tonnage
GWh	gigawatt-hour
ha	hectare (1 ha = 10 000 m²)
HC	head count
JPY	Japanese yen
kbit/s	kilobit per second
kg	kilogram
kgoe	kilogram of oil equivalent
km	kilometre
km²	square kilometre
km/h	kilometre per hour
kW	kilowatt
kWh	kilowatt hour
l	litre
LSU	livestock unit
m	metre
m³	cubic metre
mm	millimetre
MWh	megawatt-hour
NMVOC equivalent	non-methane volatile organic compounds equivalent
p/st	piece/unit
pkm	passenger-kilometre
PPS	purchasing power standard
SO_2 equivalent	sulphur dioxide equivalent
t	tonne
tkm	tonne-kilometre
toe	tonne of oil equivalent
TWh	terawatt hour
USD	United States dollar

(¹) The name of the former Yugoslav Republic of Macedonia is shown in tables and figures in this publication as FYR of Macedonia – this does not prejudge in any way the definitive nomenclature for this country, which is to be agreed following the conclusion of negotiations currently taking place on this subject at the United Nations.

Eurostat online data code(s) – easy access to the freshest data

Eurostat online data codes, such as tps00001 and nama_gdp_c (²), allow the reader to easily access the most recent data on Eurostat's website. In this yearbook these codes are given as part of the source below each table and figure.

In the PDF version of this publication, the reader is led directly to the freshest data when clicking on the hyper-links that form part of each online data code. Readers of the paper version can access the freshest data by typing a standardised hyper-link into a web browser – http://ec.europa.eu/eurostat/product?code=<data_code>&mode=view – where <data_code> is to be replaced by the online data code printed under the table or figure in question. The data is presented either in the TGM or the Data Explorer interface.

Online data codes can also be fed into the 'Search' function on Eurostat's website, which is found in the upper-right corner of the Eurostat homepage, at http://ec.europa.eu/eurostat. The results from such a search present related dataset(s) and possibly publication(s) and metadata. By clicking on these hyper-links users are taken to product page(s) (³), which provide some background information about each dataset / publication or set of metadata. For example, it is possible to move directly to the data from the data product page by clicking the TGM or Data Explorer icons presented under the 'View table' sub-heading.

Note that the data on Eurostat's website is frequently updated.

Note also that the description above presents the situation as of the end of November 2011.

Statistics Explained

Statistics Explained is part of the Eurostat website – it provides easy access to Eurostat's statistical information. It can be accessed via a link on the right-hand side of Eurostat's homepage, or directly at: http://epp.eurostat.ec.europa.eu/statistics_explained.

Statistics Explained is a wiki-based system that presents statistical topics. Together, the articles make up an encyclopaedia of European statistics, which is completed by a statistical glossary that clarifies the terms used. In addition, there are numerous links provided to the latest data and metadata, as well as further information, making Statistics Explained a portal for regular and occasional users alike.

At the end of November 2011, Statistics Explained contained more than 500 statistical articles and some 1 200 glossary pages; its content is being expanded regularly. Users may find articles using a set of navigational features in the left-hand menu; on the top-right menu bar of Statistics Explained it is possible to find options that make it possible, among others, to print, forward, cite, blog or share content easily.

(²) There are two types of online data codes:
  • Tables (accessed using the TGM interface) have 8-character codes, which consist of 3 or 5 letters – the first of which is 't' – followed by 5 or 3 digits, e.g. tps00001 and tsdph220.
  • Databases (accessed using the Data Explorer interface) have codes that use an underscore '_' within the syntax of the code, e.g. nama_gdp_c and proj_08c2150p.
(³) The product page can also be accessed by using a hyper-link, for example, http://ec.europa.eu/eurostat/product?code=<data_code>, where <data_code> is to be replaced by the online data code in question.

Health

Introduction

Health is an important priority for Europeans, who expect to have a long and healthy life, to be protected against illnesses and accidents and to receive appropriate health care. Health issues cut across a range of topics – including consumer protection (food safety issues), workplace safety, environmental or social policies. The policy areas covered within this area are under the remit of the Directorate-General for Health and Consumers and of the Directorate-General for Employment, Social Affairs and Inclusion.

The competence for the organisation and delivery of health services and healthcare is largely held by the Member States, while the European Union (EU) complements the Member States' health policies through launching actions such as those in relation to cross-border health threats and patient mobility. Gathering and assessing accurate, detailed information on health issues is vital for the EU to effectively design policies and target future actions. A first programme for Community action in the field of public health covered the period from 2003 to 2008. On 23 October 2007 the European Commission adopted a new strategy 'Together for health: a strategic approach for the EU 2008-2013' (COM(2007) 630). In order to bring about the changes identified within this new strategy, the second programme of Community action in the field of health came into force from 1 January 2008. It put in place an overarching, strategic framework for policy developments relating to health in the coming years; it has four main principles and three strategic themes for improving health in the EU. The principles are:

- taking a value-driven approach;
- recognising the links between health and economic prosperity;
- integrating health in all policies;
- strengthening the EU's voice in global health issues.

The strategic themes include:

- fostering good health in an ageing Europe;
- protecting citizens from health threats;
- looking to develop dynamic health systems and new technologies.

The programme is valued at EUR 321.5 million and will be implemented by means of annual work plans which will set out priority areas and funding criteria. In October 2011 the European Commission published a mid-term evaluation of the strategy. Within this strategy there is a strong need for comparable data on health and health-related behaviour, diseases and health systems. This needs to be based on common EU health indicators, for which there is Europe-wide agreement regarding definitions, collection and use. These include the Healthy Life Years (HLY) indicators and the European Community Health Indicators (ECHI).

Set up at the Lisbon European Council of March 2000, the open method of coordination (OMC) on social protection and social inclusion provides a framework of political coordination without legal constraints. Member States agree to identify and promote their most effective policies in the fields of social protection and social inclusion with the aim of learning from each others' experiences. The health and long-term care strand of the OMC is structured according to three objectives:

- access to care and inequalities in outcomes;
- quality of care;
- long-term sustainability of systems.

Concerning health and safety at work, the EC Treaty states that 'the Community shall support and complement the activities of the Member States in the improvement in particular of the working environment to protect workers' health and safety'. In 2007 the Council adopted Resolution 2007/C 145/01 of 25 June 2007 on a new Community strategy on health and safety at work (2007-2012). Actions in the field of health and safety at work are supported by the PROGRESS programme (2007-2013).

In December 2008 the European Parliament and the Council adopted Regulation 1338/2008 on Community statistics on public health and health and safety at work. The Regulation is designed to ensure that health statistics provide adequate information for all EU Member States to monitor Community actions in the field of public health and

health and safety at work. In April 2011 two Commission regulations were adopted specifying in detail the variables, breakdowns and metadata that

Member States must deliver: Regulation 328/2011 on statistics on causes of death and Regulation 349/2011 on statistics on accidents at work.

3.1 Healthy life years

Healthy life years, the number of years that a person is expected to continue to live in a healthy condition, is an important measure of the relative health of populations in the European Union (EU). Eurostat calculates this indicator for two ages (at birth and at the age of 65), with the indicator being presented separately for males and females.

Whether extra years of life gained through increased longevity are spent in good or bad health is a crucial question. Since life expectancy at birth is not able to fully answer this question, indicators of health expectancies, such as healthy life years (also called disability-free life expectancy) have been developed. These focus on the quality of life spent in a healthy state, rather than the quantity of life – as measured by life expectancy. The calculation of the healthy life years indicator is based on a self-perceived question which aims to measure the extent of any limitations because of a health problem that may have affected respondents as regards activities they usually do (for at least six months).

Main statistical findings

In 2009 the number of healthy life years at birth stood at 60.9 years for men and 61.6 years for women in the EU-27; this represented 79.4 % and 74.5 % of total life expectancy at birth for men and women. For survivors at the age of 65, the number of remaining healthy life years was 8.2 years for men and 8.3 years for women. These figures can be contrasted with the life expectancy of those who survive to the age of 65 – around 17 years for men and 20 years for women.

Life expectancy for women in the EU-27 was, on average, six years longer than that for men in 2009. However, most of these additional years tend to be lived with activity limitations. Indeed, the gender

gap was considerably smaller in terms of healthy life years – around one year difference in favour of women – than for overall life expectancy. On average, men therefore tend to spend a greater proportion of their shorter lives free of activity limitation.

Across the EU Member States, life expectancy at birth in 2009 ranged between 67.5 years and 79.8 years (12.3 years difference) for men and between 77.4 years and 85.0 years (7.6 years difference) for women. The corresponding healthy life years values ranged from 52.1 years to 70.5 years (18.4 years difference) for men and from 52.3 years to 70.6 years (18.3 years difference) for women. Differences between Member States therefore occur more in terms of the quality (health wise) of life, rather than the number of years of life expectancy. In six of the Member States (Denmark, Spain, Italy, the Netherlands, Portugal and Sweden), men (at birth) could expect to live longer than women without disability. In Bulgaria, Estonia, Lithuania and Poland the gender gap in healthy life years at birth was around four years in favour of women.

Life expectancy was rather stable between 2008 and 2009. However, during the same period the number of healthy life years decreased for men in nine Member States and for women in eleven Member States.

Data sources and availability

The indicator for healthy life years is calculated using mortality statistics and data on self-perceived disability. Mortality data comes from Eurostat's demographic database, while self-perceived disability data comes from a minimum European health module that is integrated within the survey on EU statistics on income and living conditions

(EU-SILC). The EU-SILC question is: for at least the past six months, to what extent have you been limited because of a health problem in activities people usually do? Would you say you have been:

- strongly limited?
- limited?
- not limited at all?

Context

Life expectancy at birth remains one of the most frequently quoted indicators of health status and economic development. Life expectancy at birth has risen rapidly in the last century due to a number of important factors, including reductions in infant mortality, rising living standards, improved lifestyles and better education, as well as advances in healthcare and medicine. While most people are aware that successive generations are living longer, less is known about the health of the EU's ageing population.

The health status of a population is difficult to measure because it is hard to define among individuals, populations, cultures, or even across time periods. As a result, the demographic measure of life expectancy has often been used as a measure of a nation's health status because it is based on a simple

and easy to understand characteristic – namely, that of death.

Indicators on healthy life years introduce the concept of the quality of life, by focusing on those years that may be enjoyed by individuals free from the limitations of illness or disability. Chronic disease, frailty, mental disorders and physical disability tend to become more prevalent in older age, and may result in a lower quality of life for those who suffer from such conditions, while the burden of these conditions may also impact on healthcare and pension provisions.

Healthy life years also monitor health as a productive or economic factor. An increase in healthy life years is one of the main goals for EU health policy, given that this would not only improve the situation of individuals (as good health and a long life are fundamental objectives of human activity) but would also lead to lower public healthcare expenditure. If healthy life years increase more rapidly than life expectancy, then not only are people living longer, but they are also living a greater proportion of their lives free from health problems. Any loss in health will, nonetheless, have significant effects. These will include an altered pattern of resource allocation within the healthcare system, as well as wider ranging effects on consumption and production throughout the economy.

Figure 3.1.1: Healthy life years at birth, females, 2007-2009
(years)

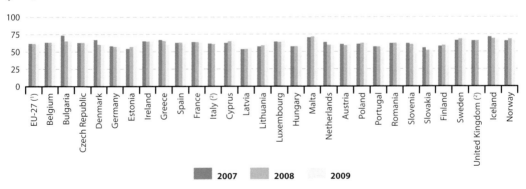

(¹) 2009, provisional.
(²) 2009, not available.

Source: Eurostat (online data code: hlth_hlye)

Figure 3.1.2: Healthy life years at birth, males, 2007-2009
(years)

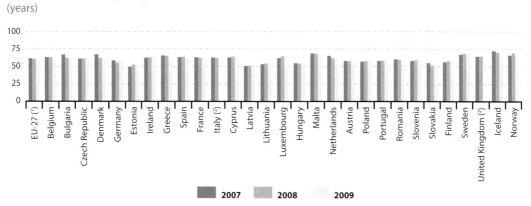

(¹) 2009, provisional.
(²) 2009, not available.

Source: Eurostat (online data code: hlth_hlye)

Figure 3.1.3: Healthy life years at age 65, females, 2007-2009
(years)

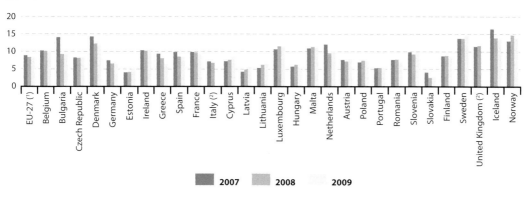

(¹) 2009, provisional.
(²) 2009, not available.

Source: Eurostat (online data code: hlth_hlye)

Figure 3.1.4: Healthy life years at age 65, males, 2007-2009
(years)

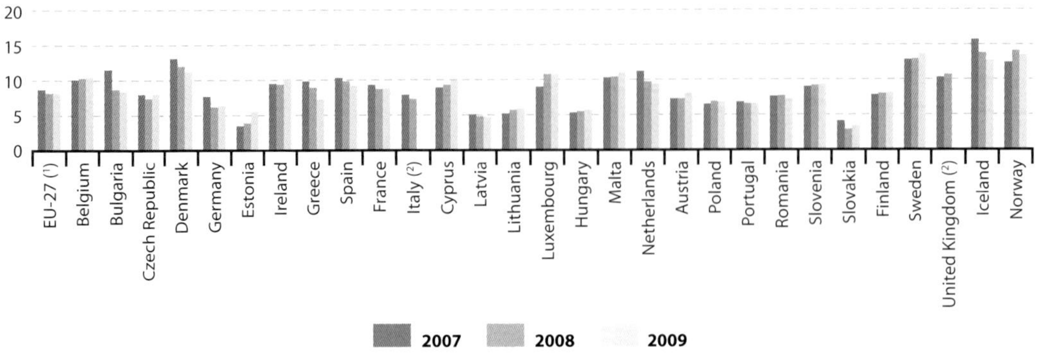

(¹) 2009, provisional.
(²) 2009, not available.

Source: Eurostat (online data code: hlth_hlye)

3.2 Causes of death

This subchapter gives an overview of recent statistics on causes of death in the European Union (EU). By relating all deaths in the population to an underlying cause of death, the risks associated with death from a range of specific diseases and other causes can be assessed; these figures can be further broken down by age, sex, nationality and region (NUTS level 2), using standardised death rates.

Statistics on causes of death are important to evaluate the state of health and healthcare in the EU. They suggest which preventive and medical-curative measures and which investments in research might increase the life expectancy of the population. These statistics, which are among the oldest medical statistics available, provide information on developments over time and differences in causes of death between Member States.

Main statistical findings

The latest information available for 2009 (¹) shows that diseases of the circulatory system and cancer were, by far, the leading causes of death in Europe. Between 2000 and 2009 there was a marked reduction in EU-27 death rates resulting from ischaemic heart disease and from transport accidents (with combined rates for men and women falling by more than 30 %), while there was a reduction of almost 10 % in the EU-27 death rate for cancer during the same period.

Diseases of the circulatory system

Diseases of the circulatory system include those related to high blood pressure, cholesterol, diabetes, and smoking; although, the most common causes of death were ischaemic heart diseases and cerebrovascular diseases. The Member States with the highest death rates from ischaemic heart disease – for men and women combined – were the Baltic Member States, Hungary and Slovakia (all above 200 deaths per 100 000 inhabitants in 2009), while France, Portugal, the Netherlands, Luxembourg and Spain had the lowest rates (below 50 deaths per 100 000 inhabitants).

(¹) France and Italy, 2008; Switzerland, 2007; Belgium, 2005.

Cancer

Cancer was a major cause of death in each of the EU Member States (averaging 169 deaths per 100 000 inhabitants across the EU-27 in 2009). Hungary, Poland, Slovenia, the Czech Republic, Slovakia, Latvia and Lithuania were most affected by this group of diseases. The most common forms of cancer in the EU-27 in 2009 included malignant neoplasms of the larynx, trachea, bronchus and lung, colon, breast, and those that the International classification of diseases (ICD) classifies as 'stated or presumed to be primary, of lymphoid, hematopoietic and related tissue'.

Analysing the figures by sex, men outnumbered women in relation to the number of deaths from cancer. Data for cancer of the larynx, trachea, bronchus and lung showed some marked differences between Member States in 2009: for men Hungary reported the highest death rate from these cancers among the EU Member States, followed by Poland, the Baltic Member States, Belgium (2005 data) and Romania; Hungary also reported a high rate for women, just behind the rate reported for Denmark. Mortality figures for this type of cancer are generally rising for women while decreasing for men.

Breast cancer as a cause of death of women was lowest (17.6 deaths per 100 000 inhabitants) in Spain in 2009, around half the rate recorded in Malta (34.4 deaths per 100 000 inhabitants). There were also relatively high death rates from breast cancer among women from Belgium, Denmark, Ireland and Hungary – see Table 3.2.1.

Respiratory diseases

The highest death rates from respiratory diseases in 2009 were recorded in Ireland, the United Kingdom, Belgium (2005 data), Denmark and Portugal. After cancer and circulatory diseases, this was the third most common cause of death in the EU-27 (with an average of 43.6 deaths per 100 000 inhabitants). Within this group of diseases, chronic lower respiratory diseases were the most common cause of mortality followed by pneumonia. Respiratory diseases are age-related with the vast majority of deaths from these diseases recorded among those aged 65 or more.

External causes of death

This category includes deaths resulting from intentional self-harm (suicide) and transport accidents. Although suicide is not a major cause of death and the data for some Member States may suffer from underreporting, it is often considered as an important indicator to be addressed by society. The lowest suicide rates in 2009 were recorded in Greece and Cyprus, and relatively low rates were also recorded in Italy (2008), Spain, the United Kingdom, Portugal and Malta. In 2009, the death rate from suicide in Lithuania was approximately three times the EU-27 average (10.3 deaths per 100 000 inhabitants), and relatively high rates (around double the EU-27 average) were recorded in Hungary and Latvia. Among women, relatively high suicide rates were recorded in Finland, Belgium (2005 data), Hungary and Lithuania – see Figure 3.2.5.

Although transport accidents occur on a daily basis, the number of deaths caused by transport accidents are fewer than, for example, the number of suicides. Romania, Greece, Lithuania and Poland had the highest death rates (in excess of 12 deaths per 100 000 inhabitants) resulting from transport accidents in 2009, while Sweden, the Netherlands and the United Kingdom reported the lowest rates (no more than four deaths from transport accidents per 100 000 inhabitants).

Gender

EU-27 death rates were higher for men than for women for all of the main causes of death in 2009 (except for breast cancer) – see Figure 3.2.3. Death rates for ischaemic heart diseases were about twice as high for men (110 deaths per 100 000 inhabitants in 2009) as for women (56 deaths per 100 000 inhabitants). Death rates for men were four to five times higher than those recorded for women for drug dependence and alcohol abuse, and three to four time higher for AIDS (HIV) and suicide (intentional self-harm).

There was a higher incidence of death from heart disease than from cancer for both sexes in the Baltic Member States, Slovakia and Romania, while in Finland there were more deaths from heart disease than from cancer among the male population.

Age

For people below 65 years of age the leading causes of mortality were somewhat different in terms of their relative importance (see Table 3.2.2). Cancer was the leading cause of death within this age group, followed by diseases of the circulatory system, external causes of mortality and morbidity, and diseases of the digestive system. However, unlike for those aged 65 years or more, diseases of the respiratory system did not figure among the four most prevalent causes of mortality.

Data sources and availability

Eurostat began collecting and disseminating mortality data in 1994, broken down by:

- a shortlist of 65 causes of death based on the International classification of diseases (ICD), developed and maintained by the World Health Organization (WHO);
- sex;
- age;
- geographical region (NUTS level 2).

Annual data are provided in absolute numbers, as crude death rates and as standardised death rates. Since most causes of death vary significantly by age and according to sex, the use of standardised death rates improves comparability over time and between countries as death rates can be measured independently of the population's age structure.

Statistics on the causes of death are based on two pillars: medical information contained on death certificates, which may be used as a basis for the ascertaining the cause of death; and the coding of causes of death following the WHO-ICD system.

The validity and reliability of statistics on the causes of death rely on the quality of the data provided by certifying physicians. Inaccuracies may result for several reasons, including:

- errors can occur with the issue of the death certificate;
- the medical diagnosis;
- the selection of the main cause of death;
- the coding of the cause of death.

Sometimes there is ambiguity in the cause of death of a person. Besides the illness leading directly to death, the medical data on the death certificate should also contain a causal chain linked to the suffering of the deceased. Other substantial health conditions may be indicated, which did not have a link to the illness leading directly to death, but may have unfavourably affected the course of a disease and thus contributed to the fatal outcome. Indeed, there is sometimes criticism that the coding of only one illness as a cause of death appears more and more unrealistic in view of the increasing life expectancy and associated changes in morbidity. For the majority of the deceased of 65 years and older the selection of just one out of a number of possible causes of death may be somewhat misleading. For this reason, some of the EU Member States have started to consider multiple-cause coding. Eurostat has supported Member States in their efforts of developing a joint automated coding system called IRIS for the improvement and better comparability of the causes of death data in Europe.

Context

Statistics on causes of death play a key role in the general information system relating to the state of health in the EU. All deaths in the population are identified by the underlying cause of death, in other words 'the disease or injury which initiated the train of morbid

events leading directly to death, or the circumstances of the accident or violence which produced the fatal injury' (a definition adopted by the World Health Assembly). The data presented in this subchapter provide information on the risks associated with death from a range of specific diseases and other causes; a breakdown by age, sex, nationality and region (NUTS level 2) of the deceased is also available.

Statistics on causes of death provide indications as to which preventive and medical-curative measures as well as investments in research have the potential to increase the life expectancy of the population. Standardised death rates may be used as a starting point for targeted epidemiological research. As there is a general lack of comprehensive European morbidity statistics, data on causes of death are often used as a tool for evaluating health systems in the EU and may also be employed for evidence-based health policy.

Figure 3.2.1: Causes of death – standardised death rate per 100 000 inhabitants, males, EU-27, 2000-2009 (¹)
(2000 = 100)

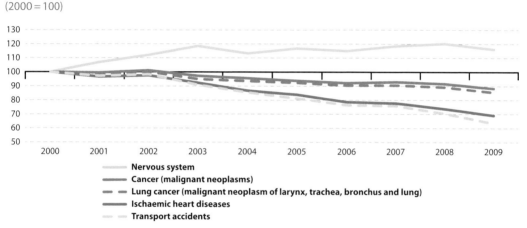

(¹) Provisional.

Source: Eurostat (online data code: hlth_cd_asdr)

Table 3.2.1: Causes of death – standardised death rate, 2009 (¹)
(per 100 000 inhabitants)

	Total							Females	
	Cancer (²)	Lung cancer (³)	Colo-rectal cancer	Circula-tory disease	Heart disease (⁴)	Respira-tory diseases	Transport accidents	Breast cancer	Uterus cancer
EU-27	*169.0*	*38.6*	*18.9*	*217.3*	*79.8*	*43.6*	*7.4*	*23.1*	*7.2*
Belgium	174.5	46.3	18.4	198.2	67.5	68.9	10.6	29.4	6.2
Bulgaria	161.2	36.3	21.8	605.0	116.1	39.7	11.0	21.3	13.5
Czech Republic	197.5	41.5	27.0	357.2	170.2	43.8	9.0	20.0	9.5
Denmark	*188.9*	*48.2*	*23.8*	*159.5*	*59.8*	*66.5*	*5.5*	*28.9*	*5.7*
Germany	159.8	34.3	18.1	217.1	84.4	39.5	5.0	24.0	5.5
Estonia	187.3	35.5	21.1	423.6	204.8	23.9	8.1	22.1	9.9
Ireland	180.8	39.9	20.1	190.1	102.3	70.6	5.9	28.1	8.0
Greece	153.5	40.1	12.4	244.6	67.4	53.7	13.6	21.1	5.3
Spain	153.0	36.1	20.0	143.2	45.4	50.3	5.7	17.6	5.8
France	166.0	36.6	16.7	124.7	33.8	27.3	6.9	24.1	6.4
Italy	161.2	35.2	17.4	173.8	60.3	28.6	8.3	23.5	5.1
Cyprus	123.1	25.0	10.0	194.4	70.7	39.4	10.5	21.5	4.2
Latvia	193.5	37.1	20.8	479.5	254.5	22.7	10.8	25.2	13.3
Lithuania	190.5	37.1	21.8	496.8	305.1	35.7	12.8	24.2	14.3
Luxembourg	165.8	40.6	19.4	186.2	44.8	44.3	9.1	24.5	4.5
Hungary	243.2	70.5	34.8	421.2	214.8	44.3	10.1	28.1	10.3
Malta	153.1	28.5	18.5	212.2	115.8	51.1	4.9	34.4	6.1
Netherlands	182.4	46.2	21.1	150.2	42.8	52.8	3.9	26.8	5.0
Austria	157.9	32.6	16.4	213.0	97.8	28.3	6.9	22.8	6.2
Poland	201.6	53.0	21.9	355.4	96.7	41.8	12.1	20.3	12.2
Portugal	156.2	26.5	22.0	177.6	42.2	63.7	9.0	20.2	8.4
Romania	181.4	42.3	19.5	548.4	188.8	50.6	15.1	22.6	17.4
Slovenia	198.5	39.0	26.5	231.7	64.4	37.8	9.3	25.5	8.4
Slovakia	197.0	37.6	28.8	450.0	270.1	51.7	9.2	21.3	12.4
Finland	134.8	25.9	13.2	218.1	122.5	24.4	6.0	19.4	5.6
Sweden	144.8	25.1	17.2	186.9	83.7	30.7	3.8	19.1	6.4
United Kingdom	172.6	40.3	17.0	169.2	80.8	69.6	4.0	25.4	5.9
Iceland	155.9	38.0	17.1	172.7	83.2	42.3	4.2	20.1	2.7
Norway	156.4	33.5	22.1	157.6	65.9	49.4	5.2	19.0	6.4
Switzerland	146.1	30.4	15.1	161.2	66.1	27.2	5.0	22.1	5.1
Croatia	211.8	49.4	28.5	387.6	158.4	33.2	12.9	25.4	9.6
FYR of Macedonia	173.8	42.5	18.8	566.4	89.7	33.4	7.2	23.7	10.5

(¹) France and Italy, 2008; Switzerland, 2007; Belgium, 2005.
(²) Malignant neoplasms.
(³) Malignant neoplasm of larynx, trachea, bronchus and lung.
(⁴) Ischaemic heart diseases.

Source: Eurostat (online data code: hlth_cd_asdr)

Figure 3.2.2: Causes of death – standardised death rate per 100 000 inhabitants, females, EU-27, 2000-2009 (¹)
(2000 = 100)

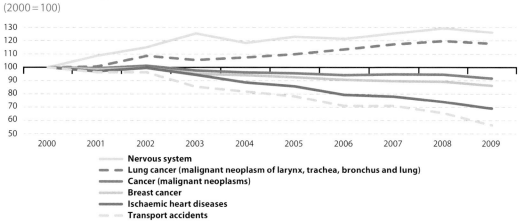

- Nervous system
- Lung cancer (malignant neoplasm of larynx, trachea, bronchus and lung)
- Cancer (malignant neoplasms)
- Breast cancer
- Ischaemic heart diseases
- Transport accidents

(¹) Provisional.

Source: Eurostat (online data code: hlth_cd_asdr)

Figure 3.2.3: Causes of death – standardised death rate, EU-27, 2009 (¹)
(per 100 000 inhabitants)

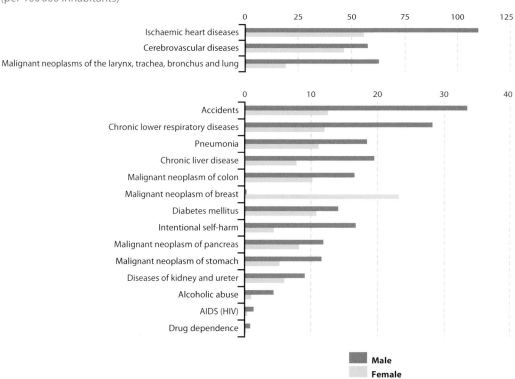

- Male
- Female

(¹) Provisional; the figure is ranked on the average of male and female; note the difference in the scales employed between the two parts of the figure.

Source: Eurostat (online data code: hlth_cd_asdr)

Figure 3.2.4: Deaths from ischaemic heart diseases – standardised death rate, 2009 (^{1})
(per 100 000 inhabitants)

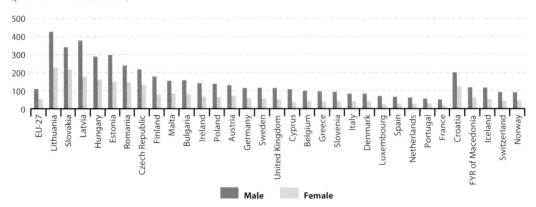

(¹) EU-27 and Denmark, provisional; the figure is ranked on the average of male and female; France and Italy, 2008; Switzerland, 2007; Belgium, 2005.

Source: Eurostat (online data code: tps00119)

Figure 3.2.5: Deaths from suicide – standardised death rate, 2009 (^{1})
(per 100 000 inhabitants)

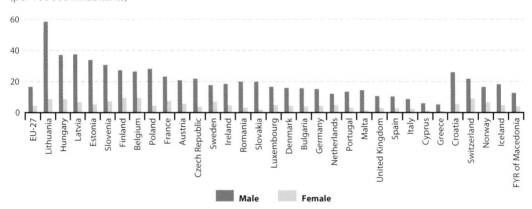

(¹) EU-27 and Denmark, provisional; the figure is ranked on the average of male and female; France and Italy, 2008; Switzerland, 2007; Belgium, 2005.

Source: Eurostat (online data code: tps00122)

Table 3.2.2: Causes of death – standardised death rate, 2009 (¹)
(per 100 000 inhabitants aged less than 65)

	Total							Females	
	Cancer (²)	Lung cancer (³)	Colo-rectal cancer	Circula-tory disease	Heart disease (⁴)	Suicide (⁵)	Transport accidents	Breast cancer	Uterus cancer
EU-27	71.9	18.5	6.3	45.0	19.4	9.5	7.1	13.3	4.2
Belgium	73.5	21.8	5.7	37.6	16.5	16.5	10.4	17.7	3.0
Bulgaria	88.3	23.7	8.8	151.1	37.1	7.7	10.8	13.1	9.8
Czech Republic	81.8	19.5	8.9	61.3	29.6	11.7	8.6	9.9	5.0
Denmark	68.7	18.3	7.2	29.2	11.2	8.7	5.2	13.7	2.8
Germany	65.9	16.5	5.9	37.0	16.7	8.3	4.7	13.0	3.0
Estonia	81.6	16.6	7.0	100.6	40.3	17.1	7.7	13.4	5.7
Ireland	65.2	14.3	6.2	34.8	21.1	11.9	5.6	15.0	5.0
Greece	61.6	18.9	3.4	46.3	28.8	2.9	13.3	10.9	2.6
Spain	65.7	18.3	6.7	26.8	11.7	5.5	5.4	10.7	3.1
France	75.0	20.7	5.4	25.6	8.9	13.5	6.8	14.3	3.3
Italy	61.9	13.7	5.8	26.6	11.5	4.8	8.0	13.6	2.5
Cyprus	46.7	10.2	3.3	35.3	22.8	3.5	9.5	13.3	1.1
Latvia	94.0	19.1	6.4	144.2	71.7	20.0	10.9	16.9	7.7
Lithuania	93.1	19.6	6.9	122.3	64.7	30.6	12.4	15.7	10.2
Luxembourg	61.5	18.1	4.7	30.8	11.4	9.8	8.6	12.2	3.1
Hungary	132.2	45.3	13.5	104.3	53.0	19.8	9.5	17.1	6.7
Malta	57.4	10.1	6.6	29.7	18.3	7.9	4.1	21.1	2.4
Netherlands	70.3	18.8	6.9	27.6	10.3	8.2	3.4	15.3	2.4
Austria	64.4	16.7	5.3	31.3	17.2	10.8	6.3	11.6	3.3
Poland	93.1	27.3	7.4	84.8	27.1	15.4	11.4	12.5	7.5
Portugal	70.6	15.0	7.5	27.6	9.7	6.3	8.2	12.9	4.4
Romania	100.4	26.6	7.7	115.9	49.2	10.5	14.0	14.4	13.4
Slovenia	79.3	18.5	8.5	36.6	17.4	16.7	8.4	12.1	4.8
Slovakia	91.1	18.9	9.9	89.2	47.4	9.8	8.8	11.5	7.3
Finland	50.7	9.8	4.2	44.9	22.2	18.2	5.3	11.5	2.6
Sweden	50.7	9.1	5.3	28.8	15.0	11.8	3.4	11.0	2.8
United Kingdom	62.8	13.6	5.6	36.2	20.4	6.7	4.0	14.5	3.0
Iceland	54.1	13.2	4.8	23.2	11.1	11.8	4.3	8.3	1.5
Norway	56.0	13.0	7.0	24.4	13.2	11.3	4.9	10.2	3.0
Switzerland	57.4	14.2	5.1	23.9	11.7	12.4	4.5	11.6	2.2
Croatia	91.3	26.6	8.9	67.3	31.7	12.5	12.1	12.7	4.5
FYR of Macedonia	86.7	24.7	7.0	95.2	31.0	6.2	5.8	13.8	6.9

(¹) France and Italy, 2008; Switzerland, 2007; Belgium, 2005.
(²) Malignant neoplasms.
(³) Malignant neoplasm of larynx, trachea, bronchus and lung.
(⁴) Ischaemic heart diseases.
(⁵) Suicide and intentional self-harm.

Source: Eurostat (online data code: hlth_cd_asdr)

Figure 3.2.6: Causes of death – standardised death rate per 100 000 inhabitants aged less than 65, EU-27, 2000-2009 (¹)
(2000 = 100)

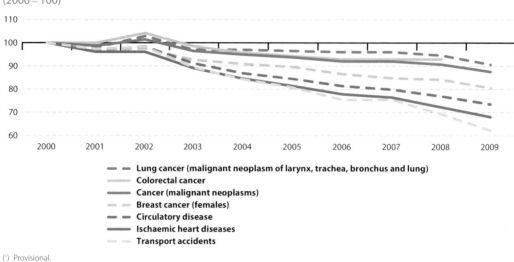

	Lung cancer (malignant neoplasm of larynx, trachea, bronchus and lung)
	Colorectal cancer
	Cancer (malignant neoplasms)
	Breast cancer (females)
	Circulatory disease
	Ischaemic heart diseases
	Transport accidents

(¹) Provisional.

Source: Eurostat (online data code: hlth_cd_asdr)

3.3 Healthcare

This subchapter presents key statistics on monetary and non-monetary aspects of healthcare in the European Union (EU) and its Member States. The state of health of individuals and of the population in general is influenced by genetic and environmental factors, cultural and socio-economical conditions, as well as the healthcare services that are available to prevent and to treat illness and disease.

Healthcare systems are organised and financed in different ways across the EU Member States, but most Europeans would agree that universal access to good healthcare, at an affordable cost to both individuals and society at large, is a basic need.

Monetary and non-monetary statistics may be used to evaluate how a country's healthcare system responds to this basic need, through measuring financial, human and technical resources within the healthcare sector and the allocation of these resources between healthcare activities (for example, preventive and curative care), groups of healthcare providers (for example, hospitals and ambulatory centres), or healthcare professionals (for example, medical and paramedical staff). It is possible to assess and measure the performance of healthcare systems by combining these data with information on technical and managerial choices that are made in relation to healthcare provision (for example, the use of inpatient or outpatient care, or the average length of stays in hospital).

Main statistical findings

Healthcare expenditure

Total current healthcare expenditure (both in relative and absolute terms) varied significantly among the EU Member States in 2009 (²). As shown in Figure 3.3.1 the share of current healthcare

(²) Bulgaria, Cyprus, Latvia, Luxembourg and Portugal, 2008.

expenditure exceeded 11 % of gross domestic product (GDP) in four EU Member States (France, the Netherlands, Germany and Denmark), which was almost double the share of healthcare expenditure relative to GDP recorded in Romania and Cyprus (below 6 % of GDP). The disparity was even bigger when comparing the level of total healthcare spending per inhabitant, which varied from PPS 608 in Romania to PPS 4 286 in Luxembourg. Notwithstanding the differences in organising and financing healthcare systems, these comparisons suggest that individuals living in those Member States with a higher average level of income per capita generally spend more on purchasing healthcare goods and services.

Public and private healthcare expenditure by financing agent

The mix of public and private funding of healthcare in the EU reflects specific arrangements in healthcare financing systems. Table 3.3.1 provides a breakdown of healthcare expenditure into public and private units that incur health expenditure. Public funding dominates the healthcare sector in the majority of EU Member States, the main exception being Cyprus, where public funding (general government and social security funds) accounted for a 42.1 % share of total funding. Among those Member States for which data are available (no information for Ireland, Greece, Italy, Malta or the United Kingdom), the share of public funding in current healthcare spending ranged from 56.2 % in Bulgaria to more than 80 % in the Netherlands, Denmark, the Czech Republic, Luxembourg and Sweden.

Public financing of healthcare is conducted through two main funding paths, social security funds and government financing. The former was somewhat more popular as a means for funding healthcare within the EU Member States and accounted for three quarters or more of overall spending on healthcare in the Czech Republic (78.2 %) and the Netherlands (76.0 %) in 2009. In contrast, Denmark and Sweden reported that government financing accounted for more than four fifths (84.5 % and 81.4 % respectively) of their total current expenditure on healthcare.

Private expenditure on healthcare is often used as an indicator to measure the accessibility of healthcare systems. The major source of private funding was direct household payments, referred to as out-of-pocket expenditure, which peaked in terms of its share of total current healthcare expenditure in Cyprus (50.2 %) and Bulgaria (42.6 %), falling to a single-digit share in France and the Netherlands (7.5 % and 6.2 % respectively). Private insurance generally represented a small share of healthcare financing among the Member States for which data are available; its relative share only exceeded 10 % in France and Slovenia.

Healthcare expenditure by function

The functional patterns of healthcare expenditure presented in Table 3.3.2 show that in 2009 curative and rehabilitative services incurred more that 50 % of current healthcare expenditure in the majority of EU Member States for which data are available, the exceptions being Hungary, Romania and Slovakia.

Medical goods dispensed to outpatients was the second largest function, with average spending accounting for around one quarter of total current healthcare expenditure – although with a significant degree of variation, from 11.5 % in Denmark up to more than one third of the total in Bulgaria (36.9 %), Slovakia (37.0 %) and Hungary (37.7 %).

Services related to long-term nursing care accounted for less than 10 % of current healthcare expenditure in more than half of the reporting Member States, but for almost a quarter of the total spend in the Netherlands (22.6 %) and Denmark (24.5 %). It should be noted that the relatively low share reported for many Member States could well be due to the main burden of long-term nursing care residing with family members with no payment being made for providing these services. In addition, limitations within the data compilation exercise also make it difficult to separate medical and social components of expenditure for long-term nursing care, leading to an inevitable impact on cross-country comparisons.

The proportion of current healthcare expenditure incurred by ancillary services to healthcare (such as laboratory testing or the transportation of patients) varies significantly among EU Member States, ranging from around 2 % in the Netherlands and Belgium to 10.1 % in Estonia. Similarly, expenditure related to prevention and public health programmes exhibits large discrepancies between Member States. In both cases these figures are likely to provide an underestimate of the true values, as part of the expenditure on these services is attributed to medical treatment and as such may be recorded under the heading of curative care. Expenditure on healthcare administration and health insurance was generally lower in those Member States with centralised social security systems or those Member States where private insurance plays a relatively restricted role, ranging from less than 1.5 % of total current healthcare expenditure in Bulgaria, Denmark, Hungary, Poland and Sweden, through to 5.5 % in Germany and 7 % in France.

Healthcare expenditure by provider

The breakdown of current healthcare expenditure by provider is shown in Table 3.3.3. Hospitals generally accounted for the highest share of current healthcare expenditure, ranging from 25.8 % of the total in Slovakia to more than 45 % in Denmark, Estonia and Sweden. The second most important category was that of ambulatory care providers, its share ranging from 13.9 % of current healthcare expenditure in Romania to more than 30 % in Belgium, Poland, Germany, Portugal, Finland and Cyprus. The share of various retail establishments and other providers of medical goods in current healthcare expenditure varied by a factor of three – with the lowest shares of between 11.2 % and 13.5 % being recorded in Luxembourg, Denmark and the Netherlands. Most of the Member States reported that retail establishments and other providers of medical goods accounted for a share of current healthcare expenditure ranging between 16 % and 27 %, a share that rose to between 36.9 % and 37.7 % in Bulgaria, Slovakia and Hungary. However, it should be borne in mind that healthcare providers classified under the same group do not necessarily perform the same set of activities. Hospitals, for example, may, in addition to inpatient services, offer outpatient, ancillary or other type of services.

Non-expenditure data on healthcare

High demand for healthcare staff in some Member States may result in qualified resources moving from other countries. One of the key indicators for measuring healthcare staff is the total number of physicians (head count), expressed per 100 000 inhabitants. In this context, Eurostat gives preference to the concept of practising physicians (although data are not available for six Member States – being replaced by the number of professionally active physicians for Greece, France, the Netherlands and Slovakia, and by the number of licensed physicians for Ireland and Portugal) – see Table 3.3.4.

In 2009 the highest number of practising physicians per 100 000 inhabitants was recorded in Austria (467.1), followed by Sweden (371.5), while Norway (399.9), Switzerland (381.2) and Iceland (372.0) also recorded relatively high ratios of practising physicians per 100 000 inhabitants; note that Greece, Ireland and Portugal also reported a relatively high number of professionally active and licensed physicians. Between 1999 and 2009 the number of physicians per 100 000 inhabitants increased in the majority of EU Member States, although modest reductions were recorded in Estonia, Lithuania, Hungary and Poland. Furthermore, the reduction of practising physicians in Poland may be explained by several breaks in the data series – for example, from 2004 onwards the Polish data excludes private practices (thought to account for about 2 000 physicians).

The number of hospital beds per 100 000 inhabitants averaged 551 in the EU-27 in 2009. Among the Member States, this ratio ranged from 277 in Sweden to 823 in Germany; among the non-member countries for which data are available Turkey (251) was the only one outside this range. During the ten years between 1999 and 2009, the number of hospital beds per 100 000 inhabitants fell in every Member State, except Greece; the average reduction in bed numbers across the whole of the EU-27 was 97 beds per 100 000 inhabitants. The largest reductions in the availability of hospital beds were recorded in the three Baltic Member States, France, Slovakia, Finland, Ireland, Belgium and Italy. These reductions may reflect, among others, economic constraints, increased efficiency through the use of technical resources

(for example, imaging equipment), a general shift from inpatient to outpatient operations, and shorter periods spent in hospital following an operation.

A closer look at the availability of hospital beds, broken down for curative care beds and psychiatric beds (see Table 3.3.5), shows a reduction in numbers for both types of beds between 1999 and 2009, with the EU-27 average falling to 308 curative care beds and 44 psychiatric care beds. The reduction was reproduced in each of the Member States for which data are available, except for an increase in the number of curative care beds in Greece and the number of psychiatric beds in Bulgaria, Germany and Austria.

In terms of healthcare activity, diseases of the circulatory system often accounted for the highest number of hospital discharges in 2009 – see Table 3.3.6. Almost one third of the Member States for which data are available reported in excess of 3 000 discharges per 100 000 inhabitants for diseases of the circulatory system. The average length of a hospital stay was generally highest among those patients suffering from cancer or problems relating to the circulatory system (see Table 3.3.7).

Data sources and availability

Eurostat, the Organisation for Economic Co-operation and Development (OECD) and the World Health Organization (WHO) have established a common framework for a joint healthcare data collection. Following this framework, EU Member States submit their data to Eurostat on the basis of a gentlemen's agreement. The data collected relates to:

- healthcare expenditure following the methodology of the system of health accounts (SHA);
- statistics on human and physical resources in healthcare – supplemented by additional Eurostat data on hospital activities (discharges and procedures).

Healthcare expenditure

Healthcare data on expenditure are based on various surveys and administrative (register-based) data sources, as well as estimations made within the Member States, reflecting country-specific ways of organising healthcare and different reporting systems for the collection of statistics pertaining to healthcare.

Total current healthcare expenditure quantifies the economic resources of both the public and private sectors dedicated to healthcare, with the exception of those related to capital investment. It reflects current expenditure of resident units on final consumption of goods and services directed at improving the health status of individuals and of the population.

The SHA provides a framework for interrelated classifications and tables relating to the international reporting of healthcare expenditure and its financing. The set of core SHA tables addresses three basic questions: i) who finances healthcare goods and services; ii) which healthcare providers deliver them, and; iii) what kinds of healthcare goods and services are consumed. Consequently, the SHA is organised around a tri-dimensional system for the recording of health expenditure, by means of the international classification for health accounts (ICHA), defining:

- healthcare expenditure by financing agents (ICHA-HF) – which provides a breakdown of public and private units that directly pay providers for their provision of healthcare goods and services;
- healthcare expenditure by provider (ICHA-HP) – which classifies units contributing to the provision of healthcare goods and services such as hospitals, various outpatients settings, diagnosis centres or retailers of medical goods;
- healthcare expenditure by function (ICHA-HC) – which details the split in healthcare expenditure following the purpose of healthcare activities – such as, health promotion, curing illnesses, rehabilitation or long-term care.

Data coverage is close to 100 % for the first-digit level of each of the three core classifications, but ranges between 75 % and 85 % at the second-digit level. However, it is possible that despite relatively high rates of coverage, there may be departures from the standard classifications. Expenditure reported under some of these ICHA categories may be under or overestimated and it is recommended to refer to specific country metadata before analysing the data.

Non-expenditure data on healthcare

Non-expenditure healthcare data are mainly based on administrative national sources; a few countries compile this information from surveys.

As a consequence, the information collected is not always comparable.

Information on the non-expenditure component of healthcare can be divided into two broad groups of data:

- resource-related healthcare data on human, physical and technical resources, including staff (such as physicians, dentists, nursing and caring professionals, pharmacists and physiotherapists) and hospital beds;
- output-related data that focuses on hospital patients and their treatment(s), in particular for inpatients.

Hospitals are defined according to the classification of healthcare providers within the SHA; all public and private hospitals should be covered.

Data on healthcare staff, in the form of human resources available for providing healthcare services, are provided irrespective of the sector of employment (in other words, regardless of whether the personnel are independent, employed by a hospital, or any other healthcare provider). Three main concepts are used for health professionals: practising, professionally active and licensed. Practising physicians provide services directly to patients; professionally active physicians include those who practice as well as those working in administration and research with their medical education being a pre-requisite for the job they carry out; physicians licensed to practice are those entitled to work as physicians plus, for example, those who are retired.

Hospital bed numbers provide information on healthcare capacities, in other words on the maximum number of patients who can be treated by hospitals. Hospital beds (occupied or unoccupied) are those which are regularly maintained and staffed and immediately available for the care of admitted patients. This indicator should ideally cover beds in all hospitals, including general hospitals, mental health and substance abuse hospitals, and other specialty hospitals. The statistics should include public as well as private sector establishments – although some Member States provide data only for the public sector – for example, Denmark (psychiatric beds), Ireland (total and curative beds),

Cyprus (curative and psychiatric beds) and the United Kingdom. Curative care (or acute care) beds are those that are available for curative care; these form a subgroup of total hospital beds.

Output-related indicators focus on hospital patients and cover the interaction between patients and healthcare systems, generally through the form of the treatment they receive. Data are available for a range of indicators including hospital discharges of inpatients and day cases by age, sex, and selected (groups of) diseases; the average length of stay of inpatients; or the medical procedures performed in hospitals. The number of hospital discharges is the most commonly used measure of the utilisation of hospital services. Discharges, rather than admissions, are used because hospital abstracts for inpatient care are based on information gathered at the time of discharge.

Context

Health outcomes across the EU are strikingly different according to where you live, your ethnicity, sex and socio-economic status. The EU promotes the coordination of national healthcare policies through an open method of coordination which places particular emphasis on the access to, and the quality and sustainability of healthcare. Some of the main objectives include: shorter waiting times; universal insurance coverage; affordable care; more patient-centred care and a higher use of outpatients; greater use of evidence-based medicine, effective prevention programmes, generic medicines, and simplified administrative procedures; and strengthening health promotion and disease prevention.

In the current economic climate, access to healthcare, the introduction of technological progress and greater patient choice is increasingly being considered against a background of financial sustainability. Many of the challenges facing governments across the EU are outlined in the European Commission's White paper, titled 'Together for health: a strategic approach for the EU 2008-2013' (COM(2007) 630).

Figure 3.3.1: Current healthcare expenditure, 2009 (¹)

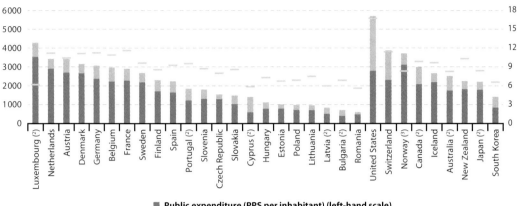

■ **Public expenditure (PPS per inhabitant) (left-hand scale)**
■ **Private expenditure (PPS per inhabitant) (left-hand scale)**
— **Current health expenditure (% of GDP) (right-hand scale)**

(¹) Countries are ranked on the total (public + private) health expenditure in PPS per inhabitant; Ireland, Greece, Italy, Malta and the United Kingdom, not available.
(²) 2008.
(³) 2007.

Source: Eurostat (online data code: hlth_sha_hf)

Table 3.3.1: Healthcare expenditure by financing agent, 2009
(% of current health expenditure)

	General government excluding social security funds	Social security funds	Private insurance enterprises (including private social insurance)	Private household out-of-pocket expenditure	Non-profit institutions serving households	Corporations (other than health insurance)	Rest of the world
Belgium	11.3	63.8	4.8	20.0	0.1	0.1	0.0
Bulgaria (¹)	17.7	38.5	0.5	42.6	0.5	0.3	0.0
Czech Republic	5.3	78.2	0.2	14.9	1.1	0.3	0.0
Denmark	84.5	0.0	1.8	13.7	0.1	0.0	0.0
Germany	6.9	70.5	9.6	12.3	0.4	0.4	0.0
Estonia	10.4	67.8	0.2	21.1	0.0	0.3	0.1
Ireland	:	:	:	:	:	:	:
Greece	:	:	:	:	:	:	:
Spain	68.6	4.6	5.5	20.7	0.6	0.0	0.0
France	5.6	72.5	13.6	7.5	0.1	0.6	0.0
Italy	:	:	:	:	:	:	:
Cyprus (¹)	42.0	0.1	5.7	50.2	2.0	0.0	0.0
Latvia (¹)	60.3	0.0	2.0	37.3	0.3	0.0	0.1
Lithuania	*11.4*	*61.7*	*0.7*	*26.2*	*0.0*	*0.1*	*0.0*
Luxembourg (¹)	8.5	73.9	3.5	13.7	0.4	0.0	0.0
Hungary	9.5	60.1	2.8	24.3	1.9	1.5	0.0
Malta	:	:	:	:	:	:	:
Netherlands	8.8	76.0	5.5	6.2	1.5	2.2	0.0
Austria (¹)	31.8	46.8	4.7	15.5	1.0	0.1	0.0
Poland	7.6	64.7	0.6	23.8	1.1	2.2	0.0
Portugal (¹)	64.3	1.3	5.2	28.7	0.1	0.5	0.0
Romania	14.1	64.6	0.1	20.9	0.0	0.3	0.0
Slovenia	*1.5*	*70.4*	*13.3*	*13.8*	*0.0*	*0.9*	*0.0*
Slovakia	6.6	62.6	0.0	26.9	1.0	2.9	0.0
Finland	58.6	15.7	2.3	20.1	1.1	2.2	0.0
Sweden	81.4	0.0	0.2	17.4	0.2	0.7	0.0
United Kingdom	:	:	:	:	:	:	:
Iceland	52.7	29.3	0.0	16.6	1.4	0.0	0.0
Norway (²)	70.6	13.1	0.0	16.1	0.0	0.2	0.0
Switzerland	*18.9*	*40.8*	*8.8*	*30.5*	*1.0*	*0.0*	*0.0*
Australia (¹)	69.0	0.0	8.5	19.2	0.3	3.0	0.0
Canada (¹)	68.1	1.5	13.5	15.5	0.0	1.5	0.0
Japan (¹)	8.5	72.0	2.5	16.0	0.0	1.0	0.0
Rep. of Korea (¹)	12.4	47.1	5.5	34.2	0.7	0.1	0.0
New Zealand	71.0	9.4	4.8	13.4	1.3	0.0	0.0
United States	*5.8*	*43.2*	*34.4*	*12.9*	*3.6*	*0.2*	*0.0*

(¹) 2008.
(²) 2007.

Source: Eurostat (online data code: hlth_sha_hf)

Table 3.3.2: Healthcare expenditure by function, 2009
(% of current health expenditure)

	Services of curative & rehabilitative care	Services of long-term nursing care	Ancillary services to healthcare	Medical goods dispensed to outpatients	Prevention & public health services	Health administration & health insurance	Not specified by kind
Belgium	52.7	19.7	2.4	17.5	2.7	4.9	0.0
Bulgaria (¹)	53.6	0.1	3.6	36.9	4.3	1.1	0.6
Czech Republic	60.0	3.5	5.8	23.1	2.7	3.4	1.5
Denmark	55.8	24.5	4.7	11.5	2.2	1.2	0.0
Germany	53.3	12.4	4.7	20.5	3.7	5.5	0.0
Estonia	54.0	4.4	10.1	26.9	2.3	2.4	0.0
Ireland	:	:	:	:	:	:	:
Greece	:	:	:	:	:	:	:
Spain	58.2	9.0	5.3	21.7	2.7	3.2	0.0
France	53.1	11.5	5.2	21.0	2.2	7.0	0.0
Italy	:	:	:	:	:	:	:
Cyprus (¹)	59.3	2.5	9.5	23.9	0.7	4.2	0.0
Latvia (¹)	55.3	3.9	9.4	24.3	1.6	5.5	0.0
Lithuania	51.5	9.1	6.0	29.6	1.2	2.7	0.0
Luxembourg (¹)	58.3	19.9	5.9	12.5	1.9	1.7	0.0
Hungary	47.4	3.9	4.4	37.7	4.4	1.3	1.1
Malta	:	:	:	:	:	:	:
Netherlands	51.7	22.6	1.9	14.5	4.3	4.0	0.9
Austria	60.3	14.0	2.8	17.5	1.8	3.6	0.0
Poland	58.2	5.4	6.2	26.4	2.3	1.4	0.0
Portugal (¹)	58.3	1.1	9.3	25.8	1.9	1.7	0.0
Romania	46.8	13.5	4.0	25.6	8.3	1.8	0.1
Slovenia	56.5	8.7	3.0	23.7	3.8	4.3	0.0
Slovakia	46.7	0.3	7.7	37.0	4.9	3.4	0.0
Finland	58.9	12.3	3.2	18.0	5.6	2.1	0.0
Sweden	66.0	7.7	4.5	16.0	3.8	1.4	0.6
United Kingdom	:	:	:	:	:	:	:
Iceland	58.5	18.0	2.3	17.9	1.5	1.9	0.0
Norway (²)	51.4	26.2	6.4	13.2	2.1	0.8	0.0
Switzerland	57.7	19.3	3.3	12.2	2.5	4.9	0.0
Australia (¹)	69.2	0.4	6.1	18.5	2.1	3.6	0.0
Canada (¹)	46.4	14.8	6.3	20.9	7.1	3.8	0.6
Japan (¹)	65.4	8.9	0.7	20.8	2.4	1.9	0.0
Rep. of Korea (¹)	57.0	10.0	0.9	25.2	3.3	3.6	0.0
New Zealand	56.5	13.9	5.2	10.6	6.7	7.2	0.0
United States	69.5	5.9	0.0	14.1	3.6	7.0	0.0

(¹) 2008.
(²) 2007.

Source: Eurostat (online data code: hlth_sha_hc)

Table 3.3.3: Healthcare expenditure by provider, 2009
(% of current health expenditure)

	Hospitals	Nursing & residential care facilities	Ambulatory health-care	Retail sale & medical goods	Admin. of public health pro-grammes	General health admin. & insurance	Other (rest of economy)	Rest of the world
Belgium	31.0	12.4	30.6	16.5	4.1	4.6	0.8	0.0
Bulgaria ([1])	41.0	0.8	16.7	36.9	1.8	1.1	1.7	0.0
Czech Republic	42.6	1.5	25.5	18.2	0.2	3.6	0.6	0.2
Denmark	45.2	13.4	28.2	11.5	0.1	1.5	0.1	0.1
Germany	29.5	7.8	30.8	21.8	0.7	5.9	3.0	0.5
Estonia	45.6	2.7	20.2	26.9	2.1	2.4	0.0	0.1
Ireland	:	:	:	:	:	:	:	:
Greece	:	:	:	:	:	:	:	:
Spain	41.0	5.5	26.3	21.7	1.3	3.2	1.0	0.0
France	35.3	7.1	27.4	21.7	0.7	7.0	0.8	0.0
Italy	:	:	:	:	:	:	:	:
Cyprus ([1])	41.9	2.5	33.4	18.8	0.2	1.9	0.0	1.2
Latvia ([1])	42.6	2.5	26.9	24.3	0.0	2.9	0.8	0.0
Lithuania	36.4	1.6	22.5	29.6	0.1	2.7	7.0	0.1
Luxembourg ([1])	32.9	15.7	26.2	11.2	0.4	1.4	2.8	9.5
Hungary	32.3	3.3	20.3	37.7	2.7	1.2	2.3	0.3
Malta	:	:	:	:	:	:	:	:
Netherlands	33.7	22.8	22.5	13.5	1.2	4.4	1.0	0.9
Austria ([1])	39.4	7.9	23.4	18.2	0.6	4.0	6.4	0.2
Poland	34.3	1.3	30.6	26.1	1.6	1.4	4.6	0.1
Portugal ([1])	37.5	1.3	31.5	25.6	0.1	1.7	1.3	1.0
Romania	41.5	2.1	13.9	25.6	2.0	1.5	13.4	0.1
Slovenia	41.1	5.8	24.0	23.1	0.7	4.3	0.9	0.1
Slovakia	25.8	0.0	27.8	37.0	2.0	3.4	3.8	0.2
Finland	35.1	8.5	32.9	18.5	1.1	1.2	2.9	0.0
Sweden	46.0	0.0	21.7	16.0	1.3	1.7	9.2	0.2
United Kingdom	:	:	:	:	:	:	:	:
Iceland	39.6	10.9	27.2	17.9	1.5	1.9	0.0	1.1
Norway ([2])	39.3	17.0	27.3	12.8	1.7	0.0	1.9	0.1
Switzerland	35.6	17.2	31.6	9.0	0.0	6.6	0.0	0.0
Australia ([1])	41.5	0.0	35.5	17.7	1.6	3.7	0.0	0.0
Canada ([1])	28.9	10.6	28.4	20.9	6.6	3.8	0.2	0.0
Japan ([1])	47.8	3.6	27.8	16.5	2.4	1.9	0.0	0.0
Rep. of Korea ([1])	41.1	3.0	28.1	21.0	2.0	3.6	1.1	0.2
New Zealand	35.9	9.3	32.0	10.6	3.6	7.3	1.4	0.0
United States	32.6	5.9	36.9	14.1	3.6	7.0	0.0	0.0

([1]) 2008.
([2]) 2007.

Source: Eurostat (online data code: hlth_sha_hp)

Table 3.3.4: Healthcare indicators, 1999-2009
(per 100 000 inhabitants)

	Practising physicians (¹)		Hospital beds		Hospital discharges of inpatients (excluding healthy new born babies)	
	1999	2009 (²)	1999 (³)	2009 (⁴)	2000 (⁵)	2009 (⁶)
EU-27	:	:	648.1	550.9	:	:
Belgium	279.7	291.3	782.3	653.4	16 252	16 284
Bulgaria	345.0	370.0	751.3	661.6	14 456	23 356
Czech Republic	308.0	355.5	774.0	710.1	22 065	19 968
Denmark	287.8	341.6	439.5	350.1	16 316	16 498
Germany	320.6	364.1	920.2	822.9	19 961	22 692
Estonia	327.7	326.7	754.9	543.9	19 947	17 567
Ireland	224.2	406.6	628.3	495.1	13 805	13 236
Greece	423.0	610.6	473.3	485.8	:	:
Spain	308.5	354.8	376.0	319.3	11 243	10 416
France	323.3	325.6	817.5	660.5	18 397	16 035
Italy	:	336.2	492.8	364.3	:	13 236
Cyprus	255.2	285.6	449.9	377.2	6 795	7 500
Latvia	272.7	300.4	906.7	638.3	:	20 290
Lithuania	372.8	366.2	898.4	682.4	22 784	21 887
Luxembourg	247.5	268.9	:	551.4	18 075	15 869
Hungary	310.9	302.3	812.6	715.0	:	19 435
Malta	:	304.4	556.0	482.6	:	10 901
Netherlands	232.2	285.9	505.6	466.9	9 088	11 279
Austria	376.3	467.1	807.2	765.0	:	27 839
Poland	226.4	217.0	:	665.0	:	15 658
Portugal	311.3	376.9	385.8	334.9	:	17 507
Romania	188.2	221.5	758.0	657.4	21 748	24 634
Slovenia	212.1	240.1	554.0	462.0	:	16 576
Slovakia	331.9	328.1	794.9	649.7	19 876	18 031
Finland	240.3	272.7	761.4	623.1	21 380	17 890
Sweden	302.3	371.5	358.6	277.1	15 266	15 200
United Kingdom	190.8	265.9	410.5	330.2	12 698	12 913
Iceland	336.1	372.0	:	*585.7*	17 085	13 027
Norway	327.5	399.9	390.2	336.6	15 409	16 637
Switzerland	:	381.2	662.7	513.2	14 646	25 868
Croatia	232.0	266.9	596.5	536.8	12 710	16 259
FYR of Macedonia	220.1	261.8	509.2	447.4	9 444	9 939
Turkey	122.6	163.5	:	251.2	:	13 345

(¹) Greece, France, the Netherlands, Slovakia, the former Yugoslav Republic of Macedonia and Turkey, professionally active physicians; Ireland and Portugal, licensed physicians.
(²) Denmark, Cyprus, the Netherlands, Romania, Finland, Sweden, Iceland and the former Yugoslav Republic of Macedonia, 2008.
(³) United Kingdom, 2000.
(⁴) Ireland, Cyprus and Romania, 2008; Iceland, 2007.
(⁵) The Czech Republic, the Netherlands, the United Kingdom and Switzerland, 2002; Lithuania, 2001.
(⁶) Belgium, Germany, Latvia and Croatia, 2008; Denmark, Cyprus and the former Yugoslav Republic of Macedonia, 2007.

Source: Eurostat (online data codes: hlth_rs_prs, tps00046 and hlth_co_disch2t)

Figure 3.3.2: Number of hospital beds, EU-27, 1999-2009
(per 100 000 inhabitants)

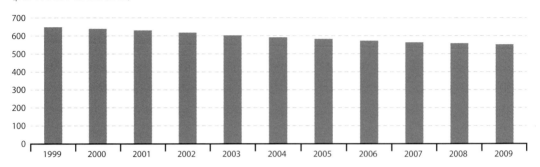

Source: Eurostat (online data code: tps00046)

Table 3.3.5: Hospital beds, 1999-2009
(per 100 000 inhabitants)

	Curative care beds in hospitals			Psychiatric care beds in hospitals		
	1999 (^{1})	2004	2009 (^{2})	1999 (^{3})	2004	2009 (^{4})
EU-27	385.9	336.8	308.2	52.1	48.3	44.0
Belgium	477.4	448.3	419.2	259.4	248.5	179.2
Bulgaria	586.1	471.4	509.1	65.0	64.7	68.5
Czech Republic	585.0	540.0	498.1	112.9	112.0	103.3
Denmark	359.0	326.2	286.7	79.0	67.6	57.9
Germany	644.8	593.0	564.8	44.3	50.8	49.0
Estonia	585.1	426.7	361.5	82.2	52.6	55.1
Ireland	282.4	280.8	257.8	143.2	102.3	77.5
Greece	376.1	380.1	406.1	97.2	89.7	79.7
Spain	290.3	263.0	247.4	53.6	48.0	41.0
France	416.1	369.0	345.3	110.7	93.7	88.0
Italy	458.1	334.8	293.8	16.2	13.1	10.6
Cyprus	394.8	389.7	351.1	55.1	31.4	26.1
Latvia	648.1	548.7	429.4	185.1	156.6	133.9
Lithuania	677.8	556.3	503.4	127.5	107.1	102.4
Luxembourg	:	505.8	428.0	:	110.1	87.5
Hungary	588.4	551.2	413.4	45.0	39.2	32.8
Malta	380.9	298.3	271.7	175.2	160.4	155.9
Netherlands	317.9	291.8	307.2	165.9	136.6	139.6
Austria	626.1	582.1	556.3	75.9	73.1	77.3
Poland	530.2	478.7	438.5	:	68.6	64.1
Portugal	315.6	298.8	275.6	69.5	65.5	58.6
Romania	520.0	443.5	451.0	88.9	76.0	80.4
Slovenia	458.5	385.1	372.8	77.7	73.7	65.9
Slovakia	584.8	483.5	479.2	92.5	86.7	79.9
Finland	249.0	226.1	183.4	106.2	96.7	80.1
Sweden	253.7	223.1	204.7	65.3	50.2	48.1
United Kingdom	312.2	303.7	264.9	93.4	78.8	60.8
Norway	319.3	291.7	239.6	70.9	107.9	86.8
Switzerland	445.0	378.2	330.1	120.5	106.9	98.8
Croatia	374.2	341.8	335.6	100.8	94.2	94.5
FYR of Macedonia	330.3	317.1	302.0	72.7	63.8	56.7
Turkey	194.2	210.3	242.2	5.4	5.3	6.6

(^{1}) Bulgaria, the United Kingdom and Turkey, 2000.
(^{2}) Ireland, Cyprus and Romania, 2008.
(^{3}) The United Kingdom and Turkey, 2000.
(^{4}) Cyprus and Romania, 2008.

Source: Eurostat (online data codes: tps00168 and tps00047)

Table 3.3.6: Hospital discharges of inpatients by diagnosis (ISHMT – international shortlist for hospital morbidity tabulation), 2009
(per 100 000 inhabitants)

	Neoplasms (cancers)	Diseases of the circulatory system	Diseases of the respiratory system	Diseases of the digestive system	Pregnancy childbirth & the puerperium	Injury poisoning & certain other consequences of external causes
Belgium (¹)	1 165.0	2 075.2	1 363.7	1 670.9	1 395.7	1 623.6
Bulgaria	1 564.6	3 867.2	3 250.1	2 092.7	2 023.2	1 372.2
Czech Republic	1 641.1	2 996.2	1 344.5	1 732.0	1 555.5	1 702.3
Denmark (²)	1 396.1	2 068.8	1 468.5	1 352.4	1 220.8	1 502.9
Germany (¹)	2 444.1	3 463.1	1 400.1	2 156.0	1 091.8	2 186.5
Estonia	1 666.9	3 326.3	1 772.7	1 475.7	1 816.5	1 168.8
Ireland	827.5	1 163.5	1 307.9	1 128.4	2 678.9	1 254.6
Greece	:	:	:	:	:	:
Spain	942.8	1 295.4	1 186.2	1 241.9	1 301.1	881.2
France	1 178.1	1 919.8	1 009.8	1 555.1	1 548.6	1 378.3
Italy	1 267.3	2 208.3	1 084.9	1 260.6	1 231.3	1 155.6
Cyprus (²)	518.6	869.9	763.0	730.8	408.9	1 019.9
Latvia (¹)	1 945.6	3 782.9	1 895.1	1 824.2	1 719.1	1 944.8
Lithuania	1 719.6	4 283.4	2 339.1	1 825.2	1 634.9	1 652.5
Luxembourg	1 473.1	1 970.1	1 241.9	1 473.5	1 352.8	1 251.5
Hungary	2 333.8	3 431.4	1 604.0	1 441.5	1 462.6	1 367.7
Malta	701.5	1 180.7	984.6	1 034.6	787.7	990.6
Netherlands	1 064.0	1 654.0	793.8	981.0	1 006.7	1 001.0
Austria	2 947.4	3 686.5	1 801.9	2 467.9	1 286.5	3 140.5
Poland	1 325.0	2 624.4	1 279.3	1 369.6	1 550.3	1 073.8
Portugal	1 075.2	1 320.4	1 078.5	1 099.6	970.2	703.9
Romania	2 016.1	3 539.1	3 281.1	2 508.1	1 836.7	1 288.0
Slovenia	1 771.9	1 988.9	1 425.4	1 422.4	1 351.0	1 545.7
Slovakia	1 573.8	2 726.6	1 471.3	1 724.6	1 615.0	1 434.2
Finland	1 682.9	2 655.4	1 419.5	1 318.7	1 258.7	1 734.1
Sweden	1 320.9	2 334.5	1 021.5	1 172.7	1 347.0	1 429.0
United Kingdom	923.7	1 287.2	1 184.6	1 197.9	1 552.1	1 277.0
Iceland	1 179.6	1 443.3	743.8	1 153.2	1 840.5	1 007.2
Norway	1 602.1	2 381.7	1 416.0	1 214.5	1 549.1	1 832.8
Switzerland	2 103.8	2 772.6	1 461.4	2 224.2	1 939.9	3 412.3
Croatia (¹)	1 934.6	2 031.7	1 077.0	1 162.6	1 406.9	1 230.9
FYR of Macedonia (²)	1 169.1	1 443.9	1 548.3	1 185.4	581.8	588.5
Turkey	852.1	1 441.7	1 684.6	1 102.1	1 591.3	588.0

(¹) 2008.
(²) 2007.

Source: Eurostat (online data code: hlth_co_disch2)

Table 3.3.7: Hospital discharges of inpatients by diagnosis (ISHMT – international shortlist for hospital morbidity tabulation), average length of stay, 2009
(days)

	Neoplasms (cancers)	Diseases of the circulatory system	Diseases of the respiratory system	Diseases of the digestive system	Pregnancy, childbirth & the puerperium	Injury, poisoning & certain other consequences of external causes
Belgium (¹)	9.1	8.1	8.0	5.8	4.7	8.6
Bulgaria	6.3	5.0	7.0	5.6	4.3	5.3
Czech Republic	9.3	12.8	8.9	7.2	5.1	10.1
Denmark (²)	6.4	5.4	5.4	5.0	3.4	5.1
Germany (¹)	10.1	10.2	8.7	7.2	4.7	9.0
Estonia	8.5	10.7	4.8	5.1	2.8	8.3
Ireland	11.1	9.5	7.2	6.2	2.8	5.6
Greece	:	:	:	:	:	:
Spain	9.0	8.2	7.0	5.8	3.1	8.2
France	0.7	0.2	0.2	1.1	0.3	0.3
Italy	9.3	9.1	8.7	6.7	3.9	8.9
Cyprus (²)	8.9	6.4	5.2	5.1	5.4	5.8
Latvia (¹)	9.3	8.6	7.7	6.2	5.2	7.9
Lithuania	8.8	8.5	6.6	6.0	4.2	6.7
Luxembourg	9.1	8.0	6.3	5.9	4.7	7.5
Hungary	5.3	7.1	5.7	5.5	4.2	5.6
Malta	6.3	9.4	5.1	4.8	3.4	6.1
Netherlands	7.3	6.7	7.0	6.0	3.3	6.5
Austria	7.5	10.8	8.4	6.6	5.4	8.6
Poland	7.2	7.4	7.4	5.8	4.8	6.1
Portugal	7.2	7.4	7.6	5.4	3.3	9.4
Romania	6.7	7.8	7.0	6.4	4.9	6.2
Slovenia	7.9	8.2	6.7	6.0	4.4	6.7
Slovakia	8.4	7.8	7.9	5.9	5.5	6.1
Finland	8.3	16.1	11.1	5.4	3.5	10.1
Sweden	7.8	6.1	5.4	4.7	2.7	5.9
United Kingdom	8.6	10.2	7.7	6.2	2.4	8.2
Iceland	7.6	7.6	7.0	4.5	2.2	6.6
Norway	6.6	4.7	6.0	4.5	1.6	4.5
Switzerland	8.7	7.7	7.2	6.0	4.9	6.2
Croatia (¹)	9.2	10.0	7.9	7.2	5.9	9.4
FYR of Macedonia (²)	7.9	10.0	7.5	5.6	4.2	9.0
Turkey	5.8	4.6	4.7	3.8	2.1	4.6

(¹) 2008.
(²) 2007.

Source: Eurostat (online data code: hlth_co_inpst)

3.4 Health and safety at work

This subchapter presents the main statistical data on serious and fatal accidents at work, as well as some statistical information in relation to work-related health problems in the European Union (EU). An accident at work is a discrete occurrence during the course of work which leads to physical or mental harm. Serious accidents at work are those that imply more than three days of absence from work. Fatal accidents at work are those that lead to the death of the victim within one year. The phrase 'in the course of work' means whilst engaged in an occupational activity or during the time spent at work. This includes cases of road traffic accidents in the course of work but excludes accidents during the journey between home and the workplace.

Main statistical findings

Serious and fatal accidents at work

In 2008, there were almost five thousand fatal accidents at work across the EU (excluding Greece and Northern Ireland) and nearly four million other accidents at work that resulted in more than three days of absence from work. These data relate to 193 million workers that were insured for accidents at work in the EU. An alternative way to analyse the information is to express the number of accidents in relation to the number of persons employed. For example, across the EU there were, on average, 2 040 serious accidents at work per 100 000 persons employed in 2008, while there were 2.53 fatal accidents per 100 000 persons employed.

Figure 3.4.1, illustrates the incidence rates of fatal accidents at work per 100 000 persons employed. Romania, with an average of 8.0 fatal work accidents per 100 000 persons employed, had the highest incidence rate followed by Lithuania and Bulgaria (6.0 and 5.2 fatal accidents per 100 000 persons employed). Denmark, Germany, the Netherlands, Sweden, Finland and France (as well as the United Kingdom, although values excluded Northern Ireland and road traffic accidents at work) had the lowest incidence rates with less than two fatal accidents at work per 100 000 persons employed in 2008.

According to the information that is available broken down by sex, men are considerably more likely to have an accident or to die at work than women. EU-27 incidence rates for serious accidents at work for men were 2.5 times higher on average than those for women in 2008. In Denmark, Sweden and Norway the average incidence rates for serious accidents at work for men were 1.5 times as high as the average incidence rate for women, while in France, Spain, Italy, Bulgaria and Finland they were 2.5 times as high and in Germany three times as high.

The number of accidents at work also varies considerably depending upon the economic activity where the victim works (see Figure 3.4.2). The construction, manufacturing and transportation and storage sectors accounted for more than 50 % of all fatal and serious accidents at work. The construction sector accounted for the largest number of fatal accidents at work (28.2 % of all fatal work accidents), followed by the manufacturing sector (18.1 %), transportation and storage (15.8 %) and agriculture, forestry and fishing (13.1 %). Most of the serious accidents at work also took place within the manufacturing and construction sectors, respectively 25.5 % and 16.5 % of all serious accidents, followed by wholesale and retail trade activities and transportation and storage, respectively 13.4 % and 8.4 % of all serious accidents.

Work-related health problems

In the EU-27, some 8.1 % of those aged 15 to 64 that worked or had previously worked reported a work-related health problem in the 12 months prior to a LFS ad-hoc survey module in 2007; this was equivalent to approximately 23 million persons.

As shown in Figure 3.4.3, musculo-skeletal problems were most often reported as the main work-related health problem (59.8 %), followed by stress, depression or anxiety (13.7 %). The occurrence of work-related health problems generally increased with age, but the rate of increase slowed down for workers aged 55 to 64 years; this may be due to unhealthy workers leaving the workforce early.

Workers with a low level of education reported work-related health problems more often than their colleagues. In particular, this group of workers were more often identified with musculoskeletal health problems as their most serious work-related health problem, whereas persons with higher levels of education most often identified stress, depression or anxiety as their main work-related health problem.

Work-related health problems were more likely to occur in agriculture, hunting and forestry, or in mining and quarrying; among women, work-related health problems were also more likely for those working in the health and social work sector. Furthermore, manual workers more often reported work-related health problems than non-manual workers.

Half (50.0 %) of all persons with a work-related health problem in the EU experienced some limitations in their ability to carry out day-to-day activities, and an additional 22.6 % experienced considerable limitations. Work-related health problems resulted in sick leave of at least one day in the past 12 months for 62.0 % of persons with a work-related health problem, and in sick leave of at least one month for 27.1 %.

It is estimated that work-related health problems resulted in at least 367 million calendar days of sick leave in the EU in 2007; this figure excludes persons that never expect to work again because of their work-related health problem.

Data sources and availability

There are two major data sources of statistics on health and safety at work: European Statistics on Accidents at Work (ESAW) and a Labour Force Survey (LFS) ad-hoc module for 2007 on accidents at work and work-related health problems.

European Statistics on Accidents at Work (ESAW) include case-by-case data on occupational accidents with more than three days of absence from work and fatal accidents. These are accidents reported to national bodies/authorities responsible for insurance against accidents at work.

The LFS ad-hoc module provides data on self-reported accidents at work and work-related health problems in the 12 months prior to the survey. The LFS module asked respondents to record all accidents leading to injuries, irrespective of whether the accident led to any absence from work. The survey module also included questions about physical or mental health problems which the respondent considered to be caused or made worse by work.

Context

A safe, healthy working environment is a crucial factor in an individual's quality of life and is also a collective concern. Member State governments across the EU recognise the social and economic benefits of better health and safety at work. Reliable, comparable, up-to-date statistical information is vital for setting policy objectives and adopting suitable policy measures and preventing actions.

The EU action in health and safety at work has its legal basis in Article 153 of the EU Treaty. The main principles governing the protection of workers' health and safety are laid down in a 1989 framework Directive 89/391/EEC, the basic objective of which is to encourage improvements in occupational health and safety. All sectors of activity, both public and private, are covered by this legislation, which establishes the principle that the employer has a duty to ensure workers' safety and health in all aspects relating to work, while the worker has an obligation to follow the employer's health and safety instructions and report potential dangers.

In this field, the policy agenda of the European Commission is set out in a Communication ((2007) 62) which details a Community strategy for 2007-2012 on health and safety at work, outlining actions to make workplaces across the EU safer and healthier. It also sets a quantitative target of a 25 % reduction in accidents at work, to be achieved through various EU and national measures.

Table 3.4.1: Number of serious and fatal accidents at work, 2008
(persons)

	Accidents at work involving more than three days of absence from work (¹)			Fatal accidents at work		
	Total	Male	Female	Total	Male	Female
EU-27	*3 942 999*	*2 923 491*	*1 018 409*	*4 898*	*4 638*	*260*
Belgium	76 514	58 445	18 024	96	92	4
Bulgaria	3 037	2 181	856	151	141	10
Czech Republic	99 477	73 444	26 033	174	166	8
Denmark	71 288	43 850	26 981	47	:	:
Germany	943 993	734 885	208 589	616	573	43
Estonia	7 228	5 143	2 085	21	:	:
Ireland	18 078	12 897	5 118	51	:	:
Greece	:	:	:	:	:	:
Spain	689 131	517 880	171 251	529	512	17
France	637 357	450 992	186 365	289	265	24
Italy	503 431	389 947	113 484	780	753	27
Cyprus	2 355	1 890	465	12	12	0
Latvia	1 705	1 121	584	43	39	4
Lithuania	3 156	2 122	1 034	79	71	8
Luxembourg	8 133	6 650	1 483	10	10	0
Hungary	22 337	15 185	7 146	117	108	9
Malta	3 213	2 818	395	:	:	0
Netherlands	184 901	119 063	65 058	106	100	6
Austria	72 990	60 119	12 871	170	159	11
Poland	96 318	69 881	26 437	520	495	25
Portugal	147 349	116 979	30 370	221	213	8
Romania	4 559	3 607	952	497	460	37
Slovenia	20 186	15 601	4 585	27	27	0
Slovakia	11 614	8 142	3 472	80	:	:
Finland	57 373	41 645	15 728	34	31	3
Sweden	34 413	21 218	13 195	68	63	5
United Kingdom (²)	223 635	147 785	75 847	157	:	:
Norway	56 518	33 928	22 590	50	:	:
Switzerland	73 640	58 967	14 673	90	85	5

(¹) EU-27: estimates made for the purpose of this publication include under-reported levels for Latvia, Poland and Romania, but exclude Greece and Northern Ireland; Latvia, Poland and Romania, data include a certain level of under-reporting.
(²) Great Britain (hence, excluding Northern Ireland).

Source: Eurostat (online data codes: hsw_n2_01 and hsw_n2_02)

Figure 3.4.1: Number of fatal accidents at work, 2008 (¹)
(incidence rates per 100 000 persons employed)

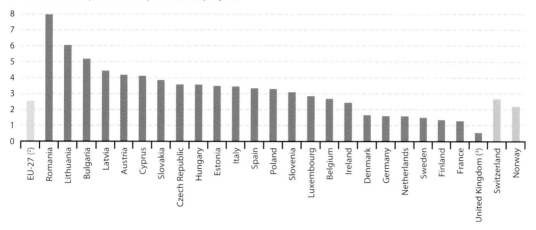

(¹) Greece, not available.
(²) Estimate made for the purpose of this publication includes under-reported levels for Latvia, Poland and Romania, but excludes Greece and Northern Ireland.
(³) Great Britain (hence, excluding Northern Ireland); also excludes road traffic accidents at work.
Source: Eurostat (online data code: hsw_n2_02)

Figure 3.4.2: Fatal and serious accidents at work by economic activity, EU, 2008
(% of serious and fatal accidents)

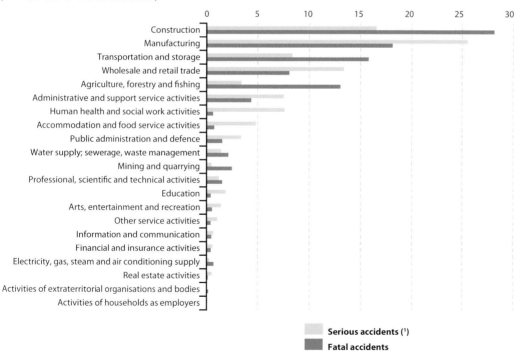

  Serious accidents (¹)
  Fatal accidents

(¹) Estimates made for the purpose of this publication including under-reported levels for Latvia, Poland and Romania, but excluding Greece and Northern Ireland.
Source: Eurostat (online data codes: hsw_n2_01 and hsw_n2_02)

Figure 3.4.3: Type of work-related health problem indicated as the most serious among persons with a work-related health problem, EU-27, 2007 (¹)
(% of persons citing each complaint)

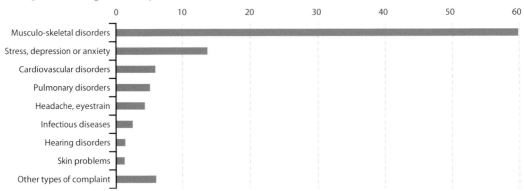

(¹) Excluding France (data are not comparable).
Source: Eurostat (online data code: hsw_pb5)

Education and training

4

Introduction

Education, vocational training and more generally lifelong learning play a vital role in both an economic and social context. The opportunities which the European Union (EU) offers its citizens for living, studying and working in other countries make a major contribution to cross-cultural understanding, personal development and the realisation of the EU's full economic potential. Each year, well over a million EU citizens of all ages benefit from EU-funded educational, vocational and citizenship-building programmes.

The Treaty establishing the European Community acknowledged the importance of these areas by stating that 'the Community shall contribute to the development of quality education by encouraging cooperation between Member States and, if necessary, by supporting and supplementing their action ... The Community shall implement a vocational training policy which shall support and supplement the action of the Member States'. As such, the European Commission follows up on policy cooperation and work with the Member States, while funding programmes such as the lifelong learning programme (LLP).

Political cooperation within the EU has been strengthened through the education and training 2010 work programme which integrated previous actions in the fields of education and training. The follow-up to this programme is the strategic framework for European cooperation in education and training (known as ET 2020) which was adopted by the Council in May 2009. This set a number of benchmarks to be achieved by 2020:

- at least 95 % of children between the age of four and the age for starting compulsory primary education should participate in early childhood education;
- the share of low-achieving 15-year-olds with insufficient abilities in reading, mathematics and science should be less than 15 %;
- the share of early leavers from education and training should be less than 10 %;
- the share of 30 to 34-year-olds with tertiary educational attainment should be at least 40 %;

- an average of at least 15 % of adults aged 25 to 64 should participate in lifelong learning.

The Bologna process put in motion a series of reforms to make European higher education more compatible, comparable, competitive and attractive for students. Its main objectives were: the introduction of a three-cycle degree system (bachelor, master and doctorate); quality assurance; and recognition of qualifications and periods of study. One of the operational goals of the process was to remove the obstacles to student mobility across Europe, and more broadly support the mobility of students, teachers and researchers.

The Bologna process set out plans to create a European higher education area and in March 2010 the Minsters of the 47 participating countries adopted the Budapest-Vienna Declaration and officially launched the European higher education area (EHEA). The next decade will be aimed at consolidating the EHEA and making it operational.

Since 2002 national authorities and social partners from 32 European countries are taking part in the Copenhagen process to help develop vocational education and training (VET) systems. In December 2010 in Bruges (Belgium) the priorities for the Copenhagen process for 2011 to 2020 were set. This established a global vision for vocational education and training to be reached by the year 2020 – see the subchapter on lifelong learning statistics.

The lifelong learning programme has been a flagship programme of the European Commission in the field of education and training since 2007, covering all learning opportunities from childhood to old age. Over the period 2007 to 2013, this programme has a budget of nearly EUR 7 000 million in order to support projects that foster exchange, cooperation and mobility between education and training systems within the EU. It is made up of four sub-programmes that focus on the different stages of education and training, each with quantified targets:

- Comenius for schools should involve at least 3 million pupils in joint educational activities over the period of the programme;

- Erasmus for higher education should reach a total of 3 million individual participants in student mobility actions since the programme began;
- Leonardo da Vinci for vocational education and training should increase placements in enterprises to 80 000 persons per year by the end of the programme;
- Grundtvig for adult education should support the mobility of 7 000 individuals involved in adult education each year by 2013.

The measurement of progress towards these objectives within the field of education policy requires a range of comparable statistics on enrolment in education and training, numbers of graduates and teachers, language learning, student and researcher mobility, educational expenditure, as well as data on educational attainment and adult learning. Education statistics cover a range of subjects, including: expenditure, personnel, participation rates, and attainment. The standards for international statistics on education are set by three international organisations:

- the United Nations Educational, Scientific, and Cultural Organization (UNESCO) institute for statistics (UIS);
- the Organisation for Economic Cooperation and Development (OECD);
- Eurostat, the statistical office of the European Union.

The main source of data is a joint UNESCO/OECD/Eurostat (UOE) questionnaire on education statistics and this is the basis for the core components of the Eurostat database on education statistics; Eurostat also collects data on regional enrolments and foreign language learning. Data on educational attainment and adult learning are mainly provided by household surveys, in particular the EU labour force survey (LFS), which is complemented by an adult education survey (AES).

4.1 School enrolment and levels of education

School helps young people acquire the basic life skills and competences necessary for their personal development. The quality of a pupil's school experience affects not only their development, but also his or her place in society, educational attainment, and employment opportunities. The quality of education may be linked to teaching standards, which in turn are related to the demands placed upon teachers, the training they receive and the roles they are asked to fill.

With this in mind, several European Union (EU) Member States are revising their school curricula in line with the changing needs of society and the economy, as well as reflecting on how to improve teacher training and evaluation. This subchapter presents statistical data on relevant aspects of teaching and education in the EU, such as class sizes and enrolments.

Main statistical findings

The level of educational enrolment depends on a wide range of factors, such as the age structure of the population, legal requirements concerning the start and end of compulsory education, and the availability of educational resources – in particular, access to specialist tertiary education may be limited in some of the smallest Member States.

In 2009, there were approximately 93.0 million pupils and students enrolled in educational establishments in the EU-27. The highest share (15.0 %) of pupils and students in the EU-27 total was accounted for by Germany, where 14.0 million pupils and students attended educational establishments in 2009; this figure was 1.2 million higher than the next largest student population in the United Kingdom, and 1.7 million higher than in France (see Table 4.1.1).

The proportion of students found in each level of education varied somewhat between the Member States, most notably for primary and lower secondary levels of education. This variation reflects, to some degree, the demographic structure of each population. However, the high proportion of pupils in primary education in Luxembourg (45.2 % in 2009) reflects the relatively undeveloped tertiary education sector in this country. At the other end of the spectrum, Greece, Slovenia, the Baltic Member States, Romania and Poland all had relatively high proportions (more than one quarter) of their student populations within the tertiary education sector.

The figures above exclude pre-primary education: just over nine out of ten (90.5 %) four-year-olds in the EU-27 were in education in 2009 (see Figure 4.1.1). The general objectives for pre-primary education are fairly similar across countries, focusing on the development of children's independence, well-being, self-confidence, citizenship, and preparation for life and learning at school. Enrolment in pre-primary education is normally voluntary and participation rates of four-year-olds ranged from 100 % in France, to less than one child in two in Ireland. The strategic framework for European cooperation in education and training adopted in May 2009 set a benchmark to be achieved by 2020 that at least 95 % of children between the age of four and the age for starting compulsory primary education should participate in early childhood education.

More than three quarters (77.6 %) of all 18-year-olds within the EU-27 remained within the education system in 2009. However, this ratio rose to above 90 % in five Member States, while just over half of all 18-year-olds were still attending an educational establishment in the United Kingdom; the ratio was lower still in Cyprus (see Figure 4.1.2). These figures may reflect a number of factors, in particular the need for students to go abroad to continue their (tertiary) education, or the practise (in some countries) of making students re-take a whole year if their performance at the end of an academic year is deemed unsatisfactory.

School expectancy is an indicator that measures the number of years that a child starting school can expect to stay within the education system. A ranking of Member States based on this indicator is broadly similar to one based on the proportion of 18-year-olds remaining within the education system, as those Member States with longer school expectancy generally have a higher proportion of 18-year-olds in education. Nevertheless, Ireland had a much larger proportion of 18-year-olds in education than the average for the EU-27, but a length of

school expectancy that was in line with the EU-27 average. Greece and Portugal had the reverse situation, as they were among those Member States with the lowest proportions of 18-year-olds in education, despite longer than average school expectancy (see Figure 4.1.3).

Pupil-teacher ratios

Pupil-teacher ratios within primary education ranged from an average of less than 10 pupils per teacher in Malta, Lithuania and Denmark in 2009, to almost double that rate in France and the United Kingdom (both above 19 pupils per teacher). Between 2004 and 2009 there was a general reduction in the average number of pupils per teacher within primary education establishments in most of the Member States. The most significant of these was recorded in Malta, where the pupil-teacher ratio was halved from 19.0 (one of the highest ratios among the Member States) to 9.4 (the lowest of all Member States); at the other end of the range, the most notable increases in pupil-teacher ratios between 2004 and 2009 were recorded in Slovenia and Luxembourg (see Table 4.1.2).

In 2009 the average number of pupils per teacher was generally lower for secondary education than for primary education. Nevertheless, nine Member States recorded higher average numbers of pupils per teacher within upper secondary education than in primary education, most notably Malta, and to a somewhat lesser extent Finland, Hungary and Poland. Luxembourg and Poland recorded notably higher pupil-teacher ratios for lower secondary education than for primary education.

Youth education attainment level and early leavers from education and training

Data on educational attainment show that, in 2010, close to four fifths (79.0 %) of the EU-27's population aged 20 to 24 had completed at least an upper secondary level of education, a figure that reached 81.8 % for women. However, 14.1 % of those aged 18 to 24 (16.0 % of men and 12.2 % of women) were early leavers from education and training, with at most a lower secondary education. The overall share of early leavers from education and training

fell by 1.7 percentage points between 2005 and 2010, down from 15.8 %, with large reductions (in percentage point terms) in Portugal, Bulgaria, Luxembourg and Cyprus (see Table 4.1.3). The strategic framework for European cooperation in education and training adopted a benchmark to be achieved by 2020 that the share of early leavers from education and training should be less than 10 %, a level already reached in 2010 by eight of the EU Member States.

Data sources and availability

The standards for international statistics on education are set by three international organisations:

- the United Nations Educational, Scientific, and Cultural Organisation (UNESCO) institute for statistics (UIS);
- the Organisation for Economic Cooperation and Development (OECD);
- Eurostat, the statistical office of the European Union.

The main source of data is a joint UNESCO/OECD/Eurostat (UOE) questionnaire on education statistics and this is the basis for the core components of Eurostat's database on education statistics; Eurostat also collects data on regional enrolments. Data on educational attainment are mainly provided by household surveys, in particular the EU labour force survey (LFS).

The international standard classification of education (ISCED) is the basis for international education statistics, describing different levels of education, as well as fields of education and training; it was first developed in 1976 by UNESCO and revised in 1997. The current version, ISCED 97, distinguishes seven levels of education: pre-primary education (level 0); primary education (level 1); lower secondary education (level 2); upper secondary education (level 3); post-secondary non-tertiary education (level 4); tertiary education (first stage) (level 5); tertiary education (second stage) (level 6). In 2007, a review of ISCED began and at the time of writing it is expected that the revised version will be presented to UNESCO's General Conference in November 2011.

The indicator for four-year-olds in education presents the percentage of four-year-olds who are enrolled in education-oriented pre-primary institutions. Day nurseries, playgroups and day care centres, where the staff are not required to hold a qualification in education, are not included.

The indicator of school expectancy corresponds to how many years, on average, a child starting in school can expect to stay at school (calculated by adding the single-year enrolment rates for all ages).

Pupil-teacher ratios are calculated by dividing the number of full-time equivalent pupils and students in each level of education by the number of full-time equivalent teachers at the same level; this ratio should not be confused with average class sizes.

Youth education attainment is defined as the proportion of the population aged 20 to 24 having completed at least an upper secondary education, in other words, those with a minimum education level of ISCED levels 3a, 3b or 3c long; the denominator consists of the total population of the same age group, excluding non-response.

The indicator for early leavers from education and training is defined as the proportion of the population aged 18 to 24 with at most a lower secondary level of education (ISCED levels 1, 2 or 3c short), who are no longer in further education or training; the denominator consists of the total population of the same age group, excluding non-response.

Context

Demographic trends in the last three decades reflect reductions in birth rates that have resulted in the structure of the EU's population ageing and the proportion of those aged under 30 decreasing in the majority of Member States. These changes can have a significant impact on human and material resources required for the sound functioning of education systems – such as average class sizes or teacher recruitment strategies.

Age is generally the sole criterion for admission to compulsory primary education, which starts at the age of five or six in most Member States, although

Bulgaria, the Baltic Member States, Finland and Sweden have a compulsory starting age of seven. In February 2011, the European Commission adopted a Communication titled 'Early childhood education and care: providing all our children with the best start for the world of tomorrow' (COM(2011) 66). This noted that early childhood education and care is an essential foundation for successful lifelong learning, social integration, personal development and later employability and that it is particularly beneficial for the disadvantaged and can help to lift children out of poverty and family dysfunction.

In general, compulsory education is completed at the end of lower secondary education, although in some countries it continues into upper secondary education. On average, compulsory education lasts nine or ten years in most of the EU, lasting longest in Hungary, the Netherlands and the United Kingdom.

Most Europeans spend significantly longer in education than the legal minimum requirement. This reflects the choice to enrol in higher education, as well as increased enrolment in pre-primary education and wider participation in life-long learning initiatives, such as mature (adult) students returning to education – often in order to retrain or equip themselves for a career change. Nevertheless around one in seven children leave school or training early and this has an impact on individuals, society and economies. In January 2011, the European Commission adopted a Communication titled 'Tackling early school leaving: a key contribution to the Europe 2020 agenda' (COM(2011) 18). This outlined the reasons why pupils decide to leave school early and gave an overview of existing and planned measures to tackle this issue across the EU.

Table 4.1.1: Pupils and students (excluding pre-primary education), 2004 and 2009 (¹)

| | Total number of pupils and students (ISCED 1-6) (1 000) | | (% of total) | | | | | | | |
| | | | Primary level of education (ISCED 1) | | Lower secondary level of education (ISCED 2) | | Upper and post-secondary non-tertiary education (ISCED 3-4) | | Tertiary education (ISCED 5-6) | |
	2004	2009	2004	2009	2004	2009	2004	2009	2004	2009
EU-27	97 893	92 958	29.7	30.2	24.1	23.8	27.5	25.0	18.7	21.0
Belgium	2 333	2 436	32.0	30.0	18.1	13.7	33.4	38.8	16.5	17.5
Bulgaria	1 250	1 111	25.1	23.5	26.4	21.7	30.2	30.1	18.3	24.7
Czech Republic	1 934	1 849	27.6	24.9	26.0	21.8	29.9	30.7	16.5	22.5
Denmark	1 127	1 160	37.2	35.1	20.0	21.4	23.5	23.3	19.3	20.2
Germany	14 583	13 984	22.8	22.7	38.5	36.1	22.7	23.7	16.1	17.5
Estonia	293	250	31.4	29.4	22.6	17.8	23.5	25.5	22.4	27.4
Ireland	1 033	1 076	43.6	46.3	17.1	16.4	21.1	20.3	18.2	17.0
Greece (²)	1 983	2 009	33.2	31.7	16.6	17.1	20.1	19.5	30.1	31.7
Spain	7 509	7 677	34.9	36.6	26.3	25.6	14.3	14.4	24.5	23.5
France	11 903	12 251	32.0	33.9	27.5	26.4	22.2	22.0	18.3	17.7
Italy	9 380	9 514	29.8	30.0	19.7	18.8	29.3	30.0	21.2	21.1
Cyprus	148	152	41.7	36.7	22.4	21.1	21.9	21.9	14.1	20.3
Latvia	502	414	18.4	27.6	33.8	17.8	22.4	24.2	25.4	30.3
Lithuania	811	719	21.0	18.0	41.2	35.8	15.3	16.9	22.5	29.3
Luxembourg	71	78	48.4	45.2	24.2	25.9	27.3	28.8	:	:
Hungary	1 988	1 825	22.5	21.4	25.0	23.8	31.2	33.1	21.2	21.8
Malta	81	75	38.3	32.9	36.4	35.1	15.6	18.2	9.7	13.8
Netherlands	3 264	3 402	39.3	37.9	24.1	22.4	19.9	21.5	16.6	18.2
Austria	1 452	1 469	25.7	22.6	27.4	25.3	30.5	31.1	16.4	21.0
Poland	9 004	8 008	31.7	28.7	18.8	17.5	26.8	27.0	22.7	26.8
Portugal	1 945	2 161	40.1	35.2	20.0	24.2	19.6	23.4	20.3	17.3
Romania	3 901	3 879	25.8	22.1	28.6	23.0	28.0	26.5	17.6	28.3
Slovenia	411	381	22.8	28.2	21.4	15.1	30.4	26.7	25.4	30.0
Slovakia	1 108	1 035	23.0	21.1	33.5	28.4	28.6	27.9	14.9	22.7
Finland	1 206	1 237	32.2	28.4	16.5	16.1	26.5	31.5	24.9	24.0
Sweden	2 123	2 028	35.4	32.8	19.2	18.9	25.2	27.5	20.2	20.8
United Kingdom	16 550	12 780	28.3	34.6	14.0	19.9	44.1	26.6	13.6	18.9
Iceland	82	87	37.8	34.3	16.9	15.7	27.4	30.7	17.9	19.4
Liechtenstein	6	6	37.3	33.8	28.6	28.1	25.3	26.2	8.8	11.9
Norway	1 052	1 081	41.1	39.5	17.3	17.5	21.3	22.7	20.3	20.3
Switzerland	1 330	1 361	40.3	37.0	22.1	21.6	22.7	24.1	14.8	17.3
Croatia	730	710	26.6	24.5	29.0	29.6	27.1	26.3	17.3	19.6
FYR of Macedonia	377	378	30.1	29.8	31.8	27.8	25.7	25.1	12.4	17.3
Turkey	16 379	17 471	64.0	61.3	–	–	24.0	22.0	12.0	16.7
Japan	19 435	18 517	37.8	39.0	19.7	19.8	21.5	20.1	21.0	21.1
United States	66 075	68 685	37.2	35.8	19.8	18.5	17.4	17.9	25.6	27.8

(¹) Refer to the Internet metadata file (http://epp.eurostat.ec.europa.eu/cache/ITY_SDDS/en/educ_esms.htm).
(²) 2008 instead of 2009.

Source: Eurostat (online data codes: tps00051 and educ_enrl1tl)

Figure 4.1.1: Four-year-olds in education, 2009 (^{1})
(% of all four-year-olds)

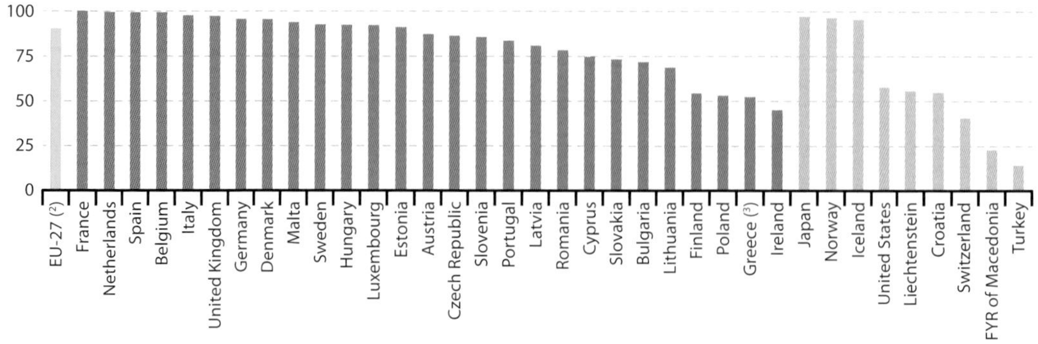

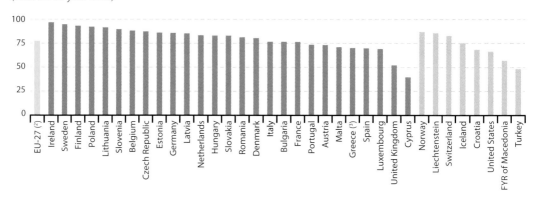

(^{1}) Refer to the Internet metadata file (http://epp.eurostat.ec.europa.eu/cache/ITY_SDDS/en/educ_esms.htm).
(^{2}) Includes Greek data for 2008.
(^{3}) 2008.

Source: Eurostat (online data code: tps00053)

Figure 4.1.2: 18-year-olds in education, 2009 (^{1})
(% of all 18-year-olds)

(^{1}) Refer to the Internet metadata file (http://epp.eurostat.ec.europa.eu/cache/ITY_SDDS/en/educ_esms.htm).
(^{2}) Includes Greek data for 2008.
(^{3}) 2008.

Source: Eurostat (online data code: tps00060)

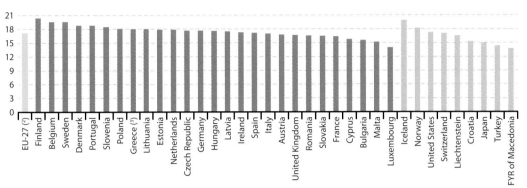

Figure 4.1.3: School expectancy, 2009 (¹)
(years)

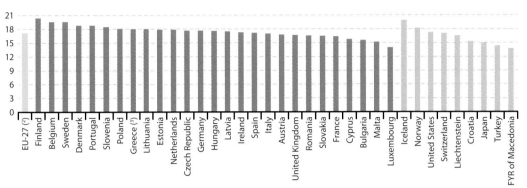

(¹) School expectancy corresponds to the expected years of education over a lifetime and has been calculated adding the single-year enrolment rates for all ages.
(²) Includes Greek data for 2008.
(³) 2008.

Source: Eurostat (online data code: tps00052)

Table 4.1.2: Pupil-teacher ratio in primary, lower and upper secondary education, 2004 and 2009 (¹)
(average number of pupils per teacher)

	Primary education (ISCED 1)		Lower secondary/ second stage of basic education (ISCED 2)		Upper secondary education (ISCED 3)	
	2004	2009	2004	2009	2004	2009
Belgium	12.9	12.5	10.6	8.1	9.2	10.2
Bulgaria	16.8	17.4	12.9	12.5	12.1	12.0
Czech Republic	17.9	18.4	13.5	11.5	12.6	12.2
Denmark	11.3	9.9	:	:	:	:
Germany	18.8	17.4	15.6	15.1	13.9	13.9
Estonia	:	16.2	:	15.7	:	16.8
Ireland	18.3	15.9	:	:	14.3	12.6
Greece (²)	11.3	10.1	8.2	7.7	8.4	7.3
Spain	14.3	13.3	12.9	10.1	8.0	9.3
France	19.4	19.7	14.1	14.9	10.3	9.6
Italy	10.7	10.7	10.3	10.0	11.5	11.8
Cyprus	17.8	14.5	12.1	10.2	11.3	10.2
Latvia	14.9	11.4	12.8	8.7	12.1	11.5
Lithuania	11.0	9.7	8.7	7.6	:	:
Luxembourg	10.7	11.6	:	18.4	9.0	9.2
Hungary	10.7	10.7	10.2	10.8	12.3	12.8
Malta	19.0	9.4	10.2	6.5	10.1	15.8
Netherlands	15.9	15.8	:	:	15.8	16.1
Austria	15.1	12.6	10.4	9.6	11.0	10.2
Poland	:	10.2	:	12.9	:	12.0
Portugal	11.1	11.3	10.0	7.6	7.3	7.7
Romania	17.8	16.4	13.4	12.2	16.8	14.4
Slovenia	15.2	16.7	11.8	7.9	14.3	14.3
Slovakia	18.9	17.7	13.9	14.0	14.2	15.1
Finland	16.3	13.6	10.0	10.1	16.2	16.6
Sweden	12.1	12.1	11.9	11.3	14.0	13.2
United Kingdom	21.1	19.9	17.1	16.1	12.6	12.3
Iceland	11.4	9.9	:	:	11.1	10.9
Liechtenstein	10.3	9.2	8.1	8.5	7.9	8.1
Norway	11.9	10.7	10.5	9.9	9.6	9.4
Croatia	18.3	15.4	13.2	11.0	11.5	10.9
FYR of Macedonia	20.1	16.5	15.2	12.0	18.0	15.1
Turkey	26.5	22.9	:	:	16.9	16.9
Japan	19.6	18.6	15.3	14.5	13.2	12.2
United States	15.0	14.8	15.2	14.3	16.0	15.1

(¹) Refer to the Internet metadata file (http://epp.eurostat.ec.europa.eu/cache/ITY_SDDS/en/educ_esms.htm).
(²) 2007 instead of 2009.

Source: Eurostat (online data codes: tps00054 and educ_iste)

Table 4.1.3: Youth education attainment level and early leavers from education and training, 2005 and 2010 ([1])
(%)

	Youth education attainment level				Early leavers from education and training			
	Total		Male	Female	Total		Male	Female
	2005	2010	2010	2010	2005	2010	2010	2010
EU-27	77.5	79.0	76.2	81.8	15.8	14.1	16.0	12.2
Euro area	74.3	76.1	72.7	79.5	17.6	15.6	18.0	13.1
Belgium	81.8	82.5	80.3	84.7	12.9	11.9	13.8	10.0
Bulgaria	76.5	84.4	85.0	83.6	20.4	13.9	13.2	14.5
Czech Republic	91.2	91.9	91.1	92.8	6.2	4.9	4.9	4.8
Denmark ([2])	77.1	68.3	61.4	75.6	8.7	10.7	13.6	7.5
Germany ([3])	71.5	74.4	72.2	76.7	13.5	11.9	12.7	11.0
Estonia ([4])	82.6	83.2	76.9	89.5	13.4	11.6	15.2	9.3
Ireland	85.8	88.0	85.3	90.6	12.5	10.5	12.6	8.4
Greece	84.1	83.4	79.5	87.2	13.6	13.7	16.5	10.8
Spain ([3])	61.8	61.2	54.7	67.9	30.8	28.4	33.5	23.1
France	83.4	82.8	79.8	85.8	12.2	12.8	15.4	10.3
Italy	73.6	76.3	72.6	80.2	22.0	18.8	22.0	15.4
Cyprus ([3])	80.4	86.3	83.2	89.0	18.2	12.6	16.2	9.8
Latvia	79.9	79.9	74.1	85.9	14.4	13.3	17.2	9.4
Lithuania ([5])	87.8	86.9	84.2	89.7	8.1	8.1	9.9	6.2
Luxembourg ([6])	71.1	73.4	67.9	78.7	13.3	7.1	8.0	6.0
Hungary	83.4	84.0	82.0	85.9	12.5	10.5	11.5	9.5
Malta	53.7	53.3	47.0	60.8	38.9	36.9	41.0	32.4
Netherlands ([2])	75.6	77.6	73.7	81.6	13.5	10.1	12.2	7.9
Austria	85.9	85.6	84.9	86.2	9.1	8.3	8.4	8.2
Poland	91.1	91.1	88.4	93.8	5.3	5.4	7.2	3.5
Portugal	49.0	58.7	54.8	62.7	38.8	28.7	32.7	24.6
Romania	76.0	78.2	77.7	78.8	19.6	18.4	18.6	18.2
Slovenia ([7])	90.5	89.1	86.1	92.8	4.9	5.0	6.4	3.3
Slovakia	91.8	93.2	93.2	93.1	6.3	4.7	4.6	4.9
Finland	83.4	84.2	82.8	85.6	10.3	10.3	11.6	9.0
Sweden	87.5	85.9	84.9	86.9	10.8	9.7	10.9	8.5
United Kingdom ([3])	78.1	80.4	78.9	82.0	11.6	14.9	15.8	14.0
Iceland	50.8	53.4	51.4	55.5	24.9	22.6	26.0	19.0
Norway ([2])	96.2	71.1	66.4	75.9	4.6	17.4	21.4	13.2
Switzerland	78.3	82.3	80.5	84.3	9.7	6.6	6.1	7.0
Croatia ([7])	93.8	95.3	94.0	96.8	5.1	3.9	4.9	2.8
FYR of Macedonia	:	82.8	86.0	79.5	:	15.5	13.7	17.5
Turkey	:	51.1	57.2	46.0	:	43.1	37.8	47.9

([1]) Refer to the Internet metadata file (http://epp.eurostat.ec.europa.eu/cache/ITY_SDDS/en/lfsi_edu_a_esms.htm); early leavers from education and training: based on annual averages of quarterly data.
([2]) Break in series between 2005 and 2010.
([3]) Early leavers from education and training: break in series between 2005 and 2010.
([4]) Male and female early leavers from education and training, unreliable or uncertain data; female early leavers from education and training, 2009.
([5]) Female early leavers from education and training: unreliable or uncertain data.
([6]) Early leavers from education and training, 2010: unreliable or uncertain data.
([7]) Early leavers from education and training: unreliable or uncertain data.

Source: Eurostat (online data codes: tsiir110 and tsisc060)

4.2 Foreign language learning

Currently there are 23 official languages recognised within the European Union (EU), in addition to which there are regional, minority languages, and languages spoken by migrant populations.

School is the main opportunity for the vast majority of people to learn these languages – although linguistic diversity is actively encouraged within schools, universities and adult education centres, as well as the workplace. This subchapter presents statistics in relation to language learning at primary and secondary schools in the EU Member States, EFTA and candidate countries.

Main statistical findings

Primary education

Within primary education, a clear majority of pupils (choose to) study English. Indeed, learning English is mandatory in several countries within secondary education institutions, and so a number of Member States have close to 100 % of pupils learning this language already in primary education, as shown in Figure 4.2.1. The highest shares of primary education pupils studying English in 2009 were recorded in Italy, Spain, Austria and Greece (2008 data), with more than nine out of every ten children studying English in each of these countries (which was also the case in Norway and Croatia). The relative importance of English as a foreign language may be further magnified because pupils tend to receive more instruction in their first foreign language than they do for any subsequent languages they (choose to) study.

The central and eastern European Member States that joined the EU in 2004 and 2007 are in a particular position with regard to language teaching, as learning Russian was compulsory for many pupils in the past. This situation has changed rapidly and these days most pupils have more choice concerning the language(s) they wish to study. In most of these countries there has been a marked increase in the proportion of pupils learning English, often above 40 % of all students and in Bulgaria, Lithuania, Poland and Estonia (2008 data) over 65 %.

Luxembourg is also of particular interest, insofar as there are three official languages, with most pupils receiving instruction in Luxembourgish, German and French at primary level; English is introduced at secondary school.

Secondary education

Turning to language learning in upper secondary education (as shown in Table 4.2.1), some 94.6 % of all EU-27 students at ISCED level 3 were studying English as a foreign language in 2009, compared with around one quarter studying German (26.5 %) or French (25.7 %).

Luxembourg and the Czech Republic stood out as the countries with the highest proportion (100 %) of secondary education students (at ISCED level 3) learning two or more languages in 2009, while there were also shares above 90 % recorded in Slovakia, Finland, Estonia (2008 data), Romania, Slovenia, Sweden and France; note this indicator includes all foreign languages, not just German, English and French.

Data sources and availability

Data on the number of pupils studying foreign languages are related to the corresponding numbers of students enrolled; mentally handicapped students enrolled in special schools are excluded.

The average number of foreign languages learned per pupil is collected for different ISCED levels. The data refer to all pupils, even if teaching languages does not start in the first years of instruction for the particular ISCED level considered. This indicator is defined as the sum of language students divided by the total number of students enrolled in the educational level considered. Each student studying a foreign language is counted once for each language he or she is studying, in other words students studying more than one language are counted as many times as the number of languages studied. The educational curriculum drawn up in each country defines the languages,

which are to be considered as foreign languages in that country and this definition is applied during data collection. Regional languages are included, if they are considered as alternatives to foreign languages by the curriculum. Only foreign languages studied as compulsory subjects or as compulsory curriculum options are included. The study of languages when the subject is offered in addition to the minimum curriculum is not included. Also data on non-nationals studying their native language in special classes or those studying the language of the host country are excluded.

Context

For several decades it has been mandatory for most European children to learn at least one foreign language during their compulsory education, with the time devoted to foreign language instruction generally increasing in recent years. In 2002, the Barcelona European Council recommended that at least two foreign languages should be taught to all pupils from a very early age. This recommendation has been implemented to varying degrees, usually for compulsory secondary

education, either by making it mandatory to teach a second language, or ensuring that pupils have the possibility to study a second foreign language as part of their curriculum. In September 2008 the European Commission adopted a Communication titled 'Multilingualism: an asset for Europe and a shared commitment' (COM(2008) 566 final), which was followed in November 2008 by a Council Resolution on a European strategy for multilingualism (2008/C 320/01). The Communication addressed languages in the wider context of social cohesion and prosperity and focused on actions to encourage and assist citizens in acquiring language skills. It explored issues such as:

- the role languages play in developing mutual understanding in a multicultural society;
- how language skills improve employability and ensure a competitive edge for European businesses;
- what to do to encourage European citizens to speak two languages in addition to their mother tongue;
- how the media and new technologies can serve as a bridge between speakers of different languages.

Figure 4.2.1: Proportion of pupils in primary education learning foreign languages, by language, 2009 (¹)
(%)

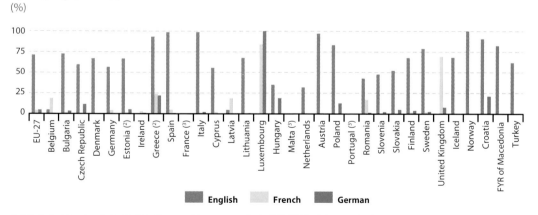

(¹) Refer to the Internet metadata file (http://epp.eurostat.ec.europa.eu/cache/ITY_SDDS/en/educ_esms.htm).
(²) 2008.
(³) Not available.

Source: Eurostat (online data code: educ_ilang), UNESCO Institute for Statistics (UIS), OECD

Table 4.2.1: Foreign languages learnt per pupil in secondary education, 2005 and 2009 (¹)
(%)

| | Proportion of students learning 2 or more languages at ISCED level 3 GEN | | Upper secondary education (ISCED 3) | | | | | |
| | | | Pupils learning English in general programmes | | Pupils learning French in general programmes | | Pupils learning German in general programmes | |
	2005	2009	2005	2009	2005	2009	2005	2009
EU-27	:	64.7	79.6	94.6	27.7	25.7	25.4	26.5
Belgium	88.7	89.3	94.4	95.0	47.8	49.3	28.4	29.3
Bulgaria	76.9	74.5	83.1	87.5	15.4	14.5	40.3	35.9
Czech Republic	100.0	100.0	98.1	100.0	22.4	24.8	72.2	60.6
Denmark	67.3	60.5	82.6	91.6	16.8	10.7	49.7	35.1
Germany	:	:	93.8	91.8	30.0	28.1	–	–
Estonia (²)	80.9	97.7	92.6	96.2	6.1	6.9	44.1	39.2
Ireland	8.9	7.8	–	–	61.7	58.2	19.1	16.4
Greece (²)	6.7	7.9	94.5	95.0	8.6	8.2	2.4	3.3
Spain	28.1	27.7	95.3	94.4	28.0	27.0	1.3	1.1
France	89.6	90.6	:	99.5	–	–	:	21.3
Italy	20.8	25.8	85.1	96.5	18.1	20.1	6.5	6.9
Cyprus	:	84.4	89.1	91.4	34.5	40.6	3.4	2.2
Latvia	74.1	77.3	93.7	97.2	3.6	3.9	38.8	28.8
Lithuania	55.0	47.6	80.2	90.8	5.9	3.8	28.4	18.8
Luxembourg	100.0	100.0	96.7	97.7	96.7	100.0	96.7	100.0
Hungary	:	44.9	73.0	79.4	6.0	6.6	51.4	48.7
Malta	14.0	:	65.6	:	6.6	:	1.7	:
Netherlands	100.0	77.8	100.0	100.0	69.5	64.2	86.2	69.8
Austria	76.2	68.2	96.9	98.5	54.1	42.5	–	–
Poland	:	73.6	96.3	92.2	12.1	8.7	72.5	54.4
Portugal	17.1	:	49.9	:	19.1	:	2.5	:
Romania	91.8	96.4	94.2	98.1	84.2	85.3	11.9	12.1
Slovenia	95.0	92.2	98.8	92.8	10.9	9.8	78.2	66.4
Slovakia	99.3	99.8	97.3	98.3	14.4	16.4	75.2	67.9
Finland	99.7	99.7	99.7	99.7	19.3	17.9	37.9	27.8
Sweden	92.6	91.8	100.0	99.9	24.2	20.0	34.5	27.0
United Kingdom	6.6	7.4	–	–	40.0	28.9	15.2	10.7
Iceland	67.8	63.3	77.2	73.2	16.4	13.7	32.4	25.4
Norway	:	:	:	44.8	:	12.8	:	20.3
Croatia	90.6	90.1	98.4	99.0	3.8	3.7	66.2	62.5
Turkey	:	:	:	81.8	:	1.4	:	14.8

(¹) Refer to the Internet metadata file (http://epp.eurostat.ec.europa.eu/cache/ITY_SDDS/en/educ_esms.htm).
(²) 2008 instead of 2009.

Source: Eurostat (online data codes: educ_thfrlan, tps00057, tps00058 and tps00059), Unesco Institute for Statistics (UIS), OECD

4.3 Educational expenditure

Expenditure on education may help foster economic growth, enhance productivity, contribute to people's personal and social development, and help reduce social inequalities. The proportion of total financial resources devoted to education is one of the key choices made by governments in each country of the European Union (EU). In a similar vein, enterprises, students and their families also make decisions on the financial resources that they will set aside for education.

Main statistical findings

Public expenditure on education in the EU-27 in 2008 was equivalent to 5.1 % of GDP, while the expenditure of both public and private sources of funds on educational institutions amounted to 5.8 % of GDP (see Table 4.3.1).

The highest public spending on education relative to GDP was observed in Denmark (7.8 % of GDP), while Cyprus (7.4 %), Sweden (6.7 %), Belgium (6.5 %), Finland (6.1 %) and Malta (6.0 %) also recorded relatively high proportions. Most Member States reported that public expenditure on education accounted for between 4 % and 6 % of their GDP, although this share was lower in Slovakia. Between 2003 and 2008 the combined public and private expenditure on education as a share of GDP rose by 1.3 percentage points in Ireland and by 0.9 percentage points in the United Kingdom; Hungary and Slovenia recorded the largest decreases, both down 0.8 percentage points. It should be noted that changes in GDP (growth or contraction) can mask significant increases or decreases made in terms of education spending.

Declining birth rates in many countries will result in reduced school age populations, which will have an effect on ratios such as the average expenditure per pupil (given that expenditure is held constant). Annual expenditure on public and private educational institutions shows that an average of PPS 6 459 was spent per pupil/student in 2008 in the EU-27. This ratio was approximately three times higher in Austria (the highest average expenditure among the Member States in 2008) than in Bulgaria (the lowest average).

Data sources and availability

The standards for international statistics on education are set by three international organisations:

- the United Nations Educational, Scientific, and Cultural Organization (UNESCO) Institute for Statistics (UIS);
- the Organisation for Economic Cooperation and Development (OECD);
- Eurostat, the statistical office of the European Union.

The main source of data is a joint UNESCO/OECD/Eurostat (UOE) questionnaire on education statistics and this is the basis for the core components of the Eurostat database on education statistics.

Indicators on education expenditure cover schools, universities and other public and private institutions involved in delivering or supporting educational services. Expenditure on institutions is not limited to that made on instructional services, but also includes public and private expenditure on ancillary services for students and families, where these services are provided through educational institutions. At the tertiary level, spending on research and development can also be significant and is included, to the extent that the research is performed by educational institutions.

Total public expenditure on education includes direct public funding for educational institutions and transfers to households and enterprises. Generally, the public sector funds education either by bearing directly the current and capital expenses of educational institutions (direct expenditure for educational institutions) or by supporting students and their families with scholarships and public loans as well as by transferring public subsidies for educational activities to private enterprises or non-profit organisations (transfers to private households and enterprises). Both types of transactions together are reported as total public expenditure on education.

Expenditure on educational institutions from private sources comprises: school fees; materials (such as textbooks and teaching equipment); transport to

school (if organised by the school); meals (if provided by the school); boarding fees, and; expenditure by employers on initial vocational training.

Expenditure per pupil/student in public and private institutions measures how much central, regional and local government, private households, religious institutions and enterprises spend per pupil/student. It includes expenditure for personnel, as well as other current and capital expenditure. Public schools/institutions are defined as those which are directly or indirectly administered by a public education authority. Private schools/institutions are directly or indirectly administered by a non-governmental organisation (such as a church, trade union, a private business concern or another body).

Context

Education accounts for a significant proportion of public expenditure in all of the EU Member States – the most important budget item being expenditure on staff. The cost of teaching increases significantly as a child moves through the education system, with expenditure per pupil/student considerably higher

in universities than in primary schools. Although tertiary education costs more per head, the highest proportion of total education spending is devoted to secondary education systems, as these teach a larger share of the total number of pupils/students.

There is an ongoing debate in many EU Member States as to how to increase or maintain funding for education, improve efficiency and promote equity – a challenge that has become harder in the context of the financial and economic crisis and, in particular, increased levels of public debt. The debate is not purely about the levels and source of finance, but also concerns proposals for reforms of education policies and systems and raises questions as to the development of labour force skills for the future, for the benefit of individuals and society. Possible approaches to funding include tuition fees, administrative or examination charges, balanced by the introduction of income-contingent grants or loans to try to stimulate enrolment rates in higher education, in particular among the less well-off members of society. Another potential fundraising source is partnerships between business and higher educational establishments.

Figure 4.3.1: Public expenditure on education, 2008 (¹)
(% of GDP)

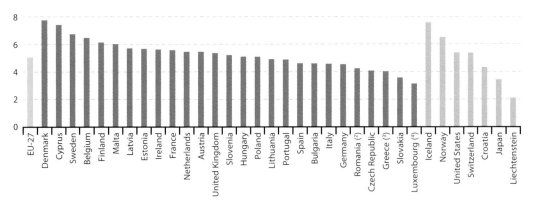

(¹) Refer to the Internet metadata file (http://epp.eurostat.ec.europa.eu/cache/ITY_SDDS/en/tsiir010_esms.htm).
(²) 2007.
(³) 2005.
(⁴) Excludes tertiary education, 2007.

Source: Eurostat (online data code: tsiir010)

Table 4.3.1: Expenditure on educational institutions, 2003 and 2008 (¹)

	Public expenditure (% of GDP)		Private expenditure (% of GDP)		Expenditure on public & private educational institutions per pupil/student (PPS for full-time equivalents)	
	2003	2008	2003	2008	2003	2008
EU-27	5.14	5.07	0.64	0.75	5414	6459
Euro area (EA–15)	5.03	4.97	:	:	:	:
Belgium	6.03	6.46	0.35	0.37	6343	7866
Bulgaria	4.23	4.61	0.67	0.58	1692	2840
Czech Republic	4.51	4.08	0.37	0.57	3354	4520
Denmark	8.33	7.75	0.32	0.55	7133	8701
Germany	4.70	4.55	0.92	0.70	6005	6953
Estonia	5.29	5.67	:	0.30	:	4226
Ireland (²)	4.38	5.62	0.31	0.34	5279	7172
Greece	3.56	:	0.20	:	3778	:
Spain	4.28	4.62	0.54	0.66	5042	6941
France	5.90	5.58	0.56	0.60	6038	7031
Italy	4.74	4.58	0.40	0.41	6118	6609
Cyprus	7.29	7.41	1.35	1.35	5968	8461
Latvia	5.32	5.71	0.83	0.60	2258	4332
Lithuania	5.16	4.91	0.46	0.52	2183	3622
Luxembourg (³)	3.77	3.15	:	:	:	:
Hungary (⁴)	5.89	5.10	0.56	0.54	:	3995
Malta (⁵)	4.70	6.01	1.40	0.31	4272	6220
Netherlands	5.42	5.46	0.94	0.92	6881	8069
Austria	5.57	5.46	0.31	0.50	7604	8836
Poland	5.35	5.09	0.66	0.74	2524	3781
Portugal	5.57	4.89	0.09	0.49	4287	4979
Romania (⁶)	3.45	4.25	:	0.50	:	:
Slovenia	5.82	5.22	0.83	0.63	5021	6529
Slovakia	4.30	3.59	0.45	0.70	2325	3523
Finland	6.44	6.13	0.13	0.15	5858	6988
Sweden	7.30	6.74	0.19	0.17	6825	8067
United Kingdom	5.24	5.36	0.95	1.72	6097	7942
Iceland	7.71	7.57	0.70	0.71	6727	8290
Liechtenstein (²)	2.46	2.11	:	:	5851	7788
Norway	7.54	6.51	0.10	0.09	8275	10084
Switzerland	6.00	5.37	0.62	0.56	:	:
Croatia	3.96	4.33	:	0.36	:	4147
FYR of Macedonia	3.39	:	:	:	:	:
Turkey (⁷)	2.96	2.86	0.04	:	:	:
Japan	3.70	3.44	1.25	1.66	6682	7530
United States	5.61	5.40	2.05	2.10	9924	11759

(¹) Refer to the Internet metadata file (http://epp.eurostat.ec.europa.eu/cache/ITY_SDDS/en/educ_esms.htm).
(²) Expenditure per pupil/student, 2007 instead of 2008.
(³) Excludes tertiary education; public expenditure, 2007 instead of 2008.
(⁴) Private expenditure and expenditure per pupil/student, 2006 instead of 2008.
(⁵) Private expenditure and expenditure per pupil/student, break in series.
(⁶) 2007 instead of 2008.
(⁷) 2006 instead of 2008.

Source: Eurostat (online data codes: educ_figdp, tps00068 and tps00067), UNESCO, OECD

4.4 Tertiary education

This subchapter presents statistics on tertiary education in the European Union (EU). Tertiary education – provided by universities and other higher education institutions – is the level of education following secondary schooling. The EU-27 has around 4 000 higher education (undergraduate and postgraduate) institutions, with around 19.5 million students. Some European universities are among the most prestigious in the world. Higher education plays an essential role in society, creating new knowledge, transferring knowledge to students and fostering innovation.

Since the introduction of the Bologna process (see the introduction for education and training) a major expansion in higher education systems has taken place, accompanied by significant reforms in degree structures and quality assurance systems. However, the financial and economic crisis has affected higher education in different ways, with some countries investing more and others making radical cutbacks in their education spending.

Main statistical findings

There were 19.5 million students active within tertiary education in the EU-27 in 2009 (see Table 4.4.1). Five Member States reported more than 2 million tertiary students in 2009, namely Germany, the United Kingdom, France, Poland and Italy; together with Spain these countries accounted for two thirds of all EU-27 students in tertiary education. Across the EU, one third (33.4 %) of the students in tertiary education were studying social sciences, business or law, with more female than male students in this field of education, as shown in Figure 4.4.1. The second largest number of students by field of education was in engineering, manufacturing and construction-related studies which accounted for 13.6 % of all students in tertiary education; male students accounted for three quarters of the students in this field.

In 2009, the median age of students in tertiary education ranged from 20.2 in Ireland to 22.4 in Spain, with the Nordic countries of Denmark, Sweden and

Finland, as well as Austria and Germany above this range (see Figure 4.4.2). The median age of students in tertiary education can be influenced by a number of factors: whether students postpone starting tertiary education either by choice (for example, by taking a break or a gap year between secondary and tertiary education) or obligation (for example, for military service); the length of the tertiary education courses studied; the extent to which mature students return to tertiary education later in life.

The strategic framework for European cooperation in education and training that was adopted in May 2009 set a number of benchmarks, including one for tertiary education, namely that by 2020 the proportion of 30 to 34-year-olds with tertiary educational attainment should be at least 40 %. Just over one third (33.6 %) of the population aged 30 to 34 in the EU-27 had a tertiary education in 2010, rising to over one third (37.2 %) among women, and falling to 30.0 % among men. In Ireland, Finland, Denmark, Sweden, Lithuania and Belgium the proportion of 30 to 34-year-old women with tertiary educational attainment was already 50 % or more in 2010 (see Figure 4.4.3); this was also the case in Norway. In contrast, less than 20 % of men in this age range had a tertiary education in the Czech Republic, Slovakia, Portugal, Romania, Italy and Malta.

Around 4.3 million students graduated from tertiary education establishments in the EU in 2009. An analysis of the number of graduates by field of education shows that 35.4 % had studied social sciences, business and law; this share was higher than the equivalent share (33.4 %) of tertiary education students still in the process of studying within this field, suggesting that less students had started this type of study in recent years, or that drop-out rates were higher in other fields. A similar situation was observed for health and welfare, which made up 15.4 % of graduates from 13.4 % of the tertiary student population, as well as in the smaller fields of services and agricultural and veterinary studies. The reverse situation was observed for the other fields of education shown in Figures 4.4.1 and 4.4.4, most notably for engineering, manufacturing and

construction-related studies, as well as science, mathematics and computing.

Within the EU, female graduates outnumbered male graduates by a ratio of approximately three to two; this ratio reached three to one for health and welfare fields of education (see Figure 4.4.4). Male graduates outnumbered female graduates slightly in agriculture and veterinary fields, more so in science, mathematics and computing fields, and by close to three to one in engineering, manufacturing and construction-related fields.

Data sources and availability

The standards for international statistics on education are set by three international organisations:

*   the United Nations Educational, Scientific, and Cultural Organisation (UNESCO) institute for statistics (UIS);
*   the Organisation for Economic Cooperation and Development (OECD);
*   Eurostat, the statistical office of the European Union.

The main source of data is a joint UNESCO/OECD/Eurostat (UOE) questionnaire on education statistics and this is the basis for the core components of the Eurostat database on education statistics.

The international standard classification of education (ISCED) is used to define levels of education: tertiary education includes both programmes which are largely theoretically based and designed to provide qualifications for entry to advanced research programmes and professions with high skills requirements, as well as programmes which are classified at the same level of competencies but are more occupationally oriented and lead to direct labour market access.

ISCED also classifies the fields of education, with 25 fields of education in all at the 2-digit level, which can be further refined at a 3-digit level. At the highest 1-digit level the following nine broad groups of fields of education are distinguished: general programmes; education; humanities and arts; social sciences, business and law; science; engineering, manufacturing and construction; agriculture; health and welfare; services.

ISCED was first developed in 1976 by UNESCO and revised in 1997. In 2007 a further review of ISCED began: at the time of writing it is expected that the revised version will be presented to UNESCO's General Conference in November 2011. Among other changes, the revised ISCED proposes four levels of tertiary education compared with two categories in the current version. A major reason behind this proposed change was to reflect better the structure of Bachelor's degrees, Master's degrees and Doctorates.

Context

While the Bologna process put in motion a series of reforms to make European higher education more compatible, comparable, competitive and attractive for students, it is only one strand of a broader effort concerning higher education. The modernisation agenda of universities is supported through the implementation of the 7th EU framework programme for research and the competitiveness and innovation programme. Furthermore, to establish synergies between the Bologna process and the Copenhagen process (for enhanced European cooperation in vocational education and training), the European Commission and EU Member States have established a European qualifications framework for lifelong learning (EQF) – see the subchapter on lifelong learning statistics.

In March 2008, the European institute of innovation and technology was established. Its aim is to bring together higher education, research and innovation through the creation of 'knowledge and innovation communities', while it should contribute towards Europe's capacity for innovation.

The integrated economic and employment guidelines were revised most recently as part of the Europe 2020 strategy for smart, sustainable and inclusive growth. Guideline 9 concerns improving the performance of education and training systems at all levels and increasing participation in tertiary education.

The Erasmus programme is one of the most well-known European programmes. Around 4 000 higher education institutions take part in it and some 2.3 million students have already participated in exchanges since it started in 1987. Erasmus became part of the EU's lifelong learning programme in 2007 and was expanded to cover student placements in enterprises, university staff training and teaching for enterprise staff. The programme seeks to expand its mobility actions in the coming years, with a target of 3 million Erasmus students by 2012.

Some of the most recent policy initiatives in this area include efforts to develop links between universities and businesses. In April 2009, the European Commission presented a Communication titled 'A new partnership for the modernisation of universities: the EU forum for university-business dialogue'. The Communication included proposals to establish a university-business forum as a European platform for dialogue, to enable and stimulate the exchange of good practice, discuss common problems, and work together on possible solutions.

Table 4.4.1: Students in tertiary education, 2009 (¹)

	Total number of students in tertiary education (1 000)	of which, studying (%)						
		Humanities & arts	Social sciences, business & law	Science, mathematics & computing	Engineering, manufacturing & construction	Agriculture & veterinary	Health & welfare	Services
EU-27 (²)	19 470	11.9	33.4	9.7	13.6	1.6	13.4	3.8
Belgium	425	10.4	29.7	5.9	10.0	2.7	19.7	1.5
Bulgaria	274	7.7	44.1	4.9	19.6	2.3	6.7	8.0
Czech Republic	417	8.8	32.7	10.8	14.7	3.7	10.2	5.1
Denmark	235	14.6	31.2	8.7	9.6	1.4	21.6	2.1
Germany (³)	2 439	14.0	26.3	14.3	15.4	1.4	18.3	2.8
Estonia	68	12.3	39.6	9.5	13.3	2.2	8.3	7.8
Ireland	183	16.0	27.4	12.9	12.6	1.4	15.6	5.0
Greece (⁴)	638	14.0	31.4	13.6	17.0	5.8	9.2	3.6
Spain	1 801	10.4	31.8	10.4	17.5	1.8	12.5	4.9
France	2 173	14.7	36.5	12.5	12.9	1.1	15.9	3.4
Italy (⁵)	2 012	15.0	34.8	7.7	15.4	2.2	13.2	2.8
Cyprus	31	10.3	51.5	8.8	8.8	0.2	6.7	5.9
Latvia	125	7.5	52.9	4.9	11.3	1.0	7.2	6.1
Lithuania	211	7.1	46.0	5.2	18.0	2.0	8.5	3.0
Luxembourg	:	:	:	:	:	:	:	:
Hungary	398	9.7	41.0	7.0	13.2	2.4	9.1	9.9
Malta	10	17.4	33.0	7.4	8.8	0.3	20.8	1.3
Netherlands	619	8.3	37.7	6.1	8.4	1.1	17.1	6.3
Austria	308	13.7	36.6	11.2	14.7	1.2	8.9	2.5
Poland	2 150	9.5	40.8	8.4	13.0	2.0	7.2	6.3
Portugal	373	8.6	32.0	7.3	22.2	1.9	16.7	6.3
Romania	1 098	7.8	57.3	4.9	17.0	2.0	6.4	3.2
Slovenia	114	8.2	38.0	6.2	19.0	3.3	8.1	9.5
Slovakia	235	6.6	30.1	8.6	14.7	2.3	18.0	6.0
Finland	297	14.5	22.5	10.4	25.2	2.2	15.3	5.1
Sweden	423	13.7	26.4	8.9	16.2	1.0	17.9	2.3
United Kingdom	2 415	16.1	26.9	12.9	8.3	1.0	18.0	1.7
Iceland	17	13.6	39.1	7.5	9.2	0.5	12.7	1.4
Liechtenstein	1	0.1	70.9	0.0	20.9	0.0	2.4	0.0
Norway	219	10.6	32.4	8.5	7.7	0.7	20.0	4.7
Switzerland	234	12.5	36.2	9.8	12.6	1.0	13.9	4.4
Croatia	139	9.0	42.9	8.0	15.9	3.8	7.3	8.8
FYR of Macedonia	65	12.2	37.0	11.6	13.3	2.7	9.7	6.1
Turkey	2 924	6.6	51.7	7.1	12.0	4.0	5.7	3.5
Japan	3 874	15.8	29.2	2.9	15.5	2.4	13.0	5.5
United States	19 103	15.1	27.7	8.6	7.2	0.7	14.9	6.2

(¹) Refer to the Internet metadata file (http://epp.eurostat.ec.europa.eu/cache/ITY_SDDS/en/educ_esms.htm).
(²) Includes Greek data for 2008.
(³) Excludes students enrolled at ISCED 6.
(⁴) 2008.
(⁵) Analysis by field of study excludes students enrolled at ISCED 6.

Source: Eurostat (online data codes: tps00062 and educ_enrl5)

Figure 4.4.1: Students in tertiary education, by field of education and sex, EU-27, 2009 (¹)
(1 000)

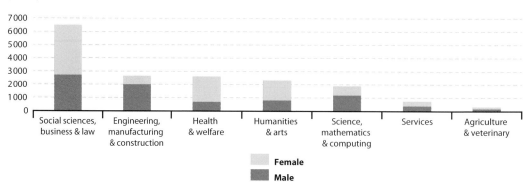

(¹) Refer to the Internet metadata file (http://epp.eurostat.ec.europa.eu/cache/ITY_SDDS/en/educ_esms.htm).

Source: Eurostat (online data code: educ_enrl5)

Figure 4.4.2: Median age in tertiary education, 2009 (¹)
(years)

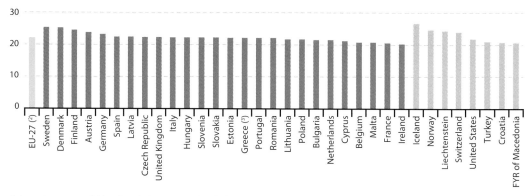

(¹) Luxembourg, not available; refer to the Internet metadata file (http://epp.eurostat.ec.europa.eu/cache/ITY_SDDS/en/educ_esms.htm).
(²) Includes Greek data for 2008.
(³) 2008.

Source: Eurostat (online data code: tps00061)

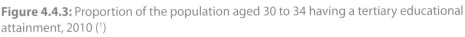

Figure 4.4.3: Proportion of the population aged 30 to 34 having a tertiary educational attainment, 2010 (¹)

(%)

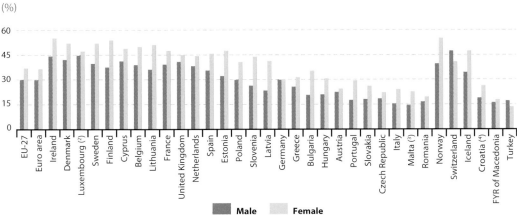

(¹) Ranked on the average shares for males and females combined; refer to the Internet metadata file
(http://epp.eurostat.ec.europa.eu/cache/ITY_SDDS/en/educ_esms.htm).
(²) Provisional.
(³) Male proportion, unreliable or uncertain data; female proportion, provisional.
(⁴) Unreliable or uncertain data.

Source: Eurostat (online data code: t2020_41)

Table 4.4.2: Graduates from tertiary education, by field of education, 2009 (¹)

	Total number of graduates from tertiary education (1 000)	of which, studying (%)							
		Humanities & arts	Teaching & training	Social sciences, business & law	Science, mathematics & computing	Engineering, manufacturing & construction	Agriculture & veterinary	Health & welfare	Services
EU-27 (²)	4 305	11.6	9.4	35.4	9.1	12.8	1.7	15.4	4.2
Belgium	99	11.1	13.0	31.3	5.6	10.7	2.6	20.5	1.4
Bulgaria	58	6.5	6.4	52.1	3.9	14.9	1.7	6.8	7.7
Czech Republic	96	6.7	14.4	33.5	9.4	14.3	3.5	9.3	4.6
Denmark	49	14.4	7.5	28.6	7.6	12.0	2.1	24.9	2.9
Germany	542	16.4	9.3	22.3	12.4	12.2	1.6	22.4	2.8
Estonia	11	11.4	8.1	38.9	8.9	10.5	2.1	11.0	9.2
Ireland	58	16.4	10.6	31.0	10.9	10.8	1.1	13.5	4.5
Greece (³)	67	12.9	8.1	30.0	10.9	14.0	4.1	11.6	8.4
Spain	310	8.9	13.2	26.1	8.9	16.4	1.7	15.7	8.0
France	628	10.3	1.5	41.6	10.6	15.6	1.5	14.9	4.0
Italy (⁴)	226	16.8	6.1	34.4	7.1	15.2	1.9	15.5	3.0
Cyprus	5	9.2	11.4	50.6	8.2	5.5	0.1	5.6	9.4
Latvia	26	7.6	11.1	53.2	4.9	8.4	0.9	7.8	6.1
Lithuania	45	7.5	12.7	43.7	5.1	16.0	1.9	9.8	3.3
Luxembourg	:	:	:	:	:	:	:	:	:
Hungary	68	12.0	13.2	41.3	6.4	8.7	2.1	9.8	8.7
Malta	3	16.1	12.8	40.6	9.4	5.6	0.8	13.3	1.2
Netherlands	127	9.0	13.6	37.3	6.2	7.8	1.3	18.8	5.5
Austria	52	9.1	13.3	33.6	10.7	18.2	1.6	10.1	3.9
Poland	575	8.2	16.1	43.6	6.8	8.8	1.7	9.0	5.7
Portugal	77	8.3	6.2	29.4	7.0	19.6	1.9	21.2	6.5
Romania	311	7.7	1.8	53.4	4.4	17.3	2.0	10.0	3.4
Slovenia	18	6.2	7.8	48.1	4.4	13.4	2.5	7.5	10.0
Slovakia	75	6.3	16.3	31.7	7.6	13.0	2.3	17.3	5.6
Finland	45	14.1	6.4	23.9	7.6	20.6	2.0	19.8	5.6
Sweden	59	6.5	16.1	24.8	7.6	17.5	1.2	26.8	3.0
United Kingdom	674	16.0	10.9	30.6	12.7	9.0	0.9	17.7	1.3
Iceland	3	11.1	20.6	39.8	6.5	8.1	0.4	12.1	1.5
Liechtenstein	0	0.3	0.0	47.0	0.0	8.8	0.0	4.0	0.0
Norway	35	8.7	17.3	28.6	7.2	8.0	1.0	24.5	4.5
Switzerland	81	7.9	9.8	37.1	8.6	13.0	1.7	14.7	6.7
Croatia	32	11.1	4.5	40.0	9.3	15.0	2.8	6.7	10.4
FYR of Macedonia	11	13.1	11.9	34.3	12.7	8.8	2.4	10.0	6.8
Turkey	489	7.2	14.6	40.7	7.9	13.1	5.6	5.8	5.1
Japan	1 015	15.0	6.9	26.5	3.0	17.5	2.4	13.0	9.3
United States	2 882	12.9	10.5	38.1	8.3	7.0	1.0	15.2	6.9

(¹) Refer to the Internet metadata file (http://epp.eurostat.ec.europa.eu/cache/ITY_SDDS/en/educ_esms.htm).
(²) Includes Greek data for 2008.
(³) 2008.
(⁴) Analysis by field of study excludes graduates from ISCED 5A (second degrees) and ISCED 6.

Source: Eurostat (online data code: educ_grad5)

Figure 4.4.4: Graduates from tertiary education, by field of education and sex, EU-27, 2009 ([1])
(1 000)

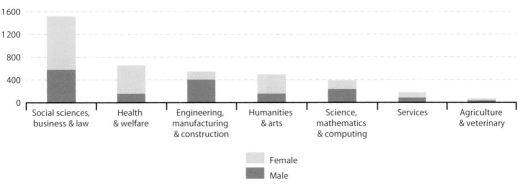

([1]) Refer to the Internet metadata file (http://epp.eurostat.ec.europa.eu/cache/ITY_SDDS/en/educ_esms.htm).

Source: Eurostat (online data code: educ_grad5)

4.5 Lifelong learning

This subchapter provides an overview of lifelong learning statistics in the European Union (EU), on the basis of data collected through the labour force survey (LFS), supplemented by the adult education survey (AES).

Main statistical findings

The strategic framework for European cooperation in education and training adopted in May 2009 sets a number of benchmarks to be achieved by 2020, including one for lifelong learning, namely that an average of at least 15 % of adults aged 25 to 64 years old should participate in lifelong learning. In 2010, the proportion of persons aged 25 to 64 in the EU receiving some form of education or training in the four weeks preceding the labour force survey was 9.1 %; a share that was 0.7 percentage points lower than the corresponding share for 2005 (see Table 4.5.1).

The proportion of the population who had participated in such lifelong learning activities was higher among women (10.0 % in 2010) than among men (8.3 %). The shares for men and women were both lower in 2010 than they had been five years earlier.

Denmark, Sweden and Finland stood out as they reported considerably higher proportions of their respective populations participating in lifelong learning, ranging between one fifth and one third; the United Kingdom, the Netherlands and Slovenia were the only other Member States where the participation rate in 2010 already exceeded the 15 % target. In contrast, Bulgaria and Romania reported lifelong learning participation rates of less than 2 %.

In addition to the data from the labour force survey, information on education and training is available from a pilot survey – the adult education survey (AES) – that was conducted on a voluntary basis between 2005 and 2008. According to this, a majority of participants took part in non-formal education and training, while most of the education and training undertaken was job-related. Indeed, the main reason given by respondents for their participation in non-formal education and training (see Table 4.5.2) was to do their job better/improve their career prospects, while getting knowledge or skills relating to interesting subjects and getting useful skills/knowledge for everyday life were also common reasons. The three most commonly cited obstacles to participation in education and training among those who wanted to participate but did

not do so were: lack of time due to family responsibilities (36.6 % of those not participating); conflict with work schedules (35.0 %); cost (28.3 %) – see Table 4.5.3.

Employers were the most common providers of non-formal education and training activities, providing close to two fifths (38.3 %) of such activities (see Table 4.5.4). Employers provided more than two thirds of non-formal education and training in Bulgaria, and half of such activities in the United Kingdom. Among the less common providers of non-formal education and training in the EU-27 as a whole, the importance of employers' organisations and chambers of commerce was particularly high in Hungary (32.8 %) and Slovenia (20.8 %), non-commercial institutions (such as libraries) were relatively frequent providers in Finland (29.5 %) and Cyprus (15.5 %), while trade unions provided a higher than average share in Hungary (13.1 %).

Data sources and availability

Lifelong learning encompasses all purposeful learning activity, whether formal, non-formal or informal, undertaken on an ongoing basis with the aim of improving knowledge, skills and competence. The intention or aim to learn is the critical point that distinguishes these activities from non-learning activities, such as cultural activities or sports activities. The information collected relates to all subjects whether they are relevant or not for the respondent's current or possible future job.

Within the domain of lifelong learning statistics, formal education corresponds to education and training in the regular system of schools, universities, colleges and other formal educational institutions that normally constitute a continuous 'ladder' of full-time education for children and young people (generally completed by the age of 25). Non-formal education and training is defined as any organised and sustained educational activities that do not correspond to the definition of formal education. Non-formal education and training may or may not take place in educational institutions and cater to persons of all ages. It may cover educational programmes to impart adult literacy, basic education for out-of-school children, life skills, work skills, and

general culture. Note that the statistics presented do not cover informal learning, which corresponds to self-learning (through the use of printed material, computer-based learning/training, (Internet) web-based education, visiting libraries, etc).

The target population for lifelong learning statistics refers to all persons in private households aged between 25 and 64 years. Data are collected through the EU's labour force survey (LFS). The denominator used for the ratios derived from LFS data consists of the total population of the same age group, excluding those who did not answer the question concerning participation in education and training.

Additional information is available from an adult education survey which was carried out by EU, EFTA and candidate countries. Surveys were carried out between 2005 and 2008 as a pilot exercise with a standard questionnaire, covering participation in education and lifelong learning activities whether formal, non-formal or informal, and included job-related activities. The survey also collected information on learning activities, self-reported skills, as well as modules on social and cultural participation. Within the context of the adult education survey, learning is defined as activities with the intention to improve an individual's knowledge, skills, and competences. Intentional learning (as opposed to random learning) is defined as a deliberate search for knowledge, skills, competences, or attitudes of lasting value. Organised learning is defined as learning planned in a pattern or sequence with explicit or implicit aims.

Context

Lifelong learning can take place in a variety of environments, both inside and outside formal education and training systems. Lifelong learning implies investing in people and knowledge; promoting the acquisition of basic skills, including digital literacy and broadening opportunities for innovative, more flexible forms of learning. The aim is to provide people of all ages with equal and open access to high-quality learning opportunities, and to a variety of learning experiences.

The integrated economic and employment guidelines were revised most recently as part of the

Europe 2020 strategy for smart, sustainable and inclusive growth. Guideline 8 concerns developing a skilled workforce responding to labour market needs, and promoting job quality and lifelong learning.

The Copenhagen process, established in 2002, lays out the basis for cooperation in vocational education and training (VET), with 33 European countries involved. The overall aim is to encourage more individuals to make wider use of vocational learning opportunities, whether at school, in higher education, in the workplace, or through private courses. The actions and tools developed as part of the process aim to allow users to link and build on learning acquired at various times, in both formal and non-formal contexts. In June 2010, the European Commission presented a ten year vision for the future of vocational education and training in a Communication titled 'A new impetus for European cooperation in vocational education and training to support the Europe 2020 strategy' (COM(2010) 296 final). In December 2010 in Bruges (Belgium) the priorities for the Copenhagen process for 2011 to 2020 were set. This established a global vision for vocational education and training to be reached by the year 2020: attractive and inclusive VET; high quality initial VET; easily accessible and career-oriented continuing VET; flexible systems of VET based on a learning outcomes approach which cater for the validation of non-formal and informal learning; a European education and training area; substantially increased opportunities for transnational mobility; easily accessible and high-quality lifelong information, guidance and counselling services. Based on this vision a total of 11 strategic objectives were set for the period between 2011 and 2020 as well as 22 short-term deliverables for the first four years.

There are a number of initiatives under development to enhance the transparency, recognition and quality of competences and qualifications, facilitating the mobility of learners and workers. These include the European Qualifications Framework (EQF), Europass, the European Credit System for VET (ECVET), and the European Quality Assurance Reference Framework for VET (EQAVET).

The launch of EQF aims to help employers and individuals compare qualifications across the EU's diverse education and training systems: it encourages countries to relate their national qualifications systems to the EQF so that all new qualifications issued from 2012 carry a reference to an appropriate EQF level. The EQF also represents a shift in European education as it is based on an approach which takes into account learning outcomes rather than the resources which are put into learning. In other words, it is a qualifications framework based on what learners are actually able to do at the end of a course of education, rather than where the learning took place and how long it took.

The Leonardo da Vinci programme in the field of vocational education and training is designed to encourage projects which give individuals the chance to improve their competences, knowledge and skills through a period spent abroad, as well as to encourage Europe-wide cooperation between training organisations.

The Grundtvig programme was launched in 2000 and now forms part of the lifelong learning programme. It aims to provide adults with ways of improving their knowledge and skills. It not only covers learners in adult education, but also the teachers, trainers, education staff and facilities that provide these services.

Table 4.5.1: Lifelong learning, 2005 and 2010 (¹)
(% of the population aged 25 to 64 participating in education and training)

	Total		Male		Female	
	2005	2010	2005	2010	2005	2010
EU-27	9.8	9.1	9.0	8.3	10.5	10.0
Euro area	8.1	7.9	7.9	7.5	8.4	8.3
Belgium	8.3	7.2	8.2	7.0	8.5	7.4
Bulgaria	1.3	1.2	1.3	1.1	1.2	1.3
Czech Republic	5.6	7.5	5.2	7.3	5.9	7.7
Denmark	27.4	32.8	23.6	26.3	31.2	39.3
Germany	7.7	7.7	8.0	7.7	7.4	7.6
Estonia (²)	5.9	10.9	4.3	8.6	7.3	13.0
Ireland	7.4	6.7	6.2	6.3	8.6	7.2
Greece	1.9	3.0	1.9	3.1	1.8	2.9
Spain (³)	10.5	10.8	9.7	10.0	11.4	11.6
France	*7.1*	5.0	*7.0*	4.6	*7.2*	5.4
Italy	5.8	6.2	5.4	5.9	6.2	6.5
Cyprus (³)	5.9	7.7	5.4	7.5	6.3	7.9
Latvia	7.9	5.0	5.0	3.4	10.6	6.5
Lithuania	6.0	4.0	4.2	3.2	7.7	4.8
Luxembourg (³)	8.5	13.4	8.5	12.8	8.5	14.0
Hungary	3.9	2.8	3.2	2.6	4.6	2.9
Malta	5.3	5.7	6.1	5.2	4.5	6.1
Netherlands (³)	15.9	16.5	15.6	15.9	16.1	17.1
Austria	12.9	13.7	12.3	12.7	13.5	14.7
Poland	4.9	5.3	4.3	4.8	5.4	5.9
Portugal	4.1	*5.8*	4.0	5.8	4.2	5.7
Romania	1.6	1.3	1.5	1.2	1.6	1.4
Slovenia	15.3	16.2	13.6	14.1	17.2	18.3
Slovakia	4.6	2.8	4.3	2.2	5.0	3.3
Finland	22.5	23.0	19.0	18.9	26.1	27.1
Sweden (³)	*17.4*	24.5	*13.0*	18.0	*21.9*	31.1
United Kingdom (³)	27.6	19.4	23.1	16.4	32.0	22.4
Iceland	25.7	25.2	21.6	21.1	29.8	29.4
Norway	17.8	17.8	16.3	16.4	19.3	19.2
Switzerland (³)	27.0	30.6	27.4	31.6	26.5	29.6
Croatia (⁴)	2.1	2.0	2.0	2.2	2.1	1.8
FYR of Macedonia	:	3.2	:	3.1	:	3.4
Turkey	:	2.5	:	2.6	:	2.4

(¹) Refer to the Internet metadata file (http://epp.eurostat.ec.europa.eu/cache/ITY_SDDS/en/lfsi_edu_a_esms.htm).
(²) 2005 male rate, unreliable or uncertain data.
(³) Break in series.
(⁴) 2010 male and female rates, unreliable or uncertain data.

Source: Eurostat (online data codes: tsiem080 and trng_lfs_01)

Table 4.5.2: Reasons for participation in non-formal education and training, 2007 (^{1})
(%)

	To get knowledge/skills relating to interesting subjects	To get knowledge/skills useful for everyday life	To increase possibility of getting a job/changing job	Obliged to participate	To be less likely to lose job	Do job better/improve career prospects	Meet new people, for fun	Obtain qualification	Start own business	Other/no resp.
Belgium	38.7	29.8	9.2	24.1	3.3	64.4	11.8	8.1	2.6	1.9
Bulgaria	38.5	40.0	20.8	22.1	22.0	77.3	9.2	34.3	1.8	1.2
Czech Republic	46.2	33.7	16.8	7.4	13.3	54.6	10.4	20.8	4.5	0.5
Denmark	:	:	:	:	:	:	:	:	:	:
Germany	45.9	14.3	15.6	25.0	19.9	68.0	10.5	11.6	3.8	5.4
Estonia	21.1	17.6	5.8	24.9	15.1	80.2	2.4	8.8	1.6	5.5
Ireland	:	:	:	:	:	:	:	:	:	:
Greece	76.7	52.4	25.5	18.1	16.0	74.8	20.6	48.6	7.9	4.3
Spain	66.6	50.8	28.4	11.8	12.7	68.4	11.8	25.0	4.8	5.0
France	:	:	:	:	:	:	:	:	:	:
Italy	43.9	20.9	10.9	13.8	2.5	47.6	13.3	13.5	2.6	3.9
Cyprus	64.3	38.2	8.7	16.9	2.1	53.6	14.7	13.3	1.6	4.4
Latvia	43.8	58.6	17.8	33.7	27.7	74.7	24.3	37.8	4.4	1.8
Lithuania	50.6	42.3	17.5	26.2	31.3	77.5	11.8	41.4	3.4	3.2
Luxembourg	:	:	:	:	:	:	:	:	:	:
Hungary	56.0	52.0	33.3	51.4	38.3	67.8	13.2	35.2	7.5	1.3
Malta	:	:	:	:	:	:	:	:	:	:
Netherlands	42.4	40.2	12.8	35.9	6.6	66.4	19.2	23.7	4.2	10.1
Austria	57.4	57.2	16.2	23.7	10.5	67.1	20.9	10.7	4.6	5.1
Poland	7.6	7.2	7.2	5.2	6.6	67.1	0.5	7.2	1.4	2.8
Portugal	80.5	81.6	31.8	12.2	16.0	69.9	23.7	47.4	6.6	6.2
Romania	:	:	:	:	:	:	:	:	:	:
Slovenia	12.5	21.2	1.7	13.1	1.0	54.4	1.8	2.3	0.3	2.5
Slovakia	34.6	30.2	23.1	66.1	26.5	63.1	8.8	19.2	4.6	1.8
Finland	62.1	41.1	16.1	35.3	14.3	69.1	30.0	13.5	3.7	9.4
Sweden	59.3	41.8	6.5	36.4	8.0	61.8	20.8	8.9	1.5	5.5
United Kingdom	82.0	44.8	18.1	57.7	2.8	55.0	9.7	33.9	9.3	86.1
Norway	67.9	33.2	9.6	43.1	12.7	71.8	16.0	18.3	1.5	7.2
Croatia	45.4	35.9	17.3	31.7	17.6	78.1	8.3	15.3	4.9	1.4

(^{1}) Multiple answers allowed; Bulgaria, the Czech Republic, Greece, Spain, Cyprus, Portugal, Finland and the United Kingdom did not interview participants taking part in guided on the job training; refer to the Internet metadata file (http://epp.eurostat.ec.europa.eu/cache/ITY_SDDS/en/trng_aes_esms.htm).

Source: Eurostat (online data code: trng_aes_142)

Table 4.5.3: Obstacles to participation in education and training, 2007 (¹)
(%)

	Health or age	None within reachable distance	No time due to family	Did not have the prerequisites	Too expensive, could not afford	Did not like idea of going back to school	Lack of employer support	Conflict with work schedule	Other/no resp.
EU	13.4	18.6	36.6	13.3	28.3	13.5	16.3	35.0	24.4
Belgium	12.8	7.7	22.5	5.6	10.5	2.8	8.6	19.4	6.2
Bulgaria	11.5	29.7	28.8	16.3	56.6	6.2	11.6	24.1	7.7
Czech Republic	11.8	16.1	38.4	7.8	19.7	2.0	22.5	36.8	3.6
Denmark	:	:	:	:	:	:	:	:	:
Germany	10.4	21.3	29.1	20.6	37.4	9.5	28.1	31.6	11.4
Estonia	17.1	32.5	36.6	2.7	50.1	8.0	8.4	30.8	40.2
Ireland	:	:	:	:	:	:	:	:	:
Greece	10.5	19.1	48.0	7.4	33.2	9.7	9.7	42.7	19.3
Spain	5.8	8.5	41.2	7.5	13.4	2.7	4.7	32.6	28.0
France	:	:	:	:	:	:	:	:	:
Italy	19.7	16.8	49.5	19.2	26.2	16.5	15.2	44.1	12.4
Cyprus	9.3	11.9	67.6	5.1	16.2	4.8	5.1	41.9	12.3
Latvia	11.9	24.1	40.1	11.2	50.8	11.9	29.7	36.8	13.7
Lithuania	13.2	19.6	34.2	3.2	45.6	4.9	16.2	48.4	13.5
Luxembourg	:	:	:	:	:	:	:	:	:
Hungary	12.5	32.4	37.4	13.9	42.3	18.9	39.9	53.2	15.0
Malta	:	:	:	:	:	:	:	:	:
Netherlands	22.8	12.4	28.6	4.0	23.9	12.9	19.2	16.8	21.8
Austria	6.2	22.2	41.4	7.1	34.2	2.8	16.0	39.3	16.8
Poland	9.1	31.0	29.2	9.2	61.3	17.5	20.4	31.4	11.5
Portugal	6.8	34.2	34.5	11.8	22.7	4.1	20.0	26.5	18.9
Romania	:	:	:	:	:	:	:	:	:
Slovenia	14.6	28.5	35.6	7.2	45.9	6.9	21.1	52.4	8.3
Slovakia	10.8	31.9	35.5	56.8	40.7	3.1	26.3	41.7	3.8
Finland	16.6	24.7	30.0	11.2	21.5	6.9	23.3	42.3	20.7
Sweden	22.9	21.2	22.2	5.6	31.4	6.7	18.4	31.3	19.8
United Kingdom	17.0	25.9	42.5	20.8	33.8	24.1	22.6	43.9	56.5
Norway	19.2	13.3	25.4	4.2	17.3	9.0	20.8	31.7	15.4
Croatia	13.4	32.1	55.5	18.4	60.6	5.2	21.0	35.0	25.3

(¹) Multiple answers allowed; Denmark, Ireland, France, Luxembourg, Malta and Romania are not included in the EU average; refer to the Internet metadata file (http://epp.eurostat.ec.europa.eu/cache/ITY_SDDS/en/trng_aes_esms.htm).

Source: Eurostat (online data code: trng_aes_176)

Table 4.5.4: Providers of non-formal education and training activities, 2007 (¹)
(%)

	Employer	Non-formal education & training institution	Formal education institution	Commercial institution where education & training is not main activity	Employers' organisation, chamber of commerce	Non-commercial institution (e.g. library)	Non-profit association	Individual	Trade union	Other
EU	38.3	16.5	10.4	8.9	5.0	4.5	4.3	4.3	1.4	4.0
Belgium	41.7	7.3	15.2	8.9	2.8	7.1	7.4	5.6	0.7	0.6
Bulgaria	68.8	14.1	3.1	3.1	3.0	5.8	0.7	1.1	0.2	0.2
Czech Republic	42.9	27.9	10.7	7.6	1.8	2.1	1.5	3.2	0.6	1.1
Denmark	:	:	:	:	:	:	:	:	:	:
Germany	42.4	14.7	4.8	13.8	4.8	6.2	5.3	5.8	1.1	0.5
Estonia	29.2	34.4	10.0	9.4	1.2	3.9	2.1	2.5	5.5	1.7
Ireland	:	:	:	:	:	:	:	:	:	:
Greece	36.0	12.1	14.6	13.6	3.3	5.2	3.2	1.4	2.3	4.8
Spain	19.9	26.2	9.7	5.0	6.7	4.5	5.4	2.9	4.2	11.5
France	:	:	:	:	:	:	:	:	:	:
Italy	27.6	8.5	12.9	8.0	12.9	2.2	4.4	6.3	1.3	11.3
Cyprus	27.1	19.3	5.4	10.1	1.3	15.5	7.1	12.9	0.9	0.3
Latvia	42.6	21.3	13.4	6.8	2.7	1.6	2.2	2.1	0.2	5.2
Lithuania	14.5	28.7	20.8	15.0	9.2	:	1.4	8.7	0.4	:
Luxembourg	:	:	:	:	:	:	:	:	:	:
Hungary	0.6	32.0	7.0	3.5	32.8	6.2	0.1	1.9	13.1	2.7
Malta	:	:	:	:	:	:	:	:	:	:
Netherlands	38.6	:	38.2	:	:	:	4.7	2.1	1.9	11.8
Austria	27.7	21.8	6.7	12.4	4.6	1.4	4.9	4.5	0.3	14.2
Poland	20.8	49.9	13.1	6.1	1.7	:	2.2	3.8	0.2	2.1
Portugal	40.7	20.9	9.1	8.4	2.3	4.5	5.5	1.4	1.4	5.8
Romania	:	:	:	:	:	:	:	:	:	:
Slovenia	11.8	44.6	8.7	8.0	20.8	:	3.9	1.9	0.3	:
Slovakia	40.0	28.2	17.0	7.5	2.8	:	0.7	1.8	0.1	1.1
Finland	36.0	10.1	8.8	1.1	6.7	29.5	0.8	3.0	3.0	:
Sweden	45.5	14.6	4.2	17.1	3.9	3.4	5.6	2.5	2.0	0.5
United Kingdom	50.2	8.2	11.1	:	7.0	1.8	1.9	4.3	0.1	5.4
Croatia	22.0	24.2	15.6	12.8	5.0	1.6	3.3	0.8	0.4	7.7
Turkey	26.4	27.0	7.3	3.2	2.8	25.4	3.8	3.6	0.4	:

(¹) Denmark, Ireland, France, Luxembourg, Malta and Romania are not included in the EU average; refer to the Internet metadata file
(http://epp.eurostat.ec.europa.eu/cache/ITY_SDDS/en/trng_aes_esms.htm).

Source: Eurostat (online data code: trng_aes_170)

Labour market

Introduction

Labour market statistics measure the involvement of individuals, households and businesses in the labour market, where the former mainly appear offering their labour in return for remuneration while the latter act as employers. The market outcomes – for example employment, unemployment, vacant posts, wage levels, labour costs – heavily affect not only the economy, but directly the personal life of virtually every citizen. Eurostat statistics cover both the supply and the demand side as well as policy interventions on the labour market. Data is collected on short-term and structural aspects, in monetary and non-monetary terms.

Labour market statistics are at the heart of many European Union (EU) policies following the introduction of an employment chapter into the Amsterdam Treaty in 1997. The European employment strategy (EES) seeks to create more and better jobs throughout the EU. A central element of the EES under the Lisbon objectives was the employment policy guidelines as part of an integrated approach based on three pillars: macro-economic policies, micro-economic reforms and employment policies.

The financial and economic crisis has however reversed much of the progress achieved in Europe since 2000. The Europe 2020 strategy for smart, sustainable and inclusive growth put forward by the European Commission is the EU's growth strategy for the coming decade. As part of the flagship initiatives, 'An agenda for new skills and jobs' and 'Youth on the move', (youth) unemployment and employment rates will be targeted through a range of policies, including proposals aimed at education and training institutions, or measures for the creation of a (work) environment conducive to higher activity rates and higher labour productivity. There are also initiatives aimed at facilitating the entry of young people into the labour market. To measure progress in meeting the Europe 2020 goals, five headline targets to be met by 2020 have been agreed; these are to be translated into national targets in each EU Member State, reflecting different situations and circumstances. One of these targets is that 75 % of 20 to 64 year-olds should be employed in the EU by 2020. The integrated economic and employment guidelines were also revised as part of the Europe 2020 strategy.

5.1 Employment

Labour market statistics are at the heart of many European Union (EU) policies following the introduction of an employment chapter into the Amsterdam Treaty in 1997. The employment rate, in other words the proportion of the working age population in employment, is a key social indicator.

This subchapter provides information on recent EU employment statistics, including an analysis based on important socio-economic dimensions: employment statistics show significant differences by sex, age and educational level attained, and there is also considerable variation across EU Member States and regions within these Member States.

Main statistical findings

Employment rates – differences by sex, age and educational attainment level

The EU-27 employment rate for persons aged 15 to 64, as measured by the EU's labour force survey (EU LFS), decreased in 2010 to 64.2 %, down from 64.6 % in 2009. This decrease of 0.4 percentage points followed on from a 1.3 percentage point fall in 2009, the first decrease recorded in the EU-27 employment rate since 2002; the EU-27 employment rate had stood at 60.7 % in 1997 (the first year data are available for this series) and peaked at 65.9 % in 2008.

Employment rates vary considerably not only across but also within the EU Member States according

to regional patterns, with a relatively high dispersion (as measured by the coefficient of variation for regions at the NUTS 2 level) observed across Italy (17.8 %) in 2010. In contrast, there was relatively little divergence in employment rates across the regions of Portugal, Austria, Greece, Sweden, the Netherlands or Denmark (all below 4 %). The dispersion of regional employment across the whole of the EU-27 was the same in 2010 as it had been five years earlier, while that of the euro area (EA-15) increased – see Figure 5.1.2.

Employment rates are generally lower among women and older workers. In 2010, the employment rate for men reached 70.1 % in the EU-27, as compared with 58.2 % for women. The rates for men and women fell in 2009 and again in 2010, such that by 2010 the rate for men was 2.7 percentage points lower than in 2008, while for women it was 0.9 percentage points lower. A longer term comparison shows that the employment rate for men was approximately the same in 2010 as it had been in 1997 (the start of the series) when it was 70.0 %, whereas for women the rate increased by 6.8 percentage points from 51.4 % in 1997.

The EU-27 employment rate for older workers (aged between 55 and 64) reached 46.3 % in 2010. In contrast to overall employment rates, the 2010 employment rate for older workers was higher than in the previous year (46.0 %), and this extended an unbroken series of increases in this rate starting in 1998 when the rate was 36.2 %. In 2010 there were eight Member States that had an employment rate for older workers in excess of 50 %, with the highest recorded in Sweden (70.5 %).

Employment rates vary considerably according to levels of educational attainment: for statistics on this issue employment rates are based on the age group 25 to 64 rather than 15 to 64. The employment rate of those who had completed a tertiary education was 83.9 % across the EU-27 in 2010, much higher than the rate (53.8 %) for those who had attained a primary or lower secondary education. The EU-27 employment rate of persons with

an upper secondary or post-secondary non-tertiary education was 73.1 %. The fall in the employment rate witnessed in 2010 for persons with a primary or lower secondary education was the third successive annual reduction, down a total of 3.4 percentage points from the 57.2 % rate recorded in 2007. For persons with an upper secondary or post-secondary non-tertiary education the rate fell 1.8 percentage points between 2008 and 2010, while for persons with a tertiary education the rate fell 1.4 percentage points over the same period.

Part-time and fixed-term contracts

The proportion of the EU-27 workforce reporting that their main job was part-time increased steadily from 16.2 % in 2000 to 19.2 % by 2010. The highest proportion of part-time workers was found in the Netherlands (48.9 % in 2010), followed by the United Kingdom, Denmark, Sweden, Germany and Austria, where part-time work accounted in each case for over a quarter (25 % to 27 %) of those in employment. In contrast, part-time employment was relatively uncommon in Bulgaria (2.4 % of employment) and Slovakia (3.9 %).

The incidence of part-time work differs significantly between men and women. Just under one third (31.9 %) of women employed in the EU-27 worked on a part-time basis in 2010, a much higher proportion than the corresponding figure for men (8.7 %). Three quarters (76.5 %) of all women employed in the Netherlands worked on a part-time basis in 2010, by far the highest rate among the Member States ([3]).

Having fallen in 2008 and 2009, the share of employees with a contract of limited duration (fixed-term employment) increased to 13.9 % in the EU-27 in 2010. One in four employees had a temporary contract in Poland and Spain in 2010 and the share was close to this level in Portugal. Among the remaining Member States, the share of employees working on a contract of limited duration ranged from 18.3 % in the Netherlands down to just 1.1 % in Romania. The considerable range in the propensity to use limited duration contracts between Member States

([3]) Anyone working fewer than 35 hours a week is considered as working part-time in the Netherlands.

may, at least to some degree, reflect national practices, the supply and demand of labour, and the ease with which employers can hire or fire.

Data sources and availability

Source statistics

The main data source for labour market statistics is the EU's labour force survey (EU LFS); another frequently used source for employment statistics is national accounts. Both of these sources use similar employment definitions based on international standards from the International Labour Organization (ILO) and the system of national accounts respectively. A third potential source for information relating to employment statistics is that of enterprise statistics.

The data source for all of the information presented in this subchapter is the EU LFS, except for the information on employment growth, which is based on national accounts. National accounts publish employment estimates with no age thresholds, nor socio-demographic breakdowns, which make data more suitable for an analysis of employment as a labour input, rather than as a social phenomenon.

The EU LFS is a quarterly sample survey covering the population in private households in the EU, EFTA (except Liechtenstein) and the candidate countries. It provides annual ([4]) and quarterly results in relation to the labour participation of persons aged 15 and over. The EU LFS collects information on labour force status (all persons being either in employment, unemployed or economically inactive), employment characteristics, working time, job search among the unemployed, levels of education, recent education and training, as well as each individuals' demographic background and family composition.

The EU LFS sample size amounts to approximately 1.5 million individuals each quarter. The quarterly sampling rates vary between 0.2 % and 3.3 % in each country. Eurostat started the collection of LFS

micro data in 1983 with one reference quarter per year (usually the spring). During the period from 1998 to 2005 the survey underwent a transition to a continuous quarterly survey; all 27 Member States now provide quarterly results.

Definition of employment and main employment characteristics

The economically active population (labour force) comprises employed and unemployed persons. The EU LFS defines persons in employment as those aged 15 and over, who, during the reference week, performed some work, even for just one hour per week, for pay, profit or family gain. The labour force also includes people who were not at work but had a job or business from which they were temporarily absent, for example, because of illness, holidays, industrial disputes, education or training.

Employment can be measured in terms of the number of persons or jobs, in full-time equivalents or in hours worked. All the estimates presented use the number of persons; the information presented for employment rates is also built on estimates for the number of persons. Employment statistics are frequently reported as employment rates to discount the changing size of countries' populations over time and to facilitate comparisons between countries of different sizes. These rates are typically published for the working age population, which is generally considered to be those aged between 15 and 64 years, although the age range of 16 to 64 is used in Spain, Sweden (only until 2001) and the United Kingdom, as well as in Iceland; this age group (15 to 64 years) is also a standard used by other international statistical organisations.

Some main employment characteristics, as defined by the EU LFS, include:

- employees are defined as those who work for a public or private employer and who receive compensation in the form of wages, salaries, payment

---

([4]) For Switzerland only spring LFS results (for the second quarter) are available and these are used as annual estimates in the respective tables and figures.

by results, or payment in kind; non-conscript members of the armed forces are also included;

- self-employed persons work in their own business, farm or professional practice. A self-employed person is considered to be working during the reference week if she/he meets one of the following criteria: works for the purpose of earning profit; spends time on the operation of a business; or is currently establishing a business;

- a full-time/part-time distinction in the main job is declared by the respondent, except in Germany, Ireland and the Netherlands, where thresholds for usual hours worked are used;

- indicators for employed persons with a second job refer only to people with more than one job at the same time; people having changed job during the reference week are not counted as having two jobs;

- an employee is considered as having a temporary job if employer and employee agree that its end is determined by objective conditions, such as a specific date, the completion of an assignment, or the return of an employee who is temporarily replaced. Typical cases include: people in seasonal employment; people engaged by an agency or employment exchange and hired to a third party to perform a specific task (unless there is a written work contract of unlimited duration); people with specific training contracts.

The dispersion of regional (NUTS level 2) employment rates shows regional differences in employment within countries and between groups of countries. This measure is zero when employment rates across all regions are identical, and will rise as the differences between regional employment rates increase. The indicator is not applicable for several countries as these comprise only one or two NUTS level 2 regions. However, the employment rates of these countries (regions) are used to compute the indicator at a European level.

Annual employment growth gives the change, in percentage terms, from one year to the next, in terms of the total number of persons employed on the economic territory of the country or the geographical area; the data source for employment growth is national accounts.

Context

Employment statistics can be used for a number of different analyses, including macro-economic (in other words, labour as a production factor), productivity or competitiveness studies. They can also be used to study a range of social and behavioural aspects related to an individual's employment situation, such as the social integration of minorities, or employment as a source of household income.

Employment is both a structural indicator and a short-term indicator. As a structural indicator, it may shed light on the structure of labour markets and economic systems, as measured through the balance of labour supply and demand, or the quality of employment. As a short-term indicator, employment follows the business cycle; however, it has limits in this respect, as employment is often referred to as a lagging indicator.

Employment statistics are at the heart of many EU policies. The European employment strategy (EES) was launched at the Luxembourg jobs summit in November 1997 and was revamped in 2005 to align the EU's employment strategy more closely to a set of revised Lisbon objectives, and in July 2008, employment policy guidelines for the period 2008 to 2010 were updated.

In March 2010, the European Commission launched the Europe 2020 strategy for smart, sustainable and inclusive growth; this was formally adopted by the European Council in June 2010. The European Council agreed on five headline targets, the first being to raise the employment rate for women and men aged 20 to 64 years old to 75 % by 2020. Member States may set their own national targets in the light of these headline targets and will draw up national reform programmes that will include the actions they aim to undertake in order to implement the strategy. The implementation of the strategy might be achieved, at least in part, through the promotion of flexible working conditions – for example, part-time work or work from home – which are thought to stimulate labour participation. Other initiatives that may encourage more people to enter the labour market include improvements in the availability of childcare facilities, providing more opportunities for lifelong learning, or facilitating job mobility. Central to this theme is the issue of 'flexicurity': policies that simultaneously address the flexibility of labour markets, work organisation and labour relations, while taking into account the reconciliation of work and private life, employment security and social protection.

Figure 5.1.1: Employment rate, age group 15-64, 2010
(%)

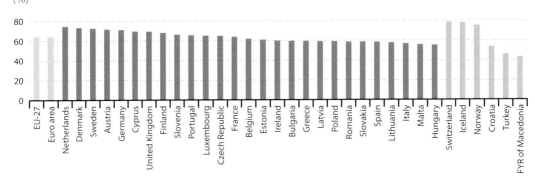

Source: Eurostat (online data code: lfsi_emp_a)

Figure 5.1.2: Dispersion of regional employment rates, 2005 and 2010 (¹)
(coefficient of variation of employment rates (of the age group 15-64) across regions (NUTS 2 level))

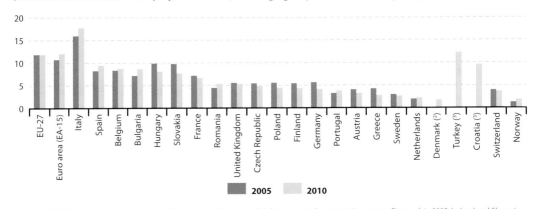

(¹) At the NUTS 2 level: Estonia, Cyprus, Latvia, Lithuania, Luxembourg and Malta are treated as one region, as was Denmark in 2005; Ireland and Slovenia have only two regions; for non-member countries statistical regions equivalent to NUTS level 2 are used.
(²) 2005, not relevant; 2009 instead of 2010.
(³) 2005, not available.

Source: Eurostat (online data code: tsisc050)

Figure 5.1.3: Employment rates by sex, 2010 (¹)
(%)

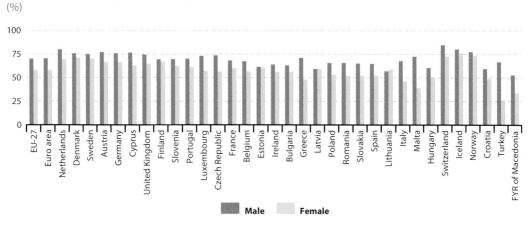

(¹) The figure is ranked on the average of employment rates for males and females.

Source: Eurostat (online data code: lfsi_emp_a)

Table 5.1.1: Employment rate, age group 15-64, 2000-2010
(%)

	2000	2001	2002	2003	2004	2005	2006	2007	2008	2009	2010
EU-27	62.2	62.6	62.4	62.6	63.0	63.5	64.5	65.4	65.9	64.6	64.2
Euro area	61.4	62.1	62.3	62.6	63.1	63.7	64.7	65.6	66.0	64.7	64.2
Belgium	60.5	59.9	59.9	59.6	60.3	61.1	61.0	62.0	62.4	61.6	62.0
Bulgaria	50.4	49.7	50.6	52.5	54.2	55.8	58.6	61.7	64.0	62.6	59.7
Czech Republic	65.0	65.0	65.4	64.7	64.2	64.8	65.3	66.1	66.6	65.4	65.0
Denmark	76.3	76.2	75.9	75.1	75.7	75.9	77.4	77.1	77.9	75.7	73.4
Germany (¹)	65.6	65.8	65.4	65.0	65.0	66.0	67.5	69.4	70.7	70.9	71.1
Estonia	60.4	61.0	62.0	62.9	63.0	64.4	68.1	69.4	69.8	63.5	61.0
Ireland	65.2	65.8	65.5	65.5	66.3	67.6	68.7	69.2	67.6	61.8	60.0
Greece	56.5	56.3	57.5	58.7	59.4	60.1	61.0	61.4	61.9	61.2	59.6
Spain (¹)	56.3	57.8	58.5	59.8	61.1	63.3	64.8	65.6	64.3	59.8	58.6
France	62.1	62.8	63.0	64.0	63.8	63.7	63.7	64.3	64.9	64.1	64.0
Italy (²)	53.7	54.8	55.5	56.1	57.6	57.6	58.4	58.7	58.7	57.5	56.9
Cyprus	65.7	67.8	68.6	69.2	68.9	68.5	69.6	71.0	70.9	69.9	69.7
Latvia	57.5	58.6	60.4	61.8	62.3	63.3	66.3	68.3	68.6	60.9	59.3
Lithuania	59.1	57.5	59.9	61.1	61.2	62.6	63.6	64.9	64.3	60.1	57.8
Luxembourg	62.7	63.1	63.4	62.2	62.5	63.6	63.6	64.2	63.4	65.2	65.2
Hungary	56.3	56.2	56.2	57.0	56.8	56.9	57.3	57.3	56.7	55.4	55.4
Malta	54.2	54.3	54.4	54.2	54.0	53.9	53.6	54.6	55.3	54.9	56.0
Netherlands (³)	72.9	74.1	74.4	73.6	73.1	73.2	74.3	76.0	77.2	77.0	74.7
Austria (²)	68.5	68.5	68.7	68.9	67.8	68.6	70.2	71.4	72.1	71.6	71.7
Poland	55.0	53.4	51.5	51.2	51.7	52.8	54.5	57.0	59.2	59.3	59.3
Portugal	68.4	69.0	68.8	68.1	67.8	67.5	67.9	67.8	68.2	66.3	65.6
Romania (⁴)	63.0	62.4	57.6	57.6	57.7	57.6	58.8	58.8	59.0	58.6	58.8
Slovenia	62.8	63.8	63.4	62.6	65.3	66.0	66.6	67.8	68.6	67.5	66.2
Slovakia	56.8	56.8	56.8	57.7	57.0	57.7	59.4	60.7	62.3	60.2	58.8
Finland	67.2	68.1	68.1	67.7	67.6	68.4	69.3	70.3	71.1	68.7	68.1
Sweden (¹)	73.0	74.0	73.6	72.9	72.1	72.5	73.1	74.2	74.3	72.2	72.7
United Kingdom	71.2	71.4	71.4	71.5	71.7	71.7	71.6	71.5	71.5	69.9	69.5
Iceland	:	:	:	83.3	82.3	83.8	84.6	85.1	83.6	78.3	78.2
Norway	77.5	77.2	76.8	75.5	75.1	74.8	75.4	76.8	78.0	76.4	75.3
Switzerland	78.3	79.1	78.9	77.9	77.4	77.2	77.9	78.6	79.5	79.0	78.6
Croatia	:	:	53.4	53.4	54.7	55.0	55.6	57.1	57.8	56.6	54.0
FYR of Macedonia	:	:	:	:	:	:	39.6	40.7	41.9	43.3	43.5
Turkey	:	:	:	:	:	:	44.6	44.6	44.9	44.3	46.3
Japan	68.9	68.8	68.2	68.4	68.7	69.3	70.0	70.7	70.7	70.0	70.1
United States	74.1	73.1	71.9	71.2	71.2	71.5	72.0	71.8	70.9	67.6	66.7

(¹) Break in series in, 2005.
(²) Break in series in, 2004.
(³) Break in series in, 2010.
(⁴) Break in series in, 2002.

Source: Eurostat (online data code: lfsi_emp_a)

Table 5.1.2: Employment rates for selected population groups, 2000-2010
(%)

	Male			Female			Older workers (55-64)		
	2000	2005	2010	2000	2005	2010	2000	2005	2010
EU-27	70.8	70.8	70.1	53.7	56.3	58.2	36.9	42.3	46.3
Euro area	71.4	71.8	70.4	51.4	55.6	57.9	34.2	40.4	45.8
Belgium	69.5	68.3	67.4	51.5	53.8	56.5	26.3	31.8	37.3
Bulgaria	54.7	60.0	63.0	46.3	51.7	56.4	20.8	34.7	43.5
Czech Republic	73.2	73.3	73.5	56.9	56.3	56.3	36.3	44.5	46.5
Denmark	80.8	79.8	75.8	71.6	71.9	71.1	55.7	59.5	57.6
Germany (¹)	72.9	71.3	76.0	58.1	60.6	66.1	37.6	45.4	57.7
Estonia	64.3	67.0	61.5	56.9	62.1	60.6	46.3	56.1	53.8
Ireland	76.3	76.9	63.9	53.9	58.3	56.0	45.3	51.6	50.0
Greece	71.5	74.2	70.9	41.7	46.1	48.1	39.0	41.6	42.3
Spain (¹)	71.2	75.2	64.7	41.3	51.2	52.3	37.0	43.1	43.6
France	69.2	69.2	68.3	55.2	58.4	59.9	29.9	38.5	39.7
Italy (¹)	68.0	69.9	67.7	39.6	45.3	46.1	27.7	31.4	36.6
Cyprus	78.7	79.2	76.6	53.5	58.4	63.0	49.4	50.6	56.8
Latvia	61.5	67.6	59.2	53.8	59.3	59.4	36.0	49.5	48.2
Lithuania	60.5	66.1	56.8	57.7	59.4	58.7	40.4	49.2	48.6
Luxembourg	75.0	73.3	73.1	50.1	53.7	57.2	26.7	31.7	39.6
Hungary	63.1	63.1	60.4	49.7	51.0	50.6	22.2	33.0	34.4
Malta	75.0	73.8	72.3	33.1	33.7	39.2	28.5	30.8	30.2
Netherlands (²)	82.1	79.9	80.0	63.5	66.4	69.3	38.2	46.1	53.7
Austria (¹)	77.3	75.4	77.1	59.6	62.0	66.4	28.8	31.8	42.4
Poland	61.2	58.9	65.6	48.9	46.8	53.0	28.4	27.2	34.0
Portugal	76.5	73.4	70.1	60.5	61.7	61.1	50.7	50.5	49.2
Romania (¹)	68.6	63.7	65.7	57.5	51.5	52.0	49.5	39.4	41.1
Slovenia	67.2	70.4	69.6	58.4	61.3	62.6	22.7	30.7	35.0
Slovakia	62.2	64.6	65.2	51.5	50.9	52.3	21.3	30.3	40.5
Finland	70.1	70.3	69.4	64.2	66.5	66.9	41.6	52.7	56.2
Sweden (¹)	75.1	74.4	75.1	70.9	70.4	70.3	64.9	69.4	70.5
United Kingdom	77.8	77.7	74.5	64.7	65.8	64.6	50.7	56.8	57.1
Iceland	:	86.9	80.1	:	80.5	76.2	:	84.3	79.8
Norway	81.3	77.8	77.3	73.6	71.7	73.3	65.2	65.5	68.6
Switzerland	87.3	83.9	84.6	69.3	70.4	72.5	63.3	65.1	68.0
Croatia	:	61.7	59.4	:	48.6	48.8	:	32.6	37.6
FYR of Macedonia	:	:	52.8	:	:	34.0	:	:	34.2
Turkey	:	:	66.7	:	:	26.2	:	:	29.6
Japan	80.9	80.4	80.0	56.7	58.1	60.1	62.8	63.9	65.2
United States	80.6	77.6	71.1	67.8	65.6	62.4	57.8	60.8	60.3

(¹) Break in series, 2000 to 2005.
(²) Break in series, 2005 to 2010.

Source: Eurostat (online data code: lfsi_emp_a)

Table 5.1.3: Employment rate by highest level of education, age group 25-64, 2010
(%)

	Pre-primary, primary & lower secondary – ISCED levels 0-2	Upper secondary & post-secondary non-tertiary – ISCED levels 3-4	Tertiary – ISCED levels 5-6
EU-27	53.8	73.1	83.9
Euro area	54.4	74.3	83.4
Belgium	48.9	74.5	84.0
Bulgaria	41.2	71.5	83.8
Czech Republic	43.2	74.5	83.3
Denmark	62.6	79.1	86.3
Germany	55.3	76.3	86.9
Estonia	45.2	68.7	79.9
Ireland	46.8	66.4	81.1
Greece	58.1	66.5	80.0
Spain	52.9	68.9	79.7
France	55.5	74.4	83.7
Italy	50.4	72.6	78.3
Cyprus	66.4	77.6	84.9
Latvia	48.5	66.1	81.1
Lithuania	32.4	63.8	86.9
Luxembourg	61.9	72.1	85.0
Hungary	37.6	66.2	78.6
Malta	49.1	81.0	85.7
Netherlands	61.4	80.3	87.2
Austria	56.1	77.9	85.7
Poland	39.9	65.6	84.8
Portugal	68.2	79.9	85.4
Romania	54.8	68.5	85.3
Slovenia	51.1	73.0	87.3
Slovakia	29.7	69.9	82.2
Finland	55.0	74.1	84.1
Sweden	65.1	83.3	88.1
United Kingdom	56.0	76.8	85.1
Iceland	76.5	82.0	89.1
Norway	63.8	81.4	90.2
Switzerland	69.3	81.2	88.4
Croatia	43.3	62.7	79.0
FYR of Macedonia	33.4	58.4	73.9
Turkey	45.6	60.0	75.7

Source: Eurostat (online data code: lfsa_ergaed)

Figure 5.1.4: Employment rates by age group, 2010 (¹)
(%)

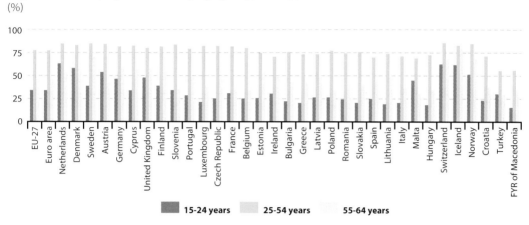

(¹) The figure is ranked on the overall employment rate.

Source: Eurostat (online data code: lfsi_emp_a)

Figure 5.1.5: Annual employment growth, 2000-2010
(% change in the number of employed persons)

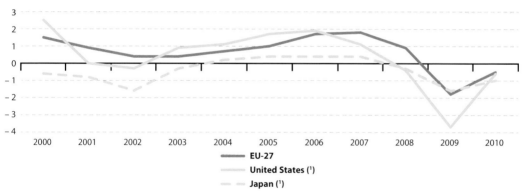

(¹) 2009 and 2010, forecasts.

Source: Eurostat (online data code: lfsi_grt_a)

Table 5.1.4: Annual employment growth by sex, 2000-2010
(% change in the number of employed persons)

	Total			Male			Female		
	2000	**2005 (¹)**	**2010 (²)**	**2000**	**2005 (³)**	**2010 (²)**	**2000**	**2005 (³)**	**2010 (²)**
EU-27	1.5	1.0	−0.5	1.0	0.7	−0.6	2.2	1.3	−0.3
Euro area	2.3	1.0	−0.5	1.9	0.4	−0.7	3.0	1.8	−0.2
Belgium	2.0	1.4	0.7	1.9	0.5	0.3	2.2	2.6	1.1
Bulgaria	−2.4	2.7	−5.9	:	3.4	−6.9	:	1.9	−4.8
Czech Republic	−0.2	1.0	−0.8	−0.2	1.7	−0.7	−0.1	0.2	−0.9
Denmark	0.5	1.0	−2.1	0.0	0.9	−2.3	1.1	1.2	−1.8
Germany	1.9	−0.1	0.5	1.4	−1.1	0.9	2.6	1.1	0.2
Estonia	−1.5	2.0	−4.8	−1.1	0.5	−5.1	−1.9	3.6	−4.5
Ireland	4.5	4.9	−4.1	3.9	4.3	−5.2	5.3	5.8	−2.9
Greece	0.5	0.8	−2.1	0.1	0.5	−2.8	1.2	1.3	−1.1
Spain	5.1	4.1	−2.3	3.6	2.7	−3.3	7.7	6.3	−0.9
France	2.6	0.7	0.2	2.5	0.2	0.2	2.7	1.2	0.1
Italy	1.9	0.6	−0.7	1.3	0.7	−1.2	3.1	0.3	0.0
Cyprus	1.7	3.6	0.1	:	3.8	−0.7	:	3.3	1.0
Latvia	−3.2	1.6	−4.8	−4.8	2.3	−5.3	−1.5	0.8	−4.3
Lithuania	−4.0	2.5	−5.1	:	2.2	−5.9	:	2.7	−4.4
Luxembourg	5.6	2.9	1.5	5.3	1.5	0.6	6.1	4.8	2.8
Hungary	1.0	−0.2	0.2	0.9	−0.3	−0.9	1.1	−0.1	1.5
Malta	:	1.5	2.0	:	0.3	0.9	:	4.2	4.2
Netherlands	2.2	0.5	−0.5	2.0	−0.3	−0.5	2.5	1.4	−0.5
Austria	0.9	1.5	1.0	0.9	1.0	1.1	1.0	2.1	0.9
Poland	−1.6	2.2	0.4	−1.5	3.1	0.1	−1.7	1.1	0.8
Portugal	2.1	−0.3	−1.5	1.9	−1.0	−1.6	2.3	0.5	−1.4
Romania	−0.8	−1.5	−1.8	−1.0	−0.6	−1.5	−0.5	−2.6	−2.1
Slovenia	1.5	−0.5	−2.0	1.4	−0.6	−1.9	1.7	−0.3	−2.2
Slovakia	−2.0	1.6	−1.4	−2.8	2.9	−2.5	−0.9	0.1	0.0
Finland	2.1	1.4	−1.4	2.2	1.0	−0.7	1.9	1.8	−2.2
Sweden	2.5	0.3	1.1	2.3	1.0	1.9	2.6	−0.5	0.3
United Kingdom (⁴)	1.3	1.3	−0.7	−0.6	1.1	−0.5	3.6	1.6	−0.9
Iceland	2.0	3.3	−0.3	:	3.7	−1.2	:	2.8	0.7
Norway	0.6	1.2	−0.2	:	1.5	0.1	:	0.9	−0.6
Croatia	4.0	0.8	−4.0	:	0.2	−4.5	:	1.5	−3.4
Turkey	−0.4	1.4	6.2	:	:	5.0	:	:	9.5
Japan	−0.6	0.4	−1.0	:	:	:	:	:	:
United States	2.5	1.7	−0.6	:	:	:	:	:	:

(¹) Austria, break in series.
(²) The Netherlands, break in series.
(³) Germany, Spain, Italy, Austria, Romania and Sweden, break in series.
(⁴) Eurostat estimates of persons employed are based on the estimates of jobs transmitted by the United Kingdom.

Source: Eurostat (online data code: lfsi_grt_a)

Table 5.1.5: Persons working part-time or with a second job, 2000-2010
(% of total employment)

	Persons working part-time			Persons with a second job		
	2000	2005	2010	2000	2005	2010
EU-27	16.2	17.8	19.2	3.9	3.7	3.7
Euro area	15.6	18.6	20.4	2.9	3.1	3.3
Belgium	18.9	22.0	24.0	3.8	3.9	4.1
Bulgaria	:	2.1	2.4	2.6	0.6	0.5
Czech Republic	5.3	4.9	5.9	2.7	2.4	2.2
Denmark	21.3	22.1	26.5	10.9	11.0	8.4
Germany (¹)	19.4	24.0	26.2	2.4	3.3	3.6
Estonia	8.1	7.8	11.0	6.3	3.3	5.0
Ireland	16.4	:	22.4	1.8	2.1	2.1
Greece	4.5	5.0	6.4	3.8	2.8	3.1
Spain (²)	7.9	12.4	13.3	1.8	2.6	2.2
France	16.7	17.2	17.8	3.5	2.9	3.4
Italy (²)	8.4	12.8	15.0	1.4	1.6	1.5
Cyprus	8.4	8.9	9.3	5.7	6.1	3.3
Latvia	11.3	8.3	9.7	4.7	5.9	4.3
Lithuania	10.2	7.1	8.1	6.9	5.7	5.1
Luxembourg	10.4	17.4	17.9	1.1	1.8	3.0
Hungary	3.5	4.1	5.8	2.0	1.9	1.8
Malta	6.8	9.6	12.4	4.4	4.5	4.9
Netherlands (³)	41.5	46.1	48.9	5.9	6.2	7.2
Austria (²)	16.3	21.1	25.2	5.5	4.0	4.0
Poland	10.5	10.8	8.3	8.5	7.8	7.3
Portugal	10.9	11.2	11.6	6.2	6.4	6.0
Romania (²)	16.5	10.2	11.0	5.3	3.1	2.7
Slovenia	6.5	9.0	11.4	2.7	3.4	3.7
Slovakia	2.1	2.5	3.9	1.0	1.4	1.2
Finland	12.3	13.7	14.6	3.8	4.0	4.5
Sweden (²)	19.5	24.7	26.4	8.8	7.3	8.4
United Kingdom	25.1	25.2	26.9	4.4	3.7	3.8
Iceland	:	22.2	22.9	17.6	10.8	8.7
Norway	25.8	28.2	28.4	8.0	5.9	8.4
Switzerland	30.5	33.1	35.3	5.9	6.4	6.7
Croatia	:	10.1	9.7	:	3.4	2.7
FYR of Macedonia	:	:	5.9	:	:	2.1
Turkey	:	:	11.7	:	:	2.8

(¹) Persons working part-time. break in series between 2000 and 2005.
(²) Break in series between 2000 and 2005.
(³) Break in series between 2005 and 2010.

Source: Eurostat (online data codes: tps00159, lfsa_e2gis and lfsa_egan)

Figure 5.1.6: Persons employed part-time, 2010
(% of total employment)

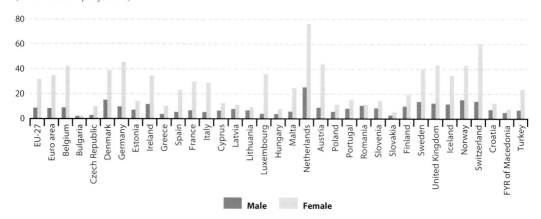

Source: Eurostat (online data code: tps00159)

Figure 5.1.7: Proportion of employees with a contract of limited duration, age group 15-64, 2010
(% of total employees)

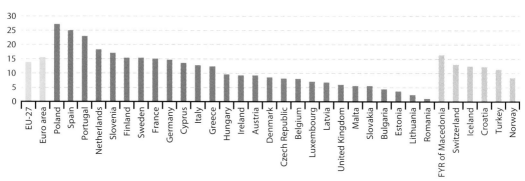

Source: Eurostat (online data code: lfsa_etpga)

5.2 Unemployment

This subchapter gives an overview of statistical information on unemployment in the European Union (EU). Unemployment levels and rates move in a cyclical way, largely related to the general business cycle. However, other factors such as labour market policies and demographic changes may influence the short and long-term development of unemployment.

Main statistical findings

Unemployment trends

In 2000, there were, on average, 19.5 million persons unemployed in the EU-27, equivalent to 8.7 % of the total labour force. This figure fell slightly in 2001, before rising slowly to 21.0 million persons by 2004. There followed a period of steadily declining unemployment within the EU-27 and the number of unemployed persons reached a low point in 2008 when 16.8 million were without a job (equivalent to 7.1 % of the labour force). In the wake of the financial and economic crisis the level of unemployment climbed rapidly, increasing by 6.3 million persons between 2008 and 2010 to reach 23.2 million persons. As such, the impact of the economic crisis on unemployment more than wiped out the steady contraction in unemployment during the period from 2004 to 2008.

The unemployment rate in the euro area followed roughly the same trend as in the EU-27. Between 2000 and 2004 the unemployment rate in the euro area was below that recorded in the EU-27. This pattern was subsequently reversed as unemployment declined more rapidly in the EU Member States outside of the euro area between 2005 and 2008. The overall impact of the financial and economic crisis on the unemployment rate in the EU-27 and the euro area was identical, as both areas reported unemployment rates rising by 2.5 percentage points between 2008 and 2010.

In 2000, the unemployment rate in the United States was 4.0 %, considerably lower than in the EU-27. It remained much lower until 2008, when unemployment in the United States started to increase rapidly. In 2009, the unemployment rate for the United States was higher (at 9.3 %) than in the EU-27 (9.0 %), although identical rates of 9.6 % were recorded for the EU-27 and the United States in 2010. Unemployment in Japan was much lower than in the EU-27; this was the case throughout the last decade, with the most recent unemployment rate – 5.1 % in 2010 – almost half that recorded in the EU-27 or the United States.

Youth unemployment trends

Youth unemployment rates are generally much higher than unemployment rates for other age groups. High youth unemployment rates reflect the difficulties faced by young people in finding jobs. However, this does not necessarily mean that the group of unemployed persons aged between 15 and 24 is large because many young people are studying full-time and are therefore neither working nor looking for a job (so they are not part of the labour force which is used as the denominator for calculating the unemployment rate).

Youth unemployment ratios use a slightly different concept: the unemployment ratio is calculated as the number of unemployed persons aged 15 to 24 divided by the total population of the same age. Table 5.2.4 shows that youth unemployment ratios in the EU-27 were much lower than youth unemployment rates; they did however rise considerably from 2008 onwards following the onset of the financial and economic crisis.

The youth unemployment rate in the EU-27 was more than double the unemployment rate for the whole population throughout the last decade. The EU-27 youth unemployment rate was systematically higher than in the euro area between 2000 and 2007; since this date, these two rates were almost identical (see Table 5.2.4).

Male and female unemployment trends

Historically, women have been more likely to be unemployed than men. In 2000, the unemployment rate for women in the EU-27 was 9.8 %, while the rate for men was 2 percentage points lower. By 2002, this sex gap had narrowed to 1.4 percentage points and between 2003 and 2007 the gap remained more or less constant. Since the start of 2008, male and female unemployment rates in the EU-27 have converged and by the second quarter of 2009 the male unemployment rate was higher than that for women. This small difference between unemployment rates by sex continued in 2010, when the rate for men was 9.7 % – just 0.1 percentage points higher than for women.

A detailed look at 2010

The overall unemployment rate in the EU-27 reached 9.6 % in 2010. In comparison to the rate during 2009, the unemployment rate rose by 0.6 percentage points; this was less than the increase in unemployment recorded between 2008 and 2009, when the unemployment rate rose by 1.9 percentage points.

In the United States, a similar pattern was observed, as the unemployment rate grew rapidly between 2008 and 2009 (climbing by 3.5 percentage points), while the rate continued to grow – albeit at a much slower pace – between 2009 and 2010, rising from 9.3 % to 9.6 %. In Japan the unemployment rate stood at 5.1 % in 2010, marking a 1.2 percentage point increase since the most recent low was recorded in 2007; as such the effect of the financial and economic crisis on Japanese unemployment levels was far less than in either the EU-27 or the United States.

The unemployment rate rose in all 27 EU Member States between 2009 and 2010, apart from Germany, Luxembourg, Malta and Austria; the biggest decrease in unemployment was recorded in Germany, where the unemployment rate dropped by 0.7 percentage points. Outside of the EU, the unemployment rate also fell in Turkey between 2009 and 2010 (down by 1.8 percentage points).

Belgium, France, Romania, Finland, Sweden and the United Kingdom each reported modest increases (below 0.5 percentage points) in their respective unemployment rates between 2009 and 2010. However, the highest increases in unemployment rates were registered in Estonia, Greece, Spain, Lithuania and Slovakia – where rates rose by in excess of 2 percentage points between 2009 and 2010.

Spain remained the Member State with the highest overall unemployment rate in the EU-27 in 2010, at 20.1 %. The dispersion of unemployment across the EU-27 continued to increase during 2010.

Long-term unemployment is one of the main concerns of policymakers. Apart from its financial and social effects on personal life, long-term unemployment negatively affects social cohesion and, ultimately, may hinder economic growth. In total, 3.8 % of the labour force in the EU-27 in 2010 had been unemployed for more than one year; almost half of these, 1.8 % of the labour force, had been unemployed for more than two years.

For the first time since the calculation of EU-27 unemployment statistics started (in 2000), the unemployment rate for women was lower than that for men in 2009, and this remained the case in 2010. Male unemployment rates were higher than the corresponding rates for women in 2010 in 14 out of the 27 EU Member States. In the euro area, the unemployment rate for women (10.3 %) remained higher than the rate for men (9.9 %). The gap between male and female unemployment rates varied from – 6.3 percentage points in Greece to + 7.2 percentage points in Ireland.

The youth unemployment rate in the EU-27 was more than double the overall unemployment rate in 2010. At 20.9 %, more than one out of every five young persons in the labour force was unemployed, but looking and available for work. In the euro area, the youth unemployment rate was marginally lower at 20.7 %. In Spain (41.6 %), Lithuania (35.1 %), Latvia (34.5 %), Slovakia (33.6 %), Greece and Estonia (both 32.9 %), youth unemployment rates were particularly high. The Netherlands (8.7 %), Austria (8.8 %) and Germany (9.9 %) were the only Member States to record youth unemployment rates in single digits in 2010.

Educational qualifications were seen to be a good insurance against unemployment, as the chances of finding a job clearly increased for those who had attained a higher level of education. This characteristic was noted in almost every Member State in 2010, as the average unemployment rate in the EU-27 for those having attained a tertiary education qualification (4.9 %) was considerably

lower than the corresponding rate for those who had obtained at most a lower secondary education (14.2 %).

Data sources and availability

The main source used by Eurostat for unemployment figures is the European Union Labour force survey (EU LFS). This household survey is carried out in all EU-27 Member States in accordance with European legislation; it provides figures at least each quarter.

There is currently no legal basis for producing and disseminating monthly unemployment data and few countries actually supply monthly unemployment figures directly from the LFS. Nevertheless, for many countries Eurostat calculates monthly data by using additional monthly figures from unemployment registers. The quarterly LFS results are always used as a benchmark to ensure international comparability.

Monthly unemployment figures are published by Eurostat as rates (as a percentage of the labour force) or levels (in thousands), by sex and for two age groups (persons aged 15-24, and those aged 25-74). The figures are available as unadjusted, seasonally adjusted and trend series. There are monthly estimates for all EU-27 Member States except for Estonia, Latvia and Lithuania. Data for the EU-27 aggregate start in 2000 and for the euro area (EA-17) in 1995; the starting point for individual Member States varies.

Quarterly and annual unemployment figures from the LFS are also published, with more detailed breakdowns (for example, a wider range of age groups, by nationality, or by educational attainment); there are also figures available on long-term unemployment (more than 12 months) and very long-term unemployment (more than 24 months).

Context

The unemployment rate is an important indicator with both social and economic dimensions. Rising unemployment results in a loss of income for affected individuals, increased pressure with respect to government spending on social benefits and a reduction in tax revenue. From an economic perspective, unemployment may be viewed as unused labour capacity.

The International Labour Organization (ILO) definition of the unemployment rate is the most widely used labour market indicator because of its international comparability and relatively timely availability. Besides the unemployment rate, indicators such as employment and job vacancies also give useful insights into labour market developments.

Time series on unemployment are used by the European Commission, other public institutions, and the media as an economic indicator; banks may use the data for business cycle analysis. Finally, the general public may also be interested in changes in unemployment.

The unemployment rate is considered to be a lagging indicator. When there is an economic downturn, it usually takes several months before the unemployment rate begins to rise. Once the economy starts to pick up again, employers usually remain cautious about hiring new staff and it may take several months before unemployment rates start to fall.

Male, youth and long-term unemployment appear to be more susceptible to cyclical economic changes than overall unemployment. Indeed, social policymakers often face the challenge of remedying these situations by designing ways to increase employment opportunities for various groups of society, those working in particular economic activities, or those living in specific regions.

Globalisation and technological progress have an ever-increasing effect on daily life, and the demand for different types of labour and skills is evolving at a rapid pace. While enterprises try to improve their productivity and become more competitive and innovative, they may well seek to pass on risk to the labour force through greater flexibility – both in relation to those already in employment, as well as those searching for a new job.

Within the context of the European employment strategy (EES), there are a number of measures that are designed to help encourage people to remain in work or find a new job, including:

the promotion of a life-cycle approach to work, encouraging lifelong learning, improving support to those seeking a job, as well as ensuring equal opportunities. The EES is in line with the Europe 2020 strategy, which sets out a vision of Europe's social market economy for the 21st century. In order to achieve the goals of the Europe 2020 strategy a number of flagship initiatives have been enacted; these include 'an agenda for new skills and jobs' and 'youth on the move' – both of which are relevant to the promotion of job creation (especially among the younger generations). These initiatives are designed to lower (youth) unemployment rates through a range of policies, including proposals aimed at education and training institutions, or measures for the creation of a (work) environment conducive to higher activity rates and higher labour productivity; there are also initiatives aimed at improving the entry rate of young people into the labour market. It is hoped that these actions will help Europe move towards three headline targets by 2020 – as part of the EES, namely, that:

- 75 % of people aged 20-64 in the EU-27 are in work;
- school drop-out rates for the EU-27 are below 10 %, and at least 40 % of those aged 30-34 have completed a third level of education;
- at least 20 million fewer people are in or at-risk-of poverty and social exclusion.

Table 5.2.1: Unemployment rate, 2000-2010
(%)

	2000	2001	2002	2003	2004	2005	2006	2007	2008	2009	2010
EU-27	8.7	8.5	8.9	9.0	9.1	9.0	8.2	7.2	7.1	9.0	9.6
Euro area	8.5	8.1	8.4	8.8	9.0	9.1	8.5	7.6	7.6	9.6	10.1
Belgium	6.9	6.6	7.5	8.2	8.4	8.5	8.3	7.5	7.0	7.9	8.3
Bulgaria	16.4	19.5	18.2	13.7	12.1	10.1	9.0	6.9	5.6	6.8	10.2
Czech Republic	8.7	8.0	7.3	7.8	8.3	7.9	7.2	5.3	4.4	6.7	7.3
Denmark	4.3	4.5	4.6	5.4	5.5	4.8	3.9	3.8	3.3	6.0	7.4
Germany	7.5	7.6	8.4	9.3	9.8	11.2	10.3	8.7	7.5	7.8	7.1
Estonia	13.6	12.6	10.3	10.0	9.7	7.9	5.9	4.7	5.5	13.8	16.9
Ireland	4.2	3.9	4.5	4.6	4.5	4.4	4.5	4.6	6.3	11.9	13.7
Greece	11.2	10.7	10.3	9.7	10.5	9.9	8.9	8.3	7.7	9.5	12.6
Spain	11.1	10.3	11.1	11.1	10.6	9.2	8.5	8.3	11.3	18.0	20.1
France	9.0	8.3	8.6	9.0	9.3	9.3	9.2	8.4	7.8	9.5	9.7
Italy	10.1	9.1	8.6	8.4	8.0	7.7	6.8	6.1	6.7	7.8	8.4
Cyprus	4.9	3.8	3.6	4.1	4.7	5.3	4.6	4.0	3.6	5.3	6.5
Latvia	13.7	12.9	12.2	10.5	10.4	8.9	6.8	6.0	7.5	17.1	18.7
Lithuania	16.4	16.5	13.5	12.5	11.4	8.3	5.6	4.3	5.8	13.7	17.8
Luxembourg	2.2	1.9	2.6	3.8	5.0	4.6	4.6	4.2	4.9	5.1	4.5
Hungary	6.4	5.7	5.8	5.9	6.1	7.2	7.5	7.4	7.8	10.0	11.2
Malta	6.7	7.6	7.5	7.6	7.4	7.2	7.1	6.4	5.9	7.0	6.8
Netherlands	3.1	2.5	3.1	4.2	5.1	5.3	4.4	3.6	3.1	3.7	4.5
Austria	3.6	3.6	4.2	4.3	4.9	5.2	4.8	4.4	3.8	4.8	4.4
Poland	16.1	18.3	20.0	19.7	19.0	17.8	13.9	9.6	7.1	8.2	9.6
Portugal	*4.5*	*4.6*	*5.7*	*7.1*	*7.5*	*8.6*	*8.6*	*8.9*	*8.5*	*10.6*	*12.0*
Romania	7.3	6.8	8.6	7.0	8.1	7.2	7.3	6.4	5.8	6.9	7.3
Slovenia	6.7	6.2	6.3	6.7	6.3	6.5	6.0	4.9	4.4	5.9	7.3
Slovakia	18.8	19.3	18.7	17.6	18.2	16.3	13.4	11.1	9.5	12.0	14.4
Finland	9.8	9.1	9.1	9.0	8.8	8.4	7.7	6.9	6.4	8.2	8.4
Sweden (¹)	5.6	5.8	6.0	6.6	7.4	7.7	7.1	6.1	6.2	8.3	8.4
United Kingdom	5.4	5.0	5.1	5.0	4.7	4.8	5.4	5.3	5.6	7.6	7.8
Norway	3.2	3.4	3.7	4.2	4.3	4.5	3.4	2.5	2.5	3.1	3.5
Croatia	:	:	14.8	14.2	13.7	12.7	11.2	9.6	8.4	9.1	11.8
Turkey (²)	:	:	:	:	:	9.2	8.7	8.8	9.7	12.5	10.7
Japan	4.7	5.0	5.4	5.3	4.7	4.4	4.1	3.9	4.0	5.1	5.1
United States	4.0	4.8	5.8	6.0	5.5	5.1	4.6	4.6	5.8	9.3	9.6

(¹) Break in series, 2001.
(²) Break in series, 2007.

Source: Eurostat (online data code: une_rt_a)

Figure 5.2.1: Unemployment rate, 2010 (¹)
(%)

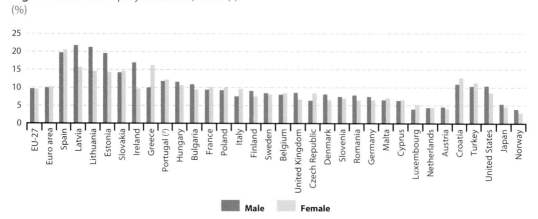

(¹) The figure is ranked on the average of male and female.
(²) Estimates.

Source: Eurostat (online data code: une_rt_a)

Figure 5.2.2: Unemployment rate by duration, 2010
(%)

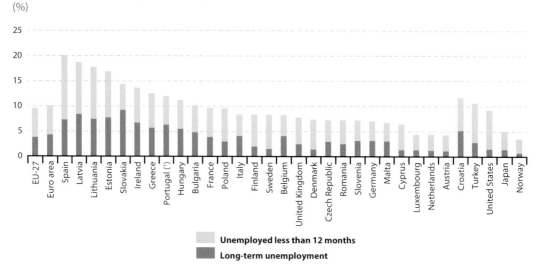

(¹) Estimates.

Source: Eurostat (online data codes: tsiem110 and tsisc070)

Table 5.2.2: Unemployment rate by sex and by age, 2005 and 2010
(%)

	Male		Female		< 25 years	25-74 years
	2005	2010	2005	2010	2010	2010
EU-27	8.3	9.7	9.8	9.6	20.9	8.3
Euro area	8.2	9.9	10.3	10.3	20.7	8.9
Belgium	7.6	8.1	9.5	8.5	22.4	7.0
Bulgaria	10.3	10.9	9.8	9.5	23.2	9.1
Czech Republic	6.5	6.4	9.8	8.5	18.3	6.4
Denmark	4.4	8.2	5.3	6.6	13.8	6.2
Germany	11.4	7.5	10.9	6.6	9.9	6.7
Estonia	8.8	19.5	7.1	14.3	32.9	15.0
Ireland	4.6	16.9	4.1	9.7	27.8	11.9
Greece	6.1	9.9	15.3	16.2	32.9	11.1
Spain	7.1	19.7	12.2	20.5	41.6	18.0
France	8.4	9.4	10.3	10.2	23.3	8.2
Italy	6.2	7.6	10.1	9.7	27.8	7.0
Cyprus	4.3	6.4	6.5	6.7	17.8	5.3
Latvia	9.1	21.7	8.7	15.7	34.5	16.6
Lithuania	8.2	21.2	8.3	14.5	35.1	16.1
Luxembourg	3.6	4.0	6.0	5.3	16.1	3.8
Hungary	7.0	11.6	7.4	10.7	26.6	10.0
Malta	6.4	6.6	8.9	7.2	12.9	5.6
Netherlands	4.9	4.4	5.8	4.5	8.7	3.7
Austria	4.9	4.6	5.5	4.2	8.8	3.7
Poland	16.6	9.3	19.2	10.0	23.7	8.1
Portugal	*8.1*	*11.8*	*9.1*	*12.2*	*27.7*	*10.6*
Romania	7.8	7.9	6.4	6.5	22.1	5.8
Slovenia	6.1	7.5	7.1	7.1	14.7	6.5
Slovakia	15.5	14.2	17.2	14.6	33.6	12.5
Finland	8.2	9.1	8.6	7.6	21.4	6.6
Sweden	7.7	8.5	7.6	8.2	25.2	5.9
United Kingdom	5.2	8.6	4.3	6.8	19.6	5.8
Norway	4.7	4.0	4.3	3.0	8.9	2.6
Croatia	11.6	11.0	13.9	12.8	30.7	9.4
Turkey	9.1	10.4	9.3	11.4	19.7	8.8
Japan	4.6	5.4	4.2	4.6	9.3	4.7
United States	5.1	10.5	5.1	8.6	18.4	8.2

Source: Eurostat (online data code: une_rt_a)

Table 5.2.3: Unemployment rate, EU-27, 2000-2010
(%)

	2000	2001	2002	2003	2004	2005	2006	2007	2008	2009	2010
Male	7.8	7.8	8.3	8.4	8.5	8.3	7.6	6.6	6.6	9.0	9.7
Female	9.8	9.4	9.7	9.7	9.8	9.8	9.0	7.9	7.6	8.9	9.6
Less than 25 years	17.3	17.4	18.0	18.2	18.6	18.7	17.4	15.6	15.7	20.0	20.9
Between 25 and 74 years	7.4	7.2	7.6	7.7	7.8	7.7	7.1	6.1	6.0	7.6	8.3
Long-term unemployment rate	4.0	3.9	4.0	4.1	4.2	4.1	3.7	3.1	2.6	3.0	3.8
Male	3.5	3.5	3.6	3.8	3.9	3.8	3.5	2.8	2.4	2.9	3.9
Female	4.6	4.4	4.5	4.5	4.6	4.5	4.0	3.3	2.8	3.1	3.7
Very long-term unemployment rate	2.4	2.3	2.3	2.4	2.4	2.4	2.2	1.8	1.5	1.5	1.8

Source: Eurostat (online data codes: une_rt_a and une_ltu_a)

Figure 5.2.3: Unemployment rate (among persons aged 25-64 years) by level of educational attainment, 2010
(%)

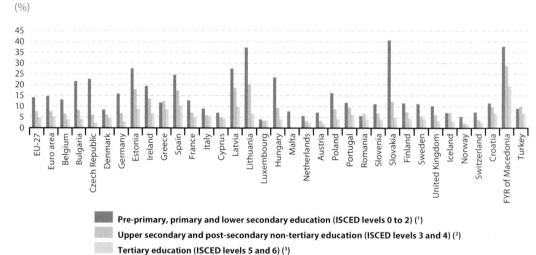

■ **Pre-primary, primary and lower secondary education (ISCED levels 0 to 2)** (^{1})
▨ **Upper secondary and post-secondary non-tertiary education (ISCED levels 3 and 4)** (^{2})
▨ **Tertiary education (ISCED levels 5 and 6)** (^{3})

(^{1}) Luxembourg and Croatia, unreliable data.
(^{2}) Malta, not available.
(^{3}) Malta, not available; Luxembourg, Slovenia and Croatia, unreliable data.

Source: Eurostat (online data code: tps00066)

Table 5.2.4: Youth unemployment rates, 2008-2011
(%)

	Youth unemployment rate				Youth unemployment ratio		
	2008	2009	2010	Q1-2011 ([1])	2008	2009	2010
EU-27	15.8	20.1	21.1	21.0	6.9	8.7	9.0
Euro area	16.0	20.2	20.9	20.6	6.9	8.7	8.7
Belgium	18.0	21.9	22.4	19.0	6.0	7.1	7.3
Bulgaria	12.7	16.2	23.2	26.8	3.8	4.8	6.7
Czech Republic	9.9	16.6	18.3	17.1	3.1	5.3	5.7
Denmark	7.6	11.2	13.8	13.5	5.5	8.0	9.3
Germany	10.6	11.2	9.9	9.0	5.5	5.8	5.1
Estonia	12.0	27.5	32.9	20.4	5.0	11.0	12.6
Ireland	13.3	24.4	27.8	28.9	6.7	11.3	11.6
Greece	22.1	25.8	32.9	38.5	6.7	8.0	10.0
Spain	24.6	37.8	41.6	44.1	11.7	17.1	17.8
France	19.3	23.9	23.7	23.4	7.2	9.2	8.9
Italy	21.3	25.4	27.8	28.6	6.6	7.4	7.9
Cyprus	8.8	14.0	17.2	19.3	3.8	5.7	6.8
Latvia	13.1	33.6	34.5	29.7	5.6	14.0	13.9
Lithuania	13.4	29.2	35.1	32.6	4.1	8.9	10.4
Luxembourg	17.3	16.5	15.6	12.8	5.2	5.5	3.5
Hungary	19.9	26.5	26.6	26.0	5.0	6.5	6.6
Malta	11.8	14.4	13.1	12.3	6.4	7.4	6.7
Netherlands ([2])	6.3	7.7	8.7	7.4	3.9	4.8	6.0
Austria	8.0	10.0	8.8	9.1	4.9	6.0	5.2
Poland	17.3	20.6	23.7	24.9	5.7	7.0	8.2
Portugal	*20.2*	*24.8*	*27.7*	26.9	*6.8*	*7.9*	*8.2*
Romania	18.6	20.8	22.1	22.8	5.7	6.4	6.9
Slovenia	10.4	13.6	14.7	16.9	4.5	5.6	5.9
Slovakia	19.0	27.3	33.6	33.2	6.2	8.6	10.4
Finland	16.5	21.5	21.4	20.5	8.8	10.9	10.6
Sweden	20.2	25.0	25.2	23.2	10.7	12.8	13.0
United Kingdom	15.0	19.1	19.6	20.0	9.2	11.4	11.6
Norway	7.2	8.9	8.9	8.9	4.6	5.3	5.3
Croatia	21.9	25.0	32.5	39.3	7.6	8.6	11.2
Turkey	18.4	22.7	19.7	17.3	6.9	8.5	7.4
Japan	7.3	9.1	9.3	:	:	:	:
United States	12.8	17.6	18.4	17.8	:	:	:

([1]) The quarterly youth unemployment rate is seasonally adjusted.
([2]) Youth unemployment ratio, break in series, 2010.

Source: Eurostat (online data codes: une_rt_a, une_rt_q and lfsi_act_a)

5   Labour market

5.3 Wages and labour costs

This subchapter compares and contrasts figures on wages and labour costs in the European Union (EU), the latter being generally defined as employers' expenditure on personnel. The level and structure of wages and labour costs are important macro-economic indicators used by policymakers, employers and trade unions to assess labour market supply and demand conditions.

Main statistical findings

Gross earnings

Among EU Member States, the mean (average) gross annual earnings of full-time employees in enterprises with ten or more employees were highest in Denmark (EUR 56 044) in 2009, followed by Luxembourg (in 2010), Ireland, the Netherlands and Germany (in 2010) – all above EUR 40 000 – while earnings were lowest in Romania (EUR 5 891 in 2010) and Bulgaria (EUR 4 085) – see Table 5.3.1.

In 2006, median annual earnings showed a broadly similar ranking of countries (see Figure 5.3.1), with mean earnings higher than median earnings in all countries except Malta. The proportion of employees considered to be low wage earners in 2006 was highest in Latvia, at 30.9 %, while more than one in four employees were also considered as low wage earners in Lithuania, Bulgaria and Romania (see Figure 5.3.2).

Gender pay gap

Despite some progress, there remains an important gap between the average earnings of men and women in the EU-27. Women were paid, on average, 17.1 % less than men in 2009. The smallest differences in average pay between the sexes were found in Slovenia, Italy, Malta, Romania, Belgium (in 2008), Poland and Portugal (at 10 % or less), the biggest in Estonia (in 2007), the Czech Republic and Austria (more than 25 %). Various effects may contribute to these gender pay gaps, such as: differences in labour force participation rates, differences in the occupations and activities that tend to be male- or female-dominated, differences in the degrees to which men and women work on a part-time basis, as well as the attitudes of personnel departments within private and public bodies towards career development and unpaid/maternity leave.

Minimum wages

In July 2011, 20 of the EU's 27 Member States (all except Denmark, Germany, Italy, Cyprus, Austria, Finland and Sweden), as well as two candidate countries (Croatia and Turkey) had national legislation setting a minimum wage by statute or by national inter-sectoral agreement.

Monthly minimum wages varied considerably in July 2011 (see Figure 5.3.4) ranging from EUR 1 758 per month in Luxembourg to EUR 158 and EUR 123 respectively in Romania and Bulgaria. When adjusted for differences in purchasing power, the disparities between the Member States were reduced from a ratio of 14:1 (highest compared with lowest) in euro terms to a ratio of 6:1 in purchasing power standard (PPS) terms. The same countries remained at either end of the range, with a high of PPS 1 466 in Luxembourg and a low of PPS 243 in Bulgaria.

Net earnings and tax rates

Tax wedge data measures the relative tax burden – within Figure 5.3.5 this information is provided in relation to low wage earners. The tax wedge for the EU-27 was 39.3 % in 2010, which was slightly lower than five years earlier. The highest tax rates on low wage earners in 2010 were recorded in Belgium, France, Germany, Hungary, Italy, Latvia, Austria and Romania.

Among the EU Member States, it was common to see tax rates lowered over the most recent five years for which data are available through to 2010. The largest reductions were recorded in the Netherlands, Cyprus (to 2007), Poland, Slovenia, Finland and the Czech Republic. On the other hand, the tax wedge rose at a relatively fast pace in France and Italy.

The other indicators presented in Table 5.3.2 provide information on the proportion of gross earnings that is 'taxed away' (higher tax rates and social security contributions and/or reduction or loss of benefits) when people return to employment or move from lower to higher incomes. The overall figures for the EU-27 show that there was generally less incentive between 2005 and 2010 for the unemployed or low wage earners to seek paid employment, as a higher proportion of their earnings would be 'taxed away'.

Labour costs

Average hourly labour costs (see Figure 5.3.6) and the structure of labour costs (see Figure 5.3.7) varied widely across the Member States in 2009. Hourly labour costs in the business economy (NACE Rev. 2 Sections B to N) ranged from a high of EUR 36.94 in Belgium and EUR 36.11 in Denmark, to EUR 4.00 in Romania and EUR 2.88 in Bulgaria in 2009 (note these figures include not only the compensation of employees, but also vocational training costs, other expenditure, taxes and subsidies incurred or received by business economy enterprises). The relative importance of wages and salaries in total labour costs was 66.2 % in Sweden (in 2007) and was also less than 70 % in Belgium and France, while it was 85 % or more in the United Kingdom, Slovenia, Luxembourg, Denmark and Malta.

Data sources and availability

Gross earnings

Gross earnings are the largest part of labour costs – information is provided on average (mean) annual gross earnings. The main definitions on earnings are provided in a European Commission Regulation 1738/2005 of 21 October 2005. Gross earnings cover remuneration in cash paid directly by the employer, before tax deductions and social security contributions payable by wage earners and retained by the employer. All bonuses, regardless of whether they are regularly paid, are included (13th or 14th month, holiday bonuses, profit-sharing, allowances for leave not taken, occasional commissions, etc.). The information is presented for full-time employees working in business economy (as covered by NACE Rev. 1.1 Sections C to K up to and including 2007, and by NACE Rev. 2 Sections B to N from 2008 onwards). The statistical unit is the enterprise or local unit. The population consists of all units, although it is limited to enterprises with at least ten employees for most countries.

Data on median earnings are based on gross annual earnings, and represent the median earnings of full-time employees in enterprises with ten or more employees. Low wage earners are full-time employees that earn less than two thirds of the median gross annual earnings.

Gender pay gap

The gender pay gap (GPG), in its unadjusted form, is defined as the difference between average gross hourly earnings of male paid employees and female paid employees, expressed as a percentage of average gross hourly earnings of male paid employees. The methodology for the compilation of this indicator has recently changed and is now based on data collected from the structure of earnings survey (SES), rather than on non-harmonised sources (as was previously the case).

According to the new methodology the unadjusted gender pay gap indicator covers all employees (there are no restrictions for age and hours worked) of enterprises (with at least ten employees) within industry, construction and services (as covered by NACE Rev. 2 Sections B to N and P to S).

Minimum wages

Minimum wage statistics refer to monthly national minimum wages; data are published showing the wage on the 1 January and the 1 July of each year. The national minimum wage is enforced by law, often after consultation with social partners, or directly by national inter-sectoral agreement (this is the case in Belgium and Greece). The national minimum wage is usually applicable for all employees, or at least for a large majority of employees in the country. Minimum wages are gross amounts, that is, before the deduction of income tax and social security contributions; such deductions vary from country to country. In some countries the basic national minimum wage is not fixed at a monthly rate but at an hourly or weekly rate. For these countries the hourly or weekly rates are converted into monthly rates according to conversion factors directly supplied by the countries:

- Ireland: hourly rate x 39 hours x 52 weeks / 12 months;
- France for data from January 1999 to January 2005: hourly rate x 39 hours x 52 weeks / 12 months; for data from July 2005: hourly rate x 35 hours x 52 weeks / 12 months;
- Malta: weekly rate x 52 weeks / 12 months;
- United Kingdom: (hourly rate x mean basic paid hours per week for full-time employees in all sectors x 52.18 weeks) / 12 months;
- United States: hourly rate x 40 hours x 52 weeks / 12 months.

In addition, when the minimum wage is paid for more than 12 months per year (as in Greece, Spain and Portugal, where it is paid for 14 months a year), data have been adjusted to take these payments into account.

Net earnings and tax rates

Net earnings are derived from gross earnings and represent the part of remuneration that employees can actually keep to spend or save. Compared with gross earnings, net earnings do not include social security contributions and taxes, but do include family allowances.

Tax rate indicators (tax wedge on labour costs, unemployment trap and low wage trap) aim to monitor work attractiveness. The tax wedge on labour costs is defined as income tax on gross wage earnings plus employee and employer social security contributions, expressed as a percentage of total labour costs. This indicator is compiled for single people without children earning 67 % of the average earnings of a worker in business economy (NACE Rev. 2 Sections B to N). The unemployment trap measures the proportion of gross earnings taxed away by higher tax and social security contributions and the withdrawal of unemployment and other benefits when an unemployed person returns to employment; it is defined as the difference between gross earnings and the increase of net income

when moving from unemployment to employment, expressed as a percentage of the gross earnings. This indicator is compiled for single persons without children earning 67 % of the average earnings of a worker in business economy (NACE Rev. 2 Sections B to N). The low wage trap measures the proportion (as a percentage) of gross earnings which is taxed away through the combined effects of income taxes, social security contributions, and any withdrawal of benefits when gross earnings increase from 33 % to 67 % of the average earnings of a worker in business economy (NACE Rev. 2 Sections B to N). This indicator is compiled for single people without children and also for single-earner couples with two children between 6 and 11 years old.

Labour costs

Labour costs are defined as employer's expenditure that is related to employing personnel. They encompass employee compensation (including wages, salaries in cash and in kind, employers' social security contributions); vocational training costs; and other expenditure (such as recruitment costs, expenditure on work clothes, and employment taxes regarded as labour costs minus any subsidies received). These labour cost components and their elements are defined in Regulation 1737/2005 of 21 October 2005. Data relate to three core indicators:

- average monthly labour costs, defined as total labour costs per month divided by the corresponding number of employees, expressed as full-time equivalent units;
- average hourly labour costs, defined as total labour costs divided by the corresponding number of hours worked;
- the structure of labour costs (wages and salaries; employers' social security contributions; other labour costs), expressed as a percentage of total labour costs.

Context

The structure and development of labour costs and earnings are important features of any labour market, reflecting labour supply from individuals and labour demand by enterprises.

Some underlying factors that may, at least in part, explain gender pay gaps include sectoral and occupational segregation, education and training, awareness and transparency, as well as direct discrimination. Gender pay gaps also reflect other inequalities – in particular, women's disproportionate share of family responsibilities and associated difficulties of reconciling work with private life. Many women work part-time or under atypical contracts: although this permits them to remain in the labour market while managing family responsibilities, it can have a negative impact on their pay, career development, promotion prospects and pensions.

The EU seeks to promote equal opportunities implying progressive elimination of the gender pay gap. Article 157(1) of the Treaty on the functioning of the European Union (TFEU) sets out the principle of equal pay for male and female workers for equal work or work of equal value, and Article 157(3) provides the legal basis for legislation on the equal treatment of men and women in employment matters. The strategy for equality between women and men (2010-2015) was adopted by the European Commission in September 2010. This builds on the experience of a roadmap (COM(2006) 0092) that was developed for the period 2006-2010 and aims to be a comprehensive framework which will commit the European Commission to promote gender equality in all of its policies. The strategy highlights the contribution of gender equality to economic growth and sustainable development, and supports the implementation of the gender equality dimension of the Europe 2020 strategy.

Table 5.3.1: Earnings in the business economy (average gross annual earnings of full-time employees), 2000-2010 ([1])
(EUR)

	2000	2001	2002	2003	2004	2005	2006	2007	2008	2009	2010
Belgium ([2])	31 644	33 109	34 330	34 643	35 704	36 673	37 674	38 659	40 698	:	:
Bulgaria ([2])	1 430	1 514	1 588	1 678	1 784	1 978	2 195	2 626	3 328	4 085	:
Czech Republic ([3])	4 616	5 142	6 016	6 137	6 569	7 405	8 284	9 071	10 930	10 596	11 312
Denmark	40 962	41 661	43 577	44 692	46 122	47 529	48 307	53 165	55 001	56 044	:
Germany	34 400	35 200	36 400	37 200	38 100	38 700	39 364	40 200	*41 400*	*41 100*	*42 400*
Estonia ([2])([3])	3 887	4 343	4 778	5 278	5 658	6 417	:	:	10 045	9 492	9 712
Ireland	:	:	:	:	:	40 462	:	39 858	45 893	45 207	:
Greece	14 723	15 431	16 278	16 739	:	:	:	:	25 915	29 160	:
Spain	17 432	17 874	18 462	19 220	19 931	20 333	21 402	21 891	25 208	26 316	:
France ([2])	26 712	27 418	28 185	28 847	29 608	30 521	31 369	32 413	33 574	34 132	:
Italy ([3])	19 991	20 583	21 076	21 494	:	22 657	23 406	:	:	:	:
Cyprus ([3])	16 086	16 736	17 431	18 165	19 290	20 549	21 310	:	:	24 775	25 251
Latvia ([2])	3 247	3 426	3 523	3 515	3 806	4 246	5 211	6 690	8 676	8 728	8 596
Lithuania ([3])([4])	3 591	3 726	4 046	4 195	4 367	4 770	5 543	6 745	7 398	7 406	7 234
Luxembourg ([2])	35 875	37 745	38 442	39 587	40 575	42 135	43 621	45 284	47 034	48 174	49 316
Hungary	4 173	4 898	5 846	6 447	7 119	7 798	7 866	8 952	10 237	9 603	10 100
Malta ([2])	13 461	13 791	14 068	14 096	14 116	14 706	15 278	15 679	16 158	:	:
Netherlands	31 901	33 900	35 200	36 600	37 900	38 700	40 800	42 000	43 146	44 412	:
Austria ([2])	:	:	:	:	34 995	36 032	36 673	37 716	32 787	33 384	:
Poland ([3])([4])	6 226	7 510	7 173	6 434	6 230	6 270	8 178	:	10 787	8 399	:
Portugal	12 620	13 338	13 322	13 350	13 700	14 042	14 893	15 345	16 691	17 129	17 352
Romania ([2])([3])	1 748	1 993	2 075	2 142	2 414	3 155	3 713	4 825	5 457	*5 450*	*5 891*
Slovenia ([3])	10 316	10 851	11 461	11 932	12 466	12 985	13 687	14 625	15 997	16 282	17 168
Slovakia	3 583	3 837	4 582	4 945	5 706	6 374	7 040	8 400	9 707	10 387	10 777
Finland ([2])	27 398	28 555	29 916	30 978	31 988	33 290	34 080	36 114	37 946	39 197	:
Sweden	31 621	30 467	31 164	32 177	33 344	34 027	35 084	36 871	37 597	34 746	40 008
United Kingdom	37 676	39 233	40 553	38 793	41 286	42 866	44 496	46 051	:	38 047	:
Iceland	37 641	34 100	:	:	:	:	:	:	:	:	:
Norway ([2])	36 202	38 604	43 750	40 883	42 152	45 560	47 221	:	:	51 343	:
Switzerland ([3])	43 682	:	48 499	:	45 760	:	46 058	:	47 088	:	:
Croatia ([3])	:	:	:	8 491	9 036	9 634	:	:	11 979	11 969	:

([1]) Enterprises with 10 or more persons employed; NACE Rev. 2 Sections B to N, 2008-2010; NACE Rev. 1.1 Sections C to K, 2000-2007.
([2]) All enterprises: Belgium, Bulgaria, Estonia, France, Malta and Finland, all years; Luxembourg, 2008-2010; Austria, 2008-2009; Romania, 2008; Norway, 2009.
([3]) All enterprises and full-time units (FTU): the Czech Republic, 2000-2001 and 2007-2010; Estonia, 2000-2005; Italy, 2000-2006; Cyprus, 2009-2010; Lithuania, all years; Poland, 2009; Romania, 2000-2003; Slovenia, 2000-2007; Switzerland, 2008; Croatia, 2008-2009.
([4]) Full-time units (FTU): Latvia, 2000-2003; Lithuania, 2000-2007 and 2009-2010; Poland, 2000, 2002-2003 and 2008.

Source: Eurostat (online data codes: earn_gr_nace2 and earn_gr_nace)

Figure 5.3.1: Median gross annual earnings of full-time employees, 2006 (¹)
(EUR)

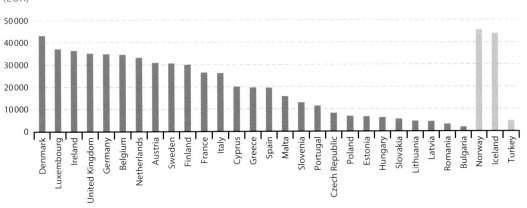

(¹) Enterprises with ten or more persons employed; excluding agriculture, fishing, public administration, private households and extra-territorial organisations.

Source: Eurostat (online data code: earn_ses_adeci)

Figure 5.3.2: Low wage earners – full-time employees earning less than two thirds of the median gross annual earnings, 2006 (¹)
(% of employees)

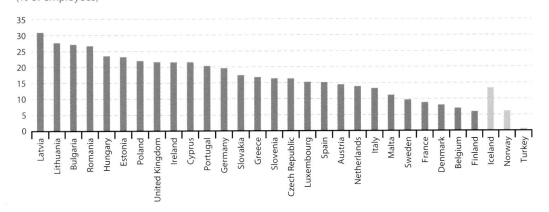

(¹) Enterprises with ten or more persons employed; excluding agriculture, fishing, public administration, private households and extra-territorial organisations.

Source: Eurostat (online data code: earn_ses_adeci)

Figure 5.3.3: Gender pay gap, 2009 (¹)
(% difference between average gross hourly earnings of male and female employees, as % of male gross earnings, unadjusted form)

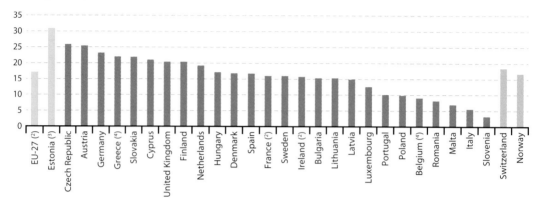

(¹) Enterprises with ten or more persons employed; NACE Rev. 2 Sections B to S excluding O.
(²) Provisional.
(³) NACE Rev. 1.1 Sections C to O excluding L; 2007.
(⁴) 2008.

Source: Eurostat (online data code: tsiem040)

Figure 5.3.4: Minimum wage, as of 1 July 2011 (¹)
(EUR per month)

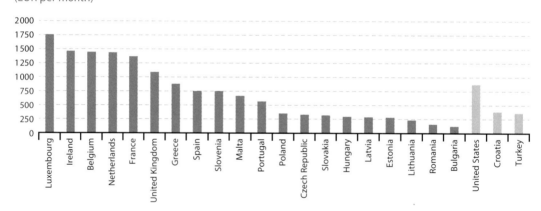

(¹) Member States not shown: not applicable.

Source: Eurostat (online data code: earn_mw_cur)

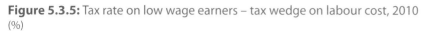

Figure 5.3.5: Tax rate on low wage earners – tax wedge on labour cost, 2010
(%)

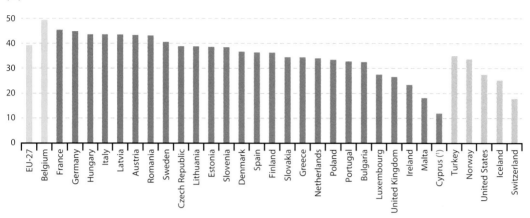

(¹) 2007.

Source: Eurostat (online data code: tsiem050), OECD, Commission services

Table 5.3.2: Tax rate indicators on low wage earners, 2004 and 2009
(%)

	Tax wedge on labour cost		Unemployment trap		Low wage trap – single person without children		Low wage trap – one earner couple with two children	
	2004	2009	2004	2009	2004	2009	2004	2009
EU-27	40	39	75	75	45	47	57	58
Belgium	49	49	85	93	57	59	45	47
Bulgaria	36	33	77	81	21	21	17	21
Czech Republic	42	39	66	80	34	48	49	88
Denmark	39	37	91	89	77	75	96	95
Germany	47	45	74	75	53	56	81	80
Estonia	38	39	64	63	26	23	22	13
Ireland	22	23	64	74	58	68	77	46
Greece	34	34	62	68	27	28	32	33
Spain	36	36	80	83	25	28	16	13
France	41	46	82	77	35	52	57	76
Italy	42	44	72	79	34	39	– 11	0
Cyprus (^{1})	12	12	62	61	6	6	110	115
Latvia	42	44	88	90	32	33	100	79
Lithuania	43	39	81	70	36	26	48	92
Luxembourg	29	27	86	86	52	56	108	107
Hungary	43	44	62	82	31	38	70	78
Malta	18	18	60	59	20	20	31	27
Netherlands	42	34	80	84	69	73	76	65
Austria	43	43	67	67	36	39	61	65
Poland	38	33	83	81	65	61	85	40
Portugal	32	33	81	79	21	22	69	60
Romania	42	43	61	59	30	31	33	32
Slovenia	42	38	83	83	51	48	76	64
Slovakia	35	34	43	42	22	26	31	45
Finland	40	36	77	73	61	54	100	100
Sweden	47	41	87	75	57	41	92	77
United Kingdom	31	30	68	64	58	49	80	79
Iceland	25	25	71	81	40	32	67	70
Norway	34	34	75	75	37	34	100	99
Switzerland	18	18	:	:	:	:	:	:
Turkey	42	35	:	:	:	:	:	:
Japan	:	:	57	50	54	60	95	94
United States	28	27	70	68	28	28	51	68

(^{1}) 2007 instead of 2009.

Source: Eurostat (online data codes: tsiem050, earn_nt_unemtrp and earn_nt_lowwtrp)

Figure 5.3.6: Average hourly labour costs in the business economy, 2009 (¹)
(EUR)

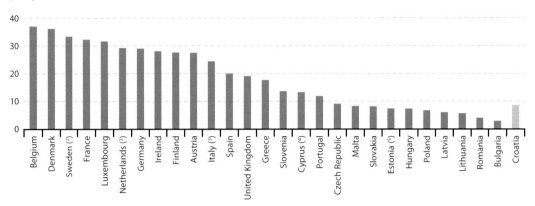

(¹) Enterprises with ten or more persons employed, NACE Rev. 2 Sections B to N.
(²) NACE Rev. 1.1 Sections C to K, 2007.
(³) 2008.
(⁴) NACE Rev. 1.1 Sections C to K, 2008.
(⁵) All enterprises.

Source: Eurostat (online data codes: lc_an_costh_r2 and lc_an_costh)

Figure 5.3.7: Breakdown of labour costs in the business economy, 2009 (¹)
(% share of total labour costs)

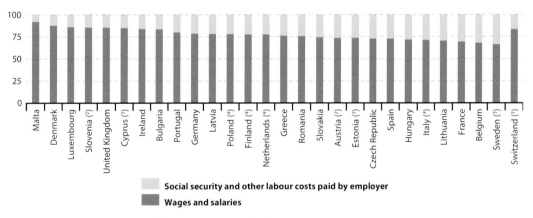

(¹) Enterprises with ten or more persons employed, NACE Rev. 2 Sections B to N.
(²) Provisional.
(³) NACE Rev. 1.1 Sections C to K, 2008.
(⁴) 2008.
(⁵) NACE Rev. 1.1 Sections C to K, 2007.

Source: Eurostat (online data codes: lc_an_struc_r2 and lc_an_struc)

5.4 Job vacancies

This subchapter gives an overview of annual job vacancy statistics in the European Union (EU), notably the job vacancy rate (JVR). Eurostat also collects quarterly job vacancy statistics.

EU policies in the area of job vacancies aim to improve the functioning of the labour market by trying to match more closely supply and demand. In order to enable job seekers to consult all vacancies publicised in each of the Member State's employment services, the European jobs and mobility portal (EURES) was set up.

Main statistical findings

There was an upward development in the job vacancy rate in the EU-27 from 2003 to 2007, with the rate peaking at 2.2 % in 2007. Thereafter, the job vacancy rate contracted in successive years, falling to 1.9 % in 2008 and a historic low of 1.4 % in 2009. The latest information available for 2010 suggests a slight recovery, as the job vacancy rate stood at 1.5 %.

The pattern of development for the euro area was similar to that recorded in the EU-27, although the job vacancy rate for the former climbed more rapidly in 2005 and 2006 (when it peaked at 2.3 %), before contracting for three consecutive years to a low of 1.4 % in 2009; the recovery in 2010 was slightly more than in the EU-27, as the job vacancy rate rose by 0.2 percentage points.

Among the Member States (no information for Belgium), the job vacancy rate in 2010 was highest in Malta (3.2 %) and Germany (2.6 %). The number of vacant posts accounted for less than 1 % of the total number of posts in 14 of the Member States in 2010, with job vacancy rates of less than 0.5 % in Ireland, France and Latvia (in other words, less than one in every 200 posts was vacant).

Data sources and availability

Data on job vacancies and occupied posts may be presented broken down by economic activity, occupation, size of enterprise and region. The national

statistical authorities responsible for compiling job vacancy statistics send these statistics to Eurostat. Their data are used to compile the job vacancy rate for the EU-27 and the euro area.

Some of the data provided by the Member States fails to match common criteria and there may be differences in the coverage of the data between countries; as a result, there are currently no EU-27 totals for the actual numbers of job vacancies or occupied posts.

The EU-27 and euro area job vacancy rates are calculated on the basis of the information that is available; no estimates are made for missing or incomplete data. It is therefore not possible, at present, to present EU-27 or euro area job vacancy rates broken down by economic activity, occupation or size of enterprise.

Context

The job vacancy rate, in part, reflects the unmet demand for labour, as well as potential mismatches between the skills and availability of those who are unemployed and those sought by employers. Job vacancy statistics are used by the European Commission and the European Central Bank (ECB) to analyse and monitor the evolution of the labour market at a national and European level. These statistics are also a key indicator for assessing the business cycle and for a structural analysis of the economy.

Policy developments in this area have mainly focused on trying to improve the labour market by more closely matching supply and demand, through:

- modernising and strengthening labour market institutions, notably employment services;
- removing obstacles to worker mobility across Europe;
- better anticipating skills needs, labour market shortages and bottlenecks;
- managing economic migration;
- improving the adaptability of workers and enterprises so that there is a greater capacity to anticipate, trigger and absorb economic and social change.

The European jobs and mobility portal (EURES) was set-up with the aim of providing job seekers in the EU with the opportunity to consult all job vacancies publicised in each of the Member States' employment services. The website provides access to a range of job vacancies from 31 European countries (the 27 EU Member States, as well as Iceland, Liechtenstein, Norway and Switzerland). In autumn 2011, there were 1.23 million job vacancies advertised by over 25 000 registered employers on the website, while more than 700 000 people had posted their CVs on the website.

European job days are another EU initiative in this domain and 2011 was the fifth edition of this programme of activities: hundreds of events were organised across Europe with the aim of raising awareness about the opportunities and practicalities of living and working in another European country, encouraging mobility throughout the EU, and putting job candidates in touch with employers who have job vacancies. The events typically include job fairs, seminars, lectures, workshops and cultural events, all aimed at improving labour mobility.

Figure 5.4.1: Job vacancy rate, 2003-2010 ([1])
(%)

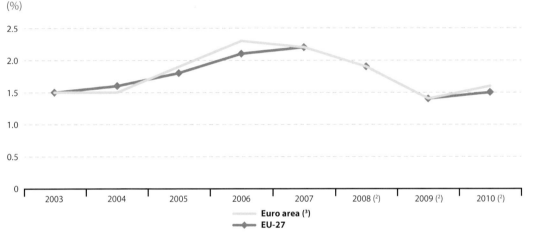

([1]) NACE Rev. 1.1 Sections A to O for 2003-2008; NACE Rev. 2 Sections B to S for 2009 and 2010.
([2]) Provisional.
([3]) EA-16 for 2003-2008; EA-17 for 2009 and 2010.
Source: Eurostat (online data codes: jvs_a_nace1 and jvs_a_nace2)

Figure 5.4.2: Job vacancy rate, 2010 (¹)
(%)

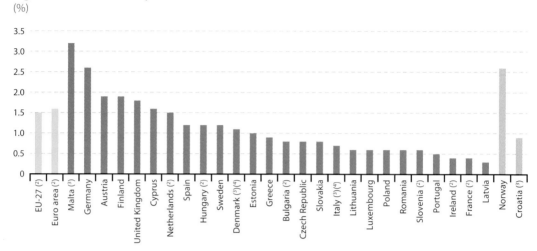

(¹) NACE Rev. 2 Sections B to S; Belgium, not available.
(²) Provisional.
(³) Enterprises with ten or more employees.
(⁴) NACE Rev. 2 Sections B to N.

Source: Eurostat (online data code: jvs_a_nace2)

5.5 Labour market policy interventions

Labour market policy (LMP) interventions are generally targeted at providing assistance to the unemployed and other groups of people who face particular difficulties to enter the labour market. In most European Union (EU) Member States the primary target group is people who are registered as unemployed by national public employment services.

However, policy objectives aimed at increasing participation in the labour market are increasingly focused on a broader range of persons who are not formally unemployed but are often receiving some other form of social benefit and are believed to be capable of working given the right support and opportunities. As a result, the types of intervention used, and the groups that are targeted, vary between Member States depending on national circumstances and priorities.

Main statistical findings

Across the EU-27, a total of 2.2 % of gross domestic product (GDP) was spent on LMP interventions in 2009. That was around 0.6 percentage points more (of GDP) than a year before in 2008, as total expenditure on LMP interventions increased by 35.4 %. The majority of this increase was derived from higher levels of expenditure on unemployment benefits as governments supported the large numbers of people that lost their jobs as a direct result of the financial and economic crisis. Indeed, the share of LMP expenditure accounted for by LMP supports rose to 64.1 % compared with 59.7 % the year before, with the share spent on LMP measures down to 25.3 % from 28.8 % and that on LMP services rather unchanged at 11 %.

The level of expenditure and the breakdown of both expenditure and participants between the different types of LMP intervention varied considerably between Member States, reflecting the diverse characteristics and problems within national labour markets, as well as the different political convictions of their respective governments.

Within the EU Member States, the highest level of relative expenditure on LMP interventions in 2009 was reported in Belgium (3.8 % of GDP), followed by Spain, Ireland and Denmark, which were the only other countries to spend more than 3.0 % of their GDP on such interventions (see Figure 5.5.1). At the other end of the scale, nine Member States spent less than 1 % of GDP on these interventions: Romania, Malta, Bulgaria, the United Kingdom, the Czech Republic, Cyprus, Slovakia, Greece and Lithuania. Relative to GDP, Spain spent the most on LMP supports (3.0 %) with Belgium and Ireland the only other countries to spend more than 2 %. Belgium, Denmark and Poland spent most on LMP measures (around 1.2 %) while Sweden and the Netherlands reported the highest relative expenditure on LMP services – around 0.4 % of GDP.

LMP measures (see Figure 5.5.2) mostly support the transition from unemployment or inactivity into employment, either: by improving employability through training or work experience; by providing incentives for employers to take on people from selected target groups; or by encouraging individuals to become self-employed. Total public expenditure on LMP measures across the EU-27 in 2009 was equivalent to 0.6 % of GDP. The largest part of this expenditure went on training (42.6 %), just less than a quarter (23.8 %) on employment incentives, while 14.4 % was accounted for by supported employment and rehabilitation (measures that promote labour market integration of people with reduced working capacity) and 12.1 % by direct job creation (which covers the provision of temporary jobs that are additional to normal market supply).

Across the EU-27 there was an average of 10.5 million people participating in LMP measures at any point during 2009, only slightly more than in 2008 (10.3 million). Of these, around 4.3 million received employment incentives, which mostly involve the use of public funds to provide a fixed-term subsidy to employers who take on people from selected target groups, either into a regular job or into a specially arranged placement for work experience. A further 3.2 million people were engaged in some form of labour market training (see Table 5.5.1).

Data sources and availability

LMP statistics cover all labour market interventions which can be described as 'public interventions in the labour market aimed at reaching its efficient functioning and correcting disequilibria and which can be distinguished from other general employment policy interventions in that they act selectively to favour particular groups in the labour market'. The scope of LMP statistics is limited to public interventions that explicitly target groups with difficulties in the labour market; this includes the unemployed, those employed but at risk of involuntary job loss, and people who are currently inactive in the labour market but would like to work.

Three types of interventions

LMP interventions are classified into three main types:

- LMP services refer to labour market interventions where the main activity of participants is job-search related and where participation usually does not result in a change in labour market status.

- LMP measures refer to labour market interventions where the main activity of participants is not job-search related and where participation usually results in a change of labour market status. In other words, a person who is unemployed typically ceases to be considered as such when participating in an LMP measure because they are temporarily in training or work and therefore not both actively seeking and immediately available for work. An activity that does not result in a change of labour market status may still be considered as a measure if the intervention fulfils the following criteria:

1. the activities undertaken are not job-search related, are supervised and constitute a full-time

or significant part-time activity of participants during a significant period of time, and;

2. the aim is to improve the vocational qualifications of participants, or;

3. the intervention provides incentives to take-up or to provide employment (including self-employment).

- LMP supports refer to interventions that provide financial assistance, directly or indirectly, to individuals for labour market reasons, or which compensate individuals for disadvantage caused by labour market circumstances.

Additional category breakdowns

The three main types of intervention are further broken down into nine detailed categories according to the type of action:

- LMP services
  1. Labour market services;
- LMP measures
  2. Training;
  3. Job rotation and job sharing;
  4. Employment incentives;
  5. Supported employment and rehabilitation;
  6. Direct job creation;
  7. Start-up incentives;
- LMP supports
  8. Out-of-work income maintenance and support;
  9. Early retirement.

The LMP methodology provides guidelines for the collection of data on LMP interventions: which interventions to cover; how to classify interventions by type of action; how to measure the expenditure associated with each intervention; and how to measure the number of participants in each intervention using observations of stocks and flows (entrants and exits).

Context

LMP interventions provide assistance to the unemployed and other groups facing difficulties entering the labour market. The LMP data collection was developed by the European Commission (EC) as an instrument to monitor the implementation and development of targeted employment policies across the EU in response to two agreements of the European Council in 1997. The first, held in Amsterdam in June 1997, confirmed that whilst employment policy should be a national responsibility, it was also an issue of common concern and that there should be a coordinated strategy at a European level. The second, held in November 1997 in Luxembourg – the so-called 'Jobs Summit' – launched the European employment strategy (EES) in which LMPs had a key role in relation to employability. Since that time, LMP statistics have been used to monitor both active and passive interventions in the labour market and, in particular, relevant areas of the employment guidelines as set out under the Lisbon strategy.

Within the new Europe 2020 strategy, the flexicurity approach aims to result in the provision and implementation of active LMPs while ensuring adequate benefits for those out of work.

This concept of flexicurity came to the forefront of the EU's employment agenda in 2007 when the European Commission released a Communication titled 'Towards common principles of flexicurity – more and better jobs through flexibility and security' (COM(2007) 359), which highlighted the idea of reconciling flexibility in the labour market with security for workers. Within this modern flexicurity approach, security refers not only to security of income (for example, through the provision of adequate unemployment benefits) but also to securing people's capacity to work by ensuring lifelong access to opportunities to develop and adapt their skills to meet new demands in the labour market. Hence, the Europe 2020 strategy specifically refers to the provision of active LMPs, which cover LMP measures and LMP services, and modern social security systems, which include LMP supports. These policies for the EU labour market are, therefore, key instruments within the Europe 2020 strategy and a series of indicators based upon LMP data continue to be used for monitoring progress.

Figure 5.5.1: Public expenditure on labour market policy interventions, 2009
(% of GDP)

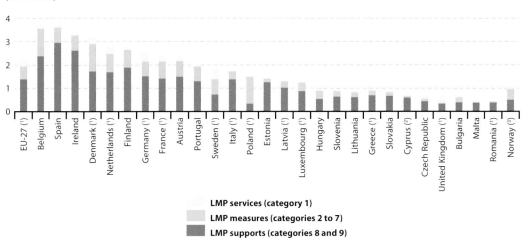

LMP services (category 1)
LMP measures (categories 2 to 7)
LMP supports (categories 8 and 9)

(¹) Includes estimates.
(²) Includes estimates and provisional data.
(³) LMP services, 2007; includes estimates.

Source: Eurostat (online data code: lmp_expsumm)

Figure 5.5.2: Public expenditure on labour market policy measures, EU-27, 2009 (¹)
(% of total)

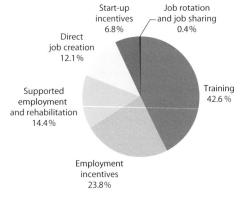

Start-up incentives
6.8%

Job rotation and job sharing
0.4%

Direct job creation
12.1%

Supported employment and rehabilitation
14.4%

Training
42.6 %

Employment incentives
23.8%

(¹) Estimates; figures do not sum to 100% due to rounding.

Source: Eurostat (online data code: tps00077)

Table 5.5.1: Labour market policy measures, participants by type of action, 2009
(annual average stock in 1 000)

	Training	Job rotation & job sharing	Employment incentives	Supported employment & rehabilita-tion	Direct job creation	Start-up incentives
EU-27 ([1])	3 240.0	117.1	4 308.4	1 199.7	894.7	782.3
Belgium	126.4	–	226.4	37.2	159.3	1.4
Bulgaria ([1])	6.1	–	7.7	0.9	43.4	2.6
Czech Republic	4.5	–	2.8	26.0	2.4	3.2
Denmark ([2])	64.9	0.2	30.8	66.5	–	–
Germany ([1])	801.4	0.2	259.7	43.5	295.5	147.4
Estonia	2.7	–	0.1	0.0	0.0	0.3
Ireland ([1])	56.1	–	2.2	3.4	24.9	5.7
Greece ([2])	1.6	–	64.7	–	–	25.5
Spain ([1])	341.6	91.0	2 183.1	53.0	:	394.3
France ([1])([3])	580.8	–	533.8	145.3	224.6	145.3
Italy ([1])	730.5	18.8	582.0	–	20.9	–
Cyprus ([1])	0.4	–	6.4	0.2	–	–
Latvia	4.9	–	1.9	–	5.1	0.1
Lithuania	5.4	0.1	:	0.2	2.7	–
Luxembourg ([1])	0.8	–	14.0	0.1	0.9	–
Hungary	13.5	–	27.5	–	13.8	1.4
Malta	0.5	–	0.1	–	0.1	0.0
Netherlands ([2])	178.3	–	27.8	154.7	–	–
Austria ([2])	113.1	0.2	69.1	1.9	7.4	3.5
Poland ([1])	3.1	–	141.1	602.8	11.1	6.7
Portugal ([1])	81.6	–	79.4	5.6	31.7	6.1
Romania	10.0	–	27.0	–	7.7	:
Slovenia ([2])	33.5	–	2.6	–	3.1	4.1
Slovakia ([1])	0.9	–	13.3	2.8	20.0	26.9
Finland ([2])	48.7	6.6	13.3	7.9	11.6	5.1
Sweden	10.5	–	87.4	44.2	–	2.8
United Kingdom ([1])([4])	21.7	–	38.2	16.2	8.0	–
Norway	25.2	–	4.8	14.3	10.3	0.3

([1]) Includes some values that are incomplete (participant data available for >80 % but <100 % of expenditure).
([2]) Includes estimates.
([3]) Employment incentives, 2008.
([4]) Training and supported employment & rehabilitation, 2008.

Source: Eurostat (online data code: lmp_partsumm)

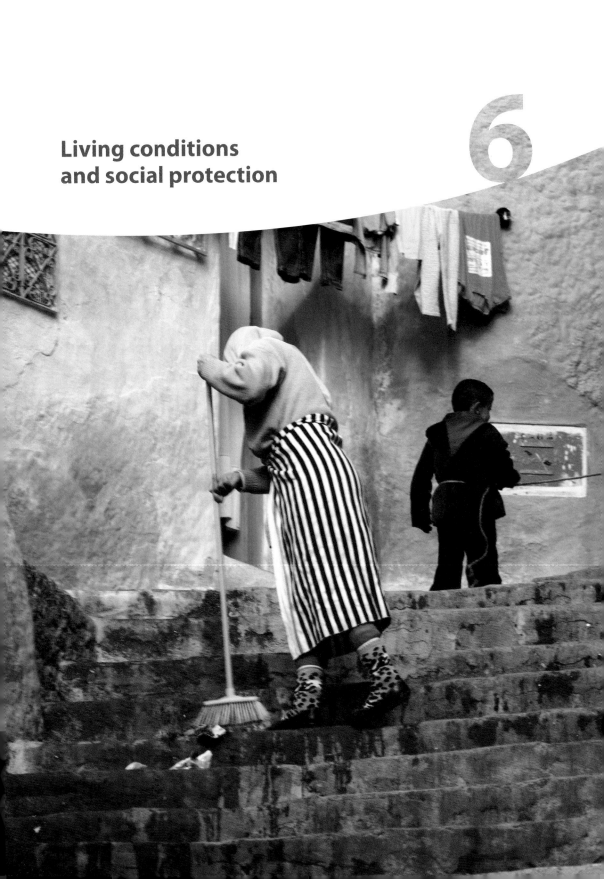

Living conditions and social protection

6

Introduction

Eurostat data on living conditions and social protection aim to show a comprehensive picture of the social situation in the European Union (EU), covering indicators related to income, housing, material deprivation, poverty, social exclusion and social protection. The demand for statistics on living conditions and social protection received a new impetus following the introduction of the social chapter of the Amsterdam Treaty (1997) which became the driving force for EU social statistics. This was reinforced by successive European Councils that have kept the social dimension high on the political agenda. Moreover, 2010 was designated as the European year for combating poverty and social exclusion.

Eurostat collects and publishes a broad portfolio of social inclusion indicators, employment and social policy indicators. Data covering living conditions and social protection come from three main sources:

- household budget surveys (HBS);
- EU statistics on income and living conditions (EU-SILC);
- the European system of integrated social protection statistics (ESSPROS).

Information is collected through an open method of coordination, designed to encourage national governments to provide regular data concerning social protection and social inclusion/exclusion, while focusing on combating poverty and social exclusion, reforming social welfare systems, and tackling the challenges posed by demographic change (in particular, population ageing). Social risks (such as unemployment, ill health or social exclusion) or actions that are undertaken to help meet social needs can be evaluated by studying data on social protection expenditure and receipts.

The Europe 2020 strategy for smart, sustainable and inclusive growth put forward by the European Commission provides a growth strategy for the coming decade. A European platform against poverty will be one of the seven flagship initiatives of this strategy. The goals are to:

- ensure economic, social and territorial cohesion;
- guarantee respect for the fundamental rights of people experiencing poverty and social exclusion, and enable them to live in dignity and take an active part in society;
- mobilise support to help people integrate into the communities where they live, get training and help them to find a job and have access to social benefits.

To measure progress in meeting the Europe 2020 goals, five headline targets to be met by 2020 have been agreed and translated into national targets in each EU Member State, reflecting different situations and circumstances. One of these targets is that for the EU as a whole there will be at least 20 million fewer people in or at-risk-of poverty and social exclusion by 2020. The integrated economic and employment guidelines, first combined in 2008, were also revised as part of the Europe 2020 strategy. Guideline 10 concerns promoting social inclusion and combating poverty.

6.1 Social inclusion

Social inclusion has long been a key part of the European Union's (EU) policies. The overriding goal is to reduce substantially the number of people at-risk-of-poverty or social exclusion, thereby creating a socially inclusive society.

However, as multi-dimensional concepts, poverty and social exclusion cannot easily be measured through statistics. As a result, both monetary and non-monetary indicators have been developed, such as the at-risk-of-poverty rate, the at-risk-of-poverty threshold, the severe material deprivation rate and the share of people living in households with very low work intensity. Other equally relevant factors should also be considered when analysing social inclusion, for example: access to education and training, health, or housing.

Main statistical findings

At-risk-of-poverty or social exclusion

In 2009, 113.7 million people in the EU-27 lived in households facing poverty or social exclusion, equivalent to 23.1 % of the entire population (see Table 6.1.1); an early estimate for 2010 (data for some Member States are not available) indicates that the number rose to 115.5 million and the share to 23.4 %. These overall figures for the EU-27 conceal considerable variations between Member States. In Bulgaria and Romania more than two fifths of the population was considered to be at-risk-of-poverty or social exclusion in 2009, while in Latvia the share was above one third. The share was above one quarter in 2009 in five other Member States, namely Hungary, Lithuania, Poland, Greece and Ireland; in 2010 the share in Lithuania also passed above one third. The lowest proportions of the population considered to be at-risk-of-poverty or social exclusion in 2009 were observed in the Czech Republic, the Netherlands and Sweden; Iceland and Norway also reported relatively low shares of their respective population at-risk-of-poverty or social exclusion. Comparing the developments during the years shown in Table 6.1.1 there was a large fall in the proportion of the population at-risk-of-poverty

or social exclusion in Poland, Bulgaria, Slovakia, Latvia, Lithuania and Estonia, although it should be noted that several Member States introduced methodological changes in 2008 causing a break in the time series. In contrast, the percentage of the population at-risk-of-poverty or social exclusion grew most notably in Germany and Sweden.

The overall risk of facing poverty or social exclusion is made up of three types of risk: being at-risk-of-poverty; facing severe material deprivation; and/or living in a household with very low work intensity. People are considered to be at-risk-of-poverty or social exclusion if they face at least one of these risks – although around 30 % of those people at-risk-of-poverty or social exclusion within the EU-27 faced a combination of two or even all three of these risks. Figure 6.1.1 provides an analysis of those persons at-risk-of-poverty or social exclusion according to the types of risk that they face. In 2009, there were 48.6 million people in the EU-27 living in households that exclusively faced income poverty (but neither severe material deprivation nor very low work intensity), while a further 18.8 million persons experienced severe material deprivation (but neither of the other two risks) and a further 12.5 million people lived in households with very low work intensity (but faced neither of the other two risks). An additional 27.1 million people lived in households facing two out of three of these risks, while a further 6.7 million people lived in households where all three of these risks were present.

Figure 6.1.2 provides an analysis for each of the Member States of the proportion of the population facing these risks. The analysis has been simplified compared to Figure 6.1.1:

- the share of people at-risk-of-poverty includes those living in households that are exclusively at-risk-of-poverty as well as those at-risk-of-poverty combined with either or both of the other two risks;
- the analysis then shows the additional share of the population experiencing severe material deprivation (either as a single risk or combined with living in a household with very low work intensity);

- the final category shows the proportion of the population that lives in households that are exclusively characterised as having a very low work intensity (those that are not at-risk-of-poverty, nor experiencing severe material deprivation).

As such, when summing the three categories shown in Figure 6.1.2, the result corresponds to the overall proportion of the population that is at-risk-of-poverty or social exclusion.

In 2009, 16.3 % of the EU-27 population was assessed to be at-risk-of-poverty, with this share ranging from 25.7 % in Latvia to 8.6 % in the Czech Republic. Social protection systems impact upon the share of the population that is considered to be at-risk-of-poverty and different groups in society are more or less vulnerable to monetary poverty (see Figure 6.1.3). More information on income and poverty is available in a subchapter on income distribution.

Material deprivation and severe material deprivation

Alongside income-related measures of poverty, a broader perspective of social inclusion can be obtained by studying a range of indicators related to other measures such as material deprivation. An analysis of material deprivation provides a more absolute approach to social inclusion rather than the relative approach used for analysis of income poverty. Material deprivation is based on the affordability of a selection of items that are considered to be necessary or desirable; the analysis distinguishes between individuals who cannot afford a certain good or service, and those who do not possess this good or service for another reason, for example because they do not want or do not need it. The material deprivation rate is defined as those persons who cannot afford to pay for at least three out of a list of nine specific items, while those who lack four or more of these items are considered to be severely materially deprived. About one in every six (17.1 %) members of the EU-27 population was materially deprived in 2009; just under half of these (8.1 % of the total population) were considered to experience severe material deprivation. The proportion of people that were materially deprived rose to around

30 % of the population in Poland, around 40 % in Latvia and Hungary, and around half or more of the population in Romania and Bulgaria – these five Member States also reported that more than half of their materially deprived population experienced severe material deprivation. Less than one in ten people in Luxembourg, the Netherlands and the Nordic Member States were materially deprived and in these Member States the proportion of the whole population that was severely materially deprived was below 3 % (see Figure 6.1.4).

Work intensity

Being in employment is generally an effective way to insulate oneself from the risk of poverty. The indicator covering people living in households with a very low work intensity is defined as those people aged 0 to 59 who are living in households where the adults worked less than 20 % of their total work potential during the year prior to the survey; these people are more likely to be exposed to social exclusion. In 2009, 9.0 % of the EU-27 population aged less than 60 lived in households with very low work intensity. Almost one fifth (19.8 %) of the population aged less than 60 in Ireland was considered to be living in a very low work intensity household (see Figure 6.1.5); this was, by far, the highest share among the Member States in 2009; double-digit shares were also recorded in the United Kingdom, Belgium, Hungary and Germany. The lowest proportions of people living in households with very low work intensity among the EU Member States were recorded in Cyprus, Slovakia, Slovenia and Estonia (less than 6 % of the population); while Iceland and Switzerland recorded even lower shares.

Data sources and availability

EU statistics on income and living conditions (EU-SILC) are the source of information for statistics relating to income, living conditions and social inclusion. More information on EU-SILC, the calculation of household disposable income, as well as the calculation of household size using the number of 'equivalent adults', is provided in a subchapter on income distribution statistics.

Context

At the Laeken European Council in December 2001, European heads of state and government endorsed a first set of common statistical indicators relating to social exclusion and poverty that were subject to a continuing process of refinement by an indicators sub-group that is part of the social protection committee. These indicators are an essential element in the open method of coordination to monitor the progress of Member States in the fight against poverty and social exclusion. The social protection committee adopted, in May 2006, a portfolio of overarching indicators complemented by specific indicators on social inclusion, pensions and health.

A European platform against poverty is one of the seven flagship initiatives of the Europe 2020 strategy for smart, sustainable and inclusive growth adopted in 2010. The goals are to:

- ensure economic, social and territorial cohesion;
- guarantee respect for the fundamental rights of people experiencing poverty and social exclusion, and enable them to live in dignity and take an active part in society;
- mobilise support to help people integrate in the communities where they live, get training and help them to find a job and have access to social benefits.

In the context of the Europe 2020 strategy, the European Council adopted in June 2010 a headline target on social inclusion. EU-SILC is the source for this indicator concerning people at-risk-of-poverty or social exclusion which combines three sub-indicators: the at-risk-of-poverty rate, severe material deprivation rate and people living in households with very low work intensity. One of the targets set to measure progress in meeting the Europe 2020 goals is that for the EU-27 as a whole there will be at least 20 million fewer people at-risk-of-poverty or social exclusion by 2020.

Table 6.1.1: Population at-risk-of-poverty or social exclusion, 2005-2010

	Percentage of the total population (%)						Number of persons (1 000)					
	2005	2006	2007	2008	2009	2010	2005	2006	2007	2008	2009	2010
EU-27	*26.0*	*25.2*	*24.5*	*23.6*	*23.1*	:	*123 893*	*122 713*	*119 449*	*115 730*	*113 668*	:
Euro area	21.4	21.7	21.7	21.4	21.2	:	67 809	69 436	69 778	69 031	68 639	:
Belgium	22.6	21.5	21.6	20.8	20.2	:	2 338	2 247	2 261	2 194	2 145	:
Bulgaria (¹)	:	61.3	60.7	44.8	46.2	:	:	4 734	4 663	3 421	3 511	:
Czech Republic	19.6	18.0	15.8	15.3	14.0	14.4	1 988	1 832	1 613	1 566	1 448	1 495
Denmark	17.2	16.7	16.8	16.3	17.4	:	921	896	905	887	952	:
Germany	18.4	20.2	20.6	20.1	20.0	:	15 022	16 444	16 760	16 345	16 217	:
Estonia	25.9	22.0	22.0	21.8	23.4	21.7	347	293	293	291	312	289
Ireland	25.0	23.3	23.1	23.7	25.7	:	1 038	991	1 005	1 050	1 150	:
Greece	29.4	29.3	28.3	28.1	27.6	:	3 131	3 154	3 064	3 046	3 007	:
Spain	23.4	23.3	23.1	22.9	23.4	:	10 045	10 155	10 257	10 340	10 652	:
France (¹)	18.9	18.8	19.0	18.6	18.4	:	11 127	11 184	11 382	11 237	11 155	:
Italy	25.0	25.9	26.1	25.3	24.7	:	14 621	15 256	15 433	15 099	14 835	:
Cyprus (¹)	25.3	25.4	25.2	22.2	22.2	:	188	193	195	174	176	:
Latvia (¹)	45.8	41.4	36.0	33.8	37.4	38.1	1 017	930	803	757	834	846
Lithuania	41.0	35.9	28.7	27.6	29.5	33.4	1 400	1 217	967	928	985	1 109
Luxembourg	17.3	16.5	15.9	15.5	17.8	:	77	74	73	72	85	:
Hungary	32.1	31.4	29.4	28.2	29.6	29.9	3 185	3 121	2 916	2 794	2 924	2 948
Malta	20.6	19.0	19.1	19.5	20.2	:	82	76	77	79	82	:
Netherlands	16.7	16.0	15.7	14.9	15.1	:	2 705	2 603	2 558	2 432	2 483	:
Austria	16.8	17.8	16.7	18.6	17.0	16.6	1 369	1 454	1 376	1 532	1 406	1 373
Poland (¹)	45.3	39.5	34.4	30.5	27.8	:	17 080	14 938	12 958	11 491	10 454	:
Portugal	26.1	25.0	25.0	26.0	24.9	:	2 745	2 640	2 653	2 757	2 648	:
Romania	:	:	45.9	44.2	43.1	:	:	:	9 904	9 418	9 112	:
Slovenia	18.5	17.1	17.1	18.5	17.1	:	362	343	335	361	339	:
Slovakia	32.0	26.7	21.3	20.6	19.6	:	1 724	1 439	1 150	1 111	1 061	:
Finland	17.2	17.2	17.4	17.4	16.9	16.9	886	891	907	910	886	890
Sweden	14.4	16.3	13.9	14.9	15.9	:	1 325	1 489	1 264	1 367	1 459	:
United Kingdom	24.8	23.8	22.9	23.2	21.9	:	14 530	14 215	13 676	14 069	13 351	:
Iceland	12.7	12.5	12.5	11.8	11.6	13.8	36	36	37	36	36	42
Norway	16.2	16.3	17.0	15.0	15.2	:	746	752	795	707	731	:
Switzerland	:	:	:	18.6	17.2	:	:	:	:	1 372	1 288	:
Turkey	:	72.4	:	:	:	:	:	48 934	:	:	:	:

(¹) Break in series, 2008.

Source: Eurostat (online data code: ilc_peps01)

Figure 6.1.1: Number of persons at-risk-of-poverty or social exclusion analysed by type of risks, EU-27, 2009 ([1])
(million)

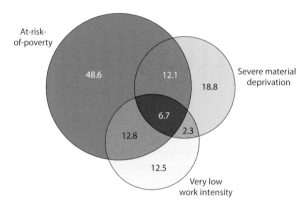

([1]) The sum of the data for the seven groups at-risk-of-poverty or social exclusion differs slightly from the total (published elsewhere) due to rounding.

Source: Eurostat (online data code: ilc_pees01)

Figure 6.1.2: Proportion of the population at-risk-of-poverty or social exclusion, 2009 ([1])
(%)

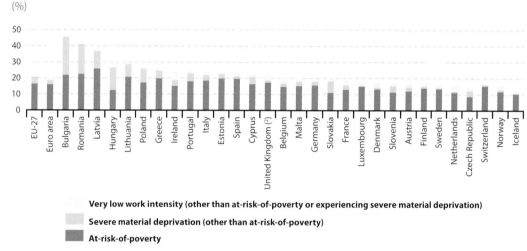

Very low work intensity (other than at-risk-of-poverty or experiencing severe material deprivation)

Severe material deprivation (other than at-risk-of-poverty)

At-risk-of-poverty

([1]) The sum of the data for the three groups at risk of poverty or social exclusion may differ slightly from the total (published elsewhere) due to rounding.
([2]) Data for severe material deprivation are not fully reliable given the high rate of missing values in some deprivation items.

Source: Eurostat (online data codes: ilc_pees01 and ilc_li02)

Figure 6.1.3: At-risk-of-poverty rate and threshold, 2009

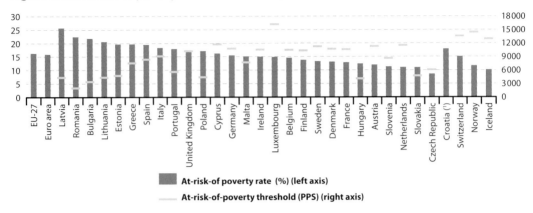

At-risk-of poverty rate (%) (left axis)

At-risk-of-poverty threshold (PPS) (right axis)

(¹) At-risk-of-poverty threshold, not available.

Source: Eurostat (online data codes: ilc_li01 and ilc_li02)

Figure 6.1.4: Material deprivation rate – proportion of persons who cannot afford to pay for selected items, 2009 (¹)
(%)

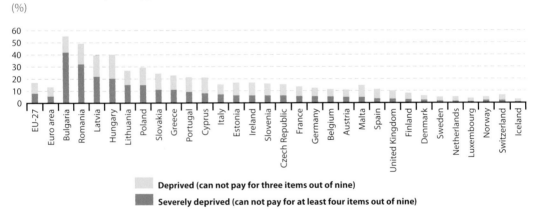

Deprived (can not pay for three items out of nine)

Severely deprived (can not pay for at least four items out of nine)

(¹) Ranked on severely deprived.

Source: Eurostat (online data code: ilc_sip8)

Figure 6.1.5: People aged less than 60 living in households with very low work intensity, 2009 (%)

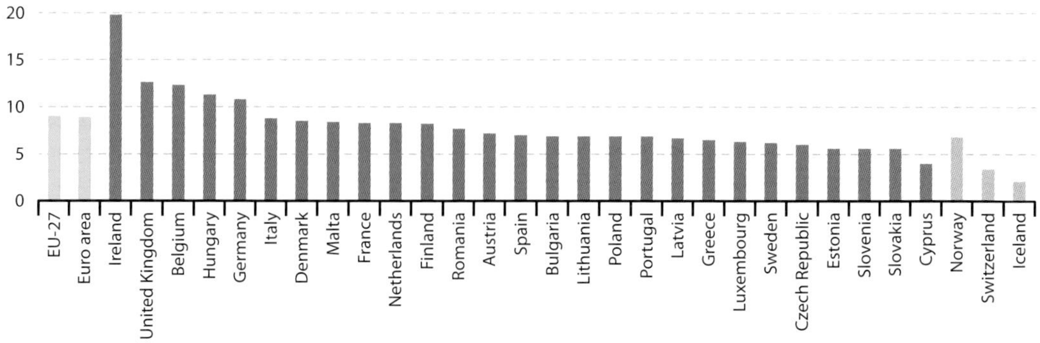

Source: Eurostat (online data code: ilc_lvhl11)

6.2 Income distribution

This subchapter analyses recent statistics on monetary poverty and income inequalities in the European Union (EU). Favourable living conditions depend on a wide range of factors, which may be divided into those that are income-related and those that are not. Income distribution within a country provides a picture of inequalities: on the one hand, inequalities may create incentives for people to improve their situation through work, innovation or acquiring new skills, while on the other, crime, poverty and social exclusion are often seen as being linked to such income inequalities.

Main statistical findings

At-risk-of-poverty rate and threshold

In 2009, 16.3 % of the EU-27 population was assessed to be at-risk-of-poverty (see Figure 6.2.1). This share, calculated as a weighted average of national results, conceals considerable variations between countries. In four of the EU Member States, namely Latvia (25.7 %), Romania (22.4 %), Bulgaria (21.8 %) and Lithuania (20.6 %), more than one fifth of the population was assessed to be at-risk-of-poverty. The lowest proportions of persons at-risk-of-poverty were observed in the Czech Republic (8.6 %), Slovakia (11.0 %), the

Netherlands (11.1 %) and Slovenia (11.3 %); Iceland (10.2 %) and Norway (11.7 %) also reported relatively low shares of their respective populations at-risk-of-poverty.

The at-risk-of-poverty threshold (also shown in Figure 6.2.1) is set at 60 % of the national median equivalised disposable income. It is often expressed in purchasing power standards (PPS) in order to take account of the differences in the cost of living across countries. It varied greatly in 2009 across the Member States from PPS 2066 in Romania and PPS 3452 in Bulgaria to a level between PPS 11000 and PPS 12000 in four Member States (Sweden, Austria, the Netherlands and Cyprus), peaking in Luxembourg above this range at PPS 16226; the poverty threshold was also relatively high in Iceland, Norway and Switzerland (above PPS 12000 in each of these countries).

In general, the at-risk-of-poverty rate (after social transfers) is stable from one year to the next (see Table 6.2.1). Between 2008 and 2009, the minor exceptions to this rule were Luxembourg (with an increase of 1.5 percentage points from 13.4 % in 2008 to 14.9 % in 2009) and the United Kingdom (with a reduction of 1.5 percentage points from 18.7 % in 2008 to 17.2 % in 2009).

Different groups in society are more or less vulnerable to monetary poverty. There was a relatively small difference in the at-risk-of-poverty rate (after social transfers) between men and women in the EU-27 in 2009 (15.4 % compared with 17.1 % respectively). However, the differences were more notable when the population was classified according to activity status (see Table 6.2.2). The unemployed are a particularly vulnerable group: almost half (45.3 %) of the unemployed were at-risk-of-poverty in the EU-27 in 2009, with the highest rates in Germany (62.0 %), Latvia (56.7 %) and Estonia (55.1 %), while four other Member States reported that more than half of the unemployed were at-risk-of-poverty. About one in six of all retired persons in the EU-27 (15.4 %) were at-risk-of-poverty in 2009; rates were much higher in Latvia, Cyprus, Estonia and Bulgaria – with more than one third of the retired population at-risk-of-poverty. Those in employment were far less likely to be at-risk-of-poverty (8.4 % in the EU-27), although there were relatively high rates in Romania (17.6 %) and Greece (13.8 %).

Social protection measures can be used as a means for reducing poverty and social exclusion. This may be achieved, for example, through the distribution of benefits. One way of evaluating the success of social protection measures is to compare at-risk-of-poverty indicators before and after social transfers (see Figure 6.2.2). In 2009, social transfers reduced the at-risk-of-poverty rate among the population of the EU-27 from 25.1 % before transfers to 16.3 % after transfers, thereby lifting 35 % of persons that would otherwise be at-risk-of-poverty above the poverty threshold. In relative terms, the impact of social benefits was lowest in Greece, Latvia, Bulgaria, Spain and Italy. In contrast, at least half of all persons who were at-risk-of poverty in Ireland, Denmark, Hungary, the Czech Republic, Austria and Sweden moved above the threshold as a result of social transfers; this was also the case in Norway.

Income inequalities

Governments, policymakers and society in general cannot combat poverty and social exclusion without analysing inequalities within society, whether they are economic in nature or social. Data on economic inequality becomes particularly important

for estimating relative poverty, because the distribution of economic resources may have a direct bearing on the extent and depth of poverty (see Figure 6.2.3). There were wide inequalities in the distribution of income among the population of the EU-27 in 2009: the 20 % of the population with the highest equivalised disposable income received 4.9 times as much income as the 20 % of the population with the lowest equivalised disposable income. This ratio varied considerably across the Member States, from 3.2 in Slovenia, 3.5 in both the Czech Republic and Hungary, to 5.8 in Greece, 5.9 in Bulgaria, 6.0 in both Spain and Portugal, 6.3 in Lithuania, 6.7 in Romania, peaking at 7.3 in Latvia.

There is policy interest in the inequalities felt by many different groups in society. One group of particular interest is that of the elderly, in part reflecting the growing proportion of the EU's population aged over 65 years. Pension systems can play an important role in addressing poverty amongst the elderly. In this respect, it is interesting to compare the incomes of the elderly with the rest of the population. Across the EU-27 as a whole, people aged 65 and more had a median income which in 2009 was around 86 % of the median income for the population under the age of 65 (see Figure 6.2.4). Hungary and Luxembourg were the only Member States where the income of the elderly was higher than the income of persons under 65. In France, Romania, Poland and Austria the median income of the elderly was more than 90 % of that recorded for people under 65; this was also the case in Iceland. In contrast, the elderly in Latvia and Cyprus had median incomes that were less than 60 % of those recorded for people under 65, with shares between 60 % and 70 % in Bulgaria and Estonia; these relatively low proportions may broadly reflect pension entitlements.

The depth of poverty, which helps to quantify just how poor the poor are, can be measured by the relative median at-risk-of-poverty gap. The median income of persons at-risk-of-poverty in the EU-27 was an average 22.4 % below the 60 % poverty threshold in 2009. Among the countries shown in Figure 6.2.5, the at-risk-of-poverty gap was widest in Romania (32.0 %), Latvia (28.9 %), Spain (27.7 %) and Bulgaria (27.4 %), but also relatively wide in

Greece (24.1 %) and Portugal (23.6 %). The lowest gap among the Member States was observed in Finland (15.1 %), followed by Ireland and Malta (both 16.2 %), Hungary (16.3 %) and the Netherlands (16.5 %); there was also a relatively low gap in Iceland (16.4 %).

Data sources and availability

EU statistics on income and living conditions (EU-SILC) were launched in 2003 on the basis of a gentlemen's agreement between Eurostat, six Member States (Austria, Belgium, Denmark, Greece, Ireland, Luxembourg) and Norway. It was formally launched in 2004 in 15 countries and expanded in 2005 to cover all of the then EU-25 Member States, together with Iceland and Norway. Bulgaria launched EU-SILC in 2006, while Romania, Switzerland and Turkey introduced the survey in 2007. Data for Croatia are based on a different data source – namely the household budget survey (HBS).

EU-SILC comprises both a cross-sectional dimension and a longitudinal dimension. Comparisons of standards of living between countries are frequently based on gross domestic product (GDP) per capita. However, such figures say little about the distribution of income within a country; this subchapter provides information on the distribution of income and relative poverty.

Household disposable income is established by summing up all monetary incomes received from any source by each member of the household (including income from work, investment and social benefits) – plus income received at the household level – and deducting taxes and social contributions paid. In order to reflect differences in household size and composition, this total is divided by the number of 'equivalent adults' using a standard (equivalence) scale, the so-called 'modified OECD' scale, which attributes a weight of 1 to the first adult in the household, a weight of 0.5 to each subsequent member of the household aged 14 and over, and a weight of 0.3 to household members aged less than 14. The resulting figure is called equivalised disposable income and is attributed to each member of the household. For the purpose of poverty indicators, the equivalised disposable income is calculated from the total disposable income of each household divided by the equivalised household size; consequently, each person in the household is considered to have the same equivalised income.

The income reference period is a fixed 12-month period (such as the previous calendar or tax year) for all countries except the United Kingdom for which the income reference period is the current year of the survey and Ireland for which the survey is continuous and income is collected for the 12 months prior to the survey.

The at-risk-of-poverty rate is defined as the share of people with an equivalised disposable income that is below the at-risk-of-poverty threshold (expressed in purchasing power standards – PPS), set at 60 % of the national median equivalised disposable income. This rate may be expressed before or after social transfers, with the difference measuring the hypothetical impact of national social transfers in reducing poverty risk. Retirement and survivors' pensions are counted as income before transfers and not as social transfers. Various analyses of this indicator are available, for example by age, sex, activity status, household type, or education level. It should be noted that the indicator does not measure wealth but is instead a measure of low current income (in comparison with other people in the same country), which does not necessarily imply a low standard of living. The EU-27 aggregate is a population-weighted average of individual national figures. In line with decisions of the European Council, the at-risk-of-poverty rate is measured relative to the situation in each country rather than applying a common threshold to all countries.

Context

At the Laeken European Council in December 2001, European heads of state and government endorsed a first set of common statistical indicators for social exclusion and poverty that are subject to a continuing process of refinement by the indicators sub-group (ISG) of the social protection committee (SPC). These indicators are an essential element in the open method of coordination to monitor the progress made by the EU's Member States in alleviating poverty and social exclusion.

EU-SILC was implemented in order to provide underlying data for these indicators. Organised under framework Regulation 1177/2003, EU-SILC is now the reference source for statistics on income and living conditions and, in particular, for indicators concerning social inclusion. In the context of the Europe 2020 strategy, the European Council adopted in June 2010 a headline target for social inclusion – namely, that by 2020 there should be at least 20 million fewer people in the EU who are at-risk-of-poverty or social exclusion. EU-SILC is the source used to monitor progress towards this headline target, which is measured through indicator that is combines of the at-risk-of-poverty rate, the severe material deprivation rate, and the proportion of people living in households with very low work intensity.

Figure 6.2.1: At-risk-of-poverty rate and threshold, 2009

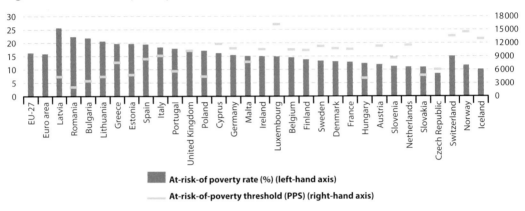

Source: Eurostat (online data codes: ilc_li01 and ilc_li02)

Table 6.2.1: At-risk-of-poverty rate after social transfers, 2007-2009
(%)

	Total			Male			Female		
	2007	2008	2009	2007	2008	2009	2007	2008	2009
EU-27	16.7	16.4	16.3	15.9	15.5	15.4	17.5	17.4	17.1
Euro area	16.1	15.8	15.9	15.1	14.8	14.9	17.1	16.8	16.8
Belgium	15.2	14.7	14.6	14.4	13.6	13.4	15.9	15.9	15.7
Bulgaria	22.0	21.4	21.8	20.9	19.8	19.8	23.0	22.9	23.7
Czech Republic	9.6	9.0	8.6	8.7	8.0	7.5	10.5	10.1	9.5
Denmark	11.7	11.8	13.1	11.3	11.7	13.0	12.0	12.0	13.3
Germany	15.2	15.2	15.5	14.1	14.2	14.7	16.3	16.2	16.3
Estonia	19.4	19.5	19.7	16.7	16.5	17.5	21.7	22.0	21.6
Ireland	17.2	15.5	15.0	16.0	14.5	14.9	18.5	16.4	15.1
Greece	20.3	20.1	19.7	19.6	19.6	19.1	20.9	20.7	20.2
Spain	19.7	19.6	19.5	18.5	18.3	18.3	20.9	21.0	20.6
France (¹)	13.1	12.7	12.9	12.8	11.9	12.0	13.4	13.4	13.7
Italy	19.9	18.7	18.4	18.4	17.1	17.0	21.3	20.1	19.8
Cyprus	15.5	16.2	16.2	13.5	14.0	14.4	17.4	18.3	17.9
Latvia	21.2	25.6	25.7	19.3	23.1	24.2	22.7	27.7	27.0
Lithuania	19.1	20.0	20.6	16.7	17.6	19.1	21.2	22.0	21.9
Luxembourg	13.5	13.4	14.9	12.9	12.5	13.8	14.1	14.3	16.0
Hungary	12.3	12.4	12.4	12.3	12.4	12.8	12.3	12.4	12.1
Malta	14.3	14.6	15.1	13.8	13.7	14.7	14.9	15.5	15.6
Netherlands	10.2	10.5	11.1	9.6	10.5	10.8	10.7	10.4	11.3
Austria	12.0	12.4	12.0	10.6	11.2	10.7	13.3	13.5	13.2
Poland	17.3	16.9	17.1	17.6	17.0	16.9	17.1	16.7	17.4
Portugal	18.1	18.5	17.9	17.2	17.9	17.3	19.0	19.1	18.4
Romania (²)	24.8	23.4	22.4	24.3	22.4	21.4	25.3	24.3	23.4
Slovenia	11.5	12.3	11.3	10.0	11.0	9.8	12.9	13.6	12.8
Slovakia	10.5	10.9	11.0	9.8	10.1	10.1	11.2	11.5	11.8
Finland	13.0	13.6	13.8	12.1	12.7	12.9	13.8	14.5	14.7
Sweden	10.5	12.2	13.3	10.5	11.3	12.0	10.6	13.0	14.5
United Kingdom	18.6	18.7	17.2	17.6	17.4	16.8	19.6	20.0	17.9
Iceland	10.1	10.1	10.2	9.1	9.5	9.3	11.0	10.7	11.1
Norway	12.4	11.4	11.7	10.6	9.9	10.1	14.1	12.9	13.2
Switzerland	:	16.2	15.1	:	14.5	13.5	:	18.0	16.7
Croatia	18.0	17.3	17.9	16.0	15.4	16.0	19.0	19.0	19.7

(¹) Break in series, 2008.
(²) Break in series, 2007.

Source: Eurostat (online data code: ilc_li02)

Table 6.2.2: At-risk-of-poverty rate after social transfers by most frequent activity status, 2009 (¹)
(%)

	Total population	Persons employed	Not employed	Unemployed	Retired	Inactive population, others
EU-27	15.2	8.4	23.0	45.3	15.4	26.9
Euro area	14.9	8.1	22.5	44.7	13.8	26.5
Belgium	14.0	4.6	23.9	33.4	17.8	26.7
Bulgaria	21.1	7.4	36.9	52.2	36.5	24.0
Czech Republic	7.4	3.1	12.9	46.9	7.1	13.0
Denmark	13.4	5.9	24.3	41.1	18.6	31.1
Germany	14.9	6.8	23.9	62.0	14.9	25.4
Estonia	19.5	8.1	36.5	55.1	37.9	30.0
Ireland	13.8	5.3	22.5	28.1	15.5	23.3
Greece	18.8	13.8	23.9	38.1	18.4	26.5
Spain	18.8	11.4	27.5	38.4	19.3	29.0
France	11.4	6.7	16.9	37.7	8.7	26.6
Italy	17.1	10.2	23.4	40.8	13.7	27.4
Cyprus	17.2	7.0	32.3	32.8	47.8	20.1
Latvia	25.4	11.1	46.4	56.7	51.2	31.9
Lithuania	19.8	10.4	32.7	54.3	27.6	33.5
Luxembourg	12.7	10.0	16.1	45.3	5.5	19.6
Hungary	10.2	6.2	14.0	47.3	4.0	18.9
Malta	13.8	6.0	20.9	33.9	19.2	20.4
Netherlands	9.6	5.0	16.0	41.7	6.7	22.3
Austria	11.6	5.9	18.7	38.0	14.2	21.0
Poland	15.9	11.0	21.2	42.1	12.3	26.8
Portugal	16.7	10.3	24.4	37.0	17.4	29.9
Romania	19.8	17.6	22.3	46.4	15.7	30.7
Slovenia	10.9	4.8	18.2	43.6	17.4	10.9
Slovakia	9.6	5.2	15.2	48.6	8.9	15.9
Finland	14.1	3.7	27.2	51.4	21.7	31.2
Sweden	13.3	6.9	23.6	39.0	17.6	33.4
United Kingdom	16.1	6.7	28.7	50.9	24.0	32.0
Iceland	9.9	7.7	17.4	29.3	14.8	18.5
Norway	11.5	5.6	22.7	38.8	13.0	31.9
Switzerland	14.6	8.3	27.3	39.7	29.6	22.0
Croatia	17.8	7.6	26.6	37.2	24.2	26.5

(¹) For persons aged 18 or over.

Source: Eurostat (online data code: ilc_li04)

Figure 6.2.2: At-risk-of-poverty rate before and after social transfers, 2009 (¹)
(%)

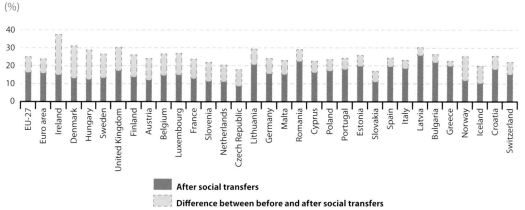

■ **After social transfers**

□ **Difference between before and after social transfers**

(¹) Ranked on the difference between before and after social transfers.

Source: Eurostat (online data codes: ilc_li02 and ilc_li10)

Figure 6.2.3: Inequality of income distribution, 2009
(income quintile share ratio)

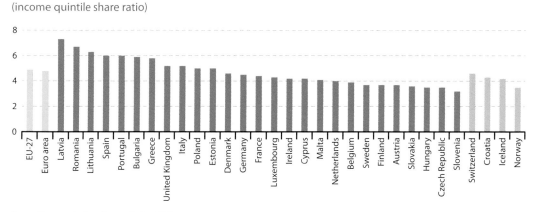

Source: Eurostat (online data code: ilc_di11)

Figure 6.2.4: Relative median income ratio, 2009
(ratio)

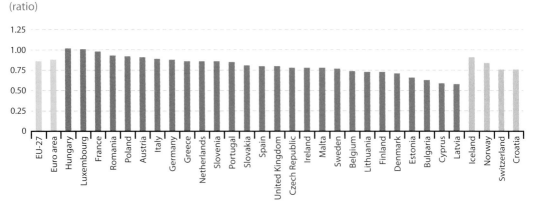

Source: Eurostat (online data code: ilc_pnp2)

Figure 6.2.5: Relative median at-risk-of-poverty gap, 2009
(%)

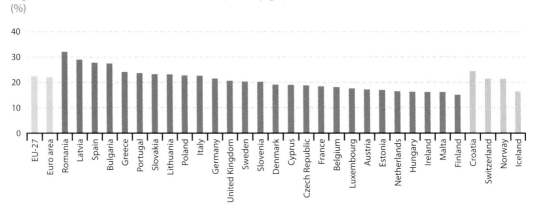

Source: Eurostat (online data code: ilc_li11)

6.3 Housing

Decent housing, at an affordable price in a safe environment, is a fundamental need and right. Ensuring this need, which is likely to alleviate poverty and social exclusion, is still a significant challenge in a number of European countries.

This subchapter provides information in relation to recent statistics on housing in the European Union (EU), focusing on dwelling types, tenure status (owning versus renting), housing quality and affordability.

Main statistical findings

Type of dwelling

In 2009, 41.8 % of the EU-27 population lived in flats, 34.4 % in detached houses and 23.0 % in semi-detached houses. The share of persons living in flats was highest in Latvia (66.2 %), Estonia (65.1 %) and Spain (64.6 %). The share of people living in detached houses peaked in Slovenia (68.7 %), Hungary (67.6 %), Romania (60.7 %) and Denmark (58.4 %); Norway also reported a high share (62.4 %) of persons living in detached houses. The highest propensity to live in semi-detached houses was reported in the Netherlands (61.4 %), the United Kingdom (60.9 %) and Ireland (57.6 %) – see Figure 6.3.1.

Tenure status

In 2009, over one quarter (27.1 %) of the EU-27 population lived in an owner-occupied home for which there was an outstanding loan or mortgage, while close to half (46.5 %) of the population lived in an owner-occupied home without a loan or mortgage. As such, a total of nearly three quarters (73.6 %) of the population lived in owner-occupied dwellings, while 13.0 % lived in dwellings with a market price rent, and 13.5 % in reduced-rent or free accommodation.

At least half of the population in each of the EU Member States (see Figure 6.3.2 – data for Germany not available) lived in owner-occupied dwellings in 2009; the share ranged from 57.5 % in

Austria to 96.5 % in Romania. In the Netherlands (59.2 %), Sweden (56.8 %) and Denmark (52.8 %) more than half of the population lived in owner-occupied dwellings with an outstanding loan or mortgage; this was also the case in Iceland (70.6 %) and Norway (61.3 %).

The share of persons living in rented dwellings with a market price rent in 2009 was less than 10 % in 12 of the EU Member States, as well as in Iceland. In Denmark, the Netherlands, Sweden and Austria more than one quarter of the population lived in rented dwellings with a market price rent. The share of the population living in a dwelling with a reduced price rent or occupying a dwelling free of charge was less than 20 % in all of the Member States except for Poland where this type of housing was lived in by 29.1 % of the population.

Housing quality

One of the key dimensions in assessing the quality of housing conditions is the availability of sufficient space in the dwelling. The overcrowding rate describes the proportion of people living in an overcrowded dwelling, as defined by the number of rooms available to the household, the household's size, as well as its members' ages and family situation.

Some 17.7 % of the EU-27 population lived in overcrowded dwellings in 2009 (see Figure 6.3.3); the highest overcrowding rates were registered in Latvia (57.7 %), Romania (55.3 %), Poland (49.1 %) and Lithuania (49.0 %). In contrast, Cyprus (1.0 %) and the Netherlands (1.7 %) recorded the lowest rates of overcrowding.

Within the population at-risk-of-poverty (in other words, people living in households where equivalised disposable income per person was below 60 % of the national median), the overcrowding rate in the EU-27 was 30.0 % in 2009, some 12.3 percentage points above the rate for the whole population. The highest overcrowding rates among the population at-risk-of-poverty were registered in Hungary (68.8 %), Poland (64.9 %) and Romania (64.8 %), while the overcrowding rate for those at-risk-of-poverty was below 6 % (see Figure 6.3.3) in Cyprus (2.7 %), Spain (5.1 %), the Netherlands (5.5 %) and Malta (5.6 %).

In addition to overcrowding, some aspects of housing deprivation – such as the lack of a bath or a toilet, a leaking roof in the dwelling, or a dwelling considered as being too dark – are taken into account to build a more complete indicator of housing quality. The severe housing deprivation rate is defined as the proportion of persons living in a dwelling which is considered as overcrowded, while having at the same time at least one of these housing deprivation measures.

Across the EU-27 as a whole, some 5.9 % of the population suffered from severe housing deprivation in 2009 (see Figure 6.3.4). In Poland, Lithuania, Slovenia, Bulgaria and Latvia more than 15 % of the population faced severe housing deprivation in 2009, rising to a high of 28.6 % in Romania. In contrast, less than 1 % of the population in Finland, the Netherlands and Cyprus lived in conditions which could be qualified as severe housing deprivation.

Housing affordability

In 2009, 12.1 % of the EU-27 population lived in households that spent 40 % or more of their equivalised disposable income on housing (see Table 6.3.1). The proportion of the population whose housing costs exceeded 40 % of their equivalised disposable income was highest for tenants with market price rents (25.6 %) and lowest for persons in owner-occupied dwellings without a loan or mortgage (5.8 %).

The EU-27 average masks significant differences between Member States: at one extreme there were a number of Member States where a relatively small proportion of the population lived in households that had housing costs in excess of 40 % of their disposable income, notably Cyprus (2.4 %), France (3.4 %), Malta (3.5 %), Luxembourg (3.7 %), Slovenia (3.9 %), Ireland (4.0 %), Estonia and Finland (both 4.4 %). At the other extreme, almost one quarter of the population in Denmark (24.4 %) and Greece (22.1 %) spent more than 40 % of their equivalised disposable income on housing, well above the next highest shares recorded in the United Kingdom (16.3 %) and Romania (15.5 %).

Data sources and availability

The data used in this section are primarily derived from micro-data from EU statistics on income and living conditions (EU-SILC). The reference population is all private households and their current members residing in the territory of the Member State at the time of data collection; persons living in collective households and in institutions are generally excluded from the target population. The EU-27 aggregate is a population-weighted average of individual national figures.

Context

Questions of social housing, homelessness or integration play an important role within the EU's social policy agenda. The charter of fundamental rights stipulates in Article II-94 that 'in order to combat social exclusion and poverty, the Union recognises and respects the right to social and housing assistance so as to ensure a decent existence for all those who lack sufficient resources, in accordance with Community law and national laws and practices'.

However, the EU does not have any responsibilities in respect of housing; rather, national governments develop their own housing policies. Many countries face similar challenges: for example, how to renew housing stocks, how to plan and combat urban sprawl, how to promote sustainable development, how to help young and disadvantage groups to get onto the housing market, or how to promote energy efficiency among house owners.

Figure 6.3.1: Distribution of population by dwelling type, 2009
(% of population)

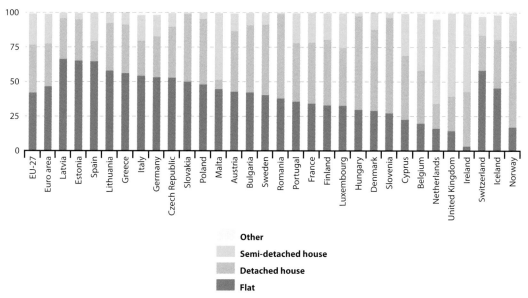

Legend:
- Other
- Semi-detached house
- Detached house
- Flat

Source: Eurostat (online data code: ilc_lvho01)

Figure 6.3.2: Population by tenure status, 2009 ([1])
(% of population)

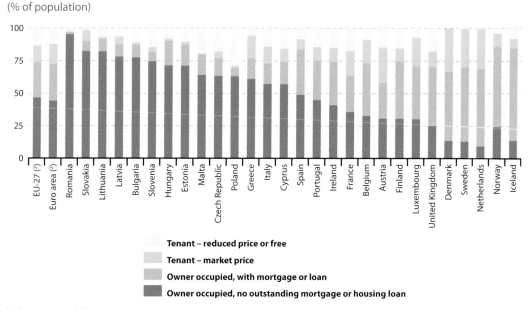

Legend:
- Tenant – reduced price or free
- Tenant – market price
- Owner occupied, with mortgage or loan
- Owner occupied, no outstanding mortgage or housing loan

([1]) Germany, not available.
([2]) Estimates.

Source: Eurostat (online data code: ilc_lvho02)

Figure 6.3.3: Overcrowding rate, 2009
(% of specified population)

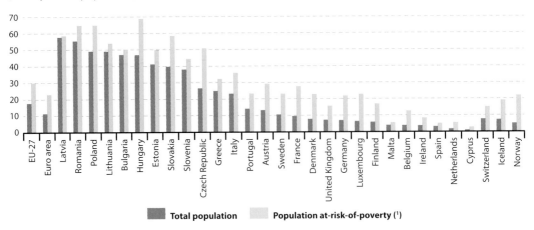

(¹) Population below 60 % of median equivalised income.

Source: Eurostat (online data code: ilc_lvho05a)

Figure 6.3.4: Severe housing deprivation, 2009
(% of population)

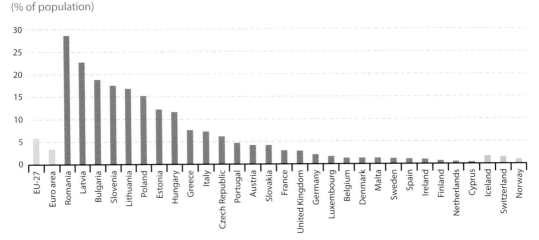

Source: Eurostat (online data code: ilc_mdho06a)

Table 6.3.1: Housing cost overburden rate by tenure status, 2009
(% of population)

	Total population	Owner occupied, with mortgage or loan	Owner occupied, no outstanding mortgage or housing loan	Tenant – market price	Tenant – reduced price or free
EU-27	12.1	8.8	5.7	25.5	11.7
Euro area	11.8	7.8	3.1	22.4	7.1
Belgium	8.7	2.5	2.9	30.6	12.7
Bulgaria	7.2	3.6	6.3	38.1	11.4
Czech Republic	8.9	10.1	6.0	23.2	14.0
Denmark	24.4	23.1	16.8	29.7	:
Germany	:	:	:	:	:
Estonia	4.4	11.5	1.9	20.9	6.3
Ireland	4.0	2.3	1.2	21.9	1.8
Greece	22.1	10.5	13.6	67.0	3.6
Spain	10.9	14.7	3.3	40.6	10.3
France	3.4	1.2	0.5	10.0	4.9
Italy	7.5	7.7	2.6	27.4	8.9
Cyprus	2.4	2.4	0.2	17.2	0.4
Latvia	8.6	14.6	7.2	14.1	11.9
Lithuania	5.5	12.2	3.9	23.4	10.9
Luxembourg	3.7	0.8	0.2	13.3	4.6
Hungary	8.9	16.4	5.2	44.0	14.5
Malta	3.5	4.6	2.7	36.5	2.9
Netherlands	13.1	12.2	4.5	17.6	5.9
Austria	5.1	1.2	1.4	12.4	6.4
Poland	8.2	6.0	7.4	32.8	8.7
Portugal	6.3	8.2	2.3	19.6	4.7
Romania	15.5	8.9	14.9	56.5	26.8
Slovenia	3.9	9.2	2.6	13.1	5.3
Slovakia	9.4	32.3	7.0	13.4	9.6
Finland	4.4	3.2	2.2	11.4	7.4
Sweden	9.6	3.9	9.7	20.1	28.9
United Kingdom	16.3	10.2	8.3	40.7	26.3
Iceland	8.5	9.0	4.9	13.3	5.8
Norway	10.9	9.7	5.8	28.2	14.6
Switzerland	12.6	7.8	:	17.0	11.9

Source: Eurostat (online data codes: ilc_lvho07c and ilc_lvho07a)

6.4 Social protection

This subchapter analyses recent statistics on social protection in the European Union (EU). Social protection encompasses all interventions from public or private bodies intended to relieve households and individuals of the burden of a defined set of risks or needs, provided that there is neither a simultaneous reciprocal nor an individual arrangement involved.

Main statistical findings

Social protection expenditure in the EU-27 was equivalent to 26.4 % of gross domestic product (GDP) in 2008 (see Table 6.4.1). Among the EU Member States, the level of social protection expenditure in relation to GDP was highest in France (30.8 %), Denmark (29.7 %) and Sweden (29.4 %), and was higher than 25 % of GDP in ten of the EU-15 Member States. In contrast, social protection expenditure represented less than 20 % of GDP in all of the Member States that joined the EU in 2004 or 2007 with the exceptions of Slovenia and Hungary.

The use of a purchasing power standard (PPS) allows a comparison of social protection expenditure per inhabitant between countries, taking account of differences in price levels. The highest level of expenditure on social protection per inhabitant in 2008 was registered for Luxembourg (PPS 14 057 per inhabitant), followed some way behind by the Netherlands, Sweden, Denmark, Austria, France and Belgium – where social protection per inhabitant was between PPS 9 600 and PPS 8 200 (see Figure 6.4.1). In contrast, expenditure in Latvia, Romania and Bulgaria was less than PPS 2 000 per inhabitant. These disparities between countries are partly related to different levels of wealth, but may also reflect differences in social protection systems, demographic trends, unemployment rates and other social, institutional and economic factors.

The highest share of social protection benefits (the largest component of social protection expenditure) was accounted for by old age and by sickness/healthcare benefits; together these two functions accounted for 68.8 % of total EU-27 social benefits

in 2008 (see Figure 6.4.2). Benefits related to family/children, disability, survivors and unemployment ranged between 5 % and 8 % each, while housing accounted for 2.1 %.

Expenditure on pensions across the EU-27 was equivalent to 11.7 % of GDP in 2008, ranging from a high of 15.0 % in Italy to lows of 6.0 % in Ireland and Latvia (see Figure 6.4.3). Expenditure on care for the elderly in the EU-27 accounted for 0.4 % of GDP in 2008, although Sweden reported a rate that was almost six times as high as the average; expenditure on the elderly fell to less than 0.1 % of GDP in Greece, Estonia, Belgium, Bulgaria, Romania and Cyprus (see Figure 6.4.4).

Average (median) pension levels of 65 to 74 year olds across the EU-27 were generally lower than average earnings for those aged 50 to 59 in 2009 (see Figure 6.4.5). This was particularly the case in Cyprus, Latvia and Bulgaria, where pensions represented around one third of the earnings among those aged 50 to 59. The aggregate replacement ratio was highest in France, Austria, Luxembourg, Hungary and Sweden, where it stood at 60 % or more. Relatively low aggregate replacement ratios may reflect low coverage and/or low income replacement from pension schemes within current pension systems, as well as incomplete careers or an under-declaration of earnings.

A breakdown of social protection receipts across the EU-27 in 2008 shows that the majority of receipts could be attributed to general government contributions (38.2 %) and employers' social contributions (37.1 %), while around one fifth (20.4 %) of social protection receipts in the EU-27 were social contributions paid by protected persons (see Figure 6.4.6).

Data sources and availability

Data on social protection expenditure and receipts are drawn up according to the European system of integrated social protection statistics (ESSPROS) methodology; this system has been designed to allow a comparison of social protection flows between EU Member States. In April 2007, a legal basis was established for the provision of ESSPROS with the delivery of data to start from reference year 2006, as provided by the European Parliament and Council Regulation 458/2007; this was later supplemented by two European Commission implementing Regulations (1322/2007 and 10/2008).

Expenditure on social protection includes: social benefits, administration costs (which represent the costs charged to the scheme for its management and administration) and other expenditure (which consists of miscellaneous expenditure by social protection schemes, principally, payment of property income).

Social protection benefits are direct transfers, in cash or in kind, by social protection schemes to households and individuals to relieve them of the burden of one or more of the defined risks or needs. Social benefits are paid to households by social security funds, other government units, non-profit institutions serving households (NPISHs), employers administering unfunded social insurance schemes, insurance enterprises, or other institutional units administering privately funded social insurance schemes.

Social protection benefits are classified according to eight social protection functions (which represent a set of risks or needs):

- sickness/healthcare benefits – including paid sick leave, medical care and the provision of pharmaceutical products;
- disability benefits – including disability pensions and the provision of goods and services (other than medical care) to the disabled;
- old age benefits – including old age pensions and the provision of goods and services (other than medical care) to the elderly;
- survivors' benefits – including income maintenance and support in connection with the death of a family member, such as a survivors' pensions;
- family/children benefits – including support (except healthcare) in connection with the costs of pregnancy, childbirth, childbearing and caring for other family members;
- unemployment benefits – including vocational training financed by public agencies;

- housing benefits – including interventions by public authorities to help households meet the cost of housing;
- social exclusion benefits not elsewhere classified – including income support, rehabilitation of alcohol and drug abusers and other miscellaneous benefits (except healthcare).

The pensions aggregate comprises part of periodic cash benefits under the disability, old age, survivors and unemployment functions. It is defined as the sum of the following social benefits: disability pensions, early-retirement benefits due to reduced capacity to work, old age pensions, anticipated old age pensions, partial pensions, survivors' pensions, and early-retirement benefits for labour market reasons.

Expenditure on care for the elderly covers care allowances, accommodation, and assistance in carrying out daily tasks; this expenditure is generally expressed in relation to GDP.

The aggregate replacement ratio measures the difference between gross retirement benefits and gross earnings. It is defined as the median individual gross pension of those aged 65 to 74 relative to median individual gross earnings of those aged 50 to 59, excluding other social benefits; it is expressed in percentage terms.

The schemes responsible for providing social protection are financed in different ways. Social protection receipts comprise social security contributions paid by employers and protected persons, contributions by general government, and other receipts from a variety of sources (for example, interest, dividends, rent and claims against third parties). Social contributions by employers are all costs incurred by employers to secure entitlement to social benefits for their employees, former employees and their dependants; they can be paid by resident or non-resident employers. They include all payments by employers to social protection institutions (actual contributions) and social benefits paid directly by employers to employees (imputed contributions). Social contributions made by protected persons comprise contributions paid by employees, by the self-employed and by pensioners and other persons.

Context

Social protection systems are highly developed in the EU: they are designed to protect people against the risks and needs associated with unemployment, parental responsibilities, sickness/healthcare and invalidity, the loss of a spouse or parent, old age, housing and social exclusion (not elsewhere classified).

Pension systems can play a role in allowing beneficiaries to maintain living standards they enjoyed in the later years of their working lives. However, as Europe's population is becoming progressively older, the main challenge social protection systems are going to face is related to their financing, as the proportion of older persons grows while the number of persons of working age decreases.

The organisation and financing of social protection systems is the responsibility of each of the EU Member States. The model used in each Member State is therefore somewhat different, while the EU plays a coordinating role to ensure that people who move across borders continue to receive adequate protection. The EU seeks to promote actions among the Member States to combat poverty and social exclusion, and to reform social protection systems on the basis of policy exchanges and mutual learning. This policy is known as the social protection and social inclusion process – it underpins the Europe 2020 strategy and will play an important role as the EU seeks to become a smart, sustainable and inclusive economy.

Table 6.4.1: Expenditure on social protection, 1998-2008
(% of GDP)

	1998	1999	2000	2001	2002	2003	2004	2005	2006	2007	2008
EU-27	:	:	26.4	26.6	26.9	27.2	27.1	27.1	26.7	25.7	26.4
Euro area (EA-16)	:	:	26.7	26.8	27.4	27.8	27.7	27.7	27.3	26.8	27.5
Belgium	27.1	27.0	26.2	27.2	28.0	29.0	29.2	29.6	30.2	26.8	28.3
Bulgaria	:	:	10.2	9.7	10.2	9.7	9.7	15.1	14.2	14.1	15.5
Czech Republic	18.5	19.2	19.5	19.4	20.2	20.2	19.3	19.2	18.7	18.6	18.7
Denmark	30.0	29.8	28.9	29.2	29.7	30.9	30.7	30.2	29.2	28.8	29.7
Germany	28.9	29.3	29.3	29.5	30.1	30.5	29.8	29.7	28.7	27.7	27.8
Estonia	:	15.4	13.9	13.0	12.7	12.5	13.0	12.6	12.1	12.3	15.1
Ireland	15.2	14.6	13.9	14.9	17.2	17.8	18.0	18.1	18.4	18.9	22.1
Greece	21.7	22.7	23.5	24.3	24.0	23.5	23.6	24.6	24.6	24.5	26.0
Spain	20.2	19.8	20.3	20.0	20.4	20.7	20.7	20.9	20.9	21.0	22.7
France	30.1	29.9	29.5	29.6	30.4	30.9	31.3	31.4	30.7	30.5	30.8
Italy	24.6	24.8	24.7	24.9	25.3	25.8	26.0	26.4	26.6	26.7	27.8
Cyprus	:	:	14.8	14.9	16.3	18.4	18.1	18.4	18.4	18.1	18.4
Latvia	16.1	17.2	15.4	14.5	14.1	13.9	13.1	12.7	12.6	11.2	12.6
Lithuania	15.1	16.3	15.8	14.8	14.1	13.6	13.4	13.3	13.4	14.5	16.2
Luxembourg	21.2	20.5	19.6	20.9	21.6	22.1	22.3	21.7	20.4	19.3	20.1
Hungary	:	20.3	19.5	19.2	20.3	21.2	20.6	21.9	22.4	22.4	22.7
Malta	17.9	17.8	16.9	17.8	17.8	18.3	18.7	18.5	18.1	18.0	18.9
Netherlands	27.8	27.1	26.4	26.5	27.6	28.3	28.3	27.9	28.8	28.3	28.4
Austria	28.5	29.0	28.4	28.8	29.2	29.6	29.3	28.9	28.4	27.9	28.2
Poland	:	:	19.7	21.0	21.1	21.0	20.1	19.7	19.4	18.1	18.6
Portugal	20.2	20.6	20.9	21.9	22.9	23.3	23.9	24.6	24.6	24.0	24.3
Romania	:	:	13.0	12.8	13.6	13.1	12.8	13.4	12.8	13.6	14.3
Slovenia	24.1	24.1	24.2	24.5	24.4	23.7	23.4	23.0	22.7	21.3	21.5
Slovakia	20.0	20.2	19.4	19.0	19.1	18.2	17.2	16.5	16.3	16.0	16.0
Finland	27.1	26.4	25.1	25.0	25.7	26.6	26.7	26.7	26.4	25.4	26.3
Sweden	31.2	30.8	29.9	30.5	31.3	32.2	31.6	31.1	30.3	29.1	29.4
United Kingdom	26.3	25.7	26.4	26.8	25.7	25.7	25.9	26.3	26.0	23.3	23.7
Iceland	18.3	18.8	19.2	19.4	21.2	23.0	22.6	21.6	21.2	21.4	22.0
Norway	26.9	26.9	24.4	25.4	26.0	27.2	25.9	23.8	22.6	22.9	22.4
Switzerland	27.4	27.4	27.0	27.7	28.5	29.2	29.3	29.3	28.0	27.3	26.4

Source: Eurostat (online data code: tps00098)

Figure 6.4.1: Expenditure on social protection per inhabitant, 2008
(PPS)

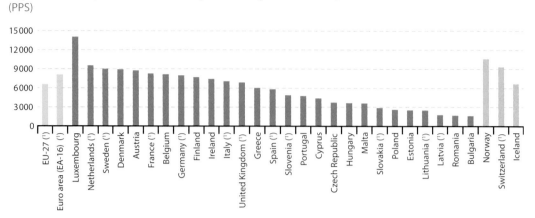

(¹) Provisional.

Source: Eurostat (online data code: tps00100)

Figure 6.4.2: Social benefits, EU-27, 2008 (¹)
(%, based on PPS)

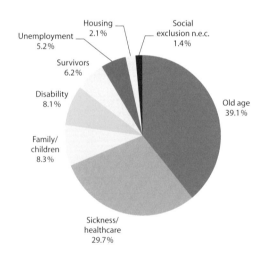

Housing
2.1%

Social
exclusion n.e.c.
1.4%

Unemployment
5.2%

Survivors
6.2%

Disability
8.1%

Family/
children
8.3%

Old age
39.1%

Sickness/
healthcare
29.7%

(¹) Provisional; figures do not sum to 100% due to rounding.

Source: Eurostat (online data code: spr_exp_sum)

Figure 6.4.3: Expenditure on pensions, 2008
(% of GDP)

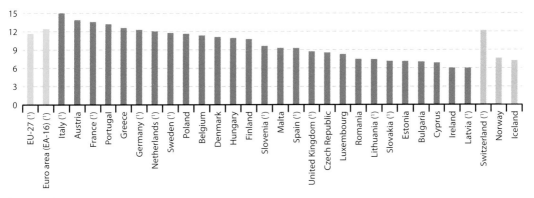

(¹) Provisional.

Source: Eurostat (online data code: tps00103)

Figure 6.4.4: Expenditure on care for the elderly, 2008
(% of GDP)

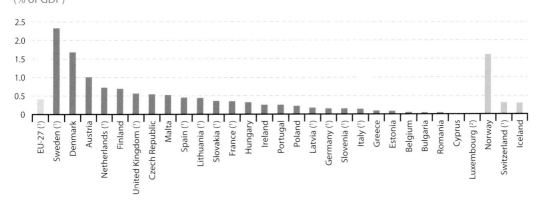

(¹) Provisional.
(²) Not available: expenditure was recorded together with similar benefits under the disability function as the split between old-age and disability was not available.

Source: Eurostat (online data code: tsdde530)

Figure 6.4.5: Aggregate replacement ratio, 2009 (¹)
(%)

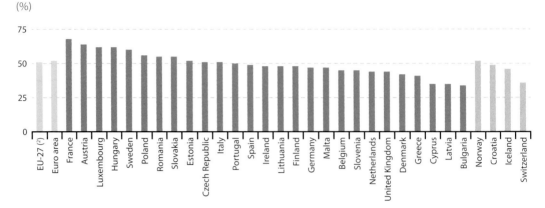

(¹) The income reference period concerns the year preceding the survey year for the majority of countries.
(²) Eurostat calculation based on population-weighted averages of national data.

Source: Eurostat (online data code: ilc_pnp3)

Figure 6.4.6: Social protection receipts, EU-27, 2008 (¹)
(% of total receipts)

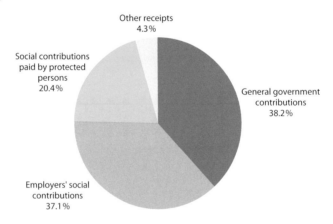

Other receipts
4.3%

Social contributions
paid by protected
persons
20.4%

General government
contributions
38.2%

Employers' social
contributions
37.1%

(¹) Provisional.

Source: Eurostat (online data code: spr_rec_sumt)

6.5 Crime

European Union (EU) statistics currently available on crime and criminal justice reflect the diversity of policing and legal systems within the EU. While the development of crime and criminal justice statistics admittedly is still in its infancy, a more comparable system is in the process of being developed.

Comparisons of crime statistics between Member States ideally should focus on trends over time, rather than directly comparing levels between countries for a specific year, given that the data can be affected by a range of factors, including different levels of criminalisation, the efficiency of criminal justice systems, and police recording practices; furthermore, it is likely that a relatively high proportion of crime remains unrecorded.

Main statistical findings

There were 1.7 million police officers in the EU-27 in 2008, which marked an overall increase of 2.5 % when compared with five years earlier (excluding Bulgaria – see Table 6.5.1). There were some quite rapid changes in the size of national police forces during the period from 1998 to 2008, as the size of the police force was reduced by more than a fifth in each of the Baltic Member States. The Czech Republic (– 4.0 %) and Austria (– 0.7 %) recorded more modest falls in police numbers. On the other hand, there were expansions in police numbers of at least 20 % recorded for Ireland and Cyprus; all of the other Member States (where an unbroken series is available) recorded increases in their respective numbers of police officers.

There were an estimated 29 million crimes recorded by the police within the EU-27 in 2008 (see Table 6.5.2). From 2000, the number of recorded crimes in the EU-27 rose to a peak around 2003, but subsequently fell each year through to 2008. From the peak in recorded crime in the EU in 2003 through to 2008 the number of recorded crimes fell by 20 % or more in Poland, Malta, and England and Wales (within the United Kingdom). Figure 6.5.1 shows the development in the number of recorded crimes between 2005 and 2008: the most substantial

fall in the number of reported crimes over this period concerned motor vehicle theft.

The EU-27 prison population rose by 1.2 % per annum during the period 1998 to 2008 to reach a total of close to 620 000, which equated to 124 prisoners per 100 000 members of the total population. When expressed in these relative terms, the Baltic Member States and Poland had the largest prison populations, with more than 200 prisoners per 100 000 inhabitants in 2008, while the relative number of prisoners in the Czech Republic was just below this level. At the other end of the range, the Nordic countries of Denmark, Finland and Sweden (as well as Iceland and Norway among non-member countries, both 2007 data), Slovenia and Ireland, each reported less than 75 prisoners per 100 000 inhabitants in 2008, with Switzerland just above this level (see Table 6.5.3).

Data sources and availability

Eurostat publishes statistics on crime and criminal justice systems from 1950 onwards for the total number of recorded crimes, and from 1993 onwards for a set of specific offences. In addition, the database also includes statistics for prison populations from 1987 onwards and the number of police officers from 1993 onwards. Figures for the United Kingdom are reported for the separate jurisdictions of England and Wales, Scotland, and Northern Ireland.

Comparisons of crime statistics between countries may be affected by a range of factors, including:

- different legal and criminal justice systems;
- the rates at which crimes are reported to the police and recorded by them;
- differences in the timing of recording crimes (for example, when reported to the police, when a suspect is identified, etc.);
- differences in the rules by which multiple offences are counted;
- differences in the list of offences that are included in the overall crime figures.

Consequently, care should be taken when analysing the information presented.

Figures for the prison population may also be affected by a range of factors, including:

- the number of cases dealt with by the courts;
- the percentage of convicted criminals given a custodial sentence;
- the length of the sentences imposed; the size of the population on remand;
- the date at which the survey was conducted (especially where amnesties or other early release arrangements might apply).

The prison population should be measured as the total number of adult and juvenile prisoners (including pre-trial detainees) as of 1 September each year. The figures include offenders held in prison administration facilities, juvenile offenders' institutions, drug addicts' institutions and psychiatric or other hospitals.

As a general rule, comparisons should be based upon trends rather than upon levels, on the assumption that the characteristics of the recording system within a country remain fairly constant over time. There are, however, a large number of breaks in time series and other methodological/definitional changes.

Context

The progressive elimination of border controls within the EU has considerably facilitated the free movement of European citizens, but may have also made it easier for criminals to operate, especially since the scope of law enforcement authorities and criminal justice systems is generally limited to the boundaries of national borders.

Since the adoption of the Amsterdam Treaty, the EU has set itself the objective of providing a common area of freedom, security and justice. This goal was further developed by the Hague programme in 2004, which outlined ten priority areas: strengthening fundamental rights and citizenship; anti-terrorist measures; defining a balanced approach to migration; developing integrated management of the EU's external borders; setting up a common

asylum procedure; maximising the positive impact of immigration; striking the right balance between privacy and security while sharing information; developing a strategic concept on tackling organised crime; ensuring a genuine European area of justice; and sharing responsibility and solidarity.

As part of the work to harmonise and develop statistics on crime and criminal justice systems, EU Member States agreed to approximate the definitions of offences and the level of sanctions for certain type of offences. Furthermore, mutual recognition of decisions taken by national judges is set to become the cornerstone of judicial cooperation in criminal matters, with a range of tools having been developed to facilitate practical cooperation across borders.

With respect to police cooperation, the EU seeks to grant law enforcement authorities in each of the Member States access to relevant information (such as DNA, fingerprint, vehicle registration or immigration databases), and to improve police cooperation within a common framework for the protection of personal data. Access to information is covered by a raft of legislation, including the Data Retention Directive 2006/24/EC, the Swedish Initiative Framework Decision 2006/960/JHA, the Prüm Council Decision 2008/615/JHA and Regulation 767/2008 concerning a visa information system (VIS) and the exchange of data between Member States.

Police cooperation has been encouraged through legislation such as Framework Decision 2002/465/JHA on Joint Investigation Teams and Council Decision 2008/617/JHA on improved cooperation between special intervention units, while a range of organisations/bodies have been created to aid cooperation between different law enforcement agencies, such as the European Police College (CEPOL), the European Police Office (Europol) or the European agency for the management of operational cooperation at the external borders of the Member States of the EU (Frontex). Furthermore, the EU supports a range of national and multi-national projects, through programmes such as the 'Prevention of and fight against crime' (Council Decision 2007/125/JHA).

The first steps towards a more comparable system of crime and criminal justice statistics were outlined in European Commission Communication (COM(2006) 437), titled 'Developing a comprehensive and coherent EU strategy to measure crime and criminal justice: an EU action plan 2006-2010'. In the short term, its objective was to collect national data and to assess its quality. However, the longer-term goal for the European Commission's Directorate-General for Home Affairs is to develop, in close collaboration with Eurostat, a harmonised methodology on which the collection of EU-wide statistics should be based, allowing comparisons of the structure and trends of crime between Member States.

Particular progress has been made in the collection of statistics related to the police and in the development of a common victimisation survey. The collection of data relating to money laundering is underway, and subsequent priorities include information on the trafficking of human beings, corruption and cybercrime. A pilot survey to assess the level and impact of crimes against businesses in EU Member States was also launched at the end of 2011.

Table 6.5.1: Police officers, 1998-2008

	Police officers (units)			Police officers (per 100 000 inhabitants)		
	1998	2003	2008	1998	2003	2008
EU-27 (¹)	:	:	1 677 846	:	:	337.1
Belgium (²)	36 419	36 318	38 068	357.3	350.7	356.9
Bulgaria	:	:	33 800	:	:	442.4
Czech Republic	43 888	46 616	42 117	426.1	456.9	405.7
Denmark	9 962	10 352	10 743	188.1	192.3	196.2
Germany	237 786	245 415	247 619	289.8	297.3	301.2
Estonia	4 089	3 553	3 218	293.5	262.0	240.0
Ireland	11 235	12 017	14 411	304.2	303.1	327.4
Greece	45 389	52 123	50 798	419.9	473.6	453.0
Spain	:	194 793	224 086	:	467.5	494.9
France (³)	223 582	233 250	228 402	383.5	388.1	367.6
Italy (⁴)	265 093	249 714	245 152	465.9	435.6	411.2
Cyprus	3 987	4 773	5 280	590.5	667.4	669.0
Latvia	10 878	9 796	8 410	449.4	420.2	370.3
Lithuania	14 181	11 910	11 018	398.1	344.0	327.3
Luxembourg (⁴)	1 136	1 304	1 555	269.2	290.9	321.4
Hungary	30 382	29 518	33 698	295.6	291.0	335.5
Malta	1 756	1 845	1 884	466.4	464.4	459.2
Netherlands	32 088	36 907	35 463	205.0	227.9	216.2
Austria	26 817	26 634	26 623	336.4	328.8	320.0
Poland	99 285	99 919	100 648	256.8	261.4	264.1
Portugal	45 484	47 417	51 584	449.9	455.6	485.8
Romania	48 803	45 690	50 339	216.7	209.8	233.8
Slovenia	6 821	7 526	7 779	343.6	377.2	387.0
Slovakia	13 988	13 667	14 059	259.6	254.1	260.3
Finland	7 889	8 323	8 191	153.3	159.9	154.5
Sweden	16 429	16 292	18 321	185.7	182.2	199.5
United Kingdom:						
England and Wales	126 814	133 366	140 230	245.6	253.2	258.4
Scotland	14 854	15 482	17 048	290.0	306.2	330.6
Northern Ireland	:	8 986	7 302	:	528.6	413.2
Iceland	:	678	646	:	235.0	204.8
Liechtenstein	:	84	83	:	248.1	234.8
Norway	7 384	8 062	7 505	167.1	177.1	158.4
Switzerland	14 367	15 155	16 326	202.5	207.2	215.0
Croatia	22 577	19 622	19 823	497.6	441.7	446.8
FYR of Macedonia	:	8 357	9 905	:	413.0	484.3
Turkey	322 766	318 189	341 770	499.3	456.1	484.2
Japan	226 401	241 732	251 939	:	:	:
United States	641 208	663 796	708 569	:	:	:

(¹) Excluding French overseas departments and territories.
(²) Break in series between 2003 and 2008.
(³) Excluding overseas departments and territories.
(⁴) Break in series between 1998 and 2003.

Source: Eurostat (online data codes: crim_plce, tps00001 and demo_r_d2jan)

Table 6.5.2: Crimes recorded by the police, 1998-2008
(1 000)

	1998	1999	2000	2001	2002	2003	2004	2005	2006	2007	2008
EU-27 ([1])	:	:	28 611	29 612	30 677	30 865	30 255	29 842	29 662	29 187	28 512
Belgium ([2])	:	:	1 003	961	1 008	1 001	1 006	991	1 012	1 017	993
Bulgaria ([2])	159	145	149	147	147	144	142	138	136	135	127
Czech Republic	426	427	391	359	372	358	352	344	336	357	344
Denmark	499	494	504	473	492	486	474	433	425	445	477
Germany	6 457	6 302	6 265	6 364	6 507	6 572	6 633	6 392	6 304	6 285	6 114
Estonia ([3])	46	52	58	58	53	54	53	53	52	50	51
Ireland ([2])	86	81	73	87	106	103	99	102	103	:	:
Greece	386	374	369	440	441	442	406	456	464	423	417
Spain ([4])	1 866	1 896	1 853	2 052	2 183	2 144	2 141	2 231	2 267	2 310	2 331
France ([5])	3 566	3 568	3 772	4 062	4 114	3 975	3 825	3 776	3 726	3 589	3 558
Italy ([6])	2 426	2 374	2 206	2 164	2 232	2 457	2 418	2 579	2 771	2 933	2 710
Cyprus ([7])	4	4	4	5	5	7	8	7	8	8	7
Latvia ([8])	37	44	50	51	49	52	62	51	62	56	57
Lithuania	78	77	82	79	73	79	84	82	75	68	72
Luxembourg ([9])	27	27	23	23	26	26	27	25	26	28	28
Hungary	601	506	451	466	421	413	419	437	426	427	408
Malta	15	16	17	16	17	18	18	19	17	15	14
Netherlands	1 235	1 303	1 329	1 379	1 402	1 369	1 319	1 255	1 218	1 215	:
Austria	480	493	560	523	592	643	644	605	589	594	573
Poland	1 073	1 122	1 267	1 390	1 404	1 467	1 461	1 380	1 288	1 153	1 082
Portugal	341	363	363	372	392	417	416	392	399	400	431
Romania	399	364	354	340	312	277	232	208	233	281	289
Slovenia ([10])	55	62	68	75	77	77	87	84	90	88	82
Slovakia	94	94	89	93	107	112	131	124	115	111	105
Finland	383	372	386	361	365	367	354	340	325	344	355
Sweden	1 181	1 194	1 215	1 189	1 235	1 255	1 249	1 242	1 225	1 306	1 378
United Kingdom:											
England and Wales ([11])	5 106	5 298	5 167	5 522	5 975	6 014	5 638	5 555	5 428	4 951	4 702
Scotland ([6])	432	436	423	421	427	407	438	418	419	386	377
Northern Ireland ([11])	109	119	120	140	142	128	118	123	121	108	110
Iceland ([4])	:	:	19	19	20	18	17	12	13	13	15
Liechtenstein	1	1	1	1	1	1	1	1	1	1	1
Norway	294	292	307	300	320	304	288	276	277	272	264
Switzerland	378	355	317	372	357	379	389	353	335	326	323
Montenegro	:	:	:	8	9	9	8	10	10	9	8
Croatia	56	58	68	78	78	80	85	80	81	76	75
FYR of Macedonia	:	:	20	17	18	23	23	23	22	26	28
Turkey ([12])	357	339	337	412	456	496	529	669	978	946	986
Japan	2 034	2 166	2 443	2 736	2 854	2 790	2 563	2 269	2 051	:	:
United States	12 486	11 634	11 608	11 877	11 879	11 827	11 679	11 565	11 402	11 252	11 150

([1]) Excluding French overseas departments and territories; the figures for 2007 and 2008 are calculated using data for Ireland for 2006 and the 2008 figures is calculated using data for the Netherlands for 2007; care should be taken in interpreting the time-series due to a large number of breaks in series.
([2]) Break in series, 1999.
([3]) Break in series, 2001 and 2005.
([4]) Break in series, 2004.
([5]) Excluding overseas departments and territories.
([6]) Break in series, 2003.
([7]) Break in series, 2002.
([8]) Break in series, 2003, 2004 and 2005.
([9]) Break in series, 1999 and 2001.
([10]) Break in series, 1999 and 2002.
([11]) Break in series, 2001.
([12]) Break in series, 2004 and 2005.

Source: Eurostat (online data code: crim_gen)

Figure 6.5.1: Offences recorded by the police, EU-27, 2005-2008
(2005 = 100)

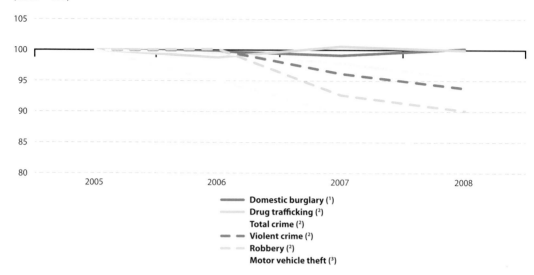

(¹) Excluding Ireland, Latvia, the Netherlands and Slovenia.
(²) Excluding Estonia, Ireland, Latvia and the Netherlands.
(³) Excluding Ireland, Latvia and the Netherlands.

Source: Eurostat (online data code: crim_gen)

Table 6.5.3: Prison population, 1998-2008

	Prison population (units)			Prison population (per 100 000 inhabitants)		
	1998	2003	2008	1998	2003	2008
EU-27 (¹)	549 399	597 450	617 676	114.2	122.8	124.1
Belgium	8 176	9 308	9 858	80.2	89.9	92.4
Bulgaria	10 779	10 056	9 922	130.1	128.2	129.9
Czech Republic	22 085	17 180	20 471	214.4	168.4	197.2
Denmark	3 422	3 641	3 530	64.6	67.6	64.5
Germany (³)	69 917	79 183	73 203	85.2	95.9	89.0
Estonia	4 791	4 352	3 656	343.9	320.9	272.6
Ireland	2 620	2 986	2 872	70.9	75.3	65.3
Greece (²) (⁴)	7 129	8 555	10 864	66.0	77.7	97.2
Spain	44 370	56 096	73 558	111.9	134.6	162.4
France (⁴)	53 667	55 407	64 003	92.1	92.2	103.0
Italy	49 173	54 237	58 127	86.4	94.6	97.5
Cyprus	226	355	646	33.5	49.6	81.8
Latvia	10 070	8 222	6 873	416.0	352.7	302.7
Lithuania	13 813	8 957	7 736	387.8	258.7	229.8
Luxembourg	392	455	673	92.9	101.5	139.1
Hungary	14 366	16 507	14 626	139.8	162.8	145.6
Malta	260	278	444	69.1	70.0	108.2
Netherlands	12 598	15 194	14 734	80.5	93.8	89.8
Austria (³)	6 891	7 816	7 899	86.4	96.5	95.0
Poland	59 180	80 692	84 549	153.1	211.1	221.8
Portugal	14 330	13 635	10 807	141.7	131.0	101.8
Romania	52 149	42 815	26 212	231.5	196.6	121.8
Slovenia	793	1 099	1 318	40.0	55.1	65.6
Slovakia	6 897	8 829	8 313	128.0	164.1	153.9
Finland	2 772	3 463	3 457	53.9	66.5	65.2
Sweden	5 279	6 726	6 806	59.7	75.2	74.1
United Kingdom:						
England and Wales	65 771	73 657	83 194	127.4	139.8	153.3
Scotland	6 029	6 621	7 835	117.7	131.0	152.0
Northern Ireland	1 454	1 128	1 490	86.3	66.4	84.3
Iceland (²)	:	112	115	:	38.8	36.5
Liechtenstein	65	67	78	207.5	197.9	220.6
Norway (²)	2 466	2 944	3 420	55.8	64.7	72.2
Switzerland (³)	5 648	5 214	5 780	79.6	71.3	76.1
Montenegro	:	744	1 255	:	120.1	200.0
Croatia	:	2 803	4 734	:	63.1	106.7
FYR of Macedonia	1 121	1 545	2 235	56.0	76.3	109.3
Turkey	60 096	63 796	103 435	93.0	91.4	146.5
Japan	51 986	71 889	:	:	:	:
United States	1 816 931	2 081 580	2 396 140	:	:	:

(¹) Excluding French overseas departments and territories; includes Greek data for 2007 instead of 2008; care should be taken in interpreting the development over time due to a large number of breaks in series.
(²) 2007 instead of 2008.
(³) Break in series between 1998 and 2003.
(⁴) Break in series between 1998 and 2003 and between 2003 and 2008.

Source: Eurostat (online data codes: crim_pris, tps00001 and demo_r_d2jan)

Industry, trade and services

7

Introduction

The European Commission's enterprise policies aim to create a favourable environment for business to thrive within the European Union (EU), thus creating higher productivity, economic growth, jobs and wealth. Policies are aimed at reducing administrative burden, stimulating innovation, encouraging sustainable production, and ensuring the smooth functioning of the EU's internal market.

European industry contributes to output, jobs, innovation and exports and is interrelated with service activities. Indeed, many service activities such as transport, information and communication depend on industry to produce the equipment and hardware which they use. The internal market for goods is one of the EU's most important and continuing priorities which aims to create a user-friendly environment for businesses and consumers. Creating a single market for the service sector – one of the main drivers of the EU's economy – relies largely on the opportunities available for businesses to provide services throughout the EU, and for other businesses and individuals to access such services.

The business environment in which enterprises operate in the EU plays a significant role in their potential success through factors such as access to capital markets (in particular for venture capital), or the openness of markets. Ensuring that businesses can compete openly and fairly is also important with respect to making Europe an attractive place in which to invest and work. Creating a positive climate in which entrepreneurs and businesses can flourish is considered by many as the key to generating growth and jobs within the EU; this is all the more important in a globalised economy, where some businesses have considerable leeway to select where they wish to operate. The regulatory environment in which businesses operate influences their competitiveness and their ability to grow and create jobs. The European Commission is committed to developing a better regulatory environment for businesses; one that is simple, understandable,

effective and enforceable. The better regulation agenda of the Commission aims to:

- implement a strategy to simplify existing legislation through a simplification programme;
- reduce administrative burdens by 25 % by 2012;
- place greater emphasis on the use of impact assessments and public consultations when drafting new rules and regulations;
- monitor the application of EU legislation.

The 20.9 million small and medium-sized enterprises (SMEs) in the EU in 2008 represented 99.8 % of enterprises in the non-financial business economy, and are regarded as a key driver for economic growth, innovation, employment and social integration. The European Commission aims to promote successful entrepreneurship and improve the business environment for SMEs, to allow them to realise their full potential in the global economy. In June 2008 the 'Small business act for Europe' (SBA) was adopted by the European Commission and endorsed by the Council in December 2008. This aims to improve the overall approach to entrepreneurship, permanently anchor the 'think small first' principle in policy making and to promote SMEs' growth. The SBA is a set of ten principles which should guide the design and implementation of national and EU policies. The results of a review of the SBA were published in February 2011, providing an overview of the progress achieved in implementing the Act and setting out new actions to respond to challenges resulting from the recent financial and economic crisis. Between 2008 and 2010, the European Commission and the EU Member States took measures to ease the administrative burden on small businesses, to facilitate SMEs' access to funding, and to support their access to global markets.

At a European Council meeting of 26 March 2010, EU leaders set out their plan for Europe 2020, a strategy to enhance the competitiveness of the EU and to create more growth and jobs. The latest revision of the integrated economic and employment guidelines (revised as part of the Europe 2020 strategy for

smart, sustainable and inclusive growth) includes a guideline to improve the business and consumer environment and modernise Europe's industrial base. In October 2010 the European Commission presented a Communication on 'An industrial policy for the globalisation era' (COM(2010) 614), which provides a blueprint to put industrial competitiveness and sustainability centre stage. This industrial policy establishes a strategic agenda and proposes some broad cross-sectoral measures, as well as tailor-made actions for specific industries, mainly targeting the so-called 'green innovation'

performance of these sectors. Furthermore, a report on Member States' competitiveness policies and performance will be published annually.

European Commission Communication titled, 'A digital agenda for Europe' (COM(2010) 245) outlines policies and actions aimed at maximising the benefit of the digital era to all sections of society. The agenda outlines seven priority areas for action – see the subchapter on information society for more detail.

7.1 Structural business statistics

This subchapter presents structural business statistics (SBS); these data describe the structure, main characteristics and performance of economic activities across the European Union (EU). While the statistics presented in this subchapter are generally analysed at the level of NACE sections readers should note that structural business statistics are available at a much more detailed level (several hundred sectors).

Structural business statistics can provide answers to questions on the wealth creation (value added), investment and labour input of different economic activities. The data can be used to analyse structural shifts, for example from industry to services, country specialisations, sectoral productivity and profitability, as well as a range of other topics. Because they arc available broken down by enterprise size-class, structural business statistics also permit a detailed analysis of small and medium-sized enterprises (SMEs), which is of particular use to EU policymakers and analysts wishing to focus on entrepreneurship and the role of SMEs. Furthermore, structural business statistics provide useful background information on which to base an interpretation of short-term statistics and the business cycle.

Main statistical findings

Sectoral analysis

Services activities accounted for the two largest shares of the enterprise population within the EU-27's non-financial business economy (industry,

construction, distributive trades and non-financial services) when analysed at the NACE section level: a little under one third (29.3 %) of the 21.0 million enterprises in the non-financial business economy were classified to distributive trades, while just under one in six (16.1 %) were in professional, scientific or technical activities – see Figure 7.1.1. Many of these business services have benefitted from the outsourcing phenomenon, which may explain, in part, the structural shift towards services.

In 2008 a total of EUR 6 155 700 million of gross value added was generated in the EU-27's non-financial business economy, which was equivalent to 63.4 % of the whole economy's value added at factor cost. The non-financial business economy workforce reached 136.3 million persons employed, around three fifths (60.2 %) of those employed in the EU-27.

Among the NACE Rev. 2 sections in the non-financial business economy, manufacturing was the largest in terms of employment and value added. Some 2.1 million manufacturing enterprises generated EUR 1 669 500 million of value added in 2008, whilst providing employment for about 33.0 million persons. Distributive trades enterprises (motor trades, wholesale trade, and retail trade) provided employment for 32.8 million persons and generated a further EUR 1 153 300 million of value added. Construction had the third largest workforce, some 15.0 million persons, and the third highest level of value added, EUR 604 400 million.

Figure 7.1.2 contrasts the value added and employment contributions of the various sectors to the non-financial business economy. The industrial activities of mining and quarrying, manufacturing, and electricity, gas, steam and air conditioning supply contributed more in terms of value added than employment to the overall non-financial business economy, indicating an above average apparent labour productivity; this was also the case in some of the service activities, namely information and communication services, real estate activities, as well as professional, scientific and technical activities. However, it should be noted that the employment data presented are head counts and not, for example, full-time equivalents, and there may be a significant proportion of persons working part-time in some of the activities covered, notably distributive trades activities, accommodation and food services, and administrative and support services (which includes cleaning and security services, as well as employment services such as the provision of temporary personnel).

Varying rates of part-time work also help explain, in part, the considerable differences in average personnel costs within the non-financial business economy of the EU-27, as shown in Table 7.1.3. Average personnel costs in the EU-27's information and communication sector and the electricity, gas steam and air conditioning supply sector were around EUR 50 000 per employee in 2008, a level that was around three times that for accommodation and food services and twice that for distributive trades. The variation in average personnel costs was even more marked between Member States. For example, within the manufacturing sector average personnel costs ranged (among those Member States for which data are available) by a factor of 15, from a high of EUR 54 600 per employee in Belgium to a low of EUR 3 700 per employee in Bulgaria.

The influence of part-time employment is largely removed in the wage adjusted labour productivity ratio, which shows the relation between average value added per person employed and average personnel costs per employee. This was particularly high for mining and quarrying activities (mainly due to a very high ratio for the extraction of crude petroleum and natural gas); it was also high for the capital-intensive

sector of real estate activities (see Figure 7.1.3). The wage adjusted labour productivity ratio fell below 100 % in the small activity of the repair of computers, personal and household goods, indicating that average personnel costs per employee were higher than average value added per person employed.

The gross operating rate shown in Figure 7.1.4 relates the gross operating surplus (value added less personnel costs) to the level of turnover and in this way indicates the extent to which sales are converted into gross operating profit (operating profit before accounting for depreciation or taxes). Due to the very high level of sales inherent in whole-saling and retailing, the distributive trades sector displayed the lowest gross operating rate. Capital-intensive activities tend to have a high gross operating rate (for example, real estate activities) as the gross operating surplus by definition does not take account of financial or extraordinary costs.

Size class analysis

Structural business statistics can be analysed by enterprise size class (defined in terms of the number of persons employed). The overwhelming majority (99.8 %) of enterprises active within the EU-27's non-financial business economy in 2008 were small and medium-sized enterprises (SMEs) – some 20.9 million – together they generated 58.6 % of value added within the non-financial business economy. More than nine out of ten (92.0 %) enterprises in the EU-27 were micro enterprises (employing less than ten persons) and their share of non-financial business economy value added was considerably lower at 21.8 %. The relative importance of SMEs was particularly high in the southern Member States of Italy, Portugal and Spain (no data available for Greece). Some of these differences may be explained by the relative importance of particular sectors in the national economy or by cultural and institutional preferences for self-employment and/or family-run businesses.

Perhaps the most striking phenomenon of SMEs is their contribution to employment. No less than two thirds (66.7 %) of the EU-27's non-financial business economy workforce was active in an SME in 2008. Some 23.3 million persons worked in SMEs in the distributive trades sector, 19.5 million in manufacturing

and 13.2 million in construction; together, these three activities provided work to 61.9 % of the non-financial business economy workforce in SMEs. Micro enterprises employed more people than any other size class in a number of service sectors. This pattern was particularly pronounced for the repair of computers, personal and household goods where an absolute majority of the workforce worked in micro enterprises. In contrast, a range of activities characterised by network supply and minimum efficient scales of production (such as mining, air or rail transport, postal and courier services) reported a considerably higher proportion of their respective workforces occupied within large enterprises.

The contribution of SMEs to non-financial business economy value added was lower than their contribution to employment, resulting in a lower level of apparent labour productivity. This pattern was particularly prevalent among activities such as manufacturing or information and communication services. However, it was also observed across most other activities and across most Member States. As a result, large enterprises tended to record higher apparent labour productivity ratios than SMEs.

Foreign-controlled enterprises

In general, foreign-controlled enterprises are few in number, but due to their larger than average size they have a significant economic impact. In those Member States for which data are available (see Figure 7.1.7), foreign-controlled enterprises generated substantial shares of value added in the non-financial business economy: the highest percentage contribution of foreign-controlled enterprises to non-financial business economy value added in 2008 was registered in Hungary where it reached 47.0 %, while shares in excess of 25 % were recorded for Poland, Sweden and Bulgaria. Employment shares of foreign-controlled enterprises were generally lower than their value added shares, ranging from 9.1 % in Spain to 23.8 % in Hungary.

Business demography

Business demography statistics are presented in Table 7.1.10, which shows enterprise birth and death rates as well as the average size of newly born

enterprises in terms of their employment. There are significant changes in the stock of enterprises within the business economy from one year to the next, reflecting the level of competition, entrepreneurial spirit and the business environment. Among the countries providing data to Eurostat, enterprise birth rates in 2008 ranged from around 3 % in Cyprus to 15 % or more in Lithuania, Estonia, Bulgaria and Slovakia. Since most new enterprises are small, the share of newly born enterprises among the whole business enterprise population is much higher than the corresponding proportion of the workforce accounted for by these enterprises. The average employment size ranged from 2.5 persons in Austria to 1.1 in Ireland, with Finland below this range at 0.5.

Data sources and availability

Eurostat's structural business statistics describe the structure, conduct and performance of economic activities, down to the most detailed activity level (several hundred sectors). Without this structural information, short-term data on the economic cycle would lack background and be hard to interpret.

The knowledge-based economy and the demand for intangibles, either for consumption or investment purposes, as well as international outsourcing, has led to a major restructuring of many European economies, with a shift away from industrial activities towards services. Traditionally, structural business statistics were concentrated on industrial and construction activities, and to a lesser extent distributive trades and services. Since the early 1990s, major developments in official statistics within the EU have seen data collection efforts focus increasingly on services.

As a result, structural business statistics now cover the 'business economy', which includes industry, construction and many services (NACE Rev. 2 Sections B to N and Division 95); financial and insurance activities (NACE Section K) are treated separately within structural business statistics because of their specific nature and the limited availability of most types of standard business statistics in this area. As such, the term 'non-financial business economy' is generally used in business statistics to refer to those

economic activities covered by NACE Rev. 2 Sections B to J and L to N and Division 95 and the units that carry out those activities. Structural business statistics do not cover agriculture, forestry and fishing, nor public administration and (largely) non-market services, such as education or health.

Structural business statistics describe the business economy through the observation of units engaged in an economic activity; the unit in structural business statistics is generally the enterprise. An enterprise carries out one or more activities, at one or more locations, and it may comprise one or more legal units. Enterprises that are active in more than one economic activity (plus the value added and turnover they generate, the people they employ, and so on) are classified under the NACE heading according to their principal activity. This is normally the one which generates the largest amount of value added.

NACE Rev. 2 was adopted at the end of 2006, and implemented in structural business statistics from the 2008 reference year. This allows a broader and more detailed collection of information to be compiled on services, while also updating the classification to identify new areas of activity better.

Structural business statistics are compiled under the legal basis provided by Parliament and Council Regulation 295/2008 on structural business statistics, and in accordance with the definitions, breakdowns, deadlines for data delivery, and various quality aspects specified in the regulations implementing it.

The structural business statistics data collection consists of a common module (Annex 1), including a set of basic statistics for all activities, as well as six sector-specific annexes covering a more extensive list of characteristics. The sector-specific annexes are: industry, trade, construction, insurance services, credit institutions, and pension funds. There were two further annexes added in 2008 covering business services and business demography.

SBS are also available with an analysis by region or by enterprise size class. In structural business statistics, size classes are defined by the number of persons employed, except for specific data series within retail trade activities where turnover size classes are also used. A limited set of the standard structural business statistics variables (for example, the number of enterprises, turnover, persons employed and value added) is analysed by size class, mostly down to the three-digit (group) level of NACE. For statistical purposes, SMEs are generally defined as those enterprises employing fewer than 250 persons. The number of size classes available varies according to the activity under consideration. However, the main groups used in this publication for presenting the results are:

- small and medium-sized enterprises (SMEs): with 1 to 249 persons employed, further divided into;
  - micro enterprises: with less than 10 persons employed;
  - small enterprises: with 10 to 49 persons employed;
  - medium-sized enterprises: with 50 to 249 persons employed;
- large enterprises: with 250 or more persons employed.

Structural business statistics contain a comprehensive set of basic variables describing business demographics and employment characteristics, as well as monetary variables (mainly concerning operating income and expenditure, or investment). In addition, a set of derived indicators has been compiled: for example, ratios of monetary characteristics or per head values.

Structural business statistics also provide information in relation to business demography, in other words, statistics that relate to the birth, survival (followed up to five years after birth) and death of enterprises within the business population; within this context the following definitions apply.

- An enterprise birth amounts to the creation of a combination of production factors, with the restriction that no other enterprises are involved in the event. Births do not include entries into the business population due to mergers, break-ups, split-offs or restructuring of a set of enterprises, nor do the statistics include entries into a sub-population that only result from a change of activity. The birth rate is the number of births relative to the stock of active enterprises.

• An enterprise death amounts to the dissolution of a combination of production factors, with the restriction that no other enterprises are involved in the event. An enterprise is only included in the count of deaths if it is not reactivated within two years. Equally, a reactivation within two years is not counted as a birth.

Structural business statistics also provide information on certain special topics, such as foreign-controlled enterprises. Statistics on foreign affiliates (FATS) provide information that can be used to assess the impact of foreign-controlled enterprises on the European economy. The data may also be used to monitor the effectiveness of the internal market and the integration of economies within the context of globalisation. A foreign affiliate, as defined in inward FATS statistics, is an enterprise resident in a country which is under the control of an institutional unit not resident in the same country. Control is determined according to the concept of the 'ultimate controlling institutional unit' which is the institutional unit, proceeding up a foreign affiliate's chain of control, which is not controlled by another institutional unit.

Context

In October 2010 the European Commission presented a Communication on a renewed industrial policy. 'An industrial policy for the globalisation era' provides a blueprint that puts industrial competitiveness and sustainability centre stage. It is a flagship initiative that forms part of the Europe 2020 strategy, and sets out a strategy that aims to boost growth and jobs by maintaining and supporting a strong, diversified and competitive industrial base in Europe offering well-paid jobs while becoming less carbon intensive. The initiative establishes a strategic agenda and proposes some broad cross-sectoral measures, as well as tailor-made actions for specific industries, mainly targeting the so-called 'green innovation' performance of these sectors.

The internal market remains one of the EU's most important priorities. The central principles governing the internal market for services were set out in the EC Treaty. This guarantees EU enterprises the freedom to establish themselves in other Member States and the freedom to provide services on the territory of another EU Member State other than the one in which they are established. The objective of the Services Directive 2006/123/EC of 12 December 2006, on services in the internal market, is to eliminate obstacles to trade in services, thus allowing the development of cross-border operations. It is intended to improve competitiveness, not just of service enterprises but also of European industry as a whole. In December 2006, this Directive was adopted by the European Parliament and the Council with transposition by the Member States required by the end of 2009. It is hoped that the Directive will help achieve potential economic growth and job creation. By providing for administrative simplification, it also supports the better regulation agenda.

SMEs are often referred to as the backbone of the European economy, providing a potential source for both jobs and economic growth. In June 2008 the European Commission adopted a Communication on SMEs referred to as the 'Small business act for Europe' (SBA). This aims to improve the overall approach to entrepreneurship, to irreversibly anchor the 'think small first' principle in policymaking from regulation to public service, and to promote SMEs' growth by helping them tackle problems which hamper their development. The Communication sets out ten principles which should guide the conception and implementation of policies both at EU and national level to create a level playing field for SMEs throughout the EU and improve the administrative and legal environment to allow these enterprises to release their full potential to create jobs and growth. It also put forward a specific and far reaching package of new measures including four legislative proposals which translate these principles into action both at EU and Member State level.

A review of the SBA was released in February 2011: it highlighted the progress made and set out a range of new actions to respond to challenges resulting from the financial and economic crisis. In doing so, it is hoped that the updated SBA will contribute towards delivering the key objectives of the Europe 2020 strategy – namely, smart, sustainable and inclusive growth.

Figure 7.1.1: Breakdown of number of enterprises within the non-financial business economy, EU-27, 2008 (¹)
(%)

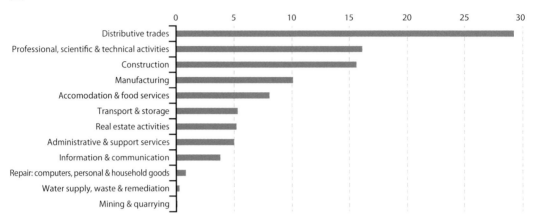

(¹) The total number of enterprises in the EU-27 non-financial business economy was estimated as 21.0 million in 2008; electricity, gas, steam and air conditioning supply, not available; estimates.

Source: Eurostat (online data codes: sbs_na_ind_r2, sbs_na_con_r2, sbs_na_dt_r2 and sbs_na_1a_se_r2)

Table 7.1.1: Value added, 2008
(EUR 1 000 million)

	Mining & quarrying	Manufacturing	Electricity, gas, steam & air conditioning supply	Water supply, waste & remediation	Construction	Distributive trades	Transport & storage	Accomodation & food services	Information & communication	Real estate activities	Professional, scientific & technical activities	Administrative & support services	Repair: computer, personal & household goods
EU-27	100.0	1 669.5	199.8	:	604.4	1 153.3	476.6	194.1	502.5	220.0	573.1	390.0	10.6
Belgium	:	49.2	:	2.4	14.5	34.9	14.4	4.2	13.1	2.9	13.2	11.8	0.2
Bulgaria	0.5	4.3	1.0	0.4	2.5	3.9	1.5	0.5	1.6	0.6	1.0	0.4	0.0
Czech Republic	2.2	31.7	5.7	1.3	7.5	14.0	6.6	1.6	6.4	2.6	6.3	2.9	0.2
Denmark	8.5	28.7	3.0	1.1	11.1	23.8	11.7	2.7	9.9	5.6	10.0	4.3	0.2
Germany	6.8	453.8	:	:	63.8	216.0	91.5	24.7	96.2	65.4	110.4	75.6	1.3
Estonia	0.1	2.2	0.3	0.1	0.9	1.7	0.9	0.2	0.6	0.3	0.5	0.4	0.0
Ireland	0.6	30.5	2.8	0.5	7.1	17.1	5.5	3.7	10.1	1.0	8.0	5.0	0.1
Greece	:	:	:	:	:	:	:	:	:	:	:	:	:
Spain	2.5	126.7	17.5	6.0	99.3	108.9	43.4	27.0	38.0	13.7	41.1	32.0	1.1
France	2.8	203.3	22.7	9.6	89.2	167.0	75.4	31.0	73.2	32.0	88.7	69.6	2.7
Italy	5.9	211.7	18.9	9.4	81.2	113.7	50.2	25.6	50.6	16.1	58.8	30.3	1.3
Cyprus	0.1	1.2	0.2	0.1	2.2	2.1	0.8	1.0	0.6	0.1	0.7	0.2	0.0
Latvia	0.1	1.9	0.5	0.2	1.3	2.6	1.5	0.3	0.7	0.7	0.6	0.4	0.0
Lithuania	0.1	2.7	0.6	0.2	1.9	3.3	1.5	0.2	0.6	0.5	0.8	0.5	0.0
Luxembourg	0.0	5.4	0.3	0.1	2.0	2.8	1.5	0.5	2.3	:	2.5	:	0.0
Hungary	0.2	19.3	2.5	0.9	3.1	9.2	3.8	0.9	4.0	1.9	3.1	2.2	0.1
Malta	:	:	:	:	:	:	:	:	:	:	:	:	:
Netherlands	8.9	59.3	5.6	3.4	29.2	65.5	26.2	7.4	23.8	10.9	35.1	21.9	0.4
Austria	1.2	46.7	5.3	1.6	15.5	28.2	13.1	6.9	7.7	7.2	11.7	9.0	0.1
Poland	8.7	57.2	9.4	2.9	18.1	40.6	13.1	2.3	12.5	4.2	9.7	5.6	0.4
Portugal	0.5	19.0	3.5	1.2	9.9	17.3	6.7	3.4	5.5	1.9	4.9	4.5	0.1
Romania	4.0	15.5	2.9	0.9	7.3	12.2	4.3	1.1	4.3	1.8	3.1	1.5	0.1
Slovenia	0.1	6.7	0.7	0.3	2.1	3.9	1.5	0.6	1.1	0.3	1.4	0.4	0.0
Slovakia	0.3	8.0	2.7	0.4	1.5	5.1	1.6	0.3	2.1	0.4	1.4	0.9	0.1
Finland	0.4	32.1	3.3	0.8	6.0	14.7	8.0	1.9	7.1	3.7	5.8	4.3	0.1
Sweden	1.9	50.3	7.5	1.2	15.4	30.3	13.1	4.0	14.7	13.1	14.9	8.7	0.2
United Kingdom	44.6	185.2	27.7	18.5	105.8	187.3	73.5	38.0	109.9	32.5	132.3	89.6	1.6
Norway	:	:	:	:	13.7	21.7	13.7	2.9	9.5	6.9	:	7.0	0.1
Croatia	:	6.1	0.7	0.8	3.1	5.2	2.1	1.1	1.8	0.3	1.9	0.6	:

Source: Eurostat (online data codes: sbs_na_ind_r2, sbs_na_con_r2, sbs_na_dt_r2 and sbs_na_1a_se_r2)

Table 7.1.2: Number of persons employed, 2008
(1 000)

	Mining & quarrying	Manufacturing	Electricity, gas, steam & air conditioning supply	Water supply, waste & remediation	Construction	Distributive trades	Transport & storage	Accomodation & food services	Information & communication	Real estate activities	Professional, scientific & technical activities	Administrative & support services	Repair: computer, personal & household goods
EU-27	*670*	32 961	*1 200*	1 266	15 047	32 816	10 863	9 612	5 798	*2 500*	10 752	11 864	377
Belgium	:	586	:	25	295	636	203	171	121	31	193	275	6
Bulgaria	30	639	36	33	260	504	161	129	61	35	82	90	5
Czech Republic	*42*	*1 366*	*33*	*54*	*413*	*685*	*303*	*164*	*111*	*58*	*232*	*194*	*12*
Denmark	4	393	13	17	220	529	321	132	108	39	154	132	5
Germany	77	7 103	221	175	1 582	4 954	1 850	1 369	1 026	491	1 906	2 452	37
Estonia	5	121	6	4	57	99	41	21	16	12	25	30	1
Ireland	6	196	9	5	105	369	87	162	70	21	119	112	2
Greece	:	:	:	:	:	:	:	:	:	:	:	:	:
Spain	37	2 408	48	99	2 232	3 348	991	1 279	439	234	1 047	1 298	50
France	:	:	:	:	:	:	:	:	:	:	:	:	:
Italy	38	4 407	84	172	2 011	3 558	1 152	1 264	575	326	1 230	1 133	55
Cyprus	1	36	1	1	40	69	20	42	9	2	15	7	1
Latvia	3	140	12	8	89	189	78	32	22	37	35	31	2
Lithuania	3	233	18	13	142	290	103	42	24	31	47	46	4
Luxembourg	0	36	1	1	40	45	23	16	14	:	25	:	0
Hungary	6	755	27	42	247	603	235	132	107	75	205	204	12
Malta	:	:	:	:	:	:	:	:	:	:	:	:	:
Netherlands	8	753	24	38	513	1 465	427	381	274	86	661	950	13
Austria	6	632	28	18	275	626	218	259	91	42	199	195	4
Poland	184	2 561	153	112	930	2 449	753	271	255	154	475	370	40
Portugal	14	773	10	28	513	830	172	289	78	51	223	320	9
Romania	87	1 403	90	78	565	*1 069*	*349*	*144*	*151*	*50*	*205*	*224*	*13*
Slovenia	3	232	8	9	90	120	54	34	22	5	45	27	2
Slovakia	9	440	22	21	84	229	102	26	40	17	51	58	1
Finland	5	422	13	8	128	298	157	63	91	19	105	121	4
Sweden	10	752	31	16	315	630	273	147	199	74	256	259	6
United Kingdom	63	2 795	121	141	1 511	4 829	1 275	1 970	1 125	419	1 937	2 240	31
Norway	:	:	:	:	195	373	156	88	85	27	:	119	3
Croatia	:	317	17	32	163	277	84	97	40	10	77	44	:

Source: Eurostat (online data codes: sbs_na_ind_r2, sbs_na_con_r2, sbs_na_dt_r2 and sbs_na_1a_se_r2)

Figure 7.1.2: Breakdown of non-financial business economy value added and employment, EU-27, 2008 (¹)
(% of non-financial business economy value added and employment)

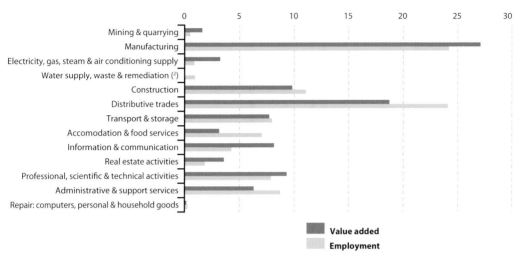

(¹) Estimates.
(²) Value added, not available.

Source: Eurostat (online data codes: sbs_na_ind_r2, sbs_na_con_r2, sbs_na_dt_r2 and sbs_na_1a_se_r2)

Table 7.1.3: Average personnel costs, 2008
(EUR 1 000 per employee)

	Mining & quarring	Manufacturing	Electricity, gas, steam & air conditioning supply	Water supply, waste & remediation	Construction	Distributive trades	Transport & storage	Accomodation & food services	Information & communication	Real estate activities	Professional, scientific & technical activities	Administrative & support services	Repair: computer, personal & household goods
EU-27	*35.0*	*34.9*	*50.0*	*31.9*	*31.4*	*25.3*	*31.6*	*16.4*	*50.2*	*30.9*	*42.8*	*23.5*	*28.8*
Belgium	:	54.6	:	54.4	41.3	42.6	49.2	19.2	67.5	42.6	62.7	32.1	46.6
Bulgaria	7.4	3.7	10.2	4.5	3.6	3.3	5.0	2.3	9.0	5.0	6.7	2.6	2.6
Czech Republic	*20.3*	*14.4*	*23.8*	*14.4*	*14.8*	*14.1*	*15.4*	*8.3*	*27.8*	*14.8*	*21.0*	*10.6*	*15.5*
Denmark	77.0	50.8	60.8	29.3	43.9	34.2	26.4	16.6	62.6	44.5	56.9	34.4	35.3
Germany	52.4	47.5	71.0	42.0	34.9	27.7	29.9	12.5	52.3	33.1	40.5	18.5	25.2
Estonia	15.0	11.9	16.4	13.5	13.4	11.8	12.9	7.8	19.1	8.7	13.9	10.9	10.6
Ireland	61.8	48.1	96.9	48.6	65.4	33.3	50.9	21.0	61.0	45.5	50.6	31.7	39.3
Greece	:	:	:	:	:	:	:	:	:	:	:	:	:
Spain	37.0	34.4	71.6	34.7	32.6	25.9	33.0	19.5	44.2	28.5	33.9	19.4	25.0
France	:	:	:	:	:	:	:	:	:	:	:	:	:
Italy	57.0	36.9	57.3	39.4	31.6	30.5	37.4	19.9	48.3	34.1	39.5	22.9	30.2
Cyprus	33.5	21.6	51.6	30.7	24.8	21.3	27.3	16.4	32.8	16.9	29.6	18.6	33.3
Latvia	9.2	8.0	14.6	9.6	8.3	7.6	9.6	5.3	14.1	6.7	10.3	8.0	4.6
Lithuania	13.0	8.8	13.6	9.0	10.2	7.8	8.7	4.8	12.3	7.2	10.8	7.7	6.4
Luxembourg	49.7	51.4	78.5	44.2	39.1	39.5	49.6	27.4	66.0	:	73.0	:	30.2
Hungary	15.6	12.7	25.9	13.2	8.9	10.1	13.5	6.4	22.4	9.9	15.9	8.3	12.2
Malta	:	:	:	:	:	:	:	:	:	:	:	:	:
Netherlands	76.6	47.7	56.1	40.5	48.8	28.0	40.7	13.0	53.2	34.9	42.7	15.5	27.5
Austria	58.3	46.7	76.3	41.9	38.9	32.8	41.2	20.6	59.8	36.4	46.9	28.1	32.5
Poland	23.8	11.6	20.7	12.3	10.8	9.2	11.5	6.4	21.3	12.3	14.0	9.5	11.1
Portugal	18.6	15.5	62.2	19.2	13.6	13.9	24.0	9.7	31.8	15.1	13.8	10.2	7.0
Romania	15.7	5.7	13.4	6.4	5.4	*4.8*	*7.0*	*3.6*	*12.0*	*5.4*	*7.0*	*3.9*	*4.0*
Slovenia	31.8	19.5	32.8	22.3	16.6	19.7	20.6	14.3	31.9	21.2	24.5	14.7	16.5
Slovakia	13.3	11.6	18.4	11.4	10.6	10.3	11.7	6.7	21.7	11.1	16.7	8.8	13.5
Finland	38.7	46.0	57.1	41.0	37.1	35.1	39.8	26.5	52.0	36.9	47.1	28.1	36.6
Sweden	58.0	53.0	67.5	47.8	45.4	41.6	0.0	0.0	0.0	0.0	0.0	0.0	0.0
United Kingdom	74.2	37.5	47.7	41.0	38.5	22.8	37.0	12.9	56.1	33.3	48.1	25.6	36.1
Norway	:	:	:	:	56.7	43.3	54.0	28.2	77.5	58.7	:	45.7	52.0
Croatia	:	12.4	19.1	15.9	11.2	11.2	17.1	8.4	19.4	13.2	15.2	9.9	:

Source: Eurostat (online data codes: sbs_na_ind_r2, sbs_na_con_r2, sbs_na_dt_r2 and sbs_na_1a_se_r2)

Figure 7.1.3: Wage adjusted labour productivity within the non-financial business economy, EU-27, 2008 (¹)
(%)

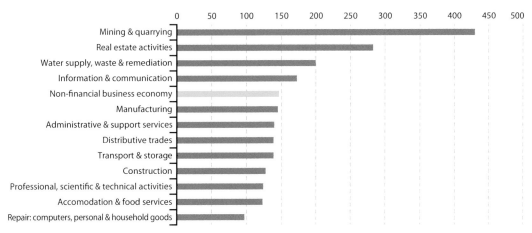

(¹) Electricity, gas, steam and air conditioning supply, not available; estimates.

Source: Eurostat (online data codes: sbs_na_ind_r2, sbs_na_con_r2, sbs_na_dt_r2 and sbs_na_1a_se_r2)

Figure 7.1.4: Gross operating rate within the non-financial business economy, EU-27, 2008 (¹)
(%)

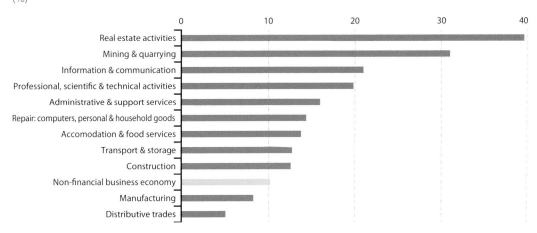

(¹) Electricity, gas, steam and air conditioning supply and water supply, waste and remediation, not available; estimates.

Source: Eurostat (online data codes: sbs_na_ind_r2, sbs_na_con_r2, sbs_na_dt_r2 and sbs_na_1a_se_r2)

Figure 7.1.5: Value added breakdown by enterprise size class, EU-27, 2008 (¹)
(% of sectoral total)

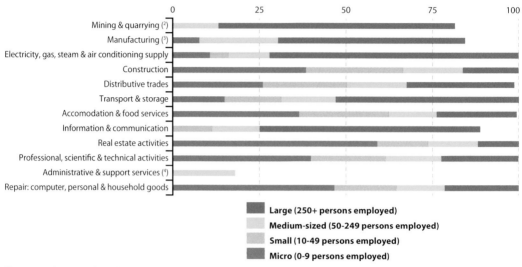

(¹) Water supply, waste and remediation, not available; estimates.
(²) Micro and small enterprises, not available.
(³) Small enterprises, not available.
(⁴) Micro, small and large enterprises, not available.
Source: Eurostat (online data codes: sbs_sc_ind_r2, sbs_sc_con_r2, sbs_sc_dt_r2 and sbs_sc_1b_se_r2)

Figure 7.1.6: Employment breakdown by enterprise size class, EU-27, 2008 (¹)
(% of sectoral total)

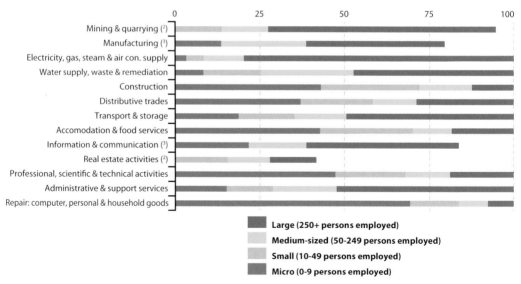

(¹) Estimates.
(²) Micro enterprises, not available.
(³) Small enterprises, not available.
Source: Eurostat (online data codes: sbs_sc_ind_r2, sbs_sc_con_r2, sbs_sc_dt_r2 and sbs_sc_1b_se_r2)

Table 7.1.4: Value added by enterprise size class, mining and quarrying and manufacturing, 2008 (¹)
(% share of size class in total sectoral value added)

	Mining & quarrying				Manufacturing			
	Micro	Small	Medium-sized	Large	Micro	Small	Medium-sized	Large
EU-27 (²)	:	:	12.5	68.8	7.0	:	23.5	53.8
Belgium	:	:	:	:	6.3	13.5	21.4	58.7
Bulgaria	−7.4	9.2	11.9	86.3	5.9	17.6	34.3	42.1
Czech Republic	1.1	2.6	10.5	85.9	9.1	11.3	24.4	55.1
Denmark	:	:	4.6	:	5.9	15.2	24.5	54.4
Germany	4.7	12.1	11.4	71.8	3.3	10.3	21.5	64.9
Estonia	3.9	21.7	:	:	6.6	20.3	42.7	30.4
Ireland	8.3	18.4	28.6	44.8	2.3	7.3	24.2	66.3
Greece	:	:	:	:	:	:	:	:
Spain	10.1	39.6	26.6	23.7	11.3	25.5	23.6	39.6
France	12.4	34.7	29.6	23.4	10.6	15.7	20.6	53.1
Italy	4.7	13.7	:	:	13.0	27.8	26.5	32.6
Cyprus	6.4	93.4	0.0	0.0	23.4	36.2	23.5	16.9
Latvia	:	:	33.1	:	5.7	20.8	42.0	31.4
Lithuania	8.2	16.7	75.1	0.0	3.4	15.8	37.7	43.2
Luxembourg	:	0.0	:	0.0	1.6	:	:	:
Hungary	9.1	38.5	:	:	4.4	9.4	17.8	68.4
Malta	:	:	:	:	:	:	:	:
Netherlands	8.9	1.5	:	:	7.9	18.9	26.4	46.8
Austria	5.3	13.6	11.3	69.8	4.6	12.0	24.1	59.3
Poland	1.0	1.5	6.1	91.5	7.3	10.0	25.3	57.3
Portugal	:	33.4	13.2	:	9.4	23.6	32.2	34.8
Romania	2.5	2.6	3.5	91.4	4.3	12.7	24.1	58.9
Slovenia	7.4	:	20.4	:	10.2	14.4	25.6	49.7
Slovakia	1.1	13.3	15.2	70.5	3.2	12.7	24.0	60.1
Finland	21.2	:	:	:	5.8	12.1	17.8	64.2
Sweden	7.6	4.7	3.6	84.1	6.3	12.5	19.4	61.6
United Kingdom	7.2	3.4	13.1	76.3	7.6	14.8	22.4	55.2
Croatia	:	:	:	:	8.7	16.0	24.2	51.0

(¹) Micro: 0-9 persons employed; small: 10-49 persons employed; medium-sized: 50-249 persons employed; large: 250+ persons employed.
(²) Estimates.

Source: Eurostat (online data code: sbs_sc_ind_r2)

Table 7.1.5: Value added by enterprise size-class, electricity, gas, steam and air conditioning supply and water supply, waste and remediation, 2008 (¹)
(% share of size class in total sectoral value added)

	Electricity, gas, steam & air conditioning supply				Water supply, waste & remediation			
	Micro	Small	Medium-sized	Large	Micro	Small	Medium-sized	Large
EU-27	*7.2*	*5.8*	*13.5*	*73.5*	:	:	:	:
Belgium	:	:	:	:	11.2	22.2	18.4	48.2
Bulgaria	1.2	1.2	11.1	86.6	1.9	6.9	15.7	75.5
Czech Republic	*0.7*	:	*15.3*	:	*9.2*	*17.1*	*29.1*	*44.6*
Denmark	47.5	7.3	7.1	38.0	23.9	15.0	:	:
Germany	:	:	:	:	:	:	:	:
Estonia	7.6	7.4	31.9	53.1	5.5	35.7	12.4	46.5
Ireland	:	:	:	:	19.7	42.7	26.3	11.3
Greece	:	:	:	:	:	:	:	:
Spain	13.6	7.3	6.9	72.1	7.7	18.0	20.7	53.6
France	38.3	1.2	1.4	59.0	11.8	15.9	19.6	52.8
Italy	8.3	10.0	6.9	74.8	8.9	25.3	:	:
Cyprus	0.0	0.0	0.0	100.0	9.9	60.4	29.7	0.0
Latvia	3.2	:	4.5	:	:	16.2	41.0	:
Lithuania	1.2	5.2	4.0	89.6	2.4	11.0	57.7	28.9
Luxembourg	:	:	:	:	12.4	:	:	:
Hungary	5.6	7.5	22.7	64.3	5.0	13.2	26.7	55.1
Malta	:	:	:	:	:	:	:	:
Netherlands	:	:	:	61.7	:	:	:	51.2
Austria	8.1	4.4	13.8	73.7	19.0	30.5	16.7	33.8
Poland	0.4	2.5	12.4	84.7	4.9	14.5	41.9	38.7
Portugal	20.9	1.5	8.6	69.1	4.0	13.7	47.5	34.9
Romania	0.7	3.7	5.6	90.0	4.4	10.5	26.8	58.3
Slovenia	3.5	2.4	20.9	73.1	6.3	:	49.5	:
Slovakia	0.5	2.5	21.1	75.9	3.5	14.2	19.6	62.8
Finland	9.2	11.8	22.0	57.0	20.2	:	:	:
Sweden	9.9	10.2	23.7	56.3	10.8	19.0	39.2	30.8
United Kingdom	2.9	1.6	6.3	89.1	6.1	8.5	9.1	76.3
Croatia	:	:	6.1	86.6	:	10.5	32.8	:

(¹) Micro: 0-9 persons employed; small: 10-49 persons employed; medium-sized: 50-249 persons employed; large: 250+ persons employed.

Source: Eurostat (online data code: sbs_sc_ind_r2)

Table 7.1.6: Value added by enterprise size-class, construction and distributive trades, 2008 (¹)
(% share of size class in total sectoral value added)

	Construction				Distributive trades			
	Micro	Small	Medium-sized	Large	Micro	Small	Medium-sized	Large
EU-27	37.6	27.7	18.2	16.5	:	24.5	:	32.0
Belgium	36.7	29.8	20.4	13.1	27.5	29.3	16.7	26.5
Bulgaria	16.1	29.7	35.0	19.1	26.8	33.4	25.6	14.2
Czech Republic	*36.4*	*22.3*	*21.0*	*20.3*	*25.4*	*27.9*	*22.8*	*24.0*
Denmark	27.6	36.8	20.2	15.4	20.1	28.8	23.5	27.5
Germany	28.3	38.6	21.5	11.6	15.8	25.4	20.9	37.9
Estonia	21.2	36.3	33.0	9.5	24.9	33.5	24.4	17.1
Ireland	41.9	18.0	21.8	18.3	17.0	40.4	21.4	21.2
Greece	:	:	:	:	:	:	:	:
Spain	38.5	27.3	18.8	15.4	35.0	24.6	14.3	26.1
France	43.7	28.5	11.9	16.0	31.8	21.4	16.6	30.1
Italy	59.1	26.1	9.3	5.5	47.2	25.3	12.1	15.4
Cyprus	38.2	30.7	16.4	14.7	33.0	31.1	23.8	12.0
Latvia	13.9	28.6	43.7	13.9	21.2	34.2	28.1	16.5
Lithuania	10.3	23.4	40.9	25.4	15.6	30.6	26.1	27.7
Luxembourg	23.7	30.4	31.4	14.5	30.5	29.3	26.0	14.2
Hungary	36.1	29.5	22.8	11.6	27.4	27.1	24.2	21.2
Malta	:	:	:	:	:	:	:	:
Netherlands	30.8	28.0	18.8	22.4	:	27.0	:	24.5
Austria	*23.6*	30.8	21.2	*24.4*	21.5	*27.1*	21.1	30.3
Poland	31.4	20.5	26.5	21.5	26.3	21.8	22.7	29.1
Portugal	30.2	28.7	20.5	20.7	30.8	28.2	19.8	21.3
Romania	*18.1*	*21.8*	*28.4*	*31.7*	*21.1*	*29.3*	*26.4*	*23.2*
Slovenia	32.5	27.8	21.7	18.0	25.0	28.4	21.6	25.0
Slovakia	11.9	36.2	28.8	23.1	24.7	40.8	18.0	16.5
Finland	51.5	27.9	8.2	12.3	25.0	24.5	16.6	33.8
Sweden	33.9	28.7	12.7	24.7	24.3	26.2	18.5	31.0
United Kingdom	36.0	22.9	18.3	22.8	17.6	16.6	16.5	49.3
Norway	32.8	32.2	15.8	19.3	24.6	30.5	19.3	25.6
Croatia	21.4	26.6	23.7	28.4	24.3	29.7	20.4	25.7

(¹) Micro: 0-9 persons employed; small: 10-49 persons employed; medium-sized: 50-249 persons employed; large: 250+ persons employed.

Source: Eurostat (online data codes: sbs_sc_con_r2 and sbs_sc_dt_r2)

Table 7.1.7: Value added by enterprise size-class, transport and storage and accomodation and food services, 2008
(% share of size class in total sectoral value added)

	Transport and storage				Accomodation and food services			
	Micro	Small	Medium-sized	Large	Micro	Small	Medium-sized	Large
EU-27	15.4	17.3	16.5	50.9	*34.1*	*26.4*	15.3	24.1
Belgium	10.9	30.3	23.9	35.0	47.9	:	10.3	:
Bulgaria	15.1	19.7	17.2	48.0	16.0	27.0	35.2	21.8
Czech Republic	*15.7*	*12.3*	*13.0*	*59.0*	*46.2*	*22.2*	*16.5*	*15.1*
Denmark	17.0	16.8	21.0	50.0	23.1	33.0	23.0	20.9
Germany	13.2	20.1	19.5	47.2	30.0	34.8	18.4	16.8
Estonia	18.7	21.7	34.4	25.2	17.4	34.8	32.2	15.5
Ireland	15.1	14.9	11.7	58.4	18.5	32.8	38.9	9.8
Greece	:	:	:	:	:	:	:	:
Spain	28.1	18.8	15.9	37.2	41.5	24.0	16.0	18.5
France	11.7	11.2	12.2	64.9	49.0	24.0	6.6	20.4
Italy	14.6	17.1	13.6	54.7	47.7	29.9	8.7	13.7
Cyprus	20.4	14.2	17.4	48.0	33.0	19.9	29.1	18.0
Latvia	12.8	24.4	16.9	46.0	:	32.1	:	:
Lithuania	9.2	24.0	24.3	42.6	10.7	38.9	29.7	20.8
Luxembourg	7.4	12.4	22.6	57.6	41.4	:	10.9	:
Hungary	17.2	19.1	14.7	49.0	29.1	25.7	21.5	23.8
Malta	:	:	:	:	:	:	:	:
Netherlands	14.7	17.7	19.2	48.4	42.4	26.3	10.0	21.3
Austria	8.2	16.2	21.4	54.2	38.7	34.9	18.4	7.9
Poland	18.5	10.7	14.9	56.0	31.1	20.1	19.2	29.6
Portugal	13.7	22.8	17.8	45.7	34.3	27.0	19.4	19.3
Romania	*12.4*	*15.7*	*14.3*	*57.7*	*16.9*	*23.3*	*27.8*	*31.9*
Slovenia	23.4	17.3	14.1	45.1	32.0	22.6	21.5	23.9
Slovakia	5.2	13.9	19.4	61.5	28.2	37.8	:	:
Finland	28.9	16.5	12.2	42.5	32.1	25.0	:	:
Sweden	20.8	18.3	15.7	45.1	37.3	31.7	14.4	16.5
United Kingdom	11.1	11.8	12.2	64.9	21.3	18.0	13.4	47.3
Norway	42.3	11.5	13.5	32.7	21.5	34.4	23.9	20.2
Croatia	13.5	16.6	20.6	49.2	24.0	16.5	24.1	35.4

(¹) Micro: 0-9 persons employed; small: 10-49 persons employed; medium-sized: 50-249 persons employed; large: 250+ persons employed.

Source: Eurostat (online data code: sbs_sc_1b_se_r2)

Table 7.1.8: Value added by enterprise size-class, information and communication and real estate activities, 2008
(% share of size class in total sectoral value added)

	Information and communication				Real estate activities			
	Micro	Small	Medium-sized	Large	Micro	Small	Medium-sized	Large
EU-27	:	*11.1*	14.1	63.6	*58.5*	*14.8*	*13.0*	:
Belgium	11.0	12.4	15.4	61.1	60.2	:	17.1	:
Bulgaria	7.3	9.7	14.2	68.8	68.8	18.5	:	:
Czech Republic	*12.3*	*10.0*	*12.2*	*65.5*	*75.9*	*13.6*	*6.3*	*4.2*
Denmark	12.5	14.0	16.9	56.6	80.9	10.9	4.5	3.7
Germany	9.6	11.9	17.4	61.1	61.5	16.1	12.7	9.7
Estonia	9.1	15.7	25.9	49.3	72.1	22.9	:	:
Ireland	5.7	10.1	:	:	65.6	16.5	:	:
Greece	:	:	:	:	:	:	:	:
Spain	6.8	9.2	11.9	72.1	76.3	14.1	7.2	2.4
France	11.8	11.7	12.8	63.7	46.2	11.6	22.7	19.5
Italy	11.2	10.0	10.9	67.8	85.0	5.3	5.9	3.9
Cyprus	7.2	10.5	20.6	61.7	75.1	:	:	0.0
Latvia	10.3	15.4	24.6	49.6	54.0	24.8	11.4	9.8
Lithuania	7.9	18.1	31.1	42.9	51.5	37.8	:	:
Luxembourg	12.7	:	:	:	:	:	:	:
Hungary	10.7	10.3	15.9	63.1	70.3	17.6	5.8	6.4
Malta	:	:	:	:	:	:	:	:
Netherlands	:	13.1	14.7	60.0	37.7	17.2	26.3	18.8
Austria	14.2	15.2	19.2	51.5	56.0	14.3	18.4	11.3
Poland	7.9	7.6	13.0	71.5	14.3	30.9	41.4	13.4
Portugal	6.5	9.0	16.7	67.8	79.5	14.7	5.7	0.0
Romania	*7.9*	*11.8*	*10.4*	*69.9*	*57.7*	*23.3*	*14.3*	*4.7*
Slovenia	14.2	18.3	17.2	50.3	56.5	:	:	0.0
Slovakia	9.8	11.1	19.7	59.4	37.3	42.0	:	:
Finland	9.2	12.3	20.7	57.8	53.6	:	:	:
Sweden	14.0	16.8	18.4	50.7	56.2	14.9	19.0	9.9
United Kingdom	14.3	9.9	11.8	64.1	43.4	13.3	11.4	31.9
Norway	12.7	16.3	22.8	48.3	90.1	6.1	:	:
Croatia	9.0	11.9	8.2	70.8	71.6	23.0	5.4	0.0

(¹) Micro: 0-9 persons employed; small: 10-49 persons employed; medium-sized: 50-249 persons employed; large: 250+ persons employed.

Source: Eurostat (online data code: sbs_sc_1b_se_r2)

Table 7.1.9: Value added by enterprise size-class, professional, scientific and technical activities and administrative and support services, 2008
(% share of size class in total sectoral value added)

	Professional, scientific & technical activities				Administrative & support services			
	Micro	Small	Medium-sized	Large	Micro	Small	Medium-sized	Large
EU-27	*39.0*	*21.1*	*16.8*	*22.8*	:	:	*19.4*	:
Belgium	44.0	21.2	19.6	15.2	14.7	12.5	17.3	55.5
Bulgaria	51.3	27.7	15.8	5.2	20.6	23.1	24.1	32.2
Czech Republic	*52.5*	*21.4*	*19.4*	*6.7*	*26.3*	*17.5*	*26.1*	*30.2*
Denmark	22.7	22.1	18.3	36.9	1.8	22.6	34.4	41.2
Germany	36.4	23.9	18.1	21.7	18.8	16.0	21.8	43.4
Estonia	41.6	38.1	20.4	0.0	20.3	27.4	23.2	29.1
Ireland	32.3	27.4	16.3	24.0	26.7	23.6	19.8	29.9
Greece	:	:	:	:	:	:	:	:
Spain	45.9	22.2	16.3	15.6	17.7	16.9	17.6	47.7
France	43.0	22.7	13.3	21.0	28.2	15.0	13.2	43.6
Italy	64.3	15.5	10.6	9.6	22.3	19.4	16.4	41.9
Cyprus	36.6	25.3	24.1	14.0	48.1	24.6	16.7	10.8
Latvia	:	35.5	17.4	:	19.7	26.7	27.6	25.9
Lithuania	40.1	30.8	21.9	7.2	21.6	13.6	30.9	33.8
Luxembourg	28.8	26.1	19.8	25.4	:	:	:	:
Hungary	43.9	23.9	19.4	12.8	24.9	23.9	23.4	27.8
Malta	:	:	:	:	:	:	:	:
Netherlands	38.6	23.7	16.5	21.2	15.6	:	:	:
Austria	42.3	28.7	19.3	9.8	25.4	20.6	24.7	29.3
Poland	48.3	14.7	19.4	17.5	19.0	14.2	22.9	43.8
Portugal	47.7	25.7	17.2	9.4	18.1	16.4	21.6	43.9
Romania	*43.1*	*21.6*	*20.8*	*14.5*	*22.3*	*20.2*	*24.5*	*33.0*
Slovenia	57.5	:	11.6	:	20.1	:	:	:
Slovakia	35.9	34.6	14.0	15.4	23.7	34.8	24.1	17.4
Finland	36.1	25.6	19.9	18.4	18.9	19.5	20.1	41.5
Sweden	39.1	23.4	17.4	20.0	19.6	18.5	18.3	43.5
United Kingdom	27.3	18.8	17.3	36.5	23.1	15.1	16.7	45.2
Norway	33.4	24.2	18.3	24.1	21.0	18.3	25.2	35.6
Croatia	46.0	30.5	14.8	8.7	23.5	24.0	21.6	30.9

(¹) Micro: 0-9 persons employed; small: 10-49 persons employed; medium-sized: 50-249 persons employed; large: 250+ persons employed.

Source: Eurostat (online data code: sbs_sc_1b_se_r2)

Figure 7.1.7: Share of value added and employment accounted for by foreign-controlled enterprises, non-financial business economy, 2008 (¹)
(%)

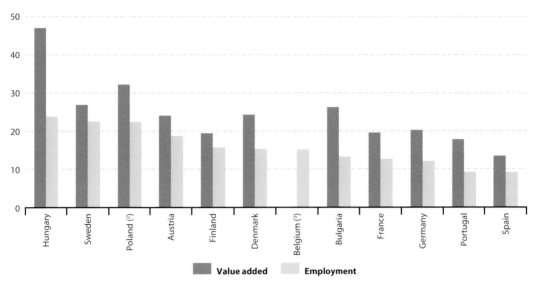

(¹) No data available for Member States not shown.
(²) A size threshold is applied excluding enterprises below the threshold.
(³) Value added, not available.

Source: Eurostat (online data code: fats_g1a_08)

Table 7.1.10: Enterprise demography, business economy, 2008 (¹)

	Enterprise birth rates (% of enterprise births among active enterprises)	Enterprise death rates (% of enterprise deaths among active enterprises)	Average employment size of newly born enterprises (number of persons employed)
Belgium	:	:	:
Bulgaria	18.2	:	2.2
Czech Republic	3.8	:	2.2
Denmark	:	:	:
Germany	9.3	:	*1.5*
Estonia (²)	18.2	:	1.5
Ireland	5.9	:	1.1
Greece	:	:	:
Spain	7.5	:	1.6
France	9.7	7.7	1.4
Italy	7.1	*7.8*	1.7
Cyprus	3.3	:	2.2
Latvia	14.0	:	2.1
Lithuania	20.0	*32.1*	1.7
Luxembourg	10.1	:	1.9
Hungary	10.2	*12.1*	1.6
Malta	:	:	:
Netherlands	14.5	:	1.9
Austria (³)	7.3	6.1	2.5
Poland	:	:	:
Portugal	10.5	:	1.6
Romania	14.7	:	2.2
Slovenia	11.7	:	1.2
Slovakia	15.5	*15.0*	1.8
Finland	10.8	:	0.5
Sweden	7.1	:	1.4
United Kingdom	13.0	:	2.2
Norway	9.6	:	0.7
Switzerland	:	:	1.9

(¹) Covers the business economy (NACE Rev. 2 Sections B to N) excluding holdings (Group 64.2).
(²) Average employment size, 2007.
(³) Enterprise death rate, 2007.

Source: Eurostat (online data code: bd_9a_l_form_r2)

7.2 Industrial production

This subchapter examines recent statistics on industrial production in the European Union (EU). PRODCOM is the name given to the EU's system of industrial production statistics which covers mining and quarrying and manufactured products.

Main statistical findings

PRODCOM covers mining and quarrying as well as manufacturing, in other words, NACE Rev. 2 Sections B and C. PRODCOM statistics are based on a list of products called the PRODCOM List which consists of about 3 900 headings and is revised every year. Products are detailed at an 8-digit level – only information at this detailed level can be found in the PRODCOM database, as production data for different products cannot always be meaningfully aggregated. The purpose of PRODCOM statistics is to report, for each product in the PRODCOM List, how much production has been sold during the reference period. This means that PRODCOM statistics relate to products (not to activities) and are therefore not strictly comparable with activity-based statistics such as structural business statistics.

PRODCOM information is currently requested for each heading in terms of the value of production sold during the survey period. Table 7.2.1 shows the level of production in the EU-27 for a selection of products. As can be seen, transport equipment products (within Divisions 29 and 30) dominated the list of the most sold manufacturing products in the EU-27 in value terms in 2010, occupying the top two places with a number of further products among the top 15 shown, while there were also several manufactured food products (within Division 10) and a couple of fabricated metal products (Division 25).

As well as data by value, information on the physical quantity (also referred to as volume) of production sold during the survey period is also requested. Table 7.2.2 shows the quantity of production sold for a selection of products. In certain circumstances this information can be supplemented by the physical quantity of actual (total) production during the survey period, including therefore any production which is used (as an intermediate product) by the enterprise in the manufacture of other products in the List.

Data sources and availability

The PRODCOM List is linked to the activity classification NACE and to the classification of products by activity (CPA): the first four digits of each PRODCOM code refer to a NACE class, the fifth and sixth digits relate to a CPA subcategory, and the seventh and eighth digits are specific to the PRODCOM List. Most headings correspond to one or more combined nomenclature (CN) codes: some headings (mostly industrial services) do not correspond to a CN heading at all. The relationship with CN enables the calculation of apparent consumption by linking production statistics to international trade statistics.

The production surveyed covers only the production actually carried out on the territory of the reporting country. This means that the production of subsidiaries which takes place outside an enterprise's territory is not included in the survey for that country. As a general principle, when a production process takes as an input a material that does not match the description of the product, and produces as an output something that does, then production of the product should be recorded. On the other hand, if the processing merely works on a product without changing the heading under which it is listed, it should not be recorded, since this would result in double-counting. This means that the link to turnover is tenuous, since some activity does not result in new products and should not be recorded in PRODCOM statistics.

PRODCOM data are available for all of the EU Member States, Iceland, Norway and Croatia, and Eurostat produces aggregates for the EU-27 and the EU-25. Data are available during the year following the reference year, with the first release by Eurostat normally in July. As more complete and revised data becomes available updates are released on a monthly basis.

Context

The development of PRODCOM dates back to 1985 when there were the first meetings of a working party on production statistics, whose objective was to harmonise the various ways industrial production statistics were collected in the EU Member States. Although statistics were collected on production in most countries, these covered the national situation, and national classifications were used and different survey methods applied. The basis of PRODCOM is to enable these national statistics to be compared and where possible aggregated geographically to give a picture relating to the output of a product within the EU context. This aim became more urgent with the creation of the single European market in 1992, such that the statistical system had to adapt.

Production statistics are used by the European Commission and national administrations for policymaking and by professional/trade associations and their members. The use of the data in climate change statistics is increasing, as well as in other environmental statistics such as the analysis of material flows or chemicals management.

Table 7.2.1: Production sold in value terms, selected products, EU-27, 2010

PRODCOM code	Product	Value (EUR million)	Rounding base (million) ([1])
29.10.22.30	Motor vehicles with a petrol engine > 1 500 cm^3	113 175	
29.10.23.30	Motor vehicles with a diesel or semi-diesel engine > 1 500 cm^3 but <= 2 500 cm^3	100 000	20 000
21.20.13.80	Other medicaments of mixed or unmixed products, p.r.s., n.e.c.	75 591	
10.00.00.Z1	Prepared and preserved meat, meat offal or blood, including prepared meat and offal dishes	48 575	
29.32.30.90	Other parts and accessories, n.e.c., for vehicles of HS 87.01 to 87.05; parts thereof	45 000	9 000
10.90.10.Z0	Preparations for animal feeds other than dog and cat food	38 382	
29.10.21.00	New vehicles with spark-ignition engine of a cylinder capacity <= 1 500 cm^3	34 024	
11.05.10.00	Beer from malt other than non-alcoholic and low-alcohol beer, excluding alcohol duty	32 000	1 000
25.11.23.60	Other structures of iron or steel	28 274	
29.32.20.90	Parts and accessories of bodies (including cabs), n.e.c.	28 098	
10.71.11.00	Fresh bread	27 691	
30.30.50.90	Parts for all types of aircraft excluding propellers, rotors, under carriages, for civil use	22 995	
25.62.20.00	Metal parts (excluding turned metal parts)	21 062	
10.51.40.50	Grated, powdered, blue-veined and other non-processed cheese	20 000	5 000
17.21.13.00	Cartons, boxes and cases, of corrugated paper or paperboard	19 128	

([1]) Indicates the magnitude of the rounding employed to protect confidential cell (in the case of PRODCOM code 29.10.23.30, the confidential value lies within the range +/- EUR 20 000 million of the reported value).

Source: Eurostat, from http://epp.eurostat.ec.europa.eu/portal/page/portal/statistics/search_database go to Data Navigation Tree/ Database by themes/Industry, trade and services/Statistics on the production of manufactured goods (prom)/NACE Rev. 2 (prodcom_n2)/ Prodcom Annual Sold (NACE Rev. 2.) (DS-066341)

Table 7.2.2: Quantity of production sold, selected products, EU-27, 2010

PRODCOM code	Product	Quantity (1 000)	Rounding base (1 000) (¹)	Unit
12.00.11.50	Cigarettes containing tobacco or mixtures of tobacco and tobacco substitutes (excluding tobacco duty)	691 236 046		p/st
18.12.14.21	Printed children's picture, drawing or colouring books	40 824		kg
20.11.11.70	Oxygen	30 540 455		m3
23.51.12.10	Portland cement	155 125 428		kg
28.29.22.10	Fire extinguishers	13 314		p/st
29.32.30.40	Road wheels and parts and accessories thereof	1 320 000	30 000	kg
32.50.13.11	Syringes, with or without needles, used in medical, surgical, dental or veterinary sciences	10 092 019		p/st
32.91.12.70	Brushes for the application of cosmetics	1 740 000	30 000	p/st
32.99.12.10	Ball-point pens	1 744 399		p/st
32.99.12.30	Felt-tipped and other porous-tipped pens and markers	1 862 435		p/st

(¹) Indicates the magnitude of the rounding employed to protect confidential cell (in the case of PRODCOM code 29.32.30.40, the confidential value lies within the range +/- 30 million kg of the reported value).

Source: Eurostat, from http://epp.eurostat.ec.europa.eu/portal/page/portal/statistics/search_database go to Data Navigation Tree/ Database by themes/Industry, trade and services/ Statistics on the production of manufactured goods (prom)/NACE Rev. 2 (prodcom_n2)/ Prodcom Annual Sold (NACE Rev. 2.) (DS-066341)

7.3 Industry and construction – short-term developments

This subchapter examines recent statistics in relation to developments for both industry and construction in the European Union (EU). Short-term business statistics (STS) are provided in the form of indices that allow the most rapid assessment of the economic climate within industry and construction, providing a first assessment of recent developments for a range of activities. STS show developments over time, and so may be used to calculate rates of change, typically showing comparisons with the month or quarter before, or the same period of the previous year. As such, STS do not provide information on the level of activity, such as the monetary value of output (value added or turnover), or actual prices.

Main statistical findings

Industry

The impact of the financial and economic crisis and the subsequent recovery of the EU-27's industrial economy can be clearly seen in two of the main industrial indicators, namely the industrial production index and the index for industrial domestic output prices. Over several years there was relatively stable output and price growth across the EU-27 (see Figure 7.3.1), which was interrupted from the second half of 2007 as price growth accelerated, while industrial output slowed. The EU-27's industrial production index saw its month-on-month rate of change turn negative in February 2008, while the index for domestic output prices peaked six months later in July 2008. The fall in output lasted more than one year, returning to a positive rate of change in April 2009, while domestic output prices started a run of relatively sustained increases from May 2009.

The decline in industrial output in the EU-27 from its relative peak in February 2008 was particularly steep, as the relative trough recorded in March 2009 was the lowest level since January 1998. By contrast, although industrial output prices in July

2009 were 8.1 % lower than at their relative peak a year earlier, they remained similar to their level recorded in October 2007 prior to the financial and economic crisis; in part, these developments continued to reflect the relatively high price of oil and associated energy-related and intermediate products.

Industrial import prices for the euro area peaked in July 2008, regardless of whether imports were from outside the euro area or from other Member States within the euro area. Thereafter, prices of imports from within the euro area fell for nine consecutive months by a total of 7.4 %, whereas the prices of imports from outside the euro area fell for one month longer, and by a total of 14.2 %. Since their low point in the spring of 2009 prices for imports from within the euro area had increased by 12.4 % (as of June 2011) and from outside the euro area by 22.0 % (as of July 2011), in both cases more than 4 % above their highest levels prior to the financial and economic crisis (see Figure 7.3.2).

The downturn in industrial activity was widespread across the EU, illustrated by the fact that every Member State recorded lower output in 2009 than in 2008, with falls ranging from –3.7 % in Poland to –23.9 % in Estonia (see Table 7.3.1). The subsequent recovery was also widespread, as only Cyprus and Greece recorded a further contraction in activity during 2010, with growth rates peaking at 20.3 % in Estonia.

The downturn in activity was also spread across almost the full range of industrial activities: in 2009 there was a single industrial activity (at the NACE Rev. 2 division level) that reported continued growth within the EU-27, as the output of pharmaceutical products and preparations rose by 3.4 % compared with the year before.. The recovery in 2010 was also relatively widespread, as output in 2010 was higher than in 2009 for most industrial activities. There were six exceptions (at the NACE Rev. 2 division level), where output continued to contract in 2010, most notably the manufacture of tobacco products, with a loss of 5.9 % (see Figure 7.3.3).

Construction

Although slightly less in magnitude, the downturn in activity for construction within the EU-27 lasted

longer than for industry. Construction output in the EU-27 peaked in March 2007 and fell gradually for five months. This initial downturn was followed by a slight, temporary recovery until January 2008, after which substantial falls were recorded, reaching a low in February 2010, just under three years after the initial downturn. Between January 2008 and February 2010 the index of production for construction in the EU-27 fell by 18.6 % overall, deteriorating to a level not seen since June 1998.

The construction of buildings is the dominant part of construction output, and unsurprisingly output for building work followed a similar path to the overall indicator for construction, although the magnitude of the contraction from the end of 2006 to the beginning of 2010 was slightly greater, totalling 20.6 % in the EU-27 (see Figure 7.3.4). For civil engineering the developments were less clear cut. From March to November 2008, civil engineering output in the EU-27 fell in a similar manner to the developments seen for building output. However, there followed renewed growth through to April 2009, perhaps reflecting increased public spending in reaction to the financial and economic crisis. Civil engineering output remained stable through much of 2009, before contracting again between November 2009 and March 2010 after which it was relatively unchanged.

The long and deep downturn in construction activity was widespread within the EU-27, illustrated by the fact that every Member State except Poland experienced at least one year of contraction in construction output during the three latest years (2008 to 2010); in ten Member States negative rates of change were recorded for all three years. The ongoing downturn has been particularly long in Denmark, Ireland and Spain where four consecutive negative annual rates of change were recorded, in Hungary where the sequence is now five years, and in Portugal where the last positive annual rate of change was recorded in 2001. Construction output declined by 20 % or more in Spain and Latvia in 2010, and by 30 % or more in Ireland and Greece. In contrast, seven Member States reported an increase in construction output in 2010, reaching highs of 7.2 % in the United Kingdom and 11.8 % in Finland.

Data sources and availability

Short-term business statistics (STS) are compiled within the scope of the STS Regulation 1165/98 of 19 May 1998 concerning short-term statistics. The STS Regulation brought major changes and improvements in the availability and timeliness of indicators which followed its implementation. The STS Regulation has been amended and adjusted to meet emerging users' needs – generally in relation to monetary union and more specifically to the specific requirements of the European Central Bank (ECB).

Indicators common to industry and construction include the production index and labour input indicators concerning employment, wages and salaries, and hours worked. For industry there are additional STS indicators concerning turnover, new orders and output prices, all three of which are compiled as a total and also distinguishing between domestic and non-domestic markets, with a further analysis of non-domestic markets between euro area and non-euro area markets. In a similar manner, there are industrial import prices, with a distinction between imports from euro area and non-euro area markets. For construction activities there is a distinction in the production index between building and civil engineering, while additional indicators are collected on building permits, as well as construction cost and price indices.

The presentation of short-term statistics may take a variety of different forms. Gross or unadjusted indices are the basic form of an index. Working-day adjustment takes into account the calendar nature of a given month in order to adjust the index. The number of working days for a given month depends on: the timing of certain public holidays (Easter can fall in March or in April depending on the year); the possible overlap of certain public holidays and non-working days (1 May can fall on a Sunday); whether or not a year is a leap year, and other reasons. Seasonal adjustment, or the adjustment of seasonal variations, aims, after adjusting for calendar effects, to take into account the impact of known seasonal factors that have been observed in the past. For example, in the case of the production index, annual summer holidays

have a negative impact on industrial production. The trend is a slow variation over a long period of years, generally associated with the structural causes of the phenomenon in question. The cycle is a quasi-periodic oscillation. It is characterised by alternating periods of higher and lower rates of change possibly, but not always, involving expansion and contraction. Generally, if this component of the time series is relatively important, the trend cycle series is a better series for the analysis of longer-term past developments. However, this advantage is less clear when analysing very recent developments. This is because trend cycle values for recent periods may have greater revisions than the equivalent seasonally adjusted values. Hence, the latter may be more appropriate for the analysis of very recent developments; this is particularly true around turning points.

Depending on the indicator in question, the EU Member States are required to transmit unadjusted or adjusted data to Eurostat. In the case that Member States transmit unadjusted data, then Eurostat calculates the seasonal adjustment. The Member States' national statistical authorities are responsible for data collection and the calculation of national time series. Eurostat is responsible for the EU-27 and euro area aggregations.

NACE Rev. 2 is the latest version of the statistical classification of economic activities and has been implemented in STS during 2009. This involved not just changing data compilation practices to use NACE Rev. 2 but also recalculating or estimating a time series in NACE Rev. 2, normally back to the year 2000. Simultaneously with the introduction of NACE Rev. 2, a new base year (2005) was adopted for STS indices to better reflect the economic structure; previously indices were presented with 2000 as the base year.

Context

The profile and use of STS is expanding rapidly, as information flows have become global and the latest news release for an indicator may have significant effects on financial markets, or decisions that are taken by central banks and business leaders. STS are

a key resource for those who follow developments in the business cycle, or for those who wish to trace recent developments within a particular industry, construction or service.

Some of the most important STS indicators are a set of Principal European Economic Indicators (PEEIs) that are essential to the ECB for conducting monetary policy within the euro area. Four PEEIs concern industrial short-term business statistics: production, new orders received, output prices of the domestic market and import prices. A further two PEEIs concern construction short-term business statistics: production and building permits.

Figure 7.3.1: Production and domestic output price indices for industry (excluding construction), EU-27, 2001-2011
(2005 = 100)

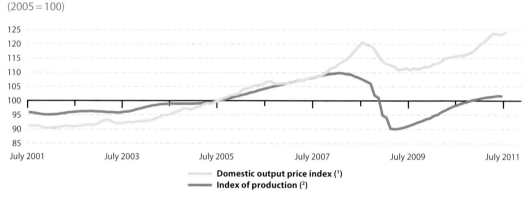

(¹) Gross series; estimates, 2001-2004 and July 2011.
(²) Trend cycle; estimates.
Source: Eurostat (online data codes: sts_inppd_m and sts_inpr_m)

Figure 7.3.2: Industrial import price index, euro area, 2005-2011 (¹)
(2005 = 100)

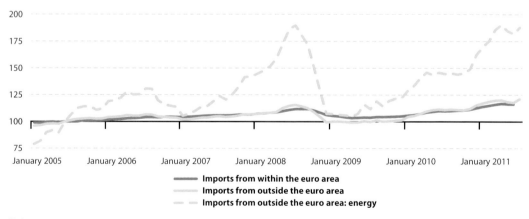

(¹) Gross series; estimates.
Source: Eurostat (online data code: sts_inpi_m)

Table 7.3.1: Annual growth rates for industry (excluding construction), 2006-2010
(%)

	Index of production (¹)					Domestic output price index (²)				
	2006	2007	2008	2009	2010	2006	2007	2008	2009	2010
EU-27	4.1	3.7	− 1.7	− 13.7	6.9	5.6	2.8	7.6	− 4.4	3.5
Euro area	4.2	3.9	−1.6	−14.7	7.5	5.1	2.7	6.1	−5.1	2.9
Belgium	4.3	6.4	3.7	−9.4	11.9	5.8	2.1	9.3	−7.2	5.4
Bulgaria	6.1	9.5	0.4	−18.2	2.2	8.7	8.0	13.2	−4.3	7.2
Czech Republic	8.7	10.1	−2.2	−12.9	9.9	1.5	4.1	4.5	−3.2	1.3
Denmark	4.1	−2.1	−1.1	−15.0	1.9	7.9	1.6	13.2	−6.7	6.4
Germany	5.7	6.1	−0.1	−16.3	10.9	5.4	1.3	5.4	−4.1	1.5
Estonia	10.1	6.4	−4.8	−23.9	20.3	4.3	9.6	9.6	−0.3	1.8
Ireland	3.2	5.2	−2.2	−4.5	7.3	3.6	2.3	6.1	−3.6	1.5
Greece	0.8	2.3	−4.2	−9.2	−6.6	7.3	4.1	10.0	−5.8	6.1
Spain	3.9	2.0	−7.3	−15.8	0.9	5.4	3.6	6.5	−3.4	3.2
France	1.1	1.3	−2.8	−12.5	5.2	3.8	2.8	5.6	−6.4	3.5
Italy	3.6	1.8	−3.5	−18.8	6.4	5.2	3.3	5.8	−5.4	3.1
Cyprus	0.6	4.5	4.0	−8.6	−1.8	5.3	3.6	11.7	−1.8	4.1
Latvia	6.5	1.1	−3.3	−17.6	14.5	9.6	18.6	15.7	−1.8	−0.2
Lithuania	6.6	2.5	5.1	−14.6	6.5	6.9	9.4	15.8	−6.6	4.1
Luxembourg	2.5	−0.7	−5.3	−15.8	10.5	12.8	4.4	15.1	−9.2	1.5
Hungary	10.6	8.1	−1.0	−17.4	10.3	8.4	6.4	11.6	1.2	7.3
Malta	8.7	9.1	−9.1	−13.8	7.3	17.9	−3.7	14.8	9.3	11.7
Netherlands	1.5	2.3	1.4	−7.6	7.1	8.6	5.2	8.9	−9.8	4.0
Austria	7.7	5.9	1.2	−11.2	6.6	2.1	4.1	4.8	−1.8	4.0
Poland	12.3	9.2	2.4	−3.7	10.8	3.4	.4.0	5.4	2.3	3.7
Portugal	3.2	0.1	−4.1	−8.5	1.6	4.4	2.8	5.2	−3.8	3.7
Romania	9.6	10.5	3.0	−6.4	5.5	10.3	8.4	12.8	2.1	5.8
Slovenia	6.3	7.4	1.6	−17.6	6.4	2.4	5.5	5.6	−0.4	2.1
Slovakia	15.6	16.9	3.2	−13.7	18.9	6.3	1.8	6.2	−2.7	−2.8
Finland	10.1	4.7	1.0	−18.1	5.5	6.3	3.9	8.6	−6.3	6.7
Sweden	3.6	3.9	−2.9	−17.9	8.7	6.1	3.6	6.1	−0.3	3.0
United Kingdom	0.5	0.3	−3.1	−10.0	2.7	8.5	2.0	16.1	−3.0	5.7
Norway	−2.1	−1.3	0.3	−3.6	−5.4	8.6	−0.6	15.2	−1.8	8.5
Switzerland	7.8	9.5	1.2	−7.7	6.1	2.7	2.5	4.1	−2.4	0.6
Croatia	4.3	5.0	0.6	−8.9	−1.5	2.7	3.4	8.3	−0.5	4.3
FYR of Macedonia	:	:	:	:	:	6.8	2.5	10.1	−7.2	8.7
Turkey	7.1	7.5	−0.8	−10.0	13.9	9.8	6.0	13.0	1.0	6.2

(¹) Working day adjusted.
(²) Gross series.

Source: Eurostat (online data codes: sts_inprgr_a and sts_inppdgr_a)

Figure 7.3.3: Annual growth rate for the industrial index of production, EU-27, 2010 (¹)
(%)

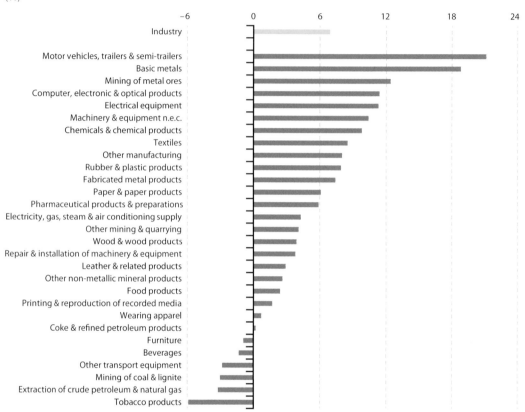

(¹) Working day adjusted; mining support service activities, not available.

Source: Eurostat (online data code: sts_inprgr_a)

Figure 7.3.4: Index of production, construction, EU-27, 2001-2011 (¹)
(2005 = 100)

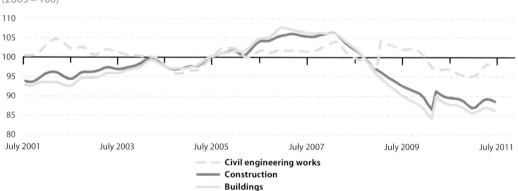

(¹) Trend cycle; estimates.

Source: Eurostat (online data code: sts_copr_m)

Table 7.3.2: Annual growth rates for construction, 2006-2010
(%)

	Index of production (¹)					Construction costs index (²)				
	2006	**2007**	**2008**	**2009**	**2010**	**2006**	**2007**	**2008**	**2009**	**2010**
EU-27	3.7	2.0	−3.8	−8.5	−4.1	4.7	4.5	3.3	−1.5	2.2
Euro area	3.7	1.3	−5.5	−7.9	−7.7	4.7	4.2	3.9	0.1	2.0
Belgium	3.3	1.5	−0.4	−3.3	−2.1	4.9	4.5	2.5	−1.1	0.0
Bulgaria	24.8	26.7	12.6	−14.2	−17.9	5.6	7.7	12.3	10.9	−0.3
Czech Republic	6.3	7.0	−0.5	−0.5	−7.3	2.1	4.8	3.5	−0.3	1.2
Denmark	3.8	−4.2	−5.6	−10.7	−8.5	4.7	6.4	2.9	−0.4	1.1
Germany	6.3	2.9	−0.7	0.1	0.3	2.3	3.2	3.3	0.2	2.2
Estonia	26.9	13.5	−13.3	−29.8	−12.4	10.5	12.7	3.5	−8.5	−2.6
Ireland	3.8	−13.5	−29.2	−36.9	−30.1	9.6	1.7	−7.7	−9.9	0.5
Greece	3.6	14.3	7.7	−17.5	−31.6	4.3	4.6	5.1	−0.3	1.8
Spain	2.2	−4.3	−16.3	−11.3	−20.2	6.9	5.0	4.7	1.0	2.5
France	4.2	2.3	−3.7	−5.9	−3.4	5.3	4.6	5.5	0.4	2.7
Italy	3.8	6.4	−1.1	−11.5	−3.4	2.8	3.6	3.8	:	:
Cyprus	4.1	6.8	2.3	−10.6	−8.0	5.0	5.0	8.0	0.8	3.2
Latvia	13.3	13.6	−3.1	−34.9	−23.4	19.5	31.6	15.6	−6.2	−9.0
Lithuania	21.7	22.2	4.1	−48.5	−7.7	10.7	16.1	9.5	−14.5	−4.8
Luxembourg	2.6	2.6	−1.8	0.8	0.1	2.9	2.9	3.2	1.4	0.8
Hungary	−0.7	−14.0	−5.2	−4.4	−10.4	6.2	7.2	7.5	3.0	−0.4
Malta	4.4	7.2	6.6	−7.9	0.2	:	:	:	:	:
Netherlands	2.3	5.6	3.2	−3.0	−11.0	3.2	4.0	4.3	0.3	0.6
Austria	5.9	3.8	−0.9	−1.6	−4.3	4.6	4.5	5.2	0.6	3.2
Poland	15.6	16.3	10.2	4.5	3.7	1.5	6.6	6.8	0.2	−0.1
Portugal	−6.3	−4.0	−1.2	−6.6	−8.5	3.0	3.4	5.2	−0.6	1.8
Romania	15.6	33.1	26.7	−15.2	−13.4	11.1	10.2	16.2	1.5	1.9
Slovenia	15.7	18.5	15.5	−20.9	−16.9	6.5	6.3	6.3	−2.8	6.6
Slovakia	15.4	5.6	11.4	−11.1	−4.4	4.0	4.1	5.8	2.0	0.0
Finland	7.8	10.2	4.0	−13.1	11.8	3.8	5.9	3.9	−1.1	1.1
Sweden	8.0	6.2	4.2	−3.5	5.9	5.1	6.1	4.9	2.0	2.5
United Kingdom	1.4	2.3	−1.3	−11.6	7.2	4.7	4.7	0.9	−7.1	3.4
Norway	6.0	5.8	1.1	−8.3	−0.1	3.7	7.4	5.7	2.3	3.2
Switzerland	2.0	1.2	2.4	1.4	1.9	:	:	:	:	:
Montenegro	46.1	−1.7	20.7	−19.3	−0.6	:	:	:	:	:
Croatia	9.3	2.6	11.8	−6.9	−15.9	:	:	:	:	:
FYR of Macedonia	−12.3	7.4	25.5	13.7	15.2	:	:	:	:	:
Turkey	18.4	5.5	−7.6	−16.3	17.5	16.0	8.3	13.6	−4.3	5.8

(¹) Working day adjusted.
(²) Gross series for new residential buildings.

Source: Eurostat (online data codes: sts_coprgr_a and sts_copigr_a)

7.4 Services statistics – short-term developments

This subchapter examines recent statistics in relation to developments for service activities in the European Union (EU). Short-term business statistics (STS) are provided in the form of indices that allow the rapid assessment of the economic climate within services, providing a first assessment of recent developments for a range of activities. Traditionally, short-term business statistics were concentrated on industrial and construction activities, and to a lesser extent retail trade. Since the middle of the 1990s, major developments in official statistics within the EU have seen short-term data collection efforts focus increasingly on services.

Main statistical findings

Services turnover fell by 8.5 % in the EU-27 in 2009 compared with the year before but rebounded in 2010 increasing by 5.0 %. Among service activities (at the NACE Rev. 2 section level), the fastest rates of turnover growth in 2010 were recorded for transportation and storage activities, as well as distributive trades, where turnover grew by around 6 % having fallen by more than 9 % in 2009.

As can be seen from Figure 7.4.1, despite strong growth in the EU-27, the level of sales for both activities in June 2011 had not quite returned to the respective peaks that had been recorded prior to the effects of the financial and economic crisis being felt; sales remained 2.1 % lower for distributive trades and 0.7 % lower for transportation and storage.

A similar pattern was observed for accommodation and food services where the June 2011 level of the index for the EU-27 was 1.7 % below its February 2008 peak. In information and communication services the level of sales in June 2011 was also very close to its pre-crisis peak, just 0.3 % lower, while for professional, scientific and technical activities the level of sales was marginally (0.1 %) above its pre-crisis peak. Administrative and support services activities was the only services section where the recent recovery had brought the level of sales clearly back above the pre-crisis peak, as sales in June 2011 stood 1.5 % higher than their February 2008 peak.

While turnover shows sales in current prices, the volume of sales indicates the situation once price changes have been removed. The decline in the volume of sales in retail trade in 2009 reached – 1.7 % in the EU-27, but this activity rebounded with growth of 0.7 % in 2010. A monthly series (see Figure 7.4.2) shows the volume of retail sales peaked in the EU-27 in January 2008 and fell a total of 2.2 % through to August 2009; positive rates of change returned with an increase of 1.1 % by September 2010, after which there was again a modest decline in the volume of sales. Figure 7.4.2 shows that some parts of retail trade were still experiencing a noticeable decline in their respective volume of sales in the first half of 2011, in particular the large activity of retailing of food, beverages and tobacco, as well as the smaller activity of the retail sale of other household equipment in specialised stores.

Among the services for which an EU-27 price index is shown in Figures 7.4.3a and 7.4.3b two stand out as having atypical developments – telecommunications and sea and coastal water transport. Since 2006 (the beginning of the series) EU-27 output prices for telecommunications have been on a steady downward path and in just over five years they fell by a total of 18.2 %. Output prices for sea and coastal water transport are remarkable for their relatively high volatility, although the net impact of these movements was that prices in the first quarter of 2011 were within 0.3 % of their level at the beginning of the series. Most of the other services recorded overall price increases in a range of 6 % to 12 % during the five years shown, with air transport output prices increasing at a faster pace, rising by an amount close to 15 %.

The developments for services turnover observed for the EU-27 as a whole in 2009 and 2010 were common across many of the individual EU Member States. Every Member State (Italy, not available) recorded a fall in services turnover in 2009 and all except Bulgaria and Greece recorded an increase in 2010, with growth exceeding 10 % in Luxembourg and Belgium.

Table 7.4.1 provides an analysis of the two latest rates of change for each of the services sections covered by short-term business statistics. Growth rates in excess of 20 % were recorded in 2010 for distributive trades in Luxembourg, for transportation and storage in Lithuania, and for administrative and supporting activities in Belgium and Poland.

The fall in the volume of sales in retail trade in 2009 and it subsequent (partial) rebound in 2010 observed for the EU-27 was not so regularly reproduced across the EU Member States. Indeed, this pattern was only reproduced in five of the Member States, but this group of five included two of the largest ones, namely Italy and Germany – the others were Cyprus, Malta and Finland. The United Kingdom and Poland were among five Member States that recorded an increase in the volume of sales in retail trade in both 2009 and 2010, while France recorded no growth in 2009 and an increase in 2010. Most Member States, 15 in total, recorded a fall in the volume of sales in retail trade in both 2009 and 2010: for Spain and four other countries, the decline in sales in 2010 was the third consecutive year of contraction for this indicator, and for Denmark and Hungary it was the fourth consecutive year. The situation in Belgium was unique insofar as it was opposed to the overall pattern of developments in the EU-27, as the volume of sales in retail trade increased in 2009 and then subsequently fell in 2010.

Data sources and availability

Short-term business statistics (STS) on services are compiled within the same methodological framework as short-term statistics on industry and construction. The subchapter on short-term developments in industry and construction provides information on: the STS Regulation; the different forms of presentation of indices, namely gross, working-day adjusted, seasonally adjusted, and trend; the implementation of NACE Rev. 2; and the exercise to rebase STS indices to a new base year of 2005 = 100.

The turnover index and the employment index are compiled for retail trade and for other services. For retail trade one additional indicator is provided, namely the volume index of retail sales, which is effectively a deflated turnover index. Furthermore, service output price indices have been developed for a selection of services in recent years.

The index of turnover shows the evolution of sales in value terms. Note that prices for some services have actually been falling, perhaps due to market liberalisation and increased competition (for example, telecommunications and other technology-related activities). In such cases, the rapid growth rates observed for turnover value indices for some activities would be even greater in volume terms.

Retail trade indices have particular importance because of the role of retail trade as an interface between producers and final customers, allowing retail sales turnover and volume of sales indices to be used as short-term indicators for final domestic demand by households. The volume measure of the retail trade turnover index is more commonly referred to as the index of the volume of (retail) sales. To eliminate the price effect on turnover in retail trade, a deflator of sales is used. This deflator is an index with a similar methodology to that of an output price index, but it is adapted specifically for retail trade; it reflects price changes in the goods sold rather than those in the retail sales service provided.

Context

Some of the most important STS indicators are a set of Principal European Economic Indicators (PEEIs) that are essential to the European Central Bank (ECB) for conducting monetary policy within the euro area. Three PEEIs concern services short-term business statistics, namely indices covering: the volume of sales in retail trade, turnover in other services, and output prices of other services.

Figure 7.4.1: Index of turnover, selected service activities, EU-27, 2001-2011 (¹)
(2005 = 100)

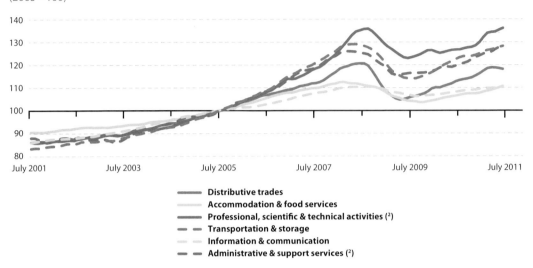

(¹) Trend cycle; estimates.
(²) As required by the STS Regulation.

Source: Eurostat (online data codes: sts_trtu_m and sts_setu_m)

Figure 7.4.2: Volume of sales index, selected retail trade activities, EU-27, 2001-2011 (¹)
(2005 = 100)

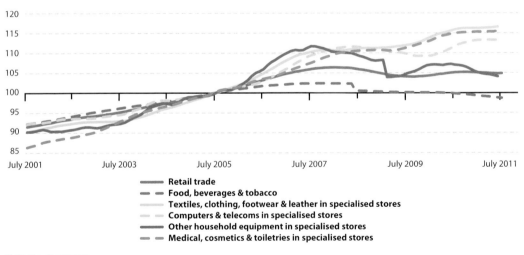

(¹) Trend cycle; estimates.

Source: Eurostat (online data code: sts_trtu_m)

Figure 7.4.3: Output price indices, selected service activities, EU-27, 2006-2011 (¹)
(2006 = 100)

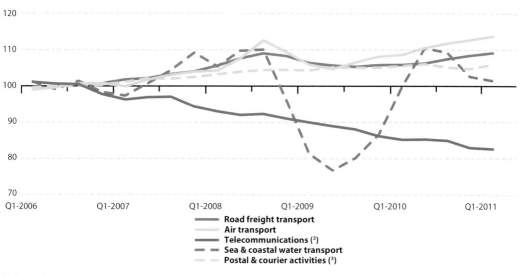

(¹) Gross series.
(²) 2006 to 2008, estimates.
(³) 2006 to 2009, estimates.

Source: Eurostat (online data code: sts_sepp_q)

Figure 7.4.4: Output price indices, selected service activities, EU-27, 2006-2011 (¹)
(2006 = 100)

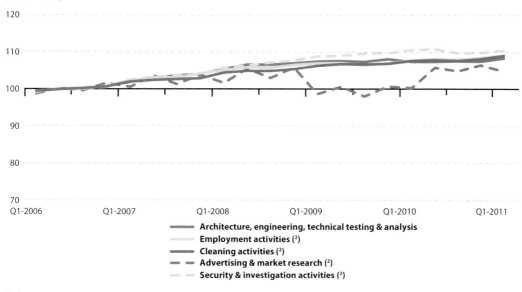

(¹) Gross series.
(²) 2006 to 2009, estimates.

Source: Eurostat (online data code: sts_sepp_q)

Table 7.4.1: Annual growth rates for the index of turnover, selected services, 2009-2010 (¹)
(%)

	Distributive trades		Transportation & storage		Accommoda- tion & food services		Information & communica- tion		Professional, scientific & technical activities (²)		Administra- tive & support services (²)	
	2009	2010	2009	2010	2009	2010	2009	2010	2009	2010	2009	2010
EU-27	−9.4	5.9	−9.5	6.0	−5.9	1.9	−3.0	1.2	−5.8	1.4	−6.4	3.5
Euro area	−10.2	5.0	−10.9	5.1	−4.6	2.3	−3.3	0.3	−5.2	2.2	−7.2	3.8
Belgium	−10.8	11.9	−15.1	8.9	0.5	6.8	1.7	1.7	−7.3	16.8	−4.0	21.0
Bulgaria	−13.1	−0.6	−16.4	−3.5	−2.7	−6.6	−0.8	−8.2	6.8	−26.2	4.3	−2.9
Czech Republic	−10.4	3.3	−13.9	5.8	−9.4	−3.3	−2.6	−2.6	−13.8	−6.8	−11.4	0.6
Denmark	−15.0	6.2	:	:	:	:	:	:	:	:	:	:
Germany	−10.5	6.3	−11.1	6.7	−5.5	2.1	−3.4	−0.1	−5.4	4.0	−7.3	6.3
Estonia	−23.1	6.2	−10.9	17.8	−20.3	5.2	−15.3	−0.1	−22.7	17.6	−17.3	1.2
Ireland	−12.9	0.2	−7.9	0.7	−18.6	12.9	−15.5	13.8	−17.5	−15.1	−19.2	−10.3
Greece	−9.9	−6.6	−27.3	−12.6	−9.0	−8.3	−8.4	−12.5	−16.9	−19.3	4.4	−8.3
Spain	−15.2	2.1	−13.3	2.8	−8.6	−1.6	−6.0	−4.8	−13.0	−2.9	−9.2	−3.1
France	−8.1	4.3	−6.2	5.4	−0.2	4.4	−0.7	3.0	0.2	0.3	−6.7	4.1
Italy	−7.8	4.4	:	:	:	:	−3.9	0.2	:	:	:	:
Cyprus	−11.0	3.7	−9.0	2.8	−3.6	5.5	−1.9	4.3	0.5	3.1	−12.6	9.7
Latvia	−33.7	13.4	−17.3	10.7	−32.5	−5.2	−15.7	−4.3	−19.6	−6.3	−19.1	5.4
Lithuania	−25.3	4.8	−25.1	27.9	−19.7	−9.6	−16.2	−5.2	−27.7	−4.2	−23.1	−0.3
Luxembourg	−18.9	22.0	−12.9	10.7	−2.7	2.8	1.7	16.9	−2.3	6.6	−8.1	0.9
Hungary	−10.4	3.0	−4.7	9.6	−6.1	1.8	3.7	−4.0	16.5	15.7	10.1	−8.5
Malta	−8.2	1.6	−7.5	4.3	−13.3	0.8	3.6	−2.6	1.1	5.2	8.3	8.9
Netherlands	−9.0	6.7	:	:	−4.8	−0.2	−3.7	0.1	−3.2	−4.3	−6.4	−0.8
Austria	−5.4	7.6	−8.4	3.3	−0.7	4.4	−4.2	−0.8	0.3	4.8	−6.9	7.2
Poland	−2.3	6.6	1.6	10.9	3.7	10.4	−1.5	7.2	5.8	6.5	11.0	22.7
Portugal	−11.5	2.9	:	:	:	:	:	:	:	:	:	:
Romania	−15.6	0.1	−18.4	12.5	−15.4	14.0	−6.9	−4.1	−8.5	−9.4	−4.1	6.8
Slovenia	−19.0	2.4	−18.8	19.8	−7.7	3.1	−6.6	1.5	−10.2	−4.0	−10.1	4.6
Slovakia	−22.4	0.9	−12.7	6.1	−22.8	−6.8	1.9	−7.4	2.5	10.4	−8.5	11.3
Finland	−15.1	8.5	−15.5	8.6	−4.0	3.2	−4.0	2.2	−9.0	2.8	−5.9	6.5
Sweden	−6.6	9.7	−9.3	6.6	−0.9	7.3	−0.5	2.2	−6.5	6.3	−3.1	8.5
United Kingdom	−6.6	9.0	−4.6	4.3	−9.7	−0.1	−2.6	3.0	−8.1	−0.4	−6.3	1.9
Croatia	−15.0	−4.1	:	:	−3.5	1.1	:	:	:	:	:	:
Turkey	:	:	:	:	−7.7	6.6	:	:	:	:	:	:

(¹) Working day adjusted.
(²) As required by the STS Regulation.

Source: Eurostat (online data codes: sts_trtu_a and sts_setu_a)

Table 7.4.2: Annual growth rates for the volume of sales index, retail trade, 2000-2010 (¹)
(%)

	2000	2001	2002	2003	2004	2005	2006	2007	2008	2009	2010
EU-27	3.3	2.5	2.2	1.8	2.6	2.4	3.2	2.5	0.2	−1.7	0.7
Euro area	2.6	2.1	1.2	0.9	1.5	2.0	2.2	1.6	−0.7	−2.4	0.8
Belgium	5.3	0.2	−0.9	−0.2	1.7	1.3	1.7	1.8	1.2	0.5	−0.6
Bulgaria	:	3.0	5.9	15.5	16.5	14.7	13.0	18.9	8.7	−7.6	−6.9
Czech Republic	−2.9	7.1	1.1	8.0	3.2	6.7	8.7	7.6	3.8	−1.4	−1.2
Denmark	0.8	4.2	3.4	3.3	4.6	8.8	4.6	−1.4	−3.1	−4.3	−1.7
Germany	1.0	0.2	−2.5	−1.0	1.5	1.4	0.4	−1.3	−0.1	−2.7	1.1
Estonia	14.2	13.2	13.0	−0.9	11.0	14.8	17.6	10.5	−4.5	−18.3	−0.3
Ireland	:	9.0	3.6	3.5	5.7	6.7	8.7	8.0	−2.2	−6.2	−0.8
Greece	7.3	3.5	5.1	4.9	4.2	4.7	9.0	2.2	1.3	−11.3	−6.3
Spain	5.8	3.2	3.9	3.0	2.2	1.3	2.3	2.7	−5.4	−5.4	−2.7
France	2.7	3.5	3.3	2.9	3.0	3.5	2.6	4.1	1.2	0.0	3.9
Italy	:	2.0	1.6	−0.1	−1.7	−0.4	1.0	−0.2	−2.6	−1.3	0.4
Cyprus	:	7.8	3.4	−0.9	3.1	4.6	6.8	7.8	5.3	−3.9	1.3
Latvia	20.2	5.7	10.7	12.6	10.2	19.7	19.9	15.5	−7.4	−27.1	−2.1
Lithuania	10.3	3.0	10.1	11.2	9.2	11.8	7.2	13.7	3.7	−21.4	−7.1
Luxembourg	10.3	5.1	5.7	6.9	3.2	1.7	3.4	4.6	1.8	2.2	8.6
Hungary	3.4	1.3	11.2	7.7	6.0	4.3	4.9	−2.0	−1.9	−5.3	−2.2
Malta	:	−3.8	−2.0	3.7	−1.3	−4.8	−3.4	8.2	−1.2	−2.0	2.9
Netherlands	−0.9	2.8	1.2	−1.0	−0.3	1.8	4.6	2.7	−0.1	−4.4	−1.0
Austria	2.0	−1.9	−0.5	−0.1	0.1	1.5	1.8	0.8	−0.8	2.1	2.1
Poland	:	1.6	0.3	5.3	5.6	−0.9	12.5	10.8	4.7	3.3	6.5
Portugal	−2.5	2.3	−0.3	−2.0	2.5	7.8	1.2	0.3	0.0	−1.7	−0.3
Romania	:	0.5	2.2	8.3	15.0	15.7	20.1	21.1	19.4	−9.9	−5.7
Slovenia	30.5	10.6	2.8	3.2	3.0	8.7	2.9	6.2	11.4	−10.5	−0.2
Slovakia	−3.0	7.6	8.3	−2.4	8.2	10.2	8.2	5.5	9.0	−10.2	−2.3
Finland	5.6	5.4	3.5	4.9	4.9	4.8	5.0	5.0	1.2	−2.6	2.8
Sweden	5.7	2.7	3.8	3.9	3.9	5.8	6.2	0.9	0.8	0.7	2.5
United Kingdom	6.1	4.2	6.0	3.3	5.6	2.2	3.9	3.7	2.0	1.3	0.4
Norway	:	1.8	5.2	2.7	3.2	3.4	5.6	6.6	1.5	0.9	1.4
Switzerland	:	2.1	−0.6	−0.2	0.8	2.2	3.4	4.2	3.0	0.6	2.3
Croatia	:	12.4	11.6	10.7	7.4	3.1	4.3	2.8	−0.4	−7.4	−2.6

(¹) Working day adjusted.

Source: Eurostat (online data code: sts_trtu_a)

7.5 Tourism

This subchapter provides information on recent statistics in relation to tourism in the European Union (EU). Tourism is important because of its economic and employment potential, as well as its social and environmental implications. Tourism statistics are not only used to monitor EU tourism policies but also its regional and sustainable development policy.

The role played by tourism, for both businesses and citizens, has grown considerably in recent decades. According to estimates from the European Commission's Directorate-General for Enterprise and Industry, tourism accounts for more than 5% of the EU-27's gross domestic product (GDP). The tourist accommodation sector employs 2.3 million people in the EU-27, and total employment within the whole of the EU-27's tourism industry is estimated to be between 12 million and 14 million people (according to preliminary estimates from tourism satellite accounts).

Main statistical findings

Tourism volume – demand and supply

Residents from the EU (excluding Malta) made more than 1 000 million holiday trips in 2010. Short trips (of one to three nights) accounted for slightly more than half (55.5%) of the trips made (see Table 7.5.1), while approximately three quarters (76.6%) of the trips made were to domestic destinations, while 23.4% were abroad.

In some Member States, over half of all holidays were spent abroad; this was the case for Luxembourg, Belgium, Slovenia and the Netherlands. However, less than 10% of holiday trips by residents of Romania, Spain, Greece, Bulgaria and Portugal were abroad. These figures appear to be influenced by both the Member State's size and its geographical location (smaller and more northerly countries tend to report a higher propensity for their residents to take holidays abroad).

It is estimated that some 51.5% of the EU-27's population took part in tourism in 2010, in other words made at least one trip of at least four overnight stays during the year. Again, large differences can be observed, as this participation rate ranged from 5.3% in Bulgaria to 87.8% in Cyprus (see Table 7.5.2).

From the supply perspective, it is estimated that nearly 204 000 hotels and similar establishments were active within the EU-27 in 2010; there were more than 256 000 other collective tourist accommodation establishments (such as campsites and holiday dwellings). Hotels and similar establishments provided more than 12.4 million bed places, of which nearly half (46.2%) were in Italy (2.3 million bed places), Spain (1.8 million bed places) or Germany (1.7 million bed places). In 2010, resident and non-resident (foreign) tourists spent over 1 500 million nights in hotels and similar establishments in the EU-27.

Over the past decade, the number of tourism nights spent in collective tourist accommodation had generally shown an upward trend. However, a decline in travel after the 2001 terrorist attacks in the United States and the financial and economic crisis caused short-term shocks: the number of tourism nights spent in collective tourist accommodation in the EU-27 fell by 0.6% in 2008 and by 2.8% in 2009. In 2010, however, the number of nights spent in collective tourist accommodation increased by 0.9%, reaching over 2 250 million nights (see Figure 7.5.1).

Top destinations

German residents spent 640.6 million nights in collective accommodation establishments outside of Germany in 2010, while residents of the United Kingdom spent 504.3 million nights abroad; residents of these two Member States accounted for almost half (49.4%) of the total number of nights spent abroad by EU-27 residents. Extending the coverage, the ten Member States whose residents spent the most nights in tourist accommodation establishments abroad made up 87.4% of the 2 315.3 million nights spent abroad in 2010 (see Table 7.5.3).

When taking into account a country's size in terms of population, Luxembourg was the Member State whose residents spent the most nights abroad per inhabitant (an average of 21.2 nights), followed by Cyprus (14.7), Ireland (11.6, data for 2009) and the Netherlands (also 11.6). At the other end of the spectrum, Romanians, Bulgarians and Greeks (data for 2009) spent, on average, less than one holiday night abroad per inhabitant in 2010 (see Figure 7.5.2).

In 2010, Spain was the most common tourism destination in the EU for non-residents (people coming from abroad), with 213.3 million nights spent in collective accommodation, or 23.2 % of the EU-27 total. The top three most popular destinations among the Member States for non-residents were Spain, Italy (167.8 million nights) and France (85.2 million nights), which together represented 50.7 % of the nights spent by non-residents in the EU-27. The least common destinations were Lithuania, Latvia and Luxembourg (data for 2009); the effect of the size of these Member States should be considered when interpreting these values (see Figure 7.5.3 and Table 7.5.4).

The number of nights spent (by residents and non-residents) can be put into perspective by making a comparison with the size of the country in population terms, providing an indicator of tourism intensity. In 2010, using this measure, the Mediterranean island destinations of Malta and Cyprus, as well as the alpine and city trip destination of Austria were the most popular tourist destinations in the EU-27 (see Figure 7.5.4).

Financial aspects of international tourism

The economic importance of tourism can be measured by looking at the ratio of international tourism receipts relative to GDP. In 2010, this was highest in Malta (13.2 %) and Cyprus (9.5 %), confirming the importance of tourism to these island nations (see Table 7.5.5); an even higher ratio was observed in Croatia (13.9 %, data for 2009). In absolute terms, the highest international tourism receipts in 2010 were recorded in Spain (EUR 39 621 million) and France (EUR 34 939 million), followed by Italy, Germany and the United Kingdom.

Germany recorded the highest level of expenditure on international tourism, totalling EUR 58 596 million in 2010, followed by the United Kingdom (EUR 36 829 million) and France (EUR 29 686 million). When analysing this expenditure relative to the size of population, Luxembourg's residents spent on average EUR 5 374 per inhabitant on travel abroad in 2010, far ahead of the second ranked country, Belgium (EUR 1 305 per inhabitant), which was followed by Ireland, Denmark and Cyprus. Not surprisingly, these five Member States were all relatively small and also among the highest ranked in terms of the share of long (in other words, four nights or more) outbound trips in the total number of holiday trips.

Data sources and availability

Tourism, in a statistical context, refers to the activity of visitors taking a trip to a destination outside their usual environment, for less than a year. It can be for any main purpose, including business, leisure or other personal reasons other than to be employed by a resident person, household or enterprise in the place visited. Tourism statistics are currently limited to at least an overnight stay; as of 2014, outbound same-day visits will be covered as well.

A system of tourism statistics was established in Council Directive 95/57/EC of 23 November 1995 on the collection of statistical information in the field of tourism. This legal basis requires Member States to provide a regular set of comparable tourism statistics. Amendments in 2004 and 2006 concerned the enlargement of the EU and recent changes in the world market for tourism. In July 2011 the European Parliament and the Council of the European Union adopted a new Regulation No 692/2011 concerning European statistics on tourism and repealing Council Directive 95/57/EC; this will come into force for reference year 2012 onwards.

Tourism statistics in the EU consist of two main components: statistics relating to capacity and occupancy in collective tourist accommodation; statistics relating to tourism demand. In most Member States, the former are collected via surveys filled in

by accommodation establishments, while the latter are mainly collected via traveller surveys at border crossings or through household surveys.

Statistics on the capacity of collective tourist accommodation include the number of establishments, the number of bedrooms and the number of bed places. These statistics are available by establishment type or by region, and are compiled annually.

Statistics on the occupancy of collective tourist accommodation refer to the number of arrivals (at accommodation establishments) and the number of nights spent by residents and non-residents, separated into establishment type or region; annual and monthly statistical series are available. In addition, statistics on the use of bed places (occupancy rates) are compiled. Statistics on tourism demand refer to tourist participation, in other words, the number of people who made at least one trip of at least four overnight stays during the reference period (quarter or year). There are statistics in relation to the number of tourism trips made (and the number of nights spent on those trips), separated by:

- destination country;
- departure month;
- length of stay;
- type of organisation for the trip;
- transport mode;
- accommodation type;
- expenditure.

The data may also be analysed by socio-demographic explanatory variables, such as age and sex.

Data from other official sources may also be used to study tourism. These statistics include:

- data on employment in the tourism accommodation sector from the labour force survey (LFS), broken down by working time (full/part-time), working status, age, level of education, sex, permanency and seniority of work with the same employer (annual and quarterly data);
- data on personal travel receipts and expenditure from the balance of payments;
- transport statistics (for example, air passenger transport);

- structural business statistics (SBS) may be used to provide additional information on tourism flows and on the economic performance of certain tourism-related sectors.

Context

The EU is a major tourist destination, with six Member States are among the world's top ten destinations for holidaymakers. Tourism is an important activity in the EU which has the potential to contribute towards employment and economic growth, as well as to development in rural, peripheral or less-developed areas. These characteristics drive the demand for reliable and harmonised statistics within this field, as well as within the wider context of regional policy and sustainable development policy areas.

Indeed, tourism can be a significant factor in the development of European regions. Infrastructure created for tourism purposes contributes to local development, while jobs that are created or maintained can help counteract industrial or rural decline. Sustainable tourism involves the preservation and enhancement of cultural and natural heritage, ranging from the arts to local gastronomy or the preservation of biodiversity.

In 2006, the European Commission adopted a Communication ((2006) 134) titled 'A renewed EU tourism policy: towards a stronger partnership for European tourism'. The document addressed a range of challenges that will shape tourism in the coming years, including Europe's ageing population, growing external competition, consumer demand for more specialised tourism, and the need to develop more sustainable and environmentally friendly tourism practices. It argued that more competitive tourism supply and sustainable destinations would help raise tourist satisfaction and secure Europe's position as the world's leading tourist destination. This was followed by a Communication ((2007) 621) in October 2007 titled, 'Agenda for a sustainable and competitive European tourism', which proposed actions in relation to the sustainable management of destinations, the integration of sustainability concerns by businesses, and the sustainability awareness of tourists.

A Communication ((2010) 352) titled, 'Europe, the world's No. 1 tourist destination – a new political framework for tourism in Europe' was adopted in June 2010. This followed the entry into force of the Lisbon Treaty, which acknowledged the importance of tourism – outlining a specific competence for the EU in this field and allowing for decisions to be taken by qualified majority. A specific Treaty article on tourism specifies that the EU 'shall complement the action of the Member States in the tourism sector, in particular by promoting the competitiveness of Union undertakings in that sector'. With its Communication in 2010, the European Commission encouraged a coordinated approach for initiatives linked to tourism and defined a new framework for action to increase the competitiveness of tourism and its capacity for sustainable growth. It proposed a number of European or multinational initiatives – including a consolidation of the socio-economic knowledge base for tourism – aimed at achieving these objectives.

Table 7.5.1: Holiday trips of residents (aged 15 years or more), 2010

	Number of trips (1 000)			Breakdown of all trips by destination and duration (%)			
	All trips	Short trips (1-3 nights)	Long trips (4+ nights)	Short domestic trips (1-3 nights)	Long domestic trips (4+ nights)	Short outbound trips (1-3 nights)	Long outbound trips (4+ nights)
EU (¹)	*1 046 804*	*580 887*	*465 916*	*50.2*	*26.4*	*5.3*	*18.1*
Belgium	*10 746*	*3 832*	*6 913*	*14.0*	*10.3*	*21.7*	*54.0*
Bulgaria	*6 280*	*4 189*	*2 090*	*63.9*	*26.7*	*2.8*	*6.6*
Czech Republic	25 735	15 546	10 189	55.2	22.8	5.2	16.8
Denmark	27 788	20 345	7 443	66.8	11.0	6.4	15.7
Germany	221 407	115 320	106 087	46.0	21.6	6.1	26.4
Estonia	2 630	1 928	702	60.4	8.4	12.8	18.3
Ireland (²)	10 638	5 559	5 079	39.7	11.3	12.6	36.4
Greece	12 159	5 525	6 635	44.2	47.3	1.2	7.3
Spain	118 931	79 804	39 127	65.1	27.3	2.0	5.6
France	197 653	103 744	93 910	50.1	39.3	2.4	8.2
Italy (²)	80 799	41 449	39 349	46.6	35.4	4.7	13.3
Cyprus	1 783	836	946	42.0	11.4	4.9	41.7
Latvia	4 114	3 261	853	72.5	7.3	6.8	13.5
Lithuania	3 270	2 170	1 101	53.8	11.9	12.6	21.7
Luxembourg	1 240	474	766	<1	<1	38.0	61.7
Hungary	18 404	12 507	5 897	60.0	19.5	7.9	12.6
Malta	:	:	:	:	:	:	:
Netherlands	29 580	10 569	19 011	25.3	22.0	10.4	42.3
Austria	16 887	7 800	9 087	31.2	19.1	15.0	34.7
Poland	*34 557*	*18 136*	*16 421*	*50.1*	*35.2*	*2.4*	*12.3*
Portugal	11 168	7 487	3 681	64.5	25.6	2.6	7.4
Romania	11 163	6 761	4 403	59.9	34.0	<1	5.4
Slovenia	4 244	2 567	1 677	34.3	9.8	26.2	29.7
Slovakia	5 947	2 571	3 375	35.0	25.4	8.3	31.3
Finland	36 125	28 186	7 939	69.9	15.1	8.2	6.9
Sweden	42 041	27 801	14 240	58.5	19.5	7.6	14.4
United Kingdom	111 515	52 521	58 994	41.4	19.9	5.7	33.0
Norway	17 552	9 951	7 601	45.5	20.1	11.1	23.2
Croatia	6 449	2 939	3 509	35.2	40.3	10.4	14.1

(¹) Estimate made for the purpose of this publication, compiled using the sum/average of the latest available data for the Member States, excluding Malta.
(²) 2009.

Source: Eurostat (online data code: tour_dem_ttq)

Table 7.5.2: Tourism indicators, 2005-2010

	Hotels & similar establishments (units)		Other collective accommo-dation establishments (units)		Bed places in hotels & similar establishments (1 000)		Nights spent in hotels & similar establishments (1 000) (¹)		Share of the population (aged 15+) taking part in tourism trips of at least 4 nights (%)	
	2005	2010	2005	2010 (²)	2005	2010 (³)	2005	2010 (⁴)	2005 (⁵)	2010 (⁶)
EU-27 (⁷)	194 199	203 854	210 881	*256 202*	11 198	*12 469*	1 481 479	*1 563 605*	55.3	*51.5*
Euro area (⁷)	144 889	143 861	162 666	*188 803*	8 848	*9 511*	1 173 090	*1 255 826*	59.7	*55.8*
Belgium	1 899	2 088	1 461	1 458	121	128	14 610	17 023	49.8	53.3
Bulgaria	1 230	1 823	325	449	201	245	15 428	15 002	:	5.3
Czech Republic	4 278	4 300	3 327	2 935	232	256	25 209	26 358	55.7	53.7
Denmark	482	482	608	584	70	82	10 100	10 939	64.1	65.6
Germany	36 575	35 867	18 756	17 665	1 621	1 722	200 767	228 302	82.1	65.5
Estonia	317	375	467	766	25	30	3 542	4 028	24.6	39.0
Ireland	4 407	3 451	4 458	4 466	149	152	25 198	23 698	:	:
Greece	9 036	9 732	341	314	682	763	54 017	*62 519*	47.0	41.2
Spain	17 607	18 635	17 151	23 318	1 580	1 785	245 637	267 147	39.8	41.6
France	18 689	17 506	10 689	11 128	1 266	1 248	198 039	195 906	61.9	64.9
Italy	33 527	33 987	96 409	116 257	2 028	2 253	240 320	254 177	48.7	48.6
Cyprus	785	690	134	149	91	84	14 939	13 599	:	87.8
Latvia	337	495	81	133	19	27	2 303	2 460	19.4	17.8
Lithuania	331	381	193	172	20	24	2 062	2 363	25.6	31.5
Luxembourg	293	285	252	241	14	16	1 360	1 282	:	61.4
Hungary	2 061	2 033	1 056	921	162	161	15 749	15 617	49.8	47.3
Malta	173	153	6	7	37	39	7 464	7 475	:	:
Netherlands	3 135	3 172	4 025	3 782	192	212	29 519	33 708	68.5	70.6
Austria	14 267	13 461	6 281	6 878	571	589	76 073	81 344	54.4	58.6
Poland	2 200	3 223	4 523	3 983	170	241	20 333	27 141	32.8	33.2
Portugal	2 012	2 011	288	307	264	280	35 521	37 391	28.3	22.8
Romania	3 608	4 724	618	498	216	258	17 471	15 418	19.7	23.6
Slovenia	344	647	358	348	30	44	4 975	5 853	59.3	56.6
Slovakia	885	1 322	1 131	1 269	57	75	6 833	6 635	:	52.6
Finland	938	842	459	467	118	121	14 275	15 737	58.1	57.9
Sweden	1 857	1 985	2 089	2 119	197	224	22 900	27 338	:	:
United Kingdom	32 926	40 184	35 395	55 605	1 062	1 411	176 835	165 143	62.5	57.3
Iceland	319	325	294	315	17	20	1 569	2 025	:	:
Liechtenstein	46	40	112	114	1	1	111	115	:	:
Norway	1 136	1 128	1 121	1 165	144	175	17 110	18 377	71.2	72.6
Switzerland	5 836	5 477	:	:	274	275	32 944	36 208	:	72.9
Croatia	1 015	841	515	1 276	203	152	21 277	19 345	38.2	38.1
FYR of Macedonia	:	172	:	221	:	13	:	705	:	:

(¹) Nights spent by residents and non-residents.
(²) France, 2009.
(³) United Kingdom, 2009.
(⁴) Ireland, Greece and the United Kingdom, monthly data was used to calculate the annual figure; Ireland and Luxembourg, 2009.
(⁵) Croatia, 2004.
(⁶) The Czech Republic, Estonia, Greece, Spain, France, Italy, the United Kingdom, Norway and Switzerland, 2009.
(⁷) Data for 2010 (in italics): estimates made for the purpose of this publication, compiled using the sum/average of the latest available data for the Member States.

Source: Eurostat (online data codes: tin00039, tin00040, tin00041, tin00043, tour_occ_nim, tin00045, tps00001 and tps00010)

Figure 7.5.1: Number of nights spent in collective tourist accommodation, EU-27, 2000-2010 (¹)
(1 000 million nights)

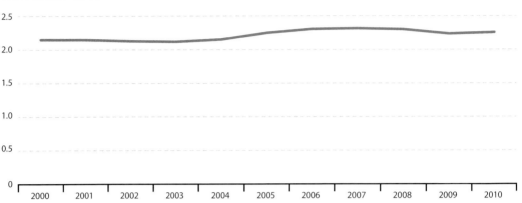

(¹) Nights spent by residents and non-residents; estimates made for the purpose of this publication.

Source: Eurostat (online data codes: tour_occ_ninat and tour_occ_nim)

Table 7.5.3: Top 10 Member States of origin for outbound holidays, 2010
(1 000 nights spent abroad by residents of the country)

		Nights abroad	Share (%)
	EU-27 (¹)	2 315 286	100.0
	Top 10	2 024 175	87.4
1	Germany	640 570	27.7
2	United Kingdom (²)	504 290	21.8
3	France (²)	192 575	8.3
4	Italy (³)	184 210	8.0
5	Netherlands	158 442	6.8
6	Spain (²)	88 028	3.8
7	Belgium	80 395	3.5
8	Sweden (³)	67 961	2.9
9	Austria	59 053	2.6
10	Poland	48 649	2.1

(¹) Estimate made for the purpose of this publication, based on annual and quarterly data.
(²) Estimate based on quarterly data.
(³) 2009.

Source: Eurostat (online data codes: tour_dem_tnw and tour_dem_tnq)

Figure 7.5.2: Country of origin for outbound holidays, 2010
(average nights spent abroad per inhabitant)

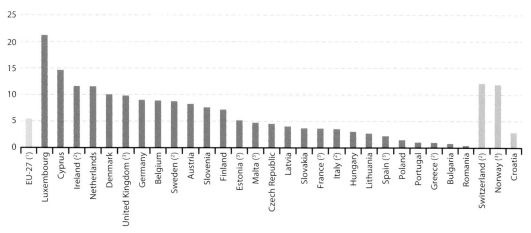

(¹) Estimate made for the purpose of this publication, using the latest available data for the Member States.
(²) 2009.
(³) Estimate based on quarterly data.

Source: Eurostat (online data codes: tour_dem_tnw, tour_dem_tnq and tps00001)

Figure 7.5.3: Tourism destinations – nights spent in collective tourist accommodation, 2010 (¹)
(1 000 nights spent in the country by non-residents)

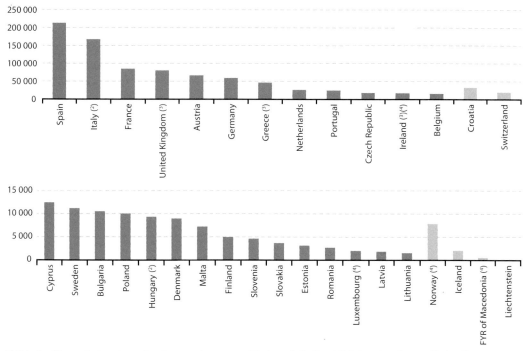

(¹) Note the differences in the scales employed between the two parts of the figure. (²) Provisional. (³) Estimate based on monthly data. (⁴) 2009.

Source: Eurostat (online data codes: tour_occ_ninat and tour_occ_nim)

Table 7.5.4: Top 10 tourism destinations – nights spent in collective tourist accommodation, 2010 (1 000 nights spent in the country by non-residents)

		Nights in country	Share (%)
	EU-27 (¹)	919 522	100.0
	Top 10	790 808	86.0
1	Spain	213 350	23.2
2	Italy	167 839	18.3
3	France	85 191	9.3
4	United Kingdom (²)	80 373	8.7
5	Austria	66 838	7.3
6	Germany	59 659	6.5
7	Greece (²)	47 007	5.1
8	Netherlands	26 800	2.9
9	Portugal	25 386	2.8
10	Czech Republic	18 366	2.0

(¹) Estimate made for the purpose of this publication, based on annual and monthly data.
(²) Estimate based on monthly data.

Source: Eurostat (online data codes: tour_occ_ninat and tour_occ_nim)

Figure 7.5.4: Tourism intensity, 2010
(nights spent by residents and non-residents in collective tourist accommodation per inhabitant)

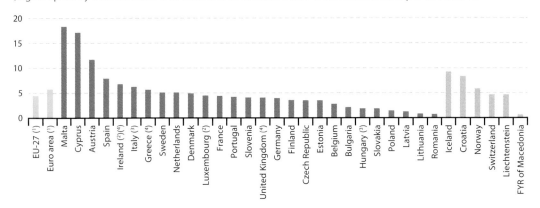

(¹) Estimate made for the purpose of this publication, based on annual and quarterly data.
(²) 2009.
(³) Provisional.
(⁴) Estimate based on monthly data.

Source: Eurostat (online data codes: tour_occ_ninat, tour_occ_nim and tps00001)

Table 7.5.5: Tourism receipts and expenditure from travel, 2000-2010

	Receipts				Expenditure			
	(EUR million)			Relative to GDP, 2010 (%)	(EUR million)			Relative to GDP, 2010 (%)
	2000	2005	2010 (¹)		2000	2005	2010 (¹)	
EU-27 (²)	:	65 737	73 028	0.6	:	84 943	87 737	0.7
Belgium	:	7 934	7 761	2.2	:	12 047	14 151	4.0
Bulgaria	1 163	1 956	2 747	7.6	582	1 053	931	2.6
Czech Republic	3 232	3 769	5 043	3.4	1 387	1 940	3 074	2.1
Denmark	4 008	4 248	4 135	1.8	5 076	5 526	6 532	2.8
Germany	20 007	23 449	26 156	1.1	57 427	59 766	58 596	2.4
Estonia	549	784	815	5.7	221	353	460	3.2
Ireland	2 886	3 863	3 075	2.0	2 858	4 898	5 826	3.7
Greece	10 068	11 037	9 611	4.2	4 947	2 446	2 156	0.9
Spain	32 446	38 558	39 621	3.8	6 454	12 125	12 664	1.2
France	33 301	35 385	34 939	1.8	19 227	25 582	29 686	1.5
Italy	29 905	28 400	29 244	1.9	17 010	17 960	20 490	1.3
Cyprus	2 101	1 875	1 655	9.5	448	750	873	5.0
Latvia	143	279	480	2.7	268	475	485	2.7
Lithuania	424	742	778	2.8	274	599	594	2.2
Luxembourg	:	2 904	3 109	7.7	:	2 398	2 698	6.7
Hungary	3 758	3 300	4 049	4.2	1 508	1 908	2 241	2.3
Malta	640	611	813	13.2	218	216	348	5.6
Netherlands (³)	7 813	8 421	9 718	1.7	13 241	12 996	14 807	2.5
Austria	10 593	12 904	14 078	4.9	6 767	7 506	7 717	2.7
Poland	6 183	5 056	7 157	2.0	3 606	4 485	6 181	1.7
Portugal	5 720	6 199	7 610	4.4	2 422	2 454	2 953	1.7
Romania	391	849	859	0.7	463	747	1 239	1.0
Slovenia	1 039	1 451	1 743	4.9	554	708	905	2.6
Slovakia	519	972	1 729	2.6	372	680	1 534	2.3
Finland (³)	1 528	1 757	2 189	1.2	2 009	2 461	3 201	1.8
Sweden	4 414	5 970	8 392	2.4	8 718	8 672	10 149	2.9
United Kingdom	23 702	24 672	23 038	1.4	41 650	47 940	36 829	2.2
Iceland (⁴)	246	332	402	4.6	509	788	383	4.4
Norway (⁴)	2 110	2 680	2 909	1.1	4 812	8 187	8 871	3.3
Switzerland (⁴)	:	8 105	9 937	2.8	:	7 141	7 619	2.1
Croatia (⁴)	:	5 961	6 367	13.9	:	604	723	1.6
Turkey (³)	8 268	14 591	15 847	2.9	1 855	2 309	3 650	0.7
Japan (⁴)	3 656	10 018	7 397	0.2	34 548	30 229	18 051	0.5
United States (³)	106 045	82 043	101 907	0.9	72 589	58 934	62 712	0.6

(¹) Provisional data.
(²) Extra EU-27 flows.
(³) 2010 estimated using quarterly data.
(⁴) 2009 instead of 2010.

Source: Eurostat (online data codes: bop_its_deth, bop_its_det, bop_q_c and nama_gdp_c)

7.6 Information society

This subchapter presents recent statistical data on many different aspects of the information society in the European Union (EU). Progress in the development of the information society is regarded as critical to improve the competitiveness of EU industry and, more generally, to meet the demands of society and the EU economy.

Information and communication technologies (ICT) affect people's everyday lives in many ways, both at work and in the home, and EU policies in this area range from regulating entire sectors to trying to protect an individual's privacy.

Main statistical findings

Households and individuals

During the last decade, ICT have become widely available to the general public, both in terms of accessibility as well as cost. A boundary was crossed in 2007, when a majority (54 %) of households in the EU-27 had internet access. This proportion continued to increase and in 2010 reached 70 %. The highest proportion (91 %) of households with internet access in 2010 was recorded in the Netherlands, the lowest (33 %) in Bulgaria (see Figure 7.6.1). Widespread and affordable broadband access is one of the means of promoting a knowledge-based and informed society. In all Member States broadband was by far the most common form of internet access, used by 61 % of all EU-27 households in 2010, approximately double the share in 2006 – see Figure 7.6.2.

Around seven out of every ten individuals in the EU-27, aged between 16 and 74 years, had used a computer in the first quarter of 2010 while a similar proportion used the internet. The proportion of individuals using a computer and using the internet in 2010 rose to 90 % in Sweden, the Netherlands and Luxembourg, and was around this level in Denmark and Finland. However, less than half of individuals used computers and the internet in Greece, Bulgaria and particularly in Romania. Well over half (56 %) of the individuals in the EU-27 used the internet for finding information on goods or

services in 2010. Large increases of 9 percentage points or more in this type of use of the internet were recorded in 2010 in several Member States that had generally low internet usage, Bulgaria and Romania in particular, and also Slovakia and Poland (see Table 7.6.1).

Among internet users, in other words, those individuals within the EU-27 using the internet in the three months before the ICT survey, more than nine in ten (92 %) accessed the internet from home, as shown in Table 7.6.2. By comparison, less than half of this subset of the population accessed the internet at work (41 %), which in turn was around double the proportion accessing the internet from a friend's, neighbour's or relative's house (23 %). Of the 69 % of individuals in the EU-27 that used the internet in 2010, more than three quarters accessed the internet on a daily or almost daily basis.

Two fifths (40 %) of individuals in the EU-27 ordered goods or services over the internet for private use during the year prior to the 2010 survey, an increase of 3 percentage points compared with the year before (see Figure 7.6.4). This proportion was around two thirds in Denmark, the Netherlands, the United Kingdom and Sweden, whereas no more than one in 20 persons made orders over the internet in Bulgaria or Romania.

Figures 7.6.5 to 7.6.7 provide an analysis of security-related issues faced by internet users. More than a half (56 %) of all internet users in the EU-27 in 2010 had (to their knowledge) received spam e-mails, a share that was as low as 18 % in Ireland but as high as 70 % in France; it was higher still (73 %) in Iceland. Nearly one third of users had been confronted by a computer virus (or similar infection), the average across the EU-27 being 31 %. In Bulgaria and Malta did even at least half of all internet users report having experienced such an infection; a much higher proportion (68 %) was reported in the former Yugoslav Republic of Macedonia. More than four fifths (84 %) of internet users in the EU-27 had an IT security software or tool installed, and more than three fifths (63 %) reported that they regularly updated their security products; backing-up data

or making safety copies of files was less common – see Figure 7.6.6. Around half (49 %) of all internet users reported having at least once avoided an activity on the internet due to security concerns (see Figure 7.6.7); the most common of these was to avoid providing personal information on social networking sites, followed by e-commerce (buying goods or services over the internet) and e-banking.

Enterprises

Only about one in 20 of all enterprises in the EU-27 did not have internet access as of the beginning of 2010 (see Figure 7.6.8). Around two thirds (67 %) of all enterprises in the EU-27 had their own website and this proportion rose to 92 % among large enterprises. By 2010, the proportion of enterprises with internet access exceeded 90 % in all Member States except Romania, Bulgaria and Cyprus, while in each of the Member States except Romania, Bulgaria and Latvia more than half of all enterprises had a website (Table 7.6.3).

In total, e-commerce accounted for around 14 % of turnover among enterprises with at least ten persons employed in the EU-27, a share that ranged from 1 % in Cyprus to 24 % in Ireland in 2009 (see Figure 7.6.9). Some 13 % of enterprises in the EU-27 received orders online during 2009, which was about half the proportion of enterprises (27 %) that made purchases online (see Figure 7.6.11). The percentage of enterprises selling online was highest in the accommodation sector (44 %), whereas the highest proportion of enterprises making online purchases was recorded for information and communication services (51 %).

By January 2010, 26 % of enterprises in the EU-27 had a formally defined ICT security policy with a plan for regular review; this share rose to over 50 % among those enterprises whose principal activity was information and communication activities. Large enterprises were more than three times as likely to have such a security policy as small ones – see Figure 7.6.12. Among the Member States, the highest shares of enterprises with a formally defined ICT security policy were recorded in Sweden and Denmark where more than two fifths of enterprises had such policies, as was also the case in Norway.

Enterprises adopt various approaches to raise awareness among employees of ICT security policy and the associated risks – see Figures 7.6.14 and 7.6.15. Voluntary training or use of generally available information was the approach most commonly reported by enterprises and around three quarters of enterprises had adopted this approach in Cyprus and Finland. Around half (48 %) of all enterprises in the EU-27 reported having used at least one of the three approaches surveyed with this share ranging from 18 % in Poland to 84 % in Cyprus.

ICT-related security incidents concern the core elements of information security, integrity, confidentiality and availability of data and IT systems. Type 1 incidents concern the unavailability of ICT services or the destruction or corruption of data due to hardware or software failures. In 2009, 16 % of enterprises in the EU-27 had experienced some kind of ICT-related security incident and 12 % had experienced a type-1 incident. Enterprises in Portugal were by far the most likely to indicate that they had experienced an ICT-related security incident, this being the case in two fifths of Portuguese enterprises in 2009 – see Figure 7.6.16.

In January 2010, the use of strong password authentication and offsite data backup were the most commonly reported procedures used by enterprises for internal ICT security, with each of these approaches used by 47 % of enterprises in the EU-27.

Data sources and availability

Statisticians are well aware of the challenges posed by rapid technological change in areas related to the internet and other new applications of ICTs. As such, there has been a considerable degree of evolution in this area, with statistical tools being adapted to satisfy new demands for data. Statistics within this domain are reassessed on an annual basis in order to meet user needs and reflect the rapid pace of technological change.

This approach is reflected in Eurostat's survey on ICT usage in households and by individuals and survey on ICT usage in enterprises. These annual surveys are used to benchmark ICT-driven developments, both by following developments for core variables

over time and by looking in greater depth at other aspects at a specific point in time. While the surveys initially concentrated on access and connectivity issues, their scope has subsequently been extended to cover a variety of subjects (for example, e-government and e-commerce) and socio-economic breakdowns, such as regional diversity, sex specificity, age, educational differences and the individual's employment situation in the household survey, or a breakdown by enterprise size (small, medium-sized, large) in the enterprise survey. The scope of the surveys with respect to different technologies is also adapted so as to cover new product groups and means of delivering communication technologies to end-users (enterprises and households).

Households and individuals

The household survey covers those households having at least one member in the age group 16 to 74 years old. Internet access of households refers to the percentage of households that have an internet access, so that anyone in the household could use the internet at home, if so desired, even simply to send an e-mail. Internet users are defined as all individuals aged 16-74 who had used the internet in the three months prior to the survey. Regular internet users are individuals who used the internet, on average, at least once a week in the three months prior to the survey. The reference period was the first quarter of 2010; the survey period was the second quarter in most countries.

The technologies most commonly used to access the internet are divided between broadband and dial-up access over a normal or an ISDN telephone line. Broadband includes digital subscriber lines (DSL) and uses technology that transports data at high speeds. Broadband lines are defined as having a capacity equal to or higher than 144 kbit/s.

A computer is defined as a personal computer powered by one of the major operating systems (Macintosh, Linux or Microsoft); handheld computers or palmtops (PDAs) are also included.

The ordering of goods and services by individuals includes confirmed reservations for accommodation, purchasing financial investments, participation in lotteries and betting, internet auctions, as well

as information services from the internet that are directly paid for. Goods and services that are obtained via the internet for free are excluded. Orders made by manually written e-mails are also excluded.

A special module on internet security was included in the 2010 ICT survey, asking individuals who had used the internet in the previous 12 months about their experience of security threats and their behaviour to avoid security incidences. The latter looked, for example, at viruses (and other infections such as worms or Trojan horses) and unsolicited e-mails (spam). Among other precautions, the use of security software (such as virus checking or anti-spyware programs) was included, as was backing-up by making copies of computer files to an external storage device such as a CD, DVD, external hard disk, USB stick or disk space on a server.

Enterprises

The survey on ICT usage and e-commerce in enterprises covers enterprises that have at least ten persons employed. The activity coverage is restricted to those enterprises whose principal activity is within manufacturing, electricity, gas, steam and water supply, sewerage and waste management, construction, wholesale and retail trade, repair of motor vehicles and motorcycles, transportation and storage, accommodation and food service activities, information and communication, real estate, professional, scientific and technical activities, administrative and support activities and repair of computers and communication equipment (NACE Rev. 2 Sections C to N excluding Division 75 plus Group 95.1); the financial and insurance activities (Section K) are covered by the survey but are excluded from the analysis presented here. A distinction is made according to the size of enterprises in terms of persons employed into small (10-49 persons employed), medium-sized (50-249) and large (250 or more persons employed) enterprises.

ICT usage data are grouped according to the year in which the survey was conducted; most data refer to the situation in January whereas some others (like e-commerce) refer to the calendar year prior to the survey year.

Context

ICT are considered as critical for improving the competitiveness of European industry and, more generally, to meet the demands of society and the economy. ICT affects many aspects of everyday lives, at both work and in the home, and EU policies in this area range from the regulation of entire sectors to the protection of an individual's privacy.

Broadband technologies are considered to be important when measuring access to and use of the internet, as they offer users the possibility to rapidly transfer large volumes of data and keep access lines open. The take-up of broadband is considered to be a key indicator within the domain of ICT policy-making. Widespread access to the internet via broadband is seen as essential for the development of advanced services on the internet, such as e-business, e-government or e-learning. Digital subscriber lines (DSL) remain the main form of delivery for broadband technology, although alternatives, such as the use of cable, satellite, fibre optics and wireless local loops are becoming more widespread.

Until 2010 the EU policy framework for ICT was the i2010 initiative called 'A European information

society for growth and employment' (COM(2005) 229 final) which sought to boost efficiency throughout the EU economy by means of the wider use of ICT. Having undergone a mid-term review, an updated i2010 strategy was presented in April 2008, addressing key challenges for the period 2008-2010.

In May 2010 the European Commission adopted its Communication concerning 'A digital agenda for Europe' (COM(2010) 245 final), a strategy for a flourishing digital economy by 2020. It outlines policies and actions aimed at maximising the benefit of the digital era to all sections of society and economy. The agenda focuses on seven priority areas for action: creating a digital single market, greater interoperability, boosting internet trust and security, providing much faster internet access, encouraging investment in research and development, enhancing digital literacy skills and inclusion, and applying ICT to address challenges facing society like climate change and the ageing population. Examples of benefits include easier electronic payments and invoicing, rapid deployment of telemedicine and energy efficient lighting. The Digital Agenda for Europe is one of the seven flagship initiatives under the Europe 2020 strategy for smart, sustainable and inclusive growth.

Figure 7.6.1: Internet access of households, 2009-2010
(% of all households)

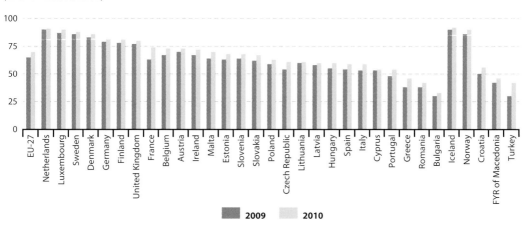

Source: Eurostat (online data code: tsiir040)

Figure 7.6.2: Internet access and broadband internet connections by households, EU-27, 2006-2010 (% of all households)

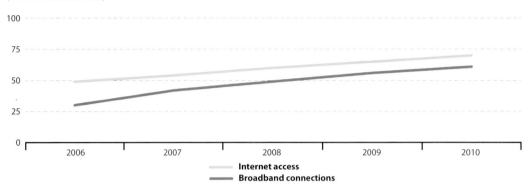

Source: Eurostat (online data codes: isoc_pibi_hiac and isoc_pibi_hba)

Table 7.6.1: Use of ICTs and use of online services, 2008-2010
(% of individuals aged 16 to 74)

	Computer use			Internet use			Used internet for finding information on goods or services		
	2008	2009	2010	2008	2009	2010	2008	2009	2010
EU-27	66	68	71	62	65	69	50	51	56
Euro area (EA-16) (¹)	66	68	72	63	65	70	52	55	59
Belgium	71	76	79	69	75	78	58	59	62
Bulgaria	40	44	45	35	42	43	22	17	26
Czech Republic	63	64	69	58	60	66	45	50	53
Denmark	86	87	89	84	86	88	73	74	78
Germany	80	81	83	75	77	80	66	69	72
Estonia	66	71	75	66	71	74	53	54	61
Ireland	67	68	70	63	65	67	46	54	57
Greece	44	47	48	38	42	44	31	33	36
Spain	61	63	67	57	60	64	46	47	54
France	71	72	79	68	69	79	57	60	65
Italy	46	49	53	42	46	51	30	33	35
Cyprus	47	53	57	39	48	52	32	39	47
Latvia	63	65	67	61	64	66	49	50	57
Lithuania	56	60	62	53	58	60	37	44	48
Luxembourg	83	88	90	81	86	90	69	75	78
Hungary	63	63	64	59	59	62	49	48	55
Malta	51	60	64	49	58	62	42	48	52
Netherlands	88	90	91	87	89	90	76	79	82
Austria	76	75	77	71	72	74	51	54	58
Poland	55	59	62	49	56	59	33	29	39
Portugal	46	51	55	42	46	51	34	40	44
Romania	35	42	41	29	33	36	17	12	26
Slovenia	60	65	70	56	62	68	48	49	57
Slovakia	72	74	78	66	70	76	49	50	62
Finland	84	84	88	83	82	86	73	73	74
Sweden	89	91	92	88	90	91	75	77	82
United Kingdom	80	84	86	76	82	83	64	64	63
Iceland	92	93	95	91	93	93	78	80	84
Norway	90	91	93	89	91	93	80	83	82
Croatia	46	50	56	42	47	54	33	33	43
FYR of Macedonia	50	55	56	42	50	52	22	26	30
Turkey	34	36	39	32	34	38	14	18	21

(¹) 2008: EA-15 instead of EA-16.

Source: Eurostat (online data codes: isoc_ci_cfp_cu, isoc_ci_ifp_iu and isoc_ci_ac_i)

Table 7.6.2: Place of internet use, 2010
(% of individuals aged 16 to 74 who used the internet in the three months prior to the survey)

	Home	Place of work (other than home)	Place of education	Neighbour, friend or relative's house	Other place
EU-27	92	41	12	23	14
Euro area (EA-16)	92	42	11	25	15
Belgium	94	41	12	20	9
Bulgaria	89	34	14	9	10
Czech Republic	92	40	16	19	3
Denmark	96	52	16	24	16
Germany	94	41	7	21	12
Estonia	92	37	15	17	9
Ireland	91	30	10	4	3
Greece	86	37	9	13	11
Spain	85	41	13	26	24
France	94	40	10	37	13
Italy	87	41	10	22	19
Cyprus	85	44	15	18	13
Latvia	85	31	15	34	21
Lithuania	90	35	19	19	10
Luxembourg	98	49	12	19	23
Hungary	91	35	18	21	10
Malta	95	36	9	9	6
Netherlands	98	52	15	21	8
Austria	92	45	13	15	11
Poland	91	32	16	19	9
Portugal	89	40	17	27	19
Romania	85	31	17	10	5
Slovenia	91	48	16	30	21
Slovakia	89	49	16	20	10
Finland	96	54	21	47	29
Sweden	97	58	14	33	23
United Kingdom	95	42	13	17	12
Iceland	97	58	28	52	15
Norway	97	61	15	28	20
Croatia	89	36	13	18	13
FYR of Macedonia	86	23	17	17	20
Turkey	63	32	7	16	21

Source: Eurostat (online data code: isoc_pibi_pai)

Figure 7.6.3: Frequency of internet use, 2010
(% of individuals aged 16 to 74)

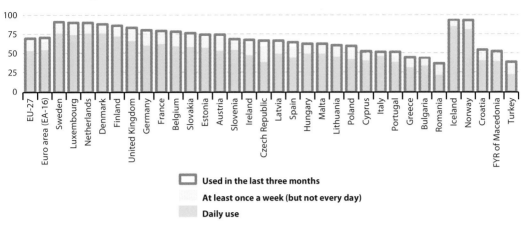

- Used in the last three months
- At least once a week (but not every day)
- Daily use

Source: Eurostat (online data codes: isoc_ci_ifp_iu and isoc_ci_ifp_fu)

Figure 7.6.4: Individuals who ordered goods or services over the internet for private use in the 12 months prior to the survey, 2009-2010
(% of individuals aged 16 to 74)

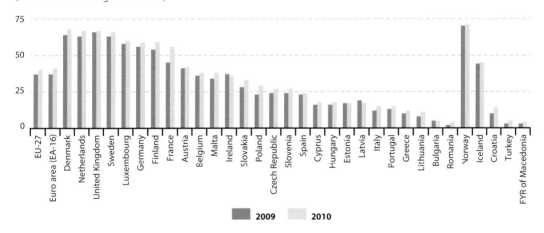

- 2009
- 2010

Source: Eurostat (online data code: isoc_ec_ibuy)

Figure 7.6.5: Security incidences (virus, spam) experienced by internet users in the 12 months prior to the survey, 2010
(% of individuals having used the internet in the 12 months prior to the survey)

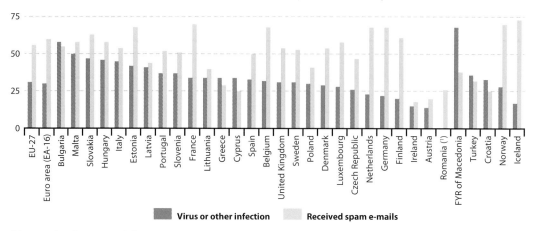

(¹) Virus or other infection, not available.

Source: Eurostat (online data code: isoc_cisci_pb)

Figure 7.6.6: Precautions taken by internet users to protect private computer and data, EU-27, 2010
(% of individuals having used the internet in the 12 months prior to the survey)

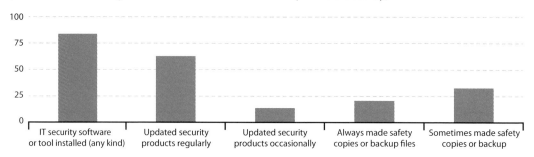

Source: Eurostat (online data codes: isoc_cisci_sw and isoc_cisci_f)

Figure 7.6.7: Activities avoided at least once in the 12 months prior to the survey by internet users due to security concerns, EU-27, 2010
(% of individuals having used the internet in the 12 months prior to the survey)

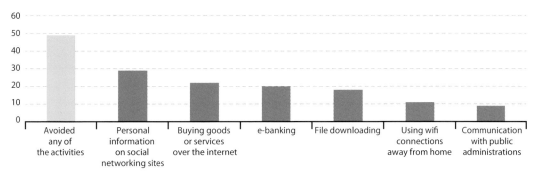

Source: Eurostat (online data code: isoc_cisci_ax)

Figure 7.6.8: Enterprise use of information technology, by size-class, EU-27, January 2010
(% of enterprises)

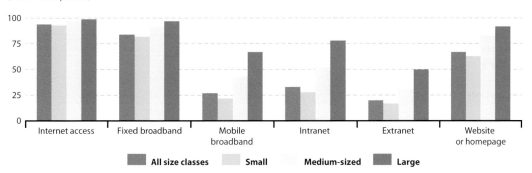

Source: Eurostat (online data codes: isoc_ci_in_en2, isoc_ci_it_en2 and isoc_ci_cd_en2)

Table 7.6.3: Enterprise use of information technology, January 2010
(% of enterprises)

	Internet access	Fixed broadband connection	Mobile broadband connection				Website or home-page
			All size classes	Small	Medium-sized	Large	
EU-27	94	84	27	22	43	67	67
Euro area (EA-16)	96	88	27	22	45	68	67
Belgium	97	89	29	24	49	70	78
Bulgaria	85	61	9	7	14	34	37
Czech Republic	95	85	18	13	35	51	74
Denmark	97	84	43	39	63	81	88
Germany	97	88	22	16	38	63	81
Estonia	96	87	9	7	13	36	70
Ireland	92	84	36	31	52	73	68
Greece	90	80	6	5	14	20	58
Spain	97	95	35	31	57	75	62
France	97	93	28	23	46	68	58
Italy	94	83	19	16	38	66	61
Cyprus	88	85	11	9	19	39	52
Latvia	91	66	12	10	19	41	48
Lithuania	96	78	20	16	32	62	65
Luxembourg	96	87	20	17	26	57	70
Hungary	90	78	22	18	36	57	57
Malta	94	91	28	24	41	62	66
Netherlands	98	90	28	23	47	68	81
Austria	97	75	46	42	65	91	80
Poland	96	66	21	16	32	64	65
Portugal	94	83	25	20	48	75	52
Romania	79	49	8	6	14	33	35
Slovenia	97	85	31	26	47	73	73
Slovakia	98	71	36	32	46	67	74
Finland	100	93	68	64	88	95	87
Sweden	96	88	55	50	76	91	89
United Kingdom	91	87	36	30	58	79	76
Iceland	98	95	43	36	74	78	77
Norway	97	84	39	35	61	84	78
Croatia	95	76	32	29	41	71	61
FYR of Macedonia	84	76	11	10	17	25	43
Turkey	91	89	16	13	25	41	53

Source: Eurostat (online data codes: isoc_ci_in_en2, isoc_ci_it_en2 and isoc_ci_cd_en2)

Figure 7.6.9: Enterprise turnover from e-commerce, 2009 (¹)
(% of total turnover)

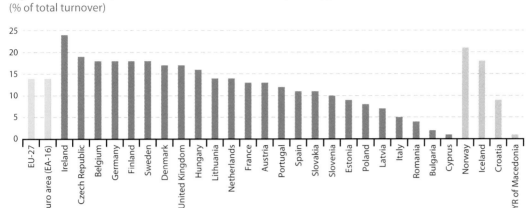

(¹) Greece, Luxembourg and Malta, not available.

Source: Eurostat (online data code: isoc_ec_evaln2)

Figure 7.6.10: Enterprises selling online (at least 1 % of turnover from electronic sales), EU-27, 2008-2009
(% of enterprises)

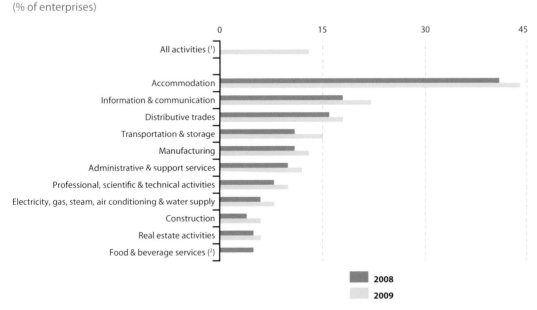

(¹) 2008, not available.
(²) 2009, not available.

Source: Eurostat (online data code: isoc_ec_eseln2)

Figure 7.6.11: Enterprises selling and buying online (at least 1 %) or having a website or homepage, EU-27, 2009
(% of enterprises)

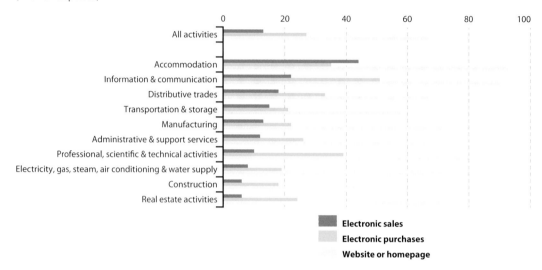

Source: Eurostat (online data codes: isoc_ec_eseln2, isoc_ec_ebuyn2 and isoc_ci_cd_en2)

Figure 7.6.12: Enterprises having a formally defined ICT security policy with a plan of regular review, EU-27, January 2010
(% of enterprises)

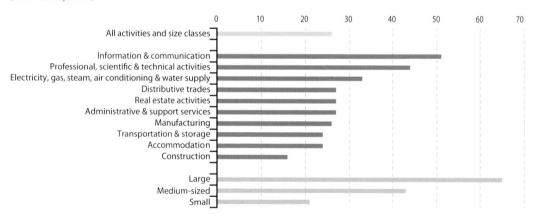

Source: Eurostat (online data code: isoc_cisce_ra)

Figure 7.6.13: Enterprises having a formally defined ICT security policy with a plan of regular review and enterprises that addressed all security risks, January 2010
(% of enterprises)

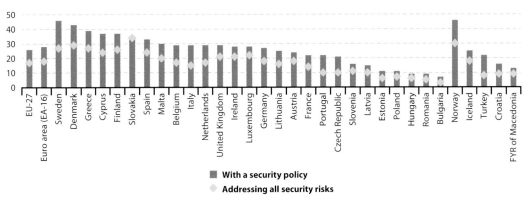

Source: Eurostat (online data code: isoc_cisce_ra)

Figure 7.6.14: Enterprises raising awareness among staff of their obligations in ICT security related issues, EU-27, January 2010
(% of enterprises)

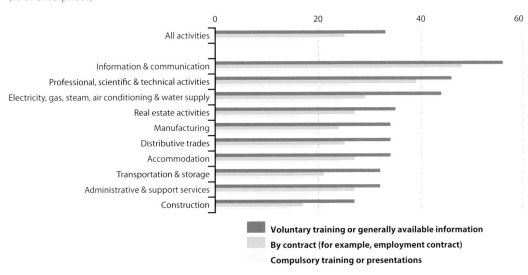

Source: Eurostat (online data code: isoc_cisce_ra)

Figure 7.6.15: Approaches adopted by enterprises to raise awareness among staff of their obligations in ICT security related issues, January 2010 (¹)
(% of enterprises)

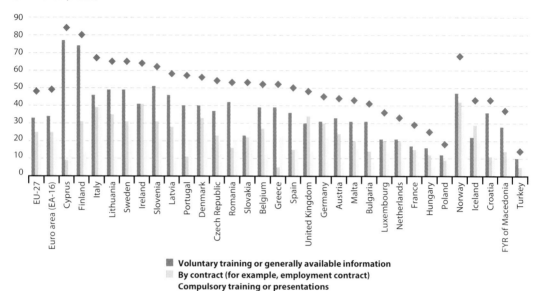

- ▨ Voluntary training or generally available information
- ▨ By contract (for example, employment contract)
- Compulsory training or presentations
- ◆ Any of the three approaches

(¹) Estonia, not available.

Source: Eurostat (online data code: isoc_cisce_ra)

Figure 7.6.16: ICT security incidents affecting the ICT systems of enterprises , 2009 (¹)
(% of enterprises)

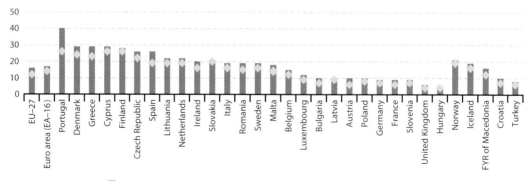

- ▨ Any reported incident
- ◈ Type 1 incidents: unavailability of ICT services, destruction or corruption of data due to hardware or software failures

(¹) Estonia, not available.

Source: Eurostat (online data code: isoc_cisce_ic)

Figure 7.6.17: Enterprises having experienced at least one ICT related security incident which affected their ICT systems, EU-27, 2009
(% of enterprises)

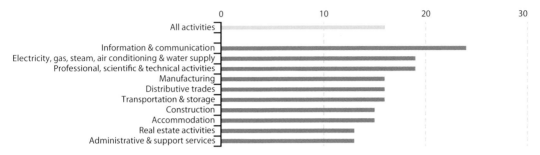

Source: Eurostat (online data code: isoc_cisce_ic)

Figure 7.6.18: Enterprises using internal security facilities or procedures, EU-27, January 2010
(% of enterprises)

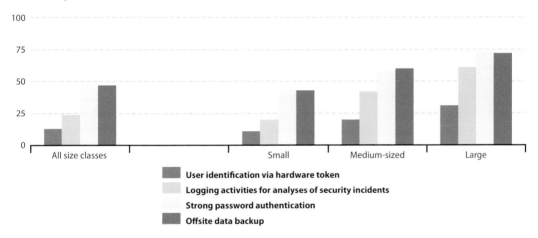

Source: Eurostat (online data code: isoc_cisce_fp)

7.7 Telecommunications

This subchapter presents data on markets and prices for telecommunication services in the European Union (EU). Telecommunication networks and services are the backbone of Europe's developing information society. Individuals, enterprises and public organisations alike depend increasingly on convenient, reliable telecommunication networks and services. During recent years a shift in the importance of various services can be noted, from wired networks to mobile networks, and from voice services to data services.

Historically, European telecommunications have been characterised by public service monopoly providers, often run in conjunction with postal services. Liberalisation of this market began in the first half of the 1980s and, at first, concerned only value added services or business users, as basic services were left in the hands of monopoly providers. By 1998, telecommunications were, in principle, fully liberalised across the EU leading to considerable reductions in prices. For Member States joining the EU in 2004 and 2007, the liberalisation process was completed at a later date.

Main statistical findings

Telecommunications expenditure accounted for 2.8 % of gross domestic product (GDP) in the EU-27 in 2010, compared with 3.3 % in the United States and 3.5 % in Japan (both 2008) – see Figure 7.7.1. The highest relative levels of expenditure were generally recorded in those Member States that joined the EU in 2004 or 2007 (data for Cyprus and Malta are not available), in particular in Estonia and Bulgaria.

The share of the total telecommunications market accounted for by fixed-line voice operations has shrunk. Growth has been concentrated in mobile telephony markets and other data services. In 2008, the incumbent ex-monopoly service providers in fixed telecommunications markets accounted for more than two fifths of international calls across those Member States for which data are available (see Table 7.7.1), a share that reached 85 % in Malta.

The share of the leading operator in the mobile market was relatively low at 38 % in the EU-27 in 2010, varying between 31 % in Poland and 76 % in Cyprus.

The average number of mobile phone subscriptions per 100 inhabitants stood at 125 in the EU-27 in 2009 (see Figure 7.7.2). It surpassed parity (100) in 24 of the Member States, where there were more subscriptions than inhabitants; the Member States where rates were below 100 subscriptions per 100 inhabitants were Austria, France and Latvia.

Total turnover in value terms is based on sales from all telecommunication services, including leased lines, fixed network services, cellular mobile telecommunication services, interconnection services, and internet service provision. In nearly all Member States (for which data are available) turnover from mobile services exceeded that from fixed network services in 2009, the main exception being Belgium (see Table 7.7.2).

The price of telecommunications fell between 2000 and 2010 in many Member States (see Table 7.7.3). Price reductions were most apparent for national long-distance calls and international calls (represented here by calls to the United States). Across the EU, the average price of a national long-distance call almost halved between 2000 and 2010, with most of this reduction occurring by 2005, as the average price fell 5 % between 2005 and 2010. The price fall between 2005 and 2010 for an international call was larger, down 19 %, whereas the price of local calls increased by 17 %.

The largest increase (in percentage terms) in the price of local calls between 2005 and 2010 was recorded in the United Kingdom, where the price more than doubled, while double-digit percentage increases were also recorded in eight other Member States. In contrast, Denmark recorded the biggest decrease in the price of local calls, down 65 %. In the majority of Member States there was a remarkable decrease of prices for international calls between 2000 and 2010; the decrease was less dynamic during the second half of the decade.

A convergence in prices for local and national long-distance calls between 2000 and 2010 was notable. Between 2000 and 2005 there was strong convergence between Member States in prices for international calls. This was followed by a slight divergence between 2005 and 2010.

Prices of local, national long-distance or international calls varied greatly across the EU Member States in 2010. Local calls were most expensive in the United Kingdom, national long-distance calls in Slovakia and Italy, while the price of international calls was highest in Latvia. The cheapest tariffs for local calls were in Denmark, Bulgaria and Cyprus, while the cheapest national long-distance calls were in Denmark and Cyprus. For international calls (to the United States), the cheapest calls, by far, were from Germany.

Data sources and availability

Data on turnover, mobile phone subscriptions and the average number of SMS come from Eurostat's collection of telecommunications statistics. The data were provided by the national statistical institutes of the EU Member States collecting information from the relevant regulatory authorities.

Indicators presented in relation to market share refer to fixed-line telecommunications and mobile telephony. The incumbent service provider for fixed-line telephony is defined as the enterprise active in the market just before liberalisation.

Indicators relating to the mobile market refer to the number of subscriptions to public cellular mobile telecommunication systems and also include active pre-paid cards. Note that many people have multiple mobile subscriptions, for example, for private and work use, or for use in different countries.

SMS messages are short-message services, traditionally sent between mobile phones, but also between a range of other SMS-enabled devices and online web services.

Data on expenditure for telecommunications cover hardware, equipment, software and other services. The data are not collected by Eurostat; further methodological information is available from the website of the European Information Technology Observatory (EITO).

Telecommunications prices are based on the price (including VAT) in euro of a 10-minute call at 11 a.m. on a weekday in August up to 2005 and September from 2006 onwards, based on normal rates. Three markets are presented, namely a local call (3 km), a national long-distance call (200 km) and an international call (to the United States). The data are not collected by Eurostat; further methodological information is available from the Teligen website.

Context

Telecommunication networks and services are the backbone of Europe's information society. Individuals, enterprises and public organisations alike have come to depend increasingly on convenient, reliable networks and services.

In recent years, the liberalisation of telecommunication markets has led to considerable reductions in prices and a wider range of services being provided. This may, in part, reflect the introduction of competition into a number of markets that were previously the domain of incumbent monopoly suppliers. In addition, it may also reflect technological change and increased capacity, which have made it possible to communicate not only by voice, but also over the internet or via messaging services. Market regulation has nonetheless continued, and the European Commission oversees this market to ensure that consumers benefit. Regulators continue to monitor the significant market power of former monopoly providers, ensure universal service provision and protect consumers. In particular, the European Commission works to ensure inclusive access to telecommunication services for all social groups.

The regulatory framework for electronic communications in the EU was updated in 2009 to take account of developments in this fast-moving field: major developments since the 2002 framework was agreed include the growth in voice-over-internet (VOIP) telephony and the uptake of television services through broadband lines. The framework covers all forms of fixed and wireless telecoms, data

transmission and broadcasting. The revised legislation aims to enable people to benefit from better and cheaper communication services throughout the EU, whether they use mobile phones, fast broadband internet connections or cable-based (television) services. To achieve this, the revised legislation aims to:

- strengthen consumer rights;
- give consumers more choice by reinforcing competition between telecoms operators;
- promote investment in new infrastructure in particular by freeing radio spectrum for wireless broadband services;
- make communication networks more reliable and more secure.

On 30 June 2007, a new set of rules on mobile phone roaming charges entered into force. These foresee that people travelling within the EU are able to make phone calls across borders at more affordable and transparent prices than before. The so-called Roaming Regulation 717/2007 of 27 June 2007 put in place a set of maximum prices for phone calls made and received while abroad (Eurotariff). The European Commission and national regulators have closely monitored price developments for text messages and data services. In July 2009 revised rules were adopted in the Roaming Regulation 544/2009 that cut roaming prices for (voice) phone calls further and introduced new caps on the tariffs for SMS (Euro SMS tariff) that will apply until the end of June 2012. In July 2011 the European Commission proposed a further revision of this legislation which aims to give customers more choice, give alternative operators easier access to the roaming market and generally bring down prices for data roaming.

Figure 7.7.1: Communications expenditure, 2010 (^{1})
(% of GDP)

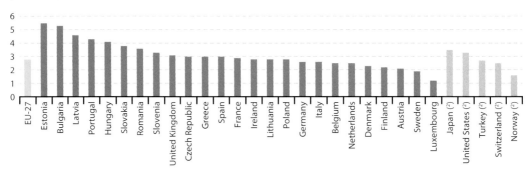

(^{1}) Cyprus and Malta, not available.
(^{2}) 2008.

Source: Eurostat (online data code: tsiir090), European Information Technology Observatory (EITO)

Table 7.7.1: Market share of incumbents in fixed telecommunications and leading operators in mobile telecommunications, 2007-2010
(% of total market)

	Fixed telecommunications: international calls		Leading operator in mobile telecommunications		
	2007	2008	2007	2008	2010
EU-27	:	:	40	39	38
Belgium	62	62	45	43	43
Bulgaria	86	82	53	49	52
Czech Republic	50	52	42	40	38
Denmark	:	:	40	46	41
Germany	:	:	37	36	33
Estonia	:	:	45	47	46
Ireland	56	54	45	42	41
Greece	74	:	38	43	54
Spain	68	55	46	45	44
France	57	56	43	44	41
Italy	44	47	40	39	33
Cyprus	79	69	89	85	76
Latvia	65	69	35	53	49
Lithuania	77	79	41	39	40
Luxembourg	:	:	57	54	51
Hungary	:	:	44	44	45
Malta	92	85	47	53	48
Netherlands	:	:	48	38	39
Austria	58	52	40	42	41
Poland	66	63	36	33	31
Portugal	:	:	46	48	44
Romania	69	62	44	45	43
Slovenia	79	75	67	72	56
Slovakia	89	80	51	55	48
Finland	:	:	41	40	38
Sweden	43	48	43	43	41
United Kingdom	48	44	24	25	34

Source: Eurostat (online data codes: tsier070 and tsier080), National Regulatory Authorities

Figure 7.7.2: Mobile phone subscriptions and the use of SMS, 2009

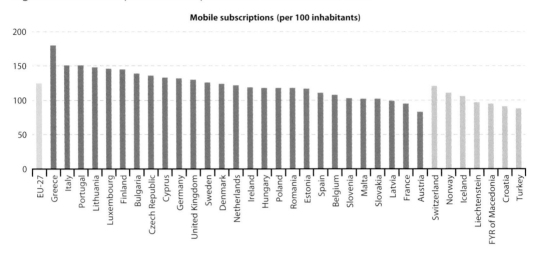

Mobile subscriptions (per 100 inhabitants)

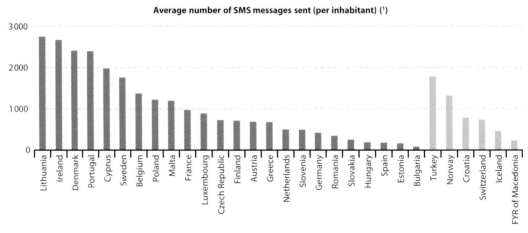

Average number of SMS messages sent (per inhabitant) (¹)

(¹) Italy, Latvia and the United Kingdom, not available; France, provisional; Norway, 2008.

Source: Eurostat (online data codes: tin00060, isoc_tc_sms and tps00001)

Table 7.7.2: Turnover from telecommunications, 2009 ([1])
(EUR million)

	Total turnover	of which:		
		Fixed network services	Cellular mobile services	Internet service provision
Belgium	10 145	6 041	4 104	:
Bulgaria	1 700	235	820	151
Czech Republic ([2])	5 071	1 809	3 059	739
Denmark	5 524	841	2 155	1 144
Germany	60 600	19 300	21 700	:
Estonia	718	263	262	100
Ireland	4 611	1 904	2 385	*482*
Greece ([3])	7 805	3 469	4 336	152
Spain	41 765	6 485	14 453	3 932
France	49 532	9 957	19 051	5 934
Italy	:	:	:	:
Cyprus ([4])	609	130	279	33
Latvia	:	:	:	:
Lithuania	835	103	326	119
Luxembourg	506	255	251	48
Hungary ([5])	3 451	591	1 590	506
Malta	249	75	132	0
Netherlands	14 013	5 109	7 176	:
Austria	5 300	1 062	3 286	780
Poland	:	:	:	:
Portugal	:	:	:	:
Romania ([6])	*4 791*	1 559	*2 433*	:
Slovenia	1 266	154	527	150
Slovakia	2 123	264	1 354	214
Finland	4 730	1 690	2 100	:
Sweden	8 080	1 449	2 095	954
United Kingdom	:	:	:	:
Iceland	250	75	97	12
Norway ([7])	3 852	816	1 919	754
Switzerland	*11 572*	*3 585*	*3 065*	:
Croatia	2 104	631	1 199	142
FYR of Macedonia	408	101	244	34
Turkey	9 557	3 560	5 997	1 128

([1]) Possibility of double-counting in the breakdown of total turnover.
([2]) Internet services, 2008.
([3]) Internet services, 2007.
([4]) Internet services, 2006.
([5]) Fixed network services, 2008.
([6]) Fixed network services, 2007.
([7]) 2008.

Source: Eurostat (online data code: isoc_tc_tur)

Table 7.7.3: Price of fixed telecommunications, 2000-2010 (¹)
(EUR per 10-minute call)

	Local calls			National long-distance calls			Calls to the United States		
	2000	2005	2010	2000	2005	2010	2000	2005	2010
EU-27	:	0.35	0.41	1.31	0.76	0.72	:	2.10	1.71
Belgium	0.49	0.57	0.63	1.74	0.57	0.63	5.95	1.98	2.17
Bulgaria	0.06	0.16	0.16	1.41	0.68	0.50	11.29	1.84	0.92
Czech Republic	0.55	0.64	0.65	1.66	1.30	0.65	:	2.36	2.34
Denmark	0.41	0.37	0.13	0.54	0.37	0.13	4.72	2.38	2.72
Germany	0.43	0.39	0.29	1.24	0.49	0.29	2.45	1.23	0.29
Estonia	0.14	0.25	0.25	0.71	0.25	0.25	10.26	2.56	2.31
Ireland	0.51	0.49	0.58	0.94	0.82	0.92	2.92	1.90	1.96
Greece	0.31	0.31	0.32	1.40	0.74	0.76	3.26	2.93	3.03
Spain	0.28	0.28	0.30	1.85	0.84	0.97	4.25	1.53	1.66
France	0.42	0.33	0.36	1.19	0.83	0.77	2.97	2.27	1.96
Italy	0.25	0.22	0.22	1.72	1.15	1.15	2.79	2.12	2.12
Cyprus	0.08	0.21	0.18	0.61	0.21	0.18	3.73	0.65	0.65
Latvia	0.35	0.35	0.36	1.01	1.01	1.04	5.81	5.83	5.98
Lithuania	0.26	0.39	0.39	1.07	0.79	0.79	11.96	4.06	4.12
Luxembourg	0.37	0.31	0.31	–	–	–	2.06	1.37	1.37
Hungary	0.34	0.41	0.46	1.22	1.07	1.12	4.24	2.93	2.40
Malta	:	0.25	0.25	–	–	–	:	1.76	1.90
Netherlands	0.30	0.33	0.60	0.42	0.49	0.60	0.78	0.85	1.82
Austria	0.69	0.49	0.54	2.30	0.59	0.54	4.32	1.90	2.20
Poland	0.36	0.36	0.51	1.49	1.30	1.02	10.72	3.79	1.24
Portugal	0.23	0.37	0.37	1.28	0.65	0.38	3.68	3.11	3.11
Romania	0.23	0.35	0.24	1.37	0.64	0.24	6.91	2.62	1.19
Slovenia	0.17	0.26	0.29	0.17	0.26	0.29	:	1.40	1.40
Slovakia	0.40	0.75	0.75	1.93	1.54	1.15	11.18	3.79	0.75
Finland	0.22	0.24	0.34	0.87	0.94	1.01	5.68	4.90	4.80
Sweden	0.30	0.30	0.29	0.30	0.30	0.29	1.12	1.08	0.89
United Kingdom	0.47	0.36	0.77	0.95	0.36	0.77	2.83	1.67	2.19
Japan	0.41	0.35	0.33	3.07	1.43	1.37	6.14	6.14	5.86
United States	0.09	0.08	0.08	0.43	1.02	0.67	–	–	–

(¹) The indicator gives the price in euro of a 10-minute call at 11 am on a weekday (including VAT) for respectively a local call (3 km), a national call (200 km) and an international call to the United States; prices refer to August for 2000 and 2005 and to September for 2010; normal tariffs without special rates are used.

Source: Eurostat (online data code: tsier030), Teligen

7.8 Postal services of universal service providers

This subchapter takes a look at European Union (EU) postal statistics covering universal service providers (USP), in other words the postal service providers operating under the universal service obligation. Eurostat restarted the collection of data on postal services in 2005.

The main priorities of EU policies on postal services are to complete the internal market and to ensure efficient, reliable and good quality services at affordable prices for citizens and enterprises. Key elements of these policies include: the gradual opening of the market to competition, guaranteed access to the universal postal service, cost transparency, a reduction of the postal reserved area, setting common quality standards, harmonisation of technical standards, and creating conditions for rapid technological progress.

Main statistical findings

Domestic postal turnover increased strongly between 2004 and 2009 in Latvia and Lithuania, doubling in both of these Member States; large increases were also recorded in Austria, Poland, Hungary and Slovenia. In relative terms, compared with GDP, domestic postal turnover also increased in most of these Member States, the exception being Poland. In contrast, the ratio of turnover to GDP fell between 2004 and 2009 by almost 40 % in Bulgaria and by more than 25 % in Luxembourg (2004 to 2008) and Estonia. In 2009 Austria had the highest turnover from its domestic postal services in relation to GDP, followed by Sweden, Denmark and Belgium, all with turnover equivalent to 0.6 % or more of GDP, as had Finland and France (latest data is from 2007). At the other end of the scale, Greece, Cyprus, Spain, Lithuania and Bulgaria recorded ratios below 0.2 %.

The postal sector in the EU-27 (excluding Italy) employed in excess of 1.1 million persons in 2008. In 2009 France had the largest workforce, totalling 242 000, far ahead of the United Kingdom's 179 000 (in 2008) or Germany's 177 000. France's postal workforce was not just large in absolute terms, it also represented a high share (0.9 %) of total employment in relative terms too – see Figure 7.8.2. Between 2004 and 2009 employment in the postal sector decreased in the majority of Member States, while in relative terms (as a share of total employment) there were also decreases in nearly every Member State (subject to data availability): in Hungary and Romania the share of the postal sector in total employment grew, while in Greece and Slovenia it was stable. In contrast, the largest reductions in employment (in relative terms) were recorded in Austria, Sweden and France.

Postal items may be deposited by customers for processing in different physical facilities. These access points include post offices, agencies and outlets, mobile post offices, letter boxes, post office boxes and places at which only stamps can be bought. Table 7.8.2 provides an overview of the number of post offices, while Figure 7.8.3 gives an indication of the density of the post office network relative to population size. The average number of inhabitants served by a post office in 2009 ranged from 1 500 or less in Sweden, Luxembourg, the Czech Republic or Cyprus to 7 700 in the Netherlands and Belgium.

In 2009, Spain and the Netherlands handled the highest number (around 4 500 million) of letter-post items; note that no recent data are available for any of the four largest Member States – aside from an estimate of 16 000 million items for Germany in 2008 (see Table 7.8.2). Between 2004 and 2009 the number of letter-post items dropped by 20 % or more in Denmark, Bulgaria and Malta, and fell in 11 other Member States. In contrast, the number of letter-post items increased in five Member States, generally by less than 10 %, although an increase of 28.4 % was recorded in Cyprus.

An analysis of postal traffic in relation to population data shows that Finland and Luxembourg recorded the highest number of letter-post items per inhabitant in 2009 (close to 375 items per inhabitant), followed by the Netherlands and Sweden (see Figure 7.8.4). In contrast, 12 Member States distributed less than 100 letter-post items per capita, with Bulgaria, Romania, Latvia, Lithuania and Poland averaging less than 50 items per capita.

Data sources and availability

The data presented in this subchapter cover postal service providers operating under the universal service obligation, known as universal service providers. In this context universal service refers to the set of general interest demands to which services such as the mail should be subject throughout society – the aim of such an obligation is to ensure that all users have access to quality services at an affordable price.

Eurostat restarted collecting data on postal services in 2005. All data presented in this subchapter are based on Eurostat's EU postal survey. The data was provided by the national regulatory authorities in each participating country, including the EU Member States, Iceland, Norway, Croatia and the former Yugoslav Republic of Macedonia.

Context

The purpose of EU policy in the postal sector is to complete the internal market for postal services and to ensure, through an appropriate regulatory framework, that efficient, reliable and good quality postal services are available throughout the EU for all citizens and enterprises at affordable prices. The importance of postal services both for the economic prosperity and social well-being and cohesion of the EU make this a priority area for EU

action. Fundamental aspects of the EU's postal policy include a desire to improve the quality of service made available, in particular in terms of delivery performance and convenient access.

The process of liberalising the postal services market in the EU was initially set in motion by a Green paper on the development of the single market for postal services in 1992. Its aim was to open-up national monopolies to competition in order to make postal services cheaper, faster, more efficient and more innovative, harmonise performance across the EU Member States, and improve the quality of cross border-services. The EU legal framework for postal services is set out in Directive 97/67 and subsequent amendments. The ongoing process of liberalisation has brought about a gradual reduction of reserved postal services. Most of the Member States were due to reach a state of complete liberalisation of their postal sectors as of 1 January 2011 while the remainder have a deadline to do so by 1 January 2013.

The European Regulators Group for Postal Services was established in August 2010 by the European Commission. This group will advise and assist the European Commission, and its establishment is expected to strengthen cooperation between the national regulatory authorities and thereby develop best regulatory practice.

Table 7.8.1: Key economic indicators for the postal sector, 2004-2009

	Domestic turnover (EUR million)				Domestic employment (number)			
	2004	2006	2008	2009	2004	2006	2008	2009
Belgium	2 001	2 092	2 218	2 200	32 311	33 378	30 551	:
Bulgaria	29	25	30	30	9 134	10 501	9 330	8 543
Czech Republic	396	:	:	:	31 681	30 175	29 125	28 431
Denmark (¹)	1 482	1 571	1 617	1 511	28 349	26 686	*24 000*	18 049
Germany (²)	14 076	*13 300*	*13 500*	12 200	201 541	*170 000*	*175 000*	*177 000*
Estonia (³)	42	37	51	42	4 222	4 358	2 910	2 631
Ireland	515	594	630	581	7 502	:	:	:
Greece	402	416	448	448	10 412	11 607	11 294	11 037
Spain	1 855	1 771	1 928	1 833	63 779	65 515	65 924	64 037
France	11 998	12 585	:	:	283 945	269 458	251 955	241 835
Italy	3 973	4 849	:	:	:	:	:	:
Cyprus	30	32	32	31	942	950	944	1 006
Latvia	20	31	38	53	7 080	7 590	7 200	6 600
Lithuania	19	38	43	40	8 164	8 168	8 243	7 744
Luxembourg	146	146	*147*	:	1 485	1 618	1 554	1 563
Hungary	269	317	390	357	27 713	27 129	32 447	31 987
Malta	:	17	20	20	625	602	570	570
Netherlands	2 660	2 596	2 751	2 658	58 000	56 997	55 648	55 176
Austria	1 668	1 736	:	2 447	26 058	23 509	22 667	21 598
Poland	922	1 207	1 476	1 239	75 986	74 791	80 192	80 977
Portugal	608	622	648	613	14 844	14 134	13 432	13 235
Romania	:	113	198	340	36 073	34 935	35 892	36 525
Slovenia	128	152	174	169	5 645	6 057	5 980	5 941
Slovakia	:	118	192	168	13 990	*13 600*	*13 500*	*13 500*
Finland	1 035	1 157	:	:	22 570	23 744	23 400	22 000
Sweden	2 753	2 670	2 795	2 184	34 299	25 316	28 550	29 242
United Kingdom	9 837	9 957	10 197	:	184 299	167 640	178 622	:
Iceland	53	64	:	:	1 257	1 323	:	:
Norway	1 104	1 164	:	:	19 650	18 300	:	:
Croatia	115	130	141	161	9 838	8 955	9 316	8 515
FYR of Macedonia	:	:	21	22	:	:	2 285	2 215

(¹) Employment, break in series, 2009.
(²) 2009, data relate to the leading operator.
(³) Employment, break in series, 2008.

Source: Eurostat (online data codes: post_ps_tur and post_ps_empn)

Figure 7.8.1: Turnover from the domestic postal sector relative to GDP, 2004 and 2009
(% of GDP)

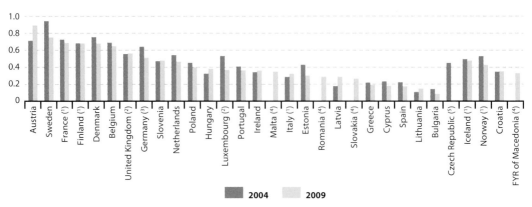

(¹) 2007 instead of 2009.
(²) 2008 instead of 2009.
(³) 2009, data relate to the leading operator.
(⁴) 2004, not available.
(⁵) 2009, not available.

Source: Eurostat (online data codes: post_ps_tur and nama_gdp_c)

Figure 7.8.2: Number of persons employed in the domestic postal sector as a share of total
employment, 2004 and 2009 (¹)
(%)

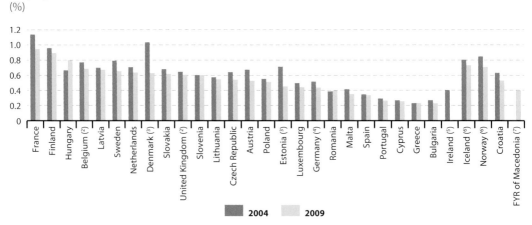

(¹) Italy, not available; Germany and Slovakia, estimates.
(²) 2008 instead of 2009.
(³) Break in series.
(⁴) 2009, data relate to the leading operator.
(⁵) 2009, not available.
(⁶) 2007 instead of 2009.
(⁷) 2004, not available.

Source: Eurostat (online data codes: post_ps_empn and nama_aux_pem)

Table 7.8.2: Post offices and postal items, 2004-2009

	Post offices (number)				Letter-post items (million)			
	2004	2006	2008	2009	2004	2006	2008	2009
EU-27	150 240	150 660	:	:	:	:	:	:
Belgium	1 308	1 348	1 351	1 403	:	:	:	:
Bulgaria	3 134	3 130	3 122	3 121	81	72	82	62
Czech Republic	13 789	13 871	13 860	13 822	955	930	947	893
Denmark	996	913	865	846	1 454	1 367	1 207	1 096
Germany (¹)	34 019	33 600	:	17 000	16 038	17 000	16 000	:
Estonia	545	545	418	380	:	117	115	100
Ireland	1 614	1 532	1 426	1 413	670	710	756	736
Greece	1 565	1 578	1 598	1 594	627	652	674	659
Spain	10 063	10 089	9 926	9 846	4 965	5 078	5 095	4 624
France	17 052	17 066	17 082	17 082	:	:	:	:
Italy	13 855	13 893	:	:	6 213	5 474	:	:
Cyprus	1 011	1 144	1 160	1 163	55	54	73	71
Latvia	967	954	701	625	64	68	79	56
Lithuania	951	940	954	880	:	120	110	94
Luxembourg	543	465	469	469	173	181	195	187
Hungary	2 820	3 197	3 098	3 095	902	824	820	785
Malta	53	53	61	61	56	54	47	44
Netherlands	2 112	2 110	2 116	2 144	5 300	4 918	4 693	4 473
Austria	1 947	1 944	1 842	1 669	:	:	:	:
Poland	8 350	8 553	8 489	8 378	1 914	1 634	1 840	1 787
Portugal	3 037	2 863	2 873	2 891	1 301	1 239	1 193	1 128
Romania	6 955	6 903	6 897	6 891	325	330	622	342
Slovenia	557	558	556	556	398	398	408	378
Slovakia	1 603	1 595	1 594	1 601	407	361	409	401
Finland	1 311	1 232	1 150	1 100	2 145	2 140	2 116	2 008
Sweden	5 474	6 365	6 350	6 410	2 444	2 450	2 350	2 168
United Kingdom	14 609	14 219	13 567	:	:	:	:	:
Iceland	189	174	:	:	:	:	:	:
Norway	3 367	3 249	:	:	1 427	1 247	:	:
Croatia	1 158	1 161	1 147	1 151	255	299	317	292
FYR of Macedonia	:	:	322	332	:	:	37	39

(¹) 2009, data relate to the leading operator.

Source: Eurostat (online data codes: post_ps_ac and post_ps_let)

Figure 7.8.3: Average number of inhabitants served by each post office, 2004 and 2009 (1 000)

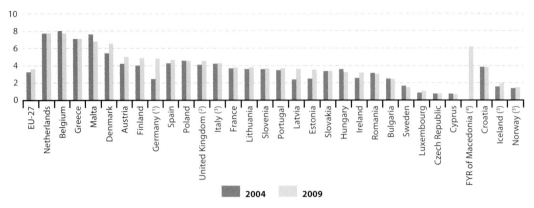

(¹) 2009, data relate to the leading operator.
(²) 2008 instead of 2009.
(³) 2007 instead of 2009.
(⁴) 2004, not available.

Source: Eurostat (online data codes: post_ps_ac and demo_gind)

Figure 7.8.4: Average number of letter-post items per inhabitant, 2004 and 2009 (¹) (number)

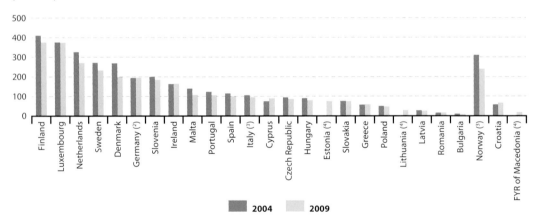

(¹) Belgium, France, Austria and the United Kingdom, not available.
(²) 2008 instead of 2009.
(³) 2007 instead of 2009.
(⁴) 2004, not available.

Source: Eurostat (online data codes: post_ps_let and demo_gind)

Agriculture, forestry and fisheries

8

Introduction

Agriculture

Agriculture was one of the first sectors of the economy (following coal and steel) to receive the attention of EU policymakers. Article 39 of the Treaty of Rome on the EEC (1957) set out the objectives for the first common agricultural policy (CAP); these were focused on increasing agricultural productivity as a way to ensure a fair standard of living for the agricultural community, stabilising markets, and ensuring security of supply at affordable prices for consumers.

As the primary objective of producing more food within Europe was realised, food surpluses accrued, distorting trade and raising environmental concerns. These were the principal drivers for changes in the common agricultural policy, a process that started in the early 1990s and which resulted in a change from support for production towards a market-oriented and a more environment-friendly and sustainable form of agriculture. Further reforms of agricultural policy have taken place in recent years, most notably in 2003 and 2008. The 2003 reform introduced a new system of direct payments, known as the single payment scheme, under which aid is no longer linked to production (decoupling). The single payment scheme aims to guarantee farmers more stable incomes. Farmers can decide what to produce in the knowledge that they will receive the same amount of aid, allowing them to adjust production to suit demand. In 2008 further changes were made, building on the reform package from 2003, such that all aid to the agricultural sector will be decoupled by 2012.

The Europe 2020 strategy offers a new perspective on economic, social, environmental, climate-related and technological challenges and future agricultural reform is likely to be made in relation to the goals of developing intelligent, sustainable and inclusive growth, while taking account of the wealth and diversity of the agricultural sector within the EU Member States. The European Commission has started a process of reviewing agricultural policy within the context of the Europe 2020 strategy and has already conducted a public debate and released proposals for legislative changes. It is expected that these will be introduced progressively following debate within the European Parliament and that a revised agricultural policy will be in place by 2013.

Forestry

Contrary to what is happening in many other parts of the world, the area covered by forests and other wooded land in the EU-27 is slowly increasing. Forests occur under a huge variety of climatic, geographic, ecological and socio-economic conditions. Ecologically, the forests of the EU belong to many different biogeographical regions and have adapted to a variety of natural conditions, ranging from bogs to steppes and from lowland to alpine forests. Socioeconomically, they vary from small family holdings to state forests or to large estates owned by companies, many as part of industrial wood supply chains. About 60 % of the EU's wooded land is privately owned.

Fisheries

Fish are a natural, biological, mobile (sometimes over wide distances) and renewable resource. Aside from fish farming, fish cannot be owned until they have been caught. For this reason, fish stocks continue to be regarded as a common resource, which therefore need to be managed collectively. This has led to a range of policies and international agreements that regulate the amount of fishing, as well as the types of fishing techniques and gear used to catch fish.

8.1 Agricultural output, price indices and income

This subchapter gives an overview of recent changes in agricultural output, gross value added and prices in the European Union (EU), and their effect on income from agricultural activity. Economic accounts for agriculture (EAA) provide statistics that may be used to analyse agricultural activity and the income it generates.

One of the principal objectives of the common agricultural policy (CAP) is to provide farmers with a reasonable standard of living. Although this concept is not defined explicitly within the CAP, a range of indicators including income development from farming activities may be used to determine the progress being made towards this objective.

Main statistical findings

The EU-27's agricultural industry generated EUR 138 721 million of gross value added at producer prices in 2010, which represented a 13.9 % increase in relation to the previous year (see Table 8.1.1). There were increases in both the value of crop output (up 9.7 % to EUR 185 186 million in 2010) and animal output (up 5.1 % to EUR 138 903 million); these were partly compensated for by a modest increase in the value of intermediate consumption of goods and services (up 3.2 %).

Changes in the value of agricultural output comprise a volume and price component: one important strand of recent changes in agricultural policy has been to move away from price support mechanisms, so that prices more accurately reflect market forces and changes in supply and demand. During the period 2005 to 2010 (see Figure 8.1.2) there were considerable differences between the Member States in the development of deflated agricultural output prices: such deflated prices show the extent to which agricultural prices have changed compared with consumer prices. Deflated output prices rose in 17 of the EU Member States, the largest increases being recorded for the United Kingdom (average growth of 5.0 % per annum), Sweden (3.3 % per annum) and Romania (2.8 % per annum), while reductions were posted in ten of the Member States,

the largest declines being in Slovakia (– 2.7 % per annum), the Czech Republic (– 2.4 % per annum) and Spain (– 1.9 % per annum).

The development of deflated agricultural input prices showed a very different picture, as prices rose in 20 of the 27 Member States. The United Kingdom (2.9 % per annum) and Portugal (2.6 % per annum) reported the highest input price increases. At the other end of the range, the largest decreases were recorded in Slovakia and Lithuania (both – 1.4 % per annum).

There was an overall 16.9 % increase in EU-27 output prices for agricultural goods between 2005 and 2010, which could be broken down for the main components into increases of 22.3 % for crop output and 11.4 % for animal output. The overall increase in output prices between 2005 and 2010 did not follow a smooth development, as there was a considerable reduction in prices between 2008 and 2009 when the price of agricultural goods fell by 11.1 %, which could be largely attributed to falling prices for cereals, milk, fruits and olive oil which all fell by between 14 % and 31 % (see Table 8.1.2).

The real net value added at factor cost of agricultural activity per unit of labour (expressed in annual work units), also known as the agricultural income indicator A, increased by 13.0 % in the EU-27 from 2009 to 2010. There were stark contrasts among the Member States, with income rising at a rapid pace in Denmark (56.5 %), Estonia (46.2 %), the Netherlands (38.9 %) and France (37.7 %), in contrast to falling income in the United Kingdom (– 6.4 %), Romania (– 3.6 %), Greece (– 3.5 %) and Italy (– 2.8 %) – see Table 8.1.3.

Data sources and availability

Economic accounts for agriculture (EAA) provide an insight into:

- the economic viability of agriculture;
- agriculture's contribution to a Member State's wealth;
- the structure and composition of agricultural production and inputs;

- the remuneration of factors of production;
- relationships between prices and quantities of both inputs and outputs.

These accounts comprise a production account, a generation of income account, an entrepreneurial income account and some elements of a capital account. For the production items, Member States transmit to Eurostat values at basic prices, as well as their components (values at producer prices, subsidies on products, and taxes on products). The data for the production account and for gross fixed capital formation are transmitted in both current prices and the prices of the previous year.

The output of agricultural activity includes output sold (including trade in agricultural goods and services between agricultural units), changes in stocks, output for own final use (own final consumption and own-account gross fixed capital formation), output produced for further processing by agricultural producers, as well as intra-unit consumption of livestock feed products. The output of the agricultural industry is made up of the sum of the output of agricultural products and of the goods and services produced in inseparable non-agricultural secondary activities; animal and crop output are the main product categories of agricultural output.

Gross value added equals the value of output less the value of intermediate consumption and is shown in producer prices (the producer price excludes subsidies less taxes on products). Intermediate consumption represents the value of all goods and services used as inputs in the production process, excluding fixed assets whose consumption is recorded as fixed capital consumption. The Member States transmit information on intermediate consumption to Eurostat using values at purchaser prices (basic prices).

Eurostat also collects annual agricultural prices (in principle net of VAT) to compare agricultural price levels between Member States and study sales channels. Quarterly and annual price indices for agricultural products and the means of agricultural production, on the other hand, are used principally to analyse price developments and their effect on agricultural income. Agricultural price indices are obtained by a base-weighted Laspeyres calculation

(2005 = 100), and are expressed in nominal terms or as deflated indices based on the use of an implicit HICP deflator.

Agricultural income indicators are presented in the form of:

- an index of real income of factors in agricultural activity per annual work unit (indicator A);
- the index of real net agricultural entrepreneurial income, per unpaid annual work unit (indicator B);
- net entrepreneurial income of agriculture (indicator C).

Context

Significant reforms of the common agricultural policy (CAP) have taken place in recent years, most notably in 2003 and 2008, with the aim of making the agricultural sector more market-oriented. The 2003 reform introduced a new system of direct payments, known as the single payment scheme, under which aid is no longer linked to production (decoupling); this single payment scheme aims to guarantee farmers more stable incomes. Farmers can decide what to produce in the knowledge that they will receive the same amount of aid, allowing them to adjust production to suit demand. In 2008 further changes were made to the CAP, building on the reform package from 2003, such that all aid to the agricultural sector will be decoupled by 2012.

The Europe 2020 strategy offers a new perspective on economic, social, environmental, climate-related and technological challenges and future agricultural reform is likely to be made in relation to the goals of developing intelligent, sustainable and inclusive growth, while taking account of the wealth and diversity of the agricultural sector within the EU Member States. As part of this process, the European Commission launched a public debate on the future of the CAP during 2010. The outcome of the debate, coupled with input from the European Council and Parliament led the Commission to present a Communication (COM(2010) 672 final) in November 2010, titled 'The CAP towards 2020: meeting the food, natural resources and territorial challenges of the future'.

Table 8.1.1: Agricultural output and gross value added at producer prices, 2005-2010
(EUR million)

	Gross value added of the agricultural industry			Crop output			Animal output		
	2005	2009	2010	2005	2009	2010	2005	2009	2010
EU-27	129497	121784	138721	157479	168860	185186	128511	132161	138903
Belgium	2153	2049	2494	2903	2994	3561	3570	3713	3987
Bulgaria	1544	1252	1404	1627	1956	2039	1129	1125	1132
Czech Republic	970	634	960	1674	1927	2160	1574	1522	1612
Denmark	2253	1505	2125	2472	2836	3182	4867	5062	5383
Germany	12920	12916	15043	18167	20902	21766	19042	19657	21394
Estonia	197	168	232	194	218	254	267	279	315
Ireland	1623	926	1512	1376	1367	1497	3651	3361	3851
Greece	6284	5334	5350	7007	6243	6490	2685	2678	2662
Spain	20345	19698	21348	21234	21770	24354	12641	12502	12393
France	21375	20046	26004	29939	33968	37668	21663	21537	22452
Italy	24410	22202	22587	25434	24569	25273	13178	14379	14347
Cyprus	332	305	318	326	312	331	301	322	332
Latvia	222	169	230	308	412	448	282	320	359
Lithuania	409	436	500	657	854	878	693	679	796
Luxembourg	107	80	95	102	94	108	151	154	166
Hungary	1793	1643	1968	3020	3233	3777	2118	2078	2139
Malta	45	55	53	39	48	46	63	69	68
Netherlands	7751	7124	8974	10131	10816	12287	7906	8567	9424
Austria	2207	2284	2606	2199	2575	2914	2543	2750	2840
Poland	5161	5437	6135	6043	7423	8603	7585	8294	8978
Portugal	1927	1846	1864	3584	3762	3971	2241	2420	2429
Romania	6003	5964	6399	7687	8414	10141	4051	3833	3811
Slovenia	397	373	391	496	547	576	468	473	484
Slovakia	382	228	316	691	851	930	760	751	720
Finland	720	1031	1152	1062	1276	1339	1703	1860	1958
Sweden	1128	926	1370	1595	1721	2108	2091	1919	2263
United Kingdom	6842	7152	7292	7512	7769	8485	11287	11858	12608
Norway	902	922	1085	1252	1270	1465	1799	1997	2217
Switzerland	2583	2656	2742	2855	3081	3227	3171	3280	3463
Croatia	883	1131	940	1181	1500	1476	921	959	941
FYR of Macedonia	490	554	:	774	768	:	212	293	:

Source: Eurostat (online data code: aact_eaa01)

Figure 8.1.1: Agricultural output and gross value added at producer prices, EU-27, 2000-2010 (2005 = 100)

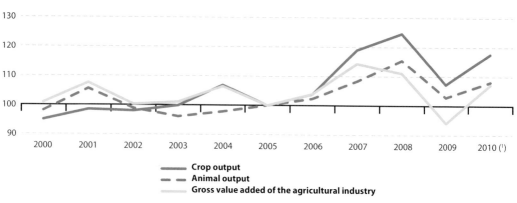

(¹) Crop output and animal output, estimates.

Source: Eurostat (online data code: aact_eaa01)

Figure 8.1.2: Change in deflated price indices of agricultural input and output, 2005-2010 (average annual rate of change, %)

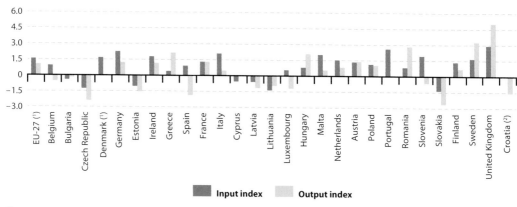

(¹) Provisional.
(²) Input index, not available.

Source: Eurostat (online data codes: apri_pi05_ina and apri_pi05_outa)

Table 8.1.2: Price indices of agricultural output (nominal), EU-27, 2006-2010
(2005 = 100)

	2006	2007	2008	2009	2010
CROP OUTPUT	107.0	123.7	126.7	108.7	122.3
Cereals	113.9	176.0	179.2	123.6	150.9
Industrial crops	99.3	113.7	119.3	104.6	125.1
Forage plants	99.6	118.9	134.7	131.4	140.2
Vegetables and horticultural products	102.6	107.1	107.6	102.6	113.4
Potatoes	154.5	149.5	133.2	124.9	148.3
Fruits	102.2	114.8	122.1	102.5	111.4
Wine	99.7	107.5	116.3	110.6	109.1
Olive oil	110.2	92.0	88.3	75.7	75.7
Other crop products	99.8	115.8	121.8	111.4	113.3
ANIMAL OUTPUT	102.8	106.0	116.2	107.9	111.4
Animals	104.5	102.8	111.6	109.9	109.4
Cattle	108.7	106.5	110.5	110.0	110.3
Cattle (excluding calves)	107.8	104.4	111.5	111.0	110.7
Calves	112.6	115.5	105.7	104.8	107.9
Pigs	104.2	95.6	107.2	103.6	101.9
Equines	110.9	113.0	141.7	144.3	139.8
Sheep and goats	100.0	95.6	103.6	113.6	117.5
Poultry	99.8	114.6	124.9	121.3	121.0
Other animals	104.7	95.1	104.8	109.6	107.5
Animal products	100.2	110.8	123.2	104.9	114.4
Milk	98.5	108.9	122.2	99.8	111.0
Eggs	109.3	128.7	136.6	148.7	139.2
Other animal products	107.8	96.8	102.7	95.5	121.4
AGRICULTURAL GOODS	105.0	115.4	121.8	108.3	116.9

Source: Eurostat (online data code: apri_pi05_outa)

Table 8.1.3: Index of income from agricultural activity (indicator A), 2000-2010
(2005 = 100)

	2000	2001	2002	2003	2004	2005	2006	2007	2008	2009	2010
EU-27	94.8	104.1	105.7	101.6	110.2	100.0	*104.0*	114.8	*109.7*	98.6	*111.4*
Belgium	118.7	108.8	96.0	104.3	109.3	100.0	123.5	134.0	109.2	107.7	*134.3*
Bulgaria	105.1	118.0	94.7	88.6	87.4	100.0	97.5	98.8	161.2	125.3	*158.7*
Czech Republic	66.4	85.0	68.8	59.2	93.2	100.0	102.7	118.6	125.1	98.5	*113.9*
Denmark	104.9	126.6	89.7	87.8	98.8	100.0	104.2	106.4	66.6	50.3	*78.7*
Germany	90.1	111.0	81.8	75.5	111.9	100.0	108.8	134.9	128.8	101.8	*124.6*
Estonia	40.5	53.2	51.6	57.6	94.8	100.0	100.4	142.1	*112.1*	94.5	*138.2*
Ireland	95.8	90.7	79.2	75.8	80.3	100.0	84.0	94.3	87.0	66.9	*85.3*
Greece	118.5	118.7	114.3	104.3	99.3	100.0	98.3	99.0	88.2	89.6	*86.5*
Spain	104.2	112.4	108.9	123.1	113.2	100.0	95.5	107.3	97.4	93.8	*101.7*
France	110.3	111.5	108.3	106.6	105.4	100.0	111.1	120.9	104.4	84.3	116.1
Italy	117.9	115.4	113.5	113.8	114.6	100.0	96.3	93.7	94.3	86.0	*83.6*
Cyprus	95.0	105.9	107.3	98.7	96.6	100.0	90.4	90.2	85.7	92.3	*92.0*
Latvia	41.1	53.4	52.5	57.6	96.0	100.0	131.8	137.8	117.2	102.4	*127.8*
Lithuania	60.8	56.4	52.3	58.7	92.5	100.0	89.0	133.4	123.4	106.6	*121.8*
Luxembourg	104.3	105.4	117.9	108.4	109.2	100.0	94.7	116.1	85.8	57.4	*70.2*
Hungary	75.1	79.3	62.7	65.4	99.1	100.0	106.6	114.3	153.4	107.2	*123.3*
Malta	78.7	91.2	90.7	85.9	82.6	100.0	97.5	94.5	90.3	99.6	*109.0*
Netherlands	124.5	116.2	100.1	108.6	101.1	100.0	122.6	121.1	99.1	87.9	*122.1*
Austria	89.9	105.9	97.2	96.9	101.9	100.0	111.1	125.1	122.0	94.3	107.8
Poland	61.0	70.2	63.4	58.5	110.3	100.0	*110.5*	134.9	108.9	134.7	*145.2*
Portugal	94.8	101.8	97.3	98.4	108.7	100.0	104.4	100.2	104.2	100.6	*109.2*
Romania	66.9	114.2	106.8	121.2	175.2	100.0	99.3	76.8	114.4	92.4	*89.1*
Slovenia	71.5	62.1	81.9	64.6	99.5	100.0	97.4	109.6	99.1	86.7	*92.8*
Slovakia	82.4	93.7	88.6	82.9	107.3	100.0	122.1	128.9	143.5	110.5	*115.2*
Finland	94.5	95.1	94.6	93.4	90.0	100.0	98.8	112.6	97.1	117.0	*126.5*
Sweden	85.0	90.6	95.5	92.8	83.9	100.0	113.5	135.7	124.2	94.8	*121.7*
United Kingdom	80.8	85.6	94.7	108.5	101.2	100.0	103.9	110.8	143.5	129.6	*121.3*
Norway	122.9	119.7	125.0	121.8	119.8	100.0	93.6	104.6	103.3	104.7	*113.4*
Switzerland	103.0	95.7	102.1	94.9	105.9	100.0	97.1	102.5	107.2	105.1	*103.0*

Source: Eurostat (online data code: aact_eaa06)

8.2 Farm structure

The structure of agriculture in the Member States of the European Union (EU) varies as a function of differences in geology, topography, climate and natural resources, as well as the diversity of regional activities, infrastructure and social customs. The survey on the structure of agricultural holdings, also known as the farm structure survey (FSS), helps assess the agricultural situation across the EU, monitoring trends and transitions in the structure of agricultural holdings, while also modelling the impact of external developments or policy proposals.

This subchapter presents some statistics from the last farm structure survey that was conducted in 2007. The results of the most recent census (2009/2010) are in the process of being validated and first results should be available at the end of 2012.

Main statistical findings

There were 7.3 million commercial agricultural holdings in the EU-27 in 2007, with a further 6.4 million small holdings (those below a threshold of one European size unit (ESU)). Almost half (48 %) of the small holdings in the EU-27, principally being subsistence in nature, were found in Romania. A little over one third of the EU-27's commercial agricultural holdings (that were greater than one ESU) were located in Poland (15.5 %) and Italy (18.9 %), while Spain (12.8 %), Romania (11.9 %) and Greece (9.7 %) also contributed about a third of the total commercial holdings in 2007.

Among most Member States and across the EU-27 as a whole, there was a steady decline in the number of agricultural holdings during the period between 2003 and 2007. In this four-year period, the number of agricultural holdings in the EU-27 declined by 1.3 million (or 8.8 %), of which almost half were commercial holdings. There were particularly fast structural changes in Estonia, where the number of holdings declined by more than one third (– 36.7 %), as well as in Bulgaria (– 25.9 %), Portugal (– 23.4 %) and Hungary (– 19.0 %).

Cattle represent close to half of the total number of livestock units in the EU. In 2007 there were 89.5 million head of cattle in the EU-27, of which more than one fifth (21.6 %) were in France. Despite being one of the smallest EU Member States, Ireland had one of the largest cattle herds, accounting for 7.3 % of the EU-27 total.

The total farm labour force in the EU-27 was the equivalent of 11.7 million full-time workers in 2007, of which 10.8 million (92 %) were regular workers (see Table 8.2.2). Agriculture remains very much a family-oriented activity in the majority of Member States; four fifths (80 %) of the total agricultural labour force in 2007 were farm holders or members of their family. The main exceptions were Slovakia (44 %) and the Czech Republic (27 %), where there is a different ownership structure compared with the majority of Member States. Just over one third (34 %) of the regular agricultural labour force in the EU-27 was female, although in the Baltic Member States this share was closer to half, reaching 50 % in Latvia. Among EU-27 agricultural holders in 2007, relatively few (6 %) were under the age of 35, while a relatively high proportion (34 %) were aged 65 years or over.

Figure 8.2.1 indicates the proportion of farm holdings with another gainful economic activity. Besides agricultural activity, other gainful activities were also conducted by about one in ten (9.9 %) of the EU's agricultural holdings in 2007, this proportion being slightly higher (13.5 %) among commercial holdings. A little over one quarter (27.6 %) of all holdings in Finland reported another gainful activity in 2007, with rates above 20 % also being recorded in Austria, Germany, the United Kingdom, Sweden, Denmark and France.

Two fifths (an estimated 40.1 %) of the total land area of the EU-27 was utilised agricultural area (UAA) in 2007. This proportion rose to two thirds (66.3 %) of the land area of the United Kingdom, but was less than one tenth of the total in Sweden and Finland. Arable land (which includes cereals and other arable land) accounted for a little less than one quarter (24.3 %) of the total land area of the EU-27, with permanent grassland (which is composed of pasture, meadow and rough grazing) accounting for 13.2 %. During the ten years through until 2007, the make-up of land use in the EU-27 did not change very much. Equally the overall area utilised by agriculture was relatively stable within the EU, although there was a slight tendency for an increase in the area among Member States that joined the EU in 2004 or 2007, with a small decrease in the EU-15 Member States.

Data sources and availability

A comprehensive farm structure survey is carried out by Member States every ten years (the full scope being the agricultural census) and intermediate sample surveys are carried out three times between these basic surveys. The Member States collect information from individual agricultural holdings. The information collected covers:

- land use;
- livestock numbers;
- rural development (for example, other gainful activities);
- management and farm labour input (including age, sex and relationship to the holder).

The survey data are aggregated to different geographic levels (Member States, regions, and for basic surveys also districts) and arranged by size class, area status, legal status of holding, objective zone and farm type.

The basic unit underlying the survey is the agricultural holding, a technical-economic unit under single management engaged in agricultural production. The survey covers all agricultural holdings with a utilised agricultural area (UAA) of at least 1 hectare (ha) and those holdings with a UAA of less than 1 hectare if their market production exceeds certain natural thresholds.

Other gainful activity is any activity other than that relating to farm work, including activities carried out on the holding itself (camp sites, accommodation for tourists, etc.) or that use its resources (machinery, etc.) or products (such as processing farm products, renewable energy production), and which have an economic impact on the holding.

Other gainful activity is carried out by the holder, his/her family members, or one or more partners on a group holding.

The farm labour force is made-up of all individuals who have completed their compulsory education (having reached school-leaving age) and who carried out farm work on the holding under survey during the 12 months up to the survey day. The figures include the holders, even when not working on the holding, whereas their spouses are counted only if they carry out farm work on the holding. The holder is the natural person (sole holder or group of individuals) or the legal person (for example, a cooperative or other institution) on whose account and in whose name the holding is operated and who is legally and economically responsible for the holding – in other words, the entity or person that takes the economic risks of the holding; for group holdings, only the main holder (one person) is counted. The regular labour force covers the family labour force and permanently employed (regular) non-family workers. The family labour force includes the holder and the members of his/her family who carried out farm work (including all persons of retiring age who continue to work on the holding). One annual work unit (AWU) corresponds to the work performed by one person who is occupied on an agricultural holding on a full-time basis. Full-time means the minimum hours required by the national provisions governing contracts of employment. If these provisions do not explicitly indicate the number of hours, then 1 800 hours are taken to be the minimum (225 working days of eight hours each).

In preparation for the 2010 survey a new legal basis was developed: Regulation (EC) 1166/2008 of the European Parliament and of the Council of 19 November 2008 on farm structure surveys and the survey on agricultural production methods.

Context

Rural development policy aims to improve: competitiveness in agriculture and forestry; the quality of the environment and countryside; and life in rural areas; and the diversification of rural economies. As agriculture has modernised and the importance of industry and services within the economy has increased, so agriculture has become much less important as a source of jobs. Consequently, increasing emphasis is placed on the role farmers can play in rural development, including forestry, biodiversity, the diversification of the rural economy to create alternative jobs and environmental protection in rural areas. The common agricultural policy (CAP) is due to be reformed by 2013 and this is likely to have an impact on rural development policies. The farm structure survey continues to be adapted with the aim of trying to provide timely and relevant data to help analyse and follow these developments.

Table 8.2.1: Agricultural holdings and cattle, 2003-2007

	Number of agricultural holdings (1 000)			Head of cattle (1 000)			Holdings with irrigable area (% of holdings)		
	2003	2005	2007	2003	2005	2007	2003	2005	2007
EU-27	15 021	14 482	13 700	92 048	90 018	89 470	:	:	:
Belgium	55	52	48	2 778	2 699	2 649	4.3	4.2	4.7
Bulgaria	666	535	493	692	609	602	20.7	14.5	15.0
Czech Republic	46	42	39	1 505	1 426	1 419	4.6	4.7	5.2
Denmark	49	52	45	1 724	1 570	1 566	19.5	17.9	15.1
Germany	412	390	370	13 639	13 034	12 675	:	:	:
Estonia	37	28	23	274	261	253	:	:	:
Ireland	136	133	128	6 990	6 869	6 573	0.0	0.0	0.0
Greece	824	834	860	733	717	732	64.5	65.2	62.7
Spain	1 141	1 079	1 044	5 973	5 866	5 741	47.8	46.4	45.6
France	614	567	527	19 454	19 132	19 350	17.5	18.0	18.2
Italy	1 964	1 729	1 679	6 261	6 180	6 364	36.2	37.6	40.4
Cyprus	45	45	40	61	59	58	75.3	77.3	78.5
Latvia	127	129	108	379	370	398	0.1	0.3	0.2
Lithuania	272	253	230	895	1 009	784	0.0	0.1	0.0
Luxembourg	2	2	2	190	185	192	0.0	:	0.0
Hungary	773	715	626	706	707	704	4.3	2.5	0.2
Malta	11	11	11	19	20	19	34.6	27.8	25.5
Netherlands	86	82	77	3 759	3 799	3 763	22.6	23.6	26.1
Austria	174	171	165	2 039	2 003	1 973	3.6	4.4	4.4
Poland	2 172	2 476	2 391	5 533	5 482	5 855	0.7	1.0	1.1
Portugal	359	324	275	1 398	1 315	1 324	62.4	62.2	62.2
Romania	4 485	4 256	3 931	2 871	2 766	2 734	5.8	3.5	2.7
Slovenia	77	77	75	478	461	472	1.5	2.3	2.3
Slovakia	72	68	69	583	514	502	6.1	10.5	2.3
Finland	75	71	68	1 000	959	927	10.6	8.1	8.5
Sweden	68	76	73	1 607	1 605	1 560	7.8	6.0	5.2
United Kingdom	281	287	300	10 507	10 400	10 280	1.8	1.4	13.9
Norway	58	53	50	957	934	906	16.5	16.8	17.5
Switzerland	:	64	62	:	1 555	1 572	:	0.0	:
Croatia	:	:	181	:	:	475	:	:	:

Source: Eurostat (online data codes: tag00001 and ef_ov_lusum)

Table 8.2.2: Farm labour force, 2007

	Farm labour force (1 000 AWU) (¹)		Analysis of labour force (% of total)				Agricultural holders (1 000)		
	Total	Regular	Regular	Full-time regular	Female regular	Family	Natural persons	Age <35 years	Age >=65 years
EU-27	11 693	10 796	92	34	34	80	13 441	823	4 584
Belgium	66	63	95	71	29	79	44	3	9
Bulgaria	491	467	95	38	39	85	490	15	222
Czech Republic	137	134	98	68	32	27	36	4	7
Denmark	56	54	96	70	23	61	44	3	9
Germany	609	555	91	50	28	69	365	28	27
Estonia	32	31	98	46	46	61	22	1	7
Ireland	148	144	98	60	21	93	128	9	32
Greece	569	489	86	22	29	82	860	60	321
Spain	968	790	82	42	20	65	988	44	361
France	805	719	89	67	25	47	428	34	66
Italy	1 302	1 169	90	37	30	84	1 664	49	741
Cyprus	26	24	94	31	32	75	40	1	12
Latvia	105	104	99	30	50	84	108	8	32
Lithuania	180	176	98	14	48	85	230	10	93
Luxembourg	4	4	98	63	27	85	2	0	0
Hungary	403	390	97	25	37	77	619	47	172
Malta	4	4	99	41	14	88	11	0	3
Netherlands	165	151	91	56	26	61	73	3	13
Austria	163	159	97	53	41	88	161	16	18
Poland	2 263	2 194	97	34	42	95	2 387	294	388
Portugal	338	315	93	35	41	82	269	5	130
Romania	2 205	2 044	93	4	42	90	3 914	167	1 762
Slovenia	84	80	96	21	41	92	75	3	26
Slovakia	91	87	96	40	32	44	67	2	22
Finland	72	68	94	56	30	83	67	6	4
Sweden	65	63	97	42	26	76	68	4	15
United Kingdom	341	318	93	55	23	67	283	7	92
Norway	56	53	94	32	25	80	50	4	4

(¹) AWU: annual work unit.

Source: Eurostat (online data codes: tag00020, tag00021, ef_so_lfwtime, ef_so_lfaa, tag00029 and tag00030)

Figure 8.2.1: Agricultural holdings with another gainful activity, 2007
(%)

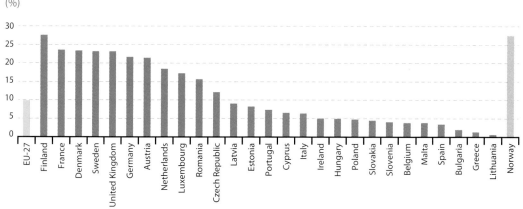

Source: Eurostat (online data code: tag00096)

Figure 8.2.2: Utilised agricultural area by land use, EU-27, 2007 (¹)
(% share of utilised agricultural area)

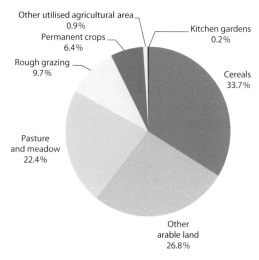

(¹) Figures do not sum to 100 % due to rounding.
Source: Eurostat (online data code: ef_lu_ovcropesu)

Table 8.2.3: Land use, 2007

| | Total land area (km²) (¹) | Utilised agricul-tural area (UAA) (km²) | Land belonging to agricultural holdings: share of total land area (%) | | | | | | |
			UAA total	Arable land	Kitchen garden	Perma-nent grassland & meadow	Perma-nent crops	Wooded area	Other (un-utilised) land
EU-27	4 299 004	1 724 851	40.1	24.3	0.1	13.2	2.6	7.2	2.8
Belgium	30 328	13 744	45.3	27.8	0.0	16.9	0.7	0.2	0.8
Bulgaria	111 002	30 507	27.5	24.0	0.2	2.5	0.8	8.6	0.8
Czech Republic	77 246	35 181	45.5	33.3	0.0	11.8	0.5	18.9	0.7
Denmark	43 098	26 626	61.8	56.9	0.0	4.7	0.2	4.8	2.5
Germany	357 108	169 319	47.4	33.3	0.0	13.5	0.6	3.8	1.1
Estonia	43 432	9 068	20.9	14.4	0.1	6.3	0.1	5.3	1.9
Ireland	68 394	41 392	60.5	14.7	0.0	45.8	0.0	1.9	2.1
Greece	130 822	40 762	31.2	16.2	0.1	6.3	8.6	0.5	2.0
Spain	501 757	248 925	49.6	23.7	0.0	17.2	8.7	9.7	6.8
France	632 834	274 769	43.4	28.9	0.0	12.8	1.7	1.5	0.8
Italy	295 114	127 442	43.2	23.5	0.1	11.7	7.9	12.9	4.3
Cyprus	9 250	1 460	15.8	11.7	0.0	0.2	3.9	0.2	3.4
Latvia	62 290	17 738	28.5	17.8	0.1	10.3	0.3	11.4	5.9
Lithuania	62 678	26 490	42.3	28.9	0.0	13.1	0.3	2.6	1.5
Luxembourg	2 586	1 309	50.6	23.6	0.0	26.4	0.6	2.5	0.3
Hungary	93 029	42 286	45.5	38.2	0.2	5.4	1.7	14.6	4.4
Malta	316	103	32.7	25.4	3.1	0.0	4.2	0.0	4.3
Netherlands	33 756	19 143	56.7	31.4	:	24.3	1.0	0.3	4.5
Austria	82 438	31 891	38.7	16.8	0.0	21.0	0.8	33.2	11.2
Poland	312 685	154 772	49.5	37.6	0.2	10.5	1.2	3.8	4.5
Portugal	92 118	34 729	37.7	11.7	0.2	19.3	6.5	7.8	2.3
Romania	229 973	137 531	59.8	37.8	0.8	19.7	1.5	4.7	1.9
Slovenia	20 141	4 888	24.3	8.6	0.1	14.3	1.3	18.8	2.7
Slovakia	49 035	19 366	39.5	27.7	0.1	11.2	0.5	21.4	1.4
Finland	304 086	22 923	7.5	7.4	0.0	0.1	0.0	10.4	2.8
Sweden	410 335	31 180	7.6	6.4	0.0	1.2	0.0	9.1	0.5
United Kingdom	243 154	161 305	66.3	24.7	0.0	41.5	0.1	2.6	1.2
Norway	304 280	10 320	3.4	2.0	0.0	1.4	0.0	7.7	9.8
Croatia	56 594	:	:	:	:	:	:	:	:

(¹) Bulgaria, Denmark, Germany, France, Cyprus, Poland and Portugal, total area; Austria, 2008; EU-27, sum of available data for the Member States.

Source: Eurostat (online data codes: demo_r_d3area and ef_lu_ovcropaa)

Map 8.2.1: Average UAA per holding, 2007
(hectares)

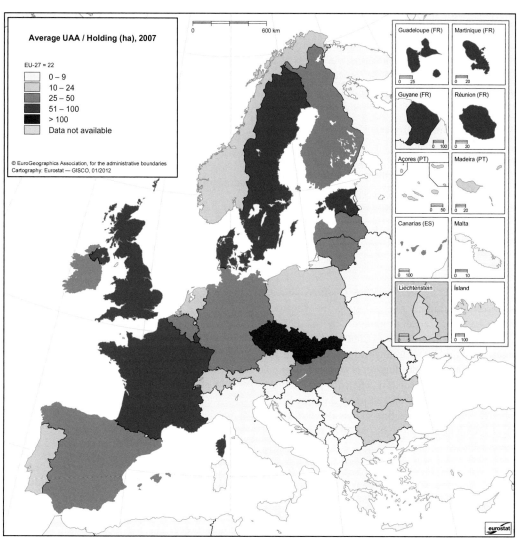

Source: Eurostat (online data code: ef_ov_kvaaesu and ef_oluaareg)

8.3 Agricultural products

There is a wide diversity of natural environments, climates and farming practices across Europe that feed into a broad array of food and drink products for human consumption and animal feed, as well as providing inputs for non-food processes. Indeed, agricultural products form a major part of the cultural identity of Europe's people and regions.

With this in mind, European Union (EU) legislation has been developed to protect particular food and drink product names which are linked to a specific territory or a specific production method, aiming to provide guarantees as to the origin and authenticity of a range of products.

Main statistical findings

Crops

In 2010, the EU-27 produced 285.2 million tonnes of cereals (including rice). Despite the vagaries of the weather, cereal production in the EU-27 was relatively stable between 2000 and 2010 (see Figure 8.3.1), albeit with notably higher harvests in 2004 and 2008. The production of cereals fell from the relative high recorded in 2008 with production falling by 6.1 % in 2009 and a further 3.6 % in 2010. Nevertheless, the production of cereals within the EU-27 remained 2.6 % higher in 2010 than it had been in 2000.

There was a large overall increase (49.9 %) in the production of oilseeds between 2000 and 2010. On the other hand, the output of potatoes declined steadily during the last decade (with production falling by 31.2 % between 2000 and 2010). The production of sugar beet also fell over the last decade (– 21.9 %), with all of the losses taking place during the second half of the decade, with output contracting considerably in 2006 and again in 2010.

An analysis of the most recent developments, based on a comparison between 2009 and 2010, shows that EU-27 production of cereals fell by 3.6 %. Sugar beet and potatoes production decreased by 6.3 % and 9.0 % respectively, while there was a small increase in the production of oilseeds (0.7 %).

France and Germany were by far the largest cereal, sugar beet and oilseed producers, together accounting for 54.8 % of the EU-27's sugar beet production, 42.9 % of its oilseeds production and 38.5 % of its cereal production in 2010 (see Table 8.3.1). The production of potatoes was more widely spread across the EU Member States, with Germany recording the highest level of production (17.9 % of the EU-27 total in 2010), while Poland, the Netherlands, France and the United Kingdom each accounted for between 15.4 % and 10.6 % of the total. France was, by far, the leading producer of pulses and textile crops in 2010.

Figure 8.3.2 presents a breakdown of the production of cereals in the EU-27 in 2010. Almost half (47.8 %) of the total production of cereals was accounted for by wheat, while around one fifth of the total was composed of grain maize (20.0 %) and barley (18.7 %); rice production in the EU-27 was considerably lower (1.1 % of the EU-27's total cereals production).

In the EU-27, the most important vegetables in terms of production were tomatoes, onions and carrots, while the most important fruits were apples, oranges and peaches (see Figures 8.3.3 and 8.3.4 respectively). In 2010, Italy and Spain had the largest vegetable and fruit production among the EU Member States. Italy produced around 14.0 million tonnes of vegetables, while Spain produced approximately 9.9 million tonnes (in 2009).

The bulk of fruit and fresh vegetable production was concentrated in a few Member States. For example, some 57.4 % of the EU-27's apple production in 2010 was located in Italy, Poland and France, while 96.8 % of oranges were produced in Spain or Italy. About two thirds of all the tomatoes produced in the EU-27 originated from Italy and Spain, while almost half (45.6 %) of the onions produced in the EU-27 came from either the Netherlands or Spain.

Meat and milk

Table 8.3.2 summarises a range of different agricultural products that are related to animals. The principal meat product in the EU-27 was pig meat

(22.0 million tonnes in 2010), where the weight of production was almost three times as high as cuts of beef/veal from cattle meat (7.9 million tonnes); the production of sheep meat in the EU-27 was relatively modest (0.7 million tonnes).

A quarter (24.7%) of the EU-27's pig meat production in 2010 came from Germany, the next highest contributions being recorded for Spain (15.3%) and France (9.1%), while the 7.9% share for Poland and the 7.6% share for Denmark were also notable. Just under one fifth (19.2%) of the beef/veal produced in the EU-27 originated from France in 2010, with Germany and Italy the only other Member States to report production in excess of one million tonnes; Ireland reported a relatively high share (7.1%) of the EU-27's production of cattle meat.

Dairy production has a diverse structure across the Member States, in terms of farm and dairy herd sizes, as well as milk yields. The total collection of cows' milk in the EU-27 in 2010 amounted to 136.1 million tonnes. Figure 8.3.5 shows that over one third (36.1%) of the whole milk that was utilised in the EU-27 in 2010 was converted into cheese, with butter accounting for the next highest proportion (28.7%); just over a tenth of the whole milk utilised in the EU-27 was used for drinking milk (12.4%) and for cream (11.5%).

Germany recorded the highest share (21.4%) of EU-27 milk collected in 2010 and also accounted for the highest proportions of EU-27 butter (23.5%) and cheese (23.3%) production.

Data sources and availability

Annual statistics on the production of a range of specific crops are covered by Council Regulations, although the data for fresh fruit and vegetables are collected under various informal agreements with the EU Member States.

The statistics on crop production in this subchapter relate to harvested production. Agricultural production of crops is synonymous with harvested production and includes marketed quantities, as well as quantities consumed directly on the farm, losses and waste on the holding, and losses during transport, storage and packaging.

Statistics on milk, eggs and meat products are compiled according to Community legislation. Milk production covers farm production of milk from cows, sheep, goats and buffaloes. A distinction is made between milk collected by dairies and milk production on the farm. Milk collection is only a part of the total use of milk production on the farm, the remainder generally includes own consumption, direct sale and cattle feed.

Meat production is based on the carcass weight of meat fit for human consumption. The concept of carcass weight is generally the weight of the slaughtered animal's cold body, although the precise definition varies according to the animal under consideration.

Context

Information on agricultural products may be used to analyse developments within agricultural markets in order to help distinguish between cycles and changing production patterns; these statistics can also be used to study how markets respond to policy actions. Agricultural product data also provides supply side information, furthering understanding as regards price developments which are of particular interest to agricultural commodity traders and policy analysts.

In October 2007, the Council adopted legislation to establish a single common market organisation for agricultural products (Regulation 1234/2007). This was designed to reduce the volume of legislation in the farming sector, to improve legislative transparency, and to make agricultural policy more easily accessible. Between the start of 2008 and the start of 2009, the single common market organisation replaced 21 individual markets for a variety of different products such as fruit and vegetables, cereals, meats, eggs, dairy products, sugar or wine.

Despite reforms of the common agricultural policy (CAP) in 2003 and 2008, farm subsidies consume more than 40% of the EU's annual spending. During the summer of 2010 a consultation process was organised in relation to the development of future agricultural policy. This identified three key areas for the stakeholders consulted, namely, food

security, environmental concerns, and rural diversity. In November 2010 the European Commission released a Communication (COM(2010) 672 final) providing a blueprint for developing agricultural policy, titled 'The CAP towards 2020: meeting the food, natural resources and territorial challenges of the future'. The document details some of the main

challenges facing the EU's agricultural sector in the coming decade – for example, how to preserve the EU's food production so as to guarantee long-term food security, while supporting farming communities that provide a diverse range of quality products, and ensuring environmental, water, animal and plant health requirements are met.

Figure 8.3.1: Indices of the agricultural production of crops, EU-27, 2000-2010 (2000 = 100)

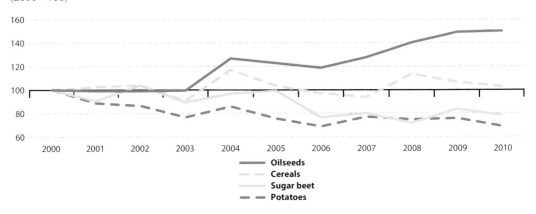

Source: Eurostat (online data code: apro_cpp_crop)

Table 8.3.1: Agricultural production of crops, 2010
(1 000 tonnes)

	Cereals	Sugar beet	Potatoes	Oilseeds	Pulses	Textile crops
EU-27	285 227	106 950	56 972	28 967	3 429	849
Belgium	3 105	4 465	3 456	54	8	64
Bulgaria	7 036	0	251	2 064	9	1
Czech Republic	6 878	3 065	665	1 160	58	0
Denmark	8 748	2 356	1 358	577	34	0
Germany	44 293	23 858	10 202	5 794	264	0
Estonia	670	0	93	131	12	0
Ireland	2 040	45	363	23	14	0
Greece	4 098	761	792	762	50	184
Spain	19 642	3 399	2 278	924	462	140
France	65 414	34 767	6 528	6 629	990	437
Italy	20 960	3 550	1 558	815	146	0
Cyprus	54	87	93	0	14	0
Latvia	1 417	0	293	168	5	0
Lithuania	2 768	723	469	178	67	0
Luxembourg	166	0	20	16	1	0
Hungary	12 300	754	440	1 623	38	0
Malta	0	0	10	0	0	0
Netherlands	1 887	5 280	6 844	109	9	17
Austria	4 818	3 132	672	332	57	3
Poland	27 299	9 823	8 766	2 103	268	3
Portugal	1 051	7	509	8	3	0
Romania	16 752	900	3 567	2 356	58	0
Slovenia	568	0	102	15	2	0
Slovakia	2 571	978	126	518	17	0
Finland	2 972	542	659	3	30	0
Sweden	4 333	1 974	816	303	85	0
United Kingdom	23 387	6 484	6 045	2 303	727	0
Croatia	2 925	1 249	179	253	3	0
FYR of Macedonia	537	:	202	13	15	:
Turkey	59 649	17 942	4 548	2 777	26	795

Source: Eurostat (online data code: apro_cpp_crop)

Figure 8.3.2: Production of cereals, EU-27, 2010 (¹)
(%, based on tonnes)

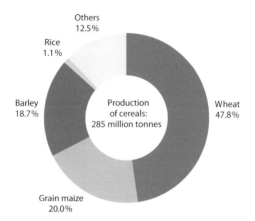

Others
12.5%

Rice
1.1%

Barley
18.7%

Production
of cereals:
285 million tonnes

Wheat
47.8%

Grain maize
20.0%

(¹) Provisional; includes Eurostat estimates made for the purpose of this publication with estimates for Italian rice production based on the area reported; figures do not sum to 100 % due to rounding.

Source: Eurostat (online data code: apro_cpp_crop)

Figure 8.3.3: Production of vegetables, EU-27, 2010 (¹)
(%, based on tonnes)

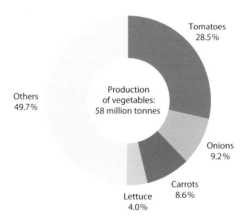

Tomatoes
28.5%

Others
49.7%

Production
of vegetables:
58 million tonnes

Onions
9.2%

Carrots
8.6%

Lettuce
4.0%

(¹) Includes Eurostat estimates made for the purpose of this publication.

Source: Eurostat (online data code: apro_cpp_fruveg)

Figure 8.3.4: Production of fruit, EU-27, 2010 (¹)
(%, based on tonnes)

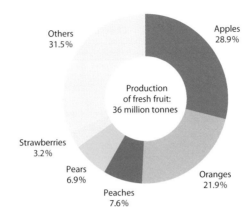

Others
31.5%

Apples
28.9%

Production
of fresh fruit:
36 million tonnes

Strawberries
3.2%

Pears
6.9%

Peaches
7.6%

Oranges
21.9%

(¹) Includes Eurostat estimates made for the purpose of this publication.

Source: Eurostat (online data code: apro_cpp_fruveg)

Table 8.3.2: Agricultural production related to animals, 2010
(1 000 tonnes)

	Collection of cows' milk	Butter	Cheese	Cattle meat	Pig meat	Sheep meat
EU-27 (¹)	136 090	*1 716*	8 953	7 918	22 011	725
Belgium	3 067	26	75	263	1 124	3
Bulgaria	565	1	69	5	37	4
Czech Republic	2 312	23	115	74	276	0
Denmark	4 830	33	292	131	1 666	2
Germany	29 076	404	2 083	1 187	5 443	20
Estonia	621	6	38	9	32	0
Ireland	:	:	:	559	214	48
Greece	673	2	209	58	114	71
Spain	5 877	31	302	607	3 369	131
France	23 558	342	1 925	1 521	2 010	83
Italy	10 500	:	1 177	1 075	1 633	36
Cyprus	151	0	14	4	57	3
Latvia	625	5	31	18	23	0
Lithuania	1 278	8	95	43	55	0
Luxembourg	282	:	:	10	10	0
Hungary	1 322	4	73	27	416	0
Malta	:	:	:	1	7	0
Netherlands	11 626	:	*753*	389	1 288	13
Austria	2 771	:	149	225	542	7
Poland	9 002	119	667	386	1 741	1
Portugal	1 829	27	69	94	384	10
Romania	904	10	64	28	234	4
Slovenia	520	:	18	36	25	0
Slovakia	800	6	29	14	69	1
Finland	2 289	45	109	82	203	1
Sweden	2 862	19	103	148	263	5
United Kingdom	13 582	:	337	925	774	281
Switzerland (²)	3 388	48	177	:	:	:
Croatia (³)	682	3	28	55	89	1

(¹) Includes Eurostat estimates made for the purpose of this publication.
(²) 2009, based on collection (apro_mk_cola).
(³) 2009 for milk, butter and cheese.

Source: Eurostat (online data codes: apro_mk_pobta, apro_mk_cola and apro_mt_pann)

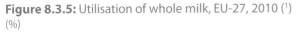
Figure 8.3.5: Utilisation of whole milk, EU-27, 2010 (¹)
(%)

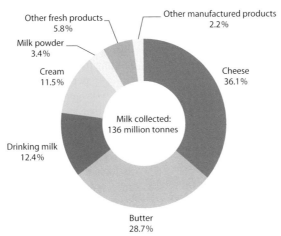

Other fresh products
5.8%

Other manufactured products
2.2%

Milk powder
3.4%

Cream
11.5%

Cheese
36.1%

Milk collected:
136 million tonnes

Drinking milk
12.4%

Butter
28.7%

(¹) Includes Eurostat estimates made for the purpose of this publication; figures do not sum to 100 % due to rounding.

Source: Eurostat (online data code: apro_mk_pobta)

8.4 Fertiliser consumption and nutrient balances

This subchapter presents data relating to fertiliser consumption and nutrient balances within the European Union (EU). Around 40 % of the EU-27's land area is farmed, highlighting the importance of farming for the EU's natural environment. Links between the natural environment and farming practices are complex: farming has contributed over the centuries to creating and maintaining a variety of valuable semi-natural habitats within which a wide range of species rely for their survival; on the other hand, inappropriate agricultural practices and land use can have an adverse effect on natural resources, through the pollution of soil, water and air, or the fragmentation of habitats and a subsequent loss of wildlife.

Main statistical findings

Fertilisers consumption

Figure 8.4.1 shows the estimated consumption of manufactured fertilisers in terms of the quantity of nutrients applied to each hectare of utilised agricultural area (UAA). Total consumption in the EU (excluding Malta) was estimated at an average 76 kg of nutrients (nitrogen, phosphorus and potassium together) per hectare in 2009 (see Figure 8.4.1).

Nitrogen-based fertilisers accounted for the vast majority (77.4 %) of the nutrients consumed, with an estimated consumption of 59 kg per hectare across the EU, ranging from 19 kg per hectare in Portugal to 125 kg per hectare in the Netherlands. EU consumption of phosphorus (in the form of manufactured fertilisers) averaged 6 kg per hectare in the EU, ranging from 2 kg per hectare in Romania to 10 kg per hectare in Poland, while potassium consumption averaged 11 kg per hectare in the EU, ranging from 2 kg per hectare in Romania to 30 kg per hectare in Belgium and Luxembourg; the consumption of potassium-based fertilisers was higher still in Norway (33 kg per hectare).

The Benelux countries reported the highest levels (over 140 kg per hectare) of nutrient consumption from manufactured fertilisers. They were followed by Norway, Germany, Ireland and Poland – the only other countries to record consumption in excess of 100 kg per hectare. In contrast, Portugal and

Romania reported the lowest levels of consumption of manufactured fertilisers, at just under 30 kg per hectare.

Some European countries produce official statistics on the use of mineral fertilisers; these are presented in Figures 8.4.2 and 8.4.3, which provide details of the average annual percentage change in fertiliser use over the period from 2000 to 2008 for nitrogen-based fertilisers and phosphorus-based fertilisers. Figure 8.4.2 shows that the consumption of nitrogen-based fertilisers increased at a rapid pace in Latvia (on average by 9.6 % per annum), while Lithuania (4.8 %) and Poland (3.6 %) reported the second and third highest growth rates. There were six additional Member States (and Norway) that reported an increase in the average tonnage of nitrogen-based fertilisers that were used during the period from 2000 to 2008, aside from Austria these were all Member States that had joined the EU in 2004 or 2007. The reduction in the use of nitrogen-based fertilisers was generally less than 4 % per annum in most of the remaining Member States (and Switzerland), although somewhat bigger declines were registered in the Netherlands (– 4.3 %), Greece (– 5.6 %) and Portugal (– 6.9 %).

Figure 8.4.3 shows that between 2000 and 2008 the consumption of phosphorus-based fertilisers increased at a relatively rapid pace in Poland (5.7 % per annum) and Hungary (4.2 %). Only two other EU Member States (and Switzerland) reported growth in the quantity of phosphorous-based fertilisers that were used during the period from 2000 to 2008; while there was no change in the consumption of phosphorus-based fertilisers in Austria. In contrast, consumption of phosphorous-based fertilisers fell by between 7.4 % and 10.2 % per annum in Ireland, the Benelux countries and Portugal.

Gross nutrient balances

A persistent surplus of nutrients indicates potential environmental problems, such as nutrient leaching (resulting in pollution of drinking water and eutrophication of surface waters), ammonia emissions (contributing to acidification, eutrophication and atmospheric particulate pollution), or emissions of nitrous oxide (a greenhouse gas). A persistent deficit in nutrients indicates, among others, a risk for declining soil fertility.

The gross nitrogen balance for the EU-27 averaged 51 kg of nitrogen per hectare of agricultural land during the period 2005 to 2008 (see Figure 8.4.4), ranging from 210 kg per hectare in the Netherlands to – 4 kg per hectare in Hungary. The nitrogen balance was generally lower among those Member States that joined the EU in 2004 or 2007, as well as in southern Europe (other than Cyprus and Malta). Comparing the average nitrogen balance for the period from 2000 to 2004 with that for 2005 to 2008, the biggest reductions in the nitrogen balance were often recorded among those Member States that reported some of the highest nitrogen surpluses; this was particularly the case for the Netherlands and for Belgium. On the other hand, there were some countries that reported an increase in their nitrogen surpluses, most notably, Poland, Romania and the Czech Republic.

The gross phosphorus balance for the EU-27 was almost at parity during the period 2005 to 2008 (see Figure 8.4.5), averaging 1.8 kg of phosphorus per hectare of agricultural land; in part this lower surplus reflected the lower use made of phosphorus-based fertilisers when compared with nitrogen-based fertilisers. The phosphorus balance ranged from 25.5 kg per hectare in Malta to – 12.2 kg per hectare in Hungary. A similar pattern (to that for nitrogen balances) was observed for the phosphorus balance, with Malta, Cyprus and several countries in north western Europe having the highest surpluses, while a deficit was recorded in eight of the Member States (all of which were either Member States that joined the EU in 2004 or 2007 or countries from southern Europe). Comparing the average phosphorus balance for the period from 2000 to 2004 with that for 2005 to 2008, the biggest reductions in the phosphorus balance were generally recorded among those Member States that reported some of the highest phosphorous surpluses; in particular, Belgium, Slovenia and the Netherlands. On the other hand, there were only two countries that reported an increase in their phosphorus surplus over the period under consideration – Poland and Norway.

Data sources and availability

Data on the estimated consumption of nutrients contained in manufactured fertilisers were provided by Fertilizers Europe, the European trade association of fertiliser manufacturers. The methodology used for the collection of these statistics is harmonised across countries and was developed as a forecasting exercise within the industry. It relies on the estimation of application rates by crop at a national and sometimes regional level by experts; figures are then multiplied by estimated cropping areas. The estimates for total consumption are reconciled with the quantities of fertilisers that are actually sold; allowance is made for changes in stocks causing differences between sales and consumption. Annual data are available for nearly all EU Member States, as well as Norway. Data on fertiliser use are broken down by nutrient type: nitrogen (N), phosphorus (P), phosphate (P_2O_5), potassium (K), potash (K_2O).

Official data on the quantities of nutrients contained in fertilisers were generally provided by national statistical offices (for Luxembourg they were provided by the Ministry of Agriculture). The data were provided under the framework of the Joint Eurostat/OECD Questionnaire on agri-environmental indicators and of the Eurostat/OECD gross nutrient balances data collection exercise. At present no harmonised European statistics on mineral fertiliser use are available from official sources. As such, different data sources were used to compile the dataset and therefore comparability may not be high. Some countries have carried out farm surveys, others have estimated consumption from statistics on production and trade of mineral fertilisers.

A gross nutrient balance is calculated as the total nutrient input to the soil minus the total nutrient output from the soil. The gross nutrient balance per hectare is derived by dividing the total balance by the reference area (in this case that of agricultural land). The reference area for the data presented in this subchapter relates to the sum of area for arable land, permanent grassland and land under permanent crops. For some countries, gross nutrient balances were estimated by Eurostat, and afterwards approved by national authorities.

Inputs for the gross nutrient balance include fertilisers (both organic and inorganic), manure production (animal excretion), manure withdrawals (exports, processed as industrial waste, non-agricultural use, etc.), changes in manure stocks and manure imports. Other inputs include seeds and planting material, atmospheric nutrient deposition and (for nitrogen only) biological fixation by leguminous crops (such as clover, soya beans, etc.).

Outputs of the gross nutrient balance include harvesting crops (for example, cereals, dried pulses, root crops, industrial crops, vegetables, fruit), the harvest and grazing of fodder (from arable land, permanent and temporary pasture), crop residuals removed from the field. Nutrient inputs and outputs are estimated for each item of the balance by multiplying basic data (such as crop area, crop production, livestock numbers) with coefficients to convert the data into nutrient contents.

Context

Fertilisers contain important nutrients, such as nitrogen (N), phosphorus (P) and potassium (K), which plants absorb from the soil for their growth. Fertilisers are often considered as an essential input in agricultural production. In addition to livestock manure (which may be used as an organic fertiliser), most non-organic farms also apply large amounts of manufactured mineral fertilisers. When the amount of fertiliser applied exceeds the plants' nutritional requirements, there is a greater risk of nutrient losses from agricultural soils into ground and surface water. The resulting higher concentration of nutrients (eutrophication) can cause serious degradation of ecosystems. In addition to the problems associated with eutrophication, fertilisers may also have adverse environmental effects resulting from their production processes. More specifically, nitrogenous fertilisers — the most commonly consumed fertilisers — require large amounts of energy to be produced leading potentially to higher levels of greenhouse gas emissions. In a different way, phosphorus and potash fertilisers also have an environmental impact, since the raw materials used to produce them are mined, therefore potentially leading to landscape destruction, water contamination, excessive water consumption or air pollution.

The gross nutrient balance provides an insight into the links between agricultural nutrient use, losses of nutrients into the environment, and the sustainable use of soil nutrient resources. In order to estimate the risk of nutrient loss, the consumption of manufactured fertilisers should be combined with other nutrient inputs. In addition, the nutrient requirements (and hence consumption) of plants are influenced by previous land management, soil type and climatic factors, and they vary from one crop to another.

The gross nutrient balance only provides an indication of the potential risks to the environment (air, water and soil), as the actual risks depend on a range of factors including climatic conditions, soil type and characteristics, soil saturation, and management practices such as drainage, tillage and irrigation. The gross nutrient balance may be used to represent the difference between nutrients applied to the soil and nutrients removed by crops; it reflects the risks associated with nutrients either leaching into the soil and water or being released into the atmosphere.

The complex relationship between agriculture and the environment has resulted in environmental concerns and safeguards being integrated within the EU's common agricultural policy (CAP), with particular attention being paid to reducing the risks of environmental degradation through cross-compliance criteria (as a condition for benefiting from direct payments, farmers must comply with certain requirements, some related to environmental protection) and targeted agri-environmental measures, in order to enhance the sustainability of agro-ecosystems.

The importance attached to assessing the interaction between agriculture and the environment is underlined by a European Commission Communication, titled 'Development of agri-environmental indicators for monitoring the integration of environmental concerns into the common agricultural policy' (COM(2006) 508 final), containing a list of 28 agri-environmental indicators which portray farming practices, agricultural production systems, pressures and risks to the environment, and the state of natural resources.

In order to limit the environmental damage associated with excess nutrient application, such as eutrophication, a number of legislative measures have been taken, such as the adoption of the nitrates Directive and the water framework Directive, covering the designation of nitrate-vulnerable zones where Member States have imposed regulatory limits on the load and timing of fertiliser spreading on agricultural land.

Figure 8.4.1: Estimated consumption of manufactured fertilisers, 2009 (¹)
(kg of nutrient per hectare of UAA)

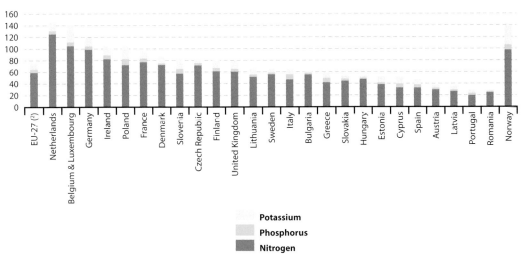

Potassium
Phosphorus
Nitrogen

(¹) Utilised agricultural area, 2007; Malta, not available.
(²) Excluding Malta.

Source: Eurostat (online data codes: aei_fm_manfert and ef_lu_ovcropaa) and Fertilizers Europe

Figure 8.4.2: Average annual change in nitrogen tonnage, 2000-2008 (¹)
(%)

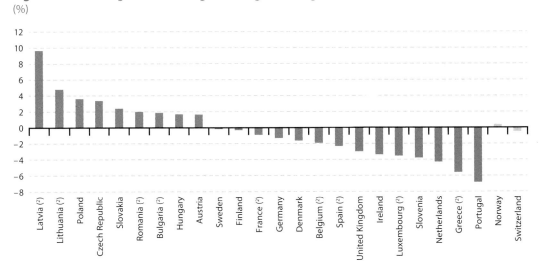

(¹) Estonia, Italy, Cyprus and Malta, not available.
(²) Estimates.

Source: Eurostat (online data code: aei_fm_usefert)

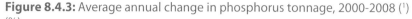

Figure 8.4.3: Average annual change in phosphorus tonnage, 2000-2008 (¹)
(%)

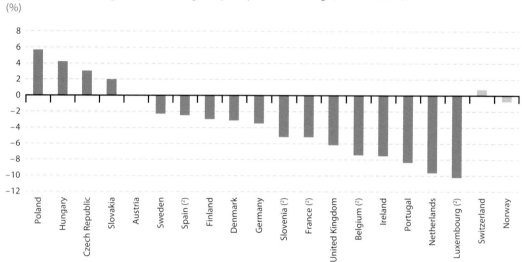

(¹) Bulgaria, Estonia, Greece, Italy, Cyprus, Latvia, Lithuania, Malta and Romania, not available.
(²) Estimates.

Source: Eurostat (online data code: aei_fm_usefert)

Figure 8.4.4: Gross nitrogen balance, 2000-2004 and 2005-2008
(kg nitrogen per hectare of agricultural land)

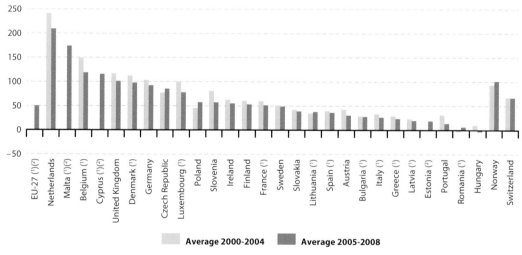

■ **Average 2000-2004**   ■ **Average 2005-2008**

(¹) Estimates.
(²) 2000-2004, not available.

Source: Eurostat (online data code: aei_pr_gnb)

Figure 8.4.5: Gross phosphorus balance, 2000-2004 and 2005-2008
(kg phosphorus per hectare of agricultural land)

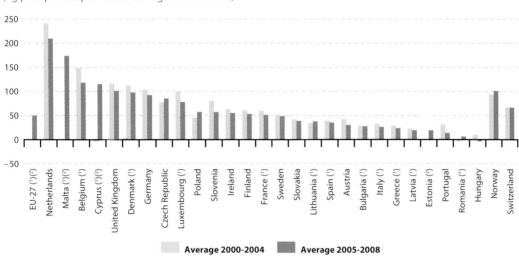

Average 2000-2004   Average 2005-2008

(¹) 2000-2004, not available.
(²) Estimates.

Source: Eurostat (online data code: aei_pr_gnb)

8.5 Forestry

This subchapter presents statistics on forestry and logging in the European Union (EU). The EU-27 has approximately 178 million hectares of forests and other wooded land, corresponding to 42 % of its land area, and forest cover is gradually increasing: over the past 20 years the forest area has increased by 5 % – approximately 0.3 % per year – although the rate varies substantially between Member States.

Main statistical findings

From 1995 to 2007, there was a relatively steady rise in the level of roundwood production in the EU-27, both for coniferous (softwood) and non-coniferous (broadleaved or hardwood) species – see Figure 8.5.1. However, the effects of the financial and economic crisis led to the level of coniferous production falling in 2008 and this was confirmed with a further reduction in 2009, when non-coniferous production also fell. Nevertheless, the overall level of roundwood production in the EU-27 in 2009 remained 25.3 million m³ higher than in 1995.

In 2010 roundwood production increased for both categories of tree species: the larger category of coniferous species recorded an increase of 13.0 % compared with 2009, while there was production growth of 8.2 % for non-coniferous species. Overall production increased by 44.1 million m³ in 2010, bringing the level of production back to 428.5 million m³, around 6.5 % below its peak level from 2007. Among the Member States, Sweden produced the most roundwood (70.2 million m³) in 2010, followed by Germany, France and Finland (each producing between 50 million and 57 million m³) – see Table 8.5.1. Some of the peaks (most recently 2000, 2005 and 2007) in roundwood production are due to forestry and logging having to cope with unplanned numbers of trees that were felled by severe storms. The 415.1 million m³ of roundwood produced in the EU-27 in 2008 was almost 10 % less than the relative peak recorded in 2007. This latest peak was due to exceptional windthrows by storms in many parts of Europe – notably in Germany and Sweden – after which many more trees had to be removed from forests than planned.

Approximately one quarter of roundwood production is used as wood for fuel and three quarters is industrial roundwood that is used either for sawnwood and veneers, or for pulp and paper production.

Some 100.4 million m³ of sawnwood were produced in the EU-27 in 2010, two fifths (39.3 %) of which came from the two largest producing Member States, namely, Germany (22.3 %) and Sweden (17.0 %); Austria, Finland and France each accounted for around 9 % of the EU-27 total. The level of sawnwood production in the EU-27 in 2010 was 10.3 % higher than in 2009.

There is a strong link between the volume of roundwood produced and the value added generated by forestry and logging – see Figure 8.5.2. There is also a link between the labour input (in terms of the number of annual work units (AWU)) and value added. However, it is worth noting that the number of AWU per area of exploited forest varies significantly between countries, ranging from more than ten AWU per 1 000 hectares in the Czech Republic to only around one AWU per 1 000 hectares in Finland (and also Norway) – see Figure 8.5.3. Forestry and logging work in mountainous areas generally requires a higher labour input than on large tracts of flat land.

Data sources and availability

Eurostat, the Timber Committee of the United Nations Economic Commission for Europe (UNECE), the Forestry Section of the United Nations Food and Agriculture Organisation (FAO) and the International Tropical Timber Organisation (ITTO) collect and collate statistics on the production and trade of wood through their Joint Forest Sector Questionnaire. Each partner collects data from a different part of the world. Eurostat is responsible for data from the EU Member States and EFTA countries.

Roundwood production is a synonym for removals; it comprises all quantities of wood removed from forests and other wooded land or other felling sites during a given period; it is reported in cubic metres (m³) underbark (in other words, excluding bark). Sawnwood production is wood that has been produced either by sawing lengthways or by a profile-chipping process and that exceeds 6 mm in thickness; it includes for example planks, beams, joists, boards, rafters, scantlings, laths, boxboards and lumber, in the following forms – unplaned, planed, and end-jointed; it is reported in cubic metres of solid volume.

Economic and employment data for forestry and logging are collected with a separate questionnaire that was developed in collaboration with Eurostat's national accountants; these statistics are part of integrated environmental and economic accounting for forests.

Context

Contrary to what is happening in many other parts of the world, the area covered by forests and other wooded land in the EU-27 is slowly increasing. The area covered by forests and other wooded land increased, on average, by 0.3 % per annum over the period 1990 to 2010, although the rates of change in individual EU Member States varied substantially. The EU-27's forests and other wooded land cover approximately the same proportion of land area as that used for agriculture.

Ecologically, the forests of the EU belong to many different biogeographical regions and have adapted to a variety of natural conditions, ranging from bogs to steppes and from lowland to alpine forests. Socioeconomically, they vary from small family holdings to state forests or to large estates owned by companies, many as part of industrial wood supply chains; about 60 % of the EU-27's wooded land is privately owned.

The EU's forestry strategy dates from 1998 and established a framework for forest-related actions in support of sustainable forest management. A report on its implementation was prepared in 2005 which led to the European Commission presenting an EU forest action plan (COM(2006) 302)

in 2006 which underpins support for sustainable forest management and the multi-functional role of forests. The plan is a framework for forest-related measures and is used to coordinate EU initiatives with the forest policies of the Member States. There are 18 key actions proposed – to be implemented jointly with the Member States. The plan focuses on four main objectives:

• improving long-term competitiveness;
• improving and protecting the environment;

• contributing to the quality of life;
• fostering coordination and communication.

In April 2011 the first steps were taken to organise a review of the forestry strategy. The current review may lead to the establishment of targets and indicators to measure progress. Equally, the common agricultural policy (CAP) is due to be reformed by 2013; this review may also have consequences for forestry policy in terms of changes to rural development policy.

Figure 8.5.1: Annual production of roundwood, EU-27, 1995-2010 (¹)
(1 000 m³)

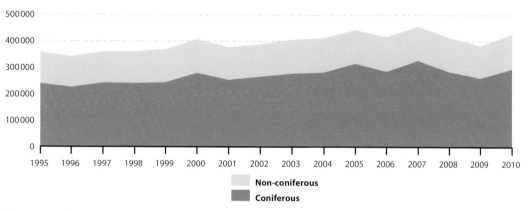

(¹) 2000, 2001 and 2007, estimates.

Source: Eurostat (online data code: for_remov)

Table 8.5.1: Wood production, 1995-2010
(1 000 m³)

	Roundwood production					Sawnwood production				
	1995	2000	2005	2009	2010	1995	2000	2005	2009	2010
EU-27	359 132	408 095	443 484	384 394	428 526	83 146	100 064	108 082	91 078	100 430
Euro area (EA-16) (¹)	212 355	236 540	232 925	214 025	240 231	52 069	61 337	66 777	54 831	60 051
Belgium	:	4 510	4 950	4 395	4 827	:	1 150	1 285	1 255	1 332
Bulgaria	2 838	4 784	5 862	4 599	5 668	257	312	569	447	633
Czech Republic	12 365	14 441	15 510	15 502	17 022	3 498	4 106	4 003	4 048	4 670
Denmark	2 282	2 952	2 962	2 813	2 669	585	364	196	441	448
Germany	39 343	53 710	56 946	48 073	54 418	14 207	16 340	21 931	20 772	22 351
Estonia	3 709	8 910	5 500	5 400	7 560	353	1 436	2 063	1 127	1 360
Ireland	2 204	2 673	2 648	2 349	2 789	678	888	1 015	774	875
Greece	1 961	2 245	1 523	1 261	1 251	337	123	191	106	118
Spain	16 075	14 321	15 531	13 980	15 648	3 312	3 760	3 660	2 072	2 038
France	60 438	65 865	52 499	54 625	57 362	10 071	10 536	9 715	7 885	8 565
Italy	9 736	9 329	8 691	8 080	7 254	1 862	1 630	1 590	1 220	1 200
Cyprus	48	21	10	10	9	15	9	4	5	4
Latvia	6 890	14 304	12 843	10 442	12 965	1 300	3 900	4 227	2 520	3 150
Lithuania	5 960	5 500	6 045	5 460	7 097	940	1 300	1 445	1 011	1 213
Luxembourg	:	260	249	274	275	:	133	133	129	94
Hungary	4 331	5 902	5 940	5 244	5 740	231	291	215	102	133
Malta	0	0	0	0	0	0	0	0	0	0
Netherlands	1 104	1 039	1 110	1 016	1 081	428	389	279	210	231
Austria	14 405	13 276	16 471	16 727	17 831	7 814	10 390	11 074	8 458	9 603
Poland	20 651	26 025	31 945	34 629	35 378	3 870	4 262	3 360	3 882	4 245
Portugal	9 350	10 831	10 746	9 564	9 648	1 831	1 427	1 010	1 093	1 045
Romania	12 178	13 148	14 501	12 557	14 333	1 777	3 396	4 321	3 598	4 349
Slovenia	1 866	2 253	2 733	2 930	2 945	513	439	527	525	596
Slovakia	5 323	6 163	9 302	9 087	13 939	661	1 265	2 621	2 254	2 524
Finland	50 219	54 542	52 250	41 653	50 952	10 007	13 420	12 269	8 072	9 473
Sweden	63 600	63 300	98 200	65 100	70 200	14 970	16 176	17 600	16 200	17 100
United Kingdom	8 146	7 791	8 519	8 624	9 662	2 446	2 622	2 780	2 871	3 078
Iceland	0	0	0	:	:	0	0	0	:	:
Liechtenstein	18	:	:	25	25	:	:	:	4	4
Norway	9 045	8 156	9 667	8 884	:	2 212	2 280	2 326	1 850	:
Switzerland	4 749	9 238	5 285	4 702	4 920	1 504	1 625	1 591	1 481	1 457
Montenegro	:	:	:	364	:	:	:	:	50	:
Croatia	2 603	3 669	4 018	4 242	:	578	642	624	653	:
FYR of Macedonia	:	:	822	639	:	:	:	18	2	:
Turkey	19 279	15 939	16 185	19 430	:	4 966	5 528	6 445	5 853	:
Brazil	:	:	255 743	256 306	:	:	:	23 557	24 987	:
Canada	188 346	201 845	203 121	107 266	:	43 838	50 465	60 187	32 820	:
China	:	:	302 028	291 850	:	:	:	18 814	29 311	:
India	:	:	328 677	330 975	:	:	:	14 789	14 789	:
Indonesia	:	:	111 291	100 585	:	:	:	4 330	4 330	:
Russia	116 510	158 100	185 000	151 400	:	27 815	20 000	22 033	18 974	:
United States	469 830	466 549	467 347	344 835	:	85 313	91 076	97 020	61 998	:

(¹) EA-11 for 1995 and 2000; EA-12 for 2005.
Source: Eurostat (online data codes: for_remov and for_swpan)

Figure 8.5.2: Roundwood production and gross value added of forestry and logging, 2008 and 2009 (¹)

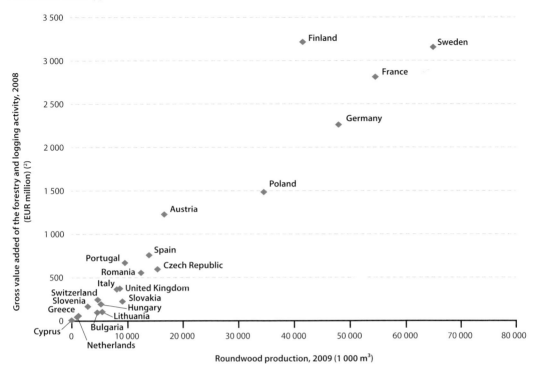

(¹) Member States that are not shown, not available.
(²) Italy, Lithuania and Netherlands, 2006; Spain and Sweden, 2007; Slovenia, Slovakia and Switzerland, 2009.

Source: Eurostat (online data codes: for_remov and for_ieeaf_cp)

Figure 8.5.3: Volume of work per area of forest available for wood supply, 2008 (¹)
(annual work units per 1 000 hectares)

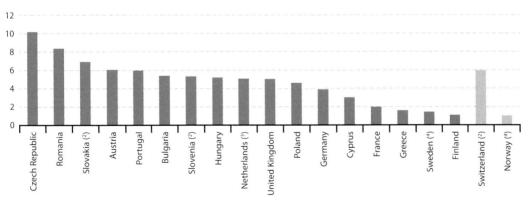

(¹) Forest available for wood supply, 2005; an annual work unit is equivalent to the work performed by one person employed full-time over a year; Member States that are not shown, not available. (²) 2009. (³) 2006. (⁴) 2007.

Source: Eurostat (online data codes: for_awu and for_area), FAO Forest Resources Assessment 2005

8.6 Fisheries

This subchapter gives an overview of recent statistics relating to fishing fleets, fish catches, and also aquaculture production in the European Union (EU). Fish are a natural, biological, mobile (sometimes over wide distances) and renewable resource. Aside from fish farming, fish cannot be owned until they have been caught. For this reason, fish stocks continue to be regarded as a common resource, which needs to be managed collectively. This has led to a range of policies that regulate the amount of fishing, as well as the types of fishing techniques and gear used in fish capture.

Main statistical findings

By far the largest fishing fleets among the EU Member States, in terms of power, were those from Italy, France, Spain and the United Kingdom; in 2010, the fishing fleets of each of these countries had a collective power of between 0.8 million kW and 1.1 million kW. In terms of tonnage, however, the Spanish fishing fleet was by far the largest (415 000 gross tonnes), which was more than twice the size of the fleets in the United Kingdom, Italy or France. The fishing fleets of Norway and Iceland were also relatively large. Indeed, the fleet in Norway had more power (1.2 million kW) than any of the fleets from the EU Member States, while in tonnage terms Norway (366 000) was second only to Spain (see Figure 8.6.1).

Total catches by the fishing fleets of Denmark, Spain, the United Kingdom and France accounted for just over half (50.6 %) of all the catches made by EU-27 fishing fleets in 2009. This share has declined in recent years from about 60 % in 2000, mainly as a result of the sharp reduction in the share of the Danish catch (see Table 8.6.1). Since 1999, the total EU-27 catch has fallen almost every year (with the exception of 2001); the total catch by the EU-27 in 2009 was 26.2 % less than in 1999. Around 70 % of the catches made by the EU-27 in 2009 were in the north east Atlantic, with the eastern central Atlantic the second largest fishing area (see Figure 8.6.2).

The level of aquaculture production in the EU-27 remained stable during the period from 1999 to 2009, with annual output of between 1.3 and 1.4 million tonnes. The five largest aquaculture producers among the EU Member States were Spain, France, the United Kingdom, Italy and Greece, which together accounted for around three quarters (75.6 %) of total aquaculture production in 2009. Among the non-member countries included in Table 8.6.2 aquaculture production was extremely large in Norway – higher than the combined output of the three largest Member States; the aquaculture output of Turkey was also quite substantial (similar in magnitude to Italy).

The development of aquaculture production between 1999 and 2009 followed different patterns across the EU Member States. Production in the Netherlands and Germany was almost halved, while there were also relatively large reductions in aquaculture output in Italy, Spain and France. In contrast, aquaculture output increased by 44.7 % in Greece during the period from 1999 to 2009 and rose by 27.0 % in the United Kingdom.

Data sources and availability

Fishery statistics are collected from official national sources either directly by Eurostat for the members of the European Economic Area (EEA) or indirectly through other international organisations for other countries. The data are collected using internationally agreed concepts and definitions developed by the coordinating working party on fishery statistics (CWP), comprising Eurostat and several other international organisations with responsibilities in fishery statistics. The flag of the fishing vessel is used as the primary indication of the nationality of the catch, though this concept may vary in certain circumstances.

In general, the data refer to the fishing fleet size on 31 December of the reference year. The data are derived from national registers of fishing vessels which are maintained pursuant to Regulation 26/2004 which contains information on the vessel

characteristics – the administrative file of fishing vessels is maintained by the European Commission's Directorate-General for Maritime Affairs and Fisheries.

There has been a transition in measuring the tonnage of the fishing fleet from gross registered tonnage (GRT) to that of gross tonnage (GT). This change, which has taken place at different speeds within the national administrations, gives rise to the possibility of non-comparability of data over time and of non-comparability between countries.

Catches of fishery products include items taken for all purposes (commercial, industrial, recreational and subsistence) by all types and classes of fishing units operating both in inland, inshore, offshore and in high-seas fishing areas. The catch is normally expressed in live weight and derived by the application of conversion factors to the landed or product weight. As such, catch statistics exclude quantities which are caught and taken from the water (that is, before processing) but which, for a variety of reasons, are not landed.

Geographical fishing areas are defined for a number of specific areas of water, including:

- the north east Atlantic, which is roughly the area to the east of 42° W longitude and north of 36° N latitude, including the waters of the Baltic Sea;
- the north west Atlantic, which is the region that is roughly the area to the west of 42° W longitude and north of 35° N latitude;
- the eastern central Atlantic, which is the region to the east of 40° W longitude between latitudes 36° N and 6° S;
- the Mediterranean and the Black Sea (also known as Food and Agriculture Organisation (FAO) major fishing area 37), which comprises the Mediterranean Sea and the adjacent Black Sea.

Aquaculture is the farming of aquatic organisms including fish, molluscs, crustaceans and aquatic plants. Farming implies some form of intervention in the rearing process to enhance production, such as regular stocking, feeding and protection from predators. Farming also implies individual or corporate ownership of, or rights resulting from contractual arrangements to, the stock being cultivated.

Context

The first common European policy measures in the fishing sector date from 1970. They set rules for access to fishing grounds, markets and structures. All these measures became more significant when, in 1976, the Member States followed an international movement and agreed to extend their rights to marine resources from 12 to 200 miles from their coasts.

After years of difficult negotiations, the common fisheries policy (CFP), the EU's instrument for the management of fisheries and aquaculture, was born in 1983. The CFP sets maximum quantities of fish that can be safely caught every year: the total allowable catch (TAC). Each country's share is called a national quota.

The CFP was reformed in 2002 to deal with the environmental, economic and social dimensions of fishing. Common measures were agreed in four areas:

- the conservation of stocks/environmental impact – to protect fish resources by regulating the amount of fish taken from the sea, by allowing young fish to reproduce, and by ensuring that measures are respected;
- structures and fleet management (such as vessels, port facilities and fish processing plants) – to help the fishing and aquaculture sectors adapt their equipment and organisations to the constraints imposed by scarce resources and the market;
- the organisation of the market for fish in the EU – to maintain a common organisation of the market in fish products and to match supply and demand for the benefit of both producers and consumers;
- and external fisheries policy – to set-up fisheries agreements and to negotiate at an international level within regional and international fisheries organisations for common conservation measures in deep-sea fisheries.

The 2002 reform identified the need to limit fishing efforts, the level of catches, and to enforce certain technical measures. To ensure sustainable fishing, it is not only the quantity of fish taken from the sea that is important, but also their species, size, and the techniques used in catching them, as well as the areas where they are caught.

The European fisheries fund (EFF) has a budget of around EUR 3 800 million and covers the period 2007 to 2013. It aims to support the objectives of the CFP by:

- supporting sustainable exploitation of fisheries resources and a stable balance between these resources and the capacity of Community fishing fleet;

- strengthening the competitiveness and the viability of operators in the sector;
- promoting environmentally-friendly fishing and production methods;
- providing adequate support to people employed in the sector;
- fostering the sustainable development of fisheries areas.

Figure 8.6.1: Fishing fleet, 2010 (¹)

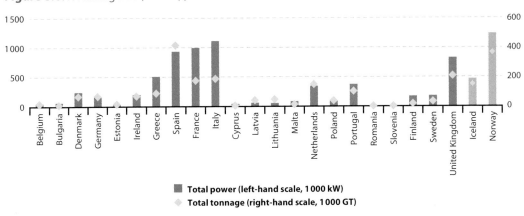

(¹) The Czech Republic, Luxembourg, Hungary, Austria and Slovakia are landlocked countries without a marine fishing fleet.

Source: Eurostat (online data code: fish_fleet)

Table 8.6.1: Total catches in all fishing regions, 1999-2009
(1 000 tonnes live weight)

	1999	2000	2001	2002	2003	2004	2005	2006	2007	2008	2009
EU-27	6 869	6 789	6 920	6 321	5 892	5 875	5 641	5 450	5 180	5 176	5 068
Belgium	30	30	30	29	27	27	25	23	25	23	22
Bulgaria	11	7	7	15	12	8	5	8	9	9	9
Czech Republic	4	5	5	5	5	5	4	5	4	4	4
Denmark	1 405	1 534	1 511	1 442	1 031	1 090	911	868	653	691	778
Germany	238	206	211	222	261	261	286	298	295	280	250
Estonia	112	113	105	101	79	88	100	87	99	101	97
Ireland	285	278	356	282	266	280	268	212	215	205	269
Greece	121	99	94	96	93	93	92	98	95	89	83
Spain	1 164	1 067	1 096	852	857	772	768	744	738	919	761
France	665	702	680	703	709	671	595	593	558	499	440
Italy	283	302	310	270	296	279	298	316	287	236	253
Cyprus	40	67	81	2	2	2	2	2	2	2	1
Latvia	125	136	128	114	115	125	151	140	155	158	163
Lithuania	73	79	151	150	157	162	140	155	187	183	173
Luxembourg	0	0	0	0	0	0	0	0	0	:	:
Hungary	8	7	7	7	7	7	8	8	7	7	6
Malta	1	1	1	1	1	1	1	1	1	1	2
Netherlands	511	496	518	464	526	522	549	470	414	417	382
Austria	0	0	0	0	0	0	0	0	0	0	0
Poland	236	218	225	223	180	192	155	145	152	142	224
Portugal	210	189	192	202	209	221	219	229	253	224	199
Romania	8	7	8	7	10	5	6	7	6	5	4
Slovenia	2	2	2	2	1	1	1	1	1	1	1
Slovakia	1	1	2	2	2	2	2	2	2	2	2
Finland	144	156	149	145	121	135	131	149	165	151	155
Sweden	351	339	312	295	287	270	256	269	238	231	203
United Kingdom	841	748	740	690	637	655	669	621	616	595	587
Iceland	1 754	2 000	2 001	2 145	2 002	1 750	1 661	1 345	1 421	1 307	1 164
Liechtenstein	0	0	0	0	0	0	0	0	0	:	:
Norway	2 628	2 700	2 687	2 740	2 549	2 525	2 393	2 256	2 378	2 431	2 524
Switzerland	2	2	2	2	2	2	1	1	1	2	2
Montenegro	:	:	:	:	:	:	:	1	1	1	2
Croatia	19	21	18	21	20	30	35	38	49	49	56
FYR of Macedonia	0	0	0	0	0	0	0	0	0	0	0
Turkey	574	503	528	567	508	550	426	533	632	494	464

Source: Eurostat (online data code: fish_ca_00)

Figure 8.6.2: Catches by fishing region, EU-27, 2009
(%, based on tonnes)

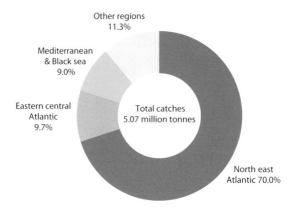

Source: Eurostat (online data code: fish_ca_main)

Table 8.6.2: Aquaculture production, 1999-2009
(1 000 tonnes live weight)

	1999	2000	2001	2002	2003	2004	2005	2006	2007	2008	2009
EU-27	1 429	1 399	1 386	1 272	1 343	1 311	1 261	1 283	1 307	1 252	1 300
Belgium	2	2	2	2	1	1	0	0	0	0	1
Bulgaria	8	4	3	2	4	2	3	3	4	5	8
Czech Republic	19	19	20	19	20	19	20	20	20	20	20
Denmark	43	44	42	32	38	43	39	28	31	37	34
Germany	80	66	53	50	74	57	45	38	45	44	41
Estonia	0	0	0	0	0	0	1	1	1	0	1
Ireland	44	51	61	63	63	58	60	53	53	45	47
Greece	84	95	98	88	101	97	106	113	113	115	122
Spain	318	309	309	255	268	293	219	295	285	252	269
France	265	267	252	252	240	243	245	238	237	238	234
Italy	210	217	218	184	192	118	181	174	181	158	162
Cyprus	1	2	2	2	2	2	2	4	3	4	3
Latvia	0	0	0	0	1	1	1	1	1	1	1
Lithuania	2	2	2	2	2	3	2	2	3	3	3
Luxembourg	:	:	:	:	:	:	:	:	:	:	:
Hungary	12	13	13	12	12	13	14	15	16	15	14
Malta	2	2	1	1	1	1	1	7	9	7	5
Netherlands	109	75	57	54	67	79	71	42	53	47	56
Austria	3	3	2	2	2	2	2	3	3	2	2
Poland	34	36	35	33	35	35	38	36	35	37	37
Portugal	6	8	8	8	8	7	7	8	7	6	7
Romania	9	10	11	9	9	8	7	9	10	12	13
Slovenia	1	1	1	1	1	2	1	1	1	1	2
Slovakia	1	1	1	1	1	1	1	1	1	1	1
Finland	15	15	16	15	13	13	14	13	13	13	14
Sweden	6	5	7	6	6	6	6	8	5	8	9
United Kingdom	155	152	171	179	182	207	173	172	174	180	197
Iceland	4	4	4	4	6	9	8	9	5	5	:
Norway	476	491	511	551	584	637	662	709	830	844	962
Switzerland	1	1	1	1	1	1	1	1	1	1	:
Montenegro	:	:	:	:	:	:	:	0	0	0	:
Croatia	6	7	10	9	8	10	11	0	0	16	:
FYR of Macedonia	2	2	1	1	1	1	1	1	1	1	:
Turkey	63	79	67	61	80	94	120	129	140	152	:

Source: Eurostat (online data code: fish_aq_q)

International trade

9

Introduction

The European Union (EU) has a common trade policy, often referred to as the common commercial policy. In other words, the EU acts as a single entity on trade issues, including issues related to the World Trade Organisation (WTO). In these cases, the European Commission negotiates trade agreements and represents Europe's interests on behalf of the EU Member States.

Main statistical findings

In 2010 the EU-27 economy returned to its previous trend of progressively more integration with the international economy in terms of its level of credits and debits relative to gross domestic product (GDP), having experienced a reversal in 2009. The average value of EU-27 trade flows of goods corresponded to 11.6 % of GDP in 2010, up from 9.8 % the previous year. The level of trade integration of services rose to 4.0 % of GDP in 2010, up from 3.9 % in 2008 and 3.8 % in 2009.

The global financial and economic crisis which started in 2007 had a considerable impact on the international exchange of goods and services and on the intensity of global financial flows and business activity. These effects are clearly evident in Figure 9.0.1, as the upward trend of EU trade in goods and services ceased in 2009. Nevertheless, the level of trade integration for goods in 2010 was the same as it had been in 2008, while for services the level of integration was slightly greater in 2010 than it had been in 2008. The EU-27 trade deficit for goods and services (see Table 9.0.1) was equivalent to −0.4 % of GDP in 2010, a smaller deficit than in the United States in 2009 (−2.7 %), whereas Japan recorded a combined goods and services surplus equivalent to 0.4 % of GDP (also in 2009). Among the Member States, the combined trade balance for goods and services in 2010 was positive in 15 Member States. Positive balances exceeded 10 % of GDP only in Ireland (18.4 %) and Luxembourg (46.6 %); in the case of Ireland this was due to a particularly large surplus for goods, while for Luxembourg it was due to a large surplus for services.

The three largest trade deficits for goods and services were recorded in Romania (−5.4 % of GDP), Portugal (−6.5 %) and Greece (−6.6 %); in each case the deficit was driven by a relatively large deficit for goods.

Data sources and availability

Trade integration of goods and services is defined as the average value of debits and credits (summed and divided by two), presented in relation to GDP: the terms credits and debits are used for international trade in services which can roughly be considered to be equivalent to exports and imports. This indicator is calculated for both goods and services, based on balance of payments data; if the values increase over time, then the reporting territory became more integrated within the international economy. It is normal that smaller countries will display a higher degree of trade integration, as they are more likely to import a range of goods and services that are not produced within their domestic markets.

Context

The EU Treaty (TEU) (also called Treaty of Maastricht) establishes the overall aims and objectives of the EU's trade policy: Article 3 sets out the general aims, including a highly competitive social market economy, aimed at full employment and social progress. Article 206 of the Treaty on the functioning of the Union (TFEU) explains how the common commercial policy must operate in principle: 'to contribute, in the common interest, to the harmonious development of world trade, the progressive abolition of restrictions on international trade and on foreign direct investment, and the lowering of customs and other barriers'. Article 207 of the TFEU sets out the scope, instruments and decision-making procedures, while Article 218 establishes the current inter-institutional procedure for the conclusion of international agreements, principally by the Council.

The EU's trade policy aims to make the EU competitive in foreign markets. Being an open economy, the EU seeks to secure improved market access for its industries, services and investments, and to enforce the rules of free and fair trade. A coordinated trade policy takes on even greater importance in an era of globalisation, when economies and borders have opened up, leading to an increase in trade and capital movements, and the spread of information, knowledge and technology, often accompanied by deregulation. The economic impact of globalisation on the EU is felt through trade in goods and services, as well as through financial flows and the movement of persons linked to cross-border economic activity.

Globalisation acquires a higher profile when it is measured by actual trade flows. Within the EU, there are two main sources of trade statistics. One is international trade in goods statistics (ITGS), providing information on trade in merchandise goods, collected on the basis of customs and Intrastat declarations. This provides highly detailed information on the value and quantity (volumes) of international trade in goods as regards the type of commodity. The second main source is balance of payments statistics (BoP), which register all the transactions of an economy with the rest of the world. The current account of the BoP provides information on external trade in goods and services, as well as income (from employment and investment) and current transfers. For all these transactions, the BoP registers the value of exports (credits) and imports (debits).

A subchapter on international trade in goods gives an overview of the EU's trade in merchandise goods (within the ITGS framework), while a subchapter on international trade in services provides an overview of its trade in services (within the BoP framework).

Figure 9.0.1: Trade integration, EU-27, 2001-2010 (¹)
(% of GDP)

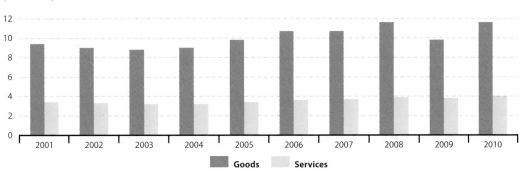

(¹) EU-25 for 2001-2003.

Source: Eurostat (online data code: tsier120)

Table 9.0.1: Trade in goods and services, 2010 ([1])
(% of GDP)

	Goods			Services		
	Exports	Imports	Balance	Exports	Imports	Balance
EU-27	11.2	12.2	− 1.0	4.3	3.7	0.6
Euro area	17.0	16.8	0.2	5.6	5.2	0.4
Belgium	60.1	60.6	− 0.5	18.3	16.8	1.5
Bulgaria	43.3	50.0	− 6.7	14.7	9.4	5.3
Czech Republic	63.9	62.5	1.4	11.0	9.2	1.7
Denmark	31.0	28.0	2.9	19.3	16.4	3.0
Germany	39.7	33.5	6.2	7.2	8.0	− 0.8
Estonia	61.7	63.1	− 1.4	23.9	14.7	9.1
Ireland	53.8	29.9	23.8	47.0	52.5	− 5.5
Greece	7.5	20.0	− 12.4	12.5	6.7	5.8
Spain	18.0	22.4	− 4.4	8.8	6.2	2.6
France	20.2	23.0	− 2.8	5.7	5.2	0.5
Italy	21.8	23.0	− 1.2	4.8	5.4	− 0.6
Cyprus	9.1	36.9	− 27.8	50.3	18.2	32.1
Latvia	37.4	43.9	− 6.4	15.4	9.2	6.2
Lithuania	57.1	61.4	− 4.3	11.3	7.8	3.6
Luxembourg	31.5	41.4	− 9.9	126.5	70.0	56.5
Hungary	72.5	67.7	4.8	14.8	12.3	2.5
Malta	37.5	52.3	− 14.7	48.8	31.5	17.3
Netherlands	62.3	55.0	7.3	12.2	11.0	1.3
Austria	38.9	40.0	− 1.1	14.4	9.7	4.7
Poland	34.5	37.0	− 2.4	6.9	6.2	0.7
Portugal	21.4	31.7	− 10.4	10.2	6.3	3.9
Romania	30.6	35.4	− 4.8	5.3	5.8	− 0.5
Slovenia	51.9	55.3	− 3.4	13.1	9.4	3.7
Slovakia	74.0	73.8	0.2	6.7	7.8	− 1.1
Finland	29.1	27.2	1.9	10.7	9.5	1.2
Sweden	34.9	32.5	2.4	14.1	10.6	3.5
United Kingdom	18.2	25.0	− 6.8	10.6	7.5	3.1
Iceland	36.6	28.8	7.8	20.2	17.2	3.0
Norway	32.1	18.0	14.1	9.6	10.4	− 0.8
Croatia	19.8	32.8	− 13.0	18.5	5.7	12.8
Turkey	16.5	24.2	− 7.7	4.7	2.7	2.0
Japan ([2])	10.8	9.9	0.8	2.6	3.0	− 0.4
United States ([2])	7.7	11.3	− 3.6	3.6	2.7	0.9

([1]) EU-27, extra-EU flows; euro area, extra-euro area flows; Member States and other countries, flows with the rest of the world.
([2]) 2009.

Source: Eurostat (online data codes: bop_q_eu, bop_q_euro, bop_q_c and tec00001)

9.1 International trade in goods

This subchapter discusses the development of the European Union's (EU) international trade in goods. It considers the EU's share in world import and export markets, intra-EU trade, the EU's main trading partners, and the most widely traded product categories.

The EU-27 accounts for just under a fifth of the world's trade in goods. The value of external trade in goods significantly exceeds that of services, which by their nature are harder to move across borders.

Main statistical findings

Total EU-27 trade with the rest of the world (the sum of extra-EU exports and imports) was valued at EUR 2 850 539 million in 2010. As such, trade activity for the EU-27 returned almost to the record levels that had been recorded in 2008. In comparison with a year before, total trade in the EU-27 increased by EUR 546 922 million in 2010.

After experiencing a sharp fall in both exports and imports in 2009, the EU-27 saw its exports rise to a record level of EUR 1 348 778 million in 2010, an increase of 23 % compared with the year before. This was largely driven by increases in the level of exports of machinery and transport equipment and other manufactured goods. Imports rose by 24 % to be valued at EUR 1 501 761 million, with the largest expansions recorded for imports of machinery and transport equipment, and energy products.

The United States remained, by far, the most important destination for goods exported from the EU-27 in 2010, although the share of EU-27 exports going to the United States fell from 28 % of the total in 2000 to 18 % of the total by 2010. The most important EU-27 exports to the United States in 2010 included machinery and transport equipment. The same group of products was also the main export category to China, which became the second most important destination market for EU-27 exports in 2010. China remained the most important supplier of goods imported into the EU-27 market in 2010, as imports from China grew by 32 % between 2009 and 2010. EU-27 imports from Russia rose at a

similar pace, and were dominated by a 35 % increase in the level of energy imports.

Trade in goods between Member States (intra-EU trade) was valued – in terms of dispatches – at EUR 2 538 393 million in 2010; this was almost twice the level of exports from the EU-27 to non-member countries. The importance of the internal EU market was underlined by the fact that for each of the Member States, intra-EU trade of goods was higher than extra-EU trade (see Figure 9.1.5). However, the proportion of total trade in goods accounted for by intra-EU and extra-EU flows varied considerably across the Member States, reflecting to some degree historical ties and geographical location. The highest shares of intra-EU trade (about 80 %) were recorded for Luxembourg, the Czech Republic and Slovakia, with this ratio falling close to 50 % in Greece and the United Kingdom.

Intra EU-27 trade – measured by dispatches – increased by 16 % in 2010; this was a lower rate of increase than that recorded for extra-EU exports (up 23 %). Considering arrivals and dispatches together, the biggest increases in intra-EU trade were registered for Estonia, Lithuania, Sweden and Latvia, up by over 25 %, while Greece (– 8 %) and Malta (– 3 %) were the only Member States to record a reduction in intra-EU trade in 2010.

Between 2009 and 2010 the EU-27's exports with all of its major trading partners increased. Exports to Switzerland, the EU-27's third largest market in 2010, were less badly affected than most by the downturn of 2009 and rose to a new record high in 2010, largely on account of exports of machinery and transport equipment, and chemicals. In contrast, EU-27 exports to Russia, which fell by almost 40 % between 2008 and 2009, did not recover fully in 2010, despite growing by over EUR 20 000 million. The highest growth rate for EU-27 exports between 2009 and 2010 among the main trading partners, was recorded for exports to Brazil (up 45 %), largely as a result of strong growth in the

level of exports of machinery and transport equipment, which reached a record level.

On the import side, the EU-27 saw an increase in the level of its imports from all of its major trading partners between 2009 and 2010. The large increase in imports from China was dominated by machinery and transport equipment, which made up over half of all the EU-27's imports from China in 2010. Imports of energy products represented just under three quarters of the EU-27's imports from Russia in 2010, although total imports and energy imports from Russia in 2010 remained below their 2008 levels.

All major product groups reported a sharp increase in their level of exports outside the EU-27 in 2010 – after exports had fallen consistently across the board the previous year. EU-27 exports of the two largest product groups, machinery and transport equipment and other manufactured goods, returned close to their 2008 levels. However, the third largest group, chemicals, saw little development in its level of exports between 2008 and 2009, before rising by 20 % in 2010. The highest growth rate for EU-27 exports in 2010 was recorded for exports of raw materials, which more than regained their losses recorded in 2009; despite a sharp increase in the value of energy exports, their level remained about 10 % below values recorded in 2008.

Imports of all major product groups also rose between 2009 and 2010, but the growth was more varied across product groups than it was for exports. The largest category of products imported by the EU-27, machinery and transport equipment, experienced growth of 30 % in 2010, resulting in a record high being posted. The largest contribution to the increase in imports of this category resulted from a rapid expansion in the level of imports for electrical machinery, which grew by 45 % between 2009 and 2010. Imports of energy products, the second largest category, also grew strongly (up 28 %), driven by a 35 % increase in the value of imported petroleum products. Just over 30 % of the EU-27's energy product imports in 2010 came from Russia, followed by Norway (12 %) and Libya (7 %).

The EU-27's trade deficit of EUR 152 983 million in 2010 was driven by the sizeable deficit in relation to petroleum products, which stood at EUR 215 348 million. This was offset by trade surpluses of EUR 82 156 million for road vehicles, and EUR 118 992 million for industrial machinery. There was also a trade surplus for the EU-27 in 2010 for chemical products (EUR 98 389 million) – part of which was due to the trade performance of pharmaceutical products (where a surplus of EUR 46 749 million was recorded).

Germany remained by far the largest player in relation to extra EU-27 trade in 2010, responsible for 28 % of the EU-27's exports to non-member countries and for almost 20 % of its imports. The next three largest exporters remained the same as in 2009 (France, Italy and the United Kingdom). The Netherlands and the United Kingdom were the second and third largest importers of goods from non-member countries, behind Germany.

Data sources and availability

Statistics on the international trade of goods measure the value and quantity of goods traded between Member States of the EU (known as intra-EU trade) and goods traded by EU Member States with non-member countries (known as extra-EU trade). These statistics are the official source of information about imports, exports and the trade balance in the EU, its Member States and the euro area.

Statistics are disseminated for each declaring country with respect to each partner country, for several product classifications. One of the most commonly used classifications is the Standard international trade classification (SITC Rev. 4) of the United Nations (UN); this allows a comparison of external trade statistics to be made on a worldwide basis.

In extra-EU trade statistics, the data shown for the EU-27 treat this entity as a single trading block and the data reported for exports relates to those exports for the whole of the EU-27 that are destined for the rest of the world, while extra-EU imports relate to imports from the rest of the world (non-member countries) into the EU. In contrast, when reporting data for individual Member States, external trade flows are generally presented in terms of world trade flows (including both intra-EU and extra-EU partners).

The definitions of extra-EU trade are as follows:

- imports are goods which enter the statistical territory of the EU from a non-member country and are placed under the customs procedure for free circulation (as a general rule goods intended for consumption), inward processing, or processing under customs control (goods for working, processing), either immediately or after a period in a customs warehouse;
- exports are goods which leave the statistical territory of the EU for a non-member country after being placed under the customs procedure for exports (definitive export), outward processing, or re-exportation following either inward processing or processing under customs control.

Statistics on trade with non-member countries do not, therefore, include goods in transit or those placed under a customs procedure for bonded warehousing or temporary entry (for fairs, exhibitions, tests, etc.), nor do they include re-export following entry under one of these procedures.

Statistics on trade between the Member States (intra-EU trade) cover the arrivals and dispatches of goods recorded by each Member State. Arrivals and dispatches are defined as follows:

- arrivals are goods in free circulation within the EU which enter the statistical territory of a given Member State;
- dispatches are goods in free circulation within the EU which leave the statistical territory of a given Member State to enter another Member State.

Customs records are the traditional source of statistical data on trade in goods. The beginning of the single market on 1 January 1993, with its removal of customs formalities between Member States, made it necessary to adopt a new data collection system, Intrastat, as the basis for statistics on intra-EU trade. In the Intrastat system, statistical data are collected directly from trade operators – who are requested to send monthly declarations to their national statistical administration.

The statistical values of extra-EU trade and intra-EU trade are recorded at their free-on-board (FOB) value for exports/dispatches and their cost, insurance and freight (CIF) value for imports/arrivals. The values reported comprise only those subsidiary costs (freight and insurance) which relate, for exports/dispatches, to the journey within the territory of the Member State from which the goods are exported/dispatched and, for imports/arrivals, to the journey outside the territory of the Member State into which the goods are imported/enter.

Context

Statistics on the international trade of goods are used extensively by public-body decision makers at an international, EU and national level. Businesses can use international trade data to carry out market research and define their commercial strategy. In the case of EU institutions, international trade statistics help in the preparation of multilateral and bilateral trade negotiations, in defining and implementing anti-dumping policies, for the purposes of macro-economic and monetary policies, and in evaluating the progress of the single market, or the integration of European economies.

The development of trade can be an opportunity for economic growth. The EU has a common trade policy, whereby the European Commission negotiates trade agreements and represents the EU's interests on behalf of its 27 Member States. The European Commission consults Member States through an advisory committee which discusses the full range of trade policy issues affecting the EU including multilateral, bilateral and unilateral instruments. As such, trade policy is an exclusive power of the EU – so only the EU, and not individual Member States, can legislate on trade matters and conclude international trade agreements. This scope extends beyond trade in goods, to cover trade in services, intellectual property and foreign direct investment.

Globally, multilateral trade issues are dealt with under the auspices of the World Trade Organization (WTO). Its membership covers 153 countries (as of July 2008), with several candidate members in the process of joining. The WTO sets the global rules for trade, provides a forum for trade negotiations,

and for settling disputes between members. The European Commission negotiates with its WTO partners and participated in the latest round of WTO multilateral trade negotiations, known as the Doha Development Agenda (DDA). However, having missed deadlines to conclude these talks in 2005 and again in 2006, the Doha round of talks broke down again at a WTO meeting in July 2008. At the time of writing, the future of the Doha round is uncertain.

Figure 9.1.1: Main players for external trade, 2010
(EUR 1 000 million)

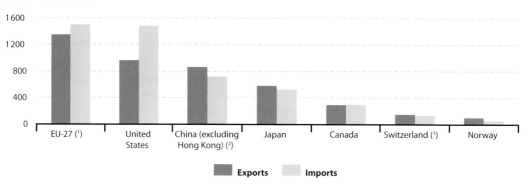

(¹) External trade flows with extra EU-27.
(²) 2009 instead of 2010.
(³) Including Liechtenstein.

Source: Eurostat (online data code: ext_lt_intertrd)

Table 9.1.1: Main players for external trade, 2000, 2005 and 2010
(EUR 1 000 million)

	Exports			Imports			Trade balance		
	2000	2005	2010	2000	2005	2010	2000	2005	2010
EU-27 (¹)	850	1 053	1 349	993	1 180	1 502	−143	−127	−153
Norway	63	84	98	37	45	57	26	39	42
Switzerland (²)	87	105	147	90	102	133	−2	4	15
Canada	300	290	291	260	253	295	40	37	−4
China (excluding Hong Kong) (³)	270	612	862	244	530	721	26	82	141
Japan	519	478	581	411	415	522	108	64	58
United States	845	727	963	1 362	1 392	1 483	−517	−666	−520

(¹) External trade flows with extra EU-27.
(²) Including Liechtenstein.
(³) 2009 instead of 2010.

Source: Eurostat (online data code: ext_lt_intertrd)

Figure 9.1.2: Shares in the world market for exports, 2009
(% share of world exports)

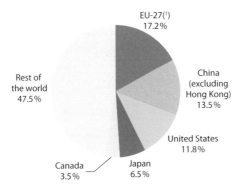

(¹) External trade flows with extra EU-27.
Source: Eurostat (online data code: ext_lt_introle)

Figure 9.1.3: Shares in the world market for imports, 2009
(% share of world imports)

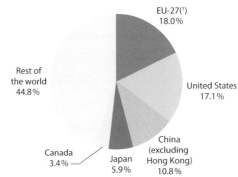

(¹) External trade flows with extra EU-27.
Source: Eurostat (online data code: ext_lt_introle)

Figure 9.1.4: Development of external trade, EU-27, 2000-2010 (¹)
(EUR 1 000 million)

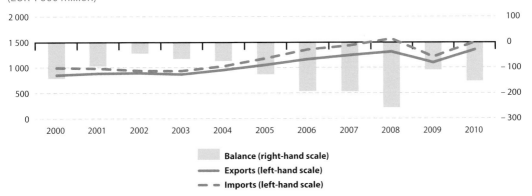

(¹) External trade flows with extra EU-27.
Source: Eurostat (online data code: ext_lt_intertrd)

Table 9.1.2: External trade, 2009-2010
(EUR 1 000 million)

	Exports			Imports			Balance	
	2009	**2010**	**2009-10 growth rate (%)**	**2009**	**2010**	**2009-10 growth rate (%)**	**2009**	**2010**
EU-27 (¹)	1 097.1	1 348.8	22.9	1 206.5	1 501.8	24.5	–109.3	–153.0
Belgium	265.2	310.9	17.3	252.3	294.5	16.7	12.8	16.4
Bulgaria	11.7	15.6	33.3	16.9	19.2	13.5	–5.2	–3.6
Czech Republic	81.0	100.2	23.7	75.3	95.2	26.4	5.7	5.0
Denmark	67.3	73.7	9.4	59.3	64.0	8.0	8.1	9.7
Germany	803.0	957.1	19.2	664.1	804.7	21.2	138.9	152.4
Estonia	6.5	8.8	34.9	7.3	9.2	27.1	–0.8	–0.5
Ireland	83.1	88.1	6.0	45.0	45.3	0.7	38.2	42.8
Greece	14.7	16.1	10.0	49.8	47.7	–4.3	–35.1	–31.5
Spain	163.0	185.3	13.7	210.2	237.1	12.8	–47.2	–51.8
France	347.4	392.7	13.0	401.5	456.9	13.8	–54.1	–64.2
Italy	291.7	337.6	15.7	297.6	365.0	22.6	–5.9	–27.4
Cyprus	0.9	1.1	18.2	5.6	6.4	14.1	–4.7	–5.3
Latvia	5.5	7.2	29.7	7.0	8.7	24.6	–1.5	–1.6
Lithuania	11.8	15.7	33.2	13.1	17.7	34.5	–1.3	–1.9
Luxembourg	15.1	14.8	–2.3	17.6	18.1	2.9	–2.4	–3.3
Hungary	59.5	72.0	21.0	55.8	66.5	19.2	3.8	5.5
Malta	1.6	1.9	18.4	3.0	3.2	6.2	–1.4	–1.2
Netherlands	357.0	432.5	21.2	317.7	389.9	22.7	39.2	42.6
Austria	98.2	114.9	17.0	102.6	119.8	16.8	–4.4	–4.9
Poland	97.9	117.5	20.0	107.2	131.0	22.2	–9.3	–13.5
Portugal	31.8	36.8	15.7	51.4	57.1	11.1	–19.6	–20.3
Romania	29.1	37.3	28.1	38.9	46.8	20.1	–9.9	–9.5
Slovenia	18.8	22.2	18.4	19.0	22.7	19.2	–0.2	–0.4
Slovakia	40.2	49.3	22.6	39.9	50.2	25.8	0.3	–0.9
Finland	45.1	52.5	16.6	43.7	51.7	18.4	1.4	0.8
Sweden	93.9	119.4	27.2	86.1	112.2	30.3	7.8	7.2
United Kingdom	253.0	306.0	21.0	346.2	422.5	22.0	–93.2	–116.5
Iceland	2.9	3.5	19.5	2.6	2.9	14.0	0.3	0.5
Norway	86.8	98.1	13.1	49.6	56.5	13.9	37.1	41.5
Switzerland (²)	124.1	147.4	18.7	111.9	132.7	18.6	12.2	14.6
Canada	226.1	291.0	28.7	230.2	295.1	28.2	–4.0	–4.1
China	861.5	:	:	720.9	:	:	140.6	:
Japan	416.3	580.7	39.5	395.7	522.5	32.0	20.6	58.2
United States	757.6	963.3	27.2	1 148.5	1 483.4	29.2	–390.9	–520.0

(¹) External trade flows with extra EU-27.
(²) Including Liechtenstein.

Source: Eurostat (online data code: tet00002)

Table 9.1.3: Extra EU-27 trade, 2010

	Exports		Imports		Trade balance
	(EUR 1 000 million)	Share of EU-27 exports (%)	(EUR 1 000 million)	Share of EU-27 imports (%)	(EUR 1 000 million)
EU-27	1 348.8	100.0	1 501.8	100.0	− 153.0
Belgium	83.5	6.2	88.3	5.9	− 4.7
Bulgaria	6.1	0.5	7.9	0.5	− 1.8
Czech Republic	16.0	1.2	24.0	1.6	− 7.9
Denmark	25.1	1.9	18.8	1.3	6.2
Germany	378.9	28.1	292.4	19.5	86.5
Estonia	2.8	0.2	1.9	0.1	0.9
Ireland	36.8	2.7	14.9	1.0	22.0
Greece	6.1	0.5	23.4	1.6	− 17.3
Spain	59.7	4.4	100.5	6.7	− 40.9
France	153.8	11.4	144.9	9.6	8.9
Italy	144.3	10.7	164.6	11.0	− 20.2
Cyprus	0.4	0.0	1.9	0.1	− 1.6
Latvia	2.4	0.2	2.1	0.1	0.2
Lithuania	6.1	0.5	7.7	0.5	− 1.5
Luxembourg	2.4	0.2	3.4	0.2	− 1.0
Hungary	16.5	1.2	21.5	1.4	− 5.0
Malta	1.1	0.1	1.1	0.1	0.0
Netherlands	99.4	7.4	208.0	13.8	− 108.5
Austria	33.1	2.5	27.0	1.8	6.1
Poland	25.2	1.9	39.2	2.6	− 14.0
Portugal	9.2	0.7	13.8	0.9	− 4.7
Romania	10.4	0.8	12.8	0.9	− 2.5
Slovenia	6.4	0.5	7.3	0.5	− 0.9
Slovakia	7.6	0.6	13.8	0.9	− 6.1
Finland	23.5	1.7	18.5	1.2	5.0
Sweden	51.0	3.8	36.9	2.5	14.1
United Kingdom	141.1	10.5	205.3	13.7	− 64.1

Source: Eurostat (online data code: ext_lt_intratrd)

Table 9.1.4: Intra EU-27 trade, 2005 and 2010
(EUR 1 000 million)

	Dispatches		Arrivals		Balance	
	2005	2010	2005	2010	2005	2010
EU-27	2 215.5	2 538.4	2 142.9	2 461.2	72.6	77.2
Belgium	206.2	227.4	184.7	206.2	21.5	21.2
Bulgaria	5.5	9.5	7.8	11.2	−2.3	−1.8
Czech Republic	53.7	84.2	50.1	71.3	3.6	12.9
Denmark	48.4	48.6	43.1	45.2	5.2	3.5
Germany	501.6	578.3	402.7	512.3	98.9	65.9
Estonia	4.8	6.0	6.3	7.4	−1.4	−1.4
Ireland	56.2	51.3	36.8	30.4	19.5	20.8
Greece	8.6	10.1	25.5	24.3	−16.9	−14.2
Spain	112.0	125.6	148.9	136.6	−36.9	−10.9
France	236.5	239.0	273.7	312.0	−37.2	−73.1
Italy	183.7	193.3	183.8	200.4	−0.2	−7.1
Cyprus	0.9	0.7	3.5	4.5	−2.6	−3.8
Latvia	3.2	4.8	5.3	6.6	−2.1	−1.8
Lithuania	6.2	9.6	7.4	10.0	−1.2	−0.4
Luxembourg	13.6	12.4	12.8	14.7	0.7	−2.3
Hungary	40.9	55.5	37.4	45.0	3.5	10.5
Malta	1.0	0.8	2.3	2.0	−1.3	−1.2
Netherlands	260.7	333.0	144.6	181.9	116.1	151.1
Austria	72.3	81.8	82.4	92.7	−10.1	−10.9
Poland	56.5	92.3	61.5	91.8	−5.0	0.5
Portugal	25.0	27.6	39.9	43.2	−14.9	−15.6
Romania	15.6	26.9	20.5	33.9	−4.9	−7.0
Slovenia	10.5	15.8	13.0	15.4	−2.4	0.5
Slovakia	22.3	41.7	21.7	36.5	0.7	5.2
Finland	29.9	29.0	31.5	33.2	−1.6	−4.2
Sweden	62.1	68.4	63.2	75.2	−1.1	−6.9
United Kingdom	177.4	164.9	232.6	217.2	−55.2	−52.4

Source: Eurostat (online data code: tet00039)

Figure 9.1.5: Intra and extra EU-27 trade, 2010
(imports plus exports, % share of total trade)

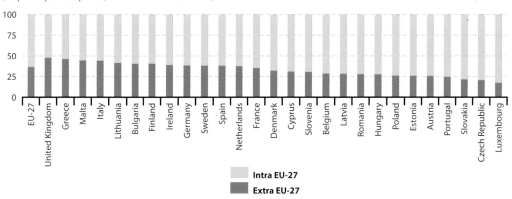

Source: Eurostat (online data code: ext_lt_intratrd)

Figure 9.1.6: Main trading partners for exports, EU-27, 2010
(% share of extra EU-27 exports)

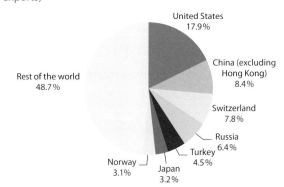

Source: Eurostat (online data code: ext_lt_maineu)

Figure 9.1.7: Main trading partners for imports, EU-27, 2010
(% share of extra EU-27 imports)

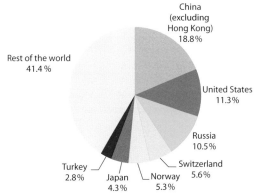

Source: Eurostat (online data code: ext_lt_maineu)

Table 9.1.5: Extra EU-27 trade by main trading partners, EU-27, 2000-2010 (¹)
(EUR 1 000 million)

	2000	2001	2002	2003	2004	2005	2006	2007	2008	2009	2010
EXPORTS											
Extra EU-27	849.7	884.7	891.9	869.2	953.0	1 052.7	1 160.1	1 240.6	1 309.9	1 097.1	1 348.8
United States	238.2	245.6	247.9	227.3	235.5	252.7	269.1	259.2	250.1	205.5	242.1
China (excl. Hong Kong)	25.9	30.7	35.1	41.5	48.4	51.8	63.8	71.8	78.4	82.4	113.1
Russia	22.7	31.6	34.4	37.2	46.0	56.7	72.3	89.1	105.0	65.6	86.5
Switzerland	72.5	76.5	72.8	71.4	75.2	82.6	87.8	92.6	98.0	88.6	105.4
Norway	26.4	27.2	28.2	27.7	30.8	33.8	38.5	43.5	43.8	37.5	41.9
Japan	45.5	45.5	43.5	41.0	43.4	43.7	44.8	43.6	42.3	36.0	43.7
Turkey	31.9	21.9	26.6	30.9	40.1	44.6	50.0	52.6	54.1	44.1	61.2
India	13.7	13.0	14.3	14.6	17.2	21.3	24.4	29.2	31.6	27.6	34.8
South Korea (Republic of)	16.7	15.8	17.7	16.4	17.9	20.2	22.9	24.7	25.6	21.6	28.0
Brazil	16.9	18.6	15.7	12.4	14.2	16.1	17.7	21.3	26.3	21.6	31.3
IMPORTS											
Extra EU-27	992.7	979.1	937.0	935.3	1 027.5	1 179.6	1 352.8	1 435.0	1 566.3	1 206.5	1 501.8
United States	206.3	203.3	182.6	158.1	159.4	163.5	175.5	174.1	186.8	159.2	169.5
China (excl. Hong Kong)	74.6	82.0	90.1	106.2	128.7	160.3	194.9	232.6	247.9	214.1	282.0
Russia	63.8	65.9	64.5	70.7	84.0	112.6	140.9	145.0	178.1	117.7	158.4
Switzerland	62.6	63.6	61.7	59.1	62.0	66.6	71.6	76.6	80.3	73.8	84.1
Norway	47.2	46.4	48.0	51.0	55.3	67.2	79.2	76.6	95.9	68.9	79.2
Japan	92.1	81.1	73.7	72.4	74.7	74.1	77.5	78.4	75.1	56.7	64.9
Turkey	18.7	22.1	24.6	27.3	32.7	36.1	41.7	47.0	46.0	36.2	42.1
India	12.8	13.5	13.7	14.1	16.4	19.1	22.6	26.6	29.5	25.4	33.1
South Korea (Republic of)	27.0	23.3	24.6	26.0	30.7	34.5	40.8	41.3	39.6	32.3	38.7
Brazil	18.7	19.6	18.4	19.1	21.7	24.1	27.2	32.5	35.9	25.7	32.3
TRADE BALANCE											
Extra EU-27	− 143.0	− 94.4	− 45.1	− 66.0	− 74.6	− 126.8	− 192.7	− 194.5	− 256.4	− 109.3	− 153.0
United States	31.9	42.3	65.3	69.2	76.1	89.2	93.6	85.1	63.3	46.3	72.6
China (excl. Hong Kong)	− 48.8	− 51.3	− 55.0	− 64.7	− 80.3	− 108.5	− 131.1	− 160.8	− 169.5	− 131.7	− 168.9
Russia	− 41.0	− 34.3	− 30.1	− 33.5	− 37.9	− 55.9	− 68.6	− 55.9	− 73.1	− 52.1	− 71.9
Switzerland	10.0	12.9	11.1	12.3	13.2	16.0	16.1	16.0	17.7	14.7	21.3
Norway	− 20.8	− 19.2	− 19.9	− 23.4	− 24.5	− 33.4	− 40.7	− 33.1	− 52.2	− 31.4	− 37.3
Japan	− 46.6	− 35.6	− 30.2	− 31.4	− 31.3	− 30.3	− 32.7	− 34.8	− 32.8	− 20.7	− 21.2
Turkey	13.2	− 0.2	2.0	3.6	7.4	8.5	8.3	5.6	8.1	8.0	19.1
India	0.8	− 0.5	0.6	0.5	0.8	2.2	1.8	2.6	2.1	2.1	1.7
South Korea (Republic of)	− 10.2	− 7.4	− 6.9	− 9.6	− 12.7	− 14.2	− 18.0	− 16.6	− 14.0	− 10.7	− 10.7
Brazil	− 1.8	− 1.0	− 2.6	− 6.7	− 7.6	− 8.1	− 9.5	− 11.3	− 9.5	− 4.1	− 1.0

(¹) Partners are sorted according to the sum of imports and exports in 2010.

Source: Eurostat (online data code: tet00040)

Table 9.1.6: Extra EU-27 trade by main products, EU-27, 2000, 2005 and 2010

	2000		2005		2010	
	(EUR 1 000 million)	(%)	(EUR 1 000 million)	(%)	(EUR 1 000 million)	(%)
EXPORTS						
Total	849.7	100.0	1 052.7	100.0	1 348.8	100.0
Food, drinks & tobacco	47.7	5.6	52.0	4.9	76.3	5.7
Raw materials	17.8	2.1	23.8	2.3	37.9	2.8
Mineral fuels, lubricants	29.1	3.4	45.9	4.4	75.6	5.6
Chemicals & related prod.	118.9	14.0	164.9	15.7	235.8	17.5
Other manufactured goods	224.1	26.4	265.8	25.3	310.4	23.0
Machinery & transport equip.	393.5	46.3	470.3	44.7	572.1	42.4
IMPORTS						
Total	992.7	100.0	1 179.6	100.0	1 501.8	100.0
Food, drinks & tobacco	54.8	5.5	63.0	5.3	80.7	5.4
Raw materials	49.2	5.0	52.7	4.5	70.4	4.7
Mineral fuels, lubricants	161.1	16.2	272.6	23.1	381.7	25.4
Chemicals & related prod.	70.5	7.1	96.4	8.2	137.4	9.1
Other manufactured goods	250.5	25.2	290.3	24.6	360.2	24.0
Machinery & transport equip.	371.5	37.4	378.7	32.1	442.4	29.5
TRADE BALANCE						
Total	− 143.0	–	− 126.8	–	− 153.0	–
Food, drinks & tobacco	− 7.1	–	− 11.0	–	− 4.4	–
Raw materials	− 31.4	–	− 28.9	–	− 32.5	–
Mineral fuels, lubricants	− 132.0	–	− 226.7	–	− 306.1	–
Chemicals & related prod.	48.4	–	68.4	–	98.4	–
Other manufactured goods	− 26.4	–	− 24.4	–	− 49.8	–
Machinery & transport equip.	21.9	–	91.6	–	129.7	–

Source: Eurostat (online data code: ext_lt_intertrd)

Figure 9.1.8: Main exports, EU-27, 2005 and 2010
(% share of extra EU-27 exports)

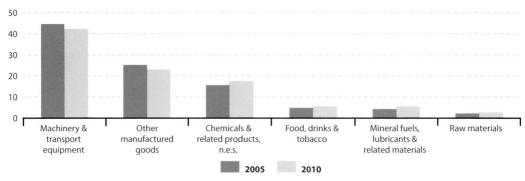

Source: Eurostat (online data code: tet00061)

Figure 9.1.9: Main imports, EU-27, 2005 and 2010
(% share of extra EU-27 imports)

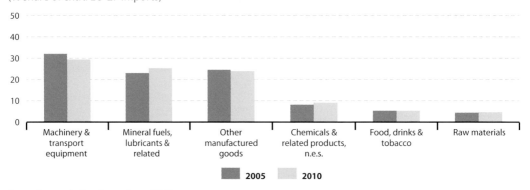

Source: Eurostat (online data code: tet00061)

9.2 International trade in services

This subchapter provides information in relation to international trade in services for the European Union (EU) and for the EU Member States. It covers the EU's main trading partners for services and the weight of different types of services in total international trade in services.

Services play a major role in all modern economies. An efficient services sector is crucial for trade and economic growth and for vibrant and resilient economies. Services provide vital support to the economy and industry as a whole, for example, through finance, logistics and communications. Increased trade in services and the widespread availability of services may boost economic growth by improving the performance of other industries, since services can provide key intermediate inputs, especially in an increasingly interlinked, globalised world.

Main statistical findings

The share of services in total exports (goods and services) was relatively stable between 28.1 % and

28.8 % from 2004 to 2008, but increased to 30.0 % in 2009 before falling back to 27.8 % in 2010. The services share of imports also increased in 2009, reaching 25.7 % having been at a level between 22.2 % and 24.7 % in the five previous years, but also fell in 2010, dropping to 23.4 %.

The EU-27 reported a surplus in service transactions of EUR 73 500 million with the rest of the world in 2010, reflecting credits of EUR 527 700 million and debits of EUR 454 200 million (see Table 9.2.1).

The United Kingdom recorded a surplus (extra and intra-EU combined) of EUR 52 200 million in service transactions in 2010, the largest value among the Member States and considerably more than the next highest levels that were recorded by Spain (EUR 27 900 million) and Luxembourg (EUR 22 800 million). In contrast, Germany recorded a deficit in service transactions of EUR 19 300 million in 2010, the largest deficit by far among the Member States. It is important to underline that most trade in services by Member States involved intra-EU transactions, amounting to 56.4 % of credits and 58.3 % of debits in 2010.

North America was the main extra-EU trading region for the EU-27's international trade in services in 2009, accounting for 27.1 % of credits and 32.5 % of debits (see Figure 9.2.1). The EU-27 had negative balances in services with North Africa, central America and north America.

More than two thirds of the EU-27's credits (67.0 %) and debits (69.8 %) in the international trade of services in 2010 were accounted for by three categories: transport, travel and other business services (see Figure 9.2.2). The surplus of EUR 32 600 million for other business services was the highest among services, followed by a surplus of EUR 26 700 million for financial services, EUR 21 900 million for computer and information services and EUR 18 900 million for transport. In contrast, the largest deficits were EUR 14 700 million for travel and EUR 11 900 million for royalties and license fees.

Data sources and availability

The main methodological references used for the production of statistics on international trade in services are the International Monetary Fund (IMF)'s fifth balance of payments manual (BPM5) and the United Nations' manual on statistics of international trade in services. The sixth edition of the balance of payments manual (BPM6) was finalised in December 2008 with implementation planned for 2014.

The transmission of data on international trade in services to Eurostat is covered by Regulation (EC) No 184/2005 of the European Parliament and of the Council. The breakdown of Eurostat statistics on international trade in services includes three main sub-items: transport, travel, and other services.

- Transport covers all transport services that are provided by residents of one economy for those of another and that involve the carriage of passengers, the movement of goods (freight), rentals (charters) of carriers with crew, and related supporting and auxiliary services. All modes of transport are considered including sea, air, space, rail, road, inland waterway, and pipelines, as are other supporting and auxiliary services (such as storage and warehousing).

- Travel covers primarily the goods and services acquired from an economy by travellers during visits of less than one year to that economy. The goods and services are purchased by, or on behalf of, the traveller or provided, without a quid pro quo (that is, are provided as a gift), for the traveller to use or give away. The transportation of travellers within the economies that they are visiting, where such transportation is provided by carriers not resident in the particular economy being visited, as well as the international carriage of travellers are excluded; both are covered in passenger services under transport. Also excluded are goods purchased by a traveller for resale in the traveller's own economy or in any other economy. Travel is divided in two sub-components: business travel and personal travel.

- Other services comprise external transactions not covered under transport or travel, specifically: communications services, construction services, insurance services, financial services, computer and information services, royalties and licence fees, other business services, personal, cultural and recreational services, and government services.

International trade in services is geographically allocated according to the residence of the trading partner, distinguishing between: intra-EU transactions which correspond to the sum of transactions declared by EU Member States with other EU Member States; extra-EU transactions which correspond to the transactions declared by EU Member States with countries outside the EU. World transactions are equal to the sum of intra-EU transactions and extra-EU transactions.

Context

The provision of services contributes an increasing share of the economic wealth of the EU, and accounts for more than 50 % of GDP in each Member State. Nevertheless, the value of exports and imports of goods is generally two to three times higher than that of services. Part of this imbalance may be due to the nature of some services: for example, professional services that are bound by distinct national legislation. Another difference between goods and services concerns the immediacy of the relationship between supplier and consumer. Many services are non-transportable, in other words, they require the physical proximity of the service provider and consumer. This proximity requirement implies that many services transactions involve factor mobility. Thus, an important feature of services is that they are provided via various modes of supply. Often services are tailored according to the client's needs and tastes and hence tend not to be homogeneous or mass-produced. For international

trade in non-transportable services to take place, either the consumer must go to the service provider or the service provider must go to the consumer. As such, services cover a heterogeneous range of products and activities that are difficult to encapsulate within a simple definition. Services are also often difficult to separate from goods with which they may be associated or bundled.

Despite the relatively low level of international trade in services, there are a number of reasons to believe that the level of trade may grow in future years. Technological developments have increased the tradability of some services, for example facilitating web-based services such as those for finance, education, health and government amongst others. Furthermore, liberalisation efforts are likely to facilitate and therefore stimulate international trade in services. Within the EU the objective of the 'Services' Directive 2006/123/EC of 12 December 2006, on services in the internal market, is to eliminate obstacles to trade in services, thus allowing the development of cross-border operations. It is intended to improve competitiveness, not just of service enterprises but also of European industry as a whole.

Globally, the inclusion of services in the Uruguay Round of trade negotiations led to the general agreement on trade in services (GATS) that entered into force in January 1995. The GATS aims at ensuring increased transparency and predictability of relevant rules and regulations, and promoting progressive liberalisation through successive rounds of negotiation.

Table 9.2.1: Trade in services, 2005 and 2010 (¹)
(EUR 1 000 million)

	Credits			Debits			Net	
	2005	2010	2009-10 growth rate (%)	2005	2010	2009-10 growth rate (%)	2005	2010
EU-27	405.2	527.7	10.4	351.9	454.2	9.6	53.3	73.5
Euro area	405.4	513.8	8.9	369.9	474.1	8.3	35.6	39.8
Belgium	45.2	64.6	9.8	41.2	59.2	12.6	4.0	5.3
Bulgaria	3.6	5.3	7.5	2.7	3.4	−6.6	0.8	1.9
Czech Republic	9.5	16.4	12.2	8.2	13.7	1.4	1.2	2.6
Denmark	35.0	45.2	13.8	29.8	38.3	4.7	5.1	6.9
Germany	134.3	179.4	8.2	170.4	198.7	8.7	−36.2	−19.3
Estonia	2.6	3.4	7.7	1.8	2.1	15.4	0.8	1.3
Ireland	48.2	73.3	10.0	57.5	81.8	9.1	−9.3	−8.5
Greece	27.6	28.5	5.5	11.9	15.2	6.2	15.7	13.2
Spain	76.2	93.7	6.4	54.0	65.7	4.8	22.2	27.9
France	98.4	108.5	5.4	86.1	98.0	7.2	12.3	10.5
Italy	71.9	74.2	8.2	72.4	83.1	6.0	−0.5	−8.9
Cyprus	5.2	8.7	22.7	2.2	3.1	6.1	3.1	5.6
Latvia	1.8	2.8	1.0	1.3	1.7	2.1	0.5	1.1
Lithuania	2.5	3.1	17.2	1.7	2.1	−0.2	0.8	1.0
Luxembourg	32.5	51.0	17.4	19.5	28.2	10.1	13.1	22.8
Hungary	10.4	14.4	8.5	9.2	12.0	0.6	1.1	2.4
Malta	1.6	3.0	19.4	1.0	1.9	26.0	0.6	1.1
Netherlands	74.0	72.0	−12.1	67.9	64.3	−17.5	6.1	7.7
Austria	34.1	41.2	4.6	24.8	27.8	5.0	9.4	13.3
Poland	13.1	24.5	18.6	12.5	21.9	26.9	0.6	2.6
Portugal	12.2	17.6	7.9	8.3	10.9	5.4	3.9	6.7
Romania	4.1	6.5	−8.3	4.4	7.1	−3.3	−0.3	−0.6
Slovenia	3.2	4.4	1.4	2.3	3.3	3.8	0.9	1.1
Slovakia	3.5	4.4	−2.5	3.3	5.1	−10.9	0.3	−0.7
Finland	13.7	18.6	−6.2	14.2	16.4	−11.0	−0.6	2.2
Sweden	34.7	48.6	14.3	28.5	36.6	11.7	6.2	12.0
United Kingdom	167.0	179.7	7.8	131.1	127.5	8.4	36.0	52.2
Iceland	1.6	1.9	14.9	2.1	1.6	12.7	−0.4	0.3
Norway	23.6	30.0	8.3	23.8	32.4	22.5	−0.2	−2.4
Croatia	8.0	8.5	0.4	2.7	2.6	−2.8	5.3	5.9
Turkey	21.5	25.9	8.1	9.2	14.9	23.3	12.3	10.9
Japan	88.8	92.4	0.4	108.1	107.0	0.2	−19.3	−14.6
United States	296.1	357.4	0.1	242.5	265.2	38.0	53.6	92.3

(¹) EU-27, extra EU-27 flows; euro area, extra EA-17 flows; Member States and other countries, flows with the rest of the world.

Source: Eurostat (online data codes: bop_q_eu, bop_q_euro and bop_q_c)

Table 9.2.2: Contribution to extra EU-27 trade in services, 2009

	Credits		Debits		Net
	(EUR 1 000 million)	Share of EU-27 credits (%)	(EUR 1 000 million)	Share of EU-27 debits (%)	(EUR 1 000 million)
EU-27 (¹)	477.8	100.0	414.6	100.0	63.3
Belgium	18.4	3.8	14.8	3.6	3.6
Bulgaria	1.4	0.3	1.2	0.3	0.2
Czech Republic	3.9	0.8	4.6	1.1	−0.7
Denmark	20.7	4.3	16.3	3.9	4.4
Germany	78.4	16.4	75.6	18.2	2.9
Estonia	0.9	0.2	0.4	0.1	0.5
Ireland	24.5	5.1	36.0	8.7	−11.5
Greece	12.1	2.5	6.3	1.5	5.8
Spain	25.9	5.4	20.7	5.0	5.1
France	51.8	10.8	44.1	10.6	7.6
Italy	29.1	6.1	33.1	8.0	−4.0
Cyprus	3.4	0.7	1.2	0.3	2.2
Latvia	1.4	0.3	0.7	0.2	0.7
Lithuania	0.9	0.2	1.0	0.2	0.0
Luxembourg	11.2	2.3	8.0	1.9	3.1
Hungary	4.2	0.9	3.7	0.9	0.5
Malta	0.7	0.1	0.4	0.1	0.2
Netherlands	32.6	6.8	37.8	9.1	−5.2
Austria	9.2	1.9	7.2	1.7	2.0
Poland	5.5	1.2	4.0	1.0	1.5
Portugal	4.3	0.9	2.9	0.7	1.4
Romania	1.7	0.3	2.0	0.5	−0.3
Slovenia	1.3	0.3	1.2	0.3	0.1
Slovakia	0.9	0.2	0.8	0.2	0.2
Finland	12.0	2.5	6.4	1.5	5.6
Sweden	20.8	4.3	12.9	3.1	7.9
United Kingdom	100.4	21.0	58.3	14.1	42.1

(¹) Data for the EU institutions are included in the aggregate information presented for the EU-27.

Source: Eurostat (online data code: bop_its_det)

Table 9.2.3: Contribution to intra EU-27 trade in services, 2009

	Credits		Debits		Net
	(EUR 1 000 million)	Share of EU-27 credits (%)	(EUR 1 000 million)	Share of EU-27 debits (%)	(EUR 1 000 million)
EU-27 (¹)	637.8	100.0	595.8	100.0	42.0
Belgium	40.4	6.3	37.8	6.3	2.6
Bulgaria	3.5	0.6	2.4	0.4	1.1
Czech Republic	10.7	1.7	9.0	1.5	1.7
Denmark	19.1	3.0	20.3	3.4	−1.2
Germany	87.4	13.7	107.3	18.0	−19.8
Estonia	2.2	0.3	1.4	0.2	0.8
Ireland	42.1	6.6	39.0	6.6	3.1
Greece	14.8	2.3	8.0	1.3	6.8
Spain	62.2	9.8	42.0	7.0	20.2
France	51.2	8.0	47.3	7.9	3.9
Italy	39.5	6.2	45.3	7.6	−5.8
Cyprus	3.7	0.6	1.8	0.3	1.9
Latvia	1.4	0.2	1.0	0.2	0.4
Lithuania	1.7	0.3	1.2	0.2	0.6
Luxembourg	32.2	5.1	17.6	3.0	14.7
Hungary	9.1	1.4	8.2	1.4	0.9
Malta	1.8	0.3	1.1	0.2	0.7
Netherlands	49.3	7.7	40.2	6.8	9.1
Austria	30.1	4.7	19.3	3.2	10.9
Poland	15.2	2.4	13.2	2.2	1.9
Portugal	12.0	1.9	7.5	1.3	4.5
Romania	5.4	0.8	5.4	0.9	0.0
Slovenia	3.0	0.5	2.0	0.3	1.0
Slovakia	3.6	0.6	5.0	0.8	−1.4
Finland	7.8	1.2	12.1	2.0	−4.3
Sweden	21.8	3.4	19.9	3.3	1.8
United Kingdom	66.3	10.4	59.4	10.0	6.9

(¹) Data for the EU institutions are included in the aggregate information presented for the EU-27.

Source: Eurostat (online data code: bop_its_det)

Figure 9.2.1: Trade in services, EU-27, 2009
(% share of extra EU-27 transactions)

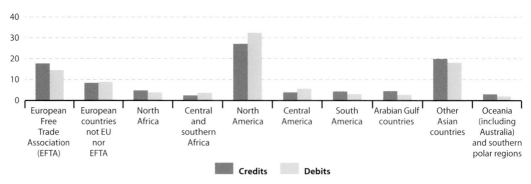

Source: Eurostat (online data code: bop_its_det)

Table 9.2.4: EU-27 credits for services, 2005-2010
(%)

	2005	2006	2007	2008	2009	2010
Extra-EU	41.9	42.0	42.4	42.7	42.8	43.6
European Free Trade Association	6.8	6.6	6.9	7.2	7.6	:
Switzerland	5.2	5.0	5.2	5.6	5.9	5.7
European countries not EU nor EFTA	3.4	3.9	3.6	3.8	3.6	:
Central and eastern Europe	0.9	0.9	0.4	0.5	0.4	:
Commonwealth of Independent States	1.8	2.0	2.2	2.5	2.3	:
Russia	1.3	1.4	1.6	1.8	1.7	1.9
Africa	2.5	2.5	2.8	3.0	3.0	:
America	16.7	16.4	15.7	15.3	15.1	:
Canada	0.9	1.0	1.0	1.0	1.0	1.0
United States	12.7	12.4	11.7	10.9	10.6	10.5
Brazil	0.5	0.5	0.6	0.8	0.8	0.8
Asia	9.9	9.9	10.5	10.4	10.4	:
China (excl. Hong Kong)	1.3	1.3	1.4	1.6	1.7	1.7
Hong Kong	0.9	0.7	0.7	0.7	0.7	0.7
India	0.6	0.7	0.7	0.7	0.8	0.8
Japan	2.1	1.8	1.7	1.6	1.5	1.5
Oceania (including Australia) and southern polar regions	1.1	1.1	1.2	1.2	1.3	:
OECD countries	81.7	80.9	79.9	79.0	78.9	:
North American Free Trade Association member countries	14.1	13.8	13.1	12.2	12.0	:
Petroleum Exporting Countries (OPEC)	2.3	2.6	3.2	3.2	3.2	:
African, Caribbean and Pacific countries, signatories of the Partnership Agreement (Cotonou agreement)	1.9	2.0	2.2	2.2	2.3	:
Association of South-East Asian Nations	1.6	1.7	1.8	1.8	1.8	:
Southern Common Market	0.7	0.7	0.8	1.1	1.1	:

Source: Eurostat (online data code: tec00080)

Table 9.2.5: EU-27 debits for services, 2005-2010
(%)

	2005	2006	2007	2008	2009	2010
Extra-EU	40.0	39.9	39.9	41.2	41.0	41.7
European Free Trade Association	5.4	5.2	5.7	5.8	5.9	:
Switzerland	4.3	4.0	4.5	4.6	4.8	4.9
European countries not EU nor EFTA	4.4	4.3	3.7	3.9	3.6	:
Central and eastern Europe	1.4	1.3	0.7	0.7	0.8	:
Commonwealth of Independent States	1.6	1.7	1.7	1.9	1.6	:
Russia	1.1	1.1	1.1	1.3	1.1	1.3
Africa	3.1	3.1	3.1	3.1	3.1	:
America	17.3	17.0	16.3	16.5	16.9	:
Canada	0.9	0.9	0.9	0.8	0.8	0.8
United States	13.4	13.0	12.4	12.1	12.5	12.2
Brazil	0.5	0.5	0.5	0.6	0.6	0.5
Asia	8.1	8.5	8.7	8.9	8.5	:
China (excl. Hong Kong)	1.1	1.3	1.3	1.4	1.3	1.5
Hong Kong	0.6	0.7	0.7	0.7	0.7	0.7
India	0.6	0.6	0.7	0.7	0.7	0.7
Japan	1.4	1.4	1.3	1.4	1.3	1.3
Oceania (including Australia) and southern polar regions	0.9	0.8	0.8	0.8	0.8	:
OECD countries	81.8	81.2	81.1	79.5	79.9	:
North American Free Trade Association member countries	14.6	14.2	13.7	13.3	13.6	:
Petroleum Exporting Countries (OPEC)	1.5	1.7	1.8	1.8	1.8	:
African, Caribbean and Pacific countries, signatories of the Partnership Agreement (Cotonou agreement)	2.1	2.0	2.0	2.0	2.1	:
Association of South-East Asian Nations	1.6	1.7	1.7	1.8	1.8	:
Southern Common Market	0.7	0.7	0.7	0.8	0.9	:

Source: Eurostat (online data code: tec00081)

Table 9.2.6: Development of trade in services, EU-27, 2005-2010
(EUR 1 000 million)

Partner	2005			2009			2010		
	Credits	Debits	Net	Credits	Debits	Net	Credits	Debits	Net
Total	405.2	351.9	53.3	477.8	414.6	63.3	527.7	454.2	73.5
United States	123.0	117.7	5.2	118.6	126.3	−7.7	126.8	133.3	−6.4
EFTA	65.7	47.8	17.9	84.3	59.9	24.4	:	:	:
Japan	19.9	12.7	7.2	17.2	12.7	4.5	18.4	14.6	3.8
Russia	12.4	9.8	2.6	18.5	11.2	7.3	22.8	14.3	8.5
China	12.5	9.9	2.6	18.7	13.3	5.4	20.4	16.4	4.0
Canada	9.1	7.5	1.6	10.8	8.1	2.7	12.4	9.2	3.2
India	5.4	5.1	0.3	8.9	7.4	1.5	10.0	8.2	1.8
Hong Kong	8.5	5.5	3.0	7.5	6.6	0.8	8.7	7.3	1.4
Brazil	4.8	4.1	0.7	9.3	6.5	2.8	10.0	5.6	4.4
Other countries	143.9	131.9	12.0	184.0	162.4	21.6	:	:	:

Source: Eurostat (online data code: bop_its_det)

Figure 9.2.2: Extra-EU trade in services, by main categories, EU-27, 2010 (¹)
(EUR 1 000 million)

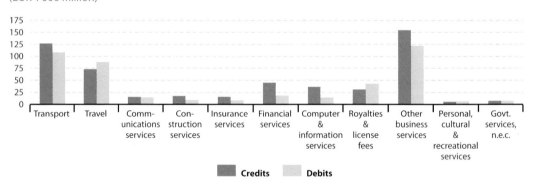

(¹) Provisional.
Source: Eurostat (online data code: bop_its_det)

Transport

Introduction

An efficient and well-functioning passenger and freight transport system is vital for European Union (EU) enterprises and inhabitants. The EU's transport policy aims to foster clean, safe and efficient travel throughout Europe, underpinning the internal market for goods (transferring them between their place of production and consumption) and the right of citizens to travel freely throughout the EU (for both work and pleasure).

Eurostat's transport statistics describe the most important features of transport, not only in terms of the quantities of freight and numbers of passengers that are moved each year, or the number of vehicles and infrastructure that are used, but also the contribution of transport services to the economy as a whole. Data collection is supported by several legal acts obliging the Member States to report statistical data, as well as voluntary agreements to supply additional data.

Transport has seen its share of greenhouse gas emissions within the EU grow from 13.8 % in 1990 to 17.9 % in 2000 and to 20.2 % in 2009 (based on data from the European Environment Agency). This development may be linked to a sizeable increase in transport volumes, as a result of (among others), trade liberalisation, globalisation, higher motorisation rates, and an increase in the number of holidays and short breaks that are taken by Europeans. Such changes have resulted in an increase in the relative share of greenhouse gas emissions accounted for by the transport sector.

On the other hand, some progress has been made in reducing air pollution within the transport sector: for example, through the application of stricter Euro emission standards. Furthermore, the energy efficiency of the transport sector has improved: for example, through the development of more efficient and hybrid vehicles, or a shift in freight transport to alternative modes such as short sea shipping. Generally, these efficiency gains have failed to outweigh

the increased volume of transport. In 2009 the EU established a binding target ([5]) for Member States, whereby 10 % of the fuel used within transport should be derived from renewable energy sources by 2020.

The European Commission's Directorate-General for Mobility and Transport is responsible for developing transport policy within the EU. Its remit is to ensure mobility in a single European transport area, integrating the needs of the population, environmental policy, and competitiveness. It aims to do so by:

- completing the European internal market: so as to ensure the seamless integration of all modes of transport into a single, competitive transport system, while protecting safety and security, and improving the rights of passengers;
- developing an agenda for innovation: promoting the development of a new generation of sustainable transport technologies, in particular for integrated traffic management systems and low-carbon vehicles;
- building a trans-European network as the backbone of a multimodal, sustainable transport system capable of delivering fast, affordable and reliable transport solutions;
- projecting these mobility and transport objectives and defending EU political and industrial interests on the world stage, within international organisations, and with strategic partners.

The European Commission's White paper titled, 'European transport policy for 2010: time to decide' (COM(2001) 370 final) was the foundation of the EU's sustainable transport policy; it was supplemented in June 2006 by a mid-term review in the form of a Communication to the Council and the European Parliament, titled 'Keep Europe moving – sustainable mobility for our continent' (COM(2006) 314 final). The mid-term review proposed that each transport mode should

([5]) Directive 2009/28/EC of the European Parliament and of the Council of 23 April 2009 on the promotion of the use of energy from renewable sources.

be: optimised to help ensure competitiveness and prosperity; more environmentally-friendly and energy-efficient; safe and secure; used efficiently on its own and in combination to achieve an optimal and sustainable utilisation of resources.

Since the 2001 White paper the European Commission has launched a range of action plans on key transport policy issues, among which: a Green paper on urban transport (COM(2007) 551 final); a proposal for a Directive on the charging of heavy goods vehicles for the use of certain infrastructures (COM(2008) 436 final); a Communication to the European Parliament and Council titled 'Greening transport' (COM(2008) 433 final); and a freight transport logistics action plan (COM(2007) 607 final).

As the ten-year period covered by the White paper drew to an end, the European Commission adopted a Communication in mid-2009, titled, 'A sustainable future for transport: towards an integrated, technology-led and user friendly system' (COM (2009) 279 final). The Communication was both consultative and strategic in nature, and underlined the challenges to be faced in the coming years, such as: the need to reduce greenhouse gas emissions, the growing demand for – but increasing scarcity of – fossil fuels, and increasing levels of congestion in many European cities, airports and ports.

Following on from this, in March 2011 the European Commission adopted a White paper titled 'Roadmap to a single European transport area – towards a competitive and resource efficient transport system' (COM(2011) 144 final). This comprehensive strategy contains 40 specific initiatives for the next decade to build a competitive transport system that aims to increase mobility, remove major barriers in key areas and fuel growth and employment. Some of these initiatives concern a specific mode of transport, such as developing a true internal market for rail services or a suitable framework for inland navigation. Several modal specific initiatives concern safety or security, including for land transport security, road safety, civil aviation safety, safer shipping and rail safety. Others concern transport terminals, notably the capacity and quality of airports and market access to ports. Freight transport is the focus of many of the initiatives, including road freight, multimodal transport of goods (e-freight), cargo security, transport of dangerous goods and multimodal freight corridors for sustainable transport networks. Equally some of the initiatives are specific to passenger transport, for example, attaining high levels of passenger security with minimum inconvenience or passengers' rights. The proposals aim to reduce dependence on imported oil and cut carbon emissions in transport by 60 % by 2050. The strategy sets different goals for different types of journey – within cities, between cities, and long distance. The key goals for 2050 include:

- no more conventionally-fuelled cars in cities;
- 40 % use of sustainable low carbon fuels in aviation; a cut of at least 40 % in shipping emissions;
- a 50 % shift of medium distance inter-city passenger and freight journeys from road to rail and waterborne transport;
- all of which should contribute towards a 60 % cut in transport emissions by the middle of the century.

10.1 Transport accidents

Safety and security are of primary concern for any transport system. According to Eurostat statistics on the causes of death, the number of people in the European Union (EU) who died as a result of transport accidents (covering all transport modes) fell by 37 % between 1999 and 2009. Transport accidents remain the largest single cause of death among people aged 15 to 29.

While rail, air, or sea transport incidents often receive considerable media coverage as they generally involve larger numbers of people, road accidents are often treated in a more mundane manner by the media, despite the fact that the vast majority of transport accidents and deaths in the EU occur on the road; the high number of deaths related to road transport reflects in part the high level of road traffic.

Main statistical findings

Road accidents

The annual number of road fatalities in the EU is falling, despite growth (prior to the financial and economic crisis) in passenger and freight transport. The reduction in road fatalities may be attributed, among others, to: improved road design and construction; stricter enforcement of drinking and driving legislation; improved vehicle safety standards; the introduction of speed limits; stricter rules on lorry and bus driving times; and reduced lorry overloads.

Indeed, the number of road fatalities in the EU-27 fell sharply during the decade between 1999 and 2009, from 57 691 deaths to an estimated 34 500 deaths (down 40.2 % overall). Nevertheless, the number of people killed on Europe's roads still accounted for almost nine out of every ten deaths resulting from transport accidents in 2009. The use of alcohol or drugs, the failure to observe speed limits, and the refusal to wear seatbelts are involved in about half of all road fatalities in the EU.

The road fatality rate, expressed as the number of deaths per million inhabitants, averaged 78 across the EU-27 in 2008, although there were stark differences between the Member States (see Figure 10.1.1).

The highest road fatality rates were recorded in Lithuania (148 deaths per million inhabitants), Poland (143), Romania (142), Bulgaria, Greece and Latvia (all 139). The rates reported by these six countries were considerably higher than in the other Member States, as the next highest figure was recorded for Slovenia (106). In contrast, road fatality rates were much lower in Sweden, the United Kingdom (both 43), the Netherlands (41) and Malta (37).

Rail accidents

Some 1 428 people were killed in railway accidents in the EU-27 in 2009 (see Table 10.1.1); this represented a slight increase (119 more victims) compared with the year before; it should be noted that the number of victims in any particular year can be greatly influenced by a small number of major accidents. Of the total number of persons killed in railway accidents in the EU-27 in 2009, around 1 in 20 (5.1 %) were either train passengers or railway employees. Approximately two thirds (63.0 %) of the lives lost in rail accidents were from incidents involving rolling stock in motion, with almost all the others (30.6 %) from incidents at level-crossings. The highest numbers of rail fatalities within the EU in 2009 occurred in Poland (365) and Germany (185).

Air accidents

In a similar manner to rail accidents, the number of air fatalities has an irregular pattern, due to the relatively low number of accidents each year and the large variations in terms of people involved in each event. In the three years covered by the average presented in Figure 10.1.2 the largest single aircraft accident within the EU-27 happened in August 2008 when a flight crashed just after take-off from Madrid's Barajas International Airport, resulting in 154 fatalities. Accidents outside of the national territory are not included in the statistics presented, regardless of whether the airport of departure or destination was in a Member State: for example, the statistics do not include the June 2009 crash in the Atlantic Ocean of a flight from Brazil to France which resulted in 228 fatalities.

Data sources and availability

Road accidents

CARE is the EU's road accident database that collects information on accidents resulting in death and/or injury. The legal basis for CARE is Council Decision 93/704/EC on the creation of a database on road accidents. Its purpose is to provide information which makes it possible to: identify and quantify road safety problems; evaluate the efficiency of road safety measures; determine the relevance of EU actions; and facilitate the exchange of experiences. Road injury accidents are defined as any accident involving at least one road vehicle in motion on a public road or private road to which the public has right of access, resulting in at least one injured or killed person. Included are: collisions between road vehicles; between road vehicles and pedestrians; between road vehicles and animals or fixed obstacles and with one road vehicle alone. Included are collisions between road and rail vehicles. Road deaths are defined as any person killed immediately or dying within 30 days as a result of an injury accident, excluding suicides.

Rail accidents

The legal basis for the collection of statistics on rail accidents is Regulation 91/2003 on rail transport statistics (Annex H), amended by Regulation 1192/2003. The data collected includes information on the number of persons killed or injured (by category of persons) and the number of accidents (by type of accident). An injury accident involves at least one rail vehicle in motion, resulting in at least one killed or injured person. Accidents in workshops, warehouses and depots are excluded. Rail deaths are defined in terms of any person who is killed immediately or dying within 30 days as a result of an accident, excluding suicides. Rail accident statistics are available from 2004 or 2006 onwards for all EU Member States, except for Malta and Cyprus (where there are no railways).

Air accidents

The questionnaire on air transport safety statistics is not supported by any legal acts. Rather, it is based on a gentlemen's agreement with the participating countries (EU Member States, EFTA and candidate countries). The final section of the questionnaire (part IV) deals with the topic of accidents. It contains requests for information on the number of injuries and the number of fatalities that take place as a result of aircraft accidents. Accidents are measured during the operation of an aircraft, which takes place between the time any person boards the aircraft with the intention of flight until such time as all such persons have disembarked (injuries sustained from natural causes or injuries that are self-inflicted are excluded). As with the other modes of transport, a fatal injury is one that results in death within 30 days of the accident.

Context

In June 2003, a European Commission Communication launched an action programme for European road safety (COM(2003) 311), which encouraged:

- road users to improve their behaviour in particular through greater respect of existing rules, initial and continuous training of private and professional drivers, and better law enforcement against dangerous behaviour;
- the use of technical progress to make vehicles safer through improved safety performance standards;
- the improvement of road infrastructure, in particular through the identification and diffusion of best practices and the elimination of black spots through the European Road Assessment Programme (EuroRAP) and the European Tunnel Assessment Programme (EuroTAP).

Railway, aviation and shipping accidents result in far fewer deaths than road accidents. The main reason for this is the limited size of these sectors, relative to the number of cars and goods vehicles that are on Europe's roads. However, when accidents involving trains, planes or ships do occur they have the potential to cause considerable environmental damage and often result in serious commercial and financial consequences. Major transport accidents are almost always investigated in great depth in order to find the cause of the accident, such that a reoccurrence may be prevented.

In March 2011 the European Commission adopted the White paper titled 'Roadmap to a single European transport area – towards a competitive and resource efficient transport system' (COM(2011) 144 final). This comprehensive strategy contains a roadmap of 40 specific initiatives for the next decade including initiatives specifically related to road safety, civil aviation safety, safer shipping and rail safety – more information on the White paper is available in the introduction for transport.

Figure 10.1.1: People killed in road accidents, 2008
(persons killed per million inhabitants)

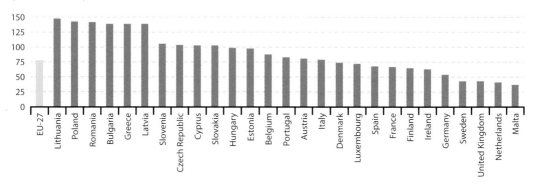

Source: Eurostat (online data code: tsdtr420), European Commission CARE database (Community Database on Road Accidents)

Table 10.1.1: Rail accidents – number of fatalities, by type of victim and accident, EU-27, 2009
(number of persons)

	Total	Passengers	Railway employees	Others
Total	1 428	37	36	1 353
Collisions (excluding level-crossing accidents)	10	0	4	6
Derailments	32	0	2	30
Accidents involving level-crossings	433	2	5	426
Accidents to persons caused by rolling stock in motion	942	34	23	883
Fire in rolling stock	0	0	0	0
Others	11	1	2	8

Source: Eurostat (online data code: rail_ac_catvict)

Figure 10.1.2: Air transport accidents – number of fatalities, annual average 2007-2009 (¹)
(persons killed)

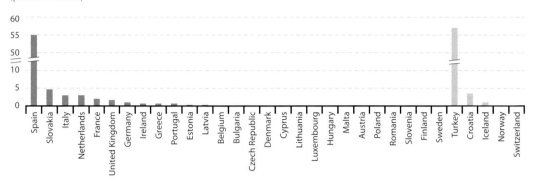

(¹) Accidents on national territory regardless of the nationality of the aircraft operator; Germany, Norway, Switzerland and Turkey, 2007 only; Croatia, average 2008-2009; Iceland, average 2007-2008.

Source: Eurostat (online data code: avia_ac_fatal)

10.2 Passenger transport

This subchapter provides details relating to recent trends for passenger transport statistics within the European Union (EU). It presents information on a range of different passenger transport modes, such as road, rail, air and maritime transport. Among these, the most dominant mode of passenger transport is that of the car, likely fuelled by a desire to have greater mobility and flexibility. The high reliance on the use of the car as a means of passenger transport across the EU has resulted in increased congestion and pollution in many urban areas and on many major transport arteries.

Main statistical findings

Passenger cars accounted for 83.3 % of inland passenger transport in the EU-27 in 2008, with buses and coaches (9.4 %) and railways, trams and metros (7.3 %) both accounting for slightly less than a tenth of the total volume of traffic (as measured by the number of inland passenger-kilometres (pkm) travelled by each mode) – see Table 10.2.1.

In the vast majority of EU Member States, gross domestic product (GDP) grew faster than the volume of inland passenger transport between 2000 and 2008 (see Table 10.2.2). This was most notably the case in Slovakia and Hungary, where GDP grew about one third faster than the rate of growth for the volume of inland passenger transport. The main exceptions to this general pattern were Lithuania and Latvia where the rate of growth in the volume of inland passenger transport was between one quarter and one third faster than the rate of growth for GDP; other exceptions were recorded for Poland, Portugal and Greece.

It should be noted that the analysis above refers only to inland transport by car, bus or train and that a significant proportion of international passenger travel is accounted for by maritime and air transport passenger services, while in some countries national (domestic) maritime and air transport passenger services may also be of note.

Road passengers

Reliance on cars for passenger transport was particularly high in Lithuania, the United Kingdom, the Netherlands and Slovenia, where it accounted for upwards of 86 % of all inland passenger-kilometres in 2008. At least 20 % of the inland passenger-kilometres travelled in Hungary and Bulgaria were by bus or coach.

Between 2000 and 2008 there was a marked increase in the use of passenger cars among many of the Member States that joined the EU in 2004 or 2007, in particular, Bulgaria and Poland, while Hungary was an exception to this development. In contrast, the relative importance of cars as a mode of inland passenger transport fell in ten of the EU-15 Member States. The most sizeable reductions in the relative importance of the car between 2000 and 2008 were recorded in Luxembourg (where the share of the car in total inland passenger transport fell 1.3 percentage points), Italy, Spain and the United Kingdom (– 1.4 points), France (– 1.9 points) and Belgium (– 5.0 points).

Rail passengers

There were 367 251 million passenger-kilometres travelled on national railway networks within the EU-27 (excluding the Netherlands) in 2008; this figure was considerably higher than the 20 388 million passenger-kilometres travelled on international journeys. More than a tenth of all inland passenger-kilometres travelled in Hungary, Austria and France were made on rail networks; these figures include trains, trams and underground railways/metros.

Approximately two thirds of all rail travel (national and international combined) was accounted for by the four largest EU Member States (note that neither Cyprus nor Malta has a railway network), with France and Germany together accounting for more than two fifths of the EU's passenger rail travel. The number of international passenger-kilometres travelled by French passengers in 2009 was, at 9 983 million passenger-kilometres, more than twice the level for Germany (4 162 million passenger-kilometres), which in turn recorded a figure that was more than double that for the United Kingdom (1 641 million passenger-kilometres). In order to compare the relative importance of rail transport between countries, the data can be normalised by expressing passenger volumes in relation to population. France, Sweden and Denmark registered the longest average distances travelled on national railways in 2009, each of these countries averaging more than 1 000 passenger-kilometres per inhabitant. In terms of international rail travel, the highest average distances covered by

rail were recorded for Luxembourg, Austria, France and Belgium (the only Member States to report averages over 100 passenger-kilometres per inhabitant). These figures may reflect, among others, the proximity of international borders, the importance of international commuters within the workforce, access to high-speed rail links, and whether or not international transport corridors run through a particular country.

Note that a subchapter on transport accidents provides more detailed information in relation to rail accidents, including a breakdown of EU-27 data according to the type of victim and accident.

Air passengers

London Heathrow was the busiest airport in the EU-27 in terms of passenger numbers in 2010 (65.7 million), followed by Paris' Charles-de-Gaulle airport (58.0 million), and then Frankfurt airport, Madrid's Barajas airport and Amsterdam's Schiphol airport (all with between 52.6 million and 45.1 million passengers) – see Figure 10.2.2.

With the exception of Barajas, the overwhelming majority (at least 88 %) of passengers through the other four largest airports in the EU were on international flights. In contrast, national (domestic) flights accounted for 37.7 % of the passengers carried through Barajas in 2010. There were also relatively high proportions of passengers on national flights to and from Paris Orly (53.0 %), Barcelona airport (39.9 %) and Roma Fiumicino (35.2 %).

Just under 800 million passengers were carried by air in 2010 in the EU-27 (see Table 10.2.4). The number of air passengers carried in the EU-27 had stagnated in 2008, fell by 5.9 % in 2009, and rebounded by 6.0 % in 2010.

The United Kingdom reported the highest number of air passengers in 2010, with almost 193 million or 3.1 passengers per inhabitant (which was approximately double the EU-27 average). Relative to population size, the importance of air travel was particularly high for the popular holiday islands of Cyprus and Malta (8.7 and 7.9 passengers carried per inhabitant).

Maritime passengers

Table 10.2.4 also shows that ports in the EU-27 handled almost 404 million maritime passengers in 2009; this marked a reduction of 2.2 % compared with 2008 following a fall of 0.3 % in 2008 (compared with 2007). Italian and Greek ports handled more passengers in 2009 than in any other Member State (accounting for 23.0 % and 21.9 % of the EU-27 total respectively); they were followed by Danish ports and then, with roughly similar numbers, ports in Sweden, the United Kingdom and Germany.

Relative to national population, the importance of maritime passenger transport was particularly high in Malta (18.9 passengers per inhabitant), followed by Denmark (7.9), Greece (7.8) and Estonia (6.8); in the remaining Member States, other than Sweden, Finland and Italy, the number of maritime passengers per inhabitant in 2009 averaged less than 1.0 in each of the remaining EU Member States.

Data sources and availability

The majority of inland passenger transport statistics are based on vehicle movements in each of the reporting countries, regardless of the nationality of the vehicle or vessel involved (the 'territoriality principle'). For this reason, the volume measure of passenger-kilometres is generally considered as a more reliable measure, as a count of passengers entails a higher risk of double-counting, particularly for international transport. The methodology used across the Member States is not harmonised for road passenger transport. As such, the figures, especially those for the smallest reporting countries, may be somewhat unreliable.

The modal split of inland passenger transport identifies transportation by passenger car, bus and coach, and train; it generally concerns movements on the national territory, regardless of the nationality of the vehicle. The modal split of passenger transport is defined as the percentage share of each mode and is expressed in passenger-kilometres (pkm), which represent one passenger travelling a distance of one kilometre. For the purpose of this subchapter, the aggregate for inland passenger transport excludes domestic air and water transport services (inland waterways and maritime).

The volume of inland passenger transport (measured in pkm) may also be expressed in relation to GDP; within this subchapter the indicator is presented in constant prices for the reference year 2000, providing information on the relationship between passenger demand and economic growth, with the series indexed on 2000 = 100, so that the annual intensity of passenger transport demand can be monitored relative to economic developments.

Rail passengers

A rail passenger is any person, excluding members of the train crew, who makes a journey by rail. Rail passenger data are not available for Malta and Cyprus (or Iceland) as they do not have railways. Annual passenger statistics for national and international breakdowns generally only cover larger rail transport enterprises, although some countries use detailed reporting for all railway operators.

Air passengers

Air transport statistics concern national and international transport, as measured by the number of passengers carried; information is collected for arrivals and departures. Air passengers carried relate to all passengers on a particular flight (with one flight number) counted once only and not repeatedly on each individual stage of that flight. Air passengers include all revenue and non-revenue passengers whose journey begins or terminates at the reporting airport and transfer passengers joining or leaving the flight at the reporting airport; but excludes direct transit passengers. Air transport statistics are collected with a monthly, quarterly and annual frequency, although only the latter are presented in this subchapter. There are also air transport passenger statistics on the number of commercial passenger flights made, as well as information relating to individual routes and the number of seats available. Annual data are available for most of the EU Member States from 2003 onwards.

Maritime passengers

Maritime transport data are available for most of the period from 2001 onwards, although some EU Member States have provided data since 1997. Maritime transport statistics are not transmitted by the Czech Republic, Luxembourg, Hungary, Austria or Slovakia, as none of these has any maritime traffic. A sea passenger is defined as any person that makes a sea journey on a merchant ship; service staff are not regarded as passengers, neither are non-fare paying crew members travelling but not assigned, while infants in arms are also excluded. Double-counting may arise when both the port of embarkation and the port of disembarkation reports data; this is quite common for the maritime transport of passengers, which is generally a relatively short distance activity.

More detailed definitions of the statistical terms used within transport statistics are available in the Illustrated glossary for transport statistics, 4th edition, 2010.

Context

EU transport policy seeks to ensure that passengers benefit from the same basic standards of treatment wherever they travel within the EU. With this in mind the EU legislates to protect passenger rights across the different modes of transport.

Legislation for aviation (Regulation 261/2004 establishing 'common rules on compensation and assistance to passengers in the event of denied boarding and of cancellation or long delays of flights') and rail travel (Regulation 1371/2007 on 'rail passengers' rights and obligations') are already in force. For bus and coach travel, Regulation 181/2011 was adopted in February 2011 and will apply from March 2013; for sea and inland waterway passenger transport, Regulation 1177/2010 was adopted in November 2010 and will apply from December 2012.

Passengers already have a range of rights covering areas as diverse as: information about their journey; reservations and ticket prices; damages to their baggage; delays and cancellations; or difficulties encountered with package holidays. Specific provisions have also been developed in order to ensure that passengers with reduced mobility are provided with necessary facilities and not refused carriage unfairly.

In March 2011 the European Commission adopted a White paper, the 'Roadmap to a single European transport area – towards a competitive and resource efficient transport system' (COM(2011) 144 final). This comprehensive strategy contains a roadmap of 40 specific initiatives for the next decade to build a competitive transport system that aims to increase mobility, remove major barriers in key areas and fuel growth and employment. More information on the White paper is available in the introduction for transport.

Table 10.2.1: Modal split of inland passenger transport, 2000 and 2008 (^{1})
(% of total inland passenger-km)

	2000			2008		
	Passenger cars	Buses	Railways, trams and metros	Passenger cars	Buses	Railways, trams and metros
EU-27	83.1	9.8	7.1	83.3	9.4	7.3
Belgium	83.4	10.5	6.1	78.4	14.4	7.2
Bulgaria	59.8	32.4	7.7	75.9	20.0	4.1
Czech Republic	73.2	18.5	8.3	76.0	16.9	7.1
Denmark	79.8	11.6	8.6	79.4	11.1	9.4
Germany	85.2	7.1	7.7	85.1	6.3	8.6
Estonia	:	:	:	79.4	18.5	2.1
Ireland	83.7	13.3	3.0	83.8	12.8	3.4
Greece	72.8	25.1	2.2	80.8	17.9	1.3
Spain	81.5	13.5	5.0	80.1	14.4	5.5
France	86.1	5.3	8.6	84.2	5.7	10.1
Italy	83.8	10.8	5.4	82.4	11.9	5.7
Cyprus	:	:	0.0	:	:	0.0
Latvia	:	:	:	80.6	14.1	5.3
Lithuania	:	:	:	90.9	8.2	1.0
Luxembourg	85.5	9.5	5.1	84.2	11.4	4.3
Hungary	62.1	25.0	12.9	62.1	25.7	12.3
Malta	:	:	0.0	:	:	0.0
Netherlands (^{2})	86.0	4.6	9.4	86.5	3.8	9.7
Austria (^{3})	79.2	11.0	9.8	78.6	10.2	11.1
Poland	72.8	15.4	11.7	85.5	8.4	6.2
Portugal	81.9	13.6	4.4	85.2	10.7	4.1
Romania	72.5	10.9	16.5	77.2	15.2	7.6
Slovenia	82.9	14.3	2.9	86.2	10.9	2.9
Slovakia	67.9	23.9	8.1	74.9	18.6	6.5
Finland	83.4	11.5	5.1	84.5	10.1	5.4
Sweden	83.7	8.7	7.6	83.3	7.4	9.3
United Kingdom	88.2	6.4	5.3	86.8	6.4	6.8
Iceland	87.0	13.0	0.0	88.6	11.4	0.0
Norway	87.0	7.7	5.3	87.6	7.3	5.1
Croatia	81.4	13.6	5.1	82.2	12.5	5.4
FYR of Macedonia	83.2	13.3	3.5	78.3	19.4	2.3
Turkey	45.9	50.7	3.4	51.0	46.8	2.2

(^{1}) Excluding powered two-wheelers.
(^{2}) Break in series.
(^{3}) The railway in Liechtenstein is owned and operated by the Austrian ÖBB and included in their statistics.

Source: Eurostat (online data code: tsdtr210)

Table 10.2.2: Volume of inland passenger transport, 1998-2008
(index of inland passenger transport volume relative to GDP (2000 = 100))

	1998	1999	2000	2001	2002	2003	2004	2005	2006	2007	2008
EU-27	:	:	100.0	:	99.8	:	:	96.3	95.7	94.7	93.5
Belgium	104.8	103.1	100.0	101.8	102.4	100.7	99.8	98.4	96.9	97.6	96.4
Bulgaria	101.0	103.0	100.0	99.8	100.0	92.7	88.1	84.0	82.7	82.4	81.8
Czech Republic	100.0	100.6	100.0	98.6	96.9	95.5	90.5	86.6	82.6	79.5	77.7
Denmark	104.7	103.5	100.0	98.0	97.7	98.0	95.7	93.8	92.3	92.7	93.9
Germany	104.6	104.7	100.0	100.9	101.4	101.1	101.5	99.4	97.8	95.9	93.1
Estonia	:	:	100.0	:	:	:	:	83.3	76.6	71.3	75.6
Ireland	113.0	105.2	100.0	98.1	93.4	91.5	89.1	86.3	84.8	84.3	88.8
Greece	94.5	97.8	100.0	101.5	102.7	101.0	99.9	102.1	102.2	102.8	104.0
Spain	101.6	102.3	100.0	98.4	97.2	95.8	96.0	94.5	90.9	90.2	89.1
France	103.8	103.3	100.0	101.6	101.6	101.0	98.8	96.2	94.1	92.9	92.3
Italy (¹)	96.4	95.5	100.0	97.4	96.4	96.4	96.1	92.7	97.1	98.2	93.9
Cyprus	:	:	100.0	:	:	:	:	:	:	:	:
Latvia	:	:	100.0	:	99.8	:	:	133.0	132.6	132.7	125.6
Lithuania	:	:	100.0	:	93.3	98.8	120.2	145.6	151.3	137.4	129.3
Luxembourg	105.3	97.5	100.0	101.3	99.8	98.6	95.9	94.3	91.7	88.9	91.8
Hungary	106.1	103.6	100.0	96.3	93.1	89.3	85.4	79.9	77.0	68.9	69.1
Malta	:	:	100.0	:	:	:	:	:	:	:	:
Netherlands (²)	106.0	103.8	100.0	98.5	99.8	99.5	100.8	97.3	94.1	91.5	88.8
Austria	104.1	102.3	100.0	100.0	99.6	100.0	98.5	97.3	95.7	93.3	93.7
Poland	103.8	100.3	100.0	101.5	103.1	101.3	99.6	102.2	104.5	105.6	112.5
Portugal	99.8	100.6	100.0	99.8	102.8	108.2	108.8	110.4	109.5	108.5	109.3
Romania	:	101.4	100.0	94.9	89.0	90.0	85.3	87.0	83.8	81.9	80.1
Slovenia	105.4	105.7	100.0	98.7	96.7	94.7	92.5	89.7	86.4	85.5	84.0
Slovakia	89.9	93.0	100.0	96.4	94.1	88.3	81.9	79.3	74.8	66.9	61.8
Finland	105.4	103.7	100.0	99.1	99.5	99.5	97.7	96.4	92.7	90.8	89.8
Sweden	104.4	102.8	100.0	99.6	99.6	99.5	95.8	93.1	89.5	89.8	89.6
United Kingdom	106.4	104.2	100.0	99.7	100.7	97.6	96.0	93.6	92.3	90.7	89.7
Iceland	89.9	89.8	100.0	103.7	106.5	107.0	102.5	101.9	102.7	88.3	88.9
Norway	102.9	102.1	100.0	99.8	100.2	101.1	98.4	97.3	95.8	95.2	92.7
Croatia	93.1	98.5	100.0	100.8	99.4	96.9	95.3	93.3	92.9	92.6	94.7
FYR of Macedonia	:	:	100.0	100.0	103.7	107.9	107.7	104.9	101.6	97.9	102.0
Turkey	:	108.1	100.0	100.6	97.0	94.1	93.3	93.0	92.7	93.5	96.8

(¹) Break in series, 2000.
(²) Break in series, 2003.

Source: Eurostat (online data code: tsien070)

Table 10.2.3: Rail passenger transport, 2008-2010

	Rail passenger transport (million passenger-km) (¹)				Rail passenger transport (passenger-km per inhabitant) (¹)				Rail accidents (number of persons)			
	National		International		National		International		Killed		Seriously injured	
	2008	2009	2008	2009	2008	2009	2008	2009	2009	2010	2009	2010
EU-27	:	:	:	:	:	:	:	:	1428	:	1145	:
Belgium	8913	9005	1226	1232	836	837	114.9	114.6	26	35	13	188
Bulgaria	2264	2089	52	49	296	275	6.8	6.4	28	16	22	22
Czech Republic	6324	6132	449	340	609	586	43.3	32.5	26	48	92	107
Denmark	5606	5590	477	377	1024	1014	87.1	68.4	15	:	15	:
Germany	78558	77044	3870	4162	955	940	47.1	50.8	185	:	138	:
Estonia	245	232	28	17	183	173	20.9	12.7	10	12	7	0
Ireland	1872	1683	104	:	425	378	23.6	:	4	8	5	0
Greece	1599	:	59	:	143	:	5.3	:	22	29	22	20
Spain	21853	21493	221	206	483	469	4.9	4.5	41	52	21	28
France	78970	78628	7546	9983	1234	1222	117.9	155.1	76	68	61	46
Italy	44708	:	1059	:	750	:	17.8	:	82	86	71	64
Cyprus	–	–	–	–	–	–	–	–	–	–	–	–
Latvia	865	686	76	62	381	303	33.5	27.4	17	22	12	15
Lithuania	235	213	22	18	70	64	6.5	5.4	33	31	12	17
Luxembourg (²)	246	246	99	101	508	490	204.6	201.2	4	0	0	0
Hungary	7912	7680	379	321	788	766	37.7	32.0	92	82	84	70
Malta	–	–	–	–	–	–	–	–	–	–	–	–
Netherlands	:	:	:	:	:	:	:	:	14	10	9	10
Austria	8235	8178	1452	1442	990	979	174.5	172.6	36	30	65	51
Poland	19324	17776	439	352	507	466	11.5	9.2	365	285	199	198
Portugal	4093	4115	120	97	385	387	11.3	9.1	32	:	18	:
Romania	6725	5842	152	133	312	272	7.1	6.2	150	139	187	182
Slovenia	713	718	53	55	355	353	26.4	27.1	11	14	14	12
Slovakia	2094	2079	202	185	388	384	37.4	34.2	73	:	35	:
Finland	3940	3785	112	91	743	711	21.1	17.1	14	13	10	8
Sweden	10609	10725	537	615	1155	1159	58.5	66.4	19	45	18	25
United Kingdom	51348	51123	1654	1641	839	830	27.0	26.6	53	25	15	23
Liechtenstein	:	:	:	:	:	:	:	:	0	0	0	0
Norway	2988	2941	31	30	631	613	6.5	6.3	3	7	4	4
Switzerland	15673	16341	912	879	2064	2122	120.1	114.1	29	19	34	38
Croatia	1703	1744	66	58	384	393	14.9	13.1	50	27	65	28
Turkey	4999	5271	98	103	71	74	1.4	1.4	89	69	303	142

(¹) The railway in Liechtenstein is owned and operated by the Austrian ÖBB and included in their rail passenger transport statistics.
(²) 2010 instead of 2009 for rail passenger transport.

Source: Eurostat (online data codes: rail_pa_typepkm, tps00001 and rail_ac_catvict)

Figure 10.2.1: Rail passenger transport, 2009 (¹)
(passenger-km per inhabitant)

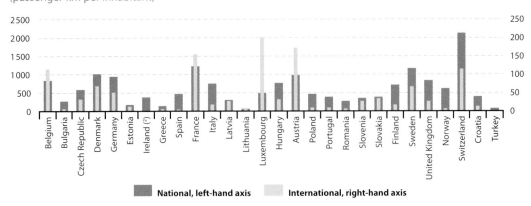

(¹) Greece and Italy, 2008; Cyprus and Malta, not applicable; the Netherlands, not available; the railway in Liechtenstein is owned and operated by the Austrian ÖBB and included in their statistics.
(²) International, not available.

Source: Eurostat (online data codes: rail_pa_typepkm and tps00001)

Figure 10.2.2: Top 15 airports, passengers carried (embarked and disembarked), EU-27, 2010
(million passengers)

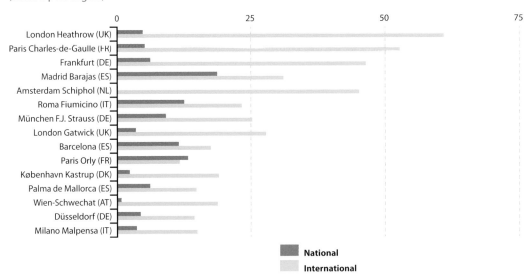

Source: Eurostat (online data code: avia_paoa)

Table 10.2.4: Air and sea passenger transport, 2009 and 2010 (¹)

	Air passengers, 2010 (²)		Maritime passengers, 2009 (³)	
	(1 000)	(passengers per inhabitant)	(1 000)	(passengers per inhabitant)
EU-27	796 396	1.6	403 752	0.8
Belgium	22 691	2.1	751	0.1
Bulgaria	6 168	0.8	0	0.0
Czech Republic	12 242	1.2	–	–
Denmark	24 331	4.4	43 561	7.9
Germany	166 131	2.0	29 573	0.4
Estonia	1 381	1.0	9 140	6.8
Ireland	23 094	5.2	2 878	0.6
Greece	32 132	2.8	88 351	7.8
Spain	153 387	3.3	21 458	0.5
France	123 021	1.9	25 067	0.4
Italy	109 174	1.8	92 707	1.5
Cyprus	6 948	8.7	96	0.1
Latvia	4 656	2.1	591	0.3
Lithuania	2 283	0.7	205	0.1
Luxembourg	1 614	3.2	–	–
Hungary	8 175	0.8	–	–
Malta	3 294	7.9	7 799	18.9
Netherlands	48 617	2.9	1 632	0.1
Austria	23 532	2.8	–	–
Poland	18 383	0.5	2 481	0.1
Portugal	25 732	2.4	833	0.1
Romania	8 849	0.4	0	0.0
Slovenia	1 382	0.7	56	0.0
Slovakia	1 882	0.3	–	–
Finland	14 221	2.7	17 226	3.2
Sweden	26 647	2.9	31 066	3.4
United Kingdom	192 885	3.1	28 281	0.5
Iceland	2 036	6.4	433	1.4
Norway	29 517	6.1	5 728	1.2
Switzerland	37 616	4.8	–	–
Croatia	4 677	1.1	26 037	5.9
Turkey	:	:	1 386	0.0

(¹) For air: aggregates exclude the double-counting impact of passengers flying between countries belonging to the same aggregate. For maritime: figures refer to the number of passengers 'handled in ports' (i.e. the sum of passengers embarked and then disembarked in ports); if both the port of embarkation and disembarkation report data to Eurostat, then these passengers are counted twice.
(²) Total passengers carried (arrivals and departures for national and international).
(³) Iceland, 2006.

Source: Eurostat (online data codes: ttr00012, tps00001 and mar_pa_aa)

10.3 Freight transport

The ability to move goods safely, quickly and cost-efficiently to markets is important for international trade, national distributive trades, and economic development. This subchapter presents information on the freight transport sector in the European Union (EU), which includes the following transport modes: road, rail, air, maritime and inland waterways.

The rapid increase in global trade up to the onset of the financial and economic crisis and the deepening integration of the enlarged EU, alongside a range of economic practices (including the concentration of production in fewer sites to reap economies of scale, delocalisation, and just-in-time deliveries), may explain the relatively fast growth of freight transport within the EU. In contrast, strains on transport infrastructure (congestion and delays), coupled with constraints over technical standards, interoperability and governance issues may slow down developments within the freight transport sector.

Main statistical findings

Total inland freight transport in the EU-27 was estimated to be close to 2 200 000 million tonne-kilometres (tkm) in 2009; a little over three quarters (77.5 %) of this freight total was transported over roads in 2009 (see Table 10.3.1). The relative importance of road freight transport, as a share of total inland freight transport, rose by 3.8 percentage points between 2000 and 2009. The volume of inland freight transported by road was a little over four times as high as the volume transported by rail (16.5 % of inland freight transported in the EU-27 in 2009), while the remainder (5.9 %) of the freight transported in the EU-27 was carried along inland waterways. It should be noted that this analysis refers only to inland freight transport and that considerable volumes of freight may be transported by maritime freight services and for some product groups by air transport or by pipelines.

The relative ascendancy of road freight transport was common in most of the Member States, with the exception of the Baltic Member States, Austria

and Sweden, where at least one third of the inland freight transported took place on the railways in 2009; in Latvia and Estonia a majority of inland freight was transported by rail, 69.8 % and 52.7 % respectively. More than 10 % of total inland freight was transported on the inland waterways of Belgium and Germany in 2009, with this share increasing to just over 20 % in Bulgaria and Romania and to more than one third (34.7 %, 2008) of the total in the Netherlands.

The volume of EU-27 inland freight transport grew at a slower pace than constant price GDP during the period from 2000 to 2009; this can be seen from the index shown in Table 10.3.2, as the index value in 2009 was 3.6 % lower than in 2000. Nevertheless, it should be noted that this was in large part due to the results for 2008 and 2009 when the index level fell sharply and that prior to this in 2007 the index had shown the volume of inland freight transport increasing more than GDP. Bulgaria and Slovenia recorded the greatest increase in inland freight transport relative to GDP, with their respective indices close to 50 % higher in 2009 than they had been in 2000. In contrast, the ratio of freight transport to GDP fell at its most rapid pace between 2000 and 2009 in Cyprus and Estonia, in both cases down by around two fifths.

Road freight

Relative to the size of their respective populations, the greatest volume of road freight transport was reported for Luxembourg, over 17 000 tonne-kilometres per inhabitant in 2010, around 2.2 times the next highest volume in Slovenia; in both cases, the vast majority of this road freight transportation was international, performed by vehicles registered in each of these Member States. Indeed, it is important to note that road freight statistics are generally based on movements in the registration country or abroad, of vehicles registered in the reporting country ('nationality principle').

Slightly more than two thirds of the goods transported on the EU-27's roads in 2010 related to the transportation of goods on national road networks.

However, this proportion varied considerably between the Member States (see Figure 10.3.1): the highest proportion of national road freight transport was in the islands of Cyprus (98.1 %) and the United Kingdom (94.3 % in 2009), while the relative importance of national freight was much lower in Slovakia (18.9 %), Slovenia (14.4 %), Lithuania (11.8 %) and Luxembourg (6.6 %). For most freight hauliers registered in the EU, international road freight transport mostly relates to exchanges with other EU Member States (intra-EU partners).

Air freight

About 14.2 million tonnes of air freight (both national and international) was carried through airports within the EU-27 in 2010 (see Figure 10.3.2). Airports in Germany dealt with 4.1 million tonnes of air freight, considerably more than in any other EU Member State – the United Kingdom had the second highest amount of air freight at 2.4 million tonnes. Some of the smaller Member States are relatively specialised in air freight, notably all of the Benelux countries, and in particular, Luxembourg (which ranked as the seventh largest air freight transporter among the EU Member States).

Maritime freight

Maritime ports in the EU-27 handled 3 445 million tonnes of seaborne goods in 2009, which marked a reduction of 12.1 % when compared with 2008. Sea ports in the United Kingdom handled 501 million tonnes of goods in 2009, more than any other Member State and equivalent to 14.5 % of the EU-27 total. Among the smaller Member States, the quantity of goods handled in maritime ports of the Netherlands, Belgium and the Nordic Member States was particularly high (see Figure 10.3.3).

Data sources and availability

The development of freight transport statistics is based upon a raft of framework legislation and implementing legislation, generally broken down according to the mode of transport under consideration.

Information on inland freight transport is available with an annual frequency and the time series generally begin in the early 1990s. The majority of inland freight transport statistics are based on movements in each reporting country, regardless of the nationality of the vehicle or vessel involved (the 'territoriality principle'). For this reason, the volume measure of tonne-kilometres is generally considered as a more reliable measure, as the use of tonnes entails a higher risk of double-counting, particularly for international transport. The methodology used across the EU Member States is not completely harmonised, for example, road freight statistics are generally based on all movements (in the registration country or abroad) of vehicles registered in the reporting country (the 'nationality principle'). Therefore, the statistics presented, especially those for the smallest reporting countries, may be somewhat unrepresentative.

The modal split of inland freight transport is based on transportation by road, rail and inland waterways, and therefore excludes air, maritime and pipeline transport. It measures the share of each transport mode in total inland freight transport and is based on the volume of goods transported in tonne-kilometres, in other words, one tonne of goods travelling a distance of one kilometre.

The volume of inland freight transport may also be expressed in relation to gross domestic product (GDP); within this subchapter the indicator is presented in constant prices for the reference year 2000, providing information on the relationship between the demand for freight transport and economic growth, with the series indexed on 2000 = 100, so that the annual intensity of freight transport demand can be monitored relative to economic developments.

Goods loaded are those goods placed on a road vehicle, a railway vehicle or a merchant ship for dispatch by road, rail or sea. The weight of goods transported by rail and inland waterways is the gross-gross weight. This includes the total weight of the goods, all packaging, and the tare weight of the container, swap-body and pallets containing goods; in the case of rail freight transport, it also

includes road goods vehicles that are carried by rail. In contrast, the weight measured for maritime and road freight transport is the gross weight (in other words, excluding the tare weight).

Road freight

Road freight transport statistics are collected under the framework provided by Regulation 1172/98 on statistical returns in respect of the carriage of goods by road, amended by Regulation 399/2009 which details implementing powers conferred on the European Commission. The data are based on sample surveys carried out in the reporting countries and record the transport of goods by road, as undertaken by vehicles registered in each of the Member States. It is important to note that almost all of the Member States apply a cut-off point for carrying capacity under which vehicles are not surveyed; this should not be greater than 3.5 tonnes carrying capacity, or 6 tonnes in terms of gross vehicle weight; some of the Member States also apply a limit on the age of the vehicles surveyed.

Rail freight

Rail freight data are collected under the framework provided by Regulation 91/2003 on rail transport statistics. The data are collected for a quarterly frequency (usually limited to larger enterprises) and for an annual frequency (which covers enterprises of all sizes). Rail freight data are not available for Malta and Cyprus (or Iceland) as they do not have a railway infrastructure. Rail statistics are also collected every five years in relation to a regional breakdown (NUTS 2 level).

Aside from the mandatory collection of data based on legal acts, Eurostat also collects rail transport statistics through a voluntary data collection exercise. The questionnaire used for this exercise provides information in relation to railway transport infrastructures, equipment, enterprises, traffic and train movements.

Maritime freight

The legal framework for the collection of statistics on maritime freight transport is Directive 2009/42/EC on statistical returns in respect of carriage of goods and passengers by sea (Recast). Maritime transport data are available for most of the period from 2001 onwards, although some EU Member States have provided data since 1997. Maritime freight statistics are not transmitted to Eurostat by the Czech Republic, Luxembourg, Hungary, Austria and Slovakia as they have no maritime ports.

Inland waterways freight

The legal framework for the collection of statistics on inland waterway freight transport is Regulation 1365/2006 on statistics of goods transport by inland waterways. Data on inland waterways are only required for those Member States with an annual quantity of goods transported that exceeds one million tonnes, namely Belgium, Bulgaria, the Czech Republic, Germany, France, Luxembourg, Hungary, the Netherlands, Austria, Poland, Romania, Slovakia and the United Kingdom; Croatia also provides data. Data collection is based on an exhaustive survey of all inland waterway undertakings for all goods that are loaded or unloaded. In the case of transit, some countries make use of sampling methods in order to estimate the quantity of goods.

Air freight

The legal framework for air transport statistics is provided by Regulation 437/2003 on statistical returns in respect of the carriage of passengers, freight and mail by air. Air freight statistics are collected for freight and mail loaded and unloaded in relation to commercial air flights. The information is broken down to cover national and international freight transport.

Air transport statistics are collected at the airport level by the EU Member States, Norway, Iceland, Switzerland and candidate countries. Annual data are available for most of the EU Member States for the period from 2003 onwards, while some countries have provided data back to 1993. The statistics that are collected are also available for a monthly and a quarterly frequency. Air freight statistics are also collected for a regional breakdown (NUTS 2 level).

More detailed definitions of the statistical terms used within transport statistics are available in the Illustrated Glossary for Transport Statistics – 4th edition, 2010.

Context

One of the main challenges identified by the 2001 White paper, titled 'European transport policy for 2010: time to decide' (COM(2001) 370) was to address the imbalance in the development of different transport modes.

A mid-term review of the White paper, titled 'Keep Europe moving – sustainable mobility for our continent' (COM(2006) 314) made a number of suggestions for new policy developments, which have been subsequently expanded upon in the form of a series of European Commission Communications, these include:

- The EU's freight transport agenda: boosting the efficiency, integration and sustainability of freight transport in Europe (COM(2007) 606);
- A freight transport logistics action plan (COM (2007) 607);
- A move towards a rail network giving priority to freight COM(2007) 608);
- A European ports policy (COM(2007) 616);
- A 'Greening transport' package (COM(2008) 433);

- A set of strategic goals and recommendations for the EU's maritime transport policy until 2018 (COM(2009) 8);
- A European maritime transport space without barriers (COM(2009) 10).

As the ten-year period covered by the White paper drew to an end, the European Commission adopted a Communication in mid-2009 titled 'A sustainable future for transport: towards an integrated, technology-led and user friendly system' (COM(2009) 279 final). Following on from this, in March 2011 the European Commission adopted a White paper titled 'Roadmap to a single European transport area – towards a competitive and resource efficient transport system' (COM(2011) 144 final). This comprehensive strategy contains a roadmap of 40 specific initiatives for the next decade to build a competitive transport system that aims to increase mobility, remove major barriers in key areas and fuel growth and employment. More information on the White paper is available in the introduction for transport.

Table 10.3.1: Modal split of inland freight transport, 2000 and 2009 (¹)
(% of total inland tkm)

	2000			2009		
	Roads	Railways	Inland waterways	Roads (²)	Railways (³)	Inland waterways (⁴)
EU-27	*73.7*	*19.7*	*6.6*	*77.5*	*16.5*	*5.9*
Belgium	77.4	11.6	10.9	72.9	15.1	14.3
Bulgaria	52.3	45.2	2.6	67.4	11.9	20.7
Czech Republic	68.0	31.9	0.2	77.8	22.1	0.1
Denmark	92.1	7.9	–	90.8	9.2	–
Germany	65.3	19.2	15.5	67.0	20.9	12.1
Estonia	37.3	62.7	0.0	47.3	52.7	0.0
Ireland	96.2	3.8	–	99.4	0.6	–
Greece	:	:	–	97.8	2.2	–
Spain	92.8	7.2	–	96.6	3.4	–
France	76.0	20.6	3.4	81.0	15.9	4.1
Italy	89.0	11.0	0.1	*91.0*	*9.0*	*0.0*
Cyprus	100.0	–	–	100.0	–	–
Latvia	26.5	73.5	0.0	30.2	69.8	0.0
Lithuania	46.6	53.4	0.0	59.9	40.1	0.0
Luxembourg	87.8	7.9	4.4	94.6	2.3	3.1
Hungary	68.1	28.8	3.1	78.8	20.6	4.1
Malta	100.0	–	–	100.0	–	–
Netherlands	63.4	3.7	32.9	63.4	4.9	34.7
Austria (⁵)	64.8	30.6	4.5	59.5	36.4	4.1
Poland	56.9	42.2	0.9	80.5	19.4	0.1
Portugal	92.5	7.5	–	94.3	5.7	–
Romania	42.9	49.1	7.9	60.0	19.4	20.6
Slovenia	*71.9*	*28.1*	–	84.0	16.0	–
Slovakia	53.0	41.7	5.3	77.9	19.6	2.5
Finland	75.8	24.0	0.3	73.3	24.1	0.2
Sweden	63.9	36.1	–	62.5	37.5	–
United Kingdom	90.0	9.8	0.1	*86.7*	*13.2*	0.1
Iceland	100.0	–	–	100.0	–	–
Norway	83.5	16.5	–	83.4	16.6	–
Croatia	:	:	:	73.7	20.6	5.7
FYR of Macedonia	86.9	13.1	–	84.3	15.7	–
Turkey	94.3	5.7	–	94.9	5.1	–

(¹) Excluding pipelines; EU-27, Bulgaria, Greece, Austria, Poland, Portugal, Romania and Croatia, break in series.
(²) Finland, 2008; FYR of Macedonia and Turkey, 2007.
(³) France, Hungary and FYR of Macedonia, 2008; Turkey, 2007.
(⁴) Netherlands, 2008; Czech Republic, Estonia, Italy and the United Kingdom, 2007.
(⁵) The railway in Liechtenstein is owned and operated by the Austrian ÖBB and included in their statistics.

Source: Eurostat (online data code: tsdtr220)

Table 10.3.2: Volume of inland freight transport, 1999-2009 ([1])
(index of inland freight transport volume relative to GDP, 2000 = 100)

	1999	2000	2001	2002	2003	2004	2005	2006	2007	2008	2009
EU-27	100.1	100.0	99.0	100.2	99.3	105.2	105.1	105.7	106.4	103.8	96.4
Belgium	80.2	100.0	102.2	101.3	97.3	91.3	84.9	82.5	80.0	73.5	67.2
Bulgaria	49.9	100.0	104.8	105.0	109.9	119.7	128.0	118.3	116.6	120.7	147.4
Czech Republic	101.5	100.0	99.6	103.9	105.2	98.6	88.5	94.0	86.2	86.6	79.2
Denmark	100.1	100.0	91.9	92.7	94.4	93.9	91.1	80.7	77.9	73.8	67.6
Germany	100.4	100.0	99.9	98.9	100.0	104.5	106.1	109.7	111.7	110.0	101.9
Estonia	91.7	100.0	89.5	92.7	84.6	90.1	87.0	76.7	66.5	61.8	61.1
Ireland	92.0	100.0	95.1	102.3	107.0	111.8	109.3	100.6	102.9	97.0	76.4
Greece	:	100.0	:	:	:	:	:	:	:	:	:
Spain	95.5	100.0	104.0	114.9	116.1	128.4	130.0	129.4	133.1	123.9	111.3
France	103.0	100.0	96.9	94.9	92.4	92.7	87.2	87.6	88.7	83.3	71.4
Italy	99.4	100.0	98.8	100.4	91.6	101.7	108.2	95.5	91.2	92.2	94.0
Cyprus	101.6	100.0	99.3	101.2	105.2	80.6	96.6	77.6	76.1	80.0	59.3
Latvia	96.7	100.0	99.9	101.9	111.0	107.2	105.0	91.6	95.2	101.0	103.6
Lithuania	96.5	100.0	89.9	107.6	109.2	106.2	116.8	118.5	120.5	119.0	117.9
Luxembourg	91.6	100.0	109.2	109.4	111.6	107.1	92.2	88.2	87.7	96.1	79.2
Hungary	101.9	100.0	93.9	89.5	85.8	93.6	105.1	118.4	132.4	131.1	131.1
Malta	:	100.0	:	:	:	:	:	:	:	:	:
Netherlands	106.9	100.0	97.4	97.8	96.2	105.6	98.7	95.2	91.4	89.1	80.3
Austria	98.1	100.0	104.7	105.7	105.2	104.3	98.5	102.2	97.7	91.4	79.1
Poland	103.0	100.0	97.6	98.4	98.4	108.2	108.9	115.2	121.6	122.5	124.4
Portugal	101.2	100.0	108.4	107.0	99.7	143.5	148.6	153.8	155.9	133.0	124.6
Romania	95.2	100.0	106.3	119.6	127.1	145.1	174.2	171.4	165.6	148.5	113.7
Slovenia	102.4	100.0	101.3	95.5	98.8	114.5	128.7	132.0	138.4	152.5	147.0
Slovakia	112.9	100.0	92.3	87.0	88.1	88.2	93.7	86.9	92.0	90.9	85.5
Finland	98.7	100.0	93.7	95.0	91.6	91.1	86.7	81.4	76.7	76.4	74.8
Sweden	98.0	100.0	95.4	96.9	96.7	94.4	95.3	94.4	94.4	97.1	87.4
United Kingdom	104.3	100.0	97.0	95.1	94.1	91.0	88.3	90.3	90.0	84.0	76.7
Iceland	103.8	100.0	105.5	108.3	108.8	109.6	113.1	119.2	:	:	:
Norway	101.5	100.0	97.8	96.6	101.4	103.1	105.9	109.9	107.6	111.9	103.7
FYR of Macedonia	:	100.0	93.5	111.8	146.1	139.0	141.5	198.5	141.2	:	:
Turkey	99.2	100.0	98.4	92.2	89.1	84.2	82.2	81.7	79.8	:	:

([1]) Excluding pipelines; breaks in series: Bulgaria, Hungary and Slovakia, 2000; Bulgaria, 2001; EU-27, Portugal and Romania, 2004.

Source: Eurostat (online data code: tsien060)

Table 10.3.3: Inland freight transport, 2010

	(million tkm)			(tkm per inhabitant)			National air freight and mail transport (tonnes) (⁴)
	Road (¹)	Rail (²)	Inland water-ways (³)	Road (¹)	Rail (²)	Inland water-ways (³)	
EU-27	:	360 636	129 516	:	722	259	575 080
Belgium	35 002	6 268	7 087	3 229	578	659	495
Bulgaria	19 433	3 064	6 048	2 569	405	800	31
Czech Republic	51 832	13 770	43	4 933	1 311	4	1 735
Denmark	15 018	1 700	–	2 716	308	–	1 045
Germany	313 104	107 317	62 278	3 828	1 312	761	119 618
Estonia	5 614	6 638	:	4 189	4 953	:	0
Ireland	10 939	92	–	2 448	21	–	9 349
Greece	28 585	435	–	2 539	38	–	11 925
Spain	210 068	8 119	–	4 568	177	–	78 922
France	182 193	29 965	9 445	2 815	463	146	134 873
Italy	175 775	18 616	:	2 913	309	:	55 859
Cyprus	1 087	–	–	1 353	–	–	0
Latvia	10 590	17 179	:	4 710	7 641	:	0
Lithuania	19 398	13 431	:	5 827	4 034	:	0
Luxembourg	8 694	200	359	17 316	405	715	0
Hungary	33 721	8 809	2 393	3 367	880	239	0
Malta	:	–	–	:	–	–	0
Netherlands	68 242	6 385	35 656	4 117	385	2 163	0
Austria	28 659	19 833	2 375	3 422	2 368	284	695
Poland	210 846	48 705	130	5 524	1 276	3	6 201
Portugal	35 368	2 174	–	3 325	205	–	18 723
Romania	25 889	12 375	14 317	1 206	577	667	185
Slovenia	15 931	3 421	:	7 783	1 671	:	0
Slovakia	27 575	6 964	899	5 083	1 287	166	0
Finland	29 532	9 750	:	5 519	1 822	:	3 133
Sweden	36 268	23 464	–	3 883	2 512	–	14 296
United Kingdom	139 536	18 576	:	2 265	299	:	117 996
Liechtenstein	303	11	:	8 442	306	:	:
Norway	19 751	3 579	–	4 065	737	–	7 412
Switzerland	12 838	323	:	1 649	41	:	3 991
Croatia	8 780	2 618	940	1 984	592	212	990
Turkey	:	11 300	–	:	156	–	:

(¹) Greece and the United Kingdom, 2009; road transport is based on movements all over the world of vehicles registered in the reporting country.
(²) EU-27, Denmark, Luxembourg, Portugal and Slovakia, 2009.
(³) EU-27, Belgium, the Netherlands and Slovakia, 2009.
(⁴) Data based on departures; France underestimated as freight transport at Paris Charles-de-Gaulle and Paris Orly is incomplete.

Source: Eurostat (online data codes: road_go_ta_tott, rail_go_typeall, ttr00007, tps00001 and avia_gooc) and Directorate-General for Mobility and Transport

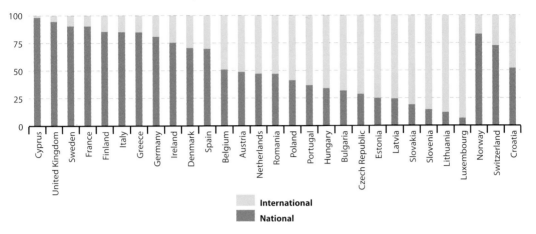

Figure 10.3.1: National and international road transport of goods, 2010 (¹)
(% based on million tkm of laden transport)

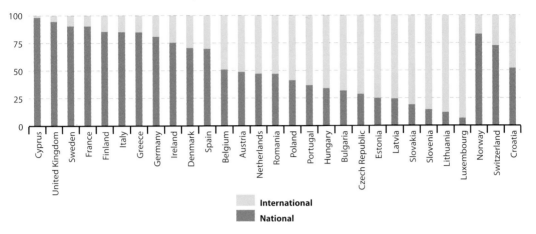

> (¹) Greece and the United Kingdom, 2009; Malta, not available.

Source: Eurostat (online data code: road_go_ta_tott)

Figure 10.3.2: Air freight transport, 2010
(1 000 tonnes)

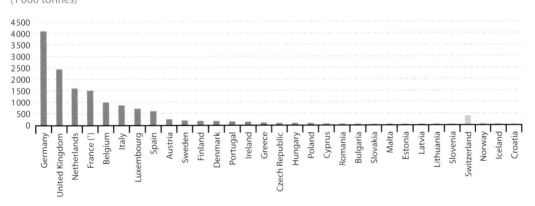

> (¹) Underestimated: freight transport at Paris Charles-de-Gaulle and Paris Orly is incomplete.

Source: Eurostat (online data code: ttr00011)

Figure 10.3.3: Gross weight of seaborne goods handled in ports, 2009 (¹)
(million tonnes)

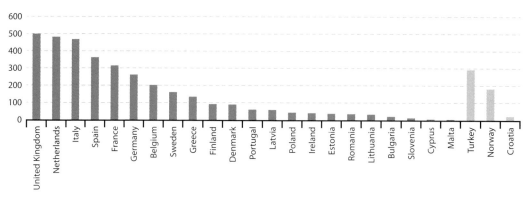

(¹) The Czech Republic, Luxembourg, Hungary, Austria and Slovakia, not applicable.

Source: Eurostat (online data code: mar_go_aa)

Environment

11

Introduction

Eurostat, in close partnership with the European Environment Agency (EEA), provides statistics and further information on environmental pressures and the state of the environment. This data supports the development, implementation, monitoring and evaluation of the European Union's (EU's) environmental policies, strategies and initiatives, including its sixth environment action programme (EAP).

Sixth environment action programme

The action programme, laid down by European Parliament and Council Decision 1600/2002/EC of 22 July 2002 is a ten-year (2002-2012) policy programme for the environment. It identifies four key priorities:

- tackling climate change;
- nature and biodiversity;
- environment and health;
- sustainable use of natural resources and the management of waste.

In order to implement the sixth EAP, the European Commission adopted seven thematic strategies: air pollution (adopted in September 2005); marine environment (October 2005); the prevention and recycling of waste (December 2005); the sustainable use of natural resources (December 2005); urban environment (January 2006); soil (September 2006); and the sustainable use of pesticides (July 2006). The data required to monitor the sixth EAP are collected in ten environmental data centres. Eurostat manages the data centres on waste, natural resources and products, while the EEA is responsible for air, climate change, water, biodiversity and land use, and the Joint Research Centre (JRC) is responsible for soil and forestry. Each strategy follows an in-depth review of existing policy and wide-ranging stakeholder consultation. The aim is to create positive synergies between the seven strategies, as well as to integrate them with existing sectoral policies and the sustainable development strategy.

Sustainable development strategy

Several environmental indicators have been chosen as sustainable development indicators (see the presentation of statistics for European policies) for the assessment of the progress achieved towards the goals of the sustainable development strategy. Examples of environmental headline indicators are the common bird index as an indicator for natural resources and greenhouse gas emissions by sector as an indicator for climate change and energy. Several others are used as indicators for sustainable consumption and production, public health, climate change and energy, sustainable transport, natural resources, and global partnership.

Europe 2020 – Europe's growth strategy

At the European Council meeting of 26 March 2010, EU leaders set out their plans for a Europe 2020 strategy for smart, sustainable and inclusive growth. The strategy includes three targets specifically related to the environment and climate change: greenhouse gas emissions 20 % lower than 1990; 20 % of energy from renewables; 20% increase in energy efficiency. As part of the sustainable growth priority one of the flagship initiatives concerns a resource-efficient Europe. The aims are to help decouple economic growth from the use of resources, support the shift towards a low-carbon economy, protect biodiversity, increase the use of renewable energy sources, modernise the transport sector, and promote energy efficiency. In the context of this initiative, several key proposals have been adopted by the European Commission.

- In March 2011 a 'Roadmap for moving to a competitive low carbon economy by 2050' (COM(2011) 112 final) was adopted. This roadmap describes a cost-effective pathway to reach the EU's objective of cutting greenhouse gas emissions by 80-95 % of 1990 levels by 2050. Based on the cost-effectiveness analysis undertaken, the roadmap gives direction to sectoral policies, national and regional low-carbon strategies and long-term investments.

- In September 2011 a further building block in this initiative was adopted in the form of the 'Roadmap to a resource efficient Europe' (COM(2011) 571 final). This builds upon and complements the other initiatives under the resource efficiency flagship, in particular the policy achievements towards a low carbon economy. It sets out a vision for the structural and technological change needed up to 2050, with milestones to be reached by 2020, proposing ways to increase resource productivity and decouple economic growth from resource use and explaining how policies interrelate and build on each other.
- An ambitious new strategy to halt the loss of biodiversity and ecosystem services in the EU by 2020 was adopted in June 2011. The 'EU 2020 Biodiversity Strategy' (COM(2011) 244 final) is built around six main targets and 20 actions to help Europe reach its goal. Biodiversity loss is an enormous challenge in the EU, with around one in four species currently threatened with extinction and 88 % of fish stocks over-exploited or significantly depleted.
- A new strategy to secure and improve access to raw materials was adopted in February 2011 titled 'Tackling the challenges in commodity markets and on raw materials' (COM(2011) 25 final). This is focused on the fair and sustainable supply of raw materials from international markets, fostering sustainable supply within the EU, and boosting resource efficiency and promoting recycling.
- A 'Roadmap to a single European transport area – towards a competitive and resource efficient transport system' (COM(2011) 144 final) was adopted in March 2011 – see the introduction for transport.
- In November 2010 the initiative 'Energy 2020 a strategy for competitive, sustainable and secure energy' (COM(2010) 639 final) was adopted, defining energy priorities for a period of ten years. In March 2011 the 'Energy efficiency plan 2011' (COM(2011) 109 final) was adopted: energy efficiency is considered to be one of the most cost effective ways to enhance security of energy supply and to reduce emissions of greenhouse gases and other pollutants. See the introduction for energy for more information.

The integrated economic and employment guidelines, first combined in 2008, were also revised as part of the Europe 2020 strategy. Guideline 5 concerns improving resource efficiency and reducing greenhouse gases.

Initiatives on water and waste

The development of a '2012 Blueprint to safeguard Europe's waters' was endorsed by the President of the European Commission on the occasion of World Water Day on 22 March 2010. The Blueprint is intended to combine a stocktaking of the achievements of the Water Framework Directive (policy assessment) with an analysis of the policy needs in the water domain for the years to come. Work on the proposed blueprint is still ongoing and may well create new data needs with respective implications for water statistics.

In January 2011 the European Commission published a review of the thematic strategy on the prevention and recycling of waste. While noting that overall recycling rates had increased, the amount of waste going to landfill decreased, and the use of hazardous substances had been reduced, the review indicated that the amount of waste produced had continued to rise in many Member States. Concerning waste statistics, the usability and policy relevance of the Waste Statistics Regulation of 2002 was improved by Regulation (EU) 849/2010. It has entered into force in 2010 and will be the basis for the collection of data in 2012. Eurostat's Environmental Data Centre on waste is a major source for data and background information on waste generation and management in the EU, presenting statistics for key waste streams by waste category and by economic activity and treatment method, such as recycling and disposal.

11.1 Land cover, land use and landscape

This subchapter presents statistical data on land cover, land use and landscapes for 23 Member States of the European Union (EU), totals exclude Bulgaria, Cyprus, Malta and Romania. The data were gathered as part of the Land use/cover area frame survey, or LUCAS, conducted during the summer of 2009. LUCAS is the largest harmonised land survey implemented in the EU.

Land is the basis for most biological and human activities on Earth. Agriculture, forestry, industries, transport, housing and other services use land as a natural and/or an economic resource. Land is also an integral part of ecosystems and indispensable for biodiversity and the carbon cycle.

Land can be divided into two interlinked concepts:

- land cover refers to the bio-physical coverage of land (for example, crops, grass, broad-leaved forest, or built-up area);
- land use indicates the socio-economic use of land (for example, agriculture, forestry, recreation or residential use).

Land cover and land use data forms the basis for spatial and territorial analyses which are increasingly important for:

- the planning and management of agricultural, forest, wetland, water and urban areas;
- nature, biodiversity and soil protection, and;
- the prevention and mitigation of natural hazards and climate change.

Main statistical findings

Land cover

Forests and other wooded areas occupied 39.1 % of the total area of the EU in 2009, cropland nearly a quarter (24.2 %) of the area and grassland almost one fifth (19.5 %), while built-up and other artificial areas, such as roads and railways, accounted for 4.3 % of the total area (see Figure 11.1.1).

Land cover varies in a significant way between countries located on the one hand in southern and northern Europe and on the other hand in western

and eastern Europe. Woodland is the prevailing land cover in northern parts of Europe and for a number of countries whose typography is dominated by mountains and hilly areas (see Figure 11.1.2). The share of woodland in the total area exceeded 60 % in Finland and, Sweden and was over 50 % in Estonia and Latvia; it was also over 60 % in Slovenia and over 40 % in Austria (both Alpine), and over 40 % in Slovakia (the Tatra mountains) and Portugal (Sistema Central). Woodland and forests in these countries have traditionally been very important ecologically, economically and socio-culturally.

Cropland (including both arable land and permanent crops) covered, on average, some 24.2 % of the total area of the EU in 2009. Denmark and Hungary were the countries that reported the highest proportion of their total area covered by cropland, its share rising close to 50 %. In most of the remaining Member States, the share of cropland was between 17 % and 35 % of overall land cover. At the bottom end of the range, cropland accounted for between 11 % and 12 % of the total area in Latvia, Estonia and Slovenia, while the lowest shares were recorded in Finland (6.0 %), Ireland (5.0 %) and Sweden (4.5 %).

Natural and agricultural grasslands dominate the landscape in Ireland, the United Kingdom and the Netherlands. In Ireland almost two thirds (64.1 %) of the country was covered in grassland in 2009, while the corresponding shares in the United Kingdom and the Netherlands were 42.4 % and 37.4 % respectively. In most of the remaining Member States for which data are available, the share of grassland in the total area was between 18 % and 33 %. However, there were six countries below this threshold: four of them (Italy, Spain, Portugal and Greece) were from southern Europe where rainfall levels are relatively low; the other two countries were Sweden and Finland, where grass covered less than 5 % of the total area.

Shrubland is a typical land cover feature of hot and arid countries such as Greece, Portugal and Spain; on the other hand, shrubland is also prevalent on the moors and heath lands of northern areas of the United Kingdom and parts of Ireland, as well as in transitional areas between forests and tundra in Sweden; these were the only Member States to report that shrubland accounted for a higher share of their total area than the EU average (5.6 %).

Artificial land composed 4.3 % of the total area of the EU in 2009. The Benelux countries had the highest proportions of built-up areas: this was particularly true in the Netherlands (which is densely populated), where artificial land accounted for 13.2 % of the total area. The four largest EU Member States in terms of population (Germany, France, Italy and the United Kingdom) also reported a higher than average share of artificial land.

On average 1.8 % of the EU was covered by wetlands and 3.4 % by inland water areas in 2009. Wetland is typically found along lakesides and in coastal areas, as well as in the form of bogs. The relative scarcity of wetlands and their importance as a habitat for various animal species (in particular, birds) often results in wetlands becoming protected areas. Sweden, Finland, Ireland and Estonia reported the highest proportions (in excess of 5 %) of their total area accounted for by wetlands; the majority of the remaining Member States had less than 1 % of their total area classified as wetlands. Inland water areas, such as lakes or rivers, covered 3.4 % of the EU in 2009. This average was highly influenced by three Member States – the Netherlands (where 11.0 % of the total area was inland water areas), Finland (10.2 %) and Sweden (9.1 %). The former is characterised by artificial lakes, several large rivers that enter the North Sea and numerous canals, while the two Nordic countries have hundreds of thousands of inland lakes.

Bare land (areas with no dominant vegetation cover) is a relatively rare in the EU, accounting for an average of 1.9 % of the total area in 2009. Spain and Portugal (5.2 % and 4.0 %) recorded the highest shares of bare land.

Land use

Agricultural land use is the most common primary ([6]) land use category in the EU; it accounted

for 43 % of the total area in 2009 (see Figure 11.1.3). Areas used for forestry covered 29.8 % of the EU's land area, while 5.0 % was used for services, residential and recreational purposes. Industrial, transport, energy production and mining purposes claimed a further 3.4 %, leaving a residual category accounting for the remaining 18.8 % of land; this was used, among others, for hunting and fishing, was under protection, or had no visible ([7]) use.

Land in agricultural use encompasses various land cover types: the most common are arable land, permanent crops and grassland. Small portions of other land cover types can also be in agricultural use, such as artificial land (farm buildings, roads, etc.) and water (for example, irrigation ponds). In 14 out of 23 EU Member States, more than half of the land area was used for agricultural purposes in 2009 (see Figure 11.1.4). The highest share of agricultural land was recorded in Ireland (73.2 %), while the United Kingdom, Denmark and Hungary each reported shares of more than 60 %. In Finland and Sweden agriculture played a minor role in terms of land use, accounting for less than 10 % of the land in both these Member States.

Unsurprisingly, forestry was often the dominant land use in those Member States which had a high degree of woodland land cover. However, not all of this land is used for forestry, with alternative land uses including recreation, hunting, protected areas, or no visible use. In Finland, Sweden and Slovenia more than 50 % of the total land area was used for forestry purposes, a share that fell to below 10 % in Ireland, the United Kingdom, and particularly the Netherlands (3.1 %).

Industry, mining and transport (which includes also energy production, waste treatment, storage and construction activities) occupied 3.4 % of the EU's territory in 2009. The most common use, among the various sub-categories, was for transport, which averaged some 70 % of the total land use within this category; some 11 % of the total for this category was accounted for by mining. The highest share of industry, mining and transport in total land use was

([6]) The same area can be used in parallel for many purposes (for example, a forest can be used for forestry, hunting and recreation); the statistics presented are based on the primary use.
([7]) The LUCAS survey is based on field visits; land use is determined on the basis of visible signs of land use.

found in the Netherlands, where 12.2 % of land was used for these purposes. The very high share in the Netherlands may be linked to a high density transport network and to large storage areas for ports and logistical services. The share of mining (which includes quarrying and the extraction of peat) in land use was relatively high in Austria, Estonia, Finland, Ireland and Latvia.

Commerce (distributive trades), community services, recreational and residential areas covered 5 % of the EU's land area in 2009. Approximately half of this total in the EU was devoted to residential areas, 30 % to recreational purposes, 10 % to community services, and less than 5 % to commerce. The share of commerce, community services, recreational and residential areas rose to above 10 % of the total area in Finland and Sweden, mainly due to larger than average areas for recreational purposes, with forest areas close to cities and towns often used for recreational purposes in these Member States.

Almost 20 % of the land in the EU in 2009 was used for other purposes or there was no visible use of the land. The most common economic uses were for fishing and hunting. However, large areas of land are excluded from any socio-economic use – for example, as a result of being in protected areas where socio-economic activities are either completely forbidden or heavily restricted; there are also remote or otherwise difficultly accessible areas which have not attracted socio-economic activities.

Landscape

The heterogeneity of land cover and the presence of linear features such as hedges, lines of trees, roads, railways, rivers and irrigation channels are two important elements characterising landscape structures. Some countries have large continuous areas of the same land cover, while others have a diversified mosaic of land cover elements. As Figure 11.1.5 shows, Slovenia, Portugal, Austria, Luxembourg, Denmark and Italy had a relatively high level of land cover diversity, characterised by a varied land cover mosaic composed of different small land cover patches. In Ireland, the United Kingdom and Estonia the landscape was dominated by larger areas composed of the same land cover type.

Structural linear green elements portray the joint role of nature and mankind in shaping the countryside. Irish landscapes, which rank lowest in terms of land cover diversity, had the second highest number of green linear features (see Figure 11.1.6). Other countries where the landscape was characterised by a high variety of green linear elements included the Netherlands and France. In Slovakia, Hungary and Sweden the landscape was characterised as having relatively few structural green elements.

The density of man-made linear elements, which have a dissecting nature (such as roads, railways, aerial cables), is closely linked to population and infrastructure developments. Countries with relatively high population densities and which act as transit countries, such as Belgium and Luxembourg, had a relatively high number of man-made infrastructure related dissection elements (see Figure 11.1.7); this was also the case in Slovenia, Portugal and France (where the population was concentrated in particular areas). At the opposite end of the scale, the Baltic States, Finland, Sweden and most eastern European Member States often reported a relatively low level of man-made linear elements, with natural land cover types prevailing.

Data sources and availability

LUCAS is a field survey based on an area-frame sampling scheme carried out by Eurostat. Data on land cover and land use are collected and landscape photographs are taken to detect any changes to land cover/use or to European landscapes. The transect, a 250-meter walk along which linear elements and land cover changes are recorded, is used for landscape analysis.

Eurostat carried out a large LUCAS campaign in 2009, covering 23 countries in the EU (Bulgaria, Cyprus, Malta and Romania were excluded). Data on land cover, land use and landscape diversity were collected for approximately 234 700 points. These points were selected from a standard 2 km grid from a total of one million points all over the EU. The land cover and the visible land use data were classified according to the harmonised LUCAS land cover and land use nomenclatures.

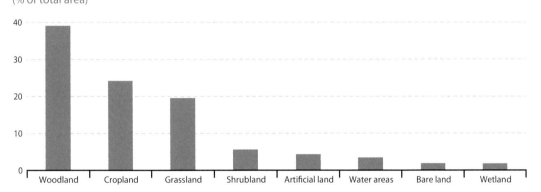
The LUCAS data set provides the basis for harmonised land cover/use statistics at European level. The data set is unique as it is comparable in terms of definitions and methodology. The data for the 2009 reference period were published, for the first time, by Eurostat and this information is freely available to users.

Context

Europe is composed of a myriad of different landscapes and land uses that reflect historical changes. While these are somewhat difficult to see on a day-to-day basis, on-going processes continually alter landscapes and the environment. Often the changes taking place may be linked to tensions arising from the conflict between the demand for more resources and infrastructure improvements on the one hand, and biodiversity and space on the other.

Land use and land cover data are important for an understanding of how environmental systems function, and their assessment over time provides a means for assessing the impact that any changes in land use may have on biodiversity and ecosystems.

Land use change is often considered to be a primary driver for changes in biodiversity and ecosystems. In recent years some of the most important land use changes have included: a decline in agricultural land use (as crop yields continue to rise); an increase in urban areas (arising from population and economic change); and a gradual increase in forest land areas (driven by the need to meet global environmental commitments in relation to climate change). The development of roads, motorways, railways, intensive agriculture and urban developments has led to Europe's landscape being increasingly broken up into small pieces. This pattern of fragmentation has the potential to affect levels of biodiversity and could result in negative impacts on flora and fauna.

Figure 11.1.1: Main land cover by land cover type, EU, 2009 (¹)
(% of total area)

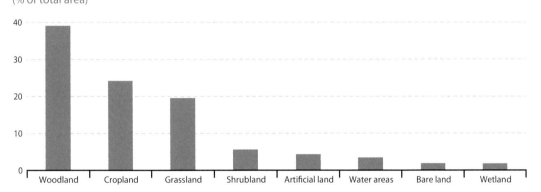

(¹) EU average excluding Bulgaria, Cyprus, Malta and Romania.

Source: Eurostat (online data code: lan_lcv)

Figure 11.1.2: Main land cover by land cover type, 2009
(% of total area)

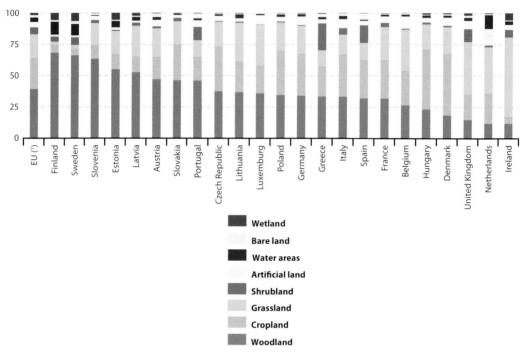

Wetland
Bare land
Water areas
Artificial land
Shrubland
Grassland
Cropland
Woodland

(¹) EU average excluding Bulgaria, Cyprus, Malta and Romania.

Source: Eurostat (online data code: lan_lcv)

Figure 11.1.3: Main land use by land use type, EU, 2009 (¹)
(% of total area)

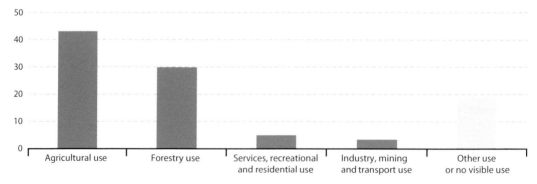

(¹) EU average excluding Bulgaria, Cyprus, Malta and Romania.

Source: Eurostat (online data code: lan_lu)

Figure 11.1.4: Primary land use by land use type, 2009
(% of total area)

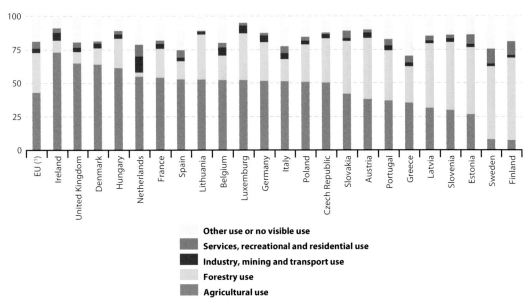

Other use or no visible use
Services, recreational and residential use
Industry, mining and transport use
Forestry use
Agricultural use

(¹) EU average excluding Bulgaria, Cyprus, Malta and Romania.

Source: Eurostat (online data code: lan_lu)

Figure 11.1.5: Land cover richness indicator – average number of different land cover types in a 250m transect, 2009 (¹)
(number)

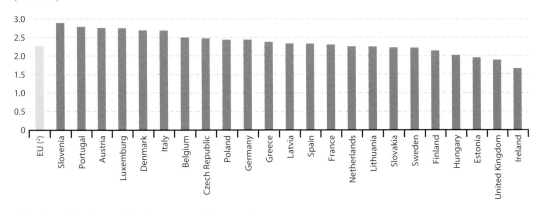

(¹) Data derived from further analysis and computation of elementary data.
(²) EU average excluding Bulgaria, Cyprus, Malta and Romania.

Source: Eurostat (online data code: lan_lcs_ric)

Figure 11.1.6: Average number of green linear structural elements in a 250m transect, 2009 ([1])
(number)

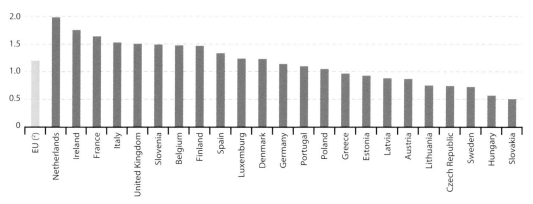

([1]) Data derived from further analysis and computation of elementary data.
([2]) EU average excluding Bulgaria, Cyprus, Malta and Romania.

Source: Eurostat (online data code: lan_lcs_str)

Figure 11.1.7: Average number of different linear dissecting elements in a 250m transect, 2009 ([1])
(number)

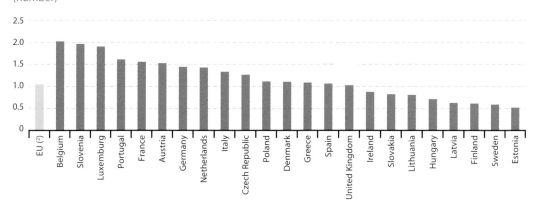

([1]) Data derived from further analysis and computation of elementary data.
([2]) EU average excluding Bulgaria, Cyprus, Malta and Romania.

Source: Eurostat (online data code: lan_lcs_diss)

11.2 Air emissions accounts

Air emissions accounts record emissions of greenhouse gases and air pollutants in the European Union (EU) showing the economic activities responsible for their production (in line with the 'polluter pays' principle), following the same classification that is used within national accounts, namely the statistical classification of economic activities in the European Community (NACE). Air emissions accounts are thus an extension of emissions inventories, such as those used for official reporting under international obligations (for example, the Kyoto Protocol).

Air emissions accounts are a statistical information system that combines air emissions data and economic data from national accounts. Their main purpose is to provide data for integrated environmental-economic analyses and modelling to supplement traditional economic data. This subchapter analyses the emissions and intensity of greenhouse gases (GHGs), acidifying substances and tropospheric ozone precursors (TOPs) in the EU-27 on the basis of an analysis of six economic activities that are responsible for their generation.

Main statistical findings

Greenhouse gas emissions

Greenhouse gas emissions for the purpose of this subchapter comprise carbon dioxide, nitrous oxide and methane; emissions of these three gases resulting from economic activities stood at 4 176 million tonnes of carbon dioxide equivalents in 2008; this was 2.4 % lower than in 1998. The development of greenhouse gas emissions over this period showed generally quite small shifts in the structure of emissions according to economic activity (see Figure 11.2.1). The biggest change was in relation to the transport, storage and communication sector (which excludes the use of private vehicles – reported under households); its share of greenhouse gas emissions rose by 3.2 percentage points.

The overall level of greenhouse gas emissions fell for four of the six activities covered in Figure 11.2.1 – by far the largest decline in emissions was

recorded for mining and quarrying, where total greenhouse gas emissions fell by 29.5 % (reflecting, at least to some degree, a reduction in mining activity as natural resources were exhausted or were no longer economically viable for extraction). The manufacturing sector saw its level of greenhouse gas emissions fall by 9.6 % between 1998 and 2008; part of the reduction resulted from a slowdown in manufacturing activity as a result of the financial and economic crisis. On the other hand, the transport, storage and communication sector reported that its greenhouse gas emissions rose overall by 29.8 % over the most recent decade for which data are available, while a much smaller increase (1.1 %) was recorded for electricity, gas and water supply.

Emissions of acidifying substances

EU-27 emissions of acidifying substances totalled 21.3 million tonnes of acid equivalents in 2008; this was 28.6 % lower than in 1998. The largest emitters of acidifying substances (which for the purpose of this subchapter comprise sulphur oxides (SO_x), nitrogen oxides (NO_x) and ammonia (NH_3)) were agriculture, hunting, forestry and fishing with a 35.8 % share of the EU-27 total in 2008 (mainly from ammonia emissions), transport, storage and communication with 22.0 % (mainly through the combustion of fossil fuels leading to emissions of nitrogen oxides and sulphur dioxide), and electricity, gas and water supply with 20.8 % (especially from thermal power plants using coal). Together they accounted for almost four fifths (78.5 %) of the EU-27's total emissions of acidifying substances in 2008. Some acidifying substances react with the water in the atmosphere and subsequently result in acid rain, which in turn can damage forests, plants, fresh waters and soils as well as buildings and infrastructure.

There was a rapid increase in the share of emissions of acidifying substances coming from transport, storage and communication activities and from agriculture, hunting, forestry and fishing between 1998 and 2008. The relative share of the former rose by 7.9 percentage points within the EU-27, while the increase for the latter was 7.0 percentage points.

In contrast, the relative importance of the electricity, gas and water supply sector fell by 12.1 percentage points during the ten-year period under consideration, as this activity cut more than half (– 54.8 %) of its emissions of acidifying substances between 1998 and 2008 (these changes may be associated with a switch in the energy mix to cleaner fuels for power generation). Indeed, the overall level of emissions of acidifying substances fell for five of the six activities covered in Figure 11.2.2, with the only exception being the transport, storage and communication sector, where emissions rose by 11.4 % overall between 1998 and 2008.

Emissions of tropospheric ozone precursors

Emissions of tropospheric ozone precursors (TOPs), substances that lead to the formation of ozone in the part of the atmosphere closest to the earth's surface as a result of photochemical reactions, have negative impacts on human health including irritation of the respiratory system, exacerbation of asthma, lung diseases, and even premature death. For the purposes of this subchapter, tropospheric ozone precursors comprise nitrogen oxides (NO_x), non-methane volatile organic compounds (NMVOCs), carbon monoxide (CO) and methane (CH_4).

There were 22.0 million tonnes of emissions of tropospheric ozone precursors in the EU-27 in 2008; this figure was 16.0 % lower than in 1998. The transport, storage and communication sector was responsible for the highest share of EU-27 tropospheric ozone precursor emissions, accounting for nearly one third (30.1 %) of the total in 2008. It was closely followed by manufacturing (27.0 %), while the shares for agriculture, hunting, forestry and fishing (15.9 %) and other services and construction (14.0 %) were somewhat lower. Unlike the other types of air emissions, the electricity, gas and water supply sector had a relatively low share of total emissions of tropospheric ozone precursors (11.0 %).

When looking at the period from 1998 to 2008, there was an overall reduction in the level of tropospheric ozone precursors for five of the six economic activities shown in Figure 11.2.3. The only exception was the transport, storage and communication sector, where emissions of tropospheric ozone precursors

rose by 9.8 % overall during the ten-year period under consideration, or by 7.1 percentage points in terms of their relative share of total emissions of tropospheric ozone precursors.

As such, the transport, storage and communication sector recorded an increase in its level of greenhouse gas, acidifying substances and tropospheric ozone precursor emissions during the period from 1998 to 2008.

Emissions intensity

Examining environmental variables together with economic ones can help identify which economic activity contributes to which environmental pressure and thus be helpful in devising specific policy measures where most needed. In order to make such comparisons it is first necessary to reflect upon the relative importance, in economic terms, of each economic activity. Across the EU-27 in 2008, by far the highest level of value added was generated by the other services and construction sector (which includes both private and public services, other than those concerning transport, storage and communication); it accounted for 71.5 % of the EU-27's gross value added. Manufacturing activities accounted for 16.5 % of the total, while transport, storage and communication had a 6.9 % share. The economic weight of electricity, gas and water supply (2.4 %) and of the primary activities of agriculture, hunting, forestry and fisheries (1.8 %) and mining and quarrying (0.9 %) was relatively small. More information on the breakdown of economic activity according to these six aggregates may be found in a subchapter on national accounts – GDP.

As shown in Figures 11.2.1 to 11.2.3, the picture was quite different when considering the relative contributions of each of these six activities to air emissions. The intensity of emissions can be used to measure the extent to which certain economic activities pollute the environment in relation to the economic value that they generate; the indicator is expressed as the ratio of emissions to gross value added and is presented in terms of the emissions produced for each monetary unit of economic output (for example, tonnes of emissions per EUR million of output).

Electricity, gas and water supply had by far the highest intensity of greenhouse gas emissions for the EU-27 among the six economic activities that are covered in Figure 11.2.4. This sector generated 7 866 tonnes of carbon dioxide equivalents for each EUR million of added value in 2008, which was almost three times as high as the next most intensive activity, namely agriculture, hunting, forestry and fishing (2 834 tonnes per EUR million). Furthermore, the electricity, gas and water supply sector was the only activity to record an increase in greenhouse gas intensity between 1998 and 2008 (up 1.9 %).

At the other end of the spectrum, the largest reductions in greenhouse gas intensity between 1998 and 2008 were recorded for manufacturing (– 26.6 %) and other services and construction (– 26.4 %).

While the electricity, gas and water supply sector also had a high level of intensity for EU-27 emissions of acidifying substances in 1998, there was a considerable reduction in its intensity rates during the following ten-year period, as the rate was more than halved from 55.0 tonnes of sulphur dioxide equivalents per EUR million of added value in 1998 to 25.1 tonnes per EUR million by 2008. This rapid change may be largely attributed to a switch from coal-fired to natural gas-fired thermal power plants and the use of industrial scrubbers that reduce emissions of sulphur oxides during energy combustion. As a result of this change, the agriculture, hunting, forestry and fishing sector became the activity with the highest level of intensity for emissions of acidifying substances by 2008 (38.1 tonnes per EUR million).

The intensity of emissions for acidifying substances in the EU-27 fell between 1998 and 2008 for all six of the economic activities covered in Figure 11.2.5; the most rapid reductions in intensity were recorded for electricity, gas and water supply (down 54.5 %), manufacturing (– 51.1 %), and other services and construction (– 42.4 %).

The intensity of tropospheric ozone precursors also fell between 1998 and 2008 for each of the six economic activities covered in Figure 11.2.6. Agriculture, hunting, forestry and fishing was the most intensive sector in both 1998 and 2008 for the EU-27, with intensity falling by 21.9 % to 17.5

tonnes of non-methane volatile organic compounds equivalents per EUR million of added value in 2008. This was the smallest reduction in percentage terms, with the intensity of tropospheric ozone precursors falling by more than a third (– 36.6 %) for manufacturing and by more than two fifths (– 43.8 %) for other services and construction.

It should also be borne in mind that these figures relating to the intensity of tropospheric ozone precursors are national averages and that regional variations could well exist. Indeed, tropospheric ozone precursors may have a pronounced local effect and it is possible for very high concentrations to be recorded at a regional level, especially in urban areas.

Data sources and availability

Air emissions accounts show data on emissions using a breakdown according to the economic activity responsible for producing them. The two main underlying data sources on emissions are two international conventions that govern efforts to reduce the release of polluting substances into the air, namely: the Kyoto Protocol for the United Nations Framework Convention on Climate Change (UNFCCC) concerning greenhouse gases; and the Gothenburg Protocol to the Convention on Long-Range Transboundary Air Pollution (CLRTAP) concerning acidifying substances. The core data from these emission inventories is published and distributed by the European Environment Agency (EEA).

Environmental accounts are subject to EU legislation, namely Regulation (EU) 691/2011 on European environmental economic accounts. The Regulation provides a framework for the development of various types of accounts, initially starting with three modules, with a view to adding other modules as they reach methodological maturity. Air emissions accounts are one of the three modules, alongside modules for material flow accounts and environmental taxes by economic activity. The aim of this legal base is to strengthen the coherence and availability of environmental accounts across the EU by providing a legal framework for their compilation, including methodology, common standards, definitions, classifications and accounting rules. The first regular annual data collection legally required under the Regulation will be in 2013.

In order to produce air emissions accounts, the emissions data are re-organised according to a breakdown by economic activity, as used within national accounts (based on the statistical classification of economic activities, NACE), which makes it possible to have an integrated environmental-economic analysis. The scope for air emissions accounts encompasses all nationally registered businesses (including those operating ships, aircrafts and other transportation equipment in other countries – the residence principle). Emissions are allocated to the economic activity responsible for producing them; unlike national emissions inventories, where the boundary for measuring the extent of emissions is the territorial border. As such, the accounting methodology used within air emissions accounts is not suited for monitoring progress towards internationally agreed emissions reduction targets, such as under the Kyoto Protocol.

The activity groups that are used in this subchapter are constructed as follows:

- Agriculture, hunting, forestry and fishing – NACE Rev. 1.1 Sections A and B;
- Mining and quarrying – NACE Rev. 1.1 Section C;
- Manufacturing – NACE Rev. 1.1 Section D;
- Electricity, gas and water supply – NACE Rev. 1.1 Section E;
- Transport, storage and communication – NACE Rev. 1.1 Section I;
- Other services and construction – NACE Rev. 1.1 Sections F, G, H, J, K, L, M, N, O and Q; as such, this grouping comprises construction, retail and wholesale trade, real estate, renting, financial services, hotels and restaurants, as well as public administration, education, health and social work.

Emissions of individual greenhouse gases and air pollutants may be converted and aggregated to provide information for three environmental pressures: greenhouse gas emissions are typically reported in terms of carbon dioxide equivalents, acidifying emissions in terms of sulphur dioxide equivalents, and ground level ozone precursors in terms of non-methane volatile organic compound equivalents. The use of a common unit allows the relative effect of different gases to be compared and combined – for example, a single kilogram of methane has 21 times the global warming effect of a kilogram of carbon dioxide (see Table 11.2.2 for more details on the conversion factors that are employed).

Air emissions accounts present information for three of the six Kyoto Protocol greenhouse gases – carbon dioxide, methane and nitrous oxide; at the time of writing no data are available for perfluorocarbons (PFCs), hydrofluorocarbons (HFCs) or sulphur hexafluoride, as most EU Member States are unable to provide a breakdown of these gases by economic activity.

Context

The need to supplement existing information on the economy with environmental indicators has been recognised in a European Commission Communication titled 'GDP and beyond' (COM(2009) 433). Furthermore, similar recommendations have been made within the so-called Stiglitz report, released by the Commission on the Measurement of Economic Performance and Social Progress. The recommendations made support the expansion of the statistical understanding of human well-being by supplementing economic indicators such as GDP with additional information, including physical indicators on the environment.

Environmental accounts are one statistical means to try to measure the interplay between the economy and the environment in order to see whether current production and consumption activities are on a sustainable path of development. Measuring sustainable development is a complex undertaking as it has to incorporate economic, social and environmental indicators without contradiction. The data obtained from environmental accounts may subsequently feed into political decision-making, underpinning policies that target both continued economic growth and sustainable development, for example, initiatives such as the Europe 2020 strategy, which aims to achieve a resource-efficient, low-carbon economy for the EU by 2020.

In order to have such a holistic view of the various aspects of sustainable development, the existing framework for measuring the economy (the system of national accounts) is supplemented by satellite accounts that cover, for example, environmental or social indicators. These satellite accounts are developed using the same concepts, definitions, classifications and accounting rules as the national accounts, bringing environmental or social data together with economic data in a coherent and comparable framework. Thus, environmental accounts serve to enhance the understanding of pressures exerted by the economy on the environment – for example, accounting for the subsequent release of

substances (such as air emissions or waste) into the environment as a result of economic activities.

Note that a reduction in one type of environmental pressure can result in an increase in another type of pressure. For example, passenger cars with diesel engines are typically more fuel efficient and therefore tend to produce less carbon dioxide emissions per kilometre travelled. However, if consumers switch to driving diesel cars then (with current engine technology) it is likely that such a switch would be accompanied by an increase in acidifying emissions and ground level ozone precursors.

Table 11.2.1: Differences between inventories and accounts

	National emissions inventories (territory principle)	**Air emissions accounts (residence principle)**
Scope of national emissions reported	Direct emissions within the geographical national territory and: – emissions from international bunkers allocated to countries where the fuel is sold and not to the nationality of the purchasing unit; – emissions/removals induced by land use change and forestry are accounted for.	Emissions within the economic territory of the country covered, for example: – emissions of entities registered in the country (e. g. ships operating abroad, residents); – CO_2 from biomass is included since these emissions arise when using these energy carriers).

Figure 11.2.1: Greenhouse gas emissions, analysis by activity, EU-27, 1998 and 2008 ([1])
(% of total, based on tonnes of CO_2 equivalents of CO_2, CH_4 and N_2O)

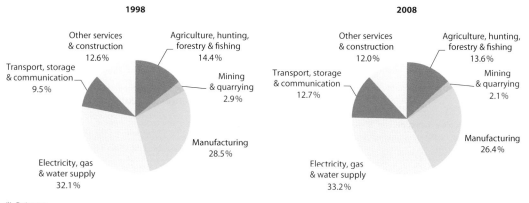

([1]) Estimates.

Source: Eurostat (online data code: env_ac_ainacehh)

Figure 11.2.2: Emissions of acidifying substances, analysis by activity, EU-27, 1998 and 2008 ([1])
(% of total, based on tonnes of SO$_2$ acid equivalents of SO$_x$, NH$_3$ and NO$_x$)

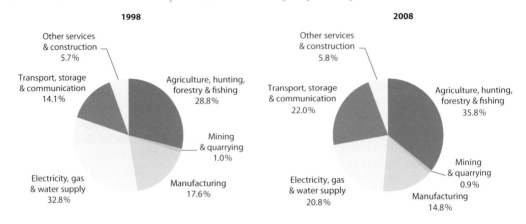

([1]) Estimates.

Source: Eurostat (online data code: env_ac_ainacehh)

Figure 11.2.3: Emissions of tropospheric ozone precursors, analysis by activity, EU-27, 1998 and 2008 ([1])
(% of total, based on tonnes of transopospheric ozone formation potential (TOFP) equivalents)

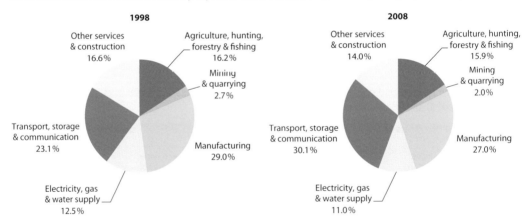

([1]) Estimates.

Source: Eurostat (online data code: env_ac_ainacehh)

Figure 11.2.4: Greenhouse gas intensity, analysis by economic activity, EU-27, 1998 and 2008 ([1])
(tonnes of CO_2-equivalents of CO_2, CH_4 and N_2O per EUR million of gross value added at basic prices)

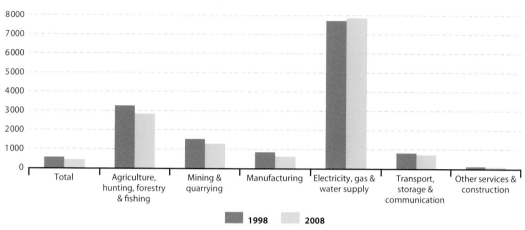

([1]) Estimates.

Source: Eurostat (online data codes: env_ac_ainacehh and nama_nace31_k)

Figure 11.2.5: Acidifying substances intensity, analysis by economic activity, EU-27, 1998 and 2008 ([1])
(tonnes of SO_2 acid equivalents of SO_x, NH_3 and NO_x per EUR million of gross value added at basic prices)

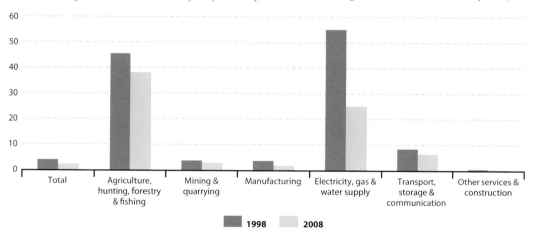

([1]) Estimates.

Source: Eurostat (online data codes: env_ac_ainacehh and nama_nace31_k)

Figure 11.2.6: Tropospheric ozone precursors intensity, analysis by economic activity, EU-27, 1998 and 2008 (^{1})
(tonnes of NMVOC-equivalents of NO_x, NMVOC, CO and CH_4 per EUR million of gross value added at basic prices)

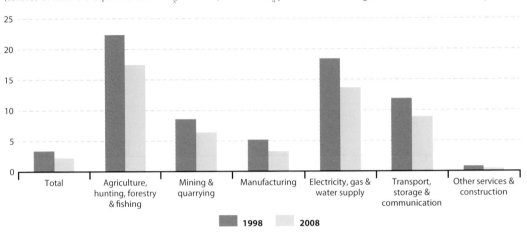

(^{1}) Estimates.

Source: Eurostat (online data codes: env_ac_ainacehh and nama_nace31_k)

Table 11.2.2: Calculation of aggregated environmental pressures

Theme	Unit	Substance	Weighting factors	Pressure
Greenhouse gases	CO_2 – equivalents	Carbon dioxide (CO_2)	1	Aggregated greenhouse gas emissions – using Global Warming Potential weighting factors for 100 years
		Methane (CH_4)	21	
		Nitrous oxide (N_2O)	310	
Acidification	SO_2 – equivalents	Sulphur dioxide (SO_2)	1	Aggregated acidification emissions
		Nitrogen oxides (NO_x)	0.7	
		Ammonia (NH_3)	1.9	
Tropospheric ozone formation	NMVOC – equivalents	Non-methane volatile organic compounds (NMVOC)	1	Aggregated emissions of tropospheric ozone forming precursors
		Nitrogen oxides (NO_x)	1.22	
		Carbon monoxide (CO)	0.11	
		Methane (CH_4)	0.014	

11.3 Carbon dioxide emissions from final consumption

This subchapter provides an estimate based on various data sets of the European Union (EU) emissions of carbon dioxide (CO_2) induced by the final use of products. Eurostat estimates the EU's CO_2 emissions from final use to be 8.9 tonnes per capita in 2007.

The modelling-estimations that are presented are based on environmentally extended input-output tables. The data provides an opportunity for analyses by researchers and policy advisors – some illustrative examples of the use that may be made of this information are presented in this subchapter.

Main statistical findings

Carbon dioxide emissions associated with EU consumption

Extended supply, use and input-output tables have been used to estimate the carbon dioxide emissions induced by the final use of products within the EU-27 in 2007; these data are also available for seven other gases. Beside the carbon dioxide that is emitted by industries within the EU while processing products for final use, the estimates presented also take into account the carbon dioxide that is 'embedded' within the EU's imports; these arise from the worldwide production chains of goods imported into the EU-27. Carbon dioxide emissions that are embedded within products that are made in the EU but exported outside of the EU-27 are, in a similar vein, included in the account of consumers abroad.

The EU-27 total of 8.9 tonnes of carbon dioxide emissions per inhabitant in 2007 was composed of three main elements (see the right-hand bar of Figure 11.3.1):

- some 5.4 tonnes per inhabitant as a result of the consumption expenditure of households and governments on goods and services;
- a further 1.8 tonnes per inhabitant from direct carbon dioxide emissions from private households in the EU-27 (for example, through burning fossil fuels for private vehicles or for heating);
- another 1.7 tonnes per inhabitant as a result of investments (gross capital formation) in the EU-27 economy.

Table 11.3.1 provides a more detailed breakdown of the carbon dioxide emissions that are induced by final use, according to a range of different product groups and categories of final use. These are ranked according to their importance in the terms of their respective share of emissions. Electrical energy, gas, steam and hot water, construction, food products and beverages, chemicals and man-made fibres, and motor vehicles ranked as the five product groups with the highest levels of emissions per inhabitant in 2007 as a result of their final use.

Carbon dioxide emissions from a production perspective

Carbon dioxide emissions may also be analysed from a production perspective, in other words, according to where the emissions were actually generated; this may be seen in the left-hand bar of Figure 11.3.1.

Using this approach, it is once again necessary to take account of the carbon dioxide emissions from private households (as above for the consumption perspective); in this case households are considered as producing units, providing their own private services, such as heating for their dwelling or the combustion of fuel for driving their own vehicles.

However, by far the biggest contributor to carbon dioxide emissions was from the production activities of domestic industries; together these emitted 7.1 tonnes of carbon dioxide per inhabitant in 2007.

Finally, the production perspective also takes account of the embedded emissions that are contained within the goods and services that are imported into the EU-27 for intermediate and final use; these were estimated to be around 1.8 tonnes per inhabitant in 2007. The latter estimate is based on the 'domestic-technology-assumption' in other words, that the imported products are produced with EU production technologies. Moreover, through the import of goods and services from the rest of the world the EU has avoided 1.8 tonnes per inhabitant of carbon dioxide emissions in its own production system. Some evidence, for example international energy statistics, indicates that the rest of the world economy may have a more carbon-intensive production system compared with the EU. Hence, the 1.8 tonnes per inhabitant may be considered as a minimum estimate.

Data sources and availability

Under the European system of national and regional accounts (ESA 95), the EU Member States transmit to Eurostat supply and use tables on an annual basis and input-output tables on a five-yearly basis. These tables formed the point of departure for a sequence of calculations leading to a consolidated data set for the EU-27 and euro area aggregates

The combination of this data allows a set of environmentally extended input-output tables to be generated. Some basic modelling and analysis steps were performed, leading to the results that are presented in this subchapter. More detailed methodological explanations are documented in a technical report available on Eurostat's website.

Eurostat's environmental accounts programme publishes information on air emissions accounts on a regular basis; these provide details of greenhouse gas emissions and air pollutants with a breakdown for various industries and households. The data are available for eight pollutants: carbon dioxide (CO_2), methane (CH_4), nitrous oxide (N_2O), sulphur oxides (SO_x), nitrogen oxides (NO_x), ammonia (NH_3), carbon monoxide (CO) and non-methane volatile organic compounds (NMVOCs). This information was added to the consolidated supply and use tables and input-output tables for the EU-27 and euro area aggregates.

Context

Supply and use tables portray production and consumption activities of national economies in a detailed manner. They form the basis for so-called input-output models and analyses. Both, the tables and the models, constitute powerful tools for addressing a range of policy areas. The focus of these models is generally made through an analysis of long-term structural changes within economies (for example, by studying value added shares, trade shares, or cumulated value added along certain production chains).

By adding environmental parameters (for example, on air emissions or the use of energy) to these input-output models, it is possible to extend their analytical scope. Environmentally extended input-output analyses are of particular relevance for policy areas such as sustainable production and consumption, sustainable use of natural resources, and resource productivity.

Figure 11.3.1: Domestic and global CO_2 emissions – production and consumption perspective, EU-27, 2007
(tonnes CO_2 per inhabitant)

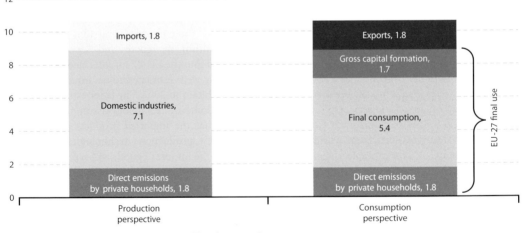

Source: Eurostat (online data codes: env_ac_ainacehh and env_ac_io)

Table 11.3.1: CO_2 emissions induced by final use, by product groups and categories of final use, EU-27, 2007
(kg of CO_2 per inhabitant)

	Final consumption	Gross capital formation	Exports	Final use	
	(kg of CO_2 per inhabitant)				(%)
Electrical energy, gas, steam and hot water	1 103	1	38	1 141	11
Construction work	38	874	2	915	9
Food products and beverages	440	13	58	511	5
Chemicals, chemical products and man-made fibres	193	6	234	433	4
Motor vehicles, trailers and semi-trailers	154	118	118	390	4
Machinery and equipment	34	181	135	350	3
Health and social work services	311	0	0	311	3
Coke, refined petroleum products and nuclear fuel	203	−8	110	305	3
Public administration and defence services; compulsory social security services	295	2	0	297	3
Retail trade services, except of motor vehicles and motor-cycles; repair services of personal and household goods	261	14	13	289	3
Hotel and restaurant services	268	0	3	271	3
Wholesale trade and commission trade services, except of motor vehicles and motorcycles	167	40	47	254	2
Land transport and transport via pipeline services	103	16	14	133	1
remaining 46 product groups	1 837	446	1 000	3 283	31
Total products	5 407	1 703	1 771	8 881	84
Direct emissions by private households	1 753			1 753	16
Total (products+direct emissions by households)	7 160	1 703	1 771	10 634	100

Source: Eurostat (online data code: env_ac_io)

11.4 Waste

This subchapter gives an overview on the development of waste generation and treatment in the European Union (EU) and several European non-member countries; it draws exclusively on data collected within the framework of Regulation 2150/2002 on waste statistics.

Waste, defined by Directive 2008/98/EC (Article 3(1) as 'any substance or object which the holder discards or intends or is required to discard', represents an enormous loss of resources in the form of both materials and energy. In addition, the management and disposal of waste can have serious environmental impacts. Landfills, for example, take up land space and may cause air, water and soil pollution, while incineration may result in emissions of dangerous air pollutants, unless properly regulated.

EU waste management policies aim to reduce the environmental and health impacts of waste and improve the EU's resource efficiency. The long-term aim of these policies is to reduce the amount of waste generated and when waste generation is unavoidable to promote it as a resource and achieve higher levels of recycling and the safe disposal of waste.

Main statistical findings

Total waste generation

In 2008, the total generation of waste from economic activities and households in the EU-27 amounted to 2 615 million tonnes; this was slightly lower than in either 2004 or 2006. Among the waste generated in the EU-27 in 2008, some 98 million tonnes (3.7 % of the total) were classified as hazardous waste. As such, inhabitants in the EU-27 generated on average about 5.2 tonnes of waste each, of which 196 kg were hazardous waste.

Table 11.4.1 shows an analysis of the total waste generated broken down by main economic activity (according to NACE Rev. 2). There were two activities that generated particularly high levels of waste across the EU-27 in 2008: they were construction (NACE Section F) accounting for 859 million tonnes (32.9 % of the total) and mining and quarrying (NACE Section B) contributing 727 million tonnes (27.8 % of the total). The vast majority of the waste that was generated within these activities was composed of mineral waste or soils (excavated earth, road construction waste, demolition waste, dredging spoil, waste rocks, tailings and so on); this explains the relatively high proportion of total waste that was accounted for by mineral waste and soils (63.0 % of the total waste generated) – see Figure 11.4.2. Manufacturing (NACE Section C) accounted for 342.7 million tonnes of waste generated in 2008 (13.1 % of the total), while households contributed a further 221 million tonnes (8.5 %). The relatively low share of total waste that was generated from agriculture, forestry and fishery activities (NACE Section A) is, at least in part, linked to manure and slurry being excluded from the data presented (as long as they are re-used within agriculture as fertiliser or a soil improver).

There was a considerable variation in the amount of waste generated in 2008 across those countries for which data are presented in Table 11.4.1 – the highest share of the EU-27 total being accounted for by Germany (14.3 %), just ahead of France and the United Kingdom. These figures may be expressed in relation to population (see Figure 11.4.1): using this measure, Latvia generated the lowest level of waste per inhabitant (660 kg) among the EU Member States, although relatively low levels of waste were also generated in Croatia, Turkey, the former Yugoslav Republic of Macedonia and Liechtenstein. Indeed, all four of these countries recorded a lower level of waste generated per inhabitant than the second lowest amount among the EU Member States, which was recorded in Hungary (an average of 2 tonnes per inhabitant). The amount of waste generated ranged between 2 and 7 tonnes per inhabitant for the majority of the EU Member States, rising to between 8 and 10 tonnes per inhabitant in Romania and Sweden, reaching 14.6 tonnes per inhabitant in Estonia, 15.4 tonnes per inhabitant in Finland, 19.6 tonnes per inhabitant in Luxembourg and peaking at 37.5 tonnes per inhabitant in Bulgaria.

Some of the large variations between countries may be linked to the differences in economic structures. For example, the extremely high level of waste that was generated in Bulgaria was strongly influenced by mineral wastes from mining and quarrying activities: Bulgaria extracts coal and lignite, metallic and non-metallic minerals, mostly by open-pit excavation. Relatively large quantities of mineral waste were generated by mining and quarrying activities in Romania, Sweden, Finland and Estonia, whereas in Luxembourg, mineral waste from construction was largely responsible for the high level of waste generated.

Non-mineral waste generation

The 919 million tonnes of non-mineral waste generated in the EU-27 in 2008 represented 35.1 % of the total waste generated; this figure was slightly less than the corresponding shares recorded in 2004 or 2006. When expressed in relation to the population, on average inhabitants of the EU-27 generated 1 843 kg of non-mineral waste each in 2008 (see Figure 11.4.3). Across the EU Member States, non-mineral waste generation ranged from an average of 606 kg per inhabitant in Latvia to 8 216 kg per inhabitant in Estonia (largely hazardous combustion waste and hazardous chemical deposits and residues from the refining and incineration of oil shale).

Figure 11.4.4 shows the origin and development of non-mineral waste broken down by economic

activity. About a quarter of the total waste generated could be attributed to manufacturing, which was around 30 million tonnes lower than in 2004. Note that the reduction in waste generated within agricultural activities between 2006 and 2008 reflects a change in coverage for manure and slurry (excluded by several countries for 2008), rather than a decrease in the actual amount of waste being generated.

Hazardous waste generation

Hazardous waste may pose a risk to human health and the environment if not managed and disposed of safely. In 2008, some 98 million tonnes of hazardous waste was generated in the EU-27; this was higher than in 2004 (89 million tonnes), but lower than in 2006 (101 million tonnes).

Figure 11.4.5 shows the amount of hazardous waste that was generated per inhabitant during 2004, 2006 and 2008; note that the figures include all hazardous waste categories, including minerals. As noted above, the high figures for Estonia (5.6 tonnes per inhabitant) may be largely attributed to oil shale, and those for Bulgaria (1.7 tonnes per inhabitant) to the mining of copper ores. Aside from these specific cases, the generation of hazardous waste in the EU Member States ranged in 2008 from 23 kg per inhabitant in Greece to 553 kg per inhabitant in Belgium.

Waste treatment

In 2008, some 2 391 million tonnes of waste was treated in the EU-27; this includes the treatment of waste that was imported into the EU. Table 11.4.2 presents more information in relation to the types of waste treatment operation that were employed, while Table 11.4.3 provides the same information for the treatment of hazardous waste.

Almost half (48.9 %) of the waste treated within the EU-27 in 2008 was subject to disposal operations other than waste incineration (this was predominantly landfills, but also included a small amount of mining waste disposed in and around mining sites and waste discharges into water bodies). A further 45.7 % of the waste treated in the EU-27 was sent to recovery operations (other than energy recovery). The remaining 5.4 % of the waste treated in the EU-27 in 2008 was sent for incineration (with or without energy recovery).

Recovery

Figure 11.4.6 shows a breakdown of the 1 093 million tonnes of waste recovered in the EU-27 in 2008 by waste categories. The recovery of non-hazardous mineral waste originating mainly from construction and mining and quarrying activities amounted to 754 million tonnes and represented 69.0 % of the total waste recovered; there was strong growth in the amount of mineral waste recovery in the EU-27 during the period from 2004 to 2008. Among the other waste categories, there was also an increase in the quantity of animal and vegetal waste that was recovered between 2004 and 2008, such that this category accounted for 6.1 % of the total waste recovered in 2008. For metals, paper and cardboard, glass and plastic wastes, which are the most common recyclable materials, growth in the quantity of material that has been treated might be expected as a result of the implementation of European waste legislation on landfills (diversion of biodegradable waste) and producer responsibility (for example, separate collection and recovery of packaging waste). In practice, only modest growth was observed during the period from 2004 to 2008 and there was even a reduction in the amount of recovered plastic wastes; these developments are thought to be linked to increasing exports of recyclable goods to non-member countries.

Incineration (including energy recovery)

Figure 11.4.7 shows an analysis of the incinerated waste (including energy recovery) for 2008. Out of a total of 129.2 million tonnes of incinerated waste in the EU-27, 38.9 % was composed of household and similar waste. Sorting residues accounted for 9.6 %, chemical wastes for 2.9 % and common sludges for 2.5 %. Hazardous waste accounted for 8.1 % of the total (some 10.5 million tonnes). Note that the miscellaneous category (38.1 %) cannot be presented in any more detail given the limited breakdown required by the waste statistics Regulation; however, this category includes wood and other biomass waste.

The total amount of incinerated waste increased steadily between 2004 and 2008, rising by 21 million tonnes (or 19.6 % overall). Approximately half of the total increase could be attributed to Germany, where the implementation of a landfill ban for untreated municipal waste led to a considerable increase in energy recovery from waste.

Landfilling

Figure 11.4.8 shows the breakdown of landfilled waste in the EU-27 for 2008. The vast majority of the waste that was destined for landfills was non-hazardous mineral waste (80.3 % of the total). Household and similar wastes accounted for 8.1 %, while hazardous wastes accounted for 3.0 % of the total.

There was a steady decrease in the quantity of non-mineral wastes going to landfills between 2004 and 2008. The disposal of household and similar waste declined by 17.3 % overall during this period, presumably reflecting changes such as the separate collection and pre-treatment of household and similar waste.

Data sources and availability

In order to monitor the implementation of waste policy, in particular compliance with the principles of recovery and safe disposal, reliable statistics on the production and management of waste from businesses and private households are required. In 2002, Regulation 2150/2002 on waste statistics was adopted, creating a framework for harmonised Community statistics on waste.

Starting with reference year 2004, the Regulation requires the EU Member States to provide data on the generation, recovery and disposal of waste every two years. Data on waste generation and treatment

are available for three reference years, namely, 2004, 2006 and 2008. There remain differences in data coverage across the Member States and methodological changes in individual countries may still have a significant impact on the comparability of waste statistics and on the time series presented, in particular at a national level.

Context

The EU's sustainable development strategy and its sixth Environment Action Programme, which identifies waste prevention and management as one of four top priorities, underline the relationship between the efficient use of resources and waste generation and management. The intention of Community policy in this area is to decouple the use of resources and the generation of waste from economic growth, while ensuring that sustainable consumption does not exceed environmental capacity.

The EU's approach to waste management is based on three principles: waste prevention, recycling and reuse, and improving final disposal and monitoring. Waste prevention can be achieved through cleaner technologies, eco-design, or more eco-efficient production and consumption patterns. Waste prevention and recycling, focused on materials technology, can also reduce the environmental impact of resources that are used through limiting raw materials extraction and transformation during production processes. Where possible, waste that cannot be recycled or reused should be safely incinerated with landfills only used as a last resort. Both these methods need close monitoring because of their potential for causing severe environmental damage.

Table 11.4.1: Waste generation, 2008
(1 000 tonnes)

	Waste from economic activities and households		Agriculture, forestry & fishing (Section A)	Mining & quarrying activities (Section B)	Manufacturing (Section C)	Energy (Section D)	Construction & demolition activities (Section F)	Other economic activities (Sections E and G to U)	Households
	Total	of which, hazardous							
EU-27 (¹)	2 615 220	97 680	45 050	726 740	342 710	90 880	859 490	328 930	220 950
Belgium	48 622	5 919	288	503	10 090	1 087	15 442	16 753	4 459
Bulgaria	286 093	13 043	754	267 559	3 447	7 655	1 829	1 943	2 907
Czech Republic	25 420	1 510	255	167	5 293	1 920	10 651	3 959	3 176
Denmark	15 155	420	41	2	1 454	1 358	5 674	4 111	2 514
Germany	372 796	22 323	1 351	28 288	52 322	11 708	197 207	46 515	35 405
Estonia	19 584	7 538	240	7 198	3 772	5 424	1 099	1 412	440
Ireland (²)	23 637	743	19	2 061	4 026	292	:	15 095	1 677
Greece (³)	68 644	253	:	38 152	5 703	11 181	6 828	2 826	3 954
Spain	149 254	3 649	11 356	25 716	19 369	4 872	44 926	18 584	24 431
France	345 002	10 893	1 313	1 195	21 640	1 004	252 980	37 559	29 311
Italy	179 034	6 655	349	1 263	43 086	3 090	69 732	29 043	32 472
Cyprus	1 843	24	127	505	138	2	431	207	433
Latvia	1 495	67	75	3	501	20	12	278	606
Lithuania	6 835	116	1 288	3	2 758	51	412	961	1 363
Luxembourg	9 592	199	2	10	673	1	8 282	347	276
Hungary	20 080	671	468	272	4 789	3 050	5 240	2 795	3 466
Malta	1 499	55	3	0	17	0	1 099	212	169
Netherlands	99 591	4 724	3 464	270	15 824	1 318	59 477	9 757	9 482
Austria	56 309	1 330	459	678	13 077	569	31 390	6 317	3 819
Poland	140 340	1 469	1 350	33 666	56 746	19 541	6 930	15 228	6 879
Portugal	36 480	3 368	160	1 891	9 001	255	8 085	11 932	5 157
Romania	189 311	524	17 035	140 677	11 064	7 058	318	4 695	8 464
Slovenia	5 038	153	132	55	1 735	354	1 376	673	714
Slovakia	11 472	527	789	151	4 469	1 151	1 302	1 838	1 772
Finland	81 793	2 163	2 739	31 796	16 948	1 531	24 455	2 648	1 674
Sweden	86 169	2 063	314	58 702	11 927	1 508	3 310	6 014	4 393
United Kingdom	334 127	7 285	681	85 963	22 837	4 885	100 999	87 223	31 539
Liechtenstein	0.35	0.01	0.00	0.01	0.03	0.00	0.00	0.30	0.00
Norway	10 427	1 336	184	113	3 689	46	1 498	2 531	2 365
Croatia	4 172	221	19	34	1 727	136	129	2 127	:
FYR of Macedonia	1 362	6	:	:	1 362	:	:	:	:
Turkey	64 770	1 024	:	:	10 741	25 525	:	50	28 454

(¹) Excluding Greece for NACE Section A and Class 46.67; excluding Ireland for NACE Sections G to U (other than Class 46.67) for other economic activities.
(²) Other economic activities excludes NACE Sections G to U, other than Class 46.67.
(³) Total and other economic activities excludes NACE Section A and NACE Class 46.67.

Source: Eurostat (online data code: env_wasgen)

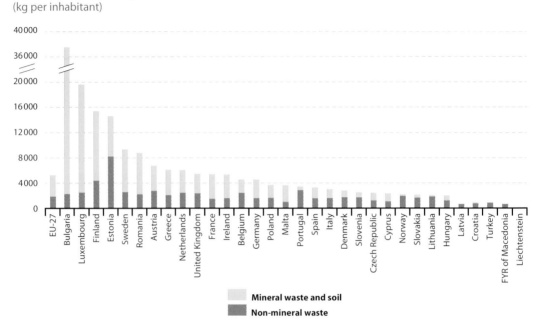
Figure 11.4.1: Waste generation, 2008
(kg per inhabitant)

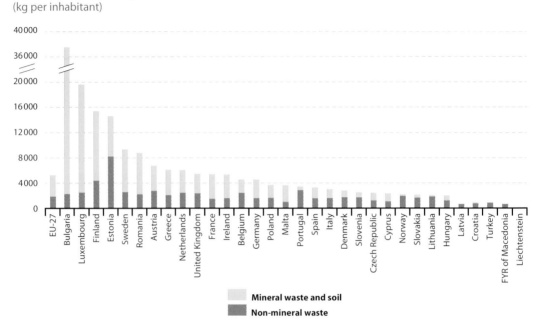

Mineral waste and soil
Non-mineral waste

Source: Eurostat (online data codes: env_wasgen and tsdpc210)

Figure 11.4.2: Waste generation, EU-27, 2008 ([1])
(%)

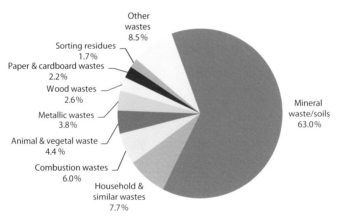

Other
wastes
8.5%

Sorting residues
1.7%
Paper & cardboard wastes
2.2%
Wood wastes
2.6%
Metallic wastes
3.8%
Animal & vegetal waste
4.4%
Combustion wastes
6.0%
Household &
similar wastes
7.7%

Mineral
waste/soils
63.0%

([1]) Figures do not sum to 100 % due to rounding.
Source: Eurostat (online data code: env_wasgen)

Figure 11.4.3: Non-mineral waste generation, 2004-2008
(kg per inhabitant)

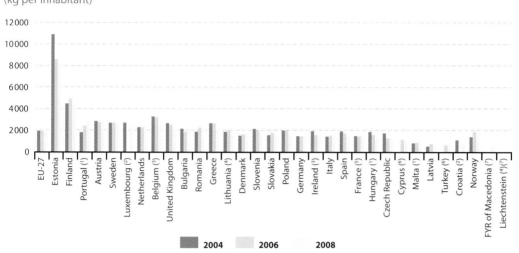

(¹) Estimates.
(²) 2006, not available.
(³) 2006, estimate.
(⁴) 2008, estimate.
(⁵) 2004 and 2006, estimates.
(⁶) 2004, not available.
(⁷) 2004 and 2006, not available.

Source: Eurostat (online data code: tsdpc210)

Figure 11.4.4: Non-mineral waste generation, EU-27, 2004-2008 (¹)
(million tonnes)

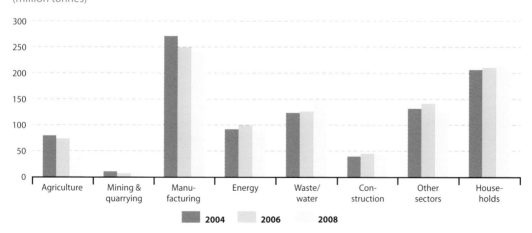

(¹) Based on NACE Rev. 2 classification.

Source: Eurostat (online data code: env_wasgen)

Figure 11.4.5: Hazardous waste generation, 2004-2008 (¹)
(kg per inhabitant)

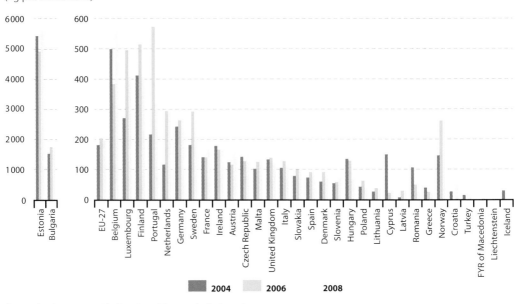

(¹) Note that the two parts of the figure have different scales for the y-axis.

Source: Eurostat (online data code: env_wasgen)

Table 11.4.2: Waste treatment, 2008
(1 000 tonnes)

	Total	Energy recovery	Incineration without energy recovery	Recovery other than energy recovery	Disposal other than incineration
EU-27	2 391 070	81 690	47 550	1 092 900	1 168 950
Belgium	28 731	4 453	3 883	17 345	3 050
Bulgaria	279 608	94	61	2 700	276 752
Czech Republic	18 864	556	69	13 442	4 798
Denmark	14 636	3 320	0	10 283	1 034
Germany	367 256	23 316	13 895	255 337	74 708
Estonia	17 388	257	0	5 456	11 675
Ireland	16 247	104	21	10 415	5 707
Greece	67 523	135	29	5 251	62 108
Spain	137 687	2 552	490	70 355	64 291
France	322 641	12 056	8 612	194 549	107 424
Italy	127 894	2 459	5 157	87 826	32 452
Cyprus	1 843	8	14	745	1 076
Latvia	1 386	18	0	646	721
Lithuania	5 417	194	52	1 361	3 810
Luxembourg	11 632	38	135	5 311	6 147
Hungary	15 823	767	65	5 307	9 684
Malta	1 419	0	6	43	1 371
Netherlands	98 049	2 456	6 369	67 619	21 606
Austria	48 353	3 904	1 594	32 150	10 706
Poland	140 456	3 122	670	107 179	29 486
Portugal	22 044	1 432	400	8 812	11 400
Romania	158 507	1 333	55	8 172	148 947
Slovenia	5 242	314	16	3 040	1 873
Slovakia	9 243	586	66	3 875	4 715
Finland	74 851	9 631	170	22 855	42 195
Sweden	81 352	8 411	87	9 818	63 036
United Kingdom	316 991	171	5 635	143 008	168 178
Norway	9 537	2 091	514	4 542	2 390
Croatia	3 351	321	25	384	2 621
FYR of Macedonia	1 503	0	0	323	1 180
Turkey	60 236	143	81	14 632	45 380

Source: Eurostat (online data code: env_wastrt)

Table 11.4.3: Hazardous waste treatment, 2008
(1 000 tonnes)

	Total	Energy recovery	Incineration without energy recovery	Recovery other than energy recovery	Disposal other than incineration
EU-27	77 860	5 760	4 730	32 260	35 120
Belgium	2 200	369	156	1 232	444
Bulgaria	13 037	0	50	141	12 846
Czech Republic	835	62	61	633	79
Denmark	416	92	0	154	170
Germany	23 824	2 390	1 544	14 674	5 215
Estonia	7 709	37	0	1 242	6 430
Ireland	193	36	21	123	13
Greece	157	8	4	129	16
Spain	3 362	342	10	1 823	1 187
France	6 841	1 031	1 229	2 462	2 120
Italy	3 277	144	449	1 994	691
Cyprus	23	1	0	9	13
Latvia	68	7	0	60	1
Lithuania	20	0	1	17	2
Luxembourg	47	:	:	:	0
Hungary	450	40	59	136	215
Malta	32	:	:	:	0
Netherlands	4 506	866	189	2 238	1 213
Austria	395	84	77	189	45
Poland	1 625	6	139	862	618
Portugal	1 623	15	18	1 464	125
Romania	260	35	32	172	21
Slovenia	116	10	11	46	49
Slovakia	356	13	47	67	228
Finland	2 178	58	113	286	1 722
Sweden	996	100	87	425	384
United Kingdom	3 314	11	433	1 600	1 271
Norway	1 338	113	45	158	1 022
Croatia	18	5	0	9	3
FYR of Macedonia	6	0	0	3	3
Turkey	1 169	122	57	252	738

Source: Eurostat (online data code: env_wastrt)

Figure 11.4.6: Recovered waste (excluding energy recovery), EU-27, 2008
(%)

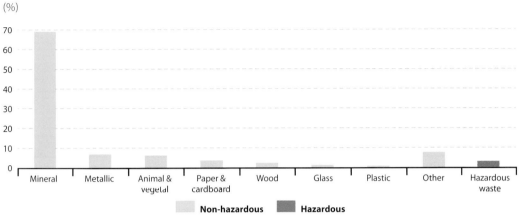

Non-hazardous   **Hazardous**

Source: Eurostat (online data code: env_wastrt)

Figure 11.4.7: Incinerated waste (including energy recovery), EU-27, 2008
(%)

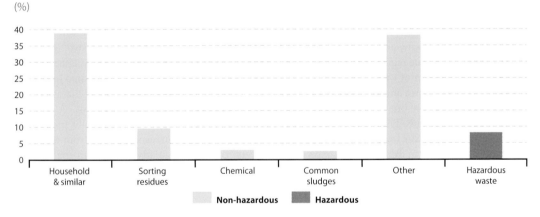

Non-hazardous   **Hazardous**

Source: Eurostat (online data code: env_wastrt)

Figure 11.4.8: Landfilled waste, EU-27, 2008
(%)

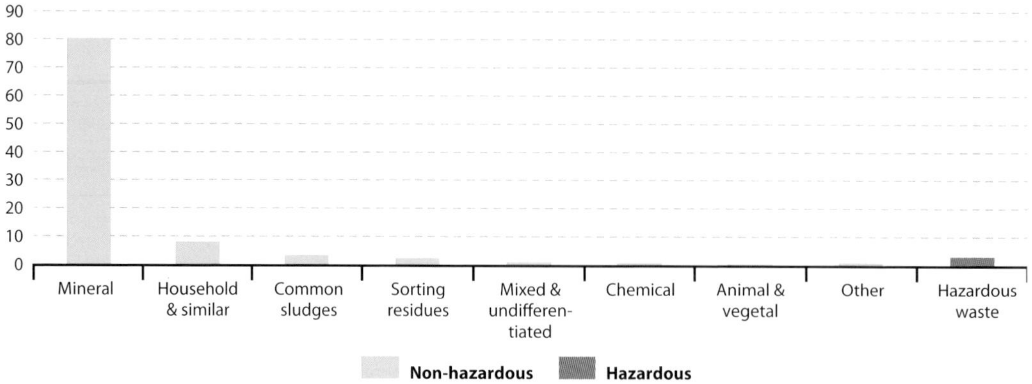

Source: Eurostat (online data code: env_wastrt)

11.5 Water

Water is essential for life, it is an indispensable resource for the economy, and also plays a fundamental role in the climate regulation cycle. The management and protection of water resources, of fresh and salt water ecosystems, and of the water we drink and bathe in is therefore one of the cornerstones of environmental protection. This subchapter on water statistics presents data on freshwater resources and the human use of water in the European Union (EU), and includes information on water abstraction and wastewater treatment and disposal.

Main statistical findings

Freshwater resources

The three main users of water are agriculture, industry and the domestic sector (households and services). The overall abstraction and use of water resources can be considered to be sustainable in the long-term in most of Europe. However, specific regions may face problems associated with water scarcity; this is especially the case in southern Europe, where it is likely that efficiency gains in relation to agricultural water use will need to be achieved in order to prevent seasonal water shortages. Regions associated with low rainfall, high population density, or intensive industrial activity may also face sustainability issues in the coming years, which may be exacerbated by natural resource endowments, geographical characteristics and freshwater management systems. A number of Member States receive a significant proportion of their water resources as inflows from upstream rivers: this is particularly the case in the Danube basin and for the Netherlands, and is also the case, to a lesser extent, in Latvia, Germany and Portugal.

One measure of sustainability in water management is the water exploitation index (WEI), calculated as water abstraction divided by long-term annual resources (Cosgrove and Rijsberman, 2000). A WEI above 20 % typically indicates water scarcity problems in a country or region, and the European Environment Agency (EEA) uses this value as a warning threshold, while WEI values of more than 40 % indicate severe stress on resources and unsustainable water use. Using this measure and subject to data availability, a relatively high degree of pressure exists on water resources in Cyprus, Belgium, Spain, Italy and Malta, with Cyprus being the only Member State to record a ratio of more than 40 %.

In absolute terms (see Table 11.5.1), total freshwater resources were broadly similar in Germany, France, Sweden, the United Kingdom and Italy, as each of these Member States reported a long-term average of annual freshwater resources of between 188 000 million m³ and 175 300 million m³. When expressed in relation to population size (see Figure 11.5.1), Finland and Sweden recorded the highest freshwater annual resources per capita (around 20 000 m³ per inhabitant or more). In contrast, relatively low levels (below 3 000 m³ per capita) were recorded in the six largest Member States (France, Italy, the United Kingdom, Spain, Germany and Poland), as well as in Belgium and the Czech Republic, with the lowest level in Cyprus (410 m³ per inhabitant).

Water abstraction

There are considerable differences in the per capita amounts of freshwater abstracted within each of the Member States, in part reflecting the resources available, but also abstraction practices for public water supply, industrial and agricultural purposes, as well as land drainage and land sealing. These differences are also apparent when looking at the breakdown of water abstraction between groundwater and surface water resources (see Table 11.5.2). In Bulgaria and Romania surface water abstraction accounted for around ten times the volume of water abstracted from groundwater resources in the year 2009, with this ratio peaking at almost 14:1 for Lithuania. At the other end of the range, larger volumes of water were abstracted from groundwater resources in Latvia, Slovakia (2007), Cyprus and Malta.

Germany, France and Spain recorded the highest amounts of groundwater extracted in 2008 (2007 in the case of France), each with 5 700 million m³ or more. Looking at the development of groundwater abstraction during the ten-year period to 2009, the volume of groundwater extracted generally fell, although Estonia, Spain and Slovenia recorded abstraction levels that were between 15 % and 30 % higher, rising to 63 % higher for Malta; a smaller increase of just over 1 % was registered in Belgium.

Spain, Germany and France headed the ranking of Member States in relation to surface water abstraction, with more than 25 000 million m³ in 2007

or 2008. Developments in surface water abstraction levels were somewhat more pronounced than for groundwater. The volume of surface water abstracted in Lithuania (2009) and Slovakia (2007) was around half the level recorded some ten years earlier. The Czech Republic and Sweden reported that their volume of surface water abstracted increased during the period from 1999 to 2009 by around 10 % (1999 to 2007 for Sweden).

Public water supply

While the share of the public water supply sector in total water abstraction depends on the economic structure of a given country and can be relatively small, it is nevertheless often the focus of public interest, as it comprises the water volumes that are directly used by the population. Most EU Member States had annual rates of freshwater abstraction of between 50 m³ and 100 m³ per capita (see Figure 11.5.2), although extremes reflect specific conditions: for example, in Ireland (141 m³ per capita) – where the use of water from the public supply is free; or Bulgaria (129 m³ per capita) – where there are particularly high losses from the public network. Abstraction rates were also rather high in some Nordic and Alpine non-member countries, notably Iceland, Norway and Switzerland, where water resources are abundant and supply is hardly restricted. At the other end of the scale, Estonia and Lithuania reported low abstraction rates, in part resulting from below-average connection rates to the public supply, while Malta and Cyprus have partially replaced groundwater by desalinated seawater.

An analysis of the development of abstraction rates over time is shown for selected Member States in Figure 11.5.3. There was a marked decrease in abstraction in a few Member States (the example of Bulgaria is shown in the figure), while there was an increase in abstraction for other Member States (for example, Portugal). Abstraction rates were relatively stable in the majority of the Member States (see the example of Belgium), with a pattern of gradually decreasing abstraction rates commonly observed (see the example of Sweden). It is likely that the reduction in abstraction is a result of various factors, including the introduction of water-saving household appliances, and an increasing level of consciousness concerning the cost or value of water and the environmental consequences of wasting it.

Wastewater treatment

The proportion of the population connected to urban wastewater treatment covers those households that are connected to any kind of sewage treatment (see Table 11.5.3). This share was above 80 % in approximately half of the Member States for which data are available (mixed reference years), rising to 99 % in the Netherlands, 97 % in England and Wales and 95 % in Germany and Luxembourg, while Switzerland (97 %) also recorded a high connection rate. At the other end of the range, less than one in two households were connected to urban wastewater treatment in Bulgaria, Malta, Cyprus and Romania; new treatment plants are under construction in Malta and it is expected that this will lead to a 100 % connection rate by 2011.

In terms of treatment levels (see Figure 11.5.4), tertiary wastewater treatment was most common (again mixed reference periods) in the Netherlands, Germany, Austria, Italy, Sweden and Greece, where at least four in every five persons were connected to this type of wastewater treatment. In contrast, no more than 1 % of the population was connected to tertiary wastewater treatment in Romania and Bulgaria.

The residual of wastewater treatment is sewage sludge. While the amount of sludge generated per capita depends on many factors and hence is quite variable across countries, the nature of this sludge – rich in nutrients, but also often loaded with high concentrations of pollutants such as heavy metals – has led countries to seek different pathways for its disposal, as illustrated in Figure 11.5.5. Typically, four different types of disposal make up a considerable share of the total volume of sewage sludge treated: more than two thirds of the total was used as fertiliser in agriculture in Cyprus, Spain, Ireland and the United Kingdom, while another five Member States (Lithuania, Bulgaria, Luxembourg, France and Latvia), as well as Norway, reported between one and two thirds of their total mass of sewage sludge being disposed of through agricultural uses.

In contrast, more than two thirds of sewage sludge was composted in Estonia, Finland and Slovakia. Otherwise, alternative forms of disposal may be used to reduce or eliminate the spread of pollutants on agricultural or gardening land; these include incineration and landfill. While the Netherlands, Slovenia, Belgium, Germany and Austria (as well as Switzerland) reported incineration as their primary pathway for disposal, its discharge into controlled landfills was practised as the primary pathway in Italy, and was used almost exclusively in Greece and Malta, as well as in Iceland.

Data sources and availability

Many of the water statistics produced by Eurostat have been used in the context of the development of EU legislation relating to water, as well as for environmental assessments, which in turn can give rise to new data needs. Water statistics are collected through the inland waters section of a joint OECD/Eurostat questionnaire which is frequently adapted to meet the demands of relevant policy frameworks. It currently reports on the following:

- freshwater resources in groundwater and surface water – these can be replenished by precipitation and external inflow (water flowing into a country from other territories);
- water abstraction – a major pressure on resources, although a large part of the water abstracted for domestic, industrial (including energy production) or agricultural use is returned to the environment and its water bodies, but often as wastewater with impaired quality;
- water use – analysed by supply category and by industrial activities;
- treatment capacities of urban wastewater treatment plants and the share of the population connected to them – which gives an overview of the development status of the infrastructure, in terms of quantity and quality, that is available for the protection of the environment from pollution by wastewater;
- sewage sludge production and disposal – an inevitable product of wastewater treatment processes, its impact on the environment depends on the methods chosen for its processing and disposal;

- generation and discharge of wastewater – pollutants present in wastewater have different source profiles and, similarly, the efficiency of treatment of any pollutant varies according to the method applied.

A large amount of data and other information on water is accessible via WISE, the water information system for Europe, which is hosted by the European Environment Agency (EEA) in Copenhagen.

Context

The central element of European water policy is a Directive for 'Community action in the field of water policy' (2000/60/EC) – often referred to as the Water Framework Directive (WFD) – which aims to achieve a good ecological and chemical status of European waters by 2015. In this respect, the Directive focuses on water management at the level of (in most cases transboundary) hydrological catchments (river basins). An important step in the course of the implementation of this legislation involved establishing river basin management plans in 2010.

A study on water saving potential conducted for the European Commission estimated that water use efficiency could be increased by nearly 40 % through technological improvements alone and that changes in human behaviour or production patterns could lead to further savings. In a scenario without changes in practices, it was estimated that water use by the public, industry and agriculture would increase by 16 % by 2030. Conversely, the use of water saving technologies and irrigation management in the industrial and agricultural sectors could reduce excesses by as much as 43 %, while water efficiency measures could decrease water wastage by up to a third.

In a Communication addressing 'water scarcity and droughts' (COM(2007) 414), the European Commission identified an initial set of policy options to be taken at European, national and regional levels to address water scarcity within the EU. This set of proposed policies aims to move the EU towards a water-efficient and water-saving economy, as both the quality and availability of water are of major concern in many regions.

A major step forward in efforts to reduce pollutants discharged into the environment with wastewater was achieved by implementing legislation on 'urban wastewater treatment' (Directive 1991/271/EC). The pollution of rivers, lakes and groundwater and water quality is affected by human activities such as industrial production, household discharges, or arable farming; a report (COM(2007) 120) on 'the protection of waters against pollution by nitrates from agricultural sources' was issued in March 2007.

Another aspect of water quality relates to coastal bathing waters. The European Commission and the EEA present an annual bathing water report – the latest of these covers information for 2010 and shows that 92.1 % of Europe's coastal bathing waters and 90.2 % of its inland bathing waters met the minimum water quality standards. It is anticipated that legislation concerning the 'management of bathing water quality' (Directive 2006/7/EC) will provide for a more proactive approach to informing the public about water quality; it was transposed into national law in 2008 but Member States have until December 2014 to implement it.

An increase of variability in weather patterns and catastrophic floods (such as those along the Danube and Elbe in 2002) prompted a review of flood risk management. This process culminated in a Directive (2007/60/EC) of the European Parliament and Council on 'the assessment and management of flood risks', which aims to reduce and manage risks to human health, the environment, cultural heritage, and economic activity.

Table 11.5.1: Water resources – long-term annual average ([1])
(1 000 million m³)

	Precipitation	Evapotrans-piration	Internal flow	External inflow	Outflow	Freshwater resources
Belgium	28.9	16.6	12.3	7.6	15.3	19.9
Bulgaria	68.6	50.5	18.1	89.1	108.5	107.2
Czech Republic	54.7	39.4	15.2	0.7	16.0	16.0
Denmark	38.5	22.1	16.3	0.0	1.9	16.3
Germany	307.0	190.0	117.0	75.0	182.0	188.0
Estonia	29.0	:	:	:	12.3	12.3
Ireland	80.0	32.5	47.5	:	:	47.5
Greece	115.0	55.0	60.0	12.0	:	72.0
Spain	346.5	235.4	111.1	0.0	111.1	111.1
France	485.7	310.4	175.3	11.0	168.0	186.3
Italy	296.0	129.0	167.0	8.0	155.0	175.0
Cyprus	3.1	2.7	0.3	0.0	0.1	0.3
Latvia	42.7	25.8	16.9	16.8	32.9	33.7
Lithuania	44.0	28.5	15.5	9.0	25.9	24.5
Luxembourg	2.0	1.1	0.9	0.7	1.6	1.6
Hungary	55.7	48.2	7.5	108.9	115.7	116.4
Malta	:	:	:	:	:	:
Netherlands	29.8	21.3	8.5	81.2	86.3	89.7
Austria	98.0	43.0	55.0	29.0	84.0	84.0
Poland	193.1	138.3	54.8	8.3	63.1	63.1
Portugal	82.2	43.6	38.6	35.0	34.0	73.6
Romania	154.0	114.6	39.4	186.3	245.6	225.7
Slovenia	31.7	13.2	18.6	13.5	32.3	32.1
Slovakia	37.4	24.3	13.1	67.3	81.7	80.3
Finland	222.0	115.0	107.0	3.2	110.0	110.0
Sweden	313.9	141.2	172.7	11.8	194.6	183.4
United Kingdom	283.7	111.2	172.5	2.8	175.3	175.3
Iceland	200.0	30.0	170.0	–	170.0	170.0
Norway	470.7	112.0	377.3	12.2	389.4	389.4
Switzerland	61.6	21.6	40.7	12.8	53.5	53.5
Croatia	63.1	40.1	23.0	:	:	:
FYR of Macedonia	19.5	:	:	1.0	6.3	:
Turkey	501.0	273.6	227.4	6.9	178.0	234.3

([1]) The minimum period taken into account for the calculation of long term annual averages is 20 years.

Source: Eurostat (online data code: env_watq1a)

Figure 11.5.1: Freshwater resources per capita – long-term average (^{1})
(1 000 m^3 per inhabitant)

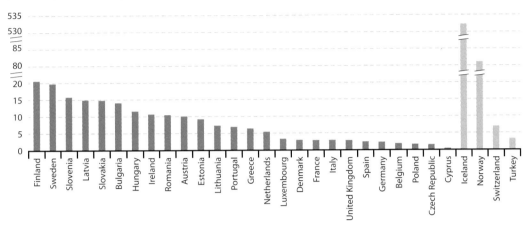

(^{1}) The minimum period taken into account for the calculation of long term annual averages is 20 years; population data are as of 1 January 2009; Malta, not available.

Source: Eurostat (online data code: env_watq1a)

Table 11.5.2: Groundwater and surface water abstraction, 1999-2009
(million m³)

	Groundwater abstraction			Surface water abstraction		
	1999	2004	2009	1999	2004	2009
Belgium (¹)	641	658	648	6 506	5 789	5 570
Bulgaria	585	601	584	6 233	5 680	5 536
Czech Republic	557	402	376	1 419	1 626	1 572
Denmark	683	660	650	18	17	10
Germany (²)	6 710	6 033	5 825	33 880	29 524	26 476
Estonia	299	310	332	1 228	1 439	1 056
Ireland (¹)	:	:	213	:	:	517
Greece (¹)	:	3 734	3 651	:	5 843	5 820
Spain (³)	4 751	6 038	5 700	33 530	30 256	26 766
France (¹)	:	6 425	5 710	:	27 289	25 905
Italy	:	:	:	:	:	:
Cyprus	155	172	145	45	95	39
Latvia (¹)	133	104	108	174	126	104
Lithuania	183	157	161	4 461	3 121	2 241
Luxembourg	32	:	27	29	:	20
Hungary (⁴)	938	708	369	:	:	4 926
Malta	19	34	31	0	0	0
Netherlands (³)	:	1 023	967	:	10 577	9 640
Austria	1 115	:	:	2 553	:	:
Poland	2 906	2 504	2 586	9 339	8 973	8 931
Portugal (⁵)	6 290	:	:	4 800	:	:
Romania	1 134	760	628	7 436	5 090	6 248
Slovenia	148	184	190	:	802	753
Slovakia (⁶)	465	386	358	697	621	330
Finland	285	285	:	2 043	:	:
Sweden (¹)	654	628	346	2 057	2 048	2 285
United Kingdom (⁷)	2 495	2 296	2 139	8 353	8 504	6 208
Iceland	157	160	:	5	5	:
Norway	:	:	:	:	:	:
Switzerland (³)	875	853	:	1 685	1 679	:
Croatia (¹)	:	:	1 162	:	:	:
FYR of Macedonia	:	247	162	:	1 428	885
Turkey (⁸)	10 050	11 443	12 096	27 840	:	:

(¹) 2007 instead of 2009.
(²) 1998 instead of 1999; 2007 instead of 2009.
(³) 2008 instead of 2009.
(⁴) 2008 instead of 2009 for surface water abstraction.
(⁵) 1998 instead of 1999.
(⁶) 2007 instead of 2009; 2003 instead of 2004 for surface water abstraction.
(⁷) England and Wales only; 2008 instead of 2009.
(⁸) 1998 instead of 1999 for surface water abstraction; 2007 instead of 2009.

Source: Eurostat (online data code: env_watq2)

Figure 11.5.2: Total freshwater abstraction by public water supply, 2009 (¹)
(m³ per inhabitant)

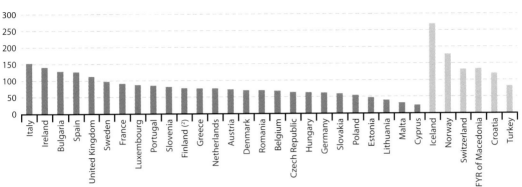

(¹) Spain, Italy, the Netherlands, Austria, Portugal, United Kingdom and Turkey, 2008; Germany, Ireland, Greece, France, Slovakia, Sweden and Norway, 2007; Switzerland, 2006; Finland and Iceland, 2005; Latvia not available.
(²) Estimate.
Source: Eurostat (online data code: env_watq2)

Figure 11.5.3: Total freshwater abstraction for public water supply, selected countries, 1990-2009
(million m³)

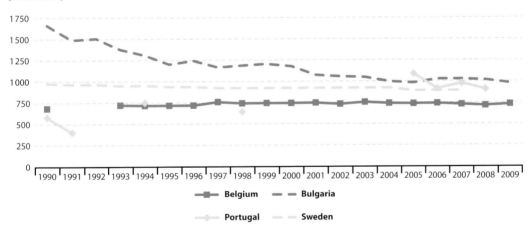

Source: Eurostat (online data code: env_watq2)

Table 11.5.3: Population connected to urban wastewater treatment, 1999-2009
(% of total)

	1999	2000	2001	2002	2003	2004	2005	2006	2007	2008	2009
Belgium	39	41	46	48	51	53	54	57	69	71	:
Bulgaria	36	37	38	39	40	40	41	41	42	44	45
Czech Republic	62	64	65	70	71	71	73	74	75	76	:
Denmark	:	:	:	:	:	:	:	:	:	:	:
Germany	:	:	93	:	:	94	:	:	95	:	:
Estonia	69	69	69	70	70	72	74	74	74	80	80
Ireland	66	:	70	:	:	:	84	:	:	:	:
Greece	:	:	:	:	:	:	:	:	85	:	87
Spain	:	:	:	:	:	:	:	91	:	92	:
France	:	:	79	:	:	80	:	:	:	:	:
Italy	69	:	:	:	:	:	:	:	:	:	:
Cyprus	13	14	16	18	23	28	30	:	:	:	:
Latvia	:	:	:	65	70	66	66	65	65	:	:
Lithuania	:	:	:	57	59	:	69	69	69	70	71
Luxembourg	93	:	:	:	95	:	:	:	:	:	:
Hungary	29	46	50	57	:	:	54	57	:	:	:
Malta	13	36	36	36	36	36	36	36	35	42	48
Netherlands	98	98	98	99	99	99	99	99	99	99	99
Austria	:	85	86	86	89	89	:	92	:	93	:
Poland	52	54	55	57	58	59	60	61	62	63	64
Portugal (¹)	:	:	:	57	60	:	65	72	69	70	:
Romania	:	:	:	:	:	27	27	28	28	29	29
Slovenia	21	23	25	25	26	34	37	52	51	52	52
Slovakia	50	51	51	52	53	54	55	55	57	:	:
Finland	80	80	81	81	:	:	:	:	:	:	:
Sweden	:	86	:	85	:	86	:	86	:	:	:
United Kingdom (²)	92	95	99	98	96	97	97	99	99	97	97
Iceland	16	33	33	50	50	50	57	:	:	:	:
Norway	73	73	74	74	75	76	77	78	78	77	79
Switzerland	96	96	96	96	:	:	97	:	:	:	:
Croatia	:	9	:	:	:	15	28	28	29	:	:
FYR of Macedonia	:	5	6	6	6	6	7	7	7	7	7
Turkey	23	26	27	28	30	36	36	42	:	46	:

(¹) The totals for urban wastewater treatment also contain values for preliminary treatment and for undefined treatment. These values refer to the public urban wastewater treatment, including collective septic tanks.
(²) England and Wales only.

Source: Eurostat (online data code: env_watq4)

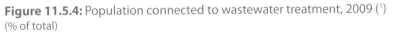

Figure 11.5.4: Population connected to wastewater treatment, 2009 (¹)
(% of total)

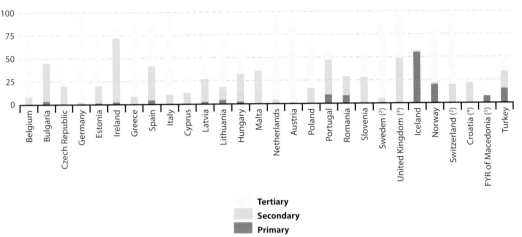

Tertiary
Secondary
Primary

(¹) Belgium, the Czech Republic, Spain, the Netherlands, Austria, Portugal and Turkey, 2008; Germany, Latvia and Croatia, 2007; Hungary and Sweden, 2006; Ireland, Italy, Cyprus, Iceland and Switzerland, 2005; Denmark, France, Luxembourg, Slovakia and Finland, not available.
(²) Primary, not available.
(³) England and Wales only.
(⁴) Primary and tertiary, not available.
(⁵) Secondary and tertiary, not available.

Source: Eurostat (online data code: env_watq4)

Figure 11.5.5: Sewage sludge disposal from urban wastewater treatment, by type of treatment, 2009 (¹)
(% of total mass)

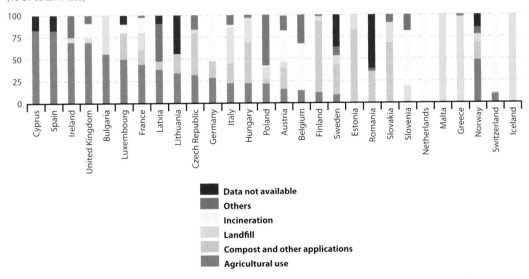

Data not available
Others
Incineration
Landfill
Compost and other applications
Agricultural use

(¹) Belgium, Germany, Luxembourg, the Netherlands and Austria, 2008; the Czech Republic, Ireland, Latvia and Slovakia, 2007; Greece and Switzerland, 2006; Italy, Cyprus and the United Kingdom, 2005; France and Hungary, 2004; Iceland, 2003; Sweden, 2002; Finland, 2000; Denmark and Portugal, not available.

Source: Eurostat (online data code: env_watq6)

11.6 Chemicals management

Work on European Union (EU) statistics concerning hazardous substances started in the mid-1990s when a set of environmental pressure indicators (EPIs) related to chemicals were developed. More recently, a set of indicators to monitor the effectiveness of the Regulation on the registration, evaluation, authorisation and restriction of chemicals (REACH) were developed. This subchapter presents two indicators developed and compiled by Eurostat that cover the production of important industrial chemicals.

Main statistical findings

Total production of chemicals

Figure 11.6.1 shows the development of EU-27 and EU-15 chemical production in terms of the level (or quantity) of output. The production of chemicals is largely concentrated in western Europe: Germany was the largest producer in the EU-27 in 2010, followed by France, Italy and the United Kingdom and these four Member States collectively generated two thirds of the EU-27's chemical production in 2010; adding Spain, the Netherlands, Belgium and Ireland, the overall share of these eight Member States was 88%.

In the EU-15, between 1995 and 2007, the total production of chemicals increased by 64.9 million tonnes (+ 26.2%) to reach a total of 313 million tonnes. In 2008, production decreased by 27.1 million tonnes (– 8.7%) and in 2009 by a further 35.8 million tonnes (– 12.5%) to reach its second lowest level of output (250 million tonnes) – just above that recorded in 1995. In 2010, total production of chemicals stood at 293 million tonnes, marking an expansion of 17.2% compared with the year before.

A shorter time series is available for the EU-27 which shows that the total production of chemicals increased continuously between 2002 and 2007, rising overall by 9.6% to reach a peak of 362 million tonnes. During the financial and economic crisis, production fell by 24 million tonnes (– 6.6%) in 2008 and by another 46 million tonnes (– 13.6%) in 2009. In 2010 the production of industrial chemicals in

the EU-27 increased by 47 million tonnes (+ 16.1%) to reach 339 million tonnes, still 23 million tonnes below the pre-crisis peak.

Production of environmentally harmful chemicals

Figure 11.6.2 presents the development of production of environmentally harmful chemicals, broken down into five environmental impact classes. Aggregated production of these chemicals in the EU-27 grew from 2002 to 2007 by 10.1% overall to a peak of 194 million tonnes. Production fell by 32 million tonnes (– 16.5%) over the next two years to a level of 162 million tonnes, which was 8.1% lower than in 2002. In 2010, the production of environmentally harmful chemicals increased by 22 million tonnes (+ 13.6%) to 184 million tonnes.

EU-15 production of environmentally harmful chemicals increased from 1996 to 2005 by 15.9% overall to record a peak in production of 168 million tonnes. After a modest reduction in 2006, production recovered again in 2007 to stand at almost the same level as in 2005 (one million tonnes lower, at 167 million tonnes). However, the output of environmentally harmful chemicals then fell (reflecting the impact of the financial and economic crisis), reaching a low point in 2009, at 138 million tonnes. There was a strong recovery in 2010, as the EU-15's output rose to 160 million tonnes, which was 15.9% higher than a year before.

The share of environmentally harmful chemicals in total EU-27 chemical output has not changed significantly, from 53.3% in 2002 to 54.3% in 2010. The 12 Member States that joined the EU in 2004 and 2007 produced 24 million tonnes of environmentally harmful chemicals in 2010, equivalent to 13.0% of the quantity of production in the EU-27 as a whole.

Production of toxic chemicals

Figure 11.6.3 presents the development of production quantities of toxic chemicals, broken down into five toxicity classes. The EU-27's production of toxic chemicals (all five toxicity classes aggregated) increased by 6.8 % between 2002 and 2007 to reach a peak of 218 million tonnes. Production fell by 15 million tonnes in 2008 (– 7.0 %) and by 23 million tonnes (– 11.3 %) in 2009 to a level of 180 million tonnes. In 2010 the production of toxic industrial chemicals increased by 25 million tonnes (+ 13.9 %) to 205 million tonnes.

EU-15 production of toxic chemicals increased from 1995 to 2005 by 21.7 % to record a peak in production of 189 million tonnes. In 2010 the EU-15's output stood at 176 million tonnes, which was still 7 % lower than in 2005.

The overall share of chemicals classified as toxic (all five classes) in total EU-27 chemicals production was 60.5 % in 2010 – which was slightly less than the ratio that had been recorded in 2002 (61.8 %). EU-27 production of the most toxic chemicals – carcinogenic, mutagenic and reprotoxic (CMR) chemicals – reached 38 million tonnes in 2004. Output fell substantially in 2008 to 32 million tonnes and increased again in 2010 to 39 million tonnes (+ 21.8 %), a figure that was comparable to the quantity of production for toxic chemicals prior to the financial and economic crisis.

The relative share of CMRs in total EU-27 chemical production fell from 10.8 % in 2004 to 9.4 % in 2008 before increasing again to 11.5 % in 2010. A more detailed analysis shows that most CMRs were produced in lower quantities; however, the production of chlorine compounds, such as vinyl chloride, compensated for these reductions.

The 12 Member States that joined the EU in 2004 or 2007 produced 14.1 % (29 million tonnes) of the EU-27's toxic chemicals in 2010, in line with the 13.6 % share of total production of all industrial chemicals.

The development of toxic chemicals production followed a similar path to that recorded for the production of all chemicals. The time series from 2002 to 2010 provides little indication that EU-27 production of chemicals – that are toxic to human health and/or harmful to ecosystems – is being significantly decoupled from the overall production of industrial chemicals.

Data sources and availability

The indicators presented in this subchapter are derived from annual statistics on the production of manufactured goods (Prodcom). EU-15 statistics on toxic chemicals cover the years from 1995 to 2010, while statistics on environmentally harmful substances start in 1996. EU-27 data are available for the years 2002 to 2010 for both of these indicators.

The information presented on the production of environmentally harmful chemicals and the production of toxic chemicals has been aggregated, in both cases, to five impact classes: these classes of environmental impacts and toxicity to human health follow official classifications in EU legislation and scientific expert judgement. It should be noted that the indicators do not describe the actual risks associated with the use of chemicals, but instead their level of production in quantity terms. Indeed, production and consumption are not synonymous with exposure, as some chemicals are handled in closed systems, or as intermediate goods in controlled supply chains.

The production of environmentally harmful chemicals is divided into five classes based on their environmental impact. The impacts, beginning with the most harmful, are:

- severe chronic environmental impacts;
- significant chronic environmental impacts;
- moderate chronic environmental impacts;
- chronic environmental impacts;
- significant acute environmental impacts.

The production of environmentally harmful chemicals – which is a sustainable development indicator – monitors progress in shifting production from more environmentally harmful to less harmful chemicals; the indicator focuses on aquatic toxicity. It seeks to take into account the inherent eco-toxicity of chemical substances, their potential for bioaccumulation and their persistence in the environment. For this purpose, substance specific data on eco-toxicity, biodegradability and bioaccumulation potential have been used. The production of environmentally harmful chemicals is primarily based on the official environmental classification of substances; certain risk-phrases related to chronic human toxicity are also included.

The indicator on toxic chemicals is also published as a sustainable development indicator within the theme for public health. Aggregated production quantities of toxic chemicals may be broken down into five toxicity classes. The classes, beginning with the most dangerous, are:

- carcinogenic, mutagenic and reprotoxic (CMR) chemicals;
- chronic toxic chemicals;
- very toxic chemicals;
- toxic chemicals;
- chemicals classified as harmful.

The indicator on the production of toxic chemicals monitors progress in shifting production from more toxic to less toxic chemicals and addresses an important objective of REACH: to reduce risks by substitution of hazardous by less hazardous substances.

Eurostat has recently, in collaboration with the Directorate-Generals of the European Commission responsible for enterprise and industry and for the environment, published a baseline study providing a set of indicators to monitor the effectiveness of the REACH Regulation.

Context

The sixth environment action programme (6th EAP), which runs from 2002 to 2012, requires a complete overhaul of EU policies on chemicals management. It is intended that REACH shall ensure a high level of protection for human health and the environment, including the promotion of alternative methods to assess the hazards of substances, the free circulation of substances on the internal market, and the enhancement of competitiveness and innovation in the EU's chemical manufacturing sector. Through increasing knowledge about the hazardous properties of chemicals, REACH is expected to enhance conditions for their safe use in supply chains and contribute towards the substitution of dangerous substances by less dangerous ones, such that there are fewer risks to human health and the environment.

For this purpose, statistical indicators that provide information on the production of toxic chemicals and chemicals that are harmful to the environment may be used to measure progress towards a number of objectives. These include the headline objective for public health established under the EU's sustainable development strategy, alongside the aim of ensuring a high level of protection for human health and the environment – an objective of the 6th EAP.

Figure 11.6.1: Total production of chemicals, 1995-2010
(million tonnes)

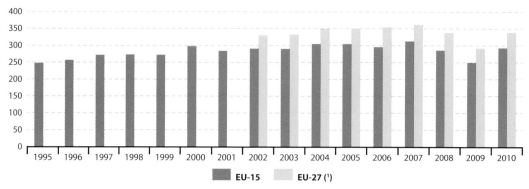

(¹) Not available, 1995 to 2001.

Source: Eurostat (online data code: tsdph320)

Figure 11.6.2: Production of environmentally harmful chemicals, 1996-2010
(million tonnes)

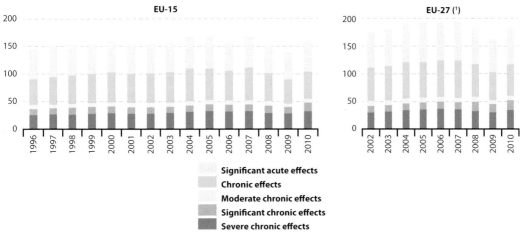

(¹) Not available, 1996 to 2001.

Source: Eurostat (online data code: ten00011)

Figure 11.6.3: Production of toxic chemicals, 1995-2010
(million tonnes)

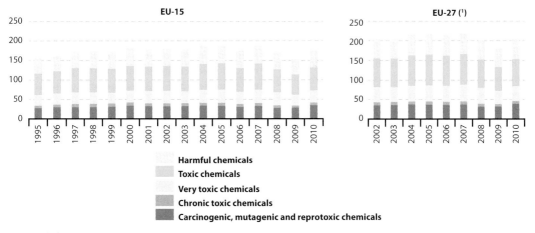

(¹) Not available, 1995 to 2001.

Source: Eurostat (online data code: tsdph320)

11.7 Environmental protection expenditure

This subchapter provides details on the expenditure carried out in the European Union (EU) with the purpose of protecting the environment, in other words, environmental protection expenditure. This covers the money spent on activities directly aimed at the prevention, reduction, and elimination of pollution or any other degradation of the environment resulting from the production or consumption of goods and services.

Nowadays, the protection of the environment is integrated into many policy fields with the general aim of attaining sustainable development. Clean air, water and soils, healthy ecosystems and biodiversity are vital for human life, and thus it is not surprising that societies devote large amounts of money to curbing pollution and preserving a healthy environment. Both business and households pay to safely dispose of waste; production activities spend money to mitigate the polluting effects of production processes; governments subsidise environmentally beneficial activities and use public funds to invest in environmental projects.

Main statistical findings

The highest level of environmental protection expenditure in the EU-27 was accounted for by specialised producers of environmental protection services (EUR 127 300 million in 2009), while the public sector and industry (which excludes recycling) had expenditure of EUR 87 000 million and EUR 51 500 million respectively.

Between 2001 and 2009, the EU-27 expenditure of specialised producers grew in value terms by almost 50 % (see Figure 11.7.1). There was a 25 % increase in environmental protection expenditure made by the public sector between 2002 and 2009, while the expenditure for industry was largely unchanged (having dipped during the early part of the decade when industrial activity was relatively weak, before rebounding between 2004 and 2008).

Contrary to the general development of rising EU-27 environmental protection expenditure over most of the last decade, the latest growth rates between 2008 and 2009 reflect, at least to some degree, the impact of the financial and economic crisis. There was a reduction of 7.6 % in the expenditure made by industry, while expenditure declined by 2.7 % for specialised producers of environmental protection services and 0.9 % for the public sector.

An alternative means to analyse the importance of environmental protection expenditure is to express its level in relation to GDP. Figure 11.7.2 shows that the EU-27 environmental protection expenditure of specialised producers of environmental protection services increased by 0.2 percentage points between 2001 and 2009 to reach 1.1 % of GDP. The relative importance of EU-27 environmental protection expenditure made by the public sector was stable around 0.7 % of GDP between 2002 and 2008, increasing somewhat in 2009. In contrast, the relative importance of EU-27 environmental protection expenditure made by industry declined between 2001 and 2003 by about 1 percentage point and then remained relatively stable though until 2009.

Between 2008 and 2009 there was a 5.8 % reduction in EU-27 GDP in current price terms. This decline in economic activity was at a more rapid pace than the reduction in EU-27 environmental protection expenditure for specialised producers of environmental protection services or the public sector, resulting in their relative shares of GDP rising in 2009 while there was a very small reduction in the relative importance of industrial environmental protection expenditure.

A breakdown of environmental protection expenditure by domain is provided in Figure 11.7.3. This shows that in 2009 the largest expenditure concerned waste management, followed by wastewater treatment. More than half of the expenditure within these two domains was accounted for by specialised producers of environmental protection services. In contrast, environmental protection expenditure related to air pollution accounted for a quarter of the total expenditure made within industry.

Environmental protection expenditure by the public sector

In most European countries, environmental protection investments and current expenditure (thus excluding subsidies) made by the public sector accounted for between 0.25 % and 0.9 % of GDP in 2009 (see Figure 11.7.4). Croatia (0.02 %), Latvia (0.08 %) and Estonia (0.16 %) were below this range, while relatively high levels of public sector investments and current expenditure were recorded in Malta (1.59 %, 2008), the Netherlands (1.58 %, 2007) and Lithuania (1.19 %).

Figure 11.7.5 provides a breakdown of the investments and current expenditure incurred by the public sector: it shows that investment across the EU-27 accounted for one quarter of the total expenditure. Investment generally accounted for a much higher share of total expenditure in most of the Member States that joined the EU in 2004 or 2007; this may reflect expenditure on fixed assets required to meet EU environmental legislation.

As noted above, waste management and wastewater treatment are generally the two main domains for expenditure and this pattern held true for most of the EU Member States in relation to their public sector spending. Figure 11.7.6 shows that this was not always the case and that in some countries the public sector spent more in other domains. For example, in Spain, the public sector principally directed its expenditure towards biodiversity and landscape protection, whereas in Cyprus, Italy, Denmark, France and Finland more than two fifths of expenditure was given over to the miscellaneous category of 'other', which includes general environmental administration and management, education, training and information relating to the environment (as well as activities leading to indivisible expenditure and activities not elsewhere classified).

Environmental protection expenditure by specialised producers of environmental protection services

The expenditure of specialised producers of environmental protection services generally ranged between 0.4 % and 1.5 %, with an EU-27 average

of 1.1 % of GDP in 2009 (see Figure 11.7.7). Below this range, Slovakia, Finland (2006), Latvia and Luxembourg had a lower level of relative expenditure among specialised producers. In contrast, the highest ratios of environmental protection expenditure for specialised producers to GDP were recorded in Estonia (2008) and Austria (2007). The differences between countries may, at least to some degree, reflect whether the public sector provides services itself, or whether these activities have been contracted out to specialised producers. The differences may also be related to the specialisation and concentration of particular industrial activities within each country. For example, wastewater treatment or waste management may be internalised within industrial plants in order to recycle or re-use some of the materials that are discarded as part of the production process.

The vast majority of the environmental protection expenditure made by specialised producers of environmental protection services was directly allocated to waste management and wastewater treatment (see Figure 11.7.8).

Environmental protection expenditure by industry

An average of 0.44 % of GDP was spent on environmental protection expenditure by industry across the EU-27 in 2009 (see Figure 11.7.9). This ratio was generally within the range of 0.2 % to 1.0 % of GDP, although Bulgaria reported a higher relative share and Cyprus (2008) and France (2007) lower shares; Turkey also had a relatively low share (2008).

Information is available for a more detailed industrial breakdown (using NACE sections) for most of the EU Member States and some non-member countries (see Figure 11.7.10). The majority of the environmental protection expenditure made within the industrial economy can be attributed to manufacturing (66.1 % of the total in the EU-27 in 2009). The manufacturing sector had the highest level of expenditure among the three industrial activities in each of the countries for which data are available, except in Latvia and Estonia (in 2008) where the electricity, gas, and water supply sector accounted for a higher share. The high manufacturing share is not surprising as this sector is far larger according to most economic measures than either mining and quarrying or the electricity, gas and water supply sector. Natural resource endowments, as well as industrial specialisation may, at least in part, explain some of the differences between countries. For example, a higher reliance on the burning of fossil fuels to generate electricity in many of the Member States that joined the EU in 2004 or 2007 may explain the relatively high degree of environmental protection expenditure within the electricity, gas and water supply sector in these countries, while natural resources of coal may explain the higher than average levels of expenditure for the mining and quarrying activity in Romania, the Czech Republic and Poland.

Figure 11.7.11 shows that 30.2 % of the environmental protection expenditure that was made within the EU-27's industrial economy in 2009 was attributed to investment; this was somewhat higher than the corresponding share recorded for public sector expenditure (25.0 %).

The environmental protection expenditure made by the industrial sector was largely concentrated among air protection measures, wastewater treatment and waste management activities (see Figure 11.7.12).

Data sources and availability

Eurostat regularly collects environmental protection expenditure data through a joint Eurostat/OECD questionnaire on environmental protection expenditure and revenues; this is based on EU methodology.

The questionnaire classifies units of the economy into four main sectors: specialised producers (in other words, public and private enterprises) of environmental protection services, the public sector (other than public specialised producers), business (other than private specialised producers) and households. In most European countries important environmental protection services (such as waste management and wastewater treatment) have evolved from being primarily provided free by the public sector (local government) to being

more commonly provided by various forms of private and public specialised producers; the methodology used for the collection of data reflects these arrangements.

The grouping of economic units is based upon the type of environmental protection activity they carry out. Units classified under the pubic sector or as specialised producers of environmental protection services are units that carry out environmental protection activities for third parties.

The public sector comprises those units which carry out non-market activities for the community as a whole. Apart from legislative and regulatory tasks, public sector units may also provide environmental public goods. They also subsidise environmental protection activities directly and indirectly, for example, by providing investment grants.

Specialised producers of environmental protection services produce market services; this group also includes producers that carry out environmental protection activities as a secondary activity. Specialised producers can be divided between public specialised producers and private specialised producers.

Units that carry out environmental protection activities for their own internal use are part of the business sector and cover internal (ancillary) activities, in other words, activities carried out on their own behalf to reduce the environmental impact of their production processes. For example, businesses can invest in equipment for cleaning up pollutants (for example, filters), cleaner production technologies that reduce emissions, or they can organise (internally) their own waste management services. The business sector includes all activities in NACE Rev. 1.1 Divisions 01 to 99, excluding the public sector (falling mainly in NACE Rev. 1.1 Division 75, public administration) and excluding the activities of specialised producers (falling mainly in NACE Rev. 1.1 Division 90, sewage and refuse disposal).

The households sector groups together those units that belong to the institutional sector of households in the national accounts, considered in their capacity as final consumers. Households mainly buy environmental services (for example, they may pay

for the collection and treatment of household waste, or the treatment of their wastewater).

Environmental protection expenditure is an indicator which comprises total investments and total current expenditure. Total current expenditure is the sum of internal current expenditure and fees and payments for environmental protection services. For the public sector, environmental protection expenditure also includes subsidies and investment grants that are paid to other sectors for related environmental protection activities. Environmental protection expenditure gives an idea of the money spent by each sector on environmental protection activities directly and indirectly, in other words, not only on environmental protection activities for their own use, but also by those buying environmental services from other economic units and financing environmental protection expenditure that is carried out by other units. Note that environmental protection expenditure is not adjusted to take account of receipts from any by-products, revenues from environmental protection services or from transfers/subsidies.

The indicators for environmental protection expenditure can be used to compare the performance of a particular sector across countries. However, these indicators should not be used to compare expenditure across sectors, as there may be cases of double-counting, for example, between specialised producers of environmental protection services and those business that purchase such services. As such, it is not possible (using the current methodology) to create a figure for the total spend on environmental protection; rather, a full satellite account to the national accounts would be necessary to perform such a calculation.

The scope of environmental protection is defined according to the Classification of Environmental Protection Activities (CEPA 2000), which distinguishes nine different environmental domains: the protection of ambient air and the climate; wastewater treatment; waste management; protection and remediation of soil, groundwater and surface water; noise and vibration abatement; protection of biodiversity and landscape; protection against radiation;

research and development, and; other environmental protection activities.

Context

The demand for goods and services to prevent or treat environmental damage encourages the supply of environmental activities and stimulates the development of a 'greener' economy. The analysis of expenditure patterns relating to environmental protection may help contribute towards an evaluation of environmental policies already in place and whether or not the 'polluter pays' principle is being implemented.

A low level of environmental protection expenditure does not necessarily mean that a country is not effectively protecting its environment. In fact, the indicator tends to emphasise clean-up costs at the expense of cost reductions which could be due to reduced emissions or more effective (less polluting) production techniques.

For many years, European statistical services have collected data on air pollution, energy and water consumption, wastewater, solid waste, and their management. The data sources can be used by policymakers to assess the environmental impact of economic activities (resource consumption, air or water pollution, waste production) and to assess the actions (investments, technologies, expenditure) that may be carried out to limit the causes and risks of pollution.

Eurostat has worked towards systematically gathering environmental statistics for all economic sectors within the EU. These statistics are used to: assess the effectiveness of new regulations and policies; analyse the links between environmental pressures and the structure of the economy.

A Regulation (691/2011) on European environmental economic accounts was adopted on 6 July 2011; it provides a framework for the development of various types of environmental accounts (also referred to as modules). Although not included in the first set of modules, the regulation does make reference to environmental protection expenditure as a future area for inclusion.

Figure 11.7.1: Total environmental protection expenditure, EU-27, 2001-2009 ([1])
(EUR million)

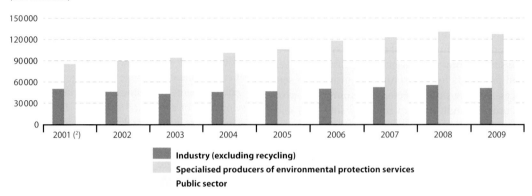

Industry (excluding recycling)
Specialised producers of environmental protection services
Public sector

([1]) Estimates.
([2]) Public sector, not available.

Source: Eurostat (online data code: env_ac_exp1)

Figure 11.7.2: Total environmental protection expenditure, EU-27, 2001-2009 ([1])
(% of GDP)

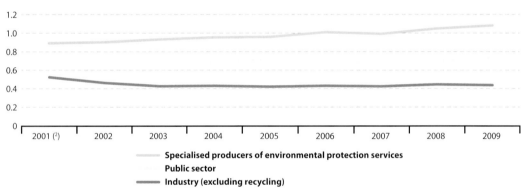

Specialised producers of environmental protection services
Public sector
Industry (excluding recycling)

([1]) Estimates.
([2]) Public sector, not available.

Source: Eurostat (online data codes: env_ac_exp1 and nama_gdp_c)

Figure 11.7.3: Total environmental protection expenditure by domain, EU-27, 2009 (¹)
(% of GDP)

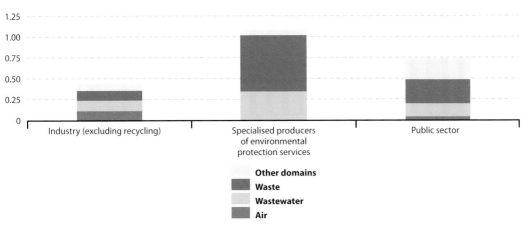

(¹) Estimates.

Source: Eurostat (online data codes: env_ac_exp1 and nama_gdp_c)

Figure 11.7.4: Public sector environmental protection investments and current expenditure, 2009 (¹)
(% of GDP)

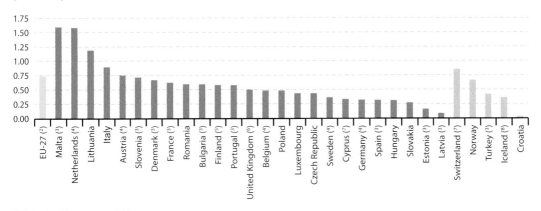

(¹) Ireland and Greece, not available.
(²) Estimate.
(³) 2008.
(⁴) 2007.
(⁵) 2006.
(⁶) 2004.
(⁷) 2003.
(⁸) 2002.

Source: Eurostat (online data codes: env_ac_exp1, env_ac_exp1r2 and nama_gdp_c)

Figure 11.7.5: Breakdown of public sector environmental protection expenditure, 2009 ([1])
(% of total)

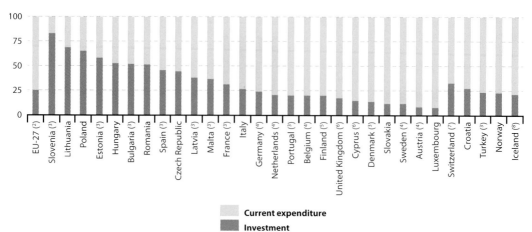

Current expenditure

Investment

([1]) Ireland and Greece, not available.
([2]) Estimates.
([3]) 2008.
([4]) 2007.
([5]) 2006.
([6]) 2004.
([7]) 2003.
([8]) 2002.

Source: Eurostat (online data codes: env_ac_exp1 and env_ac_exp1r2)

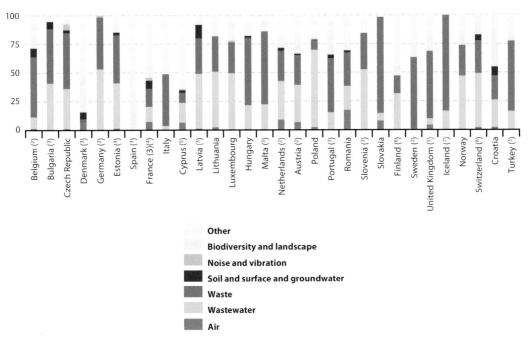

Figure 11.7.6: Breakdown of public sector environmental protection expenditure by environmental domain, 2009 (¹)
(% of total)

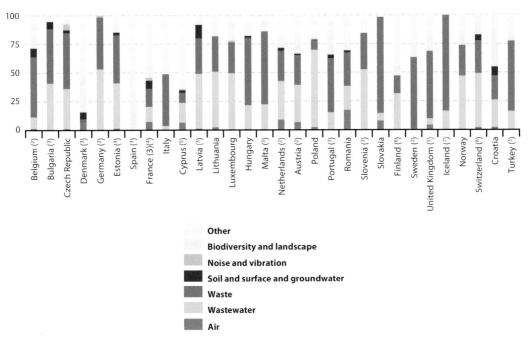

Other

Biodiversity and landscape

Noise and vibration

Soil and surface and groundwater

Waste

Wastewater

Air

(¹) Ireland and Greece, not available.
(²) 2007.
(³) 2008.
(⁴) Estimates.
(⁵) 2004.
(⁶) 2006.
(⁷) 2002.
(⁸) 2003.

Source: Eurostat (online data codes: env_ac_exp1 and env_ac_exp1r2)

Figure 11.7.7: Specialised producers of environmental protection services' environmental protection expenditure, 2009 (¹)
(% of GDP)

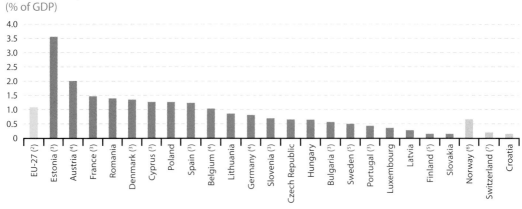

(¹) Ireland, Greece, Italy, Malta, the Netherlands and the United Kingdom, not available.
(²) Estimate.
(³) 2008.
(⁴) 2007.
(⁵) 2006.
(⁶) 2005.
(⁷) 2003.
Source: Eurostat (online data codes: env_ac_exp1, env_ac_exp1r2 and nama_gdp_c)

Figure 11.7.8: Breakdown of specialised producers of environmental protection services' environmental protection expenditure by environmental domain, 2009 (¹)
(% of total)

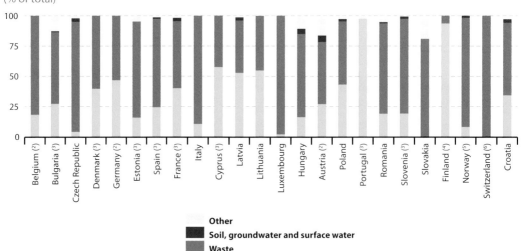

Other
Soil, groundwater and surface water
Waste
Wastewater

(¹) Greece, Ireland, Malta, the Netherlands, Sweden and the United Kingdom, not available.
(²) 2007.
(³) 2008.
(⁴) 2006.
(⁵) 2005.
(⁶) 2003.
Source: Eurostat (online data codes: env_ac_exp1 and env_ac_exp1r2)

Figure 11.7.9: Industrial (excluding recycling) environmental protection expenditure, 2009 ([1])
(% of GDP)

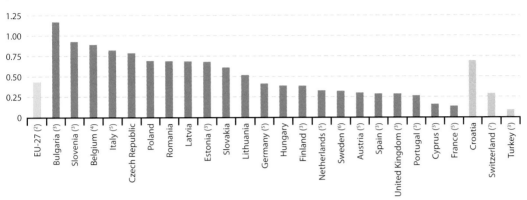

([1]) Denmark, Ireland, Greece, Luxembourg and Malta, not available.
([2]) Estimate.
([3]) 2008.
([4]) 2002.
([5]) 2007.
([6]) 2006.
([7]) 2003.

Source: Eurostat (online data codes: env_ac_exp1, env_ac_exp1r2 and nama_gdp_c)

Figure 11.7.10: Breakdown of industrial (excluding recycling) environmental protection expenditure by subsector, 2009 ([1])
(% of total)

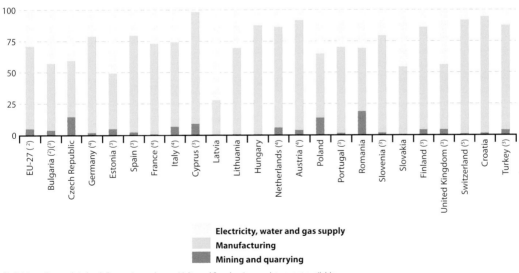

Electricity, water and gas supply
Manufacturing
Mining and quarrying

([1]) Belgium, Denmark, Ireland, Greece, Luxembourg, Malta and Sweden, incomplete or not available.
([2]) Estimates.
([3]) 2008.
([4]) 2007.
([5]) 2003.

Source: Eurostat (online data codes: env_ac_exp1 and env_ac_exp1r2)

Figure 11.7.11: Breakdown of industrial (excluding recycling) environmental protection expenditure, 2009 (¹)
(% of total)

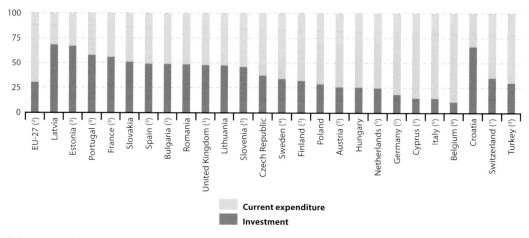

(¹) Denmark, Ireland, Greece and Malta, incomplete or not available.
(²) Estimates.
(³) 2008.
(⁴) 2006.
(⁵) 2007.
(⁶) 2002.
(⁷) 2003.

Source: Eurostat (online data codes: env_ac_exp1 and env_ac_exp1r2)

Figure 11.7.12: Breakdown of industrial (excluding recycling) environmental protection expenditure by environmental domain, 2009 (¹)
(% of total)

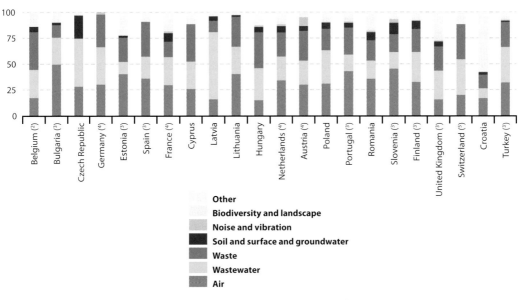

(¹) Denmark, Ireland, Greece, Italy, Luxembourg, Malta, Slovakia and Sweden, incomplete or not available.
(²) 2002.
(³) 2008.
(⁴) 2007.
(⁵) 2003.

Source: Eurostat (online data codes: env_ac_exp1 and env_ac_exp1r2)

11.8 Environmental taxes

This subchapter concerns environmentally related taxes (hereafter referred to as environmental taxes); these are taxes levied on products and activities with a proven negative impact on the environment. Environmental taxes are distinguished by four different types of tax relating to: energy, transport, pollution and resources; note that value added tax (VAT) is excluded from the definition of environmental taxes.

The subchapter examines trends in environmental taxes over the period 1999-2009 for these four categories of taxes. Its focus is on economic activities (industries and households) that pay these taxes, in order to determine who bears the biggest share of the environmental tax burden. These taxes may be viewed as a tool for implementing the 'polluter

pays' principle, since they allow environmental externalities to be taken into account. Through environmental taxes, consumers and producers may be motivated to use natural resources more responsibly and to limit or avoid environmental pollution.

Main statistical findings

Environmental taxes in the EU

Table 11.8.1 shows that the total revenue from environmental taxes in the EU-27 in 2009 was equal to EUR 286 600 million; this figure equated to 2.4 % of GDP and to 6.3 % of the total revenues derived from taxes and social contributions.

As can be seen in Figure 11.8.1, environmental tax revenue in the EU-27 increased during the period between 1999 and 2007, before the effects of the financial and economic crisis were felt, with a reduction in economic activity leading to falling revenues in 2008 and 2009. The decrease in environmental tax revenues during the last two years reversed some of the increase in revenues recorded between 1999 and 2007, although it did not fully offset it; as a result, environmental tax revenue in the EU-27 stood some EUR 42 200 million higher in 2009 than it had done in 1999 (equivalent to an overall increase of 17.3 %).

While environmental tax revenues increased in value terms between 1997 and 2007 within the EU-27, the size of these taxes relative to GDP and the share of total revenue from all taxes and social contributions fell from 2003 to 2008; this development stopped in 2009, when the relative importance of environmental taxes increased. The decline in the relative importance of environmental tax revenue during the period from 2003 to 2008 resulted from environmental tax revenues rising at a slower pace than overall economic growth; the significant increase in oil prices may have contributed to this development. While the total revenue from environmental taxes fell in 2008 and again in 2009, the losses were at a slower pace in 2009 than the reduction in general economic activity, resulting in an increase in the relative importance of environmental taxes (see Figure 11.8.2).

The level of environmental taxation varies across European countries. Comparisons should be made with caution: for instance, low revenues from environmental taxes could either be due to relatively low environmental tax rates, or could result from higher tax rates that have had the effect of changing behavioural patterns among producers and consumers. Higher levels of environmental tax revenue could be linked to individuals or businesses purchasing taxed products in countries where they are not resident if the tax rates are lower there than in the domestic market (for example, crossing a border to purchase petrol or diesel in a neighbouring country).

Map 11.8.1 shows an overall picture of relative tax revenues (both in relation to GDP and in relation

to total taxes and social contributions). Whether in relation to GDP or in relation to total taxes and social contributions, the relative importance of environmental tax revenues was high in Denmark, the Netherlands, Slovenia, Malta and Bulgaria, as these five Member States headed the rankings for both measures. At the other end of the scale, Spain and Belgium both recorded relatively low levels of environmental tax revenue (in relation to both GDP and total taxes and social contributions).

Environmental taxes by type

Energy taxes (which include taxes on transport fuels) represented, by far, the highest share of overall environmental tax revenue – accounting for 74.0 % of the EU-27 total in 2009 (see Figure 11.8.3). These taxes were particularly important in Lithuania, the Czech Republic and Luxembourg, where they accounted for upwards of 90 % of the total revenues from environmental taxes (see Figure 11.8.4). In contrast, energy taxes represented less than 60 % of total revenues from environmental taxes in Cyprus and the Netherlands, and less than 50 % in Denmark and Malta (as well as Norway).

Transport taxes made the second most important contribution to total revenues from environmental taxes, some 21.8 % of the EU-27 total in 2009. However, their relative significance was considerably higher in Malta, Cyprus, Greece and Ireland (as well as Norway), ranging between 48.4 % and 38.0 % of the environmental tax total.

Pollution/resource taxes represented a relatively small share (4.2 %) of total environmental tax revenues in the EU-27 in 2009; this pattern was repeated across most of the EU Member States, as only Estonia, the Netherlands and Denmark (as well as Iceland) reported that in excess of 10 % of their total environmental tax revenue was raised from taxes on pollution and resources; some countries did not raise any revenue from this type of tax (Greece, Luxembourg and Cyprus).

Environmental taxes by economic activity

In 2008, across those EU Member States for which data are available (see Figure 11.8.5), households paid an average of just over half (50.9 %) of the energy tax revenues collected by governments, while 46.9 % of the total was paid by enterprises and 1.4 % by non-residents; Luxembourg stood out, insofar as 44.6 % of its energy tax revenues were paid by non-residents.

Among those economic activities and Member States covered in Figure 11.8.5, the average contribution to total energy revenues from mining, manufacturing, electricity supply and construction was somewhat higher (16.1 % of the total) than that from the transport, storage and communication sector (15.5 %) or the other services sector (13.0 %). Half of the Member States for which data are available reported that the biggest contribution to energy tax revenues among enterprises came from the transport, storage and communication sector. In Denmark, Sweden and the Netherlands, it was the other services sector which paid the highest share of energy taxes among the different economic activities considered in Figure 11.8.5, while mining, manufacturing, electricity supply and construction enterprises paid the highest share of energy taxes in the Czech Republic, Italy, Germany and Lithuania.

In 2008, on average 69.4 % of the transport tax revenues collected by governments in those EU Member States for which data are available (see Figure 11.8.6) were paid by households, 20.3 % by businesses (agriculture, fishing, mining, manufacturing, electricity supply and construction, and all services), 10.2 % were non-allocated, and 0.1 % were paid by non-residents. Households accounted for more than half of total transport tax revenues in most of the Member States for which data are available, although their share of the total fell to 48.8 % in Italy and only 0.2 % in the Czech Republic. Services (other than transport, storage and communication) were often the leading contributor to transport taxes among businesses.

An analysis of pollution taxes shows that in 2008 most of the pollution tax revenues collected by governments were paid by businesses. On average for those Member States for which data are available (see Figure 11.8.7), businesses contributed 73.0 % of the total revenue stream. Households contributed almost one quarter (23.1 %) of the total revenues from pollution taxes, while the remaining 3.9 %

was not allocated. Among businesses, the highest share of pollution taxes was paid by services (other than transport, storage and communication) and by mining, manufacturing, electricity supply and construction; these two activity groupings contributed 32.0 % and 31.5 % of the total revenue.

Among the eight Member States for which data are available for resource taxes by economic activity, by far the highest receipts were collected in Denmark – some 69.3 % of the total for the eight Member States (see Figure 11.8.8). Mining, manufacturing, electricity supply and construction enterprises paid the highest share of resource taxes in five of the eight Member States for which data are available, accounting for all of the resource taxes collected in Belgium (2007), Sweden and the United Kingdom, and for upwards of 90 % of the resource taxes collected in Denmark and Lithuania in 2008. In the Netherlands and Austria the majority of resource taxes were paid by households (59.6 % and 56.1 % respectively), while in the Czech Republic resource taxes were collected in almost equal amounts from the transport, storage and communication sector, other services and households.

Data sources and availability

The European Commission's Directorate-General for Taxation and Customs Union, using Table 9 from the ESA 95 transmission programme, gathers data on environmental taxes for four categories of environmental taxes (energy, transport, pollution and resources). Eurostat validates and publishes these data.

Eurostat collects data on environmental taxes at a more detailed level, by economic activity; this data is also published. The annual collection of data concerning environmental taxes is currently based on a gentlemen's agreement. A Eurostat publication titled, 'Environmental taxes – a statistical guide' constitutes the methodological reference base for completing the questionnaire on environmental taxes.

Among the four main categories of environmental taxes, energy taxes include taxes on energy products used for both transport (for example, petrol and diesel) and stationary purposes (for example, fuel oil, natural gas, coal and electricity); in addition, carbon dioxide taxes are included under energy taxes rather than under pollution taxes. Transport taxes include taxes relating to the ownership and use of motor vehicles; these taxes may be one-off purchase taxes (for example, related to the engine size or the emissions of a particular vehicle) or recurrent taxes (such as an annual road tax). Pollution taxes include taxes for: emissions into the air (except for carbon dioxide taxes) and water; the management of waste; and noise. Taxes on resources cover taxes on the extraction of raw materials (with the exception of oil and gas). Pollution and resource taxes are generally quite small and so they are often grouped together for the purpose of analysis.

Data relating to environmental taxes provide information on the revenue stream from such taxes, as well as providing a relative measure of the importance of these taxes through the calculation of ratios relative to gross domestic product (GDP) or the total revenue from all taxes and social contributions. In the first case, the comparison helps to provide an understanding of the tax burden and identifies those activities which 'use up' the environment. In the second case, the comparison helps assess whether there is a potential shift towards 'green' taxes, in other words, shifting the tax burden from other tax bases (for example on labour income) to the most polluting behaviours.

Environmental tax revenue can also be allocated according to the different economic activities paying the tax(es). Eurostat collects data on environmental taxes using a breakdown by economic activity (using the NACE Rev. 1.1 classification supplemented by information for households, non-residents and a category not allocated).

Increasing revenues from environmental taxes should be interpreted with caution. The increases may be caused by the introduction of new taxes or an increase in tax rates, or alternatively may be linked to an increase in the tax base.

Satellite accounts are a set of accounts that can be used to supplement national accounts; they exist/are in the process of being developed in a range of areas (for example, health accounts, tourism accounts or environmental accounts). An important feature of satellite accounts is that the basic concepts and classifications of the national accounts framework are retained (ESA 95, paragraph 1.20). Regulation (691/2011) on European environmental economic accounts was adopted on 6 July 2011; this will make the collection and delivery of data obligatory from 2013. Regulation 691/2011 provides a framework for the development of various types of environmental accounts (also referred to as modules). Environmentally related taxes by economic activity are one of the three modules included in the Regulation (Annex II). The statistics on environmentally related taxes by economic activity, as stipulated in the Regulation, will record and present data from the perspective of the entities paying the taxes in a way that is fully compatible with the data reported under ESA 95.

Context

The environment is affected by existing production and consumption patterns. To counter potential environmental problems in the coming years, some commentators argue that behavioural changes will be needed – some of which may involve substantial economic costs. Environmental policy in the EU is designed to assist the Member States to attain environmental and sustainable development goals. Policymakers use incentive-based tools for targeted outcomes with the intention that these will encourage low-cost environmental solutions, which correct for externalities and/or raise revenues for specific purposes.

Economic instruments for pollution control and natural resource management are thus an increasingly important part of environmental policy in the EU Member States. The range of instruments that are available includes, among others, environmental taxes, fees and charges, tradable permits, deposit-refund systems and subsidies. Environmental taxes have been increasingly used to influence behaviour, since these taxes generate revenue that can potentially be used to promote further environmental protection. Indeed, the EU has increasingly favoured these instruments because they provide a flexible and cost-effective means for reinforcing the polluter-pays

principle and for reaching environmental policy objectives. The use of economic tools for the benefit of the environment has been promoted in the 6th Environment Action Programme (EAP), the renewed EU sustainable development strategy, and the Europe 2020 strategy.

Table 11.8.1: Total environmental tax revenue by type of tax, EU-27, 2009

	(EUR million)	(% of total environmental taxes)	(% of GDP)	(% of total revenues from taxes and social contributions)
Total environmental taxes	286 603	100.0	2.43	6.32
Energy taxes	212 189	74.0	1.80	4.68
Pollution/resources taxes	11 915	4.2	0.10	0.26
Transport taxes	62 499	21.8	0.53	1.38

Source: Eurostat (online data code: env_ac_tax)

Figure 11.8.1: Total environmental tax revenue, EU-27, 1999-2009 (EUR 1 000 million)

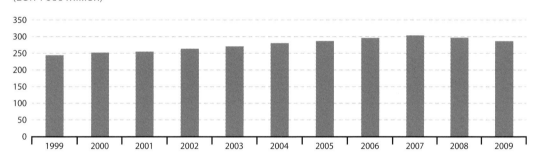

Source: Eurostat (online data code: env_ac_tax)

Figure 11.8.2: Total environmental tax revenue, EU-27, 1999-2009 (%)

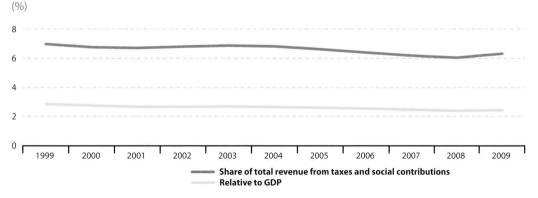

━━━ Share of total revenue from taxes and social contributions
━━━ Relative to GDP

Source: Eurostat (online data code: env_ac_tax)

Map 11.8.1: Environmental taxes as % of GDP and as % of total taxes and social contributions, 2009

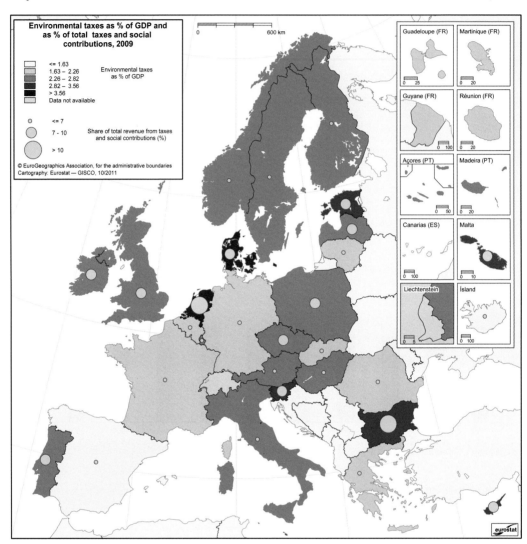

Source: Eurostat (online data code: env_ac_tax)

Figure 11.8.3: Environmental taxes by tax category, EU-27, 2009
(% of total)

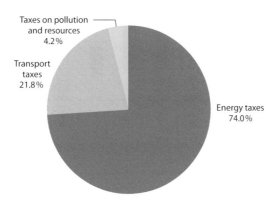

Taxes on pollution
and resources
4.2%

Transport
taxes
21.8%

Energy taxes
74.0%

Source: Eurostat (online data code: env_ac_tax)

Figure 11.8.4: Environmental taxes by tax category, 2009
(% of total environmental taxes)

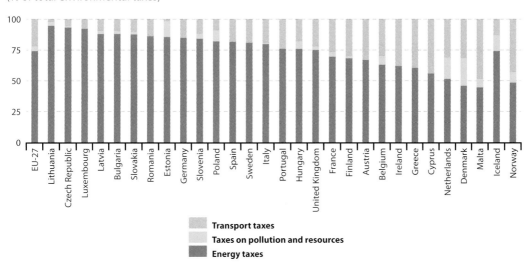

Transport taxes

Taxes on pollution and resources

Energy taxes

Source: Eurostat (online data code: env_ac_tax)

Figure 11.8.5: Energy taxes by economic activity, 2008 (¹)
(% of energy tax revenue) based on data in EUR million

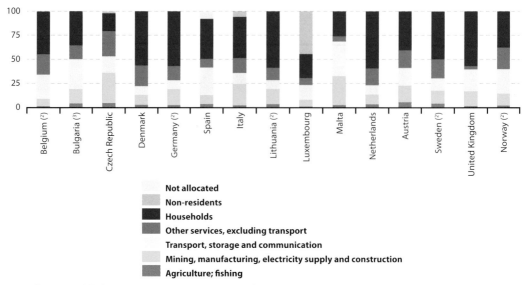

Not allocated
Non-residents
Households
Other services, excluding transport
Transport, storage and communication
Mining, manufacturing, electricity supply and construction
Agriculture; fishing

(¹) No information available for those Member States that are not shown. (²) 2007. (³) 2005.

Source: Eurostat (online data code: env_ac_taxind)

Figure 11.8.6: Transport taxes by economic activity, 2008 (¹)
(% of transport tax revenue) based on data in EUR million

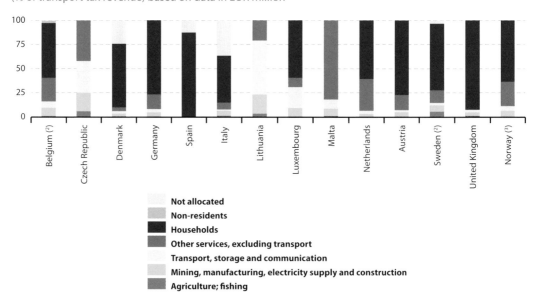

Not allocated
Non-residents
Households
Other services, excluding transport
Transport, storage and communication
Mining, manufacturing, electricity supply and construction
Agriculture; fishing

(¹) No information available for those Member States that are not shown. (²) 2007. (³) 2006.

Source: Eurostat (online data code: env_ac_taxind)

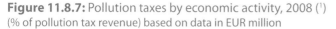

Figure 11.8.7: Pollution taxes by economic activity, 2008 (¹)
(% of pollution tax revenue) based on data in EUR million

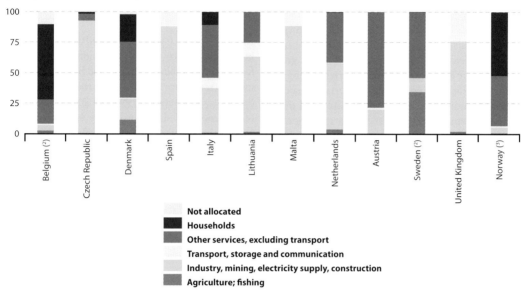

- Not allocated
- Households
- Other services, excluding transport
- Transport, storage and communication
- Industry, mining, electricity supply, construction
- Agriculture; fishing

(¹) No information available for those Member States that are not shown.
(²) 2007.
(³) 2006.

Source: Eurostat (online data code: env_ac_taxind)

Figure 11.8.8: Resource taxes by economic activity, 2008 (¹)
(% of resource tax revenue) based on data in EUR million

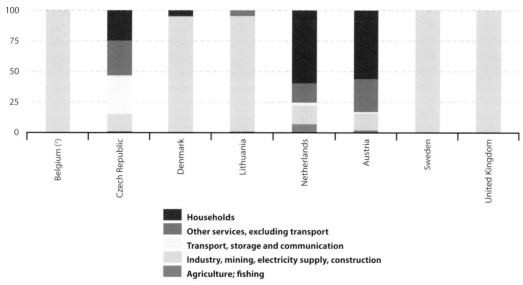

- Households
- Other services, excluding transport
- Transport, storage and communication
- Industry, mining, electricity supply, construction
- Agriculture; fishing

(¹) No information available for those Member States that are not shown.
(²) 2007.

Source: Eurostat (online data code: env_ac_taxind)

11.9 Biodiversity

Biodiversity – a contraction of biological diversity – encompasses the number, variety and variability of living organisms, including mankind. Preventing a loss of biodiversity is important for mankind, given that humans depend on the natural richness of the planet for the food, energy, raw materials, clean air and clean water that make life possible and drive economies and societies. As such, a reduction or loss of biodiversity may not only undermine the natural environment but also economic and social goals. The challenges associated with preserving biodiversity have made this topic an international issue. This subchapter presents some main indicators for biodiversity, such as the number of protected areas and bird populations, and examines the development of these indicators in the European Union (EU).

Main statistical findings

Habitats

Areas protected for the preservation of biodiversity are proposed by the Member States under the EU's Habitats Directive; they are indicated as a percentage of the total area of each country. About 14 % of the EU-27's territory was proposed for protection under the Habitats Directive as of 2010. Additional areas were proposed for protection under the Birds Directive. Since there is some overlap between the two types of protected areas, the joint area for both Directives was estimated to amount to approximately 18 % of the EU-27's terrestrial area in 2010. Figures for the Member States show that areas protected under the Habitats Directive range between 31 % of the total area of Slovenia and 30 % of that in Bulgaria to less than 10 % of the total area of France, the Netherlands, Denmark or the United Kingdom. In general, these protected areas adequately cover the biogeographical regions present in the Member States, with an EU-27 average of 89 % of sufficiently covered species and habitats in 2010; using this measure, only Cyprus reported less than 50 % sufficiency (see Figure 11.9.1).

Birds

Since 1990 there has been a general downward trend in the abundance of both common farmland and forest species of birds, as measured by common bird indices (see Figure 11.9.2). Part of the relatively steep decline (– 20 % between 1990 and 2009) in numbers of common farmland birds may be attributed to changes in land use and agricultural practices. There was a more rapid reduction in numbers of common forest birds between 1990 and 2000 across the EU (– 21 % between 1990 and 2000). However, recent years have seen a recovery in forest bird numbers, with the index rising from a relative low of 79 to reach 87 by 2009. The index of all common bird species has been relatively stable since 1995, some 10 % below its 1990 level, and stood at 90 in 2009.

Data sources and availability

Habitats

Annual data are available on areas protected under the Habitats Directive. The data are presented as the percentage of compliance with the obligation to protect habitats and species that are typical for the wider biogeographical regions of the EU. The indicator is based on the extent of the area proposed by countries for the protection of natural and semi-natural habitats, wild fauna and flora according to annexes I and II of the Habitats Directive. The index of sufficiency measures the extent to which sites of Community importance proposed by the Member States adequately cover the species and habitats listed in those annexes, in proportion to the share of the biogeographical region that falls within the territory of the country.

Birds

Birds are considered good proxies for measuring the diversity and integrity of ecosystems as they tend to be near the top of the food chain, have large ranges and the ability to move elsewhere when their environment becomes unsuitable; they are therefore responsive to changes in their habitats and ecosystems. The bird indicators presented in this subchapter measure trends of bird populations.

The indicators are designed to capture the overall, average changes in population levels of common birds to reflect the health and functioning of the ecosystems they inhabit. The population index of common birds is an aggregated index (with base year 1990 or the first year the Member State entered the scheme) of population trend estimates for a selected group of common bird species. Indices are calculated for each species independently and are then combined to create a multi-species EU indicator by averaging the indices with an equal weight using a geometric average. Indices rather than bird abundance are averaged in order to give each species an equal weight in the resulting indicator. The EU index is based on trend data from 20 Member States (Greece, Cyprus, Lithuania, Luxembourg, Malta, Romania and Slovenia, not available), derived from annually operated national breeding bird surveys collated by the Pan-European Common Bird Monitoring Scheme (PECBMS); these data are considered as a good proxy for the whole of the EU-27.

Three different indices are presented:

• common farmland birds (36 species);
• common forest birds (33 species);
• all common birds (145 species).

For the first two categories, the bird species have a high dependence on agricultural or on forest habitats in the nesting season and for feeding. Both groups comprise both year-round residents and migratory species. The aggregated index comprises farmland and forest species together with other common species that are generalists, meaning that they occur in many different habitats or are particularly adapted to life in cities.

Context

People depend on natural resources and the variety of species found on the planet for tangible goods that make life possible and drive economic development, such as food, energy, wood, raw materials, clean air and water. Many aspects of the natural environment are public goods, in other words they have no market value or price. As such, the loss of biodiversity can often go undetected by economic systems. However, the natural environment also provides a range of intangibles, such as the aesthetic pleasure derived from viewing landscapes and wildlife, or recreational opportunities. In order to protect this legacy for future generations, the EU seeks to promote policies in a range of areas to ensure that biodiversity is protected through the sustainable development of, among others, agriculture, rural and urban landscapes, energy provision and transport.

Biodiversity strategy is based on the implementation of two landmark Directives, the Habitats Directive (92/43/EEC) of 21 May 1992 and the Birds Directive (79/409/EEC) of 2 April 1979. Implementation of these Directives has involved the establishment of a coherent European ecological network of sites under the title Natura 2000. The EU wants to expand Natura 2000, which currently counts around 26 000 sites and a land area of more than 750 000 km² (and an area of almost 930 000 km² including marine sites) where plant and animal species and their habitats are protected. Establishing the Natura 2000 network may be seen as the first pillar of action relating to the conservation of natural habitats. However, EU legislation also foresees measures to establish a second pillar through strict protection regimes for certain animal species (for example, the Arctic fox and the Iberian lynx, both of which are under serious threat of extinction).

In 1998, the EU adopted a biodiversity strategy. Four action plans covering the conservation of natural resources, agriculture, fisheries, and economic and development cooperation were subsequently agreed as part of this strategy in 2001. The European Commission released a Communication ((2006) 216) on 'halting the loss of biodiversity by 2010 – and beyond'; this underlined the importance of biodiversity protection as a pre-requisite for sustainable development and set out an action plan which addressed the challenge of integrating biodiversity concerns into other policy areas.

In May 2011 the European Commission adopted the Communication 'Our life insurance, our natural capital: an EU biodiversity strategy to 2020'

(COM(2011) 244); this aims to halt the loss of bio-diversity and ecosystem services in the EU by 2020. There are six main targets and 20 actions to help reach this goal. Biodiversity loss is seen as an enormous challenge in the EU, with around one in four species currently threatened with extinction and 88 % of fish stocks over-exploited or significantly depleted. The six targets cover:

- full implementation of EU nature legislation to protect biodiversity;
- better protection for ecosystems and more use of green infrastructure;
- more sustainable agriculture and forestry;
- better management of fish stocks;
- tighter controls on invasive alien species;
- a bigger EU contribution to averting global bio-diversity loss.

The strategy is in line with two commitments made in March 2010:

- the 2020 headline target – halting the loss of biodiversity and the degradation of ecosystem

services in the EU by 2020, and restoring them insofar as feasible, while stepping up the EU contribution to averting global biodiversity loss;
- the 2050 vision – which foresees that by 2050, the EU's biodiversity and the ecosystem services it provides – its natural capital – are protected, valued and appropriately restored for biodiversity's intrinsic value, and for their essential contribution to human well-being and economic prosperity, and so that catastrophic changes caused by the loss of biodiversity are avoided.

The strategy is also in line with global commitments made in Nagoya in October 2010, in the context of the Convention on Biological Diversity, where world leaders adopted a package of measures to address global biodiversity loss over the coming decade.

Figure 11.9.1: Protected areas for biodiversity – sufficiency of sites, 2010
(%)

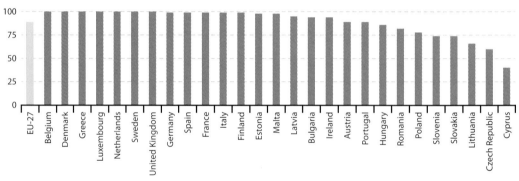

Source: EEA/European topic centre on biodiversity, Eurostat (online data code: env_bio1)

Figure 11.9.2: Common bird indices, EU, 1990-2009 ([1])
(aggregated index of population estimates of selected groups of breeding bird species, 1990 = 100)

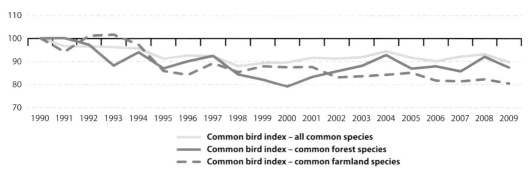

Common bird index – all common species
Common bird index – common forest species
Common bird index – common farmland species

([1]) Estimates; 'all common species' covers information on 145 different bird species; 'common farmland species' covers 36 bird species; 'common forest species' covers 33 bird species.

Source: EBCC/RSPB/BirdLife/Statistics Netherlands, Eurostat (online data code: env_bio2)

Energy

Introduction

A competitive, reliable and sustainable energy sector is essential for all advanced economies. The energy sector has been under the spotlight in recent years due to a number of issues that have pushed energy to the top of national and European Union (EU) political agendas, these include:

- the volatility of oil prices;
- interruptions to energy supplies from non-member countries;
- blackouts aggravated by inefficient connections between national electricity networks;
- the difficulties of market access for suppliers in relation to gas and electricity markets;
- increased attention to anthropogenic (human-induced) effects on climate change, in particular, increased greenhouse gas emissions.

The use of renewable energy sources is seen as a key element of the EU's energy policy and should help to: reduce dependence on fuel from non-member countries; reduce emissions from carbon-based energy sources, and; decouple energy costs from oil prices. Another key aspect of the EU's energy policy is to constrain consumption by promoting energy efficiency, both within the energy sector itself and among end-users. Indeed, the EU is putting in place an ambitious energy policy – covering a broad range of energy sources from fossil fuels (oil, gas and coal) to nuclear energy and renewables (solar, wind, biomass, geothermal, hydroelectric and tidal). This policy is designed to bring about a new industrial revolution that will result in a low-energy economy, whilst making the energy consumed more secure, competitive and sustainable, with the goal of the EU becoming a world leader in renewable energy and low-carbon technologies.

In January 2007, the European Commission adopted a Communication (COM(2007) 1) proposing a new energy policy for Europe, with the goal of combating climate change and boosting the EU's energy security and competitiveness through the development of a more sustainable and low-carbon economy. Based on the European Commission's proposal, the European Council endorsed the following targets in March 2007, namely, to:

- reduce greenhouse gas emissions by at least 20 % (compared with 1990 levels) by 2020;
- improve energy efficiency by 20 % by 2020;
- increase the share of renewable energy in final energy consumption to 20 % by 2020;
- increase the share of renewable energy sources in the fuel used by the transport sector to 10 % by 2020.

Europe 2020

At the European Council meeting of 26 March 2010, EU leaders set out their plans for a Europe 2020 strategy for smart, sustainable and inclusive growth. As part of the sustainable growth priority one of the flagship initiatives concerns a resource-efficient Europe. A number of key proposals have been adopted that are specific to energy.

In November 2010 the initiative 'Energy 2020 a strategy for competitive, sustainable and secure energy' (COM(2010) 639 final) was adopted by the European Commission. This strategy defines energy priorities for a period of ten years and proposes actions to be taken in order to tackle the challenges of saving energy, achieving a market with competitive prices and secure supplies, boosting technological leadership, and effectively negotiating with international partners.

The same month the European Commission adopted the initiative 'Energy infrastructure priorities for 2020 and beyond – a blueprint for an integrated European energy network' (COM(2010) 677 final). This defines EU priority corridors for the transport of electricity, gas and oil.

Energy efficiency is at the heart of the transition to a resource efficient economy and is considered to be one of the most cost effective ways to enhance security of energy supply and to reduce emissions of greenhouse gases and other pollutants. While substantial steps have been taken towards the target for 2020 of saving 20 % of primary energy consumption compared with projections – notably in the appliances and buildings markets – European Commission estimates indicated that the EU was on course to achieve only half of the 20 % objective. As a consequence the European Commission developed the 'Energy efficiency plan 2011' (COM(2011) 109 final) which was adopted in March 2011 – see the subchapter on the consumption of energy; the intention is to pursue this plan in conjunction with other policy actions under the Europe 2020 flagship initiative for a resource efficient Europe, including the 'Roadmap for moving to a competitive low carbon economy by 2050' (COM(2011) 112 final) – see the introduction for environment.

Energy statistics

In order to meet the increasing requirements of policymakers for energy monitoring, the legislation relating to energy statistics has in recent years undergone a period of renewal. The new legal basis is Commission Regulation (EU) 844/2010 on energy statistics. The data collection exercise covers all EU Member States, Iceland, Norway, Switzerland, Croatia, the former Yugoslav Republic of Macedonia and Turkey. Time series for energy statistics go back to 1985 for some countries, but are more generally available from 1990 onwards; monthly data are also available for certain indicators.

12.1 Energy production and imports

The dependency of the European Union (EU) on energy imports, particularly of oil and more recently of gas, forms the backdrop for policy concerns relating to the security of energy supplies. This subchapter looks at the production of primary energy in the EU and, as a result of the shortfall between production and consumption, the EU's increasing dependency on energy imports from non-member countries. Indeed, more than half (53.9 %) of the EU's gross inland energy consumption in 2009 came from imported sources.

Main statistical findings

Primary production

Production of primary energy in the EU-27 totalled 812.2 million tonnes of oil equivalent (toe) in 2009. This continued the generally downward trend of EU-27 production, as supplies of raw materials become exhausted and/or producers considered the exploitation of limited resources uneconomical. Production was dominated by the United Kingdom with a 19.2 % share of the EU-27 total, although this marked a considerable reduction when compared with a decade earlier (29.3 % of the EU-27 total in 1999). The largest producers of primary energy in 2009 were the United Kingdom, France and Germany, followed by Poland and the Netherlands (see

Table 12.1.1). The United Kingdom experienced by far the largest reduction in its output of primary energy, with production falling by 122.2 million toe over the period from 1999 to 2009; the next largest declines were recorded in Poland (16.2 million toe) and Germany (9.7 million toe). The largest expansions in the production of primary energy during the ten years to 2009 were in the Netherlands (3.7 million toe), France (2.6 million toe) and the Czech Republic (2.4 million toe).

Primary energy production in the EU-27 in 2009 was spread across a range of different energy sources, the most important of which was nuclear energy (28.4 % of the total); the significance of nuclear fuel was particularly high in Belgium, France, Lithuania and Slovakia – where it accounted for more than half of the national production of primary energy. Around one fifth of the EU-27's total production of primary energy was accounted for by solid fuels (20.4 %, largely coal), by natural gas (18.8 %) and by renewable energy sources (18.3 %), while crude oil (12.8 %) made up the remainder of the total (see Figure 12.1.1).

The growth of primary production from renewable energy sources exceeded that of all the other energy types, with particularly strong growth since 2002 (see Figure 12.1.2). Indeed, there appears to be something of a watershed since this date, as the production of renewables accelerated, rising by 52.4 % between 2002 and 2009 and an overall 60.2 % between 1999 and 2009. In contrast, the production levels for the other primary sources of energy generally fell between 1999 and 2009. The largest reductions in the production of primary energy were recorded for crude oil (– 42.3 %), solid fuels (– 26.1 %) and natural gas (– 24.6 %), with a more modest fall of 5.2 % for nuclear energy.

Imports

The downturn in the primary production of hard coal, lignite, crude oil, natural gas and more recently nuclear energy has led to a situation where the EU is increasingly reliant on primary energy imports in order to satisfy demand. The EU-27's imports of primary energy exceeded exports by some 943.6 million toe in 2009. The largest net importers of primary energy were generally the most populous Member States, with the exception of the United Kingdom and Poland (where indigenous reserves of oil/natural gas and coal remain). Since 2004 the only net exporter of primary energy among the EU Member States has been Denmark (see Table 12.1.2).

The origin of EU-27 energy imports has changed rapidly in recent years, as Russia has maintained its position as the main supplier of crude oil and natural gas and emerged as the leading supplier of hard coal (see Table 12.1.3). In 2009, some 33.1 % of the EU-27's imports of crude oil were from Russia; this was a return to the shares that it had provided in 2006 and 2007, having fallen to 31.4 % in 2008. Russia became the principal supplier of hard coal in 2006, overtaking South Africa, having overtaken Australia in 2004 and Colombia in 2002; Russia's share of EU-27 hard coal imports rose from 11.5 % in 2001 to 30.2 % by 2009, well ahead of the next highest share recorded by Colombia (17.6 %). In contrast, Russia's share of EU-27 imports of natural gas declined from 47.7 % to 34.2 % between 2001 and 2009, while Norway's share rose from 22.8 % to 30.7 %.

The security of the EU's primary energy supplies may be threatened if a high proportion of imports are concentrated among relatively few partners. Close to four fifths (79.1 %) of the EU-27's imports

of natural gas in 2009 came from Russia, Norway or Algeria. A similar analysis shows that 57.3 % of EU-27 crude oil imports came from Russia, Norway and Libya, while 77.5 % of hard coal imports were from Russia, Colombia, South Africa and the United States. Although their import volumes remain relatively small, there was some evidence of new partner countries emerging between 2001 and 2009. This was notably the case for hard coal imports from Indonesia, crude oil imports from Kazakhstan and Azerbaijan, or natural gas imports from Qatar, Libya, and Trinidad and Tobago.

EU-27 dependency on energy imports increased from less than 40 % of gross energy consumption in the 1980s to 45.1 % in 1999 and then to 53.9 % by 2009 (see Table 12.1.4). The highest energy dependency rates were recorded for crude oil (84.1 %) and for natural gas (64.2 %). The dependency on non-member countries for supplies of solid fuels and natural gas grew at a faster pace in the last decade than the dependency on crude oil (which was already at a high level). Since 2004, the EU-27's net imports of energy have been greater than its primary production; in other words, more than half of the EU-27's gross inland energy consumption was supplied by net imports.

As it was a net exporter, Denmark was the only EU-27 Member State in 2009 with a negative dependency rate (see Figure 12.1.3). Among the other Member States, the lowest dependency rates were recorded by Romania, Estonia, the United Kingdom and the Czech Republic (the only other countries to report dependency rates below 30 %); meanwhile, Malta, Luxembourg and Cyprus were almost entirely dependent on primary energy imports.

Data sources and availability

Energy commodities extracted or captured directly from natural resources are called primary energy sources, while energy commodities which are produced from primary energy sources in transformation plants are called derived products. Primary energy production covers the national production of primary energy sources and takes place when natural resources are exploited, for example, in coal mines, crude oil fields, hydropower plants, or in the fabrication of biofuels. Whenever consumption exceeds primary production, the shortfall needs to be accounted for by imports of primary or derived products.

The heat produced in a reactor as a result of nuclear fission is regarded as primary production of nuclear heat, alternatively referred to as, nuclear energy. It is calculated either on the basis of the actual heat produced or on the basis of reported gross electricity generation and the thermal efficiency of the nuclear plant. Primary production of coal and lignite consists of quantities of fuels extracted or produced, calculated after any operation for the removal of inert matter.

Transformation of energy from one form to another, such as electricity or heat generation from thermal power plants, or coke production from coke ovens is not considered as primary production.

Net imports are calculated as the quantity of imports minus the equivalent quantity of exports. Imports represent all entries into the national territory excluding transit quantities (notably via gas and oil pipelines); exports similarly cover all quantities exported from the national territory.

Context

More than half of the EU-27's energy comes from countries outside the EU – and this proportion is rising. Much of this energy comes from Russia, whose disputes with transit countries have threatened to disrupt supplies in recent years – for example, between 6 and 20 January 2009, gas flows from Russia via Ukraine were interrupted.

The European Commission adopted its second strategic energy review in November 2008. This addressed how the EU could reduce its dependency on imported energy, thereby improving its security of supply, as well as reducing its emissions of greenhouse gases. The review encouraged energy solidarity among Member States, proposed an action plan to secure sustainable energy supplies, and adopted a package of energy-efficiency proposals aimed at making energy savings in key areas, such as buildings and energy-using products.

In response to the Russian-Ukrainian gas crisis of January 2009, the legislative framework concerning the security of supplies was reviewed and in September 2009 the European Council adopted Directive 2009/119/EC imposing an obligation on Member States to maintain minimum stocks of crude oil and/or petroleum products. These measures for oil and gas markets were designed to ensure that all parties take effective action to prevent and mitigate the consequences of potential disruptions to supplies, while also creating mechanisms for Member States to work together to deal effectively with any major oil or gas disruptions which might arise; a coordination mechanism was set-up so that Member States can react uniformly and immediately in emergency cases.

A broad mix of energy sources and diversity in suppliers, transport routes and transport mechanisms may each play an important role in securing energy supplies. Building reliable partnerships with supplier, transit and consumer countries is seen as a way to reduce the risks associated with the EU's energy dependency and in September 2011 the European Commission adopted Communication COM(2011) 539 final titled 'The EU energy policy: engaging with partners beyond our borders'.

In November 2010, an initiative titled 'Energy 2020 a strategy for competitive, sustainable and secure energy' (COM(2010) 639 final) was adopted by the European Commission. This strategy defines the energy priorities for a period of ten years and sets the actions to be taken in order to tackle a variety of challenges, including achieving a market with competitive prices and secure supplies, boosting technological leadership, and effectively negotiating with international partners.

The same month the European Commission adopted an initiative titled 'Energy infrastructure priorities for 2020 and beyond – a blueprint for an integrated European energy network' (COM(2010) 677 final). This defines EU priority corridors for the transport of electricity, gas and oil. A toolbox is also proposed in order to facilitate a timely implementation of these priority infrastructures.

There are a number of on-going initiatives to develop gas pipelines between Europe and its eastern and southern neighbours. These include the Nord Stream (between Russia and the EU via the Baltic Sea) which was due to become operational in the autumn of 2011, the south stream (between Russia and the EU via the Black Sea) scheduled to be completed by 2015 and Nabucco (connecting the Caspian region and Middle East to the EU) scheduled to be operational by 2017.

Table 12.1.1: Energy production, 1999 and 2009 (million tonnes of oil equivalent)

	Total production of primary energy		Share of total production, 2009 (%)				
	1999	2009	Nuclear energy	Solid fuels	Natural gas	Crude oil	Renewable energy
EU-27	949.4	812.2	28.4	20.4	18.8	12.8	18.3
Euro area	447.9	448.4	39.8	14.6	17.1	3.3	23.4
Belgium	13.6	14.6	83.7	0.0	0.0	0.0	11.4
Bulgaria	9.1	9.7	40.8	47.0	0.1	0.3	11.6
Czech Republic	28.7	31.1	22.6	67.0	0.5	1.0	8.3
Denmark	23.8	23.9	0.0	0.0	31.5	55.4	11.5
Germany	137.2	127.5	27.3	35.9	8.7	3.6	21.7
Estonia	3.0	4.2	0.0	79.2	0.0	0.0	20.8
Ireland	2.5	1.5	0.0	38.2	20.8	0.0	40.2
Greece	9.5	10.1	0.0	81.1	0.1	0.8	17.9
Spain	30.5	29.6	46.0	12.3	0.0	0.4	40.2
France	125.8	128.5	82.3	0.0	0.6	1.0	15.2
Italy	29.4	27.3	0.0	0.2	24.0	19.0	54.0
Cyprus	0.0	0.1	0.0	0.0	0.0	0.0	91.5
Latvia	1.6	2.1	0.0	0.3	0.0	0.0	99.6
Lithuania	3.5	4.0	71.7	0.4	0.0	2.9	25.0
Luxembourg	0.1	0.1	0.0	0.0	0.0	0.0	75.5
Hungary	11.9	11.0	36.4	14.2	20.9	11.0	16.9
Malta	0.0	0.0	0.0	0.0	0.0	0.0	0.0
Netherlands	59.5	63.2	1.7	0.0	89.2	3.5	4.4
Austria	9.7	11.4	0.0	0.0	12.6	9.2	73.3
Poland	83.4	67.2	0.0	83.5	5.5	1.0	9.0
Portugal	3.4	4.9	0.0	0.0	0.0	0.0	97.2
Romania	28.1	28.5	10.6	23.0	31.4	16.4	18.5
Slovenia	2.9	3.5	42.0	32.9	0.1	0.0	24.5
Slovakia	5.5	5.7	64.5	11.4	1.5	0.3	21.4
Finland	15.4	16.4	37.1	13.3	0.0	0.9	47.8
Sweden	32.7	29.9	45.0	0.7	0.0	0.0	52.8
United Kingdom	278.6	156.3	11.4	6.4	34.4	44.2	3.3
Norway	209.7	215.9	0.0	0.8	42.0	51.5	5.6
Switzerland	12.0	12.7	56.5	0.0	0.0	0.0	37.5
Croatia	3.6	4.1	0.0	0.0	54.0	20.4	25.3
Turkey	27.5	30.3	0.0	57.3	1.9	8.1	32.7

Source: Eurostat (online data codes: ten00076, ten00080, ten00077, ten00079, ten00078 and ten00081)

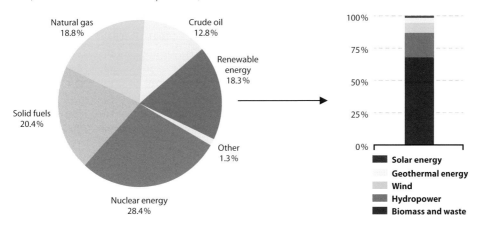

Figure 12.1.1: Production of primary energy, EU-27, 2009
(% of total, based on tonnes of oil equivalent)

Natural gas
18.8%

Crude oil
12.8%

Renewable
energy
18.3%

Solid fuels
20.4%

Other
1.3%

Nuclear energy
28.4%

Solar energy
Geothermal energy
Wind
Hydropower
Biomass and waste

Source: Eurostat (online data codes: ten00080, ten00077, ten00079, ten00078, ten00081 and ten00082)

Figure 12.1.2: Development of the production of primary energy (by fuel type), EU-27, 1999-2009
(1999 = 100, based on tonnes of oil equivalent)

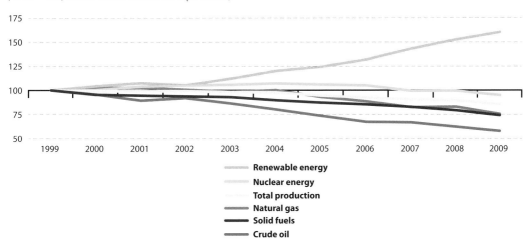

Renewable energy
Nuclear energy
Total production
Natural gas
Solid fuels
Crude oil

Source: Eurostat (online data codes: ten00076, ten00081, ten00080, ten00079, ten00078 and ten00077)

Table 12.1.2: Net imports of primary energy, 2001-2009

	(1 000 tonnes of oil equivalent)					(tonnes of oil equivalent per inhabitant)				
	2001	2003	2005	2007	2009	2001	2003	2005	2007	2009
EU-27	856 569	903 284	983 448	986 455	943 604	1.77	1.86	2.00	1.99	1.89
Euro area	806 186	836 382	866 700	842 788	794 996	2.56	2.62	2.68	2.58	2.41
Belgium	51 476	52 914	53 362	51 037	48 383	5.02	5.11	5.11	4.82	4.50
Bulgaria	9 045	9 179	9 590	10 455	8 060	1.11	1.17	1.24	1.36	1.06
Czech Republic	10 733	11 296	12 792	11 589	11 368	1.05	1.11	1.25	1.13	1.09
Denmark	−6 075	−6 895	−10 450	−5 370	−3 735	−1.14	−1.28	−1.93	−0.99	−0.68
Germany	216 740	213 397	213 906	201 278	202 708	2.63	2.59	2.59	2.45	2.47
Estonia	1 697	1 475	1 442	1 501	1 166	1.24	1.09	1.07	1.12	0.87
Ireland	13 671	13 614	13 715	14 167	13 163	3.57	3.43	3.34	3.29	2.96
Greece	22 447	22 632	23 473	24 801	22 522	2.05	2.06	2.12	2.22	2.00
Spain	99 932	109 055	123 978	123 275	110 244	2.47	2.62	2.88	2.77	2.41
France	136 296	138 688	144 391	137 802	136 002	2.24	2.24	2.30	2.17	2.11
Italy	148 272	156 335	160 223	158 591	141 905	2.60	2.73	2.74	2.68	2.36
Cyprus	2 502	2 663	2 822	2 878	2 920	3.59	3.72	3.77	3.70	3.66
Latvia	2 531	2 791	2 990	3 037	2 706	1.07	1.20	1.30	1.33	1.20
Lithuania	3 917	4 099	5 100	5 791	4 340	1.12	1.18	1.49	1.71	1.30
Luxembourg	3 728	4 153	4 684	4 487	4 260	8.49	9.26	10.16	9.42	8.63
Hungary	13 879	16 410	17 501	16 526	14 878	1.36	1.62	1.73	1.64	1.48
Malta	1 594	1 809	1 606	1 798	1 985	4.07	4.55	3.99	4.41	4.80
Netherlands	32 033	35 824	38 102	39 551	34 913	2.00	2.21	2.34	2.42	2.12
Austria	19 935	23 127	24 620	23 276	21 002	2.49	2.86	3.00	2.81	2.51
Poland	9 396	12 081	16 437	25 039	30 255	0.25	0.32	0.43	0.66	0.79
Portugal	21 844	22 391	24 768	21 939	20 584	2.13	2.15	2.35	2.07	1.94
Romania	9 817	10 229	10 848	12 790	7 190	0.44	0.47	0.50	0.59	0.33
Slovenia (¹)	3 389	3 700	3 830	3 876	3 436	1.70	1.85	1.92	1.93	1.69
Slovakia	11 711	12 196	12 491	12 239	11 164	2.18	2.27	2.32	2.27	2.06
Finland	18 919	22 410	19 289	20 293	18 637	3.65	4.30	3.68	3.85	3.50
Sweden	19 166	22 879	20 206	18 981	17 951	2.16	2.56	2.24	2.08	1.94
United Kingdom	−22 027	−15 168	31 733	44 830	55 597	−0.37	−0.26	0.53	0.74	0.90
Norway	−202 595	−206 812	−197 031	−188 179	−187 746	−44.99	−45.43	−42.77	−40.20	−39.12
Switzerland	15 262	14 739	16 254	14 129	15 646	2.12	2.02	2.19	1.88	2.03
Croatia	4 171	4 987	5 255	5 334	4 461	0.94	1.12	1.18	1.20	1.01
Turkey (²)	46 335	56 794	62 138	76 096	70 635	0.68	0.81	0.87	1.09	0.99

(¹) Tonnes of oil equivalent per inhabitant, break in series, 2009.
(²) Tonnes of oil equivalent per inhabitant, break in series, 2007.

Source: Eurostat (online data codes: nrg_100a and tps00001)

Table 12.1.3: Main origin of primary energy imports, EU-27, 2001-2009
(% of extra EU-27 imports)

Hard coal									
	2001	**2002**	**2003**	**2004**	**2005**	**2006**	**2007**	**2008**	**2009**
Russia	11.5	13.1	13.5	18.7	24.1	25.4	25.1	26.3	30.2
Colombia	12.5	12.6	12.5	12.1	12.1	12.0	13.0	12.5	17.6
South Africa	27.0	31.4	31.5	26.6	25.7	24.3	20.8	17.1	16.0
United States	11.2	8.2	7.0	7.5	7.8	8.0	9.3	14.3	13.7
Australia	16.3	16.9	17.0	15.3	13.5	12.4	13.5	12.0	7.6
Indonesia	5.7	6.7	7.1	7.0	7.4	9.7	7.9	7.4	7.1
Ukraine	1.6	2.0	1.3	2.0	2.1	1.6	1.7	2.2	1.6
Canada	3.8	3.2	2.9	2.5	3.3	2.8	3.1	2.7	1.4
Norway	0.9	1.0	1.2	0.6	0.6	0.3	0.6	0.6	0.8
Others	9.7	5.0	6.0	7.8	3.5	3.7	5.0	4.8	3.9

Crude oil									
	2001	**2002**	**2003**	**2004**	**2005**	**2006**	**2007**	**2008**	**2009**
Russia	25.5	29.2	31.1	32.2	32.5	33.4	33.2	31.4	33.1
Norway	20.1	19.4	19.2	18.8	16.9	15.5	15.1	15.1	15.2
Libya	8.2	7.5	8.4	8.8	8.8	9.2	9.8	9.9	9.0
Saudi Arabia	10.8	10.1	11.3	11.3	10.6	9.1	7.2	6.9	5.7
Kazakhstan	1.6	2.4	2.7	3.4	4.5	4.6	4.6	4.8	5.4
Iran	5.9	4.9	6.4	6.3	6.1	6.2	6.2	5.4	4.7
Nigeria	4.8	3.5	4.3	2.6	3.2	3.6	2.7	4.0	4.5
Azerbaijan	0.9	1.0	1.0	0.9	1.3	2.2	3.0	3.2	4.0
Iraq	3.8	3.0	1.6	2.2	2.1	2.9	3.4	3.3	3.8
Others	18.3	18.8	14.2	13.4	14.0	13.2	14.7	16.1	14.6

Natural gas									
	2001	**2002**	**2003**	**2004**	**2005**	**2006**	**2007**	**2008**	**2009**
Russia	47.7	45.0	45.1	43.8	40.6	39.3	38.4	37.6	34.2
Norway	22.8	26.2	25.5	25.0	24.4	25.5	28.2	28.9	30.7
Algeria	21.2	21.2	20.0	18.2	18.0	16.4	15.4	14.7	14.1
Qatar	0.3	0.9	0.7	1.4	1.6	1.8	2.2	2.2	4.6
Libya	0.4	0.3	0.3	0.4	1.7	2.5	3.0	2.9	2.9
Nigeria	2.3	2.2	3.1	3.7	3.5	4.3	4.7	4.0	2.4
Trinidad and Tobago	0.3	0.2	0.0	0.0	0.2	1.3	0.8	1.6	2.2
Egypt	0.0	0.0	0.0	0.0	1.6	2.5	1.8	1.7	2.1
Oman	0.4	0.4	0.2	0.5	0.6	0.3	0.1	0.1	0.4
Others	4.6	3.7	5.1	7.0	7.8	6.1	5.4	6.3	6.4

Source: Eurostat (online data codes: nrg_122a, nrg_123a and nrg_124a)

Table 12.1.4: Energy dependency rate, EU-27, 1999-2009
(% of net imports in gross inland consumption and bunkers, based on tonnes of oil equivalent)

	1999	2000	2001	2002	2003	2004	2005	2006	2007	2008	2009
All products	45.1	46.7	47.4	47.6	49.0	50.2	52.5	53.7	53.0	54.7	53.9
Solid fuels	27.5	30.5	33.7	33.1	34.9	38.1	39.3	41.0	41.3	44.7	41.1
Crude oil	74.2	75.6	77.7	76.4	78.7	80.9	82.4	83.9	83.6	85.0	84.1
Natural gas	47.9	48.9	47.2	51.1	52.4	53.9	57.7	60.8	60.3	62.3	64.2

Source: Eurostat (online data codes: nrg_100a, nrg_101a, nrg_102a and nrg_103a)

Figure 12.1.3: Energy dependency rate – all products, 2009
(% of net imports in gross inland consumption and bunkers, based on tonnes of oil equivalent)

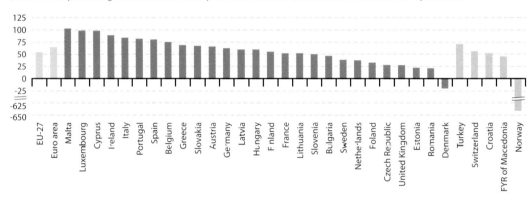

Source: Eurostat (online data codes: tsdcc310 and nrg_100a)

12.2 Consumption of energy

The European Union (EU) has pledged to cut its energy consumption by 20 % (compared with projected levels) by 2020. This subchapter explains how the consumption of energy in the EU has evolved, highlighting a gradual shift from fossil fuels to renewable energy sources, such as solar energy, wind power, and biofuels; it also looks at the evolution of energy use by various transport modes.

In tandem with supply-side policies, the EU has launched a number of initiatives which aim to increase the efficiency of energy use, reduce energy demand and attempt to decouple it from economic growth. Several instruments and implementing measures exist in this field, including the promotion of co-generation, the energy performance of buildings (whether private or public buildings), and energy labelling of domestic appliances.

Main statistical findings

Consumption

Gross inland energy consumption of primary energy within the EU-27 in 2009 was 1 703 million tonnes of oil equivalent (toe). While gross inland consumption had remained relatively unchanged throughout the period from 2003 to 2008 the data for 2009 indicate a substantial decrease, – 5.5 % compared with 2008 (see Table 12.2.1); much of the decrease may well be attributed to a lower level of economic activity as a result of the financial and economic crisis, rather than a structural shift in the pattern of energy consumption.

The gross inland consumption of each Member State depends, to a large degree, on the structure of its energy system, the availability of natural resources for primary energy production, and the structure and development of each economy (general trends in economic growth); this is true not only for conventional fuels and nuclear power, but also for renewable energy sources. Despite falls in 2009 in all EU Member States, gross inland consumption of primary energy had increased at a rapid annual average rate in Luxembourg and Cyprus throughout the period from 1999 to 2009, and at a slower average rate in Greece, Austria and Spain. The largest reduction in gross inland consumption of primary energy (during the same ten-year period) was recorded in the United Kingdom (– 10.1 %).

Over the period 1999 to 2009 there was a gradual decline in the share of crude oil and petroleum products, solid fuels, and nuclear energy in total gross inland consumption, while an increasing share of EU-27 consumption was accounted for by natural gas and renewable energy sources (see Figure 12.2.1). The combined share of crude oil, petroleum products and solid fuels fell from 57.5 % of total consumption in 1999 to 52.3 % in 2009, reflecting changes in the EU-27's energy mix and a move away from the most polluting fossil fuels. During the same period, the relative importance of natural gas rose by 2.1 percentage points, reaching 24.5 % of the EU-27's gross inland consumption by 2009 while the relative importance of renewable energy sources rose 3.5 percentage points to reach 9.0 %. The relative importance of renewable energy sources was over one third of gross inland consumption in Latvia (36.2 %) and Sweden (34.4 %), and was over one quarter of the total in Austria (27.3 %).

EU-27 final energy consumption (in other words, excluding energy used by power producers) was equivalent to just under two thirds (65.4 %) of gross inland consumption, at 1 114 million toe in 2009. Almost one fifth (19.2 %) of the EU-27's final energy consumption was accounted for by Germany (see Table 12.2.2).

The lowest levels of energy intensity – a measure of an economy's energy efficiency – were recorded for Denmark and Ireland in 2009, while the most energy-intensive Member States were Bulgaria, Estonia and Romania (see Figure 12.2.2). It should be noted that the economic structure of an economy plays an important role in determining energy intensity, as post-industrial economies with large service sectors will, a priori, have considerably lower energy use than economies characterised by heavy, traditional industrial activities. Between 1999 and 2009, substantial energy savings were made in the Bulgarian and Romanian economies, as well as in the Baltic Member States, Malta, Poland and Slovakia, as the amount of energy required to produce a unit of economic output (as measured by gross domestic product (GDP)) was reduced by 25 % or more; Ireland, Sweden and the United Kingdom also achieved reductions of just under one quarter.

End-users

An analysis of the final end use of energy shows three dominant categories, namely, transport, industry and households. The share consumed by transport was around one third of the EU-27's final energy consumption in 2009 (see Figure 12.2.3), while the shares of households and industry were nearer to one quarter. The total energy consumption of all transport modes in the EU-27 amounted to 367.6 million toe in 2009. There were, however, considerable differences in the development of energy consumption across transport modes, with the most rapid growth recorded for international aviation (18.9 % between 1999 and 2009) and an upward trend for road transport (7.3 %) and domestic aviation (5.0 %), while the energy consumption of rail fell 14.5 % and that of inland waterways by 5.6 % – see Figure 12.2.4. The largest increase in energy consumption among the different transport modes, in absolute terms, was recorded for road transport, where EU-27 consumption rose by 20.4 million toe between 1999 and 2009, compared with a 6.8 million toe increase for international aviation and a 0.4 million toe increase for domestic aviation. These changes in energy consumption reflect the use of each transport mode, but can also be influenced by technological changes, especially when these relate to fuel-efficiency gains.

Data sources and availability

Gross inland energy consumption represents the quantity of energy necessary to satisfy inland consumption of the geographical entity under consideration. It may be defined as primary production plus imports, recovered products and stock changes, less exports and fuel supply to maritime bunkers (for seagoing ships of all flags). It describes the total energy needs of a country (or entity), covering: consumption by the energy sector itself; distribution and transformation losses; final energy consumption by end-users; and statistical differences.

Final energy consumption includes the consumption of energy by all users except the energy sector itself (whether for deliveries, for transformation, and/or its own use), and includes, for example, energy consumption by agriculture, industry, services and households, as well as energy consumption for transport. It should be noted that fuel quantities transformed in the electrical power stations of industrial auto-producers and the quantities of coke transformed into blast-furnace gas are not part of overall industrial energy consumption but of the transformation sector.

Energy intensity is measured as the ratio between gross inland consumption of energy and GDP; this indicator is a key indicator for measuring progress under the Europe 2020 strategy for smart, sustainable and inclusive growth. The ratio is expressed in kilograms of oil equivalent (kgoe) per EUR 1 000, and to facilitate analysis over time the calculations are based on GDP at constant prices (currently chain-linked 2000 prices). If an economy becomes more efficient in its use of energy and its GDP remains constant, then the ratio for this indicator should fall. The economic structure of an economy plays an important role in determining energy intensity, as post-industrial economies with large service sectors will, a priori, display relatively low energy intensity rates, while developing economies may have a considerable proportion of their economic activity within industrial sectors, thus leading to higher energy intensity.

Context

As well as supply-side policies to influence the production of energy, there is a growing trend for policy initiatives to focus on improving energy efficiency in an attempt to reduce energy demand and decouple it from economic growth. This process was given impetus by the integrated energy and climate change strategy that committed the EU to cut its energy consumption by 20 % by 2020 (in relation to projected levels) and, in so doing, simultaneously address the issues of import dependency, energy-related emissions, and energy costs. The European Commission adopted the 'Energy Efficiency Plan 2011' (COM(2011) 109 final) in March 2011. The stated aim is to pursue this plan in conjunction with other policy actions under the Europe 2020 flagship initiative for a resource-efficient Europe, including the 'Roadmap for moving to a competitive low carbon economy by 2050' (COM(2011) 112 final) – see the introduction to the environment chapter. The energy efficiency plan proposes several actions to:

- promote the exemplary role of the public sector and propose a binding target to accelerate the refurbishment rate of the public sector building stock; introduce energy efficiency criteria in public procurement;
- trigger the renovation process in private buildings and improve the energy performance of appliances;
- improve the efficiency of power and heat generation;
- foresee energy efficiency requirements for industrial equipment, improved information provision for SMEs, and energy audits and energy management systems for large companies;
- focus on the roll-out of smart grids and smart meters providing consumers with the information and services necessary to optimise their energy consumption and calculate their energy savings.

The EU harmonises national measures relating to the publication of information on the consumption of energy by household appliances, thereby allowing consumers to choose appliances on the basis of their energy efficiency – a range of different products (for example, light bulbs, refrigerators, washing machines) carry the EU's energy label that details the energy efficiency of products, rating them according to a scale that ranges from A to G, with 'A' as the most energy efficient products and 'G' the least efficient.

Despite falls in the amount of energy consumed for transport in 2008 and 2009 (at least, in part, reflecting the impact of the financial and economic crisis), an analysis of a longer time series shows that transport was the fastest growing consumer of energy and producer of greenhouse gases, even if advances in transport technology and fuel have resulted in marked decreases in emissions of certain pollutants. There are many factors that impact on energy use for transport, for example, overall economic growth, the efficiency of individual transport modes, the take-up of alternative fuels, and lifestyle choices. The globalised nature of the economy has fuelled demand for international freight movements (principally by ship), while within the Single Market there has been a considerable expansion in the use of road freight transport. The growth in demand for energy for transport is not confined to business, as it has been accompanied by an expansion in personal travel. The growth of low-cost airlines, an increase in motorisation rates (the average number of motor vehicles per inhabitant), a trend for living in suburban areas, or the expansion of tourism (more frequent breaks, and more long-haul destinations) are among some of the factors that have contributed to increase the demand for energy as a result of personal travel.

Table 12.2.1: Gross inland consumption of primary energy, 1999-2009
(million tonnes of oil equivalent)

	1999	2000	2001	2002	2003	2004	2005	2006	2007	2008	2009	Share in EU-27, 2009 (%)
EU-27	1 711	1 725	1 763	1 758	1 799	1 818	1 823	1 825	1 806	1 802	1 703	100.0
Euro area	1 185	1 203	1 232	1 231	1 261	1 277	1 280	1 277	1 269	1 267	1 202	70.6
Belgium	59.0	59.2	58.6	56.4	59.6	59.2	59.0	58.4	57.0	59.6	58.2	3.4
Bulgaria	18.3	18.7	19.5	19.1	19.5	19.0	20.1	20.6	20.3	20.1	17.6	1.0
Czech Republic	39.2	41.3	42.3	42.7	44.7	45.8	45.3	46.3	46.3	45.1	42.3	2.5
Denmark	20.3	19.8	20.3	20.0	20.9	20.3	19.8	21.1	20.7	20.1	19.4	1.1
Germany	341.5	343.6	353.3	345.4	348.5	350.1	346.0	348.9	339.8	342.8	326.6	19.2
Estonia	5.0	5.0	5.2	5.0	5.5	5.7	5.6	5.4	6.1	5.9	5.3	0.3
Ireland	13.7	14.2	15.1	15.2	15.0	15.2	15.2	15.5	15.9	15.9	14.9	0.9
Greece	27.0	28.3	29.1	29.6	30.3	30.8	31.4	31.6	31.6	31.8	30.6	1.8
Spain	118.0	124.0	127.1	130.9	135.3	141.4	144.4	144.6	146.4	142.0	130.2	7.6
France	255.0	257.8	266.2	266.7	271.5	275.7	276.6	273.6	271.1	274.3	262.7	15.4
Italy	172.6	175.8	176.3	176.7	184.2	185.1	187.7	186.3	183.6	180.8	168.9	9.9
Cyprus	2.2	2.4	2.4	2.4	2.7	2.5	2.5	2.6	2.7	2.9	2.8	0.2
Latvia	4.0	3.7	4.1	4.0	4.3	4.4	4.5	4.6	4.8	4.6	4.3	0.3
Lithuania	7.9	7.1	8.2	8.7	9.1	9.2	8.7	8.5	9.2	9.2	8.3	0.5
Luxembourg	3.4	3.6	3.8	4.0	4.2	4.7	4.8	4.7	4.6	4.6	4.4	0.3
Hungary	25.9	25.3	25.9	25.9	26.5	26.2	27.7	27.5	27.0	26.8	25.3	1.5
Malta	0.8	0.8	0.9	0.8	0.9	0.9	0.9	0.9	1.0	0.9	0.8	0.0
Netherlands	74.8	76.6	78.9	79.0	81.3	82.7	82.5	80.2	85.8	83.8	81.6	4.8
Austria	29.2	29.2	30.7	31.1	32.8	33.1	34.5	34.4	33.9	34.2	32.3	1.9
Poland	93.5	89.8	90.5	89.4	91.6	91.9	93.1	97.7	97.3	99.0	95.3	5.6
Portugal	25.0	25.1	25.3	26.3	25.7	26.7	27.4	25.7	26.3	25.2	25.0	1.5
Romania	36.7	36.8	37.3	38.7	40.3	39.5	39.3	40.8	40.6	40.5	35.4	2.1
Slovenia	6.4	6.4	6.7	6.8	6.9	7.1	7.3	7.3	7.3	7.8	7.0	0.4
Slovakia	17.8	18.0	18.8	19.0	18.9	18.6	19.1	18.9	17.9	18.4	16.8	1.0
Finland	33.3	32.8	33.5	35.3	37.4	37.6	34.8	37.9	37.6	36.1	34.0	2.0
Sweden	50.2	47.7	50.6	51.7	50.7	52.8	51.7	50.5	50.3	50.0	45.9	2.7
United Kingdom	230.0	231.7	232.4	227.0	230.9	232.0	233.4	230.2	221.5	219.4	206.8	12.1
Norway	26.8	26.1	27.2	25.3	27.4	26.9	27.3	27.7	28.1	30.3	28.9	–
Switzerland	26.7	26.4	27.9	27.1	27.1	27.1	27.0	28.2	27.0	28.1	28.2	–
Croatia	8.0	7.8	8.0	8.3	8.9	8.9	9.0	9.0	9.4	9.1	8.7	–
Turkey	71.2	76.7	71.0	75.5	79.2	82.0	85.7	94.4	101.5	100.2	100.0	–

Source: Eurostat (online data code: ten00086)

Figure 12.2.1: Gross inland consumption, EU-27, 1999-2009
(% of total consumption)

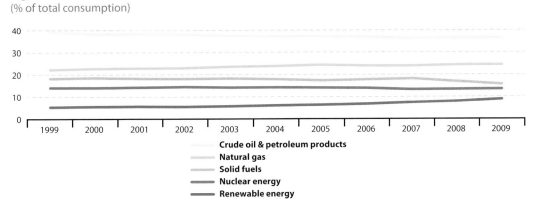

Source: Eurostat (online data codes: ten00086, nrg_102a, nrg_103a, nrg_101a, nrg_104a and nrg_1071a)

Table 12.2.2: Final energy consumption, 1999-2009
(million tonnes of oil equivalent)

	1999	2000	2001	2002	2003	2004	2005	2006	2007	2008	2009	Share in EU-27, 2009 (%)
EU-27	1 113	1 120	1 144	1 132	1 172	1 186	1 193	1 193	1 167	1 175	1 114	100.0
Euro area	774	784	804	799	831	841	845	844	821	831	789	70.9
Belgium	37.0	37.4	37.9	36.1	38.3	37.7	36.6	36.1	34.6	37.5	34.5	3.1
Bulgaria	8.9	8.8	8.8	8.9	9.5	9.4	9.9	10.4	10.1	9.9	8.6	0.8
Czech Republic	23.7	24.7	25.2	24.4	25.7	26.2	26.0	26.4	25.8	25.5	24.4	2.2
Denmark	15.0	14.7	15.1	14.8	15.1	15.4	15.5	15.7	15.7	15.5	14.8	1.3
Germany	220.8	219.1	222.7	219.2	230.8	230.9	229.6	233.3	215.7	224.2	213.3	19.2
Estonia	2.4	2.4	2.7	2.6	2.7	2.8	2.9	2.9	3.1	3.1	2.8	0.2
Ireland	9.9	10.7	11.1	11.2	11.5	11.9	12.5	13.2	13.2	13.2	11.8	1.1
Greece	18.1	18.6	19.2	19.5	20.5	20.3	20.8	21.4	21.9	21.3	20.5	1.8
Spain	74.4	79.4	83.4	84.7	90.0	94.3	97.4	96.1	98.8	95.8	89.0	8.0
France	152.4	154.5	161.0	157.6	161.2	162.8	162.3	161.5	158.6	160.7	155.5	14.0
Italy	124.5	124.7	126.0	125.5	131.0	132.5	134.4	132.3	129.3	128.3	120.9	10.9
Cyprus	1.6	1.6	1.7	1.7	1.8	1.8	1.8	1.8	1.9	2.0	1.9	0.2
Latvia	3.4	3.2	3.6	3.6	3.8	3.9	4.0	4.2	4.4	4.2	3.9	0.4
Lithuania	4.1	3.7	3.9	4.0	4.1	4.3	4.5	4.8	5.0	4.9	4.4	0.4
Luxembourg	3.3	3.5	3.7	3.7	3.9	4.4	4.5	4.4	4.3	4.4	4.1	0.4
Hungary	16.3	16.1	16.9	16.9	17.6	17.5	18.2	17.9	16.9	17.1	16.4	1.5
Malta	0.3	0.4	0.4	0.4	0.5	0.5	0.5	0.4	0.4	0.5	0.4	0.0
Netherlands	49.2	50.5	51.3	51.3	52.0	52.8	52.3	50.9	49.8	51.1	50.4	4.5
Austria	23.3	23.7	25.0	25.3	26.6	26.9	28.3	27.6	27.4	27.6	26.3	2.4
Poland	58.9	55.6	56.0	54.5	56.0	58.1	58.2	60.8	61.7	62.2	60.9	5.5
Portugal	16.8	17.7	18.0	18.4	18.4	18.9	19.0	18.7	19.0	18.5	18.2	1.6
Romania	22.5	22.5	22.9	22.9	24.0	24.4	24.7	24.9	24.1	24.6	22.1	2.0
Slovenia	4.4	4.4	4.6	4.6	4.7	4.8	4.9	4.9	4.9	5.3	4.7	0.4
Slovakia	10.9	11.0	11.5	11.6	11.2	11.1	11.5	11.4	11.2	11.5	10.7	1.0
Finland	24.2	23.9	24.3	25.3	26.0	26.4	25.5	26.9	26.7	25.9	24.0	2.2
Sweden	35.1	34.9	34.3	34.1	34.0	33.9	33.6	33.2	33.3	32.6	31.6	2.8
United Kingdom	151.0	152.4	153.3	148.8	150.5	152.3	153.3	151.2	148.7	148.2	137.5	12.3
Norway	18.6	18.1	18.4	18.1	18.0	18.5	18.6	18.5	18.9	18.9	18.1	–
Switzerland	20.8	20.6	20.9	20.4	20.9	21.0	21.3	21.2	20.6	21.5	20.9	–
Croatia	5.4	5.4	5.5	5.6	6.0	6.2	6.3	6.5	6.5	6.6	6.3	–
Turkey	49.6	56.1	50.4	55.3	59.2	61.2	63.6	69.6	74.1	73.1	68.7	–

Source: Eurostat (online data code: ten00095)

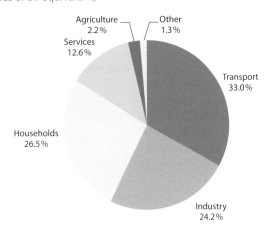

Figure 12.2.2: Energy intensity of the economy, 1999 and 2009
(kg of oil equivalent per EUR 1 000 of GDP)

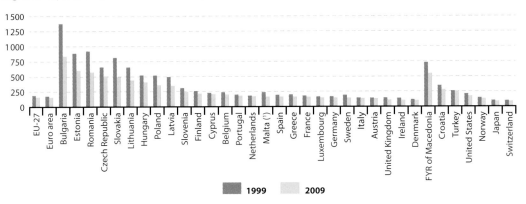

(¹) 1999, provisional.

Source: Eurostat (online data code: t2020_32)

Figure 12.2.3: Final energy consumption, EU-27, 2009 (¹)
(% of total, based on tonnes of oil equivalent)

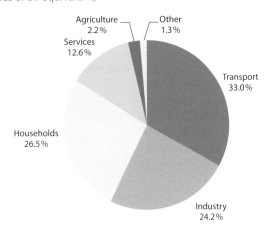

Agriculture
2.2%

Other
1.3%

Services
12.6%

Transport
33.0%

Households
26.5%

Industry
24.2%

(¹) Figures do not sum to 100 % due to rounding.

Source: Eurostat (online data code: tsdpc320)

Figure 12.2.4: Energy consumption by transport mode, EU-27, 1999-2009
(1999 = 100, based on tonnes of oil equivalent)

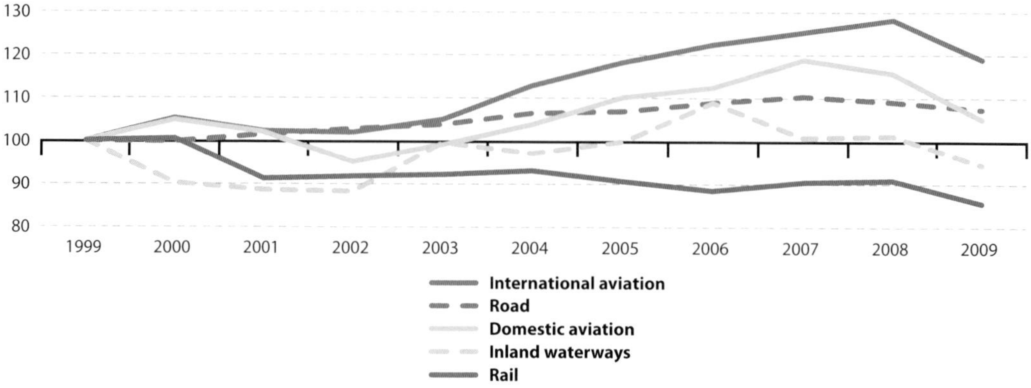

Legend:
- **International aviation**
- **- - Road**
- **Domestic aviation**
- **Inland waterways**
- **Rail**

Source: Eurostat (online data code: tsdtr250)

12.3 Electricity production, consumption and market overview

This subchapter describes the electricity market in the European Union (EU) with an analysis of electricity generation according to a range of different energy sources used for generation. It also provides statistics on the level of market liberalisation (as measured by the share of the largest generator) within electricity markets and concludes with information concerning electricity consumption by households.

The European Commission launched its third legislative package to liberalise energy markets in September 2007. The proposals were designed to: create a competitive energy market; expand consumer choice; promote fairer prices; result in cleaner energy; and promote the security of supply. In order to reach these goals, the proposals sought to: separate production and supply from transmission networks; facilitate cross-border collaboration, investment and trade in energy; introduce more effective regulation; encourage greater market transparency; and increase solidarity between EU Member States.

Main statistical findings

Electricity generation

Total net electricity generation in the EU-27 was 3.0 million gigawatt hours (GWh) in 2009 – which marked a decrease of 4.9 % compared with the year before, reflecting in part the impact of the financial and economic crisis. This large fall in the level of electricity generation effectively undid the increases built up over the five previous years, as the level of electricity generation in 2009 was approximately the same as it had been in 2003 (see Table 12.3.1). The reduction in 2009 was the first year on year fall in net electricity generation since 1992 (– 0.5 %); in the years between 1992 and 2008 net electricity generation in the EU-27 grew, on average, by 1.7 % per annum. Among the Member States the most substantial decreases in net electricity generation in 2009 (compared with 2008) were recorded in Estonia, Romania and Hungary, all in excess of 10 %. Only Lithuania (10.7 %) recorded a double-digit increase in net electricity generation in 2009, although increases in Portugal (9.3 %) and Luxembourg (9.0 %) were only slightly lower.

More than one quarter of the net electricity generated in the EU-27 in 2009 came from nuclear power plants (27.8 %) while almost exactly double this share (55.4 %) came from power stations using combustible fuels such as natural gas, coal and oil. Among the renewable energy sources shown in Figure 12.3.1, the highest share of net electricity generation in 2009 was from hydropower plants (11.6 %), followed by wind turbines (4.3 %) and solar power (0.5 %).

The relative importance of combustible fuels rose from 54.1 % in 1999 to 58.1 % in 2007, before falling back to 55.4 % in 2009. Over the same period the share of net electricity generation from nuclear energy fell from 32.1 % in 1999 to just less than 28 % in the period from 2007 to 2009. Among the renewable energy sources the share of net electricity generation from geothermal sources remained small and constant (0.15 % to 0.17 %) between 1999 and 2009, while the share from hydropower stations increased initially from 13.0 % in 1999 to 13.5 % in 2001, before stabilising in a range from 10.6 % to 11.6 % between 2002 and 2009. In contrast, the shares from solar and wind increased greatly although the share of solar remained small: the share of net electricity generation from solar power increased from close to nothing in 1999 to 0.5 % by 2009; the share from wind turbines increased from 0.5 % in 1999 to 4.3 % by 2009.

Market shares

Germany and France were the principal electricity generators in the EU-27 in 2009, with shares of 18.3 % and 17.0 % respectively, while the United Kingdom was the only other Member State to report a share in double-digits (11.8 %). The relative weight of Spain in EU-27 electricity generation rose quickly between 1999 and 2009, gaining 2.1 percentage points to reach 9.3 % (see Table 12.3.1).

One measure that is used to monitor the extent of electricity market liberalisation is the market share of the largest generator in each country (see Figure 12.3.2). The small island nations of Cyprus and Malta were both characterised by a complete monopoly in 2009, with 100 % of their electricity being generated by the largest (sole) generator. Two other Member States – Estonia and Greece – reported shares for the largest generator of 90 % or more. In 11 of the 23 Member States for which data are available, the largest generator provided less than 50 % of the total electricity generated, with the lowest share (18.1 %) being recorded in Poland.

Household electricity consumption

During the ten-year period from 1999 to 2009, the consumption of electricity by households rose in the EU-27 by 18.5 % overall (see Figure 12.3.3). There was much faster growth in a number of Member States, in particular Cyprus, Spain, Portugal, Romania and all three of the Baltic Member States where growth was at least double the EU-27 average. At the other end of the range, household electricity consumption fell in two of the Member States (Belgium and Slovakia). These figures on overall household electricity consumption are likely to be influenced, in part, by the average number of persons living in each household and by the total number of households – both of which are linked to demographic events.

Data sources and availability

Electricity is produced as a primary or secondary product in power plants. The total amount of electricity produced is called gross electricity production. However, power plants consume some electricity for their own use (in plant auxiliaries and in other transformers) and net electricity production is obtained by deducting this amount from gross production. The net production is distributed through national transmission and distribution grids to final consumers, transformed to heat in boilers or heat pumps, stored using pumped storage, or traded (exported or imported).

Final consumption of electricity covers the electricity delivered to the consumer's door (industry, transport, households and other sectors); it excludes deliveries for transformation and/or own use of energy producing activities, as well as network losses.

The market share of electricity generators is based on their net electricity production, and as such the electricity used by generators for their own consumption is not taken into account.

Context

Since July 2004, small business consumers in the EU have been free to switch their gas or electricity supplier, and in July 2007 this right was extended to all consumers. Independent national regulatory authorities have been established across the Member States to ensure that suppliers and network companies operate correctly. However, a number of shortcomings were identified in the opening-up of markets, and it was therefore decided to embark upon a third legislative package of measures with the aim of ensuring that all users could take advantage of the benefits provided by a truly competitive energy market. The European Commission launched its third legislative package to liberalise energy markets in September 2007. These proposals were designed to: create a competitive energy market; expand consumer choice; promote fairer prices; result in cleaner energy; and promote the security of supply. During 2009, a number of these

proposals were adopted by the European Parliament and the Council. This raft of legislation came into effect as of March 2011:

- Regulation 713/2009 of 13 July 2009 establishing an Agency for the Cooperation of Energy Regulators;
- Regulation 714/2009 of 13 July 2009 on conditions for access to the network for cross-border exchanges in electricity and repealing Regulation 1228/2003;
- Directive 2009/72/EC of 13 July 2009 concerning common rules for the internal market in electricity and repealing Directive 2003/54/EC.

The use of nuclear power for electricity generation has received renewed attention amid concerns about an increasing dependency on imported primary energy, rising oil and gas prices, and commitments to reduce greenhouse gas emissions. These have been balanced against long-standing concerns about safety and waste from nuclear power plants. On 25 June 2009, a European Council Directive 2009/71 was adopted concerning a framework for the nuclear safety of nuclear installations. The safety aspects of nuclear energy were highlighted by the Fukushima Dai-ichi disaster, following the Great East Japan (or Tōhoku) earthquake and subsequent tsunami in March 2011. While some Member States have continued with existing reactors or plans to construct new nuclear reactors others decided to review, and in some cases, changed policies for existing plants, as well as cancelling planned nuclear constructions.

Table 12.3.1: Net electricity generation, 1999-2009
(1 000 GWh)

	1999	2000	2001	2002	2003	2004	2005	2006	2007	2008	2009	Share in EU-27, 2009 (%)
EU-27	2 779	2 863	2 943	2 964	3 050	3 119	3 140	3 182	3 196	3 203	3 046	100.0
Euro area	1 919	1 995	2 040	2 069	2 136	2 194	2 204	2 245	2 257	2 275	2 161	70.9
Belgium	80.8	80.3	76.2	78.1	80.9	81.7	83.4	82.0	85.1	81.4	87.5	2.9
Bulgaria	34.3	36.9	39.6	38.6	38.5	37.5	40.3	41.6	39.1	40.7	38.7	1.3
Czech Republic	60.1	68.0	68.8	70.4	76.7	77.9	76.2	77.9	81.4	77.1	76.0	2.5
Denmark	37.0	34.4	36.2	37.3	43.8	38.4	34.4	43.2	37.4	34.8	34.4	1.1
Germany	518.2	538.5	548.2	549.3	567.9	576.8	581.6	597.2	598.4	598.9	556.8	18.3
Estonia	7.4	7.6	7.6	7.7	9.2	9.2	9.1	8.7	11.0	9.5	7.9	0.3
Ireland	20.9	22.7	23.7	23.9	24.1	24.4	24.8	26.1	26.9	28.9	27.1	0.9
Greece	45.8	49.9	49.7	50.6	54.3	54.9	55.7	56.5	59.1	59.4	56.1	1.8
Spain	199.1	214.4	226.0	232.7	250.2	268.7	282.1	287.7	293.2	301.5	282.9	9.3
France	500.6	516.9	526.3	534.9	542.5	549.7	550.3	549.1	544.6	549.6	518.2	17.0
Italy	252.7	263.3	266.0	270.8	280.2	290.0	290.6	301.3	301.3	307.1	281.1	9.2
Cyprus	3.0	3.2	3.4	3.6	3.8	4.0	4.1	4.4	4.6	4.8	4.9	0.2
Latvia	3.6	3.7	3.7	3.5	3.5	4.2	4.4	4.5	4.4	4.9	5.2	0.2
Lithuania	11.9	10.0	13.2	16.1	17.9	17.7	13.6	11.4	12.9	12.8	14.1	0.5
Luxembourg	1.0	1.1	1.6	3.6	3.5	4.1	4.1	4.3	4.0	3.5	3.8	0.1
Hungary	34.9	32.3	33.7	33.5	31.4	31.3	33.2	33.3	37.2	37.4	33.3	1.1
Malta	1.7	1.8	1.8	1.9	2.1	2.1	2.2	2.1	2.2	2.2	2.0	0.1
Netherlands	83.2	86.0	89.9	92.1	93.0	98.4	96.2	94.4	100.9	103.4	108.9	3.6
Austria	58.6	59.1	60.2	60.0	57.4	61.4	63.5	61.8	62.7	64.2	66.7	2.2
Poland	129.5	132.2	132.7	131.4	138.4	140.8	143.6	147.7	145.4	141.5	137.9	4.5
Portugal	41.7	42.2	44.8	44.4	45.4	43.5	45.0	47.5	45.9	44.6	48.7	1.6
Romania	46.2	48.6	50.4	51.1	51.3	52.7	55.5	58.4	56.2	60.1	52.8	1.7
Slovenia	12.5	12.8	13.6	13.7	12.9	14.3	14.1	14.1	14.0	15.4	15.4	0.5
Slovakia	25.4	27.7	29.6	30.0	28.7	28.2	29.3	28.9	25.8	26.6	24.1	0.8
Finland	66.7	67.3	71.2	71.6	80.4	82.2	67.8	78.6	77.8	74.5	69.2	2.3
Sweden	150.5	141.6	157.6	143.2	132.5	148.5	154.6	140.4	145.1	146.4	133.3	4.4
United Kingdom	351.4	360.8	367.4	370.1	380.1	376.9	380.5	378.8	379.1	372.4	359.2	11.8
Norway	121.8	139.4	118.8	130.1	106.9	109.9	137.4	121.0	136.6	141.5	131.7	–
Switzerland	67.7	65.5	70.3	65.1	65.3	63.6	57.8	62.0	65.8	66.8	66.4	–
Croatia	11.7	10.2	11.7	11.7	12.1	12.8	12.0	12.0	11.7	11.8	12.4	–
Turkey	110.7	118.7	116.3	123.7	135.2	145.1	155.5	169.5	183.3	189.8	186.6	–

Source: Eurostat (online data code: nrg_105a)

Figure 12.3.1: Net electricity generation, EU-27, 2009 (^{1})
(% of total, based on GWh)

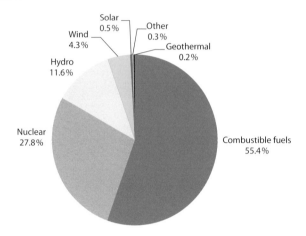

(^{1}) Figures do not sum to 100 % due to rounding.
Source: Eurostat (online data code: nrg_105a)

Figure 12.3.2: Market share of the largest generator in the electricity market, 2009 (^{1})
(% of total generation)

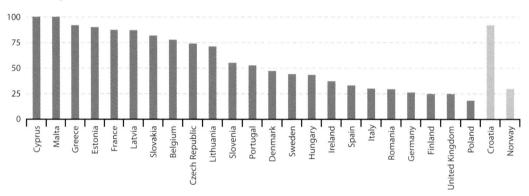

(^{1}) Bulgaria, Luxembourg, the Netherlands and Austria, not available.
Source: Eurostat (online data code: tsier060)

Figure 12.3.3: Electricity consumption by households, 2009
(1999 = 100)

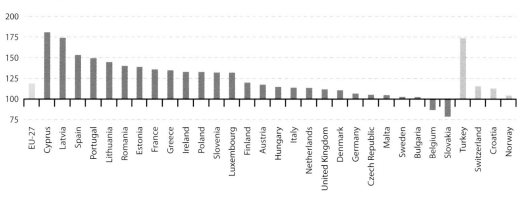

Source: Eurostat (online data code: tsdpc310)

12.4 Renewable energy

This subchapter provides recent statistics on renewable energy sources in the European Union (EU). Renewable energy sources include wind power, solar power (thermal, photovoltaic and concentrated), hydroelectric power, tidal power, geothermal energy and biomass.

The use of renewable energy has many potential benefits, including a reduction in greenhouse gas emissions, the diversification of energy supplies and a reduced dependency on fossil fuel markets (in particular, oil and gas). The growth of renewable energy sources may also have the potential to stimulate employment in the EU, through the creation of jobs in new 'green' technologies.

Main statistical findings

Primary production

The primary production of renewable energy within the EU-27 in 2009 was 148.4 million tonnes of oil equivalent (toe) – an 18.3 % share of total primary energy production. The volume of renewable energy produced within the EU-27 increased overall by 60.2 % between 1999 and 2009, equivalent to an average increase of 4.8 % per annum.

Among renewable energies, the most important source in the EU was biomass and waste, accounting for 67.7 % of primary renewables production in 2009 (see Table 12.4.1). Hydropower was the other main contributor to the renewable energy mix (19.0 % of the total). Although its level of production remains relatively low, there was a particularly rapid expansion in the output of wind energy, which accounted for 7.7 % of the EU's renewable energy produced in 2009.

The largest producer of renewable energy within the EU in 2009 was Germany, with an 18.7 % share of the EU-27 total; France (13.2 %) and Sweden (10.7 %) were the only other Member States to record double-digit shares, although Italy's share (9.9 %) was only just below this level. There were considerable differences in the renewable energy mix across the Member States, which reflect to a large degree natural endowments and climatic conditions. For example, more than three quarters (77.3 %) of the renewable energy produced in Cyprus was from solar energy, while more than a third of the renewable energy in the relatively mountainous countries of Austria, Slovenia and Sweden was from hydropower (much higher shares were recorded in Norway, Switzerland and Croatia).

Close to one third of the renewable energy production in Italy was from geothermal energy sources (where active volcanic processes still exist). The share of wind power was particularly high in Ireland (41.4 %) and also accounted for more than one fifth of renewable energy production in Spain (27.3 %) and Denmark (21.0 %).

The output of renewable energy in Germany grew at an average rate of 13.1 % per annum between 1999 and 2009, as such its share of the EU-27 total rose by 9.9 percentage points from an 8.7 % share in 1999. There were also average growth rates in excess of 10 % per annum recorded for Belgium, Ireland and Slovakia.

Consumption

Renewable energy sources accounted for 9.0 % of the EU-27's gross inland energy consumption in 2009 (see Table 12.4.2). Over one third of the energy consumed in Latvia and Sweden was derived from renewables in 2009, while in Austria more than a quarter of energy consumption was accounted for by renewables.

The EU seeks to have a 20 % share of its energy consumption from renewable sources by 2020; this target is broken down between the Member States with national action plans designed to plot a pathway for renewable energies in each Member State. Figure 12.4.1 shows the latest data available for the share of renewable energies in gross final energy consumption and the indicative targets that have been set for each country by 2020. The share of renewables in gross final energy consumption stood at 11.7 % in the EU-27 in 2009, more than half the target that has been set for 2020.

Among the Member States, the highest share of renewables in gross final energy consumption in 2009 was recorded in Sweden (47.3 %), while Latvia, Finland and Austria each reported more than a quarter of their final energy consumption derived from renewables. Compared with the most recent data available for 2009, the indicative targets for Denmark, France, Ireland and the United Kingdom require each of these Member States to increase their share of renewables in final energy consumption by at least 10 percentage points.

Electricity

The latest information available for 2009 (see Figure 12.4.2) shows that electricity generated from renewable energy sources contributed 18.2 % of the EU-27's gross electricity consumption. In Austria (66.8 %) and Sweden (56.4 %) more than half of all the electricity consumed was generated from renewable energy sources, largely as a result of hydropower and biomass.

The growth in electricity generated from renewable energy sources during the period 1999 to 2009 (see Figure 12.4.3) largely reflects an expansion in two renewable energy sources; namely, wind turbines and biomass. Although hydropower remained the single largest source for renewable electricity generation in the EU in 2009, the amount of electricity generated was somewhat lower than a decade earlier (– 2.4 %). In contrast, the volume of electricity generated from biomass more than trebled, while that from wind turbines increased more than nine-fold.

Transport

At the end of 2008, the EU agreed to set a target for each Member State, such that renewable energy sources (including biofuels, hydrogen or 'green' electricity) should account for at least 10 % of all fuel used within the transport sector by 2020. The average share of renewable energy sources across the EU-27 was 4.2 % in 2009, ranging from a high of 8.6 % in Slovakia, and 6.0 % or more in Sweden, Austria and France to less than 1 % in Bulgaria, Denmark, Estonia and Malta (see Figure 12.4.4).

Data sources and availability

The statistics presented in this subchapter are calculated on the basis of energy statistics covered by Regulation (EC) 1099/2008 on energy statistics.

The share of renewable energies in gross final energy consumption may be considered as an estimate for the purpose of monitoring Directive 2009/28/EC on the promotion of the use of energy from renewable sources – however, the statistical system for some renewable energy technologies is not yet fully developed to meet the requirements of this Directive; for example, the treatment of energy from heat pumps (and the energy used to drive the pumps). Furthermore the Directive requires hydro and wind energy to be normalised to smooth the effects of climatic variation; given the 15-year normalisation requirement for hydro production and the availability of energy statistics (for the EU-27, starting from 1990), long time series for this indicator are not available. The statistics presented for hydro and wind energy in this subchapter have not been normalised.

Electricity from renewable energy sources is defined as the ratio between electricity produced from renewable energy sources and gross national electricity consumption. Electricity produced from renewable energy sources comprises electricity generation from hydropower plants (excluding pumping), as well as electricity generated from biomass/ wastes, wind, solar and geothermal installations.

The share of renewable energies in the fuel consumed by the transport sector is calculated on the basis of energy statistics, according to the methodology as described in Directive 2009/28/EC; the contribution of all biofuels is currently included within the calculation for this indicator and the data are not restricted to biofuels satisfying the sustainability criteria.

Context

The EU has set out plans for a new energy strategy based on a more secure, sustainable and low-carbon economy. Aside from combating climate change through a reduction in greenhouse gas emissions, the use of renewable energy sources is likely to result in more secure energy supplies, greater diversity in energy supply, less air pollution, as well as the possibility for job creation in environmental and renewable energy sectors.

The integrated energy and climate change strategy adopted in December 2008 provided a further stimulus for increasing the use of renewable energy sources to 20 % of total energy consumption by 2020, while calling for energy consumption and greenhouse gas emissions to both be cut by 20 %. Directive 2009/28/EC of the European Parliament and Council on the promotion of the use of energy from renewable sources set an overall goal across the EU-27 for a 20 % share of energy consumption to be derived from renewable sources by 2020, while renewables should also account for a 10 % share of the fuel used in the transport sector by the same date. The Directive changes the legal framework for promoting renewable electricity, requires national action plans to show how renewable energies will be developed in each Member State, creates cooperation mechanisms, and establishes sustainability criteria for biofuels (following concerns over their potential adverse effects on crop prices, food supply, forest protection, biodiversity, water and soil resources).

In November 2010, the European Commission adopted a Communication titled 'Energy 2020: a strategy for competitive, sustainable and secure energy' (COM(2010) 639 final)). It defined energy priorities for the next ten years and outlined a set of actions that would need to be taken in order to tackle the challenges of: saving energy, achieving a competitive market with secure supplies, boosting technological leadership, and negotiating with international partners.

The share of renewable energy in gross final energy consumption is identified as a key indicator for measuring progress under the Europe 2020 strategy for smart, sustainable and inclusive growth – for more information see the introduction for energy.

Table 12.4.1: Primary production of renewable energy, 1999 and 2009

	Primary production (1 000 toe)		Share of total, 2009 (%)				
	1999	2009	Solar energy	Biomass & waste	Geothermal energy	Hydro-power energy	Wind energy
EU-27	92 674	148 435	1.7	67.7	3.9	19.0	7.7
Euro area	62 261	104 794	2.2	64.4	5.4	18.7	9.2
Belgium	498	1 661	1.5	91.4	0.2	1.7	5.2
Bulgaria	665	1 129	–	68.9	2.9	26.4	1.8
Czech Republic	1 409	2 593	0.5	90.5	–	8.1	1.0
Denmark	1 619	2 754	0.5	78.0	0.4	0.1	21.0
Germany	8 069	27 692	3.5	77.0	1.7	5.8	12.0
Estonia	526	864	–	97.7	–	0.3	2.0
Ireland	222	614	0.7	45.3	–	12.7	41.4
Greece	1 419	1 804	10.4	51.2	1.2	25.1	12.1
Spain	6 031	11 905	5.7	47.9	0.1	19.0	27.3
France	16 528	19 567	0.3	70.2	0.6	25.1	3.5
Italy	9 401	14 746	1.0	34.0	32.6	28.7	3.8
Cyprus	44	75	77.3	21.3	–	–	–
Latvia	1 571	2 089	–	85.6	–	14.2	0.2
Lithuania	656	992	–	94.5	0.5	3.6	1.4
Luxembourg	35	80	2.5	80.0	–	11.3	6.3
Hungary	843	1 851	0.3	92.0	5.2	1.1	1.5
Malta	0	0	:	:	:	–	–
Netherlands	1 210	2 768	0.9	84.4	0.1	0.3	14.2
Austria	6 675	8 352	1.5	54.6	0.4	41.5	2.0
Poland	3 757	6 031	0.0	94.8	0.2	3.4	1.5
Portugal	3 342	4 747	1.1	66.4	3.7	15.0	13.7
Romania	4 400	5 275	–	74.2	0.5	25.3	0.0
Slovenia	551	863	–	53.1	–	46.9	–
Slovakia	458	1 223	–	68.5	0.7	30.7	0.1
Finland	7 256	7 833	0.0	85.8	–	13.9	0.3
Sweden	13 359	15 819	0.1	62.8	–	35.8	1.4
United Kingdom	2 133	5 107	1.4	74.1	0.0	8.9	15.7
Norway	11 872	12 116	–	9.7	–	89.6	0.7
Switzerland	4 693	4 760	0.9	30.1	4.4	64.5	0.0
Croatia	900	1 030	0.5	42.6	0.3	56.2	0.5
Turkey	10 701	9 909	4.3	46.8	16.4	31.2	1.3

Source: Eurostat (online data codes: ten00081 and ten00082)

Table 12.4.2: Share of renewables in gross inland energy consumption, 2009
(%)

	Renewables total	Biomass & renewable wastes	Hydro	Geothermal	Wind	Solar
EU-27	9.0	6.1	1.7	0.3	0.7	0.1
Euro area	9.0	5.9	1.6	0.5	0.8	0.2
Belgium	3.9	3.6	0.0	0.0	0.1	0.0
Bulgaria	6.2	4.2	1.7	0.2	0.1	0.0
Czech Republic	5.7	5.2	0.5	0.0	0.1	0.0
Denmark	16.7	13.6	0.0	0.1	3.0	0.1
Germany	8.5	6.5	0.5	0.1	1.0	0.3
Estonia	13.5	13.2	0.1	0.0	0.3	0.0
Ireland	4.3	2.1	0.5	0.0	1.7	0.0
Greece	6.1	3.2	1.5	0.1	0.7	0.6
Spain	9.3	4.5	1.7	0.0	2.5	0.5
France	7.5	5.3	1.9	0.0	0.3	0.0
Italy	9.5	3.7	2.5	2.8	0.3	0.1
Cyprus	3.5	1.4	0.0	0.0	0.0	2.1
Latvia	36.2	29.2	6.9	0.0	0.1	0.0
Lithuania	10.5	9.8	0.4	0.1	0.2	0.0
Luxembourg	2.8	2.4	0.2	0.0	0.1	0.0
Hungary	7.3	6.7	0.1	0.4	0.1	0.0
Malta	0.0	0.0	0.0	:	0.0	:
Netherlands	3.9	3.3	0.0	0.0	0.5	0.0
Austria	27.3	15.5	10.7	0.1	0.5	0.4
Poland	6.6	6.2	0.2	0.0	0.1	0.0
Portugal	19.0	12.6	2.9	0.7	2.6	0.2
Romania	14.9	11.0	3.8	0.1	0.0	0.0
Slovenia	12.7	6.9	5.8	0.0	0.0	0.0
Slovakia	7.2	4.9	2.2	0.1	0.0	0.0
Finland	23.2	19.9	3.2	0.0	0.1	0.0
Sweden	34.4	21.6	12.3	0.0	0.5	0.0
United Kingdom	3.0	2.4	0.2	0.0	0.4	0.0
Norway	42.4	4.5	37.6	0.0	0.3	0.0
Switzerland	16.9	5.1	10.9	0.7	0.0	0.2
Croatia	10.9	4.1	6.6	0.0	0.1	0.1
Turkey	9.9	4.6	3.1	1.6	0.1	0.4

Source: Eurostat (online data codes: nrg_100a, nrg_1071a and nrg_1072a)

Figure 12.4.1: Share of renewables in gross final energy consumption, 2009
(%)

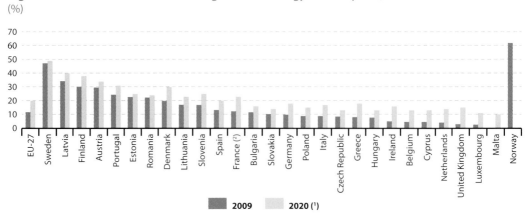

■ **2009** ☐ **2020 (¹)**

(¹) Indicative targets for 2020; not available for Norway.
(²) Excluding French overseas departments and territories.

Source: Eurostat (online data code: t2020_31)

Figure 12.4.2: Proportion of electricity generated from renewable sources, 2009
(% of gross electricity consumption)

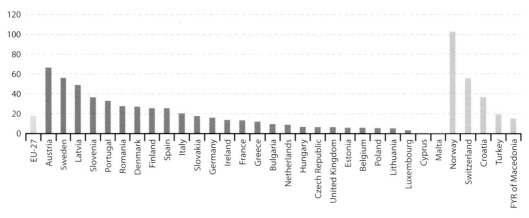

Source: Eurostat (online data code: tsien050)

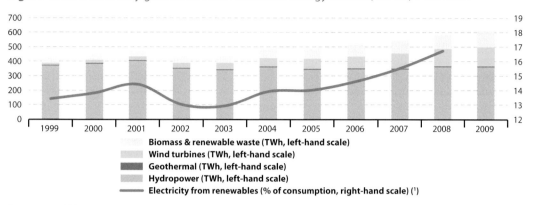

Figure 12.4.3: Electricity generated from renewable energy sources, EU-27, 1999-2009

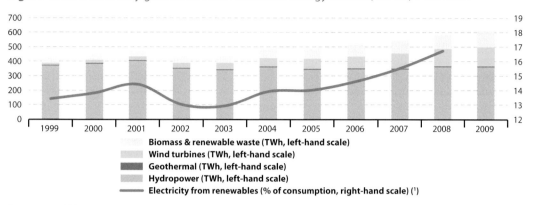

(¹) 2009, not available.

Source: Eurostat (online data codes: nrg_105a and tsdcc330)

Figure 12.4.4: Share of renewable energy in fuel consumption of transport, 2009
(%)

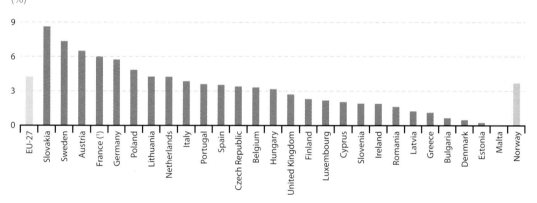

(¹) Excluding French overseas departments and territories.

Source: Eurostat (online data code: tsdcc340)

12.5 Energy prices

This subchapter highlights the level and development of electricity and natural gas prices for household consumers within the European Union (EU), Norway, Croatia, Turkey and Bosnia and Herzegovina; information on prices for industrial users is also provided.

The price of energy in the EU depends on a range of different supply and demand conditions, including the geopolitical situation, import diversification, network costs, environmental protection costs, severe weather conditions, or levels of excise and taxation; note that all of the prices presented in this subchapter include taxes and VAT for household consumers but exclude refundable taxes and VAT for industrial/business consumers.

Main statistical findings

Household consumers

An overview of the prices in euro of natural gas and electricity for the last three years (first half of each year) is presented in Table 12.5.1. The prices relate to the medium standard household consumption bands: for electricity this equates to annual consumption between 2 500 and 5 000 kilowatt hours (kWh); for natural gas (network/piped gas only) it equates to annual consumption between 5 600 and 56 000 kWh (20-200 gigajoules (GJ)).

Between the first half of 2010 and the first half of 2011, electricity prices for households increased in 24 of the EU Member States (see Table 12.5.1) and went down in two others, with prices staying roughly the same in one EU Member State. On average, the price of electricity for households in the EU-27 rose by 6.9 %. The highest price increases were experienced by households in Finland (16.2 % increase between the first half of 2010 and the first half of 2011) and Sweden (13.8 %), while decreases were recorded in the Luxembourg (– 2.8 %) and Hungary (– 1.2 %). The price of electricity for households was more than three times as high in the most expensive Member State, Denmark (EUR 0.291 per kWh), as in the cheapest Member State, Bulgaria (EUR 0.083 per kWh) – see Figure 12.5.1.

Table 12.5.2 shows the proportion of taxes in the overall electricity price for household consumers, with information for the basic price excluding all taxes, actual tax contributions in euro per kilowatt hour, as well as the relative share of the tax contribution in the final electricity price. For household consumers, the share of the tax contribution was lowest in the United Kingdom (4.75 %) where a relatively low VAT rate was applied to the basic price and no energy or other taxes were applied. The highest share of the tax contribution was charged in Denmark where more than half of the final price (56.57 %) was made up of tax contributions.

During the period from the first half of 2010 to the first half of 2011, natural gas prices for household consumers rose in all EU Member States: due to the limited size of the gas markets, gas prices are not available for Finland (for household consumers) and Greece; gas prices are not applicable for Cyprus and Malta. On average, the EU-27 price of natural gas for households rose by 6.9 % during the period considered. There were significant price increases for household users of natural gas in Latvia (up 23.2 %), Sweden (18.5 %) and Luxembourg (17.6 %). The highest prices for household consumers of natural gas were registered in Sweden (EUR 0.122 per kWh) and in Denmark (EUR 0.116 per kWh), at nearly four times the lowest price which was recorded in Romania (EUR 0.028 per kWh) – see Table 12.5.1.

Table 12.5.3 shows the proportion of taxes in the overall natural gas price for household consumers, the basic price excluding all taxes, actual tax contributions in euro per kWh, as well as the relative share of the tax contribution in the final natural gas price. As was the case for electricity, the share of the tax contribution in the total price for natural gas was lowest in the United Kingdom and highest in Denmark.

Industrial consumers

For industrial consumers (with an annual electricity consumption between 500 and 2 000 megawatt hours (MWh)), electricity prices during the first half of 2011 were highest in Malta, Cyprus and Italy (see Table 12.5.1) while the lowest prices were found in Bulgaria, Finland and Estonia: the price of electricity for industrial consumers in Malta was 2.6 times as high as that in Bulgaria. For industrial consumers with an annual natural gas consumption of between 2 778 and 27 778 MWh (10 000 and 100 000 GJ), prices in the first half of 2011 were highest in Denmark, while they were lowest in Romania and the United Kingdom. The price of natural gas for industrial consumers was 2.6 times as high in Denmark as in Romania. Between the first half of 2010 and the first half of 2011 prices for industrial consumers in the EU-27 increased on average by 5.0 % for electricity and 12.6 % for natural gas.

Data sources and availability

Due to a change in methodology from 2007 onwards, there is a break in series and hence a relatively short time series available for data relating to energy prices. Nevertheless, even in this relatively short timeframe, electricity and gas prices have fluctuated considerably – in particular, gas prices.

The transparency of energy prices is guaranteed within the EU through the obligation for EU Member States to send Eurostat information relating to prices for different categories of industrial and business users, as well as data relating to market shares, conditions of sale, and pricing systems; prices for household consumers are provided on a voluntary basis.

Electricity and gas tariffs or price schemes vary from one supplier to another. They may result from negotiated contracts, especially for large industrial users. For smaller consumers, they are generally set according to the amount of electricity or gas consumed along with a number of other characteristics; most tariffs also include some form of fixed charge. There is, therefore, no single price for electricity or gas. In order to compare prices over time and between countries, this subchapter shows information for selected consumption bands for household consumers and for industrial/business users. There are five different types of households for which electricity prices are collected following different annual consumption bands, while

for natural gas statistics information is collated for three different types of household. Across industrial/business users, electricity prices are collected for a total of seven different types of users, while for natural gas prices there are six different types of user distinguished.

Statistics on electricity and natural gas prices charged to industrial/business users are collected under the legal basis of a European Commission Decision (2007/394/EC) of 7 June 2007 amending Council Directive (90/377/EEC) with regard to the methodology to be applied for the collection of gas and electricity prices. Directive 2008/92/EC of the European Parliament and Council of 22 October 2008 concerns procedures to improve the transparency of gas and electricity prices charged to industrial end-users.

The prices presented cover average prices over a period of six months (semester) from January to June and from July to December of each year; the data presented in this subchapter cover the first half of each reference year. Prices include the basic price of the electricity/gas, transmission and distribution charges, meter rental, and other services.

Context

The price and reliability of energy supplies, electricity in particular, are key elements in a country's energy supply strategy. Electricity prices are of particular importance for international competitiveness, as electricity usually represents a significant proportion of total energy costs faced by industrial and service-providing businesses. In contrast to the price of fossil fuels, which are usually traded on global markets with relatively uniform prices, there is a much wider range of prices applied to electricity and natural gas. These prices are, to some degree, influenced by the price of primary fuels and, more recently, by the cost of carbon dioxide (CO_2) emission certificates.

These issues were touched upon in a Communication from the European Commission titled, 'Facing the challenge of higher oil prices' (COM(2008) 384), which called on the EU to become more efficient in its use of energy, and less dependent on fossil fuels – in particular, by following the approach laid out in the climate change and renewable energy package.

The EU has acted to liberalise electricity and gas markets since the second half of the 1990s. Directives adopted in 2003 established common rules for internal markets for electricity and natural gas. Deadlines were set for opening markets and allowing customers to choose their supplier: as of 1 July 2004 for business customers and as of 1 July 2007 for all consumers (including households). Certain countries anticipated the liberalisation process, while others were much slower in adopting the necessary measures. Indeed, significant barriers to entry remain in many electricity and natural gas

markets as seen through the number of markets that are still dominated by (near) monopoly suppliers. In July 2009, the European Parliament and Council adopted a third package of legislative proposals aimed at ensuring a real and effective choice of suppliers, as well as benefits for customers: this package came into effect as of March 2011. It is anticipated that increased transparency for gas and electricity prices should help promote fair competition, by encouraging consumers to choose between different energy sources (oil, coal, natural gas and renewable energy sources) and different suppliers. Energy price transparency can be made more effective by publishing and broadcasting as widely as possible prices and pricing systems.

Table 12.5.1: Half-yearly electricity and gas prices, first half of year, 2009-2011
(EUR per kWh)

	Electricity prices						Gas prices					
	Households (¹)			Industry (²)			Households (³)			Industry (⁴)		
	2009	2010	2011	2009	2010	2011	2009	2010	2011	2009	2010	2011
EU-27	0.163	0.167	0.178	0.107	0.105	0.110	0.059	0.053	0.056	0.036	0.031	0.034
Euro area (⁵)	0.171	0.176	0.187	0.111	0.109	0.116	0.066	0.058	0.062	0.038	0.032	0.036
Belgium	0.192	0.196	0.214	0.111	0.106	0.110	0.061	0.053	0.057	0.033	0.029	0.032
Bulgaria	0.082	0.081	0.083	0.065	0.065	0.065	0.047	0.037	0.043	0.031	0.024	0.029
Czech Republic	0.132	0.135	0.150	0.107	0.103	0.111	0.049	0.047	0.054	0.033	0.031	0.031
Denmark	0.270	0.267	0.291	0.086	0.094	0.099	0.092	0.107	0.116	0.056	0.057	0.067
Germany	0.228	0.238	0.253	0.113	0.112	0.125	0.065	0.057	0.059	0.043	0.036	0.046
Estonia	0.092	0.097	0.097	0.064	0.069	0.072	0.039	0.036	0.042	0.027	0.029	0.028
Ireland	0.203	0.180	0.190	0.121	0.112	0.116	0.064	0.050	0.051	0.033	0.028	0.038
Greece	0.115	0.118	0.125	0.095	0.095	0.101	:	:	:	:	:	:
Spain	0.158	0.173	0.195	0.115	0.117	0.114	0.061	0.053	0.054	0.031	0.028	0.029
France	0.121	0.128	0.138	0.073	0.085	0.085	0.055	0.052	0.058	0.036	0.033	0.037
Italy	0.210	0.197	0.201	0.153	0.139	0.153	0.076	0.062	0.069	0.040	0.030	0.031
Cyprus	0.156	0.186	0.205	0.119	0.151	0.167	:	:	:	:	:	:
Latvia	0.105	0.105	0.117	0.090	0.089	0.098	0.052	0.031	0.039	0.039	0.026	0.029
Lithuania	0.095	0.116	0.121	0.092	0.100	0.105	0.042	0.038	0.043	0.031	0.032	0.035
Luxembourg	0.188	0.173	0.168	0.116	0.102	0.100	0.049	0.043	0.051	0.040	0.037	0.042
Hungary	0.148	0.170	0.168	0.124	0.106	0.095	0.048	0.054	0.056	0.037	0.030	0.033
Malta	0.171	0.170	0.170	0.151	0.180	0.180	:	:	:	:	:	:
Netherlands	0.190	0.170	0.174	0.113	0.104	0.103	0.083	0.070	0.072	0.038	0.032	0.033
Austria	0.191	0.197	0.199	:	:	:	0.065	0.062	0.069	:	:	:
Poland	0.113	0.134	0.147	0.090	0.098	0.101	0.039	0.043	0.046	0.028	0.030	0.033
Portugal	0.151	0.158	0.165	0.094	0.094	0.099	0.060	0.059	0.061	0.035	0.027	0.034
Romania	0.098	0.103	0.108	0.081	0.085	0.080	0.029	0.027	0.028	0.023	0.022	0.023
Slovenia	0.135	0.140	0.144	0.103	0.099	0.099	0.066	0.058	0.067	0.044	0.042	0.045
Slovakia	0.154	0.152	0.168	0.142	0.117	0.128	0.046	0.044	0.047	0.041	0.033	0.035
Finland	0.130	0.133	0.154	0.069	0.069	0.076	:	:	:	0.031	0.030	0.042
Sweden	0.160	0.184	0.209	0.067	0.081	0.089	0.089	0.103	0.122	0.039	0.044	0.052
United Kingdom	0.147	0.139	0.143	0.112	0.099	0.098	0.043	0.041	0.042	0.029	0.023	0.025
Norway	0.157	0.203	0.213	0.079	0.103	0.111	:	:	:	:	:	:
Croatia	0.115	0.115	0.114	0.087	0.094	0.091	0.032	0.038	0.038	0.026	0.034	0.040
FYR of Macedonia	:	:	:	:	:	:	:	:	:	:	:	0.038
Turkey	0.114	0.134	0.122	0.078	0.089	0.079	0.039	0.032	0.029	0.029	0.024	0.022
Bosnia and Herzegovina	:	0.074	0.075	:	0.062	0.061	:	0.038	0.045	:	0.042	0.048

(¹) Annual consumption: 2 500 kWh < consumption < 5 000 kWh.
(²) Annual consumption: 500 MWh < consumption < 2 000 MWh; excluding VAT.
(³) Annual consumption: 5 600 kWh < consumption < 56 000 kWh (20-200 GJ).
(⁴) Annual consumption: 2 778 MWh < consumption < 27 778 MWh (10 000-100 000 GJ); excluding VAT.
(⁵) 2009 and 2010, EA-16.

Source: Eurostat (online data codes: nrg_pc_204, nrg_pc_205, nrg_pc_202 and nrg_pc_203)

Figure 12.5.1: Electricity prices for household consumers, first half 2011 (¹)
(EUR per kWh)

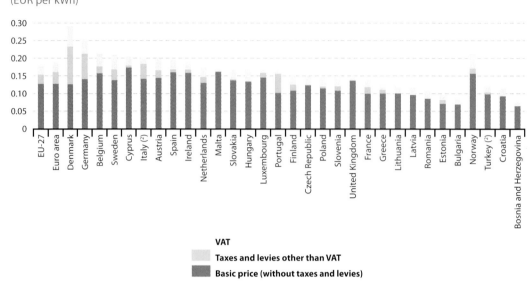

(¹) Annual consumption: 2 500 kWh < consumption < 5 000 kWh.
(²) Provisional.

Source: Eurostat (online data code: nrg_pc_204)

Figure 12.5.2: Natural gas prices for household consumers, first half 2011 (¹)
(EUR per kWh)

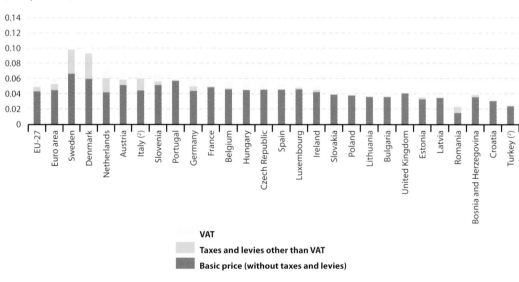

(¹) Annual consumption: 5 600 kWh < consumption < 56 000 kWh (20-200 GJ); Greece and Finland, not available; Cyprus and Malta, not applicable.
(²) Provisional.

Source: Eurostat (online data code: nrg_pc_202)

Table 12.5.2: Taxes and levies on electricity prices for household consumers; ranked on share in total price, first half 2011 (¹)

	Basic price	Taxes & levies other than VAT	VAT	Share of taxes, levies & VAT in total price
	(EUR per kWh)			(%)
EU-27	0.128	0.026	0.025	28.53
Euro area	0.128	0.033	0.027	31.91
Denmark	0.126	0.106	0.058	56.57
Germany	0.141	0.072	0.040	44.38
Portugal	0.102	0.054	0.010	38.63
Sweden	0.138	0.030	0.041	34.23
Finland	0.108	0.017	0.029	29.81
Italy	*0.142*	*0.042*	*0.018*	*29.71*
France	0.099	0.019	0.020	28.18
Estonia	0.070	0.011	0.016	27.65
Austria	0.144	0.021	0.033	27.39
Belgium	0.157	0.019	0.037	26.40
Netherlands	0.130	0.017	0.028	25.42
Slovenia	0.108	0.012	0.024	25.12
Poland	0.115	0.005	0.028	22.16
Romania	0.085	0.000	0.023	21.63
Hungary	0.134	0.001	0.034	20.58
Greece	0.100	0.011	0.014	19.92
Slovakia	0.137	0.003	0.028	18.43
Latvia	0.096	0.000	0.021	18.07
Spain	0.160	0.008	0.027	17.98
Czech Republic	0.123	0.001	0.025	17.59
Lithuania	0.100	0.000	0.021	17.30
Bulgaria	0.069	0.000	0.014	16.71
Ireland	0.158	0.009	0.023	16.68
Cyprus	0.173	0.006	0.026	15.56
Luxembourg	0.145	0.013	0.010	13.53
Malta	0.162	0.000	0.009	5.00
United Kingdom	0.137	0.000	0.007	4.75
Norway	0.156	0.014	0.043	26.72
Turkey	*0.098*	*0.005*	*0.019*	*19.57*
Croatia	0.092	0.001	0.021	19.26
Bosnia and Herzegovina	0.064	0.000	0.011	14.46

(¹) Annual consumption: 2 500 kWh < consumption < 5 000 kWh.

Source: Eurostat (online data code: nrg_pc_204)

Table 12.5.3: Taxes and levies on natural gas prices for household consumers; ranked on share in total price, first half 2011 ([1])

	Basic price	Taxes & levies other than VAT	VAT	Share of taxes, levies & VAT in total price
	(EUR per kWh)			(%)
EU-27	0.056	1.560	2.153	23.70
Euro area	0.062	2.168	2.603	27.80
Denmark	0.059	0.034	0.023	48.95
Romania	0.015	0.008	0.006	47.56
Sweden	0.066	0.032	0.025	46.05
Netherlands	0.042	0.019	0.011	41.86
Italy	*0.044*	*0.016*	*0.009*	*36.43*
Austria	0.051	0.007	0.011	26.28
Germany	0.043	0.006	0.009	26.07
Slovenia	0.051	0.004	0.011	23.33
Estonia	0.033	0.002	0.007	22.08
Hungary	0.045	0.000	0.011	20.00
Belgium	0.046	0.002	0.010	19.99
Poland	0.038	0.000	0.009	18.71
Lithuania	0.036	0.000	0.008	17.37
Ireland	0.042	0.003	0.006	17.33
Czech Republic	0.045	0.000	0.009	16.67
Bulgaria	0.036	0.000	0.007	16.65
France	0.048	0.001	0.009	16.64
Slovakia	0.039	0.000	0.008	16.63
Spain	0.045	0.000	0.008	15.25
Latvia	0.035	0.000	0.004	10.79
Luxembourg	0.046	0.002	0.003	10.36
Portugal	0.057	0.001	0.003	7.08
United Kingdom	0.040	0.000	0.002	4.78
Greece	:	:	:	:
Finland	:	:	:	:
Bosnia and Herzegovina	0.036	0.003	0.007	21.55
Croatia	0.031	0.000	0.007	18.67
Turkey	*0.023*	*0.001*	*0.004*	*18.63*

([1]) Annual consumption: 5 600 kWh < consumption < 56 000 kWh (20-200 GJ); Cyprus and Malta, not applicable.

Source: Eurostat (online data code: nrg_pc_202)

Science and technology

Introduction

Science is part of almost every aspect of our lives: at the flick of a switch, we have light; when we are ill, medicines help us get better; when we want to talk to a friend we just pick up the telephone or send a text message or e-mail. Europe has a long tradition of excellence in research and innovation, having been the birthplace of the industrial revolution. The European Union (EU) is a world leader in a range of cutting-edge industrial sectors – for example, biotechnology, pharmaceuticals, telecommunications or aerospace.

Research and development (R & D) is often considered as one of the driving forces behind growth and job creation. However, its influence extends well beyond the economic sphere, as it can potentially resolve environmental or international security threats, ensure safer food, or lead to the development of new medicines to fight illness and disease.

Since their launch in 1984, the EU's framework programmes for research have played a leading role in multidisciplinary research activities. The seventh framework programme for research and technological development (FP7) is the EU's main instrument for funding research in Europe; it runs from 2007 to 2013 and has a total budget of EUR 50 521 million, with an additional EUR 2 751 million for 2007 to 2011 for nuclear research and training activities to be carried out under the Euratom Treaty. This money is generally intended to finance grants to research actors all over Europe, usually through co-financing research, technological development and demonstration projects. FP7 is made up of four broad programmes – cooperation (collaborative research), ideas (the European Research Council), people (human potential) and capacities (research capacity). Through these programmes, FP7 aims to create European 'poles of excellence' across a wide array of scientific themes, such as information technologies, energy and climate change, health, food, and social sciences. FP7 also foresees direct research at the European Commission's own research institute (the Joint Research Centre (JRC)), whose activities are divided into 17 policy agendas, with an emphasis on understanding the relationship between the environment and health, internal and external security, and support for Europe's 2020 economic growth.

The European Research Area (ERA) was launched at the Lisbon European Council in March 2000. ERA aims to ensure open and transparent trade in scientific and technical skills, ideas and know-how. Europe's research efforts are often described as being fragmented along national and institutional lines. Indeed, individual Member States may find it difficult to play a leading role in important areas of scientific and technological advance as research is increasingly complex, interdisciplinary and expensive.

The ERA was given new impetus in April 2007 with the European Commission's Green paper on the European research area: new perspectives. In May 2008 the ERA was re-launched as part of what has become known as the Ljubljana process, including specific initiatives for five different areas: researchers' careers and mobility; research infrastructures; knowledge sharing; research programmes; and international science and technology cooperation. As a result, in the years through to 2020 the ERA will aim to establish a single European labour market for researchers, as well as single markets for knowledge and for innovative goods and services. Furthermore, the ERA should aim to: encourage trust and dialogue between society and the scientific and technological community; benefit from a strong publicly-supported research and technology base and world-class research infrastructures and capacities across Europe; provide for the joint design of research, education and innovation policies; address major challenges through strategic partnerships; and enable Europe to speak with one voice to its main international partners.

International cooperation forms an integral part of the EU's scientific policy, which includes programmes to enhance Europe's access to worldwide scientific expertise, attract top scientists to work in Europe, contribute to international responses to shared problems, and put research at the service of EU external and development policies. In December

2008, the Competitiveness Council adopted a 2020 vision for the ERA, which foresees the introduction of a 'fifth freedom' for the EU's internal market – namely, the free circulation of researchers, knowledge and technology.

In October 2010, the European Commission launched a Europe 2020 flagship initiative, titled 'innovation union' (COM(2010) 546 final) which sets out a strategic approach to a range of challenges like climate change, energy and food security, health and an ageing population. The proposals seek to use public sector intervention to stimulate the private sector and to remove bottlenecks which stop ideas reaching the market (such as access to finance, fragmented research systems and markets, under-use of public procurement for innovation, and speeding-up harmonised standards and technical specifications). European Innovation Partnerships (EIPs) form part of the innovation union and are designed to act as a framework to address major societal challenges, bringing together activities and policies from basic research through to market oriented solutions – for more information, see the subchapter on innovation statistics.

Horizon 2020 is planned as the framework programme for research and innovation after 2013, building upon FP7, the competitiveness and innovation framework programme (CIP) and the European institute of innovation and technology (EIT). A Green paper titled 'From challenges to opportunities: towards a common strategic framework for EU research and innovation funding' (COM(2011) 48) was adopted by the European Commission in February 2011 and proposed major changes to EU research and innovation funding to make participation easier, increase scientific and economic impact and provide better value for money.

Official European statistics on science and technology provide a leading example of cooperation activities between international statistical organisations.

In the domain of R & D statistics a joint survey produced by the OECD and Eurostat has been introduced, which is based on the collection of information following guidelines laid out in the Frascati manual. As regards human capital, the OECD, UNESCO and Eurostat are working towards developing internationally comparable indicators on the careers and mobility of doctorate (PhD) holders. Within the domain of innovation statistics, Eurostat conducts a Community innovation survey, which is based on the guidelines laid out within the Oslo manual (jointly produced with other European Commission services and the OECD). Together with the European Patent Office (EPO), the United States Patent and Trademark Office (USPTO) and the OECD, Eurostat has worked towards the improvement of PATSTAT, a harmonised database covering EPO patent applications and USPTO patents granted.

The innovation scoreboard used for assessing innovation performance in the Member States has been reworked to improve international comparability and to include a number of research oriented indicators in line with the purpose of monitoring the implementation of the innovation union; it has been renamed the innovation union scoreboard. This revised tool aims to provide a comparative assessment of the performance of the Member States and the relative strengths and weaknesses of their research and innovation systems. The 2010 scoreboard draws on 25 research and innovation-related indicators grouped into three main categories:

• enablers such as human resources, finance and support, open, excellent and attractive research systems;
• activities of enterprises, such as investment, linkages and entrepreneurship or intellectual assets; and
• outputs, such as innovators and economic effects.

13.1 R & D expenditure

Most European research is funded at the national level, by private and/or public sources. This subchapter presents data on R & D spending within the European Union (EU), according to the sector performing the research and according to the source of funds.

Framework programmes are the main instrument for funding R & D within the EU. The 7th framework programme (FP7) for research and technological development started in 2007 and is due to continue for a total of seven years. Horizon 2020 is planned as the framework programme for research and innovation after 2013 – see the introduction for science and technology for more information.

The European Research Area (ERA) is composed of all research and development activities, programmes and policies in Europe which involve a transnational perspective. In December 2008, the Competitiveness Council adopted a 2020 vision for the ERA, which foresees the introduction of a 'fifth freedom' – namely, the free circulation of researchers, knowledge and technology.

Main statistical findings

Gross domestic expenditure on R & D (GERD) stood at EUR 236 820 million in the EU-27 in 2009, which marked a 1.2 % decrease on the level of GERD in 2008, but was 50.3 % higher than ten years earlier (1999) – note that these rates of change are in current prices and so reflect price changes as well as real changes in the level of expenditure. In 2008 the level of expenditure on R & D in the EU-27 was 88.5 % of that recorded by the United States, although slightly more than double the level of expenditure in Japan and considerably above R & D expenditure levels in the emerging economies – for example, EU-27 expenditure was 5.3 times as high as in China.

In order to make figures more comparable, GERD is often expressed relative to gross domestic product (GDP) – see Figure 13.1.1 – or in relation to population. The ratio of GERD to GDP increased marginally in the EU-27 during the period up to 2002

reaching a high of 1.87 %, before declining modestly through to 2005 (1.82 %), and climbing again to 1.92 % by 2008 and 2.01 % by 2009. The ratio of GERD to GDP increased between 2008 and 2009 despite a fall in the absolute level of expenditure; this can be explained by GDP falling even more than GERD during the financial and economic crisis. Nevertheless, the EU-27's R & D expenditure relative to GDP remains well below the corresponding shares recorded in Japan (3.44 %) and the United States (2.77 %) in 2008; this pattern has existed for a lengthy period. There was a far higher increase in the relative importance of GERD in the Japanese economy, as its share of GDP rose by 0.42 percentage points during the period 1999 to 2008; note however that Japanese economic growth was also subdued during this period.

One of the key objectives of the EU during the last decade has been to encourage increasing levels of investment, in order to provide a stimulus to the EU's competitiveness. At the Barcelona Council in 2002, the EU agreed to a target of spending at least 3 % of gross domestic product (GDP) on research by 2010, of which two thirds was to be financed by the business sector; most of the EU Member States specified their own targets in national reform programmes. Using this measure, the highest R & D intensity in 2009 was recorded in Finland (3.96 %), Sweden (3.62 %) and Denmark (3.02 %) – see Table 13.1.1. While none of the other Member States reported GERD rising above 3 % of GDP at a national level, R & D intensity also rose to relatively high levels in a number of regions, for example in Baden-Württemberg and Berlin (Germany), the east of England (United Kingdom), and southern Austria. There were eight Member States that reported R & D expenditure accounting for less than 1 % of their GDP in 2009, with Latvia, Cyprus, Romania and Slovakia below 0.5 %. The regions with the lowest R & D intensity were generally in southern and eastern Europe.

The differences in the relative importance of R & D expenditure between countries are often explained by referring to levels of expenditure within the business enterprise sector. Table 13.1.2 shows that the share of R & D conducted within the business enterprise sector was equivalent to 1.25 % of the EU-27's GDP in 2009, compared with 2.70 % in Japan and 2.01 % in the United States (both 2008), while the relative importance of R & D expenditure in the government and higher education sector was broadly similar across all three members of the Triad. An evaluation of the data for the Member States also confirms that those countries with relatively high shares of business enterprise expenditure on R & D – namely, Finland, Sweden, Denmark, Austria and Germany – also reported relatively high levels of total GERD. Apart from Germany, these countries also tended to feature near the top-end of the ranking of expenditure by the higher education sector, where the Netherlands also had a relatively high share of R & D expenditure. Government R & D expenditure relative to GDP was highest in Germany, Slovenia, Finland and France.

A breakdown of R & D expenditure by source of funds shows that more than half (54.7 %) of the total expenditure in 2008 within the EU-27 came from business enterprises, while just over one third (33.9 %) was from government, and a further 8.7 % from abroad. Business-funded R & D accounted for 78.2 % of total R & D expenditure in Japan and 67.3 % in the United States. Table 13.1.3 confirms the relatively important role played by the business enterprise sector as a source of R & D funding in Luxembourg (2007 data), Finland (2009) and Germany (2008), as business-funded R & D accounted for over two thirds of total GERD. In contrast, a majority of the gross expenditure on R & D made in Cyprus and Bulgaria in 2008 and in Poland, Romania, Lithuania and Slovakia in 2009 was funded by the government sector. There were also considerable differences in the source of R & D funding from abroad, with relatively high shares (in excess of 15 % of total GERD) reported in the United Kingdom, Malta, Austria, Ireland and Latvia.

Data sources and availability

Statistics on science, technology and innovation (STI statistics) are based on Decision 1608/2003/ECconcerning the production and development of

Community statistics on science and technology. In close cooperation with the Member States, this Decision was implemented by Eurostat in the form of legislative measures and other work. Regulation 753/2004 on statistics on science and technology was adopted in 2004 implementing Decision 1608/2003/EC.

Eurostat's statistics on R & D expenditure are compiled using guidelines laid out in the Frascati manual, published in 2002 by the OECD. R & D expenditure is a basic measure that covers intramural expenditure, in other words, all expenditures for R & D that are performed within a statistical unit or sector of the economy.

The main breakdown of R & D statistics is by four institutional sectors of performance. These four sectors are the business enterprise sector, the government sector, the higher education sector, and the private non-profit sector (the latter is not shown in this subchapter). Gross domestic expenditure on R & D (GERD) is composed of expenditure from each of these four sectors. Expenditure data considers the research spend on the national territory, regardless of the source of funds; data are usually expressed in relation to GDP, otherwise known as R & D intensity. Additional breakdowns of R & D expenditure are available by: source of funds; field of science; type of costs; economic activity (NACE); enterprise size class; type of R & D; socio-economic objectives; and regions (NUTS).

The European Commission compiles three levels of indicators to support research and innovation policymaking. These indicators are generally grouped together as: headline indicators; innovation union scoreboard (or core) indicators; and a comprehensive set of indicators. Within the headline indicators – also referred to as Europe 2020 strategy indicators – is the measure of research intensity (with a 3 % target for investment in research across the EU). The scoreboard (or core) indicators are designed to monitor research and innovation for the Competitiveness Council, while the comprehensive set of indicators are for in-depth economic analytical purposes and Commission services to produce a science, technology and competitiveness report.

Context

The European Commission has through its Europe 2020 flagship initiative, titled 'innovation union', placed renewed emphasis on the conversion of Europe's scientific expertise into marketable products and services, through seeking to use public sector intervention to stimulate the private sector and to remove bottlenecks which stop such ideas reaching the market. Furthermore, the latest revision of the integrated economic and employment guidelines (revised as part of the Europe 2020 strategy for smart, sustainable and inclusive growth) includes a guideline to optimise support for R & D and innovation, strengthening the knowledge triangle and unleashing the potential of the digital economy.

One area that has received considerable attention in recent years is the structural difference in R & D funding between Europe and its main competitors. Policymakers in Europe have tried to increase R & D business expenditure so that it is more in line with relative contributions observed in Japan or the United States. The European Research Area (ERA) is designed to overcome some of these barriers that are thought to have hampered European research efforts, for example, by addressing geographical, institutional, disciplinary and sectoral boundaries.

Studies have been conducted in respect to business enterprises' investment in an annual report, titled the EU's industrial R & D investment scoreboard. This presents information on the top 1 000 research investors whose registered offices are in the EU and the top 1 000 investors registered elsewhere. According to this source Volkswagen (Germany) and Nokia (Finland) were among the global top ten investors in 2010, a group that was led by Roche (Switzerland) and Pfizer (the United States), and also included Novartis (Switzerland).

In December 2008, the Competitiveness Council adopted a 2020 vision for the ERA. According to the opening statement of this vision, all players should benefit from: the 'fifth freedom', introducing the free circulation of researchers, knowledge and technology across the ERA; attractive conditions for carrying out research and investing in R & D intensive sectors; Europe-wide scientific competition, together with the appropriate level of cooperation and coordination. The 2020 vision for the ERA is part of the wider picture of Europe's 2020 strategy for smart, sustainable and inclusive growth.

As part of the EU's 7th framework programme for research and technological development the European Commission announced in July 2011 nearly EUR 7 000 million of investment in research and innovation, with the aim of providing an economic stimulus expected to create around 174 000 jobs in the short-term.

Figure 13.1.1: Gross domestic expenditure on R&D in the Triad, 1999-2009 (% share of GDP)

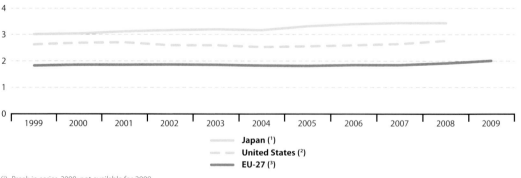

(1) Break in series, 2008; not available for 2009.
(2) Excludes most or all capital expenditure; 2008, provisional; not available for 2009.
(3) Estimates.
Source: Eurostat (online data code: t2020_20), OECD

Table 13.1.1: Gross domestic expenditure on R&D, 1999-2009
(% share of GDP)

	1999	2000	2001	2002	2003	2004	2005	2006	2007	2008	2009
EU-27	1.83	1.86	1.86	1.87	1.86	1.83	1.82	1.85	1.85	1.92	2.01
Euro area (EA-16)	1.82	1.83	1.85	1.87	1.87	1.85	1.84	1.87	1.88	1.96	2.05
Belgium	1.94	1.97	2.07	1.94	1.88	1.86	1.83	1.86	1.90	1.96	1.96
Bulgaria	0.55	0.51	0.46	0.48	0.48	0.49	0.46	0.46	0.45	0.47	0.53
Czech Republic	1.14	1.21	1.20	1.20	1.25	1.25	1.41	1.55	1.54	1.47	1.53
Denmark (¹)	2.18	2.24	2.39	2.51	2.58	2.48	2.46	2.48	2.58	2.87	3.02
Germany	2.40	2.45	2.46	2.49	2.52	2.49	2.49	2.53	2.53	2.68	2.82
Estonia	0.68	0.60	0.70	0.72	0.77	0.85	0.93	1.13	1.10	1.29	1.42
Ireland	1.18	1.12	1.10	1.10	1.17	1.23	1.25	1.25	1.29	1.45	1.77
Greece	0.60	:	0.58	:	0.57	0.55	0.59	0.58	0.58	:	:
Spain	0.86	0.91	0.91	0.99	1.05	1.06	1.12	1.20	1.27	1.35	1.38
France (²)	2.16	2.15	2.20	2.23	2.17	2.15	2.10	2.10	2.07	2.11	2.21
Italy	1.02	1.05	1.09	1.13	1.11	1.10	1.09	1.13	1.18	1.23	1.27
Cyprus	0.23	0.24	0.25	0.30	0.35	0.37	0.40	0.43	0.44	0.42	0.46
Latvia	0.36	0.44	0.41	0.42	0.38	0.42	0.56	0.70	0.59	0.61	0.46
Lithuania	0.50	0.59	0.67	0.66	0.67	0.75	0.75	0.79	0.81	0.80	0.84
Luxembourg	:	1.65	:	:	1.65	1.63	1.56	1.66	1.58	1.51	1.68
Hungary (³)	0.67	0.79	0.92	1.00	0.93	0.87	0.95	1.00	0.97	1.00	1.15
Malta (³)	:	:	:	0.26	0.26	0.53	0.56	0.61	0.58	0.57	0.54
Netherlands (⁴)	1.96	1.82	1.80	1.72	1.92	1.93	1.90	1.88	1.81	1.76	1.84
Austria	1.90	1.94	2.07	2.14	2.26	2.26	2.45	2.46	2.52	2.67	2.75
Poland	0.69	0.64	0.62	0.56	0.54	0.56	0.57	0.56	0.57	0.60	0.68
Portugal	0.69	0.73	0.77	0.73	0.71	0.75	0.78	0.99	1.17	1.50	1.66
Romania	0.40	0.37	0.39	0.38	0.39	0.39	0.41	0.45	0.52	0.58	0.47
Slovenia (⁵)	1.37	1.39	1.50	1.47	1.27	1.40	1.44	1.56	1.45	1.65	1.86
Slovakia	0.66	0.65	0.63	0.57	0.57	0.51	0.51	0.49	0.46	0.47	0.48
Finland	3.17	3.35	3.32	3.37	3.44	3.45	3.48	3.48	3.47	3.72	3.96
Sweden (⁶)	3.58	:	4.13	:	3.80	3.58	3.56	3.68	3.40	3.70	3.62
United Kingdom	1.82	1.81	1.79	1.79	1.75	1.68	1.73	1.75	1.78	1.77	1.87
Iceland	2.30	2.67	2.95	2.95	2.82	:	2.77	2.99	2.68	2.65	3.10
Norway	1.64	:	1.59	1.66	1.71	1.59	1.52	1.52	1.65	1.64	1.80
Switzerland	:	2.53	:	:	:	2.90	:	:	:	3.00	:
Croatia	:	:	:	0.96	0.96	1.05	0.87	0.75	0.80	0.90	0.84
Turkey	0.47	0.48	0.54	0.53	0.48	0.52	0.59	0.58	0.72	0.72	0.85
Japan (⁵)	3.02	3.04	3.12	3.17	3.20	3.17	3.32	3.40	3.44	3.44	:
United States	2.63	2.69	2.71	2.60	2.60	2.53	2.56	2.60	2.65	2.77	:

(¹) Break in series, 2007.
(²) Break in series, 2000 and 2004.
(³) Break in series, 2004.
(⁴) Break in series, 2003.
(⁵) Break in series, 2008.
(⁶) Break in series, 2005.

Source: Eurostat (online data code: t2020_20), OECD

Science and technology

Table 13.1.2: Gross domestic expenditure on R&D by sector, 2004 and 2009
(% share of GDP)

	Business enterprise sector (¹)		Government sector (²)		Higher education sector (³)	
	2004	2009	2004	2009	2004	2009
EU-27	*1.16*	*1.25*	*0.24*	*0.27*	*0.41*	*0.48*
Euro area (EA-16)	*1.17*	*1.27*	*0.27*	*0.29*	*0.40*	*0.47*
Belgium	1.28	*1.32*	0.14	*0.17*	0.40	*0.45*
Bulgaria	0.12	*0.16*	0.33	*0.29*	0.05	*0.07*
Czech Republic	0.78	0.92	0.28	0.33	0.18	0.28
Denmark	1.69	*2.02*	0.17	*0.09*	0.61	*0.90*
Germany	1.74	*1.92*	0.34	*0.41*	0.41	*0.49*
Estonia	0.33	*0.64*	0.11	0.16	0.39	0.60
Ireland	0.81	*1.17*	0.09	*0.08*	0.33	*0.52*
Greece (⁴)	*0.17*	0.16	*0.11*	0.12	*0.27*	0.29
Spain	0.58	0.72	0.17	0.28	0.31	0.39
France	1.36	*1.37*	0.37	*0.36*	0.40	*0.45*
Italy	0.52	*0.65*	0.20	*0.18*	0.36	0.40
Cyprus	0.08	*0.10*	0.13	*0.10*	0.13	*0.20*
Latvia	0.19	0.17	0.08	0.11	0.15	0.18
Lithuania	0.16	0.20	0.19	0.20	0.41	0.44
Luxembourg	1.43	*1.24*	0.18	*0.29*	0.02	*0.15*
Hungary	0.36	0.66	0.26	0.23	0.21	*0.24*
Malta	0.35	*0.34*	0.01	*0.03*	0.17	*0.17*
Netherlands	1.03	*0.88*	0.26	*0.23*	0.64	*0.73*
Austria	1.53	*1.94*	0.12	*0.15*	0.60	*0.66*
Poland	0.16	0.19	0.22	0.23	0.18	*0.25*
Portugal	*0.27*	0.78	*0.12*	0.12	*0.27*	0.59
Romania	0.21	0.19	0.13	0.17	0.04	0.12
Slovenia	0.94	1.20	0.28	0.39	0.18	0.27
Slovakia	0.25	0.20	0.16	0.16	0.10	0.12
Finland	2.42	2.83	0.33	0.36	0.68	0.75
Sweden	2.63	*2.55*	0.11	0.16	0.82	*0.90*
United Kingdom	1.05	*1.16*	0.18	*0.17*	0.42	*0.50*
Iceland	:	1.64	:	0.62	:	0.77
Norway	0.87	*0.95*	0.25	*0.29*	0.47	*0.57*
Switzerland (⁵)	2.14	2.20	0.03	0.02	0.66	0.72
Croatia	0.44	0.34	0.22	0.23	0.39	0.27
Turkey	0.13	0.34	0.04	0.11	0.35	0.40
Japan (⁵)	2.38	2.70	0.30	0.29	0.43	0.40
United States (⁵)	1.76	*2.01*	0.31	0.29	0.36	0.36

(¹) Break in series, Denmark, France, Slovenia and Sweden.
(²) Break in series, Denmark, Sweden and Norway.
(³) Break in series, Denmark, France, Italy, Norway and Japan.
(⁴) 2007 instead of 2009.
(⁵) 2008 instead of 2009.

Source: Eurostat (online data code: tsc00001), OECD

Table 13.1.3: Gross domestic expenditure on R&D by source of funds, 2004 and 2009
(% of total gross expenditure on R&D)

	Business enterprises [1]		Government [1]		Abroad [2]	
	2004	2009	2004	2009	2004	2009
EU-27 [3]	54.2	54.7	35.1	33.9	8.4	8.7
Euro area (EA-16) [3]	55.7	56.2	36.1	34.8	6.6	7.1
Belgium [4]	60.2	61.4	24.4	22.2	12.3	13.0
Bulgaria [3]	28.2	30.6	65.8	61.2	5.5	6.8
Czech Republic	52.8	45.8	41.9	43.9	3.7	9.2
Denmark	:	60.2	:	28.4	:	8.7
Germany [3]	66.6	67.3	30.5	28.4	2.5	4.0
Estonia	36.5	38.4	44.1	48.9	17.0	11.4
Ireland	58.6	50.8	31.1	31.5	8.6	15.6
Greece	:	:	:	:	:	:
Spain [3]	48.0	45.0	41.0	45.6	6.2	5.7
France [3]	50.7	50.7	38.7	38.9	8.8	8.0
Italy [3]	:	45.2	:	42.9	:	7.8
Cyprus [3]	18.9	17.8	64.1	64.1	11.5	14.7
Latvia	46.3	36.9	31.2	44.7	22.5	15.4
Lithuania	19.9	21.0	63.1	53.9	10.7	13.1
Luxembourg [4]	:	76.0	:	18.2	:	5.7
Hungary	37.1	46.4	51.8	42.0	10.4	10.9
Malta	:	51.4	:	31.3	:	17.2
Netherlands [4]	:	48.8	:	36.8	:	10.6
Austria	47.2	44.8	32.6	39.1	19.4	15.7
Poland	30.5	27.1	61.7	60.4	5.2	5.5
Portugal [3]	34.2	48.1	57.5	43.7	4.8	3.0
Romania	44.0	34.8	49.0	54.9	5.5	8.3
Slovenia	58.5	58.0	30.0	35.7	11.1	6.0
Slovakia	38.3	35.1	57.1	50.6	4.3	12.8
Finland	69.3	68.1	26.3	24.0	3.2	6.6
Sweden	:	58.9	:	27.3	:	10.5
United Kingdom	44.1	45.4	32.9	30.7	17.1	17.7
Iceland	:	48.5	:	41.4	:	9.9
Norway [4]	:	45.3	:	44.9	:	8.3
Switzerland [3]	69.7	68.2	22.7	22.8	5.2	6.0
Croatia	43.0	39.8	46.6	51.2	2.6	7.0
Turkey	37.9	41.0	57.0	34.0	0.4	1.1
Japan [3]	74.8	78.2	18.1	15.6	0.3	0.4
United States [3]	63.7	67.3	30.9	27.1	:	:

[1] Break in series, Denmark, Slovenia, Sweden, Turkey and Japan.
[2] Break in series, Denmark, Slovenia, Finland, Sweden and Japan.
[3] 2008 instead of 2009.
[4] 2007 instead of 2009.

Source: Eurostat (online data code: tsiir030), OECD

13.2 R & D personnel

This subchapter analyses data on research and development (R & D) personnel, researchers and human resources in science and technology in the European Union (EU). Statistics on human resources in science and technology are a key indicator for measuring the knowledge-based economy and its developments. These statistics can show the supply of, and demand for highly qualified science and technology specialists.

Main statistical findings

R & D personnel

The number of researchers in the EU-27 has increased in recent years. There were 1.6 million researchers (full-time equivalents (FTE)) employed in the EU-27 in 2009 (see Table 13.2.1), which marked an increase of almost 466 000 (or 41.6 %) when compared with 2000.

A breakdown of R & D personnel in the EU-27 by institutional sector in 2009 shows that more than two fifths of the total were concentrated in the business enterprise sector (44 %) and the higher education sector (42 %) and 12 % in the government sector. The relative importance of the different institutional sectors varied considerably across the Member States, with business enterprises accounting for more than three fifths of all researchers in Austria, Sweden and Denmark. Bulgaria reported that nearly half (49 %) of its researchers were employed within the government sector, far more than the next highest share recorded in Romania (30 %). More than two thirds of all researchers working in Latvia, Slovakia and Lithuania were employed within the higher education sector.

R & D personnel from all sectors together made up more than 1.9 % of the labour force in Finland, Luxembourg, and Denmark in 2009. Aside from these three Member States, this share ranged from less than 0.5 % in Romania, Cyprus, Poland and Latvia to just over 1.5 % in Sweden and France, with the EU-27 average estimated around 1.1 %. A gender breakdown shows that men accounted for 71 % of the EU-27's workforce of researchers in 2008, the

same as in 2007, and 2 percentage points lower than in 2000. The share of women in the total number of researchers in 2008 was close to half in Latvia, Lithuania and Bulgaria, as well as in Croatia.

Human resources in science and technology

Human resources in science and technology (HRST) provide a broad measure of the supply of, and demand for, people highly qualified in science and technology. Some 66.8 million people were employed in the EU-27 within science and technology occupations in 2010; this amounted to 31.0 % of total employment. Between 2007 and 2010 there was an increase in the relative importance of HRST within the EU-27 workforce, as their share rose by 1.1 percentage points. The HRST 'core' – which is made up of people within science and technology occupations who possess a tertiary level education (for example, university graduates) – amounted to 40.7 million persons in 2010 (or 18.9 % of the total number of persons employed).

Persons in HRST occupations accounted for around two fifths of the workforce in Sweden, Denmark and the Netherlands in 2010 and just over half in Luxembourg. The lowest shares were recorded in Portugal and Romania where persons in HRST occupations accounted for slightly less than one fifth of total employment. Concerning core HRST, in other words persons simultaneously in HRST occupations and having completed a tertiary level of education, the range between countries was similar: in Romania some 12.6 % of total employment was core HRST in 2010, while at the other end of the scale the share rose to 32.9 % in Luxembourg (see Table 13.2.2).

Within the EU-27 there were 14.3 graduates in mathematics, science and technology fields of education per 1 000 persons aged 20 to 29 years in 2009, with particularly high ratios in France, Romania, Finland and Lithuania (see Table 13.2.3). This ratio should be interpreted with care as some graduates may be foreigners who return home following their studies and so push up the ratio in the country where they studied and pull down the ratio in their country of origin; this may explain to a large extent the very low ratios recorded in two of the smallest Member States, Cyprus and Malta.

A similar but more specific measure of a country's potential research capability is provided by the number of doctoral students (see Table 13.2.4). There were 525 800 doctoral students in the EU-27 in 2007, compared with levels of 457 400 in the United States and 74 400 in Japan (these latter two figures are for 2009). In relative terms, the broad subject group of science, mathematics, computing, engineering, manufacturing and construction-related studies accounted for more than one third (36.4 %) of the doctoral students in the EU-27 in 2007, a proportion that was somewhat higher than in Japan (31.6 %, again for 2009) but lower than in the United States (38.1 %, also for 2009).

Women accounted for 47.8 % of doctoral students in the EU-27 in 2007, a share that was not too dissimilar from that recorded in the United States, where women were on a par with men (50.0 % in 2009); in contrast, men accounted for a much higher share of doctoral students in Japan (68.8 % in 2009). The gender split of doctoral students across the Member States was typically quite balanced in 2009: women accounted for more than half of all the doctoral students in the Baltic Member States, Portugal, Finland, Italy, Spain, Poland, Bulgaria and Slovenia, and at least 40 % of all doctoral students in the remaining Member States for which data are available, with the exception of Malta.

Data sources and availability

Statistics on science, technology and innovation (STI statistics) are based on Decision 1608/2003/EC concerning the production and development of Community statistics on science and technology. In close cooperation with the Member States, this Decision was implemented by Eurostat in the form of legislative measures and other work. Regulation 753/2004 was adopted in 2004 implementing Decision 1608/2003/EC.

Statistics on R & D personnel are compiled using guidelines laid out in the Frascati manual, published in 2002 by the OECD. R & D personnel include all persons employed directly within R & D, as well as persons supplying direct services to R & D, such as managers, administrative staff and clerical staff. For statistical purposes, indicators on R & D personnel who are mainly or partly employed on R & D are compiled as head counts (HC) and as full-time equivalents (FTEs). Researchers are a sub-category of R & D personnel and are professionals engaged in the conception or creation of new knowledge, products, processes, methods and systems, and in the management of the projects concerned.

Statistics on HRST are compiled using guidelines laid out in the Canberra manual, prepared in cooperation between the OECD, European Commission, UNESCO and the International Labour Organisation, and published in 1995. HRST are defined on the basis of education and/or occupation. HRST based on education are persons having successfully completed tertiary education in one or more of seven broad fields: natural sciences, engineering and technology, medical sciences, agricultural sciences, social sciences, humanities, and other fields. HRST based on occupation are persons who are employed in science and technology occupations as professionals or technicians. Persons who fulfil both education and occupation criteria are classified as the HRST 'core'. Tertiary education is defined as levels 5a, 5b or 6 of the 1997 version of the international standard classification of education (ISCED). In 2007 a review of ISCED began and, at the time of writing, it is expected that the revised version will be presented to UNESCO's General Conference in November 2011. Among other changes, the revised ISCED proposes four levels of tertiary education compared with two categories in the current version.

Science and technology occupations are covered by major groups 2 and 3 of the international standard classification of occupations (ISCO-88).

HRST data can be broken down by sex, age, region, sector of activity, occupation, educational attainment and fields of education (although it should be noted that not all combinations are possible). Data relating to stocks of HRST provide information on the characteristics of the current labour force.

Information on HRST flows from education are obtained from a UNESCO/OECD/Eurostat questionnaire on education and this can be used to provide a measure of the current and future supply of HRST from the education system, in terms of actual inflows (graduates from the reference period) and potential inflows (students participating in higher education during the reference period). Science and technology graduates are defined as the number of new graduates from all public and private institutions completing science and technology-related graduate and post-graduate studies in the reference year; the number of graduates is expressed relative to the total number of persons aged 20-29 years.

Indicators based on the number of doctoral students give an idea of the extent to which countries will have researchers at the highest level of education in the future. The data relate to the number of students in the reference year; they do not refer to the number of new graduates or to the total number (stock) of graduates in the labour market that year. The number of doctoral students is measured as students enrolled in ISCED level 6: this level concerns tertiary programmes which lead to the award of an advanced research degree, for example, a doctorate in economics. These programmes should be devoted to advanced study and original research and are not based on course-work alone; studies at the doctoral level usually require 3 to 5 years.

Context

The European Research Area (ERA) is composed of all research and development activities, programmes and policies in Europe which involve a transnational perspective. In May 2008, the European Commission adopted a Communication to launch an initiative titled, 'better careers and more mobility: a European partnership for researchers'. The goal of this initiative is to improve the mobility of researchers and to enhance the diffusion of knowledge throughout Europe, by: balancing demand and supply for researchers at a European level; helping create centres of excellence; and improving the skills of researchers in Europe.

In December 2008, the competitiveness Council adopted a 2020 vision for the ERA. According to the opening statement of this vision, all players should benefit from: the 'fifth freedom', introducing the free circulation of researchers, knowledge and technology across the ERA; attractive conditions for carrying out research and investing in R & D intensive sectors; Europe-wide scientific competition, together with the appropriate level of cooperation and coordination. The 2020 vision for the ERA is part of the wider picture of Europe's 2020 strategy for smart, sustainable and inclusive growth.

As part of the EU's 7th framework programme for research and technological development (FP7) the European Commission announced in July 2011 nearly EUR 7 000 million of investment in research and innovation, with the aim of providing an economic stimulus expected to create around 174 000 jobs.

In the FP7 the Marie Curie actions have been regrouped and reinforced within the specific programme titled people. Entirely dedicated to human resources in research, this programme has an overall budget of more than EUR 4 700 million over a seven-year period until 2013. Within this programme, efforts will be made to increase participation by women researchers, by encouraging equal opportunities in all Marie Curie actions, by designing the actions to ensure that researchers can achieve an appropriate work/life balance and by facilitating resuming a research career after a break. A number of groups are actively promoting greater sex equality. Among others these include the European association for women in science, engineering and technology (WiTEC), and the European platform of women scientists (EPWS). Horizon 2020 is planned as the framework programme for research and innovation after 2013 – see the introduction for science and technology for more information.

Table 13.2.1: Researchers, by institutional sector, 2009 (¹)

	Total	Business enterprise sector		Government sector		Higher education sector	
	(1 000 FTE)	(1 000 FTE)	(% of total)	(1 000 FTE)	(% of total)	(1 000 FTE)	(% of total)
EU-27	1 584.9	702.6	44	196.5	12	668.0	42
Euro area (EA-16)	1 101.9	526.2	48	146.5	13	416.3	38
Belgium	37.2	17.4	47	2.8	8	16.6	45
Bulgaria	12.0	1.7	14	5.8	49	4.4	37
Czech Republic	28.8	12.7	44	6.3	22	9.7	34
Denmark	35.3	21.8	62	1.3	4	12.0	34
Germany	311.5	180.0	58	49.0	16	82.5	26
Estonia	4.3	1.3	30	0.5	12	2.4	56
Ireland	14.9	7.8	53	0.6	4	6.5	44
Greece (²)	20.8	6.1	29	2.2	11	12.4	59
Spain	133.8	46.2	34	24.2	18	63.2	47
France	289.5	146.9	51	29.2	10	109.2	38
Italy	101.8	38.4	38	16.5	16	43.1	42
Cyprus	0.8	0.2	26	0.1	13	0.4	54
Latvia	3.6	0.3	9	0.7	20	2.6	72
Lithuania	8.5	1.1	13	1.7	20·	5.7	67
Luxembourg	2.4	1.4	57	0.7	27	0.4	15
Hungary	20.1	9.0	45	4.9	25	6.2	31
Malta	0.5	0.2	49	0.0	8	0.2	43
Netherlands	46.7	20.3	44	6.8	15	19.5	42
Austria	34.5	21.8	63	1.5	4	11.0	32
Poland	61.1	9.8	16	13.2	22	38.1	62
Portugal	45.9	10.8	24	3.4	7	28.1	61
Romania	19.3	6.1	32	5.7	30	7.3	38
Slovenia	7.4	3.3	44	2.2	29	2.0	27
Slovakia	13.3	1.6	12	2.8	21	8.9	67
Finland	40.8	23.6	58	4.5	11	12.3	30
Sweden	46.8	29.3	63	1.5	3	15.9	34
United Kingdom	243.3	83.3	34	8.4	3	147.6	61
Iceland	2.9	1.1	39	0.5	19	1.1	39
Norway	26.6	13.3	50	4.4	16	9.0	34
Switzerland (³)	25.1	10.3	41	0.5	2	14.3	57
Croatia	6.9	1.3	19	2.0	29	3.6	52
Turkey	57.8	21.0	36	5.7	10	31.0	54
Japan (³)	656.7	492.8	75	32.1	5	123.5	19
United States (²)	1 412.6	1 130.5	80	:	:	:	:

(¹) Shares do not sum to 100 % due to estimates, the exclusion of private non-profit sector data from the table and the conversion of data to a count in terms of FTE.
(²) 2007.
(³) 2008.

Source: Eurostat (online data code: tsc00004), OECD

Figure 13.2.1: Proportion of research and development personnel by sector, 2009 ([1])
(% of labour force)

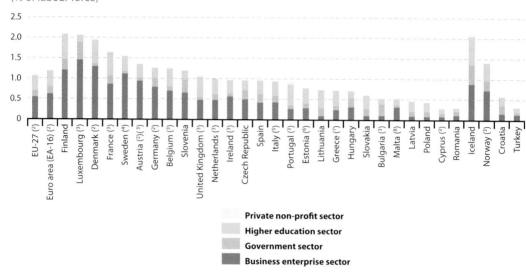

([1]) Germany, Ireland, Latvia, Lithuania, Luxembourg, Hungary, the Netherlands, Norway, Croatia and Turkey, private non-profit, not available.
([2]) Estimates.
([3]) Provisional.
([4]) Provisional, except Government.
([5]) Provisional, except higher education.
([6]) Business enterprise, provisional.
([7]) 2007, estimates.
([8]) Provisional; private non-profit, 2008.
Source: Eurostat (online data code: tsc00002)

Figure 13.2.2: Gender breakdown of researchers in all institutional sectors, 2008 ([1])
(% of total researchers, based on FTEs)

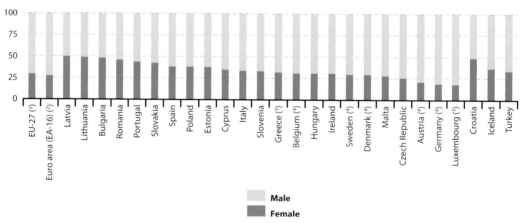

([1]) France, the Netherlands, Finland and the United Kingdom, not available.
([2]) Estimates.
([3]) 2005.
([4]) 2007.
Source: Eurostat (online data code: tsc00006)

Table 13.2.2: Human resources in science and technology, 2007-2010

	People working in an S&T occupation					People who have a tertiary education and work in an S&T occupation				
	(1 000)	(% of total employment)				(1 000)	(% of total employment)			
	2010	2007	2008	2009	2010	2010	2007	2008	2009	2010
EU-27	66 761	29.9	30.1	30.8	31.0	40 672	17.2	17.6	18.5	18.9
Belgium	1 530	33.1	32.5	33.5	34.2	1 115	23.7	22.9	23.8	24.9
Bulgaria	687	21.9	21.6	22.9	22.5	526	16.3	16.0	17.1	17.2
Czech Republic	1 721	33.3	33.8	35.6	35.3	708	11.5	11.8	13.4	14.5
Denmark	1 112	36.0	37.8	39.4	40.9	678	21.9	22.5	24.1	24.9
Germany	14 210	36.8	36.6	37.0	37.2	7 333	18.1	18.3	19.1	19.2
Estonia	179	27.3	26.7	30.0	31.4	125	18.0	17.9	21.1	21.9
Ireland	495	23.3	23.5	25.9	27.0	404	17.7	18.3	20.6	22.0
Greece	1 055	23.1	23.3	23.4	24.1	840	17.9	18.2	18.3	19.2
Spain	4 906	24.2	25.3	26.2	26.6	3 928	18.7	19.6	21.2	21.3
France	8 495	31.9	32.0	32.7	33.0	5 503	19.6	20.0	20.6	21.4
Italy	6 853	31.9	31.5	30.6	30.0	3 034	12.5	13.1	13.2	13.3
Cyprus	104	27.0	27.2	26.4	27.3	85	21.3	21.8	20.9	22.1
Latvia	284	29.8	31.1	32.4	30.2	185	15.7	17.2	19.5	19.7
Lithuania	433	26.9	29.2	30.3	32.3	336	19.0	20.5	22.1	25.0
Luxembourg	112	39.5	41.5	50.9	50.8	73	26.3	27.9	33.8	32.9
Hungary	1 063	26.6	27.8	28.3	28.1	660	15.5	16.3	17.2	17.5
Malta	45	27.3	28.1	28.7	27.6	23	13.6	14.1	14.3	14.0
Netherlands	3 231	37.6	37.9	38.0	39.3	1 904	22.0	22.5	22.9	23.1
Austria	1 280	29.7	29.9	31.2	31.4	526	11.5	11.8	12.8	12.9
Poland	4 509	26.2	26.3	27.4	28.3	3 028	16.0	16.3	17.8	19.0
Portugal	966	17.6	18.5	19.2	19.8	623	10.9	11.5	12.1	12.8
Romania	1 836	18.6	19.3	19.7	19.9	1 165	10.8	11.7	12.1	12.6
Slovenia	309	31.2	32.0	32.7	32.4	177	17.9	17.9	18.5	18.6
Slovakia	728	29.3	29.0	30.0	31.4	348	12.1	12.2	13.6	15.0
Finland	859	34.5	34.9	35.3	35.2	609	23.1	24.6	25.0	24.9
Sweden	1 878	39.3	39.6	40.6	41.4	1 187	23.9	24.4	25.5	26.1
United Kingdom	7 880	26.9	26.9	27.9	27.4	5 551	18.1	18.1	19.4	19.3
Iceland	64	33.4	36.3	38.4	38.6	37	18.9	20.6	21.8	22.2
Norway	976	36.9	37.4	38.7	39.1	703	25.9	26.3	27.7	28.2
Switzerland (¹)	1 736	39.5	40.7	41.1	:	949	20.4	21.7	22.5	:
Croatia	413	24.0	24.9	26.5	27.0	267	14.7	15.3	16.6	17.4
FYR of Macedonia	128	20.7	19.0	19.9	20.1	89	13.1	11.9	13.2	13.9
Turkey	2 945	12.5	13.4	13.4	13.1	2 034	7.7	8.6	9.0	9.0

(¹) 2009 instead of 2010 for the number of people.

Source: Eurostat (online data code: hrst_st_nocc)

Table 13.2.3: Science and technology graduates, 2004 and 2009
(tertiary graduates in science and technology per 1 000 persons aged 20-29 years)

	Total		Male		Female	
	2004	2009	2004	2009	2004	2009
EU-27	*12.5*	14.3	*16.9*	19.2	*7.9*	9.4
Belgium	11.2	12.0	16.6	17.5	5.7	6.6
Bulgaria	8.5	10.1	9.6	12.4	7.2	7.8
Czech Republic	7.4	15.3	10.2	20.5	4.4	9.8
Denmark	13.8	15.2	18.6	19.1	9.0	11.2
Germany	9.0	13.5	13.4	18.3	4.3	8.6
Estonia	8.9	10.8	10.5	12.8	7.4	8.7
Ireland	23.1	17.2	31.6	24.1	14.5	10.5
Greece (¹)	8.0	11.2	9.2	12.5	6.8	9.8
Spain	12.5	12.5	16.9	17.0	7.7	7.8
France (²)	22.8	20.2	32.7	28.9	12.9	11.5
Italy (¹)	10.8	11.3	13.4	13.6	8.1	9.0
Cyprus	4.2	4.6	5.2	5.9	3.2	3.4
Latvia	9.4	9.8	12.5	13.1	6.3	6.3
Lithuania	17.5	18.5	22.3	25.2	12.6	11.4
Luxembourg	:	:	:	:	:	:
Hungary	5.1	7.5	7.1	10.4	2.9	4.4
Malta (²)	3.4	7.0	4.6	9.4	2.1	4.5
Netherlands	7.9	8.9	12.6	14.2	3.1	3.6
Austria	8.7	14.0	13.4	21.1	4.0	6.8
Poland	9.4	14.3	12.4	17.4	6.4	11.0
Portugal	11.0	14.6	12.8	18.3	9.1	10.8
Romania	9.8	20.0	11.8	24.9	7.7	14.9
Slovenia	9.3	11.3	13.6	16.2	4.8	6.0
Slovakia	9.2	17.5	11.7	22.2	6.6	12.5
Finland	17.9	19.0	24.6	26.3	10.9	11.3
Sweden	15.9	13.0	20.6	17.1	11.0	8.7
United Kingdom	18.1	17.5	24.8	23.7	11.4	11.0
Iceland	10.8	10.3	13.2	12.6	8.3	7.8
Liechtenstein	0.9	7.0	0.9	10.1	0.9	3.7
Norway	9.0	9.0	13.4	12.4	4.4	5.5
Switzerland	14.6	18.1	24.6	28.9	4.7	7.1
Croatia	5.4	12.8	7.1	16.5	3.6	8.9
FYR of Macedonia	3.7	7.0	4.0	8.0	3.5	6.0
Turkey	5.6	8.0	7.6	11.0	3.5	4.9
Japan	13.4	14.2	22.4	23.7	4.0	4.1
United States	10.2	10.3	13.8	13.9	6.4	6.5

(¹) 2008 instead of 2009.
(²) 2005 instead of 2004.

Source: Eurostat (online data code: tsiir050)

Table 13.2.4: PhD students (ISCED level 6), 2009

	Number (1 000)			Share (% of total PhD students)					
	Total PhD students	Male	Female	Social science, business & law	Teacher training & educ.; humani- ties & arts	Science, maths & comput.; engin., manuf. & construc.	Agricul- ture & vet- erinary	Health & welfare; services	Others (¹)
EU-27 (²)	*525.8*	*274.4*	*251.4*	*21.8*	*21.0*	*36.4*	*2.9*	*14.5*	*2.0*
Belgium	12.5	7.0	5.5	21.2	12.4	43.2	7.0	16.1	0.1
Bulgaria	3.9	1.9	2.0	23.2	21.2	36.3	3.1	16.2	0.0
Czech Republic	24.9	14.7	10.2	17.5	16.9	48.3	4.2	13.1	0.0
Denmark	7.1	3.8	3.3	13.6	13.1	40.0	6.5	26.8	0.0
Germany	:	:	:	:	:	:	:	:	:
Estonia	2.5	1.1	1.4	20.5	22.8	43.5	4.8	8.4	0.0
Ireland	7.3	3.8	3.5	14.8	20.2	43.7	2.5	13.0	5.8
Greece (³)	21.6	12.1	9.5	22.6	20.4	33.1	2.6	21.3	0.0
Spain	77.2	37.1	40.1	21.7	22.3	24.4	1.9	19.5	10.2
France	71.7	38.2	33.5	27.0	24.1	46.1	0.1	2.7	0.0
Italy (⁴)	39.4	18.6	20.8	19.7	14.9	42.5	6.1	16.4	0.5
Cyprus	0.4	0.2	0.2	17.2	31.6	48.3	0.9	2.0	0.0
Latvia	2.0	0.8	1.2	33.7	22.0	32.6	2.1	9.5	0.0
Lithuania	2.9	1.2	1.7	31.6	:	40.3	4.6	:	0.0
Luxembourg	0.0	0.0	0.0	–	–	–	–	–	–
Hungary	6.9	3.5	3.4	21.6	26.7	31.6	5.1	15.0	0.0
Malta	0.1	0.1	0.0	21.6	33.8	29.7	0.0	14.9	0.0
Netherlands	7.7	4.4	3.4	:	:	:	:	:	100.0
Austria	18.5	10.1	8.4	34.2	21.2	31.2	3.2	7.9	2.3
Poland	32.5	15.6	16.9	24.9	23.9	35.8	1.9	13.5	0.0
Portugal	15.3	6.8	8.5	20.1	33.3	30.8	5.4	10.4	0.0
Romania	27.9	14.3	13.6	14.3	:	39.7	7.2	21.0	:
Slovenia	2.0	1.0	1.0	17.6	14.1	36.6	3.7	27.9	0.0
Slovakia	10.4	5.5	4.9	20.1	18.2	37.0	3.3	21.4	0.0
Finland	20.8	9.8	11.0	22.3	24.0	39.7	2.0	11.9	0.0
Sweden	19.9	10.0	9.9	11.8	11.1	41.7	2.1	33.3	0.0
United Kingdom	81.7	43.7	38.0	21.7	21.3	39.7	1.0	16.3	0.0
Iceland	0.3	0.1	0.2	18.4	24.1	34.8	1.1	21.6	0.0
Liechtenstein	0.0	0.0	0.0	33.3	3.3	0.0	0.0	63.3	0.0
Norway	6.9	3.5	3.4	19.2	11.5	39.7	1.8	26.6	1.3
Switzerland	19.1	10.9	8.2	25.7	16.3	39.1	2.3	16.2	0.4
Croatia	3.1	1.5	1.6	17.1	25.2	37.3	6.5	13.9	0.0
FYR of Macedonia	0.2	0.1	0.1	28.4	24.5	17.0	2.6	27.5	0.0
Turkey	35.9	19.9	16.0	23.6	23.5	33.3	7.6	11.9	0.0
Japan	74.4	51.2	23.2	12.8	13.9	31.6	5.5	33.0	3.1
United States	457.4	228.9	228.5	20.7	25.1	38.1	0.7	15.3	0.0

(¹) Unknown or not specified.
(²) 2007.
(³) 2008.
(⁴) Analaysis by field of education, 2007.

Source: Eurostat (online data code: educ_enrl5)

13.3 Innovation

Europe has a long-standing tradition of producing inventions. However, commentators often focus on an entrepreneurial gap in order to explain why some ideas for new products or services do not become a success in the marketplace, or why other ideas relating to new processes do not get implemented, thereby surrendering the opportunity to make efficiency gains in production or within organisations. This subchapter looks at the state of innovation in the European Union (EU) by presenting data on where innovation takes place and how many enterprises are involved.

Main statistical findings

Extent of innovation

Among the EU Member States the highest propensity to innovate in 2008 (see Figure 13.3.1) was recorded in Germany (79.9 % of all enterprises), followed by Luxembourg (64.7 %) – these were the only Member States where more than 60 % of enterprises were innovative – the EU-27 average (excluding Greece) was 51.6 %. The lowest propensities to innovate were recorded in Latvia (24.3 %), Poland (27.9 %) and Hungary (28.9 %) – the only Member States where the proportion of innovative enterprises was below 30 %. Estonia, Cyprus and the Czech Republic were the only Member States that joined the EU in 2004 to report a propensity to innovate above the EU average. Note that large enterprises tend to innovate more than small and medium-sized enterprises (SMEs) and as such these figures for the Member States may, at least to some degree, reflect the enterprise structure of each domestic economy.

New or significantly improved products contributed a relatively small proportion of total turnover among innovative enterprises in 2008, with 15 of the 25 Member States for which data are available reporting single-digit shares (see Figure 13.3.2). These products did however account for a higher proportion of sales in Malta (24.7 %), Bulgaria (17.0 %), Hungary (16.6 %), the Czech Republic (16.1 %) and Slovakia (14.9 %).

Large enterprises (with 250 or more employees) were more likely to have brought product innovations to market in 2008 than either medium-sized enterprises (50 to 249 employees) or small enterprises (10 to 49 employees); this pattern held for all of the Member States for which data are available – as shown in Table 13.3.1. Lithuania was the only Member State where the proportion of small enterprises with product innovations was above the overall proportion for all enterprises.

A similar size class breakdown for process innovations that are developed within the enterprise also showed that large innovative enterprises were generally more likely to introduce such innovations: the main exception to this was Cyprus where process innovations were much less likely to have been introduced in large enterprises than in small or medium-sized enterprises, while this was also true to a lesser extent in Bulgaria and Lithuania; in Romania, Poland, Portugal and Finland small enterprises were more likely than large enterprises to have introduced process innovations, while in Italy and Slovenia medium-sized enterprises were the most likely to have introduced process innovations.

Innovations with environmental benefits

The environmental benefits of an innovation can occur during the production of a good or service, or during the after sales use of a good or service by the end-user. Table 13.3.2 shows the proportion of innovative enterprises having introduced environmental benefits with a distinction between benefits from the production or from the use of the innovative product: six different benefits related to production are presented as well as three benefits related to use. Among the benefits from production, the most common benefits were generally a reduction in energy use or increased recycling. The main exceptions were: Estonia and Lithuania, where the most common benefit was reduced material use; Latvia, Austria and Poland (and Croatia), where the most common benefit was reduced pollution; and the Netherlands, where the most common benefit was the use of less polluting or hazardous materials.

Among the benefits from after sales use, the most common benefit was reduced energy; reduced pollution was a more common benefit in Cyprus, Latvia and Poland (as well as Croatia), whereas improved end of product life recycling was the most common benefit in Ireland and Portugal.

Table 13.3.3 focuses on innovations with reduced energy use and presents an analysis by innovator size class. In every Member State for which data are available, large enterprises were more likely than either small or medium-sized enterprises to have introduced innovations with reduced energy use during production. A similar situation can be seen for innovations which lead to reduced energy use by end-users, although there were exceptions; in Latvia such innovations were more common among small enterprises and in Lithuania they were more common among medium-sized enterprises.

The motivation for environmental innovations is presented in Table 13.3.4. The most common reason for introducing environmental innovations appears to be either because of existing environmental regulations or taxes on pollution or because of voluntary codes or agreements for environmental good practice. Current or expected market demand from customers was, however, the most common motivation in the Netherlands and Finland. Expected future environmental regulations or taxes were also often cited as a motivation, for example, in Malta. In every Member State, the availability of government financial incentives for environmental innovation was the least common motivation of the five reasons that were surveyed.

Data sources and availability

The Community innovation survey (CIS) collects information about product and process innovation, as well as organisational and marketing innovations. The legal basis for the collection of these statistics is Regulation 1450/2004 of 13 August 2004 implementing Decision 1608/2003/EC concerning the production and development of Community statistics on innovation.

Innovations are based on the results of new technological developments, new combinations of existing technology, or the use of other knowledge acquired (by the enterprise). For the purpose of the Community innovation survey an innovation is defined as a new or significantly improved product (good or service) introduced to the market, or the introduction within an enterprise of a new or significantly improved process, as well as organisational and marketing innovations, including new logistics or distribution methods. Such innovations may be developed by the innovating enterprise or by another enterprise. However, purely selling innovations wholly produced and developed by other enterprises is not included as an innovation activity, nor is introducing products with purely aesthetic changes. Innovations should therefore be new to the enterprise concerned: for product innovations they do not necessarily have to be new to the market, and for process innovations the enterprise does not necessarily have to be the first one to have introduced the process.

Enterprises with innovation activity include all types of innovator, namely product and process innovators, as well as enterprises with only on-going and/or abandoned innovation activities. Enterprises may cooperate with other parties (for example suppliers, competitors, customers, educational/research establishments) when engaging in an innovative activity. The proportion of enterprises with innovation activity is also referred to as the propensity to innovate.

An environmental innovation is an innovation that creates environmental benefits compared with alternatives. The environmental benefits can be the primary objective or motivation of the innovation or the result of other innovation objectives.

The European innovation scoreboard formerly used for assessing innovation performance in the Member States has been reworked to improve international comparability and to include a number of research-oriented indicators in line with the purpose of monitoring the implementation of the innovation union.

Context

While Europe has a tradition of producing initial ideas (inventions), it is regarded by some as not being so good at bringing them to market; as such, EU policy in this field increasingly aims to provide more focus to industry-driven, applied research and development (R & D).

Education is another area seen as key to developing an innovation-oriented society, through the acquisition of entrepreneurial, managerial, scientific, mathematical and foreign-language skills, as well as digital literacy. Policymakers express concern at the numbers of science and technology graduates who directly apply their education once they move into the labour market, while a lack of job mobility between universities and business may potentially hinder the transfer of ideas, thereby reducing the EU's innovation performance (see R & D personnel).

In October 2006, the European Parliament and the Council adopted a Decision 1639/2006/EC establishing a competitiveness and innovation framework programme (CIP) for the period 2007-2013. With SMEs as its main target, the competitiveness and innovation framework programme aims to support innovation activities (including eco-innovation), provide better access to finance and deliver business support services in the regions. It encourages the take-up and use of information and communication technologies and aims to help to develop the information society. Furthermore, it also promotes the increased use of renewable energies and energy efficiency. Horizon 2020 is planned as the framework programme for research and innovation after 2013 – see the introduction for science and technology for more information.

The European Institute of Innovation and Technology was established in March 2008 to increase sustainable growth and competitiveness by reinforcing the innovation capacity and, most importantly, the innovation impact of the EU. Its aim is to bring together higher education, research and innovation through the creation of 'knowledge and innovation communities'.

In September 2009, the European Commission adopted a Communication ((2009) 442) 'reviewing

Community innovation policy in a changing world'. In October 2010, as one of the seven flagship initiatives of the Europe 2020 strategy for smart, sustainable and inclusive growth, the European Commission adopted a Communication ((2010) 546) on an innovation union. This sets outs a comprehensive innovation strategy for Europe, focusing on major areas of concern for citizens such as climate change, energy efficiency and healthy living. It pursues a broad concept of innovation, not only technological, but also in business models, design, branding and services that add value for users. It includes public sector and social innovation as well as commercial innovation. It aims to involve all actors and all regions in the innovation cycle. The policies in the innovation union aim to do three things:

- make Europe into a world-class science performer;
- revolutionise the way public and private sectors work together, notably through innovation partnerships;
- remove bottlenecks like expensive patenting, market fragmentation, slow standard setting and skills shortages that currently prevent ideas getting quickly to market.

European innovation partnerships (EIPs) form part of the innovation union and are designed to act as a framework to address major societal challenges, bringing together activities and policies from basic research through to market-oriented solutions. The first EIP announced in February 2011 is a partnership for active and healthy ageing and has three main objectives, namely to:

- enable EU citizens to lead healthy, active and independent lives while ageing;
- improve the sustainability and efficiency of social and healthcare systems;
- boost the competitiveness and markets for innovative products and services that respond to the ageing challenge.

The partnership for active and healthy ageing is focused on prevention and health promotion, integrated care, and independent living for older persons. Its overarching target is to increase the average number of healthy life years within the EU-27 population by two years by 2020.

Figure 13.3.1: Proportion of innovative enterprises, 2008 (¹)
(% of all enterprises)

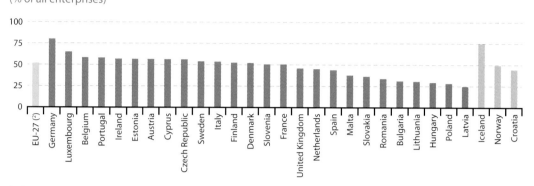

(¹) Greece, not available.
(²) Excluding Greece.

Source: Eurostat (online data code: inn_cis6_type)

Figure 13.3.2: Turnover from new or significantly improved products new to the market, 2008 (¹)
(% of total turnover of innovative enterprises)

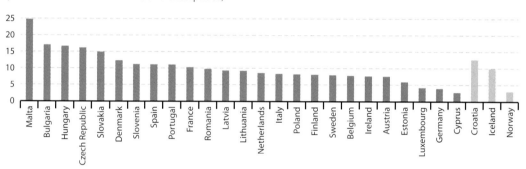

(¹) Greece and the United Kingdom, not available.

Source: Eurostat (online data code: inn_cis6_prod)

Table 13.3.1: Proportion of innovative enterprises which introduced products new to the market or own-developed process innovations, 2008
(% of enterprises within size class or total)

	Process innovations: developed by the enterprise or group				Product innovations: new to market			
	Total	With 10 to 49 employees	With 50 to 249 employees	With > 250 employees	Total	With 10 to 49 employees	With 50 to 249 employees	With > 250 employees
Belgium	42.2	42.7	39.3	47.5	47.5	47.1	45.5	59.3
Bulgaria	41.3	40.7	43.8	38.1	25.9	23.3	30.8	30.8
Czech Republic	39.0	40.1	35.4	41.2	39.1	34.0	47.0	54.1
Denmark	:	:	:	:	44.4	44.1	42.3	54.1
Germany	30.1	27.1	35.6	42.0	26.0	23.2	29.5	43.7
Estonia	40.5	37.9	44.3	56.0	25.8	24.2	28.0	36.1
Ireland	:	:	:	:	:	:	:	:
Greece	:	:	:	:	:	:	:	:
Spain	50.7	50.6	49.4	57.4	21.5	18.0	28.1	43.6
France	50.8	50.8	49.1	55.0	43.2	39.9	46.3	60.0
Italy	44.9	44.0	48.7	47.9	47.7	45.5	55.5	61.4
Cyprus	50.9	53.5	47.3	22.7	26.8	24.0	33.6	40.9
Latvia	33.9	31.3	36.1	50.6	23.4	22.7	21.5	35.6
Lithuania	51.8	55.0	47.3	46.4	37.2	40.2	28.8	47.1
Luxembourg	51.7	48.0	53.2	69.7	40.6	35.3	47.6	55.8
Hungary	24.8	25.0	21.0	32.6	33.1	31.2	32.0	45.2
Malta	47.7	46.9	46.9	55.0	39.1	38.3	32.7	60.0
Netherlands	23.4	22.0	25.7	29.4	49.2	48.1	51.3	53.6
Austria	37.6	34.9	41.7	45.8	49.5	46.3	52.1	66.4
Poland	43.7	45.8	40.7	42.7	41.5	40.1	41.6	47.5
Portugal	52.0	52.4	50.7	52.2	35.6	33.1	41.7	53.7
Romania	66.0	67.0	64.4	63.7	24.8	23.0	26.8	31.4
Slovenia	37.2	36.2	38.8	38.7	51.3	51.3	48.1	59.5
Slovakia	34.2	34.6	31.3	39.7	35.7	34.2	33.4	48.0
Finland	39.2	40.4	35.1	40.0	37.3	35.5	35.9	57.7
Sweden	33.5	33.1	33.0	39.5	50.4	48.3	53.6	62.8
United Kingdom	:	:	:	:	:	:	:	:
Norway	27.4	28.0	25.1	29.0	34.5	36.8	28.5	34.6
Croatia	37.4	36.9	39.3	36.0	37.4	36.7	38.5	39.1

Source: Eurostat (online data code: inn_cis6_prod)

Table 13.3.2: Innovations with environmental benefits — proportion of innovative enterprises introducing innovations with specified benefits, 2008
(% of innovative enterprises)

	Environmental benefits from the production of goods or services within the enterprise						Environmental benefits from the after sales use of a good or service by the end-user		
	Reduced material use per unit of output	Reduced energy use per unit of output	Reduced CO_2 'footprint' (total CO_2 production)	Replaced materials with less polluting or hazardous substitutes	Reduced air, water, soil or noise pollution	Recycled waste, water, or materials	Reduced energy use	Reduced air, water, soil or noise pollution	Improved recycling of product after use
Belgium	22.8	30.3	26.6	25.7	28.8	35.7	27.0	20.8	24.0
Bulgaria	11.6	13.6	6.0	10.0	10.5	8.6	8.8	8.1	6.1
Czech Republic	28.6	33.1	17.1	20.1	27.0	41.3	30.7	27.5	29.7
Denmark	:	:	:	:	:	:	:	:	:
Germany	38.8	46.4	38.5	25.5	41.7	41.2	44.0	35.5	30.8
Estonia	27.4	11.7	13.4	22.3	10.0	10.6	15.0	10.2	10.4
Ireland	28.2	33.5	33.1	30.9	27.1	54.3	33.1	23.8	37.1
Greece	:	:	:	:	:	:	:	:	:
Spain	:	:	:	:	:	:	:	:	:
France	27.6	28.2	21.0	26.5	24.7	38.8	23.9	17.6	17.7
Italy	13.0	16.5	13.4	15.3	23.8	25.8	23.5	23.5	23.3
Cyprus	10.8	13.6	8.6	8.2	13.5	13.2	5.4	6.1	5.6
Latvia	19.9	23.5	11.5	19.7	27.9	14.3	21.7	27.9	12.6
Lithuania	29.3	29.3	20.7	25.6	21.3	18.2	22.9	20.0	18.7
Luxembourg	20.8	24.8	27.1	26.6	22.6	41.4	30.1	18.3	29.2
Hungary	31.8	36.3	17.3	29.4	27.6	26.1	19.1	16.9	13.4
Malta	23.0	27.0	13.7	19.8	12.5	27.8	19.8	6.9	16.9
Netherlands	17.1	21.1	15.9	22.3	19.3	21.5	19.8	15.9	13.8
Austria	26.9	30.7	25.1	27.4	30.9	23.6	28.9	23.1	17.2
Poland	23.5	25.3	16.1	24.9	28.2	23.7	24.8	25.3	17.0
Portugal	37.8	41.5	31.5	41.3	46.2	58.5	39.1	38.8	41.8
Romania	31.3	32.8	22.7	21.1	31.5	32.3	30.3	29.6	20.1
Slovenia	:	:	:	:	:	:	:	:	:
Slovakia	20.2	23.7	9.2	19.5	21.9	29.3	26.2	21.0	19.0
Finland	32.0	32.9	25.9	24.0	22.8	32.2	33.0	20.3	22.2
Sweden	24.0	28.6	23.7	24.2	23.0	21.8	28.1	23.6	18.5
United Kingdom	:	:	:	:	:	:	:	:	:
Croatia	28.8	32.7	18.1	30.4	39.2	36.1	32.6	36.1	31.2

Source: Eurostat (online data code: inn_cis6_eco)

Table 13.3.3: Proportion of innovative enterprises introducing innovations with reduced energy use, 2008
(% of innovative enterprises)

	Reduced energy use per unit of output				End-user benefits, reduced energy use			
	Total	With 10 to 49 employees	With 50 to 249 employees	With > 250 employees	Total	With 10 to 49 employees	With 50 to 249 employees	With > 250 employees
Belgium	30.3	26.3	37.9	56.5	27.0	25.0	31.5	37.8
Bulgaria	13.6	11.4	15.5	24.4	8.8	8.3	8.2	15.0
Czech Republic	33.1	28.4	40.8	53.1	30.7	29.3	33.2	36.9
Denmark	:	:	:	:	:	:	:	:
Germany	46.4	42.9	54.5	60.4	44.0	41.4	49.3	55.9
Estonia	11.7	10.3	14.5	18.4	15.0	12.7	18.8	30.4
Ireland	33.5	28.0	44.7	64.4	33.1	31.8	35.1	43.1
Greece	:	:	:	:	:	:	:	:
Spain	:	:	:	:	:	:	:	:
France	28.2	23.8	35.0	50.5	23.9	21.6	27.0	38.5
Italy	16.5	14.8	22.6	34.8	23.5	21.5	30.8	43.3
Cyprus	13.6	11.5	19.3	28.0	5.4	4.8	7.3	8.0
Latvia	23.5	26.8	13.7	29.7	21.7	26.1	11.4	18.8
Lithuania	29.3	22.7	37.0	51.9	22.9	19.4	28.8	27.9
Luxembourg	24.8	17.5	33.8	54.6	30.1	28.5	28.3	48.3
Hungary	36.3	33.1	36.9	55.7	19.1	19.3	16.5	23.8
Malta	27.0	25.3	25.9	45.0	19.8	17.7	20.7	35.0
Netherlands	21.1	17.6	26.3	41.9	19.8	17.9	23.2	30.2
Austria	30.7	26.8	34.9	53.8	28.9	26.0	32.9	44.2
Poland	25.3	21.5	28.0	40.5	24.8	24.1	24.1	31.4
Portugal	41.5	40.2	43.8	55.9	39.1	40.2	34.7	40.6
Romania	32.8	29.2	37.1	50.6	30.3	28.8	32.3	37.2
Slovenia	:	:	:	:	:	:	:	:
Slovakia	23.7	18.3	31.4	45.5	26.2	24.9	27.7	32.9
Finland	32.9	28.4	38.9	56.5	33.0	29.7	35.7	55.6
Sweden	28.6	25.1	33.4	53.5	28.1	27.3	25.6	46.5
United Kingdom	:	:	:	:	:	:	:	:
Croatia	32.7	29.8	35.7	50.0	32.6	32.2	31.7	40.2

Source: Eurostat (online data code: inn_cis6_eco)

Table 13.3.4: Motivation to introduce environmental innovations — proportion of innovative enterprises reporting specified motivations, 2008
(% of innovative enterprises)

	Existing environmental regulations or taxes on pollution	Environmental regulations or taxes expected to be introduced in the future	Govern-ment grants, subsidies or other financial incentives for environmental innovation	Current or expected market demand from customers for environmental innovations	Voluntary codes or agreements for environmental good practice within sector
Belgium	20.1	16.3	7.8	13.6	26.1
Bulgaria	8.6	5.4	2.4	4.0	5.2
Czech Republic	40.6	26.8	9.5	13.6	24.3
Denmark	:	:	:	:	:
Germany	20.8	19.0	7.7	18.3	18.8
Estonia	24.1	19.3	4.4	17.2	26.3
Ireland	27.2	19.9	9.1	25.3	28.5
Greece	:	:	:	:	:
Spain	:	:	:	:	:
France	24.0	15.0	6.4	17.6	23.9
Italy	22.9	16.3	12.8	13.0	14.8
Cyprus	7.2	5.3	3.1	3.9	13.1
Latvia	19.1	11.3	8.3	13.6	34.0
Lithuania	39.3	31.8	12.5	26.8	24.5
Luxembourg	10.1	11.4	4.4	15.0	43.2
Hungary	41.3	34.5	4.1	31.9	32.8
Malta	23.8	23.8	8.1	11.3	13.3
Netherlands	10.5	9.2	6.7	13.8	12.7
Austria	:	:	:	:	:
Poland	24.1	16.1	4.9	12.7	13.3
Portugal	31.6	18.3	7.0	21.9	42.0
Romania	37.6	20.4	9.3	17.6	17.7
Slovenia	:	:	:	:	:
Slovakia	37.0	27.3	4.7	11.7	18.9
Finland	15.8	17.8	6.2	30.3	29.1
Sweden	8.4	12.3	2.7	14.7	15.1
United Kingdom	:	:	:	:	:
Croatia	35.7	28.0	8.4	19.6	30.3

Source: Eurostat (online data coed: inn_cis6_ecomot)

13.4 Patents

This subchapter provides information on patent applications in the European Union (EU). Intellectual property rights, in particular patents, provide a link between innovation, inventions and the marketplace. Applying for a patent makes an invention public, but at the same time gives it protection. A count of patents is one measure of a country's inventive activity and also shows its capacity to exploit knowledge and translate it into potential economic gains. In this context, indicators based on patent statistics are widely used to assess the inventive and innovative performance of a country.

Main statistical findings

With the exception of the years 2000 to 2002, the number of EU-27 patent applications filed with the European Patent Office (EPO) increased at a relatively fast pace from 1998 to the latest period for which data are available (2008), with annual growth averaging 7.3 % per annum between 1998 and 2000, and 2.6 % between 2002 and 2008. Over the whole of the period under consideration (1998-2008), the number of EU-27 patent applications filed with the EPO increased from 44 796 to 59 468.

Among the EU Member States, Germany had by far the highest number of patent applications to the EPO, some 24 557 in 2008 (41.3 % of the EU-27 total). In relative terms, Sweden reported the highest number of patent applications per million inhabitants (318.9), followed by Germany (298.7) and Finland (250.3). Between 2003 and 2008 the number of patent applications filed with the EPO increased in all Member States except Lithuania and the United Kingdom where small decreases were recorded; in contrast, relatively large decreases in patent applications to the EPO were recorded for Japan and the United States.

EU-27 high-technology patent applications to the EPO represented an increasing share of total patent applications up until 2001 when they accounted for 23.6 % of all applications. Their relative importance declined after this, as did their absolute number – from 12 078 high-technology patent applications in

2001, there was a relatively steady reduction through to 2007 (despite growth in 2004). This was followed by a collapse in the number of high-technology applications in 2008, with the total falling to 5 375 (provisional data). Behind Romania (which had a very small number of total patent applications) the highest shares of high-technology patent applications in total patent applications in 2008 were recorded for Finland, Belgium and France, while high-technology patent applications accounted for a low share of total applications in Luxembourg, Estonia, Austria and Italy.

Finland and Sweden registered the highest number of high-technology patent applications per million inhabitants in 2008, the figures for both countries being over 35, while Germany, the Netherlands, Denmark, Belgium, France and Austria were the only other Member States to record double-digit ratios.

The considerable reduction in high-technology patent applications filed with the EPO may reflect the length of patent procedures. Given the increasing speed of technological change and the rapid pace at which imitators are able to bring new technologies to market, it may be that enterprises increasingly choose to invest in continued innovation alongside patent protection.

Just under two fifths (38.2 %) of EU-27 patent applications to the EPO in 2008 were from a single inventor, while the remainder were co-patents (see Figure 13.4.2). By far the most common type of co-patent involved multiple inventors/applicants from a single country – in fact, such co-patents made up an overall majority (54.0 %) of all patent applications. Patent applications involving inventors from more than one country made up the remaining 7.8 % of patent applications to the EPO.

Citations in a patent application may be references to other patents or to other relevant reference material, such as scientific journals. Figure 13.4.3 shows that EU patent citations were more likely to refer to EU patent publications than to non-EU patent publications; this is an established pattern that could be observed each year between 1997 and 2007.

Data sources and availability

Since 2007 Eurostat's production of European Patent Office (EPO) data has been based almost exclusively on the EPO's worldwide statistical patent database (PATSTAT). The EPO grants European patents for the contracting states to the European Patent Convention (EPC), of which there are currently 38 – the EU Member States, the EFTA Member States, several other candidate countries (Croatia, the former Yugoslav Republic of Macedonia and Turkey), as well as Albania, Monaco, San Marino and Serbia.

European patent applications refer to applications filed directly under the EPC or to applications filed under the Patent Cooperation Treaty (PCT) and designated to the EPO (Euro-PCT). Patent applications are counted according to the year in which they are filed and are assigned to a country according to the inventor's place of residence, using fractional counting if there are multiple inventors.

In contrast, the United States Patent and Trademark Office (USPTO) data refer to patents granted; data are recorded by year of publication as opposed to the year of filing. This methodological difference implies that any comparison between EPO and USPTO patent data should be interpreted with caution.

High-technology patents are counted following criteria established by the trilateral statistical report (drafted by the EPO, USPTO and the Japan Patent Office (JPO)), where the following technical fields are defined as high-technology groups in accordance with the international patent classification (IPC): computer and automated business equipment; micro-organism and genetic engineering; aviation; communication technology; semiconductors; and lasers.

Context

Intellectual property law establishes protection over intangibles – for example, when a manufactured product is sold, the product itself becomes the property of the purchaser, however, intellectual property rights allow intangible elements to remain in the ownership of the creator; these intangibles include (among others) the idea itself, or the name or sign/logo used to distinguish the product from others.

Patents and trademarks are common ways to protect industrial property. Patents are a limited term exclusive right granted to an inventor, maintained through the payment of fees. While patents are generally used to protect research and development (R & D) results, they are also a source of technical information, which can potentially prevent re-inventing and re-developing ideas. A count of patents shows a country's capacity to exploit knowledge and translate it into potential economic gains; in this context, patent statistics are widely used to assess the inventive and innovative performance of countries. Most studies show that innovative enterprises tend to make more use of intellectual property protection than enterprises that do not innovate. Enterprise size and the economic sector in which an enterprise operates are also likely to play an important role in determining whether an enterprise chooses to protect its intellectual property; for this reason the structure of an economy plays a part in the level of patent applications.

The use of patents is relatively restricted within the EU – this may be due to a range of influences: their relative cost; the overlap between national and European procedures; or the need for translation into foreign languages. Furthermore, the increasing number and complexity of patent applications worldwide has resulted in a backlog of pending applications, while the constant expansion of the human knowledge base makes it increasingly difficult for patent offices to keep abreast of technological developments.

The European Council held in Lisbon in March 2000 called for the creation of a Community patent system to address shortcomings in the legal protection of inventions, while providing an incentive for investments in R & D. In July of the same year the European Commission made a first proposal for the creation of a Community patent: this was discussed at various levels and despite a number of proposals and amendments for a Council Regulation during 2003 and 2004 no legal basis was forthcoming. In

April 2007 the European Commission released a Communication (COM(2007) 165) titled 'Enhancing the patent system in Europe', stating that European patent systems were more expensive, uncertain and unattractive than those in non-member countries.

In July 2008 the European Commission adopted a Communication (COM(2008) 465) titled 'An industrial property rights strategy for Europe' foreseeing the development of legislation, arguing that the harmonisation of patent law should make it easier for European enterprises to patent their inventions both within and outside the EU.

On 4 December 2009, the European Council unanimously adopted conclusions on an enhanced patent system in the EU. The package agreed covers two main areas: firstly, agreement on the approach to be adopted in order to move towards an EU patent regulation; secondly, an agreement on establishing a new patent court in the EU. It is anticipated that these measures will together make it less costly for businesses to protect innovative technology and make litigation more accessible and predictable. However, the creation of the EU patent depends on a solution being found for translation arrangements which were the subject of European Commission proposal (COM(2010) 350) for a 'Council Regulation on the translation arrangements for the European Union patent' in July 2010. In December 2010 it became clear that there was not unanimous agreement on this proposal: in February 2011 the European Parliament gave its consent for the use of the enhanced cooperation procedure to make progress on this issue and this was authorised by the Council in March 2011.

Table 13.4.1: Patent applications to the EPO and patents granted by the USPTO, 2000-2008

	Patent applications to the EPO			High technology patent applications to the EPO			Patents granted by the US Patent & Trademark Office		
	(number of patent applications)		(per million inhab.)	(number of patent applications)		(per million inhab.)	(number of patents granted)		(per million inhab.)
	2003	2008	2008	2003	2008	2008	2000	2005	2005
EU-27	52318	59468	119.5	10446	5375	10.8	32009	18153	37.0
Belgium	1340	1519	142.4	278	205	19.2	772	484	46.4
Bulgaria	22	32	4.2	3	2	0.3	4	77	9.9
Czech Republic	112	200	19.3	12	15	1.5	41	57	5.6
Denmark	1071	1275	232.9	260	106	19.3	597	349	64.5
Germany	21994	24557	298.7	3537	1934	23.5	13127	7766	94.1
Estonia	11	35	25.9	7	1	0.7	3	8	6.0
Ireland	223	324	73.7	51	37	8.3	192	179	43.5
Greece	85	127	11.3	22	10	0.9	21	33	2.9
Spain	948	1545	34.1	135	126	2.8	396	229	5.3
France	7902	8557	133.7	1908	1145	17.9	4441	2759	44.0
Italy	4378	5349	89.7	489	250	4.2	2086	1152	19.7
Cyprus	6	10	13.2	3	1	1.3	5	3	3.8
Latvia	8	24	10.4	1	3	1.3	10	3	1.4
Lithuania	17	10	3.0	2	1	0.4	6	29	8.5
Luxembourg	88	115	238.1	6	2	4.2	51	43	94.0
Hungary	132	195	19.4	26	21	2.1	75	60	5.9
Malta	6	10	23.9	:	1	2.4	3	1	2.5
Netherlands	3459	3711	226.2	1012	342	20.9	1777	1227	75.3
Austria	1358	1932	232.2	224	99	11.9	709	426	52.0
Poland	111	226	5.9	14	17	0.5	33	49	1.3
Portugal	65	144	13.6	10	16	1.5	16	20	1.9
Romania	16	36	1.7	3	10	0.5	6	17	0.8
Slovenia	73	119	59.1	6	8	4.0	32	10	5.2
Slovakia	31	50	9.2	4	5	0.9	9	8	1.4
Finland	1278	1327	250.3	578	199	37.5	1060	636	121.5
Sweden	2029	2928	318.9	456	337	36.7	1783	540	59.9
United Kingdom	5555	5511	90.1	1399	482	7.9	4754	2195	36.5
Iceland	31	28	88.8	13	2	7.7	27	18	62.2
Liechtenstein	22	34	963.9	2	3	75.5	14	16	470.3
Norway	342	563	118.8	69	19	4.1	328	194	42.0
Switzerland	2762	3351	441.3	355	205	27.1	1680	896	120.8
Croatia	42	32	7.2	1	3	0.6	18	10	2.2
FYR of Macedonia	:	:	:	:	1	0.2	:	:	:
Turkey	85	270	3.8	10	14	0.2	16	12	0.2
Japan	21600	20239	158.5	7623	3317	26.0	110199	83784	253.3
United States	32601	31602	103.8	11150	2967	9.7	43396	32358	283.0

Source: Eurostat (online data codes: tsc00009, tsiir060, pat_ep_ntec, tsc00010, pat_us_ntot and tsiir070)

Figure 13.4.1: Patent applications to the EPO, EU-27, 1998-2008
(number of patent applications)

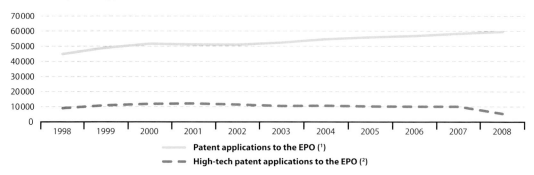

Patent applications to the EPO (¹)
High-tech patent applications to the EPO (²)

(¹) 2007 and 2008, estimates.
(²) 2008, provisional.

Source: Eurostat (online data codes: pat_ep_ntot and pat_ep_ntec)

Figure 13.4.2: Co-patenting at the EPO according to inventors' country of residence, 2008 (¹)
(% of total)

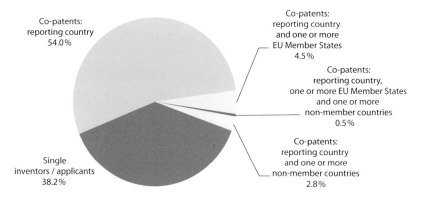

Co-patents:
reporting country
54.0%

Co-patents:
reporting country
and one or more
EU Member States
4.5%

Co-patents:
reporting country,
one or more EU Member States
and one or more
non-member countries
0.5%

Co-patents:
reporting country
and one or more
non-member countries
2.8%

Single
inventors / applicants
38.2%

(¹) Provisional.
Source: Eurostat (online data code: pat_ep_cpi)

Figure 13.4.3: EU patent citations (EPO), 1997-2007
(number)

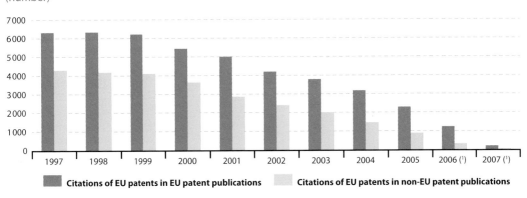

(¹) Provisional.

Source: Eurostat (online data code: pat_ep_cti)

Annex 1 — Nomenclatures and classifications

NACE Rev. 1.1 (statistical classification of economic activities in the European Community)

A   Agriculture, hunting and forestry
B   Fishing
C   Mining and quarrying
D   Manufacturing
E   Electricity, gas and water supply
F   Construction
G   Wholesale and retail trade; repair of motor vehicles, motorcycles and personal and household goods
H   Hotels and restaurants
I   Transport, storage and communication
J   Financial intermediation
K   Real estate, renting and business activities
L   Public administration and defence; compulsory social security
M   Education
N   Health and social work
O   Other community, social and personal service activities
P   Activities of households
Q   Extra-territorial organisations and bodies

A full listing of the NACE Rev. 1.1 classification is accessible on the Eurostat website (http://ec.europa.eu/eurostat/ramon/nomenclatures/index.cfm?TargetUrl=ACT_OTH_BUILD_TREE&StrNom=NACE_1_1&StrLanguageCode=EN).

NACE Rev. 2 (statistical classification of economic activities in the European Community)

A   Agriculture, forestry and fishing
B   Mining and quarrying
C   Manufacturing
D   Electricity, gas, steam and air conditioning supply
E   Water supply; sewerage, waste management and remediation activities
F   Construction
G   Wholesale and retail trade; repair of motor vehicles and motorcycles
H   Transportation and storage
I   Accommodation and food service activities
J   Information and communication
K   Financial and insurance activities
L   Real estate activities
M   Professional, scientific and technical activities
N   Administrative and support service activities
O   Public administration and defence; compulsory social security
P   Education
Q   Human health and social work activities
R   Arts, entertainment and recreation
S   Other service activities
T   Activities of households as employers; undifferentiated goods- and services-producing activities of households for own use
U   Activities of extraterritorial organisations and bodies

A full listing of the NACE Rev. 2 classification is accessible on the Eurostat website (http://ec.europa.eu/eurostat/ramon/nomenclatures/index.cfm?TargetUrl=LST_NOM_DTL&StrNom=NACE_REV2&StrLanguageCode=EN).

SITC Rev. 4 (standard international trade classification)

0   Food and live animals
1   Beverages and tobacco
2   Crude materials, inedible, except fuels
3   Mineral fuels, lubricants and related materials
4   Animal and vegetable oils, fats and waxes
5   Chemicals and related products, n.e.s.
6   Manufactured goods classified chiefly by material
7   Machinery and transport equipment
8   Miscellaneous manufactured articles
9   Commodities and transactions not classified elsewhere in the SITC

A full listing of the classification is accessible on the UN website (http://unstats.un.org/unsd/trade/sitcrev4.htm).

NUTS (nomenclature of territorial units for statistics)

A full listing of the nomenclature is accessible on the Eurostat website (http://ec.europa.eu/eurostat/ramon/nomenclatures/index.cfm?TargetUrl=LST_CLS_DLD&StrNom=NUTS_33&StrLanguageCode=EN).

ISCED 1997 (international standard classification of education)

The classification comprises 22 fields of education (at two-digit level) which can be further refined into three-digit level. The following eight broad groups (at one-digit level) are distinguished:

1   Education
2   Humanities and arts
3   Social sciences, business and law
4   Science
5   Engineering, manufacturing and construction
6   Agriculture
7   Health and welfare
8   Services

Empirically, ISCED assumes that several criteria exist which can help allocate education programmes to levels of education. The following ISCED 1997 levels can be distinguished:

0   Pre-primary education
1   Primary education (first stage of basic education)
2   Lower secondary education (second stage of basic education)
3   Upper secondary education
4   Post-secondary non-tertiary education
5   Tertiary education (first stage)
6   Tertiary education (second stage)

In 2011, a revision to ISCED was formally adopted by UNESCO Member States, taking into account significant changes in education systems worldwide since the last ISCED revision in 1997. The first data collection based on the new classification will begin in 2014.

A full listing of the classification and more details are accessible on the UNESCO website (http://www.uis.unesco.org/Education/Pages/international-standard-classification-of-education.aspx).

Annex 2 — Data presentation and abbreviations

Data presentation

Eurostat online databases contain a large amount of metadata that provides information on the status of particular values or data series. In order to improve readability, only the most significant information has been included in the tables and figures. The following notation and symbols are used, where necessary:

Italic   data value is forecasted, provisional or estimated and is likely to change;
:   not available, confidential or unreliable value;
–   not applicable.

Breaks in series are indicated in the footnotes provided under each table and figure.

In the case of the EU Member States, even when data are not available, these countries have been included in tables and figures systematically (with appropriate footnotes for figures indicating that data are not available, while in tables use has been made of the colon (:) to indicate that data are not available). For non-member countries outside the EU, when data are not available for a particular indicator the country has been removed from the table or figure in question.

Abbreviations

Geographical aggregates and names

EU	European Union
EU-27	European Union of 27 Member States including Belgium, Bulgaria, the Czech Republic, Denmark, Germany, Estonia, Ireland, Greece, Spain, France, Italy, Cyprus, Latvia, Lithuania, Luxembourg, Hungary, Malta, the Netherlands, Austria, Poland, Portugal, Romania, Slovenia, Slovakia, Finland, Sweden and the United Kingdom. Note that unless otherwise stated, the EU aggregate in this publication refers to 27 countries, as if all 27 of these had been part of the EU in periods prior to 1 January 2007
EU-25	EU-27 without Bulgaria and Romania (from 1 May 2004 to 31 December 2006)
EU-15	Belgium, Denmark, Germany, Ireland, Greece, Spain, France, Italy, Luxembourg, the Netherlands, Austria, Portugal, Finland, Sweden and the United Kingdom (from 1 January 1995 to 30 April 2004)
Euro area	Note that unless otherwise stated, the euro area (EA) aggregate in this publication refers to 17 countries (EA-17), as if all 17 of these had been part of the euro area in periods prior to 1 January 2011
EA-17	Belgium, Germany, Estonia, Ireland, Greece, Spain, France, Italy, Cyprus, Luxembourg, Malta, the Netherlands, Austria, Portugal, Slovenia, Slovakia and Finland; EA-16 plus Estonia (since 1 January 2011)
EA-16	EA-15 plus Slovakia (from 1 January 2009 to 31 December 2010)
EA-15	EA-13 plus Cyprus and Malta (from 1 January 2008 to 31 December 2008)
EA-13	EA-12 plus Slovenia (from 1 January 2007 to 31 December 2007)
EA-12	EA-11 plus Greece (from 1 January 2001 to 31 December 2006)
EA-11	Belgium, Germany, Ireland, Spain, France, Italy, Luxembourg, the Netherlands, Austria, Portugal and Finland (from 1 January 1999 to 31 December 2000)
FYR of Macedonia (¹)	the former Yugoslav Republic of Macedonia
USA	United States of America

Units of measurement

%	per cent
AWU	annual work unit
CHF	Swiss franc
cm³	cubic centimetre
CO₂ equivalent	carbon dioxide equivalent
ECU	European currency unit
ESU	economic size unit
EUR	euro
FTE	full-time equivalent
GJ	gigajoule
GRT	gross registered tonnage
GT	gross tonnage
GWh	gigawatt-hour
ha	hectare (1 ha = 10 000 m²)
HC	head count
JPY	Japanese yen
kbit/s	kilobit per second
kg	kilogram
kgoe	kilogram of oil equivalent
km	kilometre
km²	square kilometre
km/h	kilometre per hour
kW	kilowatt
kWh	kilowatt hour

(¹) The name of the former Yugoslav Republic of Macedonia is shown in tables and figures in this publication as FYR of Macedonia – this does not prejudge in any way the definitive nomenclature for this country, which is to be agreed following the conclusion of negotiations currently taking place on this subject at the United Nations.

l	litre
LSU	livestock unit
m	metre
m^3	cubic metre
mm	millimetre
MWh	megawatt-hour
NMVOC equivalent	non-methane volatile organic compounds equivalent
p/st	piece/unit
pkm	passenger-kilometre
PPS	purchasing power standard
SO_2 equivalent	sulphur dioxide equivalent
t	tonne
tkm	tonne-kilometre
toe	tonne of oil equivalent
TWh	terawatt hour
USD	United States dollar

Other abbreviations

AES	adult education survey
AIDS	acquired immune deficiency syndrome or acquired immunodeficiency syndrome
AWU	annual work unit
Benelux	Belgium, Luxembourg and the Netherlands
BoP	balance of payments
BPM5	fifth balance of payments manual
CAP	common agricultural policy
CARE	EU's road accident database of accidents resulting in death and/or injury
CD	compact disc
CEAS	common European asylum system
CEPA	classification of environmental protection activities
CEPOL	European Police College
CFP	common fisheries policy
CO	carbon monoxide
CH_4	methane
CIF	cost, insurance and freight
CIP	competitiveness and innovation framework programme
CIS	1. Commonwealth of Independent States 2. Community innovation survey

CLRTAP	convention on long-range transboundary air pollution
CMR	carcinogenic, mutagenic and reprotoxic (chemicals)
CN	combined nomenclature
CO_2	carbon dioxide
COD	codification
COFOG	classification of the functions of government
COICOP	classification of individual consumption by purpose
COM	Communication
CPA	classification of products by activity
CPI	consumer price index
DDA	Doha Development Agenda
DSL	digital subscriber line
DVD	digital versatile disk
EAA	economic accounts for agriculture
EAP	environment action programme
EC	1. European Community 2. European Commission
ECB	European Central Bank
ECOFIN	Economic and Financial Affairs Council
ECVET	European credit system for VET
EDP	excessive deficit procedure
EEA	1. European Economic Area 2. European Environment Agency
EEAICP	European Economic Area index of consumer prices
EEC	European Economic Community
EES	European employment strategy
EFC	Economic and Financial Committee
EFF	European Fisheries Fund
EFTA	European Free Trade Association
e.g.	for example
EHEA	European higher education area
EICP	European index of consumer prices
EIT	European Institute of Innovation and Technology
EITO	European Information Technology Observatory
EMU	economic and monetary union
EP	European Parliament
EPO	European Patent Office
EPC	European Patent Convention
EPI	environmental pressure indicators

EPWS	European platform of women scientists	FP7	seventh framework programme (for research and technological development)
EQAVET	European quality assurance reference framework for VET	Frontex	European agency for the management of operational cooperation at the external borders of the Member States of the EU
EQF	European qualifications framework for lifelong learning		
ERA	European research area		
ERM	exchange rate mechanism	FSS	farm structure survey
ESA	European system of national and regional accounts (ESA 95)	FTE	full-time equivalents
		FTU	full-time units
ESAC	European statistical advisory committee	GATS	general agreement on trade in services
ESAW	European statistics on accidents at work	GDP	gross domestic product
		GERD	gross domestic expenditure on R & D
ESDS	European statistical data support	GFS	government finance statistics
ESGAB	European statistical governance advisory board	GHG	greenhouse gases
		GPG	gender pay gap
ESMS	euro SDMX metadata structure	HBS	household budget survey
ESS	European statistical system	HDI	human development index
ESSC	European statistical system committee	HFCE	household final consumption expenditure
ESSPROS	European system of integrated social protection statistics	HICP	harmonised index of consumer prices
ESU	European size unit	HIV	human immunodeficiency virus
ET	education and training	HLY	healthy life years
EU	European Union	HRST	human resources in science and technology
EURES	European jobs and mobility portal		
Euribor	euro interbank offered rate	ICD	international statistical classification of diseases and related health problems
EU-SILC	European Union statistics on income and living conditions		
Europol	European Police Office	ICHA	international classification for health accounts
EUROPOP2010	Eurostat's 2010-based national population projections		
		ICT	information and communication technology
EuroRAP	European road assessment programme		
		ILO	International Labour Organisation
EuroTAP	European tunnel assessment programme	IMF	International Monetary Fund
		IPC	international patent classification
Eurotariff	(Regulation on) roaming charges	IRIS	interactive coding system for causes of death
Eurostat	statistical office of the European Union		
		ISCED	international standard classification of education
FAO	Food and Agriculture Organisation (UN)		
		ISCO	international standard classification of occupations
FATS	statistics on foreign affiliates		
FDI	foreign direct investment	ISDN	integrated services digital network
FOB	free on board	IT	information technology
		ITGS	international trade in goods statistics

ITTO	International Tropical Timber Organisation	PhD	doctoral degree
JFSQ	joint forest sector questionnaire	PLI	price level index
JHA	justice and home affairs	PPP	purchasing power parity
JRC	Joint Research Centre	PRODCOM	EU's industrial production statistics
JVR	job vacancy rate	PROGRESS	EU's employment and social solidarity programme
LFS	labour force survey		
LLP	lifelong learning programme	R & D	research and development
LMP	labour market policy	REACH	(Regulation on the) registration, evaluation, authorisation and restriction of chemicals
LUCAS	land use/cover area frame survey		
MEETS	modernisation of European enterprise and trade statistics		
		RES	renewable energy sources
MFI	monetary financial institutions	Rev.	revision
MUICP	monetary union index of consumer prices	S	south
		SBA	small business act for Europe'
N	north	SBS	structural business statistics
N_2O	nitrous oxide	SDI	sustainable development indicator
NACE	statistical classification of economic activities within the European Community	SDMX	statistical data and metadata exchange
		SDS	sustainable development strategy
n.e.s.	not elsewhere specified	SEC	Secretariat-General document; SEC documents are internal documents of the European Commission, typically staff working documents
n.e.c.	not elsewhere classified		
NGO	non-governmental organisation		
NH_3	ammonia	SES	structure of earnings survey
NMVOC	non-methane volatile organic compounds	SGP	stability and growth pact
		SHA	system of health accounts
NO_x	nitrogen oxides	SILC	statistics on income and living conditions
NPISH	non-profit institutions serving households		
		SITC	standard international trade classification
NSI/NSO	national statistical institute or office		
NUTS	hierarchical classification/nomenclature of territorial units for statistics (Eurostat) (NUTS 1, 2 and 3)	SME	small and medium-sized enterprise
		SMS	short message service
		SNA	system of national accounts
ÖBB	Österreichische Bundesbahnen (Austrian federal railways)	SO_2	sulphur dioxide
		SO_x	sulphur oxide(s)
OECD	Organisation for Economic Co-operation and Development	SPE	special purpose entities
		STI	science, technology and innovation
OMC	open method of coordination	STS	short-term (business) statistics
OPEC	Organisation of Petroleum Exporting Countries	TAC	total allowable catch
		TEU	EU Treaty
PCT	Patent Cooperation Treaty	TFEU	Treaty on the functioning of the European Union
PDA	personal digital assistant		
PDF	portable document format	TGM	tables, graphs and maps
PECBMS	pan-European common bird monitoring scheme	TOFP	tropospheric ozone formation potential
PEEI	principal European economic indicator	TOP	tropospheric ozone precursors
		UAA	utilised agricultural area
PFCs	perfluorocarbons	UIS	UNESCO institute for statistics

UN	United Nations		VAT	value added tax
UNECE	United Nations economic commission for Europe		VIS	visa information system
			VOIP	voice over internet protocol
UNESCO	United Nations educational, scientific and cultural organisation		VET	vocational education and training
			W	west
UNFCCC	United Nations framework convention on climate change		WEI	water exploitation index
			WFD	water framework Directive
UIS	UNESCO institute for statistics		WHO	World Health Organisation
UNSCR	United Nations Security Council Resolution		WISE	water information system for Europe
UNSD	United Nations Statistical Division		WiTEC	European association for women in science, engineering and technology
UOE	United Nations/OECD/Eurostat			
USB	universal serial bus			
USPTO	United States Patent and Trademark Office		WTO	World Trade Organisation

Glossary

Access points

An **access point**, in postal statistics, is a physical facility, including letter boxes provided for the public either on the public highway or at the premises of the providers of postal and related services, where postal items may be deposited by customers for processing in postal and related services.

Accident at work

An **accident at work** is a discrete occurrence during the course of work which leads to physical or mental harm. The phrase 'in the course of work' means whilst engaged in an occupational activity or during the time spent at work. This includes cases of road traffic accidents in the course of work but excludes accidents during the journey between home and the workplace.

Adult education survey (AES)

The **adult education survey**, abbreviated as **AES**, is a survey carried out by 29 European Union, EFTA and candidate countries between 2005 and 2008, collecting information on education and lifelong learning activities by individuals aged 25-64 living in private households. The AES, which uses 2007 as a reference year, was a pilot exercise, and there are plans to conduct additional surveys every five years. The survey allows for international comparisons of education, occupation and economic activity.

Aggregate

Statistics for related categories can be grouped together or **aggregated** in order to provide a broader picture. Thus, an **aggregate** is the combination of related categories, usually within a common branch of a hierarchy, to provide information at a broader level to that at which detailed observations are taken.

The aggregation is usually not done by simple addition, but taking account of the relative importance of the different categories, using weights.

Agricultural area (AA)

Agricultural area, abbreviated to **AA**, (or **utilised agricultural area**, abbreviated to **UAA**) describes the area used for farming. It includes the land categories: arable land; permanent grassland; permanent crops; other agricultural land such as kitchen gardens (even if they only represent small areas of total UAA).

The term does not include unused agricultural land, woodland and land occupied for example by buildings, farmyards, tracks or ponds.

Agricultural holding

An **agricultural holding** is a single unit, in both technical and economic terms, operating under single management, which produces agricultural products. Other supplementary (non-agricultural) products and services may also be provided by the holding.

Agricultural income

The main indicator for **agricultural income** is the factor income per labour input expressed in annual work units (AWU).

Allocation of primary income account

The **allocation of primary income account** within national accounts (NA) focuses on resident institutional units or sectors in their capacity as recipients of primary incomes rather than as producers whose activities generate primary incomes.

It lists two kinds of primary income under 'resources':

- primary incomes already recorded in the generation of income account that are receivable by resident institutional units by virtue of their direct participation in the production process (mainly

operating surplus and mixed income, compensation of employees);

- property incomes receivable by the owner of a financial asset or a tangible non-produced asset in return for providing funds to, or putting the tangible non-produced asset at the disposal of, another institutional unit (interest, dividends, withdrawals from income of quasi-corporations, reinvested earnings of foreign direct investment, rents on land).

Animal output

Animal output comprises the sales, changes in stock levels, and the products used for processing and own final use by the producers.

Annual work unit (AWU)

One **annual work unit**, abbreviated as **AWU**, corresponds to the work performed by one person who is occupied on an agricultural holding on a full-time basis. Full-time means the minimum hours required by the relevant national provisions governing contracts of employment. If the national provisions do not indicate the number of hours, then 1 800 hours are taken to be the minimum annual working hours: equivalent to 225 working days of eight hours each.

Apparent labour productivity

Apparent labour productivity is defined as value added at factor costs divided by the number of persons employed. This ratio is generally presented in thousands of euros per person employed.

Aquaculture

Aquaculture, also known as **aquafarming**, refers to the farming of aquatic (freshwater or saltwater) organisms, such as fish, molluscs, crustaceans and plants for human use or consumption, under controlled conditions. Aquaculture implies some form of intervention in the natural rearing process to enhance production, including regular stocking, feeding and protection from predators. Farming also implies individual or corporate ownership of, or contractual rights to, the stock being cultivated.

Arable land

Arable land, in agricultural statistics, is land worked (ploughed or tilled) regularly, generally under a system of crop rotation.

Asset

Assets are economic resources that have some value or usefulness (usually convertible in cash) and that are owned by enterprises or individuals, for example a piece of machinery or a house. According to the International Accounting Standards Board, assets are a result of past events and are expected to provide future economic benefits.

In the context of national accounts, economic assets can be defined as entities functioning as stores of value and over which ownership rights are enforced by institutional units, individually or collectively, and from which economic benefits may be derived by their owners through holding them, or using them, over a period of time (the economic benefits consist of primary incomes derived from the use of the asset and the value, including possible holding gains/losses, that could be realised by disposing of the asset or terminating it).

Asylum

Asylum is a form of protection given by a state on its territory based on the principle of non-refoulement and internationally or nationally recognised refugee rights. It is granted to a person who is unable to seek protection in his/her country of citizenship and/or residence in particular for fear of being persecuted for reasons of race, religion, nationality, membership of a particular social group or political opinion.

Asylum applicant

Asylum applicant means a person having submitted an application for international protection or having been included in such application as a family member during the reference period. 'Application for international protection' means an application for international protection as defined in Art.2(g) of Council Directive 2004/83/EC, in other words including requests for refugee status or for subsidiary protection status, irrespective of whether the application was lodged on arrival at a border, or from inside the country, and irrespective of whether the person entered the territory legally (for example as a tourist) or illegally.

Applications submitted by persons who are subsequently found to be a subject of a Dublin procedure (Council Regulation 343/2003) are included in the number of asylum applications. Within the same reference period every person being a subject of asylum application is counted only once, therefore repeat applications are not recorded if the first application has been lodged in the same reference period. However, such a repeat application will be recorded if lodged in a different reference month. This means that the aggregation of the monthly figures may overestimate the number of persons applying for international protection within the aggregated period (quarter or year).

At-risk-of-poverty rate

The **at-risk-of-poverty rate** is the share of persons with an equivalised disposable income (after social transfers) below the **at-risk-of-poverty threshold**, which is set at 60 % of the national median equivalised disposable income after social transfers. This indicator does not measure wealth or poverty, but low income in comparison with other residents in that country, which does not necessarily imply a low standard of living.

The **at-risk-of-poverty rate before social transfers** is calculated as the share of persons having an equivalised disposable income before social transfers that is below the at-risk-of-poverty threshold calculated after social transfers. Pensions, such as old age and survivors' (widows' and widowers') benefits, are counted as income (before social transfers) and not as social transfers. This indicator examines the hypothetical non-existence of social transfers.

The **persistent at-risk-of-poverty rate** shows the percentage of the population living in households where the equivalised disposable income was below the at-risk-of-poverty threshold for the current year and at least two out of the preceding three years. Its calculation requires a longitudinal instrument, through which individuals are followed over four years.

Balance of payments

The **balance of payments** is a statistical summary of the transactions of a given economy with the rest of the world. It comprises three elements:

- the **current account** covers international transactions in goods, services, income, and current transfers;
- the **financial account** deals with transactions involving financial claims on, or liabilities to, the rest of the world, including international purchases of securities, such as stocks and bonds;
- the **capital account** covers international capital transfers (for example, debt forgiveness) and the acquisition/disposal of non-produced, non-financial assets (such as patents).

Baltic Member States

The three Baltic Member States of the European Union are: Estonia (EE); Latvia (LV); Lithuania (LT).

Baseline study

A **baseline study** is an analysis of the current situation to identify the starting points for a programme or project. It looks at what information must be considered and analysed to establish a **baseline** or starting point, the benchmark against which future progress can be assessed or comparisons made.

Bed places

The number of **bed places** in an establishment or dwelling is determined by the number of persons who can stay overnight in beds set up in that establishment, ignoring any extra beds that may be set up following a specific customer request. The term 'bed place' applies to a single bed. A double bed is counted as two bed places. This unit serves to measure the capacity of any type of accommodation. A bed place is also defined to cover a pitch or, in a boat, a mooring that can accommodate one person. A pitch for a tent (if counted), caravan, mobile home and similar shelter, or a boat on a mooring, is usually counted as four bed places if the actual number is not known.

Benelux

The **Benelux** Member States of the European Union are: Belgium (BE); Luxembourg (LU); the Netherlands (NL).

The term 'Benelux', formed from the first two or three letters of each country's name, originally referred to a customs union established in 1948. Today, the term is used as a generic grouping of the three countries.

Biodiversity

Biodiversity, a contraction of biological diversity, refers to the number, variety and variability of living organisms, including mankind, within a given area. A reduction or loss of biodiversity undermines not only the natural environment, but also the economic and social goals of human societies, as mankind depends on natural resources for the food, energy, raw materials, clean air and clean water making life possible. The importance of preserving biodiversity, and the possible consequences of not doing so, has made it an international issue.

Biofuels

Biofuels are liquid fuels from a non-fossil biological origin and a renewable energy source, to be distinguished from fossil fuels. Biofuels can be split up into two categories, biogasoline and biodiesel.

Biomass

Biomass is organic, non-fossil material of biological origin that can be used for heat production or electricity generation. It includes: wood and wood waste; biogas; municipal solid waste; biofuels.

Births

A **birth** is defined as the start of life when a child emerges from the body of its mother. The total number of births includes both live births and stillbirths.

A **live birth** is the birth of a child who showed any sign of life; the number of live births refers to the number of births excluding stillbirths.

A **stillbirth** is the expulsion or extraction from the mother of a dead foetus after the time at which it would normally be presumed capable of independent extra-uterine existence (outside the uterus or womb). This is commonly taken to be after 24 or 28 weeks of **gestation** (the time from a child's conception to its birth).

A **live birth outside marriage** is a birth where the mother's marital status at the time of birth is other than married.

The **crude birth rate** is the ratio of the number of births during the year to the average population in that year; the value is expressed per 1 000 inhabitants.

Broadband

Broadband refers to telecommunications in which a wide band of frequencies is available to send data. Broadband telecommunication lines or connections are defined as those transporting data at high speeds, with a speed of data transfer for uploading and downloading data (also called capacity) equal to or higher than 144 kbit/s (kilobits per second or kbps).

The technologies most widely used for broadband internet access are digital subscriber line (DSL) and its variations (xDSL), or cable modem (connects a computer to a local television line).

Budget deficit

A **budget deficit** occurs when a government's spending is greater than its revenues.

In the European Union, Member States which are part of the euro area are required to keep their budget deficits below 3 % of gross domestic product to promote economic stability and sustainable public finances.

Building permit

The number (and index) of **building permits** or **construction permits** is a leading indicator in the business cycle which provides some information about the expected workload of the construction sector in the near future.

A construction or building permit is the final authorisation to start work on a building project. It is granted by public authorities in response to an application by a principal and based on a specific building plan. There are differences in the rules and procedures according to which such permits are granted among the European Union Member States.

Bunkers

Bunkers include all dutiable petroleum products loaded aboard a vessel for consumption by that vessel.

International maritime bunkers describe the quantities of fuel oil delivered to ships of all flags that are engaged in international navigation. It is the fuel used to power these ships. International navigation may take place at sea, on inland lakes and waterways, and in coastal waters.

International maritime bunkers do not include fuel oil consumption by:

- ships engaged in domestic navigation; whether a vessel is engaged in domestic or international navigation is determined only by the ship's port of departure and port of arrival – not by the flag or nationality of the ship;
- fishing vessels;
- military forces.

Business cycle

A **business cycle** describes the expansions and contractions of economic activity in an economy over a period of time.

The economy considered may be a country, or a geographical aggregate such as the euro area or the European Union. The development of economic activity is expressed as a percentage change of an economic indicator, for example production, hours worked, employment, or gross domestic product. The business cycle is usually represented in a graph showing the ups and downs of an economy over time.

Business investment rate

The **business investment rate** is defined as gross investment (fixed capital formation) divided by gross value added.

Candidate countries

At the time of writing (May 2012) Croatia (HR) is an **acceding country**, due to become a Member State of the European Union on 1 July 2013.

In addition, there are five official **candidate countries** for membership of the European Union: Iceland (IS); Montenegro (ME); the former Yugoslav Republic of Macedonia (MK) ([2]); Serbia (RS); Turkey (TR).

In addition, there are three **potential candidates**, who have applied for membership but have not yet been granted candidate country status: Albania (AL); Bosnia and Herzegovina (BA); Kosovo under UNSCR 1244/99 (XK) ([3]).

([2]) MK is a provisional code which does not prejudge in any way the definitive nomenclature for this country, which will be agreed following the conclusion of negotiations currently taking place on this subject at the United Nations.

([3]) XK is a code used for practical reasons and not an official ISO country code.

Carbon dioxide emissions (CO$_2$)

Carbon dioxide (CO$_2$) is a colourless, odourless and non-poisonous gas formed by combustion of carbon and in the respiration of living organisms and is considered a greenhouse gas. In this context emissions involve the release of greenhouse gases and/or their precursors into the atmosphere over a specified area and period of time. **Carbon dioxide emissions** or **CO$_2$emissions** are emissions stemming from the burning of fossil fuels and the manufacture of cement; they include carbon dioxide produced during consumption of solid, liquid, and gas fuels as well as gas flaring.

Carcass weight

The definition of **carcass weight** depends on the animal species under consideration.

For pigs it is the weight of the slaughtered pig's cold body, either whole or divided in half along the mid-line, after being bled and eviscerated and after removal of the tongue, bristles, hooves, genitalia, flare fat, kidneys and diaphragm.

For cattle it is the weight of the slaughtered animal's cold body after being skinned, bled and eviscerated, and after removal of the external genitalia, the limbs, the head, the tail, the kidneys and kidney fats, and the udder.

For sheep and goats it is the weight of the slaughtered animal's cold body after having been bled, skinned and eviscerated, and after removal of the head, feet, tail and genital organs. Kidneys and kidney fats are included in the carcass weight.

For poultry it is the weight of the cold body of the slaughtered farmyard poultry after being bled, plucked and eviscerated. The weight includes poultry offal, with the exception of *foie gras*.

For other species, the carcass weight is considered to be the weight of the slaughtered animal's cold body.

Carcinogenic, mutagenic and reprotoxic (CMR)

Carcinogenic, mutagenic and reprotoxic chemicals, abbreviated as **CMR** chemicals, make up the first and most toxic category of the toxicity classes into which hazardous chemicals can be subdivided, according to European Union legislation.

Carcinogenic chemicals can cause or promote cancers. Mutagenic chemicals can cause genetic mutations. Reprotoxic chemicals can damage the reproductive process.

Cattle

Cattle refers to domestic animals of the species *Bos taurus*. Cattle and water buffalo *Bubalus bubalis* together are called **bovines**.

A distinction can be made by the age of the animal (less than one year old, aged between one and two years, and two years and over), with a further division between male and female cattle. Female cattle aged two years and over are divided into **heifers** (that have not yet calved) and cows. The latter are further divided into dairy cows and others.

Cause of death

The **cause of death** is defined as the disease or injury which started the train (sequence) of morbid (disease-related) events which led directly to death, or the circumstances of the accident or violence which produced the fatal injury.

This definition is derived from the international classification of diseases (ICD) of the World Health Organisation. Although international definitions are harmonised, the statistics may not be fully comparable, among countries, as classifications may vary when the cause of death is multiple or difficult to evaluate, and because of different notification procedures.

Central government

Central government consists of all administrative departments of the state and other central agencies whose responsibilities cover the whole economic territory of a country, except for the administration of social security funds.

Cereal

Cereal includes wheat (common wheat and spelt and durum wheat), rye, maslin, barley, oats, mixed grain other than maslin, grain maize, sorghum, triticale, and other cereal crops such as buckwheat, millet, canary seed and rice.

Classification of environmental protection activities (CEPA 2000)

The European standard statistical classification of environmental protection activities, abbreviated as CEPA, is used to classify activities, products, expenditure and other transactions whose primary purpose is environmental protection. For the purposes of CEPA the following definitions are used.

Environmental protection activities are production activities using equipment, labour, manufacturing techniques, information networks or products, to create an output of goods or services.

Environmental protection products are:

- the environmental protection services produced by environmental protection activities; and
- adapted (cleaner) and connected products.

Expenditure for environmental protection includes outlays and other transactions related to:

- inputs for environmental protection activities (energy, raw materials and other intermediate inputs, wages and salaries, taxes linked to production, consumption of fixed capital);
- capital formation and the buying of land (investment) for environmental protection activities;
- users' outlays for buying environmental protection products;
- transfers for environmental protection (for example subsidies, investment grants, international

aid, donations, taxes earmarked for environmental protection).

Classification of individual consumption by purpose (COICOP)

The **classification of individual consumption by purpose**, abbreviated as **COICOP**, is a classification developed by the United Nations Statistics Division to classify and analyse individual consumption expenditures incurred by households, non-profit institutions serving households and general government according to their purpose. It includes categories such as clothing and footwear, housing, water, electricity, and gas and other fuels.

Classification of territorial units for statistics (NUTS)

The classification **of territorial units for statistics**, abbreviated as **NUTS** (from the French *Nomenclature des Unités territoriales statistiques*) is a geographical classification subdividing the territory of the European Union (EU) into regions at three different levels (NUTS 1, 2 and 3, respectively, moving from larger to smaller territorial units).

NUTS areas aim to provide a single and coherent territorial breakdown for the compilation of EU regional statistics. The 2006 version of NUTS subdivides the territory of the EU and its 27 Member States into 97 NUTS 1 regions, 271 NUTS 2 regions and 1 303 NUTS 3 regions.

The NUTS is based on Regulation 1059/2003 on the establishment of a common classification of territorial units for statistics, approved in 2003 and amended in 2006 by Regulation 105/2007. Two further amending Regulations1888/2005 and 176/2008, adopted in 2005 and 2008 respectively, extended the NUTS system to the Member States that joined the EU in 2004 and 2007.

Classification of the functions of government (COFOG)

The **classification of the functions of government**, abbreviated as **COFOG**, was developed in

its current version in 1999 by the Organisation for Economic Co-operation and Development and published by the United Nations Statistical Division as a standard classifying the purposes of government activities.

The classification has three levels of detail: divisions; groups; classes.

Divisions describe the broad objectives of government, while groups and classes both define the means by which these broad objectives are achieved.

Climate change

Climate change refers to anthropogenic (man-made) climate change that is believed to be causing an increase in global temperatures driven by emissions of gases such as carbon dioxide and methane, known as greenhouse gases.

Coefficient of variation

The **coefficient of variation** is generally defined as the standard deviation of a random variable divided by the mean.

Co-generation

Co-generation, also known as **combined heat and power** (**CHP**), describes the simultaneous production of both useful heat (that can be used, for example, in industrial processes or district heating schemes) and electricity in a single process or unit. Co-generation enables much greater plant efficiencies to be obtained in terms of energy conversion with overall efficiencies as high as 80 %-90 %. The energy savings potential of co-generation is important with regard to reducing emissions and improving energy efficiency.

COICOP/HICP

The **COICOP/HICP** is the United Nations classification of individual consumption by purpose, adapted to the compilation of the harmonised index of consumer prices of the European Union

and the euro area. Adapting COICOP to the HICP calculation involved a number of changes:

- some sub-indices of the COICOP, such as narcotics and owner-occupied housing, had to be excluded because they are not within the HICP coverage;
- certain sub-classes (those with four digits) have been combined to ensure their weight was above one part per thousand in most of the Member States.

Collective tourist accommodation establishments

A collective tourist accommodation establishment is an accommodation establishment providing overnight lodging for the traveller in a room or some other unit, with the number of places provided greater than a specified minimum for groups of persons exceeding a single family unit and all the places in the establishment must come under a common commercial-type management, even if the establishment is non-profit-making.

Combined nomenclature (CN)

The **combined nomenclature**, abbreviated as **CN**, is a classification of goods, designed to meet the needs of:

- the common customs tariff (setting import duties for products imported into the European Union (EU) and the integrated tariff of the European Communities (Taric), incorporating all EU and trade measures applied to goods imported into and exported out of the EU;
- the external trade statistics of the EU.

The CN provides the means of collecting, exchanging and publishing data on EU external trade statistics. It is also used for the collection and publication of external trade statistics in intra-EU trade.

Common agricultural policy (CAP)

The **common agricultural policy**, abbreviated as **CAP**, is the European Union's (EU's) agricultural policy. CAP is an area in which competence is shared between the EU and the Member States. Under Article 33 of the Treaty establishing the European Community, its aims are to ensure reasonable prices for Europe's consumers and fair incomes for farmers, in particular through the common organisation of agricultural markets and by enforcing compliance with the principles adopted at the Stresa Conference in 1958, namely single prices, financial solidarity and Community preference. The CAP is one of the most important EU policies from a budget point of view: agricultural spending accounts for some 45 % of the EU budget. Qualified majority voting in the Council and consultation with the European Parliament decide policy. The CAP has fulfilled its main goal of food self-sufficiency in the EU. Major policy changes, however, proved necessary in order to correct imbalances and overproduction resulting from the CAP. Therefore, its aims have changed in the course of time, and the instruments used have also evolved as a result of successive reforms.

Common fisheries policy (CFP)

The **common fisheries policy**, abbreviated as **CFP**, is the European Union (EU) policy for managing the fisheries in the waters of Member States. Its objectives are: increasing productivity; stabilising markets; ensuring security of supply and reasonable prices to the consumer.

Although a common fisheries policy was already provided for in the Treaty of Rome in 1957, it did not become a common policy in the full sense of the term until 1983. The CFP has the same legal basis (Articles 32-38 of the EC Treaty) as the common agricultural policy and shares the same aims. Like the CAP, the CFP is a shared responsibility of the EU and its Member States.

Successive reforms have added new aims to the initial goals of the CFP: sustainable exploitation of resources; protection of the environment; safeguards for a high level of human health protection; contribution to economic and social cohesion.

In particular, the protection of fish stocks and the marine environment are key issues, given the threat posed by resource depletion.

Community innovation survey (CIS)

The **Community innovation survey**, abbreviated as **CIS**, is conducted in every European Union (EU) Member State to collect data on innovation activities in enterprises, in other words on product innovation (goods or services) and process innovation (organisational and marketing).

The CIS is based on the Eurostat/OECD Oslo Manual 1997. The legal basis for CIS is Commission Regulation (EC) 1450/2004 of 13 August 2004 carrying out Decision No 1608/2003/EC of the European Parliament and of the Council on the production and development of Community statistics on innovation.

Community survey on ICT usage in enterprises

The **Community survey on ICT usage and e-commerce in enterprises** collects data on the use of information and communication technology, the internet, e-government, e-business and e-commerce in enterprises.

Community survey on ICT usage in households and by individuals

The **Community survey on ICT usage in households and by individuals** collects data on the use of information and communication technologies (ICT), the internet, e-government and electronic skills in households and by individuals.

Comparative price level

Comparative price levels are defined as the ratios of purchasing power parities (PPPs) to market exchange rates in each country. They give a measure of the difference in cross-border price levels by indicating for a given product the number of units of the common currency needed to buy the same volume of the product group in each country.

Competitiveness

Competitiveness is a measure of the comparative advantage or disadvantage of enterprises, industries, regions, countries or supranational economies like the European Union in selling its products in international markets. It refers to the ability to generate relatively high income and employment levels on a sustainable basis while competing internationally.

Computer

A **computer**, in the surveys on ICT usage in enterprises and households, is defined as a personal computer powered by one of the major operating systems (Macintosh, Linux or Microsoft); handheld computers or palmtops (PDAs) are also included.

Consumer price index (CPI)

The **consumer price index**, abbreviated as CPI, measures the change over time in the prices of consumer goods and services acquired, used or paid for by households. It is an important measure of inflation in the European Union.

CPIs aim to cover the whole set of goods and services consumed within the territory of a country by the population. To do this, a representative set is selected; the so-called consumer basket. Consumer goods and services include, for example, food and beverages, products for personal hygiene, newspapers and periodicals, expenditure on housing, water, electricity, gas and other fuels, health, transport, communications, education, restaurants and hotels.

Many of these goods and services are bought frequently or consumed on a daily basis.

CPIs may be used for a wide variety of purposes, including:

- as a guide for monetary policy;
- for the indexation of commercial contracts, wages, social protection benefits or financial instruments;
- as a tool for deflating the national accounts or calculating changes in national consumption or living standards.

Eurostat compiles harmonised indices of consumer prices (HICPs) to allow international comparisons of consumer price inflation. HICPs are used by the European Central Bank to monitor inflation in the euro area and to assess inflation convergence, as required under Article 121 of the Treaty of Amsterdam.

Convergence criteria

The **convergence criteria**, sometimes also called **Maastricht criteria**, are conditions that Member States of the European Union must fulfil to join the economic and monetary union and to use the euro as their official currency. There are four conditions, all aimed at increasing convergence of EMU participants:

- **price stability**: Member States should have a price performance that is sustainable and an average rate of inflation that does not exceed by more than 1.5 percentage points that of the three best-performing Member States in terms of price stability for a period of one year before the examination;
- **government budgetary position**: Member States are to avoid situations of excessive government deficits, that is their ratio of planned or actual government deficit to gross domestic product should be no more than 3 %, and their ratio of (general) government debt to GDP should be no more than 60 %, unless the excess over the reference value is only exceptional or temporary or the ratios have declined substantially and continuously;
- **exchange rates**: Member States should have respected the normal fluctuation margins of the exchange rate mechanism without severe tensions for at least the two years before the examination. In particular, the Member State shall not have devalued its currency's bilateral central rate against any other Member State's currency on its own initiative over the same period;
- **long-term interest rates**: Member States should have had an average nominal long-term interest rate over a period of one year before the examination that does not exceed by more than

2 percentage points that of the three best-performing Member States in terms of price stability.

Cow

A **cow** is a female bovine that has calved (including any aged less than two years). A **dairy cow** is a cow kept exclusively or principally for the production of milk for human consumption and/or other dairy produce, including cows for slaughter (whether fattened or not between last lactation and slaughter).

Credit

Credit is an amount for which there is a specific obligation of repayment. Credits include loans, trade credits, bonds, bills and other agreements that give rise to specific obligations to repay over a period of time usually, but not always, with interest. Credit is extended to finance consumption and investment expenditures, and financial transactions.

Crop output

Crop output comprises sales, changes in stock levels, and crop products used as animal feedstuffs, or for processing and own final use by the producers.

Deaths

A **death**, according to the United Nations definition, is the permanent disappearance of all vital functions without possibility of resuscitation at any time after a live birth has taken place; this definition therefore excludes foetal deaths (stillbirths).

Mortality is the number of deaths for a given area during a given period. **Infant mortality** is the mortality of live-born children aged less than one year.

The **mortality rate** or **death rate** is the mortality expressed as a proportion of the population.

The **crude mortality rate** or **crude death rate** is defined as the ratio of the number of deaths during the year to the average population in that year; the value is expressed per 1 000 inhabitants.

The **infant mortality rate** represents the ratio of the number of deaths of children under one year of age to the number of live births in the reference year. The value is expressed per 1 000 live births.

Debit

A **debit** is the opposite to a **credit** and is an expression of a debt owed in the form of a loan that must be repaid, trade credits, bonds, bills and other agreements that give rise to specific obligations to repay over a period of time usually, but not always, with interest.

Deficit

In general a **deficit** means that the sum or balance of positive and negative amounts is negative, or that the total of negatives is larger than the total of positives.

A deficit can be used in different statistical areas:

- in balance of payments statistics, it refers to the balance of credit (negative) and debit (positive) transactions of a given economy with the rest of the world, organised in two different accounts: the current account; the capital and financial account;
- in external trade statistics, it refers to the trade balance of imports (negative, as they have to be paid for) and exports (positive, because they yield revenue), which may result in a trade deficit;
- in government finance statistics, it refers to the public balance between government revenue and expenditure, a budget deficit when negative, and the resulting government debt, in the case of cumulated deficits.

Deflator

A **deflator** is a figure expressing the change in prices over a period of time for a product or a basket of products, which is used to deflate (price adjust) a measure of value changes for the same period (for example the sales of the product or basket of products), thus removing the price increases or decreases and leaving only volume changes.

A deflator compares a reference period to a base period, and it can be expressed either as an index or a percentage change.

Dial-up

A **dial-up** internet connection provides access to the internet using a modem over a normal or an integrated services digital network (ISDN) telephone line. Due to its limited bandwidth, it is often called **narrowband**.

Digital literacy

Digital literacy refers to the skills required to achieve digital competence, the confident and critical use of information and communication technology (ICT) for work, leisure, learning and communication.

Digital subscriber line (DSL)

A **digital subscriber line**, abbreviated as **DSL**, is a family of technologies that allows for digital data transmission over the wires of a local telephone network. DSL can be used at the same time and on the same telephone line as normal telephone calls since DSL operates at high-frequency bands while the telephone call uses low frequencies. The most common form of DSL technology is **ADSL**, or **asymmetric digital subscriber line**, where the bandwidth used in either direction is different.

Discharge

A **discharge** from hospital is the formal release of a patient from a hospital after a procedure or course of treatment. A discharge occurs whenever a patient leaves hospital upon completion of treatment, signing out against medical advice, transferring to another healthcare institution, or on death. A discharge includes inpatients or day cases and healthy newborn babies should also be included. Discharges should exclude transfers to another department within the same institution.

Distributive trade

Distributive trades refer to the wholesale and retail trades and the repair of motor vehicles and motorcycles (NACE Rev. 2 Section G).

Divorces

A **divorce** is defined as the final legal dissolution (ending) of a marriage. A divorce is the type of separation of husband and wife that confers on the parties the right to remarry under civil, religious or other provisions, according to the laws of each country. Divorce is possible in all European Union Member States. In almost all countries, divorces are registered at a court.

The **crude divorce rate** is the ratio of the number of divorces during the year to the average population in that year. The value is expressed per 1 000 inhabitants.

Dwelling

A **dwelling** is a room or suite of rooms – including its accessories, lobbies and corridors – in a permanent building or a structurally separated part thereof which, by the way it has been built, rebuilt or converted, is designed for habitation by one private household all year round. A dwelling can be either a one-family dwelling in a stand-alone building or detached edifice, or an apartment in a block of flats. Dwellings include garages for residential use, even when apart from the habitation or belonging to different owners.

Early leavers from education and training

The term '**early leaver from education and training**', previously named 'early school leaver', generally refers to a person aged 18-24 who has finished no more than a lower secondary education and is not involved in further education or training; the number of such persons can be expressed as a percentage of the total population aged 18-24.

For Eurostat statistical purposes, an early leaver from education and training is operationally defined as a person aged 18-24 recorded in the labour force survey (LFS):

- whose highest level of education or training attained is ISCED 0, 1, 2 or 3c short; and
- who received no education or training in the four weeks preceding the survey.

The '**early leavers from education and training**' statistical indicator is calculated by dividing the number of early leavers from education and training, as defined above, by the total population of the same age group in the LFS.

Earnings

Earnings are the wage or salary paid to an employee. There are two main types:

- **gross earnings** are paid in cash directly to an employee before any deductions for income tax and social security contributions paid by the employee. All bonuses, whether or not regularly paid, are included (for example 13th or 14th month, holiday bonuses, profit-sharing, allowances for leave not taken, and occasional commissions);
- **net earnings** represent the part of remuneration that employees can actually spend and are calculated by deducting social security contributions and income taxes payable by employees from gross earnings and by adding family allowances if there are children in the family.

E-commerce

E-commerce can be defined generally as the sale or purchase of goods or services, whether between businesses, households, individuals or private organisations, through electronic transactions conducted via the internet or other computer-mediated (online communication) networks.

The term covers the ordering of goods and services which are sent over computer networks, but the payment and the ultimate delivery of the goods or service may be conducted either on- or off-line.

For the Community survey on ICT usage in households and by individuals, e-commerce by individuals or households via the internet is defined more specifically as the placing of orders for goods or services via the internet. Also included in the definition are: buying financial investments – such as shares; confirming reservations for accommodation and travel; participating in lotteries and betting; paying for information services from the internet; buying via online auctions.

Orders via manually typed e-mails, however, are excluded.

For the Community survey on ICT usage and e-commerce in enterprises, e-commerce refers to the placement of orders (an order is a commitment to purchase goods or services) via computer networks. E-commerce may be effectively done via websites (which allow for online ordering or reservation or booking, for example using a shopping cart) or an exchange of electronic messages, EDI-type (electronic data interchange) messages. EDI-type e-commerce refers to the structured transmission of data or documents between enterprises by electronic means allowing automatic processing using for example EDI format or XML format.

Orders via manually typed e-mails, however, are excluded. Delivery or payment via electronic means is not a requirement for an e-commerce transaction.

Economic accounts for agriculture (EAA)

The **economic accounts for agriculture**, abbreviated as EAA, are a satellite account of the European system of national and regional accounts, adapted to the specific nature of the agricultural industry, providing complementary information and concepts. Although the structure of EAA matches very closely that of national accounts, their compilation requires the formulation of appropriate rules and methods.

The EAA analyse the production processes of the agricultural industry and the primary income generated by these activities. The accounts are therefore based on the industry concept. The agricultural industry, as described in the EAA, corresponds to Division 01 in NACE Rev. 1, namely agriculture, hunting and related service activities.

The EAA measure the total output of the agricultural activity which includes: output sold (including trade in agricultural goods and services between agricultural units); changes in stocks; output for own final consumption and own-account gross-fixed capital formation; output produced for further processing by other agricultural producers; intra-unit consumption of livestock feed products.

The agricultural industry's output equals the sum of the output of agricultural products plus goods and services produced in non-agricultural secondary activities.

Economic and monetary union (EMU)

Economic and monetary union, abbreviated as **EMU**, refers to the economic and monetary integration of the 27 European Union (EU) Member States. It involves three stages: coordinating economic policy; achieving economic convergence (bringing economic cycles broadly in step); adopting the euro, the EU's single currency.

All Member States are expected to participate in EMU and all, except Denmark and the United Kingdom, have committed themselves by treaty to join EMU. At the time of writing (May 2012), seventeen EU Member States have entered the third stage and adopted the euro as their currency, together making up the euro area. Denmark, Latvia, and Lithuania are the current participants in the exchange rate mechanism (ERM). Of the pre-2004 Member States, the United Kingdom and Sweden have not joined ERM II and Denmark remains in ERM without proceeding to the third stage. The five remaining Member States that joined the EU in 2004 or 2007 have yet to achieve sufficient convergence to participate. These ten EU Member States continue to use their own currencies.

The Copenhagen criteria, the current set of conditions for countries wanting to join the EU, contain the requirements a country has to fulfil in order to join economic and monetary union, as well as the time frame in which this has to be achieved.

Education

Broadly speaking, **education** refers to any act or experience that has a formative effect on an individual's mind, character, or physical ability.

In its technical sense, **education** is the formal process by which society, through schools, colleges, universities and other institutions, deliberately transmits its cultural heritage and its accumulated knowledge, values and skills to the next generation.

E-government

E-government refers to the use of information and communication technology (ICT) in public administration procedures. One aspect of e-government, on its demand side, concerns the interaction of individuals or enterprises with public administrations through ICT.

For both individuals and enterprises this interaction can consist of: obtaining information; downloading forms; returning filled-in forms; going through an administrative procedure completely electronically.

For enterprises, in addition, it can also involve submitting a proposal in an electronic tender system.

E-learning

E-learning, or **electronic learning**, also referred to as **web-based learning**, encompasses a broad range of knowledge transferred through digital technologies, sometimes as a complement to traditional education channels. The use of information and communication technology tools is especially powerful for reaching individuals with no access to traditional education and training, either because they live in remote areas or because of their socio-economic situation or special needs.

Employee

An **employee** is a person who has a contract to carry out work for an employer and receives compensation in the form of wages, salaries, fees, gratuities, piecework pay or remuneration in kind.

Employee – LFS

The labour force survey defines an **employee** as an individual who works for a public or private employer and who in return receives compensation in the form of wages, salaries, fees, gratuities, payment by results or payment in kind. Professional military staff are also included.

Employment

Employment is defined as the number of persons engaged in productive activities in an economy. The concept includes both employees and the self-employed. The two main measures used for employment are the number of persons employed and the number of employees.

More complex measures of employment are sometimes produced by measuring the number of hours worked or by converting the number of hours worked into full-time equivalent units. In addition, some particular categories of employment are measured, such as part-time employment, female employment, self-employment, apprenticeships, home-workers and unpaid employment (unpaid family workers and working proprietors).

Employment rate

The **employment rate** is the percentage of employed persons in relation to the comparable total population. For the overall employment rate, the comparison is made with the population of working age; but employment rates can also be calculated for a particular age group and/or gender in a specific geographical area (for example the males of age 15-24 employed in one of the European Union Member States).

Employment rate dispersion

Employment rate dispersion is the coefficient of variation of regional employment rates in a country, weighted by the absolute population (active population) of each region.

Energy dependency rate

The **energy dependency rate** shows the proportion of energy that an economy must import. It is defined as net energy imports divided by gross inland energy consumption plus fuel supplied to international maritime bunkers, expressed as a percentage. A negative dependency rate indicates a net exporter of energy while a dependency rate in excess of 100 % indicates that energy products have been stocked.

Energy intensity

Energy intensity measures the energy consumption of an economy relative to its output, and gives an indication of its energy efficiency. It is the ratio between gross inland consumption of energy and gross domestic product.

Enhanced cooperation

The Treaty of Amsterdam created the formal possibility of a certain number of European Union Member States establishing an enhanced cooperation between themselves on matters covered by the Treaties, using the institutions and procedures of the European Union.

The Treaty of Nice facilitates the establishment of enhanced cooperation:

- the right of veto which the Member States enjoyed over the establishment of enhanced cooperation has disappeared (except in the field of foreign policy);
- the number of Member States required for launching the procedure has changed from the majority to the fixed number of eight Member States;

- its scope has been extended to the common foreign and security policy (CFSP).

Enterprise

The **enterprise** is the smallest combination of legal units that is an organisational unit producing goods or services, which benefits from a certain degree of autonomy in decision-making, especially for the allocation of its current resources. An enterprise carries out one or more activities at one or more locations. An enterprise may be a sole legal unit.

Enterprise birth

An enterprise birth occurs when an enterprise (for example a company) starts from scratch and begins operations. An enterprise birth occurs when new production factors, in particular new jobs, are created. If a dormant unit is reactivated within two years, this event is not considered a birth. Births do not include new corporate entities created from mergers, break-ups, spin-offs or the restructuring of enterprises.

Entrepreneurial income account

The purpose of the entrepreneurial income account is to determine a balancing item corresponding to the concept of current profit before distribution and income tax, as normally used in business accounting. Entrepreneurial income corresponds to the operating surplus or mixed income (on the resources side): plus property income receivable in connection with financial and other assets belonging to the enterprise (on the resources side); minus interest on debts payable by the enterprise and rents payable on land and other non-produced tangible assets rented by the enterprise (on the uses side). Property income payable in the form of dividends or reinvested earnings on direct foreign investment is not deducted from entrepreneurial income.

Equivalised disposable income

Equivalised disposable income is the total income of a household, after tax and other deductions, that

is available for spending or saving, divided by the number of household members converted into equivalent adults; household members are made equivalent by weighting each according to their age, using the so-called modified OECD equivalence scale.

Equivalised disposable income is calculated in three steps.

1. All monetary incomes received from any source by each member of a household are added up; these include income from work, investment and social benefits, plus any other household income; taxes and social contributions that have been paid are deducted from this sum.

2. In order to reflect differences in a household's size and composition, the total (net) household income is divided by the number of equivalent adults, using a standard (equivalence) scale. The modified OECD scale gives a weight to all members of the household (and then adds these up to arrive at the **equivalised household size**): 1.0 to the first adult; 0.5 to the second and each subsequent person aged 14 and over; 0.3 to each child aged under 14.

3. Finally, the resulting figure is called the equivalised disposable income and is attributed equally to each member of the household.

For poverty indicators, the equivalised disposable income is calculated from the total disposable income of each household divided by the equivalised household size. The income reference period is a fixed 12-month period (such as the previous calendar or tax year) for all countries except the United Kingdom for which the income reference period is the current year and Ireland for which the survey is continuous and income is collected for the previous twelve months.

Erasmus programme

The **Erasmus programme**, or **European Action Scheme for the Mobility of University Students**, is the European Union (EU) student exchange programme for higher education.

Erasmus allows EU students to study in another EU Member State for part of an academic year. It is a major component of the EU's lifelong learning programme 2007–2013 and of the operational framework for the European Commission's higher education initiatives. Some 90 % of European universities participate in the programme and several million students have participated since it was launched in 1987.

Erasmus, together with several other independent programmes, was incorporated into the Socrates programme established by the European Commission in 1994.

Euro-PCT applications

Euro-PCT applications refer to applications filed under the Patent Convention Treaty (PCT) and designating the European Patent Office (EPO) for protection.

Europe 2020 strategy

The **Europe 2020 strategy** is a strategy for the European Union to develop as a smarter, knowledge-based, greener economy, growing fast and sustainably, creating high levels of employment and social progress. It has been designed as the successor to the Lisbon strategy, which was the reform strategy for the European Union for the decade from 2000 to 2010.

As in the Lisbon process, a set of structural indicators for monitoring the progress made in achieving the objectives of the Europe 2020 strategy is being used. Eurostat compiles these indicators which will be used within the annual monitoring exercise.

EU statistics on income and living conditions (EU-SILC)

EU statistics on income and living conditions, abbreviated as **EU-SILC**, is the reference source for comparative statistics on income distribution and social inclusion within the European Union. It is used for policy monitoring within the open method of coordination (OMC).

EU-SILC was launched in 2003 on the basis of a gentlemen's agreement between Eurostat, six Member States (Belgium, Denmark, Greece, Ireland, Luxembourg and Austria), and Norway. It was formally launched in 2004 in 15 countries and expanded in 2005 to cover all of the then EU-25 Member States, together with Norway and Iceland. Bulgaria launched EU-SILC in 2006 while Romania, Switzerland and Turkey introduced the survey in 2007. EU-SILC provides two types of annual data:

- cross-sectional data pertaining to a given time or a certain time period with variables on income, poverty, social exclusion and other living conditions;
- longitudinal data pertaining to individual-level changes over time, observed periodically over a four-year period.

EU-SILC is a multi-purpose instrument which focuses mainly on income. Detailed data are collected on income components, mostly on personal income, although a few household income components are included. However, information on social exclusion, housing conditions, labour, education and health information is also obtained.

EU-SILC is based on the idea of a common framework rather than a common survey. The common framework defines harmonised lists of target primary (annual) and secondary (every four years or less frequently) variables to be transmitted to Eurostat; common guidelines and procedures; common concepts (household and income) and classifications aimed at maximising comparability of the information produced.

The reference population in EU-SILC includes all private households and their current members residing in the territory of the countries at the time of data collection. Persons living in collective households and in institutions are generally excluded from the target population. Some small parts of the national territory amounting to no more than 2 % of the national population may be excluded from EU-SILC. All household members are surveyed, but only those aged 16 and more are interviewed.

Euro

The **euro** is the single, official European currency used, at the time of writing, by 17 Member States of the European Union. Together these Member States make up the euro area.

Stage III of economic and monetary union (EMU) began on 1 January 1999 with the introduction of the euro, which replaced the European currency unit on a 1:1 basis.

Until the end of 2001, the euro existed as book money only (cheque, bank transfer, payment by card) and its use was voluntary (no compulsion – no prohibition). Euro coins and notes were introduced on 1 January 2002, when use of the euro became compulsory and national currencies were progressively withdrawn.

Euro area

The **euro area** consists of those European Union Member States which have adopted the euro as their single currency.

European Central Bank (ECB)

The **European Central Bank**, abbreviated as **ECB**, is the central bank for Europe's single currency, the euro. Its main task is to maintain the euro's purchasing power and thus price stability in the European Union (EU) Member States that have introduced the euro since 1999 and form the euro area. Together, the ECB and the national central banks of all EU Member States constitute the **European System of Central Banks**.

The ECB's main decision-making body is the Governing Council; it consists of the six members of the executive board, plus the governors of the central banks of the euro area Member States.

European Commission (EC)

The **European Commission**, abbreviated as **EC**, is the executive branch of the European Union (EU). The EC is responsible for proposing legislation, implementing decisions, upholding the EU treaties and the general day-to-day running of the EU. Its official name is the **Commission of the European Communities**, but it is commonly called the European **Commission** or **Commission**.

The EC is composed of 27 Commissioners, one from each Member State, though Commissioners officially represent the interests of the EU as a whole rather than their home state. The European Commission president (one of the 27) is appointed by the European Council (the regular meeting of EU heads of state or government) with the approval of the European Parliament.

The term Commission is also often used to refer to the entire administrative body of about 25 000 European civil servants employed by the EC, based primarily in Brussels (BE).

European Council

The **European Council** refers to the regular meetings, or summits, of European Union (EU) heads of state or government.

It should not be confused with the **Council of the European Union** (also known as the *Council of Ministers* or simply the *Council* or *Consilium* in Latin), the EU's main decision-making body, with both executive and legislative powers.

European currency unit (ecu)

The ecu was the former currency unit of the European Community. It was adopted in 1979 and was the cornerstone of the European Monetary System (EMS). The ecu was used as a standard monetary unit of measurement of the market value/cost of goods, services, or assets and was composed of a basket of currencies of the Member States of the European Communities. A private market also developed for the ecu, allowing its use in monetary transactions. It was replaced by the euro at a ratio of 1:1 on 1 January 1999.

European Economic Area (EEA)

The **European Economic Area**, abbreviated as **EEA**, consists of the European Union (EU) Member

States and the EFTA Member States, except for Switzerland.

The Agreement on the EEA entered into force on 1 January 1994. It seeks to strengthen trade and economic relations between the contracting parties and is principally concerned with the four fundamental pillars of the internal market, namely: the free movement of goods, people, services and capital. The availability of comparable statistical data is considered as relevant to the four freedoms and is therefore included in the agreement.

EU enlargements had a direct impact on the EEA Agreement, and at the time of writing the enlarged EEA includes 30 countries.

European Environment Agency (EEA)

The **European Environment Agency**, abbreviated as **EEA**, located in Copenhagen (DK), is the European Union (EU) body dedicated to providing sound and independent information on the environment.

Its mission is to help the EU and its Member States in making informed decisions about improving the environment, integrating environmental considerations into economic policies and moving towards sustainability. To do this, it provides a wide range of information and assessments. These cover the state of the environment and trends in it, together with pressures on the environment and the economic and social driving forces behind them.

As EEA membership is also open to countries that are not EU Member States, it has 32 member countries: the 27 EU Member States and Iceland, Liechtenstein, Norway, Turkey and Switzerland.

European Free Trade Association (EFTA)

The **European Free Trade Association**, abbreviated as **EFTA**, is an intergovernmental organisation established in 1960 by seven European countries to promote free trade and economic integration to the benefit of its Member States. All original signatories

except Norway and Switzerland withdrew from EFTA upon joining the European Union (EU), as did Finland which had become an associate member in 1961 and full member in 1986. As Iceland joined in 1970 and Liechtenstein in 1991 EFTA currently has four Member States: Iceland (IS); Liechtenstein (LI); Norway (NO); Switzerland (CH).

The association is responsible for the management of:

- the free trade between the EFTA Member States;
- EFTA's participation in the European Economic Area, which includes the EU Member States and three EFTA countries (Iceland, Liechtenstein and Norway, but not Switzerland);
- EFTA's worldwide network of free trade agreements.

European Parliament (EP)

The **European Parliament**, abbreviated as **EP**, is the only directly elected body of the European Union (EU). Together with the Council of the European Union (EU), it forms the bicameral legislative branch of the EU's institutions. The European Parliament is composed of 736 members, who are directly elected every five years by voters in the 27 Member States.

It has had control over all areas of the EU budget (except for agriculture) since the 1970s and has a veto over the appointment of the European Commission.

The European Parliament has two meeting places:

- Strasbourg (FR), the official seat, where 12 (currently four-day) plenary sessions are held throughout the year;
- Brussels (BE), which serves for committee meetings, political groups and complementary plenary sessions.

The Secretariat, or European Parliament's administrative body, is based in Luxembourg (LU).

The most recent EU-wide elections were held in June 2009.

European Patent Convention (Munich Convention)

The **European Patent Convention**, signed in Munich (DE) in October 1973, establishes a uniform patenting system for all countries signatory to the Convention. The European patenting procedure consists of two parts; firstly, the search followed by publication of the application, and secondly, the examination which is only conducted after a formal request by the applicant. Applicants can designate as many contracting states as they want at the moment of filing the application or at the moment the Euro-PCT enters the regional (European) phase. A granted European patent is protected under national law in each of the countries designated in the application.

Twenty one countries attended the Munich Diplomatic Conference in 1973 on which the Convention is based. The Convention was (as of March 2010) in force in 36 countries. In addition to the contracting states, states may also conclude a cooperation agreement with the European Patent Office (EPO), known as an extension agreement. The state then becomes an 'extension state', which means European patents granted by the EPO may be extended to those countries by the payment of additional fees and completion of certain formalities.

European Patent Office (EPO)

The **European Patent Office**, abbreviated as **EPO**, based in Munich (DE), is the authority that grants European patents. It is the executive arm of the European Patent Organisation, an intergovernmental body set up under the European Patent Convention (EPC), which was signed in Munich on 5 October 1973 and which entered into force on 7 October 1977. The EPO's activities are supervised by the Administrative Council, composed of delegates from the contracting states.

A patent is granted on the basis of a centralised procedure. By filing a single application in one of the three official languages (English, French and German) it is possible to obtain patent protection in some or all of the EPC contracting states.

European size unit (ESU)

European size unit, abbreviated as **ESU**, is a standard gross margin of EUR 1 200 that is used to express the economic size of an agricultural holding or farm.

For each activity (or enterprise) on a farm (for example wheat production, dairy cows or the output from a vineyard), the standard gross margin (SGM) is estimated based on the area used for the particular activity (or the number of heads of livestock) and a regional coefficient. The sum of all such margins derived from activities on a particular farm is its **economic size**, which is then expressed in European size units (by dividing the total SGM in euro by 1 200).

European system of integrated social protection statistics (ESSPROS)

The **European system of integrated social protection statistics**, abbreviated as **ESSPROS**, is a common framework developed in the late 1970's by Eurostat and the European Union Member States providing a coherent comparison between European countries of social benefits to households and their financing, thus making an international comparison of the administrative national data on social protection possible.

ESSPROS is built on the concept of social protection, or the coverage of precisely defined risks and needs including health, disability, old age, family and unemployment; it records the receipts and the expenditure of the organisations or schemes involved in social protection interventions.

ESSPROS is composed of the *core system* and of *modules*. The core system contains annual data (collected by Eurostat from 1990 on):

- quantitative data: social protection receipts and expenditures by schemes (a distinct body of rules, supported by one or more institutional units, governing the provision of social protection benefits and their financing);
- qualitative data: metadata by scheme and detailed benefit.

Social protection benefits are transfers to house-holds, in cash or in kind, intended to relieve them from the financial burden of a number of risks or needs. The risks or needs of social protection included in ESSPROS are disability, sickness/healthcare, old age, survivors, family/children, unemployment, housing and social exclusion not elsewhere classified.

The modules contain supplementary statistical information on particular aspects of social protection: they relate to pensions' beneficiaries and to net social benefits.

European system of national and regional accounts (ESA95)

The **European system of national and regional accounts**, abbreviated as **ESA95** or sometimes **1995 ESA**, collects comparable, up-to-date and reliable information on the structure and developments of the economy of the Member States of the European Union (EU) and their respective regions. By providing an internationally compatible accounting framework, ESA95 makes it possible to describe the total economy of a region, country or group of countries, its components and its relation to other total economies.

The ESA95 prescribes the structure and layout of supply and use tables, symmetric input-output tables and tables linking supply and use tables to the sector accounts. These requirements refer to definitions of transactions and to concepts of classification and valuation.

ESA95 is broadly consistent with the system of national accounts of the United Nations (1993 SNA) with regards to definitions, accounting rules and classifications. But due to greater accuracy requirements for definitions and the accounting rules, it also has some specificities, particularly in its presentation, which are more in line with EU practices.

European Union (EU)

The **European Union**, abbreviated as **EU**, is an economic and political union of European countries.

The EU was established on 1 November 1993 by the Treaty on European Union (Maastricht Treaty).

Eurostat

Eurostat is the statistical office of the European Union (EU), based in Luxembourg (LU). It publishes official, harmonised statistics on the EU, the euro area and their Member States, offering a comparable, reliable and objective portrayal of Europe's society and economy.

A vast range of data is available for the EU as a whole, for Member States and in many cases also for EFTA Member States, candidate countries, and other European countries. Some data is also available for regions and cities. All users may consult or download data and publications free of charge from the Eurostat web site.

Excessive deficit procedure (EDP)

The **excessive deficit procedure**, abbreviated as **EDP**, is an action launched by the European Commission against any European Union (EU) Member State that exceeds the budgetary deficit ceiling imposed by the EU's stability and growth pact legislation. The procedure entails several steps, potentially culminating in sanctions, to encourage a Member State to get its budget deficit under control, a requirement for the smooth functioning of economic and monetary union.

According to the Protocol on the excessive deficit procedure, annexed to the Maastricht Treaty on economic and monetary union, Member States in the euro area and euro area candidate countries must demonstrate sound public finances. There are two criteria:

• the budget deficit must not exceed 3 % of gross domestic product (GDP);
• public debt must not exceed 60 % of GDP.

Exchange rate

The exchange rate is the price of one currency in relation to another.

Exchange rates are classified by the International Monetary Fund (IMF) into three broad categories, reflecting the role of the authorities in determining the exchange rates and/or the multiplicity of exchange rates in a country:

1. the **market rate** is used to describe exchange rates set largely by market forces;
2. the **official rate** is used to describe the exchange rate determined by authorities;
3. for countries maintaining multiple exchange arrangements, the rates may be labelled **principle rate**, **secondary rate** and **tertiary rate.**

A **nominal effective exchange rate** is the exchange rate of the domestic currency vis-à-vis (as compared with) other currencies weighted by their share in either the country's international trade or payments.

Real effective exchange rates take account of price level differences between trading partners. Movements in real effective exchange rates give an indication of the development of a country's aggregate (total) external price competitiveness.

Exchange rate mechanism (ERM)

The **European exchange rate (and intervention) mechanism**, abbreviated as ERM, was set up to help stabilise exchange rates and help lead Europe to become an area of monetary stability before the introduction of the single currency, the euro.

After the euro's introduction on 1 January 1999, the original ERM was replaced by ERM II (exchange rate mechanism II) at the start of stage III of economic and monetary union (EMU). This began with the irrevocable (not able to be changed) fixing of exchange rates, the transfer of monetary competence to the European Central Bank, and the introduction of the euro as the single currency. ERM II provides a framework for exchange rate policy cooperation between the Eurosystem (the central banking system of the euro area) and European Union Member States that are preparing to adopt the euro.

Expenditure approach

The **expenditure approach** of GDP is defined as private final consumption expenditure + government final consumption expenditure + gross capital formation + exports - imports.

In the system of national accounts, only households, NPISH and government have final consumption, whereas corporations have intermediate consumption. Private final consumption expenditure is defined as expenditure on goods and services for the direct satisfaction of individual needs, whereas government consumption expenditure includes goods and services produced by government, as well as purchases of goods and services by government that are supplied to households as social transfers in kind. Gross capital formation is the sum of gross fixed capital formation and the change in inventories (stocks). The external balance is the difference between exports and imports of goods and services. Depending on the size of exports and imports, it can be positive (a surplus) or negative (a deficit).

Expenditure on pensions

Expenditure on pensions comprises the following social benefits: disability pension, early retirement due to reduced capacity to work, old age pension, anticipated old age pension, partial pension, survivors' pension and early retirement due for labour market reasons.

Exports

Extra-EU exports of goods are goods which leave the statistical territory of the European Union (EU) for a non-member country after being placed under the customs procedure for exports (for definitive export) or outward processing (goods for working, further processing) or repair or following inward processing. **Intra-EU exports of goods** are goods which leave a Member State of the EU for another Member State for definitive export, outward processing or repair or following inward processing.

In **national accounts** exports consist of transactions in goods and services (sales, barter, gifts or grants) from residents to non-residents.

- An export of a good occurs when there is a change of ownership from a resident to a non-resident; this does not necessarily imply that the good in question physically crosses the frontier. If goods cross the border due to *financial leasing*, as *deliveries between affiliates of the same enterprise* or for *significant processing to order or repair* national accounts impute a change of ownership even though in legal terms no change of ownership takes place. According to the European system of accounts (ESA95) also smuggled goods must be included in exports.

- Exports of services consist of all services rendered by residents to non-residents. In national accounts any direct purchases by non-residents in the economic territory of a country are recorded as exports of services; therefore all expenditure by foreign tourists in the economic territory of a country is considered as part of the exports of services of that country. Also international flows of illegal services must be included.

Analogously, the national accounts' transactions in goods and services from non-residents to residents are **imports**.

External inflow

External inflow is the volume of water flowing into rivers and groundwater that originates in neighbouring territories.

Extra-EU

Extra-EU refers to transactions with all countries *outside of the European Union (EU)*: the rest of the world except for the EU as it is at the time of writing (May 2012), consisting of 27 Member States. The term is used in the context of external trade, balance of payments, foreign direct investment, migration, transport, tourism and similar statistical areas where goods, capital or people moving in and out of the EU are being measured and where the EU as a whole is considered in relationship to the rest of the world. Extra-EU transactions of the EU as a whole are the sum of the extra-EU transactions of the 27 Member States.

Intra-EU, on the other hand, refers to all transactions occurring *within the EU*. The term can have a different coverage, depending on the perspective taken: the EU as a whole, a Member State, a region or a city, a port or an airport, and so on.

The exports of a particular Member State, for instance, can be split into two parts, on the one hand to those countries outside the EU (extra-EU), and on the other to the 26 other Member States (intra-EU). Departures from an airport can be extra-EU or intra-EU, in the latter case they also include domestic flights, within the Member State.

To complicate matters, the EU has not always had the same composition, due to consecutive enlargements. For this reason, both terms are sometimes further qualified as extra-EU-15, intra-EU-25 and so on; extra-EU-15, for instance, refers to the rest of the world apart from the 15 Member States that in the past made up the EU-15 aggregate.

Farm structure survey (FSS)

The basic **farm structure survey**, abbreviated as **FSS**, also known as **survey on the structure of agricultural holdings** is carried out by all European Union Member States every 10 years (the full scope being the agricultural census) with intermediate sample surveys being carried out three times between the basic surveys.

The Member States collect information from individual agricultural holdings and, observing strict rules of confidentiality, data are forwarded to Eurostat. The information collected in the FSS covers land use, livestock numbers, rural development, management and farm labour input (including the age, gender and relationship to the holder of the agricultural holding). The survey data can then be aggregated by different geographic levels (Member States, regions, and for basic surveys also district level). The data can also be arranged by size class, area status, legal status of the holding, objective zone and farm type.

The basic unit underlying the FSS is the agricultural holding: a technical-economic unit, under single management, engaged in agricultural production. The FSS covers all agricultural holdings with a utilised agricultural area of at least 1 hectare (ha) and also those holdings with a UAA of less than 1 ha where their market production exceeds certain natural thresholds.

The legal basis for the FSS is Regulation 1166/2008 of 19 November 2008 on farm structure surveys and the survey on agricultural production methods, which repealed Council Regulation 571/88.

Fatal accident at work

A **fatal accident at work** is a physical or mental injury that occurs during work activities, leading to death within one year. It excludes accidents on the way to or from work, occurrences of a strictly medical origin and occupational diseases.

Feed

Feed (or **feedingstuff**) is any substance or product, including additives, whether processed, partially processed or unprocessed, intended to be used for oral feeding to animals.

Fertiliser

A **fertiliser** is a substance used in agriculture to provide crops with vital nutrients to grow (such as nitrogen (N), phosphorus (P) and potassium (K)).

Fertilisers can be divided into inorganic fertilisers (also called mineral, synthetic or manufactured) and organic fertilisers.

Inorganic fertilisers, chemical mixtures produced by fertiliser manufacturers, include:

- simple mineral fertilisers, for example urea, ammonium nitrate and sulphate;
- complex mineral fertilisers, for example NP, NK and NPK mixtures;
- mineral-organic fertilisers, for example calcium cyanamid.

Organic fertilisers include:

- manure;
- other organic fertilisers such as compost, sewage sludge, industrial waste.

Fertility

Fertility is the ability to conceive (become pregnant) and give birth to children.

The **total fertility rate** is defined as the mean number of children who would be born to a woman during her lifetime, if she were to spend her childbearing years conforming to the age-specific fertility rates that have been measured in a given year.

The **age-specific fertility rate** or the **fertility rate by age of mother** is the number of births to mothers of age x proportional to the average female population of age x.

Final consumption expenditure

Final consumption expenditure consists of expenditure by resident institutional units on goods or services that are used for the direct satisfaction of individual needs or wants or the collective needs of members of the community.

Final energy consumption

Final energy consumption is the total energy consumed by end users, such as households, industry and agriculture. It is the energy which reaches the final consumer's door and excludes that which is used by the energy sector itself.

Final energy consumption excludes energy used by the energy sector, including for deliveries, and transformation. It also excludes fuel transformed in the electrical power stations of industrial autoproducers and coke transformed into blast-furnace gas where this is not part of overall industrial consumption but of the transformation sector.

Final energy consumption in the category 'households, services, etc.' covers quantities consumed by private households, commerce, public administration, services, agriculture and fisheries.

Fish catch

Fish catch (or simply **catch**) refers to catches of fishery products including fish, molluscs, crustaceans and other aquatic animals, residues and aquatic plants that are taken:

- for all purposes (commercial, industrial, recreational and subsistence);

- by all types and classes of fishing units (including for example fishermen, vessels, gear); that are
- operating in inland, fresh and brackish water areas, and in inshore, offshore and high-seas fishing areas.

Production from aquaculture is excluded. Catch is normally expressed in live weight and derived by the application of conversion factors to the actual landed or product weight. As such, the catch statistics exclude quantities of fishery products which are caught but which, for a variety of reasons, are not landed.

Fishery products

In the context of external trade statistics, **fishery products** consist of:

- edible fishery products, including fish, crustaceans and molluscs:
- inedible products, including meals and solubles, oils and fats, sponges, corals, and so on;
- aquatic plants.

Fishing area

Geographical **fishing areas** in the European Union common fisheries policy are defined for a number of specific areas of water:

- the *north east Atlantic*, which is roughly the area to the east of 42°W longitude and north of 36°N latitude, including the waters of the Baltic Sea;
- the *north west Atlantic*, which is the region that is roughly the area to the west of 42°W longitude and north of 35°N latitude;
- the *eastern central Atlantic*, which is the region to the east of 40°W longitude between latitudes 36°N and 6°S;
- the *Mediterranean*, which is also known as the Food and Agriculture Organization Major Fishing Area 37, comprises the Mediterranean Sea and the adjacent Black Sea.

Fishing fleet

The data on the number of fishing vessels, the **fishing fleet**, in general refer to the fleet size as recorded on 31 December of the specified reference year. The data are derived from national registers of fishing vessels which are maintained according to Council Regulation 26/2004 which specifies the information on vessel characteristics to be recorded in the registers.

Food and Agriculture Organization (FAO)

The **Food and Agriculture Organization** of the United Nations, abbreviated as **FAO**, was founded in 1945. The FAO leads international efforts to combat hunger. Serving both developed and developing countries, the FAO acts as a neutral forum where all nations meet as equals to negotiate agreements and debate policy. The FAO is also a major source of knowledge and information to help developing countries, and countries in transition, to modernise and improve agriculture, forestry and fisheries practices and ensure good nutrition for all. The FAO pays special attention to development in rural areas, which are home to 70 % of the world's poor and hungry.

Foreign affiliates

Foreign affiliates statistics, abbreviated as **FATS**, describe the activities of **foreign affiliates**: enterprises resident in a country or area, such as the European Union, controlled or owned by (multinational) enterprises which are resident outside that country or area.

Foreign direct investment (FDI)

Foreign direct investment, abbreviated as **FDI**, is an international investment within the balance of payment accounts. Essentially, a resident entity in one economy seeks to obtain a lasting interest in an enterprise resident in another economy. A lasting interest implies the existence of a long-term relationship between the direct investor and the enterprise, and an investor's significant influence on the management of the enterprise.

A direct investment enterprise is one in which a direct investor owns 10 % or more of the ordinary shares or voting rights (for an incorporated enterprise) or the equivalent (for an unincorporated enterprise).

FDI flows and positions: through direct investment flows, an investor builds up a FDI position that has an impact on an economy's international investment position. This FDI position (or FDI stock) differs from the accumulated flows because of revaluation (changes in prices or exchange rates), and other adjustments like rescheduling or cancellation of loans or debt-equity swaps.

Forest

Forest is defined as land with tree crown cover (meaning all parts of the tree above ground level including for example its leaves and branches), or equivalent stocking level, of more than 10 % and with an area of more than 0.5 hectares (ha). The trees should be able to reach a minimum height of five metres at maturity *in situ*.

Fossil fuel

Fossil fuel is a generic term for non-renewable natural energy sources such as coal, natural gas and oil that were formed from plants and animals (biomass) that existed in the geological past (for example, hundreds of million of years ago). Fossil fuels are carbon-based and currently supply most human energy requirements.

Freshwater resources

Freshwater resources refers to the total volume of water available in a territory, resulting from internal flow (water from precipitation minus evapotranspiration in a territory) as well as external inflow (water inflow from neighbouring territories).

Fruit

For the purposes of European Union agricultural statistics, **fruit** includes apples, pears, stoned fruits (for example peaches or apricots), nuts (for example walnuts or hazelnuts), other top fruits (for example figs or kiwi – top fruit are fruit that grow on trees),

other soft fruit (including fruit that grow on bushes such as berries, currants), citrus fruits, grapes, olives, and wild fruits.

Full-time equivalent (FTE)

A **full-time equivalent**, sometimes abbreviated as **FTE**, is a unit to measure employment or students in a way that makes them comparable although they may work or study a different number of hours per week.

The unit is obtained by comparing the number of hours worked or studied by a person to the average number of hours of a full-time worker or student. A full-time person is therefore counted as one FTE, while a part-time person gets a score in proportion to the hours he or she works or studies. For example, a part-time worker employed for 20 hours a week where full-time work consists of 40 hours, is counted as 0.5 FTE.

The workforce of an enterprise, activity, or country for example can then be added up and expressed as the number of full-time equivalents. In the context of education the FTE unit attempts to standardise a student's actual course load in comparison with the normal course load.

Gender gap

A **gender gap** may refer to any statistical disparities between men and women. Usually, however, it refers to differences in labour market statistics, such as the gender pay gap, or differences in employment and unemployment.

Gender pay gap (GPG)

The **gender pay gap**, abbreviated as **GPG**, refers to the difference in average wages between men and women. The unadjusted gender pay gap is calculated as the difference between the average gross hourly earnings of male and female paid employees as a percentage of average gross hourly earnings of male paid employees.

From the reference year 2006 onwards, the GPG is computed annually in the European Union (EU) according to three main guidelines; the GPG is:

- unadjusted, in other words without correcting for national differences in individual characteristics of employed men and women – the main reason is that, at this stage, there is neither consensus nor scientific evidence on which adjustment method should be used;
- calculated using gross hourly earnings – this choice aims to exclude from the measurement differences among EU Member States in terms of the use of part-time work;
- based on a harmonised source across the EU, the structure of earnings survey (SES), a rich employer-employee matched data set.

The unadjusted GPG aggregates for the EU-27 and the euro area (EA-17) are calculated by Eurostat as the average of the national GPGs weighted by the corresponding number of employees, both for the overall GPG and its breakdown by main industrial grouping.

The annual data provided by the EU Member States between two SES rounds are broken down by economic activity, age class and type of economic control of the enterprise.

General government sector

The **general government sector** by convention includes all the public corporations that are not able to cover at least 50 % of their costs by sales, and, therefore, are considered non-market producers. It has four subsectors: central government; state government; local government; social security funds.

In the European system of accounts (ESA95), paragraph 2.68, the general government sector has been defined as containing 'all institutional units which are other non-market producers whose output is intended for individual and collective consumption, and mainly financed by compulsory payments made by units belonging to other sectors, and/or all institutional units principally engaged in the redistribution of national income and wealth'.

Generation of income account

The **generation of income account** of national accounts shows the types of primary incomes and the sectors, subsectors or industries in which the primary incomes originate, as distinct from the sectors or subsectors destined to receive such incomes. It includes as uses the compensation of employees and the taxes on production and imports less subsidies and as resources the gross value added (GVA) and net value added (NVA) for sectors and industries and the gross domestic product (GDP) and net domestic product (NDP) for the total economy, which are the balancing items of the production account. It analyses the extent to which value added and domestic product can cover compensation of employees and taxes on production and imports less subsidies. The balancing items of the generation of income account are the gross operating surplus (GOS), net operating surplus (NOS), gross mixed income and net mixed income, which are the surpluses/deficits on production activities before account has been taken of paid or received interest, rents or charges on financial or tangible non-produced assets.

Goods loaded

The quantity of goods loaded is defined as follows.

Goods placed on a railway vehicle and dispatched by rail. Unlike in road and inland waterway transport, transshipments from one railway vehicle directly to another and change of tractive vehicle are not regarded as unloading/loading. However, if the goods are unloaded from a railway vehicle, loaded on another mode of transport and, again loaded on another railway vehicle, this is considered as unloading from the first railway vehicle followed by loading on the second railway vehicle.

Goods placed on a road vehicle and dispatched by road. Transshipment from one goods road vehicle to another or change of the road tractor is regarded as loading after unloading.

Goods placed on an inland waterways transport (IWT) vessel and dispatched by inland waterways. Transshipment from one IWT vessel to another is regarded as loading after unloading. The same applies to changes of pusher tugs or tugs.

Goods placed on a merchant ship for transport by sea. Transshipment from one merchant ship to another is regarded as loading after unloading. Goods loaded include national goods, transshipment goods (national or foreign goods arriving in port by sea) and land transit goods (foreign goods arriving in port by road, rail, air or inland waterway).

Government

Government consists of all departments and agencies responsible for the administration of an economic territory (usually a country). According to the level, it can be further subdivided into: central government; state government; local government.

Government debt

Government debt, often referred to as **national debt** or **public debt**, is the sum of external obligations (debts) of the government and public sector agencies.

The external obligations are the debt or outstanding (unpaid) financial liabilities arising from past borrowing. Debt may be owed to foreign or domestic creditors and in the debtor's or another currency; typically, debt financing is in the form of loans or bonds.

Government debt can be broken down into:

- **government gross debt**, or all financial liabilities, primarily government bills and bonds;
- **government net debt**, equal to financial liabilities minus all financial assets; financial assets of the general government sector have a corresponding liability outside that sector; it is, however, at the government's discretion whether to list monetary gold and special drawing rights, financial assets for which there is no counterpart liability, as financial assets.

Greenhouse gas (GHG)

Greenhouse gases are a group of gases which are believed to contribute to global warming and climate change.

There are six **greenhouse gases** covered by the Kyoto Protocol, an environmental agreement adopted by many of the parties to the United Nations Framework Convention on Climate Change (UNFCCC) in 1997 to curb global warming.

The non-fluorinated gases: carbon dioxide (CO_2); methane (CH_4); nitrous oxide (N_2O).

The fluorinated gases: hydrofluorocarbons (HFCs); perfluorocarbons (PFCs); sulphur hexafluoride (SF_6).

Converting them to carbon dioxide (or CO_2) equivalents makes it possible to compare them and to determine their individual and total contributions to global warming.

Gross capital formation

Gross capital formation in the national accounts is measured by the total value of the gross fixed capital formation, changes in inventories and acquisitions less disposals of valuables for a unit or sector.

Net capital formation is reached by deducting the consumption of fixed capital.

Gross domestic expenditure on R & D (GERD)

Gross domestic expenditure on R & D (GERD) includes expenditure on research and development by business enterprises, higher education institutions, as well as government and private non-profit organisations.

Gross domestic product (GDP)

Gross domestic product, abbreviated as **GDP**, is a basic measure of a country's overall economic health.

As an aggregate measure of production, GDP is equal to the sum of the gross value added of all resident institutional units (in other words industries) engaged in production, plus any taxes, and minus any subsidies, on products not included in the value of their outputs. Gross value added is the difference between output and intermediate consumption.

GDP is also equal to:

- the sum of the final uses of goods and services (all uses except intermediate consumption) measured in purchasers' prices, minus the value of imports of goods and services;
- the sum of primary incomes distributed by resident producer units.

Gross electricity generation

Gross electricity generation or **gross electricity production** refers to the process of producing electrical energy. It is the total amount of electrical energy produced by transforming other forms of energy, for example nuclear or wind power. It is commonly expressed in gigawatt-hours (GWh) in other words one thousand million (10^9) watt-hours.

Total gross electricity generation covers gross electricity generation in all types of power plants. The **gross electricity generation at plant level** is defined as the electricity measured at the outlet of the main transformers, in other words including the amount of electricity used in the plant auxiliaries and in the transformers.

Gross fixed capital formation (GFCF)

Gross fixed capital formation (GFCF) consists of resident producers' investments, deducting disposals, in fixed assets during a given period. It also includes certain additions to the value of non-produced assets realised by producers or institutional units. Fixed assets are tangible or intangible assets produced as outputs from production processes that are used repeatedly, or continuously, for more than one year.

Gross inland energy consumption

Gross inland energy consumption, sometimes abbreviated as **gross inland consumption**, is the total energy demand of a country or region. It represents the quantity of energy necessary to satisfy inland consumption of the geographical entity under consideration.

Gross inland energy consumption covers: consumption by the energy sector itself; distribution and transformation losses; final energy consumption by end users; statistical differences (not already captured in the figures on primary energy consumption and final energy consumption).

Gross inland consumption does not include energy (fuel oil) provided to international maritime bunkers. It is calculated as follows:

- primary production + recovered products + net imports + variations of stocks – bunkers.

The difference between gross inland energy consumption and **gross (energy) consumption** is that in gross energy consumption the transformation output (electricity or heat produced from other energy sources) is included. Therefore, gross energy consumption is a product-specific consumption and does not reflect the demand for primary energy.

Gross national electricity consumption

Gross national electricity consumption includes the total gross national electricity generation from all fuels (including auto-production), plus electricity imports, minus exports. Auto-production is defined as a natural or legal person generating electricity essentially for his/her own use. Gross electricity generation is measured at the outlet of the main transformers, in other words it includes consumption in the plant auxiliaries and in transformers.

Gross national income (GNI)

Gross national income, abbreviated as **GNI**, is the sum of incomes of residents of an economy in a given period. It is equal to GDP minus primary income payable by resident units to non-resident units, plus primary income receivable from the rest of the world.

It is conceptually identical to gross national product (GNP, the concept in ESA79), though GNP was calculated differently in ESA79.

Gross operating rate – structural business statistics

The **gross operating rate** is the ratio of the gross operating surplus to turnover, expressed as a percentage.

Gross operating surplus – structural business statistics

The **gross operating surplus** or gross operating **profits** is defined, in the context of structural business statistics, as value added minus personnel costs. It is the surplus generated by operating activities after the labour factor input has been recompensed.

The gross operating surplus can be calculated from value added at factor cost. It is the balance available to a unit which allows it to recompense the providers of own funds and debt, to pay taxes and eventually to finance all or a part of its investment.

Income and expenditure classified as financial or extraordinary in company accounts is excluded from gross operating surplus.

Gross operating surplus (GOS) – national accounts

The **gross operating surplus**, abbreviated as **GOS**, can be defined in the context of national accounts as a balancing item in the generation of income account representing the excess amount of money generated by incorporated enterprises' operating activities after paying labour input costs. In other words, it is the capital available to financial and non-financial corporations which allows them to repay their creditors, to pay taxes and eventually to finance all or part of their investment.

The GOS differs from profits shown in company accounts for several reasons. Only a subset of cost items are subtracted from gross output to calculate the GOS. Essentially, GOS is gross output *less* the cost of intermediate goods and services to give gross value added, and *less* compensation of employees. It is *gross* because it makes no allowance for consumption of fixed capital (CFC). By deducting CFC from GOS one calculates the **net operating surplus (NOS)**.

A similar concept for unincorporated enterprises (for example, small family businesses like farms and retail shops or self-employed taxi drivers, lawyers and health professionals) is **gross mixed income**. Since in most such cases it is difficult to distinguish between income from labour and income from capital, the balancing item in the generation of income account is mixed by including both, the remuneration of the capital and labour (of the family members and self-employed) used in production. By deducting CFC from gross mixed income one obtains **net mixed income**.

Gross value added at market prices

Gross value added (GVA) at market prices is output at market prices minus intermediate consumption at purchaser prices; it is a balancing item of the national accounts' production account:

- **GVA at producer prices** is output at producer prices minus intermediate consumption at purchaser prices. The producer price is the amount receivable by the producer from the purchaser for a unit of a product minus *value added tax (VAT)*, or similar deductible tax, invoiced to the purchaser.
- **GVA at basic prices** is output at basic prices minus intermediate consumption at purchaser prices. The basic price is the amount receivable by the producer from the purchaser for a unit of a product minus any *tax on the product* plus any *subsidy on the product*.

GVA at factor costs is not a concept explicitly used in national accounts. It can be derived by subtracting *other taxes on production* from GVA at basic prices and adding *other subsidies on production*.

GVA can be broken down by industry. The sum of GVA at basic prices over all industries plus taxes on products minus subsidies on products gives the gross domestic product (GDP). Gross value added of the total economy usually accounts for more than 90 % of GDP.

By subtracting consumption of fixed capital from GVA the corresponding **net value added (NVA)** is obtained. NVA can also be measured at producer prices or basic prices or factor costs.

Gross-gross weight

The **gross-gross weight** includes the total weight of goods, all packaging, and the tare-weight of the transport unit (for example containers, swap bodies and pallets for containing goods as well as road goods vehicles carrying goods and transported by rail).

The **gross weight** is the total weight of goods, including all packaging but excluding the tare weight of the transport unit.

The **tare weight** is the weight of a transport unit before any cargo is loaded.

Groundwater

Groundwater is freshwater found beneath the earth's surface – specifically in the cracks and spaces in soil, sand and rock – that supplies wells and springs. The definition applies to all permanent and temporary water deposits, formed both artificially and naturally, of sufficient quality for at least seasonal use. Groundwater supplies are replenished, or recharged, by rain and melting snow, depending on climate conditions. They can usually be recovered from, or via, an underground formation.

Harmonised index of consumer prices (HICP)

The **harmonised index of consumer prices**, abbreviated as **HICP**, is the consumer price index as it is calculated in the European Union (EU), according to a harmonised approach and a single set of definitions. It is mainly used to measure inflation.

There are several types of HICP depending on the geographic area under consideration. The most important ones are:

- the **Monetary Union index of consumer prices (MUICP)** – an aggregate index covering the countries in the euro area;
- the **European index of consumer prices (EICP)** – for the whole EU (the euro area plus the other Member States);
- the national HICPs – for each of the EU Member States.

In addition to the EU HICPs, an additional HICP aggregate index for the European Economic Area is calculated:

- the **European Economic Area index of consumer prices (EEAICP)**, which in addition to the EU also covers Iceland and Norway.

Healthcare

Healthcare in a country comprises the sum of activities performed either by institutions or individuals pursuing, through the application of medical, paramedical and nursing knowledge and technology, the purposes/core functions of:

- promoting health and preventing disease;
- curing illness and reducing premature mortality;
- caring for persons affected by chronic illness who require nursing care;
- caring for persons with health-related impairment, disability, and handicaps who require nursing care;
- assisting patients to die with dignity;
- providing and administering public health;
- providing and administering health programmes, health insurance and other funding arrangements.

Health-related functions such as the education and training of the health workforce, research and development in health, and environmental health should be distinguished from the core functions; as far as possible they should be excluded when measuring activities belonging to core healthcare functions.

Healthy life years (HLY)

The number of **healthy life years**, abbreviated as **HLY,** and also called **disability-free life expectancy (DFLE)**, is defined as the number of years that a person is expected to continue to live in a healthy condition.

This statistical indicator is compiled separately for men and women, both at birth and at age 65. It is based on age-specific prevalence (proportions) of the population in healthy and unhealthy condition and age-specific mortality information. A healthy

condition is defined as one without limitation in functioning and without disability.

The indicator is calculated following the widely used Sullivan method. It is based on measures of the age-specific proportion of population with and without disability and on mortality data. Its interest lies in its simplicity, the availability of its basic data, and its independence from the size and age structure of the population. However, cultural differences in reporting disability can influence the HLY indicator.

High-speed rail

High-speed rail is a rail passenger service running at much higher speeds than normal passenger trains.

The network of the trans-European high-speed rail system includes:

- specially built high-speed lines equipped for speeds generally equal to or greater than 250 km/h;
- specially upgraded high-speed lines equipped for speeds of the order of 200 km/h;
- specially upgraded high-speed lines which have special features as a result of topographical, relief or town-planning constraints, on which the speed must be adapted to each case.

Holiday trip length

The **length of holiday or tourism trips** (involving at least one overnight stay) falls into two categories:

- **long holiday trips** are trips with at least four overnight stays;
- **short holiday trips** are trips with one to three overnight stays.

The **average length of stay** for a number of holiday trips is calculated by dividing the total number of nights spent by the total number of tourism trips.

Hospital

Hospitals include licensed establishments primarily engaged in providing medical, diagnostic and treatment services that include physician, nursing, and other health services to in-patients and the specialised accommodation services needed by in-patients.

Hospital bed

Hospital bed numbers provide information on healthcare capacities, in other words on the maximum number of patients who can be treated by hospitals. Hospital beds are those which are regularly maintained and staffed and immediately available for the care of admitted patients. They cover beds accommodating patients who are formally admitted (or hospitalised) to an institution for treatment and/or care and who stay for a minimum of one night. These include: beds in all hospitals, including general hospitals, mental health and substance abuse hospitals, and other specialty hospitals, irrespective of whether the bed is occupied or not. The statistics presented exclude surgical tables, recovery trolleys, emergency stretchers, beds for same-day care, cots for healthy infants, beds in wards which were closed for any reason, provisional and temporary beds, or beds in nursing and residential care facilities.

A **curative care bed** or **acute care bed** is a hospital bed available for curative care; these form a subgroup of total hospital beds.

Hotels and similar establishments

Hotels and similar establishments are tourist accommodation establishments offering overnight lodgings for the traveller which share common characteristics:

- the accommodation is arranged in rooms;
- the total number of rooms exceeds a specified minimum;
- the establishment comes under a common management;
- certain services are provided, including room service, daily bed-making and cleaning of sanitary facilities;
- establishments are grouped in classes and categories according to the facilities and services provided;

- the accommodation does not fall in the category of specialised establishments.

The category 'hotels and similar establishments' consists of:

- hotels, comprising:
    hotels, apartment hotels, motels, roadside inns, beach hotels, residential clubs and similar establishments providing hotel services including more than daily bed-making and cleaning of the room and sanitary facilities;
- similar establishments, comprising:
    rooming and boarding houses, tourist residences and similar accommodation arranged in rooms and providing limited hotel services including daily bed-making and cleaning of the room and sanitary facilities; this group also includes guest houses, bed & breakfast and farmhouse accommodation.

Hours worked

Hours worked is the number of hours actually worked, defined as the sum of all periods spent on direct and ancillary activities to produce goods and services.

Household – social statistics

A **household**, in the context of surveys on social conditions or income such as EU-SILC or household budget surveys, is defined as a housekeeping unit or, operationally, as a social unit that: has common arrangements; shares household expenses or daily needs; lives in a shared common residence.

A household includes either one person living alone or a group of people, not necessarily related, living at the same address with common housekeeping, in other words sharing at least one meal per day or sharing a living or sitting room.

Collective households or **institutional households** (as opposed to **private households**) are, for instance: hospitals, old people's homes, residential homes, prisons, military barracks, religious institutions, boarding houses and workers' hostels.

Household budget survey (HBS)

The **household budget survey** (HBS) is a national survey which focuses on households' expenditure on goods and services, giving a picture of living conditions in the European Union (EU). It is carried out by each Member State and is used to compile weightings for important macro-economic indicators, such as consumer price indices (which are measures of inflation) and national accounts.

The data from the survey is broken down by household characteristics, such as income, socioeconomic characteristics, size and composition, degree of urbanisation, and region.

Data collection involves a combination of one or more interviews and diaries or logs maintained by households and/or individuals, generally on a daily basis. The basic unit of data collection and analysis in the survey is the household. It is important to identify the reference person (often the head of the household) whose personal characteristics can be used in the classification and analysis of information on the household. The socioeconomic group, occupation and employment status, income, sex and age of the reference person is often used to classify and present results. Expenditure made by households to acquire goods and services is recorded at the price actually paid, which includes indirect taxes (VAT and excise duties) borne by the purchaser. Two thirds of the Member States carry out annual surveys, while the remainder have five-year or even longer intervals between surveys. Probability sampling is used in the large majority of surveys in the EU. A high incidence of non-response is a common and major problem.

Household debt-to-income ratio

The **household debt-to-income ratio** combines non-financial and financial accounts data. It is defined as the ratio of households' debt arising from loans, recorded at the end of a calendar year, to the gross disposable income earned by households in the course of that year. It thereby constitutes a

measure of the indebtedness of households, in relation with their ability to pay back their debt's principal sum. The debt-to-income ratio is calculated on the basis of gross debt – that is without taking account of any assets held by households.

Household final consumption expenditure (HFCE)

Household final consumption expenditure, abbreviated as **HCFE**, consists of the total outlay on individual goods and services by resident households, including those sold at below-market prices. HCFE includes imputed expenditures or transactions which do not occur in monetary terms and can therefore not be measured directly.

Household investment rate

The **household investment rate** is defined as gross investment (gross fixed capital formation; mainly dwellings) divided by gross disposable income of the household sector in national accounts. Consumer durables (which include passenger cars) are not considered as part of household investment.

Household net financial assets-to-income ratio

The **household net financial assets-to-income ratio** combines non-financial and financial accounts data. It is defined as the ratio of households' net financial assets – which refers to all financial assets minus all financial liabilities – at the end of a calendar year, to the gross disposable income earned by households in the course of that year. It therefore represents the accumulation of financial assets, after deduction of liabilities, of households as a proportion of their annual income. However, this ratio does not account for non-financial assets such as dwellings.

Household saving

Household saving, total savings of the household sector in national accounts, may be estimated by

subtracting consumption expenditure and the adjustment for the change in net equity of households in pension funds reserves from disposable income. The latter consists essentially of income from employment and from the operation of unincorporated enterprises, plus receipts of interest, dividends and social benefits minus payments of income taxes, interest and social security contributions.

Household saving rate

The **household saving rate** is defined as gross household saving divided by gross disposable income, with the latter being adjusted for the change in the net equity of households in pension funds reserves. Saving rates can be measured on either a gross or net basis. Net saving rates are measured after deducting consumption of fixed capital (depreciation).

Household sector

The **household sector** in national accounts encompasses all households and non-profit institutions serving households.

Housing cost overburden rate

The **housing cost overburden rate** is the percentage of the population living in households where total housing costs (net of housing allowances) represent more than 40 % of disposable income (net of housing allowances).

Human development index (HDI)

The **human development index**, abbreviated as **HDI**, is a summary composite index incorporating statistical measures of life expectancy, literacy, educational attainment and GDP per capita, calculated by the United Nations (UN) under the UN Development Programme. It measures a country's average achievements in three basic aspects of human development: health, knowledge, and a decent standard of living.

Eurostat uses the 2006 HDI classification as the basis for grouping countries by level of development.

The HDI provides an alternative to the common practice of evaluating a country's progress in development only based on per capita GDP.

Import

Imports are goods which enter the statistical territory of the European Union (EU) from a non-member country and are placed under the customs procedure for free circulation within the EU (as a general rule goods intended for consumption), inward processing or processing under customs control (goods for working, processing or repair) immediately or after bonded warehousing.

Import price index

The **industrial import price index**, abbreviated as **MPI** or sometimes **IMPR**, measures the monthly change of prices of products imported by domestic residents, mainly enterprises, in European Union (EU) Member States from other countries (including other EU Member States). The indicator distinguishes imports from the euro area from those arriving from outside the euro area.

The MPI covers mainly manufactured products. Also covered are mining, energy (gas, electricity and so on) and water (in other words products classified under sections B to E of the statistical classification of products by activity (CPA). Some product groups are however excluded (such as nuclear products, weapons, ships and aircrafts, printing, some repair services and water treatment). Excluded are also the imports by households, governments and non-profit institutions.

Import prices in the MPI:

- include cost, insurance and freight at the national border of the importing country, but not duties or import taxes;
- are actual transaction prices (not list prices) including, for example, discounts;
- are measured in the currency of the importing EU country – transactions in other currencies

have to be converted (this implies that the MPI is affected by exchange rate fluctuations);
- must take into account all price determining qualities of the imported products;
- are recorded when ownership is transferred and the index should reflect the average prices during the reference period (month).

Inactive

A person is economically **inactive**, according to the International Labour Organization definition, if he or she is not part of the labour force. So inactive persons are neither employed nor unemployed. The inactive population can include pre-school children, school children, students, pensioners and homemakers, for example, provided that they are not working at all and not available or looking for work either; some of these may be of working age.

Incineration

Incineration is a method of waste disposal that involves the combustion of waste. It may refer to incineration on land or at sea. Incineration with energy recovery refers to incineration processes where the energy created in the combustion process is harnessed for re-use, for example for power generation. Incineration without energy recovery means the heat generated by combustion is dissipated in the environment.

Income approach

The income approach to calculate GDP sums the compensation of employees, net taxes on production and imports, gross operating surplus and mixed income. The income approach shows how GDP is distributed among different participants in the production process, as the sum of:

- **compensation of employees**: the total remuneration, in cash or in kind, payable by an employer to an employee in return for work done by the latter during the accounting period; the compensation of employees is broken down into: wages and salaries (in cash and in kind); employers' social con-

tributions (employers' actual social contributions and employers' imputed social contributions);

- **gross operating surplus**: this is the surplus (or deficit) on production activities before account has been taken of the interest, rents or charges paid or received for the use of assets;
- **mixed income**: this is the remuneration for the work carried out by the owner (or by members of his/her family) of an unincorporated enterprise; this is referred to as 'mixed income' since it cannot be distinguished from the entrepreneurial profit of the owner;
- **taxes on production and imports less subsidies**: these consist of compulsory (in the case of taxes) unrequited payments to or from general government or institutions of the European Union, in respect of the production or import of goods and services, the employment of labour, and the ownership or use of land, buildings or other assets used in production.

Incumbent

In telecommunications, the **incumbent** is the company (often a regulated monopoly) active on the market just before it was liberalised, or opened to competition.

Indicator A

Indicator A of the income from agricultural activity corresponds to the deflated (real) net value added at factor cost of agriculture, per total annual work unit; the implicit price index of GDP is used as deflator.

Industrial production index

The **production index** is a business cycle indicator which aims to measure changes in value added at factor cost of industry and construction over a given reference period. It does this by measuring changes in the volume of output and activity at close and regular intervals, usually monthly.

However, the monthly data necessary for the collection of this index are often unavailable. In practice,

suitable proxy values for the calculation of the production index are needed.

The production index should also take into account:

- changes in type and quality of the commodities and of the input materials;
- changes in stocks of finished goods and services, and work in progress;
- changes in technical input-output relations (processing techniques);
- services, such as assembly of production units, repairs or planning.

Inequality of income distribution

Inequality of income distribution is the ratio of total income received by the 20 % of the population having the highest income (top quintile) to the total income of the 20 % of the population having the lowest income (bottom quintile). Income is based on equivalised disposable income.

Inflation

Inflation is an increase in the general price level of goods and services. When there is inflation in an economy, the value of money decreases because a given amount will buy fewer goods and services than before. Inflation in an economy is often calculated by examining a basket of goods and services and comparing the changes in the prices of that basket over time.

The **inflation rate** is the percentage change in the price index for a given period compared with that recorded in a previous period. It is usually calculated on a year-on-year or annual basis. For an index value of 183.1 for January of this year, and an index value of 178.4 recorded in January last year, the annual rate of inflation of January this year would be: $((183.1/178.4) - 1) * 100 = 2.6\%$

Similarly, one may compile month-on-month rates of change or average annual rates of change.

Deflation is the opposite of inflation. It is a decrease in the general price level of goods and services and represents an increase in the value of money, where

an amount of money can be exchanged for more goods and services.

Information and communication technology (ICT)

Information and communication technology, abbreviated as **ICT**, covers all technical means used to handle information and aid communication. This includes both computer and network hardware, as well as their software.

Innovation

Innovation is the use of new ideas, products or methods where they have not been used before.

For the Community innovation survey (CIS), an innovation is defined as a new or significantly improved product (good or service) introduced to the market, or the introduction within an enterprise of a new or significantly improved process. Innovations are based on the results of new technological developments, new technology combinations, or the use of other knowledge, acquired by the enterprise. The innovations may be developed by the innovating enterprise or by another enterprise. However, purely selling innovations wholly produced and developed by other enterprises is not included as an innovation activity, nor is introducing products with purely aesthetic changes. Innovations should be new to the enterprise concerned: for product innovations they do not necessarily have to be new to the market and for process innovations the enterprise does not necessarily have to be the first one to have introduced the process.

Enterprises carrying out innovation activities cover all types of innovators including product and process innovators, as well as those enterprises with only ongoing and/or abandoned innovation activities. The proportion of enterprises undertaking innovation activities is also called the propensity (tendency) to innovate.

A **product innovation** is the market introduction of a new or a significantly improved good or service. A **process innovation** is the implementation of a new or significantly improved production process, distribution method or support activity for goods or services ICHA.

Intellectual property rights

Intellectual property rights, abbreviated as IPRs, refer to the general term for the assignment of property rights through patents, copyrights and trademarks. These property rights allow the holder to exercise a monopoly on the use of the item for a set period. By restricting imitation and duplication IPRs confer monopoly power, but the social costs of monopoly power may be offset by the social benefits of higher levels of creative activity encouraged by the monopoly earnings. Ownership of ideas includes literary and artistic works (protected by copyright), inventions (protected by patents), signs for distinguishing goods of an enterprise (protected by trademarks) and other elements of industrial property.

Interest rate

An **interest rate** is the cost of borrowing or the gain from lending, normally expressed as an annual percentage amount.

Intermediate consumption

Intermediate consumption is an accounting concept which measures the value of the goods and services consumed as inputs by a process of production. It excludes fixed assets whose consumption is recorded as consumption of fixed capital. The goods and services may be either transformed or used up by the production process.

International classification for health accounts (ICHA)

The **international classification for health accounts**, abbreviated as **ICHA**, is a classification managed by the OECD. Its purpose is to define, within the context of the system of national accounts:

- healthcare **financing agents**: who is paying?
- healthcare by **function**: for which services and goods?

- healthcare **service provider industries**: who provides the services?

International classification of diseases (ICD)

The **international classification of diseases**, abbreviated as **ICD**, is used to classify diseases and other health problems on many types of health and vital (essential to life) records, as well as death certificates. As well as enabling the storage and retrieval of diagnostic information for clinical, epidemiological (which deals with the study of the causes, distribution, and control of disease in populations) and quality purposes, ICD records also form the basis for compiling national mortality and morbidity statistics by WHO Member States.

International Labour Organisation (ILO)

The **International Labour Organisation**, abbreviated as **ILO**, is the only tripartite United Nations (UN) agency that brings together governments, employers and workers of its Member States in common action to promote decent work worldwide. Its main mission is to advance opportunities for women and men to obtain decent and productive employment in conditions of freedom, equity, security and human dignity.

The ILO was founded in 1919, in the wake of World War I, to pursue a vision based on the premise that universal, lasting peace can only occur if based on the decent treatment of working women and men. The ILO became the UN's first specialised agency in 1946.

International Monetary Fund (IMF)

The **International Monetary Fund**, abbreviated as **IMF**, is an international organisation, at present counting 188 member countries, with the mission to foster global monetary cooperation, secure financial stability, facilitate international trade, promote high employment and sustainable economic growth, and reduce poverty around the world.

The IMF was conceived at the Bretton Woods conference in July 1944 (together with the World Bank), came into formal existence in December 1945 with 29 founding member countries and started operations on 1 March 1947. It is a specialised agency of the United Nations, but has its own charter, governing structure, and finances. Its members are represented through a quota system broadly based on their relative size in the global economy.

The IMF promotes international monetary cooperation and exchange rate stability, facilitates the balanced growth of international trade, and provides resources to help members in balance of payments difficulties or to assist with poverty reduction. Through its economic surveillance, the IMF keeps track of the economic health of its member countries, alerting them to risks on the horizon and providing policy advice. It also lends to countries in difficulty, and provides technical assistance and training to help countries improve economic management.

International standard classification of education (ISCED)

The **international standard classification of education (ISCED)** is an instrument for compiling internationally comparable education statistics.

The current version, ISCED 97, covers two classification variables: levels and fields of education as well as general/vocational/prevocational orientation and educational/labour market destination. ISCED 97 was implemented in European Union countries for collecting data starting with the 1997/98 school year.

There are seven levels of education in ISCED 97.

Level 0 **pre-primary education** – the initial stage of organised instruction; it is school- or centre-based and is designed for children aged at least three years.

Level 1 **primary education** – begins between five and seven years of age, is the start of compulsory education where it exists and generally covers six years of full-time schooling.

Level 2 **lower secondary education** – continues the basic programmes of the primary level, although teaching is typically more subject-focused. Usually, the end of this level coincides with the end of compulsory education.

Level 3 **upper secondary education** – generally begins at the end of compulsory education. The entrance age is typically 15 or 16 years. Entrance qualifications (end of compulsory education) and other minimum entry requirements are usually needed. Instruction is often more subject-oriented than at ISCED level 2. The typical duration of ISCED level 3 varies from two to five years.

Level 4 **post-secondary non-tertiary education** – between upper secondary and tertiary education. This level serves to broaden the knowledge of ISCED level 3 graduates. Typical examples are programmes designed to prepare pupils for studies at level 5 or programmes designed to prepare pupils for direct labour market entry.

Level 5 **tertiary education (first stage)** – entry to these programmes normally requires the successful completion of ISCED level 3 or 4. This includes tertiary programmes with academic orientation (type A) which are largely theoretical and tertiary programmes with an occupational orientation (type B). The latter are typically shorter than type A programmes and aimed at preparing students for the labour market.

Level 6 **tertiary education (second stage)** – reserved for tertiary studies that lead to an advanced research qualification (Ph.D. or doctorate).

Fields of education

The ISCED classification comprises 22 fields of education in all (at the two-digit level), which can be further refined into the three-digit level. At the highest one-digit level the following nine broad groups of fields of education are distinguished:

1 education;

2 humanities and arts;

3 social sciences, business and law;

4 science;

5 engineering, manufacturing and construction;

6 agriculture;

7 health and welfare;

8 services.

Internet access

In the context of the survey on internet use within households, **internet access** refers to the possibility for anyone in a household to access the internet from home. It does not mean connectivity, in other words whether connections can be made in the household's area or street.

Internet users

An internet user, in the context of information society statistics, is defined as a person making use of the internet in whatever way: whether at home, at work or from anywhere else; whether for private or professional purposes; and regardless of the device or type of connection used.

Invention

An **invention** is a new solution to a technical problem which satisfies the criteria of:

• novelty: the solution must be novel (new);
• inventiveness: it must involve a (non-obvious) inventive step;
• industrial applicability: it must be capable of industrial use.

Investment

Gross investment in tangible goods is defined as investment during the reference period in all tangible goods. Included are new and existing tangible capital goods, whether bought from third parties or produced for own use (in other words capitalised production of tangible capital goods), having a useful life of more than one year including non-produced tangible goods such as land. Investments in intangible and financial assets are excluded.

Job vacancy rate (JVR)

A **job vacancy** is a post, either newly created, unoccupied or about to become vacant, which the employer:

- actively seeks to fill with a suitable candidate from outside the enterprise, including any further necessary steps;
- immediately or in the near future.

Although the definition states that a job vacancy should be open to candidates from outside the enterprise, this does not exclude the possibility of appointing an internal candidate to the post. A post that is open to internal candidates only, however, is not considered a job vacancy.

The **job vacancy rate**, abbreviated as **JVR**, measures the percentage of vacant posts, as defined above, compared with the total number of occupied and unoccupied posts; it is calculated as follows:

JVR = number of job vacancies/(number of occupied posts + number of job vacancies) * 100.

An **occupied post** is a post within an organisation to which an employee has been assigned.

Data on job vacancies and occupied posts are broken down by economic activity, occupation, size of enterprise and region.

Joint forest sector questionnaire (JFSQ)

The **joint forest sector questionnaire (JFSQ)** is an initiative of the International Tropical Timber Organization (ITTO), the United Nations Economic Commission for Europe (UNECE), the Food and Agriculture Organization of the United Nations (FAO) and Eurostat to collect statistics on the world timber situation. Each agency collects data from the countries for which it is responsible, with Eurostat compiling information from European Union Member States and EFTA Member States.

Kitchen gardens

Kitchen gardens are areas of an agricultural holding devoted to the cultivation of agricultural products

not intended for selling but for consumption by the farm holder and his/her household.

Kyoto Protocol

The **Kyoto Protocol**, adopted in Kyoto (JP) in 1997, commits 37 industrialised countries and the European Union (EU) to the so-called **Kyoto target** of reducing their greenhouse gas emissions by an average of 5 % against 1990 levels, over the period from 2008 to 2012.

The Protocol was adopted at the Third Conference of the Parties to the United Nations Convention on Climate Change in December 1997 and came into force on 16 February 2005. The main distinction between the Kyoto Protocol and the **Kyoto Convention** is that while the Convention encouraged industrialised countries to stabilise emissions, the Protocol sets binding targets.

To date, there are 193 parties (192 States and the EU) that have ratified the Kyoto Protocol. Signatories must meet their targets primarily through national measures. However, the Kyoto Protocol offers an additional means of meeting targets through three market-based **Kyoto mechanisms**:

- emissions trading (also known as the carbon market);
- clean development mechanism (an emission-reduction project in the developing world);
- joint implementation (to encourage foreign investment and technology transfer).

These measures are designed to stimulate green investment and help signatories meet their emission targets in a cost-effective manner.

Labour cost

Labour cost or **total labour cost** is the total expenditure borne by employers for employing staff.

Labour cost consists of employee compensation (including wages, salaries in cash and in kind, employers' social security contributions), vocational training costs, other expenditure such as recruitment costs, spending on working clothes and

employment taxes regarded as labour costs minus any subsidies received.

The Eurostat definition closely follows the international one laid down by the International Conference of Labour Statisticians (Geneva, 1966) in its resolution on the statistics of labour cost. The labour cost includes both direct and indirect costs.

Direct costs (compensation of employees):

- gross wages and salaries paid in cash;
- direct remuneration (pay) and bonuses;
- wages and salaries in kind (for example company products, housing, company cars, meal vouchers, crèches).

Direct costs are dominated by wages and salaries paid in cash.

Indirect costs:

- employers' actual social contributions (in other words statutory, collectively agreed, contractual and voluntary social security contributions);
- employers' imputed social contributions (mostly guaranteed pay in the event of sickness or short-time working, plus severance pay and compensation instead of notice);
- vocational training costs;
- recruitment costs and work clothes given by the employer;
- taxes paid by the employer (based on their wages and salaries bill or on the numbers they employ);
- minus subsidies received by the employer (intended to refund part or all of the cost of direct pay).

Indirect costs are dominated by employers' actual social contributions, in particular by employers' statutory social security contributions.

Labour force

The **labour force** or the **economically active population**, also shortened to the **active population**, includes both employed and unemployed persons, but not the economically inactive, such as pre-school children, school children, students and pensioners.

Labour force survey (LFS)

The **labour force survey**, abbreviated as **LFS**, is an inquiry directed to households, designed to obtain information on the labour market and related issues through a series of personal interviews.

The European Union (EU) LFS covers all citizens living in private households and excludes those in collective households, such as boarding houses, residence halls and hospitals. The definitions used are common to all EU Member States and are based on international recommendations by the International Labour Organization (ILO).

Labour market

The **labour market** is the real or virtual meeting point, within an economy or market place, where people selling their labour (employees) negotiate and may reach an agreement with those who buy it (employers). Labour markets provide the structure through which workers and employers interact about jobs, working conditions and pay. Other actors are the institutions and processes of collective bargaining, including the roles played by employers' organisations and trade unions. The labour market concept also covers issues such as employment, unemployment, participation rates and wages.

Labour market policy (LMP)

The **labour market policy (LMP)** database covers all labour market measures which can be described as public interventions in the labour market aimed at reaching its efficient functioning and to correct disequilibria and which can be distinguished from other general employment policy measures in that they act selectively to favour particular groups in the labour market.

Public interventions refer to measures taken by general government in this respect which involve expenditure, either in the form of actual disbursements or of forgone revenue (reductions in taxes, social contributions or other charges normally

payable). The scope of the database is also limited to labour market measures which are explicitly targeted in some way at groups of persons with difficulties in the labour market – referred to here as target groups. In broad terms, this covers persons who are unemployed, persons in employment but at risk of involuntary job loss, and inactive persons who are currently not part of the labour force (in the sense that they are not employed or unemployed according to the ILO definitions) but who would like to enter the labour market and are disadvantaged in some way.

Labour productivity

Labour productivity measures the amount of goods and services produced by each member of the labour force or the output per input of labour. It can be measured in a variety of ways.

For structural indicators, it may be measured by gross domestic product (GDP), expressed in terms of the purchasing power standard (PPS), either relative to the number of employed persons or to the number of hours worked. In both cases, it is then expressed as an index.

Within national accounts and structural business statistics, labour productivity is often defined as the value added per employed person.

Lagging indicator

A **lagging indicator** is an economic statistical indicator that changes after macro-economic conditions have already changed. Typical examples of lagging indicators are unemployment figures, profits or interest rates. Within short-term statistics the number of persons employed is a typical lagging indicator. The lagging indicator is contrasted with the coincident indicator which changes simultaneously with economic conditions, and the leading indicator which changes in advance of expected economic developments. Lagging indicators are used to confirm economic trends that have already been predicted by leading indicators or shown by coincident indicators. Although they change after the change in the general economic conditions, they

are still useful since they are available before complete national accounts data.

Land cover

Land cover refers to the observed (bio)physical cover of the earth's surface. The main classes in the LUCAS land cover nomenclature are: artificial land; cropland; woodland; shrubland; grassland; bareland; water; wetland.

Land use

Land use refers to the socioeconomic purpose of land. Areas of land can be used for residential, industrial, agricultural, forestry, recreational, transport and other purposes. Often the same land is used for several purposes – for example, woodland can be use for forestry, hunting and recreational purposes. The main classes in the LUCAS land use nomenclature are: agriculture; forestry; fishing; mining and quarrying; hunting; energy production; industry and manufacturing; transport, communication networks, storage and protective works; water and waste treatment; construction; commerce, finance and business; community services; recreational, leisure and sport; residential; unused.

Land use/cover area frame survey (LUCAS)

The **land use/cover area frame statistical survey**, abbreviated as **LUCAS**, is a European field survey programme funded and executed by Eurostat. Its objective is to set up area frame surveys for the provision of coherent and harmonised statistics on land use and land cover in the European Union. In addition, it is designed to provide information on agriculture, the environment, landscapes and sustainable development, ground evidence for the calibration of satellite images and a register of points for specific surveys (such as soil and biodiversity) and for the core European in situ data collection network. Land cover and land use are of high importance in the definition and evaluation of common agricultural and environment policies. LUCAS was launched as a pilot in 2001 following Decision

1445/2000/EC of 22 May 2000 on the application of aerial-survey and remote-sensing techniques to the agricultural statistics.

Landfill

Landfill is the deposit of waste into or onto land. It includes specially engineered landfill sites and temporary storage of over one year on permanent sites. The definition covers both landfill in internal sites, in other words where a generator of waste is carrying out its own waste disposal at the place of generation, and in external sites. Landfill is often simply referred to as deposit.

Large enterprises

For statistical purposes, **large enterprises** are those employing 250 persons or more. Enterprises employing fewer than 250 persons are known as small and medium-sized enterprises.

Laspeyres price index

The **Laspeyres price index** is an index formula used in price statistics for measuring the price development of a basket of goods and services consumed in the base period. The question it answers is how much a basket of goods and services that consumers bought in the base period would cost in the current period. It is defined as a fixed-weight, or fixed-basket, index that uses the basket of goods and services and their weights from the base period. It is also known as a base-weighted index.

In price statistics other price index formulas may be used (Paasche price index, Fisher price index). The choice of the index formula, however, often depends on the availability of data. In contrast to the other formulas, the Laspeyres index does not require information on the composition of the basket of the current period. Therefore in practice the Laspeyres formula is usually preferred for the calculation of consumer price indices, which are typically compiled and released rapidly – before

consumption or production information for the current period could have been collected.

Liability

A **liability** is a present obligation arising from past events, in some cases specified in a written contract. A company's liabilities may include bank loans, short-term debts for goods and services received, as well as the company's loan capital and capital subscribed by shareholders. According to basic accounting principles, a company's equity is equal to assets plus liabilities.

Life expectancy

Life expectancy at a certain age is the mean additional number of years that a person of that age can expect to live, if subjected throughout the rest of his or her life to the current mortality conditions (age-specific probabilities of dying, in other words the death rates observed for the current period).

Lifelong learning

Lifelong learning is the lifelong, voluntary and self-motivated pursuit of knowledge for personal or professional reasons. The overall aim of learning is to improve knowledge, skills and competences. The intention to learn distinguishes learning activities from non-learning activities such as cultural activities or sports activities.

Within the domain of lifelong learning statistics, formal education covers education and training in the regular system of schools, universities and colleges. Non-formal education and training includes all taught learning activities which are not part of a formal education programme. The information collected relates to all education or training regardless of whether it is relevant to the respondent's current or possible future job. Lifelong learning statistics collected by Eurostat do not cover informal learning.

In contrast to lifelong learning as a concept, lifelong learning statistics do not cover informal learning, which corresponds to self-learning (for example through the use of printed material, computer-based learning/training, online internet-based web education, or visiting libraries).

Lisbon strategy

During the European Council in Lisbon in March 2000, European Union (EU) leaders launched a **Lisbon strategy** aimed at making the EU the world's most competitive economy by 2010.

This strategy, developed at subsequent meetings of the European Council, rested on three pillars.

- An **economic pillar** laying the groundwork for the transition to a competitive, dynamic, knowledge-based economy. There was a strong emphasis on adapting quickly to changes in the information society and to investing in research and development.
- A **social pillar** designed to modernise the European social model by investing in human resources and combating social exclusion. The Member States were expected to invest in education and training, and to conduct an active policy for employment, making it easier to move to a knowledge economy.
- An **environmental pillar**, added at the Gothenburg European Council in June 2001, which urged a decoupling of economic growth from the use of natural resources.

Livestock unit (LSU)

The **livestock unit**, abbreviated as **LSU** (or sometimes as **LU**), is a reference unit which facilitates the aggregation of livestock from various species and age via the use of specific coefficients established initially on the basis of the nutritional or feed requirement of each type of animal (see table below for an overview of the most commonly used coefficients). The reference unit used for the calculation of livestock units (=1 LSU) is the grazing equivalent of one adult dairy cow producing 3 000 kg of milk annually, without additional concentrated foodstuffs.

Livestock unit coefficients

Bovine animals	
Under one year old	0.400
One but less than two years old	0.700
Male, two years old and over	1.000
Heifers, two years old and over	0.800
Dairy cows	1.000
Other cows, two years old and over	0.800
Sheep and goats	0.100
Equidae	0.800
Pigs	
Piglets having a live weight of under 20 kg	0.027
Breeding sows weighing 50 kg and over	0.500
Other pigs	0.300
Poultry	
Broilers	0.007
Laying hens	0.014
Ostriches	0.350
Other poultry	0.030
Rabbits, breeding females	0.020

Local government

Local government consists of all types of public administration whose responsibility covers only a local part of the economic territory, apart from local agencies of social security funds.

Long-distance call

A **long-distance call** is a telephone call made from one local calling area or network to another.

Marriages

A **marriage** is the act, ceremony or process by which the legal relationship between two persons is formed. The legality of the union may be established by civil, religious or other means as recognised by the laws of each country.

In all European Union and other European countries, contracting a **civil marriage** (before official authorities and on a legal basis) is possible. However, the relation between a civil marriage and a **religious marriage** (before religious representative only) is not the same in all countries. In 15 countries (Denmark, Estonia, Ireland, Greece, Spain, Italy, Cyprus, Latvia, Lithuania, Poland, Slovak, Finland, Sweden and the United Kingdom, as well as Norway) a religious marriage has consequences for the civil marriage in the sense that a religious marriage is recognised by the state as equivalent to a civil marriage. France states that a religious marriage has no consequences for marital status, unless it has been contracted abroad.

The **crude marriage rate** is the ratio of the number of marriages during the year to the average population in that year. The value is expressed per 1 000 inhabitants.

Material deprivation

Material deprivation refers to a state of economic strain and durables strain, defined as the enforced inability (rather than the *choice* not to do so) to pay unexpected expenses, afford a one-week annual holiday away from home, a meal involving meat, chicken or fish every second day, the adequate heating of a dwelling, durable goods like a washing machine, colour television, telephone or car, being confronted with payment arrears (mortgage or rent, utility bills, hire purchase instalments or other loan payments).

The **material deprivation rate** is an indicator in EU-SILC that expresses the inability to afford some items considered by most people to be desirable or even necessary to lead an adequate life. The indicator distinguishes between individuals who cannot afford a certain good or service, and those who do not have this good or service for another reason, for example because they do not want or do not need it.

The indicator adopted by the Social Protection Committee measures the percentage of the population that cannot afford at least three of the following nine items: 1. to pay their rent, mortgage or utility bills; 2. to keep their home adequately warm; 3. to face unexpected expenses; 4. to eat meat or proteins regularly; 5. to go on holiday; 6. a television set; 7. a refrigerator; 8. a car; 9. a telephone.

Severe material deprivation rate is defined as the enforced inability to pay for at least four of the above-mentioned items.

Maturity

The **maturity date** or **final maturity date** is the date on which a debt obligation is to be extinguished, as agreed upon contractually.

Median

The **median** is the middle value in a group of numbers ranked in order of size.

Migration

Migration refers to the number of **migrants**, persons changing their residence to or from a given area (usually a country) during a given time period (usually one year).

Immigrants are persons arriving or returning from abroad to take up residence in a country for a certain period, having previously been resident elsewhere. According to the 1998 United Nations recommendations on the statistics of international migration (Revision 1), an individual is a **long-term immigrant** if *he/she stays in his/her country of destination for a period of 12 months or more, having previously been resident elsewhere for 12 months or more*. **Immigration** is the number of immigrants for a given area during the year.

Emigrants are persons leaving the country where they usually reside and effectively taking up residence in another country. According to the 1998 UN recommendations on the statistics of international migration (Revision 1), an individual is a **long-term emigrant** if *he/she leaves his/her country of previous usual residence for a period of 12 months or more*. **Emigration** is the number of emigrants for a given area during the year.

Net migration is the difference between immigration to and emigration from a given area during

the year (net migration is positive when there are more immigrants than emigrants and negative when there are more emigrants than immigrants). Since many countries either do not have accurate figures on immigration and emigration, or have no figures at all, net migration has to be estimated. It is usually estimated as the difference between the total population change and the natural increase during the year. Net migration gives no indication of the relative scale of the separate immigration and emigration flows to and from a country; a country may report low net migration but experience high immigration and emigration flows.

The **crude rate of net migration** is the ratio of net migration during the year to the average population in that year. The value is expressed per 1 000 inhabitants.

A **recognised non-citizen** is a person who is not a citizen of the reporting country nor of any other country, but who has established links to that country which include some but not all rights and obligations of full citizenship. Recognised non-citizens are not included in the number of European Union citizens.

Minimum wage

The **minimum wage** is the lowest wage that employers are legally obliged to pay their employees. The basic national minimum wage can be fixed at an hourly, weekly or monthly rate, and this minimum wage is enforced by law (the government), often after consultation with social partners, or directly by national intersectoral agreement (in the European Union this is the case for Belgium and Greece).

The national minimum wage usually applies to all employees, or at least to a large majority of employees in the country. Some countries have exceptions, for example for younger workers, apprentices or workers with disabilities. Gross amounts are reported, that is, before income tax and social security deductions, which vary between countries.

Mobile phone subscription

A **mobile phone subscription** refers to the use of public mobile telecommunication systems (also called mobiles or cell phones) using cellular technology. In the context of the Telecom survey on telecommunications services:

- active pre-paid cards are treated as subscriptions;
- a person may have more than one subscription.

National accounts

National accounts, often called **macro-economic accounts**, are statistics focusing on the structure and development of economies. They describe and analyse, in an accessible and reliable way, the economic interactions (transactions) within an economy. There are an almost unimaginable large number of these transactions.

The **national accounts sector** refers to the whole economy (a country, the European Union or the euro area) as a sector. All institutional units operating within an economy can be assigned to a particular **institutional sector**. Breakdowns by institutional sector are given within the sector accounts.

The institutional sectors group institutional units with broadly similar characteristics and behaviour. The following can be distinguished: households and non-profit institutions serving households; non-financial corporations; financial corporations; government.

Transactions with non-residents and the financial claims of residents on non-residents, or vice versa, are recorded in the 'rest of the world' account.

Macro-economic developments, such as economic growth and inflation, are driven by the actions of the individual economic subjects in an economy. Grouping economic subjects with similar behaviour into institutional sectors helps significantly in understanding the functioning of the economy.

Natural population change

Natural population change is the difference between the number of live births and deaths during a given time period (usually one year). It can be either positive or negative. **Natural population**

increase is a positive natural change, when the number of live births is larger than the number of deaths during the time period considered. **Natural population decrease** is the opposite, a negative natural change, when the number of deaths exceeds the number of births.

Navigable inland waterway

A **navigable inland waterway** is a stretch of water, not part of the sea, which by natural or man-made features is suitable for navigation, primarily by inland waterway vessels. This term covers navigable rivers, lakes, canals and estuaries.

The length of rivers and canals is measured in mid-channel. The length of lakes and lagoons is measured along the shortest navigable route between the most distant points to and from which transport operations are performed. A waterway forming a common frontier between two countries is reported by both.

Waterways also include river estuaries, the boundary (with the sea) being that point nearest the sea where the width of the river is both less than 3 kilometres (km) at low water and less then 5 km at high water.

Net electricity generation

Net electricity generation or **net electricity production** is equal to gross electricity generation minus the consumption of power stations' auxiliary services.

Nights spent

A **night spent** (or overnight stay) is each night a guest/tourist (resident or non-resident) actually spends (sleeps or stays) in a tourist accommodation establishment or non-rented accommodation.

Non-financial business economy

The **non-financial business economy** includes the sectors of industry, construction and distributive trades and services.

This refers to economic activities covered by Sections C to J and L to N and Division 95 of NACE Rev. 2 and the enterprises or its legal units that carry out those activities.

Non-financial services

The **non-financial services** sector includes economic activities, such as computer services, real estate, research and development, legal services and accounting. For European Union (EU) statistical purposes, it refers to activities covered by Sections G to I and K of the EU's classification system NACE Rev. 1.1 and the enterprises or parts of enterprises that carry out those activities. Based on NACE Rev. 2 it covers Sections G to J and L to N and Division 95.

Non-nationals

Non-nationals are people who are not citizens of the country in which they currently reside.

Non-profit institutions serving households (NPISH)

Non-profit institutions serving households, abbreviated as **NPISH**, make up an institutional sector in the context of national accounts consisting of non-profit institutions which are not mainly financed and controlled by government and which provide goods or services to households for free or at prices that are not economically significant. Examples include churches and religious societies, sports and other clubs, trade unions and political parties.

NPISH are private, non-market producers which are separate legal entities. Their main resources, apart from those derived from occasional sales, are derived from voluntary contributions in cash or in kind from households in their capacity as consumers, from payments made by general governments, and from property income.

Nordic Member States

The **Nordic Member States** of the European Union are Denmark (DK), Finland (FI) and Sweden (SE).

Occupancy rate

The **occupancy rate** at hotels and similar establishments is calculated as a percentage as follows:

(total number of nights for residents and non-residents at hotels and similar establishments) * 100 / (total number of bed places at hotels and similar establishments * 365).

Old age dependency ratio

The **old age dependency ratio** is the ratio of the number of elderly people at an age when they are generally economically inactive (in other words aged 65 and over), compared with the number of people of working age (in other words 15-64 years old).

Open method of coordination (OMC)

The **open method of coordination**, abbreviated as **OMC**, was created as part of the European Union's employment policy and the Luxembourg process, and was also defined as an instrument of the Lisbon strategy (2000). The OMC provides a framework for cooperation between the Member States, whose national policies can thus be directed towards certain common objectives. Under this intergovernmental method, the Member States are evaluated by one another (peer pressure), with the European Commission's role being limited to surveillance. The European Parliament and the Court of Justice play virtually no part in the OMC process.

The open method of coordination takes place in areas which fall within the competence of the Member States, such as employment, social protection, social inclusion, education, youth policy and training. It is based principally on:

- jointly identifying and defining objectives to be achieved (adopted by the Council);
- jointly established measuring instruments (statistics, indicators, guidelines);
- benchmarking, in other words a comparison of the Member States' performance and exchange of best practices (monitored by the European Commission).

Depending on the areas concerned, the OMC involves so-called 'soft law' measures which are binding on the Member States in varying degrees but which never take the form of directives, regulations or decisions. Thus, in the context of the Lisbon strategy, the OMC required the Member States to draw up national reform plans and to forward them to the European Commission. However, youth policy does not entail the setting of targets, and it is up to the Member States to decide on objectives without the need for any European-level coordination of national action plans.

Organisation for Economic Co-operation and Development (OECD)

The **Organisation for Economic Co-operation and Development**, abbreviated as the **OECD,** is based in Paris (FR). It is an international organization of 34 countries committed to democracy and the market economy. The forerunner to the OECD was the Organisation for European Economic Co-operation and Development (OEEC), formed in 1947 to administer American and Canadian aid under the auspices of the Marshall Plan following World War II. The OECD was established on 14 December 1960.

Output approach

The **output approach** to calculate GDP sums the gross value added of various sectors, plus taxes and less subsidies on products. The output of the economy is measured using gross value added. Gross value added is defined as the value of all newly generated goods and services less the value of all goods and services consumed in their creation; the depreciation of fixed assets is not included. When calculating value added, output is valued at basic prices and intermediate consumption at purchasers' prices. Taxes less subsidies on products have to be added to value added to obtain GDP at market prices.

Overcrowding rate

The **overcrowding rate** is defined as the percentage of the population living in an **overcrowded** household.

A person is considered as living in an overcrowded household if the household does not have at its disposal a minimum number of rooms equal to:

- one room for the household;
- one room per couple in the household;
- one room for each single person aged 18 or more;
- one room per pair of single people of the same gender between 12 and 17 years of age;
- one room for each single person between 12 and 17 years of age and not included in the previous category;
- one room per pair of children under 12 years of age.

Passenger car

A **passenger car** is a road motor vehicle, other than a moped or a motor cycle, intended for the carriage of passengers and designed to seat no more than nine persons (including the driver). The term passenger car also covers **microcar**s (small cars which, depending on individual Member State legislation, may need no permit to be driven and/or benefit from lower vehicle taxation), taxis and passenger hire cars, provided that they have fewer than ten seats. This category also includes vans designed and used primarily for transport of passengers, as well as ambulances and motor homes. Excluded are light goods road vehicles, as well as motor coaches and buses and mini-buses/mini-coaches.

Passenger-kilometre

A **passenger-kilometre**, abbreviated as **pkm**, is the unit of measurement representing the transport of one passenger by a defined mode of transport (for example road, rail, air, sea, or inland waterways) over a distance of one kilometre.

Patent

A **patent** is an intellectual property right, a public title of industrial property that gives its owner the exclusive right to use his/her invention in the technical field for a limited number of years.

A **patent application**, the application for a patent, needs to be for an invention, in other words a new

solution to a technical problem which satisfies the criteria of:

- novelty: the solution must be novel;
- inventiveness: it must involve a non-obvious inventive step;
- industrial applicability: it must be capable of industrial use.

A patent may be granted to a firm (enterprise), an individual or a public body by a patent office. It remains valid in a given country or area for a limited period of time.

Patent Cooperation Treaty (PCT)

The **Patent Cooperation Treaty** (PCT) allows for a filing of an international application to have the same effect as a national application in each of the contracting countries designated in the application. However, patents are still granted nationally. The PCT system is superimposed upon the national and European systems. In PCT-applications, the applicant may either designate a country, or a regional office such as the European Patent Office (EPO). These so called Euro-PCT filings may then apply for protection in a number of European countries.

Permanent crops

Permanent crops are ligneous crops not grown in rotation, but occupying the soil and yielding harvests for several (usually more than five) consecutive years. Permanent crops mainly consist of fruit and berry trees, bushes, vines and olive trees. Permanent crops are usually intended for human consumption and generally yield a higher added value per hectare than annual crops. They also play an important role in shaping the rural landscape (through orchards, vineyards and olive tree plantations) and helping to balance agriculture within the environment.

Permanent grassland

Permanent grassland and meadow is land used permanently (for several, usually more than five, consecutive years): to grow herbaceous forage

crops, through cultivation (sown) or naturally (self-seeded); not included in the crop rotation scheme on the agricultural holding. Permanent grassland and meadow can be either used for grazing by livestock, or mowed for hay or silage (stocking in a silo).

Personnel costs – structural business statistics

In the context of structural business statistics (SBS), **personnel costs** are defined as the total remuneration, in cash or in kind, payable by an employer to an employee (regular and temporary employees, as well as home-workers) in return for work done by the latter during the reference period. **Personnel costs** are made up of wages, salaries and employers' social security costs. They include taxes and employees' social security contributions retained by the employer, as well as the employer's compulsory and voluntary social contributions.

Persons employed – structural business statistics

The **number of persons employed** is defined, within the context of structural business statistics, as the total number of persons who work in the observation unit (inclusive of working proprietors, partners working regularly in the unit and unpaid family workers), as well as persons who work outside the unit who belong to it and are paid by it (for example sales representatives, delivery personnel, repair and maintenance teams). It excludes manpower supplied to the unit by other enterprises, persons carrying out repair and maintenance work in the enquiry unit on behalf of other enterprises, as well as those on compulsory military service.

Persons living in households with low work intensity

The indicator **persons living in households with low work intensity** is defined as the number of persons living in a household having a work intensity below a threshold set at 0.20.

The **work intensity of a household** is the ratio of the total number of months that all working age household members have worked during the income reference year and the total number of months that the same household members theoretically could have worked in the same period. A working age person is defined as a person aged 18-59 years, with the exclusion of students in the age group between 18 and 24 years. Households composed only of children, of students aged less than 25 and/or people aged 60 or more are totally excluded from the indicator calculation.

Physician

A **physician** or (medical) doctor has a degree in medicine. Physicians may be described as practising, professionally active or licensed.

A **practising physician** provides services directly to patients as consumers of healthcare. These services include:

- conducting medical examinations and making diagnoses;
- prescribing medication and treating diagnosed illnesses, disorders or injuries;
- giving specialised medical or surgical treatment for particular illnesses, disorders or injuries;
- giving advice on and applying preventive medical methods and treatments.

A **professionally active physician** is a practising physician or any other physician for whom medical education is a prerequisite for the execution of the job (practising medicine as defined above or, for example, verifying medical absences from work, drug testing, or medical research).

A **licensed physician** is a physician who is licensed to practise; this category includes practising physicians, professionally active physicians, as well as all registered physicians who are entitled to practise as healthcare professionals.

Pig

A **pig** is a domesticated animal of the species *Sus*. A distinction is made between pigs, piglets, fattening pigs and breeding pigs.

Police officer

Police officers generally include all ranks of police officers including criminal police, traffic police, border police, gendarmerie, uniformed police, city guard, and municipal police. They exclude civilian staff, customs officers, tax police, military police, secret service police, part-time officers, special duty police reserves, cadets, and court police.

Population

The **population figure** of a given area is the total number of people in that area at a given time.

Eurostat collects **population data as of 1 January** of each year from the European Union's Member States. The recommended definition is the 'usual resident population' and represents the number of inhabitants of a given area on 1 January of the year in question (or, in some cases, on 31 December of the previous year). The population can be based on data from the most recent census adjusted by the components of population change produced since the last census, or based on population registers.

The **average population** is calculated as the arithmetic mean of the population on 1 January of two consecutive years. The average population is further used in the calculation of demographic indicators, like crude rates per 1 000 inhabitants, and for some 'per capita' indicators.

Population change

Population change, defined generally, is the difference in the size of a population between the end and the beginning of a given time period (usually one year). Specifically, it is the difference in population size on 1 January of two consecutive years. Population change has two components: natural population change (the number of live births minus the number of deaths); net migration (the number of immigrants minus the number of emigrants, plus statistical adjustment – it should be noted that net migration as referred to in the context of population change statistics includes the statistical adjustments occurring in the annual balance of the

population and that it serves the purpose of closing this balance).

A positive population change, when the result of net migration plus live births minus deaths is positive, is referred to as **population growth**, a negative one is called a **population decrease**.

The **crude rate of population growth** is the ratio of total population growth during the year to the average population of the area in question that year. The value is expressed per 1 000 inhabitants.

Poultry

Poultry, in the context of European Union statistics, refers to domestic birds of the species: *Gallus gallus* (hens and chickens); *Meleagris spp.* (turkeys); *Anas spp.* and *Cairina moschata* (ducks); *Anser anser dom.* (geese); *Coturnix spp.* (quails); *Phasianus spp.* (pheasants); *Numida meleagris dom.* (guineafowl); *Columbinae spp.* (pigeons); *Struthio camelus* (ostriches). It excludes, however, birds raised in confinement for hunting purposes and not for meat production.

Precipitation

Precipitation is defined as the total volume of atmospheric wet precipitation (mainly rain, snow and hail) and is usually measured by meteorological or hydrological institutes.

Price level index (PLI)

The **price level index**, abbreviated as **PLI**, expresses the price level of a given country relative to another (or relative to a group of countries like the European Union (EU)), by dividing the purchasing power parities (PPPs) by the current nominal exchange rate.

If the price level index of a country is higher than 100, the country concerned is relatively expensive compared with the one to which it is compared (for example the EU), while if the price level index is lower than 100 the country is relatively cheap compared with the other country.

Price level indices are not intended to rank countries strictly. In fact, they only provide an indication of the order of magnitude of the price level in one country in relation to others, particularly when countries are clustered around a very narrow range of outcomes. The degree of uncertainty associated with the basic price data and the methods used for compiling PPPs, may affect in such a case the minor differences between the PLIs and result in differences in ranking which are not statistically or economically significant.

Primary production of energy

Primary production of energy is any extraction of energy products in a useable form from natural sources. This occurs either when natural sources are exploited (for example, in coal mines, crude oil fields, hydro power plants) or in the fabrication of biofuels.

Transforming energy from one form into another, such as electricity or heat generation in thermal power plants (where primary energy sources are burned), or coke production in coke ovens, is not primary production.

Principal European Economic Indicators (PEEI)

Principal European Economic Indicators, abbreviated as **PEEIs**, constitute a set of economic indicators for the European Union and its Member States which are essential for monitoring the euro area. In 2002, Eurostat produced an initial list of 19 principal indicators, which has since been expanded to 26 (of which 22 are currently available); they are published regularly and posted on a specific PEEI page on the Eurostat website.

Since 2002, PEEIs have been regularly monitored and improved, in terms of coverage as well as timeliness. The list of indicators currently includes gross domestic product, private final consumption, the external trade balance and three-month interest rates.

Prison population

For statistical purposes, the **prison population** is defined as the total number of adult and juvenile prisoners (including pre-trial detainees) at 1 September of a given year. The definition includes offenders held in prison administration facilities, other facilities, juvenile offenders institutions, drug addicts institutions and psychiatric or other hospitals. It excludes, however, non-criminal prisoners held for administrative purposes (for example, people held pending an investigation into their immigration status).

Prodcom

Prodcom is a survey, with a frequency that is at least annual, for the collection of statistics on the production of industrial (mainly manufactured) goods, both in value and quantity terms, in the European Union. It is abbreviated from the French term *Production Communautaire.*

The Prodcom survey is based on a list of products called the **Prodcom list** which comprises about 4 500 headings relating to industrial products. These products are detailed at an eight-digit level. The first four digits refer to the equivalent class within the statistical classification of economic activities in the European Community (NACE), and the next two digits refer to subcategories within the statistical classification of products by activity (CPA). Most Prodcom headings correspond to one or more combined nomenclature (CN) codes.

Producer price index (PPI)

The **producer price index**, abbreviated as **PPI** and also called **output price index**, is a business cycle indicator whose objective is to measure the monthly development of transaction prices of economic activities.

The PPI is not only an early indicator of inflationary pressure in the economy before it reaches the consumer, but it can also record the development of prices over longer time periods.

The domestic output price index for an economic activity measures the average price development of all goods and related services resulting from that activity and sold on the domestic market. The non-domestic price index shows the average price development (converted to local currency) of all goods and related services resulting from that activity and sold outside of the domestic market. When combined, these two indices show the average price development of all goods and related services resulting from an activity.

The following rules apply for the definition of prices:

The appropriate price is the basic price that excludes VAT and similar deductible taxes directly linked to turnover as well as all duties and taxes on the goods and services invoiced by the unit, whereas subsidies on products received by the producer, if there are any, should be added.

If transport costs are included, this should be part of the product specification.

In order to show the true development of price movements, it should be an actual transaction price, and not a list price.

The output price index should take into account quality changes in products.

The price collected in period t should refer to orders booked during period t (moment of order), not the moment when the commodities leave the factory gates.

For output prices of the non-domestic market, the price should be calculated at national frontiers, fob (free on board).

The index should in principle reflect the average price during the reference period. In practice the information actually collected may refer to a particular day in the middle of the reference period that should be determined as a representative figure for the reference period. For products with a significant impact on the national economy that are known to have, at least occasionally, a volatile price development, it is important that the index does indeed reflect average prices.

Production account

The **production account** records the activity of producing goods and services as defined within national accounts; it is drawn up for institutional sectors and for industries. Its resources include gross output and taxes on products less subsidies

on products and its uses include intermediate consumption. The production account is used to obtain one of the most important balancing items in the system – gross value added, or the value generated by any unit engaged in a production activity – and gross domestic product. Value added is economically significant for both institutional sectors and industries.

Production in construction

The **production index in construction** is a business cycle indicator which measures the monthly changes in the output of buildings (residential and non-residential) and of civil engineering work (roads, railways, bridges, tunnels, utility projects).

Conceptually the index shows changes in the volume of construction, in other words the price adjusted change in the value added by this sector. As this statistical concept is not directly measurable, the indicator is approximated by several other measures.

Mathematically the index is calculated as a Laspeyres volume index.

Productivity

Productivity is the output produced from each unit of input, for example, the number of cars assembled by one worker in a year. In statistical analysis, productivity may refer to capital productivity, labour productivity, resource productivity (of which energy productivity is a specific case), depending on the input considered.

Profit share of non-financial corporations

The **profit share of non-financial corporations** is defined as gross operating surplus divided by gross value added. Profits/gross operating surplus are the complement of wage costs that remunerate labour, plus net taxes on production that (partially) finance government services.

Profitability

Profitability refers to the degree to which an enterprise makes a financial gain from bringing goods and services to market after all expenses of doing so have been taken into consideration. Profitability may be defined as the proportion between revenues obtained from output and expenses associated with the consumption of inputs.

Public expenditure on education

Public expenditure on education generally refers to:

- direct expenditure on educational institutions: bearing directly the current and capital expenses of educational institutions;
- transfers to private households and firms: supporting students and their families with scholarships and public loans, as well as transferring public subsidies for educational activities to private firms or non-profit organisations.

Both types of transactions constitute total public expenditure on education.

Purchasing power parities (PPPs)

Purchasing power parities (PPPs) indicate how many currency units a given quantity of goods and services costs in different countries. Using PPPs to convert expenditure expressed in national currencies into an artificial common currency, the purchasing power standard (PPS), eliminates the effect of price level differences across countries created by fluctuations in currency exchange rates.

Purchasing power parities are obtained by comparing price levels for a basket of comparable goods and services that are selected to be representative of consumption patterns in the various countries. PPPs make it possible to produce meaningful indicators (based on either price or volume) required for cross-country comparisons, truly reflecting the differences in the purchasing power of, for example, households. Monetary exchange rates cannot be used to compare income or expenditure because they usually reflect more elements than just price differences, for example, the level of financial transactions between currencies and expectations in the foreign exchange markets.

Purchasing power standard (PPS)

The **purchasing power standard**, abbreviated as **PPS**, is an artificial currency unit. Theoretically, one PPS can buy the same amount of goods and services in each country. However, price differences across borders mean that different amounts of national currency units are needed for the same goods and services depending on the country. PPS are derived by dividing any economic aggregate of a country in national currency by its respective purchasing power parities. PPS is the technical term used by Eurostat for the common currency in which national accounts aggregates are expressed when adjusted for price level differences using PPPs. Thus, PPPs can be interpreted as the exchange rate of the PPS against the euro.

R & D intensity

Research and development (R & D) intensity for a country is defined as R & D expenditure as a percentage of gross domestic product (GDP). For an enterprise, R & D intensity is the ratio of an enterprise's R & D expenditure to its revenue (the percentage of revenue that is spent on R & D). R & D is the main driver of innovation, and R & D expenditure and intensity are two of the key indicators used to monitor resources devoted to science and technology worldwide. Governments are increasingly referring to international benchmarks when defining their science policies and allocating resources.

The European Council set, as part of the Lisbon strategy, an overall target for R & D intensity of 3 % of GDP by the year 2010, with industry asked to contribute two thirds of this objective; this target has been extended and is included as part of the Europe 2020 strategy.

Railway

A **railway line** is a line of communication made up by rail exclusively for the use of railway vehicles. **Lines** are one or more adjacent running tracks forming a route between two points. Where a section of network comprises two or more lines running alongside one another, there are as many lines as routes to which tracks are allotted exclusively. A **running track** is a track providing end-to-end line continuity designed for trains between stations or places indicated in tariffs as independent points of departure or arrival for the conveyance of passengers or goods. A **track** is a pair of rails over which rail borne vehicles can run.

Relative median at-risk-of-poverty gap

The **relative median at-risk-of-poverty gap** is calculated as the difference between the median equivalised disposable income of persons below the at-risk-of-poverty threshold and the at-risk-of-poverty threshold, expressed as a percentage of the at-risk-of-poverty threshold (cut-off point: 60 % of national median equivalised disposable income).

Relative median income ratio

The **relative median income ratio** is defined as the ratio of the median equivalised disposable income of persons aged 65 and over to the median equivalised disposable income of those aged below 65.

Renewable energy sources (RES)

Renewable energy sources (RES), also called **renewables**, are energy sources that replenish (or renew) themselves naturally, such as solar, wind, and tidal energy. Renewable energy sources include the following:

- **biomass and wastes**: organic, non-fossil material of biological origin, which may be used for heat production or electricity generation; comprises wood and wood waste, biogas, municipal solid waste and biofuels; includes the renewable part of industrial waste;
- **hydropower**: the electricity generated from the potential and kinetic energy of water in hydroelectric plants (the electricity generated in pumped storage plants is not included);
- **geothermal energy**: the energy available as heat from within the earth's crust, usually in the form of hot water or steam;

- **wind energy**: the kinetic energy of wind converted into electricity in wind turbines;
- **solar energy**: solar radiation exploited for solar heat (hot water) and electricity production.

Research and development (R & D)

Research and development, abbreviated as **R & D**, includes creative work carried out on a systematic basis in order to increase the stock of knowledge of man, culture and society, and the use of this knowledge to devise new applications.

Intramural research and development (R & D) expenditure is all the expenditure on R & D within a statistical unit or economic sector, whatever the source of funds. Also included is money spent outside the unit or sector but in support of intramural R & D (for example, purchase of supplies for R & D). Both current and capital expenditures are included.

Research and development (R & D) personnel and researchers

Research and development (R & D) personnel consists of all individuals employed directly in the field of R & D, including persons providing direct services, such as managers, administrators, and clerical staff.

R & D researchers can be employed in the public or the private sector – including academia – to create new knowledge, products, processes and methods, as well as to manage the projects concerned.

Researcher

A **researcher** is a professional engaged in the conception or creation of new knowledge, products, processes, methods and systems, as well as in the management of the projects concerned.

Reserve currency

A **reserve currency** is a foreign currency held by a government or central bank as part of a country's reserves. The United States dollar (USD) is the most

common global reserve currency, but the euro is increasingly widely used. **Foreign official reserves** form part of the financial assets which a country holds with respect to the rest of the world. The main parts are holdings of foreign exchange and gold.

Resident institutional unit

A **resident institutional unit** is an institutional unit that is resident because it has a centre of economic interest in the economic territory of a country (or a grouping like the European Union or the euro area).

The sectors of an economy are composed of two main types of institutional units:

- households and individuals who make up a household;
- legal and social entities, such as corporations and quasi-corporations (for example branches of foreign direct investors), non-profit institutions, and the government of that economy.

These institutional units must meet certain criteria to be considered resident units of the economy. Residence is a particularly important attribute of an institutional unit in the balance of payments because the identification of transactions between residents and non-residents underpins the system. Residence is also important in the European system of national and regional accounts (ESA95) because the residency status of producers determines the limits of domestic production and effects the measurements of gross domestic product (GDP) and many important flows. The concept of residence is based on a sectoral transactor's centre of economic interest. It is necessary to recognise the economic territory of a country as the relevant geographical area to which the concept of residence is applied. An institutional unit is a resident unit when it has a centre of economic interest in the economic territory of a country.

The institutional unit is an elementary economic decision-making centre characterised by similarity of behaviour and decision-making autonomy in the exercise of its main function. A resident unit is regarded as constituting an institutional unit if it has decision-making autonomy for its main function

and either keeps a complete set of accounts or it would be possible and meaningful, from both an economic and legal viewpoint, to make a complete set of accounts if they were needed.

Resource efficiency

Resource productivity measures the efficiency with which an economy uses energy and materials. It also shows the natural resource inputs needed to achieve a given economic output.

Risk-phrase

Risk-phrase, sometimes abbreviated as **R-phrase**, refers to the labelling, via a phrase or sentence, of dangerous substances according to the risks they present. Dangerous substances can be classified according to the type of risk and each category has a code with an associated risk-phrase, as well as a label with a standardised meaning in different languages. The list of risk-phrases for the European Union, which is also widely used outside Europe, was first published in Directive 67/548/EEC and later updated and consolidated in Annex III of Directive 59/2001 of 6 August 2001.

Road transport type

There may be different **types of transport**:

- **Transport for hire or reward**: the carriage for remuneration of persons or goods (on behalf of third parties).
- **Transport on own account**: transport which is not for hire or reward.

Roaming charge

A **roaming charge** refers to the cost of using mobile communications (typically with a mobile phone) to automatically make and receive voice calls, send and receive data, or access other services when travelling outside the geographical area of the user's home network by using a different network in the location they are visiting.

Roundwood production

Roundwood production (the term is also used as a synonym for **removals** in the context of forestry) comprises all quantities of wood removed from the forest and other wooded land, or other tree felling sites during a defined period of time.

Satellite account

Satellite accounts provide a framework linked to central (national or regional) accounts, allowing attention to be focused on a certain field or aspect of economic and social life; common examples are satellite accounts for the environment, or tourism, or unpaid household work.

Sawnwood

Sawnwood is wood that has been produced either by sawing lengthways or by a profile-chipping process and, with a few exceptions, is greater than 6 millimetres (mm) in thickness.

Seasonal adjustment

Seasonal adjustment (or the adjustment for seasonal changes) is a statistical method for removing the effects of recurring seasonal influences which have been observed in the past from an economic time series, thus showing non-seasonal trends more clearly.

The level and direction of the seasonal effects depend on several factors such as economic activity (for example the turnover of hotels typically increases during holidays, while the industrial production index develops more weakly during the summer). Seasonal effects vary between economies and countries (for example depending on which industries are particularly important in the economic structure) and between indicators.

Seasonal effects are one of the four main components that determine the development of economic indicators (apart from the general trend, cyclical effects and an irregular component) and seasonal adjustment is a central element of time series analysis.

Self-employed

A **self-employed** person is the sole or joint owner of an unincorporated enterprise (one that has not been incorporated in other words formed into a legal corporation) in which he/she works, **unless** they are also in paid employment which is their main activity (in that case, they are considered to be employees).

Self-employed persons also include:

- unpaid family workers;
- outworkers (who work outside the usual workplace, such as at home);
- workers engaged in production done entirely for their own final use or own capital formation, either individually or collectively.

Serious accident at work

A **serious accident at work** is an accident resulting in more than three days' absence of the employee involved. An accident at work is a discrete occurrence in the course of work that leads to physical or mental harm. This includes accidents outside the business premises, even if caused by a third party, and cases of acute poisoning. It excludes accidents to or from work, occurrences of a strictly medical nature, and occupational diseases.

Severe housing deprivation rate

The **severe housing deprivation rate** is defined as the percentage of population living in a dwelling which is considered as overcrowded, while also exhibiting at least one of the housing deprivation measures. Housing deprivation is a measure of poor amenities and is calculated by referring to those households with a leaking roof, no bath/shower and no indoor toilet, or a dwelling considered too dark.

Sewage sludge

Sewage sludge refers to the accumulated settled solids separated from various types of waste water, and which are either moist or partly liquefied as a result of natural or artificial processes.

Sheep

Sheep are domesticated animals of the species *Ovis aries* kept in flocks mainly for their wool or meat.

Sheep (of all ages) are divided into:

- Breeding females – which are female sheep (called **ewes**). These include: ewes that have lambed (been bred from); ewes and ewe lambs (kept) for breeding; cull cwes (unproductive ewes sent for slaughter).
- Other sheep – all sheep other than breeding females.

Short-term business statistics (STS)

Short-term business statistics, or simply **short-term statistics**, abbreviated as **STS**, are a set of indicators, usually with a monthly or quarterly frequency, used for closely tracking the business cycle of an economy (a single country, the European Union or the euro area). In order to be relevant, they have to reflect current developments with the shortest possible delays.

STS indicators are important tools for formulating and monitoring economic and monetary policies. They are in great demand by policymakers (national and regional governments), the European Commission, central banks (particularly the European Central Bank), private enterprises, professional organisations and financial markets.

The indicators covered by STS are, for example, the production index, turnover, new orders, hours worked, number of persons employed, gross wages and output prices. They are collected for the all major sectors of the non-financial business economy (industry, construction, trade and services).

Single market

The **single market**, sometimes also called the **internal market**, is one of the cornerstones of the European Union (EU). It refers to the free movement of people, goods, services and capital within the EU, the so-called 'four freedoms' laid down in the Treaty of Rome. This has been achieved by eliminating barriers and simplifying existing rules so that everyone in the EU can benefit from direct access to 27 countries and more than 500 million people.

The enabling instrument for the single market was the Single European act, which came into force in July 1987. Among other things it called for:

- extending the powers of the Community in some policy areas (social policy, research, environment);
- gradually establishing the single market over a period up to the end of 1992, by means of a vast legislative programme involving the adoption of hundreds of directives and regulations; and
- making more frequent use of majority voting in the Council of Ministers.

EU policies in the areas of transport, competition, financial services and consumer protection underpin the single market.

Small and medium-sized enterprises (SMEs)

Small and medium-sized enterprises are enterprises employing fewer than 250 persons. According to European Commission Recommendation 2003/361/EC of 6 May 2003, enterprises are defined with regard to their number of employees, annual turnover, and their independence.

For statistical purposes, small and medium-sized enterprises may be further subdivided into:

- **micro enterprises** (fewer than 10 persons employed);
- **small enterprises** (10 to 49 persons employed);
- **medium-sized enterprises** (50 to 249 persons employed).

Large enterprises are defined as those with 250 or more persons employed.

Social benefits

Social benefits other than social transfers in kind are transfers made in cash to households to relieve them of the financial burden of certain risks or needs, for example, pensions, family and child allowances, and disabled persons' allowances.

Social benefits are paid out by social security funds, other government units, non-profit institutions serving households (NPISHs), employers administering unfunded social insurance schemes, insurance enterprises or other institutional units administering privately funded social insurance schemes.

Social contributions

Social contributions are paid on a compulsory or voluntary basis by employers, employees and self- and non-employed persons. There are two types of social contributions, actual and imputed, paid by the employer for the benefit of their employees:

Actual social contributions or actual payments consist of payments made by employers for the benefit of their employees to insurers (social security funds and private funded schemes). These payments cover statutory, conventional, contractual and voluntary contributions in respect of insurance against social risks or needs.

Employers' **imputed social contributions** represent the counterpart to unfunded social benefits paid directly by employers to their employees or former employees and other eligible persons without involving an insurance enterprise or autonomous pension fund, and without creating a special fund or segregated reserve for the purpose.

Social protection

Social protection can be defined as the coverage of precisely defined risks and needs associated with: sickness/healthcare and invalidism; disability; old age; parental responsibilities; the loss of a spouse or parent; unemployment; housing; social exclusion.

Social protection benefits

Social protection benefits are transfers to households, in cash or in kind, intended to relieve them of the financial burden of several risks and needs as defined in the European system of integrated social protection statistics (ESSPROS). These include disability, sickness/healthcare, old age, survivors, family/children, unemployment, housing and social exclusion not covered elsewhere.

Social protection expenditure

Social protection expenditure is the outlay for social protection interventions. It consists mainly of:

- social benefits, or transfers in cash or in kind, to households and individuals with the aim to relieve them of the burden of a defined set of risks or needs;
- administration costs, or costs of managing or administering the social protection scheme; and
- other miscellaneous expenditure by social protection schemes (payment of property income and other).

Social security fund

A **social security fund** is a central, state or local institutional unit whose main activity is to provide social benefits. It fulfils the following two criteria:

- by law or regulation (except those about government employees), certain population groups must take part in the scheme and have to pay contributions;
- general government is responsible for the management of the institutional unit, for the payment or approval of the level of the contributions and of the benefits, independent of its role as a supervisory body or employer.

Social transfers

Social transfers cover the social help given by central, state or local institutional units. They include: old age (retirement) and survivors' (widows' and widowers') pensions; unemployment benefits; family-related benefits; sickness and invalidity benefits; education-related benefits; housing allowances; social assistance; other benefits.

Special-purpose entities (SPEs)

A special-purpose entity, abbreviated as SPE, and sometimes also called special-purpose vehicle (SPV) or financial vehicle corporation (FVC) is:

- a legal entity (an enterprise or sometimes a limited partnership or joint venture) formally registered

with a national authority and subject to the fiscal and other legal obligations of the economy in which it is resident,

- established to perform specific functions limited in scope or time, with one or a few primary creditors,
- having no or few non-financial assets and employees, little or no production or operations and sometimes no physical presence beyond a 'brass plate' confirming its place of registration,
- related to another corporation, often as a subsidiary and often resident in a territory other than the territory of residence of the related corporation (lacking any physical dimension, the residence of a SPE is determined by the economic territory under whose laws it is incorporated or registered),
- with as its core business function group financing or holding activities (the channelling of funds from non-residents to other non-residents) and only a minor role for managing and directing.

Stability and growth pact (SGP)

The **stability and growth pact**, abbreviated as **SGP**, is a rule-based framework for the coordination of national fiscal policies under economic and monetary union and the creation of the euro area with its single currency, the euro. It was established to safeguard sound public finances, an important requirement for EMU to function properly. The SGP consists of a preventive and a dissuasive arm.

The SGP has to be seen against the background of Stage III of economic and monetary union, which began on 1 January 1999. Its aim is to ensure that the Member States continued their budgetary discipline efforts once the euro was introduced.

The pact stems from a European Council resolution (adopted in Amsterdam (NL) on 17 June 1997) and two Council regulations of 7 July 1997 laying down detailed technical arrangements, one on the surveillance of budgetary positions and coordination of economic policies and the other on implementing the excessive deficit procedure (EDP).

In the medium-term, the euro area Member States undertake to achieve a balanced or nearly balanced budget and to give the Council and the European Commission a stability programme every year. Along the same lines, Member States outside the euro area are required to submit a convergence programme.

The SGP opens the way for the Council to penalise any euro area Member State that fails to take appropriate measures to end an excessive deficit. Initially, the penalty takes the form of a non-interest bearing deposit with the European Union, but it could be converted into a fine if the excessive deficit is not corrected within two years.

Standard international trade classification (SITC)

The **standard international trade classification**, abbreviated as **SITC**, is a product classification of the United Nations used for external trade statistics (export and import values and volumes of goods), allowing for international comparisons of commodities and manufactured goods.

The groupings of SITC reflect: the production materials; the processing stage; market practices and uses of the products; the importance of the goods in world trade; technological changes.

The main categories are:

- *food, drinks and tobacco* (Sections 0 and 1 – including live animals);
- *raw materials* (Sections 2 and 4);
- energy products (Section 3);
- *chemicals* (Section 5);
- machinery and transport equipment (Section 7);
- other manufactured goods (Sections 6 and 8).

SITC Revision 4 was accepted by the United Nations Statistical Commission at its 37th session in 2006 and it is currently being implemented.

Standardised death rate (SDR)

The **standardised death rate**, abbreviated as **SDR**, is the death rate of a population adjusted to a standard age distribution. It is calculated as a weighted

average of the age-specific death rates of a given population; the weights are the age distribution of that population. As most causes of death vary significantly with people's age and sex, the use of standardised death rates improves comparability over time and between countries. The reason for this is that death rates can be measured independently of the age structure of populations in different times and countries (sex ratios are usually more stable).

Standardised death rates are calculated on the basis of a standard European population defined by the World Health Organization (WHO).

State government

State government is defined as the separate institutional units that exercise some government functions below those units at central government level and above those units at local government level, excluding the administration of social security funds.

Statistical classification of economic activities in the European Community (NACE)

The **statistical classification of economic activities in the European Community**, abbreviated as **NACE**, designates the classification of economic activities in the European Union. Various NACE versions have been developed since 1970.

NACE is a four-digit classification providing the framework for collecting and presenting a large range of statistical data according to economic activity in the fields of economic statistics (for example, production, employment and national accounts) and in other statistical domains developed within the European statistical system (ESS).

NACE Rev. 2, a revised classification, was adopted at the end of 2006 and its implementation began in 2007. The first reference year for NACE Rev. 2 compatible statistics is 2008, after which NACE Rev. 2 will be consistently applied to all relevant statistical domains.

Previous versions of NACE have been:

- **NACE (1970)**, the original version of NACE (succeeding and integrating the narrower clas-

sifications NICE for industry, NCE for trade and commerce, and other specific classifications for agriculture and for services);
- **NACE Rev. 1**, the first revision of NACE (1970);
- **NACE Rev. 1.1**, a minor revision of NACE Rev. 1.

Statistical classification of products by activity (CPA)

The **statistical classification of products by activity**, abbreviated as **CPA**, is a classification of products (goods as well as services) at the level of the European Union. Product classifications are designed to categorise products that have common characteristics. They provide the basis for collecting and calculating statistics on the production, distributive trade, consumption, foreign trade and transport of such products.

CPA product categories are related to activities as defined by the statistical classification of economic activities in the European Community. Each CPA product – whether a transportable or non-transportable good or a service – is assigned to one single NACE activity. This linkage to NACE activities gives the CPA a structure parallel to that of NACE at all levels.

The CPA is part of an integrated system of statistical classifications, developed mainly under the auspices of the United Nations Statistical Division. This system makes it possible to compare statistics across countries and in different statistical domains.

Structural business statistics (SBS)

Structural business statistics, sometimes abbreviated as **SBS**, describe the structure, activity, competitiveness and performance of economic activities within the business economy down to the detailed level of several hundred sectors.

In broad terms, SBS are compiled from information concerning units engaged in economic activity; the types of statistical units observed are mainly enterprises, although local units are often used for regional SBS, and some industrial SBS data relate to the kind-of-activity unit. These data are collected within the context of Council Regulation 58/97 on

structural business statistics. SBS cover the business economy, which includes industry, construction and services. Because of their specific nature and the limited availability of most types of standard business statistics, financial services are included in SBS but treated separately. SBS do not cover agriculture, forestry and fishing, nor public administration and (to a large extent) non-market services such as education and health.

Structural funds

The **structural funds** are funding instruments that allow the European Union (EU) to grant financial assistance to specific sectors, regions, or combinations of both, to address structural economic and social problems.

At present, there are four structural funds:

- The European Regional Development Funds (ERDF), whose main objective is to promote economic and social cohesion within the EU by addressing imbalances between regions or social groups.
- The European Social Fund (ESF), the main financial instrument allowing the EU to implement its employment policy.
- The European Agricultural Guidance and Guarantee Fund (EAGGF – Guidance Section), which contributes to the structural reform of the agriculture sector and to the development of rural areas.
- The Financial Instrument for Fisheries Guidance (FTGC), the specific fund for the structural reform of the fisheries sector.

Structural indicators (SI)

During the Lisbon European Council of March 2000, the heads of state of the European Union agreed to set a strategic goal for the next decade 'of becoming the most competitive and dynamic knowledge-based economy in the world capable of sustainable economic growth with more and better jobs and greater social cohesion'.

Structural indicators (SI) were used to underpin the European Commission's analysis in an annual progress report to the European Council on the implementation of the Lisbon strategy. In 2005, the European Commission presented a new approach to the Lisbon strategy, with a greater focus on growth and jobs. From 2010 a revised set of structural indicators has been used for monitoring the Europe 2020 strategy, the successor to the Lisbon strategy.

The list of structural indicators covers six broad domains: general economic background; employment; innovation and research; economic reform; social cohesion; environment.

Structure of earnings survey (SES)

The **structure of earnings survey**, abbreviated as **SES**, is conducted every four years in the Member States of the European Union (EU) and provides comparable information at EU level on relationships between the level of earnings, individual characteristics of employees (sex, age, occupation, length of service, educational level) and their employer (for example, the economic activity or size of the enterprise) for reference years 2002 and 2006 (next survey with reference year 2010).

The data collection is based on legislation and data become available approximately two years after the end of the reference period. In the SES gross annual earnings cover remuneration in cash and in kind paid during the reference year before any tax deductions and social security contributions payable by wage earners and retained by the employer. The main difference between annual and monthly earnings in the SES is that annual earnings are not only the sum of the direct remuneration, bonuses and allowances paid to an employee in each pay period. Annual earnings hence usually exceed the figure produced by multiplying the 'standard monthly package' by 12. The 'standard monthly package' includes those bonuses and allowances which occur in every pay period, even if the amount for these regular bonuses and allowances varies, but excludes bonuses and allowances not occurring in every pay period. Furthermore, monthly earnings leave payments in kind out of consideration. However, annual earnings also cover all non-standard payments, in other words payments not occurring in each pay period, and payments in kind. The SES covers local units belonging to enterprises with at least ten employees and all economic activities defined in Sections C to K, and M to O, of the statistical classification of economic activities in the European Communities (NACE Rev. 1.1). The transmission of data covering small enterprises (below ten employees) and enterprises belonging to NACE Rev. 1.1 Section L is optional. For the survey with reference year 2010 the coverage in terms of activity and size class has changed.

The SES represents a rich microdata source for European policymaking and research purposes. Access to microdata is granted to researchers according to specific conditions and respecting statistical confidentiality.

Surface water

Fresh **surface water** flows over, or rests on the surface of a land mass, natural waterway (rivers, streams, brooks and lakes) or artificial waterway, including irrigation, industrial and navigation canals, drainage systems and artificial reservoirs.

Surface water abstraction

Surface water abstraction is the removal of water from natural or artificial waterways containing freshwater, including lakes, rivers, streams and canals.

Surplus

Surplus means in general that the sum or balance of positive and negative amounts is positive, or that the total of positives is larger than the total of negatives. A surplus can be used in different statistical areas:

- in balance of payments statistics, it refers to the balance of credit (positive) and debit (negative) transactions of a given economy with the rest of the world, organised in two different accounts: the current account; and the capital and financial account;
- in external trade statistics, it refers to the trade balance of imports (negative, as they have to be paid for) and exports (positive, because they yield revenue), which may result in a trade surplus;
- in government finance statistics, it refers to the public balance between government revenue and expenditure.

Sustainable development

Sustainable development is economic growth and social progress which is sustainable in the future, not only for the present but also for coming generations. It combines economic development with protection of the environment and social justice.

Sustainable development indicators (SDIs)

Sustainable development indicators, abbreviated as **SDIs**, aim to measure sustainable development over longer periods of time. Indicators are grouped into ten subject categories: socioeconomic development; sustainable consumption and production; social inclusion; demographic changes; public health; climate change and energy; sustainable transport; natural resources; global partnership; good governance.

System of health accounts (SHA)

The **system of health accounts**, abbreviated as **SHA**, provides for health accounting in the European Union Member States, an economic framework, and accounting rules which are methodologically compatible with the system of national accounts.

The SHA provides a standard framework for producing a set of comprehensive, consistent and internationally comparable accounts to meet the needs of public and private sector health analysts and policymakers. At present, national health accounts are at different stages of development and may not only differ in the boundaries drawn between health and other social and economic activities but also in the classifications used, the level of detail provided, and in the accounting rules. The SHA provides a framework for a family of interrelated tables for standard reporting for expenditure (spending) on health and for its financing. It has been written with

the dual aim of providing this framework for international data collections and as a possible model for redesigning and complementing national health accounts to aid policymakers.

The demand for improved health accounts is driven by an increasing complexity of healthcare systems in many countries and the rapid development in medical technology. Policymakers and observers of healthcare systems and recent reforms have questioned the adequacy of accounting practices and the ability of health accounts to monitor fast-changing healthcare systems that are becoming increasingly complex. Raising consumers' expectations of healthcare contributes to the demand for up-to-date information on healthcare systems.

Tax rate: unemployment trap

The **unemployment trap** measures the percentage of gross earnings lost to taxes when a person becomes employed. This occurs through the loss of unemployment benefits combined with higher tax and social security contributions.

Tax revenue

Total **tax revenue** is the income a government generates through the taxation of the people. It includes taxes on production and imports, current tax on income and wealth, capital gains tax, and social contributions. Total tax revenue is an aggregate comprising:

- **taxes on production and imports**, such as value added tax (VAT), import duties, excise duties and consumption taxes, stamp taxes, payroll taxes, taxes on pollution, and others;
- **current taxes on income, wealth, etc.**, such as corporate and personal income taxes, taxes on holding gains, payments by households for licences to own or use cars, hunt or fish, current taxes on capital that are paid periodically, and others;
- **capital taxes**, such as inheritance taxes, death duties and taxes on gifts and capital levies that are occasional or exceptional;
- **actual social contributions** paid on a compulsory or voluntary basis by employers or employees

or the self- or non-employed to insure against social risks (sickness, invalidity, disability, old age, survivors, family and maternity);
- **imputed or implicit social contributions** payable under unfunded social insurance schemes (in which employers pay social benefits to their employees, ex-employees or their dependants out of their own resources without creating a special reserve for the purpose).

The calculation of total tax revenue must be reduced by the amount of **taxes and social contributions assessed as unlikely to be collected**.

Tax wedge

The **tax wedge** is the difference between the employer's labour costs and the employee's net take-home pay, including any cash benefits from government welfare programmes.

Taxes on production and imports

Taxes on production and imports are compulsory, unrequited (not made for a consideration) payments, in cash or in kind, levied (charged) generally by a government or a European Union institution.

The payments are called unrequited because the government or institution provides nothing directly in return for the payment. The taxes are paid on the production and import of goods and services; the employment of labour; the ownership or use of land, buildings or other assets used in production.

Time series

A **time series** is a sequence of data which shows the value of a variable over time. Normally such data are collected on a regular periodic basis.

Tonnes of oil equivalent (toe)

Tonne(s) of oil equivalent, abbreviated as **toe**, is a normalised unit of energy. By convention it is equivalent to the approximate amount of energy that can be extracted from one tonne of crude oil. It is a standardised unit, assigned a net calorific value of 41 868 kilojoules/kg and may be used to compare the energy derived from different sources.

Other energy carriers can be converted into tonnes of oil equivalent using the following conversion factors:

- 1 tonne (t) diesel = 1.01 toe
- 1 cubic metre (m³) diesel = 0.98 toe
- 1 t petrol = 1.05 toe
- 1 m³ petrol = 0.86 toe
- 1 t biodiesel = 0.86 toe
- 1 m³ biodiesel = 0.78 toe
- 1 t bioethanol = 0.64 toe
- 1 m³ bioethanol = 0.51 toe

Total age dependency ratio

The **total age-dependency ratio** is a measure of the age structure of the population. It relates the number of individuals who are likely to be 'dependent' on the support of others for their daily living – the young and the elderly – to the number of those individuals who are capable of providing this support.

The total age-dependency ratio is the ratio of the sum of the number of young and the number of elderly people at an age when both groups are generally economically inactive, (in other words under 15 years of age and aged 65 and over), compared with the number of people of working age (in other words 15-64 years old). It is the sum of the two ratios, the young age-dependency ratio and the old age-dependency ratio.

Total general government expenditure

Total general government expenditure is all the money that a government spends.

Total general government expenditure is defined according to Commission Regulation (EC) No 1500/2000 of 10 July 2000 on general government expenditure and revenue. It comprises the following categories of the European system of accounts 1995 (ESA95): intermediate consumption; gross capital formation; compensation of employees; other taxes on production; subsidies payable; property income;

current taxes on income, wealth, etc.; social benefits other than social transfers in kind; social transfers in kind related to expenditure on products supplied to households via market producers; other current transfers; adjustments for the change in net equity of households in pension fund reserves; capital transfers payable; acquisitions less disposals of non-financial non-produced assets.

Tourism

Tourism refers to the activities of persons travelling to and staying in places outside their usual environment for not more than one consecutive year for leisure, business and other purposes.

Tourism intensity

Tourism intensity, also called **carrying capacity**, is the ratio of nights spent in hotels and similar establishments relative to the total permanent resident population of an area.

Trade balance

The **trade balance** is the difference between the value of the goods that a country (or another geographic or economic area such as the European Union or the euro area) exports and the value of the goods that it imports. If exports exceed imports then the country has a **trade surplus** and the trade balance is said to be positive. If imports exceed exports, the country or area has a **trade deficit** and its trade balance is said to be negative. However, the words 'positive' and 'negative' have only a numerical meaning and do not necessarily reflect whether the economy of a country or area is performing well or not. A trade deficit may, for instance, reflect an increase in domestic demand for goods destined for consumption and/or production. The total trade balance, including all goods exported and imported, is one of the major components of the balance of payments. A big surplus or deficit for a single product or product category can show a particular national competitive advantage or disadvantage in the world market for goods.

Trans-European networks (TENs)

The function of **trans-European networks**, abbreviated as **TENs**, is to create a modern and effective infrastructure for transport, energy and telecommunications that link European countries and regions. In the European Union they are essential to the proper operation of the single market, since they ensure free movement of goods, people and services. TENs exist in three sectors of activity.

- **Trans-European transport networks (TEN-T)** cover road and intermodal transport, waterways and seaports, and the European high-speed railway network. Intelligent transport management systems also fall into this category, as does Galileo, Europe's satellite radio navigation system.
- **Trans-European energy networks (TEN-E)** cover the electricity and natural gas sectors. They help to create a single energy market and contribute to the security of energy supply.
- **Trans-European telecommunications networks (eTEN)** have as their aim the deployment of telecommunication network-based services.

The construction of trans-European networks is also an important element for economic growth and the creation of employment.

Transport mode

A **transport mode** is the method of transport used for the carriage of goods and passengers.

Transport modes for *both passengers and goods* may include: rail; maritime (sea); road; inland waterways; air.

Transport modes for *goods only* include: pipelines.

Passenger road and rail transport include for example passenger cars, powered two wheelers (moped and motor cycles), buses, coaches, trolley-buses, trams (also known as street cars), light railways and metros (also known as subway, metropolitan railway, underground).

The **modal split** of transport describes the relative share of each mode of transport, for example by road, rail or sea. It is based on passenger-kilometres (p-km) for passenger transport and tonne-kilometres (t-km) for freight or goods transport. The modal split is usually defined for a specific geographic area and/or time period.

In practice, an analysis of the modal split may exclude certain modes of transport. For example, the analysis may be limited to inland transport and therefore exclude sea transport.

Treaties of Rome

The **Treaties of Rome** are two treaties signed in Rome on 25 March 1957 which came into force on 1 January 1958:

- the Treaty establishing the European Economic Community, also referred to as the EEC Treaty, established the European Economic Community (EEC);
- the Treaty establishing the European Atomic Energy Community, also referred to as the Euratom Treaty, established the European Atomic Energy Community (EAEC or Euratom).

Both were signed by the six founding Member States: Belgium, France, Italy, Luxembourg, the Netherlands and West Germany. The EEC Treaty is the legal basis for the European Union.

The EEC Treaty has been amended and renamed on several occasions, the most important of which were:

- the 1993 Treaty of Maastricht on European Union renaming the Treaty establishing the European Economic Community (EEC Treaty) to the **Treaty establishing the European Community** or **EC Treaty**;
- the Treaty of Lisbon, entered into force on 1 December 2009, replacing the EC Treaty with the **Treaty on the Functioning of the European Union (TFEU)**.

Treaty on European Union

The **Treaty on European Union**, abbreviated as **TEU** and also called the **Treaty of Maastricht**, was signed in Maastricht on 7 February 1992 and entered into force on 1 November 1993. It represented a new stage in European integration since it opened the way to political integration, by creating a European Union (EU) consisting of three pillars:

- the European Communities;
- Common Foreign and Security Policy (CFSP);
- police and judicial cooperation in criminal matters (JHA).

The Treaty introduced the concept of European citizenship, reinforced the powers of the European Parliament and launched economic and monetary union. Besides, the Treaty also resulted in the EEC becoming the European Community (EC).

Amendments were made to the Treaty of Maastricht by:

- the **Treaty of Amsterdam** (1997), which increased the powers of the EU by creating a Community employment policy, transferring to the Communities some of the areas which were previously subject to intergovernmental cooperation in the fields of justice and home affairs, introducing measures aimed at bringing the EU closer to its citizens and enabling closer cooperation between certain Member States (enhanced cooperation). It also extended the codecision procedure and qualified majority voting and simplified and renumbered the articles of the Treaties;
- the **Treaty of Nice** (2001) essentially dealt with the institutional problems linked to enlargement which were not resolved in the Treaty of Amsterdam: the make-up of the European Commission, the weighting of votes in the Council and the extension of the areas of qualified majority voting; it also simplified rules on the use of the enhanced cooperation procedure and made the judicial system more effective.
- the **Treaty of Lisbon** (2007), which gave legal personality to the EU, abolished pillar system, increased the power of the European Parliament and involvement of national parliaments in the legislative process of the EU, further extended areas of qualified majority voting (to be changed in 2014 into double majority voting), introduced the functions of a President of the European Council and a High Representative of the EU for Foreign Affairs and Security Policy, included the Char-

ter of Fundamental Rights of the EU into legally binding acts, introduced the European citizens' initiative and the ability of a state to voluntary withdraw from the EU.

Trend

A **trend** is the slow variation over a relatively long period of time, usually several years, generally associated with the structural causes affecting the phenomenon being measured. It is the variation left after time series analysis has removed accidental (irregular or random), working-day and seasonal variation from a time series.

In some cases, the trend shows a steady growth, decrease or stability; in others, it may fluctuate moving downwards and upwards. The cycle is a quasi (almost but not quite) periodic oscillation. It is characterised by alternating periods of higher and lower rates of change, possibly, but not always, involving expansion and contraction. In most cases, the trend is related to fluctuations in overall economic activity.

Generally, if the irregular part of the time series is relatively important, the trend cycle series is a better series for the analysis of longer-term past developments. However, this advantage is less clear when analysing recent developments. This is because trend-cycle values for recent periods may undergo greater revisions (changes) than seasonally adjusted values. Hence, the latter may be more suitable for the analysis of recent developments; this is particularly true around turning points. Trend-cycle series may, however, converge to stable results more quickly than seasonally adjusted series.

Triad

The **Triad** refers to the three centres dominating the world economy until the late 1990's: the United States (US), the European Union (EU) and Japan (JP); or, somewhat more broadly, North America, (Western) Europe and Japan.

Turnover – structural business statistics

Turnover, in the context of structural business statistics, comprises the totals invoiced by the observation unit during the reference period, and this corresponds to the total value of market sales of goods and services to third parties.

Unemployment

An **unemployed** person is defined by Eurostat, according to the guidelines of the International Labour Organization, as:

- someone aged 15-74 (in Italy, Spain, the United Kingdom, Iceland, Norway: 16-74);
- without work during the reference week;
- available to start work within the next two weeks (or has already found a job to start within the next three months);
- actively having sought employment at some time during the last four weeks.

The **unemployment rate** is the number of unemployed persons as a percentage of the labour force.

United Nations (UN)

The **United Nations**, abbreviated as the **UN**, was established on 24 October 1945 by 51 countries committed to preserving peace through international cooperation and collective security. Today, there are 193 Member States, almost every country in the world.

United Nations Economic Commission for Europe (UNECE)

The **United Nations Economic Commission for Europe**, abbreviated as **UNECE**, is one of five regional commissions of the United Nations. UNECE was set up in 1947 to promote pan-European economic integration. To do so, it groups 56 countries located in the European Union (EU), non-EU western and eastern Europe, south-eastern Europe, as well as the Commonwealth of Independent States (CIS) and North America.

United Nations Educational, Scientific and Cultural Organization (UNESCO)

The **United Nations Educational, Scientific and Cultural Organization**, abbreviated as **UNESCO**, is a specialised United Nations agency. Its mission is to promote international cooperation among its Member States and Associate Members in the fields of education, science, culture and communication. UNESCO was founded on 16 November 1945, and has 193 Member States (as of April 2012).

Universal service

Universal service refers to the practice or legal obligation of providing a baseline level of service to every resident of a country. It is mostly used in the context of regulated activities, considered by authorities as providing vital services (for example postal services, telecommunications or public transport).

Universal service providers (USP)

A **universal service provider**, abbreviated as **USP**, is defined in postal statistics as a public or private entity providing a universal service or parts thereof within a country, not specifying whether required by license, authorisation or another legal instrument.

Urban wastewater treatment

Urban wastewater treatment is all treatment of wastewater in urban wastewater treatment plants, which are usually operated by public authorities or by private companies working by order of public authorities.

Value added tax (VAT)

The **value added tax**, abbreviated as **VAT**, in the European Union (EU) is a general, broadly based consumption tax assessed on the value added to goods and services. It applies more or less to all goods and services bought and sold for use or consumption in the EU; goods sold for export or services sold to

customers abroad are normally not subject to value added tax. VAT is charged as a percentage of the price, meaning that the actual tax burden is visible at each stage in the production and distribution chain.

EU Directive 2006/112/EC, in effect since 1 January 2007, is the main piece of EU legislation relating to VAT. It guarantees that the VAT contributed by each Member State to the Community's own resources can be calculated, while allowing Member States many possible exceptions and derogations from standard VAT coverage. Rates vary between 15 % and 25 % in most Member States. There are also several temporary derogations, for example zero VAT rates for some products in Belgium, Denmark, Ireland, Italy, Malta, Finland, Sweden and the United Kingdom.

Vegetable

For Eurostat purposes **vegetables** include: brassicas (for example cabbage, cauliflower and broccoli); other leafy or stalked vegetables (for example celery, leeks, lettuce, spinach and asparagus); vegetables cultivated for fruit (for example tomatoes, cucumbers, gherkins, melons, aubergine (eggplant), pumpkins and red pepper); root and tuber vegetables (for example turnips, carrots, onions, garlic, beetroot and radishes); pulses (for example peas and beans); cultivated mushrooms; wild products; and other fresh vegetables.

Vocational education and training (VET)

Vocational education and training, abbreviated as **VET**, sometimes simply called **vocational training**, is the training in skills and teaching of knowledge related to a specific trade, occupation or vocation in which the student or employee wishes to participate. Vocational education may be undertaken at an educational institution, as part of secondary or tertiary education, or may be part of initial training during employment, for example as an apprentice, or as a combination of formal education and workplace learning.

Wage-adjusted labour productivity ratio

The **wage-adjusted labour productivity ratio** is an indicator of labour productivity that is derived from structural business statistics. It is defined as value added divided by personnel costs which is subsequently adjusted by the share of paid employees in the total number of persons employed; more simply it is apparent labour productivity divided by average personnel costs expressed as a ratio in percentage terms. Given that this indicator is based on expenditure for labour input rather than a headcount of labour input, it is more relevant for comparisons across activities (or countries) with very different incidences of part-time employment or self-employment.

Waste

Waste means any substance or object which the holder disposes of or is required to dispose of pursuant to the provisions of national law in force.

Disposal of waste means:

- the collection, sorting, transport and treatment of waste as well as its storage and tipping above or under ground;
- the transformation operations necessary for its re-use, recovery or recycling.

Wastewater

Wastewater is water that is of no further immediate value to the purpose for which it was used or in the pursuit of which it was produced because of its quality, quantity or time of occurrence. However, wastewater from one user can be a potential supply to another user elsewhere.

Water abstraction

Water abstraction is the process of taking water from a source. For European Union statistical purposes, it is the groundwater and surface water collected for use by households and enterprises.

Water use

Water use refers to water actually used by end users (for example households, services, agriculture, industry) within a territory for a specific purpose such as domestic use, irrigation or industrial processing.

Water supply, in contrast, is the delivery of water to end users including abstraction for own final use.

Weight

A **weight** in statistical terms is defined as a coefficient assigned to a number in a computation, for example when determining an average, to make the number's effect on the computation reflect its importance.

An illustration of weights and weighting is the calculation of the harmonised index of consumer prices (HICP) performed by Eurostat. The HICP is composed of prices for a selection (referred to as a basket) of items regularly purchased by consumers. However, some items are purchased more frequently than others, while the unit value of items also varies greatly. To account for these issues, the various items in the basket are assigned a weight to reflect the total consumer expenditure on these items.

Working-day adjustment

Working-day adjustment is a statistical method for removing the calendar effect from an economic time series. The **calendar effect** is the variation caused by the changing number of working days in different months or other time periods (quarters, years). Working-day adjustment is mainly used in the calculation of short-term statistics (STS), for converting gross figures or indices into their working-day adjusted equivalent. In order to adjust a figure or an index, the calendar nature of a given month is taken into account and calendar effects are removed, whatever their nature. The number of working days for a given month may depend on:

- the timing of certain public holidays (Easter can fall in March or in April, depending on the year);

- the possible overlap of certain public holidays and non-working days (1 May can fall on a Sunday);
- the occurrence of a leap year.

World Health Organization (WHO)

The **World Health Organization**, or **WHO**, is a specialised agency of the United Nations (UN) that acts as a coordinating body on public health issues. Headquartered in Geneva (CH), the WHO's main task is to fight disease, especially key infectious diseases, and provide leadership on global health matters.

World Trade Organisation (WTO)

The **World Trade Organisation**, abbreviated as **WTO**, is an international organisation with a membership covering 153 countries (as of July 2008). The WTO also has several candidate members in the process of joining.

The WTO is the only global international organisation dealing with the rules of trade between nations. The WTO sets the global rules for trade, providing a forum for trade negotiations and for settling disputes between WTO members.

Youth unemployment

Youth unemployment includes all the youth (in other words persons between the ages of 15 and 24, inclusive) who are unemployed.

Youth unemployment rate is the percentage of the unemployed in the age group 15-24 years old compared with the total labour force (both employed and unemployed) in that age group. However, it should be remembered that a large share of persons between these ages are outside the labour market (since many youths are studying full-time and thus are not available for work), which explains why youth unemployment rates are generally higher than overall unemployment rates, or those of other age groups.

Subject index

European Commission

Europe in figures — Eurostat yearbook 2012

Luxembourg: Publications Office of the European Union

2012— 692 pp. — 17.6 x 25 cm

Theme: General and regional statistics
Collection: Statistical books

ISBN 978-92-79-22085-2
ISSN 1681-4789
doi:10.2785/20539
Cat. KS-CD-12-001-EN-C

Price (excluding VAT) in Luxembourg: EUR 30